THE OXFORD HANDBOOK OF

AFRICAN
ARCHAEOLOGY

THE OXFORD HANDBOOK OF

AFRICAN ARCHAEOLOGY

Edited by

PETER MITCHELL

and

PAUL LANE

OXFORD
UNIVERSITY PRESS

UNIVERSITY PRESS

Great Clarendon Street, Oxford, OX2 6DP,
United Kingdom

Oxford University Press is a department of the University of Oxford.
It furthers the University's objective of excellence in research, scholarship,
and education by publishing worldwide. Oxford is a registered trade mark of
Oxford University Press in the UK and in certain other countries

Published in the United States of America by Oxford University Press
198 Madison Avenue, New York, NY 10016, United States of America

British Library Cataloguing in Publication Data
Data available

ISBN 978-0-19-956988-5

Contents

PART I INTRODUCTION

PART II DOING AFRICAN ARCHAEOLOGY: THEORY, METHOD, PRACTICE

PART III BECOMING HUMAN

PART IV HUNTERS, GATHERERS, AND INTENSIFIERS: THE DIVERSITY OF AFRICAN FORAGERS

PART V FOOD FOR THOUGHT: THE ARCHAEOLOGY OF AFRICAN PASTORALIST AND FARMING COMMUNITIES

PART VI POWER, PRESTIGE, AND CONSUMPTION: AFRICAN TOWNS AND STATES AND THEIR NEIGHBOURS

PART VII AFRICAN SOCIETIES AND THE MODERN WORLD SYSTEM

LIST OF FIGURES

List of Tables

LIST OF CONTRIBUTORS

Noemie Arazi Royal Museum of Central Africa, Tervuren, Belgium

Ceri Ashley Senior Lecturer in Archaeology, University of Pretoria, South Africa

Lawrence Barham Professor in Archaeology , University of Liverpool, UK

Barbara E. Barich Associate Professor of the Prehistoric Ethnography of Africa, Università di Roma 'Sapienza', Italy

Nick Barton Professor of Palaeolithic Archaeology, University of Oxford, UK

Sibel Barut Kusimba Associate Professor of Anthropology, Northern Illinois University, USA

Laura Basell Senior Lecturer in Palaeoanthropology, School of Applied Sciences, Bournemouth University, UK

Roger Blench Independent researcher, Kay Williamson Educational Foundation, Cambridge, UK

Abdeljalil Bouzouggar Maître Assistant at the Institut National des Sciences de l'Archéologie et du Patrimoine, Morocco

Colin Breen Senior Lecturer in Maritime Archaeology, University of Ulster, UK

Peter Breunig Head of African Archaeology, Johann Wolfgang Goethe University, Frankfurt-am-Main, Germany

Joanna Casey Associate Professor of Anthropology, University of South Carolina, USA

Shadreck Chirikure Senior Lecturer in Archaeology, University of Cape Town, South Africa

Graham Connah Professor Emeritus and Visiting Fellow, Australian National University, Australia

Els Cornelissen Head of Prehistory and Archaeology, Royal Museum of Central Africa, Tervuren, Belgium

Sarah Croucher Assistant Professor of Anthropology and Archaeology, Wesleyan University, USA

Matthew Curtis Associated Anthropologist, University of California, Santa Barbara, USA

Matthew Davies Research Associate, Department of Archaeology and Anthropology, University of Cambridge, UK, and Research Fellow, British Institute in Eastern Africa, Nairobi, Kenya

Manuel Domínguez-Rodrigo Professor of Prehistory, Complutense University, Spain

David N. Edwards Lecturer in Archaeology, University of Leicester, UK

Said Ennahid Associate Professor in the School of Humanities and Social Sciences, Al Akhawayn University, Morocco

Amanda Esterhuysen Senior Lecturer in Archaeology, University of the Witwatersrand, South Africa

Jeffrey Fleisher Assistant Professor of Anthropology, Rice University, Houston, USA

Robert A. Foley Leverhulme Professor of Human Evolution, University of Cambridge, UK

Dorian Fuller Professor of Archaeobotany, Institute of Archaeology, University College London, UK

Elena Garcea Researcher in Prehistory and Protohistory, Università degli Studi di Cassino, Italy

John Giblin Lecturer in Heritage and Tourism, University of Western Sydney, Australia

Diane Gifford-Gonzalez Professor of Anthropology, University of California Santa Cruz, USA

Olivier Gosselain Professor in the Department of History, Art and Archaeology and the Department of Social Science at the Université Libre de Bruxelles, Belgium, and Honorary Research Fellow in GAES, University of the Witwatersrand, South Africa

Detlef Gronenborn Curator, Roman-German Museum and Associate Professor of Archaeology, Johannes Gutenberg University, Mainz, Germany, and Honorary Research Fellow in GAES, University of the Witwatersrand, South Africa

Gunnar Haaland Professor Emeritus of Social Anthropology, University of Bergen, Norway

Randi Haaland Professor Emeritus of Archaeology, University of Bergen, Norway

Olivier Hanotte Professor of Genetics and Conservation, University of Nottingham, UK

Elisabeth Hildebrand Assistant Professor of Anthropology, Stony Brook University, New York, USA

Timothy Insoll Professor of Archaeology at the University of Manchester, UK

Kenneth G. Kelly Professor of Anthropology, University of South Carolina, USA

Carla Klehm Centre for Advanced Spatial Technologies, University of Texas at Austin, USA

Chapurukha Kusimba Curator of Anthropology, Field Museum, Chicago, USA

Marta Mirazon Lahr Lecturer in Biological Anthropology, University of Cambridge, UK

Paul Lane Senior Lecturer in Archaeology at the University of York, and Honorary Research Fellow in GAES, University of the Witwatersrand, South Africa

Adria LaViolette Associate Professor of Anthropology, University of Virginia, USA

Anna Leone Senior Lecturer in Archaeology, University of Durham, UK

Savino di Lernia Director of the Italian-Libyan Archaeological Mission in the Acacus and Messak, Università di Roma 'Sapienza', Italy, and Honorary Research Fellow in GAES, University of the Witwatersrand, South Africa

Alexandre Livingstone Smith Archaeologist, Royal Museum of Central Africa, Tervuren, Belgium

Marlize Lombard Associate Professor in Anthropology, University of Johannesburg, South Africa

Diane Lyons Associate Professor of Archaeology, University of Calgary, Canada

Kevin MacDonald Professor of African Archaeology, Institute of Archaeology, University College, London, UK

Scott MacEachern Professor of Anthropology, Bowdoin College, Maine, USA

Pierre de Maret Professor of Archaeology and Anthropology, Université Libre de Bruxelles, Belgium

Bertram B. B. Mapunda Professor of Archaeology and Principal, College of Arts and Social Sciences, University of Dar es Salaam, Tanzania

Peter Mitchell Professor of African Archaeology at the University of Oxford, UK and Honorary Research Fellow in GAES, University of the Witwatersrand, South Africa

J. Cameron Monroe Assistant Professor of Anthropology, University of California, Santa Cruz, USA

Farès K. Moussa Department of Archaeology, University of Edinburgh, UK

Akinwumi Ogundiran Professor of Africana Studies, Anthropology and History, University of North Carolina, USA

David W. Phillipson Professor Emeritus, Department of Archaeology and Anthropology, University of Cambridge, UK

Innocent Pikirayi Professor of Archaeology, University of Pretoria, South Africa

Chantal Radimilahy Director, Institut des Civilisations/Musée d'Art et d'Archéologie de l'Université d'Antananarivo, Madagascar

Andrew Reid Senior Lecturer in Eastern African Archaeology, Institute of Archaeology, University College London, UK

François Richard Assistant Professor of Anthropology, University of Chicago, USA

Michael Rogers Professor of Anthropology, Southern Connecticut State University, USA

Karim Sadr Head of the School of Geography, Archaeology and Environmental Studies, University of the Witwatersrand, South Africa

Mohamed Sahnouni Professor and Coordinator of the Prehistoric Technology Research Program, Centro Nacional de Investigación sobre la Evolución Humana, Burgos, Spain

Peter Schmidt Professor of Anthropology, University of Florida, Gainesville, USA

Alex Schoeman Lecturer in Archaeology, University of the Witwatersrand, South Africa

Sileshi Semaw Professor and Co-ordinator of the Prehistoric Technology Research Program, Centro Nacional de Investigación sobre la Evolución Humana, Burgos, Spain

Ian Shaw Senior Lecturer in Egyptian Archaeology, University of Liverpool, UK

Paul Sinclair Professor of African Archaeology, Uppsala University, Sweden

Benjamin W. Smith Professor of World Rock Art, University of Western Australia, Australia

Daryl Stump Honorary Research Fellow, Archaeology Department, University of York

Natalie Swanepoel Lecturer in Archaeology, University of South Africa, Pretoria, South Africa

Ibrahima Thiaw Director of the Archaeology Laboratory of the Institut Fondamental d'Afrique Noire, Dakar, Senegal

Christian Tryon Assistant Professor of Anthropology, New York University, USA

Lyn Wadley Professor Emeritus of Archaeology, University of the Witwatersrand, South Africa

Derek Welsby Assistant Keeper, Department of Egypt and The Sudan, The British Museum, London, UK

Stephanie Wynne-Jones Lecturer in Archaeology, University of York, UK

Intisar Soghayroun el-Zein Associate Professor of Archaeology, University of Khartoum, Sudan

PART I

INTRODUCTION

CHAPTER 1

INTRODUCING AFRICAN ARCHAEOLOGY

PETER MITCHELL AND PAUL LANE

INTRODUCTION

ONE hundred and forty years ago Charles Darwin (1871) identified Africa as the continent on which the human evolutionary story had begun. Several generations of archaeological and palaeoanthropological research have confirmed that his intuition was correct and have demonstrated that he was right on at least three counts: Africa (and specifically sub-Saharan Africa) was not only where the hominin lineage diverged from those leading to chimpanzees, bonobos, and gorillas, but also where both the genus *Homo* and—much more recently– our own species, *Homo sapiens*, evolved. In that triple, evolutionary sense, everyone everywhere is of African descent, and the long-term history of human populations on the African continent that archaeology and its cognate disciplines uncover is—or should be—of concern and interest to us all.

Traditionally, however, that is also where most general textbooks—and most university archaeology courses, at least outside Africa—have tended to stop, reflecting a belief, however understated, that once *Homo sapiens* successfully exited Africa the 'real' human story developed elsewhere, leaving Africa a cultural backwater, lit only by the material wealth of Pharaonic Egypt and the occasional reference to sites such as Great Zimbabwe or precolonial kingdoms like those of Benin and Ife in Nigeria. Despite its significant improvements in this regard, even Scarre's (2009) general overview *The Human Past* continues to give the more recent African past far less attention than other parts of the world (and notwithstanding an excellent survey by Graham Connah, one of African archaeology's leading practitioners and synthesizers). At a general level such imbalances ignore, or at least downplay, the incredible diversity and richness of Africa's experiments in food production, social complexity, urbanism, art, state formation, and international trade over the past 10,000 years. Moreover, they make it difficult for us to situate those experiments alongside those of human societies in the Americas, Eurasia, Australasia, and the Pacific, and to consider the reasons for the many similarities, and differences, between them. And for the inhabitants of Africa itself—and others whose ancestors only recently left, or were removed from, it—they form part of that more general nexus of neglect in which the rest of the world still too often views the continent.

In planning and editing the *Oxford Handbook of African Archaeology* we have been conscious of this background, just as we have been aware of—and indebted to—those colleagues who have attempted to synthesize the complexity of the African past before us. It is now several decades since a rival university press commissioned the *Cambridge History of Africa*, which included several continent- or region-wide syntheses of archaeological knowledge in its first two volumes (Fage 1978; Clark 1982), even if archaeology was increasingly lost sight of thereafter. The scale, indeed the ambition, of some of those contributions remains impressive, but much of what was written then, of necessity, has to be amended or re-evaluated in the light of new research and, indeed, of research techniques and strategies undreamt of in the 1960s and 1970s. The same holds true of the archaeological contributions to the *UNESCO History of Africa* (e.g. Ki-Zerbo 1981; Mokhtar 1981). More recent syntheses that have retained a commitment to comprehensiveness include those by Connah (2004), Phillipson (2005), and Barich (2010; in Italian), as well as Vogel's (1997) rather older *Encyclopedia of Precolonial Africa*. In partial contrast, the volume edited by Stahl (2005) provides a series of thorough, often provocative overviews on a selection of key topics and regions extending across the continent and from the Oldowan to the Kalahari debate and including some contributions of an avowedly theoretical character. In addition, the last decade or so has seen the publication of a number of more regionally, chronologically or thematically specific syntheses (e.g. Vernet 2000; Connah 2001; Mitchell 2002, 2005; Insoll 2003; Kusimba and Kusimba 2003; McIntosh 2005; Schmidt 2006; Huffman 2007; Willoughby 2007; Barham and Mitchell 2008), as well as single- and multi-author overviews for particular countries (e.g. Millogo et al. 2000; Vernet et al. 2000; Gado et al. 2001; Konaté and Vernet 2001; Bocoum et al. 2002; Edwards 2004; Finneran 2007; Insoll 2008; Schmidt et al. 2008; Gutierrez 2008; Gutron 2010).

The proliferation of these works is one of several signs attesting to the current vitality of African archaeology as a whole. Others include regular international, regional, and national conferences, the existence of three peer-reviewed journals dedicated to the subject at the pan-African scale, as well as others at more regional level, and the increasingly high profile of African archaeology in journals of broader, global remit. At the same time, it underlines the continued importance of attempting an overview of the subject that is spatially and temporally comprehensive, encompasses the theory and practice governing how African archaeology is undertaken, provides ready access to—and evaluation of—existing research, and indicates where future fieldwork, analysis, and thinking might profitably be directed. Whether the current *Handbook* succeeds, even in small measure, in attaining these goals is for its readers and reviewers to judge, but we have believed it to be worth the attempt. Our intention, then, has been to commission a series of chapters by colleagues working across the continent for incorporation within a volume that sets African archaeology within its theoretical, methodological, and historical context and simultaneously spans the entire history of human culture on the African continent, from the very earliest stone tools and cut-marked bones some 2.6 million years ago to the archaeologies of colonial intrusion and indigenous resistance and transformation of the 19th and 20th centuries. To do this, we have drawn upon the good will and generosity of 74 other individual authors, representing a broad cross-section of Africanist archaeologists within Africa and beyond. Together, they come from

16 countries (including six in Africa itself), reflect both more established and younger, newly emerging members of the academic community, and include 20 who are either based in Africa or, being of African descent, currently live and work in Europe and North America.

We have organised the *Handbook* into seven parts. Following this Introduction, 18 chapters in Part II (Doing African Archaeology: Theory, Method, Practice) examine how African archaeology is *done*: how did it emerge as a recognizable element within the broader discipline? What do cognate subjects, among them oral history, linguistics, and genetics, have to offer it, and archaeology them? How do archaeologists approach the study of particular topics (migration, religion, landscape, for instance) or the analysis of particular classes of material culture (metalworking, stone tools, ceramics, rock art)? And how is Africa's archaeological heritage managed, presented, and taught, and within what political context is this done? Our decision to put these chapters first reflects our conviction that to do otherwise would be to suggest that a straightforward narrative account of what happened when in Africa's past is unproblematic. It is not, and it would be wholly wrong to offer such a narrative without some sense of how it has been, and is being, constructed.

The rest of the volume then proceeds in broadly chronological sequence, beginning with Part III (Becoming Human), which addresses the archaeological, fossil, and genetic evidence for early human origins from the beginning of the hominin line and the earliest archaeological evidence to the evolution of the one surviving hominin species, *Homo sapiens*, some 200,000 years ago. Following this, Part IV (Hunters, Gatherers, and Intensifiers: The Diversity of African Foragers) considers the variation evident across time and space in the ways in which people structured their material and cognitive worlds while securing food and many necessary raw materials by exploiting a wide range of extraordinarily well-known plants and animals, all free of that close human control implied by the term 'domestication'. Nine chapters cover these issues.

With Part V (Food for Thought: The Archaeology of African Pastoralist and Farming Communities) the focus shifts to societies that took—or for the most part inherited and developed—a radically different approach to their subsistence needs, obtaining food from many different (and by no means always indigenously African) domesticated animals and plants combined together in a diversity of ways. After two initial chapters considering how such species were brought under effective human management and how the processes involved in this may be discerned by archaeologists, 11 further chapters trace the emergence and expansion of food production across North Africa and along the Nile, through the Sahel, the forest zone of West Africa, and the highlands of East Africa and, finally, across almost all of that enormous expanse of the continent that lies south of the Equator. Necessarily involved in the latter part of this story, too, are ongoing debates about the emergence of metallurgy south of the Sahara, the expansion of the Bantu languages, and a variety of experiments in agricultural intensification.

As elsewhere in the world, for many parts of Africa food production formed the social and economic basis on which more complex social formations were founded—formations that included both states and urban centres, though the enduring persistence of clan- and lineage-based societies in many parts of the continent emphasizes how far from universal the creation and expansion of states was before the 20th century. After introductory chapters considering the archaeology of precisely those communities, as well as the archaeologies of African urbanism and state formation, the remaining 15 chapters of Part VI (Power, Prestige, and Consumption: African Towns and States and their Neighbours) address the relations between town and state, elites and non-elites, states and states, and—an increasing theme—Africa and other parts of the world. That last topic is developed and extended in the final part of the *Handbook*, Part VII (African Societies and the Modern World System), which examines how African communities participated in the creation of the globalized world in which they now live. Along with the more 'obvious' contributions that consider European exploration of and settlement in parts of Africa and the impact of the Atlantic era trading systems (slaves, but not only slaves), the five chapters brought together here also address the place of Africa within the Ottoman 'world system', yet other colonial encounters (such as those between the Swahili and the Sultanate of Oman), and the archaeology of the African diaspora in the Americas.

The mandate given to the individual contributors was to produce essay-length overviews of their respective topics that would, as comprehensively as possible, indicate the current state of play within their research fields, as well as the directions along which future work might flow. With Lane taking primary responsibility for Parts II and VI and Mitchell that for Parts III, IV, V, and VII, for each chapter we initially sought an abstract and, after this had been agreed, invited authors to develop this into a full-length article. Once each chapter was submitted in draft form both of us read through it, identifying areas that might have been overlooked or that warranted development, and editing it for length and conformity to the *Handbook*'s overall style. Final versions of each chapter, revised in the light of these suggestions and of new work that had appeared in the interim, were then again edited by both of us before submission to the Press. During our editing we strove to insert cross-references between chapters wherever this seemed likely to be helpful to readers, for example by tying regional or period overviews to theoretical and methodological topics covered in Part II or by highlighting historical connections between different regions of the continent. We have also endeavoured to make sure that all the references cited are readily available for checking by those wishing to do so. For that reason, only in exceptional circumstances have we admitted references to doctoral theses or web-based sources, and we have completely excluded the citation of unpublished conference papers and abstracts or the 'grey' literature of contract archaeology.

While discussing the *Handbook*'s structure and our approach to its compilation, it may also be helpful to address briefly issues of chronology and geographical nomenclature. In all cases we have adhered to the standard English versions of place names, including those of Africa's modern nation-states (thus, Ivory Coast rather than Côte d'Ivoire, for example). To distinguish between the two Central African countries known as Congo we have employed their respective capitals as suffixes, thus Congo-Brazzaville and Congo-Kinshasa. Where appropriate, we have also discriminated between Somaliland and the remainder of the former Somalia.

Encompassing several million years, the story covered by this *Handbook* is one that archaeologists have dated using a great diversity of techniques with widely varying levels of resolution (see discussion in Barham and Mitchell 2008: 48–58). While encouraging individual contributors to note the specific dating methods involved at relevant points, we have sought to standardize the frameworks within which dates are expressed, as well as the abbreviations used for them. Thus, for the Pliocene and much of the Pleistocene authors frequently make use of 'mya' (for millions of years ago) and 'kya' (for thousands of years ago), but may also place events within the global framework of Marine Isotope Stages (MIS; Wright 2000). For periods postdating the Last Glacial Maximum and, in some cases, extending into the middle part of the Holocene, the preference is for BP, i.e. uncalibrated radiocarbon years counted back from the baseline of the radiocarbon method in AD 1950. All other dates are expressed in calendar years BC and AD, whether they reflect the calibration of radiocarbon determinations, actual calendrical dates, or estimates obtained by other means, such as oral histories or the presence in archaeological stratigraphies of datable imported goods.

Notwithstanding our best efforts and those of our colleagues, we are conscious that some omissions remain. The most obvious is undoubtedly the lack of any overview of Africa's palaeoclimatic and palaeoenvironmental history, although individual authors frequently make reference to aspects of this when contextualizing archaeological or palaeoanthropological data. Readily acknowledging the absence of any detailed discussion of these topics, we can only plead that to do justice to the diversity and complexity of that history, and of the scientific techniques employed to recover it, would require a Handbook of its own. Other gaps are more methodological or theoretical in nature: stable isotope analysis, in which one African university (Cape Town) is a world leader, features in many chapters but is not discussed on its own; the teaching of African archaeology at university level, both within Africa and beyond, undoubtedly merits much fuller examination than it could be given here; so too, the operation of contract archaeology and the frameworks governing cultural resource management, growing aspects of the discipline in many parts of the continent (cf. Arazi 2009). Turning to omissions in chronological or regional coverage, we are conscious that while Egypt's Pharaonic past rightly receives a chapter of its own, there is next to nothing here about its archaeology under Macedonian or Roman rule (for which, however, see Bowman 1996; Manning 2009), even less about its medieval Islamic architecture or archaeology (cf. Williams 2008). Other gaps reflect what are often genuine lacunae in (at least recent) fieldwork: Sierra Leone; Guinea Bissau; South Sudan; Somalia; the Darfur region of Sudan; much of the Congo Basin (but see Lanfranchi and Clist 1991 for an overview and, for recent work, in Gabon Oslisly 2001, Assoko Ndong 2002, and Clist 2006; in Equatorial Guinea Mercader and Marti 2003 and Gonzalez-Ruibal et al. 2011; and in Congo-Kinshasa Mercader 2003); Angola (but see Gutierrez 2008); and the continent's various islands and offshore archipelagos, such Sao Tomé and Principe, Cape Verde, and the Comoros (but see Mitchell 2004; Sørensen and Evans 2011). The coverage for Malawi, Zambia, and Mozambique, although rather better, is still less than that accorded to some of their neighbours. Sadly, the reason for many of the current gaps is all too often due to continuing or long-term political instability and military strife. Where this is not the case, or where such difficulties ease, just as much as where they do not exist at all, we hope that the review papers collated here may serve as a spur to future archaeological research.

We trust, too, that the *Oxford Handbook of African Archaeology* will prove to be of service to students of archaeology wishing to gain an initial acquaintance with the complexity of the African past and how it is being approached, as well as to colleagues—many of them perhaps non-Africanists—who, for purposes of teaching or research, require access to readable, thorough summaries of current archaeological knowledge about Africa and its history. As the reviews brought together here demonstrate, that history is of general interest way beyond the evolution of the hominin line or of *Homo sapiens* as a species. Current evidence strongly suggests that as well as being where modern humans evolved biologically, Africa is also where that nexus of complex cognitive skills and practices summarized by the term 'behavioural modernity' first crystallized, and at a date arguably before the effective dispersal of *H. sapiens* beyond the continent. If so, then Africa retains the longest archaeological record left by behaviourally modern humans on any continent, and one that— without imputing unnecessary stasis—encourages comparison between Pleistocene contexts and what is known, archaeologically and ethnographically, of much more recent hunter-gatherers.

Fast forwarding into the Holocene and we can identify several further themes of universal concern, several of them including instances where what happened in Africa may differ quite profoundly—and thus very informatively—from what happened elsewhere in the world. Examples include: the processes whereby many hunter-gatherers opted to change their subsistence base and shift to producing food (with multiple instances of an initial preference for pastoralism completely independently of cultivation, what Marshall and Hildebrand 2002 neatly term 'cattle before crops'); hitherto unsuspected complexity in the pathways by which cultivation was adopted, including several instances whereby initially chosen staples were eventually replaced by others; the possibility that, south of the Sahara, ferrous metallurgy arose independently of other parts of the world and without long, prior experience of metalworking in copper and bronze; the emergence of urbanism and of social complexity in the absence of hierarchically organised, coercive state apparatuses (cf. McIntosh 1999); and a growing appreciation of the significant role played by African societies in long-distance networks of trade and communication and of the role of such systems in the transformation of African societies themselves, including a previously unsuspected antiquity for connections across the Indian Ocean (Fuller et al. 2011) and an increasingly well-understood contribution to the formation of the Atlantic world and the post-Columbian Americas (Ogundiran and Falola 2007), including the latter's botanical landscape (Carney and Rosomoff 2009). Igor Kopytoff's (1987) conceptualization of African 'internal frontiers' also has much to contribute in a comparative sense to the study of other regions, and is one to which archaeologists have much to contribute in turn (e.g. Monroe and Ogundiran 2012). Other themes and emergent perspectives that are simultaneously beginning to shape the direction of archaeological research on the continent and contribute to wider debates within the discipline include such topics as landscape historical ecology (e.g. Lane 2010; Stump 2010), indigenous and postcolonial archaeologies (e.g. Schmidt 2009), the politics of heritage (e.g. Meskell 2012), and the intersections between history and archaeology (e.g. Stahl 2001; Swanepoel et al. 2008). At the same time, the richness of Africa's ethnographic record permits us to explore the meanings that people have given to material objects and the landscapes in which those objects and people existed—and often continue to exist—in particularly nuanced and subtle ways which go beyond simple mining for suitable analogies for use in the interpretation of the archaeological record of other regions of the world. While archaeological research in Africa must always have as its primary focus a responsibility for communicating its results to the populations among whom it is carried out and whose ancestors—in many cases—it studies, in all the areas that we have just identified African archaeology has much to say to the practice and theory of archaeology elsewhere in the world. Indeed, it is our contention that an African perspective is now essential to most debates of significance in world archaeology as a whole. We trust that this *Handbook* is a contribution to that realisation.

Finally, we should both like to express our deep gratitude to all those who have made this Handbook possible: our colleagues for their willingness to participate in writing it; the staff of Oxford University Press, who made its realisation possible, especially Hilary O'Shea, Taryn Das-Neves, Kizzy Richelieu-Taylor and Françoise Vrabel; our students, past and present, for stimulating us to think widely about the African past; our respective institutions; and, most importantly, our families for their forbearance and support during its gestation. Thank you.

REFERENCES

ARAZI, N. (2009). Cultural research management in Africa: challenges, dangers and opportunities. *Azania: Archaeological Research in Africa* 44: 95–106.

ASSOKONDONG, A. (2002). Synthèse des données archéologiques récentes sur le peuplement à l'Holocène de la réserve de faune de la Lopé, Gabon. *L'Anthropologie* 106: 135–58.

BARHAM, L. S., and MITCHELL, P. J. (2008). *The First Africans: African Archaeology from the Earliest Toolmakers to Most Recent Foragers*. Cambridge: Cambridge University Press.

BARICH, B. E. (2010). *Antica Africa: Alle Origini Delle Società*. Rome: 'L'Erma' di Bretschneider.

BOCOUM, H., VERNET, R., CAMARA, A., and DIOP, A. (2002). *Eléments d'Archéologie Ouest-Africaine V: Sénégal*. Saint Maur: Editions Sepia/Nouakchott: CRIAA.

BOWMAN, A. K. (1996). *Egypt After the Pharaohs 332 BC–AD 642*. London: British Museum Press.

CARNEY, J., and ROSOMOFF, R. (2009). *In the Shadow of Slavery: Africa's Botanical Legacy*. Berkeley: University of California Press.

CLARK, J. D. (ed.) (1982). *The Cambridge History of Africa*, vol. 1: *From the Earliest Times to c. 500 BC*. Cambridge: Cambridge University Press.

CLIST, B. (2006). Mise en évidence dans le nord-ouest du Gabon de la présence de l'homme au sein des forêts d'âge Holocène. *Journal of African Archaeology* 4: 143–52.

CONNAH, G. (2001). *African Civilizations: An Archaeological Perspective*. Cambridge: Cambridge University Press.

—— (2004). *Forgotten Africa: An Introduction to its Archaeology*. London: Routledge.

DARWIN, C. (1871). *The Descent of Man, and Selection in Relation to Sex*. London: John Murray.

EDWARDS, D. (2004). *The Nubian Past: An Archaeology of the Sudan*. London: Routledge.

FAGE, J. D. (ed.) (1978). *The Cambridge History of Africa*, vol. 2: *c. 500 BC–AD 1050*. Cambridge: Cambridge University Press.

FINNERAN, N. (2007). *The Archaeology of Ethiopia*. London: Routledge.

FULLER, D. Q., BOIVIN, N., HOOGERVORST, T., and ALLABY, R. (2011). Across the Indian Ocean: the prehistoric movement of plants and animals. *Antiquity* 85: 544–59.

GADO, B., MAGA, and OUMAROU, A. I. (2001). *Eléments d'Archéologie Ouest-Africaine IV: Niger*. Saint Maur: Editions Sepia/Nouakchott: CRIAA.

GONZALEZ-RUIBAL, A., PICOMELL GELABERT, L., and VALENCIANO MAÑE, A. (2011). Early Iron Age burials from Equatorial Guinea: the sites of Corisco Island. *Journal of African Archaeology* 9: 41–66.

GUTRON, C. (2010). *L'archéologie en Tunisie, XIXe–XXe Siècles: Jeux Généalogiques sur l'Antiquité*. Paris: Karthala.

GUTIERREZ, M. (2008). *Recherches Archéologiques en Angola: Préhistoire, Art Rupestre, Archéologie Funéraire*. Paris: L'Harmattan.

HUFFMAN, T. N. (2007). *Handbook to the Iron Age: The Archaeology of Pre-colonial Farming Societies in Southern Africa*. Scottsville: University of KwaZulu-Natal Press.

INSOLL, T. (2003). *The Archaeology of Islam in Sub-Saharan Africa*. Cambridge: Cambridge University Press.

—— (ed.) (2008). *Current Archaeological Research in Ghana*. Oxford: Archaeopress.

KI-ZERBO, J. (ed.) (1981). *General History of Africa*, vol. 1: *Methodology and African Prehistory*. Paris: UNESCO.

KONATÉ, D., and VERNET, R. (2001). *Éléments d'Archéologie Ouest-Africaine* II: *Mali*. Saint Maur: Editions Sepia/Nouakchott: CRIAA.

KOPYTOFF, I. (ed.) (1987). *The African Frontier: The Reproduction of Traditional African Societies*. Bloomington: Indiana University Press.

KUSIMBA, C. M., and KUSIMBA, S. B. (eds) (2003). *East African Archaeology: Foragers, Potters, Smiths and Traders*. Philadelphia: University of Pennsylvania Museum of Archaeology and Anthropology.

LANFRANCHI, R., and CLIST, B. (eds) (1991). *Aux Origines de l'Afrique Centrale*. Saint-Maur: Sépia/Libreville: Ministère de la Coopération et du Développement/Centre Culturel Français de Libreville.

LANE, P. J. (2010). Possibilities for a post-colonial archaeology in sub-Saharan Africa: indigenous and useable pasts. *World Archaeology* 43: 7–25.

MANNING, J. G. (2009). *The Last Pharaohs: Egypt under the Ptolemies, 305–30 BC*. Princeton, NJ: Princeton University Press.

MARSHALL, F., and HILDEBRAND, E. (2002). Cattle before crops: the beginnings of food production in Africa. *Journal of World Prehistory* 16: 99–143.

MCINTOSH, R. J. (2005). *Ancient Middle Niger: Urbanism and the Self-Organizing Landscape*. Cambridge: Cambridge University Press.

MCINTOSH, S. K. (1999). *Beyond Chiefdoms: Pathways to Complexity in Africa*. Cambridge: Cambridge University Press.

MERCADER, J. (2003). Foragers of the Congo: the early settlement of the Ituri forest. In J. Mercader (ed.), *Under the Canopy: The Archaeology of Tropical Rain Forests*. New Brunswick, NJ: Rutgers University Press, 93–116.

—— and MARTI, R. (2003). The Middle Stone Age occupations of Atlantic central Africa: new evidence from Equatorial Guinea and Cameroon. In J. Mercader (ed.), *Under the Canopy: The Archaeology of Tropical Rain Forests*. New Brunswick, NJ: Rutgers University Press, 64–92.

MESKELL, L. (2012). *The Nature of Heritage: The New South Africa*. London: Wiley-Blackwell.

MILLOGO, A. K., KOTE, L., and VERNET, R. (2000). *Eléments d'Archéologie Ouest-Africaine* I: *Burkina Faso*. Saint Maur: Editions Sepia/Nouakchott: CRIAA.

MITCHELL, P. J. (2002). *The Archaeology of Southern Africa*. Cambridge: Cambridge University Press.

—— (2004). Towards a comparative archaeology of Africa's islands. *Journal of African Archaeology* 2: 229–50.

—— (2005). *African Connections: Archaeological Perspectives on Africa and the Wider World*. Walnut Creek, Calif.: AltaMira.

MOKHTAR, G. (ed.) (1981). *General History of Africa*, vol. 1: *Ancient Civilizations of Africa*. Paris: UNESCO.

MONROE, J. C., and OGUNDIRAN, A. (eds) (2012). *Power and Landscape in Atlantic West Africa: Archaeological Perspectives*. Cambridge: Cambridge University Press.

OGUNDIRAN, A., and FALOLA, T. (eds) (2007). *Archaeology of Atlantic Africa and the African Diaspora*. Bloomington: Indiana University Press.

OSLISLY, R. (2001). The history of human settlement in the Middle Ogooué Valley (Gabon). In W. Weber, L. White, A. Vedder, and L. Naughton-Treves (eds), *African Rain Forest Ecology and Preservation*. London: Yale University Press, 101–18.

PHILLIPSON, D. W. (2005). *African Archaeology*. Cambridge: Cambridge University Press.

SCARRE, C. (ed.) (2009). *The Human Past*. London: Thames & Hudson.

SCHMIDT, P. R. (2006). *Historical Archaeology in Africa: Representation, Social Memory, and Oral Traditions*. Lanham, Md.: AltaMira.

——CURTIS, M. C., and TEKA, Z. (eds) (2008). *The Archaeology of Ancient Eritrea*. Trenton, NJ: Red Sea Press.

SØRENSEN, M. S. S., and EVANS, C. (2011). The challenges and potentials of archaeological heritage in Africa: Cape Verdean reflections. *African Archaeological Review* 28: 39–54.

STAHL, A. B. (2001). *Making History in Banda: Anthropological Visions of Africa's Past*. Cambridge: Cambridge University Press.

——(ed.) (2005). *African Archaeology: A Critical Introduction*. Oxford: Blackwell.

STUMP, D. (2010). Ancient and backward or long-lived and sustainable: the role of the past in debates concerning rural livelihoods and resource conservation in eastern Africa. *World Development* 38: 1251–62.

SWANEPOEL, N., ESTERHUYSEN, A. B., and BONNER, P. (eds) (2008). *Five Hundred Years Rediscovered: Southern African Precedents and Prospects*. Johannesburg: Wits University Press.

VERNET, R. (ed.) (2000). *L'Archéologie en Afrique de l'Ouest: Sahara et Sahel*. Saint-Maur: Editions Sépia/Nouakchott: CRIAA.

——NAFFE, B., and KHATTAR, M. (2000). *Eléments d'Archéologie Ouest-Africaine* III: *Mauritanie*. Saint Maur: Editions Sepia/Nouakchott: CRIAA.

VOGEL, J. O. (ed.) (1997). *Encyclopedia of Precolonial Africa: Archaeology, History, Languages, Cultures and Environments*. Walnut Creek, Calif.: AltaMira.

WILLIAMS, C. (2008). *Islamic Monuments in Cairo: The Practical Guide*. Cairo: American University in Cairo Press.

WILLOUGHBY, P. R. (2007). *The Evolution of Modern Humans in Africa: A Comprehensive Guide*. Lanham, Md.: AltaMira.

WRIGHT, J. D. (2000). Global climate change in Marine Stable Isotope records. In J. S. Noller, J. M. Sowers, and W. R. Lettis (eds), *Quaternary Geochronology: Methods and Applications*. Washington: American Geophysical Union, 427–33.

PART II

DOING AFRICAN ARCHAEOLOGY

Theory, Method, Practice

CHAPTER 2

....

ARCHAEOLOGICAL PRACTICE IN AFRICA
A Historical Perspective

....

GRAHAM CONNAH

INTRODUCTION

....

THE origins of archaeology were in Europe, so that its development in the African continent was initially shaped by European perceptions, subsequently modified by American influences. Only during the last half-century have indigenous Africans had a voice in the archaeologies of their own countries, which have nevertheless often retained approaches adopted from overseas. The practice of archaeology in Africa thus needs to be examined in terms of the underpinning concepts and operative models that have influenced the way that it has been carried out. The history of African archaeology should be understood as something more than a catalogue of discoveries and discoverers. Important though they have been, as demonstrated by the contributors to the leading synthesis on the subject (Robertshaw 1990a), they have merely been performances and actors. It has been the patterns of thought behind them that have decided who did what and where and how. Bruce Trigger demonstrated this when he called his general history of archaeology *A History of Archaeological Thought* (Trigger 1989). Given the diversity of influences that have impacted on African archaeological practice, it is the way that practitioners have thought that requires primary attention.

Two matters need to be considered at this point. First, in the discussion that follows, 'archaeological practice' is interpreted as meaning both the way that archaeological research is conducted in the field and laboratory and the way that it is written about in the publications that result. The subject thus has a presentational as well as an investigative aspect and, indeed, is inevitably judged by the published outcomes that constitute the only lasting record of its activities. Consequently, there exists a huge body of literature spread over at least two centuries and in a variety of languages. In the case of African archaeology, although accumulated over a shorter period, the volume of published material is also both large and linguistically varied. Selection is therefore essential, and inevitably the choice of what is considered relevant will be influenced by the way that writers think about the subject, which in turn will be influenced by their cultural background, education, professional experience, and socio-political views. The second matter that needs to be considered is affected by similar influences; this is the problem of how to interpret the geographical term 'Africa'. It has been argued that the concept is 'a European invention' (Mitchell 2005: 2), and Kwame Appiah (1992: 3–27) has discussed 'the invention of Africa' at some length. There has even been the practice of beheading the continent to produce 'sub-Saharan Africa', as if this constitutes the only 'true' Africa (cf. MacEachern 2007). In the present discussion, the whole of the continent is considered, even if some parts of it can be given only scant attention.

Archaeological beginnings

The earliest substantial archaeological investigations in Africa were along the lower Nile during the 19th century. These grew out of a long-standing European fascination with 'Ancient Egypt', that is to say the period of the Pharaonic dynasties (Baines and Malek 2000: 22–9). Research was dominated by the impressive architecture and the organic evidence preserved by the country's dry environment, including mummified human remains and extensive documentary records. Consequently, Egyptological scholarship inevitably required skills in philology, epigraphy, and art history, as well as archaeology (O'Connor 1990). In these circumstances, the quality of excavation and other field investigations lagged behind those in Europe, and research strategies concentrated on tombs and temples, giving less attention to settlements. It was only in the latter part of the 20th century that archaeology in Egypt began to adopt best international practice. Prior to that, Egyptology was characterized by esoteric, introverted scholarship. In the process, Ancient Egypt became regarded as part of the Mediterranean ancient world, divorced from the rest of Africa: the Pharaonic state had influenced parts of the Nile Valley to its south but received little of significance in return. Considering that it owed its very existence to an African river and that during its later history several of its pharaohs were Nubians, this was a remarkable case of intellectual myopia. In addition, in spite of the work of Flinders Petrie (Drower 1999) and Gertrude Caton-Thompson (Caton-Thompson and Gardner 1934), for a long time insufficient attention was given to the pre-literate origins of the Egyptian state and its hunter-gatherer and food-producing predecessors.

In the rest of Africa, however, it was stone-using hunter-gatherers who were the focus of early archaeological investigations. Nineteenth-century archaeologists regarded them as survivors from the past whose investigation could throw light on the earliest inhabitants of Europe. Furthermore, the application in Europe of the 'Three Age System' and the discovery of stone artefacts in South Africa at much the same time as their formal recognition in Europe in the 1850s (Deacon 1990: 40), inevitably led to the adoption in Africa of the European epochal model. Study of the African 'Stone Age' came to dominate African archaeology as it developed both in southern Africa and in other parts of the continent; not only was it relevant to European interests (albeit regarded as peripheral) but later periods in Africa were thought to be short and not worth archaeological investigation. Along with the use of the Three Age concept in Africa went the European idea of 'prehistory', which had emerged in the middle of the 19th century. In Africa, prehistory was thought to consist of the Stone Age and nothing else (Fig. 2.1). This remained a characteristic of African archaeology until the middle of the 20th century. H. Alimen's *Prehistory of Africa* (Alimen 1957) devoted only 10 out of 428 pages of text to later archaeology, and they were concerned with 'African megaliths' that were undatable, while even Desmond Clark's later *Prehistory of Africa* (Clark 1970) had only 35 pages on the subject of 'Farmers and present-day people' out of a total of 223.

Investigators of the African Stone Age were initially concerned to link it, so far as possible, with the European sequence. For example, the term 'Acheulean' was widely adopted in Africa, and the French Aurignacian was thought by some to have originated in the Maghreb (Sheppard 1990). Research became dominated by the classification of assemblages of stone artefacts, which were often collected from eroding surfaces rather than excavated from stratified deposits. Archaeology developed more quickly in South Africa than in most other parts of the continent. It was there during the 1920s that John Goodwin introduced a local typology and nomenclature for the Stone Age that was influential for a long time (Shepherd 2003), even in some other parts of the continent. Goodwin had been trained in Cambridge, however, and his classificatory model remained conceptually European. Significantly, two of Europe's leading prehistoric archaeologists of the early 20th century, the Abbé Breuil and Miles Burkitt, both visited South Africa and saw parallels with Europe in the African Stone Age (Burkitt 1928; Davis 1990). Breuil, in particular, believed that the rock art of southern Africa had ultimately 'descended from European cave-painting' (Davis 1990: 282), and his book *The White Lady of the Brandberg* included diffusionist views considered extreme even at the time (Breuil 1955).

The problem with both stone artefact assemblages and rock art in Africa was the same: there were no effective methods of dating. Nevertheless, strenuous efforts were made during the first half of the 20th century to provide a chronological framework for stone artefacts. Van Riet Lowe's work on the Vaal River terraces was one such, the Casablanca coastal sequence another (Fig. 2.2), but the most important was the East African system of 'pluvials' and 'interpluvials' that were long thought to correlate with glacial and interglacial periods in Europe. It was only at the end of the 1950s that the increasing availability of radiometric and other absolute methods began to provide an independent means of dating the African Stone Age that rendered previous attempts obsolete (Clark 1990: 190–91). However, there remained the problem of what it was that was being dated; did the stone artefact assemblages represent 'cultures', in the archaeological sense promoted by Gordon Childe in Europe, or were they better explained in terms of function or variations in raw material? Again, the European influence prevailed, so that Goodwin and van Riet Lowe (1929) entitled their book *The Stone Age Cultures of South Africa*, just as Louis Leakey (1931) called one of his books *The Stone Age Cultures of Kenya Colony*. As for rock art, whether in South Africa, the Sahara, or elsewhere, it provided important 'documents' of the past but, as they could neither be dated nor 'read' with any certainty, much of their investigation was limited to descriptive recording, relative sequencing and subjective interpretation. Once more the European influence was apparent.

There was, however, one aspect of the study of Africa's past that influenced European scholarship rather than being influenced by it. This was the first recognition of palaeontological and archaeological evidence for early hominins in Africa, evidence that eventually proved to be of world significance. The discovery of the australopithecines in South Africa during the 1920s and 1930s, although not generally accepted until the late 1940s, was of major importance.

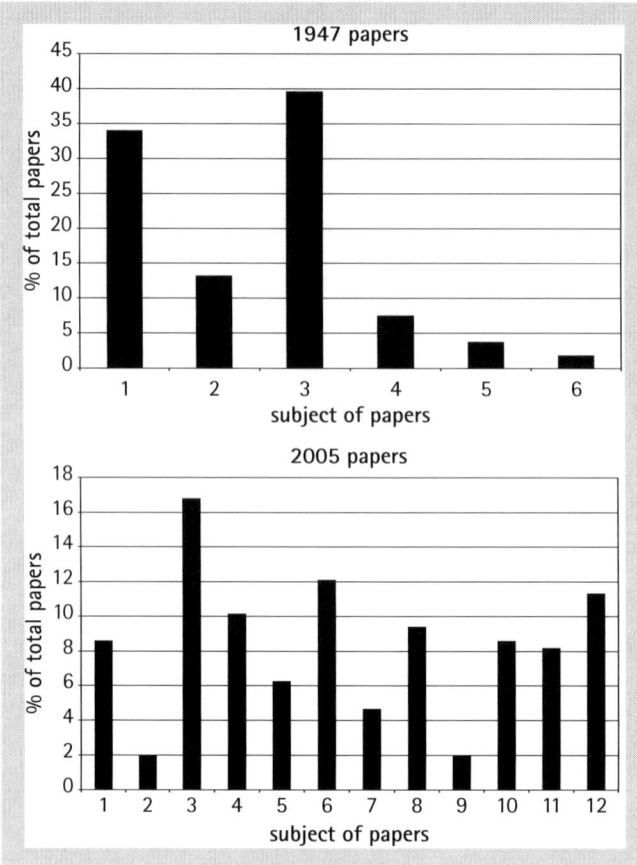

FIG. 2.1 Growth and changes in African archaeology 1947–2005: *above*, subjects of 53 papers at the 1947 Pan-African Congress on Prehistory (Nairobi); *below*, subjects of 256 papers at the 2005 Congress of the Pan-African Archaeological Association for Prehistory and Related Studies (Gaborone). Numbers for 1947 indicate: 1. Geology, general palaeontology, and climatology; 2. Human palaeontology; 3. Prehistoric archaeology (Stone Age); 4. Rock art; 5. Later archaeology; 6. Unassigned. Numbers for 2005 indicate: 1. Palaeoecology, taphonomy, and geochronology; 2. Fossil hominins; 3. Palaeolithic archaeology, hunter-gatherer communities, and Stone Age technology; 4. Later hunter-gatherer themes and transition to food production; 5. Early food production, including use of iron; 6. Development of sociopolitical complexity, also trade and contact; 7. Ethnoarchaeology; 8. Historical archaeology; 9. Archaeology and information technology; 10. Rock art and symbolic behaviour; 11. Sociopolitics of archaeology and heritage; 12. Heritage management, tourism, and development. Sources: for 1947, Leakey (1952); for 2005, Pan-African Archaeological Association for Prehistory and Related Studies (2005). Some regrouping of papers was necessary, particularly for 2005.

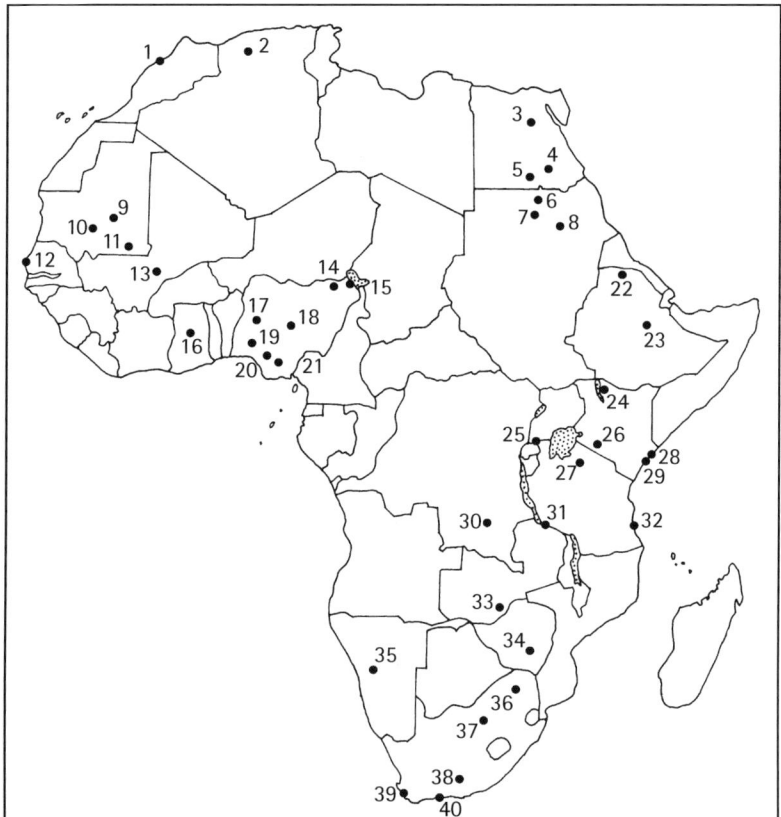

FIG. 2.2 Map of Africa showing sites, locations and areas mentioned in Chapter 2. Aksum:
22; Aswan Dam: 4; Benin City: 20; Brandberg: 35; Cape Town: 39; Casablanca: 1; Dakar: 12;
Dhar Tichitt: 9; Dufuna: 14; Gajiganna: 15; Great Zimbabwe: 34; Gwisho Hot Springs: 33;
Hadar: 23; Ife: 19; Igbo-Ukwu: 21; Interlacustrine Region: 25; Jebel Sahaba: 6; Jenné-jeno:
13; Kadero: 8; Kainji: 17; Kalambo Falls: 31; Kerma: 7; Kilwa: 32; Klasies River Mouth: 40;
Koumbi Saleh: 11; Lake Turkana: 24; Lower Nile: 3; Maghreb: 2; Makapansgat: 36; Manda:
29; Melkhoutboom: 38; Nabta Playa: 5; Olduvai: 27; Olorgesailie: 26; Shanga: 28; Taruga: 18;
Tegdaoust: 10; Upemba Depression: 30; Vaal River: 37; Volta Basin: 16.

Nevertheless, the major actors were again 'outsiders': Raymond Dart from Australia and Robert
Broom from Scotland. Both were somewhat maverick researchers, Dart particularly so
(Derricourt 2011). A hyper-diffusionist given to poorly substantiated conclusions, his most
celebrated excess was during the 1950s concerning the 'Osteodontokeratic Culture' (Dart
1957). Faunal remains from Makapansgat Cave, South Africa, were claimed on ambiguous
evidence to have been used as tools and weapons by early hominins. It is remarkable that it
was such a man who in 1925 made the first identification of an australopthithecine. Robin
Derricourt (2009a: 282) is probably justified in arguing that 'the "discovery" of *Australopithecus*
was not methodologically a scientific discovery but a fortunate stumbling on the truth'.
Whatever the case, the finding of early hominins in South Africa was of fundamental importance, because they suggested an enormous but unknown time-depth for the African past.

It was in East Africa during the 1960s, however, that the great antiquity of such evidence was eventually established. This was the achievement of Kenyan-born but Cambridge-trained Louis Leakey and his second wife, Mary Leakey, who was English. At Olduvai Gorge in Tanzania they were able to establish a stratified palaeontological and archaeological sequence some 2 million years long, containing volcanic ash that could be dated by potassium-argon. Furthermore, by excavating surfaces, the Leakeys successfully investigated the horizontal distribution of evidence relating to early hominins. This technique, pioneered by Mary Leakey at Olorgesailie in Kenya during the 1940s (Clark 1990: 198), was subsequently adopted on many early hominin sites. It led to the uncovering of what appeared to be ancient campsites and butchery sites, although some were subsequently questioned as the science of taphonomy developed. In addition, the Leakeys' son Richard, along with the South African Glynn Isaac and others, worked at various early hominin sites around Lake Turkana, in Kenya, from the 1960s onwards. Sites were also investigated in Ethiopia, of which one of the most important was Hadar, where American researcher Donald Johanson recovered the partly complete skeleton of a female *Australopithecus afarensis*, known colloquially as 'Lucy' (Johanson and Edey 1981).

The investigation of early African hominins after 1960 involved researchers from an increasingly international background, mostly external to Africa, who were usually funded from outside the continent. The quality of fieldwork, excavation, and analysis was generally high, and incorporated geological, palaeoenvironmental, chronological, and faunal evidence, as well as giving increasing attention to site-formation processes and taphonomy. Overall, their research produced a remarkable quantity of hominin fossils belonging to *Homo, Australopithecus* and other genera (Klein 2009). Typically, new discoveries were claimed to be of major importance, prominently announced in the media, and assigned to new species or even new genera. By 2005 about 7 genera and 26 species names (including subspecies) were in use. As Robin Derricourt (2009b: 193, 197) has remarked, this does 'not just reflect preferences between "lumpers" and "splitters" but nationalisms, egos and the maintenance of the image of the scientist-hero'. Subsequently, many fossils were reassigned or renamed as analyses progressed, followed by yet more claims of uniqueness for further discoveries. One of the more remarkable examples was *Tchadanthropus uxoris* (Coppens 1966), which later turned out to be a heavily eroded modern skull. It nevertheless drew attention to the possibility of early hominin discoveries outside of East and southern Africa. Significantly, since Coppens' discovery, Chad has produced two unambiguously early hominin fossils of importance (Brunet et al. 1995; Wood 2002).

Primatological research during this period also contributed to the study of early hominins. There was a long history of scientific interest in African primates (Groves 2008), but long-term detailed observations of primates in the wild were a new development. Notable examples included the work of Jane Goodall (1986) on chimpanzees, which challenged the traditional idea that humans were distinguished by the making of tools, and of Dian Fossey (1983) on gorillas, which threw light on primate social relationships. Investigations of this sort, supported by numerous laboratory studies of primate behaviour, provided a broader context for interpreting the fossil evidence of hominin evolution.

Although both palaeoanthropologists and archaeologists participated in the investigation of many early hominin sites, field practices differed to some extent from those on other Stone Age sites. In the years just before and after the Second World War a number of new researchers entered this latter field. Several made particularly significant contributions, including

Frenchman Jacques Tixier (1963) in the Maghreb, Belgian Jean de Heinzelin de Braucourt (1957) in the Belgian Congo (now Congo-Kinshasa), Englishmen Thurstan Shaw (1944) in the Gold Coast (now Ghana) and Charles McBurney (1967) in Libya, and Desmond Clark (1969, 1974, 2001), who was also English and worked in Northern Rhodesia (now Zambia) and elsewhere. The last three were Cambridge-trained, part of a trend that was to continue in African archaeology. Like others working on the African Stone Age during this period, they focused on the typology of stone artefacts and the construction of cultural stratigraphic sequences. Most remarkable were Desmond Clark's excavations at Kalambo Falls, on the border between Zambia and Tanzania, that produced a sequence commencing 300,000–400,000 years ago and continuing till the first or early second millennium AD (Phillipson 2005: 69). Excavations started in 1953, continuing for some years, and publication took from 1969 till 2001, so that this research occupied almost half a century.

INFLUENCE OF THE 'NEW ARCHAEOLOGY'

By the 1960s the 'New Archaeology' promoted in the United States and Britain had begun to affect the ideas of researchers in Africa. To some extent the Burg-Wartenstein symposium of 1965 (Bishop and Clark 1967) was a defensive reaction by those still fixated on the classification and nomenclature of stone artefact assemblages (Robertshaw 1990b: 86–7). This gathering lasted for three weeks and involved geologists and palaeontologists as well as archaeologists; these were mainly established researchers rather than those with new ideas. The symposium's terminological recommendations were influential for a while, but interest gradually faded and a nomenclature newsletter that was circulated after the symposium eventually died. As John Parkington (1993: 96) has argued, archaeologists working on the African Stone Age became less interested in 'cultural labelling' and, as dating methods improved, 'Attention could now be directed at the use of artefacts to answer behavioural questions.'

Indeed, since the 1960s there has been an increasing emphasis on the study of human behaviour and its environmental context during the African Stone Age, fuelled by a broadening both of the evidence and of the means to retrieve and investigate it. Deep-sea cores have provided information on changing climates (e.g. Weldeab et al. 2007) and established a global Marine Isotope Stage sequence that can replace the old Three Age System (Barham and Mitchell 2008). Faunal studies have become important, such as at the Klasies River Mouth excavations in South Africa (Singer and Wymer 1982) or at Nabta Playa in the Egyptian desert (Wendorf et al. 2001). Botanical evidence has received increasing attention, as at Melkhoutboom Cave, South Africa (Deacon 1976) or Dhar Tichitt, Mauritania (Neumann 2003). Similarly, pollens have been studied in order to throw light on the environments in which Stone Age people lived (e.g. Lézine and Vergnaud-Grazzini 1993). Organic evidence also includes wooden artefacts, a reminder that stone artefacts must have been used to shape many such objects that have not usually survived in archaeological contexts. At Kalambo Falls, wooden objects that had probably been worked were found in the Acheulean levels (Phillipson 2005: 71), but at Gwisho hot springs in Zambia a number of definite wooden artefacts were recovered from a Later Stone Age context (Fagan and Van

Noten 1966). Most impressive was an 8.5 m dugout canoe from Dufuna, in northeast Nigeria, found in alluvium at a depth of 5 m and dated to about 6000 cal. BC (Fig. 2.3). The oldest known boat in Africa and one of the oldest in the world, it indicates successful exploitation of aquatic resources at that time (Breunig 1996).

Other subsistence strategies of Stone Age people have also received attention, such as seasonal movements in South Africa (Parkington 2001) or molluscan exploitation in North Africa (Lubell et al. 1976). In addition, evidence of interpersonal violence has been identified, as at Jebel Sahaba in Sudan (Wendorf 1968). Furthermore, the 1966 'Man the hunter' conference and its subsequent publication (Lee and DeVore 1968) helped to focus attention on aspects of Africa's past hunter-gatherers other than stone artefacts. Subsequently, the deterministic approach of the New Archaeology's processualism began to lose favour, as many archaeologists accepted that people in the past had not been mere puppets of their environment but had repeatedly exercised choice in coping with the world around them. There was an increasing concern to understand how people had made their choices, and to seek their thoughts, symbolism, and beliefs. This cognitive emphasis formed part of archaeological approaches loosely known as post-processualism. Perhaps their most important impact was in the field of rock art studies, which had previously tended to stall. Work in southern Africa by Patricia Vinnicombe (1976) and David Lewis-Williams (1983) demonstrated that meaning could be extracted from such art by drawing on relevant ethnography. Combined with an improving chronology, these developments were to affect rock art studies worldwide.

FIG. 2.3 Many hands make light work! Recovering the dugout canoe from Dufuna, in northeastern Nigeria, found in alluvium at a depth of 5 m and dated to about 6000 BC. The oldest known boat in Africa and one of the oldest in the world, it is amongst the most significant hunter-gatherer artefacts from the continent (photograph courtesy of Peter Breunig, Johann Wolfgang Goethe Universität, Frankfurt-am-Main).

As archaeologists in Africa turned towards a broader analysis of hunter-gatherers, so the problem arose of how, why, and when they became, or were replaced by, food producers. From the 1960s onwards this was an increasingly important focus of research. Inevitably, explaining the onset of food production involved questions of indigenous development, diffusion, or even migration. The growing interest in what was often referred to as the origins of farming occurred at about the same time as a realization that the later African past did have a substantial time-depth and was worth studying. To distinguish it from the Stone Age, the unfortunate name 'Iron Age' was adopted and has continued to be used by many archaeologists, a sad relic of 19th-century thinking. Although it appeared that food production in Africa was first practised by stone-using peoples in the more northerly parts of the continent, early farming in the south seemed to be later in date and to some extent associated with the adoption of iron technology. Consequently, research concerning the earliest domesticated plants and animals in Africa concentrated on the Sahara, the Nile Valley, and adjacent areas, whereas research on early farming communities further south became associated with the expansion of Bantu-speaking peoples suggested by linguists and historians (e.g. Oliver 1966).

These developments began during the 1960s, by the end of which many European colonies in Africa had achieved independence. Political changes had an impact on archaeology—both on the identity of researchers and on the objectives of their research. In an influential paper, Bruce Trigger (1984) defined three types of world archaeology: Nationalist, Colonialist, and Imperialist. Nick Shepherd (2002) has discussed these in an African context, although he has reservations about them. Indeed, Trigger's categories are simplifications, as even he seems to have realized. Nevertheless, the history of archaeological practice in Africa is to some extent explicable in these terms. The early concentration on Stone Age studies by European scholars, who were often part of the colonial establishment in the regions that they investigated, was clearly Colonialist archaeology. Research was often more concerned with matters of relevance to analogous European evidence than with questions of importance within Africa. Furthermore, later periods were perceived as not worth investigation because colonial thinking insisted that their time-depth was limited. Nevertheless, in spite of the Colonialist label, it would be a mistake to regard such archaeologists as necessarily supportive of the regimes in which they worked; in some cases their results implicitly contributed to the demise of colonial convictions.

POST-INDEPENDENCE

With independence, Colonialist archaeology tended to be replaced by Nationalist archaeology, but the situation was often more complicated than that. Many established Africanist archaeologists of European origin continued to conduct research in newly independent African countries and, indeed, a number of new expatriate appointments were made from similar backgrounds. For example, the influence of Cambridge-trained archaeologists has already been mentioned regarding John Goodwin, Miles Burkitt, Thurstan Shaw, Charles McBurney, Desmond Clark, and Louis Leakey, to whom should be added Bernard Fagg. During the 1960s, however, a new generation of Cambridge products became involved in African archaeology, including Ray Inskeep, John Parkington, and Pat Carter in South Africa, Brian Fagan, David Phillipson, and Steve Daniels in Zambia, Merrick Posnansky in Uganda, Glynn Isaac in Kenya, Graham Connah and Robert Soper in Nigeria, and Paul Ozanne, Colin Flight, and Richard York in Ghana. In some cases these researchers later moved to other African countries or went to posts in the United States or Britain. Similarly, there were archaeologists who had been trained at other British universities, such as John Sutton, as well as archaeologists from European universities, museums, or research organizations, particularly in France and Belgium. Nevertheless, symptomatic of the end of the Colonialist period, Britain turned its back on African archaeology for several decades and offered very little employment for those with African experience. Even the Englishman Desmond Clark, the doyen of Africanist archaeologists, never held a post there.

Paradoxically, the increase in expatriate archaeologists in Africa during the 1960s was actually a product of the new Nationalist archaeology. Newly independent African governments wanted to encourage research into the past of their people, seeing this as a means of establishing a national identity that they felt had been neglected during the colonial period. In the short term few African archaeologists were available, hence the continuing involvement of outsiders. There was, however, a marked change in research objectives. In East Africa, continuing work on human origins could inspire national pride, but elsewhere stone-using people of the remote past were less relevant to modern African communities than the farming societies of the last few millennia. As a result, the domestication of plants and animals and the subsequent proliferation of food-production strategies attracted a lot of research attention. At the end of the 1960s, *The Domestication and Exploitation of Plants and Animals* (Ucko and Dimbleby 1969) contained little African subject matter, yet by 1976 a whole book could be devoted to *Origins of African Plant Domestication* (Harlan et al. 1976), and by 1984 there appeared *From Hunters to Farmers: The Causes and Consequences of Food Production in Africa* (Clark and Brandt 1984). Books on this subject have continued to appear (e.g. van der Veen 1999; Blench and MacDonald 2000; Hassan 2002).

A consequence of the growth of research in this subject has been the increasing participation of specialists other than archaeologists, such as archaeobotanists, archaeozoologists, palaeoclimatologists, geneticists, and linguists. Both they and archaeologists have been drawn from a wide variety of national backgrounds; the Blench and MacDonald book, for instance, included papers from researchers in twelve countries. There has been an internationalization of research into this aspect of Africa's past. For example, in the 1960s the American Patrick Munson (1976) conducted research at Dhar Tichitt, in Mauretania; during the 1970s Polish archaeologist Lech Krzyzaniak (1978) excavated at Kadero, Sudan; and during the 1990s German researcher Peter Breunig investigated sites around Gajiganna, in northeastern Nigeria (Breunig and Neumann 2002).

Much the same happened with another research subject that became important during the decades following independence: the investigation of African iron technology and its origins. An early excavation of relevance was by Englishman Bernard Fagg, who showed that iron smelting had been practised at Taruga, in northern Nigeria, during the late first millennium BC (Fagg 1969). Many other projects followed: Belgian archaeologist Francis van Noten (1979) investigated sites in the East African Interlacustrine Region; French archaeologist Danilo Grébénart (1988) discussed early evidence in Niger; the American Peter Schmidt (1997) conducted research in Tanzania; and Norwegian Randi Haaland (2004) carried out fieldwork in Sudan. Such investigations often included, or consisted of, re-enactments of iron smelting, when Africans who remembered former practices were encouraged by archaeologists to demonstrate how the smelting had been done. Again, participation in research projects by specialists became essential, in this case archaeometallurgists (e.g. Miller and Killick 2004). More anthropologically inclined archaeologists investigated the sociocultural and symbolic aspects of iron smelting (Bisson et al. 2000).

However, the outstanding example of internationalization in African archaeology during the 20th century occurred during rescue work in the 1960s before the construction of the Aswan High Dam in Egypt (Hassan 2007). Egyptians, Sudanese, Ghanaians, British, Germans, French, Italians, Swedes, Danes, Norwegians, Finns, Poles, Americans, and others all contributed to this massive project that continued for some years and produced literally thousands of publications. Egyptology had long appealed to scholars of many nations, and the Nubia Campaign was in some ways an extension of this attraction. Contemporary dam schemes in other parts of Africa attracted much less attention; for instance, the Volta Basin Research Project in Ghana resulted in numerous mainly small excavations but relatively little publication, and the Kainji Dam Project in Nigeria was a virtual failure (Kense 1990: 148). With the end of the Nubia Campaign, something of the international character of African archaeological research persisted, but gradually it was Imperialist archaeology that became dominant. This was because so many researchers and their funding came from the United States, although Britain, France, Germany, Canada, and some other countries played a similar role. African archaeology became a data source from which doctoral students, postdoctoral fellows, and more senior researchers from such countries could quarry material for theses and publications. Such projects usually involved only brief periods in the field, and contributed little in return to the country and its nationals that provided the subject of the research. Even the main scholarly organization of relevance, the Society of Africanist Archaeologists, was centred in North America. There were, however, notable exceptions to this general trend, the long-continued work of American researchers Susan and Roderick McIntosh in Mali and Senegal being a particularly important example (e.g. McIntosh 1998).

A third research subject that became important following African independence was the investigation of 'complex' societies, including topics such as the growth of urbanization, the formation of states, and the role of long-distance trade. Excavations at Great Zimbabwe had already demonstrated the potential of such research (Garlake 1973), but attention now turned to sites in other parts of the continent. Neville Chittick's (1974, 1984) excavations at Kilwa and Manda made major contributions to understanding the Swahili towns of the Tanzanian and Kenyan coast, as did Mark Horton's (1996) later excavations at Shanga, in Kenya. Also important was the work of Charles Bonnet (1990) at Kerma, Sudan, and of David Phillipson (2000) at Aksum, Ethiopia. On the other side of the continent, Thurstan Shaw (1970) at Igbo-Ukwu, Frank Willett (1967) in Ife, and Graham Connah (1975) in Benin City, all in Nigeria, also contributed to the investigation of social complexity, although the first two projects focused on art. To the north, in francophone West Africa, much of the relevant archaeological research was organized by the Institut Français d'Afrique Noire, in Dakar (after independence the Institut Fondamental Afrique Noire). Perhaps the most important archaeologist was Raymond Mauny (1967, 1970), whose contributions as a synthesist provided a foundation for work by others, including extensive excavations at Tegdaoust (Robert 1970) and Koumbi Saleh (Berthier 1997), both in Mauritania, and at Jenné-jeno (McIntosh 1995), in Mali. Archaeology at such urban sites often had a descriptive culture-historical emphasis, but this changed when Susan and Roderick McIntosh and others introduced a processual approach in the late 1970s (de Barros 1990; McIntosh 2005). Far to the south, Belgian archaeologists recovered extensive burial evidence of social complexity by the end of the first millennium AD, in the Upemba Depression of southeastern Congo-Kinshasa (Nenquin 1963; de Maret 1992).

Meanwhile, in southern Africa, particularly in South Africa and Southern Rhodesia, the archaeology of later periods ran into political problems. Rhodesian settlers of European origin had long insisted that Great Zimbabwe had been built by people from outside Africa, in spite of clear archaeological evidence that it was the work of the ancestors of indigenous Shona. During the period of Unilateral Independence from 1965 to 1980, the settler view was given government approval (Garlake 1982), and so serious did the matter become that two leading archaeologists who opposed the official interpretation, Roger Summers and Peter Garlake, were forced to resign their posts (Maggs 1993: 72). However, legitimate independence eventually resulted in a government to whom the indigenous origin of Great Zimbabwe was unquestionable, and the new country was named after the famous site.

Further south, in South Africa, there were also problems. Here, a long-standing obsession with the Stone Age had resulted in the neglect of what was called the 'Bantu period', which was thought to be short and of little archaeological interest. This was very convenient for the official Apartheid government view (Giblin, Ch. 19 below) that African farmers had only penetrated the southern extremity of the continent at about the same time as the arrival of the earliest Dutch settlers in the 17th century (Marks 1980). Several things changed this situation and opened up archaeological research into the last two millennia. One was the increasing availability of radiocarbon dates, which demonstrated a long tradition of farming in South Africa; other major contributions were the work of Revil Mason (1962) at the University of the Witwatersrand and of Ray Inskeep (1978), who arrived at the University of Cape Town in 1960. The latter departed for Oxford in 1972, but by then he had contributed substantially to the development of South African archaeology, particularly of its later societies (Maggs 1993; Schrire 2003).

As Apartheid dragged on through the 1960s–1980s, South African archaeologists built up a picture of the later past in their region (Fig. 2.4) that conflicted more and more with their government's view. Yet, given the prevailing repression, they understandably avoided political confrontation. It was therefore ironic that as an anti-Apartheid gesture they were excluded from a major conference in the United Kingdom in 1986, because of their tacit support of a regime that most of them found anathema (Hall 1990: 76). However, this was a complex issue concerning which many in the international archaeological community held conflicting opinions, and which led to the formation of the World Archaeological Congress when the European-based International Union of Prehistoric and Protohistoric Sciences was unable to resolve the dispute that developed (Ucko 1987). Meanwhile, by retreating into their discipline, South African archaeologists had unwittingly perpetuated Colonialist archaeology in South Africa long after it had been replaced by Nationalist archaeology in most of the continent. In South Africa this change only finally happened with the end of Apartheid in the early 1990s. Until then, archaeology remained an activity in which black South Africans played only minor roles (Shepherd 2002, 2003).

Indeed, the involvement of Africans in the archaeology of their own continent has had to overcome many problems. The earliest to be trained as archaeologists were often sent to British, European, or American universities, from which they did not always return to their own countries. Since the 1960s graduate and postgraduate study of archaeology has developed in a

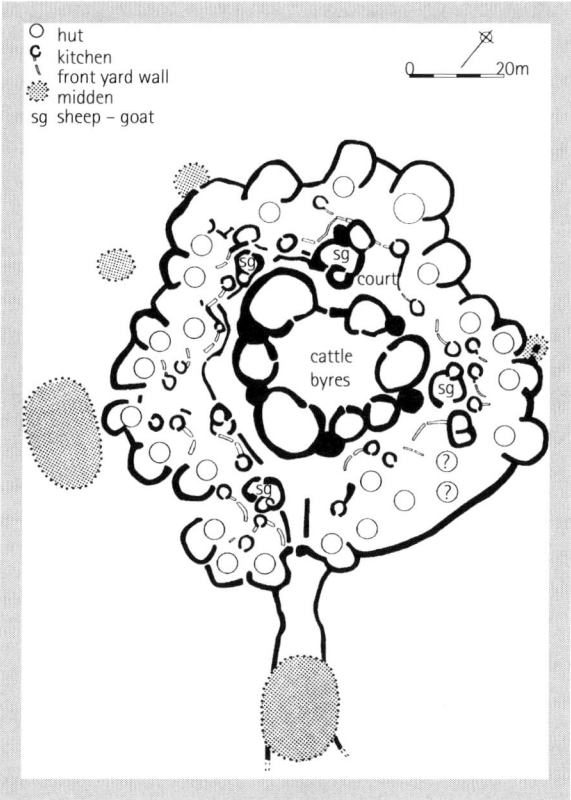

FIG. 2.4 Ground plan of the eastern unit in the stone-walled settlement at Boschoek, near Johannesburg, South Africa. Sites of this type belong approximately to the late 18th century AD, and are important because they provide substantial socioeconomic information about their former occupants (Huffman 1986: fig. 6.2) (illustration courtesy of Tom Huffman, University of the Witwatersrand, Johannesburg).

number of African universities, of which the University of Ghana, University of Ibadan, in Nigeria, Université Cheikh Anta Diop, in Senegal, University of Dar es Salaam, in Tanzania, University of Zimbabwe, University of Botswana, and the Universities of the Witwatersrand and of Cape Town, both in South Africa, are amongst the best-known examples. However, their graduates have not always stayed in the discipline. More lucrative and higher-status employment with governments or the private sector has sometimes been more attractive. Senegalese archaeologist Ibrahima Thiaw (2003: 215, 216) has commented that in his society 'What archaeologists do is locally associated with people suffering mental disability' and that 'relatives and friends who visited me . . . expressed disappointment seeing me holding a trowel and covered with dirt'. Nevertheless, although archaeology has sometimes seemed alien to the African public, many people have a great interest in their own past, particularly as presented in oral traditions. There is often a political dimension to this interest, as demonstrated by the impact of Cheikh Anta Diop's insistence during the 1960s and later that Ancient Egyptians were Black Africans and that through Ancient Greece they had influenced the whole western world (Holl 1990: 302). It did not matter that archaeologists criticized this; Diop was telling other Africans what they wanted to hear and neatly turning the diffusionist views of earlier Eurocentric archaeologists on their head.

Through no fault of their own, other African archaeologists have had only limited success in commanding international attention. Their employers (universities, museums, and government departments) have frequently suffered from chronic under-funding that has crippled research, particularly field research, and severely limited academic teaching. Without adequate transport or equipment, with indifferent access to current journals and monographs, and with limited opportunities to obtain radiometric dating or attend international conferences, it is no wonder that professional archaeologists in some countries have achieved so little. The wonder is that some have achieved so much in these circumstances: Felix Chami in Tanzania, Gilbert Pwiti and Innocent Pikirayi in Zimbabwe, Simiyo Wandibba in Kenya, Bassey Andah, Edwin Okafor, and Alex Ikechukwu Okpoko in Nigeria, James Anquandah in Ghana, Alexis Adande in the Republic of Bénin, Téréba Togola in Mali; these are just a few of the African archaeologists who stayed at home and managed to do significant work in spite of all the difficulties (Posnansky 1996). It is instructive to read both an outsider's view (Shaw 1989) and an insider's view (Musonda 1990) on the state and future of archaeology in Africa at the time that they wrote. Later, Hassan (1999) took a more positive approach to the subject.

There have also been three developments that are improving the situation. The first has been the growth of cultural resource management funding in the face of development projects. Although this has had more impact in southern Africa (Deacon 1996; van Waarden 1996) than in other parts of the continent, and has inherent weaknesses (MacEachern 2001; Arazi 2009; Arazi and Thiaw, Ch. 16 below), properly handled it can produce remarkable results. An outstanding example is the Chad to Cameroon oil pipeline project that 'resulted in location and excavation of cultural remains along a 1070-kilometre transect, in part through regions of Africa where little research had previously been undertaken' (Lavachery et al. 2005: 175). The second development has been an increasing tendency for archaeological international research projects to be conducted on a collaborative basis, in which teams from overseas provide financial and technical support but involve participation by African archaeologists whose local knowledge is often so vital and who are thus able to participate in work that would otherwise be difficult for them to undertake. Such collaboration has often included opportunities for African students to complete postgraduate studies in archaeology, funded from overseas sources, of which the Urban Origins programme directed by Paul Sinclair of Uppsala University in Sweden (SAREC 1993) is an outstanding example that assisted African archaeologists in East and Central Africa and, by publishing their theses, added substantially to the archaeological literature of those areas. The third development has been the increasing availability of journals and other publications on the Internet, bringing some relief to African archaeologists working in institutions with inadequate library resources.

Partly because of African financial difficulties, poor government infrastructures, corruption, and inadequate security, the last few decades have witnessed an increasingly intensive plundering of Africa's past (Schmidt and McIntosh 1996; Shaw 1997). Both institutions and individuals in the so-called 'developed' world have discovered a passion for African antiquities, particularly art, which has driven an illegal international trade. This has developed from a long-established trade in African art, which dealt mostly with modern reproductions particularly for the tourist market (Steiner 1994). The result has been an onslaught of looting at archaeological sites in some parts of the continent and the theft of artefacts from museums in Africa, sometimes with the connivance of staff whose wages are often inadequate or not forthcoming for lengthy periods. Without doubt, the real blame for these activities lies with the ultimate purchasers and the international dealers who supply them, often with no questions asked. It is the latter who make the big profits, not those who do their bidding in the countries concerned. There has also been a shameful reluctance by some western countries to apply adequate legislative control to this activity (Kusimba and Klehm, Ch. 17 below), although the 1993 Mali–USA Bilateral Accord is an important exception (McIntosh 1996: 788–9).

Much that has been written about African archaeology in recent years has been concerned with socioeconomic and political aspects (e.g. Stahl 2004, 2005). Less attention has been given to the theoretical and methodological problems of fieldwork and consequent analysis. Many surveys and excavations have tended to be relatively small and short-term, because they were either undertaken by visiting postgraduate students with limited funds and time or carried out by indigenous archaeologists constricted by the circumstances already discussed. Except in early hominin research, there have been few research programmes on the scale of David Phillipson's (2000, Ch. 55 below) work at Aksum, in Ethiopia, or of that of Savino di Lernia and Daniela Zampetti (2008; di Lernia, Ch. 36 below) in Libya, or of Peter Breunig and his colleagues (Magnavita et al. 2009; Breunig, Ch. 38 below) in the West African Sahel. In particular, archaeologists investigating urban sites have often had to work at too small a scale (Connah 2008). Remote sensing, physical, and electronic sub-surface prospection, rigorous sampling procedures, and open-area excavation followed by statistical analysis of recovered data have needed more attention at such sites. Indeed, archaeological science needs greater application in many cases, although the situation is improving. Similarly, ethnoarchaeology would repay more consideration at many sites (MacEachern 1996; Lyons, Ch. 7 below), and linguistics should contribute increasingly to archaeological interpretation (e.g. Blench 2006; Ch. 4 below), as also will genetics (e.g. Bradley and Loftus 2000; MacEachern, Ch. 5 below) and oral traditions (Schmidt 2006; Ch. 3 below).

An aspect of African archaeology given relatively little attention until the last few decades has been so-called 'historical archaeology'. This concerns the archaeological investigation of places and periods for which written documentation exists, although oral tradition has been treated as also relevant (Schmidt 1978, 2006). Given the variability in time and space of the boundary between 'prehistory' and 'history' in Africa, it is doubtful if the concept of historical archaeology is appropriate in this context (Connah 2007). Certainly it can mean different things to different researchers (Reid and Lane 2004). In practice, however, historical archaeology has been mainly concerned with European–African contact over the last five centuries or more, and it is therefore no surprise that it has had more attention in South Africa than elsewhere (Hall 1993). In other parts of Africa there has been less activity (although see DeCorse 1997; Horton 1997; Wesler 1998; Part VII below) and, not surprisingly, African archaeologists have been less interested in the material evidence of colonialism and other European activity in their continent than have colleagues from Europe and America. A part of historical archaeology that particularly deserves more attention is maritime archaeology (Werz 1997; Breen, Ch. 15 below), although it makes demands on funding and expertise that can be difficult to meet.

Conclusion

Much of African archaeology has been characterized by particularism; syntheses, especially at a continental level, have been relatively rare (e.g. Phillipson 2005; Stahl 2005). Even studies dealing with large parts of the continent are not that common (e.g. Connah 2001; Mitchell 2005), although areas of lesser size have received more attention (e.g. Pikirayi 2001; Mitchell 2002; Schmidt et al. 2008). At such levels, problems that plague much of African archaeological thought become particularly apparent. The Eurocentric 19th-century Three Age System and the associated concept of prehistory continue to characterize much analytical and interpretive writing. In spite of attempts to see the African past in different ways (e.g. Phillipson 1985; Barham and Mitchell 2008) and the expression of doubts about the prevailing static approach (Connah 1998: 5–6), these outmoded ideas remain current in many places. For instance, a 'total history' of Borno in northeast Nigeria (Connah 1981, 2009) was ignored by later researchers who preferred to see that part of Africa's past in traditional European terms (Breunig and Neumann 2002). Clearly, the practice of African archaeology is still haunted by its own past, and a new imaginative *African* approach is very much needed for the 21st century.

References

ALIMEN, H. (1957). *The Prehistory of Africa*. Translated by A. H. Brodrick from 1955 French edn. London: Hutchinson.

APPIAH, K. A. (1992). *In My Father's House: Africa in the Philosophy of Culture*. New York: Oxford University Press.

ARAZI, N. (2009). Cultural research management in Africa: challenges, dangers and opportunities. *Azania: Archaeological Research in Africa* 44(1): 95–106.

BAINES, J., and MALEK, J. (2000). *Cultural Atlas of Ancient Egypt*, revised edn. New York: Checkmark Books.

BARHAM, L., and MITCHELL, P. (2008). *The First Africans: African Archaeology from the Earliest Tool Makers to Most Recent Foragers*. Cambridge: Cambridge University Press.

BERTHIER, S. (1997). *Recherches Archéologiques sur la Capitale de l'Empire de Ghana*. Oxford: Archaeopress.

BISHOP, W. W., and CLARK, J. D. (eds) (1967). *Background to Evolution in Africa*. Chicago: University of Chicago Press.

BISSON, M. S., CHILDS, S. T., DE BARROS, P., and HOLL, A. F. C. (2000). *Ancient African Metallurgy: The Sociocultural Context*. Walnut Creek, Calif.: AltaMira.

BLENCH, R. M. (2006). *Archaeology, Language, and the African Past*. Lanham, Md.: AltaMira.

—— and MACDONALD, K. C. (eds) (2000). *The Origins and Development of African Livestock: Archaeology, Genetics, Linguistics and Ethnography*. London: UCL Press.

BONNET, C. (ed.) (1990). *Kerma, Royaume de Nubie*. Geneva: Mission Archéologique de l'Université de Genève au Soudan.

BRADLEY, D. G., and LOFTUS, R. (2000). Two Eves for taurus? Bovine mitochondrial DNA and African cattle domestication. In Blench and MacDonald (2000: 244–50).

BREUIL, H. (1955). *The White Lady of the Brandberg*. The Rock Paintings of Southern Africa, vol. 1. London: Trianon Press.

BREUNIG, P. (1996). The 8000-year-old dugout canoe from Dufuna (NE Nigeria). In G. Pwiti and R. Soper (eds), *Aspects of African Archaeology: Papers from the 10th Congress of the PanAfrican Association for Prehistory and Related Studies*. Harare: University of Zimbabwe, 461–8.

—— and NEUMANN, K. (2002). From hunters and gatherers to food producers: new archaeological and archaeobotanical evidence from the West African Sahel. In F. A. Hassan (ed.), *Droughts, Food and Culture: Ecological Change and Food Security in Africa's Later Prehistory*. New York: Kluwer Academic/Plenum, 123–55.

BRUNET, M., BEAUVILAIN, A., COPPENS, Y., HEINTZ, E., MOUTAYE, A. H. E., and PILBEAM, D. (1995). The first australopithecine 2,500 kilometres west of the Rift Valley (Chad). *Nature* 378: 273–5.

BURKITT, M. C. (1928). *South Africa's Past in Stone and Paint*. Cambridge: Cambridge University Press.

CATON-THOMPSON, G., and GARDNER, E. W. (1934). *The Desert Fayum*, vols 1 and 2. London: Royal Anthropological Institute.

CHITTICK, N. (1974). *Kilwa: An Islamic Trading City on the East African Coast*, vols 1 and 2. Nairobi: British Institute in Eastern Africa.

—— (1984). *Manda: Excavations at an Island Port on the Kenya Coast*. Nairobi: British Institute in Eastern Africa.

CLARK, J. D. (1969). *Kalambo Falls Prehistoric Site*, vol. 1: *The Geology, Palaeoecology and Detailed Stratigraphy of the Excavations*. Cambridge: Cambridge University Press.

—— (1970). *The Prehistory of Africa*. London: Thames & Hudson.

—— (1974). *Kalambo Falls Prehistoric Site*, vol. 2: *The Later Prehistoric Cultures*. Cambridge: Cambridge University Press.

—— (1990). A personal memoir. In Robertshaw (1990a: 189–204).

—— (2001). *Kalambo Falls Prehistoric Site*, vol. 3: *The Earlier Cultures: Middle and Earlier Stone Age*. Cambridge: Cambridge University Press.

—— and BRANDT, S. A. (eds) (1984). *From Hunters to Farmers: The Causes and Consequences of Food Production in Africa*. Berkeley: University of California Press.

CONNAH, G. (1975). *The Archaeology of Benin: Excavations and Other Researches in and around Benin City, Nigeria*. Oxford: Oxford University Press.

—— (1981). *Three Thousand Years in Africa: Man and His Environment in the Lake Chad Region of Nigeria*. Cambridge: Cambridge University Press.

—— (1998). Static image: dynamic reality. In G. Connah (ed.), *Transformations in Africa: Essays on Africa's Later Past*. London: Leicester University Press, 1–13.

—— (2001). *African Civilizations: An Archaeological Perspective*, 2nd edn. Cambridge: Cambridge University Press.

—— (2007). Historical archaeology in Africa: an appropriate concept? *African Archaeological Review* 24(1/2): 35–40.

—— (2008). Urbanism and the archaeological visibility of African complex societies. *Journal of African Archaeology* 6(2): 233–41.

—— (2009). *Three Thousand Years in Africa: Man and His Environment in the Lake Chad Region of Nigeria*. Paperback reprint, Cambridge: Cambridge University Press.

COPPENS, Y. (1966). An early hominid from Chad. *Current Anthropology* 7(5): 584–5.

DART, R. A. (1957). *The Osteodontokeratic Culture of Australopithecus prometheus*. Pretoria: Transvaal Museum.

DAVIS, W. (1990). The study of rock art in Africa. In Robertshaw (1990a: 271–95).

DEACON, H. J. (1976). *Where Hunters Gathered: A Study of Holocene Stone Age People in the Eastern Cape*. Claremont: South African Archaeological Society.

DEACON, J. (1990). Weaving the fabric of Stone Age research in Southern Africa. In Robertshaw (1990a: 39–58).

—— (1996). Cultural resources management in South Africa: legislation and practice. In G. Pwiti and R. Soper (eds), *Aspects of African Archaeology: Papers from the 10th Congress of the PanAfrican Association for Prehistory and Related Studies*. Harare: University of Zimbabwe, 839–48.

DE BARROS, P. (1990). Changing paradigms, goals and methods in the archaeology of francophone West Africa. In Robertshaw (1990a: 155–72).

DECORSE, C. (1997). Western African historical archaeology. In J. O. Vogel (ed.), *Encyclopedia of Precolonial Africa: Archaeology, History, Languages, Cultures, and Environments*. Walnut Creek, Calif.: AltaMira, 545–9.

DE MARET, P. (1992). *Fouilles Archéologiques dans la Vallée du Haut-Lualaba, Zaïre III: Kamilamba, Kikulu et Malemba-Nkulu, 1975*. I: Textes; II: Planches. Tervuren: Musée Royal de l'Afrique Centrale.

DERRICOURT, R. (2009a). The enigma of Raymond Dart. *International Journal of African Historical Studies* 42(2): 257–82.

—— (2009b). Patenting hominins: taxonomies, fossils and egos. *Critique of Anthropology* 29(2): 193–204.

—— (2011). *Inventing Africa: History, Archaeology and Ideas*. London: Pluto Press.

DI LERNIA, S., and ZAMPETTI, D. (eds) (2008). *La Memoria dell'Arte: le Pitture Rupestri dell'Acacus tra passato e futuro*. Florence: All'Insegna del Giglio.

DROWER, M. S. (1999). Sir William Matthew Flinders Petrie. In T. Murray (ed.), *Encyclopedia of Archaeology: The Great Archaeologists*, vol. 1. Santa Barbara, Calif.: ABC-CLIO, 221–32.

FAGAN, B. M., and VAN NOTEN, F. L. (1966). Wooden implements from Late Stone Age sites at Gwisho hot-springs, Lochinvar, Zambia. *Proceedings of the Prehistoric Society*, n.s., 32: 246–61.

FAGG, B. (1969). Recent work in West Africa: new light on the Nok Culture. *World Archaeology* 1(1): 41–50.

FOSSEY, D. (1983). *Gorillas in the Mist*. Boston, Mass.: Houghton Mifflin.

GARLAKE, P. S. (1973). *Great Zimbabwe*. London: Thames & Hudson.

—— (1982). Prehistory and ideology in Zimbabwe. *Africa: Journal of the International African Institute* 52(3): 1–19.

GOODALL, J. (1986). *The Chimpanzees of Gombe*. Cambridge, Mass.: Harvard University Press.

GOODWIN, A. J. H., and VAN RIET LOWE, C. (1929). *The Stone Age Cultures of South Africa*. Cape Town: Annals of the South African Museum, vol. 27.

GRÉBÉNART, D. (1988). *Les Origines de la Métallurgie en Afrique Occidentale*. Paris: Éditions Errance.

GROVES, C. (2008). *Extended Family: Long Lost Cousins: A Personal Look at the History of Primatology*. Arlington, Va.: Conservation International.

HAALAND, R. (2004). Iron smelting—a vanishing tradition: ethnographic study of this craft in south-west Ethiopia. *Journal of African Archaeology* 2(1): 65–79.

HALL, M. (1990). 'Hidden history': Iron Age archaeology in southern Africa. In Robertshaw (1990a: 59–77).

—— (1993). The archaeology of colonial settlement in southern Africa. *Annual Review of Anthropology* 22: 177–200.

HARLAN, J. R., DE WET, J. M. J., and STEMLER, A. B. L. (eds) (1976). *Origins of African Plant Domestication*. The Hague: Mouton.

HASSAN, F. A. (1999). African archaeology: the call of the future. *African Affairs* 98: 393–406.

—— (ed.) (2002). *Droughts, Food and Culture: Ecological Change and Food Security in Africa's Later Prehistory*. New York: Kluwer Academic/Plenum.

—— (2007). The Aswan High Dam and the International Rescue Nubia Campaign. *African Archaeological Review* 24(3/4): 73–94.

HEINZELIN DE BRAUCOURT, J. DE (1957). *Les Fouilles d'Ishango*. Exploration du Parc National Albert, Mission J. de Heinzelin de Braucourt (1950), 2. Brussels: Institut des Parcs Nationaux du Congo Belge.

HOLL, A. (1990). West African archaeology: colonialism and nationalism. In Robertshaw (1990a: 296–308).

HORTON, M. (1996). *Shanga: The Archaeology of a Muslim Trading Community on the Coast of East Africa*. London: British Institute in Eastern Africa.

—— (1997). Eastern African historical archaeology. In J. O. Vogel (ed.), *Encyclopedia of Precolonial Africa: Archaeology, History, Languages, Cultures, and Environments*. Walnut Creek, Calif.: AltaMira, 549–54.

HUFFMAN, T. N. (1986). Iron Age settlement patterns and the origins of class distinction in southern Africa. *Advances in World Archaeology* 5: 291–338.

INSKEEP, R. R. (1978). *The Peopling of Southern Africa*. Cape Town: David Philip.

JOHANSON, D. C., and EDEY, M. E. (1981). *Lucy: The Beginnings of Humankind*. New York: Simon & Schuster.

KENSE, F. J. (1990). Archaeology in anglophone West Africa. In Robertshaw (1990a: 135–54).

KLEIN, R. G. (2009). *The Human Career: Human Biological and Cultural Origins*, 3rd edn. Chicago: University of Chicago Press.

KRZYZANIAK, L. (1978). New light on early food-production in the Central Sudan. *Journal of African History* 19(2): 159–72.

LAVACHERY, P., MACEACHERN, S., BOUIMON, T., et al. (2005). Komé to Ebomé: archaeological research for the Chad Export Project, 1999–2003. *Journal of African Archaeology* 3: 175–93.

LEAKEY, L. S. B. (1931). *The Stone Age Cultures of Kenya Colony*. Cambridge: Cambridge University Press.

—— (ed.) (1952). *Proceedings of the Pan-African Congress on Prehistory, 1947*. Oxford: Blackwell.

LEE, R. B., and DEVORE, I. (eds) (1968). *Man the Hunter*. Chicago: Aldine.

LEWIS-WILLIAMS, J. D. (1983). *The Rock Art of Southern Africa*. Cambridge: Cambridge University Press.

LÉZINE, A.-M., and VERGNAUD-GRAZZINI, C. (1993). Evidence of forest extension in West Africa since 22,000 BP: a pollen record from the eastern tropical Atlantic. *Quaternary Science Reviews* 12: 203–10.

LUBELL, D., HASSAN, F. A., GAUTIER, A., and BALLAIS, J.-L. (1976). The Capsian escargotières. *Science* 191: 910–20.

MACEACHERN, S. (1996). Foreign countries: the development of ethnoarchaeology in sub-Saharan Africa. *Journal of World Prehistory* 10(3): 243–304.

—— (2001). Cultural resource management and Africanist archaeology. *Antiquity* 75: 866–71.

—— (2007). Where in Africa does Africa start? Identity, genetics and African Studies from the Sahara to Darfur. *Journal of Social Archaeology* 7(3): 393–412.

MAGGS, T. (1993). Three decades of Iron Age research in South Africa: some personal reflections. *South African Archaeological Bulletin* 48: 70–76.

MAGNAVITA, S., KOTÉ, L., BREUNIG, P., and IDÉ, O. A. (eds) (2009). *Crossroads/Carrefour Sahel: Cultural and Technological Developments in First Millennium BC/AD West Africa.* Frankfurt am Main: Africa Magna Verlag.

MARKS, S. (1980). The myth of the empty land. *History Today* 30(1): 7–12.

MASON, R. (1962). *Prehistory of the Transvaal: A Record of Human Activity.* Johannesburg: Witwatersrand University Press.

MAUNY, R. (1967). *Tableau Géographique de l'Ouest Africain au Moyen Âge: d'Après les Sources écrites, la Tradition et l'Archéologie.* (Mémoires de l'Institut Français d'Afrique Noire 61, 1961.) Amsterdam: Swets & Zeitlinger.

—— (1970). *Les Siècles Obscurs de l'Afrique Noire: Histoire et Archéologie.* Paris : Fayard.

MCBURNEY, C. B. M. (1967). *The Haua Fteah (Cyrenaica) and the Stone Age of the South-East Mediterranean.* Cambridge: Cambridge University Press.

MCINTOSH, R. J. (1996). Two shield Mali's past. In G. Pwiti and R. Soper (eds), *Aspects of African Archaeology: Papers from the 10th Congress of the PanAfrican Association for Prehistory and Related Studies.* Harare: University of Zimbabwe, 787–93.

—— (1998). *The Peoples of the Middle Niger: The Island of Gold.* Oxford: Blackwell.

—— (2005). *Ancient Middle Niger: Urbanism and the Self-Organizing Landscape.* Cambridge: Cambridge University Press.

MCIINTOSH, S. K. (ed.) (1995). *Excavations at Jenné-jeno, Hambarketolo, and Kaniana (Inland Niger Delta, Mali): The 1981 Season.* Berkeley: University of California Press.

MILLER, D., and KILLICK, D. (2004). Slag identification at southern African archaeological sites. *Journal of African Archaeology* 2(1): 23–47.

MITCHELL, P. (2002). *The Archaeology of Southern Africa.* Cambridge: Cambridge University Press.

—— (2005). *African Connections: An Archaeological Perspective on Africa and the Wider World.* Walnut Creek, Calif.: AltaMira.

MUNSON, P. J. (1976). Archaeological data on the origins of cultivation in the southwestern Sahara and their implications for West Africa. In J. R. Harlan, J. M. J. de Wet, and A. B. L. Stemler (eds), *Origins of African Plant Domestication.* The Hague: Mouton, 187–209.

MUSONDA, F. B. (1990). African archaeology: looking forward. *African Archaeological Review* 8: 3–22.

NENQUIN, J. (1963). *Excavations at Sanga, 1957: The Protohistoric Necropolis.* Tervuren: Musée Royal de l'Afrique Centrale.

NEUMANN, K. (2003). The late emergence of agriculture in sub-Saharan Africa: archaeobotanical evidence and ecological considerations. In K. Neumann, A. Butler, and S. Kahlheber (eds), *Food, Fuel and Fields: Progress in African Archaeobotany.* Cologne: Heinrich-Barth-Institut, 71–92.

O'CONNOR, D. (1990). Egyptology and archaeology: an African perspective. In Robertshaw (1990a: 236–51).

OLIVER, R. (1966). The problem of the Bantu expansion. *Journal of African History* 7(3): 361–76.

PAN-AFRICAN ARCHAEOLOGICAL ASSOCIATION FOR PREHISTORY AND RELATED STUDIES (2005). Unpublished programme for the 12th Congress, Gaborone, Botswana.

PARKINGTON, J. (1993). The neglected alternative: historical narrative rather than cultural labelling. *South African Archaeological Bulletin* 48: 94–7.

—— (2001). Mobility, seasonality and southern African hunter-gatherers. *South African Archaeological Bulletin* 56: 1–7.

PHILLIPSON, D. W. (1985). *African Archaeology.* Cambridge: Cambridge University Press.

—— (2000). *Archaeology at Aksum, Ethiopia, 1993–7*, vols 1 and 2. London: British Institute in Eastern Africa.

—— (2005). *African Archaeology*, 3rd edn. Cambridge: Cambridge University Press.

PIKIRAYI, I. (2001). *The Zimbabwe Culture: Origins and Decline in Southern Zambezian States.* Walnut Creek, Calif.: AltaMira.

POSNANSKY, M. (1996). Coping with collapse in the 1990s: West African museums, universities, and national patrimonies. In Schmidt and McIntosh (1996: 143–63).

REID, A. M., and LANE, P. J. (eds) (2004). *African Historical Archaeologies.* New York: Kluwer Academic/Plenum.

ROBERT, D. S. (1970). Les fouilles de Tegdaoust. *Journal of African History* 11(4): 471–93.

ROBERTSHAW, P. (ed.) (1990a). *A History of African Archaeology.* London: James Currey.

—— (1990b). The development of archaeology in East Africa. In Robertshaw (1990a: 78–94).

SAREC (1993). *Urban Origins in Eastern Africa: A SAREC-supported Archaeological Research Programme in Eastern Africa.* Stockholm: Swedish Agency for Research Cooperation with Developing Countries.

SCHMIDT, P. R. (1978). *Historical Archaeology: A Structural Approach in an African Culture.* Westport, Conn.: Greenwood.

—— (1997). *Iron Technology in East Africa: Symbolism, Science, and Archaeology.* Bloomington: Indiana University Press.

—— (2006). *Historical Archaeology in Africa: Representation, Social Memory, and Oral Traditions.* Lanham, Md.: AltaMira.

—— CURTIS, M. C., and TEKA, Z. (eds) (2008). *The Archaeology of Ancient Eritrea.* Trenton, NJ: Red Sea Press.

—— and MCINTOSH, R. J. (eds) (1996). *Plundering Africa's Past.* Bloomington: Indiana University Press.

SCHRIRE, C. (2003). Raymond Robert Inskeep. *South African Archaeological Bulletin* 58: 100–102.

SHAW, C. T. (1944). Report on excavations carried out in the cave known as 'Bosumpra' at Abetifi, Kwahu, Gold Coast Colony. *Proceedings of the Prehistoric Society*, n.s. 10: 1–67.

—— (1970). *Igbo-Ukwu: An Account of Archaeological Discoveries in Eastern Nigeria*, vols 1 and 2. London: Faber & Faber.

—— (1989). African archaeology: looking back and looking forward. *African Archaeological Review* 7: 3–31.

—— (1997). The contemporary plundering of Africa's past. *African Archaeological Review* 14(1): 1–7.

SHEPHERD, N. (2002). The politics of archaeology in Africa. *Annual Review of Anthropology* 31: 189–209.

—— (2003). State of the discipline: science, culture and identity in South African archaeology, 1870–2003. *Journal of Southern African Studies* 29(4): 823–44.

SHEPPARD, P. J. (1990). Soldiers and bureaucrats: the early history of prehistoric archaeology in the Maghreb. In Robertshaw (1990a: 173–88).

SINGER, R. J., and WYMER, J. (1982). *The Middle Stone Age at Klasies River Mouth in South Africa.* Chicago: University of Chicago Press.

STAHL, A. B. (2004). Political economic mosaics: archaeology of the last two millennia in tropical sub-Saharan Africa. *Annual Review of Anthropology* 33: 145–72.

—— (ed.) (2005). *African Archaeology: A Critical Introduction.* Oxford: Blackwell.

STEINER, C. B. (1994). *African Art in Transit.* Cambridge: Cambridge University Press.

THIAW, I. (2003). Archaeology and the public in Senegal: reflections on doing fieldwork at home. *Journal of African Archaeology* 1(2): 215–25.

TIXIER, J. (1963). Typologie de l'Épipaléolithique du Maghreb. *Mémoires du Centre de Recherches Anthropologiques, Préhistoriques et Ethnographiques* 2. Paris: Arts et Métiers Graphiques.

TRIGGER, B. G. (1984). Alternative archaeologies: nationalist, colonialist, imperialist. *Man*, n.s., 19(3): 355–70.

—— (1989). *A History of Archaeological Thought.* Cambridge: Cambridge University Press.

UCKO, P. (1987). *Academic Freedom and Apartheid: The Story of the World Archaeological Congress.* London: Duckworth.

—— and DIMBLEBY, G. W. (eds) (1969). *The Domestication and Exploitation of Plants and Animals.* London: Duckworth.

VAN DER VEEN, M. (ed.) (1999). *The Exploitation of Plant Resources in Ancient Africa.* New York: Kluwer Academic/Plenum.

VAN NOTEN, F. (1979). The Early Iron Age in the interlacustrine region: the diffusion of iron technology. *Azania* 14: 61–80.

VAN WAARDEN, C. (1996). The pre-development archaeology programme of Botswana. In G. Pwiti and R. Soper (eds), *Aspects of African Archaeology: Papers from the 10th Congress of the PanAfrican Association for Prehistory and Related Studies.* Harare: University of Zimbabwe, 829–36.

VINNICOMBE, P. (1976). *People of the Eland: Rock Paintings of the Drakensberg Bushmen as a Reflection of their Life and Thought.* Pietermaritzburg: University of Natal Press.

WELDEAB, S., LEA, D. W., SCHNEIDER, R. R., and ANDERSEN, N. (2007). 155,000 years of West African monsoon and ocean thermal evolution. *Science* 316: 1303–7.

WENDORF, F. (1968). Site 117: a Nubian Final Paleolithic graveyard near Jebel Sahaba, Sudan. In F. Wendorf (ed.), *The Prehistory of Nubia*, vol. 2. Dallas, Tex.: Southern Methodist University Press, 954–95.

—— SCHILD, R., and associates (2001). *Holocene Settlement of the Egyptian Sahara*, vol. 1: *The Archaeology of Nabta Playa.* New York: Kluwer Academic/Plenum.

WERZ, B. E. J. S. (1997). Maritime archaeology. In J. O. Vogel (ed.), *Encyclopedia of Precolonial Africa: Archaeology, History, Languages, Cultures, and Environments.* Walnut Creek, Calif.: AltaMira, 558–60.

WESLER, K. W. (ed.) (1998). *Historical Archaeology in Nigeria.* Trenton, NJ: Africa World Press.

WILLETT, F. (1967). *Ife in the History of West African Sculpture.* London: Thames & Hudson.

WOOD, B. (2002). Palaeoanthropology: hominid revelations from Chad. *Nature* 418: 133–5.

CHAPTER 3

ORAL HISTORY, ORAL TRADITIONS, AND ARCHAEOLOGY

The Application of Structural Analyses

PETER SCHMIDT

SINCE historical archaeology gained a foothold in Africa during the late colonial era, the use of oral traditions and oral histories has been a hallmark of African archaeology (Schmidt 1983, 1990, 2006). Pioneering efforts by Lanning (1966) and Posnansky (1966, 1968, 1969) on the historical traditions associated with sites such as Bigo and Mubende Hill (Fig. 3.1) set the scene for an experimental approach in East Africa that complemented a burgeoning interest in histories written from local oral perspectives. Archaeologists in many other regions of Africa soon turned to oral testimonies, both traditions and direct historical accounts, to supplement and question documentary records pertaining to the African past of the last several millennia (Willet 1970; van der Merwe and Scully 1971; Sutton 1973; Andah and Okpoko 1976; Maggs 1976; Keteku 1978; Scully 1979; Wright and Kus 1979). Most attempted to verify oral accounts by using archaeological evidence (cf. Schmidt 1983), an approach that often led to ambiguous results, compelling investigators to pay greater attention to oral traditions not only as symbolic commentaries about social and political contests but also as ways to view structural change in societies over time. Several methods arose to account for such non-literal narratives about the African past, among them structural analysis.

Coeval with Lanning and Posnansky's pioneering efforts, Africanist historian Jan Vansina (1965) argued that scholars could valorize local oral traditions through a multidisciplinary approach that evaluated oral testimonies using critical comparative analyses, including archaeology. He employed Posnansky's (1968) research at an Ankole capital site, the Bweyorere palace (cf. Reid, Ch. 61 below), as an example of how oral traditions could be brought together with archaeology to sort out the significance of oral texts and affirm their historical veracity, including evidence for a destructive fire that was identified with that

FIG. 3.1 Interlacustrine East Africa, with the Bigo and Rugomora Mahe sites highlighted in Uganda and Tanzania, respectively.

discussed in the royal genealogy during the second of its four claimed occupations of the site. While this 'verification' of oral tradition produced positive results, we now know that archaeology was unable to answer many other questions about the site (Schmidt 2006). At the time, however, Vansina (1965) nevertheless enthusiastically advocated the use of archaeology to verify oral traditions, although his optimism had waned by the publication of a later landmark text, *Oral Tradition as History*, in which archaeological data play only a minor role (Vansina 1985).

In the meantime, important strides had been made by others, best exemplified perhaps by the research of Susan and Roderick McIntosh (1980, 1986) into oral traditions and archaeology in Mali. This research showed the importance of bringing multiple sources of evidence to bear upon widely accepted historical narratives and opened important insights into Mali's history by showing how European and Arab ethnohistoric accounts about the origins of the town of Jenné-jeno, fixed to the 13th century AD, were contradicted by indigenous oral traditions pointing to a much earlier genesis for this ancient community (MacDonald, Ch. 57 below). The material evidence excavated at Jenné-jeno affirmed a mid-first-millennium rise of urbanism, a finding that escaped the clichéd representations of the published litera-ture while rewriting history bolstered by material evidence. This important work, among others, fell outside Vansina's (1985) gaze when his archaeological discussions reduced com-plex studies to summaries, glossing their contributions to history-making.

At broadly the same time, Schmidt's (1978) study of Haya oral texts in northwestern Tanzania used a detailed structural exegesis of several oral traditions about both the ancient Bacwezi rulers supposed to have ruled in the Interlacustrine region and the more recent royal Hinda clan (Fig. 3.2). As one of the first Vansina-inspired systematic examinations of how oral traditions may be used with archaeology, this explored the importance of the iron tower in the Rugomora Mahe oral traditions (Fig. 3.3). This is an origin myth for iron that uses the structural outline of the Tower of Babel myth. It is a *specific* origin or aetiological myth that has borrowed a transformed Tower of Babel cliché to do its work in communicat-ing about the origins and memorializing ancient ironworking in the region. It does not relate to differences between people, an interpretive position imposed upon the Haya text by refer-ence to more universal meanings for Babel-like tales. To impose a universal interpretation, such as favoured by Vansina (1985) on the Katuruka iron tower tale, we would be left without any sense of the myth's place in the symbolic life of the Haya and other peoples of East and Central Africa, especially when such stories are explicitly associated with iron production and human reproduction. As an aetiological story that memorializes the role and antiquity

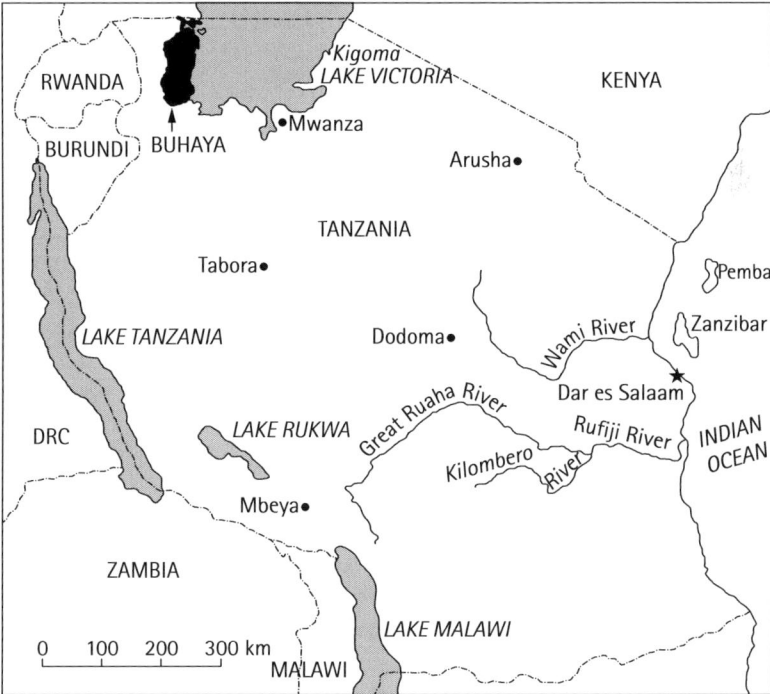

FIG. 3.2 Buhaya is located in the far northwestern corner of Tanzania, now known as Kagera Region.

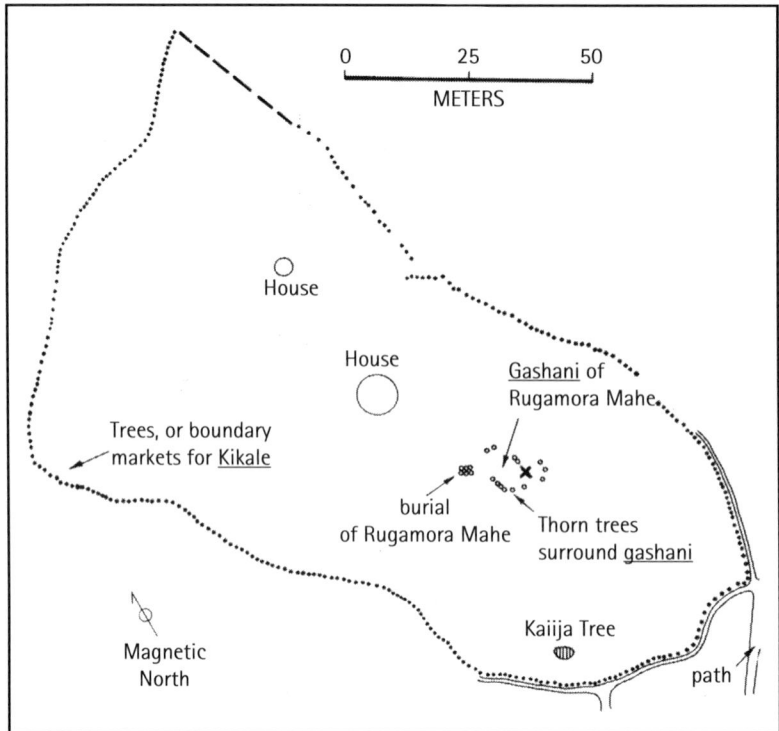

FIG. 3.3 The *kikale* or palace of Rugomora Mahe (1650–1675) is marked by his *gashani* or burial estate and the *Kaiija* shrine tree, incorporated into the precincts of the royal palace. The ancient forge was excavated just north of *Kaiija* tree.

of iron, the iron tower myth also captures the central symbolic reproductive role of iron among the Haya. For a deeper understanding of what the iron tower myth means for Haya sexual practices and human reproduction, and how these related meanings are linked to technology and history, it is instructive to review some of the history of the Katuruka research. In particular, this illustrates how more diverse ways of thinking about how aetiological myths are configured to encapsulate local histories as well as how they function as timeless principles of human reproduction, powerful tropes in symbolic armatures that confer enhanced legitimacy and power when controlled by specific social groups.

The *Kaiija* tree—the place of the iron forge—was far more than a mnemonic of great importance; it was also the focal point of identity for different social groups, among them the Hinda royal clan and the indigenous ironworking clan known as the Bayango (Fig. 3.4). Iron production and the symbolic landscape are two of the most important cultural features of Katuruka and surrounding villages. The *Kaiija* tree is linked to a local myth that says that the first Hinda king in this area, Rugomora Mahe, had his ironworkers build an iron tower to the heavens to observe Kazoba, the sun god. Before reaching the sun, the iron tower collapsed and beat upon Katerero, a village known for its ironworking and located on a ridge to the west across a swamp. This landscape is filled with place names the meanings of which are potent sexual tropes that repeat those found in ironworking—the furnace as a fertile bride

FIG. 3.4 The *Kaiija* tree (about 1970). *Kaiija* was purposefully killed during the late 1990s and early 2000s, but remains a vital place and the central feature of a heritage museum at the site (photograph, Peter Schmidt).

who gives birth to multiple foetuses (iron blooms), and iron smelters using blow pipes and bellows metaphorically referenced as phalluses and testicles.

The *Kaiija* tree is not only a very ancient monument to the genesis of iron production but is also linked with these landscape-based tropes, the most prominent of which is *katerero*— beating, beating—the rhythmic pounding of the hammer upon the forge and also the rhyth-mic beating of a penis upon a clitoris prior to sexual penetration (Schmidt 1983, 1997, 2006). To practise *katerero* during sex is to create vaginal fluid. Significantly, the stream located just below *Kaiija* (the iron tower/phallus) is named *Kiizi*, or vaginal fluid. Passing through the village of Katerero leads one to a descent into Kanyinya, or, pushing, pushing—the place of entry. Thus *Kaiija*, the iron phallus, the wellspring of human reproduction, celebrates iron production that ensures agricultural production and the reproduction of society (Fig. 3.5). These, then, are the embedded meanings held in the iron tower myth and preserved by its

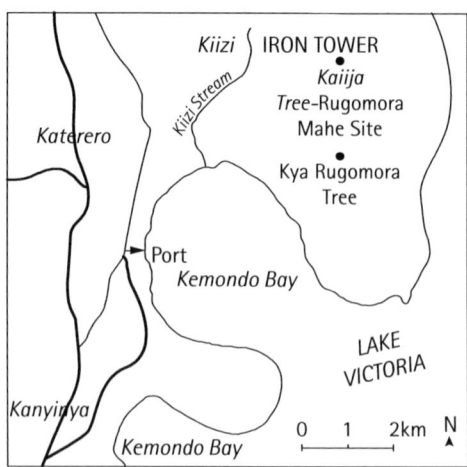

FIG. 3.5 The landscape around the *Kaiija* tree (which is paired with the Kya Rugomora shrine) is filled with symbolic meanings attached to ironworking, including the iron tower's collapse onto Katerero.

concrete mnemonic setting, a set of conditions and insights that cannot be obscured by a Tower of Babel gloss.

Contrary to what anthropological convention has maintained over the last several decades, Lévi-Strauss's development of a structuralist approach opened ways to see and better understand structural change and similarity when applied to various periods, especially when genealogically organized. By placing this study in broader comparative perspective, it should be possible to recognize reordering of cult influence and practice over time if oral traditions providing different structural readings over time are ordered by, say, genealogy. To affirm the usefulness of structural analysis in historical studies, however, contradicts the thinking of many historians and anthropologists who have (mostly correctly I believe) maintained that the structural method is arbitrary and not replicable. The chief objection is that structuralism treats myth and other oral traditions as synchronic, timeless expressions, disconnected from historical process (e.g. Barnes 1971; Leach 1966, 1970), a view shared by Vansina (1983, 1985).

The absence of a thorough and more exhaustive discussion within African history and archaeology about using structuralism for important historical insights is mystifying. Both Feierman (1974) and Atkinson (1975) in history and Schmidt (1978) in archaeology made historically profitable use of structural analysis. Feierman's (1974) treatment of the Mbegha myth among the Shambaa about the kingdom's founder (a hunter), for example, draws on structural analysis to demonstrate the affinities between the Mbegha story and an earlier myth about Sheuta, also a hunter who became chief of the Shambaa.

Feierman's analysis was a harbinger in African history in its use of structuralism to strip away mystifications and relate a tale to rites of passage and a much more ancient myth. That his method was not openly discussed in methodological debates in African history is informative. The utility of structuralism was kept under wraps, not to be taken up in a discourse about analysis of oral texts in Africa. We see a similar but more explicit treatment with Atkinson's (1975) analysis of early Buganda myth, which sorted out narrative patterns in early

Buganda mythology through structural analysis. Even though these patterns were logical and persuasive—'[Atkinson] . . . documents the full extent of the structuring'—the analysis remains unacceptable because 'Unfortunately, he interprets the contents away in structuralist fashion' (Vansina 1985: 170). This is an important moment, with the most eminent practitioner and critic of oral tradition analysis finding value in such analyses but simultaneously denying them through either silence or rejection. Perhaps such critiques cast a chill on other experimental attempts.

Nearly two decades before Vansina proffered his opinion on these innovative attempts to make sense out of oral texts, anthropologists had been examining other ways of applying structural analysis to historical and folk texts. One of the first was Hammel (1972), who argued that folk texts reflect the times, institutions, and social contests during which they were told and, sometimes, recorded. Hammel reasoned that with some diachronic control over the text, we should be able to observe important historical processes, changing values, behaviour, and struggles over institutions. Of the early experiments with structural analysis, Hammel's research into a well-known European folk tale 'The Three Bears' provides more explicit signposts for textual analysis. His treatment demonstrates how dated texts showed elaboration through time, particularly in the addition of more elaborate binary relationships—the paradigmatic elements of tales distilled from content. Hammel's innovative treatments also show how elaboration in the sequencing of tale elements—the syntagmatic component of his structural analysis—could be discerned. Thus for Hammel, elaboration and increased perfection of a text through time marked critical periods in western life, changing values, behaviour, and institutions. It would appear that the concept of increased perfection, given that it is premissed on tightly dated published texts, has little utility for African oral traditions; but rapid increases in binary elements clearly held promise as diagnostic markers for social change, particularly when different social groups hold similar evidence that is structured by genealogical ordering.

With reference to Biblical texts, Leach (1966) then asked how this essential diachrony of the traditional hermeneutic related to the synchrony of a structural analysis, and showed how structural analyses of Old Testament texts demonstrate a three-phase unit in which the same characters appear but in different costumes. Showing how myth history is consistently structured over the chronology set out by the Biblical texts, with variation and different themes such as endogamy/exogamy and Israelite/Foreigner integral to all phases of the stories, he put structural analysis to work in explaining sociological and political relations and how these reverberate in the way the texts are fabricated. Both Leach and Hammel thus developed ingenious ways to finesse the structuralist conundrum of synchronic dominance, creating instructive signposts for understanding the potentials and possibilities of such analyses for African oral texts.

When anthropologists of African oral tradition tried to apply Leach's insights to oral texts, they met the barricades erected in African history best illustrated when Willis (1976) used structural analysis to create insights into historical process among the Fipa of southwestern Tanzania. Acknowledging Feierman's influence and arguing that his analyses revealed three structurally distinct levels of traditional lore, with myth expressing cosmological symbolism as the deepest strata, Willis observed that the middle stratum of tales from three different ritual-political sources are randomized and lack the binary relationships found in the first. The third period, during which there were two centralized states, is marked by significant structural change, a change in texts manifest by the absence of symbolic elements and a regular sequencing of events, what we might consider as increased arbitrariness, thus fitting Willis's observations with those of Hammel and, later, Eva Hunt (1977). Recognizing that his construct lacked a firm chronological framework, Willis called for archaeological research to provide it, but his call failed to receive a positive response, at least from other historians (e.g. Vansina 1983: 308).

Hammel's (1972) monograph opened new possibilities for structural analyses at the same time as Atkinson and Feierman were taking up related but as yet undisclosed pathways. Drawing on these insights, Schmidt (1978) reasoned that, since genealogical ordering is highly valued by the Haya in their oral traditions concerning social groups (clans as well as larger political entities such as kingdoms), structural analysis seeking rapid expansion of binary relationships should point to significant social change. The first analysis focused on various genealogical representations by different social groups about Kiziba royal history in far northern Buhaya. Different clan histories agreed that a moment of significant social experimentation and institutional development occurred around the seventh generation of royal history. Structural analysis of these texts revealed a proliferation of binary oppositions that pointed to and affirmed the creation of a new royal cult. The paradigmatic relations arising from the content related to oppositions between expensive/cheap, white/black, dangerous/benign, Bacwezi/Bito royal, etc. A significant increase in these oppositions related to the creation of a new cult to counter the influence of Bacwezi spirit mediums who had steadfastly been opposing the throne for generations. The structural analysis stretched across many generations of oral traditions, bringing together patterns of opposition that would otherwise have gone unnoticed within the context of individual generations. Once the proliferation of symbolic oppositions arising out of new cult creation had been acknowledged, it was then easier to recognize parallel processes in the more southerly kingdom of Kyamutwara at a similar generational moment.

The second focus in structural analysis of Haya oral traditions takes inspiration from both Hammel and Leach. The large corpus of tales from different social groups in the kingdom of Greater Kyamutwara exhibits similar sequencing in the structure of the oral traditions of King Rugomora Mahe and those associated with the ancient Bacwezi. A syntagmatic analysis of the sequencing of events in some of the Rugomora stories showed a pattern that mimics some but not all of Bacwezi myth. These sequences were drawn from bits and pieces of Bacwezi myth but clearly testified to a significant complexity in the genesis of the Rugomora myth. The second analysis also examined paradigmatic relationships between the various elements in the story, revealing paradigmatic relationships that often bore significant affinities between Bacwezi myth and the Rugomora legend. Again, it was not a wholesale adoption of Bacwezi mythology but rather Bacwezi myth that structured part of the content and form of the Rugomora legend. The names of the actors were, of course, changed, along with some other details; yet without structural analysis applied to this synthesis we would have inappropriately concluded that the history of Rugomora was a bounded history relatively free of other influences.

The reasons for these changes relate to the hegemony of the Hinda royal clan being extended over territory and sacred shrines that were previously controlled by indigenous groups. The adoption of myth sequences taken directly from Bacwezi myth related to royal appropriation of the oral genres of the most powerful practitioners of religion and ritual, the *embandwa* spirit mediums of the Bacwezi. This appropriation not only helped neutralize their political influence but also created the illusion that the royal usurpers had a continuous link to the ancient past, a key constituent in their legitimacy as the new ruling group.

Decoding the Rugomora stories and their rootedness in the Bacwezi past has been closely linked to unveiling the deeper meanings associated with the iron tower myth and the geography of the tower. The iron tower myth, linked to the *Kaiija* shrine and reproductive iron symbolism, assumed a different kind of potency when archaeology revealed an ancient iron forge dating to 500 BC, directly tied to the construction of the tower, the earliest ironworking evidence found in East or Central Africa (see Chirikure and Mapunda, Chs 10 and 42 below). The Hinda royals, archaeology disclosed, took over this ancient shrine about 1675, a date congruent with royal and other clan genealogies. As Vansina (1985) observes, memory and concrete, physical place have much to do with such deep time preservation.

Lévi-Strauss (1978) also suggested drawing on archaeology as a way to solve conflicting tales, while the structural anthropologist Eva Hunt (1977) used archaeology as a metaphor in discussing how structuralism could be used together with historical texts to isolate key social change. Most useful in her analysis is her examination of arbitrariness and elaboration, both clear signposts of change such as the growth of new cults and the overthrow of institutions like priestly hierarchies. Since much African oral tradition touches upon institutional history interpenetrated by ritual and myth, the methods she proposes resonate with the goals of isolating major periods of change that may have been inscribed in the material record. As a way forward, Schmidt (1997, 2006) suggested that an analysis of tropes—symbolic language in metaphor and metonymy—will reveal moments of elaboration, particularly when texts are genealogically ordered. The most arbitrary trope (graded by its transformational effect) is metonymy (Fernandez 1977; Ricoeur 1977; Tilley 1999), often expressed in naming, e.g. 'the saxophone led the band'. When metonymy proliferates in oral texts, it signals major social realignments, i.e. 'that significant changes in the patterning of history or the abrupt rise of altered symbol systems mark periods of rapid historical change' (Schmidt 2006: 107). This can be illustrated by the renaming of indigenous ruling groups with the royal Hinda clan name—for example, the Bayango become the Hinda-Bayango. This transformation of an indigenous group (into foreign interloper) through naming is accompanied by the renaming of other social groups; for example, ironworkers became the Bahuge or 'forgetful ones' because they failed to pay proper respect to the Hinda king. These metonymies point to deeper shifts in hierarchical relationships, the displacement of powerful social groups who control the productive economy.

As an instrument of 'integrative identity' (Ricoeur 1977), metonymy depends on contiguity for its transformation programme. The saxophone—an object contiguous to the player—comes to represent the player, with the player taking on the identity of the saxophone. The unfolding of integrative identity under conditions of contiguity, a hallmark of metonymy, may also play out across space. When Rugomora Mahe incorporated the *Kaiija* shrine into the precincts of his palace, he created a relationship of contiguity in which the identity of the Hinda royals came to be characterized by the iron tower and its associated symbology. So, too, the mixing of fragments of Bacwezi mythology into Rugomora Mahe's history created a new historical syntax, a metonymic relationship of contiguity allowing Hinda history to be understood through the lens of ancient symbolic armatures tied to human reproduction and the productive economy.

Finally, an examination of ritual history reveals that the Hinda also manipulated this domain to create the illusion of legitimacy in the sea of indigenous groups. Because the Hinda were cattle keepers, they lacked the identity of ironworkers and their mystical transformational power. This conundrum was solved by the institutionalization of a ritual process at the installation of a new king when the king was made to work iron, declaring at the end of the ritual, 'I am Iron'—a metonymic process that reiterates Hinda skill at creating new relationships through contiguity and naming. Structural analysis links together these processes in different domains—mythological, ritual, geographic—to reveal a major point in Haya history, with change in all these domains signalling larger political and economic change. In this manner, then, structural analysis applied to text and landscape exposes historical processes and negotiations among social groups that would otherwise remain hidden.

A retrospective view of Lévi-Strauss's contributions to historical studies reopens more potent treatments of oral texts and promises to enrich and expand our repertoire of analytical methods appropriate to uncovering relationships to deep pasts studied by archaeologists. It is now clear that Lévi-Strauss was misunderstood, that he did not see an antimony between diachrony and synchrony, that in fact 'It should be possible to study in terms of structure the passage from one state to another in any system or society' (Gaboriau 1970: 162). Certainly those who have sought to put such a perspective into practice and derive historical insights from structural analyses—Leach, Hammel, Feierman, Atkinson, and Willis—have left us a legacy that remains hidden and unfortunately forgotten in the study of African history and archaeology. Victor Turner (1977) and others sympathetic to the use of structural analyses in historical studies would be discouraged to learn of the consequences of such strictly enforced orthodoxy at the expense of deeper understanding of historical processes.

References

ANDAH, B. W., and OKPOKO, A. (1979). Oral traditions and West African culture history: a new direction. *West African Journal of Archaeology* 9: 201–24.

ATKINSON, R. (1975). The traditions of the early kings of Buganda: myth, history and structural analysis. *History in Africa* 2: 17–58.

BARNES, J. A. (1971). Time flies like an arrow. *Man* 6: 537–52.

BELCHER, S. (2004). Myth. In P. M. Peek and K. Yankah (eds), *African Folklore: An Encyclopedia*. New York: Routledge, 280–81.

FEIERMAN, S. (1974). *The Shambaa Kingdom: A History*. Madison: University of Wisconsin Press.

FERNANDEZ, J. (1977). Edification by puzzlement. In I. Karp and C. S. Bird (eds), *Exploration in African Systems of Thought*. Washington, DC: Smithsonian Institution Press, 44–59.

HAMMEL, E. A. (1972). *The Myth of Structural Analysis: Lévi-Strauss and the Three Bears*. Reading, Mass.: Addison-Wesley.

HUNT, E. (1977). *Transformation of the Hummingbird*. Ithaca, NY: Cornell University Press.

KETEKU, E. (1978). Akwamu empire at Nyanawase: myth or reality? *Nyame Akuma* 13: 11–13.

LANNING, E. C. (1966). Excavations at Mubende Hill. *Uganda Journal* 30: 153–63.

LEACH, E. (1966). The legitimacy of Solomon: some structural aspect of Old Testament history. *European Journal of Sociology* 7: 58–101.

—— (1970). *Claude Lévi-Strauss*. New York: Viking Press.

LÉVI-STRAUSS, C. (1978). *Myth and Meaning*. New York: Shocken Books.

MAGGS, T. M. O'C. (1976). Iron Age patterns and Sotho history on the southern high veld. *World Archaeology* 7: 318–32.

MCINTOSH, S. K., and MCINTOSH, R. J. (1980). *Prehistoric Investigations in the Region of Jenne, Mali*. Oxford: British Archaeological Reports.

—— —— (1986). Recent archaeological research and dates from West Africa. *Journal of African History* 27: 423–42.

POSNANSKY, M. (1966). Kingship, archaeology, and historical myth. *Uganda Journal* 30: 1–12.

—— (1968). The excavation of an Ankole capital site at Bweyorere. *Uganda Journal* 32: 165–82.

—— (1969). Bigo bya Mugenyi. *Uganda Journal* 33: 125–50.

RICOEUR, P. (1977). *The Rule of Metaphor: Multidisciplinary Studies of the Creation of Meaning in Language*. Toronto: University of Toronto Press.

SCHMIDT, P. R. (1978). *Historical Archaeology: A Structural Approach in an African Culture*. Westport, Conn.: Greenwood Press.

—— (1983). An alternative to a strictly materialist perspective: a review of historical archaeology, ethnoarchaeology, and symbolic approaches in African archaeology. *American Antiquity* 48: 62–81.

—— (1990). Oral traditions, archaeology and history: a short reflective history. In P. Robertshaw (ed.), *A History of African Archaeology*. London: James Currey, 252–70.

—— (1997). *Iron Technology in East Africa: Symbolism, Science, and Archaeology*. Bloomington: Indiana University Press.

—— (2006). *Historical Archaeology in Africa: Representation, Social Memory, and Oral Traditions*. Lanham, Md.: AltaMira.

SCULLY, R. T. K. (1979). Nineteenth century settlement sites and related oral traditions from the Bungoma area, western Kenya. *Azania* 14: 81–96.

SUTTON, J. E. G. (1973). *The Archaeology of the Western Highlands of Kenya*. Nairobi: British Institute in Eastern Africa.

TILLEY, C. (1999). *Metaphor and Material Culture*. Oxford: Blackwell.

TURNER, V. (1977). Foreword. In E. Hunt, *Transformation of the Hummingbird*. Ithaca, NY: Cornell University Press, 7–9.

VAN DER MERWE, N. J., and SCULLY, R. T. K. (1971). The Phalaborwa story: archaeological and ethnographic investigations of a South African Iron Age group. *World Archaeology* 3: 178–96.

VAN NOTEN, F. L. (1972). *Les Tombes du Roi Cyirima Rujugira et de la Reine-Mère Nyirayuhi Kanjogera*. Tervuren: Musée Royale de l'Afrique Centrale.

VANSINA, J. (1965). *Oral Tradition: A Study in Historical Methodology*. Chicago: Aldine.

VANSINA, J. (1983) Is elegance proof? Structuralism and African history. *History in Africa* 10: 317–47.

—— (1985). *Oral Tradition as History*. Madison: University of Wisconsin Press.

WILLET, F. (1970). Archaeology. In J. O. Biobaku (ed.), *Sources of Yoruba History*. Oxford: Clarendon Press, 111–39.

WILLIS, R. G. (1976). *On Historical Reconstruction from Oral-Traditional Sources: A Structuralist Approach*. Evanston, Ill.: Northwestern University Program of African Studies.

WRIGHT, H. T., and KUS, S. (1979). An archaeological reconnaissance of ancient Imerina. In R. J. Kent (ed.), *Madagascar in History*. Albany, CA: Foundation for Malagasy Studies, 1–31.

CHAPTER 4

LANGUAGE, LINGUISTICS, AND ARCHAEOLOGY

Their Integration in the Study of African Prehistory

ROGER BLENCH

INTRODUCTION

AFRICA constitutes a mosaic of some 2,000 languages (Lewis 2013), falling into four major phyla and a few isolates. The density of languages and their patterns call for interpretation and explanation in terms of prehistory. Linguists would like to understand and model the processes responsible for the synchronic situation, and have typically turned to archaeology and, more recently, genetics. Archaeologists have been more circumspect, with many ignoring the results of linguistic research or actively opposing any conjunction of the disciplines (e.g. Eggert et al. 2006). Interest can be highly selective, for example in discussions of the Bantu expansion (de Maret, Ch. 43 below), while bypassing many other significant problems, such as the homeland and expansion of the Mande peoples (MacDonald, Ch. 57 below). This failure to explore integrated prehistory does not necessarily operate elsewhere the world: the Indo-European and Oceanic regions offer more encouraging examples of a willingness to synthesize.

Despite this, the study of African languages should have much to teach us about the continent's prehistory. Languages are spoken by peoples, and human migration is as much a fact of the past as it is visible in the present. Not only does the pattern of languages testify to these movements on a broad scale (Fig. 4.1), but embedded in the lexicon of individual languages is a complex texture of reconstructible terms relating to subsistence and loanwords that can provide rich evidence for micro-level case histories. This chapter outlines the major methodological issues around relating language to other disciplines in African prehistory, and sketches some recent case histories that illustrate these procedures.

Mediterranean

Atlantic Ocean

KEY

Austronesian

Afroasiatic

Niger-Congo

Nilo-Saharan

Khoesan

♦   Isolated Languages
     Jalaa, Laal

───   Major Rivers

      Lakes

Indian
Ocean

KWEF Graphic Services March 2012

FIG. 4.1 Outline distribution of Africa's language families.

THE GENERAL PATTERN

African languages are conventionally divided into four continental phyla: Niger-Congo, Nilo-Saharan, Afroasiatic, Khoesan, as well as Austronesian on Madagascar (Greenberg 1963; Blench 2006). Two of these have significant numbers of speakers outside Africa; Afro-Asiatic,

Table 4.1 Numbers of African languages by phylum

Phylum	Number	Source
Niger-Congo	1524	Lewis (2013)
Afroasiatic	332	Lewis (2013)*
Nilo-Saharan	198	Lewis (2013)
Khoesan	24	Lewis (2013)°
Austronesian	1 (in Africa)	Lewis (2013)
Unclassified	7	Author

* Arrived at by deducting 34 Arabic dialects from total.
° Living languages only. With extinct languages, total was c. 70.

because of the expansion of Arabic northwards and eastwards, and Austronesian, which is mainly centred in Southeast Asia and Oceania. Language numbers are distributed very unevenly across the phyla (Table 4.1). This division into phyla owes much to the work of Joseph Greenberg (1963), although there have been many changes and additions since his proposals were first set out. The coherence of the first three phyla is generally accepted, although single, authoritative sources that provide the type of proof usual in Indo-Europeanist or Austronesianist circles are lacking. Until recently, most Khoesan scholars were sceptical of the unity of Khoesan, partly because of the inadequate documentation of so many languages and partly because of the wayward transcription of clicks (Westphal 1962, 1963; Köhler 1981). However, following new research in the 1980s and a clearer perception of how sound correspondences work with clicks, most now consider that Southern African Khoesan does form a group (Traill 1986; Vossen 1997). Two languages, Kwadi and Eastern ‡Hõã, resist integration in the North/Central/South scheme now widely adopted. In both cases, poor documentation makes any final judgement provisional. Hadza and Sandawe, both spoken in Tanzania, are often assigned to Khoesan because of the presence of clicks, but evidence for joining them to Southern African Khoesan is sorely lacking.

Apart from the well-known and largely established phyla, a few African languages defy easy classification, although it is surprising that their number should be so small. In other regions with high language diversity, notably the New World, New Guinea, Australia, and Siberia, isolates are common. Assuming modern humans originated in Africa (Lahr, Ch. 23 below), there should be many more. The synchronic pattern of African language phyla must therefore reflect large-scale population movements, change, and assimilation in a relatively recent period. Table 4.2 lists those languages that remain unclassified. Except for Bangi Me, these peoples are either foragers or were so until recently, suggesting that they were marginalized communities, relics of a once more widespread network of hunter-gatherers. The broad pattern is thus of a small number of phyla expanding relatively recently and assimilating a complex mosaic of forager peoples speaking highly diverse languages.

A general problem for archaeologists attempting to make sense of linguistic hypotheses is that linguists by no means all agree. Although there is a general consensus on the four established phyla just mentioned, beyond that their internal classification and membership remain much disputed. For example, in the case of Nilo-Saharan, for example, Ehret (2001)

Table 4.2 African language isolates

Language name	Location	Source	Comments
Bangi Me	Mali	Blench (2007a)	
Hadza	Tanzania	Sands (1998)	
Jalaa (= Cuŋ Tuum)	Nigeria	Kleinwillinghöfer (2001)	Probably extinct
Kujarge	Sudan	Doornbos and Bender (1983); Lovestrand (p.c.)	Probably East Chadic
Kwadi	Angola	Westphal (1963), Güldemann (2008)	Perhaps Khoesan
Laal	Chad	Boyeldieu (1977)	
Ongota	Ethiopia	Fleming (2006), Sava and Tosco (2000)	Perhaps Afroasiatic
Oropom	Uganda	Wilson (1970)	Existence unconfirmed
Sandawe	Tanzania	Sands (1998)	Probably Khoesan

reconstructs >1,700 roots for proto-Nilo-Saharan, whereas Bender (1996) could only find around 100 (Blench 2002). Ehret includes names for cultivated plants while Bender finds none; clearly the trust placed in an individual author reflects the reader's presuppositions about the antiquity of a language family. Similarly at odds are reconstructions of Afroasiatic by Ehret (1995) and Orel and Stolbova (1995), a case where there is a fundamental dispute between those who believe it to be associated with the terminal Pleistocene Natufian culture of the Levant (e.g. Militarev 2003; cf. Bellwood 2005) and those who canvass Ethiopia and the Horn of Africa—almost certainly the correct solution, as Ethiopia is home to the greatest diversity of Afroasiatic languages. The issue here is that all types of large-scale phylum level reconstruction are highly preliminary; the type of scholarly honing characteristic of Indo-European or Austronesian has yet to be undertaken in Africa. The datasets are vast and constantly under revision. The archaeologist is probably better off regarding proposals on this scale as tools for thinking, rather than as some finished product that can be picked up and interpreted.

METHODOLOGIES

The classification of African language phyla has a wayward history, in part because of the simultaneous use of very different paradigms. Four main strategies can be distinguished (Table 4.3), but in fact they tend to slide into one another. For example, Niger-Congo is often said to be characterized by the presence of nominal affixes marking noun classes, and Greenberg (1963) used this as a major feature in assigning the Kordofanian languages to Niger-Congo. But alternating nominal affixes also occur in scattered Nilo-Saharan languages (Daju, Koman, Kadu); thus, a feature once considered an indicator of genetic affiliation turns out to be purely typological. When Doke (1945) and Guthrie (1948) first developed their classification of Bantu, it was an explicitly referential, numerical, and geographical scheme

Table 4.3 Types of classification applied to African language phyla

Category	Sense
Areal	Languages that are geographically proximate and may share features but which do not constitute evidence for genetic affiliation
Genetic	Languages that go back to a common ancestor
Referential	Systems that assign a classification purely for reference purposes
Typological	Languages that share common features (phonological, morphological, etc.) but which have no necessary genetic connection

intended to help bring order to a large number of languages the relationships of which were then unknown. Later, as Herbert and Huffman (1993) point out, Guthrie (1967–71) began referring to his numbered zones *as if* they were genetic, i.e. as if the historical relations between the alphanumeric groups had somehow been demonstrated. The Nuba Hills in Sudan represent a clear example of areal features confounding perceptions of genetic affiliation. Although their languages include both Niger-Congo and several quite different groups of Nilo-Saharan, a common lifestyle and extensive intermarriage and cultural interaction has created a zone with many areal features in common. There is thus a tendency to refer to 'Nuba Hills Languages' as if they represented a genetic unity.

Lexicostatistics is the counting of cognate words in a standardized list and assigning a numerical value to their relationship. Despite some 19th-century precursors, it was not until Swadesh (1952) that this idea made a significant impact on the scholarly community. Lexicostatistics initially proved attractive to Africanist researchers as a way of ordering a large mass of languages of uncertain relationship, with one early use of it to classify the Gur languages (Swadesh et al. 1966). Related to lexicostatistics is glottochronology, the hypothesis that languages change at a standard rate over time and that by applying an algorithm to lexicostatistical results, the approximate ages of language families can estimated. Armstrong (1964) applied glottochronological methods to estimate the time-depth of southern Nigeria's Kwa languages. Although there is a long list of sceptical evaluations of lexicostatistics, its mathematical presentation is very alluring and there have been many attempts to modernize it (e.g. Lamb and Mitchell 1991; Ehret 2002). Its most recent incarnation is the Automated Similarity Judgement Programme (AJSP) proposed by the Max Planck Institute, which eliminates human cognacy judgements (Müller et al. 2009). Although its output is somewhat idiosyncratic (e.g. linking Dogon with the Caddoan family of North America), advocates see it as a major advance in modelling language relationships. It is safe to say that, as they have virtually no empirical content, such methods will continue to be promoted by their advocates but be ignored by researchers espousing field-based approaches.

Much of the interplay between linguistics and archaeology in Africa depends upon assigning genetic affiliations to the languages under consideration. Where we place individual languages in the global mosaic of language phyla is essential to developing archaeological interpretations. The key strategy in determining genetic affiliation is the identification of shared innovations. When any new speech form develops, it is marked by innovation. Changes occur in the speech of individuals and may spread to the whole community over time. These changes can be extended by analogy to other sounds, lexemes, or clauses, according to rules internal to the language. The methodology of reconstruction is usually known as the comparative method, and has a venerable, if controversial, history (Durie and Ross 1996). The key element in the mutual interplay of historical linguistics and archaeology is the identification of reconstructible lexical items with potential links to archaeology.

Shared innovations are sets of changes that have occurred at the level of a protolanguage, and are reflected in its daughter languages, allowing linguists to assign a particular language to a genetic grouping. However, protoforms can also encode cultural information directly relevant to the reconstruction of prehistory. For example, terms for livestock species such as 'goat' or crops such as 'Bambara groundnut' can be reconstructed to proto-Bantu, and it is thus a reasonable assumption that the Bantu began their journey across the equatorial forest with these species as part of their subsistence repertoire.

A distinctive feature of the history of African language classification has been a widespread unwillingness to analyse commonalties between languages as the result of contact and borrowing, except in the case of transparent and recent loanwords. Historical linguists seek reconstructions that can be assigned to protolanguages. Shared words common to a group of languages may indicate relatedness, but may also point to the spread of new technologies or social change. How we interpret a common form exists in a feedback relationship with our historical understanding of its cultural role and chronology. We assume that people have always eaten and drunk, slept and died, and that where we find a widespread root referring to these concepts it can be used in historical reconstruction. By contrast, words for 'tobacco' in Africa all resemble one another, partly because they were adopted from contact languages when tobacco was introduced from the New World (Pasch 1980). Tracking loanwords can provide much information that is unavailable through other means. The nautical vocabulary of Swahili, for instance, shows clear evidence of borrowing from both Old Malay and Portuguese (Table 4.4), and linguistics can also be used to track the spread of introduced crops, including vegetative species that leave no archaeological trace (Blench et al. 1997; Bahuchet and Philippson 1998; Blench 2009a).

Table 4.4 Sources of Swahili nautical vocabulary

Swahili	Gloss	Source language	Source word	Gloss
sambo	ship (archaic)	Old Malay	sambaw	seagoing vessel
sapʰa	raft	Javanese	sampan	harbour boat; canoe
taliki	rope to lift cargo	Malay	tarik ~ tarek	pull, haul, drag
utari	ship's cable	Malay	tali	rope, cord, line
barakinya	schooner	Portuguese	barraquinha	
batela	small boat	Portuguese	batel	
bereu	tar	Portuguese	breu	
bunta	pontoon	Portuguese	bunta	
furutile	dock	Portuguese	flotilha	
gana	tiller	Portuguese	cana	

Sources: Martin Walsh (pers comm.), Kiraithe and Baden (1976)

As with language shift, trajectories of language change observable today clearly also occurred in the past, although they muddy the waters of conventional language diversification models. One such process is pidginization and its relative, creolization (Thomason and Kaufman 1988). The characteristic of pidgins and creoles is that they mix vocabulary, phonology, and syntax from their source languages. Earlier descriptions often characterize them as 'simplified', but this is a culturally loaded term. A language may be simplified from the point of view of speakers of a particular language, partly because they do not recognize complexity in an area that is underdeveloped in their own language. Contact languages have developed in Africa in a variety of situations, most notably for trade, as a consequence of slavery or in armies (Heine 1982), and for communication between employers and employees (Mesthrie 1989).

GENETICS, MATERIAL CULTURE, AND OTHER PARALLEL DISCIPLINES

Since the 1990s publications on the human genetics of Africa have grown substantially. An overview of African mtDNA observes that 'Africa presents the most complex genetic picture of any continent, with a time depth for mitochondrial DNA (mtDNA) lineages >100,000 years' (Salas et al. 2002), while Tishkoff et al. (2009) claim to observe strong associations between genetic and linguistic diversity, reflecting the concomitant spread of languages, genes, and culture. Sadly, the attractiveness of this congruence is unsupported by the unequal distribution and small number (N = 121) of sampling points used (Tishkoff et al. 2009: Supporting Material Map A) and by systematic omission of contrary arguments (cf. MacEachern, Ch. 5 below).

Despite this optimism, convincing large-scale correlations with archaeology and linguistics are probably still far in the future. On a smaller scale, the potential for correlations between the distribution of the Bantu languages, archaeology, and genetics would seem to be high, with Underhill et al. (2001) suggesting the haplotypes defined by M2/PN1/M180 polymorphisms as markers of that expansion. Their evidence of strong founder effects in that sub-clade (40% of the members share the M191 mutation) is independently supported by results from Y-STR haplotypes in a South African Bantu population (Thomas et al. 2000), where the proportion of YAP $^+$/sY81G lineages was 80 ± 5%, of which more than half shared the same 6 Y-STR based haplotype or its one-step neighbours. In other studies, Pereira et al. (2001) have tracked the mtDNA of Mozambican populations both within the Bantu heartland and in its outliers in the diaspora, while Beleza et al. (2005) established possible patterns of the Bantu 'western stream' focusing on a movement down the coast to Angola. Ribot (2011) has argued that the Bantu expansion can also be detected using classic osteometric techniques.

Greater knowledge of African biogeography can also increasingly be linked to the expansion of language families, especially in constrained environments such as islands or deserts. A well-known example concerns the correlation of the current distribution of Nilo-Saharan languages with archaeological finds of bone harpoons (Table 4.5) and other evidence of aquatic resource exploitation dating to the early Holocene when more plentiful rains

Table 4.5 Cognate words for 'hippopotamus' in Nilo–Saharan languages

Family	Subgroup	Language	Attestation
Central Sudanic	Sara	Nar	àbà
Gumuz		Kokit	ba a
Maba		Aiki	bùngùr
Songhay		Kaado	bà à
Songhay		Koyra Chiini	ba a

supported lakes and rivers in currently hyperarid regions (Sutton 1974; Drake et al. 2010; Barich, Ch. 31 below).

Case histories

Space does not permit detailed discussion of individual case studies, but a brief examination of a few may be useful. First, the Bantu languages, which have well-attested links, share a large number of phonological, morphological, and lexical isoglosses and certainly represent a recent expansion, generally accepted to have involved a major element of migration— 'demic diffusion' in archaeological language (Ashley, Ch. 6 below). From an origin near the Cameroon/Nigeria border, the widely accepted model has Bantu splitting into at least two groups, one heading east along the northern edge of the rainforest and the other staying in the west and moving south and southeast through the rainforest (Blench 2010b). The relatively recent date of these events has made it possible to link particular groupings with pottery styles in a manner not yet possible elsewhere in Africa (Phillipson 1977; Huffman 2007; but see Eggert 1992 for a critical approach to simplistic correspondences between pottery styles and Bantu subclassification; also Lavachery et al. 2010; de Maret, Ch. 43 below).

Both livestock and pottery appear in the southern African archaeological record prior to the arrival of the Bantu. Sadr and Sampson (2006) conclude: 'Thin-walled, fibre tempered pottery appears [in southern Africa] two to four centuries before the arrival of Iron Age agro-pastoralists who were uniformly associated with thick-walled ceramics.' Despite being archetypical foragers, Khoesan languages incorporate deep-level etymons for livestock-related activities (Vossen 2007). Pastoral systems in southwest Africa show evident cultural features similar to those of Cushitic herders in northeast Africa (Blench 2009c). This argues that there was a 'lost' branch of the Cushitic family whose speakers encountered the early Khoe and transferred basic herding skills as well as the animals (fat-tailed sheep and long-horn taurine cattle). Fig. 4.2 depicts this interaction somewhere in present-day Zambia, a region now entirely occupied by Bantu speakers. Cushitic languages have almost entirely disappeared, overwhelmed by the expansion of Neolithic farmers in a later period.

A second example concerns Austronesian, not usually considered an African language phylum, but spoken today throughout Madagascar and on the Comoros. Earlier models of the peopling of Madagascar relied on a simple migration from insular Southeast Asia, where

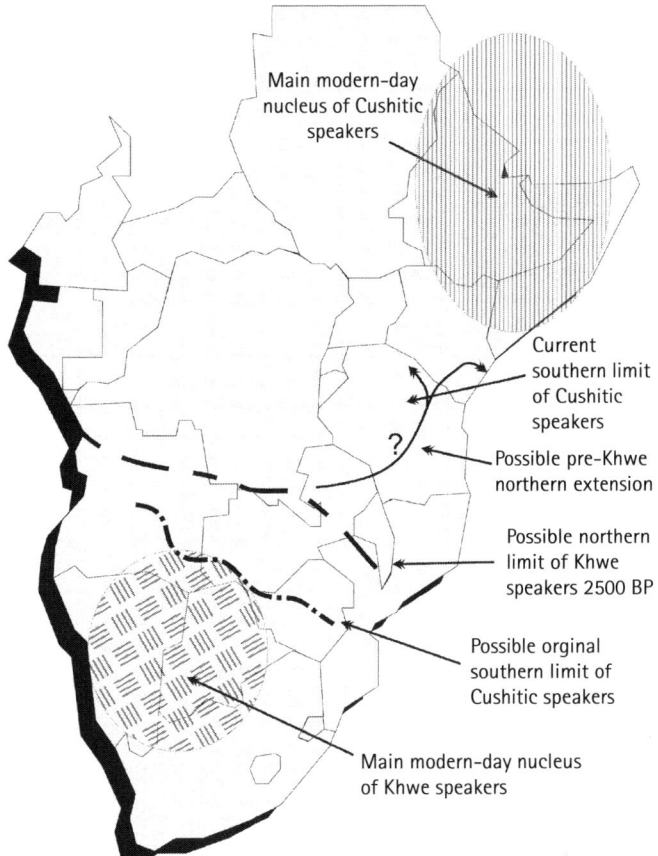

FIG. 4.2 Potential overlaps between the distributions of Cushitic and Khoe speakers.

Malagasy's closest links are with Barito languages on Kalimantan (Dahl 1951). However, it has also been considerably influenced by Malay, acquiring many nautical and other technical terms (Adelaar 1996). There are also numerous loans from the Bantu languages of the East African coast, especially the Sabaki group (Table 4.6), showing that early Austronesian mariners must have been in direct contact with African coastal populations at a date preceding the earliest archaeological evidence for Austronesian settlement on Madagascar (Blench 2010a; cf. Radimilahy, Ch. 65 below). Combining archaeology with a better knowledge of East African Bantu languages produces a more complex three-way model for Malagasy's development that includes multiple interactions between various migrant and resident populations at different periods, as well as layers of loanwords from diverse regions (Beaujard 2003; Walsh 2007; Blench 2007b, 2009b).

   Finally, let us consider an even more recent case, the movement of languages associated with the Atlantic slave trade. Slavers were obviously not concerned with the languages of their victims, but speakers of Niger-Congo predominated in the Americas, since Afroasiatic and Nilo-Saharan languages tend to be spoken inland and so were less affected by the trade. Slaves carried their languages to the New World, in many cases continuing to speak them for some considerable time. In some cases, well-established Niger-Congo languages like Yoruba

Table 4.6 Malagasy mammal names of Sabaki origin

Malagasy	English	Scientific name	Etymology
ampongy	Eastern avahi	*Avahi laniger*	cf. Swahili (Unguja) kʰima punju 'Zanzibar red colobus, *Colobus kirkii*'; Nyakyusa kipunji 'Highland mangabey, *Rungwecebus kipunji*'
ankomba, komba	Crowned lemur (& related lemur spp.)	*Eulemur coronatus*	cf. Swahili (Unguja) kʰomba 'galago spp.'< Proto-Sabaki **nkomba** 'galago'
antsanga	Bushpig	*Potamochoerus larvatus*	cf. Swahili (Unguja) **kitanga** 'solitary male bushpig'
antsangy	rice tenrecs	*Oryzorictes* spp.	cf. Swahili (Tanzanian mainland) **sange** 'elephant shrew spp.'; Mijikenda (Giryama) tsᵗʰanje 'Four-toed elephant shrew, *Petrodomus tetradactylus*'
gidro	Crowned lemur	*Eulemur coronatus*	cf. Swahili (southern dialects) **ngedere** 'Blue monkey, *Cercopithecus mitis*'

Table 4.7 Americanisms of probable African origin

American term	Gloss	First citation	Etymology
chigger, jiga, jigger	sandfly	1756	W. Indies chigoe (1668) (cf. Wolof and Yoruba jigà 'insect', Luba njiga)
cooter*	turtle	1835	kuta root is widespread in Africa, e.g. Bambara kuta, Luba kuda
gombay	cow	?	cf. proto-Bantu* gombe
goober	peanut	1833	Bantu (cf. Kikongo and Kimbundu nguba 'peanut').
gumbo	okra stew	1805	Luba kingumbo, Mbundu ngombo for 'okra'
jive (talk)	insincere, inflated speech	1928	Wolof jev, jeu talk about someone absent, especially in a disparaging manner
okra	okra	1679	Twi and similar Kwa languages kr mā
pinda, pinder	peanut	1794	mbenda in many coastal languages of southern Cameroun and Gabon (Pasch 1980)
tote	to carry	1677	Kikongo tota 'pick up', Kimbundu tuta 'carry, load'
yam	sweet potato	1588	< Port. inhame or Sp. igname, from a W. African language (cf. Fulfulde nyami 'to eat', Twi anyinam 'species of yam')
zombie	living dead	1871	Kikongo zumbi 'fetish', Kimbundu nzambi 'god'

* Also cooter-grass, cooter-back road, cooter-log 'bench for idlers', and box-cooter 'uncommunicative person'.

and Kikongo were parlayed into ritual languages used in the ceremonies of syncretic religions such as Santería. Haiti and Cuba, in particular, remain reservoirs of these languages today. We know too that Nupe, spoken today by up to a million people in west-central Nigeria, was also spoken in Brazil in the 1850s under its Yoruba name, Tapa (Rodrigues 1932). However, most of the transplanted languages died out, though often leaving lexical and grammatical traces in the modern creoles spoken in many regions—for example Berbice Dutch in Surinam, which draws its vocabulary fairly evenly from four distinct sources, Kalabari (in Nigeria's Niger Delta), Arawakan, Dutch, and English (Kouwenberg 1993).

The possible African origin of words and place names in the southern United States has been the subject of much controversy. Early identifications of exotic-soundings toponyms with Amerindian words sometimes concocted strained etymologies (Vass 1979), but the turning point was probably the identification of 'Africanisms' in the dialect of the Gullah people of Georgia's Sea Islands (Georgia Writers' Project 1940; Turner 1949). Westcott (1974) subsequently demonstrated a Bini origin for almost thirty Gullah personal names, precipitating a reversal of the earlier pattern such that seeking an African heritage became fashionable, with the consequence that elaborate claims for African sources were put forward, some dependent on very contorted etymological chains (e.g. Vass 1979). That said, detailed comparison with individual languages can often yield plausible etymologies. Table 4.7 shows a number of words in American English of fairly uncontroversial origin.

Conclusion

Africa's language map provides an important starting point for a broad-brush history of the continent over the last 20,000 years. The pattern of phyla points to large-scale movements, particularly the gradual assimilation of diverse foraging populations by expanding agriculturalists. Historical reconstruction can provide striking insights into the economic history of particular regions, for example in relation to agriculture or pastoralism. Loanwords allow us to track the spread of innovations that may not be reflected in the archaeological record. New techniques in human and animal genetics are providing fresh insights into migration and domestication, although the claims of their proponents still frequently outrun their evidential value.

The classification of African languages is not without controversy, and new discoveries and fresh analyses ensure that the picture is constantly evolving. For archaeologists to make sense of the large-scale patterns of migration and cultural evolution, they need to maintain an informed but sceptical awareness of the current picture, and to incorporate linguistics in the broader reconstruction of prehistory.

References

ADELAAR, K. A. (1996). Malagasy culture-history: some linguistic evidence. In J. Reade (ed.), *The Indian Ocean in Antiquity*. London: British Museum, 487–500.

ARMSTRONG, R. G. (1964). The use of linguistic and ethnographic data in the study of Idoma and Yoruba history. In J. Vansina, R. Mauny, and L. V. Thomas (eds), *The Historian in Tropical Africa*. London: Oxford University Press, 127–39.

BAHUCHET, S., and PHILIPPSON, G. (1998). Les plantes d'origine américaine en Afrique Bantoue. In M. Chastenet (ed.), *Plantes et Paysages d'Afrique*. Paris: Karthala, 82–116.

BEAUJARD, P. (2003). Les arrivées austronésiennes à Madagascar: vagues ou continuum? (parts 1 and 2). *Études Océan Indien* 35–36: 59–147.

BELEZA, S., GUSMÃO, L., AMORIM, A., CARRACEDO, A., and SALAS, A. (2005). The genetic legacy of western Bantu migrations. *Human Genetics* 117: 366–75.

BELLWOOD, P. (2005). *First Farmers: The Origins of Agricultural Societies*. Oxford: Blackwell.

BENDER, M. L. (1996). *The Nilo-Saharan Languages: A Comparative Essay*. Munich: Lincom Europa.

BLENCH, R. M. (2002). Besprechungsartikel: The classification of Nilo-Saharan. *Afrika und Übersee* 83: 293–307.

—— (2006). *Archaeology, Language and the African Past*. Lanham, Md.: AltaMira.

—— (2007a). Bangi Me: a language of unknown affiliation in northern Mali. *Mother Tongue* 12: 147–78.

—— (2007b). New palaeozoogeographical evidence for the settlement of Madagascar. *Azania* 42: 69–82.

—— (2009a). Bananas and plantains in Africa: re-interpreting the linguistic evidence. *Ethnobotany Research and Applications* 7: 363–80.

—— (2009b). The Austronesians in Madagascar and their interaction with the Bantu of the East African coast: surveying the linguistic evidence for domestic and translocated animals. *Philippines Journal of Linguistics* 18: 18–43.

—— (2010a). New evidence for the Austronesian impact on the East African coast. In A. Anderson, J. H. Barrett, and K. V. Boyle (eds), *Global Origins and the Development of Seafaring*. Cambridge: McDonald Institute, 239–48.

—— (2010b). The linguistic geography of Nigeria and its implications for prehistory. In Philip Allsworth-Jones (ed.), *West African Archaeology: New Developments, New Perspectives*. Oxford: Archaeopress, 161–70.

—— WILLIAMSON, K., and CONNELL, B. (1997). The diffusion of maize in Nigeria: a historical and linguistic investigation. *Sprache und Geschichte in Afrika* 14: 19–46.

BOYELDIEU, P. (1977). Éléments pour une phonologie de Laal de Gori. In J.-P. Caprile (ed.), *Études Phonologiques Tchadiennes*. Paris: SELAF, 186–98.

DAHL, O. C. (1951). *Malgache et Maanjan: Une Comparaison Linguistique*. Oslo: Egede Instituttet.

DOKE, C. M. (1945). *Bantu: Modern Grammatical, Phonetical, Lexicographical Studies since 1860*. London: Lund Humphries.

DOORNBOS, P., and BENDER, M. L. (1983). Languages of Wadai-Darfur. In M. L. Bender (ed.), *Nilo-Saharan Language Studies*. East Lansing: Michigan State University Press, 43–79.

DRAKE, N. A., BLENCH, R. M., ARMITAGE, S. J., BRISTOW, C. S., and WHITE, K. H. (2010). How fish swam across the green Sahara: implications for the peopling of the desert and the 'out of Africa' hypothesis. *Proceedings of the National Academy of Sciences of the United States of America* 108(2): 458–62.

DURIE, M., and ROSS, M. (eds) (1996). *The Comparative Method Reviewed: Regularity and Irregularity in Language Change*. Oxford: Oxford University Press.

EGGERT, M. K. H. (1992). The Central African rain forest: historical speculation and archaeological facts. *World Archaeology* 24: 1–24.

—— HÖHN, A., KAHLHEBER, S., MEISTER, C., NEUMANN, K., and SCHWEIZER, A. (2006). Pits, graves and grains: archaeological and archaeobotanical research in southern Cameroon. *Journal of African Archaeology* 4: 273–98.

EHRET, C. (1995). *Reconstructing Proto-Afroasiatic (Proto-Afrasian): Consonants, Vowels, Tone and Vocabulary*. Berkeley: University of California Press.

EHRET, C. (2001). *A Historical-Comparative Reconstruction of Nilo-Saharan*. Cologne: Rudiger Köppe.

——(2002). Language family expansion: broadening our understandings of cause from an African perspective. In P. Bellwood and A. C. Renfrew (eds), *Examining the Farming/Language Dispersal Hypothesis*. Cambridge: McDonald Institute, 163–76.

FLEMING, H. C. (2006). *Ongota: A Decisive Language in African Prehistory*. Mainz: Harassowitz.

GEORGIA WRITERS' PROJECT (1940). *Drums and Shadows: Survival Studies among the Georgia Coastal Negroes*. Athens: University of Georgia Press.

GREENBERG, J. H. (1963). *Languages of Africa*. The Hague: Mouton.

GÜLDEMANN, T. (2008). A linguist's view: Khoe-Kwadi speakers as the earliest food-producers of southern Africa. *Southern African Humanities* 20(1): 93–132.

—— and VOSSEN, R. (2000). Khoisan. In B. Heine and D. Nurse (eds), *African Languages: An Introduction*. Cambridge: Cambridge University Press.

GUTHRIE, M. (1948). *The Classification of the Bantu Languages*. London: International African Institute.

——(1967–71). *Comparative Bantu: An Introduction to Comparative Linguistics and Prehistory of the Bantu Languages*. Farnborough: Gregg.

HEINE, B. (1982). *The Nubi Language of Kibera: An Arabic Creole*. Berlin: Reimer.

HERBERT, R. K., and HUFFMAN, T. N. (1993). A new perspective on Bantu expansion and classification: linguistic and archaeological evidence fifty years after Doke. *African Studies* 52: 37–61.

HUFFMAN, T. N. (2007). *Handbook to the Iron Age of Southern Africa*. Pietermaritzburg: University of KwaZulu-Natal Press

KIRAITHE, J. M., and BADEN, N. T. (1976). Portuguese influences in East African languages. *African Studies* 35: 3–31.

KLEINEWILLINGHÖFER, U. (2001). Jalaa—an almost forgotten language of northeastern Nigeria: a language isolate? *Sprache und Geschichte in Afrika* 16/17: 239–71.

KÖHLER, O. (1981). Les langues Khoesan. In G. Massey (ed.), *Les Langues de l'Afrique Subsaharienne*. Paris: CNRS, 455–615.

KOUWENBERG, S. (1993). *A Grammar of Berbice Dutch Creole*. The Hague: Mouton de Gruyter.

LAMB, S. M., and MITCHELL, E. D. (eds) (1991). *Sprung from some Common Source: Investigations into the Prehistory of Languages*. Palo Alto, Calif.: Stanford University Press.

LAVACHERY, P., MACEACHERN, S., BOUIMON, T., and MBIDA MINDZIE C. (2010). *Komé-Kribi: Rescue Archaeology Along the Chad-Cameroon Oil Pipeline, 1999–2004/De Komé à Kribi: Archéologie Preventive le Long le l'Oléoduc Tchad-Cameroun, 1999–2004*. Frankfurt: Afrika Magna Verlag.

LEWIS, M. P. (ed.) (2013). *Ethnologue: Languages of the World*. 17th Edition. Dallas, Tex.: SIL.

MESTHRIE, R. (1989). The origins of Fanagalo. *Journal of Pidgin and Creole Languages* 4:211–40.

MILITAREV, A. J. (2003). Prehistory of dispersal: Proto-Afrasian (Afroasiatic) farming lexicon. In P. Bellwood and A. C. Renfrew (eds), *Examining the Farming/Language Dispersal Hypothesis*. Cambridge: McDonald Institute, 135–50.

MÜLLER, A., VELUPILLAI, V., WICHMANN, S., et al. (2009). *ASJP World Language Tree: Version I*. Leipzig: Max Planck Institute.

OREL, V., and STOLBOVA, O. (1995). *Hamito-Semitic Etymological Dictionary*. Leiden: Brill.

PASCH, H. (1980). *Linguistische Aspekte der Verbreitung Lateinamerikanischer Nutzpflanzen in Afrika*. Magisterarbeit, Universität zu Köln.

PEREIRA, L., MACAULAY, V., TORRONI, A., SCOZZARI, R., PRATA, M. J., and AMORIM, A. (2001). Prehistoric and historic traces in the mtDNA of Mozambique: insights into the Bantu expansions and the slave trade. *Annals of Human Genetics* 65: 439–58.

PHILLIPSON, D. W. (1977). *The Later Prehistory of Eastern and Southern Africa*. London: Heinemann.

RIBOT, I. (2011). *A Study through Skull Morphology on the Diversity of Holocene African Populations in a Historical Perspective*. Oxford: Archaeopress.

RODRIGUES, N. (1932). *Os Africanos no Brasil*. São Paulo: Companhia Editora Nacional.

SADR, K., and SAMPSON, C. G. (2006). Through thick and thin: early pottery in Southern Africa. *Journal of African Archaeology* 4 (2): 235–52.

SALAS, A., et al. (2002). The making of the African mtDNA Landscape. *American Journal of Human Genetics* 71: 1082–1111.

SANDS, B. (1998). *Eastern and Southern African Khoesan: Evaluating Claims of a Distant Linguistic Relationship*. Cologne: Rüdiger Köppe.

SAVÀ, G., and TOSCO, T. (2000). A sketch of Ongota: a dying language of southwest Ethiopia. *Studies in African Linguistics* 29(2): 59–135.

SUTTON, J. E. G. (1974). The aquatic civilization of Middle Africa. *Journal of African History* 15: 527–46.

SWADESH, M. (1952). Lexicostatistic dating of prehistoric ethnic contacts. *Proceedings of the American Philosophical Society* 96: 453–62.

—— ARAÑA, E., BENDOR-SAMUEL, J. T., and WILSON, W. A. A. (1966). A preliminary glottochronology of Gur languages. *Journal of West African Languages* 3: 27–65.

THOMAS, M. G., PARFITT, T., WEISS, D. A., et al. (2000). Y Chromosomes traveling south: the Cohen modal haplotype and the origins of the Lemba—the 'Black Jews of southern Africa'. *American Journal of Human Genetics* 66: 674–86.

THOMASON, S. G., and KAUFMAN, T. (1988). *Language Contact, Creolization and Genetic Linguistics*. Berkeley: University of California Press.

TISHKOFF, S. A., et al. (2009). The genetic structure and history of Africans and African Americans. *Science* 324: 1035–44.

TRAILL, A. (1986). Do the Khoi have a place in the San? New data on Khoesan linguistic relationships. *Sprache und Geschichte in Afrika* 7: 407–30.

TURNER, L. D. (1949). *Africanisms in the Gullah Dialect*. Chicago: University of Chicago Press.

UNDERHILL, P. A., PASSARINO, G., LIN, A. A., et al. (2001). The phylogeography of Y chromosome binary haplotypes and the origins of modern human populations. *Annals of Human Genetics* 65: 43–62.

VASS, W. K. (1979). *The Bantu Speaking Heritage of the United States*. Los Angeles, Calif.: Center for Afro-American Studies.

VOSSEN, R. (1997). *Die Khoe-sprachen*. Cologne: Rudiger Köppe.

—— (2007). Languages of the desert…and what they can tell us about the economic history of southern Africa. *Sprache und Geschichte in Afrika* 18: 175–85.

WALSH, M. T. (2007). Island subsistence: hunting, trapping and the translocation of wildlife in the western Indian Ocean. *Azania* 42: 83–113.

WESTCOTT, R. W. (1974). Bini names in Nigeria and Georgia. *Linguistics* 124: 21–32.

WESTPHAL, E. O. J. (1962). A re-classification of southern African non-Bantu languages. *Journal of African Languages* 1: 1–8.

WESTPHAL, E. O. J. (1963). The linguistic prehistory of southern Africa: Bush, Kwadi, Hottentot and Bantu linguistic relationships. *Africa* 33: 237–265.

WILSON, J. G. (1970). Preliminary observations on the Oropom people of Karamoja, their ethnic status, culture and postulated relation to the peoples of the late stone age. *Uganda Journal* 34: 125–45.

WOTZKA, H.-P. (1995). *Studien zur Archäologie des zentral-afrikanischen Regenwaldes*. Cologne: Heinrich-Barth Institut.

CHAPTER 5

GENETICS AND ARCHAEOLOGY

SCOTT MACEACHERN

INTRODUCTION

THE last fifteen years have witnessed a vast increase in information on genetic relationships among human populations. Beyond all its other scientific and medical implications, this research provides an extraordinary body of data for testing against archaeological reconstructions of the African past. Generation of historical reconstructions based upon the biological relations of modern African populations allows researchers to juxtapose such reconstructions (presumably derived from population movements, marriage patterns, etc.) with those based upon cultural variation (expressed e.g. through similarities or differences in language or material culture). Comparisons between patterning revealed using these different approaches might indicate that genetic and cultural variability run in parallel, indicating that biological and cultural interactions went hand in hand. In other cases, genetic and cultural patterning might be quite different, revealing biological interactions not directly reflected in cultural variability or vice versa. Both outcomes would be interesting and informative for African history and prehistory.

Such approaches have obvious potential to impact a great variety of research problems in African archaeology, but they also generate significant challenges. While serious questions about interdisciplinarity and sociopolitical power relationships are nothing new, the potentials and difficulties of collaboration between archaeologists and geneticists—and the African people in whose communities both work—may be particularly fraught (Nyika 2009). In many ways, the relationship between genetic research and archaeology now is comparable to that between radiocarbon and archaeological research fifty years ago, when the initial appearance of radiocarbon dating was marked by the same extremes of rejection and uncritical acceptance among archaeologists that often accompany the results of genetic research (Pollard and Bray 2007). It seems likely that the iterative and interactive relationship between genetics and archaeology will ultimately effect transformations similar to those that took place in the case of radiocarbon, but that point has not yet arrived.

VARIETIES OF GENETIC ANALYSES

Different kinds of genetic analyses have been undertaken among African (and other human) populations through time, and these differences can have significant effects on research results. Until the early 1990s, most such research involved the so-called classical polymorphisms: genetic variants expressed serologically or immunologically or detected through analysis of blood proteins (ABO, Rh factors, haemoglobin variants, etc.; Cavalli-Sforza et al. 1994). Variability in these polymorphisms was relatively easy to study before the development of more fine-grained analytical techniques (especially the polymerase chain reaction [PCR]) over the last twenty-five years, and a substantial literature on these classical markers exists. Some of these genetic systems have significant adaptive consequences (e.g. haemoglobin S in the presence of malaria, or the human leukocyte antigen [HLA] system), which limits their utility for studying ancient population relations. Note too that samples originally gathered in the course of this research are still being used as genetic sources in more recent studies, and so uncertainties in data-gathering procedures and ethnic identifications from some decades ago may still be embedded in much more recent genetic reconstructions of African history.

Over the last two decades, a great deal of genetic research into the human past has taken the form of lineage-based analyses involving the study of genetic systems that do not undergo recombination and are thus passed down untransformed from one generation to the next. This lack of recombination makes the definition of historical lineages relatively straightforward. The best-known such system is the mitochondrial DNA [mtDNA] genome, which is inherited maternally, although research on the non-recombining region of the Y-chromosome (NRY), inherited through the paternal line, is also now extremely significant. Besides the simplicity of phylogenetic reconstructions that non-recombination makes possible, the smaller effective population size and rapid mutation rates for both mtDNA and NRY allow studies of relations among human populations at spatial and temporal scales that are useful archaeologically (i.e. over the period of evolution and dispersal of modern humans in Africa and across the globe). The fact that mtDNA and NRY are respectively passed down maternally and paternally means that their comparison can inform researchers on demographic processes that differentially affected women and men, such as variation in marriage patterns (see below on the 'Bantu expansion').

For all their undoubted utility, lineage-based analyses have two major limitations. First, and most obviously, they illuminate only a single line of maternal or paternal descent among the vast number of ancestors of any individual. Second, the fact that mtDNA and NRY are non-recombining means that each acts as single genetic loci and correspondingly each generates only single phylogenetic trees. There is a randomizing component in the structure of any single gene tree, based on variations in sampling and the vagaries of conservation and disappearance of different alleles through generations, and such randomizing factors cannot easily be accounted for through lineage-based methods. Analysis of autosomal DNA (i.e. DNA from the recombining portions of the human genome) partially avoids these disadvantages, since each sampled position on the autosome potentially acts as a different genetic locus. Phylogenetic trees derived from analyses of many different loci can thus be compared and random errors at any one locus corrected, at least to some degree. The disadvantage of autosomal analysis is, of course, that definition of historical lineages is impossible over significant time periods: instead, the result is a biogeographic comparison of sampled modern populations.

Geneticists have studied autosomal variation for decades—indirectly in the case of the classical markers—but such research has been significantly enhanced over about the last five years by advances in analytical techniques, especially in the automation of analysis of single-nucleotide polymorphisms (SNPs), with accompanying advances in bio-informatics. These techniques allow simultaneous comparison of variation at tens or hundreds of thousands of loci on genetic material gathered from thousands of individuals, in 'genome-wide' or 'whole-genome' scans (e.g. Bryc et al. 2010). This allows a more complete examination of similarities and differences across the autosome, and potentially more detailed and reliable accounts of the relations of modern populations. Genome-wide scans will probably become significantly more common in the study of genetic relations among populations, as the necessary technology becomes more widely available and affordable, and it is important for archaeologists to remember that these approaches vary in significant ways from lineage-based analyses. It should also be noted that SNPs are only one form of DNA sequence variation (albeit an extremely important form) used in population studies, based upon research problem orientation, the perceived advantages of different systems, and data availability.

Challenges to collaboration: data comparability and the Last Paragraphs Problem

Substantive collaboration between geneticists and archaeologists will occur when reasonably comparable data sources deriving from the two fields can be tested against one another. Without such comparability, insights gained from one discipline may generally inform research agendas in the other, but advances will be piecemeal and it will remain extremely difficult to establish with any confidence that patterning in one dataset has anything to do with patterning in the other. 'Comparable' in such a case may mean various things. First, data from both fields must simply exist for the area under study, which in Africa is by no means a given. Thus, a considerable amount of genetic research has been undertaken on modern African forager groups, especially Khoisan and Pygmy/BaTwa populations, because of their putative relevance to the study of prehistoric inhabitants of Africa and the origins of modern humans (see below). Populations in certain geographical areas, like the southern Lake Chad Basin, are reasonably well known genetically. On the other hand, research on farming populations in most of central, southwestern, and southern Africa is restricted to a relatively small number of Bantu-speaking groups, few populations have been sampled in West Africa between Senegambia and the Lake Chad Basin, very little genetic research has been undertaken on Saharan populations, and in eastern Africa many Bantu-, Cushitic-, and Nilotic- speaking groups have never been studied.

Archaeologists' knowledge of the African past is similarly geographically patterned, with some areas much more extensively investigated through survey and excavation than others.

Congruencies in our state of knowledge for different regions exist, often involving criteria of access, political circumstances, or resources: for example, east-central Africa is not very well known either archaeologically or genetically, while significant research in both disciplines has taken place in the Lake Chad Basin, Senegambia, and the Nile Valley. However, some areas are comparatively well known genetically but not archaeologically, or vice versa. Compounding these differences in coverage is the fact that genetic research typically involves only one of a number of genetic systems and their expressions, as noted above. Few regions of Africa currently offer comparable data from different genetic systems for the same population (see e.g. Wood et al. 2005; Tishkoff et al. 2007). This is a significant problem, given that different systems may have been subject to quite different selection pressures and may inform us about different sociocultural processes (e.g. asymmetrical mating patterns or male–female mobility).

Even if congruent genetic and archaeological data exist for a particular area or population, basic issues of data evaluation remain: how does one systematically compare variation in biological characteristics (e.g. genetic polymorphisms) with variation in some elements of material culture, and how does one then establish that these very different kinds of data reflect common historical processes (MacEachern 2000; cf. Pluciennik 2006)? In the past, such comparisons were sometimes impressionistic, when for example the different coordinates in principal-components analyses of genetic variation across space were associated with different events in African history, like the Bantu Expansion and the invention of agriculture (Cavalli-Sforza et al. 1994: 189–92; cf. Novembre and Stephens 2008). More recent historical interpretations of genetic data have been more systematic, more modest, and better founded in data, but the challenge of establishing associations between genetic and material culture (and, perhaps, linguistic) patterning remains significant (Blench, Ch. 4 above). In addition, techniques for estimating the time-depths of genetic processes—the occurrence of a particular mutation, for example—remain less precise than radiocarbon dating, which sometimes renders comparison of genetic and archaeological reconstructions difficult.

Significant issues of scale also exist. Archaeologists work at a variety of spatiotemporal and cultural scales, from the continental to very local levels. Most would probably acknowledge that these different scales of research are all valuable to the overall project of investigating African history and Africa's historic role in the world. To this point, genetic research in Africa has been almost exclusively concerned with large-scale questions, with historical reconstructions that operate regionally or across the whole continent and over significant time-scales. To a degree, this orientation can be traced back to limitations of data coverage, with usually small samples of varying (and often unknown) representativeness from different ethnic groups, and to the poor temporal resolution of genetic reconstructions noted above. In addition, genetics research has become Big Science, directed toward Big Questions, with more modest questions perhaps falling by the wayside. Researchers therefore know relatively little about the structuring of genetic variability within ethnic groups across Africa or the relationships between ethnolinguistic boundaries and changes in the states of different genetic systems. Indeed, it is entirely unclear what the 'genetic boundary' between the ethnic groups forming the basis of geneticists' interpretations in Africa would look like. Remarkably few examples of more detailed research on intragroup variability exist in Africa (but see Veeramah et al. 2008), and it is notable that some of the few papers examining this topic have done so for reasons largely unconnected with specifically African history (Thomas et al. 2000; Kaplan 2006; Parfitt 2006).

Interdisciplinary research in archaeology and genetics is frequently hobbled by conceptual misunderstandings in both directions, as researchers working in Africa do not take sufficient account of research perspectives outside their own disciplines. We might designate this the 'Last Paragraphs Problem', as it is in the concluding paragraphs of genetics papers, in which genetic patterning is linked to historical process, that many of the problems arise. Archaeologists and other social scientists are often intimidated by the specialized terminologies and complex procedures associated with genetic research. The result is an unfortunate tendency either to more or less disregard genetics research when trying to understand the human past in Africa and elsewhere, or to accept the results of genetic research somewhat uncritically, skipping to the last paragraphs of research papers in historical genetics (where the historical reconstructions usually reside) and trying to reconcile those reconstructions with pre-existing culture histories derived from more familiar sources. Current syntheses of African prehistory (see e.g. Phillipson 2005; Stahl 2005) give notably little consideration to genetic research, especially for recent periods.

Geneticists, on the other hand, often do not appear to appreciate the scope or pace of research in the social sciences, including African archaeology, and in some cases employ inadequate or dated sources in formulating their own historical constructions—the other side of the Last Paragraphs Problem. The contrast between the sophistication of genetic analysis and the superficial knowledge of African history, prehistoric archaeology, and/or ethnography displayed in some (but by no means all) genetics papers can be quite striking. Encyclopedia entries, mass-media texts on African history and archaeology, academic texts written fifty or more years ago, and passed-on claims about African prehistory made in earlier papers by other geneticists are simply not sufficient resources for any serious historical contextualization of the results of genetic research. It is difficult to avoid the impression that some geneticists rely for their understandings of the African past upon distant memories (and perhaps hoarded textbooks) from introductory undergraduate courses in anthropology or archaeology (cf. Mitchell 2010).

At the same time, effective historical reconstructions do get made. In Africanist research, archaeologists and geneticists do not often converse with one another, but neither do they entirely talk past one another. Rather, they speak at disciplinary tangents: at the intersection of those tangents new understandings are formed, but opportunities for effective collaboration are also often missed. It is to these more positive, and often extraordinarily informative, cases that we now turn.

Modern human origins and modern hunter-gatherers

Some of the earliest, and certainly best-known, genetic research in Africa involved the use of mtDNA and subsequently NRY data to respectively establish maternal and paternal lineages that link modern peoples around the world to small ancestral populations of females and males living in Africa (Cann et al. 1987; Underhill et al. 2000). Originally undertaken to test conflicting models of modern human origins, this work effectively supported a recent African origin model (Lahr, Ch. 23 below). Establishing the time-depth of these ancient populations is complicated by assumptions about effective population sizes for males and females through time, and the much larger size of and lack of knowledge of variation across the NRY genome when compared to mtDNA. Current estimates for the most recent common ancestor of modern humans based on mtDNA data yield a date of approximately 160,000 years (Soares et al. 2009), in good agreement with palaeoanthropological evidence for the appearance of *Homo sapiens idaltu*, with a subsequent expansion of modern humans out of Africa approximately 70,000–50,000 years ago.

Research on the origins of modern human populations in Africa is undertaken chiefly using data from modern African forager populations, and illustrates both the potentials and difficulties of deriving historical inferences from genetic data. That research seems to indicate that members of San and Pygmy/BaTwa populations tend to exhibit mtDNA and NRY lineages that exist close to the roots of phylogenetic trees for these genetic systems, and that (for mtDNA at least) there was substantial genetic isolation of these lineages in Africa during much of the Middle/Upper Pleistocene, with other lineages appearing and decreasing levels of genetic isolation after 60,000–70,000 years ago (e.g. Behar et al. 2008). Even the Sandawe and Hadza, living only about 150 km apart, are claimed to have been genetically isolated for 15,000–20,000 years, with such isolation ending only within perhaps the last 4,000 years (Tishkoff et al. 2007). If these claims are supported by future research, genetic isolation may be partly explained by palaeoenvironmental data suggesting periodic and exceptionally severe mega-droughts in tropical Africa over generally the same period (Behar et al. 2008; cf. Cohen et al. 2007). Such data have obvious implications for how archaeologists view the cultural evolution of modern humans during the Pleistocene (cf. Barham, Ch. 24 below). They are especially significant for understanding widespread Middle Stone Age industrial traditions like the Lupemban, since they imply the existence of only small and isolated human populations in eastern and southern Africa over much of the period of modern human evolution. A number of archaeological models have identified regional differentiation in MSA stone tool traditions with widening social networks and the development of stylistic or symbolic behaviour (e.g. Brooks and McBrearty 2000), but these genetic data raise the possibility that such differentiation was due to cultural and biological isolation instead.

At the same time, there are substantial challenges to reconciling these interpretations with archaeological and other reconstructions. Isolation of small African populations over multiple tens of millennia is not obvious archaeologically for the late Pleistocene, although that might partly be due to assumptions that archaeologists have brought to their data. It is difficult to envisage how periodic episodes of even extreme drought could have enforced population separations on the order of 50,000–100,000 years, as interpreted from the mtDNA data. More problematical—because harder to test—are assumptions made about human identities and the historical status of African forager groups. Thus, the claim that a genetic differentiation of Khoisan, Hadza, and Sandawe populations over the period 30,000–50,000 BP (at least) implies a similar time-depth for click phonemes common to these different languages (Knight et al. 2003; Tishkoff et al. 2007) offers no model for linguistic conservativism over such extraordinary time-scales, and risks conflating modern and very ancient linguistic and cultural identities.

One important side effect of these genetic investigations of modern African foragers has been the Western reinscription of San, Pygmy/BaTwa, and other African populations as fossilized remnants of ancient times, holdovers from the Pleistocene. The mtDNA and NRY variations used to generate these phylogenetic trees do not appear to have major adaptive significance—if they had, they would be correspondingly less useful for indicating ancient population relations—and these genetic studies in no way indicate that the people with DNA from these ancient lineages are 'less modern' than other humans. However, these modern forager communities have been directly identified with early modern humans from the period before the expansion out of Africa, both by geneticists (e.g. Wells and Read 2002) and by journalists disseminating this research to western publics (e.g. Wade 2006). When a significant paper in human genetics identifies Biaka Pygmies as 'one of the oldest distinct African populations and, hence, one of the oldest human populations in the world' (Chen et al. 2000: 1372), with the phrase 'oldest human population' widely repeated in the media, it bespeaks a fundamental conflation of genetic variability and historical identity that Africanist researchers must resist when possible. More recent debates over the functioning of particular genes for brain development provide another example of the assumption of African ahistoricity: Mekel-Bobrov et al. (2005), for example, take a lack of cultural advance on the continent in the late Pleistocene and Holocene as given, and assume it in turn to be explained by the distribution of particular variants of the ASPM gene, a classic example of the Last Paragraphs Problem.

LATE PLEISTOCENE AND HOLOCENE
POPULATION DYNAMICS

Genetic analyses of most non-forager populations in Africa (excepting groups like the Sandawe, because of their putative linguistic connections to San-speaking forager groups; Güldemann and Stoneking 2008) are most often used to generate evidence for prehistoric population expansions and migrations in different parts of the continent. As with research on modern human origins, problem orientations for geneticists tend to derive explicitly or implicitly from prior research in other disciplines. In both modern human origins research and more recent analyses, this involves using palaeoanthropological and archaeological data, but for more recent periods problem orientations from historical linguistics predominate. This is perhaps not surprising, given Africa's linguistic diversity, the broad commonality involved in some phylogenetic approaches in the two disciplines, and the lack of archaeological data in many areas. One widely held assumption in such research has been that such population expansions frequently occur as well-integrated 'packages' often associated with initial spreads of farmers into a region (e.g. Diamond and Bellwood 2003). Genetic reconstructions are then most often understood as the result of the dispersals of named linguistic groups.

Thus, the Holocene social/cultural phenomenon most intensively studied in African genetic research is the 'Bantu expansion'. A substantial number of studies exist on the genetic legacy of migrations associated with Bantu-speaking populations (Beleza et al. 2005; Quintana-Murci et al. 2008; Berniell-Lee et al. 2009; cf. Bostoen et al. 2009), although as noted above their geographical distribution is extremely patchy. There is, of course, a significant preceding literature on the nature of the processes through which Bantu languages came to be spoken over large areas of Africa, based upon linguistic, archaeological, and ethnographic evidence (de Maret, Ch. 43 below). Genetic data certainly indicate that these processes involved substantial movements of people at some places and at some times, i.e. that the 'Bantu expansion' was indeed a demographic phenomenon, as well as a linguistic and cultural one. This may, however, be something of proving a commonplace: previous researchers had accepted that at least part of this vast and complex process would have involved actual population movements, although they might have disagreed on the extent and dynamics of such movements. At this point, genetic data are not sufficiently fine-grained to inform us about the origins of such population movements, and so geneticists (and archaeologists) use historical linguistic reconstructions to locate their origins in the southern borderlands between Nigeria and Cameroon. Perhaps the most important contribution of genetic research to this point has been in analysis of the dynamics of the Western Bantu expansion (Beleza et al. 2005), in an area little known archaeologically and where those dynamics have not been well understood.

Genetic data can very usefully inform us about some of the large-scale past demographic processes that have left traces among Bantu-speaking populations, and may illuminate ancient population movements. Thus, diversity in NRY lineages among modern Bantu-speaking populations is significantly lower than is mtDNA diversity (Salas et al. 2002; Wood et al. 2005; Bostoen et al. 2009), an observation that led researchers to conclude that the 'Bantu expansion' involved asymmetrical reproduction patterns between immigrating farmer and indigenous forager populations. This might have involved females from forager communities disproportionately reproducing with men from Bantu-speaking farmer communities and thus contributing to mtDNA diversity, while polygyny would have lessened the diversity of paternal lineages. These processes would presumably have been associated with adoption of Bantu languages by in-marrying woman, and by the children of these couples (Wood et al. 2005). However, this observation highlights the disjuncture between description and explanation: while these genetic data may indeed illuminate ancient demographic interactions in early Bantu-speaking populations, they do not provide an *explanation* for the spread of Bantu languages on a macro-scale. The picture becomes particularly complicated when we consider that Yoruba, a non-Bantu language of the Niger-Congo family and a language not (as far as we know) associated with comparable range expansions, exhibits the same asymmetrical pattern of mtDNA and NRY diversity as do the Bantu languages (Tishkoff et al. 2007).

Thus, late Pleistocene and Holocene genetic reconstructions over much of Africa are dominated by accounts of a variety of encounters between proto-Bantu and (putatively Pygmy/San) foragers. Only in areas beyond those where Bantu is spoken, such as the Sahelian and Sudanian environmental belts running east–west to the south of the Sahara, do other ancient population relationships receive much attention. One particular nexus for research has been the southern Lake Chad Basin, an area of great linguistic and cultural diversity, probably because of its central location along routes of migration and trade linking the Atlantic with the Nile and North Africa with areas south of the Sahara. In and around the Mandara Mountains, along the basin's southern peripheries, ethnic diversity is greater than almost anywhere else in Africa, especially among Chadic-speaking montagnard populations that have been one focus of genetic investigations for more than two decades (e.g. Spedini et al. 1999; Cruciani et al. 2002, 2010; Coia et al. 2005; Cerny et al. 2009; Tishkoff et al. 2009). The region's location and cultural characteristics have also encouraged significant ethnographic, archaeological, and linguistic research during the last sixty years, making it one of the few areas of sub-Saharan Africa where detailed comparisons between the findings of these different disciplines may be feasible.

Genetic research here over the last decade highlights the advances and challenges inherent in such multidisciplinary undertakings. Using classical polymorphisms, Spedini et al. (1999) still identified Mandara montagnard populations as *paléonigritique*, an entirely obsolete designation dating to before the Second World War implying more or less unchanged remnants of an ancient stratum of African culture, pushed into refuge areas by more advanced societies and accompanied by assumptions about the historical isolation of populations that, in some cases, lived only kilometres apart. At more or less the same time, however, other researchers used NRY data to posit long-range connections between some of these 'isolated' Chadic-speaking montagnard groups and West Asian/North African populations (Cruciani et al. 2002), a connection which, if verified, would probably be associated with early Holocene human movements across a 'Green Sahara'.

Ten years later, genetic understandings are appreciably richer. Data exist on mtDNA, NRY, and autosomal genetic variation for many Lake Chad Basin and neighbouring populations (although too often without comparable data in these different systems for the same groups), allowing very interesting, albeit tentative, reconstructions of population relationships and migrations over the last 7,000–8,000 years, informed by historical linguistic and (to a lesser extent) archaeological and palaeoenvironmental reconstructions. In the context of increasing rainfall levels and environmental changes, these involve an early Holocene movement into the region from the Nile Valley of ancestral Nilo-Saharan speakers, and their subsequent interactions with ancestral Chadic-speaking groups moving out of a desiccating Sahara in the mid-Holocene (e.g. Tishkoff et al. 2009). Other genetic investigations have productively examined more recent population interactions in the region (Hassan et al. 2008; Keita et al. 2010). One contribution of genetic research to these issues lies in its identification of significant east–west migrations and interactions south of the Sahara, especially between East Africa, the Nile, and Lake Chad. Archaeologists working in this area have tended to examine north–south interactions between Saharan and sub-Saharan regions; they have done so in part because of the lack of archaeological data available east of Lake Chad and in southern Sudan. The genetic research thus provides valuable orientation for future archaeological fieldwork.

In this region, the goal of combining data from a variety of different sources into integrated models of African history is probably as close as anywhere on the continent, as far as data quality is concerned. Significant challenges still exist, however, including the perennial basic issues of data comparability: how can researchers establish linkages between patterning in genetic, archaeological, and linguistic data, and to what extent would this be furthered by common data formats and analytical approaches in these different fields of study? How do geneticists best account for rather different results when different genetic systems are being studied (a problem not unfamiliar to archaeologists comparing different realms of material culture)? Perhaps most fundamentally, how do researchers reconcile the ethnohistorical evidence for diversity of origins among populations in this area, with small genetic samples often gathered under assumptions of low in-group genetic variability? While genetic contributions from different ancestral populations are frequently acknowledged (e.g. Tishkoff et al. 2009: figs 3 and 4), no intermediate level of genetic identity between the individual and the ethnic group is allowed for in these studies, even though the internal historical diversity of many modern (and presumably ancient) African populations is widely accepted by anthropologists and archaeologists alike.

These challenges—and others like them faced by researchers working elsewhere in Africa—are significant, making the elucidation of the complex relations between genetic variation and variation in different aspects of human culture certainly a long-term process. Still more challenging will be the formulation of procedures for interpreting such relations in the distant past. However, archaeologists should not let these difficulties obscure the tremendous capabilities that exist in genetic studies of African history, capabilities that are being demonstrated almost daily. The development of truly interdisciplinary research initiatives, involving genetics, archaeology, historical linguistics, and related disciplines, undoubtedly has the potential to transform our understanding of the African past.

References

BEHAR, D. M., VILLEMS, R., SOODYALL, H., et al. (2008). The dawn of human matrilineal diversity. *American Journal of Human Genetics* 82: 1130–40.

BELEZA, S., GUSMAO, L., AMORIM, A., CARRACEDO, A., and SALAS, A. (2005). The genetic heritage of western Bantu migrations. *Human Genetics* 117: 366–75.

BERNIELL-LEE, G., CALAFELL, F., BOSCH, E., et al. (2009). Genetic and demographic implications of the Bantu expansion: insights from human paternal lineages. *Molecular Biology and Evolution* 26: 1581–9.

BOSTOEN, K., DE FILIPPO, C., and PAKENDORF, B. (2009). Molecular anthropological perspectives on the Bantu expansion: facts and fiction. Paper presented at the annual meeting of the African Studies Association, New Orleans.

BROOKS, A. S., and MCBREARTY, S. (2000). The revolution that wasn't: a new interpretation of the origin of modern human behavior. *Journal of Human Evolution* 39: 453–563.

BRYC, K., AUTON, A., NELSON, M. R., et al. (2010). Genome-wide patterns of population structure and admixture in West Africans and African Americans. *Proceedings of the National Academy of Sciences (USA)* 107: 786–91.

CANN, R., STONEKING, M., and WILSON, A. (1987). Mitochondrial DNA and human evolution. *Nature* 325: 31–6.

CAVALLI-SFORZA, L. L., MENOZZI, P., and PIAZZA, A. (1994). *The History and Geography of Human Genes.* Princeton, NJ: Princeton University Press.

CERNY, V., FERNANDES, V., COSTA, M., HAJEK, M., MULLIGAN, C., and PEREIRA, L. (2009). Migration of Chadic speaking pastoralists within Africa based on population structure of Chad Basin and phylogeography of mitochondrial L3f haplogroup. *BMC Evolutionary Biology* 9: 63.

CHEN, Y.-S., OLCKERS, A., SCHURR, T., KOGELNIK, A., HUOPONEN, K., and WALLACE, D. (2000). mtDNA variation in the South African Kung and Khwe—and their genetic relationships to other African populations. *American Journal of Human Genetics* 66: 1362–83.

COHEN, A. S., STONE, J. R., BEUNING, K. R.M., et al. (2007). Ecological consequences of early late Pleistocene megadroughts in tropical Africa. *Proceedings of the National Academy of Sciences (USA)* 104: 16422–7.

COIA, V., DESTRO-BISOL, G., VERGINELLI, F., et al. (2005). mtDNA variation in north Cameroon: lack of Asian lineages and implications for back migration from Asia to sub-Saharan Africa. *American Journal of Physical Anthropology* 128: 678–81.

CRUCIANI, F., SANTOLAMAZZA, P., SHEN, P., et al. (2002). A back migration from Asia to sub-Saharan Africa is supported by high-resolution analysis of human Y-chromosome haplotypes. *American Journal of Human Genetics* 70: 1197–1214.

CRUCIANI, F., TROMBETTA, B., SELLITTO, D., et al. (2010). Human Y chromosome haplogroup R-V88: a paternal genetic record of early mid Holocene trans-Saharan connections and the spread of Chadic languages. *European Journal of Human Genetics* 18: 800–807.

DIAMOND, J., and BELLWOOD, P. (2003). Farmers and their languages: the first expansions. *Science* 300: 597–603.

GÜLDEMANN, T., and STONEKING, M. (2008). A historical appraisal of clicks: a linguistic and genetic population perspective. *Annual Review of Anthropology* 37: 93–109.

HASSAN, H., UNDERHILL, P., CAVALLI-SFORZA, L. L., and IBRAHIM, M. (2008). Y-chromosome variation among Sudanese: restricted gene glow, concordance with language, geography, and history. *American Journal of Physical Anthropology* 137: 316–23.

KAPLAN, S. (2006). Genealogies and gene-ideologies: the legitimacy of the Beta Israel (Falasha). *Social Identities: Journal for the Study of Race, Nation and Culture* 12: 447–55.

KEITA, S. O. Y., FATIMAH, L. C. J., LATIFA, F. J. B., and KOFFI, N. M. (2010). Commentary on the Fulani: history, genetics, and linguistics [an adjunct to Hassan et al. 2008]. *American Journal of Physical Anthropology* 141: 665–7.

KNIGHT, A., UNDERHILL, P., MORTENSEN, H., et al. (2003). African Y chromosome and mtDNA convergence provide insight into the history of click languages. *Current Biology* 13: 464–73.

MACEACHERN, S. (2000). Genes, tribes, and African history. *Current Anthropology* 41: 357–84.

MEKEL-BOBROV, N., GILBERT, S. L., EVANS, P. D., et al. (2005). Ongoing adaptive evolution of ASPM, a brain size determinant in *Homo sapiens*. *Science* 309: 1720–22.

MITCHELL, P. (2010). Genetics and southern African prehistory: an archaeological view. *Journal of Anthropological Sciences* 88: 73–92.

NOVEMBRE, J., and STEPHENS, M. (2008). Interpreting principal component analyses of spatial population genetic variation. *Nature Genetics* 40: 646–9.

NYIKA, A. (2009) Ethical and practical challenges surrounding genetic and genomic research in developing countries. *Acta Tropica* 112: S21–31.

PARFITT, T. (2006). *Genetics, Mass Media and Identity: A Case Study of the Genetic Research on the Lemba and Bene Israel.* London: Routledge.

PHILLIPSON, D. W. (2005). *African Archaeology.* Cambridge: Cambridge University Press.

PLUCIENNIK, M. (2006). Clash of cultures? Archaeology and genetics. *Documenta Praehistorica* 33: 39–49.

POLLARD, A. M., and BRAY, P. (2007). A bicycle made for two? The integration of scientific techniques into archaeological interpretation. *Annual Review of Anthropology* 36: 245–59.

QUINTANA-MURCI, L., QUACH, H., HARMANT, C., et al. (2008). Maternal traces of deep common ancestry and asymmetric gene flow between Pygmy hunter-gatherers and Bantu-speaking farmers. *Proceedings of the National Academy of Sciences (USA)* 105: 1596–1601.

SALAS, A., RICHARDS, M., DE LA FE, T., et al. (2002). The making of the African mtDNA landscape. *American Journal of Human Genetics* 71: 1082–1111.

SOARES, P., ERMINI, L., THOMSON, N., et al. (2009) Correcting for purifying selection: an improved human mitochondrial molecular clock. *American Journal of Human Genetics* 84: 740–59.

SPEDINI, G., MONDOVI, S., PAOLI, G., and DESTRO-BISOL, G. (1999). The peopling of sub-Saharan Africa: the case of Cameroon. *American Journal of Physical Anthropology* 110: 143–62.

STAHL, A. (ed.) (2005). *African Archaeology: A Critical Introduction.* Oxford: Blackwell.

THOMAS, M., PARFITT, T., WEISS, D., et al. (2000). Y chromosomes traveling south: the Cohen modal haplotype and the origins of the Lemba—the 'Black Jews of Southern Africa'. *American Journal of Human Genetics* 66: 674–86.

TISHKOFF, S. A., GONDER, M. K., HENN, B. M., et al. (2007). History of click-speaking populations of Africa inferred from mtDNA and Y chromosome genetic variation. *Molecular Biology and Evolution* 24: 2180–95.

TISHKOFF, S. A., REED, F. A., FRIEDLAENDER, F. R., et al. (2009). The genetic structure and history of Africans and African Americans. *Science* 324: 1035–44.

UNDERHILL, P., SHEN, P., LIN, A., et al. (2000). Y chromosome sequence variation and the history of human populations. *Nature Genetics* 26: 358–61.

VEERAMAH, K. R., ZEITLYN, D., FANSO, V. K., et al. (2008). Sex-specific genetic data support one of two alternative versions of the foundation of the ruling dynasty of the Nso in Cameroon. *Current Anthropology* 49: 707–14.

WADE, N. (2006). *Before the Dawn: Recovering the Lost History of Our Ancestors.* New York: Penguin Press.

WELLS, S., and READ, M. (2002). *The Journey of Man: A Genetic Odyssey.* Princeton, NJ: Princeton University Press.

WOOD, E., STOVER, D., EHRET, C., et al. (2005). Contrasting patterns of Y chromosome and mtDNA variation in Africa: evidence for sex-biased demographic processes. *European Journal of Human Genetics* 13: 867–76.

......

CHAPTER 6

ARCHAEOLOGY AND MIGRATION IN AFRICA

......

CERI ASHLEY

INTRODUCTION

......

THE archaeology of Africa is littered with migration narratives. Indeed, key migration events from Africa have shaped global history, from the hominin dispersal 'Out of Africa' (Barham, Ch. 24 below) to the more recent forced exodus of the Atlantic slave trade (Thiaw and Richard, Ch. 68 below). Closer to home, local and regional migrations within Africa are a recurring leitmotiv within archaeology and history, from the grand narratives of the sub-continental Bantu Migration hypothesis (de Maret, Ch. 43 below) to local origin histories that talk of the impact of 'outsiders' (Kopytoff 1987). However, despite this prominence and seeming ubiquity, African archaeology has often had a complicated and contested relationship with migration, and it remains a potentially divisive issue. As an introduction to some of the key trends in archaeological approaches to migration, this chapter outlines some of the past archaeological uses of migration paradigms, as well as exploring theoretical and methodological issues associated with its application to African archaeological contexts.

ARCHAEOLOGY AND MIGRATION

......

Migration and its twin, diffusion, came to prominence in archaeology in late 19th-/early 20th-century Europe, where they became the interpretive cornerstone of the culture historical approach to archaeology. Culture history embraced a local historical scale of analysis, and sought to trace individual cultures as they interacted and intermixed through the migration of people, or the diffusion of ideas (Daniel 1950). It was arguably with Gordon Childe, the 'organising genius of European migrations' (Adams et al. 1978: 493), that migration truly came to the fore. At the heart of Childean culture history was the notion of the archaeological culture and the idea that past societies produced culturally distinct objects and practices. Any change in this material manifestation was believed to reflect significant cultural disruption, typically as the result of outside influence, either the migration of another culture or the diffusion of a new technology or style. The culture historical approach suffered from a well-documented theoretical backlash with the rise of processual archaeology (Shennan 1989), which rejected its specificity in favour of modelling and testing cross-cultural processes. As the linchpin of culture history, migration similarly suffered in what has been described as the 'retreat from migrationism' (Adams et al. 1978). As a result, for a long time and for many, migration effectively fell off the archaeological agenda in favour of 'indigenist' or 'immobilist' modelling (Chapman and Hamerow 1997; Härke 1998).

Recent decades, however, have seen the slow re-emergence of migration as a respectable topic of archaeological enquiry. In 1987, in a theoretical turnabout, Renfrew (1987: 3) asked whether archaeology had, in rejecting migration, 'thrown the baby out with the bathwater', prompting a new wave of research led by Anthony (1990, 1997; cf. Chapman and Hamerow 1997; Härke 1998; Burmeister 2000) that has seen archaeologists from a broad range of theoretical backgrounds and methodologies embrace the topic once more. Recent work has also covered a wide chronological span, with for example an important debate in European palaeolithic archaeology between migration versus regionalism (Gamble 1993; Otte and Keeley 1990). Regional research trajectories have also been noted (Härke 1998), with one of the most successful and active arenas of migration research emerging in the American Southwest (Cameron 1995). Sustained archaeological investigations of colonization, in effect studies of the impact of migration rather than of the process, have also emerged, again in a wide variety of contexts, from the settlement of previously empty landscapes to the period of European colonial expansion (e.g. Lyons and Papadopoulos 2002; Rockman and Steele 2003; Gosden 2004; Stein 2005).

Discussion

Despite this recent re-engagement with migration and breadth of research, fundamental theoretical and methodological issues still remain, central to which is the question of definition. The ad hoc use of migration in culture history contributed to its earlier demise (Adams et al. 1978), whilst its frequently axiomatic application remains an issue (Burmeister 2000). Attempts to categorize and define migration have emerged, but with little consensus (Chapman and Hamerow 1997); definitions can be split into narrow and broad categories. Anthony (1990, 1997; cf. Tilley 1978), for example, argues that migration involves a broad spectrum of activities and actions that can include seasonal movement such as transhumance, whilst Adams et al. (1978) demand a tighter definition in which migration requires large-scale, permanent, and intentional relocation. Indeed, some researchers question the very idea that a single, all-encompassing definition is even possible given archaeology's vast chronological, political, and demographic range (e.g. Chapman and Dolukhanov 1992; Cameron 1995).

The issue of how and why past communities migrated is similarly problematic. In the past, archaeology tended to use the 'wave-of-advance' model for demographic spread, in which the build-up of population density forced relocation in a search for fresh resources. Recent research has, however, emphasized a wider range of migratory movement, with Anthony (1990) drawing on Lee's (1966) 'Laws of Migration' to include circular or tethered migration alongside career, coerced, and chain migration. The question of incentive and motivation also remain complex, with Anthony (1990, 1997) again drawing on Lee (1966) to develop the 'push–pull' model in which the decision to move is governed by the balance of negative factors in the home area against positive factors in the migrant destination (cf. Burmeister 2000). Migration has returned to the archaeological agenda, but is clearly still subject to intense debate.

ARCHAEOLOGY AND MIGRATION IN AFRICA

The idea of migration and external demographic influence was deeply embedded in early European encounters with Africa, and became a central pillar of colonial rhetoric. Following prevalent Enlightenment thinking, African society was regarded as inherently primitive and backward; any indication of civilization and advancement must, therefore, logically come from outside. This approach was clearly steeped in a broader moral philosophy, but also suited the very specific demands of colonial ideology, which sought to legitimize European expansion into, and rule over, Africa. Invoking migration as a long-term historical phenomenon could justify ongoing incursions by Europeans, as well as reiterating the notion that Africa needed such influxes to advance and develop. This rhetoric was perhaps most perniciously applied in southern Africa, where early commentators such as Stow and Theal developed the idea of 'empty lands' to which migrating Europeans and Africans were equally entitled (Dubow 1995: 66–74). The case of the Hamites provides another illustrative example of such an approach. Believed to descend from Noah's cursed son Ham, the Hamites came to be regarded as a quasi-racial, linguistic, and cultural entity (Sanders 1969), who spread from the Near East across Africa, bringing superior technologies, skills, and intellect (e.g. Johnston 1913). Portrayed as a branch of the Caucasian 'race' (Sanders 1969), they were allegedly responsible for a raft of innovations; as Seligman (1957: 85) famously stated, 'the civilisations of Africa are the civilisations of the Hamites' (cf. Reid, Ch. 61 below).

Such racist thinking remained powerful for a long time, but lost favour in the post-Nazi era (Sanders 1969) as a new generation of professional archaeologists approached African independence. Despite the decline of this 'outsider' paradigm, migration remained highly influential within archaeological and historical reconstructions. Perhaps unsurprisingly, given the European training of many of the period's practitioners, culture-history was the archaeological mainstay and migration thus took its place as a primary agent of change. Culture-history provided a convenient tool to link disparate pockets of archaeological data, whilst migration could explain the diffuse spread of such cultural features. Sutton (1977), for example, sought to understand the distribution of dotted wavy line ceramics across eastern Africa and the Sahara, suggesting that it reflected an interconnected 'Aqualithic' culture that had spread west from the Rift Valley (cf. Barich, Ch. 31 below). Still more influential has been the link made between the Early Iron Age cultural package and the spread of Bantu languages (cf. de Maret, Ch. 43 below).

Nevertheless, despite the centrality of migration as an explanatory device at this time, an emerging undercurrent of scholarship soon challenged its automatic use. Unlike New Archaeology's epistemological rejection of migration as the handmaiden of culture history, the theoretical implications of migration were generally not the prime concern in sub-Saharan Africa. Rather, the enduring reliance on the idea of 'outsiders', even intra-African ones, grated in the new nation states, and growing voices emphasized *in situ* development and self-determination instead (Lwanga-Lunyiigo 1976; Gramly 1978). By the 1980s, migration was therefore increasingly melting away from its position as the de facto explanation of culture change.

Within the Bantu migration hypothesis some very specific concerns emerged. Alongside allegations of interdisciplinary tautology, some began questioning the essential viability of such large-scale population movements (Eggert 2005). Vansina (1995), for instance, challenged the very premiss of the migration, arguing for pulses of small-scale, local dialect-chaining that cumulatively led to the wide dispersal of Bantu languages. Robertson and Bradley (2000: 287) voiced similar disquiet when suggesting that the drawing of 'large arrows scything across big blank maps' of Africa took no account of its complex topographical and environmental mosaic, and that migration's enduring appeal was linked to a neo-colonial mindset. While these concerns are well known from the Bantu migration literature, they are not alone; Sutton's (1977) Aqualithic suffered a comparable fate, with Holl (2005), for example, critiquing its empirical foundations and arguing for parallel evolution rather than migration *per se*. For many, migration remains intimately connected to colonial era rhetoric and comes with too much historical baggage to be suitably applied; as Chami (1994: 32) states, 'it is difficult to disentangle the mind from the diffusionistic/migrationist/Hamitic paradigm.'

Paradoxically, however, migration remains a central organizing device within African archaeology, whether openly acknowledged or implicitly applied. Perhaps most vocal in its continued promotion is Tom Huffman, who continues to embrace large-scale migration narratives in explaining the history of farming communities in southern Africa (Huffman 2002, 2006, 2007; cf. Mitchell and Schoeman, Chapters 33 and 64 below). The issue of migration within African archaeology is therefore clearly divisive, and has the potential to polarize broader discussion down the pro/anti-migration divide. Such an approach is not always useful, and can unduly simplify a complex situation and created an artificial intellectual rift.

The Kintampo debate

An excellent case study that encapsulates the to-and-fro fortune of migration within African archaeological thought is that of early agricultural Kintampo communities in central Ghana (Casey, Ch. 41 below). Having identified a suite of microliths and comb-impressed ceramics, Davies (1962) drew on typological similarities to Sahelian material to argue for a southerly invasion of Sudanic intruders *c.* 3600 BP. Stahl (1985) later challenged this culture-historical model, arguing that the chronological overlap between Kintampo material culture and that of earlier Punpun hunter-gatherers indicated *in situ* development and economic intensification rather than large-scale migration. More recently, Watson (2005a) critiqued Stahl's approach, arguing that the presence of two distinct ceramic technologies clearly indicated discrete potting communities, and thus the migration of a new population into the area. Unlike Davies, however, Watson's approach moved beyond simplistic 'invasions', speculating that the migrants may have moved from the Sahara in a 'leap-frogging' motion (cf. Anthony 1997), as each group clears the path for the following migrants. The adversarial tone of Stahl's

(2005) response and Watson's (2005b) counter-response reiterate how divisive an issue migration can be, although a recent paper sounds a somewhat more conciliatory note (Watson 2010: 155).

Discussion

Migration has thus clearly played a fluctuating role within African archaeology, simultaneously being reviled, embraced, and ignored within the discipline. Existing polemics arguably leave a gap in the middle ground that must be embraced for migration to be shorn of simplistic modelling or political baggage. In order to do this, key areas of debate and future enquiry need to be addressed. Three are tackled here.

Definition

All too often migrations are implicitly assumed without being specifically defined. This is, of course, a broader issue within archaeology, but remains critical in African archaeology. Some forms of population movement are easier to discern and less contentious. Colonization of Africa's islands, for example, required a degree of deliberate and active movement over some distance (Mitchell 2004), whilst responses to environmental change such as the Holocene repopulation of the Sahara after the hyperarid Last Glacial Maximum cannot be disputed (MacDonald 1998; Barich, Ch. 31 below); as Mitchell (2004: 236) notes, 'Colonising new environments is rarely anything other than a purposeful, informed undertaking.' Such types of migration, or perhaps more accurately, colonization, can be taken as read. However, human mobility is a daily occurrence, and what constitutes migration within the African context requires clarification; can, for example, Anthony's economic migration be equally applied to mobile Hausa merchants and Rift Valley pastoralists? Should Robertson and Bradley's (2000: 288) assertion that the topography of Africa would probably only have allowed mass migrations in the last 400 years be taken seriously? Africanists need to be clearer in what they mean by migration, deciding whether models developed outside the continent are appropriate and whether a single definition can ever be applied.

Having recognized that migration occurs, there is also an urgent need to understand and explain more clearly its mechanisms. Current debate is often polarized, but much of this can be attributed to sometimes polemical approaches; the sweeping black arrows antagonize anti-migrationists who resort to extreme localism, parallel evolution, and reductive immobilism. This essentializes and simplifies what is a complex and multi-faceted phenomenon. Indeed, there may be a strong case to argue that the particularities of Africa mean that specific forms of migratory activity occurred; Kopytoff's (1987) treatise on the 'Internal African Frontier', for example, draws on the relatively low population density of precolonial Africa, as a result of which wealth in people, not land, was the path to power. Within such a scenario, the prevalent wave of advance model, reliant as it is on growing population density, becomes potentially redundant. It is therefore essential that new research addresses specific local conditions in order to develop appropriate models.

Identifying migration: material culture and identity

Like wider migration research, African archaeology has typically recognized migrating peoples through their diagnostic, and intrusive, material debris. Ceramics, in particular, have become a proxy for past population movement, with the Bantu migration hypothesis structured almost entirely around ceramic distributions. This is perhaps not surprising; Childe long ago recognized the value of ceramics, as everyday domestic artefacts, in reflecting migrant identity. However, Childe (1951) also emphasized the need to use a polythetic assemblage of multiple recurring objects in recognizing archaeological cultures. In contrast, for much of African archaeology ceramic data is often the primary, if not the sole, *fossile directeur*. Supporters of this method argue that ceramics are a perfect tool for expressing identity; 'because of the vital relationship between language and material culture, ceramics can be used to recognise and trace movements of groups' (Huffman 2002: 3). However, critics argue that this approach is too deterministic, and that material culture does not behave so predictably, or in such neat concert with nebulous sociocultural identities (e.g. Pikirayi 2007). Moreover, the specific behaviour of ceramics, or of material culture in general, in a migration environment is poorly studied in African archaeology. One of the few studies is that of Collett's (1987) examination of migrating Kololo and Nguni material signatures in southern Africa during the 19th century *Mfecane* (cf. Schoeman, Ch. 64 below). Intriguingly, Collett found that ceramic variability did not behave uniformly, with migrant Nguni communities losing their ceramic style, while the Kololo introduced their own Linyanti ceramics to the Barotse kingdom of western Zambia. The role that material culture plays within a migrant society thus needs to be reviewed more closely, and existing frameworks re-examined; it is perhaps dangerous to assume that ceramics alone can reflect population movement.

After migration: frontiers and boundaries

The idea that 'migration is a process, not an event' (Anthony 1990: 905) requires archaeologists to explore its long-term impact, recognizing that the journey itself is perhaps not as important as the new social situations created by relocation. This is arguably one area where African archaeology has been more successful, particularly in studying frontier relations and responses; as Kopytoff (1987: 7) notes, 'Africa has been a "frontier continent".' For instance, Alexander's (1978) model of frontier relations between hunter-gatherers and farmers, in which a porous boundary, or 'moving frontier', between pioneer farmers and endogamous foragers allowed considerable contact and interaction, has been applied in both southern and eastern Africa (Alexander 1984; Lane 2004).

Another highly influential frontier model to have emerged from Africa is Kopytoff's (1987) 'Internal African Frontier', which has been applied in numerous archaeological contexts, both in Africa (e.g. Usman 2009) and beyond (e.g. Schlegel 1992; cf. Anthony 1997; Chapman 1997; Burmeister 2000). As noted, Kopytoff's thesis focuses around the idea of wealth-in-people, not land, creating a dynamic in which mobility shaped political authority, as leaders sought to retain followers and stop defection to other polities, or the establishment of new communities. Fission, according to Kopytoff, was thus a regular political strategy, a means by which to challenge or escape authority. Whereas Alexander's frontier model centres around early contact phases, Kopytoff's model has been used to explore a wide range of political contexts, from farming communities to state-level societies. Exploring the archaeology of frontiers and the effects of migration therefore seems to have been a more successful pursuit in African archaeology than perhaps the search for the migration itself.

Conclusions

Global archaeology is slowly re-engaging with migration as an explanatory device, overcoming some of the earlier theoretical divisions that 'banished it from centre-stage' (Chapman and Hamerow 1997: 1) and beginning a new chapter of targeted research. In Africa, migration never really left archaeological discourse, but it did become a highly divisive issue that split researchers and arguably led to polemical and undue simplification of a nuanced debate. Migration is clearly a central dynamic within African society, and therefore a new era of engagement is needed. In particular, researchers need to develop new theoretical approaches to migration, making it much clearer what is meant by the term, as well as reviewing how it is identified archaeologically. While wider archaeological investigations of migration may be a useful resource, such work should not simply be imported direct to the African context, as migratory behaviour can be affected by time and place, and it is thus essential that appropriate models be developed for African archaeology. It is also apparent that one of the more successful and interesting outcomes of migration research has been exploration of the long-term effects of such movement, and the archaeology of contact situations. It may be that attention should therefore shift from the contested and problematic identification of migration and focus instead on what happens after such events.

References

Adams, W. Y., Van Gerven, D. P, and Levy, R. S. (1978). The retreat from migrationism. *Annual Review of Anthropology* 7: 483–532.

Alexander, J. A. (1978). Frontier studies and the earliest farmers in Europe. In D. Green, C. Haselgrove, and M. Spriggs (eds), *Social Organisation and Settlement*. Oxford: British Archaeological Reports, 13–29.

——(1984). Early frontiers in Southern Africa. In M. Hall, G. Avery, W. L. Wilson, and A. J. B. Humphreys (eds), *Frontiers: Southern African Archaeology Today*. Oxford: British Archaeological Reports, 12–23.

Anthony, D. W. (1990). Migration in archaeology: the baby and the bathwater. *American Anthropologist* 92: 895–914.

——(1997). Prehistoric migration as social process. In J. Chapman and H. Hamerow (eds), *Migrations and Invasions in Archaeological Perspective*. Oxford: British Archaeological Reports, 21–32.

Burmeister, S. (2000). Archaeology and migration: approaches to an archaeological proof of migration. *Current Anthropology* 41: 539–67.

Cameron, C. (1995). Migration and the movement of southwest peoples. *Journal of Anthropological Archaeology* 14: 104–24.

CHAMI, F. (1994). *The Tanzanian Coast in the First Millennium AD: An Archaeology of the Iron-Working-Farming Communities*. Uppsala: Societas Archaeological Upsaliensis.

CHAPMAN, J. (1997). The impact of modern invasions and migrations on archaeological explanation. In J. Chapman and H. Hamerow (eds), *Migrations and Invasions in Archaeological Perspective*. Oxford: British Archaeological Reports, 11–20.

—— and DOLUKHANOV, P. M. (1992). The baby and the bathwater: pulling the plug on migrations. *American Anthropologist* 94: 169–74.

—— and HAMEROW, H. (eds) (1997). *Migrations and Invasions in Archaeological Perspective*. Oxford: British Archaeological Reports.

CHILDE, V. G. (1951). *Social Evolution*. London: C. A. Watts.

COLLETT, D. P. (1987). A contribution to the study of migrations in the archaeological record: the Ngoni and Kololo migrations as a case study. In I. Hodder (ed.), *Archaeology as Long-Term History*. Cambridge: Cambridge University Press, 105–16.

DANIEL, G. (1950). *A Hundred Years of Archaeology*. London: Gerald Duckworth.

DAVIES, O. (1962). Neolithic cultures of Ghana. In G. Mortelmans and J. Nenquin (eds), *Proceedings of the IVth Panafrican Congress*. Tervuren: Musée Royale de l'Afrique Centrale, 291–302.

DUBOW, S. (1995). *Scientific Racism in Modern South Africa*. Cambridge: Cambridge University Press.

GAMBLE, C. (1993). People on the move: interpretation of regional variation in Palaeolithic Europe. In J. Chapman and P. Dolukhanov (eds), *Cultural Transformations and Interactions in Eastern Europe*. Aldershot: Avebury, 37–55.

GOSDEN, C. (2004). *Archaeology and Colonialism: Cultural Contact from 5000 BC to the Present*. Cambridge: Cambridge University Press.

GRAMLY, R. M. (1978). Expansion of Bantu-speakers versus development of Bantu languages and African culture *in situ*: an archaeologist's perspective. *South African Archaeological Bulletin* 33: 107–12.

HÄRKE, H. (1998). Archaeologists and migration: a problem of attitude? *Current Anthropology* 39: 19–45.

HOLL, A. (2005). Holocene 'aquatic' adaptations in north tropical Africa. In A. B. Stahl (ed.), *African Archaeology: A Critical Introduction*. Oxford: Blackwell, 174–86.

HUFFMAN, T. N. (1989). Ceramics, settlements and Late Iron Age migrations. *African Archaeological Review* 7: 155–82.

—— (2002). Regionality in the Iron Age: the case of the Sotho-Tswana. *Southern African Humanities* 14: 1–22.

—— (2006). Bantu migrations in southern Africa. In H. Soodyall (ed.), *The Prehistory of Africa: Tracing the Lineage of Modern Man*. Johannesburg: Jonathan Ball, 97–108.

—— (2007). *Handbook to the Southern African Iron Age*. Pietermaritzburg: University of KwaZulu-Natal Press.

JOHNSTON, H. (1913). A survey of the ethnography of Africa: and the former racial and tribal migrations in that continent. *Journal of the Royal Anthropological Institute* 43: 375–421.

KOPYTOFF, I. (1987). The internal African frontier: the making of an African political culture. In I. Kopytoff (ed.), *The African Frontier: The Reproduction of Traditional African Societies*. Bloomington: Indiana University Press, 3–88.

LANE, P. J. (2004). The 'moving frontier' and the transition to food production in Kenya. *Azania* 39: 243–64.

LEE, E. S. (1966). A theory of migration. *Demography* 3: 47–57.

LWANGA-LUNYIIGO, S. (1976). The Bantu problem reconsidered. *Current Anthropology* 17: 282–6.

LYONS, C. L., and PAPADOPOULOS, J. K. (eds) (2002). *The Archaeology of Colonialism*. Los Angeles, Calif.: Getty Publications.

MITCHELL, P. J. (2004). Towards a comparative archaeology of Africa's islands. *Journal of African Archaeology* 2: 229–50.

OTTE, M., and KEELEY, L.H. (1990). The impact of regionalism on palaeolithic studies. *Current Anthropology* 31: 577–82.

PIKIRAYI, I. (2007). Ceramics and group identities: towards a social archaeology in southern African Iron Age ceramic studies. *Journal of Social Archaeology* 7: 286–301.

RENFREW, A. C. (1987). *Archaeology and Language: The Puzzle of Indo-European Origins*. London: Jonathan Cape.

ROBERTSON, J. H., and BRADLEY, R. (2000). A new paradigm: the African Early Iron Age without Bantu migrations. *History in Africa* 27: 287–323.

ROCKMAN, M., and STEELE, J. (eds) (2003). *Colonization of Unfamiliar Landscapes: The Archaeology of Adaptation*. London: Routledge.

SANDERS, E. R. (1969). The Hamitic hypothesis: its origin and functions in the time perspective. *Journal of African History* 10: 521–32.

SCHLEGEL, A. (1992). African political models in the American Southwest: Hopi as an Internal Frontier Society. *American Anthropologist* 94: 376–97

SELIGMAN, C. G. (1957). *Races of Africa*. London. Oxford University Press.

SHENNAN, S. J. (1989). Introduction. In S. Shennan (ed.), *Archaeological Approaches to Cultural Identity*. London: Unwin Hyman, 1–32.

STAHL, A. B. (1985). Reinvestigation of Kintampo 6 Rockshelter, Ghana: implications for the nature of culture change. *African Archaeological Review* 3: 117–50.

—— (2005). Glass houses under the rocks: a reply to Watson. *Journal of African Archaeology* 3: 57–64.

STEIN, G. J. (ed) (2005). *The Archaeology of Colonial Encounters: Comparative Perspectives*. Santa Fe, NM: School of Advanced Research.

SUTTON, J. E. G. (1977). The African Aqualithic. *Antiquity* 51: 25–34.

TILLEY, C. (1978). Migration in modern European history. In W. McNeill and R. Adams (eds), *Human Migration: Patterns and Policies*. Bloomington: Indiana University Press, 48–74.

USMAN, A. (2009). Precolonial regional migrations and settlement abandonment in Yorubaland, Nigeria. In T. Falola and A. Usman (eds), *Movement, Borders, and Identities in Africa*. Rochester, NY: University of Rochester Press, 99–125.

VANSINA, J. (1995). New linguistic evidence and 'the Bantu Expansion'. *Journal of African History* 36: 173–95.

WATSON, D. J. (2005a). Under the rocks: reconsidering the origin of the Kintampo Tradition and the development of food production in the savanna-forest/forest of West Africa. *Journal of African Archaeology* 3: 3–55.

—— (2005b). Straws within a glass house: a reply to Stahl. *Journal of African Archaeology* 3: 65–8.

—— (2010). Within savanna and forest: a review of the Late Stone Age Kintampo Tradition, Ghana. *Azania: Archaeological Research from Africa* 45: 141–74.

CHAPTER 7

....

ETHNOARCHAEOLOGICAL RESEARCH IN AFRICA

....

DIANE LYONS

INTRODUCTION

....

ETHNOARCHAEOLOGY examines the relationship between people and their material worlds in ways that are useful to archaeological interpretation. As a research strategy, practitioners apply it with diverse theoretical and topical interests but are bound by a common concern: constructing strong analogy (Cunningham 2003, 2009; Lane 2005). This goal distinguishes ethnoarchaeology from the broader field of material culture studies, to which it is an important contributor. Ethnoarchaeology is also distinct from experimental archaeology lacking direct ethnographic context.

Africanist ethnoarchaeology has dominated the ethnoarchaeological literature since the 1970s and has engaged in key archaeological debates and interests. Here I provide a brief overview of ethnoarchaeological approaches, and summarize four major research foci and the debates to which they contribute: human evolution; social interpretations of settlement; style and identity; and technology.

ETHNOGRAPHIC ANALOGY

....

Ethnographic analogy as an inductive methodology is subject to a degree of uncertainty, and for this reason some archaeologists rejected it in the late 1970s. However, analogy plays an important role in all sciences, and without ethnographic analogy archaeologists can do little more than describe the past (Wylie 1985). Ethnographic analogies derive from two sources. The direct historical approach holds that direct living descendants are appropriate analogues for interpreting their ancestors because they share a common cultural tradition. General analogies are based in considerations of relevance between an ethnographic source and archaeological subject that are historically unrelated but causally linked by multiple shared boundary conditions such as similar ecological settings, subsistence practices, and social organizations. The presumption that direct historical analogies are stronger than general ones is unfounded. Both must be developed using multiple lines of evidence that demonstrate relevant connections between source and subject, and a comparative approach must be applied to reveal how source and subject are similar *and* different in order to consider cultural continuity and change (Stahl 1993; Fewster 2006). Using ethnographic analogy always carries the danger of presenting Africans as perpetually traditional (Fewster 2001; Cruz 2011), so it is essential that ethnographic sources be historically situated in order to assess how colonialism and other historic processes have affected contemporary practice. In so doing, ethnoarchaeology contributes to the documentation of African history.

THEORY

Ethnoarchaeology is framed in positivist and post-positivist theory that contributes to different but essential understandings of the human past. These perspectives are described elsewhere (David and Kramer 2001) and summarized only briefly here. Early positivist ethnoarchaeology argued that humans adapt to their ecological circumstances through behaviours that are predictable, cross-culturally relevant, and reflected in material patterning. Hodder's (1982) ethnoarchaeological research in East Africa challenged the causal role of ecological factors in culture process. His research initiated the post-positivist critique that investigates how humans think about their world and, as social agents constrained by social structures, constitute and negotiate identity, meaning, and power through material practice. From this perspective, material culture does not reflect human behaviour, it constitutes social action. Despite criticisms of Hodder's methodology (MacEachern 1996), his ideas profoundly affected archaeological theory and the consideration of social and ideological factors in interpreting the past. After heated debate, theoreticians have demonstrated that post-positivist research is as scientific in its agenda as positivism (VanPool and VanPool 1999), and Kosso (1991) shows that positivists and post-positivists conduct research using a similar methodology. For example, positivist middle-range theory and post-positivist hermeneutic or contextual approaches both test their respective theories by tacking between theory and material evidence of human behaviours. Ultimately, interpretations framed in either theory are equally constrained by the material evidence and the plausibility of their interpretation (VanPool and VanPool 1999). Criticisms that post-positivist ethnoarchaeology is particularist in nature is inaccurate. While specific meaning is context-dependent (as are aspects of positivist interpretations), post-positivists commonly use general principles from their studies to interpret other cultures. For instance, Hodder (1992) developed a hypothesis with material expectations from his research in Africa to interpret Neolithic remains in Europe; Betsileo practices in Madagascar inspired Parker Pearson and Ramilisonina (1998) to reinterpret Stonehenge; and Insoll's (2008) study of Tallensi shrines is a model for interpreting Bronze Age deposits in Britain. In addition to their contribution to general archaeological concerns, the following four research foci illustrate positivist and post-positivist approaches in Africanist ethnoarchaeology.

HUMAN EVOLUTION

Isaac (1968) once asserted that ethnoarchaeology of African hunter-gatherers could offer 'inspiration' to develop hypotheses with which to investigate Pleistocene foragers and test archaeological assumptions. Such research is limited so far to southern, eastern, and central African foragers and does not represent the continent's diverse hunter-gatherer populations. These studies challenge models of human behaviour developed by archaeologists from archaeological materials and non-human predator behaviours, and take the stance that contemporary human hunters are the best analogues to interpret Pleistocene foragers because they face common ecological concerns (e.g. O'Connell et al. 2002; Hawkes et al. 2001b). This research addresses taphonomic processes, what can be inferred from faunal assemblages, and actualistic critiques of evolutionary models based on the importance of big game hunting.

Pleistocene hominin behaviour is inferred partly from the composition and alteration of archaeological bone assemblages. Until Yellen's (1977) study in the Kalahari, archaeologists incorrectly assumed that faunal assemblages directly reflected diet and the spatial locations of specific types of activities. Beginning in the 1980s, studies of the Hadza of Tanzania (Bunn et al. 1988; O'Connell et al. 1988) tested a widely used model of carcass transport and expectations of bone element compositions at kill and base camps that were used to infer site function. It became clear that variables affecting the formation of bone assemblages are more complex than previously realized. For example, in addition to transport costs, bone assemblages are affected by food sharing (Marshall 1994; Kelly et al. 2005) and cooking practices (Kent 1993; Lupo 1995).

Studies of the Hadza were used to critique the widely applied hypothesis that early human evolution was based on increasingly effective big-game hunting. Lupo and O'Connell (2002) tested archaeological models used to infer scavenging and hunting practices with Hadza-generated faunal assemblages. Their study supported the principles of these models, but evidence for these behaviours varied dramatically in their Hadza control sample, suggesting that simplistic interpretations of archaeological assemblages are misleading. The question emerging from this research was not how hominins got their meat, but whether hunting big game was a reliable feeding strategy. The Hadza's staple diet is made up of smaller game and tubers, and the assumption that food sharing reduces risk inherent in big-game hunting was not supported in practice (O'Connell et al. 1992; 2002; Hawkes et al. 2001a). Instead, hunting big game was socially valuable in enhancing men's status and attracting wives who were successful gatherers (Lupo and Schmitt 2002, 2005). The unreliability of big-game hunting challenged assumptions that men provide their families with meat allowing their wives to produce more infants more often. Men contribute some food, but women (and their dependent children) are provisioned by their own mothers during pregnancy and lactation (Hawkes et al. 1997, 2001b; Marlowe 2003). Unfortunately, plant food collection practices have low archaeological visibility while big game is over-represented in archaeological assemblages, an important transform in the inference of forager diets.

These studies provide rich insights into taphonomic processes and problems in inferring diet and behaviour from bone assemblages. But reliance on common ecological concerns of contemporary and past foragers as the basis for analogical relevance is problematic. Few if any of these studies provide substantive consideration of how Pleistocene foragers differ from contemporary ones or the historical or cultural processes that impact the distribution of resources and hunters in modern landscapes.

SOCIAL INTERPRETATIONS OF SETTLEMENT

Positivist studies of settlement focus on the fit between social group, household space, and architectural investment, anticipated and actual length of stay, and the need to settle near kin or friends in order to share labour or resources (e.g. David 1971; Kent and Vierich 1989; Stone 1993). While settlement is shaped by these concerns, it also actively constitutes meaning. For this reason, settlement has been an important area of post-positivist research. These studies show how power and meaning are negotiated through spatial metaphors and architecture (see Wynne-Jones, Ch. 13 below).

Domestic spatial order is an important context for investigating gender relations. Moore's (1986) *Space, Text and Gender* is a seminal study in gender archaeology. Moore demonstrates how patrilineages of Kenya's Endo reproduce an ideology of male values and authority over resources in domestic spatial order, concluding that women's perspectives are not represented in domestic spatial texts because women negotiate their interests within the same patrilineal ideology. However, Lyons (1998) found that in northern Cameroon, Mura women participate actively in constructing the dominant patrilineal ideology, including the perspective that women are witches. Women use this perception of themselves as potentially dangerous as a strategy to negotiate their own interests, an ideology materialized in different building materials and site formation processes in men's and women's areas of compounds. Fredriksen (2007) reminds us that gender relations and their expression in household material and spatial contexts are dynamic—a direct challenge to the static use of ethnographic analogy which underpins the Central Cattle Pattern, a model widely used to interpret social organization in southern Africa's Iron Age settlements (see also Lane 2005; Fewster 2006).

Lane (2006) observes that the Dogon of Mali use domestic space and architecture as a way of *presencing* the past (Ray 1987). By this he means that the material traces of abandoned and occupied houses are a tangible record to which the Dogon refer in remembering patrilineage history and claiming land and settlement. Women and men are moved through space differently and use material culture to construct their histories and identities differently, an observation generally applicable to the Mura, the Endo, the Luo of Kenya (Herbich and Dietler 2009), the Tigrayans of Ethiopia (Lyons 2009), and perhaps to a widespread practice for legitimating control over resources in sedentary societies.

Spatial metaphor is also important in negotiating societal power. For example, Smith and David (1995) investigate political power in the house of the chief of Sukur in northeastern Nigeria. Sukur's chiefly power needed constant renegotiation partly through spatial strategies that legitimated and mystified chiefly authority. While the chief's domestic compound is spatially organized according to gendered principles that structure other Sukur compounds, his house is located downhill from Sukur's council house, metaphorically representing him as the 'wife of Sukur' serving his people (Fig. 7.1).

FIG. 7.1 The chief of Sukur's compound, enclosed by a monumental wall and located below Sukur's council house (photograph courtesy of N. David, Mandara Archaeological Project).

Control of occult forces is fundamental to power in many African societies. Spirits are materially engaged through shrines that are often made of durable materials and maintained after compound abandonment (Agorsah 1985; Insoll 2008). In some societies shrines are integral to group territorial expansion (Dawson 2009). For example, the Bafut kingdom of Cameroon is built peacefully by elevating villages into sub-chiefdoms that are tied to the ritual centre by the construction of two emblems of status: a monolith and a shrine built atop materials franchised from the polity's central shrine (Asombang 1999).

States also negotiate power by manipulating architectural and spatial meaning. Kus and Raharijaona (1998, 2000) demonstrate how Madagascar's former Imerina state inserted itself into the daily life and cosmological beliefs of rural people partly through manipulating vernacular house symbolism. Symbolizing the centre of the four cardinal directions, the central house pillar is used metaphorically as a position of strength in life. The Imerina palace was located in the polity's geographical centre; its central pillar was the state's centre and the metaphor for a strong ruler. Similarly, nobles in northern Ethiopia manipulated the vernacular architectural aesthetic in which houses embodied the ambitions and qualities of their builders, and were used by owners, regardless of social class, as platforms to negotiate status and land tenure (Lyons 2007). Clay house models and elite stone stelae carved as multi-storied houses are part of the material symbolism of the region's early Aksumite polity (Phillipson, Ch. 55 below), and houses may represent a long-term practice for claiming land and power.

STYLE AND SOCIAL IDENTITY

Ethnoarchaeology contributes significantly to the understanding of how social identities are materialized, a concept fundamental to archaeological interpretation. Prior to the post-positivist critique, archaeologists assumed that the spatial-temporal distribution of artefact styles reflected bounded social entities. For instance, Wobst's (1977) information exchange theory proposed that stylistic meaning encoded in highly visible objects is a cost-effective means to signal ethnic identity and maintain territorial boundaries with other groups. Wiessner's (1983, 1984) study of Kalahari projectile points and beaded headbands further distinguished information exchange as having an emblemic style, which signals corporate group identity, and an assertive style, which communicates individual and informal group identity. An implication of this theory is that groups decode stylistic messages as representing ethnic identities, a fact that was not demonstrated for Kalahari foragers. Hodder's (1979, 1982, 1985) ethnoarchaeological investigations in East Africa understood style as an active strategy used by ethnic groups to negotiate their interests, differentiating them from their neighbours when social and economic relations were strained, but suppressing stylistic differences when relations were more reciprocal. Thus, style only demarcates ethnic boundaries if groups deem that this strategy furthers their interests.

In a study of material style in the Mandara Mountains region of northern Cameroon and Nigeria, David et al. (1988) concluded that human bodies and pots are perceived and decorated similarly, and that decoration protects the contents of pots and bodies from dangerous occult forces. They suggest that both features might be found in a considerable range of societies. While stressing that not all decoration is protective or even meaningful, some style expresses the underlying structures of a social group's worldview and is used consistently across multiple artefact categories (Gavua 1989; Lyons 1998) (Fig. 7.2). Contrary to Wobst, Sterner (1989) found that stylistic investment was greatest in objects only seen by members of the same social group, and that any signalling of ethnic identity to outsiders was either an unintended by-product of within-group messaging or transmitted by pot morphology or usage.

Stylistic borrowing that blurs distinctions between neighbouring groups further muddies the relationship between style and ethnic group boundaries (Larick 1986, 1991; MacEachern 1998). Where multiple ethnic groups interact over long periods of time, they may come to share a 'symbolic reservoir' (after McIntosh 1989: 77) of core symbols (Sterner 1992) that renders them archaeologically indistinguishable. From these investigations emerged a new understanding of ethnic identity as situational, fluid, and malleable, and of ethnic boundaries as permeable (e.g. MacEachern 1994).

Yet inferring social group identity from material evidence remains a fundamental problem in interpreting culture history and social interactions in the past. In the 1990s ethnoarchaeologists turned to technological style to investigate social identities using *chaîne opératoire*, a concept borrowed and modified from the *technologie* school. In Africanist ethnoarchaeology, *chaîne opératoire* recognizes that artisans' technological choices at each stage in craft production are social choices learned as members of a social group of producers and consumers. The suite of choices of a particular artisan commu-

FIG. 7.2 Mura potters in northern Cameroon apply red paint and twisted roulette designs to vessels that are widely perceived to protect vessel content from the manipulation of witches, a perception and practice that crosses ethnic boundaries (photograph, Diane Lyons, Mandara Archaeological Project directed by N. David).

nity constitutes their technological style—a material signature of their identity (Dietler and Herbich 1998; Livingstone Smith 2000). Learning networks play an important role in artisan choice, and some choices, once learned, are resistant to change (Fig. 7.3). For instance, Gosselain (2001) found that sub-Saharan pottery-forming techniques are particularly resistant, an observation supported in other work (Sterner and David 2003; Livingstone-Smith and Van der Veke 2007–9; Fowler 2008; Guèye 2011). Because technological styles are ethnographically and archaeologically accessible, *chaînes opératoires* research holds particular promise in unravelling historical relationships between contemporary and archaeological social groups (Gosselain and Livingstone Smith, Ch. 9 below). For example, ethnoarchaeologists have discerned five main ceramic traditions with different *chaînes opératoires* correlated with specific ethnolinguistic groups in Mali's Dogon country, with the mechanisms that produce these different traditions in the present explaining patterning found in archaeological materials over the past millennium (Mayor et al. 2005; Mayor 2010). However, there are conditions in which technological styles change (e.g. Gosselain 2008; Herbich and Dietler 2008). Wynne-Jones and Mapunda (2008) show that on Mafia Island on the Swahili Coast, technological style is related to identity in place rather than ethnic group, as ethnolinguistically different potters who emigrate from the mainland adopt a common technological style as part of a cosmopolitan coastal identity.

FIG. 7.3 Learning networks guide potters' choices at every stage of production. Here a daughter learns from her mother to make pots through a lifetime of assisting in different stages of the *chaîne opératoire* (photograph, Diane Lyons, Eastern Tigray Pottery Project).

TECHNOLOGY

The organization of craft production is important in archaeological interpretations of social complexity. In many African societies craft workers, especially blacksmiths and potters, are marginalized because they are believed to possess dangerous powers (Tobert 1988; Sterner and David 1991; La Violette 2000; Haaland 2004). Considerable variation exists in the degree of marginalization experienced by different categories of artisans within and between societies, and researchers disagree on the use of the term 'caste' in African contexts. Nevertheless, artisans are sometimes segregated into endogamous communities and prohibited from owning land, holding political office, and eating with others (but see Lane 2008). Despite this widespread practice, inferring craft workers' status from material evidence is not straightforward, and is subject to current ethnoarchaeological interest (Weedman 2002, 2006; Arthur 2006, 2009; Lyons and Freeman 2009).

Ironworking has received major ethnoarchaeological attention since the 1970s, and has played a role in deconstructing colonialist agendas that represented Africans as technologically and culturally backward. The ethnoarchaeology of ironworking shows us the value of using a broad range of sources, theoretical perspectives, and methodologies to understand African technological knowledge. This work is invaluable because, except for southwest

FIG. 7.4 Observations of iron smelting in northern Cameroon contributed to the understanding of technical, social, and ideological aspects of iron production (photograph, Diane Lyons, Mandara Archaeological Project directed by N. David).

Ethiopia, the direct observation of ironworking is no longer possible (Haaland et al. 2004; Killick 2004).

Because symbolic and material practices are integrated in African ironworking, many researchers use a *chaîne opératoire* approach to investigate ironworking traditions (e.g. Fluzin et al. 2001; Huysecom 2001). David (2001) suggests that Peter Schmidt's research (an ethnoarchaeological project that integrates archaeology, oral history, and metallurgy) is the most comprehensive of ironworking studies and falls within the spirit of *chaîne opératoire*. Long-term projects such as David's (e.g. David 2012) in Cameroon and Nigeria and Schmidt's (e.g. 1996, 1997) in Tanzania have combined cross-disciplinary expertise to understand not only how African smelters made iron but how ironmaking was understood by its practitioners within their social and ideological perspectives (Fig. 7.4). In sub-Saharan Africa, these perspectives frequently involve the use of metaphors and metonyms of human reproduction (or broader perceptions of fertile forces) to ensure smelting success (e.g. Barndon 1996; Goucher and Herbert 1996; Rowlands and Warnier 1996; Bekaert 1998; David 2001; Schmidt 2009). Importantly, Schmidt and Mapunda (1997) have tacked between ethnoarchaeological observations and archaeological evidence in the Great Lakes Region and found that material aspects of observed rituals occur in the region's early Iron Age sites, suggesting a long tradition of material symbols if not practice. Ironworking is the subject of Chirikure's chapter, this volume.

CONCLUSIONS

Ethnoarchaeology has contributed to the deconstruction of colonial ideologies of African social and technological achievements, and to the documentation of African history. This body of research not only has enriched the understanding of African material practices but also contributes to archaeological inference generally. Africanist ethnoarchaeology has tested and shaped positivist and post-positivist theory since the 1970s, but greater synergy between ethnoarchaeologists and archaeologists is needed. In a previous summary, Lane (2005) concluded that, despite the body of ethnoarchaeological work, many Africanist archaeologists persist in interpreting material style as representing bounded social entities and present ancient foragers as ahistoric exploiters of landscapes occupying worlds devoid of meaning, something clearly contradicted by the wealth of rock art they produced (see Smith, Ch. 11 below). The way forward is through collaborative projects that incorporate ethnoarchaeological and archaeological components, as has been done in the study of African ironworking. David and Kramer (2001: 41) advise that this requires that researchers accept that different theories may be necessary to interpret different kinds of behaviour. African material practices are complex, and we should anticipate that inferences drawn from these practices will be so as well.

REFERENCES

AGORSAH, E. K. (1985). Archeological implications of traditional house construction among the Nchumuru of northern Ghana. *Current Anthropology* 26: 103–15.

ARTHUR, J. (2006). *Living with Pottery*. Salt Lake City: University of Utah Press.

——(2009). Understanding household population through ceramic assemblage formation: ceramic ethnoarchaeology among the Gamo of southwestern Ethiopia. *American Antiquity* 74: 31–48.

ASOMBANG, R. (1999). Sacred centers and urbanization in west central Africa. In S. K. McIntosh (ed.), *Beyond Chiefdoms: Pathways to Complexity in Africa*. Cambridge: Cambridge University Press, 80–87.

BARNDON, R. (1996). Fipa ironworking and its technological style. In P. Schmidt (ed.), *The Culture and Technology of African Iron Production*. Gainesville: University Press of Florida, 40–57.

BEKAERT, S. (1998). Multiple levels of meaning and the tension of consciousness: how to interpret iron technology in Bantu Africa. *Archaeological Dialogues* 5: 6–29.

BUNN, H., BARTRAM, L., and KROLL, E. (1988). Variability in bone assemblage formation from Hadza hunting, scavenging and carcass processing. *Journal of Anthropological Archaeology* 7: 412–57.

CRUZ, M. D. (2011). 'Pots are pots, not people': material culture and ethnic identity in the Banda Area (Ghana), nineteenth and twentieth centuries. *Azania: Archaeological Research in Africa* 46: 336–57.

CUNNINGHAM, J. (2003). Transcending the 'obnoxious spectator': a case for processual pluralism in ethnoarchaeology. *Journal of Anthropological Archaeology* 22: 389–410.

——(2009). Ethnoarchaeology beyond correlates. *Journal of Ethnoarchaeology* 1: 115–36.

DAVID, N. (1971). The Fulani compound and the archaeologist. *World Archaeology* 3: 111–31.

—— (2001). Lost in the third hermeneutic? Theory and methodology, objects and representations in the ethnoarchaeology of African metallurgy. *Mediterranean Archaeology* 14: 49–72.

—— (ed.) (2012). *Metals in Mandara Mountains' Society and Culture*. Trenton, NJ: Africa World Press.

—— and KRAMER, C. (2001). *Ethnoarchaeology in Action*. Cambridge: Cambridge University Press.

—— STERNER, J., and GAVUA, K. (1988). Why pots are decorated. *Current Anthropology* 29: 365–89.

DAWSON, A. (ed.) (2009). *Shrines in Africa*. Calgary: University of Calgary Press.

DIETLER, M., and HERBICH, I. (1998). Habitus, techniques, style: an integrated approach to the social understanding of material culture and boundaries. In M. Stark (ed.), *The Archaeology of Social Boundaries*. Washington, DC: Smithsonian Institution Press, 232–63.

FEWSTER, K. (2001). The responsibilities of ethnoarchaeologists. In M. Pluciennik (ed.), *The Responsibilities of Archaeologists*. Oxford: Archaeopress, 65–73.

—— (2006). The potential of analogy in post-processual archaeologies: a case study from Basimane ward, Serowe, Botswana. *Journal of the Royal Anthropological Institute* 12: 61–87.

FLUZIN, P., SERNEELS, V., HUYSECOM, E., BENOIT, P., and KIENON, H. (2001). Reconstitution of the operating chain in paleo-iron and steel metallurgy from archaeological remains: comparative studies with the African ethno-archaeology. In S. Beyries and P. Pétrequin (eds), *Ethno-archaeology and its Transfers*. Oxford: Archaeopress, 113–22.

FOWLER, K. (2008). Zulu pottery production in the Lower Thukela Basin, Kwa-Zulu Natal, South Africa. *Southern African Humanities* 20: 477–511.

FREDRIKSEN, P. (2007). Approaching intimacy: interpretations of changes in Moloko household space. *South African Archaeological Bulletin* 62: 126–39.

GAVUA, K. (1989). Goat skins versus wax prints: an analysis of Mafa costume. In D. Tkaczuk and B. Vivian (eds), *Cultures in Conflict*. Calgary: Archaeological Association of the University of Calgary, 293–6.

GOSSELAIN, O. (2001). Globalizing local pottery studies. In S. Beyries and P. Pétrequin (eds), *Ethno-archaeology and its Transfers*. Oxford: Archaeopress, 95–112.

—— (2008). Mother Bella was not a bella: inherited and transformed traditions in southwestern Niger. In M. Stark, B. Bowser, and L. Horne (eds.), *Cultural Transmission and Material Culture*. Tucson: University of Arizona Press, 150–77.

GOUCHER, C., and HERBERT, E. (1996). 'The blooms of Banajeli': technology and gender in West African iron making. In P. Schmidt (ed.), *The Culture and Technology of African Iron Production*. Gainesville: University of Florida Press, 40–57.

GUEYE, N. S. (2011). Dis-moi quel pot tu as et je te dirai qui tu es! Matérialiser les identités sociales dans les décors céramiques de la moyenne vallée du fleuve Sénégal (nord du Sénégal). *Azania: Archaeological Research in Africa* 46: 20–35.

HAALAND, G., HAALAND, R., and DEA, D. (2004). Smelting iron: caste and its symbolism in south-western Ethiopia. In T. Insoll (ed.), *Belief in the Past*. Oxford: Oxbow Books, 75–6.

HAALAND, R. (2004). Iron smelting—a vanishing tradition: ethnographic study of this craft in south-west Ethiopia. *Journal of African Archaeology* 2: 65–80.

HAOUR, A. (2011). Putting pots and people in the Sahelian empires. *Azania: Archaeological Research in Africa* 46: 36–48.

HAWKES, K., O'CONNELL, J. F., and BLURTON JONES, N. (1997). Hadza women's time allocation, offspring provisioning, and the evolution of long postmenopausal life spans. *Current Anthropology* 38: 551–77.

HAWKES K., O'CONNELL, J. F., and BLURTON JONES, N. (2001a). Hadza meat sharing. *Evolution and Human Behavior* 22: 113–42.

—— —— —— (2001b). Hunting and nuclear families. *Current Anthropology* 42: 681–709.

HERBICH, I., and DIETLER, M. (2008). The long arm of the mother-in-law: learning, postmarital resocialization of women, and material culture style. In M. Stark, B. Bowser, and L. Horne (eds), *Cultural Transmission and Material Culture Breaking Down Boundaries*. Tucson: University of Arizona Press, 233–44.

—— —— (2009) Domestic space, social life and settlement biography: theoretical reflections from the ethnography of a rural African landscape. *Arqueo Mediterrània* 11: 11–23.

HODDER, I. (1979). Economic and social stress and material culture patterning. *American Antiquity* 44: 446–54.

—— (1982). *Symbols in Action*. Cambridge: Cambridge University Press.

—— (1985). Boundaries as strategies: an ethnoarchaeological study. In S. Green and S. Periman (eds), *The Archaeology of Frontiers and Boundaries*. New York: Academic Press, 141–59.

—— (1992). Burials, houses, women and men in the European Neolithic. In I. Hodder (ed.), *Theory and Practice in Archaeology*. London: Routledge, 45–80.

HUYSECOM, E. (2001). Technique et croyance des forgerons africains: élements pour une approche ethnoarchéologique. *Mediterranean Archaeology* 14: 73–82.

INSOLL, T. (2008). Negotiating the archaeology of destiny. *Journal of Social Archaeology* 8: 380–403.

ISAAC, G. (1968). Traces of Pleistocene hunters: an East African example. In R. B. Lee and I. Devore (eds), *Man the Hunter*. New York: Aldine, 253–61.

KELLY, R., POYER, L., and TUCKER, B. (2005). An ethnoarchaeological study of mobility, architectural investment, and food sharing along Madagascar's Mikea. *American Anthropologist*, 107: 403–16.

KENT, S. (1993). Variability in faunal assemblages: the influence of hunting skill, sharing, dogs and mode of cooking on faunal remains at a sedentary Kalahari community. *Journal of Anthropological Archaeology* 12: 323–85.

—— and VIERICH, H. (1989). The myth of ecological determinism: anticipated mobility and site spatial organization. In S. Kent (ed.), *Farmers as Hunters: the Implications of Sedentism*. Cambridge: Cambridge University Press, 96–130.

KILLICK, D. (2004). What do we know about African iron working? *Journal of African Archaeology* 2: 97–112.

KOSSO, P. (1991). Method in archaeology: middle range theory as hermeneutics. *American Antiquity* 56: 621–7.

KUS, S., and RAHARIJAONA, V. (1998). Between earth and sky there are only a few large boulders: sovereignty and monumentality in central Madagascar. *Journal of Anthropological Archaeology* 17: 53–79.

—— —— (2000). House to palace, village to state: scaling up architecture and ideology. *American Anthropologist* 102: 98–113.

LANE, P. J. (2005). Barbarous tribes and unrewarding gyrations? The changing role of ethnographic imagination in African archaeology. In A.B. Stahl (ed.), *African Archaeology*. Oxford: Blackwell, 24–54.

—— (2006). Household assemblages, lifecycles and the remembrance of things past among the Dogon of Mali. *South African Archaeological Bulletin* 61: 40–56.

—— (2008). The social production and symbolism of cloth and clothing among the Dogon of Mali. *Anthropos* 103: 77–98.

LARICK, R. (1986). Age grading and ethnicity in the style of Loikop (Samburu) spears. *World Archaeology* 18: 269–83.

—— (1991). Warriors and blacksmiths: mediating ethnicity in East African spears. *Journal of Anthropological Archaeology* 10: 299–331.

LA VIOLETTE, A. (2000). *Ethno-archaeology in Jenné, Mali*. Oxford: Archaeopress.

LIVINGSTONE SMITH, A. (2000). Processing clay for pottery in northern Cameroon: social and technical requirements. *Archaeometry* 42: 41–2.

—— and VAN DER VEKE, A. (2007–9). The 'Crossing Borders Project': pottery traditions in Katanga (DRC). *Afrique: Archéologie & Arts* 5: 141–8.

LUPO, K. (1995). Hadza bone assemblages and hyena attrition: an ethnographic example of the influence of cooking and mode of discard on the intensity of scavenger ravaging. *Journal of Anthropological Archaeology* 14: 288–314.

—— and O'CONNELL, J. F. (2002). Cut and tooth mark of distributions on large animal bones: ethnoarchaeological data from the Hadza and their implications for current ideas about early human carnivory. *Journal of Archaeological Science* 29: 85–109.

—— and SCHMITT, D. (2002). Upper Paleolithic net-hunting, small prey exploitation, and women's work effort: a view from the ethnographic and ethnoarchaeological record of the Congo Basin. *Journal of Archaeological Method and Theory* 9: 147–79.

—— —— (2005). Small prey hunting technology and zooarchaeological measures of taxonomic diversity and abundance: ethnoarchaeological evidence from Central African forest foragers. *Journal of Anthropological Archaeology* 24: 335–53.

LYONS, D. (1998). Witchcraft, gender, power and intimate relations in Mura compounds in Déla, northern Cameroon. *World Archaeology* 29: 344–62.

—— (2007). Building power in rural hinterlands: an ethnoarchaeological study of vernacular architecture in Tigray, Ethiopia. *Journal of Archaeological Method and Theory* 14: 179–207.

—— (2009). How I built my house: an ethnoarchaeological study of gendered technical practice in Tigray, Ethiopia. *Ethnoarchaeology* 1: 137–61.

—— and FREEMAN, A. (2009). 'I'm not evil': materialising identities of marginalised potters in Tigray Region, Ethiopia. *Azania: Archaeological Research in Africa* 44: 75–93.

MACEACHERN, S. (1994). 'Symbolic reservoirs' and inter-group relations: West African examples. *African Archaeological Review* 12: 205–24.

—— (1996). Foreign countries: the development of ethnoarchaeology in sub-Saharan Africa. *Journal of World Prehistory* 10: 243–304.

—— (1998). Scale, style and cultural variation: technological traditions in the northern Mandara Mountains. In M. Stark (ed.), *The Archaeology of Social Boundaries*. Washington, DC: Smithsonian Institution Press, 107–31.

MARLOWE, F. (2003). A critical period for provisioning by Hadza men: implications for pair bonding. *Evolution and Human Behavior* 24: 217–29.

MARSHALL, F. (1994). Food sharing and body part representation in Okiek faunal assemblages. *Journal of Archaeological Science* 21: 65–77.

MAYOR, A. (2010). Ceramic traditions and ethnicity in the Niger Bend, West Africa. *Ethnoarchaeology* 2: 5–48.

—— HUYSECOM, E., GALLAY, A., RASSE, M., and BALLOUCHE, A. (2005). Population dynamics and paleoclimate over the past 3000 years in the Dogon Country, Mali. *Journal of Anthropological Archaeology* 24: 25–61.

MCINTOSH, R. (1989). Middle Niger terracottas before the Symplegades gateway. *African Arts* 22: 74–83.

MOORE, H. (1986). *Space, Text and Gender*. Cambridge: Cambridge University Press.

O'CONNELL, J. F., HAWKES, K., and BLURTON JONES, N. (1988). Hadza hunting, butchering, and bone transport and their archaeological implications. *Journal of Anthropological Research* 44: 113–62.

——— ——— ———(1992). Patterns in the distribution, site structure and assemblage composition of Hadza kill-butchering sites. *Journal of Archaeological Science* 19: 319–45.

——— ———LUPO, K., and BLURTON JONES, N. (2002). Male strategies and Plio-Pleistocene archaeology. *Journal of Human Evolution* 43: 831–72.

PARKER PEARSON, M., and RAMILISONINA (1998). Stonehenge for the ancestors: the stones pass on the message. *Antiquity* 72: 308–26.

RAY, K. W. (1987). Material metaphor, social interaction and historical reconstructions: exploring patterns of association and symbolism in the Igbo-Ukwu corpus. In I. Hodder (ed.), *The Archaeology of Contextual Meanings*. Cambridge: Cambridge University Press, 66–78.

ROWLANDS, M., and WARNIER, J.-P. (1996). Magical iron technology in the Cameroon Grassfields. In M.-J. Arnoldi, C. Geary, and K. Hardin (eds), *African Material Culture*. Bloomington: Indiana University Press, 51–72.

SCHMIDT, P. (1996). Reconfiguring the Barongo: reproductive symbolism and reproduction among a work association of iron smelters. In P. Schmidt (ed.), *The Culture and Technology of African Iron Production*. Gainesville: University Press of Florida, 74–127.

——— (1997). *Iron Technology in East Africa*. Bloomington: Indiana University Press.

——— (2009). Tropes, materiality, and ritual embodiment of African iron smelting furnaces as human figures. *Journal of Archaeological Method and Theory* 16: 262–82.

——— and MAPUNDA, B. B. B. (1997). Ideology and the archaeological record in Africa: interpreting symbolism in iron smelting technology. *Journal of Anthropological Archaeology* 16: 73–102.

SMITH, A., and DAVID, N. (1995). The production of space and the house of Xidi Sukur. *Current Anthropology* 36: 442–71.

STAHL, A. B. (1993). Concepts of time and approaches to analogical reasoning in historical perspective. *American Antiquity* 58: 235–60.

STERNER, J. (1989). Who is signaling whom? Ceramic style, ethnicity and taphonomy among the Sirak Bulahay. *Antiquity* 63: 451–9.

——— (1992). Sacred pots and 'symbolic reservoirs' in the Mandara highlands of northern Cameroon. In J. Sterner and N. David (eds), *An African Commitment: Papers in honour of Peter Lewis Shinnie*. Calgary: University of Calgary Press, 171–80.

——— and DAVID, N. (1991). Gender and caste in the Mandara highlands: northeastern Nigeria and northern Cameroon. *Ethnology* 30: 355–69.

——— ———(2003). Action on matter: the history of the uniquely African tamper and concave anvil pot-forming technique. *Journal of African Archaeology* 1: 3–38.

STONE, G. D. (1993). Agrarian settlement and the spatial disposition of labor. In A. Holl and T. Levy (eds), *Spatial Boundaries and Social Dynamics*. Ann Arbor, Mich.: International Monographs in Prehistory, 25–38.

TOBERT, N. 1988. *The Ethnoarchaeology of the Zaghawa of Darfur (Sudan)*. Oxford: British Archaeological Reports.

VANPOOL, C., and VANPOOL, T. (1999). The scientific nature of postprocessualism. *American Antiquity* 64: 33–53.

WEEDMAN, K. (2002). On the spur of the moment: effects of age and experience on hafted stone scraper morphology. *American Antiquity* 67: 731–44.

—— (2006). An ethnoarchaeological study of hafting and stone tool diversity among the Gamo of Ethiopia. *Journal of Archaeological Method and Theory* 13: 189–238.

WIESSNER, P. (1983). Style and social information in Kalahari San projectile points. *American Antiquity* 48: 253–76.

—— (1984). Reconsidering the behavioral basis for style: a case study among the Kalahari San. *Journal of Anthropological Archaeology* 3: 190–234.

WOBST, H. M. (1977). Stylistic behavior and information exchange. In C. Cleland (ed.), *Papers for the Director: Research Essays in Honor of James B. Griffin.* Ann Arbor: Museum of Anthropology, University of Michigan, 317–42.

WYLIE, A. (1985). The reaction against analogy. *Advances in Archaeological Method and Theory* 8: 63–111.

WYNNE-JONES, S., and MAPUNDA, B. B. B. (2008). 'This is what pots look like here': ceramics, tradition and consumption on Mafia Island, Tanzania. *Azania* 43: 2–17.

YELLEN, J. E. (1977). *Archaeological Approaches to the Present.* New York: Academic Press.

CHAPTER 8

STUDYING AFRICAN STONE TOOLS

CHRISTIAN TRYON

INTRODUCTION

THE archaeological record demonstrates that some hominin populations began experimenting with making and using stone tools more than 2.5 million years ago in eastern Africa. The diversity of the African lithic record is the outcome of the antiquity and durability of stone artefacts, and their use by multiple populations in varied environmental and social contexts (Fig. 8.1). Before widespread application of radiometric dating techniques, the same factors also encouraged the use of stone artefacts as basic chronological tools for ordering much of African prehistory. In its broadest outlines, the temporal framework first developed by Goodwin and van Riet Lowe (1929) still offers a simple means for understanding basic trends in African lithic technology, although its numerous problems encourage some workers (e.g. Phillipson 2005; Barham and Mitchell 2008) to employ Clark's (1977) alternative 'modal' terminology, and the assumption that stone tools can be associated with specific hominin populations is also controversial (Foley and Lahr 1997).

Archaeologists have learned about stone tool production from a variety of sources, including the study of historical and recent populations that manufacture(d) or use(d) stone tools, laboratory-based investigations of the physics behind tool production, and a variety of experimental approaches, including modern replications of ancient artefacts to understand their methods of manufacture (see Whittaker 1994). These experimental approaches have helped shift the study of stone tools from one of finished products to an emphasis on the process of manufacture (Inizan et al. 1999). This begins with the raw material: unmodified naturally occurring stone that typically occurs either as primary deposits such as outcrops, or as secondary deposits, where material has been eroded from outcrops and redeposited elsewhere (e.g. rounded cobbles in a riverbed derived from upstream sources). After careful selection of pieces of the appropriate material, size, shape, and quality, stone tool manufacture is a reductive process using a number of different means, broadly divisible into percussion, pressure, and grinding. Drawing on a range of African examples, this chapter discusses

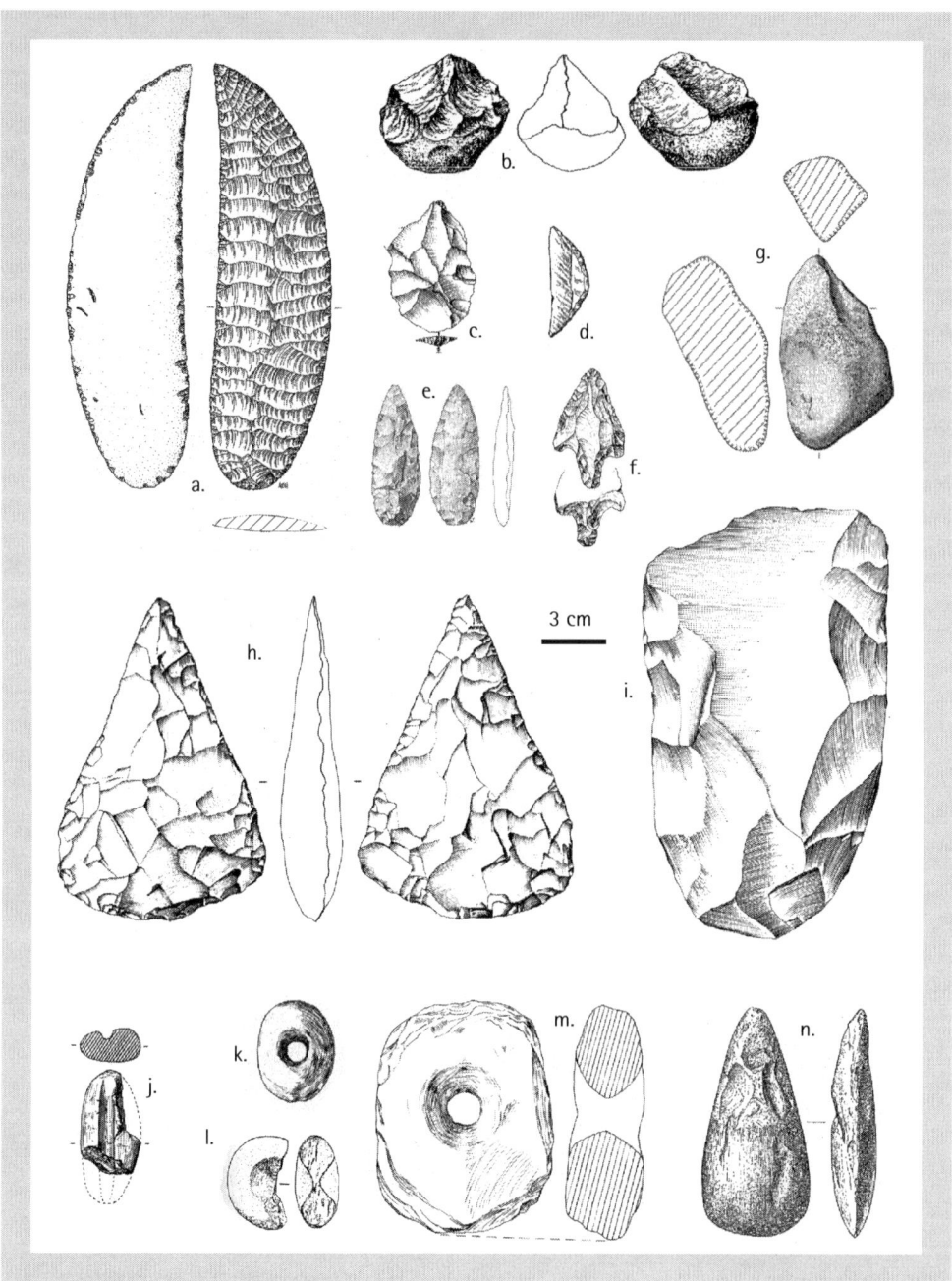

FIG. 8.1 Examples of African stone artefacts: **a.** Gerzean knife, Predynastic Egypt, from John C. Whittaker, *Flintknapping: Making and Understanding Stone Tools*, © 1994 by permission of the University of Texas Press; **b.** Oldowan bifacial chopper, Koobi Fora, Kenya, from K. Schick and N. Toth, *Making Silent Stones Speak*, © 1993 by permission of K. Schick and N. Toth; **c.** Levallois flake, Nazlet Khater 2, Egypt, with kind permission from Springer Science + Business Media: P. M. Vermeersch et al., 'Paleolithic chert exploitation in the limestone stretch of the Egyptian Nile Valley', *African Archaeological Review* 8: 77–102, © 1990; **d.** Howiesons Poort backed piece, Klasies River, South Africa, from R. Singer and J. Wymer, *The Middle Stone Age at Klasies River Mouth in South Africa*, © 1982 by permission of the University of Chicago Press; **e.** Still Bay point, Blombos Cave, South Africa, reprinted from

the kinds of raw materials employed by African stone tool makers and then the techniques of manufacture employed. It adopts an approach grounded in anthropological archaeology that seeks to identify the environmental and social factors that led to the diversity of the stone artefact record in Africa. Chapters in Parts III and IV of this Handbook outline temporal geographic trends in the use of stone tools in Africa over the last 2.5 million years. Andrefsky (2005) gives further information on the basic mechanics of stone tool manufacture and the key terms and concepts used in their description and interpretation, while Schick and Toth (1993), Whittaker (1994), and Inizan et al. (1999) are particularly helpful for the analysis of African lithic technologies.

Note that throughout, the terms 'tool' and 'stone tool' are used rather loosely. Shaped tools such as hand-axes (Fig. 8.1h) are more obviously implements to the untrained eye, and many classification schemes (typologies) are devoted to shaped tools. In contrast, such typologies rarely devote comparable attention to the many smaller unmodified flakes that can be produced during any knapping session, variably termed 'debris' or (from the French) *débitage*. However, archaeological and experimental evidence show that such flakes often provided the sharpest cutting edges and were routinely used in a variety of cutting and scraping tasks (Schick and Toth 1993). Thus, 'tool' as used here refers to those detached and flaked pieces with the potential for use, whether or not we can detect if that potential was realized. For some, the term 'blank' refers to unmodified flakes that are potential tools (often meaning that they are large enough to be held in the hand), but the identification of blanks and the criteria to identify them are frequently arbitrary and vary between authors.

FIG. 8.1 (*continued*)

P. Villa et al. (2009), 'The Still Bay points of Blombos Cave (South Africa)', *Journal of Archaeological Science* 36: 441–60, with permission from Elsevier; **f.** Aterian point, Oued Djebbana (Bir-el-Ater), Algeria, reprinted from J. Morel (1974), 'La station éponyme de l'Oued Djebbana à Bir-el-Ater (est Algérien): contribution à la connaissance de son industrie et de sa faune', *L'Anthropologie* 78: 53–80, with permission from Elsevier; **g.** Oldowan hammerstone, Lokalelei, Kenya, reprinted from A. Delagnes and H. Roche (2005), 'Late Pliocene hominid knapping skills: the case of Lokalalei 2C, West Turkana, Kenya', *Journal of Human Evolution* 48: 435–72, with permission from Elsevier; **h.** Acheulean handaxe, Kapthurin Formation, Kenya, reproduced with permission from E. Cornelissen (1992), *Site GnJh-17 and Its Implications for the Archaeology of the Middle Kapthurin Formation, Baringo, Kenya*, © Musée Royal de l'Afrique Centrale, Tervuren, Belgique; **i.** Acheulean cleaver, Kamoa, Congo-Kinshasa, reproduced with permission from D. Cahen (1975), *Le site archéologique de la Kamoa (région du Shaba, République du Zaïre) de l'Âge de la Pierre ancien a l'Âge du fer*, © Musée Royal de l'Afrique Centrale, Tervuren, Belgique; **j.** Later Stone Age grooved stone fragment, Klasies River, South Africa, from R. Singer and J. Wymer, *The Middle Stone Age at Klasies River Mouth in South Africa*, © 1982, by permission of the University of Chicago Press; **k.** Later Stone Age bored stone, Nachikufu Cave, Zambia, after Clark (1970); **l, m.** two Later Stone Age bored stones in various stages of manufacture, Kalambo Falls, Zambia, reproduced with permission from J. D. Clark (ed.), *Kalambo Falls Prehistoric Site*, vol. 2, © 1974 Cambridge University Press; **n.** Later Stone Age ground stone axe, Poko, Congo-Kinshasa, reproduced with permission from F. L. van Noten (1968), *The Uelian. A Culture with a Neolithic Aspect, Uele-Basin (N.E. Congo Republic: An Archaeological Study*, © Musée Royal de l'Afrique Centrale, Tervuren, Belgique.

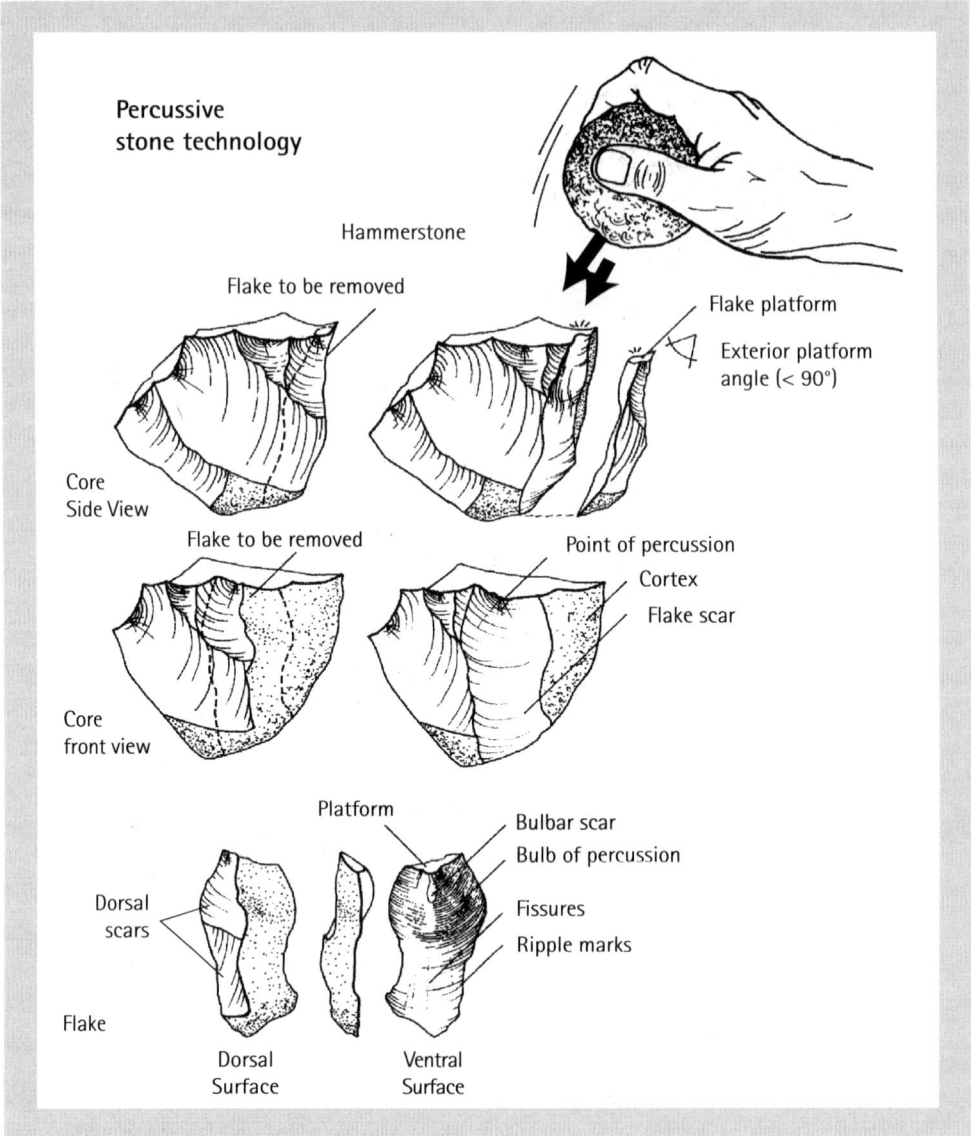

FIG. 8.2 Key processes and terms involved in percussion flaking where detached pieces (flakes) are removed from flaked pieces (cores) by percussion, in this case through direct hard hammer percussion (after Schick and Toth 1993 and reproduced with the kind permission of K. Schick and N. Toth).

Distinguishing humanly modified stone artefacts from those produced by natural processes is a critical archaeological endeavour. In addition to contextual data a number of other criteria diagnostic of humanly modified stone exist (Fig. 8.2). For artefacts, repeated successful flake removals can only be achieved through good hand–eye coordination and a complex visual and spatial understanding of core morphology, which changes as the core is reduced

(Stout et al. 2005). Sequential human flaking produces patterns that can thus be readily distinguished in most cases from breakage produced in natural settings (cf. Clark 1958).

STONE RAW MATERIAL

Although a wide variety of rock types is exposed at the Earth's crust, relatively few are suitable for making stone tools, with preference typically given to those that are fine-grained, hard, and fracture in a predictable manner, the latter criterion being more important for flaked than for ground stone tools. Rocks that show good conchoidal fracture are relatively homogenous in composition and texturally isotropic, i.e. they fracture equally well in any direction.

Even the earliest (> 2 mya) archaeological sites show that hominins could select high-quality raw material from a range of options. At Gona (Ethiopia) and Lokalalei (Kenya), for example, hominins preferentially selected relatively fine-grained lavas that exhibit good conchoidal fracture, although these rocks are rare in the cobble bars used as raw material sources in the adjacent streams (Stout et al. 2005; Harmand 2007). In contrast, at the ~2 mya site of Kanjera (Kenya) rocks that maintained a sharp edge even after repeated use as cutting devices were selected over those that flaked more readily (Braun et al. 2009). There are thus clear trade-offs among different rock types in their usefulness as tools (e.g. 'durability' vs 'flakability'). However, in many regions of Africa during later time periods, particularly in the Middle and Later Stone Ages, toolmakers clearly sought out and preferentially used the finest-grained raw materials available (especially obsidian), despite their low durability. By 164,000 years ago, some in South Africa were even applying complex methods of heat treatment to rocks to modify and improve their knapping qualities (Brown et al. 2009).

Despite the overall rarity in the geological record of rocks suitable for tool manufacture, African populations used a surprising diversity of sedimentary, metamorphic, and igneous rocks (Clark 1980). They include chert or flint, quartzite, quartz, hornfels, and a variety of lavas ranging from coarse-grained, durable basalt to very fine-grained, brittle, and sharp obsidian (volcanic glass). In more recent periods, manufactured bottle glass was also occasionally used (Gramly 1970). Identifications of raw material type employ several different methods, including comparison to specimens of known composition using the naked eye or low-power (10×) magnification to the use of petrographic thin sections and a variety of chemical techniques (Church 1994; Shackley 2008). The latter can also help to identify the source of the rock used, taking advantage of the fact that the complexity of the processes involved in rock formation may provide a distinctive geochemical signature or 'fingerprint' determinable using techniques like electron probe microanalysis, X-ray fluorescence, or instrumental neutron activation analysis. Site-to-source distances then provide a rough measure of the extent to which hominins transported tools across the landscape, either through direct movement or as down-the-line trade and exchange. These data, mostly available from eastern Africa, show that by ~2 mya some hominins were transporting stone artefacts > 10 km about the landscape (Braun et al. 2008a), while by 130,000 years ago some obsidian artefacts were transported ~300 km from their source, perhaps through exchange

(Merrick et al. 1994). Long-distance movement of stone raw material and tools incurs costs for mobile foragers (Beck et al. 2002), and the rarity of residual cortex and other raw material portions that are of little use as tools at sites with increasing distances from stone sources, provide relative measures of reduction intensity and raw-material economization (Braun et al. 2008b).

Techniques of stone tool manufacture

Technique is the means by which force is applied in order to remove pieces of stone by knapping or grinding, a definition based on that originally formulated by Tixier (1967) in his detailed study of Late Pleistocene and Holocene lithic assemblages from northern Africa. The different knapping techniques vary according to the type of percussor used and the manner in which force is applied, as detailed below. Ground stone tools vary in the extent to which grinding is used to deliberately shape pieces, as in the case of some axes. Alternatively, it may be the outcome of repeated use as with handstones used to grind grain or other materials. In many cases, grinding is preceded by additional techniques of stone shaping, including knapping (Fig. 8.1n).

Much of our knowledge of the types of techniques used in the past derives from recent experimentation (e.g. Schick and Toth 1993; Jones 1994; Pelcin 1997; Inizan et al. 1999), and only to a much lesser extent from direct observation of populations that make or use stone tools today, or did so in the recent past (e.g. Clark 1984; David 1998; Weedman 2006). Some percussors are preserved in the archaeological record, particularly those made of stone (Fig. 8.1g). However, inferring use of a particular technique in the past is often controversial and difficult to interpret from traces left on stone flakes or tools. Experimental and archaeological evidence strongly suggests that multiple techniques were often involved in the manufacture of even a single stone tool (e.g. Toth 1997; Tryon et al. 2005; Soriano et al. 2009).

Hard hammer (stone on stone) percussion is one of the most widespread and oldest knapping techniques known (Fig. 8.2). Such hammerstones are identified in the archaeological record by the presence of cobbles or other stones with localized pitting or battering resulting from repeated striking, and have been found among sites > 2 mya old in eastern Africa (e.g. Roche et al. 1999; Fig. 8.1g). Throwing one stone against another is another way to initiate stone fracture, as is the use of the anvil technique, where a core is struck against a stationary stone 'anvil' to produce flakes. Anvils can also be used in the bipolar technique, where a (typically small) core is struck while held stationary on a hard substrate. The resulting shock initiates fractures on both ends (poles) of the core, traces of which are visible on the characteristic flakes produced. Each of these techniques appears early in the archaeological record and persists throughout the history of stone tool manufacture (Barham 1987; Jones 1994; Toth 1997).

Soft hammer percussion, in contrast, involves flake removal using a hammer or percussor that is softer than the piece being struck. These include organic materials like bone or hard wood, as well as certain types of relatively soft stone, such as limestone or haematite. Soft hammers typically produce thin flakes with small platforms and diffuse bulbs of percussion, unlike the larger platforms and more prominent bulbs of percussion present on many flakes made by hard hammer percussion (but see Pelcin 1997 on the difficulty of uniformly applying these criteria). There is little direct archaeological evidence for organic hammers in Africa because they are unlikely to survive in the archaeological record, although Texier's (1996) experiments suggest their use in biface manufacture at Isenya, Kenya, by 700,000 years ago. Other experiments suggest the use of soft stone hammers to manufacture blades and other elongated flakes at the South African site of Rose Cottage Cave from strata ~50,000–65,000 years old (Soriano et al. 2007). These observations are supported by the remarkable recovery from another South African site, Sibudu, of traces of soft stone (ochre or haematite) hammers that rubbed off onto and are preserved on the striking platforms of flakes used in the manufacture of ~70,000-year-old bifacial Still Bay spear points (Soriano et al. 2009).

In indirect percussion, on the other hand, the hammer does not strike the core directly, but rather an intermediate tool (a pointed cylinder of bone or wood) is held against the surface of the core. The use of this punch guides the force of the blow, and is particularly useful in making long, thin blades that require a precise strike and carefully guided force. The archaeological existence of this technique is difficult to demonstrate, but it may have been used in some later (Holocene) blade and bladelet assemblages (Ambrose 2002).

In addition to percussion, stone may also be fractured by the pressure technique in which the piece of stone to be worked is typically held in the hand (supported on a piece of thick leather by modern experimenters), with pressure applied to the edge of the stone to remove flakes using a piece of bone or other material. Pressure flaking is typically used for small, detailed flake removals. Gerzean knives from Predynastic Egypt are some of the most remarkable examples, probably made using copper-tipped pressure flaking tools (Whittaker 1994; Fig. 8.1a). Like indirect percussion, pressure flaking becomes widespread relatively late in the history of stone tool production, although its earliest use was for the final shaping of Still Bay points more than 70,000 years ago (Mourre et al. 2010).

Grinding, polishing, and pecking are additional techniques for the shaping of stone tools, but rely on the removal of small fragments through abrasion instead of flakes through percussion. Many ground stone tools form as a result of incidental rather than intentional shape modifications through use in grinding or otherwise modifying other objects (Adams 2002). Handstones that become rounded as a result of repeated use to grind grain are one common example. Many ground stone tools are first roughly shaped by flaking, with the grinding occurring as a final step in their manufacture. This is in part because deliberately manufactured ground stone tools, such as axes (Fig. 8.1n), represent a substantial investment of time and effort that is offset by the ability of ground stone tools to retain a functioning edge for longer than flaked tools (Hayden 1987). In Africa, deliberately shaped ground stone tools appear late. Except for the bored stones (Fig. 8.1k, l, m), commonly found across southern Africa and principally used to weight digging sticks (Ouzman 1997), these are mostly associated with increasingly sedentary populations, including the ground stone axes found in much of Central Africa (e.g. van Noten 1968; Fig. 8.1n). Ground stone tools formed incidentally as a result of grinding or processing vegetal matter or pigments, on the other hand, date back to at least the Middle Pleistocene (Barham 2000).

METHODS OF STONE TOOL MANUFACTURE

Again following suggestions by Tixier (1967), 'method' refers to the patterned sequence of gestures involved in sequentially removing pieces of stone in the manufacture of flakes or tools. From an anthropological perspective, methods are normative guidelines that are the outcome of learned, shared ways of doing familiar tasks or making objects. The study of the cultural variation in particular sequences of gestures and actions, or *chaînes opéra-toires*, is an established part of the anthropology of technology (Lemonnier 1992), and links objects to the social habits of past hominin communities. Socially patterned and varying cross-culturally, most gestures or actions leave no detectable trace in the archaeological record, but this is not the case for lithic technology, and the reductive process of stone knapping is particularly useful for reconstructing past methods of tool production (Inizan et al. 1999; Bar-Yosef and Van Peer 2009). The order and pattern of removals can often be deduced from careful reading of the scar patterns on many knapped artefacts, while more convincing evidence comes when flakes removed from cores can be refitted back onto the core by matching the outline of the flake with its negative scar preserved on the core's surface. In remarkable instances, large numbers of flakes can be refitted onto a single core, allowing incredibly detailed, literally blow-by-blow reconstructions of the gestures used by ancient toolmakers (Vermeersch 2002). Moreover, refitting of artefacts from Oldowan contexts at Lokalalei, Kenya, shows that mastery of the technical skills and sophisticated visual imaging needed to deal with complex shapes was already in place ≥ 2 mya (Delagnes and Roche 2005), while in other cases (e.g. Bunn et al. 1980) refitting identifies artefacts that were transported to and away from sites, indicating anticipation of future needs.

The particular method used by ancient knappers is not always apparent from the recovered artefacts. Simple approaches that exploit all available flakable core edges are common throughout prehistory. Other methods are identified by their very particular gestures and flake removal patterns. For example, triangular Levallois points are created by the prior removal of two elongated flakes with convergent terminations (Fig. 8.3). The scars formed by these flakes form a guiding ridge (with an area termed the 'basal triangle') that controls the pointed shape of the subsequent flake, termed a 'Levallois point', one of many methods that fall under the broader Levallois concept.

Detailed refitting sequences are also particularly important for illuminating flexible approaches to flaking within a method adopted by ancient stone workers (Bar-Yosef and Van Peer 2009). Although an established sequence of actions (method) may exist for producing certain types of flakes (e.g. Van Peer 1992), each piece of stone worked is unique in shape and other characteristics, and knapping is a one-way, reductive process. Thus, even a single poorly placed blow can radically alter the piece's shape, requiring a further series of removals to rectify the mistake, the patterns of which may deviate from the normal sequence that characterizes the method. As such, although there exist certain well-defined methods of stone tool production, these are more like recipes, the details of which change as needed, and considerable variation exists in how the method is actually carried out.

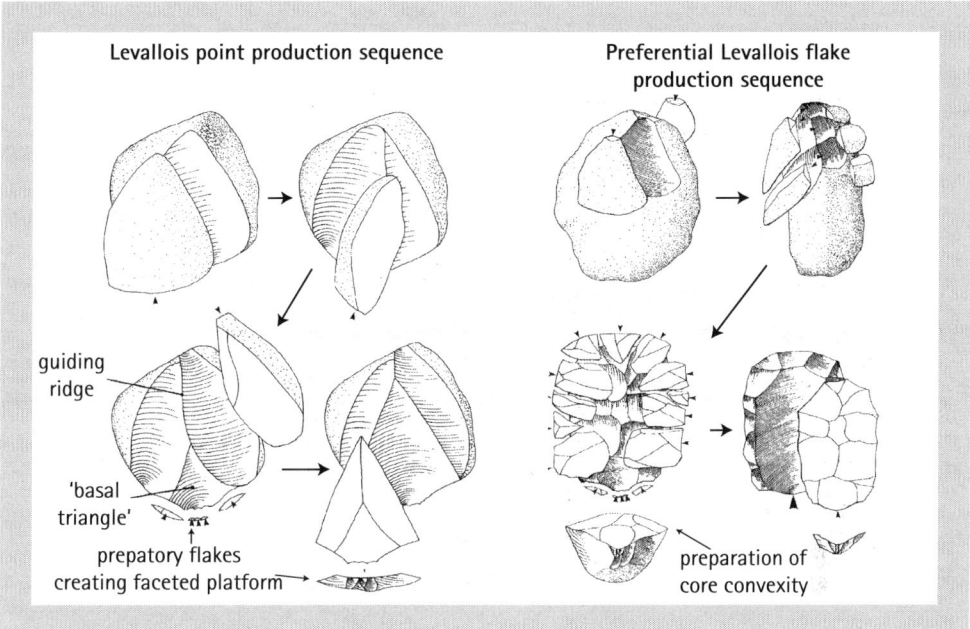

FIG. 8.3 Schematic representation of the process of manufacturing a Levallois point and a Levallois flake by the preferential method. Each sequence begins with an unmodified cobble of stone raw material. Also noted are the different elements that control the shape of the Levallois point or flake, including ridges from previous flake removals and the convexity of the upper core surface (after Inizan et al. 1999, reproduced with the kind permission of Hélène Roche and the Cercle de Recherches et d'Etudes Préhistoriques).

TOOL TYPE AND FUNCTION

Typology refers to the means by which archaeologists classify tools according to their shape or form. Artefact classification is an important task because it provides a grammar for communicating among archaeologists (Adams and Adams 1991), but it is often a difficult one because the normative approaches used are frequently at odds with the variation manifest in the archaeological record. Among the many stone tool typologies currently in use, the terms employed often describe an artefact's shape as well as its inferred function, as in the 'convergent pointed picks' of the typology devised for Kalambo Falls, Zambia (Clark and Kleindienst 1974).

However, despite such seemingly clear functional terms as 'scraper' or 'point', tool function is rarely known with certainty (e.g. Lane 2006). What we do know is generally derived from experimental studies that determine the feasibility of certain tools for particular tasks (e.g. Schick and Toth 1993), comparison with ethnographic or ethnohistoric examples (Clark et al. 1974; Deacon and Deacon 1980; Weedman 2006), or microscopic studies of edge damage on stone tools. Such microwear or usewear studies proceed from the observation that stone tool damage acquired through repeated use can be diagnostic of the action performed or material worked, and in rare cases, portions of that material (skin, grass cuticles, etc.) may adhere to the tool surface. Comparing these traces or materials to detailed comparative collections made under controlled conditions leads to inferences about past tool function (e.g. Keeley and Toth 1981; Binneman and Deacon 1986; Dominguez-Rodrigo et al. 2001; Rots and Williamson 2004; Mercader 2009). Particular progress has recently been made through combining residue studies, microwear analyses, and experimental approaches in determining the function of Howiesons Poort, Still Bay, and other Middle Stone Age stone tools in South Africa and the ways in which they were hafted (see Lombard, Ch. 26 below).

Changes in the types of tools made, and the range of tasks they performed, provide important information on behavioural shifts in the role of stone tools among the populations that made them. Stone-tipped hunting equipment provides one example. Stone-tipped spears, javelins, or arrows are complex, multi-part tools that represent a substantial investment of time and effort, most of which goes into making the wooden shaft and the binding material rather than the stone tip. Stone-tipped weaponry provides greater penetrating power than wooden or bone points, but stone points are prone to breakage with even limited use. The widespread adoption of stone-tipped weaponry may indicate increased reliance on big-game hunting, where the improved success rates provided by stone tips outweigh the costs of frequent repair (Ellis 1997). The frequencies of different kinds of projectiles, from triangular stone points to microlithic barbs to bone projectiles, may then often co-vary, perhaps in relation to the type of game targeted or the type of weapons delivery system used (Ellis 1997; Bousman 2005).

CONCLUSION

The onset of stone tool production currently marks the beginning of the archaeological record, and evidence for this behaviour first appears in Africa. The making and using of stone tools persists among a very few African populations today. Throughout more than 2.5 million years of experimentation with stone working, hominins have shown a remarkable diversity of approaches to transforming stone raw material into useful tools. Stone tools allowed access to a range of different resources, and the occasional movement of this material across great distances attests to its value among some ancient societies. New approaches to lithic analysis are constantly being developed and new archaeological finds continue to alter our perceptions of the past. However, the foundations for the analysis of stone tools outlined here should provide the basis for integrating lithic data into broader anthropological questions.

ACKNOWLEDGEMENTS

I would like to thank Paul Lane and Peter Mitchell for their invitation to contribute to this book. Every effort has been made to contact the holders of copyright in materials reproduced here. I would also like to thank Dave George and Sally McBrearty, who first taught me lithic analysis, and Rhonda Kauffman and Violet Tryon for their patience during the completion of this manuscript.

REFERENCES

ADAMS, J. L. (2002). *Ground Stone Analysis: A Technological Approach*. Salt Lake City: University of Utah Press.

ADAMS, W. Y., and ADAMS, E. W. (1991). *Archaeological Typology and Practical Reality*. Cambridge: Cambridge University Press.

AMBROSE, S. H. (2002). Small things remembered: origins of early microlithic industries in sub-Saharan Africa. *Archaeological Papers of the American Anthropological Association* 12: 9–29.

ANDREFSKY, W. (2005). *Lithics: Macroscopic Approaches to Analysis*. Cambridge: Cambridge University Press.

BAR-YOSEF, O., and VAN PEER, P. (2009). The *chaîne opératoire* approach in Middle Paleolithic archaeology. *Current Anthropology* 50: 103–31.

BARHAM, L. S. (1987). The bipolar technique in southern Africa. *South African Archaeological Bulletin* 42: 45–50.

—— (2000). *The Middle Stone Age of Zambia, South-Central Africa*. Bristol: Western Academic & Specialist Press.

—— and MITCHELL, P. J. (2008). *The First Africans: African Archaeology from the Earliest Toolmakers to Most Recent Foragers*. Cambridge: Cambridge University Press.

BECK, C., TAYLOR, A. K., JONES, G. T., FADEM, C. M., COOK, C. R., and MILLWARD, S. A. (2002). Rocks are heavy: transport costs and Paleoarchaic quarry behavior in the Great Basin. *Journal of Anthropological Archaeology* 21: 481–507.

BINNEMAN, J. N. F., and DEACON, J. (1986). Experimental determination of usewear on stone adzes from Boomplaas Cave, South Africa. *Journal of Archaeological Science* 13: 219–28.

BOUSMAN, C. B. (2005). Coping with risk: Later Stone Age technological strategies at Blydefontein Rock Shelter, South Africa. *Journal of Anthropological Archaeology* 24: 193–226.

BRAUN, D. R., PLUMMER, T., DITCHFIELD, P., et al. (2008a). Oldowan behavior and raw material transport: perspectives from the Kanjera Formation. *Journal of Archaeological Science* 35: 2329–45.

—— —— FERRARO, J. V., DITCHFIELD, P., and BISHOP, L. C. (2009). Raw material quality and Oldowan hominin toolstone preferences: evidence from Kanjera South, Kenya. *Journal of Archaeological Science* 36: 1605–14.

—— ROGERS, M. J., HARRIS, J. W. K., and WALKER, S. J. (2008b). Landscape-scale variation in hominin tool use: evidence from the Developed Oldowan. *Journal of Human Evolution* 55: 1053–63.

BROWN, K. S., MAREAN, C.W., HERRIES, A. I. R., et al. (2009). Fire as an engineering tool of early modern humans. *Science* 325: 859–62.

BUNN, H., HARRIS, J. W. K., ISAAC, G., et al. (1980). FxJj50: an early Pleistocene site in northern Kenya. *World Archaeology* 12: 109–36.

CAHEN, D. (1975). *Le Site Archéologique de la Kamoa (Région du Shaba, République du Zaïre) de l'Âge de la Pierre Ancien à l'Âge du Fer*. Tervuren: Museé Royal de l'Afrique Centrale.

CHURCH, T. (1994). *Lithic Resource Studies: A Sourcebook for Archaeologists*. Tulsa, Okla.: University of Tulsa Press.

CLARK, J. D. (1958). The natural fracture of pebbles from the Batoka Gorge, Northern Rhodesia, and its bearing on the Kafuan Industries of Africa. *Proceedings of the Prehistoric Society* 24: 64–77.

CLARK, J. D. (1970). *The Prehistory of Africa*. New York: Praeger.

—— (ed.) (1974). *Kalambo Falls Prehistoric Site*, vol. 2. Cambridge: Cambridge University Press.

—— (1980). Raw material and African lithic technology. *Man and Environment* 4: 44–55.

—— (1984). Old stone tools and recent knappers: Late Pleistocene stone technology and current flaking techniques in the Zaire basin. *Zimbabwea* 1: 8–22.

—— and KLEINDIENST, M. R. (1974). The Stone Age cultural sequence: terminology, typology and raw material. In Clark (1974: 71–106).

—— PHILLIPS, J. L., and STALEY, P. S. (1974). Interpretations of prehistoric technology from ancient Egyptian and other Sources, part I: Ancient Egyptian bows and arrows and their relevance for African prehistory. *Paléorient* 2: 323–88.

CLARK, J. G. D. (1977). *World Prehistory: A New Outline*. Cambridge: Cambridge University Press.

CORNELISSEN, E. (1992). *Site GnJh-17 and Its Implications for the Archaeology of the Middle Kapthurin Formation, Baringo, Kenya*. Tervuren: Musée Royale de l'Afrique Centrale.

DAVID, N. (1998). The ethnoarchaeology and field archaeology of grinding at Sukur, Adamawa State, Nigeria. *African Archaeological Review* 15: 13–63.

DEACON, H. J., and DEACON, J. (1980). The hafting, function and distribution of small convex scrapers with an example from Boomplaas Cave. *South African Archaeological Bulletin* 35: 31–7.

DELAGNES, A., and ROCHE, H. (2005). Late Pliocene hominid knapping skills: the case of Lokalalei 2C, West Turkana, Kenya. *Journal of Human Evolution* 48: 435–72.

DOMINGUEZ-RODRIGO, M., SERRALLONGA, J., JUAN-TRESSERRAS, J., ALCALA, L., and LUQYE, L. (2001). Woodworking activities by early humans: a plant residue analysis on Acheulian stone tools from Peninj (Tanzania). *Journal of Human Evolution* 40: 289–99.

—— PICKERING, T. R., SEMAW, S., and ROGERS, M. J. (2005). Cutmarked bones from Pliocene archaeological sites at Gona, Afar, Ethiopia: implications for the functions of the world's oldest stone tools. *Journal of Human Evolution* 48: 109–21.

EDWARDS, S. W. (2001). A modern knapper's assessment of the technical skills of the Late Acheulian biface workers at Kalambo Falls. In J. D. Clark (ed.), *Kalambo Falls Prehistoric Site*, vol. 3: *The Earlier Cultures: Middle and Earlier Stone Age*. Cambridge: Cambridge University Press, 605–11.

ELLIS, C. J. (1997). Factors influencing the use of stone projectile tips: an ethnographic perspective. In H. Knecht (ed.), *Projectile Technology*. New York: Plenum Press, 37–74.

FOLEY, R., and LAHR, M. M. (1997). Mode 3 technologies and the evolution of modern humans. *Cambridge Archaeological Journal* 7: 3–36.

GOODWIN, A. J. H., and VAN RIET LOWE, C. (1929). The Stone Age cultures of South Africa. *Annals of the South African Museum* 27: 1–289.

GRAMLY, R. M. (1970). Tools of bottle glass from near Nairobi. *Azania* 5: 179–82.

HARMAND, S. (2007). Economic behaviors and cognitive capacities of early hominins between 2.34 Ma and 0.7 Ma in West Turkana, Kenya. *Mitteilungen der Gesellschaft für Urgeschichte* 16: 11–23.

HAYDEN, B. (1987). From chopper to celt: the evolution of resharpening techniques. *Lithic Technology* 16: 33–43.

INIZAN, M.-L., REDURON-BALLINGER, M., ROCHE, H., and TIXIER, J. (1999). *Technology and Terminology of Knapped Stone*. Nanterre: CREP.

JONES, P. R. (1994). Results of experimental work in relation to the stone industries of Olduvai Gorge. In M. D. Leakey and D. A. Roe (eds), *Olduvai Gorge*, vol. 5: *Excavations in Beds III, IV and the Masek Beds, 1968–1971*. Cambridge: Cambridge University Press, 254–96.

KEELEY, L. H., and TOTH, N. (1981). Microwear polishes on early stone tools from Koobi Fora, Kenya. *Nature* 293: 464–5.

LANE, P. (2006) Present to past: ethnoarchaeology. In C. Tilley, W. Keane, S. Küchler, M. Rowlands, and P. Spyer (eds), *Handbook of Material Culture*. London: Sage, 402–24.

LEMONNIER, P. (1992). *Elements for an Anthropology of Technology*. Ann Arbor: University of Michigan Museum of Anthropology.

LOMBARD, M. (2008). Finding resolution for the Howiesons Poort through the microscope: micro-residue analysis of segments from Sibudu Cave, South Africa. *Journal of Archaeological Science* 35: 26–41.

MERCADER, J. (2009). Mozambican grass seed consumption during the Middle Stone Age. *Science* 326: 1680–83.

MERRICK, H. V., BROWN, F. H., and NASH, W. P. (1994). Use and movement of obsidian in the Early and Middle Stone Ages of Kenya and northern Tanzania. In S. T. Childs (ed.), *Society, Culture, and Technology in Africa*. Philadelphia : MASCA, 29–44.

MOREL, J. (1974). La station éponyme de l'Oued Djebbana à bir-el-Ater (est Algérien): contribution à la connaissance de son industrie et de sa faune. *L'Anthropologie* 78: 53–80.

MOURRE, V., VILLA, P., and HENSHILWOOD, C. S. (2010). Early use of pressure flaking on lithic artefacts at Blombos Cave, South Africa. *Science* 330: 659–62.

OUZMAN, S. (1997). Between margin and centre: the archaeology of southern African bored stones. In L. Wadley (ed.), *Our Gendered Past: Archaeological Studies of Gender in Southern Africa*. Johannesburg: Witwatersrand University Press, 71–106.

PELCIN, A. W. (1997). The effect of indentor type on flake attributes: evidence from a controlled experiment. *Journal of Archaeological Science* 24: 613–21.

PHILLIPSON, D. W. (2005). *African Archaeology*. Cambridge: Cambridge University Press.

ROCHE, H., DELAGNES, A., BRUGAL, J.-P., et al. (1999). Early hominid stone tool production and technical skill 2.34 Myr ago in West Turkana, Kenya. *Nature* 399: 57–60.

ROTS, V., and WILLIAMSON, B. S. (2004). Microwear and residue analyses in perspective: the contribution of ethnoarchaeological evidence. *Journal of Archaeological Science* 31: 1287–99.

SCHICK, K. D., and TOTH, N. (1993). *Making Silent Stones Speak: Human Evolution and the Dawn of Technology*. New York: Simon & Schuster.

SHACKLEY, M. S. (2008). Archaeological petrology and the archaeometry of lithic materials. *Archaeometry* 50: 194–215.

SINGER, R., and WYMER, J. (1982). *The Middle Stone Age at Klasies River Mouth*. Chicago: University of Chicago Press.

SORIANO, S., VILLA, P., and WADLEY, L. (2007). Blade technology and tool forms in the Middle Stone Age of South Africa: the Howiesons Poort and post-Howiesons Poort at Rose Cottage Cave. *Journal of Archaeological Science* 34: 681–703.

—— —— —— (2009). Ochre for the toolmaker: shaping the Still Bay points at Sibudu (KwaZulu-Natal, South Africa). *Journal of African Archaeology* 7: 41–54.

STOUT, D., QUADE, J., SEMAW, S., ROGERS, M. J., and LEVIN, N. E. (2005). Raw material selectivity of the earliest stone toolmakers at Gona, Afar, Ethiopia. *Journal of Human Evolution* 48: 365–80.

TEXIER, P.-J. (1996). Evolution and diversity in flaking techniques and methods in the Palaeolithic. In C. Andreoni, C. Giunchi, C. Petetto, and I. Zavatti (eds), *Proceedings of the XIIIth UISPP Congress*. Forlì: ABACO Edizioni, 297–325.

TIXIER, J. (1967). Procédés d' analyse et questions de terminologie dans l'étude des ensembles industriels du Paléolithique récent et de l' Epipaléolithique en Afrique du Nord-Ouest. In

W. W. Bishop and J. D. Clark (eds), *Background to Evolution in Africa*. Chicago: University of Chicago Press, 771–820.

TOTH, N. (1997). The artefact assemblages in the light of experimental studies. In G. L. Isaac and B. Isaac (eds), *Koobi Fora Research Project*, vol. 5: *Plio-Pleistocene Archaeology*. Oxford: Clarendon Press, 363–401.

TRYON, C. A., MCBREARTY, S., and TEXIER, P.-J. (2005). Levallois lithic technology from the Kapthurin Formation, Kenya: Acheulian origin and Middle Stone Age diversity. *African Archaeological Review* 22: 199–229.

VAN NOTEN, F. L. (1968). *The Uelian. A Culture with a Neolithic Aspect, Uele-Basin (N.E. Congo Republic): An Archaeological Study*. Tervuren: Musée Royale de l'Afrique Centrale.

VAN PEER, P. (1992). *The Levallois Reduction Strategy*. Madison, Wis.: Prehistory Press.

VERMEERSCH, P. M. (ed.) (2002). *Palaeolithic Quarrying Sites in Upper and Middle Egypt*. Leuven: Leuven University Press.

—— PAULISSEN, E., and VAN PEER, P. (1990). Paleolithic chert exploitation in the limestone stretch of the Egyptian Nile Valley. *African Archaeological Review* 8: 77–102.

VILLA, P., SORESSI, M., HENSHILWOOD, C. S., and MOURRE, V. (2009). The Still Bay points of Blombos Cave (South Africa). *Journal of Archaeological Science* 36: 441–60.

WADLEY, L., HODGSKISS, T., and GRANT, M. (2009). Implications for complex cognition from the hafting of tools with compound adhesives in the Middle Stone Age, South Africa. *Proceedings of the National Academy of Sciences USA* 106: 9590–94.

WEEDMAN, K. J. (2006). An ethnoarchaeological study of hafting and stone tool diversity among the Gamo of Ethiopia. *Journal of Archaeological Method and Theory* 13: 189–238.

WHITTAKER, J. C. (1994). *Flintknapping: Making and Understanding Stone Tools*. Austin: University of Texas Press.

WURZ, S., VAN PEER, P., LE ROUX, N., GARDNER, S., and DEACON, H. J. (2005). Continental patterns in stone tools: a technological and biplot-based comparison of early Late Pleistocene assemblages from northern and southern Africa. *African Archaeological Review* 22: 1–24.

CHAPTER 9

A CENTURY OF CERAMIC STUDIES IN AFRICA

OLIVIER GOSSELAIN AND
ALEXANDRE LIVINGSTONE SMITH

INTRODUCTION

OVER a century ago, one of the first monographs devoted to African pottery (Coart and de Haulleville 1907) announced many further developments in ceramic studies. To identify cultural facies, for instance, its authors relied on an intuitive multivariate analysis, eschewing the 'tribal' paradigm typical of 20th-century art history. Embracing the evolutionist theories of the time, they also viewed Congolese potters as modern equivalents of European 'prehistoric' ones, seeing this as an opportunity to develop a better understanding of the ancient potter's art (Fig. 9.1). They thus paid considerable attention to tools, gestures, and recipes, looking for technical residues on finished products and even providing the mineralogical compositions of some potters' clays.

The modernity of a publication whose overall tone and presentation are grounded in early colonial ideology should not be exaggerated, but it nevertheless heralded some major directions in African ceramic studies: close association with prevailing theories in social science; interest in large-scale comparisons; use of ethnographic analogy in archaeology; attention to technical processes. Completely missing, however, were considerations of the cultural history of those among whom pots and technical information were collected. This only started to change once western scholars acknowledged not only that African people had a past but that that past was worth attention.

This chapter summarizes the evolution of Africanist ceramic studies in ethnography and archaeology. Since they developed mainly independently in both fields, only starting to merge during the 1970s, they require separate consideration, which we structure in three chronological subdivisions. Detailed reviews of ceramic studies as a whole include Devisse (1984), Hegmon (2000), David and Kramer (2001), and Stark (2003).

POTERIES DE LA RÉGION MARITIME.

FIG. 9.1 Pottery collected from the coastal region of Congo-Kinshasa (now in the Royal Museum for Central Africa, Tervuren, Belgium), early 20th century. Source: Plate III of Coart and de Hauleville's *Notes Analytiques sur les Collections Ethnographiques du Musée du Congo*, reproduced with permission from the Royal Museum for Central Africa.

DEVELOPING AN INTEREST (1900–1945)

Ethnography

Soon after Coart and de Haulleville's volume, another compilation of ethnographic data was published by the French archaeologist Franchet (1911a), who conceived of ethnography as an auxiliary to European archaeology. His evolutionist agenda compelled him to sort techniques according to their 'degree of evolution' and to look for the ancestors of some technical devices (Franchet 1911b). Unsatisfied by the quality of available data, he also devised a field enquiry form for travellers and ethnographers. Questions focused on the manufacturing process, but also considered sociological and religious aspects.

Serious work could have started at this point, but into the 1930s pottery was mainly relegated to the back sections of ethnographic monographs, even though the development of colonial museums and the intellectual impact of the German school of cultural diffusionism (*Kulturkreise*) generated increased attention for African material culture. Nevertheless, of at least thirty studies published before 1939, some stand out in regard to the details provided and/or the quality of their illustrations (e.g. Nicholson 1929; Arkell 1939). Most authors, however, lacked the experience needed to describe technical actions and especially the shaping process, severely hampering their modern use.

Dominated largely by English-speaking and Belgian scholars, most fieldwork was undertaken in relation to museum collections (Bentley and Crowfoot 1924) or in order to depict 'native customs', though the intrinsic importance of pottery making was also recognized (Macfie 1913), not least by colonial authorities concerned to improve the diversity and quality of its products and to find new openings for local crafts (Maquet-Tombu 1938). Sadly, much of the data recovered at this time remains unexplored in European museums (but see Drost 1967), and despite a few tentative suggestions (e.g. Braunholtz 1934), little was done to understand spatial patterning in ceramic techniques as the result of historical processes.

Archaeology

Archaeological studies first developed among Egyptologists, most famously with Petrie's (1921) seriation of Predynastic pottery, though this pioneer work defined types according to a confusing mix of technical, ornamental, and morphological parameters (Peet 1933). Most early Africanist archaeologists were not concerned with pottery, however, focusing instead on Stone Age contexts and ignoring the history of extant African populations (Robertshaw 1990). The first classification of sub-Saharan pottery was thus that of Laidler (1929), who attempted to reconstruct the recent prehistory of southern African 'native' populations. Although infused with racist conceptions (Hall 1984), this was among the first attempts at using pottery remains for approaching African history, and at seeking connections between archaeological and ethnographical contexts.

Trained in Egyptology, Caton-Thompson (1931), who undertook systematic excavations at Great Zimbabwe and related sites in 1929, devised a classification of associated ceramics that helped prove the African origin of the complex. Her contribution was followed by those of Fouché (1937) at Mapungubwe and Wells (1939) at Mumbwa Cave. Connections between ancient pottery styles and modern social entities played an important part in these southern African studies, and also in Uganda, where Wayland et al. (1934) related the presence of plaited roulette impression on archaeological potsherds to contemporary Baganda ceramics. Hubert et al. (1921) likewise exploited local ethnographic references in devising a decorative typology for ancient Mauritanian pottery, as did Griaule and Lebeuf in the Lake Chad area, their combination of archaeology and ethnography including a specific emphasis on techniques (Lebeuf 1937). Nevertheless, archaeological analyses remained essentially descriptive throughout the first half of the 20th century and largely isolated from contemporary studies of extant pottery traditions.

Broadening the scope (1945–1970)

Ethnography

Although things initially remained much the same after the Second World War, new areas benefited from scholarly interest, especially in West Africa, paralleling a shift in the geographical origin of researchers, who included not only more French but also Spanish (Panyella and Sabater 1955) and Portuguese (Dias 1960) scholars, as well as the Malian Boubou Niakaté (1946), whose note on Soninke pottery was probably the first publication by an African scholar on such a topic; other contributions from African colleagues only appeared after independence (Nizurugero 1966; Eyo 1968). Field research was also increasingly professionalized. In France, Leroi-Gourhan's (1943, 1945) classification of techniques and the subsequent creation of the Department of Comparative Technology at the Musée de l'Homme had an evident impact on technological studies. Professionalism was also increased by a generalization of enquiry forms used in museums, anthropology departments, or Christian missions. A 1947 exemplar held at the Royal Museum for Central Africa (Belgium) shows that information on rituals, taboos, social organization of the craft, location and characteristics of the workshop, names of tools and materials, and trading modalities were now supposedly recorded, together with a description of the manufacturing sequence (but see Trowell and Wachsmann 1953 for an example of lesser professional standards).

The postwar period also witnessed the development of large-scale surveys. In some cases, such as the collection made by S. Leith-Ross at the request of the Federal Department of Antiquities in Nigeria, this resulted in the development of pottery galleries at museums (Jos), as well as comprehensive regional catalogues (Leith-Ross 1970). In others, it involved compilation of earlier ethnographic accounts. Drost (1967), for example, sought to identify distribution areas, the size and positioning of which would provide information on the origin of specific technical traits (Fig. 9.2), though in this case an anaemic theoretical and methodological toolkit resulted in largely uninspiring interpretations. Lawton's (1967) study of 'Bantu pottery in southern Africa' also focused largely on second-hand data, but nevertheless made some interesting observations regarding how the shaping techniques used could be broken down into a 'basic' method and several technical 'developments', the distribution of which could help to subdivide or regroup ethnolinguistic groupings. Regrettably, the opportunity to discuss why the spatial distribution of formal and ornamental attributes did not match that of other—technical—aspects remained unseized.

FIG. 9.2 Image of an Ila (Zambia) potter employing the coil-building technique, early 20th century, used by Drost (1967) in his book on African pottery to illustrate this technique. This copy of a photograph taken from Edwin W. Smith and Andrew M. Dale, *The Ila-Speaking People of Northern Rhodesia* (London: Macmillan, 1920, p. 192) was found in the archives of the section of prehistory at the Royal Museum for Central Africa, Tervuren, Belgium. Pencil marks outlining the potter and her work confirm Drost's use of the photograph.

ARCHAEOLOGY

The postwar period saw a surge of archaeological discoveries and a shift in research focus, with Africa's post-Stone Age history becoming increasingly fashionable. This placed pottery analysis in a better position, but again without drastically changing the way it was carried out.

West Africa stands out in regard to methodological developments. Although the region saw the first publication of pottery remains made by an African scholar (Nunoo 1948), there was for a long time only a remote interest in ceramic analysis (Devisse 1984). Most archaeologists considered pottery in combination with a large body of data, including written and oral sources. While this helped avoid fragmented views of the past, it also weakened historical reconstructions that were too often built on ad hoc typologies. Things started to change during the 1960s, with the publication of regional classifications such as that devised by Camps-Fabrer (1966) for North African and Saharan ceramics, which used both archaeological and experimental materials. With these works, pottery started to be used as a relative dating tool, even for rock art (Bailloud 1969).

Further south, archaeologists' interest in the Bantu 'problem' (de Maret, Ch. 43 below) had a strong impact. At first, the aim was to characterize pottery shapes and decorations in order to fill the gap of the 'protohistoric period' (Leakey et al. 1948; Schofield 1948; Hiernaux and Maquet 1957). Following major developments in the classification of Bantu languages (Guthrie 1948), some also started to view the simultaneous appearance of pottery and iron production as indicating the arrival of a new population. At the end of the 1950s, several authors made an explicit connection with the Bantu expansion, opening a research avenue that still survives. Some references were made to extant pottery traditions or oral history (Nenquin 1963: 272), but these topics never benefited from serious enquiries. With pottery analyses restricted to typological descriptions, archaeologists lacked a methodological framework for exploring relationships between archaeological remains and language expansion. As data accumulated, many felt a need to improve their understanding of pottery artefacts, and thought that they could achieve that in turning toward anthropology. This explains the plea for ethnographic enquiries made at the 1965 Burg-Wartenstein Conference (Clark et al. 1966: 117).

Some theoretical advances were, however, made during the period. Posnansky (1961), for instance, proposed to access past socioeconomic contexts through combining the analysis of the context of discovery with that of pottery stylistic and functional diversity. In a key paper Adams (1968) rejected the 'invasion' paradigm in explanations of culture change, and later pleaded for a more careful handling of archaeological data in the reconstruction of history (Adams 1979).

All in all, Africanist archaeologists' Zeitgeist at the end of the 1960s was dominated by methodological and theoretical concerns, with an increasing demand for revising former tools and developing new ones, among them regional typologies and terminologies. As a consequence of the Burg-Wartenstein meeting, further discussion on the classification of African pottery took place at the Second Conference of West African Archaeologists in Ibadan (Willet 1967). Compared to other parts of the world, however, Africanists' methods and theories remained undeveloped.

BUILDING A FIELD (SINCE 1970)

Ethnography

Major changes in African pottery studies were connected to the development of ethnoarchaeology. Not only did pottery benefit from professional enquiries, but data also reached a broader audience. At least two independent factors explain such development. First, western archaeologists saw the African continent as a good laboratory for testing new theories. Second, postcolonial politics led many western governments (including the United States) to invest in Africanist studies. This attracted scholars with new research interests and theoretical backgrounds.

Although the roots of ethnoarchaeological approaches run back earlier, 1970 was a pivotal date in regard to African pottery studies, as it saw Swiss archaeologist Gallay (1970) publish a detailed study of pottery production in two Sarakolé localities in Mali, slightly before David and Hennig (1972) did the same for a Fulani village in Cameroon. Both studies proved extraordinarily inspirational for a generation of archaeologists. For the first time, minute descriptions of pottery making were provided, from production to consumption and discard, and new research topics considered (e.g. distribution networks, household inventories, lifespan of vessels). What differentiated the authors had less to do with theoretical positions than with research interests and training. In step with the burgeoning field of technical studies in France, Gallay offered a meticulous description of the manufacturing process. David and Hennig were more superficial in that regard, but made a detailed exploration of the consumption and use of vessels. Such differences were not purely coincidental. They illustrated diverging traditions in French and British approaches to material culture which developed from the 1970s onward, irrespective of the archaeological agenda (Coupaye and Douny 2009).

In the following years, archaeologists who had so far frequented potters during their leisure time paid them more attention. Pottery studies gradually expanded. An early and enduring example of ethnoarchaeology is the 'direct historical approach', in which modern pottery traditions are used for interpreting historically related archaeological remains. This developed initially in connection with existing archaeological projects and major archaeological departments. English-speaking Africa was especially well represented during the 1970s and early 1980s (e.g. Huffman 1972; Blackburn 1973; Crossland and Posnansky 1978). Perhaps the 'first truly ethnoarchaeological study by a non-Westerner' (David and Kramer 2001: 21) was made in Ghana by Effah-Gyamfi (1980), and there, as in Nigeria, an increasing number of African scholars found in the direct historical approach a way of exploring the past that was both scientifically sound and capable of including elements of living traditions. French-speaking Africa followed in the next decade (e.g. Bedaux and Lange 1983; Gallay et al. 1990). The geography of these contributions illustrates the changing fortune of post-independence archaeology research centres and teaching programmes, yet some poles emerged and strengthened through the years, among them the University of Ouagadougou and the National Museums of Kenya, where J.-B. Kiethega and S. Wandibba respectively initiated and directed dozens of pottery studies.

Two research projects using the direct historical approach stand out in terms of their geographical and historical importance and their theoretical sophistication. The first developed in the Banda area of Ghana (Stahl 2001), the second in the Inner Niger Delta in Mali (Mayor 2010). Both were long-term projects that involved painstaking and eclectic data collection, and maintained separation from the models produced by more theoretically oriented ethnoarchaeological research.

The latter are typically associated with research into material culture patterning. As critical discussions are available elsewhere (David and Kramer 2001; Lane 2006), we do not go into details here. A fashionable issue at the end of the 1970s, 'style' was the focus of early ethnoarchaeological explorations. It was subsequently considered as a visible channel through which information about identity was deliberately communicated to foreign groups (Hodder 1979, 1982), a reification of worldviews aimed primarily at those who made and used the vessels (David et al. 1988; Sterner 1989), a materialization of social interaction networks developing at various scales (Herbich 1987), and a repertoire of technical, formal, and ornamental elements reflecting various facets of social identity (Dietler and Herbich 1989; Gosselain 1992; Gallay et al. 1998). Discussions about style faded out at the end of the 1990s as interests shifted to symbolic dimensions (Barley 1994) and broader considerations of social interactions (Dietler and Herbich 1998). Neither of these contributions led to the big 'law-like' models archaeologists had in mind when engaging in ethnographic research. Yet ethnoarchaeological studies have considerably increased our knowledge of the potter's world in Africa, and contributed to the building of invaluable

reference collections that currently allow for better reconstruction of ancient tools and techniques (Haour et al. 2010). Another legacy is a series of contemporary studies that explore how
African potters actively shape their social world through manipulating techniques and materials (Fowler 2008; Gosselain 2008; Lyons and Freeman 2009; Mayor 2010).

The last decades have also witnessed increasing involvement by art historians. Crucial
contributions from this field are culture-historical approaches that treat elements of pottery
traditions as historical documents, comparing them at local or regional levels (Berns 1989;
Schildkrout et al. 1989; Frank 2007). These studies join a growing body of history-oriented
works in various parts of the continent (Pinçon and Ngoie-Ngalla 1990; Gallay 1994; Sall
1996). Although largely avoiding theoretical fashions, and choosing to publish mainly in
German, German researchers must be singled out for having maintained a tradition of 'thick
description' that confers a particularly high value on their publications (e.g. Hahn 1991; Platte
and Steigerwald 1999).

Archaeology

On the archaeological side, an explosion of research and theoretical discussion has also been
witnessed since the 1970s. Pottery assemblages have become the backbone of long-term
sequences and large-scale syntheses. Regions previously ignored, such as West Africa
(Shinnie and Kense 1989; McIntosh 1994), the Sahel (Jesse 2010), and Congo (de Maret 1985;
Wotzka 1995), have entered the picture. Sub-continental syntheses have also appeared,
largely built on stylistic variations in pottery (e.g. Phillipson 1977). Analytical systems and
tools vary considerably, but are usually detailed in publications, contrary to previous
practice. A more recent body of regional studies focused on specific aspects of pottery
(decorations, form–function relationships) is allowing for new historical interpretations
(Desmedt 1991; Livingstone Smith 2007; Ashley 2010).

Strikingly, all these contributions have emerged nearly independently of one another. The
only manifestation of an interest in broader theoretical debates comes from South Africa
(Hall 1983; Huffman 1983) and an isolated criticism of the growing distance between theory
and practice in archaeological classifications (Adams 1988). A recent field manual for identifying and classifying African pottery roulette may be indicative of a shift, as it results from
the joint effort of a dozen scholars from various horizons (Haour et al. 2010); while the idea
that classification methods have shaped archaeologists' perception of identities (Huffman
1980; cf. Lane 2006) is also of interest.

The second major advance concerns pottery technology. Two independent traditions are
attested in Africa. The first follows the American school of pottery ecology, as in Nordström's
(1972) study of Sudanese pottery, while the second is directly or indirectly connected to the French
school of technological studies. So far, the latter's impact has been more pronounced, with contributions devoted especially to ornamental techniques (Bedaux and Lange 1983; Caneva 1987) and
shaping techniques (Huysecom 1996; van Doosselaere 2005; Livingstone Smith and Vysserias
2010). As regards decoration, technical analyses have also been combined with a reconstruction
of ornamental 'grammars' or 'structures' (Assoko Ndong 2002; Gallin 2002).

Finally, a major issue such as the Bantu expansion remains mainly unresolved. Pottery
analyses have played their part (see de Maret, Ch. 43 below), but still have to be fully
integrated in historical reconstructions. What we need, more than ever, is to improve our

understanding of the relationships between language, societies, and material culture. As pottery is one the few media allowing for an interface between the past and the present, and between archaeology, history, anthropology, and linguistics, the future may be bright. But this means becoming even more scrupulous and innovative in our daily handling of data, analytical methods, and theories.

REFERENCES

ADAMS, W. Y. (1968). Invasion, diffusion, evolution? *Antiquity* 42: 194–215.

—— (1979). On the argument from ceramics to history: a challenge based on evidence from Medieval Nubia. *Current Anthropology* 20: 727–44.

—— (1988). Archaeological classification: theory versus practice. *Antiquity* 61: 40–56.

ARKELL, A. J. (1939). Darfur pottery. *Sudan Notes and Records* 22: 79–88.

ASHLEY, C. Z. (2010). Towards a socialised archaeology of ceramics in Great Lakes Africa. *African Archaeological Review* 27: 135–63.

ASSOKO NDONG, A. (2002). Synthèse des données archéologiques récentes sur le peuplement à l'Holocène de la réserve de faune de la Lopé, Gabon. *L'Anthropologie* 106: 135–58.

BAILLOUD, G. 1969. L'évolution des styles céramiques en Ennedi (République du Tchad). In J.-P. Lebeuf (ed.), *Actes du Premier Colloque International d'Archéologie Africaine (Fort Lamy, 11–26 Décembre 1966)*. Fort-Lamy: Institut National Tchadien pour les Sciences Humaines, 31–45.

BARLEY, N. (1994). *Smashing Pots: Feats of Clay from Africa*. London: British Museum.

BEDAUX, R. M. A., and LANGE, A. G. (1983). Tellem: reconnaissance archéologique d'une culture de l'Ouest Africain au Moyen-Âge: la poterie. *Journal des Africanistes* 53: 5–59.

BENTLEY, O., and CROWFOOT, J. W. (1924). Nuba pots in the Gordon College. *Sudan Notes and Records* 7: 18–28.

BERNS, M. C. (1989). Ceramic clues: art history in the Gongola Valley. *African Arts* 22: 48–59.

BLACKBURN, R. H. (1973). Okiek ceramics: evidence for central Kenya prehistory. *Azania* 8: 55–70.

BRAUNHOLTZ, H. J. (1934). Pottery methods in East and Central Africa: classification and distribution. In *Congrès International des Sciences Anthropologiques et Ethnologiques*, vol. 1. London: Royal Anthropological Institute, 253–4.

CAMPS-FABRER, H. (1966). *Matière et Art Mobilier dans la Préhistoire Nord-Africaine et Saharienne*. Paris: Arts et Métiers Graphiques.

CANEVA, I. (1987). Pottery decoration in prehistoric Sahara and upper Nile: a new perspective. In B. E. Barich (ed.), *Archaeology and the Environment in the Libyan Sahara: The Excavations in the Tadrart Acacus, 1978–1983*. Oxford: British Archaeological Reports, 231–54.

CATON-THOMPSON, G. (1931). *The Zimbabwe Culture*. Oxford: Clarendon Press.

CLARK, J. D., COLE, G. H., ISAAC, G. L., and KLEINDIENST, M. R. (1966). Precision and definition in African archaeology. *South African Archaeological Bulletin* 21: 114–21.

COART, E., and DE HAULLEVILLE, A. (1907). *Notes analytiques sur les collections ethnographiques du Congo Belge*, vol. 2: *Les Industries Indigènes*, part 1: *La céramique*. Tervuren: Royal Museum for Central Africa.

COUPAYE, L., and DOUNY, L. (2009). Dans la trajectoire des choses: comparaison des approches francophones et anglophones contemporaines en anthropologie des techniques. *Techniques et Culture* 52/53: 12–39.

CROSSLAND, L. B., and POSNANSKY, M. (1978). Pottery, people and trade at Begho. In I. Hodder (ed.), *The Spatial Organisation of Culture*. London: Duckworth, 77–89.

DAVID, N., and HENNIG, H. (1972). The ethnography of pottery: a Fulani case seen in archaeological perspective. *MacCaleb Module in Anthropology* 21: 1–29.

—— and KRAMER, C. (2001). *Ethnoarchaeology in Action*. Cambridge: Cambridge University Press.

—— STERNER, J., and GAVUA, K. B. (1988). Why pots are decorated. *Current Anthropology* 29: 365–89.

DE MARET, P. (1985). *Fouilles Archéologiques dans la Vallée du Haut-Lualaba, Zaïre*, II: *Sanga et Katongo 1974*. Tervuren: Royal Museum for Central Africa.

DESMEDT, C. (1991). Poteries anciennes décorées à la roulette dans la région des Grands Lacs. *African Archaeological Review* 9: 161–96.

DEVISSE, J. (1984). Pour une histoire globale de la céramique africaine. In J. Devisse, C. H. Perrot, Y. Person, and J.-P. Chrétien (eds), *Le Sol, la Parole et l'Écrit: 2000 ans d'histoire africaine. Mélanges en hommage à Raymond Mauny*. Paris: L'Harmattan, 179–203.

DIAS, M. (1960). Aspectos técnicos e sociais da olaria dos Chopes. *Garcia de Orta* 8: 779–85.

DIETLER, M., and HERBICH, I. (1989). Tich Matek: the technology of Luo pottery production and the definition of ceramic style. *World Archaeology* 21: 148–64.

—— —— (1998). Habitus, techniques, style: an integrated approach to the social understanding of material culture and boundaries. In M. T. Stark (ed.), *The Archaeology of Social Boundaries*. Washington, DC: Smithsonian Institution Press, 232–63.

DROST, D. (1967). *Töpferei in Afrika: Technologie*. Leipzig: Akademieverlag.

EFFAH-GYAMFI, K. (1980). Traditional pottery technology at Krobo Takyiman (Techniman), Ghana: an ethnoarchaeological study. *West African Journal of Archaeology* 10: 103–16.

EYO, E. (1968). Ritual pots from Apomu Forest, Ondo Province, western Nigeria. *West African Archaeological Newsletter* 8: 9–14.

FOUCHÉ, L. (1937). The pottery of the Mapungubwe district. In L. Fouché (ed.), *Mapungubwe: Ancient Bantu Civilisation on the Limpopo*. Cambridge: Cambridge University Press, 32–102.

FOWLER, K. D. (2008). Zulu pottery production in the Lower Thukela Basin, KwaZulu-Natal, South Africa. *Southern African Humanities* 20: 477–511.

FRANCHET, L. (1911a). Instructions: première partie—la céramique. *L'Homme Préhistorique*, 9: 1–24.

—— (1911b). *Instructions Destinées aux Archéologues et Ethnographes dans le But de Recueillir des Renseignements Relatifs à la Technique Céramique, Verrière et Métallurgique chez les Peuples Primitifs*. Paris: Schleicher Frères.

FRANK, B. E. (2007). Marks of identity: potters of the Folona (Mali) and their 'mothers'. *African Arts* 40: 30–41.

GALLAY, A. (1970). La poterie en pays Sarakolé (Mali, Afrique Occidentale). *Journal des Africanistes* 40: 7–84.

—— (1994). Société englobées et traditions céramiques : le cas du Pays dogon (Mali) depuis le XIIIe siècle. In F. Audouze and D. Binder (eds), *Terre Cuite et Société: Document Technique, Économique, Culturel*. Juan-les-Pins: APDCA, 435–57.

—— HUYSECOM, E., HONEGGER, M., and MAYOR, A. (1990). *Hamdallahi: Capitale de l'Empire Peul du Massina, Mali*. Stuttgart: Franz Steiner.

—— —— and MAYOR, A. (1998). *Peuples et céramiques du Delta Intérieur du Niger (Mali): un bilan de cinq années de missions (1988–1993)*. Mainz: Philipp.

GALLIN, A. (2002). Proposition d'une étude stylistique de la céramique imprimée de Kobadi: définition de classes morphométriques des vases et analyse de la composition de leurs décors. *Préhistoire Anthropologie Méditerranéennes* 10–11: 117–34.

GOSSELAIN, O. P. (1992). Technology and style: potters and pottery among Bafia of Cameroon. *Man*, n.s., 27: 559–86.

—— (2008). Thoughts and adjustments in the potter's backyard. In I. Berg (ed.), *Breaking the Mould: Challenging the Past through Pottery*. Oxford: Archaeopress, 67–79.

GUTHRIE, M. (1948). *The Classification of the Bantu Languages*. Oxford: Oxford University Press.

HAHN, H. P. (1991). Die Töpferei der Bassar, Konkomba, Kabyè und Lamba. *Paideuma* 37: 25–51.

HALL, M. (1983). Tribes, traditions and numbers: the American model in southern African Iron Age ceramic studies. *South African Archaeological Bulletin* 38: 51–7.

—— (1984). Pots and politics: ceramic interpretations in southern Africa. *World Archaeology* 15: 262–73.

HAOUR, A., MANNING, K., ARAZI, N., et al. (2010). *African Impressed Pottery Past and Present: Techniques, Identification and Distribution*. Oxford: Oxbow.

HEGMON, M. (2000). Advances in ceramic ethnoarchaeology. *Journal of Archaeological Method and Theory* 7: 129–37.

HERBICH, I. (1987). Learning patterns, potter interaction and ceramic style among the Luo of Kenya. *African Archaeological Review* 5: 153–204.

HIERNAUX, J., and MAQUET, E. (1957). Cultures préhistoriques de l'âge des métaux au Ruanda-Urundi et au Kivu (Congo belge), part 1. *Académie Royale Sciences Coloniales Bulletin des Séances* 1 (1956–7): 1126–49.

HODDER, I. (1979). Economic and social stress and material culture patterning. *American Antiquity* 44: 446–54.

—— (1982). *Symbols in Action: Ethnoarchaeological Studies of Material Culture*. Cambridge: Cambridge University Press.

HUBERT, H., LAFORGUE, P., and VANELSCHE, G. (1921). Objets anciens de l'Aouker. *Bulletin du Comité d'Études Historiques et Scientifiques de l'Afrique Occidentale Française* 4: 371–444.

HUFFMAN, T. N. (1972). Shona pottery from Pumula Township, Bulawayo, Rhodesia. *South African Archaeological Bulletin* 27: 66–81.

—— (1980). Ceramics, classification and Iron Age entities. *African Studies* 39: 123–74.

—— (1983). Hypothesis evaluation: a reply to Hall. *South African Archaeological Bulletin* 38: 57–61.

HUYSECOM, E. (1996). Iron Age terracotta pestles in the Sahel area: an ethnoarchaeological approach. In L. Krzyzaniak, K. Kroeper, and M. Kobusiewicz (eds), *Inter-Regional Contacts in the Later Prehistory of Northeastern Africa*. Poznán: Poznán Archaeological Museum, 419–58.

JESSE, F. (2010). Early pottery in northern Africa: an overview. *Journal of African Archaeology* 8: 219–38.

LAIDLER, P. W. (1929). Hottentot and Bushman pottery of South Africa. *South African Journal of Science* 26: 758–86.

LANE, P. J. (2006). Present to past: ethnoarchaeology. In C. Tilley, W. Keane, S. Kuechler, M. Rowlands, and P. Spyer (eds), *Handbook of Material Culture*. London: Sage, 402–24.

LAWTON, A. C. (1967). Bantu pottery of Southern Africa. *Annals of the South African Museum* 49: 1–434.

LEAKEY, M. D., OWEN, W. E., and LEAKEY, L. S. B. (1948). *Dimple-Based Pottery from Central Kavirondo*. Nairobi: Corydon Memorial Museum.

LEBEUF, J.-P. (1937). Rapport sur les travaux de la 4e mission Griaule, Sahara-Cameroun (10 juillet 1936–16 octobre 1937). *Journal de la Société des Africanistes* 7: 213–19.

LEITH-ROSS, S. (1970). *Nigerian Pottery*. Lagos: Ibadan Univerity Press.

LEROI-GOURHAN, H. (1943). *L'Homme et la Matière*. Paris: Albin Michel.

—— (1945). *Milieu et Techniques*. Paris: Albin Michel.

LIVINGSTONE SMITH, A. (2007). Histoire du décor à la roulette en Afrique subsaharienne. *Journal of African Archaeology* 5: 189–216.

—— and VYSSERIAS, A. (2010). Shaping Kabambian pottery: identification and definition of technical features. *Open Anthropology Journal* 3: 124–41.

LYONS, D., and FREEMAN, A. (2009). 'I'm not evil': materialising identities of marginalised potters in Tigray Region, Ethiopia. *Azania: Archaeological Research in Africa* 44: 75–93.

MACFIE, J. W. S. (1913). The pottery industry of Ilorin, northern Nigeria. *Bulletin of the Imperial Institute* 11: 110–21.

MAQUET-TOMBU, J. (1938). Les arts et métiers indigènes tels qu'ils sont représentés à l'Office de Vente de Léopoldville. *Arts et Métiers Indigènes* 8: 6–16.

MAYOR, A. (2010). Ceramic traditions and ethnicity in the Niger Bend, West Africa. *Ethnoarchaeology* 2: 5–48.

MCINTOSH, S. K. (1994). Pottery. In S. K. McIntosh (ed.), *Excavations at Jenné-Jeno, Hambarketolo, and Kaniana (Inland Niger Delta, Mali): The 1981 Season*. Berkeley: University of California Press.

NENQUIN, J. A. E. (1963). *Excavations at Sanga 1957: The Protohistoric Necropolis*. Tervuren: Royal Museum for Central Africa.

NIAKATÉ, B. (1946). Industrie potière en pays Sarakolé. *Notes Africaines* 32: 10.

NICHOLSON, W. E. (1929). The potters of Sokoto, northern Nigeria. *Man* 29: 45–50.

NIZURUGERO, J. (1966). *La Poterie de Luxe Rwandaise: sa technologie, sa Morphologie et ses Aspects Socio-Culturels*. Louvain: Institut Africaniste.

NORDSTRÖM, H.-A. (1972). *Cultural Ecology and Ceramic Technology: Early Nubian Cultures from the Fifth and the Fourth Millennia BC*. Stockholm: Almqvist & Wiksell.

NUNOO, R. B. (1948). A report on excavations at Nsuta Hill, Gold Coast. *Man* 48: 73–6.

PANYELLA, A., and SABATER, J. (1955). *Estudio del Proceso Técnico de la Cerámica Fang (Guinea Epañola y Camarones) e su Relación con la Estructura Social*. Madrid: Consejo Superior de Investigaciones Cientificas.

PEET, T. E. (1933). The classification of Egyptian pottery. *Journal of Egyptian Archaeology* 19: 62–4.

PETRIE, W. M. F. (1921). *Corpus of Prehistoric Pottery and Palettes*. London: Bernard Quaritch.

PHILLIPSON, D. W. (1977). *The Earlier Prehistory of Eastern and Southern Africa*. London: Heinemann.

PINÇON, B., and NGOIE-NGALLA, B. (1990). L'unité culturelle Kongo à la fin du XIXème siècle : l'apport des études céramologiques. *Cahiers d'Études Africaines* 118: 157–78.

PLATTE, E., and STEIGERWALD, P. (1999). Afrikanische Keramiek in der ethnographischen Sammlung des Frobenius-Instituts (1952–1993). *Tribus* 48: 127–45.

POSNANSKY, M. (1961). Pottery types from archaeological sites in East Africa. *Journal of African History* 2: 177–98.

ROBERTSHAW, P. T. (1990). *A History of African Archaeology*. London: James Currey.

SALL, M. (1996). *La Poterie en Pays Serere (Sénégal: Étude Ethnographique des Procédés de Façonnage et des Modes de Distribution Céramique au Mbadane, Dieghem et au Sine.* Tervuren: Royal Museum for Central Africa.

SCHILDKROUT, E., HELLMAN, J., and KEIM, C. (1989). Mangbetu pottery: tradition and innovation in northeast Zaïre. *African Arts* 22: 38–47.

SCHOFIELD, J. F. (1948). *Primitive Pottery: An Introduction to South African Ceramics, Prehistoric and Protohistoric.* Cape Town: South African Archaeological Society.

SHINNIE, P. L., and KENSE, F. J. (1989). *Archaeology of Gonja, Ghana: Excavations at Daboya.* Calgary: University of Calgary Press.

STAHL, A. B. (2001). *Making History in Banda: Anthropological Visions of Africa's Past.* Cambridge: Cambridge University Press.

STARK, M. T. (2003). Current issues in ceramic ethnoarchaeology. *Journal of Archaeological Research* 11: 193–242.

STERNER, J. (1989). Who is signalling whom? Ceramic style, ethnicity and taphonomy among the Sirak Bulahay. *Antiquity* 63: 451–9.

TROWELL, K. M., and WACHSMANN, K. (1953). *Tribal Crafts of Uganda.* Oxford: Oxford University Press.

VAN DOOSSELAERE, B. (2005). Technologie de la poterie à Kumbi Saleh: premiers résultats, premiers enjeux. *Afrique–Archéologie–Arts* 3: 63–80.

WAYLAND, E. J., BURKITT, M. C., and BRAUNHOLTZ, H. J. (1934). Archaeological discoveries at Lutzira, Uganda. *Man* 33: 25–9, 55.

WELLS, L. H. (1939). 146. A study of the ceramics from the deeper levels of the Mumbwa Cave, Northern Rhodesia. *Man* 39: 150–52.

WILLET, F. (1967). Pottery classification in African archaeology. *West African Archaeological Newsletter* 7: 44–55.

WOTZKA, H.-P. (1995). *Studien zur Besiedlungsgeschichte des Aquatorialen Regenwaldes Zaïres: Die Archäologische Keramik des Inneren Zaïre-Beckens und ihre Stellung im Kontext der Bantu-Expansion.* Cologne: Heinrich Barth Institut.

CHAPTER 10

THE ARCHAEOLOGY OF AFRICAN METALWORKING

SHADRECK CHIRIKURE

INTRODUCTION

METALWORKING encompasses both the reductive smelting of ores to produce metal and its refining and forging to create usable objects (Miller 2002; Miller and Killick 2004; Chirikure 2010). The advent of this process is one of the most significant technological progressions in human history. In Africa, especially south of the Sahara, not only was the socioeconomic and political landscape transformed by metalworking, but even the physical landscape was affected (Childs and Killick 1993): metalworking changed humanity's relationship with both the cultural and the physical environment. Given this broadly encompassing effect, it is not surprising that much effort has been invested in understanding this crucial dimension of Africa's past (Cline 1937; van der Merwe and Avery 1987; Miller and van der Merwe 1994; Schmidt 1997; Vogel 2000; Killick 2004; Chirikure 2010). When compared to other aspects of the African past, however, the archaeology of metalworking is not as popular as it should be. Its interdisciplinary nature requires skills from disparate disciplines, a requirement that may deter potential entrants to the field.

Material remains from past activities are the staple of archaeology. Indeed, the archaeology of metalworking is no exception to this generalization; it thrives on studying residues from past metallurgical activities (e.g. Friede and Steel 1976; Okafor 1993; Miller and Killick 2004). Most frequently encountered are those relating to both the primary production and secondary working of metals. Often, production debris appear in the form of collapsed furnaces, broken tuyères, slags, blooms, fragments of charcoal, and pieces of ore (Fig 10.1) (Rehren et al. 2007). Typical material traces of secondary metalworking include dilapidated forges, smithing slag, casting moulds, and finished objects (Miller 2002). As such, the archaeology of metalworking is all about using the material and sociological evidence from the field to address a set of research questions. Given the distinct cultural developments, at least metallurgically, between areas north and south of the Sahara, the emphasis here is on sub-Saharan Africa, although connections between the two may have been important for the emergence of metalworking in different parts of the continent (Mapunda, Ch. 42 below).

FIG. 10.1 Example of a typical iron-smelting site characterized by multiply fused tuyères, fragments of slag, pieces of pottery, and remnant furnace wall, Tswapong Hills, Botswana (photograph courtesy of Per Detlef Frederiksen).

The archaeology of metalworking has evolved in various directions (Chirikure 2010). Earlier studies were mainly inspired by ethnographic observations of metalworking traditions, with the archaeology tailored to fit established ethnographic classifications (Kense and Okoro 1993). As more data became available, the limitations of this approach became self-evident. Archaeologists could not identify furnace types enumerated ethnographically, for example, nor was it possible to separate low from tall shaft furnaces archaeologically or to establish a chronological scheme of furnace types (Kense and Okoro 1993). As the 20th century progressed, some researchers became interested in excavating and dating sites with the hope of establishing the earliest dates for sub-Saharan metallurgy. The origin of metallurgy debate still rages, without any solution or middle ground in sight (Pringle 2009; Mapunda, Ch. 42 below). More importantly, numerous insightful studies have focused on the sociological and physico-chemical aspects of past metalworking activities, with modern research tending increasingly to consider these together while integrating fieldwork-based studies and laboratory investigations within the same continuum of research.

WHAT METALS AND HOW WERE THEY WORKED?

When compared to the present, the inventory of metals worked in the archaeological record of sub-Saharan Africa is limited (Chirikure 2010). Metals such as platinum were unknown and precolonial metallurgists worked iron, copper, tin, gold, bronze, and brass. More importantly, these metals and alloys were adopted at different times depending on the region. For instance, while Egypt opened its metalworking stage with the working of copper, then bronze, and then iron, the picture in sub-Saharan Africa is remarkably different. Iron and copper were the first metals to be worked, with gold, tin, bronze, and brass following centuries, if not a millennium or more, later.

This beginning of metalworking with iron has generated controversy over the origins of sub-Saharan metallurgy (Holl 2009). In the Middle East the development of metallurgy followed a clear path of increasing technological complexity, beginning with the working of native copper, progressing through the smelting of copper and the working of bronze until the widespread adoption of iron (Killick 2009). Given this situation, some archaeologists have posited that because sub-Saharan African metallurgy started with iron, the knowledge to work it was imported from the Middle East (Phillipson 2005), despite the fact that so far the evidence for such a technological transfer is hazy at best (Holl 2009). Other scholars therefore look within the region for the origins of sub-Saharan metallurgy, deriving support from seemingly very early dates of iron working going back as far as 3000 BC, older than the earliest episodes of iron smelting in the Middle East (Holl 2009). However, these very early dates and the contexts from which the dated samples were retrieved are heavily contested on technical grounds (Pringle 2009). Issues to do with well-resolved methods of dating are therefore critical in the archaeology of metalworking, particularly when it comes to identifying sites with the earliest evidence (Killick 2004). Leaving these controversies aside, iron and copper metallurgy were clearly well established in West Africa by 500 BC with gold, bronze, and brass following in the mid-first millennium AD. The earliest appearance of metallurgy in East Africa dates to the closing centuries of the last millennium BC. In southern Africa, the southward migration of Bantu-speaking farmers introduced iron and copper around AD 200, with gold, tin, bronze, and brass appearing towards the beginning of the second millennium (Miller 2002). Thus the absolute chronology for metallurgy in sub-Saharan Africa shows a gradual progression of dates, with the more northerly areas being comparatively older than the more southerly areas.

Just as the inventory of metals worked differs between the precolonial and industrial (colonial/postcolonial) periods, so too did the technology of metalworking (Chirikure 2010). Before European conquest, the reductive smelting of iron, copper, and tin was conducted in comparatively small furnaces of different types (Friede and Steel 1975, 1976). Metal ores were charged into these furnaces together with a combustible material (charcoal) and heated to a point where the ore was reduced to metal (Rehren et al. 2007). While part of the ore was converted to metal, the rest combined with waste impurities to form slag (Miller and Killick 2004). Although the melting points of iron, tin, and copper differ, the technology of smelting available required more or less the same temperatures to be achieved. This was occasioned by the need to mop away the impurities from the ore through slag formation, and regardless of the metal smelted, these slags formed at temperatures exceeding 1000°C (Killick 2001; Chirikure et al. 2010). Because gold is a noble metal, gold ores were crushed, washed, and panned to separate the earthy gangue from the ore. The resulting gold nuggets or dust were melted in crucibles to consolidate them into bigger nuggets (Miller 2002).

At the end of the individual smelts, the metal was subjected to refining to expel impurities as well as to fashion desired objects, a process known as smithing. This involved placing lumps of metal in a forge and repeatedly hammering them on the anvils to shape them. Because of their physical properties, copper, tin, and gold were sometimes cast to produce ingots and well-crafted finished objects. Examples include the spectacular *musuku* and *lerale* tin and cop-per ingots widely used in precolonial southern Zambezia (Miller 2002). Often, copper was mixed with tin to produce bronze, which was treated in the same way as copper. The most prominent bronze objects in sub-Saharan Africa include the famous cast objects from places such as Igbo Ukwu, Benin, and Ife, all in Nigeria (Ogundiran, Ch. 59 below).

THE ETHNOGRAPHY/ETHNOARCHAEOLOGY OF METALWORKING AND THE FRAGMENTARY ARCHAEOLOGICAL RECORD

From the late 19th century, sub-Saharan metalworking practices attracted the attention of European scholars and observers alike. For example, Bellamy and Harbord (1904) described contemporary iron smelting at Oyo in Nigeria, recording the types of ores used, how air was provided to the furnace and the organization of production. Similar observations were made for both iron and copper working in East, Central, and southern Africa, with the ethnograph-ically most comprehensive record being that of Cline (1937), who surveyed the primary and secondary working of metals in different regions, noting mining techniques, ores types, fur-nace types, bellows types, and methods of metal fabrication. He then outlined the distribution of different metalworking techniques, enumerating three types of furnace—bowl, low shaft, and tall shaft—and showing that their distribution varied by region (Figs 10.2, 10.3, and 10.4). For instance, tall shaft furnaces operated by natural draught had no presence in Africa south of the Zambezi. Also interesting was the fact that copper-smelting furnaces closely resembled those for iron and tin, although the smelting of copper in natural draught furnaces is very

FIG. 10.2 Natural draught furnaces, Bassar, Togo (photograph courtesy of Phillip De Barros).

FIG. 10.3 Low shaft furnace, Zimbabwe (photograph Shadreck Chirikure).

FIG. 10.4 A pair of bowl furnaces excavated from Mabhija, KwaZulu-Natal, South Africa (photograph courtesy of Tim Maggs, after Maggs 1982: 131).

rare. Cline's work represented a watershed in the development of studies of sub-Saharan metalworking in that his summary of what was known challenged archaeologists in ethnographical terms to probe the archaeological record. Examples of questions emerging from his work include: What furnace types are the earliest? Why is there such a great deal of diversity in metalworking practices in sub-Saharan Africa, and can they be attested archaeologically?

Archaeological research on iron-using societies in sub-Saharan Africa gathered momentum in the 1960s. At the same time, several studies were undertaken to record and preserve knowledge of traditional metalworking practices before it disappeared, work that included experiments in both smelting and forging. For example, Schmidt (1997) conducted a series of ethnographic experiments among the Buhaya of Tanzania based on the experiences of those who remembered the process of iron production, recording important details such as the amount of ore sufficient for individual smelts, their duration, and the quantities of raw materials consumed. He also subjected the remains to scientific studies, thus gaining insights into the reduction process that allowed him to make statements about iron smelting in the past. Childs and Killick's (1993) study of iron smelting among the Chewa and Phoka of Malawi also paid attention to the technology and sociology of the process; while the former conformed to the bloomery process, iron production was also associated with the use of medicines to neutralize the power of witches. Other ethnoarchaeological studies documented unique smelting practices, such as those employed by the Mafa of Cameroon's Mandara Mountains. Using down-draft furnaces, the Mafa produced cast iron together with soft iron, highlighting the variation and complexity of sub-Saharan metalworking processes (David et al. 1989). These ethnographic studies show that archaeologists cannot generalize about sub-Saharan metallurgy from one or two communities alone.

Because of the fragmentary nature of the archaeological record, features of ethnographic practices of metalworking were often extended into the past. For example, the ethnographic classification of furnaces was extended far back in time, leading van der Merwe (1980) to argue that the earliest furnace types in sub-Saharan Africa were simple bowl furnaces. These were followed by non-slag-tapping low shaft furnaces, slag tapping low shaft furnaces, and finally the tall natural draught type. Further attempts were made to plot the distribution of different furnace types to illustrate the diachronic development of smelting practices over time (Kense 1985). These exercises were not that successful because of the complexities presented by both the archaeological and ethnographic records. For example, the distribution of furnace types in the recent past was mixed, with neighbouring groups using different furnaces while widely separated peoples used similar furnace types (Cline 1937). Furthermore, while this furnace classification worked satisfactorily in the ethnographic record, recognizing different furnace types presented formidable challenges archaeologically, especially in separating bowl furnaces from low shaft furnaces with bowls. Neither is it easy to distinguish tall shaft furnaces from low shaft ones on the basis of furnace structure. In a few instances, however, it may be possible to identify natural draught furnaces archaeologically using the presence of multiple fused tuyères. Given the contrasting fortunes of the archaeological and the ethnographic records, we need more archaeological research to understand the development of practices of metalworking over time.

Like smelting, smithing has also been studied both ethnographically and archaeologically. Unlike smelting, which had large installations in the form of furnaces, smithing was conducted in smaller structures known as forges in which pieces of metal were heated and repeatedly hammered to shape to produce the desired object. Although the process of smithing leaves slags, it is difficult to detect archaeologically, since forges rarely survived (but see Pringle 2009). Furthermore, smithing slag is notoriously difficult to separate from that of smithing, implying that in most cases it is the finished objects that are our best testimonies of the process of smithing (Brown 1995). While the smithing of copper, gold, and bronze was the same as that for iron, they were sometimes melted in crucibles and cast to produce a variety of objects, as at Mapungubwe in northernmost South Africa (Miller 2001; Pikirayi, Ch. 63 below).

Air supply was fundamental to the success of both smelting and forging. In smelting, air was either provided by bellows or drawn in naturally using the principle of convection, producing a distinction between bellows-driven and natural draught furnaces. Bellows were exclusively used when forging and smelting using bowl and low shaft furnaces. Two types were known in precolonial Africa (Brown 1995; Chirikure et al. 2009): bag bellows consist of sacks that were pumped to generate air, while bowl bellows used a pot with animal skin diaphragm. Because of their perishable nature, bag bellows have rarely survived archaeologically, though Shinnie (1985) excavated pots used as cylinders at Meroë in Sudan. For the greater part of Africa, however, we do not know what types of bellows were used, though their presence can be inferred from the existence of tuyères.

The anthropology of African metalworking

The process of precolonial metalworking is often recognized by the presence of material fingerprints such as slags, remains of blooms, or finished objects. However, the whole process of metalworking was associated with a wealth of significant sociocultural beliefs that were integral to its success. Once dismissed as magic and unimportant in the success of activities like smelting, such a purely materialist approach ignores a fundamental aspect of the African past (Collett 1993) and has witnessed significant research over the past two decades and more.

Across sub-Saharan Africa, at least among farmers, the gaining of metal from its ores was universally viewed as an act of transformation (Herbert 1993). By comparison, we know much less about the social significance of metalworking among pastoralists, although in many such societies smiths and smelters are regarded as potentially polluting. Not surprisingly, indigenous smelting is metaphorically linked to human reproduction and childbirth. According to Collett (1993), for example, Chishinga smelters in southern Africa regarded furnaces as smelters' wives. As such, they often practised sexual abstinence during smelting because they believed that sex with their real wives would lead to failed smelts. Still in the same region, among the Shona of Zimbabwe, iron-smelting furnaces were decorated with female anatomical body parts such as breasts and navels. At Ziwa in eastern Zimbabwe, some were decorated with pictures of women giving birth. This association with reproduction, which is a private activity, often led to the seclusion of smelting from living areas, and a similar procreational paradigm is also recorded elsewhere, for example in West Africa among groups such as the Bassari of Togo (De Barros 2000).

The sexual symbolism and taboos that accompanied smelting were often expressed through the exclusion of certain social groups, such as women and children, from the smelting progress. Rituals such as the slaughtering of animals and the use of medicines were also often performed during the smelting process. While rituals and taboos are difficult to recover archaeologically, probable medicine holes at the base of furnaces have been excavated in eastern, central, and southern Africa (Rowlands and Warnier 1993). This association with magic sometimes empowered smelters by conferring on them positions of authority, as among the Njanja of south-central Zimbabwe (Chirikure 2006). Elsewhere, however, as among the Tsara of Ethiopia, associations with acts of transformation and use of medicines disempowered smelters, placing them at the lowest societal level (Haaland 2004). This variable position of smiths has been recorded amongst the agriculturalists (high status) and pastoralists (low status) of Kenya (Brown 1995).

Unlike smelting, which was heavily ritualized, the process of secondary metalworking or smithing was hardly so. It could be practised in the centre of villages in full view of women and children, groups excluded from the smelting process. Inasmuch as smithing was public and less ritualized, the resultant metal objects were often loaded with deep social and symbolic meanings. For example, iron hoes were frequently important in negotiating social relationships such as marriage (Herbert 1993; Childs and Killick 1993). Other objects, such as the Benin 'bronzes' of West Africa (actually made of brass; Ben-Amos 1980) and, from southern Africa, the famous golden rhinoceros from Mapungubwe and the bronze spearheads from Great Zimbabwe (Miller 2001) were ceremonial and status objects used to enhance the legitimacy and power of rulers.

Although easier to detect ethnographically and in the recent past, reconstructing such beliefs becomes more difficult the further back in time we get. This presents formidable challenges to sub-Saharan archaeologists, who often use analogies from ethnography to explain past metalworking practices (see also Lyons, Ch. 7 above). Perhaps, the best example of this is the spatial organization of metal smelting in relation to settlements in the archaeological record of southern Africa. Archaeologists have argued that the 'smelting outside settlements and smithing inside settlements' dichotomy observed in the recent past was also characteristic of the Early Iron Age some 2,000 years ago (Huffman 2007; Mitchell, Ch. 33 below). Because of this belief, slags and tuyères from settlements have been classified as smelting and smithing without any technical studies being carried out. In some cases, the difficulty of separating smithing from smelting slags has been cited as one of the reasons why ethnographically derived interpretations should hold. The cases of Ndondondwane and Broederstroom in South Africa readily come to mind. Huffman (2007) argues that slags and other metalworking remains from Broederstroom were remnants from smithing, since in the ethnographic record smithing was done outside villages. This is despite the fact that on the site there are remains of ores, and slagged tuyères, that are unequivocally associated with smelting only. At Ndondondwane, a multi-component site in KwaZulu-Natal, Greenfield and Miller (2004) detected the presence of smelting, but concluded that this cannot have been contemporary with the Early Iron Age occupation, despite their failure to demonstrate this stratigraphically.

Not surprisingly, several archaeologists have challenged this rather uncritical application of ethnographic models. This is because several sites have now been found that contain remains of ore, vitrified tuyères, and collapsed furnace walls, all consistent with smelting inside Early Iron Age villages (Maggs 1992; Haaland 1993; Swan 2005; Chirikure 2007). The dating and mapping of sites such as Kwali and Swart Village in Zimbabwe shows that smelting *was* sometimes conducted inside settlements during the Early Iron Age, with the spatial separation of smelting from settlements being characteristic of some, but not all, Late Iron Age sites—a difference that argues for cultural change over time. It is therefore important for archaeologists to consider metallurgical interpretations when reconstructing the past, as analogies drawn from the present without additional supporting evidence can be misleading.

FIELDWORK AND LABORATORY-BASED
STUDIES OF METALWORKING

The archaeology of metalworking also involves the scientific study of both production and smithing remains in the laboratory. Known as archaeometallurgy, this aspect of investigation is based on the fact that remains from high-temperature processes such as slags, tuyères, and finished objects contain within their macro- and microstructures partial histories of the processes that they have undergone (Miller and Killick 2004; Chirikure 2006). This information is obtainable using techniques such as reflected and transmitted light optical microscopy (Fig. 10.5), X-ray fluorescence analyses, and X-ray diffraction. Using some of these techniques, Okafor (1993) analysed iron-smelting remains from the Leija sites in Nigeria's Nsukka Division. Late Iron Age (LIA) slags contained less free iron oxide when compared to those from the Early Iron Age (EIA), suggesting that Late Iron Age smelting was more efficient in terms of iron extraction. This interpretation was consistent with the field observations that, while EIA furnaces were non-slag-tapping, their LIA counterparts were slag-tapping. Apart from morphological characteristics, when viewed under the microscope, LIA slags had well-developed magnetite skins or oxidation layers consistent with slag-tapping, a clear contrast with EIA slags. To place this technical study in a cultural framework, Okafor conducted ethnographic studies and also discovered that the location of iron ores determined the siting of the smelting industry.

Miller and Killick (2004) have undertaken comparable studies in southern Africa that characterized the different slags from metal processing in this region. Around Phalaborwa in eastern South Africa, they observed that locally available magnetite ores were high-grade with negligible amounts of gangue minerals, making it difficult to smelt them using the

FIG. 10.5 Transmitted plane polarized photomicrograph of Late Iron Age tin slag from the Rooiberg, South Africa, showing magnetite and stannous spinels forming dendrites in the glassy matrix. The spinels mopped away all the metal from the glass (photograph courtesy of Robert Heimann).

bloomery process. In response to this technological challenge, Phalaborwa smelters developed a technique of adding sand to the furnaces as a flux during smelting, an innovation that enabled them to surpass the limitations imposed by their technology (Rehren et al. 2007).

In another study Miller (2002) conducted extensive laboratory investigations in order to explore the fabrication methods invested in fashioning objects from a large corpus of materials from both elite and non-elite sites belonging to southern African farmers in the first and second millennia AD. His work revealed that the technology of fabrication was stable for the Early and Late Iron Age periods, with no major differences in the techniques of metalworking used in the two periods. More importantly, Miller's work revealed that the techniques for fabricating iron, copper, and bronze were largely the same, with the exception that non-ferrous metals could be cast to produce a wide variety of objects. The techniques employed proved to be mostly indigenous, despite a marked presence of imported metal in the form of imported high-zinc brasses of East Asian origin. The paucity of any foreign techniques suggests that imported metal was recycled and worked using local techniques.

In recent years, archaeological studies of precolonial metalworking have undergone major change. No longer do archaeometallurgists see themselves as technicians waiting for archaeologists to dig up materials for them to study. They now embark on active programmes to address fundamental questions relating to metalworking and its role in society. For example, Chirikure (2006) investigated specialist iron production amongst the Njanja of central Zimbabwe within a combined framework of ethnohistory, archaeological fieldwork, and laboratory studies. Historical data suggested that the Njanja were renowned specialist metalworkers who supplied iron to much of Zimbabwe and adjacent parts of Mozambique. The most interesting observation was that the Njanja supplied metal to areas with their own smiths. The results from this integrated study revealed that Njanja success derived partly from their superior organizational ability and partly from their mastery of technological skills. They introduced many tuyères and bellows to their furnaces—techniques that increased air supply and combustion and resulted in more efficient metal recovery. It was this technological and organizational efficiency that sustained their specialist production.

The issue of innovation features prominently in studies of precolonial African metalworking. In the 1980s, Schmidt and Avery (1983) advanced the hypothesis that East African iron smelters practised the technique of preheating the air in the furnace before smelting began, thereby raising temperatures to produce high-carbon steels. This preheating technique is central to the blast furnace method prevalent today, and its postulation emphasized the high technical skill of traditional African metallurgists. This hypothesis is not, however, widely accepted today, as experimental work revealed that the so-called preheating observed did not, in fact, significantly raise furnace temperatures (Rehder 2000). Elsewhere in East Africa, the claim that the Swahili made crucible steel, both for export across the Indian Ocean and for mundane items such as nails (Kusimba et al. 1994), is also not universally accepted, with some researchers thinking that the metal is likely to have been imported (Killick 2009). Given the sad history of the outside world's engagement with Africa, consideration of the technological capabilities of its inhabitants is frequently informed by a perception of Africa as 'the Dark Continent'. Perhaps it is therefore worth considering Schmidt (2001)'s call for researchers to resist homogenizing African metalworking and to start considering processes of local innovation as well as local developments. This is critical because so far very few things can be accepted as innovations in the sub-Saharan metallurgical record. Obviously, researchers should also desist from making claims that cannot be backed up by the evidence.

Given the fragmentary nature of what we know, only more research can provide answers to elusive questions such as those relating to innovations.

CONCLUSION

There is no doubt that the archaeology of metalworking is now growing in both stature and importance. But ethnographies still have an important role in interpretation, alongside the techniques of the physical sciences and their ability to provide information on what was happening inside furnaces and forges. However, lack of an adequate comparative database still hinders our comprehension of this aspect of the past. With more data, researchers will also be better placed to resolve highly contentious issues surrounding origins and innovations in the African metallurgical record.

REFERENCES

BELLAMY, C. V., and HARBORD, F. W. (1904). West African smelting house. *Journal of the Iron and Steel Institute* 66: 99–126.

BEN-AMOS, P. (1980). *The Art of Benin*. London: Thames & Hudson.

BROWN, J. (1995). *Traditional Metalworking in Kenya*. Oxford: Oxbow.

CHILDS, S. T., and KILLICK, D. J. (1993). Indigenous African metallurgy: nature and culture. *Annual Review of Anthropology* 22: 317–37.

CHIRIKURE, S. (2006). New light on Njanja iron working: towards a systematic encounter between ethnohistory and archaeometallurgy. *South African Archaeological Bulletin* 61: 142–51.

—— (2007). Metals in society: iron production and its position in Iron Age communities of southern Africa. *Journal of Social Archaeology* 7: 72–100.

—— (2010). *Indigenous Mining and Metallurgy in Africa*. Cambridge: Cambridge University Press.

—— BURRET, R., and HEIMANN, R. B. 2009. Beyond furnaces and slags: a review study of bellows and their role in indigenous African metallurgical processes. *Azania: Archaeological Research in Africa* 44: 195–215.

—— HEIMANN, R. B., and KILLICK, D. J. (2010). The technology of tin smelting in the Rooiberg Valley, Limpopo Province, South Africa, *ca.* 1650–1850 ce. *Journal of Archaeological Science* 37: 1656–69.

CLINE, W. (1937). *Mining and Metallurgy in Negro Africa*. Menasha: George Banta.

COLLETT, D. P. (1993). Metaphors and representations associated with pre-colonial iron-smelting in eastern and southern Africa. In T. Shaw, P. J. J. Sinclair, B. Andah, and A. Okpoko (eds), *The Archaeology of Africa: Food, Metals and Towns*. London: Routledge, 499–511.

DAVID, N., HEIMAN, R., KILLICK, D., and WAYMAN, M. (1989). Between bloomery and blast furnace: Mafa iron smelting technology in northern Cameroon. *African Archaeological Review* 7: 183–207.

DE BARROS, P. (2000). Iron metallurgy: social cultural context. In M. Bisson, S. T. Childs, P. De Barros, and A. Holl (eds), *Ancient African Metallurgy: The Socio-cultural Context*. Walnut Creek, Calif.: Altamira Press, 147–99.

FRIEDE, H. M., and STEEL, R. H. (1975). Notes on Iron Age copper-smelting technology in the Transvaal. *Journal of the South African Institute of Mining and Metallurgy* 76: 212–31.

—— —— (1976). Tin mining and smelting in the Transvaal during the Iron Age. *Journal of the South African Institute of Mining and Metallurgy* 76: 461–70.

—— —— (1988). Notes on an iron smelting pit furnace found at Bultfontein Iron Age Site 41/85 (Central Transvaal) and on general features of pit furnaces. *South African Archaeological Bulletin* 43: 38–42.

GREENFIELD, H. J., and MILLER, D. E. (2004). Metal production at Ndondondwane, an Early Iron Age site in KwaZulu-Natal, South Africa. *Journal of Archaeological Science* 31: 1511–32.

HAALAND, R. (1993). Excavations at Dakawa, an Early Iron age site in East-central Tanzania. *Nyame Akuma* 40: 47–57.

—— (2004). Iron smelting—a vanishing tradition: ethnographic study of this craft in south western Ethiopia. *Journal of African Archaeology* 2: 65–81.

HERBERT, E. (1993). *Iron, Gender and Power: Rituals of Transformations in African Iron Working*. Bloomington: Indiana University Press.

HOLL, A. F. C. (2009). Early West African metallurgies: new data and old orthodoxy. *Journal of World Prehistory* 22: 415–38.

HUFFMAN, T. N. (2007). *Handbook to the Southern African Iron Age*. Pietermaritzburg: University of KwaZulu-Natal Press.

KENSE, F. J. (1985). The initial diffusion of iron to Africa. In R. Haaland and P. Shinnie (eds), *African Iron-Working Ancient and Traditional*. Oslo: Norwegian University Press, 1–27.

—— and OKORO, J. A. (1993). Changing perspectives on traditional iron production in west Africa. In T. Shaw, P. J. J. Sinclair, B. Andah, and A. Okpoko (eds), *The Archaeology of Africa: Food, Metals and Towns*. London: Routledge, 449–58.

KILLICK, D. J. (2001). Science, speculation, and the origins of extractive metallurgy. In D. R. Brothwell and A. M. Pollard (eds), *Handbook of Archaeological Sciences*. Chichester: Wiley, 479–88.

—— (2004). What do we know about African iron working? *Journal of African Archaeology* 2: 97–113.

—— (2009). Cairo to Cape: the spread of metallurgy through eastern and southern Africa. *Journal of World Prehistory* 22: 399–414.

KUSIMBA, C. M. KILLICK, D. J., and CRESSWELL, R. (1994). Indigenous and imported metals at Swahili sites on the coast of Kenya. In S. T. Childs (ed.), *Society, Culture and Technology in Africa*, vol. 11. Philadelphia: University of Pennysylvania Press, 68–78.

—— and KUSIMBA, S. B. (eds) (2003). *East African Archaeology: Foragers, Potters, Smiths, and Traders*. Philadelphia: University of Pennsylvania Museum Press.

MAGGS, T. O'C. (1992). 'My father's hammer never ceased its song day and night': the Zulu ferrous metalworking industry. *Natal Museum Journal of Humanities* 4, 65–87.

—— (1982). Mabhija: pre-colonial industrial development in the Tugela Basin. *Annals of the Natal Museum* 25: 123–42.

MILLER, D. E. (2001). Metal assemblages from Greefswald areas K2, Mapungubwe Hill and Mapungubwe Southern Terrace. *South African Archaeological Society Bulletin* 56: 83–103.

—— (2002). Smelter and smith: metal fabrication technology in the Southern African Early and Late Iron Age. *Journal of Archaeological Science* 29: 1083–1131.

—— and KILLICK, D. J. (2004). Slag identification at southern African archaeological sites. *Journal of African Archaeology* 2: 23–48.

—— and VAN DER MERWE, N. J. (1994). Early metalworking in sub-Saharan Africa: a review of recent research. *Journal of African History* 35: 1–36.

OKAFOR, E. E. (1993). New evidence on early iron-smelting from southeastern Nigeria. In T. Shaw, P. J. J. Sinclair, B. Andah, and A. Okpoko (eds), *The Archaeology of Africa: Food, Metals and Towns*. London: Routledge, 432–48.

PHILLIPSON, D. W. (2005). *African Archaeology*. Cambridge: Cambridge University Press.

PRINGLE, H. (2009). Seeking Africa's first iron men. *Science* 323: 200–202.

REHDER, J. E. (2000). *The Mastery and Uses of Fire in Antiquity*. Kingston: McGill-Queens University Press.

REHREN, T., CHARLTON, M., CHIRIKURE, S., HUMPHRIS, J., IGE, A., and VELDHUIJZEN, A. (2007). The human factor in African iron working. In S. Laniece, D. Hook, and P. Craddock (eds), *Mines and Metals: Studies in Archaeometallurgy*. London: Archetype, 211–18.

ROWLANDS, M., and WARNIER, J.-P. (1993). The magical production of iron in the Cameroon Grassfields. In T. Shaw, P. J. J. Sinclair, B. Andah, and A. Okpoko (eds), *The Archaeology of Africa: Food, Metals and Towns*. London: Routledge, 512–49.

SCHMIDT, P. R. (1996). *The Culture and Technology of African Iron Production*. Gainesville: University of Florida Press.

—— (1997). *Iron Technology in East Africa: Symbolism, Science, and Archaeology*. Bloomington: Indiana University Press.

—— (2001). Resisting homogenisation and recovering variation and innovation in African iron smelting. *Mediterranean Archaeology* 14: 219–27.

—— and AVERY, D. H. (1983). More evidence for an advanced prehistoric iron technology in Africa. *Journal of Field Archaeology* 10: 421–34.

SHINNIE, P. (1985). Iron working at Meroe. In R. Haaland and P. Shinnie (eds), *African Iron-Working Ancient and Traditional*. Oslo: Norwegian University Press, 28–35.

SWAN, L. (2005). Iron ore as a long term resource in south-eastern Zimbabwe. *Zimbabwean Prehistory* 26: 11–16.

VAN DER MERWE, N. J. (1980). The advent of iron in Africa. In T. Wertime and R. Muhly (eds), *The Coming of the Age of Iron*. New Haven, Conn.: Yale University Press, 463–506.

—— and AVERY, D. H. (1987). Science and magic in African technology: traditional iron smelting in Malawi. *Africa* 57: 142–77.

VOGEL, J. (ed.) (2000). *Ancient African Metallurgy: The Socio-Cultural Context*. Walnut Creek, Calif.: AltaMira Press.

CHAPTER 11

ROCK ART RESEARCH IN AFRICA

BENJAMIN W. SMITH

EARLY REPORTS

THE first report of rock art in Africa is generally ascribed to a Portuguese missionary who, in 1721, reported on the existence of paintings of 'dogs, camels, other animals and Abyssinian writing' on rocks in Mozambique (Willcox 1984: 1). As became a common feature of early writings, he had not looked carefully at the art, because there are no rock paintings of camels or dogs in Mozambique. The animal images in question were depictions of kudu and other small buck made in the classic fineline San rock art tradition that typifies hunter-gatherer rock art south of the Zambezi. The so-called 'Abyssinian writing' was actually a panel of a type of geometric rock art that is found north of the Zambezi and is typical of the hunter-gatherer rock art of central Africa (Fig. 11.1).

The second African report, in 1752 by August Beutler, also concerned San rock art, this time along the Fish River in South Africa (Theal 1897: 133). After this there was a steady stream of rock art reports from southern Africa (e.g. Barrow 1801), all by European travellers and/or colonists. Most stuck to simplistic description, a few attempted to copy the art onto paper (e.g. Alexander 1837), but attention to the meaning and motivation behind the art was scant. Where attempts were made to read the art, these typically assumed that the images reflected daily life and that the motivation was either art for art's sake or hunting magic (Lewis-Williams 1990). It is tragic that, at a time when many hundreds of San speakers were still practising their painting and engraving traditions, no one attempted to collect direct testimonies concerning the art. It was only later, in the 1870s, a time at which second- or third-hand sources had become the best available, that the first San commentaries about the art were recorded (Orpen 1874; Stow and Bleek 1930; Lewis-Williams and Challis 2011).

By contrast, when French army officers reported rock engravings in Algeria in 1847 and when Heinrich Barth recorded rock engravings in the Fezzan of Libya in 1850 (Willcox 1984: 2; Le Quellec 2004: 14), most of the north African rock paintings and engravings were many thousands of years old and knowledge of their makers was already long gone. Unlike in

FIG. 11.1 The so-called panel of 'Abyssian writing'. In fact, this is a typical example of central African geometric tradition art including rare examples of handprints (after Staudinger 1911; RARI Archives).

southern Africa, it was immediately clear that there was a long internal stratigraphy to Saharan rock art, with obvious and major stylistic variations. Many of the first writers on Saharan rock art therefore concentrated their efforts on description and upon defining regional and temporal traditions (or what they called Schools) of art (e.g. Flamond 1921; Frobenius and Obermaier 1925; Monod 1938).

Since these early reports, discoveries of both painted and engraved rock art have been made in nearly every country of Africa. Around 50,000 rock art sites are now formally on record at universities, museums, and heritage agencies. Ongoing discoveries suggest that this figure may represent as little as 10 per cent of the actual total number of sites. New surveys report hundreds of additional sites each year. For example, in an intensive survey of the northern section of the northernmost province of South Africa, an area not previously considered especially rich in rock art, Ed Eastwood has recorded more than 1,000 previously unreported sites (Eastwood and Eastwood 2006). Similarly, in two small study areas in a part of central Africa not well known for rock art, surveys recorded just over 700 previously unreported sites (Smith 1997). Large parts of West Africa and some areas in the Sahara, such as the western desert of Egypt and the Ennedi along the Chad–Sudan border, also contain thousands of unrecorded sites.

This vast quantity of sites has led researchers progressively to concentrate upon more intensive and more localized rock art studies and more specific time periods. Gone are the days of writers such as Henri Breuil and Leo Frobenius, who worked at sites across the length and breadth of Africa on rock art of all eras. Most researchers today focus on rock art in a small section of a single country and usually specifically on hunter-gatherer, pastoralist, or agriculturalist rock art. But this tightening of focus reflects more than research practicalities: underlying it are fundamental paradigm shifts in the ways in which we work with rock art.

CHANGING PARADIGMS

Whilst each section of Africa has its own particular history of research, certain widespread trends can be discerned. Early research was empirically focused and much of it was empiricist. The value of this research lay in detailed recording work and in observations of things such as subject matter, manners of depiction, and superimpositions; however, much of the work remained at the level of assertion. The quality of the recording work varied greatly, with some early copyists omitting much fine detail and/or shifting the relative positions of images (e.g. Stow and Bleek 1930; Breuil 1955) and later work tending to be more detailed and more accurate (e.g. Pager 1971; Leakey 1983). Many of the early copies are therefore of questionable value for analysis today because they lack or misrepresent important details. Where the early works were more useful was in laying down relative sequences of traditions, and in establishing the approximate age and authorship of many traditions.

But working from observation to explanation proved to be an ill-founded way to move towards an understanding of the meaning and motivation of rock art, not least because the empiricist method was flawed (Lewis-Williams 1984). As David Lewis-Williams has rightly noted, we can gaze at rock art for as long as we like, but this will not help us to make better guesses at its meanings; indeed, it is more likely that any flawed sense of understanding of the art will simply be a reflection of our own preconceptions, expectations, and prejudices (Lewis-Williams 2006a). People expecting hunter-gatherers to make art for hunting-magic purposes therefore saw depictions of men pointing bows and arrows at animals as supporting evidence. Others who expected the art simply to depict 'primitive' everyday life found confirmation in exactly the same depictions.

In the 1970s the only way to move beyond gaze-and-guess towards a more scientific understanding of the art seemed to be through numerical quantification and statistical analysis of associations. Much rock art research therefore became dominated by statistics. It was demonstrated that particular animals occurred more frequently in the art than others, that certain human forms occurred with certain animals, and that some classes of figures tended to overlay others (see e.g. Pager 1971; Lewis-Williams 1972; Vinnicombe 1976; Striedter 1983; Leakey 1983). This work exposed a series of interesting and demonstrable painted choices, but each still required explanation. The statistics alone could not explain why the choices were made. It also became clear that there was considerable variation between areas—for example, giraffe dominates the hunter-gatherer rock art of Tanzania (Leakey 1983) whereas kudu dominates in Zimbabwe (Tucker and Baird 1983) and eland in South Africa (Lewis-Williams 1972; Vinnicombe 1976). Comparison of painted animal frequencies with natural prevalence and archaeological finds immediately made it clear that the art was neither a direct depiction of the natural environment nor a depiction of local diet. The differences between areas could only be explained by local cultural difference.

In the late 1970s and 1980s researchers in most areas therefore turned to local ethnographies to try to understand the patterns they had identified in the art. It was specifically the work of Patricia Vinnicombe (1976) and David Lewis-Williams (1981) concerning the San art of southern Africa that pioneered this move and demonstrated the potential of using African ethnographies to unlock hidden meanings behind the patterns in the art. Whilst these specific findings were of relevance only to southern Africa, this type of hermeneutic

FIG. 11.2 Panels such as this from the southern uKhahlamba-Drakensberg in South Africa have formed the focus of recent research looking at agency, interaction, and change within later San rock art (redrawing, Patricia Vinnicombe and Justine Olofsson; RARI Archives).

approach has come to dominate rock art studies in all parts of Africa except the Sahara. In southern Africa one can chart a progressive growth in sophistication through time, with researchers working to address early concerns over the use and relevance of ethnographies as well as giving increasing consideration to issues of individual agency, gender, change through time, and multivocality (Solomon 1992; Dowson 1994; Lewis-Williams 2001, 2006b; Blundell 2004) (Fig. 11.2). These shifts have influenced rock art work in all parts of Africa, as we will see in the following regional overviews.

THE CURRENT STATE OF REGIONAL RESEARCH

Southern Africa

In Africa south of the Zambezi River research has been dominated by San rock art studies. Since the 1980s there has been a near consensus that San rock art played a part in San religious experiences, beliefs, and rituals. More specifically, the art is recognized as depicting the negotiation of supernatural potency and the control of the relationships between the material and spiritual worlds (Fig. 11.3). This means that the art played a specific role within San society, predominantly relating to the control of things such as health, rain, and the movement of animals. Within this general understanding, researchers have forged their own particular emphases, often by interpreting regionally specific sets of paintings (e.g. Eastwood and Eastwood 2006; Hollmann 2006; Mguni 2006).

Recently some researchers have suggested that the importance of myth has been neglected in ethnographic understandings of the art (e.g. Solomon 1997, 2008; Le Quellec 2004). This is a somewhat nebulous debate, as it is an incontestable fact that the art does not illustrate any of the known San myths. The question is simply whether the symbolism of the art can be understood better by considering the symbolism used within San myths, and on this point there is actually no disagreement, as myths have been used by almost all researchers since the early work of Patricia Vinnicombe and David Lewis-Williams in elucidating San rock art symbolism.

More productive lines of recent research have suggested that, rather than write in terms of western conceptions of culture and nature, material and spiritual, mind and body, ritual and myth, we would do better to write in terms of those San understandings and ways of thinking that we can discern from the ethnographies and in which there are few such clear-cut ontological distinctions (Dowson 2007). Many writers have sought to move away from generalized understandings of San symbolism to more localized and historically particular understandings. The success of these efforts has varied according to the availability of local histories/ethnographies/archaeologies and the ability to locate the rock art in time (Smith 2010). Some of the most revealing research has focused on linking specific developments in the art to contextual interactions and processes of cultural hybridity, creolization, and identity formation amongst historically known San and mixed groups (Jolly 1996; Blundell 2004; Ouzman 2006; Mallen 2008; Challis 2009, 2012; Henry 2010) (e.g. Fig. 11.2).

Alongside this growing understanding of historical changes in San rock art has also come a better understanding of the role played by rock art amongst other groups who lived and interacted with the San. A tradition of geometric art that is spread along the watercourses and sources of southern Africa, in both painted and engraved form (Fig. 11.4), has been convincingly linked to Khoekhoen speakers and to groups of mixed Khoekhoen descent (Smith and Ouzman 2004; Eastwood and Smith 2005). This art has profound implications for the origins

FIG. 11.3 David Lewis-Williams used panels such as this to demonstrate that symbolism related to the negotiation and control of supernatural potency is a repeated theme in San rock. Here a dying eland is releasing its potency and this is being harnessed by a line of ritual specialists (redrawing, Thomas Dowson; RARI Archives).

FIG. 11.4 A dense panel of Khoekhoen tradition rock engravings from the central interior of South Africa (photograph, Benjamin Smith; RARI Archives).

of herding in South Africa, shifting the weight of evidence in favour of a migratory model. Rock arts of farmer groups have also received increasing attention. White finger-painted images in northern South Africa have been tied to Northern Sotho speaking farmer groups (Fig. 11.5). This art was originally made as part of boys' and girls' initiation ceremonies and, in the 19th century developed into a powerful political protest art (Prins and Hall 1994; Smith and van Schalkwyk 2002; van Schalkwyk and Smith 2004; Namono and Eastwood 2005; Moodley 2008). Cattle settlement pattern rock engravings in Mpumalanga (Fig. 11.6) have been shown to have been made by Nguni speakers, for reasons which remain obscure (Mbewe 2007).

Central Africa

The central African rock art zone extends from the part of Mozambique that lies north of the Zambezi, across to the Angolan Atlantic coast, spanning the central African rainforests and reaching as far north as Cameroon and Uganda. The hunter-gatherer rock art of this region is dominated by a finger-painted red geometric tradition of rock art; Desmond Clark (1959) called this the 'schematic rock art zone'. About 90 per cent of all 'schematic' rock art sites comprise geometric designs such as concentric circles, sausage shapes, parallel lines, grids, and finger strokes as well as a few examples of handprints (Figs 11.1, 11.7). The other 10 per cent contain highly stylized animal depictions in which the belly of the animal is strongly emphasized and the extremities such as legs and head are dwarfed or

FIG. 11.5 Northern Sotho boys' initiation rock art from northern South Africa (photograph, Benjamin Smith; RARI Archives).

FIG. 11.6 Settlement pattern rock engraving from eastern South Africa. Note the central pecked area representing the cattle kraal. Around this are dots representing the houses, and around these is a circle representing the perimeter fence of the settlement. The line leading out from the top represents the cattle track (photograph, Benjamin Smith; RARI Archives).

omitted entirely, surrounded by rows of finger dots. The animals are generally painted in separate sites from the geometrics, as if intentionally kept apart; on some major hills one can find animal and geometric sites a few hundred metres apart but with no overlap in imagery (Smith 1997). It is argued that the geometric images were made by women and the animals made by men (Smith 1997). Recent research has argued that the painters and engravers were culturally ancestral to the so-called 'Pygmies' or forest hunter-gatherers of central Africa, and that their rock art is dominated by forms of sexual symbolism (Fig. 11.7) aimed at maintaining harmony and balance in the forest and therefore wellbeing within society (Namono 2010, 2011).

Eastern Zambia, central Malawi, and adjacent parts of Mozambique are also rich in farmer rock art. This is different from hunter-gatherer art in that it is dominantly white. The pigment used is riverine clay and it is applied thickly by daubing. This rock art was made by ancestors of modern-day Chewa speakers. It was primarily made as part of the girls' initiation ceremony known as *chinamwali* (Phillipson 1976; Prins and Hall 1994; Smith 1997; Zubieta 2006). This art continued to be made into the 20th century; the images were used for didactic and mnemonic purposes so as to help the girls assimilate the huge quantity of information passed on during the ceremony (Zubieta 2009). A smaller section of art, also daubed in white (Fig. 11.8), has been linked to boys' initiation and to the Chewa secret society known as *nyau* (Lindgren and Schoffeleers 1978; Smith 2001). This art was painted in the late 19th and early 20th century when *nyau* was suppressed by Ngoni invaders, early missionaries and the colonial government (Smith 2001).

Other rock art sites made by Bantu-speaking farmer groups are found in a thin scatter throughout central Africa, but remain poorly researched. These are typically made in white and are dominated by spreadeagled designs with the appearance of an animal skin seen from above. Some of the most extensive examples are found in central and southern Angola. They were probably linked, like the Chewa art, to initiation ceremonies, but their specific meanings and motivations remain uncertain (Gutierrez 1996). A group of engravings in eastern Angola, using unusual patterns of interwoven lines and dots, has been linked to the Chokwe and to other related Bantu language speakers (Kubik 1989). These engravings are still readily understood by groups in this area today. They are called *tusona* and each symbol is used to evoke a proverb or societal teaching (Kubik 1989).

FIG. 11.7 Red geometric tradition rock paintings from central Malawi. This panel combines the theme of weather divination with sexual symbolism (e.g. Smith 1995; redrawing, Benjamin Smith; RARI Archives).

FIG. 11.8 Boys' initiation rock art from central Malawi linked to the *nyau* secret society (Smith 2001; photograph, Benjamin Smith; RARI Archives).

East Africa

The Central African geometric art tradition is found spread throughout Uganda as well as in western parts of Kenya and Tanzania. However, in Singida and Kondoa Districts of Tanzania there is a separate and localized hunter-gatherer rock art tradition. Unlike the finger-painted geometric art surrounding it, this art is dominated by brush-painted human and animal forms. The forms are made in outline or using an assortment of fill types, the most common being solid, grid fill, and dot fill. The giraffe is the most frequently painted animal, but many types of antelope, zebra, elephant, rhino, feline, and ostrich are also depicted (Leakey 1983). Particularly characteristic of this tradition are some highly distinctive stylized human head forms (Fig. 11.9).

This art was made by East African click speakers ancestral to modern groups such as the Hadza and Sandawe. Eric Ten Raa observed Sandawe making rock paintings in the mid twentieth century (Ten Raa 1971, 1974). On the basis of oral traditions, Ten Raa argued that the rock art was made for three main purposes: (1) casual art; (2) magic art—either for hunting purposes or connected to the *simbó* ceremony and therefore to health and fertility; (3) sacrificial art made to appease clan spirits. David Lewis-Williams (1987) drew upon Sandawe ethnography and parallels with southern African San rock art to argue that a much greater percentage of the art was connected to *simbó* and to experiences of altered states of consciousness than Ten Raa realized. Whilst this art is no longer made today, Imogene Lim has argued that modern site use and the use of mobile art in modern ceremonies can be used to help us further to understand the use and symbolism of the rock art (Lim 2010).

In addition to the hunter-gatherer art traditions, a number of paintings in Kenya and Tanzania have been linked to pastoralist and farmer groups. A specific group of

FIG. 11.9 Characteristic stylized human forms from the hunter-gatherer tradition of central Tanzania (photograph, Benjamin Smith; RARI Archives).

FIG. 11.10 Paintings of Maa-speaker cattle brands from western Kenya that have been linked to meat-feasting rituals (photograph, Benjamin Smith; RARI Archives).

finger-painted images depicts the cattle brands and shields of Maa speakers (Fig. 11.10). It is argued that these paintings were linked to traditional Maa speaker meat-feasting sites and practices (Gramly 1975; Lynch and Robbins 1977). Other images show stylized solid-filled representations of long- and short-horned cattle, using both side-on profile and as seen from above (Wright 1961; Chaplin 1974; Leakey 1983). It is assumed that these paintings and engravings were made either by Cushitic or Nilotic speaking groups, but their exact authorship and meaning remains unclear. The only part of East Africa known to have a significant number of sites made by Bantu language speakers is Kondoa (Leakey 1983; Anati 1986). This art was painted by daubing, mostly using white, as is typical of Bantu speaker rock art across sub-Saharan Africa. It seems to have played a role in local initiation ceremonies (Anati 1986).

The Horn

All the rock art so far reported in the Horn of Africa seems to fall within a single tradition of art, what Pavel Červíček has called the 'Ethiopian-Arabian' tradition (Červíček 1971). This art spans the Horn and the whole of the Arabian Peninsula. It comprises principally images of long-horned, humpless cattle, human figures (Fig. 11.11), items of material culture, and rare depictions of sheep/goat, dogs, and camels (Brandt and Carder 1987; Gutherz et al. 2003). Dates of between 5,000 and 3,000 years ago have been tentatively assigned to much of the art (Červíček 1979), though the images of camels must date to the last 2,000 years. Given the great age of the art, interpretation of its meanings has proven difficult. Most researchers have concentrated on developing temporal sequences and on defining regional variation, but recent studies have emphasized the need for further research into the symbolism of the detail in the cattle forms and the highly selective choice of images for depiction (Mire 2008).

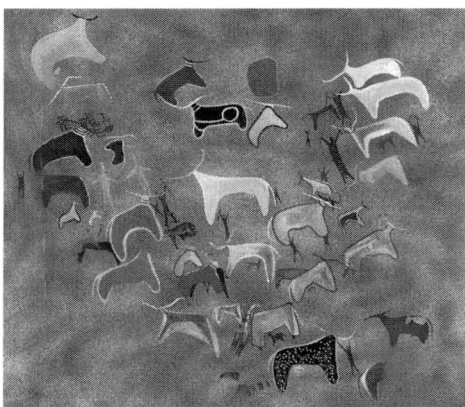

FIG. 11.11 Typical panel of 'Ethiopian-Arabian' tradition rock art from Ethiopia depicting cattle, human forms, and a few material culture items (redrawing, Patricia Vinnicombe and Justine Olofsson; RARI Archives).

North and West Africa

Stretching from the Atlas mountains in the west, down through Mali, across the central Sahara as far south as Lake Chad and then up as far east as the Nile Delta is the huge arc of West and North African rock art. Over the past century French, Italian, German, and other international teams have recorded art in almost every country within the Sahara region. It is thought that this area may contain as many as 100,000 rock engraving and rock painting sites. The art is found in a series of stone plateaux and mountain massifs that are scattered throughout the Sahara sands. Major concentrations of sites are found in: the Atlas mountains in Morocco and Algeria; Adrar des Ifoghas in Mali; Aïr and Ténéré in Niger; Ahaggar and Tassili n'Ajjer in Algeria; Tadrart Acacus and Fezzan in Libya; Tibesti and Ennedi in Chad; Jebel Uweinat on the Libyan–Sudanese–Egyptian border; and Gilf Kebir in Egypt.

The bulk of Saharan rock art research has been concerned with classifying and sequencing. Researchers divide between 'lumpers' and 'splitters', with earlier researchers more prone to lumping together traditions across most of the Sahara (e.g. Flamand 1921; Frobenius and Obermaier 1925; Monod 1938; Lhote 1961) and later researchers seeing the need to split the art into more exactly defined regional traditions (e.g. Mori 1965; Muzzolini 1995; Le Quellec 1998). Classifications have been made according to both time and manner of depiction, and this has led to some confusion. One set of classifications is solely chronological. In this the art is divided according to the animal that typified the time, for example: the bubaline (wild buffalo) period from around 12000 BP to c. 5500 BP; the bovidian (domesticated cattle) period from c. 5500 BP to c. 3500 BP (Fig. 11.12); the caballine (horse) period from c. 3500 BP to 2300 BP, and the camel (dromedary) period following this. These divisions, because they are temporal, are pan-Saharan. The exact date range of each period necessarily varies between areas depending on the age of the appearance or extinction of each species. The date of the start of the bovidian period remains much debated and may vary considerably between countries.

FIG. 11.12 Bovidian period scene of cattle and pastoralists from the Sahara region of south-eastern Algeria (photograph, Lucas Smits; RARI Archives).

Another set of classifications uses changes in the manner of depiction, usually of the human form or facial features, to define 'Schools' of art. Examples include: the Round Head School; the Abaniora School; the Iheren-Tahilahi School; the Ti-n-Anneuin Herdsmen School; and the Libyan Warrior School. A smaller number of Schools are defined around the manner of depiction of animals, for example the Naturalistic Bubaline School and the Tazina School. All the Schools are necessarily localized, often particular to one or a group of mountain massifs, and each has temporal limits. Each School therefore fits, at least in theory, within a period in the broader chronological sequence. The Round Head School, for example, is found in Algeria and Libya; it is early and was probably made during the bovidian period. The Libyan Warrior School is found in Mali and Niger; it is late and was made during the end of the horse period and throughout the camel period. To a certain extent the Schools and periods can therefore be meshed.

But this combination of classifications derived using manner of depiction, subject matter, and age has created a bewildering array of classificatory schema. Each researcher working in a particular massif has created a local schema, and whilst some broad trends can be identified between most, there have been acrimonious debates as to how different schema can be related, if at all (see e.g. Muzzolini 1995). In comparison to other parts of Africa, North African rock art research remains overly fixated upon classification, and this has not allowed sufficient movement away from an old archaeological style of cultural history. How the Schools of art link to past ethnic, archaeological, or other identities, for example, remains under-theorized. Interpretations of meaning and motivations have tended to follow European trends and so have included ideas about hunting magic, totemism, fertility divination, and shamanism, but such interpretations tend to be confined to brief speculative 'discussion' sections near the ends of books and papers, instead of forming the kind of fully integrated hermeneutic study typical of other parts of Africa. Attempts to link panels to specific local traditions or to broad cross-cultural mythological themes currently lie at the vanguard of recent interpretations (e.g. Smith 1993; Le Quellec 1993, 2004; Gauthier et al. 1996; Holl 2004), but these have not provided convincing detailed understandings of painted symbolism—perhaps unavoidably, given the great age of much of the art.

The place of African rock art research within African archaeology

In the late 1960s, rock art research lay at the periphery of African archaeology, largely the preserve of amateurs and bedevilled by poor-quality recording work and wildly speculative interpretations. The last fifty years have seen a transformation in the application of both method and theory in rock art studies, and this has allowed for reintegration within main-stream archaeology. A professional MSc. degree in Rock Art Studies was developed at Wits University in South Africa in the 1990s, and there are now dozens of Africans who have writ-ten Master's and Ph.D theses in rock art studies at many universities around the world. Problems of dating rock art remain (but see Mazel 2009), but this has not stopped the devel-opment of historically particular and regionally specific contextual understandings of the role and symbolism of rock art in many parts of Africa (e.g. Blundell 2004; Hollmann 2006; Moodley 2008; Zubieta 2009; Henry 2010; Namono 2010, 2011; Challis 2012). The days of gazing at rock art and guessing its meaning are over. Rock art studies now have a central place in the study of cognition, hermeneutics, and identity formation throughout Africa. They have usefully shifted the study of the African past from a focus on the workings of past African hands to consideration of the complexities of past African minds.

References

ALEXANDER, J. E. (1837). *A Narrative of a Voyage of Observation: Among the Colonies of Western Africa, in the Flagship Thalia.* London: Colburn.

ANATI, E. (1986). The rock art of Tanzania and the East African sequence. *Bollettino del Centro Camuno di Studi Preistorici* 23: 15–68.

BARROW, J. (1801). *An Account of Travels into the Interior of Southern Africa in the Years 1797 and 1798.* London: Cadell & Davies.

BLUNDELL, G. (2004). *Nqabayo's Nomansland: San Rock Art and the Somatic Past.* Uppsala: Uppsala University Press.

BRANDT, S. A., and CARDER, N. (1987). Pastoral rock art in the Horn of Africa: making sense of udder chaos. *World Archaeology* 19: 194–213.

BREUIL, H. (1955). *The White Lady of the Brandberg.* Paris: Trianon Press.

ČERVÍČEK, P. (1971). Rock paintings of Laga Oda (Ethiopia). *Paideuma* 17: 121–36.

—— (1979). Some African affinities of Arabian rock art. *Rassegna di studi etiopici* 27: 5–12.

CHALLIS, W. (2009). Taking the reins: the introduction of the horse in the 19th century Maloti-Drakensberg and the protective medicine of baboons. In P. Mitchell and B. W. Smith (eds), *The Eland's People: New Perspectives in the Rock Art of the Maloti-Drakensberg Bushmen.* Johannesburg: Wits University Press, 104–7.

—— (2012). Creolisation on the nineteenth-century frontiers of southern Africa: a case study of the AmaTola 'Bushmen' in the Maloti-Drakensberg. *Journal of Southern African Studies* 38: 265–80.

CHAMBERLAIN, N. (2006). Report on rock art of south west Samburu District, Kenya. *Azania* 41: 139–57.

CHAPLIN, J. H. (1974). The prehistoric rock art of the Lake Victoria region. *Azania* 9: 1–50.

CLARK, J. D. (1959). The rock paintings of Northern Rhodesia and Nyasaland; The rock engravings of Northern Rhodesia and Nyasaland. In R. Summers (ed.), *Prehistoric Rock Art of the Federation of Rhodesia and Nyasaland*. Glasgow: National Publications Trust, 163–220, 231–44.

DOWSON, T. A. (1994). Reading art, writing history: rock art and social change in southern Africa. *World Archaeology* 25: 332–44.

—— (2007). Debating shamanism in southern African rock art: time to move on. *South African Archaeological Bulletin* 62: 49–61.

EASTWOOD, E. B., and EASTWOOD, C. (2006). *Capturing the Spoor: An Exploration of Southern African Rock Art*. Cape Town: David Philip.

—— and SMITH, B. W. (2005). Finger prints of the Khoekhoen: geometric and handprinted rock art in the Central Limpopo Basin, South Africa. *South African Archaeological Society Goodwin Series* 9: 63–76.

FLAMAND, G.-B.-M. (1921). *Les Pierres Ecrites (Hadjrat-Maktoubat): gravures et inscriptions rupestres du Nord Africain*. Paris: Masson.

FROBENIUS, L., and OBERMAIER, H. (1925). *Haschra Maktuba: Urzeitliche felsbilder Kleinafricas*. Munich: Kurt Wolff.

GAUTHIER, Y., GAUTHIER, C., MOREL, A., and TILLET, T. (1996). *L'Art du Sahara*. Paris: Le Seuil.

GRAMLY, R. M. (1975). Meat-feasting sites and cattle brands: patterns of rock-shelter utilization in East Africa. *Azania* 10: 107–21.

GUTHERZ, X., CROS, J.-P, and LESUR, J. (2003). The discovery of new rock paintings in the Horn of Africa: the rockshelters of Las Geel, Republic of Somaliland. *Journal of African Archaeology* 1: 227–36.

GUTIERREZ, M. (1996). *L'Art Pariétal de l'Angola*. Paris: Harmattan.

HENRY, L. (2010). Rock art and the contested landscape of the North-Eastern Cape, South Africa. MA thesis, University of the Witwatersrand. http://wiredspace.wits.ac.za/bitstream/handle/10539/8307/Leila%20Henry%20MA%20Dissertation.pdf?sequence=1. Site accessed 21 Jan. 2011.

HOLLMANN, J. (2006). 'Swift-people': therianthropes and bird symbolism in hunter-gatherer rock paintings, Western and Eastern Cape Province, South Africa. *South African Archaeological Society Goodwin Series* 9: 21–33.

HUYGE, D, WATCHMAN, A., DE DAPPER, M., and MARCHI, E. (2001). Dating Egypt's oldest 'art': AMS ^{14}C age determination of rock varnishes covering petroglyphs at El-Hosh (Upper Egypt). *Antiquity* 75: 68–72.

JOLLY, P. (1996). Symbiotic interaction between Black farmers and south-eastern San. *Current Anthropology* 37: 277–305.

KLEINITZ, C. (2001). Rock art in sub-Saharan Mali. *Antiquity* 75: 799–800.

—— and DIETZ, B. (2004). Art rupestre au Pays Dogon: l'auvent de Songo. In R. Bedaux and D. Van der Waals (eds), *Regards sur les Dogon du Mali*. Leiden: Rijksmuseum voor Volkenkunde/Gand: Éditions Snoeck, 138–45.

KUBIK, G. (1989). Tusona ideographs: a lesson in interpretative objectivity. In I. Hodder (ed.), *The Meaning of Things: Material Culture and Symbolic Expression*. London: Routledge, 210–31.

LEAKEY, M. (1983). *Africa's Vanishing Art: The Rock Paintings of Tanzania*. New York: Doubleday.

LE QUELLEC, J.-L. (1993). *Symbolisme et Art Rupestre au Sahara*. Paris: Harmattan.

—— (1998). *Art Rupestre et Préhistoire du Sahara*. Paris: Peyot & Rivages.

—— (2004). *Rock Art in Africa: Mythology and Legend*. Paris: Flammarion.

LEWIS-WILLIAMS, J. D. (1972). The syntax and function of the Giant's Castle rock paintings. *South African Archaeological Bulletin* 27: 49–65.

—— (1981). *Believing and Seeing: Symbolic Meanings in Southern San Rock Painting*. London: Academic Press.

—— (1984). The empiricist impasse in southern African rock art studies. *South African Archaeological Bulletin* 39: 58–66.

—— (1987). Beyond style and portrait: a comparison of Tanzanian and southern African rock art. In R. Vossen, and K. Keuthmann (eds), *Contemporary Studies on Khoisan*. Hamburg: Helmut Buske, 93–159.

—— (1990). *Discovering Southern African Rock Art*. Cape Town: David Philip.

—— (2001). Monolithism and polysemy: Scylla and Charybdis in rock art research. In K. Helskog (ed.), *Theoretical Perspectives in Rock Art Research*. Oslo: Novus, 23–39.

—— (2006a). The evolution of theory, method and technique in southern African rock art research. *Journal of Archaeological Method and Theory* 13: 343–77.

—— (2006b). Debating rock art: myth and ritual, theories and facts. *South African Archaeological Bulletin* 61: 105–14.

—— and CHALLIS, W. (2011). *Deciphering Ancient Minds: The Mystery of San Bushman Rock Art*. London: Thames & Hudson.

LHOTE, H. (1961). The rock art of the Maghreb and Sahara. In H.-G. Bandi, H. Breuil, L. Berger-Kirchner, H. Lhote, E. Holm, and A. Lommel, *The Art of the Stone Age: Forty Thousand Years of Rock Art*. New York: Crown, 99–152.

LIM, I. (2010). Archaeology, ethnography and rock art: a modern-day study from Tanzania. In G. Blundell, C. Chippindale, and B. Smith (eds), *Seeing and Knowing: Understanding Rock Art With and Without Ethnography*. Johannesburg: Wits University Press, 99–115.

LINDGREN, N. E., and SCHOFFELEERS, J. M. (1978). *Rock Art and Nyau Symbolism in Malawi*. Zomba: Malawi Government Printers.

LYNCH, M., and ROBBINS, L. H. (1977). Animal brands and the interpretation of rock art in East Africa. *Current Anthropology* 18: 538–9.

MABULLA, A. Z. P. (2005). Rock art of the Mara region, Tanzania. *Azania* 40: 19–42.

MALLEN, L. (2008). Rock art and identity in the north Eastern Cape Province. MA thesis, University of the Witwatersrand. http://wiredspace.wits.ac.za/bitstream/handle/10539/5968/Lara%20Mallen%20MA%20Dissertation.pdf?sequence=1 Site accessed 21 Jan. 2011.

MAZEL, A. D. (2009). Images in time: advances in the dating of Maloti-Drakensberg rock art since the 1970s. In P. J. Mitchell and B. W. Smith (eds.), *The Eland's People: New Perspectives in the Rock Art of the Maloti-Drakensberg Bushmen*. Johannesburg: Wits University Press, 81–97.

MBEWE, R. (2007). Engraved rocks at Boomplaats farm: farmer settlement rock engravings of Mpumalanga Province, South Africa. MSc. thesis, University of the Witwatersrand. http://wiredspace.wits.ac.za/bitstream/handle/10539/5943/THESIS%20MAIN%20BODY.pdf?sequence=1. Site accessed 21 Jan. 2011

MGUNI, S. (2006). Iconography of termites' nests and termites: symbolic nuances of formlings in southern African San rock art. *Cambridge Archaeological Journal* 16: 53–71.

MIRE, S. (2008). The discovery of Dhambalin rock art site, Somaliland. *African Archaeological Review* 25: 153–68.

MONOD, T. (1938). *Contributions à l'Étude du Sahara Occidental, 1: Gravures, Peintures et Inscriptions Rupestres*. Paris: Larose.

MOODLEY, S. (2008). Koma: the crocodile motif in the rock art of the northern Sotho. *South African Archaeological Bulletin* 63: 116–24.

MORI, F. (1965). *Tadrart Acacus: Arte Rupestre e Culture del Sahara Preistorico*. Turin: Einaudi.

MUZZOLINI, A. (1995). *Les Images Rupestres du Sahara*. Toulouse: Préhistoire du Sahara.

NAMONO, C. (2010). Resolving the authorship of the geometric rock art of Uganda. *Journal of African Archaeology* 8: 239–57.

—— (2011). *Pongo* symbolism in the geometric rock art of Uganda. *Antiquity* 85: 1209–24.

—— and EASTWOOD, E. B. (2005). Art, authorship and female issues in a northern Sotho rock painting site. *South African Archaeological Society Goodwin Series*, 9: 77–85.

NOOTER, N. I. (1986). The Late Whites of Kondoa: an interpretation of Tanzanian rock art. *RES: Anthropology and Aesthetics* 12: 97–108.

ORPEN, J. M. (1874). A glimpse into the mythology of the Maluti Bushmen. *Cape Monthly Magazine* 9: 1–13.

OUZMAN, S. (2006). The magical arts of a raider nation: central South Africa's Korana rock art. *South African Archaeological Society Goodwin Series* 9: 101–13.

PAGER, H. (1971). *Ndedema*. Graz: Akademische Druck.

PHILLIPSON, D. W. (1976). *The Prehistory of Eastern Zambia*. Nairobi: British Institute in Eastern Africa.

PRINS, F. E., and HALL, S. (1994). Expressions of fertility in the rock art of Bantu-speaking agriculturists. *African Archaeological Review* 12: 171–203.

SKOTNES, P. (2007). *Claim to the Country: The Archive of Lucy Lloyd and Wilhelm Bleek*. Johannesburg: Jacana.

SMITH, A. B. (1993). New approaches to Saharan rock art. *Memorie della Società Italiana di Scienze Naturali e del Museo Civico di Storia Naturale di Milano* 26: 467–78.

SMITH, B. W. (1997). *Zambia's Ancient Rock Art*. Livingstone: National Heritage Conservation Commission of Zambia.

—— (2001). Forbidden images: rock paintings and the *Nyau* secret society of central Malawi and eastern Zambia. *African Archaeological Review* 18: 187–212.

—— (2010). Envisioning San history: problems in the reading of history in the rock art of the Maloti-Drakensberg Mountains of South Africa. *African Studies* 69: 345–59.

—— and OUZMAN, S. (2004). Taking stock: identifying Khoekhoen herder rock art in southern Africa. *Current Anthropology* 45: 499–526.

—— and VAN SCHALKWYK, J. A. (2002). The White Camel of the Magkabeng. *Journal of African History* 43: 235–54.

SOLOMON, A. (1992). Gender, representation and power in San ethnography and rock art. *Journal of Anthropological Archaeology* 11: 291–329.

—— (1997). The myth of ritual origins? Ethnography, mythology and interpretation of San rock art. *South African Archaeological Bulletin* 52: 3–13.

—— (2008). Myths, making and consciousness: differences and dynamics in San rock art. *Current Anthropology* 49: 59–86.

STAUDINGER, P. (1911). Funde und Abbildungen von Felszeichnungen aus den alten Goldgebieten von Portugiesisch-Südostafrika. *Zeitschrift für Ethnologie* 43: 140–46.

STOW, G. W., and BLEEK, D. F. (1930). *Rock Paintings in South Africa: From Parts of the Eastern Province and Orange Free State*. London: Methuen.

STRIEDTER, K. H. (1983). *Felsbilder Nordafrikas und der Sahara*. Wiesbaden: Franz Steiner.

TEN RAA, E. (1971). Dead art and living society: a study of rock paintings in a social context. *Mankind* 8: 42–58.

—— (1974). A record of some pre-historic and some recent Sandawe rock paintings, *Tanzania Notes and Records* 75: 9–27.

THEAL, G. M. (1897). *History of South Africa under the Administration of the Dutch East India Company 1652 to 1795*, vol 2. London: Swan Sonnenschien.

TUCKER, M., and BAIRD, R. C. (1983). The Trelawney/Darwendale rock art survey. *Zimbabwean Prehistory* 19: 26–58

VAN SCHALKWYK, J. A., and SMITH, B. W. (2004). Insiders and outsiders: sources for reinterpreting an historical event. In D. A. M. Reid and P. J. Lane (eds), *African Historical Archaeologies*. London: Kluwer Academic/Plenum, 325–46.

VINNICOMBE, P. (1976). *People of the Eland: Rock Paintings of the Drakensberg Bushmen as a Reflection of their Life and Thought*. Pietermaritzburg: Natal University Press.

WILLCOX, A. (1984). *The Rock Art of Africa*. Johannesburg: Macmillan.

WRIGHT, R. (1961). A painted shelter on Mount Elgon, Kenya. *Proceedings of the Prehistoric Society* 27: 28–34.

ZUBIETA, L. (2006). *The Rock Art of Mwana wa Chentcherere II Rock Shelter, Malawi*. Leiden: African Studies Centre.

—— (2009). The rock art of Chinamwali: material culture and girls' initiation in south-central Africa. Ph.D thesis, University of the Witwatersrand. http://wiredspace.wits.ac.za/bitstream/handle/10539/8137/PHDZubietaCalvertFINcompressed.pdf?sequence=1

CHAPTER 12

THE ARCHAEOLOGY OF RITUAL AND RELIGIONS IN AFRICA

TIMOTHY INSOLL

INTRODUCTION

THE archaeology of ritual and religions in Africa is extremely rich though little researched (Insoll 2011). Exceptions exist, but the most intensively studied material relates to either rock art, predominantly in the southern portion of the continent and often conceptualized under the framework of 'shamanism' (Smith, Ch. 11 above), and that of world religions, primarily Christianity (Finneran 2002; Phillipson 2009) or Islam (Horton 1996; Insoll 2003). In contrast, the archaeology of indigenous religions and prehistoric ritual practices in large areas of the continent remains under investigated. This is unfortunate, as sub-Saharan Africa in particular has much to contribute to our understanding of religions, empirically within the continent itself, but also hermeneutically in providing analogies and new perspectives potentially relevant elsewhere.

Defining the parameters of study—the archaeology of ritual and religion itself—is itself not unproblematic. How far religiosity can be presumed to imbue both African thought and life (Mbiti 1989: Morris 2006) has direct implications for how the archaeological record is conceptualized as to what constitutes the residue of the 'sacred' or the 'profane' (Insoll 2004). A theoretical approach that regards religion in African life as an 'ontological phenomenon' (Mbiti 1989: 15) and opens all aspects of material culture to archaeological consideration of it seems most useful. Such an approach is facilitated by emphasizing context in identifying, within specific archaeological situations, how broadly the notion of 'religion' or religiosity extends into the domain of material culture. As the emergence of early forms of symbolic behaviour is considered elsewhere (Barham, Ch. 24 below), the emphasis here is on ritual and religion in later periods of African prehistory and history.

Much of the material discussed relates to what might be described as the archaeology of African indigenous or traditional religions. Whether this concept is applicable and whether, if so, it refers to a singular religion (Idowu 1973) or multiple religions (Mbiti 1989) has been extensively debated (Shaw 1990; Morris 2006). Commonsense dictates thinking in the plural, but recognizing certain key recurring elements that might have material correlates. Such elements include: a belief in a high or sky God, beliefs in a lesser tier of spirits or divinities, ancestral veneration and propitiation, belief in the power of certain material substances, and the recognition of witchcraft as 'a constituent part of African religious culture' (Morris 2006: 151), something more broadly framed by Mbiti (1989: 189) as 'mystical power, magic, witchcraft and sorcery'.

Direct recognition of these anthropologically known categories in the archaeological record is unlikely, but it is not improbable that similar beliefs and practices, singly or in combination, and perhaps allied with now unknown or forgotten elements, underpinned the archaeological material. Our reconstructions will only ever be partial, and great diversity is evident in how rituals and religions are manifested materially; but following de Maret (1994) certain recurring categories can be isolated.

PORTABLE RITUAL OBJECTS

In comparison to rock art (Smith, Ch. 11 above), archaeological research on 'portable ritual objects' is less prolific. For example, our understanding of the clay figurines assumed to have ritual purposes from Jenné-jeno, Mali, or various sites associated with the so-called Sao in Chad, is still meagre. At Jenné-jeno, over seventy human or animal representations have been found dating from between the 11th and 15th centuries AD (McIntosh 1995). Some may have functioned as toys, but others probably served ritual purposes, including a single kneeling figure with arms crossed over its torso, perhaps associated with 'ancestor worship' (McIntosh and McIntosh 1979: 53). Other terracotta figurines were associated with funerary urns and what are termed 'rain-making altars' (McIntosh and McIntosh 1988: 156), but the great majority are from looted sites and thus without context (Schmidt and McIntosh 1996).

Also largely unknown is the function of 10th–16th- century AD Sao figurines (Lebeuf et al. 1980) that include human heads, torsos, full figures, masks, and animals such as hippopotami, lizards, sheep, and porcupines modelled in clay. Their overall context is thought to have encompassed ancestor veneration, totemism, and belief in various spirits, with a possible shrine from Tago comprising a group of three human figurines placed facing east, with one atop a funerary jar accompanied by four balls of fired clay at the cardinal points and, surrounding this arrangement, other figurines, some with zoomorphic masks, stone pounders, ochre, animal bone, and a 'ritual' hearth (Lebeuf and Masson Detourbet (1950). The function and meaning of the Lydenburg heads from Mpumalanga in South Africa similarly remains unclear. One suggestion is that these seven terracotta heads dating from c. AD 500–700, two of which are large enough to have been used as helmet masks, might have functioned in the performance of initiation rituals (Davison 1995: 195).

Elsewhere, renewed investigations are beginning to place such terracotta figurines within a fuller archaeological context. This is true, for example, of the Nok terracotta figurines from

FIG. 12.1 Ritual figurines *in situ*, Yikpabongo, Ghana (photograph, Timothy Insoll, 2010).

central Nigeria, among sub-Saharan Africa's earliest figurative sculptures (Rupp et al. 2005; Breunig, Ch. 38 below), which date from *c.* 500 BC to AD 200. Further west, in Komaland, northern Ghana, recent research suggests that terracotta figurines (Fig. 12.1) there did not have a mainly funerary role (*pace* Anquandah 1998), but involved links with fertility, witchcraft, and curing (Kankpeyeng and Nkumbaan 2008), and principally date to between the 6th and 12th, rather than 13th–17th, centuries AD (Kankpeyeng and Nkumbaan 2009: 200). Recent research has also been adding contextual data, which was previously lacking, to the Luzira Head, a pottery figurine from Uganda. This research has indicated that it belongs within the period of political centralization that occurred in the region at the end of the first millennium AD (Reid and Ashley 2008).

Though perhaps constituting the majority of portable ritual objects, by their perishable nature sculptures, figurines, 'fetishes', shrines, and ritual objects made in wood and other plant materials, cloth, leather and skins, and animal parts (bones, blood, feathers) rarely survive in the archaeological record. An exception is provided by a zoomorphic wooden head dated to the 8th/9th centuries AD from Angola that may represent an aardvark (de Maret 1995), an animal known ethnographically to be thought of as an anomalous creature, 'good to think' (de Maret 2005).

MATERIALITY AND TECHNOLOGY

Substances, materials, and technologies are not necessarily conceptually inert. They can function within religious systems of belief and be subject to ritual sanction, and it is now well established that technology should not be divorced from its social and symbolic contexts (Hodder 1982). These points have perhaps been most fully explored in relation to iron production and technology (Herbert 1993; Reid and MacLean 1995; Schmidt 1997; Chirikure, Ch. 10 above), and analogies drawing on African experience have also had significant impacts on archaeological interpretations of metallurgy elsewhere in the world (Blakely 2006; Giles 2007; Haaland 2007).

Less well known but potentially as significant are ceramics (Herbert 1993; Gosselain and Livingstone Smith 2005, Ch. 9 above). Prohibitions and taboos can exist in regard to how clay is extracted and handled, as Frank (1998: 79) relates for the Mande of Mali, who believe that it has *nyama*, 'a kind of vital energy or "heat" that pervades all things'. Clay can be seen as a powerful substance and this, besides technical considerations, may help explain why old pots were often ground down as grog and used to temper new ones; for the Fulani/Gurma of Burkina Faso and Songhai/Zarma of Niger this is done explicitly to link new vessels with those of the ancestors (Gosselain and Livingstone Smith 2005: 41). Such beliefs are less universal than those surrounding ironworking, but offer their own possibilities for archaeological interpretation, as in understanding the deposition of a large spread of pottery at Tallensi earth shrines in northern Ghana (Insoll et al. 2007) (Fig. 12.2).

Both ceramic and metallurgical technologies also explicitly relate to gender, and to pollution and taboo. Hence ceramics might be used in the negotiation of gender identities, and possibly disposed of or treated in special ways if associated with polluting activities as Bedaux and Lane (2003) have discussed in relation to menstruation amongst the Dogon of Mali (see also Douny 2007). In ironworking, Herbert (1993: 25) states that 'the smith and smelter are always male', and describes how furnaces can be modelled upon the female form with the provision of clay breasts, incised scarification marks, navels, and a gynecomorphic parallel often evident in how the bloom in the furnace is thought of as analogous to the foetus in the womb, with the furnace opening sometimes considered similar to the vulva, in giving birth (access) to the iron (cf. Collett 1993: 503; Barndon 2004). In contrast to male-dominated iron production, women produce pots in the vast majority of sub-Saharan societies (Berns 1993; Frank 1998; Gosselain 1999) with the link between women and pots connected with the Earth

FIG. 12.2 Ceramic spread and accompanying stone arrangements, Nyoo Shrine, Tong Hills, Ghana (photograph, Timothy Insoll, 2006).

and the metaphor of fertility all over sub-Saharan Africa (Jacobson-Widding and Van Beek 1990).

Death and burial

Death and burial constitute a further realm of enquiry, with an immense and varied body of archaeological evidence. Gaining inferences about how 'ancestors' are created based on archaeology alone is difficult, though hypotheses can be developed through ethnography. David's (1992) ethnoarchaeological study of the funerary practices of various non-hierarchical agricultural societies in Cameroon's central Mandara Mountains is useful in this respect, for all these groups have ancestor cults. He shows, for example, how the grave's form has symbolic connotations, with the bell- or flagon-shaped tombs of the Mofa or Kapsiki signifying 'hut, granary, pot and uterus, all appropriate abodes for the process of ancestralization through germination, gestation and conceivably also fermentation' (David 1992: 193). The concept of secondary burial can also be significant in constructing and attaining ancestral status, with perhaps the most influential ethnographic work here being that of Metcalf and Huntington (1991), which both draws upon African material, notably from Madagascar, and has influenced work elsewhere on the continent by others (e.g. David 1992).

Shrines and monuments

Significant research has also been undertaken on the archaeology and ethnoarchaeology of African shrines and sacred groves (Sheridan and Nyamweru 2008; Dawson 2009; Apoh and Gavua 2010). Mathers (2003), for example, has explored the relationship between shrines, 'land gods' as places of power, the founding of settlements, and the domestication of the landscape amongst the Kusasi of northern Ghana, while Chouin (2002, 2008) has worked on sacred groves in southern Ghana. The recurring relationship between sacred groves and former settlements has been explored within the framework of perceiving groves as anthropogenic 'creations' and *lieux de mémoire*, rather than as just shrines or places of sacrifice (Chouin 2002: 42, 45). Ethnobotanical research in Tallensi sacred groves indicates similar processes in operation at groves where species composition may have been affected by human agency (Insoll 2007).

Shrines and the substances from which they are made also offer possibilities for exploring ritual relationships and obligations and religious links and influences. This is because shrines can be 'franchised', creating extensive ritual networks actualized through movements of ideas and tangible materials such as stone, clay, other medicinal substances or animal remains from the 'parent' shrine (Insoll 2006). Kuba and Lentz (2002: 393) show, for example, how the stone that forms the centre of Dagara earth shrines in the regions of southwest Burkina Faso and northwest Ghana 'is a surprisingly mobile object', and how power is transferred to other stones surrounding it, thus producing 'children' of the mother shrine that can in turn form shrines elsewhere. Similarly, among the Tallensi powerful shrines such as

Tonna'ab Yaane are franchized (Allman and Parker 2005) via the *Boarbii*, 'the shrine's child' and the *Boarchii*, 'the shrine gourd' constructed from elements that include medicinal substances, cow horns, skin, gourds, feathers, and blood. Such processes carry profound implications for thinking about archaeological materials elsewhere—for example, why 'exotic' rock is found in British Neolithic ritual contexts at sites like Stonehenge and West Kennet Long Barrow (Insoll 2006).

Where the category of 'shrines' ends and that of 'monuments' begins is inevitably arbitrary. Great Zimbabwe, a massive site in Zimbabwe principally dating from AD 1270 to 1450 (Pikirayi, Ch. 63 below), might be better defined as a 'monument', though it equally contains shrines linked to the role of the king as rainmaker, a connection vital in the emergence of social complexity in the region (Huffman 2009). Drawing upon ethnographic analogy and other sources, Huffman (1996) has also developed interesting, if debatable, hypotheses that contextualize the site, its components, setting, architecture, and small finds in relation to each other in seeking to interpret its symbolic, ritual, and ultimately religious purpose. One example concerns perhaps the most famous objects recovered from Great Zimbabwe, carved soapstone birds that seem to represent raptors, and probably symbolized the mediating role of royal ancestors between God and man (Huffman 1996: 134–5).

Megaliths are an important but little-understood category of African ritual monuments that connect many of the categories already described such as death, burial, materiality, and technology. Four main distributions exist, in Central Africa, West Africa, Ethiopia, and Madagascar (Joussaume 1988). In western Central African Republic and eastern highland Cameroon, for example, at least 200 such monuments exist, usually formed of oval mounds or tumuli of earth and granite rubble ranging in size from 25 to 2,000 m², some containing interior cists, some later exterior ones, and topped with up to 100 standing stones that can be up to 4 m high. Dating from the first millennium BC to the mid-second millennium AD, they were probably funerary monuments, though not necessarily tombs (David 1982; Zangato 1999). Not all such standing stone arrangements, however, need be ritual in nature; in northwestern Cameroon, for instance, the 3×3 m rectangular stone alignments found within megalithic monuments find parallels in granary bases (Asombang 2004).

WORLD RELIGIONS

Separating world religions from indigenous religions is somewhat arbitrary, for it denies processes of syncretism (Insoll 2001). World religions have also undeniably been made indigenous in Africa, as the diverse forms of Christianity and Islam practised there show. I consider Islam first, as it is by far the more widespread of the two.

Islam

Islam's spread in Africa began with the Arab conquest of Egypt in 642, quickly followed by its expansion across North Africa and simultaneous move across the Red Sea. By the early 9th century it had reached the East African coast and, almost contemporaneously, the western Sahel. Subsequently, in the 11th century, the first tangible evidence of Islamization is found in the central Sudan, while in the West African Sudan this dates from the 12th century. Finally, from the mid-17th century in the Cape area of South Africa, but largely in the 19th century, its impact was also felt in parts of east-central and southern Africa (Levtzion and Pouwels 2000). Dynamic processes of conversion were incorporated within this historical sequence.

South of the Sahara, the archaeology of Islam in each of the regions just defined is also a continuation of their Iron Age archaeology. This pre-Islamic background was crucial in dictating the degree of Islamization and the impact of Islam upon the various societies that existed (Insoll 2003). In parts of Ethiopia and the Horn, notably Harar, for instance, the cult of saints was important, with over 150 saints' shrines known in and around the city (Foucher 1994). These vary in form and size, with some linked with pre-Islamic sacred sites, such as trees or pools (Insoll 2003: 80). Islam's spread in the Sudanese Nile Valley and Nubia was similarly dominated by holy men (McHugh 1994). Fired-brick architecture—secular (palace) and religious (mosques, tombs)—also recurs in the trade centres of the western Sahel as at Gao (Fig. 12.3). Here, trans-Saharan trade flourished, and extensive archaeological evidence for contacts with the Muslim world was found dating especially from the 11th–12th centuries (Insoll 1996). This included five inscribed Muslim tombstones apparently imported ready-carved from the vicinity of Almeria in Muslim Spain (Farias 1990). A cache of over fifty hippopotamus tusks, possibly destined for the ivory workshops of North Africa (Insoll 1995), as well as glazed Spanish, Egyptian, and Tunisian pottery, numerous glass beads, and fragments from glass vessels, all also attested to the lively north–south commerce between Muslim North Africa and the increasingly Islamized urban population of Gao. This is a picture mirrored at other sites in the western Sahel, as at Tegdaoust in Mauritania (Devisse 1983), and broad parallels can also be drawn with the entrepots operating on the other side of the continent on the East African coast (Insoll 2003: 402). This and other archaeological and architectural evidence from across sub-Saharan Africa attest to how Islam was 'Africanized' and adapted to suit local contexts gradually over time, reflecting indigenous conversion processes rather than external imposition.

FIG. 12.3 Possible aisle of a mosque, Gao Ancien, Mali (photograph, Timothy Insoll, 1993).

These parallels exist in their respective geographical (coastal Sahara and Indian Ocean) situations and chronological contemporaneity, and in the role of trade as an agent of Islamisation—but significant differences are also seemingly evident. This is apparent in the degree of cultural unity of the 'Swahili' East African coastal settlements (stone mosque and other architecture, similar trade goods from long-distance trade) lacking in the western Sahel. But look deeper and the polities on the East African coast appear as dissimilar as they were similar, and traces of experimentation with different sects and schools of Islam exist in the archaeological record (Horton and Middleton 2000). For example, at Shanga on the Kenyan coast the excavated mosque sequence dating from before AD 1000 indicates a progression towards orthodoxy in the *qiblah* angle employed, i.e. the direction of prayer towards Mecca (Horton 1996). Burial orientation also shows a similar initial confusion and correct alignment over time, and this would seem to physically represent the adoption and integration of Islam within Swahili society as a whole (Insoll 2003: 164).

In the central Sudan the narrative of Islamic archaeology again differs, and this was a region in which important empires, kingdoms, city-states, and emirates flourished and disappeared. These contributed significantly to the character of Islam, and to the existence of warfare and jihad, as attested by a rash of fortified towns and cities scattered across the central Sudan. Archaeology repeatedly attests to the large fortified urban centres built, as at Birni Ngazargamo, a capital of the Kanem-Borno kingdom founded during the reign of Ali Dunamami (*c.* 1472–1504). An area of 2 km across was defended by an earthern rampart up to 7 m in height with five entrances (Bivar and Shinnie 1962; Gronenborn 2001). Similarly within the Hausa kingdoms, cities such as Kano and Zaria were defended. At Zaria various phases of wall building have been isolated (Sutton 1976), but unfortunately many of the Hausa monuments belonging to the early phase of Islamization were deliberately destroyed following the Fulani jihads at the outset of the 19th century (Insoll 2003: 296).

In contrast, within the West African Sudan and forest, Islam spread in an essentially peaceful process, primarily via the agency of Mande traders, who established links between the termini of the trans-Saharan trade routes such as Timbuktu and Gao and forest and savannah regions to the south (Levtzion 1986). Trading in, for example, gold and kola nuts, they established a presence at centres such as Begho, Buipe, and Daboya in northern Ghana from the 15th/16th centuries. At Kramo, the 'strangers' quarter at Begho, evidence seemingly indicating a Muslim presence included burials, and northern-derived architecture and technology (Posnansky 1987).

Finally, in southern and east-central Africa the archaeological evidence again differs. Here, trade goods originating from the Muslim world are found in parts of the region, as with glass beads from Great Zimbabwe of probable 14th-century date (Garlake 1973) or in parts of Uganda dating from between AD 900–1200 (Robertshaw 1997). However, it is noticeable that Muslims themselves, apart from small bands of Arab and Swahili traders and slavers, were largely absent until the arrival of Europeans in the late 19th century (Insoll 2003: 402).

Christianity

The archaeology of Christianity in Africa is more geographically restricted than that of Islam, with the main areas being Ethiopia, Nubia and North Africa. Chronologically, as Finneran (2002: 11) notes, 'Christianity has had a foothold in the African continent for almost two thousand years', as old as the religion itself. Christianity's earliest presence in Africa, now replaced by Islam except for the Coptic communities of Egypt, was in North Africa (Frend 1996), and it was introduced to Ethiopia and Nubia in the 4th and 6th centuries respectively (Edwards 2004; Finneran 2007).

According to tradition, Ezana, king of Aksum, converted to Christianity in 330, (Phillipson 2009, Ch. 55 below), a process signalled materially, on coins by the replacement of the sun and crescent symbols of earlier religion by the cross (Munro-Hay 1991). Subsequently, other aspects of material culture also gradually changed or appeared as the religion percolated downwards from the elite (Finneran 2002: 133–7). For example, nearly 50 per cent of the motif types on Brown Aksumite burnished wares by the 6th century are of crosses, bifurcate plain ones or the flared-top Aksumite cross. Churches also appear, converted from pre-Christian temples as at Yeha, or built anew as at Qohaito, Quiha, Tekondo, and Matara. Drawing on Aksumite roots, later buildings include some of the most famous Christian monuments in the world, notably the rock-cut churches at Lalibela that took on their final form in the 13th century but have been rebuilt and modified up to the present (Phillipson 2009, Ch. 53 below).

Further north, in Christian Nubia, numerous churches and other religious buildings survive, as at Soba, capital of the kingdom of Alwa (Welsby 1998; Edwards, Ch. 54 below) and, in Lower Nubia, in the extraordinarily well-preserved murals at Faras. Also in Lower Nubia, exceptional preservation of organic materials at Qasr Ibrim provides insights into Christian (and subsequent Muslim) communities usually denied the archaeologist. Finds include numerous manuscripts, as well as palm crosses, crucifixes, fragments of icons and amulets, and even the body of a bishop, Timotheus, along with his testimonial letters from the Pope of Alexandria, Gabriel IV (1370–78) (Adams 1996; Frend 1996; see also Edwards, Ch. 54 below).

Finally, at the other end of Christianity's history in Africa, interesting research has been completed on the relationship between the London Missionary Society and various Tswana communities in southern Africa in the late 19th/early 20th centuries. This indicates the ambivalent nature of the encounters between the two (Lane 2001) but, in a pattern already repeatedly referred to here, also shows continuities in the organization of space and in vernacular architectural form, rather than simple replacement by new 'Christianized' models (Lane 1999). Similar patterns have been charted elsewhere in Africa by Crossland (2006), with reference to the impact of the first Welsh missionaries to enter highland Madagascar in the 19th century. Conversely, whereas one of the earliest instances of European missionary activity in Africa—the conversion of the Kingdom of Kongo in the late 15th century—is known historically (Vansina 1966), it has yet to be the subject of archaeological investigation.

CONCLUSIONS

The archaeology of ritual and religions in Africa is complex and variably understood, but has enormous research potential. It is to be hoped that the database of earliest evidence for symbolic and ritual behaviours will continue to grow, along with understanding of them. Future foci for archaeological investigation could include charting trajectories of religious change, fusion, and syncretism in relation to past material culture. Neither world nor African indigenous religions have ever been static phenomena, but have instead been adapted and reworked to suit different contexts, circumstances, and environments over time. A more anthropologically informed approach to the archaeological investigation of indigenous sub-Saharan African rituals and religions is emerging (Insoll 2008, 2009; Stahl 2008). Similar possibilities exist for the archaeology of world religions, where material culture could be treated less passively and descriptively and more as the outcome of active processes and agents.

References

ADAMS, W. Y. (1996). *Qasr Ibrim: The Late Medieval Period*. London: Egypt Exploration Society.

ALLMAN, J., and PARKER, J. (2005). *Tongnaab*. Bloomington: Indiana University Press.

APOH, W., and GAVUA, K. (2010). Material culture and indigenous spiritism: the Katamansu archaeological 'otutu' (shrine). *African Archaeological Review* 27: 211–35.

ASOMBANG, R. N. (2004). Interpreting standing stones in Africa: a case study in north-west Cameroon. *Antiquity* 78: 294–305.

BARNDON, R. (2004). A discussion of magic and medicines in East African iron working: actors and artefacts in technology. *Norwegian Archaeological Review* 37: 21–40.

BEDAUX, R. M., and LANE, P. (2003). L'attitude des Dogon vis-à-vis des Dechets. In R. M. Bedaux and J. D. Van Der Waals (eds), *Regards sur les Dogon du Mali*. Leiden: Rijksmuseum, 83–91.

BERNS, M. (1993). Art, history, and gender: women and clay in West Africa. *African Archaeological Review* 11: 129–48.

BIVAR, A. D. H., and SHINNIE, P. (1962). Old Kanuri capitals. *Journal of African History* 3: 1–10.

BLAKELY, S. (2006). *Myth, Ritual and Metallurgy in Ancient Greece and Recent Africa*. Cambridge: Cambridge University Press.

CHOUIN, G. (2002). Sacred groves in history: pathways to the social shaping of forest landscapes in coastal Ghana. *IDS Bulletin* 33: 39–46.

—— (2008). Archaeological perspectives on sacred groves in Ghana. In M. J. Sheridan and C. Nyamweru (eds), *African Sacred Groves: Ecological Dynamics and Social Change*. Oxford: James Currey, 178–94.

COLLETT, D. P. (1993). Metaphors and representations associated with pre-colonial iron-smelting in eastern and southern Africa. In T. Shaw, B. Andah, P. Sinclair, and A. Okpoko (eds), *The Archaeology of Africa: Foods, Metals, and Towns*. London: Routledge, 499–511.

CROSSLAND, Z. (2006). Landscape and mission in Madagascar and Wales in the early nineteenth century: 'sowing the seeds of knowledge'. *Landscapes* 1: 93–121.

DAVID, N. (1982). *Tazunu*: megalithic monuments of Central Africa. *Azania* 17: 43–77.

—— (1992). The archaeology of ideology: mortuary practices in the central Mandara Highlands, northern Cameroon. In J. Sterner and N. David (eds), *An African Commitment*. Calgary: University of Calgary Press, 181–210.

DAVISON, P. (1995). Lydenburg Head. In T. Phillips (ed.), *Africa: The Art of a Continent*. London: Royal Academy of Arts, 194–5.

DAWSON, A. (ed.) (2009). *Shrines in Africa*. Calgary: University of Calgary Press.

DE MARET, P. (1994). Archaeological and other prehistoric evidence of traditional African religious expression. In T. D. Blakely, W. E. A. Van Beek, and D. L. Thomson (eds), *Religion in Africa*. London: James Currey, 182–95.

—— (1995). Zoomorphic head. In T. Phillips (ed.), *Africa: The Art of a Continent*. London: Royal Academy of Arts, 240.

—— (2005). L'Orycterope, un animal 'bon à penser' pour les Africains, est-il a l'origine du dieu égyptien Seth? *Bulletin de l'Institut Français d'Archéologie Orientale* 105: 107–28.

DEVISSE, J. (ed.). (1983). *Tegdaoust III*. Paris: Association Diffusion Pensée Francais.

DOUNY, L. (2007). The materiality of domestic waste: the recycled cosmology of the Dogon. *Journal of Material Culture* 12: 309–31.

EDWARDS, D. (1999). Christianity and Islam in the Middle Nile: towards a study of religion and social change in the long term. In T. Insoll (ed.), *Case Studies in Archaeology and World Religion*. Oxford: British Archaeological Reports, 94–104.

—— (2004). *The Nubian Past*. London: Routledge.

FINNERAN, N. (2002). *The Archaeology of Christianity in Africa*. Stroud: Tempus.

—— (2007). *The Archaeology of Ethiopia*. London: Routledge.

FOUCHER, E. (1994). The cult of Muslim saints in Harar: religious dimension. In B. Zewde, R. Pankhurst, and T. Beyne (eds), *Proceedings of the Eleventh International Conference of Ethiopian Studies*. Addis Ababa: Institute of Ethiopian Studies, 71–9.

FRANK, B. (1998). *Mande Potters and Leather-Workers*. Washington, DC: Smithsonian Institution Press.

FREND, W. H. C. (1996). *The Archaeology of Early Christianity*. London: Geoffrey Chapman.

GARLAKE, P. (1973). *Great Zimbabwe*. London: Thames & Hudson.

GILES, M. (2007). Making metal and forging relations: ironworking in the British Iron Age. *Oxford Journal of Archaeology* 26: 395–413.

GOSSELAIN, O. (1999). In pots we trust: the processing of clay and symbols in sub-Saharan Africa. *Journal of Material Culture* 4: 205–30.

—— and LIVINGSTONE SMITH, A. (2005). The source: clay selection and processing practices in sub-Saharan Africa. In A. Livingstone Smith, D. Bosquet, and R. Martineau (eds), *Pottery Manufacturing Processes: Reconstitution and Interpretation*. Oxford: British Archaeological Reports, 33–47.

GRONENBORN, D. (2001). A brief summary of the history and archaeology of an empire in the central *Bilad al-Sudan*. In C. DeCorse (ed.), *West Africa During the Atlantic Slave Trade: Archaeological Perspectives*. Leicester: Leicester University Press, 101–30.

HAALAND, R. (2007). Say it in iron: symbols of transformation and reproduction in the European Iron Age. *Current Swedish Archaeology* 15: 1–20.

HERBERT, E. (1993). *Iron, Gender and Power*. Bloomington: Indiana University Press.

HODDER, I. (1982). *Symbols in Action*. Cambridge: Cambridge University Press.

HORTON, M. (1996). *Shanga*. Nairobi: British Institute in Eastern Africa.

—— and MIDDLETON, J. (2000). *The Swahili*. Oxford: Blackwell.

HUFFMAN, T. N. (1996). *Snakes and Crocodiles: Power and Symbolism in Ancient Zimbabwe*. Johannesburg: Witwatersrand University Press.

—— (2009). Mapungubwe and Great Zimbabwe: the origin and spread of social complexity in southern Africa. *Journal of Anthropological Archaeology* 28: 37–54.

IDOWU, E. B. (1973). *African Traditional Religion: A Definition*. London: SCM Press.

INSOLL, T. (1995). A cache of hippopotamus ivory at Gao, Mali; and a hypothesis of its use. *Antiquity* 69: 327–36.

—— (1996). *Islam, Archaeology and History: Gao Region (Mali) Ca.AD 900–1250*. Oxford: Tempus Reparatum.

—— (2001). Introduction: the archaeology of world religion. In T. Insoll (ed.), *Archaeology and World Religion*. London: Routledge, 1–32.

INSOLL, T. (2003). *The Archaeology of Islam in Sub-Saharan Africa*. Cambridge: Cambridge University Press.

—— (2004). *Archaeology, Ritual, Religion*. London: Routledge.

—— (2006). Shrine franchising and the Neolithic in the British Isles: some observations based upon the Tallensi, northern Ghana. *Cambridge Archaeological Journal* 16: 223–38.

—— (2007). Natural or human spaces? Tallensi sacred groves and shrines and their potential implications for aspects of northern European prehistory and phenomenological interpretation. *Norwegian Archaeological Review* 40: 138–58.

—— (2008). Negotiating the archaeology of destiny: an exploration of interpretive possibilities through Tallensi shrines. *Journal of Social Archaeology* 8: 380–403.

—— (2009). Materialising performance and ritual: decoding the archaeology of shrines in northern Ghana. *Material Religion* 5: 288–311.

—— (2011). Sub-Saharan Africa. In T. Insoll (ed.), *Oxford Handbook of the Archaeology of Ritual and Religion*. Oxford: Oxford University Press, 425–41.

—— KANKPEYENG, B., and MACLEAN, R. (2007). Shrines, rituals, and archaeology in northern Ghana. *Current World Archaeology* 26: 29–36.

JACOBSON-WIDDING, A., and VAN BEEK, W. (1990). Chaos, order, and communion in African models of fertility. In A. Jacobson-Widding and W. van Beek (eds), *The Creative Communion: African Folk Models of Fertility and the Regeneration of Life*. Uppsala: Uppsala University Press, 15–43.

JOUSSAUME, R. (1988). *Dolmens for the Dead*. London: Guild Publishing.

KANKPEYENG, B., and NKUMBAAN, S. N. (2008). Rethinking the stone circles of Komaland: a preliminary report on the 2007/2008 fieldwork at Yikpabongo, northern region, Ghana. In T. Insoll (ed.), *Current Archaeological Research in Ghana*. Oxford: British Archaeological Reports, 95–102.

—— —— (2009). Ancient shrines? New insights on the Komaland sites of northern Ghana. In S. Magnavita (ed.), *Crossroads/Carrefour Sahel*. Frankfurt: Africa Magna, 193–202.

KUBA, R., and LENTZ, C. (2002). Arrows and earth shrines: towards a history of Dagara expansion in southern Burkina Faso. *Journal of African History* 43: 377–406.

LANE, P. J. (1999). Archaeology, nonconformist missions and the 'colonisation of consciousness' in southern Africa, *c.* 1820–1900. In T. Insoll (ed.), *Case Studies in Archaeology and World Religion*. Oxford: British Archaeological Reports, 153–65.

—— (2001). The archaeology of Christianity in global perspective. In T. Insoll (ed.), *Archaeology and World Religion*. London: Routledge, 148–81.

LEBEUF, J.-P., and MASSON DETOURBET, A. (1950). *La Civilisation du Tchad*. Paris: Payot.

—— TREINEN-CLAUSTRE, F., and COURTIN, J. (1980). *Le Gisement Sao de Mdaga*. Paris: Société d'Ethnographie.

LEVTZION, N. (1986). Rural and urban Islam in West Africa: an introductory essay. *Asian and African Studies* 20: 7–26.

—— and POUWELS, R. (eds) (2000). *The History of Islam in Africa*. Oxford: James Currey.

MATHERS, C. (2003). Shrines and the domestication of landscape. *Journal of Anthropological Research* 59: 23–45.

MBITI, J. S. (1989). *African Religions and Philosophy*. Oxford: Heinemann.

MCHUGH, N. (1994). *Holymen of the Blue Nile*. Evanston, Ill.: Northwestern University Press.

MCINTOSH, R. J., and MCINTOSH, S. K. (1979). Terracotta statuettes from Mali. *African Arts* 12: 51–3.

—— —— (1988). From *siècles obscurs* to revolutionary centuries in the Middle Niger. *World Archaeology* 20: 141–65.

McINTOSH, S. K. (ed.) (1995). *Excavations at Jenne-jeno, Hambarketolo, and Kaniana (Inland Niger Delta, Mali), the 1981 Season*. Los Angeles: University of California Press.

METCALF, P., and HUNTINGTON, R. (1991). *Celebrations of Death: The Anthropology of Mortuary Ritual*. Cambridge: Cambridge University Press.

MORRIS, B. (2006). *Religion and Anthropology. A Critical Introduction*. Cambridge: Cambridge University Press.

MUNRO-HAY, S. (1991). *Aksum: An African Civilisation of Late Antiquity*. Edinburgh: Edinburgh University Press.

PHILLIPSON, D. W. (2009). *Ancient Churches of Ethiopia*. London: Yale University Press.

POSNANSKY, M. (1987). Prelude to Akan civilisation. In E. Schildkrout (ed.), *The Golden Stool*. New York: American Museum of Natural History, 14–22.

REID, A., and ASHLEY, C. (2008). A context for the Luzira Head. *Antiquity* 82: 99–112.

—— and MacLEAN, R. (1995). Symbolism and the social contexts of iron production in Karagwe. *World Archaeology* 27: 144–61.

ROBERTSHAW, P. (1997). Munsa earthworks: a preliminary report on recent excavations. *Azania* 32: 1–20.

RUPP, N., AMEJE, J., and BREUNIG, P. (2005). New studies on the Nok Culture of central Nigeria. *Journal of African Archaeology* 3: 283–90.

SCHMIDT, P. (1997). *Iron Technology in East Africa*. Oxford: James Currey.

—— and MCINTOSH, R. J. (eds) (1996). *Plundering Africa's Past*. Oxford: James Currey.

SHAW, R. (1990). The invention of 'African traditional religion'. *Religion* 20: 339–53.

SHERIDAN, M. J., and NYAMWERU, C. (eds) (2008). *African Sacred Groves: Ecological Dynamics and Social Change*. Oxford: James Currey.

STAHL, A. B. (2008). Dogs, pythons, pots and beads: the dynamics of shrines and sacrificial practices in Banda, Ghana, AD 1400–1900. In B. Mills and W. Walker (eds), *Memory Work: The Materiality of Depositional Practice*. Sante Fe, NM: SAR Press, 159–86.

VANSINA, J. (1966). *Kingdoms of the Savanna*. Madison: University of Wisconsin Press.

WELSBY, D. A. (1998). *Soba II: Renewed Excavations within the Metropolis of the Kingdom of Alwa in Central Sudan*. Nairobi: British Institute in Eastern Africa.

ZANGATO, E. (1999). *Sociétés Préhistoriques et Mégalithes dans le Nord-Ouest de la République Centrafricaine*. Oxford: British Archaeological Reports.

CHAPTER 13

MATERIAL CULTURE, SPACE, AND IDENTITY

STEPHANIE WYNNE-JONES

INTRODUCTION

THE African material record offers both challenge and opportunity. On the one hand, researchers grapple with patchily known typologies over large geographical distances, but on the other they consider societies among whom material culture has an important and fascinating role that often challenges and refines archaeological assumptions. African material culture has a contemporary vibrancy that shapes the ways it has been conceived for past populations, and object studies on the continent explore a wide range of artefacts that are only partially recoverable in the archaeological record. Most archaeological effort has been directed towards either lithics or ceramics; in particular, pots have been the central focus of studies of material identities with the links between style and identity explored both archaeologically and in the ethnographic literature on production and technology (Gosselain and Livingstone Smith, Ch. 9 above). Still, anthropological and art historical studies have developed an emphasis on social meanings or 'object efficacies' (Hardin and Arnoldi 1996: 1) which accords with a emphasis on 'social' rather than 'aesthetic' approaches to materiality in archaeology (Sofaer 2007: 3). In fact, it is African material ethnographies that informed this turn towards object meanings in the discipline as a whole (Hodder 1982, 1990; Wiessner 1983; Moore 1986). In addition, studies of contemporary African objects encompass a long-standing interest in culture history, which remains the backbone of archaeological interpretation in some regions (Lagercrantz 1950; Dias and Dias 1964; Sundström 1965). Thus the interplay between the ethnographic and archaeological records is a key feature of the ways that material culture, space, and identity have been explored, creating one of the most distinctive aspects of African archaeological reconstructions.

This chapter cannot do justice to the richness of archaeological work on these topics. Instead, it will explore two themes among the many ways that material culture, space and identity have been construed in the African past. First, studies that have taken the 'social' approach to materialities are discussed, in which object analysis has been linked overwhelm-

FIG. 13.1 Map of Africa showing the sites and regions discussed in Chapter 13.

ingly to individual, household, and community aspects of identity, and to the construction of social space in daily practice. Then, this chapter will consider the large-scale archaeological entities or cultures that have most often been understood through the lens of ethnicity. We consider a series of decidedly Africanist explorations of the ways that ethnicity and materiality interrelate (Fig. 13.1). Although these seem to be opposite ends of a spectrum in the conceptualization of identities, it is argued that there are similarities in the ways that both draw on the interplay between ethnographic and archaeological interpretations.

SOCIAL OBJECTS

One of the more influential studies of objects and spaces in African archaeology has explored the social life of the Swahili house (Fig. 13.2), and the ways that meaning was negotiated through practice (Donley 1982; Donley-Reid 1987, 1990a, 1990b). Ethnographic research in Lamu town on the northern Kenya coast examined the ways that both objects and people were given meaning through the activities in which they were implicated. These understandings were combined into a conceptual map of the Swahili stonehouse that positioned and defined both things and people. The binding concept was the notion of practice, drawing on theoretical frameworks derived from Giddens (1984) and Bourdieu (1977); there are striking similarities with the latter's exploration of the Kabyle house (Bourdieu 1979: 133–53), also a key ethnographic case study from the African context. The major strength of Donley-Reid's work, however, was her illustration of the longevity of some of these spatial practices through the excavation of the back rooms of three 18th- and 19th-century houses. These excavations recovered the remains predicted by the ethnographies, including a ditch used for washing away polluted water, a goat sacrifice, and several infant burials (Donley-Reid 1987). These seem to demonstrate a substantial time-depth to the scale of ascending privacy that Donley-Reid postulates for stonehouses, and for the concern with purity that saw much of women's activity, and other sources of possible pollution, confined to the back rooms. In reference to objects, Donley-Reid mainly focused on imported ceramics and beads, which were seen to have protective powers and were therefore linked to these sensitive parts of the house (cf. Fleisher and La Violette 2007). Both these objects and the inhabitants of the house were given meaning through the repeated uses of the space, and particularly the rituals that mediated Swahili self-identification. This is epitomized in the ritual of *kutolewande*, during which a newborn baby is taken around the house, introduced to the spaces, the associated objects, and the people who occupy and use those areas, simultaneously reinscribing those associations. The richness of her data allowed Donley-Reid (1982, 1990b) to explore the deeper meaning of such practices, linking them to cosmological principles of order, purity, and Islam.

The influence of Donley-Reid's work has been particularly great because of its elegant application of universalizing practice approaches, tying objects into networks of activity that define the social world. In an African context, these studies are also important as an application of the notion of gender, and the ways that gendered identities can be made manifest in the material record. Despite the importance of gender in approaching identity, archaeological treatments of female and male roles are surprisingly few in Africanist research (but see Wadley 1997; Kent 1998a). Kent (1998b: 15–19) suggests several reasons for this, not least the difficulties of identifying women archaeologically, avoiding the teleology of equating past and present practices. Lane (1998) also suggests that this lack may be due to an overemphasis on other axes of identity, particularly ethnic groupings. The practice approach brings gender roles to the forefront, as it concentrates at the level of daily life and the structure of life within a settlement. A nuanced approach to these aspects will highlight a social world in which individuals had complex lives, sometimes structured according to gendered principles and sometimes according to cross-cutting principles of ethnic, linguistic, or age affiliations.

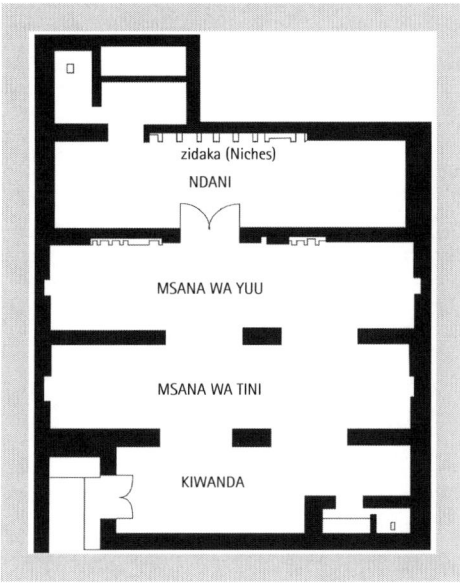

FIG. 13.2 Idealized plan of the ground floor of a Swahili stonehouse (redrawn after Donley-Reid 1990b: 121).

Casey (1998) explores this complexity in a neat case study based on lithic assemblages from Kintampo sites in Ghana. Drawing on evidence from sites on the Gambaga Escarpment of northern Ghana (Casey 2000), she argues that a move towards 'basic' lithic tools from 3,500 BP links to a developing agricultural complex. In a sedentary context, the more formal tools associated with hunting and thought to be linked to male status display became, she argues, less important. Both men and women were increasingly integrated into more domestic economic activities, represented by the simpler toolkit, as change in the sphere of operations would have created new social roles and opportunities for both men and women. Thus, instead of looking for distinct genders in the archaeological record, Casey instead 'thinks gender into the past' (Sørenson 1996) by considering gender roles as part of the changing society she identifies through lithic remains. She envisions a Kintampo society in which both genders were involved in ongoing production and subsistence processes, thereby creating a more diverse imagined population.

Nevertheless, diversity among past populations tends to be recognized between broad groups or social distinctions. Individuals are only rarely sought, despite the implication of individual agency in these meaning-oriented reconstructions. One route through which more individual forms of identity might be thought through is in the archaeology of death and burial. At Deir el Medina in New Kingdom Egypt, Meskell (1999) has used the archaeology of the forty houses and their substantial associated cemetery to explore individual identities in the archaeology of the site. Her approach builds explicitly on third-wave feminist thought and hence adopts a performative approach to gender, class, and age; impressive quantities of information on the occupants of the tombs in the town allows a picture of New Kingdom life to be built up that resists the general and demonstrates how objects were part of the ways individuals operated within the world. For example, it was often possible to access aspects of individuals' professions through the incorporation of sculptor's and builder's tools into several male graves, and bronze sewing implements into female. Some graves also complicated this gender dichotomy, with one man (Grave 1389) having chosen to incorporate both a needle and a papyrus suggestive of work as a scribe (Meskell 1999: 182). Likewise, items of personal adornment reflected individual tastes and class differences, and items relating to magical practice—particularly figurines—give an insight into the beliefs and fears of the individuals or their families. This study begins to show how broad-scale patterning and archaeological understandings about a society are built up through a multiplicity of individual choices, tastes, activities, and beliefs. Beyond the Nile Valley, the excavation of substantial graveyards and the level of preservation found at Deir el Medina are both rare, but the case study stands as a key example of the ways that these webs of meaning are constituted through individual object interactions and habituations.

OBJECT WORLDS

Moving away from identity negotiations, researchers have also sought the meanings of objects themselves through the activities in which they were caught up. Ritualized contexts have been particularly fertile ground for such explorations, positioning things within new realms of meaning. Often, the objects bound up into offerings and ritual practices are relatively mundane, distinguished only by their context, or by precise associations with individual histories

FIG. 13.3 Esu figure, Lakaaye Chambers, 2011, Nigeria (photograph courtesy of Akin Ogundiran).

(Insoll 2004, 2008: 386). This makes recognizing them more difficult, but potentially extremely rewarding, as it can give clearer insights into how everyday objects can become socially significant. Stahl (2008), for example, identifies ritual deposits in the archaeology of Banda, Ghana, through the association of ordinary local ceramics and esoteric deposits, particularly recurring associations with buried ceramics and the bones of dogs and of pythons. Although neither of these animals is linked with contemporary ritual, such unexpected associations for everyday items cast them in a specialized role, with implications for past practice and performance. Similar buried offerings among 17th-/18th-century Hueda settlement deposits in Bénin led Norman (2009) to consider changing practices linked to the Vodun religion, these offerings forming a bridging mechanism between past and present.

In both of these studies, objects are entwined in networks of meaning that have greater longevity than the individual parts; they tie people, through practice, to spaces and social worlds. These insights resonate with Ray's (1987) use of the concept of 'material metaphors' in his analysis of the symbolic meanings of the Igbo-Ukwu corpus of metal, ceramic, ivory, and other objects recovered from a sequence of 8th–11th century AD sites near Akwa, southeastern Nigeria. Critical to his arguments is the notion of 'presencing', which he defined as 'the remote introduction [by means of material culture] of individuals or categories of person into contexts and interactions they are not directly involved in' (Ray 1987: 68).

Specialized uses of objects can also relate to more worldly concerns. Several studies have emphasized the implication of objects into the enactment and constitution of power. Aspects such as feasting (Ashley 2010; Fleisher 2010) and display (Kus and Raharijaona 2000) can give meaning to both objects and people, as the specialized uses of particular items create a set of relationships that enable and define social interaction. A particularly elegant exploration of this is Ogundiran's (2002) study of beads and cowries in precolonial Yorubaland. Ritual practices here were both maintained and transformed through time as new trade goods became available, and were incorporated into existing webs of meaning. As cowries became more plentiful from the 17th century onwards, they appear increasingly in the archaeology, replacing beads in ritual and domestic contexts. Rather than simply reflecting changing fashions, or incorporation into existing value systems, Ogundiran argues that this material change fundamentally altered existing object logics. Cowries were an embodiment of wealth, their ownership linked to developing notions of individual accumulation. The challenge offered by shrines decorated with cowries in individual homes (Fig. 13.3) to the bead-laden shrines of royal courts was therefore also a challenge to the established modes of ritual power that they referenced. The materials thus had a direct effect on the meaning of ritual practices into which they were incorporated and—ultimately—on the identities of the gods and people bound up in them. Ogundiran elaborates the paradox of how it was the role that beads had in the local ritual economy that enabled cowries to become important and later to supplant them; rather than being important ritual objects simply due to their rarity, they fitted into an established mode of object-person relations.

PRACTICE AND PRACTICALITIES OF SCALE

Recognizing the active engagement between people and objects profoundly affects how archaeological 'cultures' are conceived as the result of human action. In Africa, however, while some practice-based approaches have been developed, culture-historical mapping has been hard to supersede. Partly, this reflects a paucity of data that can lead to comparisons across great distances, as archaeologists attempt to understand their site's position within large-scale chronologies and cultural sequences. Yet the continued importance of typology and culture-history is also a function of the existence of large-scale patterns that do need to be explained. Engaging with identity writ large in material culture can also be seen in the longevity of large-scale models, such as that associating the start of the Early Iron Age with the movement of Bantu-speaking farmers (Ashley; de Maret, Ch. 43 below) or the Swahili origins debate (Chami 1994, 1998, 2007; Horton 1996; Fleisher and Wynne-Jones 2011; La Violette, Ch. 62 below). Large-scale social phenomena of this kind clearly exist at a different scale from those explored through household archaeologies or models of daily practice.

It is now rare for studies to equate archaeological cultures directly with ethnic groups, and yet ethnicity still predominates as an explanatory device for broad similarities in materials such as ceramics. Here, too, the influence of ethnography is seen, as ethnicity can be a primary factor in the ways that people define themselves today. Yet ethnographic studies and archaeologies of the recent past have also argued against a simplistic equation between material and ethnic identities (Croucher and Wynne-Jones 2006). The notion of a somewhat separate stylistic identity has emerged, that may not necessarily correspond to other linguistic, ethnic, or social models. Instead, the 'human environment of actions and materials within which we live our lives' (MacEachern 1994: 206) may itself be a structuring factor akin to aspects such as ethnicity or linguistics. This has been recognized in the 'style systems' of the southern African Iron Age, and most comprehensively discussed in the concept of a symbolic reservoir.

Southern Africa's Iron Age (Huffman 2007; Mitchell, Pikirayi, Schoeman, Chs 33, 63, 64 below) is traditionally understood through a series of ceramic traditions and migrations, which have been linked with particular settlement types and technologies in an attempt to create more nuanced understandings of the links between society and style (Huffman 1989a). The 'style system' concept (Huffman 1986) draws on ethnographic analogy alongside archaeological data to argue for 'repetitive and integrated codes of cultural symbols learned and transmitted within groups of people' (Huffman 1989b: 156) that reflect interaction and identity negotiation. As similar designs are often repeated across different media, shared sets of design principles may inform all aspects of life, from house design to ceramics and bodily adornment.

These systems are correlated by Huffman (1989b: 157–8) with language clusters, but the fact that this might be the case among contemporary populations is no guarantee that similar material practices operated in the past (Lane 1994/5, 1998). Yet, even laying aside the correlation with language or ethnicity, the idea of a common set of design principles, and the sense that these principles would have structured all material media, is interesting for archaeology, representing the quintessential archaeological 'culture'. Pikirayi (1999, 2007) takes this up when advocating 'interaction studies' to explore material similarities among Later Iron Age assemblages while appreciating the nebulous nature of ethnic identities and the fact that different types of interaction network can cross-cut linguistic and ethnic groupings. Observing the repetition of shared motifs across the entire material repertoire, he proposes the existence of stylistic groupings as part of zones of shared aesthetic principles. Regarding style as communicative, citing Wiessner (1983) and arguing for aspects of verbal, non-verbal, and symbolic communication (as implied by Huffman), Pikirayi further suggests that stylistic motifs would have been even more widely distributed, probably as part of bodily decorations, basketry, and other less permanent forms of material culture. Motifs like the chevron would thus have formed commonly acknowledged visual leitmotifs signalling inclusion within a wider shared identity, and explicitly linked to bodily decoration and hence to embodied identities (Pikirayi 2007: 290). Collett (1993) and Ndoro (1991) also recognize this in the decoration of the region's iron-smelting furnaces, although their technological style is seen as a separate realm of identification, again opening the way for multiple material identities to have operated simultaneously.

These concepts recall the notion of a symbolic reservoir, developed through archaeological and ethnoarchaeological fieldwork in West Africa. First outlined for the heterogeneous society of Jenné-Jeno, Mali (McIntosh 1989), the concept of 'symbolic reservoirs' is now most commonly associated with Cameroon's Mandara Mountains (Sterner 1992; MacEachern 1994). Symbolic reservoirs 'contain' or represent a series of aesthetic and technological understandings about style, which are differentially drawn upon by interacting groups. Thus, material style does not correspond to a particular ethnic or linguistic identity but represents a common and long-standing shared system of symbols and cosmology, utilized during the process of creating objects and artworks, a pool from which people draw. The aesthetic understandings represented by the reservoir colour every aspect of life. Unlike the southern

African example, its proponents *have* attempted to explain the decoration of pottery in particular and of material culture in general, advocating an approach that sees the decoration of objects as an extension of bodily decoration, with explicit equivalences drawn between certain objects and persons (David et al. 1988). Ceramic decoration is seen as having an active role in signalling identity, transmitting messages about gender, age, and social identities through metaphorical association with the body.

Both of these approaches use culture-historical understandings in new ways. Rather than assuming equivalence between material culture patterning and identities as they are constructed socially, linguistically, or racially, they think about archaeological cultures as specific entities in their own right. Though this seemingly represents a challenge to the whole basis of archaeological understandings, in fact it is an enabling move, allowing appreciation of large-scale patterns across time and space, as well as avoiding essentialization by correlating ethnic or social identities with material patterns. The result is a more dynamic model than seen in previous attitudes to material culture. MacEachern (2002: 214), for example, refers to the symbolic reservoir as part of an ongoing process of reciprocal production, rather than the external conceptual referent that might be suggested by the metaphor.

MATERIAL CULTURE, SPACE, AND IDENTITY IN AFRICAN ARCHAEOLOGY

There are links, then, between the developing archaeologies of large-scale style systems and more agent-focused approaches to object worlds. Both increasingly emphasize the implication of objects into networks of use, performance, and practice as a means to understand both the patterning of the archaeological record and the meanings that objects may have had in past communities. Both are also inspired by contemporary observations of material ethnographies that continually provide inspiration for archaeologists to consider the complex and varied relationships that people have with their material world. It is these ethnographies that inspired the dialectical studies of materiality that suggest that only through practice are the identities of *both* objects and people produced (Hodder 1990: 45). In an African context, they have also inspired new approaches to the old problem of explaining the archaeological culture, with the style system and the symbolic reservoir emerging as characteristically Africanist approaches to the archaeological record. The notion of a material identity, distinct from other forms of identity, opens the way for links to be drawn with food systems and consumption (Haaland 2007) or with understandings of changing tastes (Stahl 2002), rather than simply reflecting some kind of primordial identity.

Africanist archaeology therefore retains its position as an innovator in the field of material culture studies through a combination of the particular factors that make the continent's archaeology unique. The large-scale and patchy coverage of research led researchers to a continuing engagement with culture histories as well as the small-scale agent-focused archaeologies that have derived from African examples but come to define archaeology elsewhere. The rich ethnoarchaeological tradition on the continent (Lyons, Ch. 7 above) instead continues to provide the means for archaeologists to think through the place of material culture in past societies, whether through direct analogy (Wylie 1985) or through indirect insight into the dialectical nature of material worlds and individual identities. Whether at the level of the household or across large regions, the ways that material practices were implicated in social worlds are subject to enquiry, shaped by the unique strengths and limitations of the African record.

REFERENCES

ASHLEY, C. (2010). Towards a socialised archaeology of ceramics in Great Lakes Africa. *African Archaeological Review* 27: 135–63.

BOURDIEU, P. (1977). *Outline of a Theory of Practice*. Cambridge: Cambridge University Press.

—— (1979). *Essays by Pierre Bourdieu*. Cambridge: Cambridge University Press.

CASEY, J. (1998). Just a formality: the presence of fancy projectiles in a basic tool assemblage. In Kent (1998a: 77–95).

—— (2000). *The Kintampo Complex: The Late Holocene on the Gambaga Escarpment, Northern Ghana*. Oxford: Archaeopress.

CHAMI, F. A. (1994). *The Tanzanian Coast in the Early First Millennium AD: An Archaeology of the Iron-Working, Farming Communities*. Uppsala: Societas Archaeologica Upsaliensis.

—— (1998). A review of Swahili archaeology. *African Archaeological Review* 15: 199–218.

—— (2007). Diffusion in the studies of the African past: reflections from new archaeological findings. *African Archaeological Review* 24: 1–14.

COLLETT, D. (1993). Metaphors and representations associated with precolonial iron-smelting in eastern and southern Africa. In T. Shaw, P. Sinclair, B. Andah, and A. Okpoko (eds), *The Archaeology of Africa: Food, Metals and Towns*. London: Routledge, 499–511.

CROUCHER, S., and WYNNE-JONES, S. (2006). People not pots: locally-produced ceramics and identity on the nineteenth-century East African coast. *International Journal of African Historical Studies* 39: 107–24.

DAVID, N., STERNER, J., and GAVUA, K. (1988). Why pots are decorated. *Current Anthropology* 29: 365–89.

DIAS, A. J., and DIAS, M. (1964). *Os Macondes de Mocambique*, vol. 2: *Cultura Material*. Lisbon: Junta de Investigacoes do Ultramar.

DIETLER, M., and HERBICH, I. (1989). Tich Matek: the technology of Luo pottery production and the definition of ceramic style. *World Archaeology* 21: 148–64.

DONLEY, L. (1982). House power: Swahili space and symbolic markers. In I. Hodder (ed.), *Symbolic and Structural Archaeology*. Cambridge: Cambridge University Press, 63–73.

—— (1987). Life in the Swahili town house reveals the symbolic meaning of spaces and artefact assemblages. *African Archaeological Review* 5: 181–92.

DONLEY-REID, L. (1990a). The power of Swahili porcelain, beads and pottery. *Archaeological Papers of the American Anthropological Association* 2: 47–59.

—— (1990b). A structuring structure: the Swahili house. In S. Kent (ed.), *Domestic Architecture and the Use of Space: An Interdisciplinary Cross-Cultural Study*. Cambridge: Cambridge University Press, 114–26.

FLEISHER, J. B. (2010). Rituals of consumption and the politics of feasting on the eastern African coast, AD 700–1500. *Journal of World Prehistory* 23: 195–217.

—— and LA VIOLETTE, A. (2007). The changing power of Swahili houses, fourteenth to nineteenth centuries A.D. In R. Beck (ed.), *The Durable House*. Carbondale: Southern Illinois University Press, 175–97.

FLEISHER, J. B. and WYNNE-JONES, S. (2011). Ceramics and the Early Swahili: deconstructing the Early Tana Tradition. *African Archaeological Review* 28: 245–78.

GIDDENS, A. (1984). *Constitution of Society: Outline of a Theory of Structuration*. Cambridge: Polity Press.

HAALAND, R. (2007). Porridge and pot, bread and oven: food ways and symbolism in Africa and the Near East from the Neolithic to the present. *Cambridge Archaeological Journal* 17: 167–83.

HARDIN, K. L., and ARNOLDI, M. J. (1996) Introduction. Efficacy and objects. In M. J. Arnoldi, C. M. Geary, and K. L. Hardin (eds), *African Material Culture*. Washington, DC: Smithsonian Institution Press, 1–28.

HODDER, I. (1982). *Symbols in Action*. Cambridge: Cambridge University Press.

—— (1990). Style as historical quality. In M. Conkey and C. Hastorf (eds), *Uses of Style in Archaeology*. Cambridge: Cambridge University Press, 44–51.

HORTON, M. C. (1996). *Shanga: The Archaeology of a Muslim Trading Community on the Coast of East Africa*. Nairobi: British Institute in Eastern Africa.

HUFFMAN, T. N. (1986). Iron Age settlement patterns and the origins of class distinction in southern Africa. *Advances in World Archaeology* 5: 291–338.

—— (1989a). *Iron Age Migrations: The Ceramic Sequence in Southern Zambia*. Johannesburg: Witwatersrand University Press.

—— (1989b). Ceramics, settlements and Late Iron Age migrations. *African Archaeological Review* 7: 155–82.

—— (2007). *Handbook to the Iron Age*. Pietermaritzburg: University of KwaZulu-Natal Press.

INSOLL, T. (2004). *Archaeology, Ritual, Religion*. London: Routledge.

—— (2008). Negotiating the archaeology of destiny: an exploration of interpretive possibilities through Tallensi shrines. *Journal of Social Archaeology* 8: 380–403.

KENT, S. (ed.) (1998a). *Gender in African Prehistory*. Walnut Creek, Calif.: AltaMira Press.

—— (1998b). Gender and Prehistory in Africa. In Kent (1998a: 9–21).

KUS, S., and RAHARIJAONA, V. (2000) House to palace, village to state: scaling up architecture and ideology. *American Anthropologist* 102(1): 98–113.

LAGERCRANTZ, S. (1950). *Contribution to the Ethnography of Africa*. Lund: Hékan Ohlssons Boktryckeri.

LANE, P. J. (1994/5). The use and abuse of ethnography in the study of the southern African Iron Age. *Azania* 29/30: 51–64.

—— (1998). Engendered spaces and bodily practices in the Iron Age of Southern Africa. In Kent (1998a: 180–203).

—— (2005). Barbarous tribes and unrewarding gyrations? The changing role of ethnographic imagination in African archaeology. In A. B. Stahl (ed.), *African Archaeology: A Critical Introduction*. Oxford: Blackwell, 24–54.

MACEACHERN, S. (1994). 'Symbolic reservoirs' and inter-group relations: West African examples. *African Archaeological Review* 12: 205–24.

—— (2002). Beyond the belly of the house: space and power around the Mandara Mountains. *Journal of Social Archaeology* 2: 197–219.

MCINTOSH, R. (1989). Middle Niger terracottas before the Symplegades gateway. *African Arts* 22: 74–83, 103–4.

MESKELL, L. (1999). *Archaeologies of Social Life: Age, Sex, Class et cetera in Ancient Egypt*. Oxford: Wiley-Blackwell.

MOORE, H. (1986). *Space, Text, and Gender: An Anthropological Study of the Marakwet of Kenya.* Cambridge: Cambridge University Press.

NDORO, W. (1991). Why decorate her? *Zimbabwea* 3: 60–65.

NORMAN, N. L. (2009). Powerful pots, humbling holes, and regional ritual processes: towards an archaeology of Huedan Vodun, *ca.* 1650–1727. *African Archaeological Review* 26: 187–216.

OGUNDIRAN, A. (2002). Of small things remembered: beads, cowries, and cultural translations of the Atlantic experience in Yorubaland. *International Journal of African Historical Studies* 35: 427–57.

PIKIRAYI, I. (1999). Taking southern African ceramic studies into the twenty-first century: a Zimbabwean perspective. *African Archaeological Review* 16: 185–9.

—— (2007). Ceramics and group identities: towards a social archaeology in southern African Iron Age ceramic studies. *Journal of Social Archaeology* 7: 286–301.

RAY, K. W. (1987). Material metaphor, social interaction and historical reconstructions: exploring patterns of association and symbolism in the Igbo-Ukwu corpus. In I. Hodder (ed.), *The Archaeology of Contextual Meanings.* Cambridge: Cambridge University Press, 66–78.

SOFAER, J. (2007). Introduction: materiality and identity. In J. Sofaer (ed.), *Material Identities.* Oxford: Blackwell, 1–9.

SØRENSEN, M.-L. S. (1996). Identifying or including: approaches to the engendering of archaeology. *Kvinner Arkaeologi Norge* 21: 51–60.

STAHL, A. B. (1994). Change and continuity in the Banda area, Ghana: the direct historical approach. *Journal of Field Archaeology* 21: 181–203.

—— (2002). Colonial entanglements and the practices of taste: an alternative to logocentric approaches. *American Anthropologist* 104: 827–45.

—— (2008). Dogs, pythons, pots and beads: the dynamics of shrines and sacrificial practices in Banda, Ghana, ad 1400–1900. In B. Mills and W. Walker (eds), *Memory Work: The Materiality of Depositional Practice.* Sante Fe, NM: School of Advanced Research Press, 159–86.

STERNER, J. (1992). Sacred pots and 'symbolic reservoirs' in the Mandara Highlands of Northern Cameroon. In J. Sterner and N. David (eds), *An African Commitment: Papers in Honour of Peter Lewis Shinnie.* Calgary: University of Calgary Press, 171–9.

SUNDSTRÖM, L. (1965). *The Exchange Economy of Pre-colonial Tropical Africa.* New York: St. Martin's Press.

WADLEY, L. (ed.) (1997). *Our Gendered Past: Archaeological Studies of Gender in Southern Africa.* Johannesburg: Witwatersrand University Press.

WIESSNER, P. (1983). Style and social information in Kalahari San projectile points. *American Antiquity* 48: 253–76.

WYLIE, A. (1985). The reaction against analogy. *Advances in Archaeological Method and Theory* 8: 63–111.

CHAPTER 14

LANDSCAPE ARCHAEOLOGY

JEFFREY FLEISHER

INTRODUCTION

IN recent years, landscape archaeology has become a recognized subfield in global archaeology, spawning a robust literature on its theoretical and methodological aspects (for reviews see Anschuetz et al. 2001; David and Thomas 2008). Perhaps the most surprising aspect of this new emphasis is its heterogeneity, with widely diverging theoretical concerns claiming the moniker 'landscape archaeology'; some argue that the ambiguity of terminology is the subfield's strength (Gosden and Head 1994), while others have sought clearer definitions (Anschuetz et al. 2001). Contrast, for example, Rossignol and Wandsnider (1992), who argue for an intensified off-site or non-site approach, with Thomas (2001: 173), who describes landscapes as 'networks of places...gradually revealed through people's habitual activities and interactions'. This distinction, between envisioning landscapes as the canvas on which human action unfolds and as the product of human action, represents the ends of a theoretical continuum between which most research resides.

Research on landscape archaeology in Africa has often stood on the sidelines of these larger debates, and only rarely has the term itself even been invoked, although that is changing (Schmidt 1994; Norman and Kelly 2004; McIntosh 2005; Monroe and Ogundiran 2012). On a continent with so much landscape, why have space and spatial practices not been the focus of research? In some ways, this may be a terminological matter, as many African archaeologists *have* taken up the concerns of what has been defined as 'landscape archaeology' in the West, but without engaging specifically with that theory.

Landscape archaeology is primarily the inclusion of a broader spatial scale into archaeological interpretations to include regions, territories, areas of land use that surround sites and settlements, and more ephemeral features not normally included when discussing 'sites' (roads, paths, fields, shrines, graves). For African archaeology, however, work focused on landscape concerns has always meant more than just a wider spatial scale. A broader approach to space has changed archaeological interpretations in crucial ways:

- First, landscape approaches have helped to put past actors in 'action', both through research that explores how they used and moved through extensive landscapes and through investigating how past people (and ideas) served to transform the environment, remaking it into a 'landscape.'

- Landscape archaeology has also allowed for important insights into the way spatial practices mattered, both through how people structured the world in a practical sense, through foraging ranges and farming, but also for those individuals seeking and retaining power and authority.

- Finally, the expansion of archaeology to a landscape perspective has had a dramatic effect on how we view the African past and its importance for the present. Through documenting and describing African forms of spatial complexity, landscape archaeology in Africa can serve as an important generator of models and corollaries in global archaeological discussions. These novel forms of spatial complexity challenge colonial assumptions about a stagnant and primitive African past. Landscape approaches can also have practical applications, offering deep-time histories that can be used in formulating environmental and social policies, thus linking contemporary issues to long-term patterns of continuity and change.

To review these implications of landscape archaeology in Africa, this chapter is organized around three topics: (1) research on settlement or territorial archaeology; (2) historical ecology and dialectical approaches to landscape; and (3) landscapes of power and perception, including symbolic and ritual understandings of landscapes.

LANDSCAPE AS TERRITORY: MOVING 'OFF-SITE' AND INTO THE 'REGION'

A common lament is that so much of Africa remains profoundly unstudied archaeologically (Bower 1986). Related to this is the way that archaeological research had tended to focus on the foremost sites in a region: those with the most obtrusive remains, significant oral histories, or richest finds. In the 1970s and 1980s, research sought to address these issues by emphasizing the larger territory within which archaeological remains were found. For early hominin or hunter-gatherer studies, this was achieved through an off-site approach (Foley 1981), and for Iron Age studies via an expanding interest in territorial (Sinclair 1987) and regional approaches (McIntosh and McIntosh 1980). As elsewhere, all these approaches relied substantially on archaeological survey (Bower 1986). Many studies have employed the rigorous and systematic survey approaches of processual archaeology to great effect (e.g. McIntosh and McIntosh 1980; Sinclair 1987; Fawcett and LaViolette 1990; Curtis and Schmidt 2008; Fleisher 2010). However, most archaeological survey carried out in Africa remains unsystematic, and has focused more on the discovery of sites than on more comprehensive understandings of the relationship between sites in a region. While reconnaissance is a crucial first step in any project, archaeological surveys need to be systematic for their results to be considered representative of regional and landscape patterns.

Contrasting approaches are also adopted depending on the time period and social contexts under investigation. For instance, archaeological surveys increasingly focus on the rural components of complex societies (Usman 2000; Kusimba and Kusimba 2005; Wynne-Jones 2007; Swanepoel 2008; Norman 2009; Fleisher 2010). While earlier territorial studies included rural settlements as a way of delineating the functions of the settlement system, these recent studies examine rural areas and peripheries to understand how urbanism was experienced from them. For example, Wynne-Jones (2007) describes the complex ways through which rural settlers in the region surrounding the coastal town of Kilwa Kisiwani, southern Tanzania, interacted with an expanding urban landscape. At times they were incorporated into urban expansion, but at others they struggled to maintain political economic and religious/ritual autonomy. This has been supplemented by surveys of Kilwa's 'seascape', resulting in discovery of previously unsuspected features in the intertidal zone and greater awareness of the influence of maritime concerns and the sea on the positioning of various features, including mosques, in the landscape (Pollard 2008).

Conversely, in palaeoanthropological research, territorial studies have focused more on off-site materials than on sites and settlement patterns—using those 'archaeological features and material outside the context of the site to deduce hypotheses about past behaviour' (Foley 1981: 29). This is often classified under the term 'land use' (Potts 1994), but has increasingly taken up the terminology of 'landscape'. Data from the Lake Turkana region have been central to these debates, allowing Isaac (1989) to formulate his home-base and subsequent central-place foraging models, which added a dynamic dimension to hominin studies through which foraging and ranging behaviour could be reconstructed. Urging researchers to think about hominins 'in action', he argued that palaeoanthropological data should be analysed as distributions across a landscape, and that the 'value of stone tools lies not so much in the details of morphology as in the fact that these objects are crucial markers of the places where early man was active' (Isaac 1989: 77). These land-use patterns have invariably dealt with how early hominins exploited the natural resources of a region. While Isaac focused on the way foraging was carried out in relationship to a central place, others working with Koobi Fora data have adopted Binford's (1984) 'routed' foraging model, where hominins moved through the landscape, feeding along the way (e.g. Bunn 1994). More recently, Cachel and Harris (2006) have suggested that Early Pleistocene artefact distributions may also be indicative of hominid movement related to resource acquisition, and Sinclair et al. (2003) have investigated the environmental aesthetics in the South African Makapansgat landscape to begin exploring the cognitive dimensions of hominin landscape use. Through the evaluation of different 'scenes'—particular perspectives of the landscape—they aim to understand how perception structured individual choices in moving around the landscape. These studies are enriching our understanding of land use for these early periods of the African past, making landscape—as land use and resource acquisition—crucial frameworks of study.

Similar types of studies can be found in archaeological research on hunter-gatherers and efforts by archaeologists to determine seasonal mobility in Stone Age contexts. Here, 'landscape' represents the ecological context through which hunter-gatherers lived and traversed (e.g. Parkington 1999) and the way they sought to exploit variable ecological niches. Like palaeoanthropological studies, this work uses landscape as a setting for the movement of people, cast largely in functional terms as necessary to survival. Early hypotheses about hunter-gatherer movements were based on ethnographic case studies of contemporary groups, but archaeological techniques developed to determine whether groups moved seasonally (or not) have been central to debates in southern African hunter-gatherer archaeology

(Mitchell 2005). Parkington's (2001) work in South Africa, in particular, employs a variety of faunal and botanical indicators to this end, although results remain at odds with those obtained from stable isotope analysis of human skeletal remains (Sealy and van der Merwe 1992).

All these studies provide means of animating distant people and moving the discussion away from the mapping of typologies and technologies toward understandings of how people moved across space, made decisions about the environments in which they lived, and exploited the environmental opportunities that they encountered; by putting people into 'action', such an approach makes past narratives more active as well.

LANDSCAPE AS DIALECTIC: HISTORICAL ECOLOGY

A more recent approach to landscape in archaeology is historical ecology (Balée 1998), a sub-field that understands landscapes as 'the material manifestation of the relationship between humans and the environment' (Crumley 1994: 6). Foregrounding human agency in the relationship between people and environment, historical ecologists seek to counter more adaptationist approaches in which humans are seen as simply responding and reacting to environmental changes. Historical ecology has been aided by using geoarchaeology (French 2002) to reconstruct ancient landscapes and land use (French et al. 2009), and to delineate spatial practices within archaeological sites themselves (Shahack-Gross et al. 2004). Historical ecology is particularly valuable for African archaeology in that it actively works to counter problematic images of the relationship between people and the environment (Lane 2010). These include simplistic images of 'natural natives' living fully balanced in 'pristine' environments (McIntosh 2005: 46; Erickson 2006); the idea that indigenous people unwittingly overexploit their landscape, creating environmental problems that they cannot solve themselves; and the notion that people passively respond to environmental change rather than actively engaging with it through cultural understandings (Schmidt 1994). Historical ecologists also hope that deep-time reconstructions of the human–environment dialectic will allow contemporary policymakers more ably and responsibly to confront contemporary problems and concerns (cf. Hardesty 2007; Stump 2010).

Schmidt's (1994) work west of Lake Victoria in Tanzania offers a rich, multi-faceted study of historical ecological landscape change that reconstructs not only the historical ecology of a tropical ecosystem but also the role of cultural perceptions in landscape management. The region's transformation from 'bountiful' forest in the Early Iron Age to a denuded landscape in the early colonial period is put down to human action, including increased agricultural settlement, farming practices (on fragile soils), and deforestation related to charcoal production for industrial iron smelting. People thereby 'remade the landscape' (Schmidt 1994: 111) with dire consequences, including severe erosion and ultimately an inability to continue to live and work in the area, with settlements shifting to the lakeshore. If this study had ended here, it would have been a significant contribution to understandings of prehistoric landscapes—one that helps counter the dual notions of Africans living within 'wild' and 'natural' settings (the myth of the pristine) and as functioning in harmonious balance with them (the myth of the noble savage). However, Schmidt extends his argument onward to the Late Iron

Age, showing how, after forests and swamps had regenerated, they were once again assaulted through renewed iron production, increased settlements and farming, and the introduction of cattle. During the Late Iron Age, however, a series of technological adaptations and ritual sanctions worked to manage scarce resources. These interpretations come from a perspective that understands that iron production was carried out through elaborate, sacred rituals that reaffirmed the very essence of the human experience: the reproduction of labour and the regeneration of life. The integration of this belief system with industrial activity established an abiding perception of the landscape as an abundant, sustaining, and responsive mother, in which ritual proscriptions and protection of particular species as shrines may have served to manage important resources at times when they were most fragile (Schmidt 1994).

Lane's (2009) work further south in Kondoa has similarly aimed at contextualizing the role of human agency in the history of erosion in the region, employing a combination of survey, excavation, and informant interviews, as well as rich geomorphological studies. Colonial and postcolonial officials blamed local farming and herding practices for the region's significant erosion, claiming that this reflected recent failures to manage a landscape that had once been sustained (and sustainable). Archaeological, geomorphological, and pedological research shows that these assumptions were overly simplistic, and that the causes of erosion, including climate change, iron smelting, and farming and herding activities, are multi-faceted and variable over time. Archaeological research of this kind that follows an historical ecological approach thus helps not only to dispel myths about the deficiencies of native ecologies and management practices but also to provide crucial long-term patterns of landscape change which can help policymakers understand the complex causes of environmental problems.

A historical ecological approach has also been used to explore the self-organizing urban landscape around Jenné-jeno in Mali's Inland Niger Delta (IND) (McIntosh and McIntosh 1980). In this case, McIntosh (2005: 52–3) draws out another key feature of historical ecologists—close attention to issues of spatial and temporal scale and the way that these matter to humans and their perceptions of, and actions upon, the world (Crumley and Marquardt 1990). For the IND, specialized subsistence niches linked by exchange and interdependence gave the landscape the ability to maintain an urban centre without the normal expectation of agricultural intensification (what McIntosh (1999: 74) terms 'diversification within specialisation'), matching in many ways Erickson's (2006: 241) notion of the 'domestication of landscape' that he defines as 'all nongenetic, intentional and unintentional activities and practices of humans that transform local and regional environments into productive and physically patterned cultural landscapes for humans and other species'. Useful for African archaeologists as they work to overturn entrenched notions of Africans living 'within' nature, subject to its whims, this alternative vision of urbanism has proved to be a major contribution to global studies of urban form, forcing a rethinking of the way urban regions function and are spatially organized (e.g. Ur et al. 2007).

Landscape archaeology, especially as framed within historical ecology, offers the possibility of making archaeological research relevant and practical. Archaeological reconstructions of long-term human action and its role in landscape transformation can aid development projects in the present by providing a firm historical foundation for environmental assessments. Additionally, in seeing humans as crucial agents in the construction and alteration of the environments and landscapes, historical ecologists are well suited to uncovering ancient human behaviours that may be useful in tackling problems of today. As both Lane and Schmidt have demonstrated, populations that lived within degraded environments developed strategies for dealing with them—adaptations that allowed them to change environmental conditions and complex mechanisms to manage scarce resources. Similarly, McIntosh's (2005) description of the way the Mande conceptualize and manage climate change in a relatively unpredictable environment provides a crucial deep-time emic perspective that must be taken into account if contemporary development projects are to succeed. In this way, historical ecologists may be able to make archaeology 'matter' (Sabloff 2008), as they seek to 'drain the past to irrigate the present' (Crumley 1994: 4).

LANDSCAPES OF POWER AND PERCEPTION: SYMBOLIC AND RITUAL LANDSCAPES

One realm of landscape archaeology that has not had particular salience within African archaeology is that which emphasises experience and perception (Tilley 1994; Van Dyke 2008). This school, influenced by the phenomenology of Heidegger and Merleau-Ponty, seeks to explore past subjectivity by reconstructing how past actors experienced the landscape. It argues that western images of 'landscape' emerged through a particular gaze that was detached, elevated, and privileged, linked to landscape painting as this emerged in the 15th century (Thomas 2001). In this way, the *idea* of landscape is saturated with a particular western view of the world that, when applied to other landscapes, can only reproduce those Cartesian fantasies. The way out, it is argued, is through efforts to imagine the experience of a past individual within the landscape—their orientation, vision and senses—as a way to reconstruct past meanings. This must grow from 'being-in-the-world' in the landscape itself, rather than imposed on it by a vision reckoned through settlement pattern maps and artefact distributions, the exact tools that structure a detached vision of the world.

Debates on the phenomenology of landscape are polemic, with detractors arguing either that past landscape experiences are unobtainable through the lens of late capitalist vision (Smith and Blundell 2004) or that phenomenological interpretations have been narrowly conceived without thought of the age, gender, or ability of past individuals (Brück 2005). While phenomenological approaches have been central in landscape discussions in Europe, especially in relation to Neolithic landscapes, they have had few adherents in African archaeology. One reason may be that theoretical developments often lag in African archaeology, related most likely to scarce resources and an emphasis on more foundational cultural historical research. Additionally, the rich corpus of ethnographic data in Africa has offered a deep mine of local conceptions that archaeologists can access, without recourse to more speculative approaches emphasizing experience.

Smith and Blundell (2004) have, however, attempted to explore the utility of a phenomenology of landscape for southern African rock art studies, experimenting with this approach in the northern part of South Africa. Because rock art landscapes are well understood through ethnographic studies, they attempted to reconstruct what might be gained through an experiential approach to rock 'places' through immersion in the surrounding topography of the region. Their hope was to provide a contrast with previous ideas about rock art landscapes that focused on how rock art was understood to simply mark functional places on the Khoisan landscape. Emphasizing the closeness of paintings to material resources such as food, water, and shelter, this 'naive approach' to rock art landscapes, worked well, they argue, with an ecologically oriented settlement pattern approach, but was less able to comprehend the richer symbolic and conceptual understandings of rock art. However, as they began working through their own deep understanding of 'being-in-the-world' that came from repeated visits to their study area, they were deeply troubled by the way that the phenomenological approach simply disguised 'simplistic "gaze and guess" type assertions about rock art and landscape' (Smith and Blundell 2004: 259). The problem, they argue, was twofold. First, interpretations of rock art within landscapes often recapitulated western visions of landscape, preconceptions of the landscape, rather than drawing out novel interpretations based on experiences within the landscape. Second, ethnographic understandings of this particular rock art indicates that the places where it was created were places of spiritual negotiation for San religious specialists, which means they were chosen not because of their importance in this world, but rather as a means to access another.

This cautionary tale is not meant to discredit entirely the experiential approaches offered through phenomenology, but rather to show how it does not offer a simple panacea to constructing symbolic and experiential landscapes. It also suggests that African archaeology has at its disposal a rich alternative means toward reconstructing conceptual landscapes: that of ethnographic and ethnoarchaeological data. Such richness allows not only a greater sense of meaning and perception of past ritual landscapes but also an important intervention into studies of symbolic landscapes more generally.

The work of Insoll et al. (2009) is important here, with a multi-pronged study of Tallensi shrines in Ghana. Using archaeological surveys and excavations, they document the ancient ritual landscape, replete with shrines, sacred groves, and otherwise 'natural' features. Their success lies in discovering and delineating particular shrines and a degree of archaeological complexity that suggests long-term use. Excavations at the Nyoo shrine, in particular, have demonstrated the complex ritual activities that were once associated with it as a location at which ancestors and/or deceased members of society were honoured and commemorated, or as an assembly place for ritual activities.

This research is important on a number of fronts. First, in seeking out and documenting shrine sites, the project aims to recover more ephemeral parts of human landscapes, moving away from traditional 'sites' of habitation (cf. Schoeman 2006). Landscape archaeology in other parts of the world has focused on paths and roads, earthworks, water, and sacred sites as a means to more fully reconstruct past conceptual and sacred landscapes. However, Insoll et al.'s (2009) research in Ghana also helps question the existence of universal concepts such as 'nature' or universal notions of materiality, including the distinction made between natural and anthropogenic features often made in studies of symbolic or ritual landscapes (Insoll 2007). Sacred groves of trees, for example, were converted through consecration and sustenance from natural to social entities (Chouin 2002; cf. Abungu 1994; Mutoro 1994), a notion that mirrors Erickson's (2006) idea of domesticated landscapes. This work thus provides crucial insight into the pitfalls to which symbolic approaches may be subject when only the 'bones of the land' and not the 'skin' are considered (Tilley 1994: 73–74).

Other approaches to symbolic and ritual landscapes examine the way that they are constructed, conceptualized, and ideologically infused (Ashmore and Knapp 1999), emphasizing how landscapes were part of ritual practice and the enactment of power. Norman and

Kelly (2004) explore the way massive ditches in southern Bénin were efforts to materialize cosmological forces in order to influence and negotiate the political landscape. Previous research on ditch systems in West Africa had described their remarkable extent and the way they seemed to represent significant control over large labour pools (Connah 2000). Colonial administrators, interpreting the ditches through their own models, saw them as evidence of defensive systems and military prowess. Norman and Kelly, however, see these more functional explanations as problematic, especially given the connections drawn between the ditches and Dangbe, a python deity important in political and social life. Subsequent negotiations of power and authority in the kingdom of Dahomey drew on these perceptions and used them to demonstrate political and religious authority over conquered groups. The ditches, then, were not simply work projects to control the labour of defeated populations, but rather physical representations of control over religious and political space. This type of research follows Smith's (2003) call to take seriously the political landscape not only in the way that monuments and constructions *materialized* power, but in terms of how spatial practice—and linked performance—was crucial to the *construction* of power and authority.

CONCLUSION

Landscape archaeology in Africa is an active subfield through which new understandings of past societies have been achieved through broadening the spatial scale. It also offers insights that challenge troubling notions of an African past, as well as making archaeology relevant to contemporary concerns, forcing policymakers to take seriously both deep-time patterns of human–environmental interactions and the culturally relative ways through which local populations conceive of, manage, and construct their own landscapes.

REFERENCES

ABUNGU, G. H. O. (1994). Islam on the Kenya coast: an overview of Kenyan coastal sacred sites. In D. Carmichael, J. Hubert, B. Reeves, and A. Schanche (eds), *Sacred Sites, Sacred Places*. London: Routledge, 152–62.

ANSCHUETZ, K. F., WILSHUSEN, R. H., and SCHEICK, C. L. (2001). An archaeology of landscapes: perspectives and directions. *Journal of Archaeological Research* 9: 157–207.

ASHMORE, W., and KNAPP, A. B. (1999). *Archaeologies of Landscape: Contemporary Perspectives*. Oxford: Blackwell.

BALÉE, W. (1998). *Advances in Historical Ecology*. New York: Columbia University Press.

BINFORD, L. R. (1984). *Faunal Remains from Klasies River Mouth*. London: Academic Press.

BOWER, J. (1986). A survey of surveys: aspects of surface archaeology in sub-Saharan Africa. *African Archaeological Review* 4: 21–40.

BRÜCK, J. (2005). Experiencing the past? The development of a phenomenological archaeology in British prehistory. *Archaeological Dialogues* 12: 45–72.

BUNN, H. T. (1994). Early Pleistocene hominid foraging strategies along the ancestral Omo River at Koobi Fora, Kenya. *Journal of Human Evolution* 27: 247–66.

CACHEL, S. M., and HARRIS, J. W. K. (2006). The behavioural ecology of Early Pleistocene hominids in the Koobi Fora region, East Turkana Basin, northern Kenya. In E. C. Robertson, J. D. Seibert, D. C. Fernandez, and M. U. Zender (eds), *Space and Spatial Analysis in Archaeology*. Calgary: University of Calgary Press, 49–59.

CHOUIN, G. (2002) Sacred groves in history: pathways to the social shaping of the forest landscapes in coastal Ghana. *IDS Bulletin* 33, 39–46.

CONNAH, G. (2000). African city walls: a neglected source? In D. M. Anderson and R. Rathbone (eds), *Africa's Urban Past*. Oxford: James Currey, 36–51.

CRUMLEY, C. L. (1994). Historical ecology: a multidimensional ecological orientation. In C. L. Crumley (ed.), *Historical Ecology: Cultural Knowledge and Changing Landscapes*. Santa Fe, NM: SAR Press, 1–16.

—— and MARQUARDT, W. H. (1990). Landscape: a unifying concept in regional analysis. In K. M. S. Allen, S. W. Green, and E. B. W. Zubrow (eds), *Interpreting Space: GIS and Archaeology*. London: Taylor & Francis, 73–9.

CURTIS, M. C., and SCHMIDT, P. R. (2008). Landscape, people and places on the ancient Asmara Plateau. In P. R. Schmidt, M. C. Curtis, and Z. Teka (eds), *The Archaeology of Ancient Eritrea*. Trenton, NJ: Red Sea Press, 65–108.

DAVID, B., and THOMAS, J., (eds) (2008). *Handbook of Landscape Archaeology*. Walnut Creek, Calif.: Left Coast Press.

ERICKSON, C. L. (2006). The domesticated landscapes of the Bolivian Amazon. In W. Balée and C. L. Erickson (eds), *Time and Complexity in Historical Ecology: Studies in the Neotropical Lowlands*. New York: Columbia University Press, 235–78.

FAWCETT, W., and LA VIOLETTE, A. (1990). Iron Age Settlement around Mkiu, south-eastern Tanzania. *Azania* 25: 19–26.

FLEISHER, J. (2010). Swahili synoecism: rural settlements and town formation on the central East African coast, AD 750–1500. *Journal of Field Archaeology* 35: 265–82.

FOLEY, R. (1981). *Off-Site Archaeology and Human Adaptation in Eastern Africa*. Oxford: British Archaeological Reports.

FRENCH, C. A. I. (2002). *Geoarchaeology in Action: Studies in Soil Micromorphology and Landscape Evolution*. London: Routledge.

—— SULAS, F., and MADELLA, M. (2009). New geoarchaeological investigations of the valley systems in the Aksum area of northern Ethiopia. *Catena* 78: 218–33.

GOSDEN, C., and HEAD, L. (1994). Landscape: a usefully ambiguous concept. *Archaeology in Oceania* 29: 113–16.

HARDESTY, D. L. (2007). Perspectives on global change archaeology. *American Anthropologist* 109: 1–7.

INSOLL, T. (2007). Natural or human spaces? Tallensi sacred groves and shrines and their potential implications for aspects of northern European prehistory and phenomenological interpretation. *Norwegian Archaeological Review* 40: 138–58.

—— KANKPEYENG, B., and MACLEAN, R. (2009). The archaeology of shrines among the Tallensi of northern Ghana: materiality and interpretative relevance. In A. Dawson (ed.), *Shrines in Africa*. Calgary: University of Calgary Press, 41–70.

ISAAC, G. LL. (1989). Early hominids in action: a commentary on the contribution of archaeology to understanding the fossil record in East Africa. In N. Isaac (ed.), *The Archaeology of Human Origins: Papers by Glynn Isaac*. Cambridge: Cambridge University Press, 77–95.

KUSIMBA, C. M., and KUSIMBA, S. B. (2005). Mosaics and interactions: East Africa, 2000 B.P. to the present. In A. B. Stahl (ed.), *African Archaeology: A Critical Introduction*. Oxford: Blackwell, 392–419.

LANE, P. J. (2009). Environmental narratives and the history of soil erosion in Kondoa District, Tanzania: an archaeological perspective. *International Journal of African Historical Studies* 42: 457–83.

—— (2010). Developing landscape historical ecologies in Eastern Africa: an outline of current research and potential future directions. *African Studies* 69: 299–322.

MCINTOSH, R.J. (2005). *Ancient Middle Niger: Urbanism and the Self-Organizing Landscape*. Cambridge: Cambridge University Press.

MCINTOSH, S. K. (1999). Modelling political organization in large-scale settlement clusters: a case study from the Inland Niger Delta. In S. K. McIntosh (ed.), *Beyond Chiefdoms: Pathways to Complexity in Africa*. Cambridge: Cambridge University Press, 66–79.

—— and MCINTOSH, R. J. (1980). *Prehistoric Investigations in the Region of Jenne, Mali*. Oxford: British Archaeological Reports.

MITCHELL, P. J. (2005). Modelling Later Stone Age societies in southern Africa. In A. B. Stahl (ed.), *African Archaeology: A Critical Introduction*. Oxford: Blackwell, 150–73.

MONROE, J. C., and OGUNDIRAN, A. (eds) (2012) *Power and Landscape in Atlantic West Africa*. Cambridge: Cambridge University Press.

MUTORO, H. W. (1994). The Mijikenda kaya as a sacred site. In D. L. Carmichael, J. Hubert, B. Reeves, and A. Schanche (eds), *Sacred Sites, Sacred Places*. London: Routlege, 132–9.

NORMAN, N. L. (2009). Hueda (Whydah) country and town: archaeological perspectives on the rise and collapse of an African Atlantic kingdom. *International Journal of African Historical Studies* 42: 387–410.

—— and KELLY, K. (2004). Landscape politics: the serpent ditch and the rainbow. *American Anthropologist* 106: 98–110.

PARKINGTON, J. E. (1999). Western Cape landscapes. *Proceedings of the British Academy* 99: 25–35.

—— (2001). Mobility, seasonality and southern African hunter-gatherers. *South African Archaeological Bulletin* 56: 1–7.

POLLARD, E. J. (2008) The maritime landscape of Kilwa Kisiwani and its region, Tanzania, 11th to 15th century AD. *Journal of Anthropological Archaeology* 27: 265–80.

POTTS, R. (1994). Variables versus models of early Pleistocene hominid land use. *Journal of Human Evolution* 27: 7–24.

ROSSIGNOL, J., and WANDSNIDER, L. (1992). *Space, Time and Archaeological Landscapes*. New York: Springer.

SABLOFF, J. A. (2008). *Archaeology Matters: Action Archaeology in the Modern World*. Walnut Creek, Calif.: Left Coast Press.

SCHMIDT, P. R. (1994). Historical ecology and landscape transformation in eastern Equatorial Africa. In C. L. Crumley (ed.), *Historical Ecology: Cultural Knowledge and Changing Landscapes*. Santa Fe, NM: SAR Press, 99–126.

SCHOEMAN, M. H. (2006). Imagining rain places: rain-control and changing ritual landscapes in the Shashe–Limpopo confluence area, South Africa. *South African Archaeological Bulletin* 61: 152–65.

SEALY, J., and VAN DER MERWE, N. J. (1992). On 'Approaches to dietary reconstruction in the Western Cape: are you what you have eaten?' A reply to Parkington. *Journal of Archaeological Science* 19: 459–66.

SHAHACK-GROSS, R., MARSHALL, F., RYAN, K., and WEINER, S. (2004). Reconstruction of spatial organization in abandoned Maasai settlements: implications for site structure in the Pastoral Neolithic of East Africa. *Journal of Archaeological Science* 31: 1395–1411.

SINCLAIR, A., MCCRAITH, L., and NELSON, E. (2003). Understanding hominid landscapes at Makapansgat, South Africa. In P. Mitchell, A. Haour, and J. Hobart (eds), *Researching Africa's Past: New Contributions from British Archaeologists*. Oxford: Oxford University School of Archaeology, 11–24.

SINCLAIR, P. J. J. (1987). *Space, Time, and Social Formation: A Territorial Approach to the Archaeology and Anthropology of Zimbabwe and Mozambique c 0–1700 AD*. Uppsala: Societas Archaeologica Upsaliensis.

SMITH, A. T. (2003). *The Political Landscape: Constellations of Authority in Early Complex Societies*. Berkeley: University of California Press.

SMITH, B. W., and BLUNDELL, G. (2004). Dangerous ground: a critique of landscape in rock art studies. In C. Chippindale and G. Nash (eds), *Pictures in Place: The Figured Landscape of Rock Art*. Cambridge: Cambridge University Press, 239–62.

STUMP, D. (2010). Ancient and backward or long-lived and sustainable: the role of the past in debates concerning rural livelihoods and resource conservation in eastern Africa. *World Development* 38: 1251–62.

SWANEPOEL, N. (2008). View from the village: changing settlement patterns in Sisalaland, northern Ghana. *International Journal of African Historical Studies* 41: 1–27.

THOMAS, J. (2001). Archaeologies of place and landscape. In I. Hodder (ed.), *Archaeological Theory Today*. Cambridge: Polity, 165–86.

TILLEY, C. (1994). *A Phenomenology of Landscape: Places, Paths and Monuments*. Oxford: Berg.

UR, J. A., KARSGAARD, P., and OATES, J. (2007). Urban development in the Ancient Near East. *Science* 317: 1188.

USMAN, A. A. (2000). A view from the periphery: northern Yoruba villages during the Old Oyo empire, Nigeria. *Journal of Field Archaeology* 27: 27–61.

VAN DYKE, R. M. (2008). *The Chaco Experience: Landscape and Ideology at the Center Place*. Santa Fe, NM: SAR Press.

WYNNE-JONES, S. (2007). It's what you do with it that counts: performed identities in the East African coastal landscape. *Journal of Social Archaeology* 7: 325–45.

CHAPTER 15

MARITIME ARCHAEOLOGY IN AFRICA

COLIN BREEN

INTRODUCTION

MARITIME archaeology has, until recently, been regarded as a peripheral branch of archaeology, concerned largely with ships, marine infrastructure, and nautical traditions. Originating with the emergence of diving technologies after the Second World War, it quickly became associated with western researchers interested in investigating submerged vessels associated with the great naval empires of the past. While it has developed along significantly more nuanced and informed lines, the subject is still largely regarded as dealing with European expansion and the emergence of western capitalist expressions of trade, industry and modernity (Gibbins and Adams 2001). In Africa, however, it has been more inclusive and integrated, dealing with coastal landscapes and the cultural remains of past settlement, trade, and movement, as well as intertidal and underwater remains including shipwrecks and drowned landscapes (Breen and Lane 2003). Maritime archaeology is, then, the integrated study of past maritime communities and peoples and their interaction with the environment and seascapes.

Dealing with Africa's maritime past is, however, hugely difficult given its understudied nature and the sheer diversity of African maritime histories and traditions. Any statement can only be labelled as interim, though requiring some form of framework with which to contextualize and survey the maritime archaeology of such an expansive area. One possibility is a marine systems approach that would document the cultural chronologies of people, traditions, and landscapes across the continent's many different coastlines: its Mediterranean north coast, its west coast and the Atlantic world, South Africa and the southern seas, East Africa and the Indian Ocean, and, finally, the Red Sea (cf. Mitchell 2005) (Fig. 15.1). While useful in terms of categorization, this may be overly formulaic and downplay the interconnectedness of different parts of the continent and the multiplicity of influences that have moulded the cultural character of its coasts. For present purposes, a thematic approach is more useful. General themes central to maritime research include resource availability,

FIG. 15.1 Map of Africa showing the principal places mentioned in Chapter 15.

settlement, colonialism, and globalization. More abstract concepts of movement, displacement, and connections would recognize the complexity of Africa's past and the need to move away from western-led research agendas that govern the construction of African traditions and identities. Recent innovative surveys have begun to address some of these issues, including the pioneering terrestrial and underwater investigations on the Farasan Islands examining the process of anatomically modern humans exiting Africa (Bailey et al. 2007) through to archaeologies of identity and movement associated with the Hajj (cf. Petersen 1994).

RESOURCE AVAILABILITY

Resource availability is central to the sustainability of coastal settlements, and Africa's coastlines and seas contain a plethora of resources that people have systematically exploited for millennia. Oldest among these is the evidence for shellfish exploitation from coastal sites in

Eritrea (Walter et al. 2000) and South Africa (Marean et al. 2007), while Blombos Cave also documents surprisingly early evidence of fishing (Henshilwood et al. 2001). These activities are, in effect, the earliest tangible evidence for human engagement with the marine environment (Erlandson 2001). Whether or not access to high-quality lipids from these marine resources was indeed instrumental in the evolution of modern cognitive capacities (Broadhurst et al. 2002) is still debated. Yet, at least from the onset of the Holocene, shell middens are one of the most characteristic archaeological signatures along Africa's coasts (Parkington 2006; Bar-Yosef Mayer and Beyin 2009). Landscapes associated with them sometimes also retain other indicators of past maritime activity in the form of settlements and fishing structures, with several studies documenting the often long history of usage of fish traps in particular (Avery 1975; Cairns 1975; Parkington 1976; McConkey and McErlean 2007; Pollard 2008a; Hine et al. 2010). Other coastal resources also continued to be utilized throughout the historic period. Mangroves, for example, operate as breeding grounds for fish stocks and protect the coast against erosion and storm surges. Extensively exploited on the East African coast for construction during the height of the Swahili era, when they were shipped to the Persian Gulf ports for use in local buildings, mangrove poles are still exported from the continent today (Horton and Middleton 2000). Coral reefs along the same coast are likewise important for fishing, while on the Swahili coast, coral blocks on exposed and raised reefs provided a widely used building material (Horton and Middleton 2000; La Violette, Ch. 62 below).

MERCHANTS AND MARINERS IN PHARAONIC AND CLASSICAL TIMES

Africa's northern and Red Sea coasts have long been important avenues of trade and communications. While the Nile was the central focus of waterborne traffic during the Pharaonic period, the Ancient Egyptians also traded and travelled by sea and shipping and maritime activity are well documented. Reliefs at the Medinet Habu temple show Rameses III's (1184–1153 BC) naval battle against the 'Sea Peoples' in the early 12th century BC, for example, while wooden river-going vessels, including the Cheops boat dating to c. 2570 BC, have been recovered from the Old Kingdom pyramid complex on the Giza plateau (Lipke 1984). Voyages down the Red Sea to the land of Punt toward its southern end are most famously recorded at the Deir el-Bahri funerary temple of Queen Hatshepsut (1473–1458 BC). Excavations at Mersa/Wadi Gawasis on the Red Sea have now identified a beach harbour that facilitated this trade (Bard and Fattovich 2007). Well-preserved ship parts, including cordage, ship timbers, oars, and stone anchors, most probably of Middle Kingdom date (2055–1650 BC), consistent with nearby inscriptions recording successful voyages to Punt, have been identified in artificial caves at the site (Ward and Zazzaro 2010).

Carthage, on Africa's north coast, first developed by the Phoenicians in the 9th century BC, quickly emerged as a significant port controlling maritime trade across the western/central Mediterranean. Large-scale infrastructural works to accommodate shipping activity included two harbours, one for the navy, the second for mercantile ships of the kind represented by the later Mahdia shipwreck, found by sponge divers off Tunisia in 1907. Some 1,900

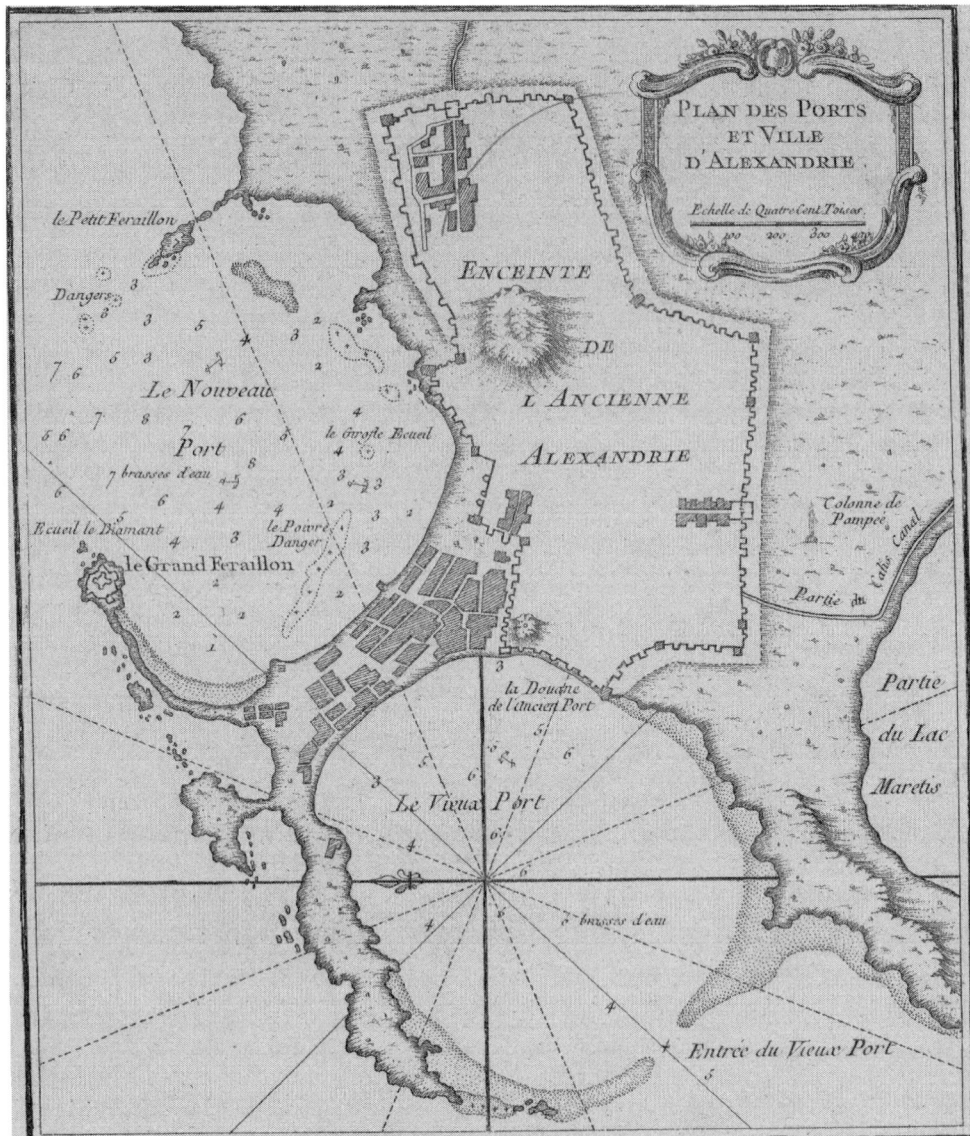

FIG. 15.2 A Bellin 1764 coastal chart of the historic port of Alexandria, Egypt.

tonnes of architectural fragments and art recovered from the seabed here were likely en route from Greece to Italy when the vessel was lost between 60 and 80 BC (Kapitän 1983).

With the expansion of Alexander the Great's empire (336–323 BC) another major port was established on Egypt's Mediterranean coast. Alexandria consisted of a series of harbours of which the Great Harbour is the best documented (Fig. 15.2). Subject to significant subsidence activity in the 4th century AD, substantial sections of harbour works and associated structures, including possible basal elements of the Pharos lighthouse, have been identified on the seabed (Empereur 2000). Large quantities of stonework including columns, statues, and sphinxes have also been recorded, while shipwrecks dating from both the Greek and

Roman periods have been examined in the broader region (Goddio 2007). On Egypt's Red Sea coast, several Roman-era harbour locations have also been investigated, including Berenike, which linked the Red Sea to the Nile from the 3rd century BC to the 6th century AD via caravan routes across the Eastern Desert. A graffito on an amphora sherd dating to the second half of the first century AD depicts a merchant vessel clearly designed for the open sea and suitable for moving commodities like wine, textiles, and ceramics between the eastern Roman Empire and the Indian subcontinent (Sidebotham and Wendrich 1996). Additional research has been undertaken at Berenike's sister port of Quseir al-Qadim, equated with the harbour of Myos Hormos mentioned by many Classical historians, where sections of the Roman-period waterfront and buildings were excavated and the topography of the original harbour mapped (Peacock and Blue 2006).

Further south in Eritrea, Adulis was the primary port for Aksumite trade from the 4th to the 7th centuries AD, but is already mentioned in this connection by the *Periplus of the Erythraean Sea*, a mariner's guide dating to the 1st century AD, when it serviced the trade to India and exported ivory and shell (Peacock and Blue 2007). Not far away, a 4th–7th- century shipwreck has been identified on Black Assarca Island off the Eritrean coast (Pedersen 2000). Although no structural remains survived because of the site's exposed nature and the rapid deterioration of wood remains in the warm waters of the Red Sea, pottery was recovered, including varying forms of amphorae likely to be of Byzantine Palestinian origin, as well as a glass sherd and a lead counterbalance weight for a steelyard. A further series of port towns were present along the Swahili coast, stretching from modern-day Somalia to northern Mozambique. These were significant centres of settlement and trade along the Western Indian Ocean littoral. Survey work at one of these major trade and settlements centres, at Kilwa in Tanzania, has identified a number of intertidal causeways and platforms associated with the 13th–16th-century town and harbour (Pollard 2008b).

COLONIALISM AND GLOBALIZATION

From the mid-15th century the Portuguese began exploring Africa's coasts, seeking gold, new markets and access to the Indies unimpeded by Muslim powers. Their search bore fruit in 1498, when Vasco da Gama, building on earlier voyages, reached India and initiated over a century of Portuguese dominance in the Indian Ocean (Pearson 1998). Offshore, relevant evidence includes the remains of an early 16th-century Portuguese outward-bound vessel, found near Oranjemund, Namibia, during near-shore mining operations (Werz 2009). Sections of the vessel's lower hull and a concentration of cast metal ingots were uncovered during rescue investigations, as well as three bronze cannon; adjacent areas yielded ivory, coins, and navigational instruments (Chirikure et al. 2010). On land, the Portuguese established a series of fortified sites to protect and promote their new economic interests at strategic positions along the African coast. First established (in 1482) was São Jorge de Mina (Elmina) on the Gold Coast (modern Ghana), later a central element in a network of European fortifications along this littoral (Swanepoel, Ch. 67 below). Many of these sites were established where good natural harbours existed and access to the hinterland was facilitated by local groupings or by river courses. Although other forts have also been investigated, Elmina has received particular attention. A trading and settlement centre since at least the

15th century AD, at Portuguese arrival it was one of several small ports and fishing settlements associated with the Akan (DeCorse 1992, 2001a; Thiaw and Richard, Ch. 68 below). To begin with, Europeans valued gold and ivory most highly as exports, but trade in people quickly emerged and by the 17th century slaves were the primary commodity of West African trade (DeCorse 2001b). Work at Elmina adopted an inclusive approach towards the landscape, combining both terrestrial and underwater investigations and including geophysical and diver surveys of the harbour's approaches. Several potential wreck sites were located, with one 19th-century European vessel producing ceramics, beads, brass, and lead sheathing, although its involvement in the slave trade is unconfirmed (Webster 2008a).

While the Transatlantic Slave Trade Database records nearly 200 vessels lost while engaged in slaving activity, only a handful of wreck sites have actually been identified (Eltis et al. 1999; Webster 2008b). Although lying far beyond African waters, they represent an integral part of the continent's heritage within the broader Atlantic social world. One example is the *Fredensborg*, lost off Tromoy, southern Norway, while returning from a slaving voyage from the Gold Coast following the sale of 265 slaves in 1768. The objects recovered from this Danish West India Guinea Company ship make important personal connections with the slaves' homeland, including possible amulets and a large quern used in food processing (Svalesen 2000). Another wreck, the *Henrietta Marie*, located off Key West, Florida, is that of an English merchant trader lost in 1700; investigations uncovered sections of its hull, containing large amounts of material culture and artefacts directly related to the slave trade, including numerous shackles (Moore and Malcom 2008). The wreck of the French slaver *Adelaïde*, lost while sailing from Ouidah on the Bight of Benin to Haiti with 300 slaves, has also been provisionally identified, this time on reefs off Haiti, where sections of the vessel's hull and rigging have been recorded on the seabed (Webster 2008b).

The trans-oceanic slave trade had a significantly longer, more complex history along Africa's east coast. By the 9th century AD slaves were being traded to Iraq via centres such as Pemba, and their export continued across the Indian Ocean region for more than a millennium (Alexander 2001). A similar trade existed in the Red Sea, where ports like Suakin emerged as key centres (Mallinson et al. 2009). As along the Atlantic, Portuguese arrival heralded an era of European expansion marked by the construction of coastal forts that displaced and subjugated earlier settlements. By the late 17th century Portuguese power in the northwestern Indian Ocean was seriously threatened by Oman, which besieged the largest of these forts, Fort Jesus at Mombasa, in 1696, taking it in 1698. One of several ships sent from Portuguese India to assist the fort, the *Santo Antonio da Tanna*, built in 1681, was lost during the siege. Excavation of its wreck yielded important information relating to late 17th-century naval architecture and indicated that, instead of sending a highly armed squadron to Mombasa, the Portuguese had hastily put together four lightly armed vessels that, in some cases, were still carrying trading goods (Sassoon 1981; Piercy 1982, 2005). Recent survey work in the harbour has further identified a number of 18th- and 19th-century vessels in the harbour, and documented the port's historic landscape (Forsythe et al. 2003; Quinn et al 2007).

By the late 18th century Oman dominated the East African coast, and in the 1820s its sultan transferred his capital to Zanzibar (Horton and Middleton 2000) (Fig. 15.3). Over the next eight decades the Zanzibar sultanate became the focus for maritime-based trade across the whole region, with slavery, along with ivory and cloves, an integral part of its growth (Croucher, Ch. 70 below). Physical manifestations of this trade include the expansion of port facilities at places like Zanzibar's Stonetown, Mombasa, and Malindi. Waterfront palaces and

FIG. 15.3 'Zanzibar Town from the Sea' from Richard Burton's 1872 *Zanzibar; City, Island and Coast*. London.

associated European administrative and residential buildings provided a highly visible expression of the prestige of the merchants and rulers involved with the trade and an overt demonstration of their growing wealth (Rhodes 2010). No slave-carrying dhows have yet been identified archaeologically, but, as with West Africa, little systematic marine survey has taken place (for details, see Lane 2012). Surveys have, however, been undertaken on the wreck of the French East India vessel *L'Utile*, engaged in the Atlantic slave trade and lost on Tromelin Island in 1761 while on passage to Mauritius; the associated settlement established by marooned slaves has also been investigated (Webster 2008b; Marriner, Guerout and Romon, 2010).

Maritime trade, East India companies, and Africa

From the start of the 17th century other European countries established trading companies to gain footholds in the highly lucrative Indian Ocean commerce dominated by the Portuguese. The Dutch East India Company (VOC) initially had limited interests in Africa, but the supply station established at the Cape of Good Hope in 1652 later grew into a full colony (Swanepoel, Ch. 67 below). Important waterfront excavations in Cape Town document its development through to the construction of a series of wharfs in 1839 (Saitowitz et al. 1993). Nearby underwater projects include South Africa's first scientifically investigated shipwreck, the Dutch East Indiaman *Oosterland*, lost in Table Bay in 1697. Spices, tropical hardwoods, cowries, Chinese export porcelain and stoneware and Japanese and Persian porcelain all document the range and diversity of VOC trade (Werz 1993, 1999). Other possible wreck sites with VOC links include one in Meob Bay, Namibia, where coins, identified as VOC doits minted in the Netherlands in 1746 have washed ashore, perhaps from the *Vlissingen*, lost in 1747 (Werz 2008). The potential site of the *Meermin*, a Dutch East India Company slaver that ran aground off Cape Town in 1766, has also been investigated (Webster 2008b).

Competing with the Dutch, the French East India Company initially failed to plant a colony on Madagascar but did initiate ports on Réunion and Mauritius. The English East India Company likewise had little direct involvement with the African mainland, but plunder by salvage divers of one of its vessels, the *Doddington*, lost in South Africa's Algoa Bay in 1755, sparked an important legal case that resulted in clarification of international maritime law with regard to the ownership of marine archaeological materials (Hoffman 2006).

Europe's East India companies came to dominate much of the continent's trade with East and South Asia, but at broadly the same time Ottoman mercantile expansion took place on a similar scale across the northeast of Africa. Many Red Sea ports became important Ottoman outposts, and facilitated both trade and administration (Elzein, Ch. 66 below). Excavations at Suakin (Sudan) have uncovered Ottoman-period buildings and waterfront structures (Mallinson et al. 2009), while underwater investigations have focused on a mid-18th-century vessel wrecked *c.* 1765 at Sadana Island off the Egyptian coast (Ward 2005). This large mercantile ship was probably travelling northwards, possibly from Jeddah or Mocha on the Arabian side of the Red Sea, when it sank, losing a valuable cargo of coffee, spices, and Chinese export porcelain manufactured for Middle Eastern markets. Together, the vessel and its cargo provide tangible links to the expanding mercantile world of the Ottomans and a physical manifestation of early modern globalization.

CONFLICT ARCHAEOLOGY

Africa's coasts have witnessed many conflicts, with naval battles, military campaigns, and associated events resulting in construction of coastal forts and protected harbours, as well as the loss of numerous vessels in battle. While the northern Mediterranean and Red Sea coasts probably contain many Classical-era vessels, most such shipwrecks are of more recent date. They include the French Océan-class 118-gun ship of the line *L'Orient*, originally Napoleon's vessel during the French invasion of Egypt, which was sunk near Alexandria in 1798 during the Battle of the Nile. Discovered in 1983, its remains include a 14 m-long rudder that had been braced in bronze, and sections of a copper-sheathed hull. The German warship *Konigsberg*, lost in Tanzania's Rufiji Delta during the First World War, exemplifies the potential of African maritime archaeology to address even more recent conflicts (Lane 2005).

CONCLUSION

Africa's maritime past encompasses a hugely diverse and complex set of sites, landscapes, and narratives that involve multiple players and perspectives centred not only on trade but also subsistence, regional development, and belief systems. It is an understudied subject area that sadly still involves few African voices, providing obvious opportunities and challenges for redressing this imbalance to build capacity within the continent and reorient the subject to an African-led examination of a complex, often exploitative past. It is to be hoped that such an inclusive approach will engage with a more critical view of western expansion, but also reveal more of the multitude of other peoples and cultural layers present along the continent's coastlines. The many (and growing) natural and human threats to the survival of Africa's maritime heritage, both on land and under water, do however demand the urgent implementation of measures for its protection and future management. Intensive coastal development coupled with expanding coastal population, increasing marine resource exploitation, and climate change are all having a negative impact on the maritime cultural resource. Improved legislation and enforcement in individual countries, combined with implementation of the UNESCO Convention on the Protection of the Underwater Cultural Heritage, will aid countries in dealing with the challenges the next decade poses in safeguarding the maritime archaeology of the continent (cf. Lane 2007).

REFERENCES

ALEXANDER, J. (2001). Islam, archaeology and slavery in Africa. *World Archaeology* 33: 44–60.

AVERY, G. (1975) Discussion on the age and use of tidal fish-traps (*visvywers*). *South African Archaeological Bulletin* 119/120: 105–13.

BAILEY, G. N., FLEMMING, N. C., KING, G. C. P., et al. (2007). Coastlines, submerged landscapes, and human evolution: the Red Sea Basin and the Farasan Islands. *Journal of Island and Coastal Archaeology* 2: 127–60.

BARD, K. A., and FATTOVICH, R. (eds) (2007). *Harbor of the Pharaohs to the Land of Punt: Archaeological Investigations at Mersa/Wadi Gawasis, Egypt, 2001–2005*. Naples: Università degli Studi di Napoli 'L'Oriente', Dipartimento di Studi e Ricerche su Africa e Paesi Arabi, Laboratorio di Archeologia.

BAR-YOSEF MAYER, D. E., and BEYIN, A. (2009). Late Stone Age shell middens on the Red Sea coast of Eritrea. *Journal of Island and Coastal Archaeology* 4: 108–24.

BREEN, C., and LANE, P. J. (2003). Archaeological approaches to East Africa's changing seascapes. *World Archaeology* 33: 469–92.

BROADHURST, C. L., WANG, Y., CRAWFORD, M. A., CUNNANE, S. C., PARKINGTON, J. E., and SCHMIDT, W. F. (2002). Brain-specific lipids from marine, lacustrine or terrestrial food resources: potential impact on early *Homo sapiens*. *Comparative Biochemistry and Physiology Part B*, 131: 653–73.

CAIRNS, P. (1975) A report on circular stone features associated with coastal shell middens at Cape St. Francis. *South African Archaeological Bulletin* 117: 36–9.

CHIRIKURE, S., SINAMAI, A., GOAGOSES, E., MUBUSISI, M., and NDORO, W. (2010) Maritime archaeology and trans-oceanic trade: a case study of the Oranjemund shipwreck cargo, Namibia. *Journal of Maritime Archaeology* 5: 37–55.

DeCORSE, C. R. (1991). West African archaeology and the Atlantic slave trade. *Slavery and Abolition* 12: 92–6.

——(1992). Culture contact, continuity, and change on the Gold Coast, AD 1400–1900. *African Archaeological Review* 10: 163–96.

——(2001a). *An Archaeology of Elmina: Africans and Europeans on the Gold Coast, 1400–1900*. Washington, DC: Smithsonian Institution Press.

DeCorse, C. R. (ed.) (2001b). *West Africa during the Atlantic Slave Trade: Archaeological Perspectives*. Leicester: Leicester University Press.

Erlandson, J. M. (2001). The archaeology of aquatic adaptations: paradigms for a new millennium. *Journal of Archaeological Research* 9:287–350.

Eltis, D., Behrendt, S. D., Richardson, D., and Klein, H. S. (1999). *The Trans-Atlantic Slave Trade Database*. Cambridge: Cambridge University Press.

Empereur, J. (2000). Underwater archaeological investigations of the ancient Pharos. In M. H. Mostafa, N. Grimal, and D. Nakashima (eds), *Underwater Archaeology and Coastal Management: Focus on Alexandria*. Paris: UNESCO Coastal Management Sourcebooks 2, 54–9.

Forsythe, W., Quinn, R., and Breen, C. (2003) Subtidal archaeological investigations in Mombasa's Old Port. In A. Haour, P. Mitchell, and J. Hobart (eds), *Researching Africa's Past: New Contributions from British Archaeologists*. Oxford: Oxbow Books, 133–8.

Gibbons, D., and Adams, J. (2001). Shipwrecks and maritime archaeology. *World Archaeology* 32: 279–91.

Goddio, F. (2007). *The Topography and Excavation of Heracleion-Thonis and East Canopus (1996–2006): Underwater Archaeology in the Canopic Region in Egypt*. Oxford: Oxford Centre for Maritime Archaeology.

Henshilwood, C. S., Sealy, J. C., Yates, R., et al. (2001). Blombos Cave, southern Cape, South Africa: preliminary report on the 1992–1999 excavations of the Middle Stone Age levels. *Journal of Archaeological Science* 28: 421–48.

Hine, P., Sealy, J., Halkett, D., and Hart, T. (2010) Antiquity of stone-walled tidal fish traps on the Cape Coast, South Africa. *South African Archaeological Bulletin* 191: 68–96.

Hoffman, B. T. (2006). *Art and Cultural Heritage: The Case of the Doddington Coins*. Cambridge: Cambridge University Press.

Horton, M., and Middleton, J. (2000). *The Swahili*. Oxford: Blackwell Publishers.

Kapitän, G. (1983). Toothed gear and water-drawing pendulum from the Mahdia wreck. *International Journal of Nautical Archaeology* 12: 145–53.

Lane, P. J. (2005). Maritime archaeology: a prospective research avenue in Tanzania. In B. B. B. Mapunda and P. Msemwa (eds), *Salvaging Tanzania's Cultural Heritage*. Dar es Salaam: Dar es Salaam University Press, 96–132.

—— (2007). New international frameworks for the protection of underwater cultural heritage in the Western Indian Ocean. *Azania* 42: 115–36.

—— (2012). Maritime and shipwreck archaeology in the Western Indian Ocean and southern Red Sea: an overview of past and current research. *Journal of Maritime Archaeology* 7: 9–41.

La Riche, W. (1997). *Alexandria: The Sunken City*. London: Weidenfeld & Nicolson.

Lipke, P. (1984). *The Royal Ship of Cheops*. Oxford: British Archaeological Reports.

Mallinson, M., Smith, L., Breen, C., Forsythe, W., and Phillips, J. (2009). Ottoman Suakin 1540–1865: lost and found. In A. C. S. Peacock (ed.), *The Frontiers of the Ottoman World*. Oxford: Oxford University Press, 469–92.

Marean, C. W., Bar-Matthews, M., Bernatchez, J., et al. (2007). Early human use of marine resources and pigment in South Africa during the Middle Pleistocene. *Nature* 449: 905–8.

Marriner, N., Guerout, M., and Romon, T. (2010). The forgotten slaves of Tromelin (Indian Ocean): new geoarchaeological data. *Journal of Archaeological Science* 37: 1293–304.

McConkey, R, and McErlean, T. (2007). Mombasa Island: a maritime perspective. *International Journal of Historical Archaeology* 11: 99–121.

Mitchell, P. J. (2005). *African Connections: Archaeological Perspectives on Africa and the Wider World*. Walnut Creek, Calif.: AltaMira Press.

MOORE, D. D., and MALCOM, C. (2008). Seventeenth-century vehicle of the Middle Passage: archaeological and historical investigations on the *Henrietta Marie* shipwreck site. *International Journal of Historical Archaeology* 12: 20–38.

PARKINGTON, J. (1976). Coastal settlement between the mouths of the Berg and Olifants Rivers, Cape Province. *South African Archaeological Bulletin* 123/124; 127–40.

PEACOCK, D., and BLUE, L. (2006). *Myos Hormos–Quseir al-Qadim: Roman and Islamic Ports on the Red Sea*. Oxford: Oxbow.

—— —— (eds) (2007). *The Ancient Red Sea Port of Adulis, Eritrea*. Oxford: Oxbow.

PEARSON, M. N. (1998). *Port Cities and Intruders: The Swahili Coast, India and Portugal in the Early Modern Era*. Baltimore, Md.: Johns Hopkins University Press.

PEDERSEN, R. K. (2000). Under the Erythraean Sea: an ancient shipwreck in Eritrea. *Institute of Nautical Archaeology Quarterly* 27: 3–12.

PETERSEN, A. (1994). The archaeology of the Syrian and Iraqi Hajj routes. *World Archaeology* 26: 47–56.

PHILLIPSON, D. W. (2005). *African Archaeology*, 3rd edn. Cambridge: Cambridge University Press.

PIERCY, R. C. M. (1982). Excavation of a shipwreck in Mombasa Harbour, Kenya. *National Geographic Society Research Reports*, 1976 Projects: 17–30.

—— (2005). The tragedy of the Santo Antonio de Tanna: Mombasa, Kenya. In G. G. Bass (ed.), *Beneath the Seven Seas*. London: Thames & Hudson, 172–9.

POLLARD, E. J. D. (2008a). *The Archaeology of Tanzanian Coastal Landscapes in the 6th to 15th Centuries AD: the Middle Iron Age of the Region*. Oxford: British Archaeological Reports.

—— (2008b). Inter-tidal causeways and platforms of the 13th- to 16th-century city-state of Kilwa Kisiwani, Tanzania. *International Journal of Nautical Archaeology* 37: 98–114.

QUINN, R., FORSYTHE, W., BREEN, C., BOLAND, D., LANE, P., and OMAR, A. L. (2007). Process-based models for port evolution and wreck formation at Mombasa, Kenya. *Journal of Archaeological Science* 34: 1449–60.

RHODES, D. (2010). *Historical Archaeologies of Nineteenth-Century Colonial Tanzania: A Comparative Study*. Oxford: British Archaeological Reports.

SAITOWITZ, S., SEEMANN, U., and HALL, M. (1993). The development of Cape Town's waterfront in the earlier nineteenth century: history and archaeology of the North Wharf. South African Archaeological Society Goodwin Series 7: 98–103.

SASSOON, H. (1981). Ceramics from the wreck of a Portuguese ship at Mombasa. Azania 16: 98–130.

SIDEBOTHAM, S. E., and WENDRICH, W. Z. (1996). *Preliminary Report of the Excavations at Berenike and the Survey of the Eastern Desert*. Leiden: CNWS.

SVALESEN, L. (2000). *The Slave Ship Fredensborg*. Kingston: Ian Randle.

WALTER, R. C., BUFFLER, R. T., BRUGGEMAN, H., et al. (2000). Early human occupation of the Red Sea coast of Eritrea during the last interglacial. *Nature* 405: 65–9.

WARD, C. (2005). Chinese porcelain for the Ottoman court: Sadana Island, Egypt. In G. F. Bass (ed.), *Beneath the Seven Seas*. London: Thames & Hudson, 186–91.

—— and ZARRARO, C. (2010). Evidence for Pharaonic seagoing ships at Mersa/Wadi Gawasis, Egypt. *International Journal of Nautical Archaeology* 38: 27–43.

WEBSTER, J. (2008a). Historical archaeology and the slave ship. *International Journal of Historical Archaeology* 12: 1–5.

—— (2008b). Slave ships and maritime archaeology: an overview. *International Journal of Historical Archaeology* 12: 6–19.

WERZ, B. E. J. S. (1993). South African shipwrecks and salvage: the need for improved management. *International Journal of Nautical Archaeology* 22: 237–44.

——(1999). *Digging up the Past: Perspectives of Maritime Archaeology with Specific Reference to Developments in South Africa until 1999*. Oxford: British Archaeological Reports.

——(2008). Not lost without a trace. The DEIC ship *Vlissingen*, assumed to have foundered near Meob Bay in 1747. *Journal of Namibian Studies* 4: 47–74.

——(2009). The Oranjemund shipwreck, Namibia. The excavation of sub-Saharan Africa's oldest discovered wreck. *Journal of Namibian Studies* 6: 81–106.

CHAPTER 16

···

MANAGING AFRICA'S ARCHAEOLOGICAL HERITAGE

···

NOEMIE ARAZI AND IBRAHIMA THIAW

INTRODUCTION

ARCHAEOLOGICAL resources constitute the major source material for the study of the pre-colonial history of most African countries, and have largely contributed to revising Africa's portrayal as the 'dark continent'. Instead, over the past century, archaeology has placed Africa at the forefront of all major debates in world prehistory and history including hominin evolution, the emergence of food production and other technological innovations, elite formation and the development of complex societies, and long-distance trade.

However, while archaeology has given Africa a greater voice in world prehistory and history, it is curious that the archaeological resources that made this possible are still neglected in the cultural heritage policies of many of the continent's nations. This might be partly explained by the fact that Africa's legal heritage was much structured by colonial powers, which defined heritage along a western perspective that emphasized the monumental and the aesthetic, leaving the bulk of archaeological sites, which do not fit into these categories, unprotected and exposed to neglect and destruction by both natural and human activities (Abungu and Ndoro 2009). Moreover, although the concept of preserving natural and cultural heritage is well established in many African societies, traditional notions of preservation tend to privilege *immaterial* cultural heritage and the material heritage of sacred or ritual sites (Togola 2004). Again, much of the archaeological record may be omitted.

Thirty years ago, Merrick Posnansky (1982) estimated the number of full-time archaeologists for the entire sub-Saharan African region as fewer than 100. While this number has expanded significantly since, it is still pitifully small compared to even a small western country. It is not, therefore, unreasonable to say that the state of archaeology and archaeological heritage management in Africa is precarious. Moreover, local archaeologists are generally overwhelmed with either administrative or teaching responsibilities and unable to engage in extensive fieldwork. Although lack of funding and trained personnel continue to plague the development of archaeological heritage management in Africa (Mabulla 2000), there is also a sense that archaeology has failed to demonstrate its potential to contribute significantly to the social and economic advancement of many of the communities where it operates (Thiaw 2003; Gavua 2006). Africa's archaeological heritage remains subject to rapid and massive destruction as a result of unbridled exploration and exploitation of minerals and energy resources, urbanization, irrigation, agriculture, and the expansion of facilities for tourism, as well as looting, while archaeological collections are poorly curated and preserved in many parts of the continent and continue to feed the illicit art trade (Schmidt and McIntosh 1996; see also Kusimba and Klehm, Ch. 17 below).

However, this gloomy picture of African archaeological heritage management is not universally true, and numerous positive developments, especially in the last decade, should not be overlooked. This chapter reflects on and analyses practices, politics, and policies in the preservation, valorization, and dissemination of archaeological resources and, examines the opportunities and challenges of heritage management in Africa. It then uses this diagnosis to look to the future of archaeological heritage management in Africa.

Management in precolonial Africa

Although heritage management in Africa is often thought to have started with colonialism, this assumption is wrong, for many heritage sites encountered by Europeans had only survived intact because of local forms of traditional management (Ndoro 2004). Custody of sites tended to focus on places that were held sacred by local communities, such as rain-making shrines, rockshelters, royal and chiefly burials, perennial springs, trench systems, and tree groves and forests (Mahachi and Kamuhangire 2009). Abandoned villages and homesteads often became the abodes of the spirits of former inhabitants, and were generally held intact by avoiding those sites, while others became shrines for religious functions. Great Zimbabwe is one of the best-known examples that had permanent resident site custodians (Sinamai 2003; Ndoro 2005). Usually a set of rules governed access to or behaviour at such sites. At Great Zimbabwe, for instance, designated entrances called *mijejeje* were ritually opened and closed upon entry and exit (Mahachi and Kamuhangire 2008: 44).

The tombs of the Baganda kings at Kasubi, Uganda, were another important example of a site that had witnessed sophisticated management structures since precolonial times, with a variety of specialists responsible for their welfare and particular clans dedicated to different aspects of their maintenance (Munjeri 2004)—tragically, these were burned down as a result of arson in March 2010. The importance of such traditional and customary systems lies in the fact that sites were protected as part of people's lives on a day-to-day basis. With the advent of colonialism, previously existing structures of heritage protection underwent drastic changes. New legal systems were introduced, resulting in the transfer of power and responsibilities from communities to central colonial governments. This often led to the centralization of heritage management, while emphasizing the beauty, uniqueness, and physical attributes of sites also resulted in restriction and denial of access to local communities (Abungu and Ndoro 2009).

Archaeological heritage and colonial rule

Such changes were particularly the case in areas under direct (rather than indirect) colonial rule. Tangible (or movable and immovable) heritage was disconnected from the intangible, and access and ownership to sites restricted and/or denied (Ndoro et al. 2009). This signalled the beginning of a long process of alienation and loss by local communities vis-à-vis their heritage resources, but also a new era, as explorations, often undertaken by military officials, colonial administrators, and amateurs, led to identification, research, preservation, and wider dissemination of Africa's archaeological resources (Robertshaw 1990). Nevertheless archaeological findings and their interpretation and uses were generally informed by the colonial paradigm that attributed sites and material cultures deemed 'sophisticated' to external forces and those deemed 'backward' and 'primitive' to Africans (cf. Trigger 1984; Hall 1995). These early efforts were also shaped by western interests in using ancient art and antiquities to fill European museums, then considered one of the primary goals of archaeology (Posnansky 1982).

Museum displays are an important component of heritage management and public outreach to ensure appropriation of archaeological resources (Fig. 16.1; see also Kusimba and Klehm, Ch. 17 below). The earliest museums in most of Africa date to the 1920s and 1930s, and as the first generation of Africanist archaeologists was affiliated to them they became sites for safeguarding and disseminating archaeological heritage for the wider public. Although this strengthened their role as centres for research and education,

FIG. 16.1 Art students drawing exhibition models to appropriate and valorize precolonial heritage in the context of the decolonization movements in the 1950s (copyright IFAN Archive, Guitat 1951, reproduced with permission).

museums mainly attracted white expatriate elites (Abungu 2001). Displays of archaeological collections were inspired by the same paradigm as ethnographic museums, and
emphasized essentialist views of African societies (Lane 1996). Local populations had little or no voice at any stage of the process, from research design and data recovery to curation, publications, and displays. Although these negative perceptions of African heritage
are long gone, they have had long-term impacts on archaeological heritage management
in Africa.

ARCHAEOLOGICAL HERITAGE MANAGEMENT
IN INDEPENDENT AFRICA

As Mire (2007) points out in the case of Somalia, not only did colonial archaeology
primarily extract material without record, but it was also dominated by expatriate
archaeologists who invested little in capacity building and infrastructure for the development of archaeological heritage management. As a result, even after independence, both
the new elite and the general population showed little interest in an archaeological heritage that was viewed as 'backward', aspiring instead to the new opportunities conferred by
modern urban life. Archaeology was a reminder of the old practices and material cultures
attributable to the rural areas. While this may still be true in the context of Somalia today,
in many other parts of the continent aspects and elements of the archaeological past have
been mobilized by the new elites of independent Africa to rebuild identities that were
profoundly shattered by the colonial experience (Posnansky 1982; Ndoro 2001; Folorunso
2008).

Although most archaeologists operating in Africa from the 1950s until the 1970s were still
European expatriates, this era of independence was characterized by the development of
local universities with departments of archaeology, antiquity services, and museums, and
was particularly favourable to the expansion and strengthening of archaeological heritage
programmes (Robertshaw 1990). Subsequently, old and recent monuments, archaeological
sites, and museums, along with music, songs, dances, food, archives, and even clothing and
hairstyles, were mobilized to create a sense of pride, self-achievement, national identity,
unity, and hope for the future (Fig. 16.2; Heath 1992; Abungu 2001; Ndoro 2001). National
museums, national heroes, and national heritage sites were created to transcend ethnic par-
ticularisms and to forge homogeneous forms of identity and citizenship. As Segobye (2008:
169) notes, 'some leaders like former president of Zambia Kenneth Kaunda promoted a "One
Zambia One Nation" philosophy which attempted to ensure that Zambian citizenry completely identified with the national culture and its heritage rather than ethnic or other identities' (see also, for Nigeria, Nzewunwa 1984).

International agencies and NGOs such as UNESCO, ICOM, ICCROM, and ICOMOS
contributed their fair share to the modern heritage concern by allocating important resources
to collections, sites, monuments, and archives in order to promote and valorize them and to
elevate some of them to the status of World Heritage sites. At this time, keywords such as
reparation, repatriation (of human remains, artefacts, and even monuments), ethnic rights,
and collective or community ownership also started to enter popular imagination and

FIG. 16.2 Senegalese models reaffirming African beauty via clothing, hairstyle and jewellery in the context of the decolonization movements of the 1950s (copyright IFAN Archive, Chérif 1951, reproduced with permission).

language. As a result of the economic, social, and political crises that affected many African countries in the 1970s and 1980s, however, resources allocated to heritage preservation by states and international communities alike were considerably reduced. To some extent, culture lost its aura in national policies, once again accelerating deprivation and degradation of archaeological heritage resources.

In this context, which coincided with weak legislatures, insufficient or poorly trained personnel, and inadequate or inexistent policies, looting and the sale of antiquities were widespread, expropriating many African countries of valuable archaeological resources (Schmidt and McIntosh 1996). In Senegal, for instance, large archaeological shell middens on the Atlantic coast were exploited as building material for road pavements, housing, and hotels embellishments (Thiaw 2008). At Pate, Kenya, many historical buildings were dismantled to retrieve coral rag used either for construction or for the production of lime (Kusimba 1996), while Mali suffered severe losses as archaeological sites were systematically mined for terracottas (Brent 1996; McIntosh 1996; Sanogo 1999). Mijikenda carved grave posts in coastal Kenya were likewise fed into the maw of western art markets (Wilson 1996; Udvardy et al. 2003). At the same time, rapid urbanization and development projects (dam and road constructions, irrigation projects) were implemented without taking into account the negative impacts on archaeological heritage resources (McIntosh 1993; Kankpeyeng and DeCorse 2004; Bocoum 2008; Folorunso 2008; Nao 2008). Except for countries in southern and North Africa, few African nations proved capable of responding to these changes, with most lacking site inventory records and databases and having little information on the nature and location of archaeological sites (McIntosh 1993; de Maret 1994).

Recently, concerns that local African populations are still marginalized and ill-informed about the importance and role of archaeology in social, political, cultural, and economic development have again been raised (e.g. Thiaw 2003, 2008; Gavua 2006; Mire 2007). Indeed, archaeology has been charged with not being very responsive to the social and economic interests of Africans (Gavua 2006). As a result, archaeological heritage is sometimes unclaimed (Thiaw 2003), and is attributed to 'aliens', 'giants', or a 'backward' population from the countryside with whom some post-independence African urban elites did not wish to be affiliated (Mire 2007). Archaeologists themselves are, in some cases, publicly ridiculed (Gavua 2006) and in others seen as cannibals whose activity is hazardous or useless to the community (Thiaw 2003). In countries torn by war, archaeology museums continue to be looted and pillaged to fund war efforts (Mire 2007). Religious fundamentalism and zealotry have also taken their toll, with the deliberate burning and destruction of monuments, shrines, and sacred places considered offensive and heretical to the new belief systems of resurgent religions (see also Giblin, Ch. 19 below). Even in politically stable countries local governments continue to neglect archaeology, as it is not considered a viable cultural resource worthy of investment (Naffé et al. 2008).

The actions of international agencies such as UNESCO have made little difference, because they followed a top-down approach that barely involved local populations who did not endorse their programmes and policies (Munjeri 2004; Mire 2007; Segobye 2008). Clearly, it is not always the lack of funds, as we generally tend to think, but rather the lack of dialogue between the different stakeholders and the local population that is the primary cause of the mismanagement of Africa's archaeological heritage.

CURRENT TRENDS

The last two decades have witnessed a resurgent interest of both African states and the international community in preserving the continent's cultural heritage. Pressure and motivation to advance the state of cultural heritage management resulted from the African Cultural Renaissance,[1] UNESCO's recognition that Africa was severely underrepresented on its World Heritage List, and the international community's recognition of the importance of integrating culture into development policies (Serageldin and Taboroff 1994). Regional centres were born such as the École du Patrimoine Africain (EPA), based in Porto-Novo, Bénin, and the Centre for Heritage Development (CHDA), based in Mombasa, Kenya. Both focus on the preservation, management, and promotion of movable and immovable cultural heritage. Under the impetus of the AFRICA 2009 programme and its partners, they have also provided capacity-building programmes for heritage professionals in francophone and anglophone sub-Saharan African countries respectively, sharing the coverage of Portuguese-speaking sub-Saharan Africa. EPA, for instance, has trained more than 600 African heritage professionals since its creation in 1998—a major advance, given that one of the most frequently cited problems is the lack of experienced staff to carry out cultural heritage activities (de Maret 1994; Taboroff 1994). Moreover, both EPA and CHDA enjoy close relationships with and support from UNESCO and ICCROM (the International Centre for the Study of the Preservation and Restoration of Cultural Property), which provide them with direct contact to cultural cooperation programmes and contributions from bi- and multilateral donors.

---

[1] The term 'African Renaissance' was first coined in the 1990s by Thabo Mbeki, former President of South Africa, but before that there already existed the Cultural Charter of Africa, which was adopted by the heads of state and government of the Organization of African Unity in 1976 but only entered into force in 1990 (available at www.dfa.gov.za). This has now been replaced by the Charter for African Cultural Renaissance, signed by African Union heads of state in 2006 (available at www.africa-union.org).

However, management of Africa's archaeological heritage seems to have become synonymous with the activities of the World Heritage Centre. Most efforts focus on sites inscribed on the World Heritage List and on increasing this number, of which Africa currently accounts for less than 10 per cent, though an alarming 45 per cent of those are on the List of World Heritage in Danger (UNESCO 2010). This grim situation led to the establishment of the African World Heritage Fund (AWHF) in 2006, whose objectives include increasing the number of African sites on the List, helping with conservation and management efforts, and rehabilitating sites inscribed on the List of World Heritage in Danger. Doubts persist, however, about whether the status of World Heritage Site constitutes the most effective option for site protection, sustainable conservation, and management, given the high costs of inscription and the lack of guaranteed funds for long-term conservation and management (Breen 2007). Such developments also leave unaddressed the question of what protection can be provided for the non-monumental sites that make up the bulk of the continent's archaeological resources.

The last decade has also seen a flurry of regional and bilateral agreements that should equally advance the protection and valorization of Africa's cultural and archaeological heritage. The Second Pan-African Cultural Congress of the African Union (PACC2), held in November 2009 at the headquarters of the African Union Commission (AUC), Addis Ababa, concluded with a common statement of intent to protect Africa's cultural heritage and goods. The most pressing issues identified were: the need for African countries to have legislation that regulates both the local sale and export of cultural goods; the need for each African country to conduct a national audit of its cultural goods and to take an inventory of its cultural objects outside the country; the need to ratify international conventions that protect and promote cultural heritage; and the need for capacity building of museums (Department of Social Affairs, African Union 2010). Much attention was also directed to the return of stolen or illicitly exported African goods—a goal likely to encounter strong opposition, especially by the Universal Museums and their reluctance to engage in dialogue with communities affected by issues of repatriation (ICOM News 2004). Indeed, a large number of African objects are nowadays housed in museum collections outside the continent, especially in western museums, which has led to an international polemic engaging not only museum experts and archaeologists but also political activists, artists, journalists, philosophers, etc. (e.g. Traoré 2007; Nurkin 2009).

In the framework of the European Union's (EU) development cooperation with ACP (African, Caribbean, and Pacific) countries, culture, and cultural heritage more specifically, were firmly integrated in 2000 by what is known as the Cotonou Agreement. Projects financed by the EU–ACP cultural industry support programme have included work on Ethiopia's Lalibela churches, the National Museum of Kenya, the Elmina and Old Accra preservation project in Ghana, and both national and regional museums in Mali. In this context, most attention is directed towards the preservation and conservation of World Heritage sites, the rehabilitation of historic city centres, and the enhancement of museums and their collections. This indicates that international funding schemes are driven by the old concepts of 'monumentality' and 'aesthetics', which brings us back to the question of the role and place of Africa's non-monumental heritage. Whereas the EU is less explicit on the economic gains of cultural heritage programmes, other major lending institutions such as the World Bank are much more outspoken concerning their potential role in reducing poverty.

Economic growth remains one of the strongest means of arousing the World Bank's interest in cultural heritage projects (Cernea 2001), but numerous setbacks in its MENA (Middle East and North Africa) region project, including political disagreements, bankruptcy of the project's executing agency, and the displacement of residents, indicate that dealing with culture and heritage from an overly economic and quantitative perspective may be as fallacious as projects that fail to consider sustainability after project funds have expired. A recently funded cultural resource management programme concerning Lesotho's Metolong Dam indicates that the World Bank has been revising its priorities towards funding mitigation activities (cultural heritage surveys and archaeological excavations) and capacity building of national experts and institutions (Mitchell and Arthur 2010).

The management of cultural resources is indeed 'subject to changing political and financial climates' (Schaafsma 2000: 38). However, nowhere have these political and financial climates, influencing the conservation ethic or lack of it, been as disparate as in Africa. Problems of repatriation and looting illustrate this well. On the one hand, irrefutable progress has been made—115 countries have ratified UNESCO's Convention on the Means of Prohibiting and Preventing the Illicit Import, Export and Transfer of Ownership of Cultural Property, including some that have historically been the least favourable to it, such as Japan, Switzerland, the United Kingdom, Sweden, Denmark, Norway, and Germany. The International Council of Museums (ICOM) has also produced a 'Red List of Antiquities at Risk', as well as a 'Code of Professional Ethics' that lays down a set of principles governing museums and the museum profession in general, and acquisitions and transfers of ownership of collections in particular. The United States has an agreement with Mali to restrict the importation of specified objects that are in danger of being looted from archaeological sites, and important contributions have been made by archaeologists and museum professionals in publicizing the illicit traffic in archaeological and other heritage objects (Fig. 16.3; R. McIntosh et al. 1989; Schmidt and McIntosh 1996; Sanogo 1999; Panella 2002; Polet 2005). However, these achievements

FIG. 16.3 The looted site of Gao-Saney, located approximately 6 km to the east of the modern city of Gao, Mali (photograph, Noemie Arazi, 1998).

have so far done little to diminish demand for these objects on the international art markets (for a recent example, consider the exhibition of African terracottas held in 2009 at the Barbier-Mueller Museum in Geneva; Huysecom 2009). Such high-profile public and private collections stand in stark contrast to the ever-increasing number of requests from countries for the return of objects preserved outside their borders, as well as for assistance in reconstituting their cultural memory and traditional knowledge. Holders of these objects, such as the British Museum, typically prefer to turn the argument on its head, emphasizing access rather than property rights, and have recently provided part of their East African ethnographic collection on loan to the National Museums of Kenya. Nevertheless, repatriation seems likely to remain an ongoing issue (e.g. Anastassopoulos 2008).

Another critical issue in the management of Africa's archaeological heritage relates to legislation. Outdated laws have failed to meet the contemporary realities of integrated development, especially regarding environment, land planning, urban and rural development, traditional and cultural rights, and community values (Eboreime 2009). As long as this remains the case, the gains of the last decades will be lost. As Munjeri (2009: 21) stipulates, 'harmonization of domestic laws, community-based traditional systems and international treaties is an a priori condition for the future of culture, nature and the environment in Africa south of the Sahara.'

THE FUTURE OF ARCHAEOLOGICAL HERITAGE MANAGEMENT IN AFRICA

One way forward is by integrating cultural heritage policy and law into all areas of national life, especially in regard to physical planning, environmental management, and land use. This calls for the implementation of an effective mechanism for the prior assessment of the potential impacts on the cultural heritage of proposed development activities (Taboroff 1994; Naffé et al. 2008; Arazi 2009, 2011). This will, however, only be achieved with improved coordination and dialogue between the agencies responsible for cultural heritage and those responsible for the environment and planning (Fig. 16.4). In line with an increasing recognition that all heritage resources are at risk from modern development, there is also a need to establish and/or upgrade information systems for archaeological resources, especially if they are to be used by other ministries in their project planning (McIntosh 1993; Taboroff 1994). Attention has also been directed to Africa's urban explosion and for national and visiting research teams to focus part of their work on urban and peri-urban areas, as otherwise a hitherto neglected research field might be lost forever (Lane 2011). There is also a need to raise awareness of the research potential of, and threats to, the continent's underwater cultural heritage (Breen, Ch. 15 above) and for coastal states to sign the 2001 UNESCO Convention on the Protection of Underwater Cultural Heritage (Lane 2007).

Museums have lately been in the spotlight through various programmes that have concentrated on redefining their role and rendering them more accessible to local populations (e.g. Bouttiaux 2007). Various roundtables and international cooperation programmes have recognized the need to establish regional and local museums, providing the opportunity for communities to reappropriate their own cultures and provide easier access to museum spaces, which are usually located in distant capitals. It has also been acknowledged that museums in

FIG. 16.4 Salvage excavation at the future site of a gas-fired power plant at Kribi, Cameroon (photograph, Noemie Arazi, 2010).

Africa need to transform themselves from 'dead' places into 'living' spaces. South–South cooperation constitutes another important theme, which contrasts with the usual North-South exchanges. Positive developments have included loan exhibitions from Europe to museums in Africa (e.g. the exhibition 'Behanzin, King of Abomey' between the Musée du Quai Branly, Paris, and the Zinsou Foundation, Cotonou), and vice versa (the 'Kingdom of Ife: Sculptures from West Africa' exhibition organized between various museums in Nigeria and the British Museum). However, the issues of repatriation and of who owns Africa's cultural patrimony are far from resolved, and continue to be thorny issues within a wide spectrum of stakeholders.

Another theme, steadily gaining in profile, concerns the role and active involvement of local communities in heritage management. Indeed, new legislation in Botswana, South Africa, and Namibia has made important concessions in favour of local communities (e.g. Mahachi and Kamuhangire 2008). In practice, however, the accommodation of local communities remains contentious, as their knowledge often collides with that of the scientific community (see Lane, Ch. 40 below). The general tendency to screen indigenous knowledge by the scientific community before it becomes acceptable does little to contribute to improving relations between them. Universities, museums, governments, lending institutions, and international agencies are increasingly confronted with issues of community participation as they seek to bridge the gap between their objectives and sustainable practices, and the World Summit on Sustainable Development (2002) has clearly highlighted the importance of broad public participation in decision-making and of communities having access to information. Future developments in the management of archaeological resources will have to move in the same direction if archaeologists and heritage professionals want to make those resources more relevant to local communities and governments, collaborating with civil groups and communities in a process that could also contribute significantly to the future of Africa's archaeological heritage by releasing archaeological resources from the usual confines of museums, academic research, and conferences toward alternative spaces and publics.

REFERENCES

ABUNGU, G. (2001). Museums: arenas for dialogue or confrontation. *ICOM News*, Special Issue, 1–18.

—— and NDORO, W. (2009). Introduction. In Ndoro et al. (2009: vi–ix).

ANASTASSOPOULOS, G. (2008). Statement by the President of UNESCO's General Conference on the occasion of the international conference 'The Return of Cultural Property to its Countries of Origin'. www.unesco.org

ARAZI, N. (2009). Cultural research management in Africa: challenges, dangers and opportunities. *Azania* 44: 95–106.

—— (2011). Safeguarding archaeological cultural resources in Africa: policies, methods and issues of (non) compliance. *African Archaeological Review* 28: 27–38.

BOCOUM, H. (2008). Aménagement du territoire et archéologie préventive au Sénégal: quels enjeux pour la recherche? In Naffé et al. (2008: 75–85).

BOUTTIAUX, A. M. (2007). *Afrique: Musées et Patrimoines Pour Quels Publics?* Tervuren: Musée Royale de l'Afrique Centrale.

BREEN, C. (2007). Advocacy, international development and World Heritage Sites in sub-Saharan Africa. *World Archaeology* 39: 355–70.

BRENT, M. (1996). A view inside the illicit trade in African antiquities. In Schmidt and McIntosh (1996: 63–78).

CERNEA, M. M. (2001). *Cultural Heritage and Development: A Framework for Action in the Middle East and North Africa*. Washington, DC: World Bank.

DE MARET, P. (1994). Archaeological research, site protection, and employment generation: Central African perspectives. In Serageldin and Taboroff (1994: 371–86).

EBOREIME, J. (2009). Challenges of heritage management in Africa. In Ndoro et al. (2009: 1–6).

FOLORUNSO, C. A. (2008). Archaeological sites and heritage in the face of socio-economic development in Nigeria, since independence. In Naffé et al. (2008: 135–41).

GAVUA, K. (2006). Rethinking African archaeology from inside-out. http://cohesion.rice.edu/CentersAndInst/SAFA/emplibrary/Gavua,K.SAfA2006.pdf

HALL, M. (1995). Great Zimbabwe and the Lost City. In P. J. Ucko (ed.), *Theory in Archaeology*. London: Routledge, 28–45.

HEATH, D. (1992). Fashion, anti-fashion and heteroglossia in urban Senegal. *American Ethnologist* 19: 19–33.

HUYSECOM, E. (2009). Le pillage de l'histoire africaine. *Le Temps*, 1 May.

ICOM NEWS (2004). *Universal Museums* 57(1). http://icom.museum/media/icom-news-magazine/icom-news-2004-no1/

KANKPEYENG, B. W., and DECORSE, C. R. (2004). Ghana's vanishing past: development, antiquities, and the destruction of the archaeological record. *African Archaeological Review* 21: 89–128.

KUSIMBA, C. M. (1996). Kenya's destruction of the Swahili cultural heritage. In Schmidt and McIntosh (1994: 201–24).

LANE, P. J. (1996). Breaking the mould? Exhibiting Khoisan in southern African museums. *Anthropology Today* 12(5): 3–10.

—— (2007). New international frameworks for the protection of underwater cultural heritage in the Western Indian Ocean. *Azania* 42: 115–35.

—— (2011). Future urban growth and archaeological heritage management: some implications for research activity in Africa. *Conservation and Management of Archaeological Sites* 13: 134–59.

MABULLA, A. Z. P. (2000). Strategy for cultural heritage management in Africa (CHM): a case study. *African Archaeological Review* 17: 211–33.

MAHACHI, G., and KAMUHANGIRE, E. (2009). Administrative arrangements for heritage resource management in sub-Saharan Africa. In Ndoro et al. (2009: 43–51).

MCINTOSH, R. J. (1996). Just say shame: excising the rot of cultural genocide. In Schmidt and McIntosh (1994: 45–62).

—— MCINTOSH, S. K., and TOGOLA, T. (1989). People without history. *Archaeology* 42: 74–80.

MCINTOSH, S. K. (1993). Archaeological heritage management and site inventory systems in Africa. *Journal of Field Archaeology* 20: 500–504.

MIRE, S. (2007). Preserving knowledge, not objects: a Somali perspective for heritage management and archaeological research. *African Archaeological Review* 24: 49–71.

MITCHELL, P. R., and ARTHUR, C. (2010). Archaeological fieldwork in the Metolong Dam catchment, Lesotho, 2008–10. *Nyame Akuma* 74: 51–62.

MUNJERI, D. (2004). Anchoring African cultural and natural heritage: the significance of local community awareness in the context of capacity building. In E. De Merode, R. Smeets, and C. Westrik (eds), *Linking Universal and Local Values: Managing a Sustainable Future for World Heritage*. Paris: UNESCO World Heritage Center, 75–80.

—— (2009). Introduction to international conventions and charters on immovable heritage. In Ndoro et al. (2009: 13–23).

NAFFÉ, B. O. M., LANFRANCHI, R., and SCHLANGER, N. (eds) (2008). *L'Archéologie Préventive en Afrique: Enjeux et Perspectives*. Saint-Maur: Editions Sépia.

NAO, O. (2008). Archéologie preventive et préservation du patrimoine culturel au Burkina-Faso. In Naffé et al. (2008: 100–2).

NDORO, W. (2001). *Your Monument Our Shrine: The Preservation of Great Zimbabwe*. Uppsala: Acta Universitatis Upsaliensis.

—— (2004). Traditional and customary heritage systems: nostalgia or reality? The implications of managing heritage sites in Africa. In E. De Merode, R. Smeets, and C. Westrik (eds), *Linking Universal and Local Values: Managing a Sustainable Future for World Heritage*. Paris: UNESCO World Heritage Center: 81–4.

—— (2005). *The Preservation of Great Zimbabwe: Your Monument, Our Shrine*. Rome: ICCROM.

—— MUMMA, A., and ABUNGU, G. (eds) (2009). *Cultural Heritage and the Law. Protecting Immovable Heritage in English-Speaking Countries of Sub-Saharan Africa*. Rome: ICCROM.

NURKIN, G. (2009). Would Western museums return looted objects if Nigeria and other states would be ruled by angels? Restitution and corruption. http://www.culturalheritagelaw.org/news-issues/news-issues-in-cultural heritage. Accessed 6 December 2009.

NZEWUNWA, N. (1984). Nigeria. In H. Cleere (ed.), *Approaches to the Archaeological Heritage: A Comparative Study*. Cambridge: Cambridge University Press, 101–8.

PANELLA, C. (2002). *Les Terres Cuites de la Discorde: Déterrement et Écoulement des Terres Cuites Anthropomorphes du Mali. Les Réseaux Rocaux*. Leiden: CNWS.

POLET, J. (2005). Recherches archéologiques à Dia et Thial. In *Archéologies: Vingt Ans de Recherches Françaises dans le Monde*. Paris: Maisonneuve & Larose, 321–4.

POSNANSKY, M. (1982). African archaeology comes of age. *World Archaeology* 13: 345–58.

ROBERTSHAW, P. (ed.) (1990). *A History of African Archaeology*. London: James Currey.

SANOGO, K. (1999). The looting of cultural material in Mali: culture without context. http://www.mcdonald.cam.ac.uk/projects/iarc/culturewithoutcontext/issue4/sanogo.htm Accessed 1 Feb. 2010.

SCHAAFSMA, C. F. (2000). Significant until proven otherwise: problems versus representative samples. In H. Cleere (ed.), *Archaeological Heritage Management in the Modern World*. London: Routledge, 38–51.

SCHMIDT, P. R., and MCINTOSH, R. J. (eds) (1996). *Plundering Africa's Past*. Bloomington: Indiana University Press.

SEGOBYE, A. K. (2008). Layered histories and identities in the development of public archaeology in southern Africa. In Naffé et al. (2008: 164–86).

SERAGELDIN, I., and TABOROFF, J. (eds) (1994). *Culture and Development in Africa. Proceedings of an International Conference held at the World Bank, Washington D.C.* Washington, DC: World Bank.

SINAMAI, A. (2003). Cultural shifting sands: changing meanings of Zimbabwe sites in Zimbabwe, South Africa and Botswana. http://www.international.icomos.org/victoria-falls2003/papers.htm Accessed 10 Feb. 2010.

TABOROFF, J. (1994). Bringing cultural heritage into the development agenda: summary findings of a report of cultural heritage in environmental assessments in sub-Saharan Africa. In Serageldin and Taboroff (1994: 319–64).

THIAW, I. (2003). Archaeology and the public in Senegal: reflections on doing fieldwork at home *Journal of African Archaeology* 1: 27–35.

—— (2008). Développement touristique et malgestion des ressources culturelles archéologiques dans le Delta du Saloum. In Naffé et al. (2008: 86–96).

TOGOLA, T. (2004). Sauvegarde et valorisation du patrimoine au Mali: bref aperçu historique. In K. Sanogo and T. Togola (eds), *XIth Congress of the Panafrican Association for Prehistory and Related Fields*. Bamako: ACTS, 455–61.

TRAORÉ, A. (2007). Ainsi nos œuvres d'art ont droit de cité là où nous sommes, dans l'ensemble, interdits de séjour. http://www.afriblog.com/blog.asp?code=aminatatraore Accessed 18 Jan. 2010.

TRIGGER, B. G. (1984). Alternative archaeologies: nationalist, colonialist, imperialist. *Man* 19: 355–70.

UDVARDY, M. L., GILES, L. L., and MITSANZE, J. B. (2003). The transatlantic trade in African ancestors: Mijikenda memorial statues *(vigango)* and the ethics of collecting and curating non-Western cultural property. *American Anthropologist* 105: 566–80.

UNESCO (2010). *Convention Concerning the Protection of the World Cultural and Natural Heritage: State of Conservation of World Heritage Properties Inscribed on the World Heritage List*. Brasilia: World Heritage Committee 34.

WILSON, T. H. (1996). The loss of cultural heritage in Mali: a perspective from Kenya. *AfricanArts* 29: 36–41, 103–4.

WORLD SUMMIT ON SUSTAINABLE DEVELOPMENT (2002). *Report of the World Summit on Sustainable Development, Johannesburg, South Africa: 26 August–4 September 2002*. New York: United Nations.

CHAPTER 17

MUSEUMS AND PUBLIC ARCHAEOLOGY IN AFRICA

CHAPURUKHA KUSIMBA AND CARLA KLEHM

INTRODUCTION

MUSEUMS teach ideas and advance knowledge through field-, laboratory-, and collection-based research and exhibitions. Although definitions vary, the general view is that museum institutions educate the public, as well as care for, own, and use tangible and intangible objects, which they exhibit on a regular basis to the public. Through systematic research, museum curators and other specialists discern new knowledge that enables museums to mount permanent and temporary exhibitions to advance knowledge and public understanding. Since museums serve public interests, they are typically owned and administered by a group of individuals (usually a board of trustees) on behalf of the public (Smith 2000). Tending to specialize in specific subjects, such as natural history, cultural history, or art history, they have increasingly adopted more active leadership and education agendas in addition to their traditional collection-centred responsibilities (Edson and Dean 1996; Macdonald 2011).

In the context of a primarily non-written African past, the paucity of documentary sources is critically informed and enhanced by archaeological evidence. Museums are necessary to curate past and future archaeological evidence: in many instances, museums in Africa were prefigured by the presence of large volumes of archaeological and ethnological collections that needed to be temporarily stored pending analysis. These temporary storerooms eventually became more permanent as the need to systematically organize and display these objects was recognized. Archaeology thus has an important taxonomic base in museum collections (Sturtevant 1969).

MUSEUMS AND ARCHAEOLOGY: A BRIEF HISTORY

Anthropological archaeology owes its foundation and wellbeing to museums. Sturtevant's (1969) classification of anthropology in North America and Europe into three major periods is relevant for understanding archaeology in Africa. During his first period (c. 1840–90), anthropological practitioners were all based in museums, lacked formal training, and focused on cultural evolution. In his second (*c.* 1890–1920), anthropology began to be established as a university-based discipline, with museums the primary source of employment for anthropologists and museum collections the core component of research into issues of diffusion vs independent invention and the relations between cultures and their environments. Since the 1920s, however, anthropology has shifted increasingly away from museums and a strictly collections-based approach and toward a more theoretically oriented, university-based practice.

The African situation is similar in the sense that African archaeologists have primarily been trained in museum archaeology and museums are still their primary employers. With the exception of South Africa, universities in postcolonial Africa were quite critical of the role anthropology had played in enabling the colonial agenda (p'Bitek 1971; Mafeje 1991; cf. Nicholas 2010 for a global perspective). Many removed traditional anthropology from university curricula in favour of history and sociology. Wherever it was taught, archaeology was treated as a handmaiden of history, playing a minor place as a unit in departments of history. Museums were the only places where students interested in archaeology could be trained (Kusimba 2009). Happily, anthropology has now been rehabilitated and fully incorporated into the curriculum in many universities. Expansion of university education has also opened more opportunities for teaching and learning about archaeology. Thus, although museums still serve as the main depository where archaeological collections are documented and curated, many archaeologists are becoming more engaged with universities. Indeed, in some countries, for example Kenya, all archaeologists trained through the national museums in the period 1980–2000 have since left to teach in universities. The situation was similar in Zimbabwe and in Botswana until recently. Reasons include reduced research funding, low salaries, low prestige, and interfering politics (Ndoro 2001).

African museums

Museums in Africa are a product of colonization. Almost all were founded through the efforts of the continent's pioneer anthropologists, historians, naturalists, palaeontologists, and palaeoanthropologists (Clark 1990; Deacon 1990; Morell 1995); some, such as Cape Town (1825), Cairo (1869), and Antananarivo (1897), in the 19th century (Prösler 1996). Museums initially served as repositories of material culture of 'native cultures', but through the work and vision of early curators quickly developed into major research centres dedicated to the study, publication, preservation, and display of treasures of precolonial and contemporary Africa (Leakey 1990). At independence, museums were the only places where indigenous material cultures could be found, and thus institutions that initially served colonial interests increasingly became symbols of national unity, where the diversity and dynamism of new independent nations could be displayed and celebrated. Despite criticism that they primarily served the elite, foreign tourists, and schoolchildren, there is no denying the critical role museums have played and continue to play in the formation of modernity, the nation-state, and global relations. Ardouin (2000) has emphasized the crucial engagement museums need to have with history, in particular recent history, since they are the only institutions responsible for imparting and increasing knowledge and thereby affecting the society's perceptions of the past African communities relationships with each other. He is critical of museums in terms of lack of engagement with more recent (political) history and a limiting of displays to archaeological and ethnographic artefacts. In Ardouin's (2000: 1) words, 'in every era, events, upheavals, peaceful or conflict relations have been carried on, experienced, and understood in different ways by communities and individuals. This has been expressed, directly or indirectly, in material culture, which are then carriers of data and memories.'

With six million years (and counting) of human evolution, most of which is confined to the continent, Africans are caretakers of one of the longest and richest heritages of our species. The continent's more recent history stretching over the last 10,000 years is also extremely complex, while diverse ethnic groups each have claims to notions of ever-changing self-identity. African archaeologists and museums thus have a daunting task in developing flexible and multivocal cultural histories that can satisfy these varied stakeholders. Separating the museum from, and shedding the image of, the museum's original colonial linkages further complicates these issues. We think it is possible for this to be achieved locally and responsibly, in spite of the lack of resources at so many African museums.

Some of the most challenging problems museums face today include: curbing illicit excavation of important archaeological sites and trafficking of antiquities; maintaining collections at both national and regional levels despite the lack of adequate, climate-controlled storage facilities; protecting, preserving, and conserving archaeological sites, especially monumental sites; building viable community support for archaeology and museums; making archaeology an attractive career option for young people; and forging national reconciliation, cohesion, tolerance, and unity in diversity through exhibits.

Because most museums, including those in Africa, depend on governmental and private funding, they tend to be vulnerable to fluctuations in the funding base. Budget cuts often affect cultural institutions more than others, in part due to ill-informed perceptions that culture is not a priority but a luxury to be discarded during tough economic times. Also, budgetary cuts often deeply affect the smaller community and regional museums. Unless such museums have politically and economically powerful trustees, they tend to be left out and almost forgotten, partly because they do not bring in much revenue and are thus less self-sustaining. When museums are not well funded, they almost inevitably became less attractive as career options. This is even more so in Africa, where museums have a less than stellar history and have until lately been viewed as symbols of the colonial past that is best forgotten. Hence, those who are unfortunate enough to find employment in museums will tend to be those who took that career path as a last resort. But of course, this is not true any longer.

Museums as guardians of the continent's archaeological resources

In Africa today, countries realize the important role museums play in dispersing knowledge about cultural heritage and its potential to promote cultural diversity and to heal ethnic divisions. Hence, exhibits are increasingly geared towards schoolchildren and families, as well as tourists. Moreover, there is the colonial past that the African museums are trying to reject; African museums were often founded by the colonial powers, mostly visited by European elites, and often exoticized African culture by removing it from its cultural context. Forums elsewhere in Africa have recognized that the idea of museums as a neutral space is false; 'culture is in politics and politics in culture' (Coombes 2003: 151). This leads to a specific call for 'monuments, museums, and other cultural spaces [to] embody the history, experiences, and values of different groups and classes from their perspectives, not only those of the previously or currently dominant' (Tomaselli and Ramgobin 1988: 106–7). National museums (Fig. 17.1) are among the most important heritage institutions in Africa, since they are statutory bodies empowered to regulate archaeological and palaeontological sites and monuments as well as serving as national repositories of cultural and biological specimens, and play an important role in conservation. However, they all too frequently have more administrators than professional staff, are severely under-funded, and are unable to discharge their responsibilities.

Often smaller, regional museums are particularly stressed in terms of resources. These museums are often located in rural areas, focus on a specific topic, and thus address mostly regional or highly specialized audiences. Sites of archaeological significance frequently fall into this category. In Kenya, for example, palaeoanthropological sites like Kariandusi, Koobi Fora, and Olorgesailie are of international significance, yet they command a very low turn-out, usually of scholars, a few tourists, and schoolchildren. Their revenue is minimal, and therefore they have to rely almost entirely on governmental funding to remain open. There are other smaller regional museums that focus on the local cultural and natural histories of the regions. These museums are often located away from the cities and are supported by local volunteers and cultural enthusiasts, many of whom are not museum professionals. Attention

FIG. 17.1 Entrance to the Nairobi National Museum, the flagship museum of the National Museums of Kenya (photograph, Carla Klehm, July 2008).

to these museums is particularly critical, since their audience is primarily the local community. Funding issues are endemic, as much of their audience is smaller and generally comprising fewer tourists, and these collections are therefore not the revenue powerhouses that the national museums are. Increased representation in these regional museums, along with the professionalization and training of their staff by national museums and centralized funding bodies, will build an infrastructure that reaches out and invests in the education of the country as a whole. These museums have the potential to play an important role in national unity from the grassroots by increasing community awareness in preserving and safeguarding their heritage, including archaeological, ethnological, and sacred sites, for contemporary and future generations.

Attention to programmes that target and integrate the community into heritage conservation should be at a prime. This may include everything from building the museum into a communally functional space—as at the Khama III Museum in Serowe (Figs 17.2 and 17.3), Botswana, where local musicians gather and interact with local children, teaching them traditional music and dance—to educational programmes, such as those at the National Museums of Kenya, whose Education Department is dedicated to providing programmes for communities to maximize the museum's resources. These programmes include workshops for students and teachers; public lectures to schools and the general public; and the organization of city-wide .competitions in art, traditional dances, and essay writing. In Botswana, one of the National Museum of Botswana's more impressive and successful programmes has been the travelling exhibition known as *Pitse ya Naga*, or 'Zebra on Wheels'. In a country with a low population and a traditionally dispersed community, going 'to the people' is particularly important. The programme has expanded from private schools in rural areas to include towns, and targets primary and early secondary schoolchildren (a half-day programme for each), with educational films for the community in the evenings, and through its history has now reached nearly every primary school in the country. A decline

FIG. 17.2 Exterior of the Khama III Museum in Serowe, Botswana (photograph, Carla Klehm, September 2011).

FIG. 17.3 Community interactive space at the Khama III Museum in Serowe, Botswana (photograph, Carla Klehm, September 2011).

from 2005 to 2011 in funding and organization led to a gap during this period, and again highlights why these initiatives and success stories must be encouraged and supported. Outreach programmes such as those in Kenya and Botswana have had a huge impact on educating the local communities about pride in cultural heritage and the importance of each member of the community as a custodian of their national heritage.

International collaborations are indispensable for developing museums, exhibitions, and programmes: while the resources and/or infrastructure are often lacking or insufficient, well-structured partnerships can build a dialogue and equal relationship between African museums and professionals and foreign museums worldwide. These relationships are beneficial to both collaborating partners and stakeholders. When they are well developed, they have to remain sustainable even after funding ends. One such programme of huge importance to the development of museums in Africa is the International Council of Museums, AFRICOM. Founded primarily to identify, address, and rectify problems facing museums in Africa, AFRICOM's primary goals are to manage the continent's intangible heritage, train museum professionals, and promote continental networking. Thus, rather than continually looking towards Europe and North America for the training of museum professionals, AFRICOM regularly organizes training workshops held in different African countries. These workshops and training sessions enhance the skills and knowledge of African heritage professionals, increase the effectiveness with which they solve their problems, and create a support network based upon mutual interests, trust, and friendship arising from shared experiences. Since its founding less than a decade ago, AFRICOM's success can now be seen in a large cohort of museum professionals. There is now a much greater appreciation of and commitment to the promotion and protection of Africa's archaeological and natural heritage. Museum professionals now work more closely with local communities and with law enforcement officials in monitoring archaeological resources, including excavations. Efforts to monitor illegal excavations of archaeological sites funded by the illicit antiquities markets have improved in many member states. Through the efforts of the African Archaeological Network, AAN, archaeologists from Kenya, Tanzania, Mozambique, Botswana, Nigeria, and Ghana have built local collaborative teams and networks. Most archaeological expeditions concerned with the later prehistory of these countries now have representatives from these countries as well. Master's and doctoral research programmes are now collaborative efforts involving advisers from member countries. These efforts need to be emulated in other regions of the continent as well. Through AFRICOM, museum professionals in Africa have found an 'African voice' to address issues of African concern and seek solutions that are homegrown. The success of AAN in the training of young archaeologists from the region at home institutions is especially deserving of praise, as this addresses one of the core problems that African archaeology faces: that of provincialism. As African archaeologists work across international boundaries for their master's and doctoral research, they gain a level of knowledge that has hitherto been the preserve of their western counterparts. These efforts will translate into the creation of an African perspective, and perhaps voice, that has been lacking in the discipline.

Collaborations with international museums need to continue to be enhanced through the signing of memoranda of understanding between museums. Both African and foreign museums can learn from each other and enhance each others' programmes in terms of joint research, curation, collecting and conservation, outreach, training, loans, and exhibit development. Organizations such as the African Swedish Museum Network (SAMP) and the ALAS network (Africa–Latin America–Africa–Sweden) bring together over forty museums from four continents to create joint projects, build capacity, and tackle mutually frustrating issues, such as increasing appeal to and attendance of the local community.

One particularly successful example is that between the Musée National de Lubumbashi (MNL) (Fig. 17.4) in the Democratic Republic of the Congo and the Royal Museum for

FIG. 17.4 Christian Kaweme of the education department of the National Museum of Lubumbashi, Congo-Kinshasa, guiding schoolchildren at the exhibition 'Congo: Nature & Culture', 2007 (© Bart Deputter, RMCA, reproduced with permission).

Central Africa (RMCA) in Belgium. Through collaboration across divisions, including archaeology and ethnography, and via permanent exhibitions, collections, and internships, these museums were able to revive and reopen the permanent exhibition at MNL and begin a digital inventory of its collections. Since 2000, the Congolese-oriented projects have focused on protecting artefacts, creating cultural and educational programmes, and developing a sustainable plan. They have expanded through institutional cooperation, in 2004 with Lubumbashi and 2011 with Kinshasa, to eventually involve Kinshasa University, the National Museums of Congo in Kinshasa, Lubumbashi University, and the National Archives of Congo. Subjects developed range from culture to traditional healing knowledge and human–environmental interactions. For example, one exhibition project in 2007, 'The Congolese Society: History and Memory', stressed the importance and richness of Congolese history, and set out to better educate the public about misrepresentations and stereotypes. These exhibitions paid attention to differences in African educational systems as well as showing sensitivity to religion in subjects such as evolution. This sensitivity in the creation and implementation of the exhibits even extended to the topic of ethnic tensions, in which the power of language plays a strong part. The Democratic Republic of Congo has four official languages, but in this geographically large and divided country with 23 minor languages and over 200 other spoken languages, language choice is often politically and ethnically charged. To combat this, the MNL and RMCA compromised as such: they created an entrance where each visitor is greeted by recordings in each of these minor languages, while the signs inside the museum are written in three languages: English, French, and the Congolese dialect of Swahili. Noteworthy, and part of the reason these programmes are particularly commendable, is the power balance among the partners involved: the RMCA acts in an advisory role, and the African partners have discretion in planning the content of the exhibitions. Even in its infancy, the scheme achieved admirable success: in 2006, 320 schools and 8000 students visited the MNL. Unfortunately, it has encountered great difficulties since its reopening, but it remains accessible on appointment. However, the collaboration between the RMCA's Education Department and the MNL continues to this day, and an exhibition panel on Kinshasa was exported in February 2011 to encourage further south–south collaboration between institutions in Kinshasa and Lubumbashi.

THE FUTURE OF AFRICAN ARCHAEOLOGY
IN MUSEUMS

African archaeology has made great strides. Every African nation today has trained archaeologists. Many of these professionals received their training in western institutions and continue to conduct collaborative research with their western colleagues. These collaborative efforts are good, and must be encouraged. They are especially important in providing an opportunity for re-engagement which rebuilds historical ties that have been obfuscated by the often tenuous histories between the colonizer and the colony. In such collaborations, professionals from both institutions should be cognizant of the history and, rather than seek to distance themselves from it, learn from it and possibly embrace it through exhibits that incorporate both voices—those of the colonial master and the colonial subject (cf. Lionnet 2001). Even with all these good intentions, organizing exhibitions about Africa without the involvement of African museum professionals can have the unfortunate outcome of appearing paternalistic or simply being misunderstood (e.g. Cannizzo 1989).

The training of African archaeologists on the continent has increased. More and more African nationals are now receiving their training locally, and the numbers of PhDs from African universities has steadily grown (Schmidt 2009). This trend will certainly continue, with the Universities of Dar es Salaam, the Witwatersrand, Cape Town, Pretoria, and Ibadan, Cheikh Anta Diop University-Dakar, and the University of Ghana among others continuing to provide training to the bulk of students. Museums and universities will still continue to provide most of the employment for archaeologists. The hiring of African professionals in South African universities such as Pretoria and Cape Town in recent years bodes well for attracting local black South African students to pursue academic careers in a discipline until recently seen as a preserve of western intellectuals (Ndukuyakhe 2009; Schmidt 2009). To address the problem of funding, museums and universities will need to explore the possibilities of developing cultural resource management (CRM) programmes within archaeology departments. CRM will become involved in development-funded programmes that will enhance the mapping of nations' archaeological heritage. With the rare exception of southern Africa, there are almost no CRM programmes in African countries today. Many development initiatives do not request CRM surveys. And in situations when it is requested, expertise has often been sought outside Africa, for large-scale projects like pipelines and road and rail construction (see Arazi and Thiaw, Ch. 16 above).

With regard to exhibitions, emphasis ought to be placed on developing a narrative that embraces the local, regional, and global. Exhibition developers must continue to think across communities while simultaneously engaging them. The 'Zebra on Wheels' example drawn from Botswana illustrates the potential success of reaching out to rural communities and why this should be emulated in other countries. It has also demonstrated that funding across the board should be the hallmark of doing business in museums. Both national and regional museums contribute to larger national questions of identity and heritage.

Efforts to conserve the archaeological heritage in African countries will continue to be hamstrung by the still underdeveloped infrastructure, especially in the remote regions. Larger national museums do have a presence in the capital cities, for example in Nairobi, Cape Town, Johannesburg, Cairo, and Dakar, but regional and rural museums still remain woefully underfunded and understaffed. Without addressing this imbalance, monitoring and protection of archaeological sites will continue to be weak. The good news is that more African nations have ratified the UNESCO 1970 Convention. They must now take the next step to promulgate and pass antiquities laws that criminalize the destruction of archaeological sites, including illegal excavation and export of the archaeological artefacts and ecofacts (Shaw 1986; Inskeep 1993; Schmidt and McIntosh 1996; Atwood 2004; Kusimba and Agbaje-Williams 2006). Efforts by PMDA, CHDA, and the École du Patrimoine Africaine (EPA) have increased awareness of this problem, and this bodes well for the future of the continent's archaeological heritage. As Lavine and Karp (1990) correctly intimated two decades ago, museums are historically and socially located and, as such, inevitably bear the imprint of social relations beyond their walls and beyond the present. Yet museums are never *just* spaces for the playing out of wider social relationships: a museum is a process as well as a structure, a creative agency as well as a 'contested terrain'. Since museums have a formulative as well as a reflective role in social relations, they have a major role to play in shaping the future political and cultural landscape of the new Africa. Archaeology and archaeologists have, and will continue to have, a major role in shaping that terrain.

REFERENCES

ARDOUIN, C. D. (2000). Introduction. In Ardouin and Arinze (2000: 1–2).

—— and ARINZE, E. (eds) (2000). *Museums and History in West Africa*. Oxford: James Currey.

ATWOOD, R. (2004). *Stealing History: Tomb Raiders, Smugglers, and the Looting of the Ancient World*. New York: St. Martins Press.

CANNIZZO, J. (1989). *Into the Heart of Africa*. Toronto: Royal Ontario Museum.

CLARK, J. D. (1990). The development of archaeology in East Africa. In P. Robertshaw (ed.), *A History of African Archaeology*. London: James Currey, 78–94.

COOMBES, A. E. (2003). *Visual Culture and Public Memory in a Democratic South Africa*. Durham, NC: Duke University Press.

DEACON, J. (1990). The development of archaeology in South Africa. In P. Robertshaw (ed.), *A History of African Archaeology*. London: James Currey, 78–94.

EDSON, G., and DEAN, D. (1996). *The Handbook for Museums*. London: Routledge.

INSKEEP, R. R. (1993). Making an honest man of Oxford: good news for Mali. *Antiquity* 66: 114.

KUSIMBA, C. M. (2009). Practicing postcolonial archaeology in eastern Africa from the United States. In Schmidt (2009: 57–76).

—— and AGBAJE-WILLIAMS, B. (2006). Trade in African antiquities. *Journal of Environment and Culture* 3: 129–38.

LAVINE, S. D., and KARP, I. (1990). Introduction: museums and multiculturalism. In I. Karp and S. D. Lavine (eds), *Exhibiting Cultures: The Poetics and Politics of Museum Display*. Washington, DC: Smithsonian Institution Press, 1–10.

LEAKEY, R. E. (1990). A centre of excellence. *Weekly Review*, 21 Sept., 32.

LIONNET, F. (2001). The mirror and the tomb: Africa, museums, and memory. *African Arts* 34: 50–55, 93.

MACDONALD, S. (2011). *A Companion to Museum Studies*. Malden: Wiley-Blackwell.

MAFEJE, A. (1991). *The Theory and Ethnography of Social Formations: The Case of the Interlacustrine Kingdoms*. Dakar: Codesria Books Series.

MORELL, V. (1995). *Ancestral Passions: The Leakey Family and the Quest for Humankind's Beginnings*. New York: Simon and Schuster.

NDUKUYAKHE, N. (2009) Decolonizing the mind-set: South African archaeology in a post-colonial, post-Apartheid era. In Schmidt (2009: 177–92).

NDORO, W. (2001). *Your Monument Our Shrine: The Preservation of Great Zimbabwe*. Uppsala: Uppsala University Press.

NICHOLAS, G. (ed.) (2010). *Being and Becoming Indigenous Archaeologists*. Walnut Creek, Calif.: Left Coast Press.

P'BITEK, O. (1971). *African Religions in Western Scholarship*. Nairobi: East African Literature Bureau.

PRÖSLER, M. (1996). Museums and globalization: representing identity and diversity in a changing world. In S. Macdonald and G. Fyfe (eds), *Theorizing Museums*. Oxford: Blackwell, 21–44.

SHAW, T. (1986). Restitution of cultural property: elements of the dossier. *Museum* 146: 46–8.

SCHMIDT, P. R. (ed.) (2009). *Postcolonial Archaeologies in Africa*. Bloomington: Indiana University Press.

—— and MCINTOSH, R. J. (eds) (1996). *Plundering Africa's Past*. Bloomington: Indiana University Press.

SMITH, C. S. (2000). Museums, artefacts and meanings. In P. Vergo (ed.), *The New Museology*. London: Reaktion Books, 6–21.

STURTEVANT, W. C. (1969). Does anthropology need museums? *Proceedings of the Biological Society of Washington* 82: 619–49.

TOMASELLI, K. T., and RAMGOBIN, M. (1988). Culture and conservation: whose interests? In I. Coetzee and G.-M. Van Der Waal (eds), *The Conservation of Culture*. Pretoria: South African Conference on the Conservation of Culture, 106–7.

WILSON, D. M. (2002). *The British Museum: A History*. London: British Museum Press.

CHAPTER 18

ARCHAEOLOGY AND EDUCATION

AMANDA ESTERHUYSEN AND PAUL LANE

INTRODUCTION

THE links between archaeology and education take many forms, ranging from the formal teaching of archaeology at primary, secondary, and tertiary levels, or as part of various categories of adult education, or the use of archaeology in teaching across the school curriculum, to informal education of members of the public through different media, or the more structured education programmes of museums which are typically aimed at school-age children. In this chapter we focus on efforts to promote more formal teaching of archaeology, especially at primary and secondary level although with some passing reference also to university teaching. Some of the approaches and challenges associated with the role of museums and other forms of public education are discussed elsewhere (Kusimba and Klehm, Ch. 17 above). However, it is worth stressing that an integrated strategy toward archaeology and education, that exploits different opportunities, develops resources and methods appropriate to different learning ages, constituencies, and contexts, and deploys the different elements so as to complement each other is likely to be the most successful. Moreover, this must begin with children, since it is in childhood that the foundations of education are laid from which a life-long engagement with archaeology and heritage is most likely to emerge.

Unfortunately, while the links between archaeology and education have long been a matter of interest in the wider discipline, only rarely have they been given the degree of attention they warrant, either by archaeologists or educationalists. In the United Kingdom, early calls for closer integration of archaeology into school curricula were made by, among others, Grahame Clark (1943) and Aileen Fox (1944). Clark (1943: 113) took the view that because of its temporal and spatial reach, its focus on humanity's evolutionary trajectory and relationship with nature, and the history and development of human society and social institutions, archaeology was ideally suited to helping people everywhere appreciate their 'inheritance as a citizen of the world' and their power to mould their own destinies. Fox, on the other hand, emphasized the range of skills that an archaeological education can impart, the training it provides in careful observation and recording, and opportunities to exercise 'the imagination and common sense' (Fox 1944: 156). She also held that the introduction of archaeology as a core subject in primary and secondary school curricula, along with greater collaboration between schools and museums in the teaching of the discipline, could have 'far-reaching and cumulative results' (Fox 1944: 157), including better preparation of those planning to take a university degree in archaeology and wider public support for the conservation of the material traces of the past.

Given the circumstances under which they were made, it might be easy to dismiss such remarks as mere wishful thinking—a necessary reaction to the blatant misuse of archaeological evidence on the part of the Nazi Party in 1930s/1940s Germany to further its own racist and anti-Semitic ideology (Arnold 1990). However, even against changing political, economic, and social conditions, as the discipline has grown and diversified several of the themes raised by Clark and Fox have continued to be reiterated. For instance, Stone (1994: 15) has noted that the case for teaching archaeology in schools is still made in terms of three criteria—the discipline's strengths in promoting 'understanding of the development and progress of the human species'; its suitability as a means to enhance analytical skills and critical judgement; and 'as a preparation for the study of archaeology at university'. Despite such apparent strengths, however, by the end of the 20th century the 'educational role of archaeology' had still not been 'accepted by those in control of teaching about the past' (Stone 1994: 17), in no small part because of an insistence that the study of the past is accomplished primarily through the analysis of documentary sources (Stone 1994: 16).

Such a text-based approach, as Stone and MacKenzie (1990) have observed, excludes consideration of the interpretation of the past through material remains or oral sources as legitimate practices; and as long as this perception persists so too will the incorporation of archaeology into mainstream school curricula be limited. On the other hand, as Stone points out, simple statements on the part of archaeologists that the kind of knowledge archaeology imparts 'will enhance contemporary, and future, society as a whole', or that the skills gained through the study of archaeology better equip pupils with more general life and work skills, in the absence of any sustained substantiation, do little to convince those in charge of setting school curricula (Stone 1994: 16). Recent developments in Europe, Australia and North America indicate much closer engagement with the need to demonstrate the educational benefits of archaeology at the tertiary level (e.g. Colley 2004; Smith 2008), and in primary and secondary education via closer collaboration between schools, museums, and the archaeological profession (e.g. Malone et al. 2000; Moe et al. 2002; Cohen et al. 2006). In Britain, for instance the Council for British Archaeology (CBA) has provided support for many years to Key Stage 3 (the first three years of secondary education) teachers wishing to include archaeology in their teaching activities (Cracknell and Corbishley 1986; Pearson 2001), as do the various national archaeology bodies such as English Heritage (Corbishley 1999). The CBA also helps to promote the single A-level (the subject-based, higher secondary school leaving qualifications in England, Wales, and Northern Ireland) course in Archaeology offered by the AQA awarding body (Corbishley and Stone 1994), and hosts a regular conference and hosts, with partners, a regular on archaeology and education.

There have been comparable developments in North America in recent decades (Black 2001). The Society for American Archaeology, for example, has developed with educators a series of lesson plans aimed at different grades for school teachers and, like the CBA, runs periodic professional development workshops for teachers. Following a major study (Bender and Smith 2000), it has also made a number of recommendations concerning ways to make archaeological teaching in the tertiary sector relevant in the 21st century. Across the border, the Canadian Archaeological Association has developed a similar 'Archaeology Canada' curriculum, which also entailed close consultation with teachers. Important though such initiatives have been, their impact on formal school curricula remains limited, however, and in many situations more energy is now invested in developing public and community archaeology education programmes than in trying to influence the educational establishment.

ARCHAEOLOGY AND EDUCATION IN AFRICA

Many of the same arguments still used in western countries to promote closer integration of archaeology into school curricula have been used in Africa (Fig. 18.1), and for almost as long. As early as 1955, for instance, Miles Burkitt proposed at the Third Congress of the Panafrican Archaeological Association (PAA) that archaeology should be included on the curricula of teachers' training colleges (Burkitt 1957). At the Seventh PAA Congress in 1971, Merrick Posnansky (1976) returned to the topic, with a more specific focus on the establishment of an archaeology degree at the University of Legon, Ghana—the first full degree programme to be taught in sub-Saharan Africa outside South Africa. The subsequent decades witnessed an expansion of university courses in archaeology throughout much of Africa (see regional overviews in Robertshaw 1990), and a corresponding increase in initiatives to embed archaeology in national curricula for primary and secondary school education, and in some cases also to promote public awareness and understanding through adult education programmes (e.g. Afigbo 1976; Okpoko 1986; Nzewunwa 1990; Adandé and Zevonou 1994; Kiyaga-Mulindwa and Segobye 1994; Mbunwe-Samba et al. 1994; Pwiti 1994).

FIG. 18.1 Pupils and staff from Baawa Primary School, Maralal District, Kenya, visiting the excavation of a Pastoral Neolithic/Pastoral Iron Age burial cairn, July 2008 (photograph, Paul Lane).

Different strategies have been followed and different problems and challenges have been encountered. One common theme, nonetheless, has been the legacy of European colonial rule and how this has shaped educational policy (e.g. Nzewunwa 1990: 195; Adandé and Zevounou 1994: 316). This has determined until quite recently the range of historical topics and themes that have been taught and examined (e.g. Kiyaga-Mulindwa and Segobye 1994: 50–51), and has discouraged engagement with 'the past' through material remains as opposed to indigenous oral histories and other informal means of learning (e.g. Nzewunwa 1990: 197; Kiyaga-Mulindwa and Segobye 1994: 46). Overcoming such legacies has been particularly acute in countries that were subject to colonial rule by more than one European power, such as Cameroon (Mbunwe-Samba et al. 1994: 326). Even where formal education systems were restructured with specific nation-building objectives in mind and with an emphasis on celebrating precolonial achievements, as in Kenya (Wandibba 1994: 353–4) and Zimbabwe (Pwiti 1994: 340–42), archaeologists have struggled to get their discipline treated as anything other than an 'adjunct of history' of no instrumental value, and irrelevant to the goals of national economic development. Likewise, recent attempts to include archaeology in school curricula through the introduction of more 'integrated' subjects such as 'social studies' (as has been attempted e.g. in Nigeria, Botswana, and Kenya) appear to have met with limited success, in no small part due to what Kiyaga-Mulindwa and Segobye (1994: 46) describe as the general 'conservatism of education and development philosophies' (see also Nzewunwa 1994: 285).

This general lack of success is surprising, given that at the tertiary level, because the teaching of archaeology is often embedded in university history departments, there is a related expectation that most graduates from these programmes will become secondary or primary schoolteachers. This was certainly a key premise behind the establishment of an archaeology degree at the University of Ghana, Legon in 1968—the first to be taught at university level in sub-Saharan Africa (Posnansky 1976: 329). It also remains one of the guiding principles underpinning archaeology degree courses in many contemporary African universities, including those in Botswana (Kiyaga-Mulindwa and Segobye 1994), Kenya (Wandibba 1994), Tanzania (LaViolette 2002), and Nigeria (Nzewunwa 1990). As a consequence, one might expect that many of the citizens of these countries would have at least a moderate awareness of the goals of archaeology, its methods, and perhaps even some of the more significant regional sites and landscapes, since these future teachers are potentially an effective way of passing on such information to school children (Nzewunwa 1990: 197). Yet, in fact, in all of these countries public awareness of archaeology remains minimal, and despite early exposure to archaeology, even the most committed graduate finds it difficult to incorporate this knowledge into the school curriculum, because of a lack of further training on how to do this (e.g. Pwiti 1994: 345; Wandibba 1994: 353), a lack of relevant resources for use in the classroom (e.g. Mbunwe-Samba et al. 1994: 329), and, particularly because of pressures to restrict their classroom activities to covering what national education boards consider to be more important essentials (e.g. Kiyaga-Mulindwa and Segobye 1994: 50). Consequently, as Mbunwe-Samba and colleagues (1994: 328) note with reference to Cameroon, 'few actually end up using their knowledge for the promotion of the subject, either in the classroom or elsewhere.'

In light of the above discussion, it is instructive to consider in more detail the one case on the continent where a more concerted effort has been made, with government backing, to fully integrate the teaching of archaeology into school curricula, and why even this has only been partially successful. The example concerns South Africa, where following the 1994 elections these initiatives were begun under the remit of what became known as 'Educational Archaeology'. This generally refers to the way in which archaeology is made available or taught to learners in primary and secondary schools. Very little research has been conducted into pedagogical strategies implemented at a university level. Nevertheless the impetus (and inertia) that gave form to Educational Archaeology in South Africa grew out of the efforts of researchers in universities and museums to produce a more archaeologically informed school-leaving public, more often than not in response to international and local political pressures.

EDUCATIONAL ARCHAEOLOGY IN SOUTH AFRICA

In 1948, when the Afrikaner National Party came to power, its policies were strongly influenced by orthodox Protestant-Calvinist principles. Fundamental to this Christian National Policy was the notion of *apartheid* or separate development. There was to be 'no mixing of languages, no mixing of cultures, no mixing of religions and no mixing of races' (SPRO-CAS 1971: 74). When the National Education Policy Act was passed for whites in 1967, the Christian character of National Education (known as Christian National Education (CNE)) was made explicit. It was 'education founded on the Bible and imprinted through religious instruction as a compulsory non-examination subject, and the spirit and manner in which all teaching and education as well as administration and organisation shall be conducted' (Malherbe 1977: 147, cited in Christie 1991: 176).

Separate education became a useful means of implementing unequal education and a way of determining the level of employment to which members of different race groups could aspire. But while CNE enforced separate education and different subject matter at different schools, all pupils were taught the same history syllabi. In schools, presentations of the past were used in a calculated manner to foster racial, ethnic or cultural difference and to justify white minority dominance. Children were force-fed 'white superiority' and came to regard anything 'African' as technologically and ideologically primitive. The role of black, 'coloured', and Asian South Africans in the country's past was systematically distorted, trivialized, or erased. The psychological impact of this was devastating, and its impact on the discipline of archaeology was, and continues to be, significant. On the one hand, white Nationalists had no interest in the depth and complexity of African prehistory, giving rise to, among other things, a 'myth of an empty land' (Marks 1980). On the other hand, black intellectuals came to regard the work of the predominantly white archaeological fraternity with suspicion. Many felt that archaeologists were out to prove that black people were primitive, or found it distasteful that African history found prominence and acceptance through the work of white intellectuals trained in a western paradigm. In 2006 the controversial 'Native Club' was launched in South Africa to develop a platform for African intellectuals. Strongly supported by President Mbeki's cabinet, the group aimed to decolonize the South African mindset and establish new and critical insights through indigenous knowledge systems (Ndlovu-Gatsheni 2007). While this foregrounded debate around Eurocentricism, Africanism, and Nativism (both white and black), these different and often distinct frames of reference continue to bedevil and weaken the heritage sector.

The discipline of archaeology took shape in South Africa during the first decades of the 20th century (Deacon 1990), but it was not until the 1960s and 1970s that it truly began to flourish, with many universities and museums establishing departments and supporting archaeological studies. However, unlike the preceding decades, when archaeologists' work had often suited the ideals of the Afrikaner Nationalist government, advances in science and the growing body of archaeological evidence and theory increasingly came into conflict with the official history constructed and disseminated by the government, especially as the study of the Iron Age Farming Communities rose in prominence (Hall 1990). For this reason information about archaeology or its findings was excluded from mainstream school curricula.

During the 1980s there was a worldwide re-emergence of radical history inspired mainly by the Marxist revisionist historiography of the time. In South Africa this revival took place at the more progressive academic institutions and within anti-apartheid social movements (Callinicos 1986). This alternative movement focused for the most part on capturing the history of the working class and oral histories. Historians and archaeologists alike began to draw attention to and expose the fallacy of the myths perpetuated in the school history curriculum. In particular, they criticized the Eurocentric bias in state school curricula and the role that it played in perpetuating racist myths about indigenous people (see e.g. Marks 1980, 1981; Smith 1983; Mason 1986; Mazel and Stewart 1987), dispelled the myth that Bantu-speaking people had arrived at much the same time as the whites, and similarly dispatched the misapprehension that the delineation of the 'tribal' homelands was based on the historical position of 'tribes' documented by whites on their arrival (Marks 1980). Researchers also cast a critical eye over museum displays and spoke out about how such displays represented and reinforced the ideology of the ruling class (Wright and Mazel 1987). A number of teachers, mostly in private institutions, also began to collaborate with archaeologists and to experiment with alternative histories in the classroom. In 1987, Revil Mason (1987) produced an educational book, *Origins of African People of the Johannesburg Area*, but these efforts gained little purchase in government schools.

By the early 1990s it was clear that the decades of white minority rule were coming to an end and that the South African school system would undergo radical change. Historians anticipated the need for reform and began to debate the content of the new history curricula. It was widely accepted that there was a need to include precolonial history; however, historians felt that they were best placed to write these sections because they could interpret and explain the otherwise opaque archaeological data. Archaeologists were spurred on by this to

FIG. 18.2 Education programmes allow learners to participate in excavations (photograph, Amanda Esterhuysen).

make their analyses accessible to the general public, and to engage with the curriculum reform process. University and museum archaeology departments began to offer school outreach programmes (Fig. 18.2), and a number of archaeologists began to write popular materials for newspapers and magazines.

POST-1994 DEVELOPMENTS IN SOUTH AFRICA

Following the 1994 elections and the victory of the African National Congress (ANC), a new National Qualification Framework (NQF) was launched in 1995. This introduced an Outcomes Based (OBE) system of life-long learning. The OBE policy was borrowed quite liberally, and some would argue uncritically, from Australia, Canada, and England. The global influence in education was also evident in the integration of general education and vocational training. The new curriculum had a strong vocational slant that underwrote the need for education to focus on and support economic growth (Chisholm 1997). The NQF eliminated the traditional divisions between 'mental' and 'manual' labour (Chisholm 1997: 59) so that people with little or no formal education could be assessed and accredited, and linked into the education framework.

The NQF's dual focus created two separate opportunities for archaeology to enter the education system: first, through formal schooling, and secondly through the informal education sector, which allowed people to train on the job or to receive accreditation for prior experience. Between 2002 and 2004, a group of professionals coordinated by Janette Deacon identified and registered core and elective unit standards to provide people with archaeological experience the opportunity to obtain a grade 11 and 12 equivalent qualification. Thus, field assistants and fossil preparators with no schooling could receive certification and recognition for their abilities and expertise. These unit standards also became incorporated into 'tourist guide' and other heritage-related courses.

The ANC policy framework also called for a radical and hasty reconstruction of school curricula. In 1995 the new government introduced its new schools education plan. Syllabi for the junior levels were to be written first, and implementation of the junior curriculum would begin while the senior phase was being formulated. All phases were to be in operation by 2005; this curriculum became known as Curriculum-2005 (C2005).

In August 1995 Aron Mazel, the then chair of the South African Archaeological Association (now the Association of Southern African Professional Archaeologists, ASAPA), spearheaded an initiative to produce a supplementary document to guide and inform curriculum developers. The intention was to provide a set of subject matters that teachers could use to develop an understanding of archaeological methods and an appreciation of the antiquity of human endeavour in South Africa (Fig. 18.3). This document was presented to members of parliament, and discussed with the then deputy director of curriculum development. In 1996, the University of the Witwatersrand archaeology department created a part-time post for an educational archaeologist (Esterhuysen), who launched a research project to investigate the potential for, and impact of, teaching evolution and archaeology in the classroom. By 1998 archaeologists were identified as a critical interest group, and were invited to participate in the establishment of the Human and Social Sciences (HSS) Learning Area Committee (LAC) (Esterhuysen 1999). Curriculum developers had decided that from Grade 1–10 history, geography and civics would be collapsed together under the rubric of the HSS.

FIG. 18.3 One of the many posters distributed by the South African government in celebration of the Cradle of Humankind World Heritage Site (photograph, Amanda Esterhuysen).

Research carried out in classrooms and at teacher workshops exposed how the capitalist economy in South Africa had produced a 'core' urban and a 'peripheral' rural and informal economic sector. Schools within the 'core' were predominantly multiracial ex-white schools with adequate facilities, while schools at the periphery were completely under-resourced. The 'core' also retained highly skilled teachers, while poorly trained teachers, who were insecure about their own knowledge base and found the notion of outcomes-based teaching intimidating, occupied the periphery (Chisholm 1997). The response to workshops about archaeology and evolution was consequently very varied. In urban areas most children had heard about dinosaurs and had some frame of reference to begin to comprehend deep time and evolution, while in some rural areas neither teacher nor learner had ever heard of dinosaurs. Additionally, introducing dinosaurs or extinct creatures in these situations often only served to confuse matters further. Many confused them with mythical creatures that their elders had told them came from the sea and caused cyclones. Language too was (and continues to be) a stumbling block. Concepts would often get mistranslated: for example, on one occasion the earth's 'magnetic field' was interpreted as a 'mealie (maize) field'. Generally, rural learners had never heard of archaeologists or about archaeological research. It was clear that a vast range and scope of materials would be required to address this deficit. Textbooks alone could not sustain the in-depth analysis required to provide an adequate understanding of the precolonial past.

Urban children and teachers responded well to the application of archaeology in the classroom. Studies showed that archaeological enquiry was well suited to achieving the end of outcomes-based curricula (Esterhuysen 1999). Students developed skills of observation, inference, and logical argument. Archaeological study provided an excellent way of introducing children to the nature of evidence, helping to underscore the fact that not all things preserve, that multiple explanations may exist, and interpretations may be biased. Teachers who introduced archaeology found that it was an innovative way of presenting history. Importantly, it proved an effective means through which teachers could introduce and dispel issues of race, equip learners with tools to challenge and question negative images of an African past, and acquaint pupils with sections of history unique to South Africa (Esterhuysen and Smith 1998; Esterhuysen 2000).

Despite the positive outcome of the various studies, archaeology was disappointingly reduced to one statement in the Grade 1–10 Human and Social Sciences curriculum: 'precolonial—from earliest hominids'. Curriculum-2005 had resorted to crude periodization. The syllabus was divided into sociopolitical categories: precolonial, colonial, postcolonial, apartheid, and post-apartheid. In many ways C2005 did not deviate much from old curricula and in effect reinforced the old *apartheid* stereotypes because the notion of progress was still implicit in the categories; precolonial societies were 'less developed' than 'colonial societies'. Furthermore, by compressing three million years of time into one category, the precolonial past was reduced to a blur of hominids, hunter-gatherers, and African farmers evidenced only by large-scale technological shifts. Smaller-scale social dynamics, ideas, and interactions were absent (Esterhuysen 1999: 87). It became clear that archaeologists were going to have to employ more creative measures to introduce archaeology to learners in the classroom.

Martin Hall (Multimedia Education Group, University of Cape Town) and students of John Parkington (University of Cape Town Archaeology Department) began to experiment with computer-mediated education (CME) as a means of introducing archaeology into the classroom. In a collaborative Rock Art Information Exchange Project organized by archaeologists at the Universities of Cape Town and the Witwatersrand, schools in Cape Town were linked up with schools in Johannesburg. Learners completed modules about rock art on computer and then exchanged key pieces of information via e-mail with each other (Esterhuysen 2002; Loopuyt 2002). Museums and universities, often in collaboration, obtained funding to develop community-run museums, and several projects were undertaken to encourage children from all levels of society—from private schools to street children—to visit and enjoy sites. Some of these community-based projects include the Living Landscape Project in Clanwilliam (Western Cape Province) (http://www.clip.uct.ac.za) and the Wildebeest Kuil Rock Art Centre in Kimberley (Northern Cape Province) (http:/www.wildebeestkuil.itgo.com/).

Recent developments in South Africa

Between 1999 and 2005, a number of different events conspired to increase the profile of archaeology in schools in South Africa. First, a range of different archaeological sites was granted World Heritage status. These sites were individually fêted by the media and celebrated by the government, which procured educational materials for schools, libraries, and community centres. Secondly, C2005 began to falter.

By 2000, for example, it was becoming increasingly clear that the curriculum was not particularly well suited to schools in South Africa, especially those in rural areas where sociopolitical traditions rallied against encouraging individuality in learners, and large class sizes coupled with poor resources negated learner-centred education (Jansen 2009: 240). OBE reinforced rather than altered educational inequalities. Partially in response to this, the then Minister of Education, Kadar Asmal, unilaterally appointed a review committee. The manner in which this was carried out caused major ructions within the ANC, whose members saw it as undermining the legacy of the first post-apartheid minister of education and possibly an attempt to return to the past (Chisholm 2005: 88). However, although some recommendations were rejected outright, in the end the cabinet accepted the report, which paved the way for a more consultative process of curriculum review. The product of this assessment was the Revised National Curriculum Statement (RNCS). In this version, learning areas were cut and the global epistemologies that underpinned the NQF were toned down. However, the ANC was not yet ready to admit complete defeat and OBE was retained. Poorly trained and resourced teachers were to receive retraining.

One of the many recommendations made by the review was that *history* should be reintroduced as a subject. Historians took this as lifeline because history's loss of subject status had begun to affect the numbers of students taking history at university level (Sieborger 2000: 4). At much the same time, a report by a working group, titled 'Values, Education and Democracy', called for the Minister of Education to establish a panel of historians and archaeologists to advise the Minister on how to strengthen the teaching of these subjects in South African schools. This report suggested that amongst other things the History and Archaeology Panel should review the teaching of evolution in schools, the state of teacher training, and the quality of support materials (Report of the History and Archaeology Panel 2002). A panel of eleven people was appointed. The panel was heavily biased towards historians and only one archaeologist was appointed (Esterhuysen), which inevitably led to partiality in approach and content. For example, the historians were deeply perturbed about the request to include evolution in the report because they felt that it could further damage the image of an already beleaguered subject. They decided that evolution should be dealt with by other more 'relevant' scientific disciplines (Report of the History and Archaeology Panel

2002: 3). Despite this restricted input, archaeology as a discipline entered the discourse of mainstream education.

The report that was delivered in 2000 (Fig. 18.4) argued that history, along with archaeology, offered a key learning area for understanding the nature and manifestation of South Africa's different cultures and identities. It further stressed the need for the country, with its fractured national memory, to develop a historical memory that invokes pride, humanity, and achievement. Following on from this report, a ministerial committee was appointed to facilitate the development of materials and promote the teaching of history in the country. In 2001, a committee of several historians, an archaeologist, and a journalist was appointed by the Minister to advise members of the South African History Project, an initiative based in the National Department of Education (Race and Values Directorate). The History Project conducted a number of teacher workshops and helped to coordinate the writing and distribution of resource materials, which ironically included six posters on evolution and the Cradle of Humankind. The ministerial committee also commented and advised on the content of the history syllabi for senior phases. By 2005 the History Project had run its course, and with the installation of a new Education Minister, history lost its champion.

In 2006, global educational strategies and ideas began to take hold in South African Universities. The market-oriented discourse placed an emphasis on measurable outputs. Unfortunately, outreach projects, although encouraged, did not find the same favour as research publication and student throughput. As a result many, if not all, of the universities' educational archaeology and heritage management initiatives ended, or came under heavy censure for not producing publishable research.

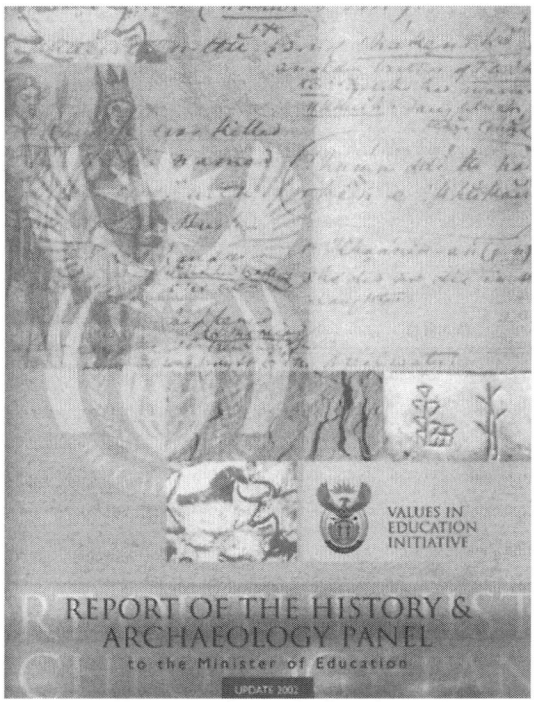

FIG. 18.4 Report of South Africa's history/archaeology working group (photograph, Amanda Esterhuysen).

Summary and conclusion

This chapter on educational archaeology thus ends, with specific reference to South Africa, at a low point in Educational Archaeology, but also at the point that the South African Ministry of Education has decided to throw in the towel on OBE and announce its demise (July 2010). Due to the poor pass rates in rural areas and falling performance of learners at university, the ANC was forced to admit that OBE was inappropriate, cumbersome, complicated, and administratively burdensome. There is nonetheless an expectation that the government will shortly unveil a comprehensive new action plan aimed 'towards the realization of schooling' by 2025. In the interim, schools will return to an education system that has subjects, marks, and symbols—all markers of a traditional, modernist epistemology. It now remains to be seen whether history will become another collection of 'correct nationalist facts' and whether archaeology will feature in a meaningful way. Either way, this new development will no doubt stimulate a new chapter in Educational Archaeology.

On a wider, more continental scale, archaeology departments and divisions at African universities need to include educational archaeologists on their staff so as to better link the two disciplines, provide a critical approach to the way in which archaeology is taught at university level, and determine how it is being implemented at school level—especially by graduates from their own programmes, many of whom go on to train as schoolteachers but are poorly empowered to communicate their knowledge and understanding of the subject to their pupils. One emerging opportunity which might facilitate this is to make use of social media technologies—while not as widespread as in western countries, take-up is growing rapidly. Further research on these possibilities, and also on the role of social media in developing broad-based communities of support and interest, would be particularly beneficial. Additionally, archaeologists need to encourage trained educationists to investigate how archaeology can best be taught in schools, and to establish also whether archaeologists should be developing stronger links with the physical sciences (given the general push in schools to develop the sciences) in the same way as archaeologists have tried to do with history and social studies.

References

ADANDÉ, A. B. A., and ZEVENOU, I. (1994). Education and heritage: an example of new work in the schools of Bénin. In Stone and Molyneaux (1994: 315–25).

AFIGBO, A. E. (1976). History, archaeology and schools in Nigeria. *West African Journal of Education* 20: 407–17.

ARNOLD, B. (1990). The past as propaganda: totalitarian archaeology in Nazi Germany. *Antiquity* 64: 464–78.

BENDER, S. J., and SMITH, G. S. (eds) (2000). *Teaching Archaeology in the Twenty-First Century*. Washington, DC: Society for American Archaeology.

BLACK, M. S. (2001). Maturing gracefully? Curriculum standards for history and archaeology. *Social Studies* 92: 103–8.

BURKITT, M. (1957). Archaeology and education. In J. D. Clark (ed.), *The Third Pan-African Congress on Prehistory, Livingstone 1955*. London: Chatto & Windus, 433–40.

CALLINICOS, L. (1986). The people's past: towards transforming the present. *Critical Arts* 4(2): 21–39.

CHISHOLM, L. (1997). The restructuring of South African education and training in comparative context. In P. Kallaway, G. Kruss, A. Fataar, and G. Donn (eds), *Education After Apartheid: South African Education in Transition*. Cape Town: University of Cape Town Press, 50–67.

—— (2005). The politics of curriculum review and revision in South Africa in regional context. *Compare* 35: 79–100.

CHRISTIE, P. (1991). *The Right to Learn: The Struggle for Education in South Africa*. Johannesburg: SachedTrust/Ravan Press.

CLARK, J. G. D. (1943). Education and the study of Man. *Antiquity* 17: 113–21.

COHEN, C., MARQUET, J.-C., and PATHY-BARKER, C. (eds) (2006). *L'Archéologie et l'Éducation/ Archaeology and Education*. Oxford: Archaeopress.

COLLEY, J. (2004). University-based archaeology teaching and learning and professionalism in Australia. *World Archaeology* 36: 189–202.

CORBISHLEY, M. (ed.) (1999). *Primary History: Using the Evidence of the Historic Environment*. London: English Heritage.

—— and STONE, P. G. (1994). The teaching of the past in formal school curricula in England. In Stone and Molyneaux (1994: 383–94).

CRACKNELL, S., and CORBISHLEY, M. (eds) (1986). *Presenting Archaeology to Young People*. York: Council for British Archaeology.

DEACON, J. (1990). Weaving the fabric of Stone Age research in southern Africa. In Robertshaw (1990: 39–58).

ESTERHUYSEN, A. B. (1999). Archaeology, time and space and the human and social sciences: curriculum 2005. *Perspectives in Education* 18: 83–9.

—— (2000). The birth of educational archaeology in South Africa. *Antiquity* 74: 159–65.

—— (2002). Virtually educated. In K. Asmal and W. James (eds), *Spirit of the Nation*. Cape Town: New Africa Education, 53–6.

—— and SMITH, J. M. (1998). Evolution: 'the forbidden word'? *South African Archaeological Bulletin* 53: 135–7.

FOX, A. (1944). The place of archaeology in British education. *Antiquity* 18: 153–7.

HALL, M. (1990). 'Hidden history': Iron Age archaeology in southern Africa. In Robertshaw (1990: 59–77).

JANSEN, J. (2009). Big change question: can and should school change in the developing world be guided by research from the developed world? *Journal of Educational Change* 10: 239–43.

KIYAGA-MULINDWA, D., and SEGOBYE, A. K. (1994). Archaeology and education in Botswana. In Stone and Molyneaux (1994: 46–60).

LAVIOLETTE, A. (2002). Encountering archaeology in Tanzania: education, development, and dialogue at the University of Dar es Salaam. *Anthropological Quarterly* 75: 355–74.

LOOPUYT, M. (2002). Rock Art Information Exchange Project, Unpublished Honours Project, University of Cape Town.

MALONE, C., STONE, P., and BAXTER, M. (2000). Special section: education in archaeology. *Antiquity* 74: 122–6.

MARKS, S. (1980). South Africa: 'the myth of the empty land'. *History Today* 30: 8–12.

—— (1981). 'Bold, thievish, and not to be trusted': racial stereotypes in South Africa in historical perspective. *History Today* 31: 15–21.

MASON, R. (1986). *Origins of Black People of Johannesburg and the Southern Western Central Transvaal AD 350–1880*. Johannesburg: Archaeological Research Unit, University of the Witwatersrand.

MASON, R. (1987). *Origins of the African People of the Johannesburg Area*. Johannesburg: Skotaville.

MAZEL, A. D., and STEWART, P. M. (1987). Meddling with the mind: the treatment of San hunter-gatherers and the origin of South Africa's black population in recent South African school history textbooks. *South African Archaeological Bulletin* 42: 166–70.

MBUNWE-SAMBA, P., NIBA, N. L., and AKENJI, N. I. (1994). Archaeology in the schools and museums of Cameroon. In Stone and Molyneaux (1994: 326–37).

MOE, J. M., COLEMAN, C., FINK, K., and KREJS, K. (2002). Archaeology, ethics, and character: using our cultural heritage to teach citizenship. *Social Studies* 93: 109–12.

NDLOVU-GATSHENI, S. J. (2007). *Tracking the Historical Roots of Post-Apartheid Citizenship Problems in South Africa*. Leiden: African Studies Centre.

NZEWUNWA, N. (1990). Cultural education in West Africa: archaeological perspectives. In P. Gathercole and D. Lowenthal (eds), *The Politics of the Past*. London: Unwin Hyman, 189–202.

—— (1994). The Nigerian teacher and museum culture. In Stone and Molyneaux (1994: 283–9).

OKPOKO, A. I. (1986). Archaeology education in Nigeria. *West African Journal of Archaeology* 16: 147–53.

PEARSON, V. (ed). (2001). *Teaching the Past: A Practical Guide for Archaeologists*. York: Council for British Archaeology.

POSNANSKY, M. (1976). Archaeology as a university discipline: Ghana, 1967–71. In B. Abebe, N. Chavaillon, and J. E. G. Sutton (eds), *Proceedings of the Seventh Panafrican Congress of Prehistory and Quaternary Studies, 1971, Addis Ababa*. Addis Ababa: Ministry of Culture, 329–31.

PWITI, G. (1994). Prehistory, archaeology and education in Zimbabwe. In Stone and Molyneaux (1994: 338–47).

REPORT OF THE HISTORY AND ARCHAEOLOGY PANEL TO THE MINISTER OF EDUCATION (2002) (update). Pretoria: Values in Education Initiative, Ministry of Education.

ROBERTSHAW, P. T. (ed.) (1990). *A History of African Archaeology*. London: James Currey.

SIEBORGER, R. (2000). History and the emerging nation: the South African experience. *International Journal of Historical Learning, Teaching and Research* 1: 39–48.

SMITH, A. B. (1983). The Hotnot syndrome: myth-making in South African school textbooks. *Social Dynamics* 9: 37–49.

SMITH, G. S. (2008) Teaching and learning archaeology: skills, knowledge and abilities for the twenty-first century. *Research in Archaeological Education Journal* 1: 6–14.

SPRO-CAS (1971). *Education Beyond Apartheid: Report of the Education Commission on Christianity in Apartheid Society*. Johannesburg: Christian Institute of South Africa.

STONE, P. G. (1994). Introduction: a framework for discussion. In Stone and Molyneaux (1994: 15–28).

—— and MACKENZIE, B. L. (1990). Introduction: the concept of the excluded past. In P. G. Stone and B. Molyneaux (eds), *The Excluded Past: Archaeology in Education*. London: Unwin Hyman, 1–11.

—— and MOLYNEAUX, B. (eds) (1994). *The Presented Past: Heritage, Museums and Education*. London: Routledge.

WANDIBBA, S. (1994). Archaeology and education in Kenya: the present and the future. In Stone and Molyneaux (1994: 349–58).

WRIGHT, J. B., and MAZEL, A. D. (1987). Bastions of ideology: the depiction of precolonial history in the museums of Natal and KwaZulu. *South African Museums Association Bulletin* 17: 301–10.

CHAPTER 19

POLITICS, IDEOLOGY, AND INDIGENOUS PERSPECTIVES

JOHN GIBLIN

INTRODUCTION

SINCE its inception, African archaeology has been influenced and harnessed by various political ideologies. From European colonialism, when at times archaeological narratives reproduced racist colonial dogma, to African nationalism and the celebration of an African past, African archaeology has been used for ideological legitimation. More recently, archaeologists working in Africa have reflected on the political nature of the discipline. They have identified the inherent colonialism of previous archaeologies and now seek to undertake postcolonial ones that have contemporary relevance for the societies in which they work. This includes the identification and incorporation of indigenous knowledge systems—something that is, in turn, leading to new indigenous archaeological drivers.

African archaeology thus continues to exist in overtly political contexts. Yet archaeological interpretation is not simply dictated by political biases. It may also be influenced by methodological, logistical, and theoretical developments, as well as by the availability and nature of archaeological data (Trigger 1990). However, ignorance of political influences in, and political use of, archaeology neglects the discipline's subjectivity and agency beyond the academy. Thus, while this chapter describes political trends in African archaeology, it recognizes that its history is also the product of non-political factors.

COLONIAL ORIGINS OF AFRICAN ARCHAEOLOGY

Isolated examples of archaeological research in Africa exist from the 18th century (Trigger 2006: 195). However, the appearance of archaeology as a discipline, albeit one practised by amateurs, is typically traced to the arrival of European colonialism (Robertshaw 1990a; Shepherd 2002; Lane 2011). In late 19th-century Europe, racial unilinear cultural evolution, which arranged cultures in stages from simplest to most complex, with industrial societies at the top and 'savagery at the bottom', became the dominant anthropological paradigm (Holl 1990: 299). Earlier evolutionary approaches promoted the essential equality of all human cultures and their inherent potential for change and development. However, due to a growing sense of European nationalism, in the later model cultural characteristics became unchangeable biological differences, with the simplest cultures doomed to racial inferiority (Trigger 2006: 173–4). Thus, colonial action by superior races was imperative if less culturally evolved peoples of the world were to be saved from cultural oblivion. Nowhere was this more pronounced than in Africa, where the explicit colonial mission was to bring civilization to the otherwise culturally condemned and 'backward' African masses (Holl 1990: 297).

Because it was believed that the ethnographic record preserved living examples of the various stages of man, archaeology could explain little new about humanity. Instead it became an important tool through which unilinear cultural evolution could be demonstrated to have occurred (Trigger 2006: 208). For example, African hunter-gatherers were identified as unevolved survivors from the Palaeolithic era (Robertshaw 1990b: 4).

The political bias of the first practitioners has been used as an explanation for the colonial nature of early African archaeologies (e.g. Trigger 1990). Amateur enthusiasts were typically employed in other professions attached to the colonial mission and thus had a vested interest in the promotion of colonial ideologies (de Barros 1990: 158; Holl 1990: 297–8; Robertshaw 1990b: 4; Shepherd 2002: 193). For example, Mrs Boutakoff (1937), the wife of a geological prospector, published some of the first archaeological finds from Rwanda, while E. J. Wayland (1934), himself a geologist, conducted some of the first archaeological research in Uganda. However, 'colonial archaeologies' (*sensu* Trigger 1984, 1990) persisted well after the arrival of professional archaeologists in the 1920s (Holl 1990: 298), and even beyond the end of colonialism into the late 20th century. The first African archaeologies, thus, were colonial not simply because Europeans practised the discipline, but also because African archaeology was built on similar ideological foundations.

In this manner colonial ideology shaped early archaeological research trajectories. Amateur and professional archaeologists alike focused their attentions on Palaeolithic studies, believing the recent past to be one of 'cultural isolation, stagnation, and general degeneracy' (Robertshaw 1990b: 4). Consequently, the archaeologies produced reinforced the view that nothing of any significance had occurred in Africa until the arrival of Europeans. Archaeology thereby contributed toward the denial of an African past (Robertshaw 1990b: 4) and 'provided a powerful legitimation for the colonial project itself' (Shepherd 2002: 194).

Implicit colonial-era biases

As archaeology developed in Africa, culture-historical diffusionism, which suggested that all cultural similarities were the product of cultural connections resulting from migration and diffusion, became the dominant archaeological paradigm in Europe (Trigger 1990: 311). Within Africa, diffusionism supported unilinear cultural evolution, whilst also providing an explanation for the presence of 'unexpected' cultural accomplishments (Holl 1990: 300). It suggested that the Sahara was a cultural barrier that allowed 'higher' cultures from the north to penetrate south, but prevented 'lower' cultures from the south from movement north (Deacon 1990: 46). This denied Africans the potential for independent invention or cultural development without European or Asian influence (de Barros 1990: 160). Although diffusionism encouraged archaeologists to investigate post-Palaeolithic periods, in eastern and southern Africa 'this was largely intended to demonstrate that pastoral groups were descended from more civilised peoples to the north' (Robertshaw 1990c: 84), or, in West Africa, to prove that historical empires were Arabic or Jewish in origin (de Barros 1990: 162, 164; Holl 1990: 300).

Seligman's (1930) Hamitic Hypothesis exemplified colonial diffusionist arguments by 'explaining' how every African cultural accomplishment was the result of a migration of prehistoric Hamitic, Caucasoid colonists from Egypt and the Middle East. This model, and others like it, appropriated all cultural accomplishments from Africa. Consequently, Maasai pastoralists became wandering Jews, Saharan and Sahelian settlements became Negro, Hamite, or Berber based on lithics or rock art, Maghrebi lithic traditions were given European antecedents, and Egyptian influence was identified in West African stone ruins and lithic industries, while ancient Greeks became the colonizers of Ife, southern African rock art, Asian or European, and metallurgy in sub-Saharan Africa Arabian, and Swahili coastal states and monuments in the east African interior the products of a northeastern Azanian civilization (Robertshaw 1990a).

Trigger (1990: 312) defends the use of diffusionism in early African archaeologies as an ethnographic theory applied by amateurs that was produced in the absence of an archaeological or historical record. However, this position cannot be maintained past the early 20th century, as the materials and expertise available to archaeologists expanded. Diffusionist explanations in African archaeology nevertheless persisted well into the later 20th century. One reason for this is that diffusionism was also a common explanation of cultural change in Europe at this time. Indeed, extreme, early examples such as Smith and Perry's Hyper-Diffusionism (Daniel 1962) denied invention not only to Africans south of the Sahara but to all humanity in the continent outside the Nile Valley (Robertshaw 1990c: 84). Furthermore, in the absence of an African cultural chronology (and particularly before the widespread availability of radiocarbon dating), the attempted location of Africa within an international framework is understandable.

However, diffusionism was more pronounced in Africa than it was in Europe (Holl 1990) because, it is suggested, it benefited colonialism. Diffusionism provided colonial precedents by constructing a past in which positive change for 'backward' Africans only occurred through contact with external civilizing forces (de Barros 1990: 160; Robertshaw 1990c: 84). Thus, diffusionist explanations in African archaeology helped legitimize the colonial mission: they were not simply academic products of their time but also products of covert political biases.

OVERT COLONIAL-ERA BIASES

Great Zimbabwe

Early interpretations of Great Zimbabwe helped legitimize white settler ideology by suggesting that non-Africans, such as the Queen of Sheba, King Solomon, or the Phoenicians, were its builders (Hall 1990: 61). It was not until twenty years later that this was seriously challenged by Caton-Thompson (1931), who presented extensive stratigraphic evidence to disprove Great Zimbabwe's external origins. However, she did not escape the pervading colonial ideology and, while meticulous in her fieldwork and clear about the stratigraphic evidence (Fontein 2006: 13), nevertheless suggested that Great Zimbabwe was 'the product of an infantile mind' (Caton-Thompson 1931: 103). Perhaps not surprisingly, the persistence of white settler ideologies and the lack of an African political voice in the then Rhodesia prevented until much later the development of a new agenda, one concerned with promoting African cultural accomplishments. Consequently, within white-ruled Rhodesia, Great Zimbabwe continued to be presented to the public as an exotic structure, unable therefore to question the legitimacy of the prevailing political system, until Zimbabwe achieved independence in 1980 (Hall 1990: 77; Shepherd 2002: 196; Fontein 2006: 8, 10).

Apartheid

Marks (1980) described how the 'myth of an empty land' underpinned the ideology of apartheid in post-1948 South Africa. This legend described how in the 17th century 'barbaric, black hordes' swept into the region at the same time that white settlers moved north from the Cape (Hall 1990: 65). Archaeology was well placed to challenge this fanciful construction and undermine apartheid by demonstrating that the country had, in fact, been occupied by African farmers, let alone herders or hunter-gatherers, well before the arrival of any Europeans (Marks 1980; Hall 1990: 72; Trigger 1990: 316). However, this opportunity was rarely realized.

One reason was that following the election victory of the National Party in 1948 and the imposition of apartheid, archaeology lost government support because of its potential to challenge the state's version of history (Deacon 1990: 48; Hall 1990: 76; Shepherd 2002: 197). Even when archaeology was expanded as a university and museum discipline from the 1960s as part of official efforts to create a feeling of academic normality (Hall 1990: 68; Shepherd 2002: 198; Lucas 2006: 56), many South African archaeologists, however much they despised the regime, typically avoided conflict by investigating less controversial periods or retreating into an inaccessible technical world (Hall 1990: 73, 75). Indeed, Trigger (1990: 317) suggests that they bought 'government support and freedom to carry out research at the cost of maintaining political neutrality and apparent irrelevance to social issues'. In their defence, however, Martin Hall explains that even when archaeologists challenged the apartheid state the government were not interested in academic debates (Lucas 2006: 56). Furthermore, as all school texts were government-controlled there was no scope for altering their content, whilst the presence of white archaeologists in non-white areas and schools was illegal before 1990. Unfortunately, however, the retreat into scientific obscurity led to the exclusion of the very groups that archaeology might have empowered, such as the Black Consciousness movement, which instead resorted to 'an abstract, utopian vision of the pre-colonial past' (Hall 1990: 73).

The failure to challenge apartheid by South African archaeologists was not confined to South Africa and the immediate pressures of the apartheid government. At the Southern African Association of Archaeologists in Gaborone, Botswana, in 1983, the participants, mostly South African, refused to condemn apartheid, leading to the resignation of delegates from Mozambique and Zimbabwe (Holl 1990; Shepherd 2002). Indeed, the most famous clash between archaeology and apartheid occurred outside Africa in 1986, when South

African archaeologists were 'disinvited' from the first World Archaeological Congress (WAC) (Shepherd 2002: 201). The organizers' stance was intended to prevent archaeologists from other African nations boycotting the congress and to protest against apartheid. Consequently, however, over 400 academics boycotted the congress in protest at its perceived politicization, political discrimination, and the silencing of fellow academics (see Tobias 1985). The divisions created by the events preceding the first WAC were not formally closed until 1999, when the fourth such conference was held in Cape Town.

In summary, the political power of the apartheid state thus led to the self-obscuration of a discipline well placed to challenge it—something that allowed political groups from both sides to fill the interpretive vacuum.

Pan-Africanism, Negritude, and Black Consciousness

The reaction against European colonialism in Africa ultimately climaxed with the achievement of independence from the mid-20th century onwards. However, the intellectual and political movements that led to these events began much earlier, and enjoyed a shared aim to reappropriate African precolonial cultural accomplishments.

Pan-Africanism was founded around the turn of the 19th/20th centuries to protest against British colonialism, promote the unity and rights of all African peoples, challenge European denigration, or appropriation, of African cultural accomplishments and fight for African self-determinism (Contee 1969). An important figure in the Pan-African movement was William Du Bois, an American history professor, who challenged European diffusionism, promoted African precolonial culture, and was a major influence in the development of a professional African history (Contee 1969: 48; Miller 1999: 5–6). However, like his counterparts, he continued to suggest that contemporary Africa was backward by European and American standards, although he explained this as the result of European and Muslim slave trading (Miller 1999: 6).

In 1900 Du Bois attended the first Pan-African Congress, out of which the Pan African Association was formed. Unfortunately, as Contee (1969: 59) describes, 'The movement was forty-five years away from being in the hands of Africans living on African soil . . . who could convert an elitist movement into a mass one.' In francophone Africa the Negritude movement provided a different platform for African Nationalism. Negritude campaigned for black relocation within French society whilst also actively constructing a black personality and cultural identity, which was harnessed by African Nationalists (Lambert 1993: 239). Subsequently, Negritude proponents such as Leopold Senghor (the future president of Senegal) challenged European diffusionism by promoting the Africanness of Ancient Egypt and thus the global cultural impact of Africans (Lambert 1993: 240).

Cheik Anta Diop (1960), a Senegalese physicist, was undoubtedly the most famous African scholar to adopt Senghor's pan-African diffusionism, using archaeological information to argue that Ancient Egypt was the cradle of all black Africans, who had subsequently migrated out of the Nile Valley. Furthermore, he suggested that because Ancient Egypt was the source of world civilization, as suggested by early 20th-century hyperdiffusionism, Africans should appropriate it for themselves (Holl 1990: 302–4). However, Diop's arguments were based on limited evidence and, like European diffusionism, served to underestimate African creativity outside Egypt (Trigger 2006: 203). Less extreme refutations of European diffusionism include the work of historians Abdullah Lauroui and Marcel Bènabou, both of whom promoted the indigenous dimension of Roman North Africa (van Dommelen 2006: 105–6). Within Egypt, however, the Pharaonic past continues to be used to promote modern Egyptian nationalism (see Wood 1998).

In contrast, due to the political obscurity of archaeology under apartheid, and despite a willingness to rewrite African history (Hall 1990: 73; Shepherd 2002: 196), the Black Consciousness movement in South Africa did not harness archaeology to counter white-settler ideologies, although holding up Great Zimbabwe as a symbol of black achievement.

EARLY INDEPENDENCE LEADERS AND THE CELEBRATION OF AFRICA'S PAST

Following independence, activists from the Pan-African, Negritude, and Black Consciousness movements became Africa's national leaders. In their new role they continued to promote precolonial African accomplishments and the revision of the past to produce African national histories. This is most clearly visible in the naming of the republics of Ghana and Zimbabwe (previously Gold Coast and Rhodesia) after a precolonial kingdom and the country's largest archaeological site respectively. It was also prominent in the policies of their respective post-independence presidents, Kwame Nkrumah and Robert Mugabe. As Kankpeyeng and DeCorse (2004: 94–5) suggest, the creation of the Ghana Museums and Monuments Board 'to manage archaeological and cultural resources was part of nationalists' desire to develop a national identity for the emerging nation state'. Nkrumah also expressed his Pan-Africanist ideology through the national heritage service by encouraging the collection and display of objects from other African nations. However, in contrast to Nkrumah, who promoted ethnic diversity through museum displays (Kankpeyeng and DeCorse 2004: 95), Mugabe's government sought to replace ethnic identities with a single Zimbabwean national identity (Ucko 1983).

Nevertheless, despite differences in approach, several themes recur in the policies of Africa's early independence leaders. For example, many promoted the reconstruction of the precolonial past to aid the construction of new national narratives, as famously expressed in 1970 by Sir Seretswe Khama, Botswana's first president:

> We should write our own history books to prove that we did have a past, and that it was a past that was just as worth writing and learning about as any other. We must do this for the simple reason that a nation without a past is a lost nation, and a people without a past are a people without a soul. (Cited in Lane 2011: 12)

The importance of African history was also expressed by Julius Nyerere, then president of Tanzania, at the International Congress on African History held at Dar es Salaam University College in 1965:

> We in Tanzania have devoted what is for us a lot of time and money in organising this gathering. We have done so for one reason only: because we believe that a

knowledge of African history is important for the growth of our continent. (Nyerere 1968: 85).

Thus, a new political mission for archaeology was set. From this moment onward the explicit exploration and celebration of the pasts of Africa's peoples to contribute toward post-independent nation building and to counter colonial constructions became the political *raison d'être* for archaeology in Africa.

Postcolonialism

Nationalism

Notwithstanding the political call to rewrite the African past, explicitly nationalist archaeologies were rare (Robertshaw 1990c: 78; although for a contrasting view see Trigger 1990). Indeed, many archaeologies of this period maintained overt colonial influences, such as in Rwanda (e.g. Hiernaux 1968), while others that explicitly countered colonial ideologies such as the Hamitic Myth were transnational in scope (e.g. Posnansky 1968). Furthermore, since the early independence period archaeology in Africa has diversified into a variety of approaches, most recently influenced by postcolonialism (e.g. Schmidt 2009; Lane 2011). However, overt nationalism did exist in African archaeologies and can be seen in Ken Mufuka's (1983) *Dzimbahwe: Life and Politics in the Golden Age, 1100–1500* AD, which suggested that life in precolonial Zimbabwe was a socialist utopia.

In contrast, and more typical of early post-independence archaeology, was the covert support of nationalist aims through the exploration and celebration of the 'Iron Age' and the early African origins of the features that constituted it. In East Africa this involved the indigenous development of pastoralism, iron smelting, pottery production, and coastal statehood. Although not an explicit attempt to support nationalism, the archaeologists involved were not 'slow in grasping the implications of their results for promoting nationalist perspectives about the past' (Robertshaw 1990c: 92–3). However, archaeologists have also directly challenged official national pasts. For example, Robertshaw (1996: 8) used archaeological evidence to question the Ugandan government's repeated invocation of 'the notion of a Cwezi empire in the precolonial era as a symbol of Uganda's glorious and united past', suggesting instead, and despite concerns regarding the undermining of government attempts to promote national unity, that the supposed Cwezi empire was actually composed of 'small and possibly competing polities'.

More recently, some African archaeologists have begun to re-engage with Pan-Africanist romanticism, which has re-emerged under the guise of the African Union's New Partnership for Africa's Development programme (Segobye 2005), while other archaeologists have identified its persistence within national archaeologies, such as in Ethiopia (Finneran 2003).

Postcolonialism

Despite the end of colonial rule and the subsequent implicit support of nationalist aims by some archaeologists, African archaeology retained elements of colonialism in purpose,

practice, and interpretation. This has been highlighted by post-processual political reflections and can be traced to the non-African origins of the majority of archaeologists working
in Africa and the unconscious retention of colonial disciplinary paradigms. Put simply,
African archaeology in the postcolonial era typically remained an elite, white endeavour in
which foreign academics with their own interests continued to appropriate the past, largely
for the benefit of a non-indigenous audience. In response, archaeologists have begun to
engage with the postcolonial critique, highlighting the need to expose uncomfortable colonial legacies and to decolonize the discipline. This is being achieved by engaging with contemporary concerns within community-sensitive methodological and theoretical
frameworks to construct explicitly postcolonial archaeologies, although criticisms of colonial power structures, as reproduced by non-African archaeologists working in Africa,
remain (Schmidt 2009; for a critical review of this work see Stahl 2010).

Archaeological engagement with the postcolonial critique and the recognition of the
inherent colonialism of African archaeology has produced two positive archaeological
responses, the 'usable past model' and the 'indigenous epistemologies model' (Lane 2011: 9).
The usable past model may be compared to nationalist approaches because in its commonest
form it harnesses archaeology to challenge colonially influenced constructions of the past.
However, the usable pasts model is much broader. It includes applied archaeologies that
address practical, contemporary concerns such as human rights, the environment, and
socioeconomic development (e.g. Lane 2009; Schmidt 2009; Stump 2010), as well as the
way in which methodologies engage with community sensitivities, such as in post-conflict
archaeologies (e.g. Mire 2011).

Post-conflict archaeologies

This term refers here to the practice of archaeology following the cessation of violence, such
as liberation struggles, civil war, and/or genocide within and between African nations. In
these contexts, it is often not simply the revision of colonially constructed derogatory narratives that is of archaeological concern, although their legacy is very relevant. Instead, the
need to justify archaeological research is intensified, and concerns regarding archaeological
interpretation where competing interest groups within national historical narratives exist
are paramount. This may include both the investigation of the recent past, including crimes
against humanity (e.g. Connor 1996), and the investigation of longer-term issues, such as the
mutability of precolonial identities (Giblin in press).

Post-conflict archaeology has been highlighted here because it is an intensely political,
emergent form of postcolonial archaeology (Fig. 19.1). The negotiation of social identities
within post-conflict contexts may exert specific pressures over the practice, interpretation,
and use of archaeology, presenting serious ethical concerns for the discipline. Nevertheless,
the reconstruction of the past often exists in post-conflict arenas. In response, archaeologists
in Africa have considered their political and ethical role within post-conflict societies. This
concerns, among other issues, the moral justification of research in post-conflict regions that
may draw resources away from more important reconstruction projects, the employment of
methodologies sensitive to logistical constraints as well as community emotions, the development of research questions that reflect the concerns of indigenous community groups
alongside interpretations that may clash with post-conflict reconciliation strategies, and the

FIG. 19.1 Photograph showing archaeological excavation of a *c.* 4th-century AD burial in Rwanda. Due to the specific post-genocide context in Rwanda, the investigation of the past, and especially the excavation of human burials, is a highly political and visible activity, even when the remains are over 1,500 years old (photograph, John Giblin).

possibility that research results will be 'used' politically to legitimate post-conflict governments and may inadvertently foster conflict in the future.

The post-conflict, usable past approach to archaeology in Africa has been most extensively, if not always explicitly, explored in post-apartheid South Africa. For example, Dowson (1994) has promoted the use of rock art to counter apartheid myths, Esterhuysen (2000; Esterhuysen and Lane, Ch. 18 above) has discussed the revisionary and reconciliatory role of educational archaeology; Martin Hall (2005) has investigated the politicization, responsibility, and ethics of archaeology; Shepherd (2007) has considered conflict-era cultural heritage management issues in a post-conflict context; Blundell (2002) has highlighted the need for post-apartheid archaeologies that have a practical benefit beyond research; Meskell (2005, 2007) has discussed the heritage implications of current ethnic diversity policies and the impact of archaeological research on local communities; and Smith (2009) and Ndlovu (2009) have both highlighted the importance of an engaged racial transformation programme in South African archaeology.

Thus, just as the end of colonialism challenged archaeology in Africa to reconsider its political underpinnings and its role within newly independent nations, the practice of archaeology in post-conflict contexts is now challenging practitioners to consider their contemporary political context and responsibilities. Unfortunately, as several African countries are still suffering or emerging from episodes of violent conflict, post-conflict politics are likely to be relevant for some time.

Indigenous perspectives

Perhaps the most important contemporary development in the shifting political and ideological world of African archaeology is the emergence and adoption of what Lane (2011: 9) terms 'indigenous epistemologies'. The gradual rise in the number of indigenous African archaeologists working in the continent has had a direct influence over the deconstruction of colonialist archaeology and the promotion of indigenous perspectives (e.g. Mire 2011). However, due to the persistence of colonial epistemologies this has only recently begun to take shape, having been facilitated by archaeological engagement with the postcolonial critique (Schmidt 2009).

The stated purpose of the indigenous epistemologies model is to celebrate 'alternative strategies; challenge long held assumptions about who has the right, authority and power to interpret the past; and wrest exclusive control over the production and use of archaeological knowledge from the discipline of Archaeology and its self-identifying practitioners' (Lane 2011: 15). Considering the inherent colonialism of many African archaeologies and the consequent need for such an approach, it is unfortunate that it has met with reluctance and only rarely been comprehensively undertaken. Shepherd (2002: 200), drawing on a statement by Andah et al. (1994), suggests that this is because African archaeologists have lacked control over research agendas, priorities, and resources due to the overwhelming power that non-African scholars continue to have over the African past.

Lane (2011: 15) has also identified a lack of indigenous epistemologies in African archaeology, which he suggests is the result of 'contrasting understandings and definitions of "indigenous people"' in a continent where most people would consider themselves indigenous. In addition, because all knowledge systems are hybrids, the value in distinguishing between scientific archaeological knowledge and traditional indigenous knowledge systems is questionable (Lane 2011: 17). However, without the development and employment of indigenous epistemologies, it is suggested, African archaeology will remain inherently colonial. Furthermore, it is unacceptable simply to associate local community engagement with indigenous archaeology when the community remains excluded from interpretation. Although community engagement may represent a laudable attempt to consider community needs and a valuable public relations exercise, while interpretation and management continue to be controlled solely by western archaeological traditions, colonial ideologies will persist.

A notable example of an indigenous epistemological approach is nevertheless Mire's (2011) work in Somaliland. Mire suggests that, alongside the destruction caused by two decades of civil war, a lack of qualified Somali archaeologists, heritage professionals, and legislation resulted in a lack of dialogue with local communities and a failure to incorporate their understandings, leading to the destruction of much of the cultural heritage of both Somaliland and Somalia. In response she identifies distinct Somali heritage perspectives that focus on the preservation of knowledge and not objects and promotes their implementation by trained local groups, who, she suggests, should henceforth lead all archaeological research and heritage management.

Although the idea of indigenous, local community, heritage management is not contentious and must be supported, the practicalities of Mire's response, in terms of archaeological research, are challenging and no doubt uncomfortable for many archaeologists. However, if a contemporary political concern of African archaeology is relevance and decolonization, then indigenous epistemologies of the kind that she advocates should be explored and engaged with by all archaeologists working in Africa. The development and employment of indigenous epistemologies is thus likely to be a major political influence in African archaeology in future years.

REFERENCES

ANDAH, B., ALANDE, A., FOLORUNSO, C. and BAGADO, O. (1994). African archaeology in the 21st century; or, Africa, cultural puppet on a string? *West African Journal of Archaeology* 24: 152–9.

BLUNDELL, G. (2002). *The Unseen Landscape: A Journey to Game Pass Shelter* (guide booklet). Johannesburg: Rock Art Research Institute.

BOUTAKOFF, I. (1937). Premières exploration méthodiques des gisements de l'âge de la pierre au Ruanda-Urundi: abris sous roche, ateliers et stations en plein air. *Institut Colonial Belge, Bulletin des Séances* 8: 179–201.

CATON-THOMPSON, G. (1931). *The Zimbabwe Culture: Ruins and Reactions.* Oxford: Clarendon Press.

CONNOR, M. (1996). The archaeology of contemporary mass graves. *Society of American Archaeology Bulletin* 14: 6–31.

CONTEE, C. (1969). The emergence of Du Bois as an African nationalist. *Journal of Negro History* 54: 48–63.

DANIEL, G. (1962). *The Idea of Prehistory.* London: Watts.

DE BARROS, P. (1990). Changing paradigms, goals and methods in the archaeology of francophone West Africa. In Robertshaw (1990a: 155–72).

DEACON, J. (1990). Weaving the fabric of Stone Age research in southern Africa. In Robertshaw (1990a: 39–58).

DIOP, C. A. (1960). *L'Afrique Noire Précoloniale: Étude Comparée des Systèmes Politiques et Sociaux de l'Europe et de l'Afrique Noire, de l'Antiquité à la Formation des États Modernes.* Paris: Présence Africaine.

DOWSON, T. A. (1994). Reading art, writing history: rock art and social change in southern Africa. *World Archaeology* 25: 332–45.

ESTERHUYSEN, A. B. (2000). The birth of educational archaeology in South Africa. *Antiquity* 74: 159–65.

FINNERAN, N. (2003). The persistence of memory: nationalism, identity and the represented past. The Ethiopian experience in a global context. *Studies in Ethnicity and Nationalism* 3: 21–37.

FONTEIN, J. (2006). *The Silence of Great Zimbabwe: Contested Landscapes and the Power of Heritage.* London: UCL Press.

GIBLIN, J. (in press). The archaeological identification of pre-colonial Twa, Tutsi and Hutu in Rwanda. In F. Richard and K. C. Macdonald (eds), *Ethnic Ambiguities in African Archaeology: Materiality, History and the Shaping of Cultural Identities.* Walnut Creek, Ca.: Left Coast Press.

HALL, M. (1990). 'Hidden history': Iron Age archaeology in southern Africa. In Robertshaw (1990a: 59–77).

——— (2005). Situational ethics and engaged practice: the case of archaeology in Africa. In L. Meskell and P. Pels (eds), *Embedding Ethics: Shifting the Boundaries of the Anthropological Profession.* Oxford: Berg, 169–94.

HIERNAUX, J. (1968). Bantu expansion: the evidence from physical anthropology confronted with linguistic and archaeological evidence. *Journal of African History* 9: 505–15.

HOLL, A. F. C. (1990). West African archaeology: colonialism and nationalism. In Robertshaw (1990a: 296–308).

KANKPEYENG, W., and DeCORSE, C. R. (2004). Ghana's vanishing past: development, antiquities, and the destruction of the archaeological record. *African Archaeological Review* 21: 89–128.

LAMBERT, M. (1993). From citizenship to negritude: 'making a difference' in elite ideologies of colonized francophone West Africa. *Comparative Studies in Society and History* 35: 239–62.

LANE, P. J. (2009). Environmental narratives and the history of soil erosion in Kondoa District, Tanzania: an archaeological perspective. *International Journal of African Historical Studies* 42: 457–83.

—— (2011). Possibilities for a postcolonial archaeology in sub-Saharan Africa: indigenous and useable pasts. *World Archaeology* 43: 7–25.

LUCAS, G. (2006). Archaeology at the edge: an archaeological dialogue with Martin Hall. *Archaeological Dialogues* 13: 55–67.

MARKS, S. (1980). South Africa: 'the myth of the empty land'. *History Today* 30: 7–12.

MESKELL, L. (2005). Recognition, restitution and the potentials of postcolonial liberalism for South African heritage. *South African Archaeological Bulletin* 60: 72–8.

—— (2007). Falling walls and mending fences: archaeological ethnography in the Limpopo. *Journal of Southern African Studies* 33: 383–400.

MILLER, J. C. (1999). History and Africa/Africa and history. *American Historical Review* 104: 1–32.

MIRE, S. (2011). The knowledge-centred approach to the Somali cultural emergency and heritage development assistance in Somaliland. *African Archaeological Review* 28: 71–9.

MUFUKA, K. (1983). *Dzimbahwe: Life and Politics in the Golden Age, 1100–1500*. Harare: Harare publishers.

NDLOVU, N. (2009). Transformation challenges in South African archaeology. *South African Archaeological Bulletin* 64: 91–3.

NKRUMAH, K. (1973). *Revolutionary Path*. London: Panaf Books.

NYERERE, J. (1968). *Freedom and Socialism/Uhuru na Ujamaa: A Selection from Writings and Speeches 1965–1967*. Dar es Salaam: Oxford University Press.

POSNANSKY, M. (1968). Bantu genesis: archaeological reflections. *Journal of African History* 9: 1–11

ROBERTSHAW, P. T. (ed.) (1990a). *A History of African Archaeology*. Oxford: James Currey.

—— (1990b). A history of African archaeology: an introduction. In Robertshaw (1990a: 3–12).

—— (1990c). The development of archaeology in East Africa. In Robertshaw (1990a: 78–94).

—— (1996). Knowledge and power. *African Archaeological Review* 13: 7–9.

SEGOBYE, A. K. (2005). Weaving fragments of the past for a united Africa: reflections on the place of African archaeology in the development of the continent in the 21st century. *South African Archaeological Bulletin* 60: 79–83.

SCHMIDT, P. R. (ed.) (2009). *Postcolonial Archaeologies in Africa*. Santa Fe, NM: School for Advanced Research Press.

SELIGMAN, C. G. (1930). *Races of Africa*. London: Oxford University Press.

SHEPHERD, N. (2002). The politics of archaeology in Africa. *Annual Review of Anthropology* 31: 189–209.

—— (2007). Archaeology dreaming: post-apartheid urban imaginaries and the bones of the Prestwich Street dead. *Journal of Social Archaeology* 7: 3–28.

SMITH, B. W. (2009). A Transformation Charter for South African archaeology. *South African Archaeological Bulletin* 64: 87–9.

STAHL, A. B. (2010). Review of Peter R. Schmidt (ed.), *Postcolonial Archaeologies in Africa*. *African Archaeological Review* 27: 165–68.

STUMP, D. (2010). Ancient and backward or long-lived and sustainable: the role of the past in developmental debates in eastern Africa. *World Development* 38: 1251–62.

TOBIAS, P. V. (1985). Prehistory and political discrimination. *South African Journal of Science* 81: 667–71.

TRIGGER, B. G. (1984). Alternative archaeologies: nationalist, colonialist, imperialist. In R. Preucel and I. Hodder (eds), *Contemporary Archaeology in Theory: A Reader*. Oxford: Blackwell, 615–31.

—— (1990). The history of African archaeology in world perspective. In Robertshaw (1990a: 303–19).

—— (2006). *A History of Archaeological Thought*. Cambridge: Cambridge University Press.

UCKO, P. J. (1983). The politics of the indigenous minority. *Journal of Biosocial Science* 8: 25–40.

VAN DOMMELEN, P. (2006). Colonial matters: material culture and postcolonial theory in colonial situations. In C. Tilley, W. Keane, S. Küchler, M. Rowlands, and P. Spyer (eds), *Handbook of Material Culture*. London: Sage, 104–24.

WAYLAND, E. J. (1934). Rifts, rivers, rain and early man in Uganda. *Journal of the Royal Anthropological Institute of Great Britain and Ireland* 64: 333–52.

WOOD, M. (1998). The use of the Pharaonic past in modern Egyptian nationalism. *Journal of the American Research Center in Egypt* 35: 179–96.

PART III

BECOMING HUMAN

CHAPTER 20

HOMININ EVOLUTION AS THE CONTEXT FOR AFRICAN PREHISTORY

ROBERT A. FOLEY

INTRODUCTION

CONSENSUS is rare in the field of human evolution, but there is one overriding agreement—that Africa is central to all aspects of it. This may seem almost platitudinous, but we should remember that it was not always so. Prior to the 1920s, Africa was assumed to be an unlikely place for human origins, and there was certainly no fossil evidence to support such a view. Asia and Europe seemed considerably stronger possibilities, both on a priori grounds and because there was fossil evidence (albeit, in the case of Piltdown man, fraudulent). Even after the discovery of the South African australopithecines, claims for an African origin were subject to doubts about the humanness of the fossils, dating, and the relative merits of fossils from elsewhere. To find a strong backer for Africa one has to go back to Darwin (1871) himself, who pointed to the presence in Africa of humanity's closest relatives, gorillas and chimpanzees. However, spectacular discoveries since 1960 make it hard to consider anywhere other than Africa as the primary source of hominin species; and for this reason African archaeology is integrally related to human evolution, and the bulk of the archaeological record exists in Africa rather than elsewhere. The earliest African stone tools are at least a million years earlier than any found elsewhere (~2.5 mya; Semaw et al. 1997; Domínguez-Rodrigo, Ch. 21 below) and the 'human' lineage stretches back in Africa for possibly seven million years (Brunet et al. 2002).

Hominin evolution is therefore the context for much of African archaeology. I describe its evolutionary context first and then present the fossil evidence before briefly discussing hominin evolutionary patterns in Africa and their implications for prehistory.

THE PHYLOGENETIC FRAMEWORK FOR HOMININS

Primate evolution

Primates emerged as a distinct mammalian order towards the end of the Cretaceous (65 mya), and subsequently diversified into several thousand species, most of which are now extinct (Fleagle 1999). Currently over 250 species are recognized, with humans belonging to the anthropoid clade and, in turn, to the Catarrhini, the Old World monkeys and apes. The catarrhines are divided into two superfamilies, the Cercopithecoidea (Old World monkeys) and the Hominoidea (apes and humans). Current fossil and molecular evidence suggest that these separated 29–24 mya (Zalmout et al. 2010) Classically, the Hominoidea have been considered to be three families—the Hylobatidae (lesser apes), Pongidae (great apes), and Hominidae (humans)—but molecular and palaeontological research has completely transformed this perspective in ways that provide an important framework for human origins and significantly change the systematic nomenclature.

Humans, we now know, share a unique relationship with chimpanzees and bonobos (*Pan*), and the African apes as a whole (including gorillas) are a clade or branch relative to the Asian great ape, the orang-utan (*Pongo*) (Goodman et al. 1990). This has forced a change in nomenclature: the term traditionally reserved for humans and their close, extinct relatives, 'hominid' (from the family Hominidae) is no longer appropriate, as it now refers to all great apes and humans. Relative to *Pan*, the human lineage has been relegated to a lower taxonomic rank (tribe), and so the term 'hominin' (from Hominini) is now used (Fig. 20.1). Extinct and living forms subsequent to the divergence from chimpanzees are thus referred to here as hominins.

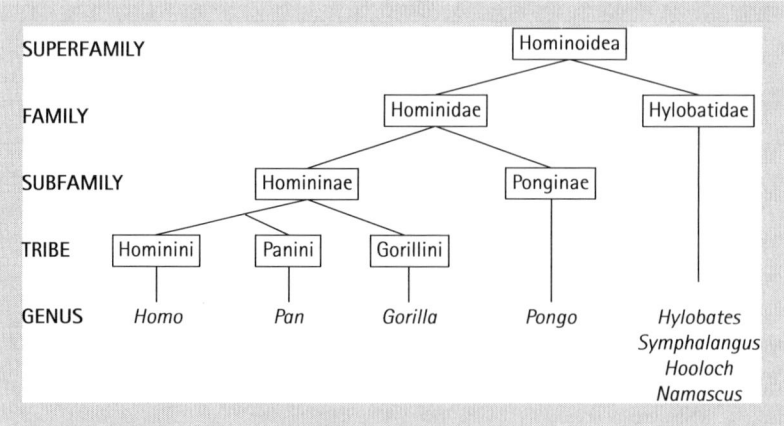

FIG. 20.1 Classification and nomenclature for human evolution. As evolutionary genetics has shown a close and private relationship between humans and chimpanzees, it has become necessary to change nomenclature to reflect this. Consequently, whereas humans and their ancestors were once placed into a separate family (Hominidae) and so became 'hominids', now they are confined to a 'sub-family' or 'tribe'—and hence become 'hominins'.

These changes in phylogeny and systematics are not just a matter of terminology. The close relationship between humans and African apes, and the more divergent position of the orang-utan, confirms Darwin's original proposal, making it probable that the last common ancestor (LCA) of humans and chimpanzees/bonobos was in Africa. Molecular evidence, which strongly supports this African clade model, dates this divergence to between 4 and 6 million years ago. Hominins therefore probably originated among a group of apes resident in (equatorial?) Africa 8–4 million years ago (Kumar et al. 2005), although the common ancestor of that group may have arrived in Africa from Asia in the late Miocene (Begun 2010). Whether this is the case or not, there is now general consensus that we should seek the origin of hominins in the later Miocene and early Pliocene of Africa, a period of changing climates, dwindling and fragmenting forests, and increased aridity and seasonality.

THE FOSSIL RECORD FOR HOMININ EVOLUTION

The hominin fossil record comes from several different geological and geographical contexts. As the focus here is on hominin evolution as a context, rather than the palaeontological details, only a few general points can be made (see Klein 2009 for a recent summary of individual sites). First, while the hominin record is excellent, it is also patchy, and any interpretation must allow for that. From the later Miocene to the Middle Pleistocene, one major physiographic feature dominates: the East African Rift System (EARS). Highly fossiliferous, this vast tectonic system provides many windows into the past and is susceptible to accurate radiometric dating. As a

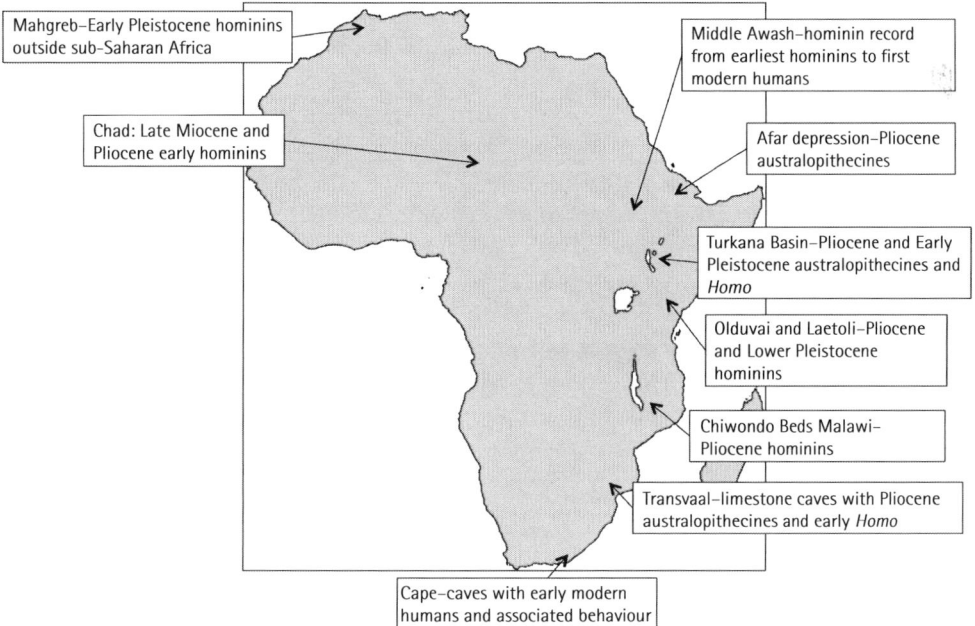

FIG. 20.2 Principal areas for sources of information about human evolution in Africa.

result it is probably fair to say that this area, stretching from Eritrea through Ethiopia, Kenya and Tanzania to Malawi, has provided the bulk of the information available. Secondary to this are the limestone regions of the Transvaal in South Africa, which have provided a rich source of fossils since the 1920s. New areas are being exposed—of which the best example is the central Chad desert—but large parts of the continent, especially equatorial and western regions, remain relatively unknown. For later periods, beyond the Middle Pleistocene, other areas such as the North African coastal region and the Cape Province become as significant. Fig. 20.2 shows a very schematic map of the primary sources of information for human evolution in Africa, and reminds us that what we know may be less than complete.

Fossil hominins

There are now more than 3,000 specimens of hominin from Africa, and a review such as this must organize these in a comprehensible manner. The most obvious way of doing this remains by taxonomic assignment, but this is often controversial and lacks consensus. For example, some authorities would reduce the variation in 'early *Homo*' to a single species, some would place it in at least two, and some would argue that these specimens should be placed into the genus *Australopithecus*. Even at generic level there is considerable confusion; most researchers use the broad genus *Australopithecus* to include a number of species, including *A. afarensis*, but others would use the genus *Praeanthropus*. The group widely known as 'robust australopithecines' have been variously placed into one (*Australopithecus*), two (+ *Paranthropus*), or three (+ *Zinjanthropus*) genera. Even for *Homo* there is lack of consensus; Wolpoff has proposed that everything beyond *Homo habilis* should be *H. sapiens*; more reasonably Rightmire has suggested three species (*H. erectus*, *H. heidelbergensis*, and *H. sapiens*) (Rightmire 1998); some recognize *H. helmei* as a later species (Foley and Lahr 1997), or *H. rhodesiensis* as a particular African lineage distinct from the European *H. heidelbergensis* (Howell 1999), and others employ the taxon *H. ergaster* to describe a uniquely African Lower to Middle Pleistocene lineage, distinct from the 'Asian *H. erectus*' (Andrews 1984). To some this lack of terminological consensus might seem like an irritating academic game, but there are important issues involved, ranging from the correct use of the Linnaean rules to disagreements about morphological interpretations, to different uses of the species concepts, to issues about principles and processes of evolution. In the end, it should be remembered that species assignments are hypotheses about biology and phylogeny. Taxonomy is used here to outline the general patterns, but this caveat should be borne in mind.

Table 20.1 provides a table of hominin taxa (for the sake of completeness, non-African ones are included, and it is important to bear in mind that despite the central importance of Africa in hominin evolution, the continent cannot be treated in isolation when considering human evolution, despite claims to the contrary (McBrearty and Brooks 2000)). In summary, there are currently seven genera of hominin widely recognized. Within these seven genera, there are around twenty-six species which could be recognized (for various fuller descriptions of this issue, see Wood and Lonergan 2008). Fig. 20.3 shows the distribution of the species within the genera. It also tries to indicate how the nomenclature would vary if the various species were lumped into progressively larger taxa. Such an exercise might appeal to those who are more interested in the broad patterns than the phylogenetic details, but it is fraught with difficulty. The extreme lumped scheme shown on the right of the figure, with

Table 20.1 Principal taxa of hominin evolution. A problem with hominin evolution is that there is no full consensus about nomenclature, and especially the amount of splitting and lumping of species. In the table below it is possible to either start from the left, and see the homomin lineage with a maximal number of taxa, or from the left with a minimal one.

Genus	Progressive splitting		Progressive lumping		Genus
	1	2	3	4	
Sahelanthropus	tchadensis	tchadensis	tchadensis	tchadensis	Sahelanthropus
Ororrin	tugenensis	tugenensis	tugenensis	tugenensis	Ororrin
Ardipthecus	kadabba	ramidus	ramidus	ramidus	Ardipthecus
	ramidus				
Paranthopus	aethiopicus	aethiopicus	robustus	robustus	Paranthopus
	robustus	robustus			
	boisei				
Australopithecus	anamensis	anamensis	afarensis	africanus	Australopithecus
	afarensis	afarensis			
	bahrelghazali				
	africanus	africanus	africanus		
	garhi	garhi			
	sediba	sediba			
Kenyanthropus	platyops	platyops			
Homo	habilis	habilis	habilis	habilis	Homo
	rudolfensis				
	ergaster	erectus	erectus	erectus	
	erectus				
	georgicus				
	antecessor	antecessor	heidelbergensis	heildelbergensis	
	rhodesiensis	heidelbergensis			
	heidelbergensis				
	helmei	helmei			
	neanderthalensis	neanderthalensis	neanderthalensis		
	sapiens	sapiens	sapiens	sapiens	

three basic genera (*Ardipithecus* as a genus of very primitive forms; *Australopithecus* as a more progressive hominin with bipedal adaptations; and *Homo* as a more encephalized hominin) is almost certainly untenable on any rigorous phylogenetic analysis.

Fig. 20.3 shows the distribution of the fossil hominin taxa through time (for reviews, see Tattersall 2000; Wood and Richmond 2000; Foley 2005; Wood and Lonagan 2008; Foley and Gamble 2009; Klein 2009). Hominin taxa are grouped informally into four broad chronological and evolutionary units. The first are the earliest hominins, which are entirely later Miocene and early Pliocene, and are both controversial and ape-like. The second are the broad grouping of the australopithecines, including the robust ones (paranthropines), all of which are probably bipedal in some form or other, and occur between 4.2 mya and around 1.7 mya. The third are the earlier members of *Homo*, with brain sizes of less than 1,000 cc. These occur

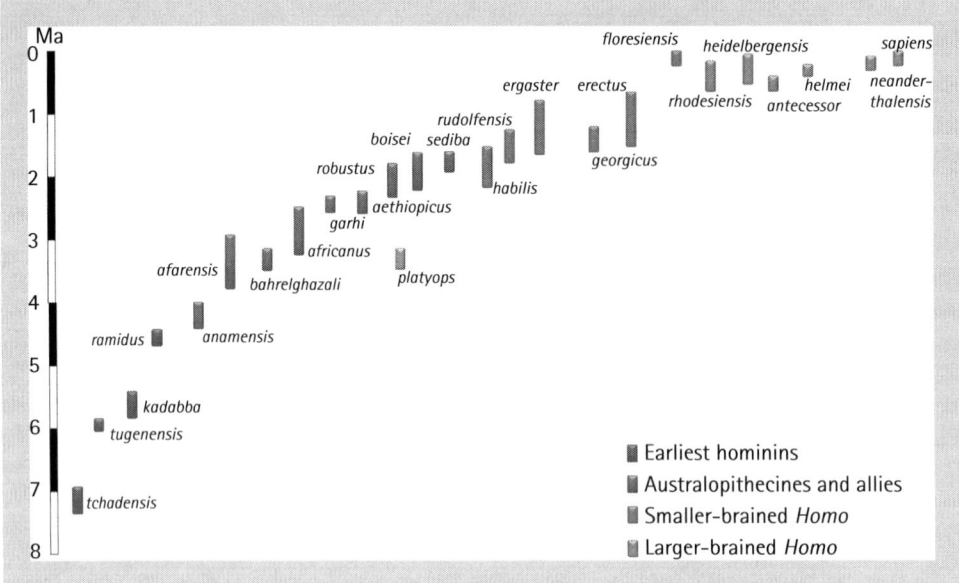

FIG. 20.3 Chronological distribution of hominins. Each bar represents a species and their first and last appearance dates indicate their chronological range (redrawn from Foley and Gamble 2009).

between approximately 2.3 mya and around 700 kya (excluding *H. floresiensis*, which is an exception to most of the generalities of human evolution). Finally, there are the later and larger-brained members of *Homo*, which are all younger than one million years old.

It should be noted that while there is a clear chronological trend, there is significant overlap between these units. It can also be seen that for virtually the whole period there was in existence more than one species of hominin, and that the solitary position of *Homo sapiens* is probably less than 20 kya old. Finally, virtually all the taxa shown here have an African origin; only Neanderthals, *H. antecessor*, and *H. floresiensis* are unambiguously non-African (Brown et al. 2004; de Castro et al. 1997; Hublin and Pääbo 2006); *H. georgicus* is not African, but has been seen as an early disperser from Africa (Rightmire et al. 2006), and the Asian nature of *H. erectus* depends to a very large extent on its definition (Antón 2003). *H. heidelbergensis*, the later European form, can also be seen as European when defined narrowly (Howell 1999).

HOMININ EVOLUTION THROUGH TIME

Later Miocene and early Pliocene (< 7.0—~4.4 mya)

The fossil evidence for the emergence of the hominin clade does fit broadly with the phylogenetic and molecular expectations. A very plausible model would see the period after about 8 mya seeing the dispersals and divergence of the African ape clade (itself, perhaps, an 'African exotic', Stewart and Disotell 1998) across the equatorial regions. That radiation would have included the ancestors of both gorillas and chimpanzees, but the fossil evidence for hominins is also an indication that there was greater diversity still (White et al. 2009). What is perhaps most noticeable about the whole group (gorilla, chimpanzee, bonobo, and the earliest hominins *Sahelanthropus*, *Ororrin*, and *Ardipithecus*) is that they all show a considerable element of terrestrial adaptation. This is consistent with the environmental evidence, which shows a decline in global temperatures, increased tropical seasonality, and growing aridity (Bobe 2006). The impact on the African environment was not, as is often supposed, a massive expansion of grassland savannah, but rather a break-up of tropical rainforests and their replacement by woodlands with grasslands present (Cerling et al. 2010). Closed environments did not disappear, but became more fragmented.

At one level this evidence is straightforward and compelling, a match between changing environments and the evolution of the hominin clade, all as a part of a general catarrhine trend towards terrestriality. There are, however, a number of areas where the evidence requires more evaluation. One issue is the chronology. The earliest claimed hominin is *Sahelanthropus* from Chad, dated to 7.2 mya (Brunet et al. 2002). The features that support a hominin affinity are the relatively flat face and the rounded cranium, with brow ridges reminiscent of later hominins; the canine is also reduced. There have been claims for bipedalism on the basis of the foramen magnum. However, the proposed date is right at the boundaries for what is consistent with the molecular evidence for the LCA of chimpanzees and hominins (Kumar et al. 2005). This difficulty becomes compounded when *Sahelanthropus* is compared to the latest of the three very early hominins, *Ar. Ramidus*. Work on this hominin has been extensively published recently (White et al. 2009), and the broad claims made are that it is a hominin, that it is bipedal, and that it is very unlike a chimpanzee. Lovejoy has therefore argued that the links between early hominins and chimpanzees are overstated (Lovejoy 2009). However, the interpretation of *Ardipithecus* is not straightforward. The inference of bipedalism is based on a heavily reconstructed pelvis, and in contrast the hallux (big toe) is highly divergent, a characteristic of non-bipedal apes. Without that the primary feature for a hominin is the reduced canine. Overall, many would interpret *Ardipithecus* as rather less hominin-like than *Sahelanthropus*, and indeed, very distant from the first australopithecine, which occurs only 200,000 years later. In between these two, chronologically, lies *Orrorin*. Here there does seem to be substantial evidence for bipedalism, but with little cranial material it is difficult to compare it with the other early hominins (Richmond and Jungers 2008).

The fossil evidence does show quite clearly that hominins emerged in Africa in the latest Miocene or early Pliocene. The fossil evidence cannot be simply interpreted as a gradual lineage of evolving hominins from seven million years. What is far more likely is that these relatively newly discovered fossils are opening a window on a high degree of diversity among the African apes, and that adaptations to terrestriality—locomotor, behavioural, ecological, or social—may well have evolved in more than one lineage. The urge to place all fossils in the hominin line is probably what is limiting our ability to understand the diversity of the patterns of African ape evolution.

Plio-Pleistocene (4.4–1.6 mya)

While there remains an element of uncertainty as to which, if any, of the early genera belong to the hominin clade, rather than being part of a broader ape radiation, after 4.2 mya there is indubitable evidence for hominins. The basis for this is twofold: first, the existence of a fossil species, *A. anamensis*, that has clear evidence for bipedalism, and second, that this species, unlike *Ardipithecus*, shows strong continuity with later hominins and so suggests a more continuous lineage (Brown et al. 2001; Leakey et al. 1998; Ward et al. 1999; Ward et al. 2001; Ward et al. 2003).

The overall pattern for the Plio-Pleistocene is one of high hominin diversity. Across this period there are as many as fourteen possible species. It has become standard to refer to hominin evolution as an adaptive radiation (Foley 2002a), and this is the period which would demonstrate this most clearly. In terms of trends across time, the earliest of the australopithecines are what have often been termed the 'gracile' ones—this should not be interpreted too literally, but rather refers to the lack of cranial and dental specializations of later hominins which lead to extreme musculature (Aiello and Andrews 2000). *A. anamensis*, known from northern Kenya (4.2–3.9 mya), is the earliest taxon (Brown et al. 2001), and has a lower limb with strong bipedal elements (Ward et al. 2001). *A. afarensis* is almost certainly a descendent lineage (Kimbel et al. 2006), and the best way of interpreting this group as a whole is probably to see them as local variants of each other, with an element of temporal change. So, for example, *A. africanus* would be the South African version, and *A. afarensis* is the East African one (Foley 1999; Strait and Wood 1999); *A. bahrelghazali* may be the biogeographical variant from the more central parts of Africa (Brunet et al. 1996).

It is probably the case that all australopithecines are bipedal; the anatomical evidence suggests not that this is identical to the full striding gait of modern humans, but that these creatures were capable of facultative upright walking to a greater extent than any living ape. The palaeoenvironmental evidence suggests that they occupied riparian and lacustrine woodland and bushland, rather than open grassland. No stone tools have been associated with them with any degree of certainty. Dental morphology, dental wear, isotopes, and associational studies all tend to suggest that the australopithecines had a relatively broad-based, largely frugivorous diet, compatible with a woodland, wooded savannah habitat (Grine et al. 2006; Scott et al. 2005).

The most significant trend across this period is towards larger dental adaptations, and the associated musculature and cranial superstructures. The earliest appearance of this trend is in *Paranthropus aethiopicus* (2.6 mya), but it can be argued that the South African *A. africanus* display the trend as well. Later forms of these 'robust australopithecines' are found in both East and South Africa, and are probably allospecies (*P. boisei* and *P. robustus* respectively) (Aiello and Andrews 2000; Grine 1989). The very large molars, molarized premolars, extensive wear on thick-enamelled crowns, and reduced anterior dentition, with the associated very large mandibles, short broad faces, and sagittal and nuchal crests, were all adaptations to hard, coarse, gritty, or fibrous plant foods, and the most probable interpretation is that this trend reflects the increasingly arid and open environments, and the more specialized, seasonal resources with which they were living and on which they depended.

This trend is not, it must be stressed, in what might be referred to as a human direction; on the contrary, the robust australopithecines or paranthropines are in many ways hyperaustralopithecines, and there is a strong continuity from the early to the later forms, with an adaptive basis to it. There is, however, another trend, although it is harder to delineate clearly. Among a number of fossils dated to younger than 2.3 mya, there is evidence for large brains and reduced dentition—two traits associated with the genus *Homo*. These occur in Olduvai Gorge and at Turkana, and perhaps indicate that the genus may be as old as 2.3 mya

(Ackermann 2002; Tobias 1991; Wood 1992). However, the level of encephalization is not very marked, and more importantly, it is associated with a rather diverse set of morphologies (Wood and Collard 1999b).

In broad terms the Plio-Pleistocene clearly shows a hominin adaptive radiation; for most of the period the dominant trend is towards megadonty, but there is a secondary one which either retains more primitive australopithecine traits or develops more derived ones associated with *Homo*. There remain, though, many uncertainties and complexities. Principal among these is that the origins of *Homo* are unclear. The very early evidence, prior to 2.0 mya, is ephemeral, and does not provide more than an indication of the presence of trends that are similar to those seen in later *Homo*. The material after 2.0 mya is much more complete (especially from Olduvai and Koobi Fora), but in contrast suffers from very high variability and mixed characters. The material that has been classically placed into *H. habilis sensu stricto* shares with *Homo* the reduced face and dentition, and many elements of the facial morphology; however, if correctly assigned, the associated post-crania are remarkably primitive. Conversely, the material referred to as *Homo rudolfensis* shares with later *Homo* the greater level of encephalization and a relatively flat face, but retains the larger gnathic morphology associated with the robust australopithecines. Furthermore, as Wood and Collard have argued (1999a), both taxa are in many ways more similar to the preceding and ancestral australopithecines (*sensu lato*) rather than to later *Homo*. Perhaps the point to emphasize, given the present evidence, is that the period of the Plio-Pleistocene is one of remarkable diversity and also divergent trends— ones that later become clearly established through the extinction of the australopithecines and the evolution of *Homo*.

Lower Pleistocene (1.8–0.79 mya)

There are two competing definitions for the beginning of the Lower Pleistocene: 2.6 and 1.8 mya. The latter is used here, as it is the more widely adopted. This period can be seen as the point in which 'human' as opposed to simply 'hominin' evolution occurs. While the Pliocene is dominated by australopithecines of various sorts, and the emergence of forms that may or may not be the beginnings of *Homo*, the period from around 1.9 mya shows novel trends. The key taxon is *Homo erectus*. This is at once the core of Pleistocene human evolution, and a taxonomic problem. One interpretation is that *H. erectus* is a very wide-ranging species, occurring from about 1.9 mya in Africa, dispersing widely across Eurasia, and surviving through to the end of the Middle Pleistocene in parts of Asia (Andrews 1984; Antón 2003; Bilsborough 2005). However, for some this is too broad a definition, and the term has been limited to the Asian forms, with other names being applied to material from Africa (*H. ergaster*) (Wood 1984), and Georgia (*H. georgicus*) (Lordkipanidze et al. 2006).

The earliest material of this taxon is from eastern Africa. The key specimens are primarily from Lake Turkana (Wood 1991). Two virtually complete crania—KNM-ER3733 and KNM-ER3883—show features that are incontrovertibly *Homo*—a smaller and more orthographic face, prominent nasal bones, a more rounded vault with a larger brain, and reduced dentition. However, the key specimen is WT-15000, which is the most complete skeleton of an early hominin (Walker and Leakey 1993). Although it is a juvenile, nonetheless it provides clear evidence for a reorganization of the post-cranial skeleton in line with that seen in modern humans (a more linear arrangement, with narrow hips, vertebral curvature, extended legs, and shortened arms, and evidence for a full striding gait). The evidence from these three specimens alone is enough to indicate a grade shift in hominins, away from the australopithecine mode, towards a human one.

These key specimens are dated between 1.8 and 1.5 mya; there is some suggestion that there may be older specimens (1.9 mya). The lower end of the range is harder to estimate, as it is very sensitive to nomenclature. Buia, dated to 0.9 mya, is very similar (Abbate et al. 1998), and is among the younger specimens, as are those from North Africa (Terginif) and the Middle Awash. In his review, Klein (2009) suggests that no *H. erectus* fossils belong unambiguously to the Middle Pleistocene. It can be argued that across this time period the dominant African hominin is adaptively different from both australopithecines and modern humans. It has an encephalization quotient of 3.66–4.11 (Rightmire 2004), compared to ~3 in australopithecines and >5 in modern humans (McHenry 1976); its growth patterns are intermediate; its locomotion was clearly functionally equivalent to that of modern humans, with net energetic savings coming from leg length extension; in addition, it is strongly associated with stone tools, and with the greater complexity of those tools.

However, perhaps the most significant element of this taxon is that it—or its related descendants—occurs outside Africa. The earliest securely dated specimens are found in Georgia (1.6 mya), and in Java there are strong claims for dates of similar ages. From 1.0 mya there is broader evidence for *H. erectus* in the cooler parts of the Old World (Antón 2003). This wider distribution has been associated with technology and increased dependence upon meat (Foley 2001).

This simple model of the evolution of African *H. erectus* and its dispersal into the Old World (or alternatively, of *H. ergaster* in Africa, and the subsequent dispersal and diversification of descendent species such as *H. erectus*) is useful, but it is increasingly clear that it hides considerable complexity. In brief, within Africa there is growing evidence for diversity of forms—for example, the diminutive hominin from Ileret (Spoor et al. 2007), suggesting that body size at least was an adaptive dimension for *H. erectus* as much as in modern humans; beyond Africa, the Dmanisi specimens show variation which is not only very considerable, but also overlaps with earlier hominins such as *H. habilis*, challenging the simple monophyletic origin of *H. ergaster*; and the evidence for persistence of the taxon in eastern Asia long after it had disappeared in Africa. The observations indicate that while a broad 'grade of humanity' may have been achieved, nonetheless it shows very strong geographical, temporal, and phylogenetic patterns that must reflect divergent evolutionary histories. In broad terms, early *Homo* evolved in Africa at some time towards the end of the Pliocene, and developed adaptations that enabled them to disperse more widely both within Africa and beyond. From that point, hominin evolutionary history must have consisted of widely dispersed populations, existing in considerable isolation one from another at a continental scale, and evolving private trajectories, so that each continent, and even subcontinent, had different histories. In Africa this certainly involved the transformation into a later, larger-brained species in the Middle Pleistocene; in many parts of Asia, on the other hand, the archaic forms persisted.

Middle Pleistocene (0.78–0.125 mya)

The middle Pleistocene in Africa broadly coincides with a number of developments. Specimens such as Bodo do retain some of the primitive traits of *Homo erectus* but they also have a number of more derived ones—especially a higher and more rounded cranium, a frontal which is less flattened, and more heavily arched brow ridges (Asfaw 1983). Above all, there is a larger brain size (Conroy et al. 2000). Once again, nomenclature can be problematic. For some this creature belongs to a broader grouping of what was historically often referred to as archaic *Homo sapiens*, a poorly defined taxon that basically included all larger-brained hominins that were neither modern human nor *erectus*, but which has more recently been referred to as *H. heidelbergensis*. This species would occur in Africa and Europe (the 'Mauer jaw' is the type specimen), and it spans the period from around 800 kya to 200 kya. Within Africa the record of this period is very sparse, and only a handful of specimens provide information: Elandsfontein (South Africa), Kabwe (Zambia), Kapthurin (Kenya), and Cave of Hearths (South Africa) (see (Klein 2009) and (Barham and Mitchell 2008)). Given the variety of specimens, especially when eastern Asia is taken into account, it may be that the African specimens can be considered to be a separate species or at least subspecies/palaeodeme—*Homo rhodesiensis*.

A very scarce fossil record for much of the Middle Pleistocene, especially the early parts, means that it is possible to see only a single lineage (*H. heidelbergensis* or *H. rhodesiensis*) across much of this time. However, the later part of the period shows that there is greater diversity, even if it is not clear how this should be managed taxonomically. First, there are a group of larger-brained hominins that occur after about 350 kya, and show generalized features that may form the ancestral morphology for *H. sapiens*. It has been proposed that these be placed in a separate taxon, *H. helmei* (Foley and Lahr 1997), although this has not been universally accepted (McBrearty and Brooks 2000). The type specimen would be from Florisbad (South Africa), and other specimens assigned to it would include Eliye Springs, Jebel Irhoud, Singa, and possibly others outside Africa. This group is elusive, but may be a useful term for the forms that are neither classic *H. heidelbergensis* nor modern humans. Some would consider it to be a clade relative to earlier and later forms, but others see it simply as part of a phase in the evolution of a lineage.

The other taxon of the Middle Pleistocene is *Homo sapiens*, or anatomically modern humans. Unlike most other taxa, *H. sapiens* is often assumed to be a clearly demarcated species, with an easily distinguishable set of traits—higher frontal, maximum cranial breadth high on the cranium, a rounded occipital, reduction or loss of brow ridges, and other robust elements. However, the Pleistocene fossils of *Homo sapiens* show a much more complex pattern, with combinations of primitive and derived features, so that one should be wary of treating this as a clear evolutionary rubicon. This is evident from an examination of the two earliest *H. sapiens* samples, Omo Kibish (Day and Stringer 1991) and Herto (White et al. 2003). The former, probably dating to 194 kya (McDougall et al. 2005), shows a combination of traits not just within individuals but also between specimens (Omo Kibish 1 and 2). Herto, younger at 160 kya, is also remarkably robust, with a large broad face, which is not particularly characteristic of later human populations.

The primary point about these earlier modern human fossils is that they show continuity within Africa between more archaic forms (*H. helmei*) and later modern humans (e.g. Klasies River Mouth) (see Lahr, Ch. 23 below). They indicate that the evolution of modern humans is an event that occurs in the Middle Pleistocene within Africa (probably eastern Africa), and that it was part of the overall diversity of the hominin lineage at that time.

PATTERNS OF EVOLUTIONARY CHANGE

The succession of fossils shows the 'story' of human evolution, from ape-like ancestors to modern humans. There are a number of ways in which this succession can be used to infer actual evolutionary patterns, and thus a better understanding of the underlying reasons for it. Three such patterns can be proposed: phylogenetic, evolutionary trends, and evolutionary geography and adaptive radiations.

Phylogeny

A major goal of evolutionary analysis is to reconstruct the relationships by descent of the lineages and taxa involved, and such trees are iconic of human evolution. Phylogenetic reconstructions have, over the years, become more technical (as cladistic algorithms and software have been used), more complex (as the fossil record has increased), and more uncertain (a combination of the two). This can lead to an abandonment of phylogenetic considerations. However, as one of the most powerful developments in evolutionary biology is the greater understanding of the relationship between phylogeny and adaptation (Harvey and Pagel 1991), this is a mistake. Phylogeny, even if it is uncertain, is central to understanding evolutionary patterns. Fig. 20.4 shows three phylogenies, one for earliest hominins, one for australopithecines and early *Homo*, and one for later *Homo*. These are not formal, cladistically built evolutionary trees, but ones that attempt to indicate areas of uncertainty and certainty. Phylogenetically speaking, the greatest confidence is associated with the broad set of relationships among the australopithecines/paranthropines, and for the monophyletic nature of *Homo* subsequent to 1.8 mya. At the opposite extreme, there is little confidence with regard either to the relationships among the earliest potential hominins (*Sahelanthropus*, *Orrorin*, and *Ardipithecus*) or to their relationship to australopithecines; the origins of *Homo* are also poorly understood.

Evolutionary trends

Evolutionary trends are notoriously difficult to define, and are inevitably a selective perspective on evolution. Nonetheless, it is clear that there is an overall adaptive pattern of hominin evolution from a biological perspective. Three major adaptive patterns should be emphasized. The first of these is the fundamental importance of bipedalism and terrestrial commitment for the hominins. It is clear that this is not only the major adaptive element of the early African hominins, but also that it forms the basis for major skeletal and other biological change. While there may be arguments about the onset of this (australopithecines or earlier?), the different forms of bipedalism (australopithecine vs *Homo*), and its adaptive advantage (feeding behaviour, energetic, thermoregulation?), none would question its ultimate significance and centrality to early hominin evolution.

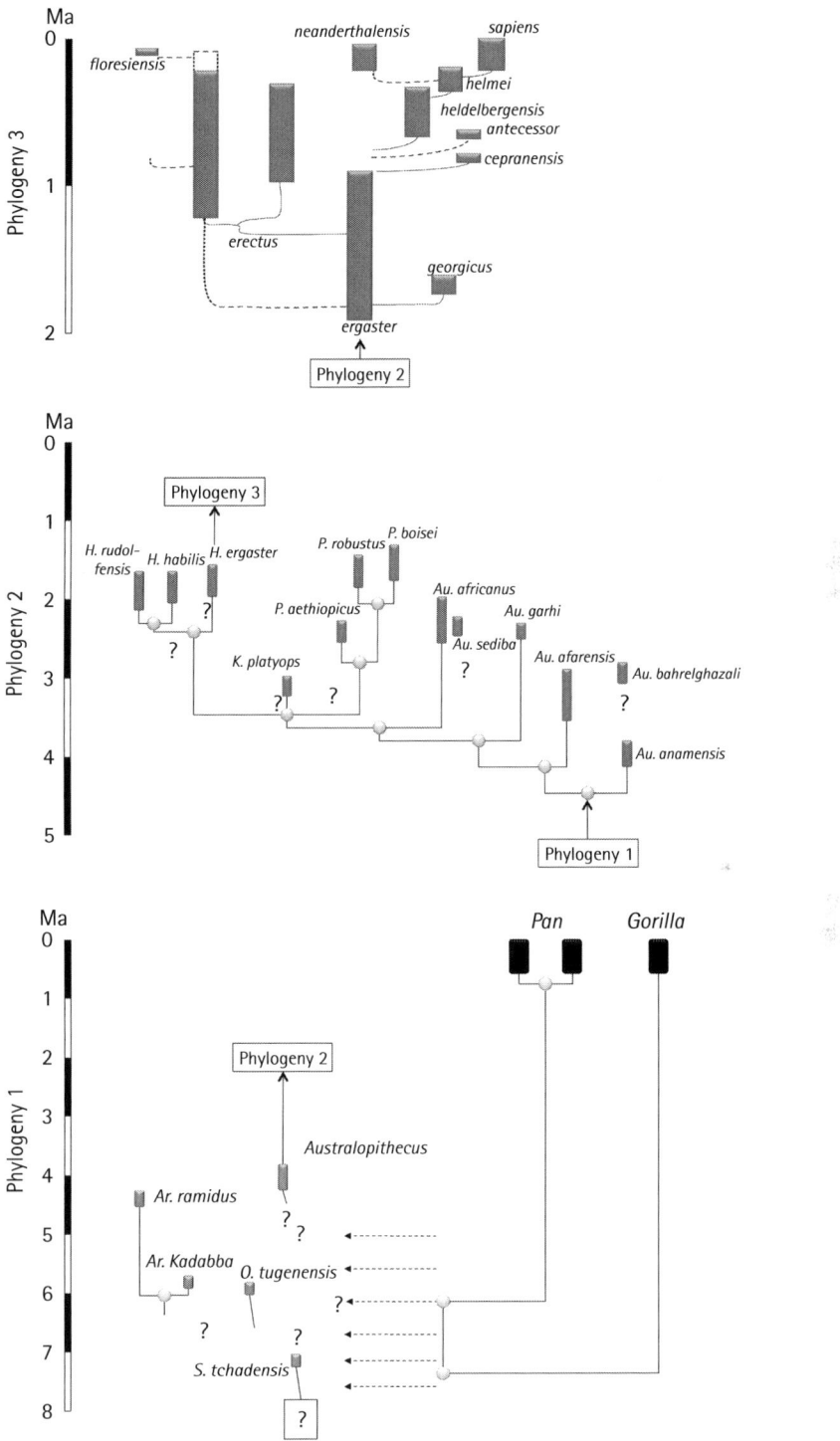

FIG. 20.4 Hominin phylogeny. There is no consensus phylogeny for hominin evolution, due to the many difficulties in reconstruction. The phylogeny presented here is informal and tentative only, and based primarily on (Strait and Grine 2004); see also (Wood and Lonergan 2008).

The second is that the pattern is ecological. There is little doubt that the evolution of hominins is more closely associated with what can be called the more seasonal and open environments of Africa than with closed forested ones (deMenocal 2004). This is a carefully phrased statement, as it is often assumed that savannah is the same as grassland, and that hominins evolved in grasslands. This is not the case, but neither did human evolution occur in forest. The gradient from woodlands through to open grasslands represents the range of habitats that shaped hominin ecology. The adaptive consequences are significant—a greater dependence upon animal resources, a high level of adaptability to a range of environments, increased diet breadth, and most probably more and more dependence upon technology to gain access to otherwise inaccessible resources (large game, underground plants, etc.). The bulk of these are associated with *Homo* and later hominin evolution, and it remains to be seen how far australopithecine diet shifted significantly. Indeed, it could be argued that a major trend in hominin evolution is that seen in paranthropines (see above), with their megadontic specializations.

The third pattern is geographical. As the hominins evolved they underwent major shifts in distribution, and these almost certainly structured populational and species diversity. Phylogeny is very largely an outcome of spatial patterns, and so fossil hominin distributions are critical in interpreting human evolution. We are almost certainly severely constrained in understanding evolutionary geography by the limited fossil record (the archaeological record is a much richer source in this respect). Two broad points can be made, however. The first is that it is clear that the eastern quadrant of Africa is critical for hominin origins, and that this probably fits well with our understanding of the relationships between hominins and other African hominoids. Second, that the broad homeland for hominins appears to be the higher and more arid eastern and southern half of the continent. Third, that although there is this 'east to south' continuity pattern, it is likely that there is also a recurrent process of divergence between eastern and southern hominins, and that phylogeny should reflect that (Foley 1999). And lastly, that early hominin evolution prior to 2 million years at least is clearly an African event, and that even after this period, when Eurasian dispersals begin to occur, Africa remains one of the primary sources of evolutionary novelty, through to and including, the origins of modern humans.

The final pattern is the most obvious: the evolution of larger brains, and associated complexity of behaviour. This has been well documented and discussed, and hardly needs reiterating (Sherwood et al. 2008): large brains, and their associated life history parameters, are the human evolutionary trademark. What should be emphasized is that this increase is not constant across the whole period of hominin evolution. While there may be some encephalization among australopithecines, it is not very marked. Brain size increases occur with the genus *Homo*, and in general it is during the last half million years or so in which both the rate of increase accelerates and brain sizes become more than double that which would be expected for an equivalent-sized ape.

Climate, environment, and evolution

Phylogeny, species diversity, foraging behaviour, locomotor behaviour and structure, encephalization, and life history, as well as geographical dispersals, are the patterns of hominin evolution, reflecting how selection and adaptation have operated and developed over millions of years. While there have been a number of debates about the causality and driving forces for these patterns, it is certainly the case that hominin evolution occurs in the context of major climatic change. From the late Miocene there is a marked drop in temperature, and from the middle of the Pliocene large parts of Africa become more arid (Vrba 1996a). During the Pleistocene there are marked temperature reductions, as well as major climatic fluctuations. A number of climatic cycles become superimposed, producing the well-known glacial and interglacial phases of the higher latitudes. The later parts of these changes are moderately well understood, with a relationship between reduced global temperatures and drier environments in Africa; earlier phases are less clear. However, mapping both biological and behavioural change in the hominins during this period must take into account climatic factors. Some evolutionary biologists have seen a strong causal relationship between climate and evolution (Vrba 1996b; Potts 2007), others less so (Foley 1994). However, even if the role of climate is indirect, it remains a fundamental part of the process.

Archaeological implications

For much of the latter half of the 20th century the archaeological and fossil records were considered to be rather independent, telling different stories of our past. The last two decades have seen considerable convergence between archaeologists and palaeontologists in their attempts to reconstruct evolutionary history (Foley 2002b). It is now generally accepted that human biological evolution provides the appropriate framework for understanding Pleistocene prehistory, and equally, that behaviour, as seen through the archaeological record, plays a very significant role in biological evolution. There are a number of ways in which this interdependence is significant.

The role of phylogeny

Darwin defined evolution as descent with modification. This provides a critical framework for looking at any aspect of the past, as the 'modifications' (be they new tools, new diets, new anatomies) occur in the context of existing ones. Phylogeny, or alternatively the existing phenotype, is that context. Evolutionary biologists have thus become proficient at placing new adaptive patterns in an evolutionary context, or more technically, using a cladistic framework for analysing behaviour. This approach is becoming more common in archaeology (e.g. Lycett 2009), and should be particularly important for understanding human evolution in Africa. One example where this may be important is considering the phylogeny of early *Homo*: are the first Eurasians *H. erectus* or *H. habilis*, and does this help explain why only Mode 1 technologies occur? Do technologies track biological populations, or are they the product of repeated local change and convergence? Whichever is the answer, it is impossible to consider lithic technology in Africa without considering the role of biological populations (Foley and Lahr 2003).

The role of Africa

The fossil record and genetic evidence clearly gives a central role to Africa in human evolution, and the Eurasian record is largely a product of dispersal from Africa. This means that tackling any archaeological problems in the African Pleistocene needs to build on this evolutionary constraint, and seek to relate non-African patterns to an African source. This is most probably the case for both Mode 1 and Mode 2. Above all, though, is the need to link the pattern of human evolution to the continental history (Kingdon 1989).

The role of archaic fossils in the evolution of modern humans

Perhaps the key finding of recent years is that modern humans evolved in Africa (see Lahr, Ch. 23 below). This seems to be well substantiated in the fossil record, and there is growing evidence for the early appearance of more modern forms of behaviour in Africa (Barham, Ch. 24 below). On current evidence it seems that the biological changes—the development of modern human anatomy and the demographic evidence for bottlenecks at the base of the human lineage—preceded any changes in behaviour by tens of thousands of years. Current research would seem to suggest that the evolution of modern behaviour occurred in the African Middle Stone Age, and that this archaeological phase overlapped with both modern and more archaic populations. This firmly roots the archaeological studies of the last 200,000 years in the evolutionary history of African lineages. The origins of modern humans, and their subsequent evolutionary history in Africa, render the boundaries between archaeology and human palaeontology obsolete.

References

Abbate, E., Albianelli, A., Azzaroli, A., et al. (1998). A one-million-year-old *Homo* cranium from the Danakil (Afar) Depression of Eritrea. *Nature* 393: 458–60.

Ackermann, R. R. (2002). Patterns of covariation in the hominoid craniofacial skeleton: implications for paleoanthropological models. *Journal of Human Evolution* 43: 167–87.

Aiello, L. C., and Andrews, P. J. (2000). The Australopithecines in review. *Human Evolution* 15: 17–38.

Andrews, P. J. (1984). An alternative interpretation of the characters used to define *Homo erectus*. *Courier Forschunginstitut Seckenbergensis* 69: 167–75.

Antón, S. (2003). Natural history of *Homo erectus*. *Yearbook of Physical Anthropology* 46: 126–70.

Asfaw, B. (1983). A new hominid parietal from Bodo, Middle Awash Valley, Ethiopia. *American Journal of Physical Anthropology* 61: 367–71.

Barham, L. S., and Mitchell, P. J. (2008). *The First Africans: African Archaeology from the Earliest Toolmakers to Most Recent Foragers*. Cambridge: Cambridge University Press.

Begun, D. R. (2010). Miocene hominids and the origins of the African apes and humans. *Annual Review of Anthropology* 39: 67–84.

Bilsborough, A. (2005). *Homo erectus* revisited: aspects of affinity and diversity in a Pleistocene hominin species. *L'Anthropologie* 43: 129–58.

Bobe, R. (2006). The evolution of arid ecosystems in eastern Africa. *Journal of Arid Environments* 66: 564–84.

Brown, B., Brown, F. H., and Walker, A. (2001). New hominids from the Lake Turkana Basin, Kenya. *Journal of Human Evolution* 41: 29–44.

BROWN, P., SUTIKNA, T., MORWOOD, M., et al. (2004). A new small bodied hominin from the late Pleistocene of Flores, Indonesia. *Nature* 431: 1055–61.

BRUNET, M., BEAUVILAIN, A., COPPENS, Y., HEINTZ, E., MOUTAYE, A.H.E., and PILBEAM, D. (1996). *Australopithecus bahrelghazali*, a new species of early hominid from Koro Toro region, Chad. *Comptes Rendus de l'Académie des Sciences, série II-A* 322: 907–13.

BRUNET, M., GUY, F., PILBEAM, D., et al. (2002). A new hominid from the upper Miocene of Chad, central Africa. *Nature* 418: 145–51.

CERLING, T. E., LEVIN, N. E., QUADE, J., et al. (2010). Comment on the paleoenvironment of *Ardipithecus ramidus*. *Science* 328: 1105.

CONROY, G. C., WEBER, G. W., SEIDLER, H., RECHEIS, W., ZUR NEDDEN, D., and MARIAM, J. H. (2000). Endocranial capacity of the Bodo cranium determined from three-dimensional computed tomography. *American Journal of Physical Anthropology* 113: 111–18.

DARWIN, C. (1871). *Descent of Man and Selection in Relation to Sex.* London: Murray.

DAY, M. H., and STRINGER, C. B. (1991). The Omo Kibish cranial remains and classification within the genus Homo. *L'Anthropologie* 95: 573–94.

DE CASTRO, J. M. B., ARSUAGA, J. L., CARBONELL, E., ROSAS, A., MARTINEZ, I., and MOSQUERA, M (1997). A hominid from the lower Pleistocene of Atapuerca, Spain: possible ancestor to Neanderthals and modern humans. *Science* 276: 1392–5.

DEMENOCAL, P. B. (2004). African climate change and faunal evolution during the Pliocene-Pleistocene. *Earth and Planetary Science Letters* 220: 3–24.

DENNELL, R., and ROEBROEKS, W. (2005). An Asian perspective on early human dispersal from Africa. *Nature* 438: 1099–104.

FLEAGLE, J. (1999). *Primate Adaptations and Evolution.* London: Academic Press.

FOLEY, R. A. (1994). Speciation, extinction and climatic change in hominid evolution. *Journal of Human Evolution* 26: 275–89.

—— (1999). The evolutionary geography of Pliocene hominids. In T. Bromage and F. Schrenk (eds), *African Biogeography, Climatic Change, and Hominid Evolution.* Oxford: Oxford University Press, 328–48.

—— (2001). The evolutionary consequences of increased carnivory in hominids. In C. B. Stanford (ed.), *The Early Human Diet: The role of Meat.* Oxford: Oxford University Press, 305–31.

—— (2002a). Adaptive radiations and dispersals in hominin evolutionary ecology. *Evolutionary Anthropology* 11: 32–7.

—— (2002b). Parallel tracks in time: archaeology and human evolution. In B. W. Cunliffe, A. C. Renfrew, and W. Davies (eds), *Archaeology: The Widening Debate.* Oxford: Oxford University Press, 3–42.

—— (2005). Species diversity in human evolution: challenges and opportunities. *Transactions of the Royal Society of South Africa* 60: 67–72.

—— and GAMBLE, C. S. (2009). The ecology of social transitions in human evolution. *Philosophical Transactions of the Royal Society,* series B, 364: 3267–79.

—— and LAHR, M. M. (1997). Mode 3 technologies and the evolution of modern humans. *Cambridge Archaeological Journal* 7: 3–36.

—— —— (2003). On stony ground: lithic technology, human evolution, and the emergence of culture. *Evolutionary Anthropology* 12: 109–22.

GOODMAN, M., TAGLE, D. A., FITCH, D. H. A., et al. (1990). Primate evolution at the DNA level and a classification of hominoids. *Journal of Molecular Evolution* 30: 260–66.

GRINE, F. E. (ed.) (1989). *The Evolutionary History of the 'Robust' Australopithecines*. Chicago: Aldine de Gruyter.

—— UNGAR, P. S., and TEAFORD, M. F. (2006). Was the Early Pliocene hominin 'Australopithecus' anamensis a hard object feeder? *South African Journal of Science* 102: 301–10.

HARVEY, P., and PAGEL, M. (1991). *The Comparative Method in Evolutionary Biology*. Oxford: Oxford University Press.

HOWELL, F. C. (1999). Paleo-demes, species clades, and extinctions in the Pleistocene hominin record. *Journal of Anthropological Research* 55: 191–243.

HUBLIN, J. J., and PÄÄBO, S. (2006). Neandertals. *Current Biology* 16: R113–14.

KIMBEL, W. H., LOCKWOOD, C. A., WARD, C. V., LEAKEY, M. G., RAK, Y., and JOHANSON, D. C. (2006). Was *Australopithecus anamensis* ancestral to *A. afarensis*? A case of anagenesis in the hominin fossil record. *Journal of Human Evolution* 51: 134–52.

KINGDON, J. (1989). *Island Africa*. London: Academic Press.

KLEIN, R. G. (2009). *The Human Career*. Chicago: University Press of Chicago.

KUMAR, S., FILIPSKI, A., SWARNA, V., WALKER, A., and HEDGES, S. B. (2005). Placing confidence limits on the molecular age of the human-chimpanzee divergence. *Proceedings of the National Academy of Sciences (USA)* 102: 18842–7.

LEAKEY, M. G., FEIBEL, C. S., MCDOUGALL, I., WARD, C., and WALKER, A. (1998). New specimens and confirmation of an early age for *Australopithecus anamensis*. *Nature* 393: 62–6.

LORDKIPANIDIZE, D., VEKUA, A., FERRING, R., et al. (2006). A fourth hominin skull from Dmanisi, Georgia: anatomical record, part A. *Discoveries in Molecular, Cellular, and Evolutionary Biology* 288: 1146–57.

LOVEJOY, C. O. (2009). Re-examining human origins in light of *Ardipithecus ramidus*. *Science* 326: 74e1–e8.

LYCETT, S. J. (2009) Are Victoria West cores 'proto-Levallois'? A phylogenetic assessment. *Journal of Human Evolution* 56: 175–91

MCBREARTY, S., and BROOKS, A. S. (2000). The revolution that wasn't: a new interpretation of the origin of modern human behavior. *Journal of Human Evolution* 39: 453–563.

MCDOUGALL, I., BROWN, F., and FLEAGLE, J. (2005). Stratigraphic placement and age of modern humans from Kibish, Ethiopia. *Nature* 433: 733–6.

MCHENRY, H. M. (1976). Early hominid body weight and encephalization. *American Journal of Physical Anthropology* 45: 77–84.

POTTS, R. (2007). Paleoclimate and human evolution. *Evolutionary Anthropology*, 16: 1–3.

READER, J. (1988). *Missing Links*. London: Pelican.

RICHMOND, B. G., and JUNGERS, W. L. (2008). *Orrorin tugenensis* femoral morphology and the evolution of hominin bipedalism. *Science* 319: 1662–5.

RIGHTMIRE, G. P. (1998). Human evolution in the middle Pleistocene: the role of *Homo heidelbergensis*. *Evolutionary Anthropology* 6: 218–27.

—— (2004). Brain size and encephalization in early to Mid-Pleistocene *Homo*. *American Journal of Physical Anthropology* 124: 109–23.

—— LORDKIPANIDIZE, D., and VEKUA, A. (2006). Anatomical descriptions, comparative studies and evolutionary significance of the hominin skulls from Dmanisi, Republic of Georgia. *Journal of Human Evolution* 50: 115–41.

SCOTT, R. S., UNGAR, P. S., BERGSTROM, T. S., et al. (2005). Dental microwear texture analysis shows within-species diet variability in fossil hominins. *Nature* 436: 693–5.

SEMAW, S., RENNE, P., HARRIS, J. W. K., et al. (1997). 2.5-million-year-old stone tools from Gona, Ethiopia. *Nature* 385: 333–6.

SHERWOOD, C. C., SUBIAUL, F., and ZAWIDZKI, T. W. (2008). A natural history of the human mind: tracing evolutionary changes in brain and cognition. *Journal of Anatomy* 212: 426–54.

SPOOR, F., LEAKEY, M. G., GATHOGO, P. N., et al. (2007). Implications of new early *Homo* fossils from Ileret, east of Lake Turkana, Kenya. *Nature* 448: 688–91.

STEWART, C. B., and DISOTELL, T. R. (1998) Primate evolution—in and out of Africa. *Current Biology* 8: R582–8.

STRAIT, D. S., and GRINE, F. E. (2004). Inferring hominoid and early hominid phylogeny using craniodental characters: the role of fossil taxa. *Journal of Human Evolution* 47: 399–452.

—— and WOOD, B. A. (1999). Early hominid biogeography. *Proceedings of the National Academy of Sciences (USA)* 96: 9196–200.

TATTERSALL, I. (2000). Paleoanthropology: the last half-century. *Evolutionary Anthropology* 9: 2–16.

TOBIAS, P. V. (1991.) *Olduvai Gorge*, vol. 4: *The Skulls, Teeth, and Endocasts of Homo habilis.* Cambridge: Cambridge University Press.

VRBA, E. S. (ed.) (1996a). *Palaeoclimate and Neogene Evolution.* New Haven, Conn.: Yale University Press.

—— (1996b). Climate, heterochrony, and human evolution. *Journal of Anthropological Research* 52: 1–28.

WALKER, A. C., and LEAKEY, R. E. (1993). *The Nariokotome* Homo erectus *Skeleton.* Springer.

WARD, C. V., LEAKEY, M., and WALKER, A. (1999). The new hominid species *Australopithecus anamensis. Evolutionary Anthropology* 7: 197–205.

—— —— —— (2001). Morphology of *Australopithecus anamensis* from Kanapoi and Allia Bay, Kenya. *Journal of Human Evolution* 41: 255–368.

—— LOCKWOOD, C. A., KIMBEL, W. H., et al. (2003). Was *Australopithecus anamensis* ancestral to *A-afarensis? American Journal of Physical Anthropology* 36: 219–20.

WHITE, T. D., ASFAW, B., BEYENE, Y., et al. (2009). *Ardipithecus ramidus* and the paleobiology of early hominids. *Science* 326: 75–86.

—— —— DEGUSTA, D., et al. (2003). Pleistocene *Homo sapiens* from Middle Awash, Ethiopia. *Nature* 423: 742–7.

WOOD, B. A. (1984). The origins of *Homo erectus. Courier Foschungsinstitut Senckenberg* 69: 99–111.

—— (1991). *Koobi Fora Research Project*, vol. 4: *The Hominid Cranial Remains.* Oxford: Clarendon Press.

—— (1992). Origin and evolution of the genus *Homo. Nature* 355: 783–90.

—— and COLLARD, M. (1999a). Anthropology: the human genus. *Science* 284: 65–9.

—— —— (1999b). The changing face of genus *Homo. Evolutionary Anthropology* 8: 195–207.

—— and LONERGAN, N. (2008). The hominin fossil record: taxa, grades and clades. *Journal of Anatomy* 212: 354–76.

—— and RICHMOND, B. (2000). Human evolution: taxonomy and paleobiology. *Journal of Anatomy* 196: 19–60.

ZALMOUT, I. S., SANDERS, W. J., MACLATCHY, L. M., et al. (2010). New Oligocene primate from Saudi Arabia and the divergence of apes and Old World monkeys. *Nature* 466: 360–4.

CHAPTER 21

THE OLDOWAN

Early Hominins and the Beginning of Human Culture

MANUEL DOMÍNGUEZ-RODRIGO

THE OLDOWAN TOOL KIT

AT the boundary between the Late Pliocene and Early Pleistocene (2.6 mya), during the transition from the more ape-like australopithecines to the earliest representatives of the genus *Homo* (Foley, Ch. 20 above), one of the most significant elements in the human evolutionary process appeared: the use of stone tools and their accumulation at the earliest archaeological sites. Called Oldowan from the eponymous site of Olduvai Gorge, Tanzania, this industry was first formally defined by Louis Leakey (1951), though foreshadowed by his reference two decades previously to a primitive industry composed of nodular bifacially flaked artefacts and their debitage (flakes) and thought to be younger than the Kafuan Industry in the oldest terraces of the Kafu River, Uganda (Leakey 1934). This early definition was expanded by Mary Leakey (1967), influenced by Kleindienst (1967), and adopted its definitive form with Leakey's (1971) typology. The concept of an older Kafuan industry has long been abandoned, given its ecofactual nature, rendering the Oldowan the oldest known stone tool kit. Its typology identifies several types of artefacts: unmodified cobblestones and nodules used for battering (hammerstones), modified cobblestones and nodules (cores), and the pieces detached from them (variously called debitage, flakes and debris). Cobblestones and nodules were flaked in various ways: flaking occurred unidirectionally along one edge (resulting in unifacial and bifacial choppers and discoids) or multidirectionally along various edges (resulting in polyhedrons and subspheroids). The flake pieces detached from these cobbles usually consist of fragments with one striking platform (i.e. point of impact) and a sharp-edged perimeter (Fig. 21.1). The oldest known Oldowan stone tools come from Gona in the Afar region of Ethiopia and date to 2.6 mya (Semaw et al. 1997, 2003). Oldowan sites are widespread in East Africa (e.g. Gona, Omo (Ethiopia), Koobi Fora, Kanjera (Kenya), Olduvai Gorge, Peninj (Tanzania)), but they are also documented in some localities in Southern Africa (e.g. Swartkrans) and North Africa (e.g. Ain Hanech) (Kuman 2007; Sahnouni 2006) (Fig. 21.2).

FIG. 21.1 Some examples of stone tools from the oldest archaeological site in the world: OGS7 at Gona (Ethiopia). **A.** Some examples of refitting of flakes to a core. **B.** End-struck flake. **C.** Core/chopper. **D.** Side-struck flake. Arrows show striking platform and impact point areas (images courtesy of S. Semaw).

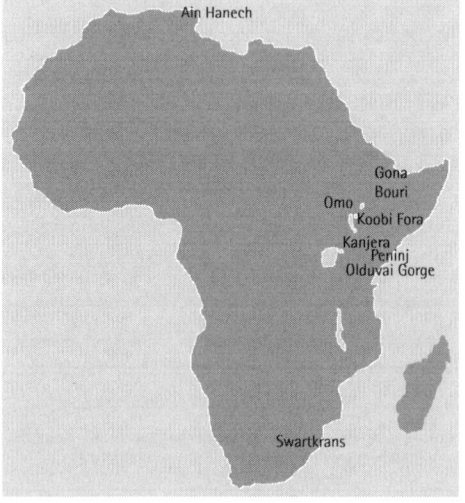

FIG. 21.2 Map of Africa displaying the archaeological localities mentioned in the text.

As defined by Mary Leakey (1971), the Oldowan is highly variable. Only sites at Olduvai Gorge show the diversity of types she recognized (Schick and Toth 1993) and most sites older than 2 mya show a more reduced variety of forms, with flakes, choppers, and moderately knapped cores being the most abundant forms (Semaw 2000). In some cases, a larger variety of knapped forms is documented, as at Kanjera (Kenya) (Braun et al. 2009a).

In the *Prehistory of Uganda Protectorate*, O'Brien (1939) noticed that the evolution of the Oldowan was progressive and remarked that the Oldowan and the Acheulean were at some point in their evolution contemporary and context-dependent. This was confirmed later by Hay (1976), who stressed that Oldowan sites seemed to be mostly restricted to lake environments, with Acheulean sites occurring more frequently in fluvial contexts. Mary Leakey (1971) herself divided the Oldowan at Olduvai Gorge into Oldowan (Bed I), Developed Oldowan A (lower Bed II), Developed Oldowan B (upper Bed II), and Developed Oldowan C (Bed III). Each type depended on the proportion of choppers and chopping tools, which decreased through time as the proportion of polyhedrons, spheroids, and retouched tools increased.

Oldowan technology and chimpanzee stone tool making

Some Oldowan core artefacts and flakes were used as tools. In the beginning, as can be observed at Gona (Ethiopia), most of the cobbles were used as cores to produce flakes. However, pitting on the end opposite the flaked area suggests that some were also initially used as hammerstones. It was previously assumed that stone tools were developed for animal butchery, but most archaeological sites earlier than 2 mya lack evidence of this (Domínguez-Rodrigo 2009). Nonetheless, the discovery of cut-marked bones at Gona and in the nearby area of Bouri has yielded evidence of stone tools used for butchery as early as 2.6 mya (Domínguez-Rodrigo et al. 2005). In Bouri, no stone tools were found in association with the cut-marked bones, and sources of raw material are several kilometres away (Heinzelin et al. 1999). This suggests that hominins were transporting stone tools over much longer distances than reported for chimpanzees, who also use and transport stone tools (Carvalho et al. 2008).

Technological analysis of the earliest stone tools suggests that early Pleistocene hominins differed from chimpanzees in planning and flaking skills. They therefore represent the earliest documented evidence of behavioural complexity in the human evolutionary process beyond that observed in extant apes. In order to obtain a usable flake it is necessary to select a striking platform neither too close nor too far from the edge of the core, so that angular fragments, usually devoid of sharp edges, are not produced. The hammerstone must hit the striking platform with a certain force and at a certain angle, which varies with the size of the core and the hammerstone (see also Tryon, Ch. 8 above). Experiments with chimpanzees suggest that this degree of precision is highly unusual. Most of their flaking takes place in the form of multiple strikes on the core surface, usually near the core's edge. This frequently results in small and useless debris fragments or in core fragmentation. Once chimpanzees obtain a flake, they do not usually rotate the core to produce a new one; rather, they tend to abandon the core or to continue flaking a different part of it (Toth et al. 2006).

Early hominins were more sophisticated than their chimpanzee-like ancestors. They selected raw materials according to their flaking and functional properties (Semaw 2006). Most of the Gona archaeological sites were created a few metres from the source of raw material, in contrast with the Bouri cut-marked bones. Comparison of several of the Gona artefact assemblages with random cobble samples taken from associated conglomerates that record raw material availability in the region at the time of occupation proves that hominins were selecting specific fine-grained materials over others (Stout et al. 2005). Some of these fine-grained materials have a limited representation in the conglomerates The selection of raw materials, together with their regular transport over long distances, again clearly differentiates early hominins from chimpanzees. This is further confirmed by research undertaken at Kanjera (Kenya), where around 2 mya raw materials were selected from various sources based on their durability and fracture predictability and transported over distances spanning several kilometres (Braun et al. 2009b).

The Oldowan can thus be differentiated from what chimpanzees are able to knap by the following characteristics: control of conchoidal fracture, orderly sequential extraction of flakes, control of impact and knapping (less edge battering on cores and less debris), extraction of end-struck flakes, a higher proportion of side-struck choppers, more heavily reduced cores, more flake scars per core, more functional flakes (longer relative to breadth), higher selection and exploitation of raw materials, and higher degree of planning (Toth et al. 2006).

FUNCTIONALITY

While the first stone tools at 2.5 mya were likely used for butchering animal carcasses (Plummer 2004), this does not imply that animal butchery was their main or only function. Among all sites dated to >2 mya, slightly more than a dozen cut-marked bones have been found (Domínguez-Rodrigo 2009) and in most of them bones are not present at all. Instead, pitting on cores suggests that pounding activities (e.g. of plant foods) may have also taken place. This is suggested by recent analyses of sites at Olduvai Gorge dating to 1.9–1.3 mya, where the most widely represented activity is heavy-duty pounding unrelated to carcass exploitation (Mora and de la Torre 2005; Domínguez-Rodrigo et al. 2007).

WHO CRAFTED THESE TOOLS?

The identity of the hominin(s) responsible for creating the earliest stone tools is still debated. At Bouri, the cut-marked bones are associated with *Australopithecus garhi*, the brain size of which is the same as that of other australopithecines and not much larger than that of apes. There is no indication in the fossil record that this hominin had neurophysiological skills different from those documented in chimpanzees, and until it is more fully reconstructed it will remain difficult to assign the earliest stone tools to a specific hominin. However, considering that these stone tools are part of a new behavioural repertoire that included the creation of special referential places where they accumulated, a substantial amount of planning,

and the beginning of animal butchery, stone tools should probably be associated with a hominin that shows significant physiological differences from earlier hominins. These features
are observable in the genus *Homo* at 2 mya (Foley, Ch. 20 above) and may have emerged earlier as indicated by fragmentary remains of early *Homo* dating to 2.4–2.3 mya retrieved at
Hadar (Ethiopia) and West Turkana (Kenya) (Kimbel et al. 1996).

THE BEHAVIOURAL MEANING OF OLDOWAN
ARCHAEOLOGICAL SITES

As important as the emergence of stone tools is the appearance of the sites in which they are
found. While chimpanzees move linearly from one eating place to the next, hominins began
to select specific *loci* (referential places) in the landscape to which they brought raw material
and transformed it into tools. Some raw materials and tools were then transported away
from these spots. Sometimes, hominins also bought animal carcasses to the same sites (central places). This selection of specific places in which certain activities (including animal
butchery) are performed and radial movement to and from these locations to other points
on the landscape are still seen among living hunter-gatherers. What do these early sites represent in terms of hominin behaviour? Several models have been proposed over the past
thirty years for the most widely debated type of site, those showing a spatial association of
stone tools and bones from multiple animals in discrete archaeological horizons. However,
these models have different heuristics. Taphonomic studies have discarded most of them
(Table 21.1). Presently, only two models survive with unequal heuristics: central-spot models
(in the form either of a central-foraging place or a resource-defence place) (Isaac 1983; Rose
and Marshall 1996) and refuge models (Blumenschine et al. 1994). The former conceive of
sites as referential spots that result from radial movements of hominins around them to
which animal food is brought to be processed and shared in the absence of carnivore competition. This implies a degree of behavioural complexity not documented in other primates.
The latter models assume that sites were places in or near carnivore-competitive areas that
hominins used as temporary refuges, within a foraging behaviour that did not need to be
radial but rather linear, as understood in ethological terms; i.e. hominin behaviour was similar to the foraging behaviour of other primates. Hominins used these refuge spots, presumably, to escape predation and carnivore competition in order individually to consume carcass
remains without the need for intensive cooperation or food-sharing.

These two model groups carry different palaeoecological and taphonomic implications.
Central-spot models require that sites were formed in low-competition settings, which in
modern savannahs are mostly restricted to alluvial woodland habitats. They also require that
the amount of food transported to sites exceeded the needs of one individual in order for food
sharing to have been feasible. For this reason, these models rely on meat-eating as key to hominin subsistence and on primary access to carcass resources, whether in the form of hunting or
aggressive confrontational scavenging, as the main way of obtaining meat (Rose and Marshall
1996; Domínguez-Rodrigo 2002; Bunn 2007; Domínguez-Rodrigo et al. 2007). Strict refuge
models posit that hominins may have accidentally used the same spots because they provided a
temporary safe haven for the consumption of carcass remains obtained while competing with

Table 21.1 Arguments of the least heuristic models provided to account for early site formation, focusing on FLK Zinj

Model	Argument	Taphonomic testing	Technological testing	Palaeoecological testing
Marginal scavenger (Binford 1981)	Sites were formed by animals dying or being predated in certain spots (static concept of site formation) or transported to dens (dynamic concept of site formation) and marginally scavenged by hominins.	The 'static' concept in part of the model was disproved by neo-actualistic studies (see Potts 1988). The model was rejected because: scavenging would only have been feasible after felids and prior to canids or hyenids (Blumenschine 1986); no evidence of den burrowing was found in any of the Olduvai sites; denning by hyenas (the only important bone accumulators in modern savannahs) is reflected in high frequency of tooth-marked and broken bones; no resource can be scavenged in a hyena den; hominins did not target the poorest elements from carcasses (Bunn and Kroll 1986); meat and not marrow was the goal of carcass exploitation (as documented by skeletal part profiles, cut-mark frequencies, and anatomical distribution), and therefore, no marginal scavenging strategy would have resulted in the taphonomic signatures documented at FLK Zinj.	This model would have required only bone-breaking tools and not cutting artefacts. At Zinj, the bulk of artefacts were elaborated with the intention of producing flakes (e.g. cutting tools).	Sites would have been formed in the habitats where carnivores are most active. This is proved wrong in the recent reconstruction of the palaeoecology of the site (Ashley et al. 2010; Domínguez-Rodrigo et al. 2010)

The stone-cache or resource provisioning model (Potts 1988)	Hominins simultaneously used not one but several spots, which they used to store raw material in order to process carcasses obtained nearby efficiently to avoid carnivores. This behaviour over vast time spans could eventually generate the concentrations of fossils and stone artefacts documented in the Olduvai sites.	Faunal remains should reflect the local fauna (in this case given the new palaeoecological reconstruction, woodland taxa). In contrast, there is a mix of taxa from open and closed vegetation habitats. The carnivore damage documented on bones can be taphonomically defended as the results of carnivores post-depositionally ravaging remains abandoned by hominins, instead of carnivores interfering with hominin processing of carcasses. Other activities, besides carcass processing, have been documented in some of these sites (Toth and Keeley 1981), which indicates that the places were not solely carcass butchery and consumption spots but multi-task spots where hominins delayed their stay. The prolonged use of the spot over years (decades) was based on the misinterpretation at FLK Zinj of bones chemically modified by diagenetic soil conditions, with bone showing various stages of subaerial weathering (Domínguez-Rodrigo et al. 2007).	The evidence of raw material storage in the form of manuports as shown by Potts (1988) was argued to be equivocal (de la Torre and Mora 2005). Most manuports were ecofacts, and their poor quality contrasts with the good quality of the basaltic and quartz/quartzite that hominins knapped and used at the site. Complete reduction sequences of raw materials should be represented at the site and, in contrast, only incomplete sequences have been documented.	Sites would occur in diverse ecological settings. and all of them would be subjected to a significant degree of carnivore competition. The recent reconstruction of the palaeoecological setting of FLK Zinj shows a dense riparian woodland around a spring, with minimal carnivore presence (Ashley et al. 2010). No carnivore competition can be defended from the available data. and no other type of setting has been documented for any other Olduvai Bed I site. Riparian woodlands in modern savannahs show the lowest degree of carnivore presence (Blumenschine, 1986; Domínguez-Rodrigo, 2001). Hominins did not need to hurriedly abandon the site because of carnivore interference.

(continued)

Table 21.1 Continued

Model	Argument	Taphonomic testing	Technological testing	Palaeoecological testing
The passive scavenger and the refuge model (Blumenschine 1991; Blumenschine et al. 1994)	Hominins were passively scavenging carcasses at felid kills and occasionally bringing them under a tree for consumption. No food-sharing or cooperation beyond what is ethologically observed was at play.	This model is based on an overestimate of tooth marks at FLK Zinj, by lumping biochemical marks with tooth marks (Dominguez-Rodrigo and Barba 2006). It disregards the evidence of primary access to carcasses provided by cutmarks. It is almost exclusively based on frequencies of tooth marks on long bone mid-shaft sections, to the exclusion of any other taphonomic evidence. For a detailed critique see Dominguez-Rodrigo (2009) and Dominguez-Rodrigo et al. (2007).	Flakes would have been used for removing the marginal flesh abandoned by carnivores, and battering tools would have been used for breaking bones open. However, battering tools are very marginally represented in anthropogenic sites such as FLK Zinj, where carcass butchery is documented. In contrast, they abound in other sites for which Blumenschine and colleagues have inferred primary access (such as FLK N 1–2), to the virtual lack of proper flakes and in absence of taphonomic evidence (cutmarks, percussion marks, dynamic bone loading in bone breakage, etc.) of systematic carcass exploitation by hominins (see Dominguez-Rodrigo et al. 2007)	FLK Zinj was conceived of as occurring in a barren lacustrine floodplain. The available evidence based on soil carbon isotopes (Sikes 1994) suggests otherwise: the setting must have been wooded. Recent evidence indicates the presence of an important woodland, supported by the discovery of a spring nearby and abundant tree phytoliths at the site (Ashley et al. 2010).

The favoured-place model (Schick 1987)	Hominins are presented as being dependent on raw materials for stone tool production and discard, which would have conditioned the *loci* on the landscape where stone tools and bones were more likely to accumulate. According to Schick (1987), repeatedly visited sites with nearby lithic sources would have a net import of artefacts (and potentially food residue, like carcass parts) greater than on other parts of the landscape, because the need to transport stone was less immediate and artefact discard rates were increased, due both to the proximity of raw material sources and to the use of tools on these *loci*.	This model does not present any taphonomic requirements regarding the accumulation of faunal remains at the site. However, if applied to FLK Zinj, it does not explain why butchery activities are concentrated in one single clearly defined cluster, in contrast with a more wide-spread immediate area. If lithic resources were abundant nearby, carcasses do not need to be systematically accumulated on the same spot. The model does not explain why almost 50 animals were processed in the same place.	The model was created with the Koobi Fora sites in mind, most of them being situated in fluvial environments. If applied to FLK Zinj, the model presents several contradictions, the most important being that the location of the site does not show any greater proximity to stone raw sources that any other point along the eastern Olduvai palaeo-lake shoreline. The concentration of lithic remains in one determined spot is in stark contrast with the surrounding environment (Domínguez-Rodrigo et al. 2010) somewhat contradicts the model, especially given that no source of raw materials is known to be in the proximity of the site.	Not specified.

(continued)

Table 21.1 Continued

Model	Argument	Taphonomic testing	Technological testing	Palaeoecological testing
Chimpanzee nesting models (Sept 1992; Hernández-Aguilar 2009)	Nest sites could have been the antecedent or equivalent of carcass-processing sites. Hominins could have created them following a strictly ethological adaptation, as documented among chimpanzees.	There is no epistemological link between chimpanzee nesting sites and Oldowan hominin carcass-processing sites. Redundancy in the occupation of a site is neither an exclusive quality of chimpanzees or of hominins (sleeping sites of many mammals, ranging from denning creatures (e.g. rodents), nesting creatures (e.g. birds) to several other species of primates (e.g. baboons)) repeatedly use the same sites for sleeping. However, most of them do not use these sites for carcass consumption. Only those animals, such as certain denning carnivores, will also use these places for carcass consumption when food is brought to be communally consumed (shared) with other group members (i.e. offspring). Oldowan hominins selected carcass-processing spots either for similar reasons to the latter group of animals or for some other reason non-structurally related to the sleeping behaviour of a large array of mammals, chimpanzees included.	Technology at Oldowan sites indicates that there is a lot of foresight and planning in the way raw materials are brought into sites, transformed, used, and discarded, or further transported away from sites. None of this behaviour is hinted at in chimpanzee sleeping sites.	Chimpanzees repeatedly select the same nest because they are selective with the tree taxa where they choose to build nests (Sept 1992). None of the taxa (or types) of trees chimpanzees select has been documented in the fossil record. In savannahs, chimpanzees tend to select habitats for repeated nesting situated in slopes and away from alluvial settings (Hernández-Aguilar 2009). Oldowan hominins in Plio-Pleistocene savannahs selected the former type of habitat, in contrast, for creating some of their carcass-processing sites.

carnivores in broadly open environments. The presence of one or just a few trees in an overall grassy habitat could have promoted the repeated use of such spots. Hominins did not share food because cooperation in obtaining animal resources was not relevant (as in the previous model set), given that most of them would have been scavenged and food supplies (mostly restricted to within-bone nutrients) would have been insufficient to have been shared (Blumenschine 1991; Blumenschine and Masao 1991; Blumenschine et al. 1994).

These and most of the other models shown in Table 21.1 were tested against the empirical information provided by the Olduvai Bed I sites, the most crucial being FLK Zinj (Domínguez-Rodrigo et al. 2007). A thorough review of the taphonomic evidence for functional association between stone tools and bones in most Oldowan sites shows that no Early Pleistocene site older than 1.5 mya, other than FLK Zinj, provides compelling taphonomic evidence of an anthropogenic origin (Domínguez-Rodrigo 2009). When applying a comprehensive taphonomic approach to the Olduvai sites, FLK Zinj clearly stands out as unique in its taphonomic properties and is the most similar site to human-made assemblages that can be documented in Olduvai Bed I, whereas the remaining sites cluster around modern analogical assemblages created by carnivores (Fig. 21.3).

By using FLK Zinj as the testing ground for both model types, taphonomic analyses have shown that:

1. Passive scavenging models were supported by an over-interpretation of tooth-marked bones at the site, which was artificially inflated by confusing tooth marks made by

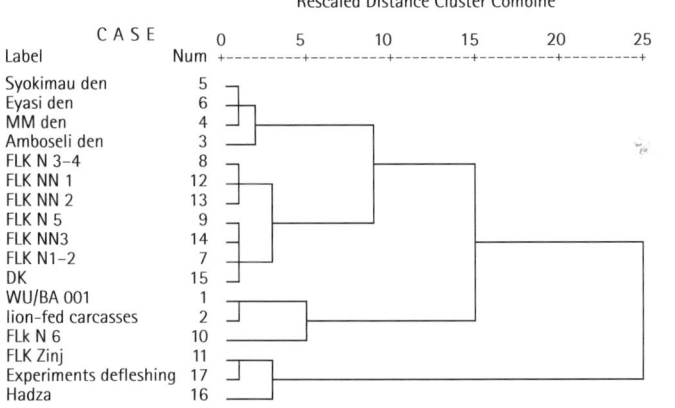

FIG. 21.3 Hierarchical agglomerative cluster analyses of several bone assemblages from spotted hyena dens, leopard dens, lion-consumed carcasses, and the Olduvai Bed I sites. The proximity matrix was obtained using the square Euclidean distance and the dendrogram was made using the method of average linkage between groups (UPGMA). The taphonomic variables used are related to bone breakage (% of complete long bones, shaft circumference types) and bone surface modification (tooth mark, cutmark and percussion mark distribution on shafts). Data for this analysis are summed up in Domínguez-Rodrigo et al. (2007) and Domínguez-Rodrigo and Pickering (2010). Notice how the Olduvai sites are clustered between hyena den and felid-accumulated assemblages showing the interaction of both agents in their taphonomic signatures. FLK Zinj is clearly distinct, and is clustered with modern human hunter-gatherer data (Hadza) and experiments modelling primary access to fleshed carcasses.

carnivores with biochemical marks caused mostly by fungi and bacteria adhering to plant roots (Domínguez-Rodrigo and Barba 2006; 2007). The corrected frequency of tooth-marked bones is much lower than initially estimated—more than three times lower than the carnivore-human experimental models of the 1980s and 1990s—and within the range of variation of human-carnivore experimental models (Domínguez-Rodrigo et al. 2007).

2. Some researchers have cast doubt on the study of cutmarks (Blumenschine 1991; Capaldo 1997), whereas experimental research has convincingly shown that they can provide great resolution in the interpretation of hominin butchery practices (Domínguez-Rodrigo 2009). Cutmarks in the FLK Zinj assemblage are mostly situated on meaty bones and more specifically on mid-shaft long bone portions. Experiments carried out in savannah ecosystems in East Africa show that flesh availability in carcasses abandoned by felids is minimal, and especially on long bones is mostly restricted to the ends and metadiaphyses in the form of flesh scraps; scavenging such remains would thus produce cutmarks on those sections rather than on shafts. Cut-mark frequencies on meaty bones and on their mid-shafts like those documented at FLK Zinj have only been confidently reproduced in carcass butchery experiments reproducing human-carnivore models (Domínguez-Rodrigo and Pickering 2003; Domínguez-Rodrigo et al. 2007). Furthermore, the exact location of marks on each long bone type also reflects primary access to fleshed carcasses, since a substantial portion of cutmarks occur on areas where no flesh scrap survives initial consumption of carcasses by carnivores (Domínguez-Rodrigo et al. 2007). For discussion of other actualistic scenarios and their limitations, see Domínguez-Rodrigo (2008).

3. Disarticulation cutmarks on FLK Zinj bones also suggest butchery of fleshed carcasses from an optimal foraging point of view (why dismember defleshed carcasses if that does not provide any energetic advantage and blunts tool edges?). In addition, the presence of some ribs with cutmarks on their ventral side supports interpretations of early access to carcasses by hominins, since viscera are the first resources to disappear from carcasses after carnivores' initial access to them.

4. Survival of a substantial number of complete marrow-bearing long bones in the other Olduvai sites, where hominin participation is detected through the presence of stone tools in clear spatial non-functional association with faunal remains, argues against passive scavenging behaviour by hominins at Olduvai. The existence of sites with bone assemblages accumulated by carnivores without a single trace of hominin modification, despite the presence of marrow-bearing complete bones and evidence that hominins had visited the sites for stone tool battering activities, suggests that hominins were not interested in defleshed carcasses from carnivore kills, and that they were using other primary-access strategies for carcass acquisition.

5. The discovery of similar taphonomic signatures to those seen at FLK Zinj in slightly younger sites dating to 1.5–1.2 mya, such as BK (upper Bed II, Olduvai) and ST4 (Humbu Formation, Peninj), where tooth-mark frequencies are marginal and cutmarks abundantly represented in upper meaty long bones and their diaphyses, supports primary access to fleshed carcasses over a vast time period. The anatomical distribution and frequency of cutmarks found at these sites, as well as in three others recently found at Koobi Fora (FwJj14A, FwJj14B, and GaJi14), also cluster together with

experimental and ethnoarchaeological assemblages where fleshed carcasses were obtained through primary access when multivariate statistics are applied (Domínguez-Rodrigo, Mabulla, Diez-Martín, et al. 2009; Domínguez-Rodrigo, Bunn, Mabulla, et al. 2009).

In sum, taphonomic evidence indicates that hominins at the few early Oldowan sites that can be defended as anthropogenic targeted meat instead of just marrow when exploiting carcass resources. This refutes traditional passive scavenging scenarios and supports the hunting hypothesis, long held in quarantine since revisionism entered early hominin archaeology. Recent studies on age mortality profiles grant this hypothesis more support, since they show that the age profiles of the taxa present at FLK Zinj and those from various types of potentially scavengeable carnivore kills (aggressively or passively) are dissimilar (Bunn and Pickering 2010).

Hominins were therefore not only targeting meat in their exploitation of animal resources but regularly obtaining carcasses that were too large to satisfy the needs of one or two individuals, since the most widely exploited carcass size at these anthropogenic sites ranged between 100 and 400 kg. They repeatedly transported large carcasses (or carcass portions) to the same spot, where food supplies could easily have been communally consumed. The nature of those Oldowan sites therefore also suggests another function beyond just a refuge for individual food consumption.

The currently available palaeoecological information permits us to define the function of these sites better. FLK Zinj's situation in a near-lake setting prompted some supporters of the scavenging hypothesis to argue that it occupied an undetermined spot in a barren lacustrine floodplain (Blumenschine and Masao 1991), based on Hay's (1976) original interpretation of its geological context as a 'near-lake' location. In addition, it has also been claimed that this site, as well as others from Beds I and II at Olduvai, were not necessarily high-density anomalies in the landscape—since they were initially conceived of as patches (localized concentrations of bones and lithics) in contrast to the surrounding, low-density scatters of materials—but rather were spots where materials accumulated in densities similar to the nearby environments (Blumenschine and Masao 1991). If true, this would mean that the biotic agents responsible for the accumulation of bones at the site did not specifically select one spot over others to carry out documented activities, given the lack of trees or their very patchy distribution. The paucity of arboreal refuges in mudflats would suggest that any visit by hominins must have been brief and limited to the fast processing of some carcass parts.

Those interpretations were described by Blumenschine and Masao (1991) as refutable if the following premises were confirmed:

1. *Stable carbon and oxygen isotope analysis of organic carbon and inorganic carbonates indicates the presence at the site of woody vegetation that might have offered refuge and/or plant foods.* The presence of a wooded habitat at FLK-Zinj was confirmed by carbon and oxygen analyses (Sikes 1994). In addition, recent research at Olduvai clearly documents the existence of palm and tree phytoliths at FLK Zinj within an area surrounding the site of about 2,000 m², thus showing the presence of a closed woodland (Ashley et al. 2010).

2. *A higher density and more laterally extensive excavated sample shows that spatially discrete density anomalies can be detected within the laterally continuous archaeological record of the lake margin.* Recent excavations have shown that FLK-Zinj is actually a

302 MANUEL DOMÍNGUEZ-RODRIGO

density anomaly, with a sharp contrast in the number of stone tools and fossil bones accumulated at the site vs those documented in the surrounding landscape (Domínguez-Rodrigo et al. 2010).

3. *The spatially discrete high-density patches are also shown to contain a greater diversity of stone artefacts and, for example, more completely butchered animal bones than are found in lower density samples.* This has also been documented in recent fieldwork, with FLK-Zinj containing a higher diversity of stone tool types. For instance, few quartz and quartzite artefacts have been found outside FLK-Zinj, and flakes are uncommon away from the site. Furthermore, *all* cut-marked bones occur at the site: none has been documented in excavations of the surrounding landscape. Carcass butchering activities were thus restricted to the site (Domínguez-Rodrigo et al. 2010).

Hominins at FLK Zinj (as well as at the younger ST4 site in Peninj; Domínguez-Rodrigo, Alcalá, and Luque 2009) intentionally selected wooded environments where they processed meat, which represented a high-quality moveable resource transported to focal places offering spatially fixed, defensible resources such as fresh water, trees and plant foods, and where predation risk was very low. Some Oldowan sites, therefore, seem to have constituted the focus of complex hominin behaviours not documented in other primates, specifically communal use of resources and sharing of animal food.

Archaeologists still do not know how representative this behaviour, painfully reconstructed over 30 years of research at FLK Zinj, is of other Oldowan sites. It should not surprise us if other sites tell us different stories. The more sites that are discovered with good preservation, and the more thorough the taphonomic studies applied to them, the more we shall know of early human behavioural variability. The degree of complexity inferred from such a small window (FLK Zinj) to the past will be widened and refined.

Summary

Archaeologists have reconstructed how the earliest Oldowan stone tools were created. They have also discovered that sometimes they were used for butchering animals. The location of the cut and percussion marks created on bones by the use of stone flakes has allowed the identification of several butchery activities: skinning, dismembering, filleting, and demarrowing. The distribution of cutmarks created through defleshing has also been used to suggest that as early as 2.6 mya hominins might have had primary access to fleshed carcasses (in contrast to secondary access, i.e. scavenging). This is more scientifically supported at later sites such as FLK Zinj and BK at Olduvai Gorge.

However, there is still a long way to go towards understanding the range of activities for which stone tools might have been used. We do not yet know if animal butchery at that time was an important or marginal part of hominin activities, i.e. the extent to which meat formed part of the diet. Finally, the behavioural meaning of most early archaeological sites where these stone tools are found continues to elude us. This is partly because most research on Oldowan site modelling has focused on those sites where stone tools appear associated with faunal remains from multiple animals in thin horizons, mostly in one particular area:

Olduvai Gorge. However, other types of sites exist (as well as other archaeologically rich areas) for which there is insufficient analogical work (and archaeological research). Some sites, such as those occurring on vertically thin horizons and containing only stone artefacts, indicate brief occupational episodes, and their functionality beyond stone tool making is not known. Others span thick vertical deposits, such as FLK North in Olduvai Gorge, where more than one dozen archaeological levels (more correctly, lithological units) have been discovered spanning a thickness of more than five metres. Sites like this suggest very prolonged occupation of the same site in between sedimentary episodes, probably spanning many hundreds of years. Intentional reoccupation of the same site also occurs during the Oldowan, indicating that hominins intentionally selected specific places in the landscape and used them repeatedly. This occurs at both early Oldowan sites like EG 10 at Gona (Semaw 2000) and later Oldowan sites such as FLK Zinj (Domínguez-Rodrigo, Bunn, Mabulla, et al. 2009), where sterile stratigraphic hiatuses clearly separate different archaeological levels. This brings up the issue of multi-functionality of Oldowan sites, i.e. the likelihood that a range of different behaviours produced a diverse archaeological record. Despite decades of work, we are just beginning to understand this diversity from a behavioural point of view.

The Oldowan hominins, therefore, showed a higher neurophysiological complexity than modern chimpanzees, as inferred from the way they crafted their tools. They also displayed a different adaptive behaviour by eating meat from a more diverse range of animal sizes (probably entering the predatory guild) and establishing referential places in which they carried out specific activities. Sometimes, they reused the same sites. One type of site can be interpreted as a 'central place', to which food was transported from the place of obtainment (postponing its consumption; Isaac 1983), processed, and consumed. Stone raw materials were also transported there and transformed into tools, with some discarded after use.

The Oldowan shows an evolution from its earlier stages, where reduction sequences of cores are orthogonal and discoid, to later periods, where bifacial and multifacial reduction sequences are more widespread (although early 2.6 mya sites, like OGS7 in Gona, exceptionally display intense reduction sequences). The first phase has been called the variability period, the second the diversity period (Carbonell et al. 2009). This leaves the door open for a previous stage, still archaeologically undocumented, during which tool use evolved prior to the transformation of lithic artefacts. It is to this hypothetical stage that tool use by chimpanzees would apply as a proper analogue (McGrew 1992). However, this remains to be archaeologically documented. If it existed, it would probably be the result of plant exploitation, as with chimpanzees. We should expect that this activity preceded the processing of carcass resources in the use of stone tools, and that plant exploitation was one of the activities for which the Oldowan stone tool tradition emerged. Butchery could explain the intensive production of cutting tools (flakes), and plant processing the important presence of battering tools from the beginning of this stone tool industry.

References

Ashley, G. M., Dominguez-Rodrigo, M., Bunn, H. T., Mabulla, A. Z. P., and Diez-Martín, F. (2010). A spring and woodland habitat: new paleoenvironmental reconstruction of FLK-Zinj, Olduvai Gorge, Tanzania. *Quaternary Research* 74: 304–14.

Binford, L. R. (1981). *Bones: Ancient Men, Modern Myths*. New York: Academic Press.

BLUMENSCHINE, R. J. (1986). *Early Hominid Scavenging Opportunities: Implications of Carcass Availability in the Serengeti and Ngorongoro Ecosystems*. Oxford: British Archaeological Reports.

—— (1991). Hominid carnivory and foraging strategies, and the socio-economic function of early archaeological sites. *Philosophical Transactions of the Royal Society* (London) 334: 211–21.

—— CAVALLO, J. A., and CAPALDO, S. D. (1994). Competition for carcasses and early hominid behavioral ecology: a case study and a conceptual framework. *Journal of Human Evolution* 27: 197–213.

—— and MASAO, F. T. (1991). Living sites at Olduvai Gorge, Tanzania? Preliminary landscape archaeology results in the basal Bed II lake margin zone. *Journal of Human Evolution* 21: 451–62.

—— PRASSACK, K. A., KREGER, C. D., and PANTE, M. C. V. (2007). Carnivore tooth-marks, microbial bioerosion, and the invalidation of Domínguez-Rodrigo and Barba's (2006) test of Oldowan hominin scavenging behavior. *Journal of Human Evolution* 53: 420–26.

BRAUN, D. R., PLUMMER, T., DITCHFIELD, P., BISHOP, L., and FERRARO, J., (2009a). Oldowan technology and raw material variability at Kanjera South. In E. Hovers and D. R. Braun (eds), *Interdisciplinary Approaches to the Oldowan*. New York: Springer, 99–110.

—— —— FERRARO, J., DITCHFIELD, P., and BISHOP, L. (2009b). Raw material quality and Oldowan hominid toolstone preferences: evidence from Kanjera South, Kenya. *Journal of Archaeological Science* 36: 1605–14.

BUNN, H. T. (2007). Butchering backstraps and bearing backbones: insights from Hadza foragers and implications for Paleolithic archaeology. In T. R. Pickering, K. D. Schick, and N. Toth (eds), *Breathing Life into Fossils: Taphonomic Studies in Honor of C. K.(Bob) Brain*. Bloomington: Stone Age Institute Press, 269–80.

—— and KROLL, E. M. (1986). Systematic butchery by Plio-Pleistocene hominids at Olduvai Gorge, Tanzania. *Current Anthropology* 27: 431–52.

—— and PICKERING, T. R. (2010). Bovid mortality profiles in paleoecological context falsify hypotheses of endurance running–hunting and passive scavenging by Plio-Pleistocene hominids. *Quaternary Research* 74: 395–404.

CARBONELL, E., SALA, R., BARSKY, D., and CELIBERTO, V. (2009). From homogeneity to multiplicity: a new approach to the study of archaic stone tools. In E. Hovers and D. Braun (eds), *Interdisciplinary Approaches to the Oldowan*. New York: Springer, 25–37.

CAPALDO, S. D. (1997). Experimental determinations of carcass processing by Plio-Pleistocene hominids and carnivores at FLK 22 (Zinjanthropus), Olduvai Gorge, Tanzania. *Journal of Human Evolution* 33, 555–97.

CARVALHO S., CUNHA E., SOUSA C., and MATSUZAWA, T. (2008). *Chaînes opératoires* and resource exploitation strategies in chimpanzee nut-cracking (*Pan troglodytes*). *Journal of Human Evolution* 55: 148–63.

DE LA TORRE, I., and MORA, R. (2005). Unmodified lithic material at Olduvai Bed I: manuports or ecofacts? *Journal of Archaeological Science* 32: 273–85.

DOMÍNGUEZ-RODRIGO, M. (2001). A study of carnivore competition in riparian and open habitats of modern savannas and its implications for hominid behavioural modelling. *Journal of Human Evolution* 40: 77–98.

—— (2002). Hunting and scavenging by early humans: the state of the debate. *Journal of World Prehistory* 16: 1–54.

—— (2008). Conceptual premises in experimental design and their bearing on the use of analogy: an example from experiments on cutmarks. *World Archaeology* 40: 67–82.

—— (2009). Are all Oldowan sites palimpsests? If so, what can they tell us of hominid carnivory? In E. Hovers and D. Braun (eds), *Interdisciplinary Approaches to the Oldowan*. New York: Springer, 129–48.

—— ALCALÁ, L., and LUQUE, L. (2009). *Peninj: A Research Project on Human Origins 1995–2005*. Oxford: Oxbow Books.

—— and BARBA, R. (2006). New estimates of tooth marks and percussion marks from FLK Zinj, Olduvai Gorge (Tanzania): the carnivore–hominid–carnivore hypothesis falsified. *Journal of Human Evolution* 50: 170–94.

—— —— (2007). Five more arguments to invalidate the passive scavenging version of the carnivore–hominid–carnivore model: a reply to Blumenschine et al. [2007]. *Journal of Human Evolution* 53: 427–33.

—— —— and EGELAND, C. P. (2007). *Deconstructing Olduvai*. New York: Springer.

—— —— —— et al. (2010). New excavations at the FLK *Zinjanthropus* site and its surrounding landscape and their behavioral interpretations. *Quaternary Research* 74: 315–32.

—— MABULLA, A., DIEZ-MARTÍN, F., et al. (2009). Unraveling hominid behavior at another anthropogenic site from Olduvai Gorge (Tanzania): new archaeological and taphonomic research at BK, Upper Bed II. *Journal of Human Evolution* 57: 260–83.

—— and PICKERING, T. R. (2003). Early hominids, hunting and scavenging: a summary of the discussion. *Evolutionary Anthropology* 12: 275–82.

—— —— (2010). A multivariate approach for discriminating bone accumulations created by spotted hyenas and leopards: harnessing actualistic data from East and Southern Africa. *Journal of Taphonomy* 8: 155–80.

—— —— SEMAW, S., and ROGERS, M. (2005). Cutmarked bones from Pliocene archaeological sites at Gona, Afar, Ethiopia: implications for the function of the world's oldest stone tools. *Journal of Human Evolution* 48: 109–21.

HAY, R. (1976). *Geology of the Olduvai Gorge*. Berkeley: University of California Press.

HERNÁNDEZ-AGUILAR, A. (2009). Chimpanzee nest distribution and site reuse in a dry habitat: implications for early hominid ranging. *Journal of Human Evolution* 57: 350–64.

HEINZELIN, J. DE, CLARK, J. D., WHITE, T., et al. (1999). Environment and behavior of 2.5-million-yearold Bouri hominids. *Science* 284: 625–9.

ISAAC, G. L. (1983). Bones in contention: competing explanations for the juxtaposition of Early Pleistocene artifacts and faunal remains. In J. Clutton-Brock and C. Grigson (eds), *Animals and Archaeology*, 1: *Hunters and Their Prey*. Oxford: British Archaeological Reports, 3–19.

KIMBEL, W. H., WALTER, R. C., JOHANSON, D. C., et al. (1996). Late Pliocene *Homo* and Oldowan tools from the Hadar Formation (Kada Hadar Member), Ethiopia. *Journal of Human Evolution* 31: 549–61.

KLEINDIENST, M. R. (1967). Questions of terminology in regard to the study of Stone Age industries of Eastern Africa: 'cultural stratigraphic units'. In W. Bishop and J. D. Clark (eds), *Background to Evolution in Africa*. Chicago: University of Chicago Press, 821–60

KUMAN, K. (2007). The earlier stone age in South Africa: site context and the influence of cave studies. In T. Pickering, K. D. Schick, and N. J. Toth (eds), *Breathing Life into Fossils: Taphonomic Studies in Honor of C.K. 'Bob' Brain*. Gosport: Stone Age Institute Press, 181–98.

LEAKEY, L. S. B. (1934). *Adam's Ancestors: The Evolution of Man and His Culture*. London: Peter Smith.

—— (1951). *Olduvai Gorge*. Cambridge: Cambridge University Press.

LEAKEY, M. (1966). A review of the Oldowan culture from Olduvai Gorge, Tanzania. *Nature* 210: 462–6.

—— (1967). Preliminary survey of cultural material from Beds I and II, Olduvai Gorge, Tanzania. In W. Bishop and J. D. Clark (eds), *Background to Evolution in Africa*. Chicago: University of Chicago Press, 417–46.

—— (1971). *Olduvai Gorge: Excavations in Bed I and II, 1961–1963*. Cambridge: Cambridge University Press.

MCGREW, W. C. (1992). *Chimpanzee Material Culture*. Cambridge: Cambridge University Press.

MORA, R., and DE LA TORRE, I. (2005). Percussion tools in Olduvai Bed I and II (Tanzania): implications for early human activities. *Journal of Anthropological Archaeology* 24: 179–92.

O'BRIEN, T. P. (1939). *The Prehistory of Uganda Protectorate*. Cambridge: Cambridge University Press.

PLUMMER, T. (2004). Flaked stones and old bones: biological and cultural evolution at the dawn of technology. *Yearbook of Physical Anthropology* 47: 177–204.

POTTS, R. (1988). *Early Hominid Activities at Olduvai*. New York: Aldine.

ROSE, L., and MARSHALL, F. (1996). Meat eating, hominid sociality, and home bases revisited. *Current Anthropology* 37: 307–38.

SAHNOUNI M., (2006). The North African Early Stone Age and the sites at Ain Hanech, Algeria. In N. J. Toth and K. D. Schick (eds), *The Oldowan: Case Studies into the Earliest Stone Age*. Gosport: Stone Age Institute Press, 77–111.

SCHICK, K. D. (1987). Modeling the formation of early stone age artifact concentrations. *Journal of Human Evolution* 16: 789–808.

—— and TOTH, N. (1993). *Making Silent Stones Speak: Human Evolution and the Dawn of Technology*. New York: Simon & Schuster.

SEMAW, S. (2000). The world's oldest stone artefacts from Gona, Ethiopia: their implications for understanding stone technology and patterns of human evolution between 2.6–2.5 million years ago. *Journal of Archaeological Science* 27: 1197–1214.

—— (2006). The oldest stone artefacts from Gona (2.6–2.5 Ma) Afar, Ethiopia: implications for understanding the earliest stages of stone knapping. In N. Toth and K. D. Schick (eds), *The Oldowan: Case Studies into the Earliest Stone Age*. Bloomington: Stone Age Institute Press, 43–76.

—— RENNE, P., HARRIS, J. W. K., et al. (1997). 2. 5 million-year-old stone tools from Gona, Ethiopia. *Nature* 385: 333–8.

—— ROGERS, M., QUADE, J., et al. (2003). 2.6-million-year-old stone tools and associated bones from OGS-6 and OGS-7, Gona, Afar, Ethiopia. *Journal of Human Evolution* 45: 160–77.

SEPT, J. (1992). Was there no place like home? A new perspective on early hominid archaeological sites from the mapping of chimpanzee nests. *Current Anthropology* 33: 187-207.

SIKES, N. (1994). Early hominid habitat preferences in East Africa: paleosol carbonate isotopic evidence. *Journal of Human Evolution* 27: 25–45.

STOUT, D., QUADE, J., SEMAW, S., ROGERS, M. J., and LEVIN, N. (2005). Raw material selectivity of the earliest stone tool makers at Gona, Afar, Ethiopia. *Journal of Human Evolution* 48: 365–80.

TOTH, N., and KEELEY, L. (1981). Microwear polishes on early stone tools from Koobi Fora, Kenya. *Nature* 292: 464–5.

—— SCHICK, K. D., and SEMAW, S. (2006). A comparative study of the stone tool-making skills of *Pan*, *Australopithecus* and *Homo sapiens*. In N. Toth and K. D. Schick (eds), *The Oldowan: Case Studies into the Earliest Stone Age*. Bloomington: Stone Age Institute Press, 155–222.

CHAPTER 22

THE AFRICAN ACHEULEAN

An Archaeological Summary

MOHAMED SAHNOUNI, SILESHI SEMAW
AND MICHAEL ROGERS

INTRODUCTION

ACHEULEAN technology (Mode 2 of Clark 1969) emerged ~1.76 mya in East Africa (Lepre et al. 2011; Beyene et al 2013), broadly coinciding with the appearance of *H. erectus* (*H. ergaster*), a larger-brained hominin known at this time from Koobi Fora in Kenya, and outside Africa, at Dmanisi in Georgia (Gabunia et al. 2000). During the preceding Oldowan (Mode 1), toolmakers mainly sought sharp-edged cutting flakes (made preferably on fine-grained raw materials), whereas Acheulean toolmakers were primarily interested in large-sized, purposefully-shaped 'cutting' tools—namely, handaxes, cleavers and picks—seemingly irrespective of stone flaking quality or workability (Sharon 2008; Semaw et al. 2009). Handaxes, for some the very symbol of the Palaeolithic, are large (>10cm) tools/cores made from cobbles or flakes that have been flaked into a triangular or teardrop shape, with one narrow pointed end and the other end wider and often rounded. Cleavers are similarly large, but instead of a pointed end, they have a broad straight edge oriented transversely or obliquely to the long axis of the tool. Both handaxes and cleavers are usually, but not always, bifacially flaked, and the informal term 'biface' is often applied to them both, but particularly to handaxes. Picks are similar to handaxes in plan view, but are thicker tools that often have a tip created by the intersection of three flaking planes. Though their function is unclear from the archaeological record, there is some evidence to suggest that these large tools were effective for large animal butchery and may have been used for other tasks, such as digging and/or woodworking (Keeley 1980; Domínguez-Rodrigo et al. 2001).

Archaeologists have classified the Acheulean into different phases (e.g. Isaac 1982: 172), but the temporal and technological boundaries between these are vaguely defined, in part due to a lack of good radiometric dates and in part because the degree of refinement shown by handaxes, in particular, is likely to have been strongly influenced by raw material quality. Some trends can nevertheless be discerned, and this chapter therefore separates the

Acheulean into Early (1.75–1.0 mya), Middle (~1.0–0.6 mya), and Late (~0.6–0.3 mya) phases, while acknowledging that these divisions are somewhat arbitrary and prone to revision (or even discard) as more sites are discovered and dating is refined.

In the Early Acheulean, handaxes were simply made with a rounded, thick edge (or butt, and in many cases cortical) on one extremity and a narrow pointed tip at the other. After about 1 mya, oval, triangular, and other forms of handaxes were made with predetermined shape and with more emphasis on symmetry and balance. By the mid-Pleistocene, Acheulean toolmakers crafted very thin and smaller bifaces, and numerous sites in Africa show that the Levallois technique (Tryon, Ch. 8 above) was also used, presaging the transition to Mode 3 (Middle Stone Age) traditions ~ 300,000 years ago (Tryon and McBrearty 2002). Hence, Acheulean technology persisted close to 1.5 million years. It has also been documented across much of Europe and Asia. As far as Africa is concerned, before about 1 mya the hominin fossils associated with it are assignable to *Homo erectus* (or *H. ergaster*; Wood 1984), while specimens of Middle Pleistocene age are more varied and taxonomically more challenging. The term *H. heidelbergensis* refers broadly to such fossils, with those postdating 350 kya and showing further increases in brain size perhaps classifiable under a different name, *H. helmei* (Foley and Lahr 1997). Foley (Ch. 20 above) provides further discussion of the issues and fossils involved.

THE CONCEPTUAL LEAP OF THE FIRST ACHEULEAN

On current archaeological evidence, the Acheulean emerged in Africa by ~1.76 mya, its appearance signalling an important step in hominin technological innovation and behavioural evolution. Despite this, simple core-flake artefacts of Mode 1 type of the kind associated with the preceding Oldowan (Domínguez-Rodrigo, Ch. 21 above) remained ubiquitous in the archaeological record throughout the Palaeolithic (Clark et al. 1994).

Still puzzling are the mode and tempo of the Oldowan-Acheulean transition (Semaw et al. 2009). Analysing the artefacts from Beds I and II at Olduvai Gorge, Leakey (1971) proposed an 'advanced Oldowan' tradition that she named the 'Developed Oldowan' and divided it into three stages (A, B, and C). Oldowan assemblages with spheroids/subspheroids and so called 'proto-bifaces' (dated to ~1.7 mya) were assigned to the Developed Oldowan A, while those that included handaxes (dated to ~1.5 mya) were labelled Developed Oldowan B. A number of stone assemblages from Africa and the Levant were subsequently assigned to this tradition, which was generally accepted as transitional between the Oldowan and the Acheulean (e.g. Chavaillon et al. 1979; Clark and Kurashina 1979; Bar-Yosef 1994). Although this classification still appears in the literature (e.g. Harris et al. 2007), similarities in techniques of artefact manufacture and temporal overlap now make it sensible to include the Developed Oldowan A within the Oldowan, and the Developed Oldowan B within the Early Acheulean (Stiles 1979; de la Torre and Mora 2005; Semaw et al. 2009). In this framework, the Developed Oldowan C assemblages from Upper Bed IV Olduvai are also subsumed within the Acheulean (see also Jones 1994).

The Oldowan–Acheulean transition seems to have been rapid, and few transitional artefact assemblages can be identified (Isaac 1969; Semaw et al. 2009). The cognitive processes involved in conceptualizing Acheulean tool forms and the techniques employed for making handaxes/bifaces differ drastically from those used in the Oldowan. Oldowan flakes were generally struck from fist-sized cobbles (usually by selecting those with fine-grained texture). Acheulean toolmakers chose instead to select large cobbles or boulder cores for removing large (usually >10 cm) flake blanks to produce handaxes, picks, and cleavers. Based on experimental work, they could have successfully removed large flake blanks while supporting the core on an anvil or on the ground, in contrast with the handheld percussion technique generally practised by Oldowan hominins (Toth et al. 1992; Stout 2002). Compared to the Oldowan, then, the hominins responsible for the Acheulean had different objectives, different raw material selection strategies, and generally focused on producing larger artefacts using a different flaking strategy that required much greater force, as well as excellent coordination and precision (Semaw et al. 2009). It should be said, though, that while we view the differences between Oldowan and Acheulean stone tools as marked and reflecting differences in kind, others have suggested that the differences are only in degree— for example, that bifaces may simply be the by-product of an allometric trend towards larger, more elongated cores that can produce more cutting edge per volume of stone (e.g. Jones 1994; Shea 2010).

THE EARLY ACHEULEAN

A large number of archaeological sites with well-documented Acheulean artefacts are known in much of Africa (Fig. 22.1). In East Africa, well-investigated sites with *in situ* archaeological materials such as Kokiselei in Kenya show that the Early Acheulean dates back to 1.76 mya (Lepre et al. 2011). Slightly later (1.7 mya), are the materials from Konso in Ethiopia (Beyene et al. 2013) and the *in situ* large handaxes (Fig. 22.2a), picks, debitage, and fossilized fauna dated to ~1.7 mya from Gona, Ethiopia (Quade et al. 2004; Semaw et al. 2009). All these sites await full description and publication, while the Early Acheulean assemblage from Melka Kunture (also in Ethiopia), which was originally labelled Developed Oldowan due to its low density of handaxes and cleavers, has an approximate age of 1.5–1.4 mya (Piperno 2001). Technologically advanced Mode 1 stone assemblages with large flake blanks and/or standardized core forms that nevertheless lack bifaces date to ~1.6–1.5 mya at Koobi Fora (the Karari Industry in the Okote Member; Harris and Isaac 1997) and to ~1.5–1.2 mya at Peninj (de la Torre et al. 2003), but how they relate to the Early Acheulean is unclear. The earliest clearly Acheulean artefacts at Peninj occur in layers dated to ~1.2–1.1 mya (de la Torre et al. 2008; Domínguez-Rodrigo et al. 2009), whereas at Koobi Fora they date to 1.4–1.2 mya (Harris and Isaac 1997). Other important Early Acheulean sites in East Africa include Gadeb (Clark 1987) and Daka Member assemblages in the Middle Awash (~1.0 mya; Schick and Clark 2003).

Unlike the Oldowan, which is restricted to Sterkfontein and Kromdraai B southwest of Johannesburg (Kuman 2007), the Acheulean is widespread across southern Africa. Although some sites are assigned to the Middle Acheulean, most authorities discern two major

FIG. 22.1 Map showing the major Acheulean sites in Africa mentioned in the text.

Acheulean phases in southern Africa: an Early Acheulean that postdates the Oldowan around 1.7–1.4 mya, and a Late Acheulean broadly younger than 1 mya (Klein 2000; Kuman 2007). The South African sites suffer, however, from a lack of radiometric dates due to the rarity of sound datable material. Absolute dating is thus limited to a handful of sites including the Rietputs Formation (Gibbon et al. 2009), Wonderwerk Cave (Beaumont and Vogel 2006; Chazan et al. 2008), Duinefontein 2 (Feathers 2002), and Rooidam (Szabo and Butzer 1979). The antiquity of the remaining Acheulean sites is estimated from faunal biochronological comparisons with East Africa or from the technology and typology of the artefacts themselves. In the Sterkfontein Valley potentially Early Acheulean artefacts are dated between 1.7 and 1.4 mya, but diagnostic specimens are extremely few (Kuman et al. 2005; Kuman 2007), as is also the case for the two crude bifaces now dated to ~1.6 mya at Wonderwerk (Chazan et al. 2008). The rather larger (N = 465) assemblage from the Rietputs Formation in the Vaal Basin, which includes picks, crude handaxes, and a cleaver, is also dated to 1.57 mya (Gibbon et al. 2009).

(a)

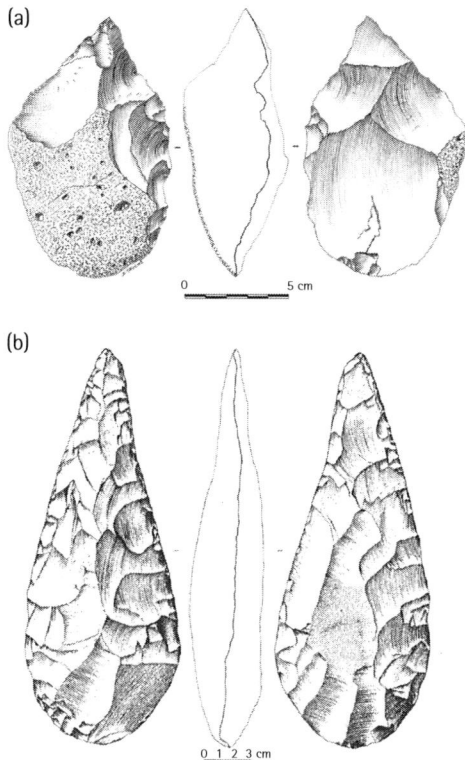

(b)

FIG. 22.2 Acheulean bifaces: **A.** Early Acheulean biface on a flake made of trachyte from Gona, Ethiopia (OGS12–102); **B.** Late Acheulean biface from Kamoa, Katanga, Congo (K.70 A.41), redrawn after Cahen (1973).

In North Africa, Early Acheulean assemblages are well illustrated near Casablanca in Atlantic Morocco, where the sequence (Biberson 1961) begins with the Early Acheulean at Thomas Quarry 1 Unit L (Raynal et al. 2002), which is associated with a late Lower Pleistocene fauna. The artefacts are made of quartzite and flint and include trihedrons, partially flaked bifaces, cleavers, large flakes obtained from boulder cores, unifacial and bifacial choppers, polyhedrons, and spheroids, plus a few denticulates. The site has an OSL date of 989 ± 208 kya (Rhodes et al. 2006), making this the oldest securely dated Acheulean assemblage in the region and significantly younger than Oldowan occurrences such as that at Ain Hanech, Algeria, from which it is separated by a long hiatus. The site of Tighennif in northwestern Algeria is another landmark site, discovered in the 19th century during the course of sand quarry exploitation. From 1954 to 1956 large-scale excavations led to the discovery of *H. erectus* remains associated with a rich Middle Pleistocene fauna and Acheulean assemblage (Arambourg 1955; Arambourg and Hoffstetter 1963). The lithic assemblage comprises both Oldowan and Acheulean artefacts, including choppers, polyhedrons, bifaces, cleavers, trihedrons, cores, and retouched pieces, as well as large and small flakes, made from quartzite, sandstone, limestone, and flint. It is assigned to the Lower (Early) Acheulean based on the use of hard hammer percussion and the proportions of 'pebble-tools', trihedrons and bifaces with a cortical base, and 'proto-cleavers' (Balout et al. 1967).

THE MIDDLE ACHEULEAN

The Middle Acheulean (~1.0–0.6 mya) is not a well-defined cultural/technological 'stage', either chronologically or technologically, but some researchers see modest refinement in biface manufacture (e.g. Isaac 1977: 213; Schick and Clark 2003), perhaps coinciding with global climate change at ~1.0 mya (e.g. deMenocal 2004; Barham and Mitchell 2008).

Olorgesailie, from Kenya, is an important archaeological and palaeontological site with several different strata dated to ~1.0–0.5 mya, many of which contain Acheulean artefacts (Isaac 1977; Potts et al. 1999; 2003). Although there are assemblage differences among the many sites excavated at Olorgesailie, they are not patterned in a way that shows clear sequential change through time (Isaac 1982: 198–9). Rather, variability in biface size/shape and reduction intensity seems to be conditioned by strategic land use (Potts et al. 1999). Moreover, even though most raw materials used in lithic manufacture were local, the mapping of the sources of rare but significant raw materials at Olorgesailie suggests a threefold increase in the maximum transport distance compared to the earlier Oldowan and Early Acheulean (~45 km versus ~15 km; Potts and Teague 2010).

Elsewhere in East Africa, important sites with Middle Acheulean assemblages include Gombore II (~0.84 mya; Piperno 2001), the Dawaitoli Member in the Middle Awash (~0.7–0.6 mya; Schick and Clark 2003) in Ethiopia, and Kilombe and Kariandusi in Kenya, for which palaeomagnetic profiles suggest ages of 1.0–0.7 mya (Gowlett and Crompton 1994). Several researchers note the presence of contemporaneous Mode I assemblages at this time, as well as associations with isolated large mammals: e.g. hippopotami in the Middle Awash, and an elephant at the Kenyan site of Nadung'a 4 (Delagnes et al. 2006).

In Atlantic Morocco, the Middle Acheulean is illustrated at Rhinoceros Cave and Thomas Quarry Hominin Cave; ESR dates at the former show a wide range: 435 ± 85 kya for early uptake and 735 ± 129 kya for linear uptake models (Rhodes et al. 2006). The excavations yielded a faunal assemblage in which white rhinoceros remains are abundant and the associated lithic assemblage is characterized by abundant discoid cores, flakes, rare cleavers, and large bifaces. Other Middle Acheulean sites in the Casablanca sequence include Sidi Al Khadir-Hélaoui Quarry, STIC Quarry, Bears Cave, Littorines Cave, and Cap Chatelier.

THE LATE ACHEULEAN

The term 'Late Acheulean' refers to the time from ~600–500 kya until the beginning of the Middle Stone Age ~300 kya (Clark 2001a), when bifaces certainly become more refined (i.e. thinner, more symmetrical, with more flake scars), probably in part due to the introduction of soft hammer percussion. Among the oldest sites is Bodo from the Middle Awash of Ethiopia, dated to ~600 kya and well known for its cut-marked hominin cranium associated with Acheulean and Mode 1 artefacts (Clark et al. 1994). Isimila in Tanzania (Howell 1961;

Howell et al. 1972) and Isenya in Kenya (Roche et al. 1988) may also be of this same broad age, while in the Kapthurin Formation at Baringo, also in Kenya, an informal flake industry made on small cobbles associated with rare handaxes has been documented ~500 kya (Deino and McBrearty 2002). Middle Pleistocene hominin remains slightly younger than those from Bodo are also documented there, but Baringo is better known for producing some of the earliest Middle Stone Age artefacts known in Africa, dated to 284 kya (Tryon and McBrearty 2006). Recent investigations at Baringo also show the presence of blade technology even before that, around 500 kya (Johnson and McBrearty 2009). The MSA site of Gademotta in Ethiopia parallels the Baringo evidence, with a date of 276 kya (Morgan and Renne 2008).

The Acheulean–Middle Stone Age transition, then, appears to have been complex, with Mode 2 technologies persisting for much of the Middle Stone Age, when we see the appearance of Mode 3 and Mode 4 technologies. For example, at Herto, in the Middle Awash, both Acheulean and Middle Stone Age artefacts are dated to ~160 kya. Their contemporaneity there with fossil material assigned to *Homo sapiens* (Clark et al. 2003) underlines the complex associations, or lack thereof, between hominin type and stone tool technology that the Acheulean (and indeed, most of the Palaeolithic) demands we consider.

Both Mode 2 and Mode 3 assemblages are also found at Kalambo Falls, Zambia, perhaps as recent as ~200–150 kya (Clark 2001b). The preservation of wood (possibly shaped) and other plant remains at Kalambo is unusual, and provides a reminder that stone was not the only material used at this time for tool manufacture.

In southern Africa, all Acheulean sites younger than 1.0 mya are usually lumped into the Late Acheulean (Klein 2000). Faunally and radiometrically well-dated Late Acheulean sites include: Cornelia (1.0–0.7 mya); Elandsfontein (1.0–0.6 mya); Power's Site, Kathu Pan and Namib IV (1.0–0.5 mya); Wonderwerk (~0.8–0.3 mya); Cave of Hearths Bed I–III (0.5 mya); Duinefontein 2 (0.29–0.27 mya); and Rooidam 1 and 2 (0.6–0.5 mya). The Late Acheulean at these sites is usually characterized by thin and finely made symmetrical bifaces (Fig. 22.2b), probably due to the use of soft hammers. Bifaces are also accompanied by flake tools, probably signalling the emergence of MSA industries. Indeed, Late Acheulean toolmakers invented the Levallois technique for producing flakes with predetermined size and shape. A variant of the Levallois technique in southern Africa is the 'Victoria West' technique utilized for producing large flakes that are shaped into bifaces and cleavers. Such very finely made Late Acheulean artefacts are sometimes called Fauresmith (after a town in South Africa's Free State Province), indicating the closing of the Acheulean Industrial Tradition.

In North Africa the Late Acheulean occurs at several sites. Lac Karâr in northwestern Algeria produced lanceolate and cordiform bifaces, cleavers, and large and small flakes (Boule 1900), while Sidi Zin in northwestern Tunisia contains a sequence of three archaeological levels sealed by a tuff deposit (Gobert 1950). The lower and middle levels yielded Acheulean assemblages dominated by lanceolate and cordiform bifaces, while the upper level is rich in unifacial points and cleavers. In the tuff stratum the Acheulean elements disappear entirely and are replaced by a Middle Palaeolithic-like assemblage. Sidi Abederrahman, dated to ~200 kya (Raynal et al. 2002), closes the Casablanca Acheulean sequence with an assemblage characterized by predetermined flake productions, thin and small bifaces, and rare cleavers.

THE SAHARA

Thus far we have not mentioned the Sahara, but in fact the Acheulean is overwhelmingly present there, suggesting that it was a highly desirable habitat for hominins during periods of more favourable climate. The richest region by far is the western part of the Sahara, which is well known for its long sequence of Acheulean sites, especially at Saoura and Tabelbala-Tachenghit (Tixier 1957, 1958–9; Chavaillon 1964; Alimen 1978). Here the lithic assemblages are made of local metamorphic rocks and occur in both gravel terraces and fine- and coarse-grained sediments. The sites show a developmental sequence of the local Acheulean tradition more or less equivalent to the early, middle, and late phases employed here (Alimen 1978). The earliest period is characterized by large frequencies of 'pebble tools', crude trihedrons, rare bifaces, cores, and flakes. The second period is rich in Acheulean assemblages with many fewer 'pebble tools', but the bifaces are thick and still produced using the hard hammer technique. Cleavers are numerous, and Levallois flakes are already present. There are also assorted types of cores, including Kombewa, Victoria West, and Levallois variants. In spite of some technical differences between these cores, they all relate to technological novelties entailing the production of preferential flakes, suggesting a higher level of hominin skill and intelligence. The third period is characterized by thin and finely made bifaces, with cleavers predominating, especially those made by utilizing the Tabelbala–Tachenghit technique (Tixier 1957). This is an effective Proto-Levallois method for producing a preformed cleaver before the flake is detached from the core. Slightly to the west, in the Tarfaya area, a Late Acheulean assemblage is characterized by a preponderant use of the Levallois technique and by tools on flakes, but the paucity of bifaces and cleavers probably signals the closing of the Acheulean in this region (Nocairi 2000). Further south, in the Adrar area of Mauritania, Acheulean artefacts are found in wadi terraces (Biberson 1963).

In the Central Sahara, Tihodaine, bordering Algeria's Tassili n'Ajjer plateau, is among the rare Saharan sites to yield an abundant Upper Acheulean industry associated with a mammalian fauna (Arambourg and Balout 1955; Thomas 1977). The site consists of residual buttes partially covered by dune sands of the current era. The archaeological assemblages were contained in lacustrine sediments, with diatomite and a high proportion of kaolinite deposited during a lacustrine episode. Equivalent to the middle level at Sidi Zin in Tunisia, the site's age is estimated as ≥ 250 kya (Thomas 1977). There is no precise account of the bifaces and cleavers collected from the surface from the earlier expeditions. However, analysis of 300 bifaces shows that they are primarily ovate and cordiform, and appear finer and thinner than those of the Early Acheulean of Tighennif (Oussedik 1972).

Along the Nile Valley numerous localities cover the entire Acheulean sequence, with the Abbassia gravel deposits, formed during the hot-humid period OIS 11 (approximately 400 kya), yielding the oldest artefacts in this area, consisting of core-tools and bifaces (Vermeersch 2006). However, the only excavated Acheulean site is Nag'Ahmed el Khalifa near Abydos (Vermeersch et al. 1980). Although in secondary context, its artefacts appear to form a homogeneous assemblage primarily comprising amygdaloid, cordiform, and oval bifaces; Levallois debitage is entirely absent. In the Eastern Sahara too, none of the Late Acheulean assemblages encountered by Wendorf and Schild (1980) was in primary position, including the well-known sites of Bir Sahara and Bir Tarfawi. Fossil spring sites at modern oases such as Dakhla and Kharga have also yielded a number of bifaces and cleavers assigned to the Late Acheulean, but of unknown age (Caton-Thompson 1952; Churcher et al. 1999).

THE CONGO BASIN AND WEST AFRICA

West and Central Africa are also little known, with the Congo Basin yet to yield Acheulean sites that are well dated to the Early or Mid-Pleistocene. The Early Acheulean and Middle Acheulean are very hypothetically dated; and the majority of industries, from the Late Acheulean to the end of the Middle Stone Age, post-date 100 kya (Lanfranchi 1991). Sporadic instances of crudely made bifaces have been reported, but are probably Sangoan or even later in affiliation, although Kalambo Falls, southeast of the Congo Basin in Zambia, is a clear exception to this generalization (Isaac 1982: 214). Tropical West Africa also lacks clear sites, except for Nigeria's Jos Plateau, where definite Middle or Late Acheulean artefacts have been documented, though they lack precise dating. While it is possible that these regions were sparsely occupied by Early Pleistocene hominins, it is also conceivable that stone tools made during this time were too crude to be recognized as tools and/or that weathering and erosion may have destroyed them. The relative scarcity of archaeological research in many areas must also be a factor.

BROAD BEHAVIOURAL AND EVOLUTIONARY ISSUES

What were handaxes used for?

There is compelling evidence that Acheulean handaxes were used for large animal butchery and/or woodworking. A number of butchery experiments (e.g. Jones 1980, 1994; Schick and Toth 1993; Machin et al. 2005) have shown that handaxes are effective for butchering large animals such as hippopotamus and elephant. Unlike small flakes, large bifacial cutting tools bear weight, have long cutting edges, and are perhaps more convenient for holding. Tools from a limited number of sites have been subjected to microwear studies, with the edges of handaxes preserving evidence of animal butchery and soft plant tissue processing (Keeley 1980), and *Acacia* phytolith residues have been documented at Peninj (Domínguez-Rodrigo et al. 2001). Furthermore, the Gesher Benot Ya'aqov Acheulean site in Israel preserves evidence of pitted hammers and anvils used for pounding nuts (Goren-Inbar et al. 2002).

Most archaeologists consider the handaxe to be an all-purpose tool that could also have served as an efficient source of sharp flakes. Suggestions that handaxes may have been used as a throwing device (Calvin 2002) or as a signal in sexual selection (Kohn and Mithen 1999) are not as readily testable. However, a majority of researchers think that handaxes were intentionally designed with imposed shape and symmetry, which became more elaborate and thinner through time, and with clear aesthetic features seen towards the end of the Acheulean (Wynn 1995).

Indeed, the consistent shape and symmetry of handaxes through time and across space has long intrigued archaeologists, several of whom have begun testing aspects of Acheulean tool variability and how factors including function, raw materials, and reduction intensity impacted this tradition. For example, Lycett (2008), based on an analysis of widely separated assemblages from Africa, Europe, and Asia, shows that Acheulean handaxe symmetry varies across space, implying some sort of selective force at play, be it functional, sexual, and/or aesthetic.

Much more work needs to be done to understand better the various functions of handaxes, as well as those of cleavers and picks, and it seems likely that they could have served different functions in different settings and at different times. For example, while some suggest handaxes were used for woodworking, others doubt the effectiveness of thin biface edges on such hard material (e.g. Jones 1994). It does seem clear, however, that Acheulean toolmakers were interested in large tools, for whatever purpose.

Did diet and subsistence change during the Acheulean?

From about 1.5 mya the fossilized remains of large animal bones (such as those of hippopotamus) have been recovered from several Acheulean sites, including Olduvai Gorge (Leakey 1971) and the Middle Awash (Clark et al. 1984), although the frequency of large mammal, single-carcass sites seems to increase in the Middle and Late Acheulean. More research needs to be done, though, to establish the timing and conditions of the first habitual use of such large animal resources (see, however, Domínguez-Rodrigo, Ch. 21 above), as well as the use of various plants. The site of Kalambo Falls provides extraordinary direct evidence of plant use during the Late Acheulean. Presumably, early hominins also used plant resources as tools as well as for food, but evidence is indirect and rare.

Controlled use of fire has been suggested for various times within the Acheulean, from the Early Pleistocene (possibly at Swartkrans, Koobi Fora, or Chesowanja) to the Middle Pleistocene (Cave of Hearths and Montagu Cave). However, none of these sites provides definitive evidence, and arguably the controlled use of fire in Africa does not appear until the MSA. Since, however, it is documented at 790,000 years ago at Gesher Benot Ya'aqov in Israel (Goren-Inbar et al. 2004), we feel that it will also eventually be confirmed within the African Acheulean at some future time.

What role did environmental change play in the emergence and evolution of *H. erectus* and/or the Acheulean?

Most Oldowan sites in Africa are found in lake margin or floodplain settings (mainly along major rivers/drainages) and mainly in low-lying areas of the Rift, whereas Acheulean toolmakers occupied a wide range of habitats including drier and higher elevated areas. They were also probably the first hominins to venture out of Africa in large numbers, although Acheulean technology itself did not become widespread in Eurasia until much later, after 1.0 mya (see Shea 2010). The diversity of non-African Acheulean assemblages is currently being debated. For example, Norton et al. (2006) have suggested that the so called 'Movius line' (*sensu stricto*), the traditional boundary that separates the lithic industries of east and southeast Asia from the Acheulean of the west, can no longer be supported, due to the few sites recently documented in east Asia with handaxe-like artefacts. Comparison of Korean artefacts with those from India and Olorgesailie in East Africa showed marked technological differences, though, particularly in their thickness, and the inclusion of the East Asian assemblages in the Acheulean has yet to be resolved (Lycett and Gowlett, 2008).

Major changes in global climate took place around 1.9–1.7 mya, with stable carbon isotope analyses of ungulate teeth and palaeosol carbonates suggesting an expansion of grassland in East Africa (Cerling 1992; Wynn 2004), and deep sea cores in the Gulf of Aden showing increased aeolian dust that suggests cooling and drying episodes (deMenocal 2004). Studies of fossil fauna and East African lake history reinforce this global pattern, and indicate not only drying but also extreme environmental variability (including high lake levels) at 1.9–1.7 mya (Vrba 1995; Trauth et al. 2007). While it seems likely that these environmental changes (increased aridity, spread of grassland) and increased seasonality and variability played a significant role in the emergence of both *H. erectus* and the Acheulean, and perhaps also in the changing adaptations of the Middle and Late Acheulean as well, it is still not clear what specific selective agents spurred these biological and technological changes. Much more work needs to be done in integrating global and regional environmental records with the palaeontological and archaeological records in Africa (Antón 2004; Rogers and Semaw 2009).

Conclusion

The Acheulean is perhaps the longest lasting cultural-technological tradition in human history, dating from ~1.7–0.3 mya and roughly corresponding to the time during which *H. erectus* (*H. ergaster*) and *H. heidelbergensis* lived in Africa. Unlike earlier Oldowan technology, Acheulean cores—primarily handaxes, cleavers, and picks—were standardized, of predetermined shape, and made on large cobbles and flakes. The extensive Acheulean archaeological record throughout Africa over 1.4 million years described here is testimony to the success of this technology's practitioners in different habitats, altitudes, and settings, but also to its apparent conservative cultural nature: a learned tradition passed on through thousands of generations of highly mobile hominin groups with small population sizes, perhaps by means of a conservative 'many-to-one' type of social transmission (Lycett and Gowlett 2008). Although there are differences between Early and Late Acheulean technology, the makers of these tools may have undergone more significant change with respect to the use of other technologies (e.g. the use of wood and bone, even fire), strategic land use, and social life (e.g. group size, organization, mode of cultural transmission). On the other hand, a number of researchers (including Pope et al. 2006; Lycett and Gowlett 2008) suggest technological 'stasis' for the Acheulean, which also characterizes the preceding Oldowan (Semaw et al. 2009). Pope et al. (2006) also argue that, although technologically static, the symmetry and standardization of a semiotic Acheulean set the stage for the later development of symbolism and language. As we discover new sites and refine our knowledge of those already discovered, we shall certainly need to revisit many of the issues summarized here.

REFERENCES

ALIMEN, H. (1978). *L'évolution de l'Acheuléen au Sahara Nord-Occidental (Saoura, Ougarta, Tabelbala)*. Meudon: CNRS.

ANTÓN, S. C. (2004). A natural history of *H. erectus. Yearbook of Physical Anthropology* 46: 126–70.

ARAMBOURG, C. (1955). A recent discovery in human paleontology: Atlantropus of Ternifine (Algeria). *American Journal of Physical Anthropology* 13: 191–202.

—— and BALOUT, L. (1955). L'ancien lac de Tihodaïne et ses gisements préhistoriques. In L. Balout (ed.), *Actes du IIème Congrès Panafricain de Préhistoire, Session II, Alger*. Paris: Arts et Métiers Graphiques, 281–92.

—— and HOFFSTETTER, R. (1963). *Le Gisement de Ternifine*. Paris: Archives de l'Institut de Paléontologie Humaine.

BALOUT, L., BIBERSON, P., and TIXIER, J, (1967). L' Acheuléen de Ternifine. *L'Anthropologie* 71: 217–37.

BAR-YOSEF, O. (1994). The Lower Paleolithic of the Near East. *Journal of World Prehistory* 8: 211–65.

BARHAM, L. S. and MITCHELL, P. J. (2008). *The First Africans: African Archaeology from the Earliest Toolmakers to Most Recent Foragers*. Cambridge: Cambridge University Press.

BEAUMONT, P. B., and VOGEL, J. C. (2006). On a timescale for the past million years of human history in central South Africa. *South African Journal of Science* 102: 217–28.

BEYENE, Y., KATOH, S., WOLDEGABRIEL, G., et al. (2013). The characteristics and chronology of the earliest Acheulean at Konso, Ethiopia. *Proceedings of the National Academy of Sciences* 110: 1584–1591.

BIBERSON, P. (1961). *Le Paléolithique Inférieur du Maroc Atlantique*. Rabat: Service des Antiquités du Maroc.

—— (1963). Recherches sur le Paléolithique inférieur de l'Adrar de Mauritanie. In G. Mortelmans and J. Nenquin (eds), *Actes du IV Congrès Panafricain de Préhistoire et de l'Étude du Quaternaire, Léopoldville 1959*. Tervuren: Musée Royal d'Afrique Central, 179–93.

BOULE, M. (1900). Étude paléontologique et archéologique sur la station paléolithique du Lac Karar (Algérie). *L'Anthropologie* 11: 1–21.

CAHEN, D. (1973). Le site archéologique de la Kamoa (région du Shaba, République du Zaire): de l'âge de la pierre ancien à l'âge du fer. Ph.D thesis, Université Libre de Bruxelles.

CALVIN, W. H. (2002). *A Brain for all Seasons: Human Evolution and Abrupt Climate Change*. Chicago: University of Chicago Press.

CATON-THOMPSON, G. (1952). *Kharga Oasis in Prehistory*. London: Athlone Press.

CERLING, T. E. (1992). Development of grasslands and savannas in East Africa during the Neogene. *Palaeogeography, Palaeoclimatology, Palaeoecology* 5: 241–7.

CHAVAILLON, J. (1964). *Les Formations Quaternaires du Sahara Nord-Occidental*. Paris: CNRS.

—— CHAVAILLON, N., HOURS, F., and PIPERNO, M. (1979). From the Oldowan to the Middle Stone Age at Melka-Kunture (Ethiopia): understanding cultural changes. *Quaternaria* 21: 87–114.

CHAZAN, M., RON, H., MATMON, A., et al. (2008). Radiometric dating of the earlier Stone Age sequence in Excavation I at Wonderwerk Cave, South Africa: preliminary results. *Journal of Human Evolution* 55: 1–11.

CHURCHER, C. S., KLEINDIENST, M. R., and SCHWARCZ, H. P. (1999). Faunal remains from a Middle Pleistocene lacustrine marl in Dakhleh Oasis, Egypt: palaeoenvironmental reconstructions. *Palaeogeography, Palaeoclimatology, Palaeoecology* 154: 301–12.

CLARK, J. D. (1987). Transitions: *Homo erectus* and the Acheulian: the Ethiopian sites of Gadeb and the Middle Awash. *Journal of Human Evolution* 16: 809–26.

—— (2001a). Variability in primary and secondary technologies of the later Acheulian in Africa. In S. Milliken and J. Cook (eds), *A Very Remote Period Indeed: Papers on the Palaeolithic Presented to Derek Roe*. Oxford: Oxbow Books, 1–18.

—— (2001b). *Kalambo Falls Prehistoric Site*, vol. 3: *The Earlier Cultures: Middle and Earlier Stone Age*. Cambridge: Cambridge University Press.

—— ASFAW, B., ASSEFA, G., et al. (1984). Paleoanthropological discoveries in the Middle Awash Valley, Ethiopia. *Nature* 307: 423–8.

—— BEYENE, Y., WOLDEGABRIEL, G., et al. (2003). Stratigraphic, chronological and behavioural contexts of Pleistocene *Homo sapiens* from Middle Awash, Ethiopia. *Nature* 423: 747–52.

—— HEINZELIN, J., SCHICK, K. D., et al. (1994). African *Homo erectus*: old radiometric ages and young Oldowan assemblages in the Middle Awash Valley, Ethiopia. *Science* 264: 1907–9.

—— and KURASHINA, H. (1979). Hominid occupation of the East Central Highlands of Ethiopia in the Plio-Pleistocene. *Nature* 282; 33–9.

CLARK, J. G. D. (1969). *World Prehistory*. Cambridge: Cambridge University Press.

DEINO, A. L., and MCBREARTY, S. (2002). ^{40}Ar/^{39}Ar dating of the Kapthurin Formation, Baringo. *Journal of Human Evolution* 42: 185–210.

DELAGNES, A., LENOBLE, A., HARMAND, S., et al. (2006). Interpreting pachyderm single carcass sites in the African Lower and Early Middle Pleistocene record: a multidisciplinary approach to the site of Nadung'a 4 (Kenya). *Journal of Anthropological Archaeology* 25: 448–65.

DE LA TORRE, I., and MORA, R. (2005). *Technological Strategies in the Lower Pleistocene at Olduvai Beds I and II*. Liège: ERAUL.

—— —— DOMÍNGUEZ-RODRIGO, M., LUQUE, L., and ALCALA, L. (2003). The Oldowan industry of Peninj and its bearing on the reconstruction of the technological skills of Lower Pleistocene hominids. *Journal of Human Evolution* 44: 203–24.

—— —— and MARTINEZ-MORENO, J. (2008). The early Acheulian in Peninj (Lake Natron, Tanzania). *Journal of Anthropological Archaeology* 27: 244–64.

DEMENOCAL, P. B. (2004). African climate change and faunal evolution during the Pliocene-Pleistocene. *Earth and Planetary Sciences Letters* 220: 3–24.

DOMÍNGUEZ-RODRIGO, M., ALCALA, L., and LUQUE, L. (eds) (2009). *Peninj: A Research Project on Human Origins 1995–2005*. Oxford: Oxbow Books.

—— SERRALLONGA, J., JUAN-TRESSERRAS, J., ALCALA, L., and LUQUE, L. (2001). Woodworking activities by early humans: a plant residue analysis on Acheulian stone tools from Peninj (Tanzania). *Journal of Human Evolution* 40: 289–99.

FEATHERS, J. K. (2002). Luminescence dating in less than ideal conditions: case studies from Klasies River Main site and Duinefontein, South Africa. *Journal of Archaeological Science* 29: 177–94.

FOLEY, R., and LAHR, M. (1997). Mode 3 technologies and the evolution of modern humans. *Cambridge Archaeological Journal* 7: 3–36.

GABUNIA, L., VEKUA, A., LORDKIPANIDZE, D., et al. (2000). Earliest Pleistocene hominid cranial remains from Dmanisi, Republic of Georgia: taxonomy, geological setting, and age. *Science* 288: 1019–25.

GIBBON, R. J., GRANGER, D. E., KUMAN, K., and PARTRIDGE, T. C. (2009). Early Acheulean technology in the Rietputs Formation, South Africa, dated with cosmogenic nuclides. *Journal of Human Evolution* 56: 152–60.

GOBERT, E. (1950). Le gisement paléolithique de Sidi Zin. *Karthago* 1: 1–51.

GOREN-INBAR, N., ALPERSON, N., KISLEV, M. E., et al. (2004). Evidence of hominin control of fire at Gesher Benot Ya'aqov, Israel. *Science* 304: 725–7.

—— SHARON, G., MELAMED, Y., and KISLEV, M. (2002). Nuts, nut cracking, and pitted stones at Gesher Benot Ya'aqov, Israel. *Proceedings of the National Academy of Sciences* (USA) 99: 2455–60.

GOWLETT, J. A. J., and CROMPTON, R. H. (1994). Kariandusi: Acheulian morphology and the question of allometry. *African Archaeological Review* 12: 3–42.

HARRIS, J. W. K., and ISAAC, G. L. (1997). Sites in the Upper KBS, Okote, and Chari Members: reports. In G. L. Isaac (ed.), *Koobi Fora Research Project*, vol. 5: *Plio-Pleistocene Archaeology*. Cambridge: Cambridge University Press, 115–236.

—— BRAUN, D., and PANTE, M. (2007). 2.7 MYR–300,000 years ago in Africa. In S. A. Elias (ed.), *Encyclopedia of Quaternary Science*. New York: Elsevier Science, 63–72.

HOWELL, F. C. (1961). Isimila: a Paleolithic site in Africa. *Scientific American* 205: 118–29.

—— COLE, G. H., KLEINDIENST, M. R., SZABO, B. J., and OAKLEY, K. P. (1972). Uranium-series dating of bone from the Isimila prehistoric site, Tanzania. *Nature* 237: 51–2.

ISAAC, G. L. (1969). Studies of early culture in East Africa. *World Archaeology* 1: 1–28.

—— (1977). *Olorgesailie*. Chicago: University of Chicago Press.

—— (1982). The earliest archaeological traces. In J. D. Clark (ed.), *The Cambridge History of Africa*, vol. 1: *From the Earliest Times to c. 500 B.C.* Cambridge: Cambridge University Press, 157–247.

JOHNSON, C. R., and MCBREARTY, S. (2009). 500,000 year old blades from the Kapthurin Formation, Kenya. *Journal of Human Evolution* 58: 193–200.

JONES, P. R. (1980). Experimental butchery with modern stone tools and its relevance for Palaeolithic archaeology. *World Archaeology* 12:153–65.

—— (1994). Results of experimental work in relation to the stone industries of Olduvai Gorge. In M. D. Leakey (ed.), *Olduvai Gorge*, vol. 5: *Excavations in Beds III, IV and the Masek Beds, 1968–1971*. Cambridge: Cambridge University Press, 254–98.

KEELEY, L. (1980). *Experimental Determination of Stone Tool Uses: A Microwear Analysis*. Chicago: University of Chicago Press.

KLEIN, R. G. (2000). The earlier Stone Age of southern Africa. *South African Archaeological Bulletin* 55: 107–22.

KOHN, M., and MITHEN, S. (1999). Handaxes: products of sexual selection? *Antiquity* 73: 518–26.

KUMAN, K. (2007). The earlier Stone Age in South Africa: site context and the influence of cave studies. In T. Pickering, K. Schick, and N. Toth (eds), *Breathing Life into Fossils: Taphonomic Studies in Honor of C. K. (Bob) Brain*. Bloomington: Stone Age Institute Press.

—— FIELD, A. S., and MCNABB, A. J. (2005). La préhistoire ancienne de l'Afrique méridionale: contribution des sites à hominidés d'Afrique du Sud. In M. Sahnouni (ed.), *Le Paléolithique d'Afrique: l'Histoire la Plus Longue*. Paris: Artcom/Errance, 53–82.

LANFRANCHI, R. (1991). Synthèse régionale des âges de la pierre ancien et moyen. In R. Lanfranchi and B. Clist (eds), *Aux Origines de l'Afrique Centrale*. Paris: SEPIA Éditions, 89–90.

LEAKEY, M. D. (1971). *Olduvai Gorge*, vol. 3: *Excavations in Beds I and II, 1960–1963*. Cambridge: Cambridge University Press.

LEPRE, C. J., ROCHE, H., KENT, D. V., HARMAND. S., QUINN, R. L., BRUGAL, J-P., TEXIER, P-J., ARNAUD LENOBLE A., and FEIBEL C. S. (2011). An earlier origin for the Acheulian. *Nature* 477: 82–5.

LYCETT, S. J. (2008). Acheulean variation and selection: does handaxe symmetry fit neutral expectations? *Journal of Archaeological Science* 35: 2640–8.

—— and GOWLETT, A. J. (2008). On questions surrounding the Acheulean 'tradition'. *World Archaeology* 400: 295–315.

MACHIN, A. J., HOSFIELD, R., and MITHEN, S. J. (2005). Testing the functional utility of handaxe symmetry: fallow deer butchery with replica handaxes. *Lithics* 26: 23–37.

MORGAN, L. E., and RENNE, P. R. (2008). Diachronous dawn of Africa's Middle Stone Age: new ^{40}Ar/^{39}Ar ages from the Ethiopian Rift. *Geology* 36: 967–70.

NOCAIRI, M. (2000). *Paléolithique Inférieur du Bassin Côtier de Tarfaya (SW du Maroc): analyse techno-typologique*. Oxford: Archaeopress.

NORTON, C. J., BAE, K., HARRIS, J. W. K., and LEE, H. (2006). Middle Pleistocene handaxes from the Korean Peninsula. *Journal of Human Evolution* 51: 527–36.

OUSSEDIK, O. (1972). Les bifaces acheuléens de l'Erg Tihodaine (Sahara Central Algérien): analyse typométrique. *Libyca* 20: 153–61.

PIPERNO, M. (2001). The prehistory of Melka Kunture (Ethiopia). *Bulletin du Centre de Recherche Français de Jérusalem* 8: 135–45.

POPE, M., RUSSEL, K., and WATSON, K. (2006). Biface form and structured behaviour in the Acheulean. *Lithics* 27: 44–57.

POTTS, R., BEHRENSMEYER, A. K., DEINO, A., DITCHFIELD, P., and CLARK, J. (2003). Small Mid-Pleistocene hominin associated with East African Acheulean technology. *Science* 305: 75–8.

—— —— and DITCHFIELD, P. (1999). Paleolandscape variation and Early Pleistocene hominid activities: Members 1 and 7, Olorgesailie Formation, Kenya. *Journal of Human Evolution* 37: 747–88.

—— and TEAGUE, R. (2010). Behavioral and environmental background to 'Out-of-Africa I' and the arrival of *Homo erectus* in East Asia. In J. G. Fleagle, J. J. Shea, F. E. Grine, A. L. Baden, and R. E. Leakey (eds), *Out of Africa I: The First Hominin Colonization of Eurasia*. New York: Springer, 67–85.

QUADE, J., LEVIN, N., SEMAW, S., et al. (2004). Paleoenvironments of the earliest stone toolmakers, Gona, Ethiopia. *Geological Society of America Bulletin* 16: 1529–44.

RAYNAL, J. P., SBIHI ALAOUI, F. Z., MAGOGA, L., MOHIB, A., and ZOUAK, M. (2002). Casablanca and the earliest occupation of North Atlantic Morocco. *Quaternaire* 13: 65–77.

RHODES, E. J., SINGARAYER, J. S., RAYNAL, J. P., WESTAWAY, K. E., and SBIHI-ALAOUI, F. Z. (2006). New age estimates for the Palaeolithic assemblages and Pleistocene succession of Casablanca, Morocco. *Quaternary Science Reviews* 25: 2569–85.

ROCHE, H., BRUGAL, J.-P., LEFEVRE, D., PLOUX, S., and TEXIER, P.-J. (1988). Isenya: état des Recherches sur un nouveau site acheuléen d'Afrique orientale. *African Archaeological Review* 6: 27–55.

ROGERS, M. J., and SEMAW, S. (2009). From nothing to something: the appearance and context of the earliest archaeological record. In M. Camps and P. Chauhan (eds), *A Sourcebook of Paleolithic Transitions: Methods, Theories, and Interpretations*. New York: Springer, 155–71.

SCHICK, K., and CLARK, J. D. (2003). Biface technological development and variability in the Acheulean industrial complex in the Middle Awash region of the Afar rift, Ethiopia. In M. Soressi and H. L. Dibble (eds), *Multiple Approaches to the Study of Bifacial Technologies*. Philadelphia: University of Pennsylvania Museum of Archaeology and Anthropology, 1–30.

—— and TOTH, N. (1993). *Making Silent Stones Speak: Human Evolution and the Dawn of Technology*. New York: Simon & Schuster.

SEMAW, S., ROGERS, M., and STOUT, D. (2009). The Oldowan–Acheulian transition: is there a 'Developed Oldowan' artifact tradition? In M. Camps and P. Chauhan (eds), *A Sourcebook of Paleolithic Transitions: Methods, Theories, and Interpretations*. New York: Springer, 173–90.

SHARON, G. (2008). The impact of raw material on Acheulian large flake production. *Journal of Archaeological Science* 35: 1344–29.

SHEA, J. J. (2010). Stone Age visiting cards revisited: a strategic perspective on the lithic technology of early hominin dispersal. In J. G. Fleagle, J. J. Shea, F. E. Grine, A. L. Baden, and R. E. Leakey (eds), *Out of Africa I: The First Hominin Colonization of Eurasia*. New York: Springer, 47–64.

STILES, D. (1979). Early Acheulian and Developed Oldowan. *Current Anthropology* 20: 126–9.

STOUT, D. (2002). Skill and cognition in stone tool production: an ethnographic case study from Irian Jaya. *Current Anthropology* 45: 693–722.

SZABO, B. J., and BUTZER, K. W. (1979). Uranium-series dating of lacustrine limestones from pan deposits with Final Acheulean assemblages at Rooidam, Kimberley District, South Africa. *Quaternary Research* 11: 257–60.

THOMAS, H. (1977). *Géologie et Paléontologie du Gisement Acheuléen de l'Erg Tihodaine, Ahhagar-Sahara Algérien*. Algiers: Société Nationale d'Édition et de Diffusion.

TIXIER, J. (1957). Le hachereau dans l'Acheuléen nord-africain: notes typologiques. In E. Patte (ed.), *Congrès Préhistorique de France, XVème session*. Poitiers: Angoulême, 914–23.

—— (1958–9). Les industries lithiques d'Ain Fritissa (Maroc Oriental). *Bulletin d'Archéologie Marocaine* 3: 107–248.

TOTH, N., CLARK, J. D., and LIGABUE, G. (1992). The last stone ax makers. *Scientific American* 267: 88–93.

TRAUTH, M. H., MASLIN, M. A., DEINO, A. L., et al. (2007). High-and low-latitude forcing of Plio-Pleistocene East African climate and human evolution. *Journal of Human Evolution* 53: 475–86.

TRYON, C. A., and MCBREARTY, S. (2002). Tephrostratigraphy and the Acheulian to Middle Stone Age transition in the Kapthurin Formation, Kenya. *Journal of Human Evolution* 42: 211–35.

—— —— (2006). Tephrostratigraphy of the bedded Tuff Member (Kapthurin Formation, Kenya) and the nature of archaeological change in the later middle Pleistocene. *Quaternary Research* 65: 492–507.

VRBA, E. S. (1995). The fossil record of African antelopes (Mammalia, Bovidae) in relation to human evolution and paleoclimate. In E. S. Vrba, G. H. Denton, T. C. Partridge, and L. H. Burckle (eds), *Paleoclimate and Evolution, with Emphasis on Human Origins*. New Haven, Conn.: Yale University Press, 385–424.

VERMEERSCH, P. M. (2006). La vallée du Nil et le Sahara oriental: une population préhistorique fluctuante sous l'effet des variations climatiques. *Comptes Rendus Palévol* 5: 255–62.

—— PAULISSEN, E., OTTE, M., GUSELINGS, G., and DRAPPIER, D. (1980). Acheulian in the Middle Egypt. In R. E. Leakey and B. A. Ogot (eds), *Proceedings of the 8th Panafrican Congress of Prehistory and Quaternary Studies*. Nairobi: International Louis Leakey Memorial Institute for African Prehistory, 218–21.

WENDORF, F., and SCHILD, R. (1980). *Prehistory of the Eastern Sahara*. New York: Academic Press.

WOOD, B. (1984). The origins of *Homo erectus. Courier Forschunginstitut Senckenberg* 69: 99–111.

WYNN, J. G. (2004). Influence of Plio-Pleistocene aridification on human evolution: evidence from paleosols of the Turkana Basin, Kenya. *American Journal of Physical Anthropology* 123: 106–18.

WYNN, T. (1995). Handaxe enigmas. *World Archaeology* 27: 10–24.

CHAPTER 23

GENETIC AND FOSSIL EVIDENCE FOR MODERN HUMAN ORIGINS

MARTA MIRAZON LAHR

INTRODUCTION

STUDYING the origins of our own species, *Homo sapiens*, should be straightforward: we know what we look like and how we behave, and it should simply be a matter of pinpointing the moment when these human biological and cultural characteristics are in place. In practice, this is not the case. Evolution is a relentless process, and the characteristics that make us so obviously human today appeared in fits and bursts. To complicate matters further, circumstances can make evolutionary change happen faster and more haphazardly, and at least two of these—sharp demographic fluctuations and exposure to new environments—characterize our recent history. The inevitable outcome is that the last population ancestral to all humans, that to which we can trace our origins, did not look or behave like anyone alive today. So how can we tell which, among the various hominin populations that once existed in Africa, is the one ancestral to us?

To answer this question we need to look for when the 'precursors' of modernity first evolved—in other words, the morphologies or behaviours that most approximate ours, even though they are not yet what we would call typical of humans today. In the past, researchers focused on the modern precursors of traits that characterized different human populations, Chinese, European, or African, for instance. This led them to propose that each of these groups had evolved from local archaic hominins (Weidenreich 1943; Wolpoff 1989), and consequently that the last population to whom all humans could be traced was in fact not human at all, but rather a different hominin species that probably existed around two million years ago. Today, most researchers believe that this is incorrect.

Studies of recent and fossil skeletons showed that the focus should have been on the modern precursors of the traits that characterize *all* humans rather than different human groups. Several such traits have been identified (Howells 1989; Day and Stringer 1991; Lahr 1996), suggesting that people today—independent of how different they look otherwise—must have inherited them from the last population common to all. Yet these traits are absent in all archaic hominin fossils except a few relatively recent ones from Africa, inconsistent with the regional origin of human groups from local archaic hominin ancestors (Lahr 1994). This led to the hypothesis that the last common ancestor of humans lived in Africa, and colonized the rest of the world recently (Stringer and Andrews 1988). As described below, this hypothesis is strongly supported by discoveries relating to human genetic diversity. Together, morphological and genetic evidence now congruently indicate that we should search for human origins among African hominin populations in the last 250,000 years. However, Africa is very large and 250,000 years a very long period of time. Most importantly, the particular list of features that truly represent the modern precursors of human morphology and behaviour is controversial and the correlation of genetic and historical events in space and time extremely difficult. Lastly, the number of fossil finds of the right age in Africa is extremely small. These issues make the study of modern human origins challenging. Yet results from genetic studies give us temporal and demographic boundaries to the early history of humans on the basis of which we may assess the place of individual fossils within that history, while other genetic data give us insights into the first events that shaped the human species.

THE GENETIC ORIGINS OF *HOMO SAPIENS*

The genetic make-up of each individual is the sum of genetic events accumulated throughout the entire history of life such that two classes of genes are informative about the specific history of our species. The first are those genes that, in the last few tens and hundreds of thousands of years, accumulated mutations that altered their function and consequently contributed to making *Homo sapiens* adaptively different from all other hominins. The second are genes, or parts of the genome, that accumulated mutations that did not affect gene function, and thus simply track the genealogy of those individuals who survived. The first of these groups can throw light onto key adaptive moments in human evolutionary history, but the lack of resolution on gene function and differential mutation rates makes interpretation of the patterns still tentative outside the realm of medicine. The second, in the form of studies of mitochondrial DNA (mtDNA) and the non-recombinant portion of the Y-chromosome (NRY), have been the major source of information on human genetic history and human diversity (e.g. Salas et al. 2002; Semino et al. 2002; Wood et al. 2005; Gonder et al. 2007; Tishkoff et al. 2007; Behar et al. 2008; Batini et al. 2011). These uniparental genetic systems are particularly useful in reconstructing genetic history as, in contrast to autosomal genes, they coalesce over time back to a single ancestor, thus preserving ancestry more clearly. On the other hand, it must be remembered that these are only a small part of the genome and so give a partial, and in each case sex-biased, perspective. Recently, analysis of large numbers of genomic single base-pair mutations (SNPs) has further enhanced our understanding of population structure and admixture (e.g. Tishkoff et al. 2009). Finally, the sequencing of most of the Neanderthal genome has provided critical insights into hominin evolution in Europe and Africa during the Middle Pleistocene (Green et al. 2010), as has publication of the first complete genomic sequences of Africans (Schuster et al. 2010).

Although the evolutionary study of human genetics continues to reveal aspects of the population and adaptive history of our species, a number of facts about those histories have become accepted. Among these, four are critical to reconstructing human origins: the comparative lack of diversity in living humans; the comparatively larger amount of diversity in African populations; evidence for early population differentiation and dispersals; and the role of natural selection in shaping human history.

That *Homo sapiens* as a species is relatively homogenous, indicating that living humans descend from a comparatively small ancestral population in the not too-distant past, has been known for some time. These results were long interpreted as evidence of a severe population bottleneck. However, the data from our nuclear genes suggest that this was not the case, and instead point towards a long, continuous period of small to very small population size, followed by a relatively recent expansion of the effective (reproducing) population of *Homo sapiens* (Garrigan and Hammer 2006). Using coalescent theory, the dates obtained for the last common ancestor of humans along the mtDNA and Y chromosome genealogies are between 200,000 and 100,000 years ago (Thomson et al. 2000; Repping et al. 2006; Behar et al. 2008; Soares et al. 2009). Combined, these data tell us that all living humans derive from a single small (or very small) late Middle Pleistocene population that was part of a hominin lineage that had been small throughout its evolutionary past.

Besides being small in comparison to other animals, human genetic variation is not distributed equally across populations. Some, such as those found on some islands, have very little variation, reflecting a small number of founding individuals and relatively endogamic traditions. To unravel the evolution of human diversity as a whole, scientists compare the amount of variation, as well as the historical sequence of mutations, among large continental or regional groups. These studies have revealed that Africans are significantly more diverse genetically than people anywhere else in the world (Rosenberg et al. 2002; Tishkoff et al. 2009). This means that the descendants of the first populations to split and diversify from the last common ancestor (and which consequently have had longer time and larger cumulative number of individuals to accumulate mutations) all live in Africa today. This is very strong evidence that the ancestral population to all humans lived there too. Indeed, the first few branches of both the mtDNA and Y-chromosome trees are exclusively found among Africans. Finally, analyses of how human genetic diversity is distributed across the world shows that variation declines with distance from East Africa (Ramachandran et al. 2005) and that Linkage Disequilibrium (a measure of lack of recombination across sections of the genome) increases linearly with distance from Africa (Jakobsson et al. 2008), best explained by a model of serial founder effects (Deshpande et al. 2009; Hunley et al. 2009). In other words, the evidence from human genetic variation across the world suggests that several small groups left Africa towards Eurasia, often from the same ancestral population; once in Eurasia they colonized new lands, admixed with existing or other dispersing groups, and grew in numbers.

These two insights—that all humans share a common ancestor in a small African population who first began to diversify within Africa, and that African groups colonized Eurasia through a series of dispersals and expansions of small, often related groups—provide critical information for building a biological history of our species. The third complementary piece of evidence derives from the pattern of genetic diversity within Africa itself, i.e. what the genetic structure of African populations tells us about the evolution of humans in general.

Africa is both large and environmentally complex. Climate change over the last 200,000 years led to demographic fluctuations in human populations which, through time, have redistributed genes more than once. The last of these fluctuations, associated with the expansion of food-producing communities, had a profound impact on the distribution of genetic diversity across the continent (e.g. Underhill et al. 2001; Salas et al. 2002; Coelho et al. 2009). This is important as, when searching for the evidence of early modern human evolution in the genes of African groups today, we must take into account how far the geographical distribution of African genes is recent. Until 2010, two worldwide genomic studies had included African populations (Jakobsson et al. 2008; Li et al. 2008), plus one more completely focused on Africa (Tishkoff et al. 2009). They show that, despite the very high levels of admixture observed among African populations, patterns of association between genetic diversity and language are significant, while African female diversity also shows a geographic patterning that is absent in males (presumably because migrations were demographically dominated by men dispersing and acquiring local mates). They also confirm results from mtDNA and Y chromosome studies (Gonder et al. 2007; Behar et al. 2008) that clearly point to southern African hunter-gatherer populations, often called Khoisan (but see Mitchell 2010), having the greatest number of private alleles among human groups (Jakobsson et al. 2008). In other words, their genomes have unique variants that are completely absent in others and give them the most diversified lineages. However, the greatest diversity of lineages and greatest regional sub-structure are found in East Africa, including that private to the Hadza and Sandawe populations, the first of which is distinct from other groups at a worldwide level (Tishkoff et al. 2009), consistent with its unique language (Ehret and Posnansky 1982). In fact, genetic data, both genomic SNPs and mtDNA/Y chromosome data, indicate that present-day African hunter-gatherers—the Khoisan from southern Africa, the Hadza and Sandawe (mostly farming now) from Tanzania, and the western (Baka, Biaka) and eastern (Mbuti, Efe) Pygmies of Central Africa, uniquely share aspects of their gene pool, leading to the suggestion that they represent the comparatively unmixed descendants of an early modern human population. However, their genetic affinities are not simple. Khoisan, Sandawe, and to some extent Mbuti share a unique genetic signature (reflected in their clustering in the genomic *Structure* analyses), consistent with their L0d mtDNA lineages (Gonder et al. 2007; Tishkoff et al. 2007). The Sandawe also share unique genes with the Hadza that are not seen among the Khoisan and cannot be attributed to recent gene flow (Tishkoff et al. 2009), while the Khoisan and Pygmies also have a unique set of genes in common, consistent with their shared Y-chromosome signature (Wood et al. 2005) and, fascinatingly, shared musical patterns (Frisbie 1971; Fürniss and Olivier 1997). However, in terms of most of the genome, all Pygmies share a common ancestor with people who today speak Bantu languages, having diverged from them some 70,000 years ago and remained relatively isolated (Batini et al. 2011). Western and eastern Pygmies remained a single population until approximately 20,000 years ago (Batini et al. 2007, 2011; Quintana-Murci et al. 2008; Patin et al. 2009), while the fact that they do not share mtDNA lineages suggests important differences in their demographic histories.

This complex genetic history of African hunter-gatherers is not only intrinsically interesting but, together with the occurrence of their deep lineages in a very small number of individuals throughout Africa, provides critical insights into the early diversification of our species (Fig. 23.1). It tells us that the ancestral human population fragmented during the glacial period known as Marine Isotope Stage (MIS) 6 (200–130 kya), and that some of the genetic differences observed among African groups today—such as between Khoisan and Bantu-speaking groups—have been accumulating since then. It also tells us that during the Last Interglacial (MIS 5, 130–70 kya), modern human populations underwent an important demographic and geographic expansion so that the entire framework of human mtDNA diversity (all the existing stem lineages) had evolved by then. Just after this period, one of these populations expanded again—including the ancestors of the Bantu and the small sub-branch representing the ancestors of all non-African peoples of the world. Finally, this history suggests that, besides extensive population admixture throughout the continent, there has been very substantial population extinction as food-producing economies overtook hunting and gathering strategies in the recent past.

The final aspect of the genetic history of the early evolution of our species is the identification of its adaptive dimension: to what extent did natural selection shape our evolution, and can we identify the features that shaped our adaptive strategy? Research on this topic, made possible by genome-wide scans of variation and, recently, new generation sequencing, is only a few years old, and many theoretical and statistical challenges remain for identifying the effects of natural selection on the genome. The most important aspect of this research to date is the strong change in paradigm: whilst for decades it had been assumed that the main mode of genetic evolution was neutrality (Kimura 1983), present estimates suggest that at least 10–15 per cent, if not as many as 40 per cent, of all amino-acid changes between chimpanzees and humans were adaptive (Boyko et al. 2008; Eyre-Walker and Keightley 2009).

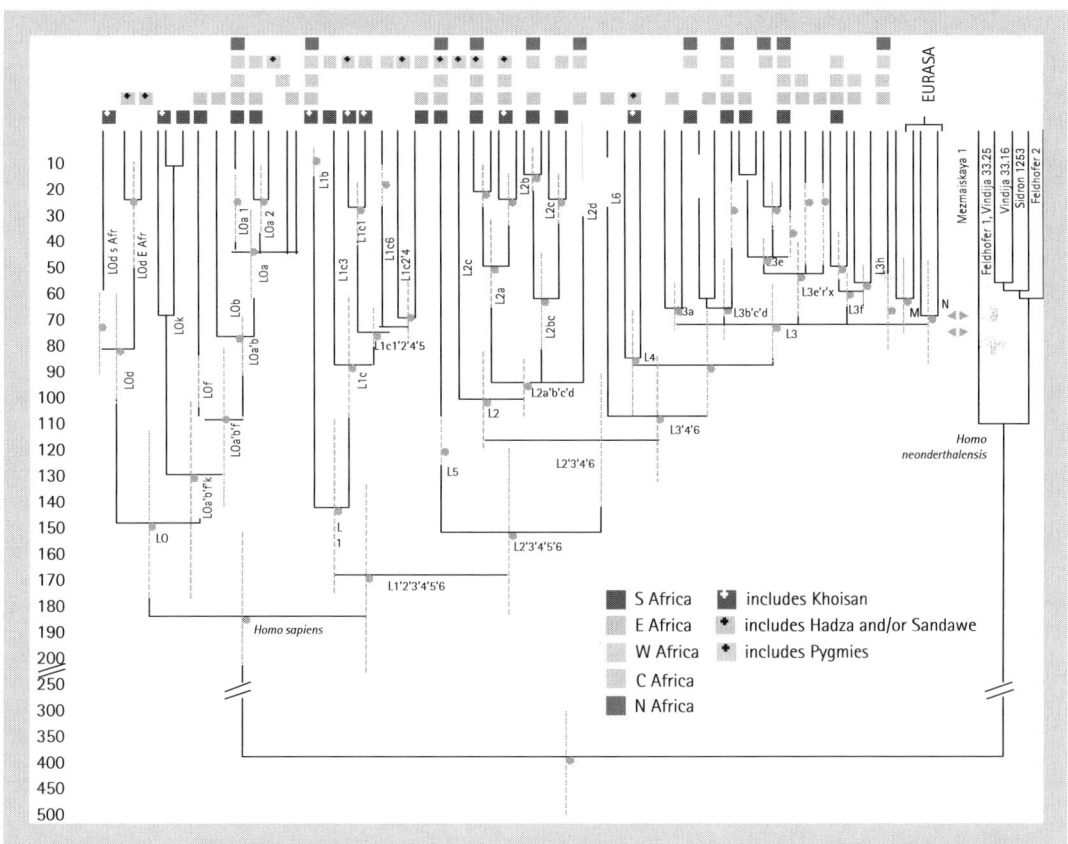

FIG. 23.1 Schematic phylogenetic tree of human mitochondrial DNA, highlighting the distribution of lineages in time throughout Africa.

More than 2,000 genes have been identified as potential targets of selection (Sabeti et al. 2006; Barreiro et al. 2008; Akey 2009). Some are clearly the result of positive selection leading to selective sweeps (e.g. the LCT gene), while others may be the outcome of selection on standing variation or multiple beneficial alleles (thus explaining inter-populational differences in allele frequencies and/or haplotype backgrounds), or of selection on polygenic traits (Nielsen et al. 2007; Sabeti et al. 2007; Hernandez et al. 2011). The function of many of these genes is still unknown, but the recurrent identification of genes or gene clusters associated with certain functional pathways creates an emerging pattern (Voight et al. 2006; Barreiro et al. 2008). The gene category with the strongest evidence for selection is immunity, including genes that provide partial immunity to malaria such as the G6PD (Tishkoff et al. 2001; Nielsen et al. 2005), followed by genes related to reproduction (particularly spermatogenesis— Wyckoff et al. 2000). Genes related to diet also show signs of selection—in the form of single genes, such as the lactose tolerance (LCT) multiple mutation adaptation (Beja-Pereira et al. 2003; Tishkoff et al. 2007), or as differential gene expression due to copy number differences, such as the Amylase gene (AMY1), where increase in copy number is associated with increased salivary amylase secretion (which acts on starch metabolism), which is found in populations of high-starch diets (Perry et al. 2007). Other strongly selected genes are related to smell, skin pigmentation, and cell-cycle regulating genes in which mutations that lead to loss of function have major phenotypic effects, including changes in brain size. However, most of those identified as targets of selection have been evolving in the recent past (Hawks et al. 2007) and are thus private to a portion of humans (either for being advantageous only in one particular human environment or for not having had time to realize a selective sweep) (Coop et al. 2009). Therefore, few of these could have given our ancestors a particular advantage in relation to other hominins or the late Middle Pleistocene world.

One candidate for the latter category is a gene known as FOXP2, mutations in which cause problems of speech, as they affect the motor control of craniofacial muscles, and cognitive language skills, as they affect grammatical competence (Fisher et al. 1998; Lai et al. 2001). This is a very strongly conserved gene, in which only four mutations have become fixed throughout the genealogy of mice and primates, two of them specific to humans (Enard et al. 2002; Zhang et al. 2002). Although it was suggested that the derived human form of FOXP2 had evolved early in the history of *Homo sapiens* (~200 kya) associated with the evolution of language, the timing of this event, and its unique role in modern human evolution, are challenged by the discovery of human FOXP2 in Neanderthals (Krause et al. 2007) and (convergently) of one of the mutations in carnivores (Stajich and Hahn 2005). Together with the fact that FOXP2 expresses in many tissues, this may suggest that its variants are not strictly related to differences in speech and cognition. Thus, while genomic studies are beginning to provide the adaptive background for the evolution of human diversity, it is not yet possible to identify exactly which genes increased the fitness of our ancestors in relation to other hominins.

THE MORPHOLOGICAL ORIGINS OF *HOMO SAPIENS*

Given the dearth of fossil specimens from Africa for the last 250,000 years, the genetic history of our species could be used as the framework within which to place and interpret the few fossils that have been found. However, that history is inferred from the present extent and distribution of genetic diversity; in other words, it is a history of people alive today, not of our species as a whole. Considering the level of population extinction and replacement in the last few millennia, it is clear that the history inferred from the genes of living people only partially reflects that of early humans. In the absence of genetic data from the fossils themselves, therefore, integrating the genetic and fossil records of early humans in Africa remains a challenge.

Hominin fossils from sub-Saharan Africa of Middle (780–130 kya) and Upper Pleistocene (130–10 kya) age, the time when the modern human morphology evolved, are few and comparatively poorly dated (Tables 23.1 and 23.2). They nevertheless show a pattern of morphological affinities and diversity broadly consistent with the genetic history discussed above (Foley, Ch. 20 above), changing during the early to mid-Middle Pleistocene in relation to earlier forms (*Homo erectus* in the wider sense). Interestingly from a biogeographic perspective, fossils from Morocco (Salé, Thomas Quarry I, Oulad Hamida I, Littorina Cave) still show morphological affinities to *Homo erectus* (Rightmire 1988; Debénath 2000; Hublin 2001), suggesting that the Maghreb may have been biogeographically marginal to sub-Saharan evolutionary events at this time. Note, however, that interpretation of the fossil of Salé is hampered by its likely pathological condition (Hublin 2001). The sub-Saharan hominins, represented by specimens such as Bodo (Ethiopia), Kabwe (Zambia), and Elandsfontein (South Africa), are termed *Homo heidelbergensis* in recognition of their affinities with the broadly contemporary hominins living in Europe at that time. They share a number of derived characteristics with later *Homo*, such as increased encephalization also reflected in the arched frontal and temporal profiles of their crania, supraorbital tori divided into medial and lateral portions, the morphology of the lower margin of the nasal cavity, and the palate opening of the incisive canal, all of which differentiate this group and its descendants from earlier *Homo erectus* and identify them as the population that gave rise to humans in Africa and Neanderthals in Europe (Rightmire 2009).

Late African Middle Pleistocene hominin evolution is represented by a very small number of poorly dated fossils: Eliye Springs, Guomde, Florisbad, Ngaloba, and Djebel Irhoud. Their morphology is varied, but each shows (often different) traits that link them to earlier African *Homo heidelbergensis* and later *Homo sapiens*. The small number of remains, the geographic area covered, and the length of time involved (some 150,000 years) make interpretations regarding particular affinities and taxonomy speculative. What can be said is that Middle Pleistocene human evolution in Africa was characterized by both chronological phases (reminiscent of the concepts of early or late archaic *Homo sapiens* populations) and local and/or regional differentiation. Although the available fossil data do not presently allow us to test evolutionary models, this spatio-temporal pattern of variation is the same observed in modern human genetics, whereby clines at continental or even inter-continental level are formed by dispersal events (isolation by distance mechanisms together with serial founder structure), over which regional patterns evolve through adaptation and drift. In the case of modern humans, we know the pattern was created by a particular dynamic demography of population expansion followed by fragmentation and partial isolation largely driven by the combined effects of climate change and human adaptation (biological and cultural). The genetic evidence for long-term small population size in the lineage ancestral to *H. sapiens*, together with the level of climatic variability throughout the Middle Pleistocene, suggest that such dynamic demography probably characterized the evolution of *Homo* in Africa for most of the last million years (Lahr and Foley 1998).

Table 23.1 Middle Pleistocene sub–Saharan African hominin fossils

Site	Age	Comment
Elandsfontein, South Africa	> 600 kya (fauna, lithics)	A cranial vault and mandibular fragment. The cranium has several traits typically seen in *H. erectus*, such as a supraorbital sulcus and moderately angled occipital. It shows an increased cranial capacity at 1225 cm³ (Rightmire 1988; Klein et al. 2007).
Bodo d'Ar, Middle Awash, Ethiopia	630 kya (⁴⁰Ar/³⁹Ar)	A large partial cranium, with estimated 1,250cc cranial capacity, a broken parietal and humerus. The cranium has a very broad, robust face, with an extremely broad nose (the largest of any Pleistocene hominin) with no marked lower nasal margins. It has an expanded maxilla, and an associated lack of a canine fossa, with the robust zygomatic arches angling backwards. It has a thick, continuous supraorbital torus and pronounced flexion of the cranial base (Clark et al. 1994; Rightmire 1996)
Broken Hill, Kabwe, Zambia	~ 600? kya (?fauna)	Complete cranium and other fragmentary remains (a cranial fragment, a right maxilla, a fragmentary humerus, two pelvises, six femoral fragments, a fragment of tibia); the associations among the fossils, and between them and the fauna and stone tools are uncertain. The cranium (1325 cm³) combines archaic *Homo* features (e.g. forward setting of the face in relation to the anterior cranial fossa, reduced cranial basal flexion, very large supraorbital tori) with derived traits (e.g. vertical nasal margin, palatal anatomy and brain size) (Stringer 1986; Rightmire 1988, 2009).
Kapthurin GnJh-01 and GnJh-19, Kenya	543–509 kya (⁴⁰Ar/³⁹Ar)	Several hominin fossils from at least two individuals (mandibles: KNM–BK67 and KNM–BK63, right metatarsal: KNM–BK63, right ulna: KNM–BK65) (Deino and McBrearty 2002)
Ndutu, Tanzania	500–300 kya ? (lithics)	A relatively small cranium (1100 cm³), with anatomical details that differentiate it from *H. erectus* (e.g. size of the articular tubercle in the mandibular fossa, thickness of the tympanic plate, small supraorbital tori, and absence of strong muscular markings (Clarke 1976; Leakey and Hay 1982)
Berg Aukas, Otavi Mtns, Namibia	500–200 kya ?	The proximal half of a very robust hominin femur. It has a flatter neck in antero–posterior dimensions than is typical of *Homo erectus*, while its sub-trochanteric antero–posterior flattening differentiates it from modern femora; its most striking feature is the level of cortical thickness, which at mid-shaft is the greatest recorded (Grine et al. 1995).

Site	Date	Description
Lainyamok, Kenya	392–330 kya (^{40}Ar/^{39}Ar)	Teeth and a fragment of femoral shaft (Potts et al. 1988)
Wadi Dagadlé, Djibouti	~400–250 kya ? (fauna, TL)	Partial maxilla (Bonis et al. 1984, 1988)
Garba III, Melka Kunturé, Ethiopia	400–250 kya ? (fauna, lithics)	Cranial fragments associated with fauna and lithics (Chavaillon et al. 1987)
Eyasi, Tanzania	400–200 kya ? (fauna, lithics)	Fragmentary remains of several hominins (Eyasi I: cranium, II: partial occipital bone, III: partial occipital bone, IV: partial occipital bone) (Mehlman 1987; Trinkaus 2004)
Cave of Hearths, South Africa	400–200 kya ? (fauna, lithics)	Mandibular fragment with teeth (Pearson and Grine 1997; Latham and Herries 2004)
KNM-ES11693, Eliye Springs, Kenya	300–200 kya ?	Well-preserved cranium, but pathology makes interpretations difficult (Bräuer and Leakey 1986; Bräuer et al. 2003)
Hoedjies Punt, South Africa	300–200 kya ? (TL, ISL, fauna)	Fragments of cranial and post-cranial bones, and teeth (Berger and Parkington 1995; Stynder et al. 2001)
KNM-ER3884 Guomde, Kenya	270 kya (γ-ray spectrometry)	A partial cranium and femur; the occipital bone is comparatively derived, and like LH18, resembles a modern human anatomy (Bräuer et al. 1992, 1997).
Florisbad, Free State, South Africa	259 ± 35 kya (ESR)	A fragmentary cranium with a partial face, which has had several reconstructions. The remains show some derived features, such as a relatively broad frontal bone and a possible canine fossa, but the latter may not be homologous with the human condition (Clarke 1985, Grün et al. 1996, Maddux and Franciscus 2009, Rightmire 2009).
Kébibat, Rabat, Morocco	~200–130 kya (U-s on shell)	Fragments of the cranium and mandible of a juvenile hominin, found in association with a mammalian fauna that suggests a late Middle Pleistocene age (Debénath 2000)
Ngaloba, Laetoli, Tanzania	200–120 kya ? (U-s, fauna, lithics)	A relatively complete cranium, in which a combination of derived and archaic features are seen (e.g. thick supraorbital tori, which are nevertheless clearly separated into medial and lateral sections, overall cranial breadth, and a curved occipital) (Day et al. 1980, Rightmire 1988)

Table 23.2 Late Middle (200–130 kya) and early Upper Pleistocene (130–60 kya) African human fossils

Site	Age	Comment
Omo Kibish, Ethiopia	~ 195 kya (^{40}Ar/^{39}Ar, sapropel stratigraphy)	Omo I: Fragmentary cranium, reconstructed by Day and Stringer, including fragments of the face. Very large (>1,400cm^3), but comparatively gracile skull, with a relatively narrow face, high frontal bone, and mandible with a chin. The post-crania shows long limbs, and estimated body mass is approximately 70kg; Omo II: Large cranium, lacking a face, with a comparatively angled occipital morphology and a cranial capacity of 1,435cm^3. The skull was a surface find, which may derive from the same sediments as Omo I (Day and Stringer 1991; McDougall et al. 2008; Pearson et al. 2008).
BOU-VP-16/1; 2; 5 – *Homo sapiens idaltu*	160–154 kya (^{40}Ar/^{39}Ar)	16/1: An almost complete adult cranium—very large and robust, with 1,450 cm^3. The skull is long and high in lateral view, and has a number of features near or beyond the limit of modern human variation (the occipital angle, mastoid height, palate breadth). It has derived traits in the height of the vault, and its supraorbital morphology. 16/2: consists of portions of another adult cranium which appears to have been even larger than the previous specimen. 16/5: consists of most of a skull case from a child, probably about 6 or 7 years of age judging by its teeth (Clark et al. 2003; White et al. 2003).
Jebel Irhoud, Morocco	160 kya (190–90 kya) (ESR, U–s)	Several individuals, including a nearly complete cranium (Irhoud 1), a cranial vault, a partial mandible, and a juvenile mandible and humerus shaft. The Irhoud 1 skull has a short face, but the vault is comparatively low (similar in Irhoud 2), it has thick supraorbital tori that do not clearly divide into medial and lateral sections and have a slight sulcus depression behind them; the child's mandible has been shown recently to have a modern human dental maturation pattern and by inference, life-history (Grün and Stringer 1991; Hublin 2001; Smith et al. 2007).
Singa, Sudan	>133 kya (ESR, U–s, fauna)	A fairly complete cranium, with a curved frontal bone, a high vault, and very broad parietals that show distinct bossing; it has been suggested that the latter feature, together with thickness of the temporal bone, are pathological (Grün and Stringer 1991; McDermott et al. 1996; Spoor et al. 1998)
Klasies River Main site, South Africa	115–60 kya (ESR, fauna)	Fragments of several individuals of clear modern human affinities: five partial mandibles of strikingly different size, facial and vault fragments, isolated teeth, and fragments of post-crania (Rightmire and Deacon 1991; Deacon 1995; Pearson and Grine 1997)
Mugharet el'Aliya, Morocco	128–60 kya ?? (?Aterian lithics)	Juvenile maxillary fragment and isolated teeth (Wrinn and Rink 2003)

Site	Date	Description
Dar-es Soltan 2, Morocco	128–60 kya ?? (Aterian lithics)	An incomplete adult cranium and partial mandible, as well as fragments of a child's skull and of fragmentary mandible/maxilla of a juvenile. The adult skull has a very broad and robust face, which is positioned under the vault, and has large supraorbital tori and pronounced glabella (Debénath 2000; Hublin 2001)
El Harhoura 1, Zouhrah Cave, Morocco	128–60 kya ?? (Aterian lithics)	Mandible and isolated tooth (canine) (Debénath 2000)
Témara, Morocco	128–60 kya ?? (Aterian lithics)	Fragments of a cranium (Debénath 2000; Hublin 2001)
Haua Fteah, Libya	130–50 kya ?? (lithics, stratigraphy)	Fragments of two mandibles (McBurney et al. 1953)
Mumba Shelter, Tanzania	130–109 kya (U–s)	Isolated teeth from MSA levels (Bräuer and Mehlman 1988)
Aduma, Middle Awash, Ethiopia	105–79 kya (^{40}Ar/^{39}Ar, Us, OSL, TL)	Four incomplete crania; ADU-VP-1/3 is a vault with similar occipital morphology and proportions to Omo 1, LH18 and Skhul 5 (Haile-Selassie et al. 2004a; Rightmire 2009).
Border Cave, South Africa	80–60 kya (ESR, U–s)	Remains of at least six individuals (BC1: an adult skull, BC2: partial mandible, BC3: child skeleton, BC5: partial mandible, BC6: R humerus shaft, BC7: R proximal ulna, CB8a + b: R metatarsals) (de Villiers 1973; Pearson and Grine 1996; Grün et al. 2003).
Taramsa Hill, Egypt	80–50 kya (lithics, OSL)	Skeleton of a child, 8–10 years of age, which is unfortunately poorly preserved (Vermeersch et al. 1998).
Blombos Cave, South Africa	75 kya (OSL, TL)	A few isolated teeth (Henshilwood 2005).
Die Kelders Cave 1, South Africa	75–65 kya (ESR, fauna, lithics)	Isolated teeth and two phalanges (Avery et al. 1997).
Equus Cave, South Africa	75–30 kya (fauna, stratigraphy)	A partial mandible and teeth (Klein et al. 1991)
Diré-Dawa, Ethiopia	> 60 kya	Fragment of a mandible; dating of associated MSA lithics (Assefa 2006)

Late Middle Pleistocene fossils from two Ethiopian sites—Omo Kibish and Herto, dated to *c.* 200 and 160 kya respectively (Clark et al. 2003; McDougall et al. 2008)—show derived features of the cranium and face that group them with later modern humans. In particular, the first evidence for a high cranial vault, the relative position of the face in relation to it, as well as the presence of a chin, clearly place these specimens within the modern human evolutionary line. Unfortunately, the small number and comparatively fragmentary nature of early Upper Pleistocene fossils in Africa make it difficult to trace the evolutionary changes that followed. However, during MIS 5 modern human fossils are found in East (Mumba), South (Border Cave, Klasies River) and North (el'Aliya, El Harhoura, Témara, Haua Fteah) Africa, as well as at the continent's edge in the Levant (Skhul and Qafzeh, Israel), consistent with a model of expansions associated with improved climatic conditions (Lahr and Foley 1998) and a time-depth of >70,000 years for the genetic differences observed among major clusters of African variation today. However, the fact that southern African hunter-gatherers share an ancestry with other East Africans at the end of this period, while current North African populations have affinities to groups who dispersed there more recently, suggests that most of the human populations alive during MIS 5, particularly in southern and North Africa, probably became extinct in the subsequent 100–70,000 years.

Evolving humans

This chapter has briefly reviewed the biological evidence for the evolution of *Homo sapiens*. That evidence derives from both genetic and morphological data, which together throw light onto different aspects of a continuous process. Genetic inferences are largely drawn from patterns of variation in living people today, and thus reflect the history of those populations and individuals who survived the vicissitudes of climate change and population competition over the last 200,000 years. Most individuals alive before 100,000 years ago did not survive this process, and disappeared in the face of either competition with other hominins in Africa and Eurasia, extreme climatic adversity in parts of Africa during glacial maxima, or competition with other human populations with more successful immunity, communication, and economies. Their history is told by fossils (and stone tools) that allow us to place particular morphological trends in time and space.

Together, genetic and morphological data allow us to build a relatively confident picture of the process that led to the evolution of modern humans. That picture has no defined beginning, as humans appear to be the most recent phase of an evolutionary process characterized by demographic change as the main adaptive response to rapidly changing environments. The process itself created a population that repeatedly expanded geographically, leading to differentiation and drift, but the daughter populations of which followed private or separate evolutionary trajectories once isolated. This resulted in an ancestral line shaped genetically by small (or very small) population size, from which populations dispersed through time to colonize various regions in Africa and Eurasia. Given the paucity and lack of chronological resolution of fossil remains, the morphological evolution of this lineage at the regional level is not yet visible, making it difficult to identify the anatomical adaptations that underlay the expansion of hominins in the Middle and Upper Pleistocene. Nevertheless, the first appearance of a set of morphological features in Ethiopia 200–160 kya that is only observed among recent humans allows us to begin to trace the history of our lineage within Africa and to unravel the evolutionary novelties that shaped it. Genetics is presently the most powerful source of information of what happened to those early people, and what mutations shaped their differences. However, only new fossils will allow us truly to understand the evolutionary landscape of modern human origins.

REFERENCES

AKEY, J. M. (2009). Constructing genomic maps of positive selection in humans: where do we go from here? *Genome Research* 19: 711–22.

BARREIRO, L. B., LAVAL, G., QUACH, H., PATIN, E., and QUINTANA-MURCI, L. (2008). Natural selection has driven population differentiation in modern humans. *Nature Genetics* 40: 340–45.

BATINI, C., COIA, V., BATTAGGIA, C., et al. (2007). Phylogeography of the human mitochondrial L1c haplogroup: genetic signatures of the prehistory of Central Africa. *Molecular Phylogenetics and Evolution* 43: 635–44.

BATINI, C., LOPES, J., BEHAR, D. M., et al. (2011). Insights into the demographic history of African pygmies from complete mitochondrial genomes. *Molecular Biology and Evolution* 28: 1099–1110.

BEHAR, D. M., VILLEMS, R., SOODYALL, H., et al. (2008). The dawn of human matrilineal diversity. *American Journal of Human Genetics* 82: 1130–40.

BEJA-PEREIRA, A., LUIKART, G., ENGLAND, P. R., et al. (2003). Gene-culture coevolution between cattle milk protein genes and human lactase genes. *Nature Genetics* 35: 311–13.

BOYKO, A. R., WILLIAMSON, S. H., INDAP, A. R., et al. (2008). Assessing the evolutionary impact of amino acid mutations in the human genome. *PLoS Genetics* 4(5).

CLARK, J. D., BEYENE, Y., WOLDEGABRIEL, G., et al. (2003). Stratigraphic, chronological and behavioural contexts of Pleistocene *Homo sapiens* from Middle Awash, Ethiopia. *Nature* 423: 747–52.

COELHO, M., SEQUEIRA, F., LUISELLI, D., BELEZA, S., and ROCHA, J. (2009). On the edge of Bantu expansions: mtDNA, Y chromosome and lactase persistence genetic variation in southwestern Angola. *BMC Evolutionary Biology* 9(1).

COOP, G., PICKRELL, J. K., NOVEMBRE, J., et al. (2009). The role of geography in human adaptation. *PLoS Genetics* 5(6): e1000500.

DAY, M. H., and STRINGER, C. B. (1991). Les restes crâniens d'Omo-Kibish et leur classification à l'intérieur du genre *Homo*. *L'Anthropologie* 95: 573–94.

DEBÉNATH, A. (2000). Le peuplement préhistorique du Maroc: données récentes et problèmes. *L'Anthropologie* 104: 131–45.

DESHPANDE, O., BATZOGLOU, S., FELDMAN, M. W., and CAVALLI-SFORZA, L. L. (2009). A serial founder effect model for human settlement out of Africa. *Proceedings of the Royal Society B: Biological Sciences* 276: 291–300.

EHRET, C., and POSNANSKY, M. (eds) (1982). *The Archaeological and Linguistic Reconstruction of African History*. Berkeley: University of California Press.

ENARD, W., PRZEWORSKI, M., FISHER, S. E., et al. (2002). Molecular evolution of FOXP2, a gene involved in speech and language. *Nature* 418: 869–72.

EYRE-WALKER, A., and KEIGHTLEY, P. D. (2009). Estimating the rate of adaptive molecular evolution in the presence of slightly deleterious mutations and population size change. *Molecular Biology and Evolution* 26: 2097–2108.

FISHER, S. E., VARGHA-KHADEM, F., WATKINS, K. E., MONACO, A. P., and PEMBREY, M. E. (1998). Localisation of a gene implicated in a severe speech and language disorder. *Nature Genetics* 18: 168–70.

FRISBIE, C. J. (1971). Anthropological and ethnomusicological implications of a comparative analysis of Bushmen and African Pygmy music. *Ethnology* 10: 265–90.

FURNISS, S., and OLIVIER, E. (1997). Systématique musicale pygmée et Bochiman: deux conceptions africaines du contrepoint. *Musurgia* 4: 9–30

GARRIGAN, D., and HAMMER, M. F. (2006). Reconstructing human origins in the genomic era. *Nature Reviews Genetics* 7: 669–80

GONDER, M. K., MORTENSEN, H. M., REED, F. A., DE SOUSA, A., and TISHKOFF, S. A. (2007). Whole-mtDNA genome sequence analysis of ancient African lineages. *Molecular Biology and Evolution* 24: 757–68.

GREEN, R. E., KRAUSE, J., BRIGGS, A.W., et al. (2010). A draft sequence of the neandertal genome. *Science* 328: 710–22.

HAWKS, J., WANG, E. T., COCHRAN, G. M., HARPENDING, H. C., and MOYZIS, R. K. (2007). Recent acceleration of human adaptive evolution. *Proceedings of the National Academy of Sciences (USA)* 104: 20753–8.

HERNANDEZ, R. D., KELLEY, J. L., ELYASHIV, E., et al. (2011). Classic selective sweeps were rare in recent human evolution. *Science* 331: 920–24.

HOWELLS, W. W. (1989). *Skull Shapes and the Map: Craniometric Analyses in the Dispersion of Modern* Homo. Cambridge, Mass.: Harvard University Press.

HUBLIN, J.-J. (2001). Northwest African Middle Pleistocene hominids and their bearing on the emergence of *Homo sapiens*. In L. S. Barham and K. Robson-Brown (eds), *Human Roots: Africa and Asia in the Middle Pleistocene*. Bristol: Western Academic Press, 99–121.

HUNLEY, K. L., HEALY, M. E., and LONG, J. C. (2009). The global pattern of gene identity variation reveals a history of long-range migrations, bottlenecks, and local mate exchange: implications for biological race. *American Journal of Physical Anthropology* 139: 35–46.

JAKOBSSON, M., SCHOLZ, S. W., SCHEET, P., et al. (2008). Genotype, haplotype and copy-number variation in worldwide human populations. *Nature* 451: 998–1003.

KIMURA, M. (1983). *The Neutral Theory of Molecular Evolution*. Cambridge: Cambridge University Press.

KLEIN, R. G., AVERY, G., CRUZ-URIBE, K., and STEELE, T. E. (2007). The mammalian fauna associated with an archaic hominin skullcap and later Acheulean artifacts at Elandsfontein, Western Cape Province, South Africa. *Journal of Human Evolution* 52: 164–86.

KRAUSE, J., LALUEZA-FOX, C., ORLANDO, L., et al. (2007). The derived FOXP2 variant of Modern Humans was shared with Neandertals. *Current Biology* 17: 1908–12.

LAHR, M. M. (1994). The multiregional model of modern human origins: a reassessment of its morphological basis. *Journal of Human Evolution* 26: 23–56.

—— (1996). *The Evolution of Human Diversity*. Cambridge: Cambridge University Press.

—— and FOLEY, R. A. (1998). Towards a theory of modern human origins: geography, demography and diversity in recent human evolution. *Yearbook of Physical Anthropology* 41: 137–76.

LAI, C. S. L., FISHER, S. E., HURST, J. A., VARGHA-KHADEM, F., and MONACO, A. P. (2001). A forkhead-domain gene is mutated in a severe speech and language disorder. *Nature* 413: 519–23.

LI, J. Z., ABSHER, D. M., TANG, H., et al. (2008). Worldwide human relationships inferred from genome-wide patterns of variation. *Science* 319: 1100–104.

McDougall, I., Brown, F. H., and Fleagle, J. G. (2008). Sapropels and the age of hominins Omo I and II, Kibish, Ethiopia. *Journal of Human Evolution* 55: 409–20.

Mitchell, P. J. (2010). Genetics and southern African prehistory: an archaeological view. *Journal of Anthropological Science* 88: 73–92.

Nielsen, R., Bustamante, C., Clark, A. G., et al. (2005). A scan for positively selected genes in the genomes of humans and chimpanzees. *PLoS Biology* 3: 0976–85.

—— Hellmann, I., Hubisz, M., Bustamante, C., and Clark, A. G. (2007). Recent and ongoing selection in the human genome. *Nature Reviews Genetics* 8: 857–68.

Patin, E., Laval, G., Barreiro, L. B., et al. (2009). Inferring the demographic history of African farmers and Pygmy hunter-gatherers using a multilocus resequencing data set. *PLoS Genetics* 5(4).

Perry, G. H., Dominy, N. J., Claw, K. G., et al. (2007). Diet and the evolution of human amylase gene copy number variation. *Nature Genetics* 39: 1256–60.

Quintana-Murci, L., Quach, H., Harmant, C., et al. (2008). Maternal traces of deep common ancestry and asymmetric gene flow between Pygmy hunter-gatherers and Bantu-speaking farmers. *Proceedings of the National Academy of Sciences (USA)* 105: 1596–1601.

Ramachandran, S., Deshpande, O., Roseman, C.C., Rosenberg, N. A., Feldman, M. W., and Cavalli-Sforza, L. L. (2005). Support from the relationship of genetic and geographic in human populations for a serial founder effect originating in Africa. *Proceedings of the National Academy of Sciences (USA)* 102: 15942–7.

Repping, S., Van Daalen, S. K. M., Brown, L. G., et al. (2006). High mutation rates have driven extensive structural polymorphism among human Y chromosomes. *Nature Genetics* 38(4): 463–7.

Rightmire, G. P. (1988). *Homo erectus* and later middle Pleistocene humans. *Annual Review of Anthropology* 17: 239–59.

—— (2009). Middle and later Pleistocene hominins in Africa and southwest Asia. *Proceedings of the National Academy of Sciences* (USA) 106: 16046–50.

Rosenberg, N. A., Pritchard, J. K., Weber, J. L., et al. (2002). Genetic structure of human populations. *Science* 298: 2381–5.

Sabeti, P. C., Schaffner, S. F., Fry, B., et al. (2006). Positive natural selection in the human lineage. *Science* 312: 1614–20.

—— Varilly, P., Fry, B., et al. (2007). Genome-wide detection and characterization of positive selection in human populations. *Nature* 449: 913–18.

Salas, A., Richards, M., de la Fe, T., et al. (2002). The making of the African mtDNA landscape. *American Journal of Human Genetics* 71: 1082–111.

Schuster, S. C., Miller, W., Ratan, A., et al. (2010). Complete Khoisan and Bantu genomes from southern Africa. *Nature* 463: 943–7.

Semino, O., Santachiara-Benerecetti, A. S., Falaschi, F., Cavalli-Sforza, L. L., and Underhill, P. A. (2002). Ethiopians and Khoisan share the deepest clades of the human Y-chromosome phylogeny. *American Journal of Human Genetics* 70: 265–8.

Soares, P., Ermini, L., Thomson, N., et al. (2009). Correcting for purifying selection: an improved human mitochondrial molecular clock. *American Journal of Human Genetics* 84: 740–59.

Stajich, J. E., and Hahn, M. W. (2005). Disentangling the effects of demography and selection in human history. *Molecular Biology and Evolution* 22: 63–73.

Stringer, C. B., and Andrews, P. J. (1988). Genetic and fossil evidence for the origin of modern humans. *Science* 239: 1263–8.

THOMSON, R., PRITCHARD, J. K., SHEN, P., OEFNER, P. J., and FELDMAN, M. W. (2000). Recent common ancestry of human Y chromosomes: evidence from DNA sequence data. *Proceedings of the National Academy of Sciences (USA)* 97: 7360–65.

TISHKOFF, S. A., GONDER, M. K., HENN, B. M., et al. (2007). History of click-speaking populations of Africa inferred from mtDNA and Y chromosome genetic variation. *Molecular Biology and Evolution* 24: 2180–95.

—— REED, F. A., FRIEDLAENDER, F. R., et al. (2009). The genetic structure and history of Africans and African Americans. *Science* 324: 1035–44.

—— —— RANCIARO, A., et al. (2007). Convergent adaptation of human lactase persistence in Africa and Europe. *Nature Genetics* 39: 31–40.

—— VARKONYI, R., CAHINHINAN, N., et al. (2001). Haplotype diversity and linkage disequilibrium at human G6PD: recent origin of alleles that confer malarial resistance. *Science* 293: 455–62.

UNDERHILL, P. A., PASSARINO, G., LIN, A. A., et al. (2001). The phylogeography of Y chromosome binary haplotypes and the origins of modern human populations. *Annals of Human Genetics* 1: 43–62.

VOIGHT, B. F., KUDARAVALLI, S., WEN, X., and PRITCHARD, J. K. (2006). A map of recent positive selection in the human genome. *PLoS Biology* 4: 0446–58.

WEIDENREICH, F. (1943). *The Skull of Sinanthropus pekinensis: A Comparative Study of a Primitive Hominid Skull.* Beijing: Geological Survey of China.

WOLPOFF, M. H. (1989). Multiregional evolution: the fossil alternative to Eden. In P. Mellars and C. B. Stringer (eds), *The Human Revolution*. Edinburgh: Edinburgh University Press, 62–108.

WOOD, E. T., STOVER, D. A., EHRET, C., et al. (2005). Contrasting patterns of Y chromosome and mtDNA variation in Africa: evidence for sex-biased demographic processes. *European Journal of Human Genetics* 13: 867–76.

WYCKOFF, G. J., WANG, W., and WU, C. (2000). Rapid evolution of male reproductive genes in the descent of man. *Nature* 403: 304–9.

ZHANG, J., WEBB, D. M., and PODLAHA, O. (2002). Accelerated protein evolution and origins of human-specific features: FOXP2 as an example. *Genetics* 162: 1825–35.

CHAPTER 24

···

BEYOND MODERNITY

···

LAWRENCE BARHAM

INTRODUCTION

THIS chapter highlights the impact of relatively recent developments in dating techniques and genetic analyses on the study of the evolution of modern humans in Africa. A secondary aim is to provide a historical context within which to view the emergence of the current working consensus of what constitutes modern human behaviour. That context is presented using Kuhn's (1970) well-known model of paradigm change in the natural sciences. The concept of paradigm shift provides a foundation for anticipating the inevitable challenges to the existing consensus—some raised here—and for predicting directions for further research. The emphasis on change also throws into relief underlying continuities in the conceptualization of the process and tempo of modern human evolution. Awareness of these deep-seated continuities helps contextualize the immediacy of current debates and minimizes the risk of presentism for those new to the field.

THE MAKING OF MODERNITY

Behavioural modernity as a concept has a relatively recent history. It appeared in the late 1980s as part of the synthesis of fossil, genetic, and archaeological data that came to be known as the 'Out of Africa II' model, described below (Stringer and Andrews 1988). The concept's roots though lie in the preceding generation of Africanist archaeologists, who did not make explicit reference to behavioural modernity but referred to 'modern man' (*sic*) as a biological entity with a distinctive artefactual record (e.g. Clark 1970). Behavioural and anatomical modernity were implicitly assumed to have evolved together. That assumption reflected the dominance of the European Upper Palaeolithic as the benchmark of human innovation and symbolic expression, especially when compared with the uniformity of Middle Palaeolithic technology and the apparent limitations of Neanderthal behaviour generally (Bordes 1968). For Africanists, at issue were the place and timing of the origins of *Homo sapiens*, whether among subspecies of *Homo* within Africa or as an immigrant species entering from the Near East.

Sites in Israel (Kebara, Qafzeh, Skhul, and Tabun) provided the anatomical evidence for a likely transitional phase from Neanderthals to anatomically modern humans and a potential source of African moderns. In the absence of direct dating methods, this lineal evolutionary sequence seemed the most parsimonious explanation of what appeared to be a gradual morphological development of the modern human form. Weidenreich (1947: 83–91), among others, championed a model of multiple centres of modern human origins across the Old World with populations ultimately linked by hybridization (gene flow). In southern Africa, he traced an evolutionary sequence that linked contemporary Bushman groups to a distant ancestor '*H. rhodesiensis*' (from Broken Hill, now Kabwe, Zambia) through intermediate stages represented by progressively more modern fossil crania. The multiple origins or multiregional model in its current form (Wolpoff 1989) recognized a potential African origin of *H. sapiens*, though not an exclusively African origin as Darwin (1871) had predicted in the absence of supporting fossil evidence. Boule and Vallois (1957: 455) offered a dissenting view that saw no evolutionary contribution from the likes of *H. rhodesiensis* or from Neanderthals generally to modern humans, and viewed *H. sapiens* as a separate lineage, of uncertain origin, that swept across the Old World marked by the spread of Upper Palaeolithic technology from Europe to Africa and elsewhere. Africa, in this scheme, was the recipient continent and one that retained several living archaic human forms 'on the point of extermination' (Boule and Vallois 1957: 455). The negative implications of this view of Africa's past at the very time that African countries were seeking, and obtaining, independence should not be ignored.

COLE AND CLARK: BEFORE THE GREAT TRANSFORMATION

Two influential English language textbooks of the time, Sonia Cole's (1963) *The Prehistory of East Africa* and Desmond Clark's (1970) *The Prehistory of Africa*, reflect current methodological approaches to the study of modern human origins and reveal the constraints posed by the then available dating methods. Their respective models of regional and continental processes of behavioural change were based on a small number of radiocarbon-dated sites, many with effectively infinite ages beyond the reliable range of the technique (~40 kya). Both researchers were engaged primarily in building culture histories of the Stone Age, but they avoided the culture historians' recourse to diffusion as an explanatory device, offering instead models of technological, social, and biological adaptations to regional patterns in biogeography, primarily vegetation. Significant aspects of their eco-functional framework remain current today. Also current are their respective positions on the evolution of behavioural modernity, with Cole taking a gradualist perspective and Clark highlighting the importance of a constellation of symbolic behaviours, founded on language, as the necessary markers of modernity.

Summarizing the East African record, Cole (1963: 200, 335) drew tentative correlations between contemporary hunter-gatherer populations (i.e. Bushmen, Hadza), their apparent racial affinities ('Bushmanoid' and 'Negroid'), and two long-lived regional archaeological traditions ('Stillbay–Magosian–Wilton' and 'Sangoan–Lupemban–Tshitolian' respectively). Cultural and biological identities coincided and each tradition marked a distinctive techno-logical response to enduring ecological conditions, the Bushmen an ancient adaptation to dry savannah, the Hadza to tropical woodlands. Linking culture, environment, and race was part of the methodology of culture-historical archaeology into the 1950s (Trigger 1989), though already abandoned by cultural anthropologists, who recognized its inherently static and racist view of cultural patterning (Stocking 1968). Cole (1963: 170), with her background in geology, explained cultural change in Darwinian terms, stimulated by competition rather than migration or diffusion. She also recognized the potential for technological convergence as opposed to a normative view of cultural inheritance. Human groups, separated in space and time, were capable of producing similar responses to similar environmental challenges. As a case in point, making flakes from prepared cores (Levallois technology) transcended cultural, chronological, and species boundaries (Cole 1963: 182).

On the issue of the origin of modern human behaviour, Cole emphasized continuity and incremental change rather than replacement and rapid innovation. She drew attention to the accumulation of a wider range of tools forms at the end of the Acheulean—not just in East Africa—as the precursor to the transition to the Middle Stone Age (MSA) with its character-istic points. No single place of origin could be identified nor single period of change be sin-gled out as the start of behavioural modernity. This gradualist view has its current advocates (McBrearty 2007), as does Cole's (1963: 168) emphasis on hafting as the significant innova-tion that marked the transition (Barham 2010).

The associated hominin was equally difficult to identify, given the poor chronological res-olution available for specimens with widely differing morphologies including robust, pre-sumably ancestral forms (*H. rhodesiensis* from Broken Hill/Kabwe, Zambia) to intermediate cranial morphologies (Florisbad, South Africa) and fully modern *H. sapiens* (Kanjera, Kenya). What Cole (1963: 166) called a 'very awkward problem' was subsequently resolved with the application of new radiometric techniques and closer analyses of geological con-texts of discovery (e.g. Plummer and Potts 1995; Grün et al. 1996). Making the best of a con-fusing situation, Cole argued, without chronological support, for a generalized form of *Homo* as the ancestor of both Neanderthals and *H. sapiens* in Africa and Europe. Thought responsible for the innovations seen in the late Acheulean and early MSA, today this ances-tral clade is recognized by some as *H. heidelbergensis*, which incorporates the Kabwe material (Rightmire 2004; Foley, Ch. 20 above).

Clark (1970) expanded on Cole's eco-functionalism, moving African archaeology further away from culture historical frameworks. Like her, he followed in a long tradition among Palaeolithic archaeologists of applying scientific principles and methods derived from geol-ogy and palaeontology (e.g. stratigraphic correlation). Darwin's legacy was also evident in Clark's expectation of likely associations between habitat type and human technological response, but the most direct influence on his ecological approach derived from develop-ments in British archaeology in the 1950s led by Grahame Clark (1954). Desmond Clark's (1959) first regional synthesis of the African record employed an environmental framework to examine cultural variability, that later featured in his grand overview of 1970. Like Cole, Clark recognized coeval regional adaptations to general ecological conditions, those of grassland and forest habitats. With the benefit of more data and a continental-sized canvas on which to portray Africa's past, he mapped the distribution of archaeological cultures against current and past vegetation patterns. Desmond Clark's (1967) *Atlas of African*

Prehistory provided the spatial evidence to support the observation that *H. sapiens* was the first species to regularly inhabit rainforests and deserts (Clark 1970: 107). Language was the cognitive foundation for the ecological flexibility of modern humans, and enabled the subsequent elaboration of regional artefact traditions, including ritual behaviours. This equation of behavioural plasticity with language, symbol use, and anatomical modernity foreshadowed current views of what constitutes behavioural modernity (see below).

Unlike Africanists today, Cole and Clark had to contend with the then-accepted fact that Neanderthals had ranged across North Africa from Morocco to Ethiopia. The skeletal evidence from Jebel Irhoud (Morocco), Haua Fteah (Libya), and Porc Epic (Ethiopia) has since been reanalysed and attributed to variability within *H. sapiens* (Hublin 2001). As Cole argued, the use of Levallois technology could not be considered a cultural or biological marker and, by extension, the 'Mousterian' tradition of North Africa could not be attributed with certainty to Neanderthals. Clark, too, argued that the persistence of prepared core use in Africa after its abandonment in Europe reflected neither a late survival of Neanderthals on the continent nor a lack of innovation among African *H. sapiens*. It was simply one of several effective flaking techniques employed by modern humans. The African record displayed regional combinations of prepared flake and blade tools not seen in the European Middle or Upper Palaeolithic. Cole (1963: 169) grouped these variants into the MSA, including those attributed to the ill-defined 'First Intermediate' phase that bridged the Early and Middle Stone Ages. The phase concept and name had been formally abandoned by 1970 (Bishop and Clark 1967: 897), though Clark retained the terminology of a Middle and Upper Palaeolithic as applied across francophone North Africa. The terminological separation between Saharan and sub-Saharan African records contributed to a perception of separate trajectories, including a Neanderthal stage in the north.

Separate developmental trajectories also seemed to exist between Africa and Europe. Boule and Vallois' (1957) argument for an earlier European origin of *H. sapiens* and the Upper Palaeolithic appeared to be supported by the limited number of radiocarbon dates available from Africa for the early MSA. With hindsight, these dates were effectively infinite ages that reflected the limitations of the technique rather than archaeological reality. In Desmond Clark's (1970) synthesis, the MSA (thought to date ~35–15 kya) began as the European Middle Palaeolithic ended, making it contemporary with the Upper Palaeolithic. This continental mismatch confirmed the long-held perception of Africa as a marginal continent in its contribution to later human evolution.

Five years later that view was challenged fundamentally in a seminal paper entitled 'Africa in prehistory: peripheral or paramount?' (Clark 1975) that marshalled radiocarbon dates from 18 MSA sites in sub-Saharan and North Africa and compared them to radiometric dates from 16 Middle Palaeolithic sites in the Near East and Europe. The results showed an unexpected chronological parity between regions. No longer could Africa be perceived as the poor relation on the receiving end of change; if anything, it might just predate the Eurasian record. Newly published radiocarbon results from Border Cave (South Africa), known for its long sequence and fossils of *H. sapiens*, demonstrated that the *end* of the MSA sequence was beyond the effective age range of the technique (>48 kya) (Beaumont and Vogel 1972). At the other end of the time-scale, the late Acheulean to early MSA transition was substantially earlier than expected, with potassium-argon results from the Kapthurin Formation, Kenya, and Gademotta, Ethiopia, ranging from 220–180 kya (Wendorf et al. 1975).

Potassium-argon dating was one of thirteen dating techniques, mostly radiometric, with potential application to archaeological contexts in Africa of relevance to modern human origins (Curtis 1981). By the early 1990s, electron spin resonance, luminescence, and optically stimulated luminescence combined with Uranium-series dating had emerged as the most transformative in extending the potential age range of the MSA and dating the ESA/MSA transition, using materials routinely found in both cave and open sites (Schwarcz 2001). Palpable excitement accompanied each publication or conference announcement of ever older dates from Africa. Radiometric dating of the Israeli cave sites of Tabun, Qafzeh, and Skhul also contributed to the changing perception of Africa's role in modern human origins with Uranium-series results showing that *H. sapiens* predated Neanderthals in this region, or were at least coeval (McDermott et al. 1993). The yoke of a European source for *H. sapiens* in Africa lifted and the prospect of an African origin became more realistic. That expectation was realized with the recovery of fossil *H. sapiens* from datable contexts in South Africa (Klasies River, ~120 kya; H. Deacon 1992). Subsequent discoveries in Ethiopia confirmed an early African origin of anatomically modern humans, extended their age range into the later Middle Pleistocene (Omo I, Ethiopia ~195 kya; McDougall et al. 2005). The age of the MSA has expanded even more radically with the application of radiometric techniques to stratified cave sequences in southern Africa and open sites in eastern Africa. Moreover, the behavioural and fossil records are no longer in step chronologically, with the MSA now pre-dating the development of anatomical modernity by at least 60–80 kya in Kenya (285 kya, Kapthurin Formation; Tryon and McBrearty 2002), Zambia (~265 kya, Twin Rivers; Barham 2000), and South Africa (>276 kya, Wonderwerk Cave; Beaumont and Vogel 2006).

OUT OF AFRICA II

Desmond Clark's (1975) demonstration of chronological parity between Africa and Eurasia laid the foundations for the acceptance of bold claims soon to arise from a new source—genetics—of an African origin for all modern humans. By the mid-1980s, techniques of DNA analysis had moved beyond the study of indirect genetic markers, such as blood proteins, to the direct analysis of DNA base-pair sequences (MacEachern, Ch. 5 above). Mitochondrial DNA (mtDNA) provided the genetic basis of the first, and still the most spectacular, challenge to the prevailing consensus of modern human origins. The African MSA rivalled, if it did not exceed, the age of the European Middle Palaeolithic, but still uncertain in the 1980s was the time and place of origin of anatomically modern humans. In a pioneering paper, Cann et al. (1987) argued that all mtDNA in living humans owed its origins to a single female ancestor who lived in sub-Saharan Africa ~200,000 years ago, a date derived from calculating an assumed constant rate of mutation in a small proportion of the mtDNA genome. Broad age estimates were also calculated for the dispersal of modern humans from Africa into Eurasia, and a further inference was made that little or no interbreeding took place between dispersing and indigenous populations. Some attempt was made to integrate the fossil and archaeological records to support an African origin and spread of modern humans, but the real impact for archaeologists came shortly afterwards.

Stringer and Andrews (1988) combined the mtDNA results with a more thorough review of the fossil evidence for the origin of *H. sapiens*, concluding that Africa was indeed the single centre of origin from which modern humans dispersed across the Old World. The Out of Africa II or Recent African Origin model was born. Critical responses from multi-regionalists (e.g. Wolpoff 1989) and initial uncertainties about the interpretation of the mtDNA data (Templeton 1992) have since largely given way to an impressive and still growing body of data from a variety of genetic sources (whole mtDNA genomes, the non-recombining Y-chromosome, and autosomal DNA) that collectively support a single African origin of modern humans (Campbell and Tishkoff 2010; Lahr, Ch. 23 above).

For archaeologists, the impact of the Out of Africa model was profound. The MSA archaeological record became by default the testing ground for the proposed behavioural advantages that enabled modern humans to disperse so widely. The new focus on Africa as the centre of modern human origins was embodied in the two volumes that emerged from the 'Human Revolution' conference held in Cambridge in 1987, just weeks after the publication of Cann et al.'s pioneering study. Africanist archaeologists drove the debate, arguing for an African origin of behavioural modernity, though disagreeing about the criteria that signalled modernity and therefore the timing and processes underlying its development (cf. Clark 1989; Deacon 1989; Klein 1989). The European Upper Palaeolithic retained a potent intellectual grip on the proceedings; if the Out of Africa model was correct in its predictions, then Upper Palaeolithic behaviours should first appear in Africa. The search was on for early examples in Africa of blades, backed blades, beads, art, pigment use, bone tools, structured hearths, burials with grave goods, big-game hunting, and long-distance exchange networks, as might be expected of behaviourally modern hunter-gatherers. The quest culminated in a landmark publication by McBrearty and Brooks (2000), who compiled a continent-wide list of behavioural traits and their first appearances. They combined these with a review of the human fossil record, and concluded that there was no particular time or place in which modernity emerged. Its evolution was regionally variable but the record still supported an African origin, with early occurrences of many behaviours considered distinctively modern in the European context. A logical offshoot of the Out of Africa model was a likely source of the European Upper Palaeolithic among some MSA population of moderns that dispersed into Eurasia during the late Pleistocene. Routes of dispersal and entry were hypothesized via the Nile through the Near East (Van Peer 1998) and climate change posited as the trigger for population movements (Ambrose 1998). The most extreme version of the new diffusionism traced the origins of the Upper Palaeolithic to South Africa and the makers of the Howiesons Poort industry (~65–60 kya; Lombard, Ch. 26 below) (Mellars 2005). The transformation was now complete: Africa was the donor rather than the recipient of modernity.

FORAGING THEORY AS CRITIQUE

The conflicting models of modern human origins debated at the 'Human Revolution' conference had become well entrenched by the start of the new millennium with little common ground between them (Deacon and Wurz 2001). McBrearty and Brooks' (2000) gradualist model provided an alternative to the polarized early and late origin models, but no consensus had been reached about what constituted behavioural modernity and how to recognize it archaeologically. To this cacophony Henshilwood and Marean (2003) brought much-needed conceptual and methodological rigour. They demonstrated the conceptual inadequacy of behavioural trait lists as the means of identifying the appearance of modernity. Many supposedly universal behaviours could be discounted as local responses to specific ecological conditions. Foraging theory provided an elegant predictive model that accounted for much regional variability in the archaeological record (Torrence 2001). Ethnographic research showed that high-latitude hunter-gatherers faced markedly different resource stresses from those living in the tropics, and accordingly their social and technological responses differed (Hayden 1981). Trait lists derived from the European record were thus inappropriate markers of modernity for assessing the African record. In their place, Henshilwood and Marean offered a general behavioural definition of modernity allied with a methodology for recognizing its appearance.

The essence of modern human behaviour, they argued, lies in the construction of social lives through the use of symbols. Language is a symbol-based form of communication, but symbols in material form provide a visual and more lasting means of transmitting conventions, codes, and agreed actions that define a particular group or culture. Henshilwood and Marean established a material threshold for recognizing the unambiguous expression of socially agreed conventions in the archaeological record. Art, artefact style, and the socially organized use of space together constituted the essential markers of external symbolic storage that in turn reflected 'fully symbolic *sapiens* behaviour' (Henshilwood and Marean 2003: 644). The concept and its material correlates have been developed further (Henshilwood 2007; Marean 2007) and found support among those who had previously called for a more rigorous set of criteria for recognizing modernity in the archaeological record (Wadley 2001). For those uncomfortable with modernity as a vaguely defined term, the phrase 'fully symbolic *sapiens* behaviour' provided a means of avoiding its usage whilst conveying a linkage with anatomical modernity. The gradualist and late origins models retain their proponents (e.g. McBrearty 2007; Klein 2009), but on balance a consensus has crystallized around symbol use as the marker of modernity, with the earliest unambiguous evidence for its expression coming from Africa and the Near East, all within the time-frame (< 200 kya) of *H. sapiens* (Marean 2007).

PARADIGM GAINED AND CHALLENGED

This chapter has charted the changing perceptions of Africa's role in later human evolution, arising in part from new analytical techniques, and the subsequent development of a consensus of what constitutes behavioural modernity. The history of science tells us, however, that Henshilwood and Marean's framework will, sooner or later, be replaced by a new construct arising from conflicting data. Kuhn (1970) outlines a cyclical process of paradigm change in which a body of theory and practice that guides research until sufficient evidence to the contrary emerges that can no longer be accommodated within the existing framework. Paradigm change then follows, a new consensus forms, and normal science resumes until the weight of anomalous data tips the scales again. The fully symbolic *sapiens* concept is approaching paradigm status, though it remains a working hypothesis rather than a fully developed theory. As an hypothesis it offers a testable prediction: fully symbolic behaviour emerged only with *H. sapiens*. This can be refuted by the discovery of fully symbolic behaviours among other species of *Homo*. It offers a clearly defined set of criteria for recognizing modernity (external symbolic storage), but lacks a fully articulated theory of cause and effect that predicts when and where fully symbolic *sapiens* behaviour will appear, and why.

The first challenge arises from the limited but growing evidence for symbolic behaviours among later Neanderthals (d'Errico 2003), including art in the form of personal ornamentation (Zilhão et al. 2010). The explicit species linkage of this model seems unlikely to hold over time. An equally serious challenge lies in the charge of inductivism that Henshilwood and Marean levied against those who used a trait list approach to recognize modernity. The appearance of all the markers of external symbolic storage at any one place and time may in itself be a contingent behaviour rather than an essential feature of modernity.

Some elements of external symbolic storage pre-date *H. sapiens*, such as artefact style and the structured use of space (e.g. Barham 2000; Van Peer et al. 2004). Ochre use also pre-dates the evolution of anatomical modernity (McBrearty 2001; Barham 2002), but for most archaeologists it cannot be considered unequivocal evidence of symbol use given its potential functional properties (Wadley 2001). The coalescence of art, artefact style, and socially structured use of space seen in parts of southern and northern Africa (Bouzouggar et al. 2007; Lombard 2009) and the Near East (Vanhaeren et al. 2006) between 120 and 60 kya is notably episodic rather than cumulative and sustained (d'Errico and Vanhaeren 2007). The relatively brief interludes in which external symbolic storage appears suggest that this phenomenon reflects the confluence of demographic, ecological, and social factors (Powell et al. 2009), rather than being an inherent property of modern humans expressed at all times and places. If an external force such as population pressure drives the extent of symbolic signalling, then the term 'demographic modernity' better reflects the contingency of these behaviours. The Last Interglacial with its climatically variable sub-stages (Marine Isotope Stages 5e–5a) may have been the first time in African prehistory that population levels had grown to the extent that competition for limited resources led to the systematic use of symbolic markers of identity (Barham and Mitchell 2008: 238).

Another potential challenge to the consensus resides among the minority of researchers who retain a gradualist perspective on the evolution of modernity. As a group, they are examining other complex behaviours, such as hierarchical technologies, as sources of indirect evidence of socially mediated rules founded on language (and a large brain) that also pre-date *H. sapiens* (e.g. Gowlett 2009; Barham 2010; Shea 2011). Further challenges to the model of a late and *sapiens*-specific expression of modernity can be expected from this quarter, and from archaeological discoveries to come.

References

Ambrose, S. (1998). Late Pleistocene human population bottlenecks, volcanic winter, and differentiation of modern humans. *Journal of Human Evolution* 34: 623–51.

Barham, L. S. (2000). *The Middle Stone Age of Zambia, South-Central Africa*. Bristol: Western & Academic Specialist Press.

—— (2002). Systematic pigment use in the Middle Pleistocene of South-Central Africa. *Current Anthropology* 43: 181–90.

——(2010). A technological solution to Dunbar's dilemma? *Proceedings of the British Academy* 158: 371–94.

—— and MITCHELL, P. J. (2008). *The First Africans: African Archaeology from the Earliest Toolmakers to Most Recent Foragers*. Cambridge: Cambridge University Press.

BEAUMONT, P. B., and VOGEL, J.C. (1972). On a new radiocarbon chronology for Africa south of the Equator. *African Studies* 31: 155–82.

—— —— (2006). On a timescale for the past million years of human history in central South Africa. *South African Journal of Science* 102: 217–28.

BISHOP, W. W., and CLARK, J. D. (eds) (1967). *Background to Evolution in Africa*. Chicago: University of Chicago Press.

BORDES, F. (1968). *The Old Stone Age*. New York: McGraw-Hill.

BOULE, M., and VALLOIS, H. (1957). *Fossil Men*. London: Thames & Hudson.

BOUZOUGGAR, A., BARTON, N., VANHAEREN, M., et al. (2007). 82,000-year-old shell beads from North Africa and implications for the origins of modern human behaviour. *Proceedings of the National Academy of Sciences* (USA) 104: 207–48.

CAMPBELL, M. C., and TISHKOFF, S. A. (2010). The evolution of human genetic phenotypic variations in Africa. *Current Biology* 20: 166–73.

CANN, R. L. M., STONEKING, M., and WILSON, A. C. (1987). Mitochondrial DNA and human evolution. *Nature* 325: 31–6.

CLARK, J. D. (1959). *The Prehistory of Southern Africa*. Harmondsworth: Penguin.

——(1967). *Atlas of African Prehistory*. Chicago: University of Chicago Press.

——(1970). *The Prehistory of Africa*. London: Thames & Hudson.

——(1975). Africa in prehistory: peripheral or paramount? *Man* 10: 175–98.

——(1989). The origins and spread of modern humans: a broad perspective on the African evidence. In: P. Mellars and C. B. Stringer (eds), *The Human Revolution: Behavioural and Biological Perspectives on the Origins of Modern Humans*. Edinburgh: Edinburgh University Press, 565–88.

CLARK, J. G. D. (1954). *Excavations at Star Carr*. Cambridge: Cambridge University Press.

COLE, S. (1963). *The Prehistory of East Africa*. London: Weidenfeld & Nicolson.

CURTIS, G. H. (1981). Man's immediate forerunner: establishing a relevant time scale in anthropological and archaeological research. *Philosophical Transactions of the Royal Society* (London) B, 292: 7–20.

DARWIN, C. (1871). *The Descent of Man, and Selection in Relation to Sex*. London: James Murray.

DEACON, H. J. (1989). The Late Pleistocene palaeoecology and archaeology in the southern Cape, South Africa. In: P. Mellars and C. B. Stringer (eds), *The Human Revolution: Behavioural and Biological Perspectives on the Origins of Modern Humans*. Edinburgh: Edinburgh University Press, 547–64.

—— (1992). Southern Africa and modern human origins. *Philosophical Transactions of the Royal Society* (London) B, 337: 177–83.

—— and WURZ, S. (2001). Middle Pleistocene populations of southern Africa and the emergence of modern behaviour. In L. S. Barham and K. Robson-Brown (eds), *Human Roots: Africa and Asia and in the Middle Pleistocene*. Bristol: Western Academic & Specialist Press, 55–63.

D'ERRICO, F. (2003). The invisible frontier: a multiple species model for the origin of behavioral modernity. *Evolutionary Anthropology* 12: 188–202.

D' ERRICO, F. and VANHAEREN, M. (2007). New evidence for the origin of symbolic behaviour in and out of Africa. In P. Mellars, K. Boyle, O. Bar-Yosef, and C. B. Stringer (eds), *Rethinking The Human Revolution: New Behavioural and Biological Perspectives on the Origin and Dispersal of Modern Humans*. Cambridge: McDonald Institute, 275–86.

GOWLETT, J. A. J. (2009). The longest transition or multiple revolutions? Curves and steps in the record of human origins. In M. Camps and P. Chauhan (eds), *Sourcebook of Paleolithic Transitions*. London: Springer Science, 65–78.

GRÜN, R., BRINK, J. S., SPOONER, N., et al. (1996). Direct dating of Florisbad hominid. *Nature* 382: 500–501.

HAYDEN, B. (1981). Subsistence and ecological adaptations of modern hunter-gatherers. In R. S. O. Harding and G. Teleki (eds), *Omnivorous Primates: Gathering and Hunting in Human Evolution*. New York: Columbia University Press, 344–421.

HENSHILWOOD, C. S. (2007). Fully symbolic *sapiens* behaviour: innovations in the Middle Stone Age at Blombos Cave, South Africa. In P. Mellars, K. Boyle, O. Bar-Yosef, and C. B. Stringer (eds), *Rethinking the Human Revolution: New Behavioural and Biological Perspectives on the Origin and Dispersal of Modern Humans*. Cambridge: McDonald Institute, 123–32.

—— and MAREAN, C. W. (2003). The origin of modern human behaviour: critique of the models and their test implications. *Current Anthropology* 44: 627–51.

HUBLIN, J.-J. (2001). Northwestern African Middle Pleistocene hominids and their bearing on the emergence of *Homo sapiens*. In L. S. Barham and K. Robson-Brown (eds), *Human Roots: Africa and Asia in the Middle Pleistocene*. Bristol: Western Academic & Specialist Press, 99–121.

KLEIN, R. G. (1989). Biological and behavioural perspectives on modern human origins in southern Africa. In P. Mellars and C. B. Stringer (eds), *The Human Revolution: Behavioural and Biological Perspectives on the Origins of Modern Humans*. Edinburgh: Edinburgh University Press, 529–46.

—— (2009). *The Human Career*. Chicago: University of Chicago Press.

KUHN, T. S. (1970). *The Structure of Scientific Revolutions*. Chicago: University of Chicago Press.

LOMBARD, M. (2009). The Howieson's Poort of South Africa amplified. *South African Archaeological Bulletin* 64: 4–12.

MCBREARTY, S. (2001). The Middle Pleistocene of East Africa. In L. S. Barham and K. Robson-Brown (eds), *Human Roots: Africa and Asia in the Middle Pleistocene*. Bristol: Western Academic & Specialist Press, 81–98.

——(2007). Down with the revolution. In P. Mellars, K. Boyle, O. Bar-Yosef, and C. B. Stringer (eds), *Rethinking the Human Revolution: New Behavioural and Biological Perspectives on the Origin and Dispersal of Modern Humans*. Cambridge: McDonald Institute, 133–51.

—— and BROOKS, A. S. (2000). The revolution that wasn't: a new interpretation of the origin of modern human behavior. *Journal of Human Evolution* 39: 453–563.

MCDERMOTT, F., GRÜN, R., STRINGER, C. B., and HAWKESWORTH, C. J. (1993). Mass-spectrometric U-series dates for Israeli Neanderthal/early modern hominid sites. *Nature* 363: 252–5.

MCDOUGALL, I., BROWN, F. H., and FLEAGLE, J. (2005). Stratigraphic placement and age of modern humans from Kibish, Ethiopia. *Nature* 433: 733–6.

MAREAN, C. W. (2007). Heading north: an Africanist perspective on the replacement of Neanderthals by modern humans. In P. Mellars, K. Boyle, O. Bar-Yosef, and C. B. Stringer (eds), *Rethinking the Human Revolution: New Behavioural and Biological Perspectives on the Origin and Dispersal of Modern Humans*. Cambridge: McDonald Institute, 367–79.

MELLARS, P. A. (2005). The impossible coincidence: a single-species model for the origins of modern human behaviour. *Evolutionary Anthropology* 14: 12–27.

PLUMMER, T., and POTTS, R. (1995). Hominid fossil sample from Kanjera, Kenya: description, provenance, and implications of new and earlier discoveries. *American Journal of Physical Anthropology* 96: 7–23.

POWELL, A., SHENNAN, S., and THOMAS, M. G. (2009). Late Pleistocene demography and the appearance of modern human behavior. *Science* 324: 1298–1301.

RIGHTMIRE, P. (2004). Brain size and encephalization in early to mid-Pleistocene *Homo*. *American Journal of Physical Anthropology* 124: 109–23.

ROBERTSHAW, P. T. (ed.) (1990). *A History of African Archaeology*. London: James Currey.

SCHWARCZ, H. P. (2001). Chronometric dating of the Middle Pleistocene. In L. S. Barham and K. Robson-Brown (eds), *Human Roots: Africa and Asia in the Middle Pleistocene*. Bristol: Western Academic & Specialist Press, 41–53.

SHEA, J. J. (2011). *Homo sapiens* is as *Homo sapiens* was. *Current Anthropology* 52:1–35.

STOCKING, G. W. (1968). *Race, Culture, and Evolution: Essays in the History of Anthropology*. New York: Free Press.

STRINGER, C. B., and ANDREWS, P. (1988). Genetic and fossil evidence for the origin of modern humans. *Science* 239: 1263–8.

TEMPLETON, A. R. (1992). Human origins and analysis of mitochondrial DNA sequences. *Science* 255: 737.

TORRENCE, R. (2001). Hunter-gatherer technology viewed at different scales. In C. Panter-Brick, R. Layton, and P. Rowley-Conwy (eds), *Hunter-Gatherers: An Interdisciplinary Perspective*. Cambridge: Cambridge University Press, 73–98.

TRIGGER, B. G. (1989). *A History of Archaeological Thought*. Cambridge: Cambridge University Press.

TRYON, C. A., and MCBREARTY, S. (2002). Tephrostratigraphy and the Acheulian to Middle Stone Age transition in the Kapthurin Formation, Kenya. *Journal of Human Evolution* 42: 211–35.

VAN PEER, P. (1998). The Nile corridor and the Out-of-Africa model: an examination of the archaeological record. *Current Anthropology* 39: S115–20.

——, ROTS, V., and VROOMANS, J.-M. (2004). A story of colourful diggers and grinders: the Sangoan and Lupemban at site 8-B-11, Sai Island, northern Sudan. *Before Farming* 3: 139–66.

VANHAEREN, M., D'ERRICO, F., STRINGER, C., JAMES, S. L., TODD, J., and MIENSIS, H. K. (2006). Middle Palaeolithic shell beads in Israel and Algeria. *Science* 312: 1785–8.

WADLEY, L. (2001). What is cultural modernity? A general view and a South African perspective from Rose Cottage Cave. *Cambridge Archaeological Journal* 11: 201–21.

WEIDENREICH, F. (1947). *Apes, Giants and Man*. Chicago: University of Chicago Press.

WENDORF, F., LAURY, I., ALBRITTON, C. C., et al. (1975). Dates for the Middle Stone Age in East Africa. *Science* 187: 740–42.

WHITE, T. D., ASFAW, B., DEGUSTA, D., et al. (2003). Pleistocene *Homo sapiens* from Middle Awash, Ethiopia. *Nature* 432: 742–7.

WOLPOFF, M. (1989). Multiregional evolution: the fossil alternative to Eden. In P. Mellars and C. B. Stringer (eds) *The Human Revolution: Behavioural and Biological Perspectives on the Origins of Modern Humans*. Edinburgh: Edinburgh University Press, 62–108.

ZILHÃO, J., ANGELUCCI, D. E., BADAL GARCIA, E., et al. (2010). Symbolic use of marine shells and mineral pigments by Iberian Neanderthals. *Proceedings of the National Academy of Science* (USA) 107: 1023–8.

PART IV

HUNTERS, GATHERERS, AND INTENSIFIERS: THE DIVERSITY OF AFRICAN FORAGERS

CHAPTER 25

THEORETICAL FRAMEWORKS FOR UNDERSTANDING AFRICAN HUNTER-GATHERERS

LYN WADLEY

INTRODUCTION

ARCHAEOLOGISTS use theory from many disciplines. Theories embody premises, tenets, and other concepts used to answer questions. Within the scientific paradigm, they provide the foundation for hypotheses that apply concepts to data. Models of human behaviour are, in turn, hypotheses derived from theory. Interpretations need to be based on inferences that involve bridging arguments or theory that must be grounded and warranted. Grounding requires that there is evidence to support the inference, while warranting requires that this is relevant to connecting the data and the inference. Links between interpretations of human behaviour and archaeological data can sometimes be made through experiments that include replication or ethnoarchaeological studies that are part of what Binford (1977) called 'middle range theory'. Such an approach increases the strands of evidence available; using multiple lines of evidence can decrease the level of ambiguity and reinforce the strength of arguments and interpretations (Wylie 1989; Atici 2006). These principles apply, of course, not only to the interpretation of past hunter-gatherer behaviour but more broadly to inferences about any class of archaeological data.

Anthropological theory helps explain behavioural variation amongst living humans (Blurton Jones et al. 1996); archaeologists add a time dimension to this aim. Nevertheless, no single theory used by archaeologists can account for why or how there is change through time. Indeed, although time is central to the business of archaeologists, this seemingly straightforward matter requires theoretical and methodological deliberation. Time, as construed in this volume, is a Eurocentric construct, yet even within a single cultural vision of what time means, there are different methodological approaches for measuring time in archaeological sites (Stern 1994; Bailey 2007). Eurocentrism inevitably affects other aspects of research into the African past (see e.g. Deacon 1995). To some extent this problem has been countered by the increasing use of methods such as DNA analysis, isotope analysis, and use trace analysis. Employment of these methods shows that science can provide direct answers to some questions that archaeologists ask, reducing the usefulness of traditional ethnographic analogy for many aspects of archaeological interpretation and placing some aspects of archaeology firmly within the realm of the scientific paradigm. In the process, changing research emphases have become evident. Thus, while the consensus view of a sub-Saharan origin for modern human origins has publicized the Middle Stone Age (MSA) and used it to speak for the past of all living humans, it may concurrently have contributed to the decline in Later Stone Age (LSA) studies (Mitchell 2005).

Societies still largely dependent on indigenous animals and plants live in widely separated parts of Africa. People such as the Ju/'hoansi Bushmen have become archetypes of a hunter-gatherer way of life and have long been central to archaeologists' hypotheses (Barham and Mitchell 2008). Loosely used in all types of literature, the term 'hunter-gatherer' nevertheless needs proper definition to separate human from animal hunter-gatherers. Distinctively human are the harvesting of plants and small animals into containers and hunting using out-of-body and deliberately fashioned weapons. Archaeological finds of wooden spears at Schoeningen, Germany, dating to about 400 kya (Thieme 1997) and of stone points that were almost certainly the tips of hunting weapons at East African MSA sites such as Aduma (Brooks et al. 2006) and Kapthurin (Deino and McBrearty 2002; Tryon and McBrearty 2002, 2006) dated to >350 kya show that hunting and gathering as a subsistence mode is not restricted to *Homo sapiens,* the oldest specimens of which are no more than 200,000 years old (Foley, Ch. 20 above).

The early advent of hunting with 'out-of-body' weapons and the associated social corollaries suggests that there is no reason to separate theoretical approaches used for MSA and LSA hunter-gatherers, notwithstanding the 'grand moment' (Barham and Mitchell 2008: 6) represented by the evolution of 'modern behaviour' during the MSA. Consequently, this chapter moves seamlessly between discussions of theoretical frameworks used for the interpretation of African hunter-gatherers who lived at any time between 300,000 and 100 years ago. Although global theoretical perspectives such as processualism, post-processualism, structural-functionalism, and structural Marxism have been used separately to interpret at least some African archaeological materials, it would be oversimplistic to pigeonhole all African hunter-gatherer research in this way. Indeed, the theoretical frameworks referred to here include not only anthropological ones but also some derived from psychologists, neuroscientists, cognitive scientists, and ecologists. Likewise, the thematic divisions are heuristic rather than rigid: many of the themes are linked and there is much overlap between them.

THE USE OF ETHNOGRAPHY

Ethnographic analogy: opposing and supporting perspectives

Attitudes to using ethnography for interpreting ancient hunter-gatherer behaviour vary considerably between those who champion it and those who disregard it. Like any tool, ethnographic analogy is useful when used wisely and it would be injudicious to ignore the insights it provides (Lyons, Ch. 7 above). One way in which ethnographic records have been especially valuable is in providing evidence that communities, no matter how impoverished by western standards, do not necessarily behave in ways that optimize resources or personnel. People are first and foremost social beings who operate according to cultural mores. For example, Bofi and Aka hunters in the Central African Republic are most successful at capturing duiker with snares, yet largely ignore this technique and opt instead for net hunting (Lupo and Schmitt 2005). Although relatively inefficient, net hunts are public activities at which a hunter's accomplishments are seen by all, and they thereby provide 'nonconsumptive benefits'. In East Africa, too, a large component of men's hunting seems to take place for social reasons: for 'showing-off', competing between men, attracting mates, or gaining status or allies (Hawkes et al. 2001; Hawkes and Bliege Bird 2002; O'Connell et al. 2002).

Wobst (1978: 303) refers to the 'tyranny of the ethnographic record in archaeology', and Wylie (1985) points to the difficulties associated with inductive analogical reasoning, not least the problem of deciding whether observed similarities have relevance. Kuhn and Stiner (2006) suggest that modern human analogues show us most specifically how our ancestors were *not* like us and what we still need to explain about human evolution. Thus, they say, recent hunter-gatherer overviews are most useful when they expose disagreement between the historical record of hunter-gatherer behaviour and the archaeological reconstruction of behaviour in the deep past. One problem with archaeological interpretations based on ethnographic models is that they can lead to oversimplified conclusions and an assumption that uniformitarian principles of behaviour apply to all hunter-gatherers, past and present. An example is the assumption that ochre that occurs in archaeological sites automatically implies rituals such as body-painting. This stems from analogy with modern hunter-gatherers, including southern African Bushmen (Bleek and Lloyd 1911; Marshall 1976), but there is presently no way of testing whether MSA or LSA hunter-gatherers in Africa also practised body painting.

More insidiously, ethnographic analogy can unintentionally imply that living hunter-gatherers are 'human fossils' (Headland and Reid 1989)—a criticism also made by revisionists such as Wilmsen (1989) as part of the 'Kalahari Debate'. Studies of living hunter-gatherers have demonstrated a wealth of behavioural diversity between groups (e.g. Kent 1996; Hawkes et al. 2001; Hawkes and Bliege Bird 2002; Lupo and Schmitt 2002), and there is every likelihood that this was also true of hunter-gatherer communities in the past. Revisionist scholars also challenge portrayals of Kalahari foragers as autonomous or pristine communities (Wilmsen and Denbow 1990)—an issue of particular relevance when pastoral and farming communities entered the African stage. The use of ethnographic analogy contributed to the assumption that foragers and farmers were polarized, although archaeological research has helped counter this by demonstrating the variety of farmer/pastoralist and hunter-gatherer interactions in Africa during the past 2,000 years. Symbiotic relationships formed in areas as divergent as the forests of Central Africa and the deserts of southern Africa (Headland and Reid 1989; Wadley 1996; Robbins et al. 1998; van der Ryst 1998; Casey 2005; van Doornum 2008). The facility with which some hunter-gatherers either adopted livestock or became assimilated into farming communities contradicts interpretations that they were inherently conservative or unwilling to change. Hunter-gatherers living in Africa before 2,000 years ago may have been equally adaptable about other kinds of change. Archaeologists clearly need to explore the specific historical context of ethnographic records before using them to construct models about the past. Indeed, there can be no expectation that archaeological data should be explained by ethnography or historical records (Stahl 2005), and archaeologically retrieved data may suggest past behaviour for which there are no known modern correlates. As an example, LSA burial practices in some coastal sites in South Africa's Western and Eastern Cape Provinces were more complex than those of contemporary or recent Kalahari hunter-gatherers (Hall and Binneman 1987; Wadley 1997).

Gendered behaviour

Linked to the discussion of ethnographic models is the issue of gender attribution. One view sees a gender/age-based division of labour as a unique and universal attribute of *Homo sapiens* behaviour (Shea 2006). Others, such as Hovers (2006), are more cautious. Whether or not a division of labour is specific to modern humans, it seems problematic to seek gender attributions for tasks in the archaeological record (Dobres 1995; Conkey and Gero 1997), even though some cognitive differences do appear to exist between men and women (Schenker et al. 2005). Some gender stereotypes derived from the ethnographic literature about hunter-gatherer social behaviour have been exploded, such as egalitarian food-sharing practices between the sexes. Dietary practices can sometimes be detected through stable isotope analysis of human bone. Sealy's (2006) study of 74 Western Cape skeletons (most postdating 3000 BP) showed, for example, that men's diets were enriched with marine foods such as seal and fish compared to those of women, but that before 3000 BP this was less evident, thus demonstrating social change through time. Furthermore, modern examples of women who hunt or otherwise contribute to the meat quest invalidate any simple 'man-the-hunter' model (Estioko-Griffin and Griffin 1981; Wadley 1998; Kuhn and Stiner 2006).

Material culture theory

'Material culture theory' deals with the meanings of things and places and their roles in determining social values. Some archaeologists view material culture as an active rather than passive participant in human culture; others regard it differently, though they may agree that style and social boundaries coincide only under particular circumstances (Lane 2005; Wynne-Jones, this volume). Symbolism is potentially an important group marker (Donald 1998), though symbolic meanings can crosscut groups, and also maintains, negotiates, legitimizes, and transmits information about relationships such as those based on kinship, gender, and age (Wadley 2001). Artefacts are not automatically imbued with symbolism; that happens once they are used to define or mediate social relationships. It is only when technology begins to participate in the social and ideological realms of life that it takes on a symbolic role (Kuhn and Stiner 1998: 155–6). The interpretation by some archaeologists of ancient stone or bone weapons as symbolic has almost certainly been inspired by San hunting equipment being closely associated with male sexual symbolism. In the absence of bridging theory to link this ethnographically derived model to the archaeological data, such a leap of faith is unwise.

'Art' is the most obvious example of symbolic storage outside the human brain, yet is not universally practised by hunter-gatherers and cannot be used as an essential attribute that marks symbolic behaviour. There is really no consensus about what art is, but Conkey (2001) incorporates beadwork into an art category that includes visual images, and suggests that all such representations are modes of knowledge. Certainly beads can be characterized as part of a shared system of communication, even as information technology, and they allow the same data to be expressed over large spatial and temporal domains (Kuhn et al. 2001; Kuhn and Stiner 2007: 51). Early shell beads occur in the MSA in North and South Africa (d'Errico et al. 2009) as well as very commonly in the LSA, where ostrich eggshell beads are also abundant (Deacon and Deacon 1999). Some archaeologists believe that the engraved ochre pieces dated older than 70 kya from Blombos, South Africa, also represent art and early symbolic expression (Henshilwood et al. 2009; cf. Barham, Lombard, Chs 24 and 26 this volume). Symbolic items need to be part of a tradition in order to reach a wide audience and have any impact as a cultural marker (Mellars 1996). The engraved ostrich eggshell from the Howiesons Poort Industry (>60 kya) at Diepkloof represents one such early repeated cultural item, albeit at a single site (Coolidge and Wynn 2008), and similar engraved eggshell is extremely common in LSA sites from about 15 kya (Deacon and Deacon 1999).

MIDDLE-RANGE THEORY

Binford (1977) pioneered archaeological middle-range theory, which he envisaged would operate in conjunction with general theories. It belongs more in the realm of methods than theory, but is a particularly useful bridging mechanism between archaeological data, theory, and interpretation. Actualistic research on spatial patterning in hunter-gatherer campsites, such as that by Yellen (1977), has made intrasite and intersite spatial analysis of ancient campsites possible. The concept of *chaîne opératoire* is another good illustration of the use of middle-range theory because it links empirically grounded analytic methods with established anthropological theory (Dobres 2000). Apart from the effective application of *chaîne opératoire* to the analysis of lithic assemblages (Tryon, Ch. 8 above), it has been used for establishing the procedural strategies for the manufacture of bone tools and engraved ochre (e.g. d'Errico and Henshilwood 2007; Backwell and d'Errico 2008). Residue and use trace analyses provide similar advantages because they combine experimental work with fine-grained examination of material culture items. A combination of ethnographic research with microscopy on scrapers has confirmed stylistic hafting differences among East African groups (Rots and Williamson 2004), while Williamson (2004) and Lombard (2005, 2007, 2008) have unequivocally demonstrated the use as weaponry of MSA stone tools such as retouched points and backed segments. Further experiments have shown the complexity of cognition required to produce the compound adhesives needed to haft them (Wadley et al. 2009; Lombard, Ch. 26 below).

COGNITIVE ARCHAEOLOGY

As the social world of hunter-gatherers became more complex, as it did in the LSA, its management would have required progressively demanding social rituals. Indeed, the evidence for social ritual or symbolic expression does appear to increase gradually through time in

African prehistory. Ostrich eggshell beads appear about 40 kya in East Africa (Ambrose 1998a) and South Africa (Beaumont et al. 1978), and early representational art at about 27 kya in Apollo 11, Namibia (Wendt 1976; Vogelsang et al. 2010). This and the subsequent florescence of art in the LSA is the subject of many interpretive models (Smith, this volume). A combination of theory derived from neuropsychology, historical accounts, and ethnography underlies the seminal interpretations of rock art by Lewis-Williams (1981). Notwithstanding the heuristic value of what is sometimes called the 'shamanistic hypothesis' for explaining the imagery, and its wide use by other rock art specialists (cf. Mitchell 2002: 199–210), the model's detractors (e.g. Solomon 1997; McCall 2007) contend that it is too restrictive in scope.

Many cognitive theoretical frameworks concentrate on the abilities of the individual. When contemplating cultural innovation we tend to think of an inventor or a lone genius, yet humans are social creatures that evolved in groups. The need to operate in groups is sometimes reflected in aspects of human cognitive abilities. Experiments show that thinking in groups produces results superior to those from individuals, but only for cognitive tasks that are sufficiently challenging to exceed the capacity of an individual (Wilson et al. 2004). Furthermore, psychologists demonstrate that individuals who frequently engage socially perform better on tests of cognitive performance than those who do not; this supports the perception that social factors, more than technological ones, were responsible for the development of modern cognition (Rossano 2009). The desire for social solutions to problems (including those that may have originated in the natural world) may be reflected in some archaeological data. Mazel (1989), for example, used models of alliance networks to explain hunter-gatherer behaviour and social reproduction in the Holocene occupations of the Thukela Basin, South Africa. Gift exchange is frequently used to facilitate hunter-gatherer social interactions, particularly when groups meet, and there seems to be some evidence in Africa for its practice in the past (Mitchell 2003). Band fluidity, in the form of aggregation and dispersal, is a universal hunter-gatherer practice that seems recognizable in some LSA sites (Wadley 1987). Fission–fusion behaviour may have developed as a combination of environmental constraints and the overwhelming need amongst hunter-gatherers for periodic large-group interaction.

ECOLOGICAL AND DEMOGRAPHIC THEORIES

There is a fine line between environmental reconstructions that set the stage for human action and environmental determinism, which controls behaviour. The situation is complicated by ethnographic accounts of hunter-gatherers who themselves cite environmental causes for aspects of their social behaviour. The archaeological literature abounds with theories and models that use the environment and/or climate change to explain subsistence behaviour, demography, and population movements. These include optimal foraging (Winterhalder 2001), diet breadth (Stiner and Munro 2002), group-size models, and transport-cost models (Holl 1989). Optimal foraging theory predicts that hunter-gatherers will rely on resources that provide the best return for effort, so that people use low-ranked resources only when the cost of searching for higher-ranked foods becomes excessive (Kuhn and Stiner 2001; Winterhalder 2001). It is clear that environments set constraints on what is available to eat, and that people need calories to survive, but cultural mores can play a large role in determining how people go about obtaining their food. People sometimes ignore economic logic in the face of social demands for less productive methods, even though these may run the risk of failure. Thus, patterns recognized in faunal assemblages at archaeological sites may sometimes be more strongly linked to people's social needs than to meat-getting strategies designed to deliver reliable protein supplies. The difficulty for archaeologists is to make the distinction between economic and social intent, and for much of the time this may not be possible. The link between demography and environments is potentially less problematic.

Demographic shifts appear to have taken place repeatedly in Africa, increasing social constraints and, at least on some occasions, marking group boundaries (Barham 2007). They continued into the Holocene, with several areas being sparsely occupied at times (e.g. J. Deacon 1984), some until symbiotic social relationships with farmers enabled hunter-gatherers to occupy them (van der Ryst 1998). African populations probably waxed and waned several times, with Premo and Hublin (2009) using mitochondrial DNA sequences and a model of 'culturally mediated migration' to demonstrate that, during part of the MSA, sub-Saharan Africa did not have a geographically continuous population; instead, sub-populations remained partially isolated. Group isolation in refugia and population bottlenecks is generally given an environmental explanation (most dramatically, the population bottleneck postulated to have followed the Toba eruption ~70 kya; Ambrose 1998b). Between about 190 and 130 kya, human numbers may have been severely reduced, with isolated groups surviving around lake margins, rivers, and in well-watered highlands (Parkington 2006). Basell (2008) suggests that such dramatic, rapid climate swings may have influenced cultural evolution because hominins possessing the creative ingenuity required for adaptation and survival would have had the edge over those who lacked it. Simulations imply that innovation is of low value in small local populations, but of high value in large populations; this suggests that demographic fluctuations may indeed be important factors in explaining how and why modern human culture emerged when it did (Shennan 2001: 15). If so, innovation should be scarce during times of low population density, though Walker (1995) argues for the opposite effect in LSA sites in the Matopo Hills of Zimbabwe. Stiner and Munro (2002) too place demographic forces squarely in the evolutionary arena, as does Klein (2008), who suggests that when population density crossed a critical threshold social reorganization would have been forced. In southern Africa, the large average size of marine shells and tortoise bones from several MSA coastal sites implies that MSA populations were smaller than LSA ones living under similar conditions (Klein 2008). Large group size is costly in energetic terms and obliges hunter-gatherers to remain highly mobile; this conclusion supports the ecological constraints theory, which in turn suggests a possible evolutionary stimulus for fission–fusion social systems (Grove 2009).

Endnote

The questions asked by an archaeologist before the start of a project ultimately determine the choice of theory. Those questions are in turn framed by the paradigm embraced by the archaeologist. Satisfying answers to enquiries about the past depend on the choice of an appropriate theoretical framework, but more is generally required. Interpretation is seldom satisfactorily concluded using theory alone; the greater the number of supporting strands of evidence, the more convincing will be the narrative. Theory needs support from 'middle-range' methodology that might include experiments, data analyses, or other types of empirical evidence. The choice of robust theory and a carefully structured programme linking this to archaeological data through inferential steps and bridging theories is the basic requirement for telling the story of Africa's hunter-gatherer past.

References

AMBROSE, S.H. (1998a). Chronology of the Later Stone Age and food production in East Africa. *Journal of Archaeological Science* 25: 377–92.

—— (1998b). Late Pleistocene human population bottlenecks, volcanic winter and the differentiation of modern humans. *Journal of Human Evolution* 34: 623–51.

ATICI, A. L. (2006). Middle-range theory in Paleolithic archaeology: the past and the present. *Journal of Taphonomy* 4: 29–45.

BACKWELL, L. R., and D'ERRICO, F. (2008). Early hominin bone tools from Drimolen. *Journal of Archaeological Science* 35: 2880–94.

BAILEY, G. N. (2007). Time perspectives, palimpsests and the archaeology of time. *Journal of Anthropological Archaeology* 26: 198–223.

BARHAM, L. S. (2007). Modern is as modern does? Technological trends and thresholds in the south-central African record. In P. Mellars, K. Boyle, O. Bar-Yosef, and C. B. Stringer (eds), *Rethinking the Human Revolution*. Cambridge: McDonald Institute for Archaeological Research, 165–76.

—— and MITCHELL, P. J. (2008). *The First Africans: African Archaeology from the Earliest Toolmakers to Most Recent Foragers*. Cambridge: Cambridge University Press.

BASELL, L. S. (2008). Middle Stone Age (MSA) site distributions in eastern Africa and their relationship to Quaternary environmental change, refugia and the evolution of *Homo sapiens*. *Quaternary Science Reviews* 27: 2484–98.

BEAUMONT, P. B., DE VILLIERS, H., and VOGEL, J. C. (1978). Modern man in sub-Saharan Africa prior to 49000 years BP: a review and evaluation with particular reference to Border Cave. *South African Journal of Science* 74: 409–19.

BINFORD, L. R. (1977). *For Theory Building in Archaeology*. New York: Academic Press.

BLEEK, W. H. I., and LLOYD, L. (1911). *Specimens of Bushman Folklore*. London: Allen.

BLURTON JONES, N., HAWKES, K., and O'CONNELL, J. F. (1996). The global process and local ecology: how should we explain differences between the Hadza and the !Kung? In S. Kent (ed.), *Cultural Diversity Among Twentieth-Century Foragers: An African Perspective*. Cambridge: Cambridge University Press, 159–87.

BROOKS, A. S, YELLEN, J. E., NEVELL, N., and HARTMAN, G. (2006). Projectile technologies of the African MSA: implications for modern human origins. In E. Hovers and S. L. Kuhn (eds), *Transitions Before the Transition: Evolution and Stability in the Middle Paleolithic and Middle Stone Age*. New York: Springer, 257–5.

CASEY, J. (2005). Holocene occupations of the forest and savanna. In A. B. Stahl (ed.), *African Archaeology: A Critical Introduction*. Oxford: Blackwell, 225–48.

CONKEY, M. W. (2001). Hunting for images, gathering up meanings: art for life in hunting-gathering societies. In C. Banter-Brick, R. H. Layton, and P. Rowley-Conwy (eds),

Hunter-Gatherers: An Interdisciplinary Perspective. Cambridge: Cambridge University Press, 267–91.

—— and GERO, J. M. (1997). Programme to practice: gender and feminism in archaeology. *Annual Review of Anthropology* 26: 411–37.

COOLIDGE, F. L., and WYNN, T. (2008). The role of episodic memory and autonoetic thought in Upper Paleolithic life. *PaleoAnthropology* 2008: 212–17.

DEACON, H. J. (1995). Two late Pleistocene-Holocene archaeological depositories from the southern Cape, South Africa. *South African Archaeological Bulletin* 50: 121–31.

—— and DEACON, J. (1999). *Human Beginnings in South Africa: Uncovering the Secrets of the Stone Age.* Walnut Creek, Calif.: AltaMira Press.

DEACON, J. (1984). *The Later Stone Age of Southernmost Africa.* Oxford: British Archaeological Reports.

DEINO, A. and MCBREARTY, S. (2002). ^{40}Ar/^{39}Ar chronology for the Kapthurin Formation, Baringo, Kenya. *Journal of Human Evolution* 42: 185–210.

D'ERRICO, F., and HENSHILWOOD, C. S. (2007). Additional evidence for bone technology in the southern African Middle Stone Age. *Journal of Human Evolution* 52: 142–63.

D'ERRICO, F., VANHAEREN, M., BARTON, N., et al. (2009). Additional evidence on the use of personal ornaments in the Middle Paleolithic of North Africa. *Proceedings of the National Academy of Sciences* (USA) 106: 651–5.

DOBRES, M.-A. (1995). Gender and prehistoric technology: on the social agency of technical strategies. *World Archaeology* 27: 25–49.

—— (2000). *Technology and Social Agency: Outlining a Practice Framework for Archaeology.* Oxford: Blackwell.

DONALD, M. (1998). Material culture and cognition: concluding thoughts. In A. C. Renfrew and C. Scarre (eds), *Cognition and Material Culture: The Archaeology of Symbolic Storage.* Cambridge: McDonald Institute, 181–7.

ESTIOKO-GRIFFIN, A., and GRIFFIN, P. B. (1981). Woman the hunter: the Agta. In F. Dahlberg (ed.), *Woman the Gatherer.* New Haven, Conn.: Yale University Press, 121–51.

GROVE, M. (2009). Hunter–gatherer movement patterns: causes and constraints. *Journal of Anthropological Archaeology* 28: 222–33.

HALL, S. L., and BINNEMAN, J. N. F. (1987). Later Stone Age burial variability in the Cape: a social interpretation. *South African Archaeological Bulletin* 42: 140–52.

HAWKES, K., and BLIEGE BIRD, R. (2002). Showing off, handicap signaling, and the evolution of men's work. *Evolutionary Anthropology* 11: 58–67.

—— ——O'CONNELL, J. F., and BLURTON JONES, N. G. (2001). Hadza meat sharing. *Evolution and Human Behavior* 22: 113–42.

HEADLAND, T., and REID, L. (1989). Hunter-gatherers and their neighbours from prehistory to the present. *Current Anthropology* 37: 43–66.

HENSHILWOOD, C. S., D'ERRICO, F., and WATTS, I. (2009). Engraved ochres from the Middle Stone Age levels at Blombos Cave, South Africa. *Journal of Human Evolution* 57: 27–47.

HOLL, A. (1989). Social issues in Saharan prehistory. *Journal of Anthropological Archaeology* 8: 313–54.

HOVERS, E. (2006). Comment on Kuhn and Stiner (2006). *Current Anthropology* 47: 965–6.

KENT, S. (ed.) (1996). *Cultural Diversity Among Twentieth-Century Foragers: An African Perspective.* Cambridge: Cambridge University Press.

KLEIN, R. G. (2008). Out of Africa and the evolution of human behavior. *Evolutionary Anthropology* 17: 267–81.

KUHN, S. L., and STINER, M. C. (1998). Middle Palaeolithic 'creativity'. In S. Mithen (ed.), *Creativity in Human Evolution and Prehistory*. New York: Routledge, 143–64.

—— —— (2001). The antiquity of hunter-gatherers. In C. Panter-Brick, R. H. Layton, and P. Rowley-Conwy (eds), *Hunter-Gatherers: An Interdisciplinary Perspective*. Cambridge: Cambridge University Press, 99–142.

—— —— (2006). What's a mother to do? The division of labor among Neanderthals and modern humans in Eurasia. *Current Anthropology* 47: 953–63.

—— —— (2007). Body ornamentation as information technology: towards an understanding of the significance of early beads. In P. Mellars, K. Boyle, O. Bar-Yosef, and C. B. Stringer (eds), *Rethinking the Human Revolution*. Cambridge: McDonald Institute for Archaeological Research, 45–54.

—— —— REESE, D. S., and GÜLEÇ, E. (2001). Ornaments of the earliest Upper Paleolithic: new insights from the Levant. *Proceedings of the National Academy of Sciences (USA)* 98: 7641–6.

LANE, P. J. (2005). Barbarous tribes and unrewarding gyrations? The changing role of ethnographic imagination in African archaeology. In A. B. Stahl (ed.), *African Archaeology: A Critical Introduction*. Oxford: Blackwell, 24–54.

LEWIS WILLIAMS, J. D. (1981). *Believing and Seeing: Symbolic Meanings in Southern San Rock Paintings*. Cambridge: Cambridge University Press.

LOMBARD, M. (2005). Evidence of hunting and hafting during the Middle Stone Age at Sibudu Cave, KwaZulu-Natal, South Africa: a multianalytical approach. *Journal of Human Evolution* 48: 279–300.

—— (2007). The gripping nature of ochre: the association of ochre with Howiesons Poort adhesives and Later Stone Age mastics from South Africa. *Journal of Human Evolution* 53: 406–19.

—— (2008). Finding resolution for the Howiesons Poort through the microscope: microresidue analysis of segments from Sibudu Cave, South Africa. *Journal of Archaeological Science* 35: 26–41.

LUPO, K. D., and SCHMITT, D. N. (2002). Upper Paleolithic net-hunting, small prey exploitation, and women's work effort: a view from the ethnographic and ethnoarchaeological record of the Congo Basin. *Journal of Archaeological Method and Theory* 9: 147–79.

—— —— (2005). Small prey hunting technology and zooarchaeological measures of taxonomic diversity and abundance: ethnoarchaeological evidence from Central African forest foragers. *Journal of Anthropological Archaeology* 24: 335–53.

MARSHALL, L. (1976). *The !Kung of Nyae Nyae*. Cambridge, Mass.: Harvard University Press.

MAZEL, A. D. (1989). People making history: the last ten thousand years of hunter-gatherer communities in the Thukela Basin. *Natal Museum Journal of Humanities* 1: 1–168.

MCCALL, G. S. (2007). Add shamans and stir? A critical review of the shamanism model of forager rock art production. *Journal of Anthropological Archaeology* 26: 224–33.

MELLARS, P. A. (1996). *The Neanderthal Legacy: An Archaeological Perspective from Western Europe*. Princeton, NJ: Princeton University Press.

MITCHELL, P. J. (2002). *The Archaeology of Southern Africa*. Cambridge: Cambridge University Press.

—— (2003). Anyone for *hxaro*? Thoughts on the theory and practice of exchange in southern African Later Stone Age archaeology. In P. J. Mitchell, A. Haour, and J. H. Hobart (eds), *Researching Africa's Past: New Perspectives from British Archaeologists*. Oxford: Oxford University School of Archaeology, 35–43.

—— (2005). Why hunter-gatherer archaeology matters: a personal perspective on renaissance and renewal in southern African Later Stone Age research. *South African Archaeological Bulletin* 60: 64–71.

O'CONNELL, J. F., HAWKES, K., LUPO, K. D., and BLURTON JONES, N. G. (2002). Male strategies and Plio-Pleistocene archaeology. *Journal of Human Evolution* 43: 831–72.

PARKINGTON, J. E. (2006). The archaeology of Late Pleistocene encephalisation in the Cape, Southern Africa. In H. Soodyall (ed.), *The Prehistory of Africa*. Johannesburg: Jonathan Ball, 64–75.

PREMO, L. S. and HUBLIN, J.-J. (2009). Culture, population structure, and low genetic diversity in Pleistocene hominins. *Proceedings of the National Academy of Sciences (USA)* 106: 33–7.

ROBBINS, L. H., MURPHY, M. L., CAMPBELL, A. C., and BROOK, G. A. (1998). Intensive mining of specular hematite in the Kalahari ca. A.D. 800–1000. *Current Anthropology* 39: 144–50.

ROSSANO, M. J. (2009). Ritual behaviour and the origins of modern cognition. *Cambridge Archaeological Journal* 19: 243–56.

ROTS, V., and WILLIAMSON, B. S. (2004). Microwear and residue analyses in perspective: the contribution of ethnographical evidence. *Journal of Archaeological Science* 31: 1287–99.

SCHENKER, N. M., DESGOUTTES, A.-M., and SEMENDEFERI, K. (2005). Neural connectivity and cortical substrates of cognition in hominoids. *Journal of Human Evolution* 49: 547–69.

SEALY, J. C. (2006). Diet, mobility and settlement pattern among Holocene hunter-gatherers in southernmost Africa. *Current Anthropology* 47: 569–95.

SHEA, J. J. (2006). Comment on Kuhn and Stiner (2006). *Current Anthropology* 47: 968.

SHENNAN, S. (2001). Demography and cultural innovation: a model and its implications for the emergence of modern human culture. *Cambridge Archaeological Journal* 11: 5–16.

SOLOMON, A. C. (1997). The myth of ritual origins? Ethnography, mythology and interpretation of San rock art. *South African Archaeological Bulletin* 52: 3–13.

STAHL, A. B. (2005). Introduction: changing perspectives on Africa's past. In A. B. Stahl (ed.), *African Archaeology: A Critical Introduction*. Oxford: Blackwell, 1–23.

STERN, N. (1994). The implications of time-averaging for reconstructing the landuse patterns of early tool-using hominids. In J. S. Oliver, N. E. Sikes, and K. M. Stewart (eds), *Early Hominid Behavioural Ecology*. New York: Academic Press, 89–106.

STINER, M. C., and MUNRO, N. D. (2002). Approaches to prehistoric diet breadth, demography, and prey ranking systems in time and space. *Journal of Archaeological Method and Theory* 9: 181–214.

THIEME, H. (1997). Lower Palaeolithic hunting spears from Germany. *Nature* 385: 807–10.

TRYON, C. A., and MCBREARTY, S. (2002). Tephrostratigraphy and the Acheulian to Middle Stone Age transition in the Kapthurin Formation, Kenya. *Journal of Human Evolution* 42: 211–35.

—— —— (2006). Tephrostratigraphy of the Bed Tuff Member (Kapthurin Formation, Kenya) and the nature of archaeological change in the later middle Pleistocene. *Quaternary Research* 65: 492–507.

VAN DER RYST, M. (1998). *The Waterberg Plateaux in the Northern Province, Republic of South Africa, in the Later Stone Age*. Oxford: British Archaeological Reports.

VAN DOORNUM, B. (2008). Sheltered from change: hunter-gatherer occupation of Balerno Main Shelter, Shashe–Limpopo confluence area, South Africa. *Southern African Humanities* 20: 249–84.

VOGELSANG, R., RICHTER, J., JACOBS, Z., EICHHORN, B., LINSEELE, V., and ROBERTS, R. G. (2010). New excavations of Middle Stone Age deposits at Apollo 11 rockshelter, Namibia:

stratigraphy, archaeology, chronology and past environments. *Journal of African Archaeology* 8: 185–218.

WADLEY, L. (1987). *Later Stone Age Hunters and Gatherers of the Southern Transvaal: Social and Economic Interpretation.* Oxford: British Archaeological Reports.

—— (1996). Changes in the social relations of precolonial hunter-gatherers after agro-pastoralist contact: an example from the Magaliesberg, South Africa. *Journal of Anthropological Archaeology* 15: 205–17.

—— (1997). Where have all the dead men gone? Stone Age burial practices in South Africa. In L. Wadley (ed.), *Our Gendered Past: Archaeological Studies of Gender in South Africa.* Johannesburg: Witwatersrand University Press, 107–34.

—— (1998). The invisible meat providers: women in the Stone Age of South Africa. In S. Kent (ed.), *Gender in African Prehistory.* Walnut Creek, Calif.: AltaMira Press, 69–81.

——(2001). What is cultural modernity? A general view and a South African perspective from Rose Cottage Cave. *Cambridge Archaeological Journal* 11: 201–21.

—— HODGSKISS T., and GRANT M. (2009). Implications for complex cognition from the hafting of tools with compound adhesives in the Middle Stone Age, South Africa. *Proceedings of the National Academy of Sciences (USA)* 106: 9590–94.

WALKER, N. J. (1995). *Late Pleistocene and Holocene Hunter-Gatherers of the Matopos.* Uppsala: Societas Archaeologica Upsaliensis.

WENDT, W. E. (1976). 'Art mobilier' from the Apollo 11 Cave, South West Africa: Africa's oldest dated works of art. *South African Archaeological Bulletin* 31: 5–11.

WILLIAMSON, B. S. (2004). Middle Stone Age tool function from residue analysis at Sibudu Cave. *South African Journal of Science* 100: 174–8.

WILMSEN, E. N. (1989). *Land Filled with Flies: A Political Economy of the Kalahari.* Chicago: University of Chicago Press.

—— and DENBOW, J. R. (1990). Paradigmatic history of San-speaking peoples and current attempts at revision. *Current Anthropology* 31: 489–524.

WILSON, D. S., TIMMEL, J. J., and MILLER, R. R. (2004). Cognitive cooperation: when the going gets tough, think as a group. *Human Nature* 15: 225–50.

WINTERHALDER, B. (2001). The behavioural ecology of hunter-gatherers. In C. Panter-Brick, R. H. Layton, and P. Rowley-Conwy (eds), *Hunter-Gatherers: An Interdisciplinary Perspective.* Cambridge: Cambridge University Press, 12–38.

WOBST, M. (1978). The archaeo-ethnology of hunter-gatherers or the tyranny of the ethnographic record in archaeology. *American Antiquity* 43: 303–9.

WYLIE, A. (1985). The reaction against analogy. *Advances in Archaeological Method and Theory* 8: 63–111.

—— (1989). Archaeological cables and tacking: the implications of practice for Bernstein's 'options beyond objectivism and relativism'. *Philosophy of the Social Sciences* 19: 1–18.

YELLEN, J. E. (1977). *Archaeological Approaches to the Present: Models for Reconstructing the Past.* New York: Academic Press.

CHAPTER 26

HUNTER-GATHERERS IN SOUTHERN AFRICA BEFORE 20,000 YEARS AGO

MARLIZE LOMBARD

INTRODUCTION

HUNTER-GATHERER archaeology does not represent a unilinear history, but explores a complex record with differences of emphasis and a diversity of problems and points of view (Barnard 2004). This chapter focuses on late Pleistocene hunter-gatherer archaeologies in southern Africa (Fig. 26.1) between ~130 kya and the Last Glacial Maximum at ~20 kya. The topic concerns both the Middle Stone Age (MSA) and a possible MSA/LSA (Later Stone Age) transitional phase. The former covers a plethora of localized lithic sub-stages, cultures, industries, or techno-complexes (Table 26.1), and encompasses both flake and blade tool industries that often include Levallois cores and points, and sometimes unifacial points, bifacial points, and/or backed tools.

Attention turned towards Africa and the MSA during the late 1980s as an outcome of DNA studies that suggest a recent sub-Saharan origin for *Homo sapiens* (Lahr, Ch. 23 above). The MSA, and particular that of southern Africa, became central to discussions about the origins of anatomically, cognitively, and culturally modern humans (McBrearty and Brooks 2000; Henshilwood and Marean 2003). Whether this was a unique evolutionary trajectory is debated, but deliberation of it being true for the particular period and region under discussion is closed. Other chapters (Foley, Lahr, Chs 20 and 23 above) discuss the relevant fossil and genetic evidence, but only archaeology gives glimpses of the cognitive, behavioural and cultural evolution of early hunter-gatherer societies.

Table 26.1. Overview of some Middle Stone Age sites in southern Africa with available age estimations and stone tool cultural affiliations. Abbreviations in brackets relate to the map in Fig. 26.1

Country	Site	Age	Stone tool cultural affiliation
BOTSWANA	Depression Cave (Dc)	~ 37 ka	MSA affiliation uncertain (Willoughby 2007)
	≠Gi (Gi)	~ 65-85 ka	Generic MSA (Robbins & Murphy 1998)
	White Paintings Shelter (Wp)	~ 48-65 ka	MSA/LSA transitional (possible Howieson's Poort, Robbins & Murphy 1998)
		~ 65-85 ka	Generic MSA (Willoughby 2007)
LESOTHO	Melikane (Mk)	~ 20 ka	Final MSA (Stewart pers. comm.)
		~ 33-42 ka	Late MSA (Stewart pers. comm.)
		~ 50 ka	Post-Howieson's Poort (Jacobs & Roberts 2008)
		~ 61 ka	Howieson's Poort Industry (Jacobs & Roberts 2008)
		~ 79 ka	Pre-Howieson's Poort MSA (Jacobs & Roberts 2008)
	Ntloana Tsoana (Nt)	~ 56 ka	Post-Howieson's Poort (Jacobs & Roberts 2008)
		~ 61 ka	Howieson's Poort Industry (Jacobs & Roberts 2008)
	Sehonghong (Sg)	~ 57 ka	Post-Howieson's Poort (Jacobs & Roberts 2008)
		Unreported	Possible Howieson's Poort (Mitchell 1992)
NAMIBIA	Apollo 11 (Ap)	~ 58 ka	Late MSA (Jacobs & Roberts 2008)
		~ 63 ka	Howieson's Poort Industry (Jacobs & Roberts 2008)
		~ 71 ka	Still Bay Industry (Jacobs & Roberts 2008)
		Unreported	Early MSA (Vogelsang et al. 2010)
	Pockenbank (Pb)	~ 29-49 ka	MSA Complex 3 (Vogelsang 1998)
		> 39 ka	MSA Complex 2 (Vogelsang 1998)
		Unreported	MSA Complex 1 (Vogelsang 1998)
	Zebrarivier (Zr)	~ 37->48 ka	Generic MSA (Vogelsang 1998)

SOUTH AFRICA			
	Blombos Cave (Bc)	~ 77-70 ka	Still Bay Industry (Villa et al. 2009)
	Boomplaas (Bp)	~ 84-100 ka	Pre-Still Bay (Henshilwood et al. 2009)
		~ 34 ka	Post-Howieson's Poort MSA (Willoughby 2007)
	Border Cave (Bo)	~ 62 ka	Howieson's Poort (Willoughby 2007)
		~ 35-42 ka	MSA/LSA transition or Early LSA (Mitchell 2008)
		< 54 ka	Post-Howieson's Poort (Willoughby 2007)
		~ > 54 ka–<75 ka	Howieson's Poort Industry (Willoughby 2007)
		> 75 ka	MSA I (Willoughby 2007)
	Cave of Hearths (Ch)	Unreported	Howieson's Poort Industry (McNabb et al. 2009)
		Unreported	Later Pietersburg/Mossel Bay Industry (McNabb et al. 2009)
		Unreported	Early and Middle Pietersburg/Klasies River sub-stage (McNabb et al. 2009)
	Diepkloof (Df)	~ 55 ka	Post-Howieson's Poort (Jacobs & Roberts 2008)
		~ 63-58 ka	Howieson's Poort Industry (Jacobs & Roberts 2008)
		~ 70-73 ka	Still Bay Industry (Jacobs & Roberts 2008)
	Florisbad (Fb)	Unreported ~ 121 ka	Final MSA (Willoughby 2007) MSA with little retouch (Willoughby 2007)
		~ 157 ka	MSA highly retouched (Willoughby 2007)
		~ 279 ka	Early MSA (Willoughby 2007)
	Klasies River (Kr)	Unreported	MIS IV (Mitchell 2008)
		~ 57 ka	Post-Howieson's Poort (Jacobs & Roberts 2008)
		~ 65-63 ka	Howieson's Poort Industry (Jacobs & Roberts 2008)
		~ 71-94 ka	Mossel Bay/MSA II (Jacobs & Roberts 2008)
		~ 115-90 ka	Klasies River sub-stage/MSA I (Wurz 2002)
	Klein Kliphuis (Kk)	Unreported	MSA/LSA transition or Early LSA (Mitchell 2008)
		~ 55-57 ka	Post-Howieson's Poort Industry (Jacobs & Roberts 2008)
		~ 59-64 ka	Howieson's Poort (Jacobs & Roberts 2008)

(Continued)

Table 26.1 Continued

Country	Site	Age	Stone tool cultural affiliation
	Peers Cave (Pc)	Unreported	MSA III (Volman 1984)
		Unreported	Howieson's Poort Industry (Jolly 1948)
		Unreported	Still Bay (Jolly 1948)
		Unreported	MSA 1 (Volman 1984)
	Pinnacle Point (Pp)	MIS 5b–MIS	Generic MSA (Thompson et al. 2010)
		MIS 5e–MIS 5c	Generic MSA (Thompson et al. 2010)
		4MIS 6	Generic MSA (Thompson et al. 2010)
	Rose Cottage Cave (Rc)	~ 20–27 ka	MSA/LSA transition (Pienaar et al. 2008)
		~ >27–35 ka	MSA IV (Pienaar et al. 2008)
		~ 56 ka	Post-Howieson's Poort (Jacobs & Roberts 2008)
		~ 63–65 ka	Howieson's Poort (Jacobs & Roberts 2008)
		~ 70–96 ka	Pre-Howieson's Poort (Pienaar et al. 2008)
	Sibudu Cave (Sc)	~ 38 ka	Final MSA (Jacobs et al. 2008)
		~ 39–49 ka	Late MSA (Jacobs et al. 2008)
		~ 56–59 ka	Post-Howieson's Poort (Jacobs & Roberts 2008)
		~ 64–61 ka	Howieson's Poort Industry (Jacobs & Roberts 2008)
		~ 72 ka	Still Bay Industry (Jacobs & Roberts 2008)
		~ 73–77 ka	Pre-Still Bay (Jacobs & Roberts 2008)
	Umhlatuzana (Um)	~ 32–40	MSA/LSA transition (Lombard et al. 2010)
		~ 42 ka	Post-Howieson's Poort (Lombard et al. 2010)
		~ 60 ka	Howieson's Poort Industry (Lombard et al. 2010)
		~ 71 ka	Still Bay Industry (Lombard et al. 2010)

SWAZILAND		
Loin Cavern (Lc)	~ 43 ka	Generic MSA (Volman 1984)
Sibebe (Si)	~ 23 ka	Generic MSA (Mitchell 2008)
ZIMBABWE		
Amadzimba (Am)	Unreported	Bambatan Industry (Volman 1984)
Bambata Cave (Ba)	Unreported	Possible Tshangula (Volman 1984)
	Unreported	Bambatan Industry /Mode 3 Industry (Volman 1984))
	Unreported	Charma (Volman 1984)
Ntswatugi Cave (Nt)	> 41 ka	Generic MSA with backed pieces (Willoughby 2007)
Pomongwe Cave (Po)	Estimated ages are reported for the sequence between 11-30 ka, but need revision	Tshangula Industry (Willoughby 2007)
		Magosioan (probably MSA/LSA mix) (Willoughby 2007)
		Bambatan/Still Bay-like Industry (Willoughby 2007)
		Proto-Still Bay Industry (Willoughby 2007)
Tshangula Cave (Ts)	Unreported	Magoisian-like debitage (probably MSA/LSA mix) (Willoughby 2007)
	Unreported	Late MSA/MSA/LSA transitional Tshangula (Willoughby 2007)
	Unreported	Bambatan/Still Bay-like Industry (Willoughby 2007)
Zombepata (Zo)	Unreported	Possible Tshangula (Volman 1984)
	Unreported	Bambatan Industry (Volman 1984)

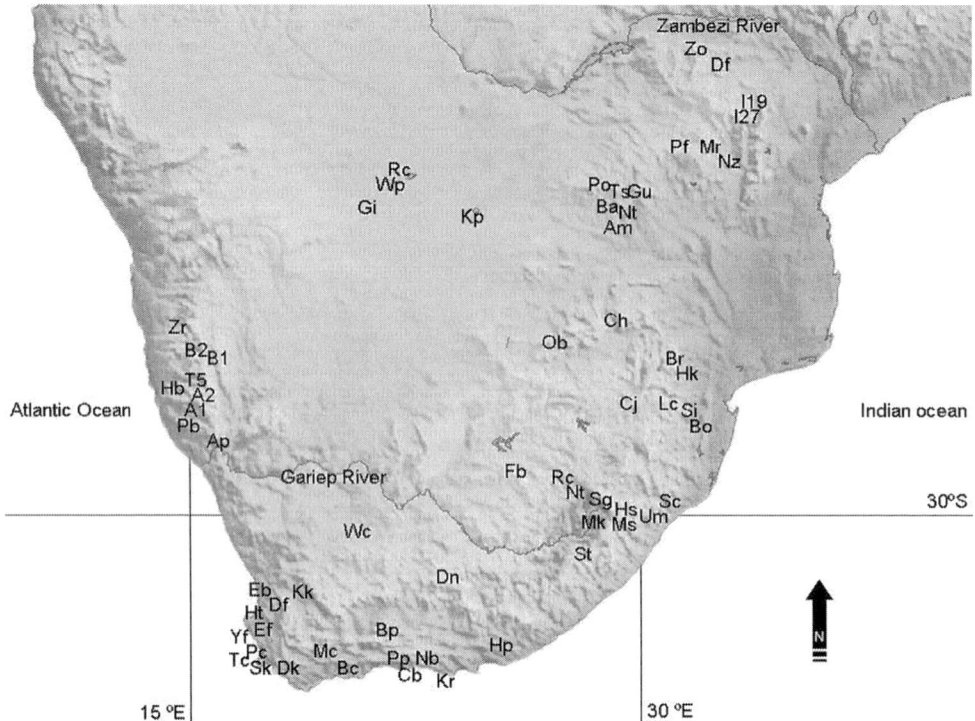

FIG. 26.1 Approximate locations of sites mentioned in the text and in Table 26.1. Abbreviations used on the map correspond to those provided in Table 26.1.

LITHIC TECHNOLOGY: A WORK IN PROGRESS

For most of prehistory, archaeologists rely on interpretations of stone tool assemblages to reconstruct cultural sequences and behavioural repertoires. Yet directly linking lithic technology to levels of behavioural evolution or cognitive complexity is not trouble-free, as the frequent recurrence of Oldowan, Levallois, and blade technologies shows (Conard 2007). Likewise, laminar and backed geometric tool assemblages have been interpreted as indicators of modern cognition, but marked fluctuations in their production rates during the Holocene are not matched by changes in cognitive complexity (Lombard and Parsons 2010). Although sometimes useful, the straightforward equation of the MSA with J. G. D. Clark's (1977) Mode 3 technology is inaccurate (McBrearty and Brooks 2000), and the division of the MSA into informal sub-stages (Singer and Wymer 1982; Volman 1984) fails to explain the complex nature of adaptive processes.

Previously, the MSA of southern Africa was interpreted as representing a supposed stasis, sameness, and lack of complexity based on sweeping conclusions drawn from limited, contextualized material for which the culture chronology was poorly understood, and the general lack of complete typological/technological analyses of artefact sequences still hampers comparative studies (see Lombard 2008). Finding resolution for early hunter-gatherer behavioural evolution requires focus on subtle changes between and within techno-complexes. The only way to gain such resolution is to define, name, and date assemblages in ways that do not obscure spatio-temporal change and variability. Progress has been made in this direction with the reinstatement of the Still Bay Industry and improved understanding of its technological subtleties (Henshilwood et al 2001;Villa et al. 2009; Lombard et al. 2010), after it was dropped from the cultural sequence in the 1980s (Volman 1984). Ages for the Still Bay at several sites converge at ~70–75 kya, pre-dating the Howieson's Poort Industry (Jacobs and Roberts 2008; Jacobs et al. 2008). The latter is currently the best-understood MSA phase regarding lithic technology, age (~59–65 kya), palaeoenvironment, subsistence, and levels of cognitive complexity (Lombard 2009). Sound technological foundations and clear definitions have also been provided for the Mossel Bay Industry, ~71–94 kya (previously MSA II or MSA 2b) and the Klasies River substage, ~90–120 kya (previously MSA I or MSA 2a) (Wurz 2002; in press). These four techno-complexes contain subtle internal variation, yet maintain some technological continuity, so that during the Howieson's Poort, techniques that were already part of the technological repertoire ~110 kya were used by highly adaptable hunter-gatherer groups. Adjustments in production technology reflect shifts in preferred technological configurations and conventions (Wurz 2008; in press), dispensing with the notion of unchanging, stagnant technology, and human behaviour between ~120 and 60 kya.

Stone tool assemblages immediately postdating the Howieson's Poort are often informally referred to as MSA III or post-Howieson's Poort (Table 26.1). Production of backed artefacts made on small blades seemingly stopped after ~59 kya, resulting in these assemblages once being described as reverting to type, reminiscent of Mossel Bay/MSA II assemblages—a change explained in terms of technological/behavioural reversal and territorial population displacement (Mellars 2007). It is, however, becoming evident that similarities between Mossel Bay/MSA II and post-Howieson's Poort assemblages at Klasies River, at least—on which most interpretations were based—are probably overemphasized and oversimplified. The transition to younger stone tool technologies may also have occurred more gradually than previously thought (Wurz 2002; Villa et al. 2010), and data from well-dated, stratified sites with extensive deposits post-dating the Howieson's Poort, such as Sibudu in KwaZulu-Natal, provide records for technological and behavioural flexibility not much different from that of recent hunter-gatherers (Wadley 2006; Lombard and Parsons 2010).

Although shifts within and between traditions can no longer be considered simple, unidirectional processes, many questions remain for the interval ~35–120 kya, and even larger gaps exist in our knowledge of the preceding and following phases (Mitchell 2008; Thompson et al. 2010). The challenge is to redate, redescribe, reinterpret, and/or re-excavate many previously excavated sites and assemblages, particularly those outside South Africa. Moreover, until nomenclature and methods are standardized, and unless comparisons are based on directly comparable data, the MSA will retain its 'muddle in the middle' reputation. It is therefore fortunate that new discoveries and novel interpretations are now reshaping our perceptions of hunter-gatherer behaviour and cognition during the MSA.

MSA BONE TOOL TECHNOLOGIES

Formal bone tools used to be associated with behaviourally modern *Homo sapiens* during the Eurasian Upper Palaeolithic and African LSA. In the past most MSA bone artefacts, such as the point from Klasies River (Fig. 26.2d), were brushed aside as late aberrations or the result of mixing (Klein 2000), but there can be no doubt about the presence of a MSA bone tool industry between ~72–80 kya at Blombos Cave (d'Errico and Henshilwood 2007) (Fig. 26.2a–c). Artefacts include awls made on long-bone shaft fragments or bird bone that

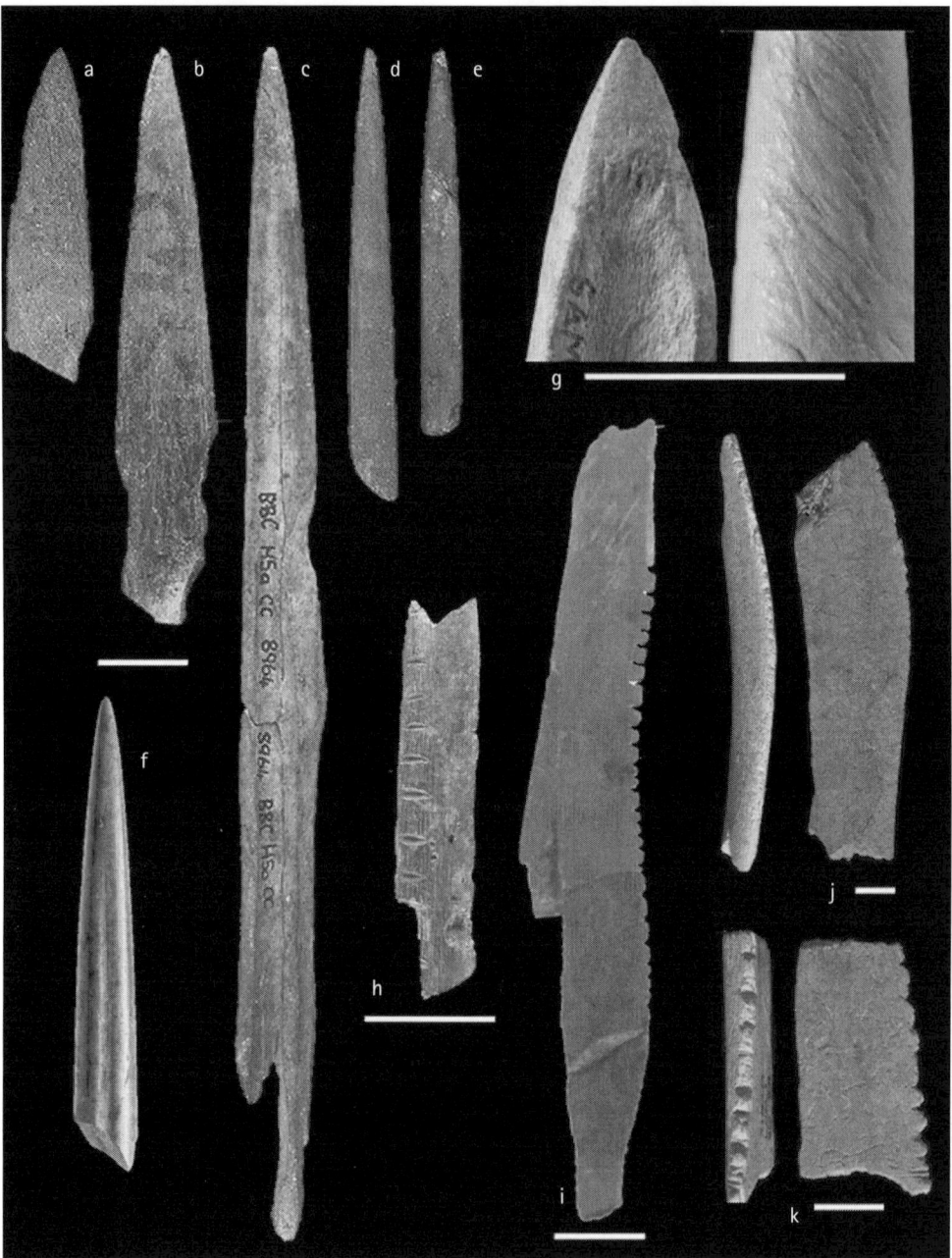

FIG. 26.2 Bone tools from MSA contexts, scale bars = 1cm. Bone points from Blombos (2a–c), Klasies River (2d), and Sibudu (2e). Polished bone point from Blombos (2f). Microscopic details of bone tool manufacture recorded on points from Blombos (2g). Notched bone from; Sibudu (2h), Apollo 11 (2i), Klasies River (2j & k). The images are reproduced with the courtesy of the following copyright holders: Chris Henshilwood and Francesco d'Errico for Blombos; Lyn Wadley and Lucinda Backwell for Sibudu; Ralph Vogelsang for Apollo 11; and Sarah Wurz for Klasies River.

were probably used to pierce leather or shells and carefully polished points possibly hafted as weapon tips; one (Fig. 26.2b) has a tang. Another site with bone tools from well-dated, stratified contexts is Sibudu. Here several bone points come from layers dated to 64–61 kya, one of them interpreted as a potential arrowhead (Backwell et al. 2008) (Fig. 26.2e). Bone working may be intimately tied to the development of mechanically projected weaponry, which could explain its presence in some MSA contexts (McBrearty and Brooks 2000).

Notched and engraved bone objects have also been reported from MSA contexts. In South Africa, two possibly engraved bone fragments from Blombos date to ~72–80 kya, while two notched bone objects from Klasies River (Fig. 26.2j and k) dated ~80–100 kya, are interpreted as tools used on soft materials; a third object from the Howieson's Poort context at this site bears potential symbolic engravings (d'Errico and Henshilwood 2007). At Sibudu, a post-Howieson's Poort layer with an age of ~60 kya yielded a fragment of caudal rib with ten evenly spaced notches (Wadley 2006) (Fig. 26.2h), and two rib fragments with notches are known from ~70,000 year old layers at Apollo 11, Namibia (Vogelsang et al. 2010) (Fig. 26.2i). The possibility that these are cut-marks from deboning can be excluded, but whether the notches were functional, decorative, or contained symbolic meaning remains unclear.

Although still few, instances of bone artefacts unambiguously attributable to the MSA are increasing, and there is evidence for contextualized, systematic bone tool manufacture and use at some sites from ~80 kya. However, while the bone tool assemblages demonstrate technical ability and competence, little is known about the relationship between bone working and behaviour considered 'modern' (d'Errico and Henshilwood 2007). Inferring the significance of bone tool manufacture for the hunter-gatherers who occupied southern Africa during the MSA, and determining whether and how bone tool manufacture changed in different social, geographic, and environmental settings remains a challenge. Although faint, the presence of deliberate, arguably symbolic markings on MSA bone objects indicates that bone was a suitable medium to embody symbolic markings. Thus, some bone tools may have formed part of a symbolically mediated society (d'Errico and Henshilwood 2007).

THE OLDEST KNOWN PERSONAL ORNAMENTS IN SOUTHERN AFRICA

Personal ornaments, such as beads, are considered unambiguous expressions of symbolism, and accepted as evidence of modern human behaviour in Africa and Eurasia after ~40 kya (Wadley 2001; Henshilwood and Marean 2003). The manufacture and use of ostrich eggshell beads are widespread during the LSA, but their presence during the MSA is restricted to a handful of sites, none with unequivocal contexts or recently produced ages. The region's oldest known beads are, instead, made from the estuarine mollusc *Nassarius kraussianus* and come from Blombos with an age of ~72 kya (Henshilwood et al. 2004) (Fig. 26.3a). Taphonomic, morphometric, and microscopic analyses show that they were deliberately manufactured and worn as personal ornaments, as use-wear patterns (Fig. 26.3b) are consistent with friction from rubbing against thread, clothes, and/or other beads. Almost all were found in closely clustered groups of similar size, shade, use-wear, and perforation patterns that may represent artefacts coming from the same beadwork item, lost or disposed during a single event (d'Errico et al. 2005).

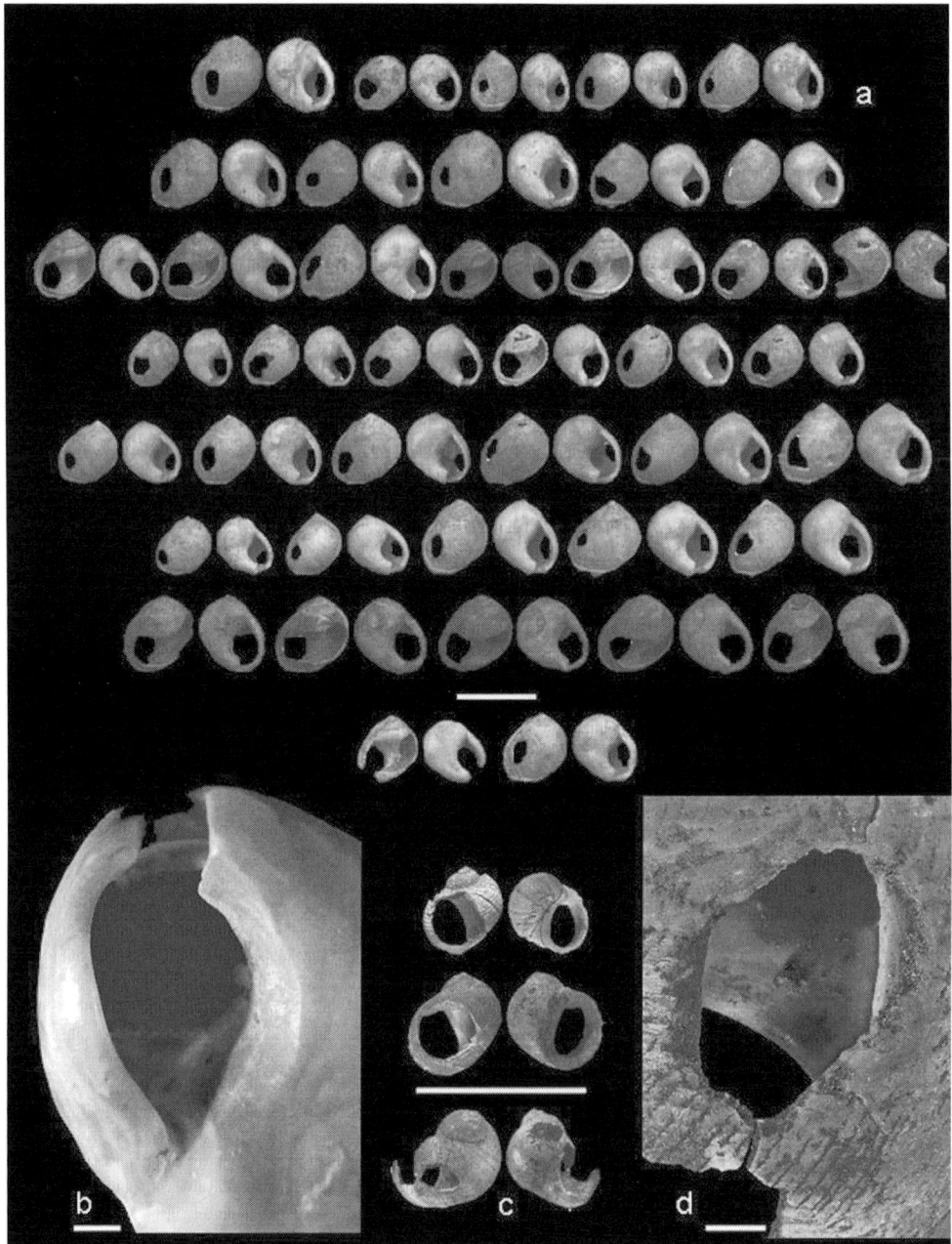

FIG. 26.3 Marine shell beads from MSA contexts, scale bars for 3a and 3c = 1cm and scale bars for 3b and 3d = 1mm. *Nassarius kraussianus* beads from Blombos (3a) with microscopic detail of abraded surfaces (3b). *Afrolittorina Africana* beads from Sibudu (3c) with microscopic detail of perforation (3d). The images are reproduced with the courtesy of the following copyright holders: Chris Henshilwood and Francesco d'Errico for Blombos; Lyn Wadley and Francesco d'Errico for Sibudu.

Blombos is not unique in producing such evidence, with even older beads known (for instance) from MSA contexts in North Africa (Bouzouggar et al. 2007; Barton and Bouzouggar, Ch. 30 below). In South Africa six *Afrolittorina africana* shells, three of them perforated, were recovered at Sibudu from a context with an estimated date of ~71 kya (d'Errico *et al.* 2008) (Fig. 26.3c). Taphonomic analysis, microscopic examination (Fig. 26.3d), morphometry, experimental work, and a review of the natural agents that may accumulate marine shells at inland sites indicate human involvement in the collection, transport, modification, and abandonment of these shells and thus their possible use as beads. Little is known about the mechanisms that triggered the use of personal ornaments, or of the role that early beadwork played in the creation and maintenance of early symbolic traditions (d'Errico et al. 2008). Fully syntactical language was, however, surely indispensable for sharing and transmitting the meaning of beads, and possibly other artefacts, within and beyond the group (d'Errico et al. 2005).

ART IN THE MIDDLE STONE AGE?

Art is another expression of symbolism, and accepted as evidence of modern human behaviour after ~40 kya. The discovery of engraved ochre nodules at Blombos, ~72–100 kya, unsettled accepted wisdom regarding the origins of 'art' (Henshilwood et al. 2009). Although some pieces are ambiguous, and it is sometimes possible to create scoring on ground ochre when stone flakes or other tools are used to remove ochre powder (Wadley 2005; Hodgskiss 2010), at least eight engraved ochre nodules from Blombos have complex geometric patterns made within limited, predetermined areas (Fig. 26.4a–c). Their production required focused attention and was clearly deliberate. Moreover, to produce such abstract images implies that the artists must have had a referent symbolic system that included image-making/interpretation, or the cognitive setting enabling their creation (Henshilwood et al. 2009).

Importantly, the engraved ochres from Blombos are recognized as a tradition of geometric engraving that lasted at least 25,000 years, straddling striking changes in stone tool technologies at the site (Henshilwood et al. 2009; Lombard and Parsons 2010). Further support for a tradition of engraving during the MSA derives from motifs on ochre nodules from Pinnacle Point, ~100 kya (Watts 2010) and Klein Kliphuis, >50 kya (Mackay and Welz 2008); parallel-line incisions on a bone fragment from Klasies River, ~80–100 kya (Henshilwood et al. 2009) (Fig. 26.4f); and parallel-line and cross-hatched engravings on ostrich eggshell fragments from Diepkloof, ~55–65 kya (Rigaud et al. 2006; Texier et al. 2010) (Fig. 26.4d). Less well contextualized are line engravings on ochre nodules from Bushman Rock Shelter, and a pebble fragment with a cross-hatched pattern from Palmenhorst (Henshilwood et al. 2009). Though still rare, collectively these examples suggest a tradition of producing geometric engraved motifs going back to at least 100 kya. That they were created with deliberate intent suggests they functioned as artefacts within a society where behaviour was mediated by symbols (Henshilwood et al. 2009).

A symbolic interpretation of these MSA engravings is widely accepted, but there is some concern about whether they should be considered 'art'. The presence of figurative art has been suggested as the 'gold standard' by which behavioural modernity can be identified (Conard 2007). In southern Africa the earliest figurative art comes from a late MSA context at Apollo 11 dated to ~27 kya (Vogelsang et al. 2010). The painted slabs in question depict a number of animals, geometric forms, and a possible therianthrope (Fig. 26.4g and h), resemble Holocene hunter-gatherer rock art, and probably represent a sustained behavioural

FIG. 26.4 Engraved and painted objects from MSA contexts, scale bars = 1cm. Engraved ochre nodules from Blombos (4a, b & c). Engraved ostrich egg shell fragments from Diepkloof (4d). Painted ostrich egg shell fragment from Apollo 11 (4e). Engraved bone fragment from Klasies River (4f). Painted slabs from Apollo 11 (4g and 4h). The images are reproduced with the courtesy of the following copyright holders: Chris Henshilwood and Francesco d'Errico for Blombos; Pierre-Jean Texier and colleagues for Diepkloof; Ralph Vogelsang for Apollo 11; and Sarah Wurz for Klasies River.

development over time. They do, however, remain a unique find, awaiting support from future discoveries of similar age and context.

HAFTING TECHNOLOGIES AND HUMAN COGNITION

It is not essential to rely solely on evidence for symbolically mediated behaviour to assess levels of past cognitive complexity. Stone points, and sometimes backed geometric tools, are the characteristic implements of the MSA. This transition is technologically significant, because it probably represents the transition from handheld to hafted artefacts (McBrearty and Brooks 2000). On an evolutionary level, the progression of tool-making from simple to composite could be seen as the archaeological reflection of the transition from proto-language to language with a more complex structure. A composite tool may be analogous to a sentence, but explaining how to make one is the equivalent of a recipe or short story (Ambrose 2001; 2010). Producing compound adhesives is particularly complex, and could reflect a capacity for novel, sustained multilevel cognitive operations, similar to our own (Wadley 2010a).

Attaching stone tools to hafts with compound, ochre-enriched adhesives persisted over time and space during the late Pleistocene MSA (Fig. 26.5a and b). Presently, the earliest direct evidence comes from ~70 kya contexts at Sibudu, but the practice continued until the final MSA ~35 kya and is represented at several sites (Lombard 2007). Replication studies suggest that early artisans did not merely colour their glues red; they deliberately effected physical transformations involving chemical changes from acidic to less acidic pH, dehydration of the adhesive near wood fires, and changes to mechanical workability and electrostatic forces. This shows that, by at least 70 kya, hunter-gatherer populations in southern Africa were competent chemists and pyrotechnologists, who understood the properties of their adhesive ingredients and were able to manipulate them knowingly (Wadley et al. 2009).

The steps required for compound-adhesive manufacture demonstrate multitasking and the use of abstraction and recursion. As is the case in recursive language, the artisan needed to hold in mind what was previously done in order to carry out what was still needed. Cognitive fluidity enabled people to do and think several things at the same time—for example, mix glue from disparate ingredients, mentally rotate segments (Fig. 26.5c), talk, and maintain fire temperature. Thus, there is a case for attributing advanced mental abilities to people who lived 70,000 years ago in Africa without necessarily invoking symbolic behaviour (Wadley 2010a).

EARLY TRACES OF MECHANICALLY
PROJECTED WEAPON SYSTEMS

The invention of the bow and arrow used to be closely linked to the late Upper Palaeolithic in Europe, and was thought to be a recent invention in Eurasia and the Americas (Shea 2009). Since southern Africa became a focus region for studying various aspects of *Homo sapiens* evolution, its archaeological record is vigorously debated. Opinions regarding the

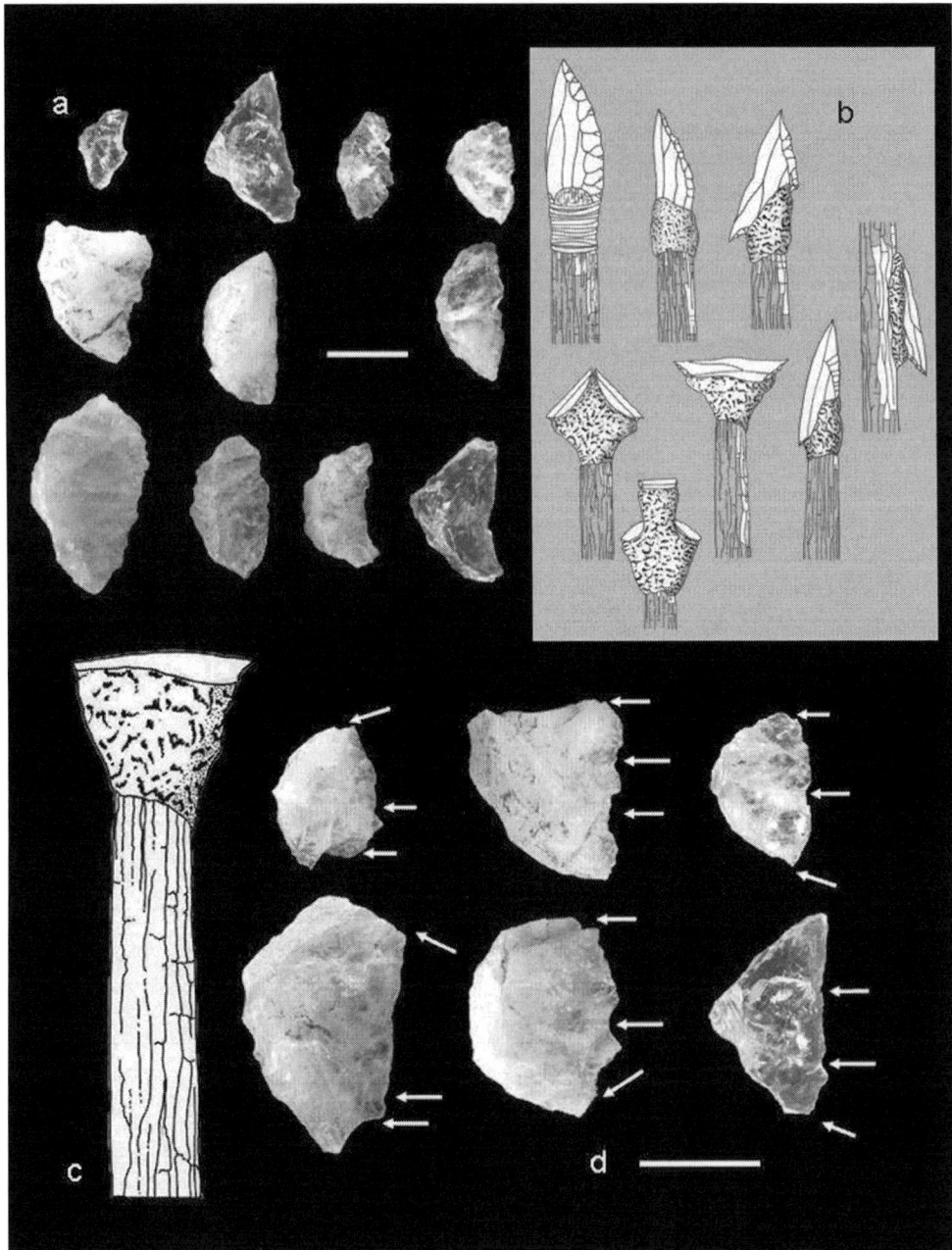

FIG. 26.5 Hafting and hunting technologies associated with backed pieces from the Howieson's Poort, South Africa, ~60–64 ka, scale bars = 1cm. a hornfels segment from Sibudu with ochre-loaded adhesive along the backed portion (5a). Micrograph, 200x, of ochre-loaded tree gum adhesive recorded on a Howieson's Poort segment (Fig. 5b). Potential hafting configurations of segments could include use as spear- and arrowheads (5c). Hypothetical reconstruction of transversely hafted arrowhead (5d). Macrofractures indicating potential use of small quartz segments and backed pieces as transversely hafted arrowheads (5e). The images are reproduced with the courtesy of the following copyright holder: Marlize Lombard.

inception of mechanically projected weaponry also vary considerably. Some maintain that the bone points and hafted microliths of the Early Later Stone Age at Border Cave, South Africa, ~ 40–35 kya, suggest the advent of the bow and arrow (Villa et al. 2010); others claim that dart and spearthrower technology could have existed by ~ 100 kya elsewhere in the region (Brooks et al. 2006). As research resolution and methods are refined, some researchers are shifting their predictions for the early apperance of mechanically projected weaponry. For example, Shea (2006) initially did not find support for the widespread use of mechanically projected weaponry before ~ 50 kya, but has recently suggested that bow-and-arrow technology developed in sub-Saharan Africa between ~ 100–50 kya (Shea 2009; Shea and Sisk 2010).

Providing unambiguous evidence for the use of mechanically projected weapon systems remains challenging (Lombard and Phillipson 2010). There are several ways to explore potential or hypothetical use (Sisk and Shea 2009; Brooks et al. 2006; Wadley and Mohapi 2008), but few that can be considered dependable records of application and mode of delivery. Multi-stranded, direct and circumstantial evidence that indicate the use of stone-tipped arrows, and by implication bows, comes from Howieson's Poort contexts at Sibudu and Umhlatuzan dated between 60 and 64 kya (Figs 26.5a and d) (Lombard and Phillipson 2010; Lombard et al. 2010). This supports previous suggestions that a bone point from the slightly younger, overlaying context at Sibudu signifies bow-and-arrow hunting at the time (Backwell et al. 2008). Currently these artefacts, and the information they carry, embody the most direct and convincing evidence for mechanically projected weaponry during the MSA. If Shea (2009) is correct in the inference that bow and arrow technology is exclusive to *Homo sapiens*, and if the artefacts from Sibudu signal the earliest known use of the technology in southern Africa during the MSA, it has significance for studies that aim to trace human cognitive and behavioural evolution over time and space (Ambrose 2010; Haidle 2010).

Trapping complex cognition

The creation and use of snares and traps as other ways of securing protein can also be used to recognize enhanced working memory and complex cognition, and may be a more reliable indicator of levels of cognitive complexity than encounter hunting, for example with spears, because it involves the concept of remote animal capture (Wadley 2010b). The challenge for archaeologists is to work backwards from this interpretive window to make additional bridging assumptions between archaeological data and remote capture technology. Snares and traps are difficult to recognize archaeologically because they are generally made from perishable materials. To infer their presence in the past, we must therefore rely on circumstantial evidence. A multistranded approach applied to material from the ~61–70 kya contexts at Sibudu shows that snares or other non-selective capture techniques may have been used there. Evidence consists of high-frequency representations of animals that prefer forested environments including the tiny blue duiker (*Philantomba monticola*) and the dangerous bush-pig (*Potamochoerus porcus*), high frequencies of small mammals, high taxonomic diversity, and the presence of small carnivores (Wadley 2010b).

The concept of a snare necessitates brainpower of the kind that we value so highly when hypothesizing about complex cognition (Wadley 2010b). Whereas the technology used for creating and setting traps or snares is relatively simple, the idea of remote capture, which enabled the invention of such equipment, is complicated, and provides evidence for the ability to integrate action across space and through time in ways that engage modern executive functions of the brain, which in turn characterize enhanced working memory and modern cognition.

Fire as an engineering tool

In addition to evidence for complex hunting and hafting technologies, the application of pyrotechnology during the MSA also attests to advanced technical proficiency (Brown et al. 2009; Mourre et al. 2010). The controlled use of fire was a breakthrough invention that allowed cooking, the production of warmth and light, and protection from predators, and eventually also more complex technologies such as producing compound adhesives, firing clay for ceramics, and heating ores for metallurgy. However, the technological links between using fire for simple tasks of light and heat production and using it as an engineering tool to alter raw materials remain poorly documented and understood.

Three independent analytical methods (archaeomagnetism, thermoluminescence, and maximum gloss) for recognizing heated silcrete from Pinnacle Point site 5–6 show that by ~71 kya early modern humans regularly employed pyrotechnology to increase the quality and efficiency of their stone tool manufacture processes (Brown et al. 2009). This technology required associations between fire, its heat, and a structural change in stone with consequent flaking benefits that once again may signal complex cognition. Gloss analysis of the Pinnacle Point 13B lithics suggests that this technology had originated by ~164 kya. Heat treatment technology in southern Africa may explain the presence of advanced tools during the MSA and their rarity in the Eurasian Middle Palaeolithic, where Neanderthals predominated. As early modern hunter-gatherers moved from Africa into Eurasia, the ability to alter and improve available raw materials and increase the quality and efficiency of stone tool manufacture may have been a behavioural advantage (Brown et al. 2009).

Middle Stone Age housekeeping

It is not only in the more durable materials such as stone, bone, and adhesives that we observe evidence for social and behavioural complexity. Plant materials from MSA contexts are rarely preserved, and even when present are difficult to interpret behaviourally. Recent work on sediment micromorphology and seed remains from Sibudu does, however, provide direct evidence for the construction and maintenance of sedge-covered sleeping areas or bedding between ~50–60 kya (Goldberg et al. 2009). The identification of different and distinct microfacies at the site also provided evidence for hearth construction and for sweeping and dumping events relating to their maintenance. Construction and maintenance of fireplaces and bedding occurred during single occupations and in localized spaces of the site from at least ~58 kya. These behaviours are well recorded from more recent hunter-gatherer occupation contexts in the caves and rock shelters of southern Africa, including Strathalan A in a very late MSA context dated to 29–21 kya (Opperman 1996). Such deliberate use and arrangement of living space reflects complexity in social organization, and has been suggested as an important trait of culturally modern behaviour (H. Deacon 1995; Wadley 2001).

CONCLUDING REMARKS

This chapter has presented some of the archaeological finds that toppled the accepted wisdom that 'modern culture' and complex cognition evolved first in Europe, or not before ~50–40 kya in Africa. Many questions and challenges remain, but southern Africa has a remarkable archaeological record that enables us to trace significant cognitive and behavioural trends in the evolution of hunter-gatherer societies. The ability of *Homo sapiens* to evolve complex cultural traditions, albeit over a very long period, allowed these hunter-gatherers to penetrate a vacant 'cognitive niche'. This advantage arguably allowed them to expand globally and replace all other hominins (Henshilwood 2007; Shea 2009).

Material manifestations took the form of a mosaic of innovative behaviours during the MSA, some omnipresent, others discontinuous. Tracing and interpreting these innovative/cognitive advances is proving extraordinarily intricate, based on rare finds or enduring, fine-grained research programmes. This is not surprising given the subcontinent's size, the relatively small number of well-excavated, preserved, and dated sites, and the potential inadequacy of our methods for recognizing cognitive complexity or symbolic behaviour. Notwithstanding such challenges, the evidence discussed here shows that the modern hunter-gatherer behavioural repertoire evolved during the MSA in southern Africa.

REFERENCES

AMBROSE, S. (2001). Paleolithic technology and human evolution. *Science* 291: 1748–53.

—— (2010). Coevolution of composite-tool technology, constructive memory, and language. *Current Anthropology* 51: S135–47.

BARNARD, A. (ed.) (2004). *Hunter-Gatherers in History, Archaeology and Anthropology*. Oxford: Berg.

BACKWELL, L., d'ERRICO, F., and WADLEY, L. (2008). Middle Stone Age bone tools from the Howiesons Poort layers, Sibudu Cave, South Africa. *Journal of Archaeological Science* 35: 566–80.

BOUZOUGGAR, A., BARTON, N., VANHAEREN, M., et al. (2007). 82,000-year-old shell beads from North Africa and implications for the origins of modern human behaviour. *Proceedings of the National Academy of Sciences (USA)* 207: 9964–9.

BROOKS, A. S., NEVELL, L., YELLEN, J. E. and HARTMAN, G. (2006). Projectile technologies of the African MSA: implications for modern human origins. In E. Hovers and S. L. Kuhn (eds), *Transitions Before the Transition; Evolution and Stability in the Middle Palaeolithic and MSA*. New York: Springer, 233–55.

BROWN, K., MAREAN, C. W., HERRIES, A. I. R., et al. (2009). Fire as an engineering tool of early modern humans. *Science* 325: 859–62.

CLARK, J. G. D. (1977). *World Prehistory: A New Outline*. Cambridge: Cambridge University Press.

CONARD, N. J. (2007). Cultural evolution in Africa and Eurasia during the Middle and Late Pleistocene. In W. Henke and I. Tattersall (eds), *Handbook of Palaeoanthropology*, vol. 3: *Phylogeny of Hominids*. Berlin: Springer, 2001–37.

DEACON, H. J. (1995). Two Late Pleistocene-Holocene archaeological depositories from the southern Cape, South Africa. *South African Archaeological Bulletin* 50: 121–31.

D'ERRICO, F., and HENSHILWOOD, C. S. (2007). Additional evidence for bone technology in the South African Middle Stone Age. *Journal of Human Evolution* 52:142–63.

—— ——VANHAEREN, M., and VAN NIEKERK, K. (2005). *Nassarius kraussianus* shell beads from Blombos Cave: evidence for symbolic behaviour in the Middle Stone Age. *Journal of Human Evolution* 48:3–24.

—— VANHAEREN, M., and WADLEY, L. (2008). Possible shell beads from the Middle Stone Age layers of Sibudu Cave, South Africa. *Journal of Archaeological Science* 35: 2675–85.

GOLDBERG, P., MILLER, C. E., SCHIEGL, S., et al. (2009). Bedding, hearths and site maintenance in the Middle Stone Age of Sibudu Cave, KwaZulu-Natal, South Africa. *Archaeological and Anthropological Sciences* 1: 95–122.

HAIDLE, M. N. (2010). Working-memory capacity and the evolution of modern cognitive potential. *Current Anthropology* 51: S149–66.

HENSHILWOOD, C. S. (2007). Fully symbolic Sapiens behaviour: innovations in the Middle Stone Age at Blombos Cave, South Africa. In P. A. Mellars, K. Boyle, O. Bar-Yosef, and C. B. Stringer (eds), *Rethinking the Revolution*. Cambridge: McDonald Institute, 123–32.

—— D'ERRICO, F., VANHAEREN, VAN NIEKERK, K., and JACOBS, Z. (2004). Middle Stone Age shell beads from South Africa. *Science* 304: 404.

—— —— and WATTS, I. (2009). Engraved ochres from the Middle Stone Age levels at Blombos Cave, South Africa. *Journal of Human Evolution* 57: 27–47.

—— and MAREAN, C. W. (2003). The origin of modern human behaviour: a critique of the models and their test implications. *Current Anthropology* 44: 627–51.

—— SEALY, J. C., YATES, R. J., et al. (2001). Blombos Cave, southern Cape: preliminary report on the 1992–1999 excavations of the Middle Stone Age levels. *Journal of Archaeological Science* 28:421–48.

HODGSKISS, T. (2010). Identifying grinding, scoring and rubbing use-wear on experimental ochre pieces. *Journal of Archaeological Science* 37: 3344–58.

JACOBS, Z., and ROBERTS, R. G. (2008). Testing times: old and new chronologies for the Howieson's Poort and Still Bay Industries in environmental context. *South African Archaeological Society Goodwin Series* 10: 9–34.

—— GALBRAITH, R. F., et al. (2008). Ages for Middle Stone Age innovations in southern Africa: implications for modern human behavior and dispersal. *Science* 322: 733–5.

JOLLY, K. (1948). The development of the Cape Middle Stone Age in the Skildegat Cave, Fish Hoek. *South African Archaeological Bulletin* 3: 106–7.

KLEIN, R. G. (2000). Archaeology and the evolution of human behaviour. *Evolutionary Anthropology* 9: 17–36.

LOMBARD, M. (2007). The gripping nature of ochre: the association of ochre with Howiesons Poort adhesives and Later Stone Age mastics from South Africa. *Journal of Human Evolution* 53: 406–19.

—— (2008). From testing times to high resolution: the late Pleistocene Middle Stone Age of South Africa and beyond. *South African Archaeological Society Goodwin Series* 10: 180–88.

—— (2009). The Howieson's Poort of South Africa amplified. *South African Archaeological Bulletin* 64: 4–12.

—— and PARSONS, I. (2010). Fact or fiction? Behavioral and technological reversal after 60 ka in southern Africa. *South African Archaeological Bulletin* 65: 224–8.

—— and PHILLIPSON, L. (2010). Indications of bone and stone-tipped arrow use 64 000 years ago in KwaZulu-Natal, South Africa. *Antiquity* 84: 635–48.

—— WADLEY, L., JACOBS, Z., MOHAPI, M., and ROBERTS, R. G. (2010). Still Bay and serrated points from Umhlatuzana Rock Shelter, Kwazulu-Natal, South Africa. *Journal of Archaeological Science* 37: 1773–84.

MACKAY, A., and WELZ, A. (2008). Engraved ochre from a Middle Stone Age context at Klein Kliphuis in the Western Cape. *South African Archaeological Bulletin* 61: 181–8.

MCBREARTY, S., and BROOKS, A. S. (2000). The revolution that wasn't: a new interpretation of the origin of modern human behaviour. *Journal of Human Evolution* 39: 453–563.

MCNABB, J., and SINCLAIR, A. (eds) (2009). *The Cave of Hearths: Makapan Middle Pleistocene Project*. Oxford: Archaeopress.

MELLARS, P. A. (2007). Rethinking the revolution: Eurasian and African perspectives. In P. Mellars, K. Boyle, O. Bar-Yosef, and C. Stringer (eds), *Rethinking the Revolution*. Cambridge: McDonald Institute, 1–14.

MITCHELL, P. J. (1992). Archaeological research in Lesotho: a review of 120 years. *African Archaeological Review* 10: 3–34.

—— (2008). Developing the archaeology of Marine Isotope Stage 3. *South African Archaeological Society Goodwin Series* 10: 52–65.

MOURRE, V., VILLA, P., and HENSHILWOOD, C. S. (2010). Early use of pressure flaking on lithic artefacts at Blombos Cave, South Africa. *Science* 330: 659–62.

OPPERMAN, H. (1996). Strathalan Cave B, north-eastern Cape Province, South Africa: evidence for human behaviour 29,000–26,000 years ago. *Quaternary International* 33: 45–54.

PIENAAR, M., WOODBORNE, S., and WADLEY, L. (2008). Optically stimulated luminescence dating at Rose Cottage Cave. *South African Journal of Science* 104: 65–70.

RIGAUD, J-P., TEXIER, P.-J., POGGENPOEL, C., and PARKINGTON, J. E. (2006). Le mobilier Stillbay et Howiesons Poort de l'abri Diepkloof: la chronologie du Middle Stone Age sud-africain et ses implications. *Comptes Rendus Palé* vol. 5: 839–49.

ROBBINS, L. H., and MURPHY, M. L. (1998). The Early and Middle Stone Age. In P. J. Lane, A. Reid, and A. K. Segobye (eds), *Ditswa Mmung: The Archaeology of Botswana*. Gaborone: Pula Press, 50–64.

SHEA, J. J. (2006). The origins of lithic projectile point technology: evidence from Africa, the Levant, and Europe. *Journal of Archaeological Science* 33: 823–46.

—— (2009). The impact of projectile weaponry on Late Pleistocene hominin evolution. In J. J. Hublin and M. P. Richards (eds), *The Evolution of Hominin Diets: Integrating Approaches to the Study of Palaeolithic Subsistence*. Leipzig: Springer Science, 189–99.

—— and SISK, M. L. (2010). Complex projectile technology and *Homo sapiens* dispersal from Africa to western Eurasia. *PaleoAnthropology* 2010: 100–122.

SINGER, R., and WYMER, J. (1982). *The Middle Stone Age at Klasies River Mouth in South Africa*. Chicago: University of Chicago Press.

SISK, M. L., and SHEA, J. J. (2009). Experimental use and quantitative performance analysis of triangular flakes (Levallois points) used as arrowheads. *Journal of Archaeological Science* 36: 2039–47.

TEXIER, P.-J., PORRAZ, G., PARKINGTON, J., et al. (2010). A Howiesons Poort tradition of engraving ostrich eggshell containers dated to 60,000 years ago at Diepkloof Rock Shelter, South Africa. *Proceedings of the National Academy of Sciences (USA)* 107: 6180–85.

THOMPSON, E., WILLIAMS, H. M., and MINICHILLO, T. (2010). Middle and late Pleistocene Middle Stone Age (MSA) lithic technology from Pinnacle Point 13B, Mossel Bay, Western Cape Province, South Africa. *Journal of Human Evolution* 59: 358–77.

VILLA, P., SORESSI, M., HENSHILWOOD, C. S., and MOURRE, V. (2009). The Still Bay points of Blombos Cave (South Africa). *Journal of Archaeological Science* 36: 441–60.

—— SORIANO, S., TEYSSANDIER, N., and WURZ, S. (2010). The Howiesons Poort and MSA III at Klasies River Mouth, Cave 1A. *Journal of Archaeological Science* 37: 630–55.

VOGELSANG, R. (1998). *Middle-Stone-Age Fundstellen in Südwest-Namibia*. Cologne: Heinrich Barth Institut.

—— RICHTER, J., JACOBS, Z., EICHHORN, E., LINSEELE, V., and ROBERTS, R. (2010). New excavations of Middle Stone Age deposits at Apollo 11 rockshelter, Namibia: stratigraphy, archaeology, chronology and past environments. *Journal of African Archaeology* 8: 185–218.

VOLMAN, T. P. (1984). Early prehistory of southern Africa. In R. G. Klein (ed.), *Southern African Prehistory and Palaeoenvironments*. Rotterdam: Balkema, 169–220.

WADLEY, L. (2001). What is cultural modernity? A general view and South African perspective from Rose Cottage Cave. *Cambridge Archaeological Journal* 11:201–21.

—— (2005). Ochre crayons or waste products? Replications compared with MSA 'crayons' from Sibudu Cave, South Africa. *Before Farming* 3: 1–12.

—— (2006). Partners in grime: results of multi-disciplinary archaeology at Sibudu Cave. *Southern African Humanities* 18(1): 315–41.

—— (2010a). Compound-adhesive manufacture as a behavioral proxy for complex cognition in the Middle Stone Age. *Current Anthropology* 51: S111–19.

—— (2010b). Were snares used in the Middle Stone age and does it matter? A review and case study from Sibudu, South Africa. *Journal of Human Evolution* 58: 179–92.

——, HODGSKISS, T., and GRANT, M., (2009). Implications for complex cognition from the hafting of tools with compound adhesives in the Middle Stone Age, South Africa. *Proceedings of the National Academy of Sciences (USA)* 106: 9590–94.

—— and MOHAPI, M. (2008). A segment is not a monolith: evidence from the Howiesons Poort of Sibudu, South Africa. *Journal of Archaeological Science* 35: 2594–2605.

WATTS, I. (2010). The pigments from Pinnacle Point Cave 13B, Western Cape, South Africa. *Journal of Human Evolution* 59: 392–411.

WILLOUGHBY, P. (2007). *The Evolution of Modern Humans in Africa: A Comprehensive Guide*. Lanham, Md.: AltaMira Press.

WURZ, S. (2002). Variability in the Middle Stone Age lithic sequence, 115,000–60,000 years ago at Klasies River, South Africa. *Journal of Archaeological Science* 29: 1001–15.

—— (2008). Modern behaviour at Klasies River. *South African Archaeological Society Goodwin Series* 10: 150–6.

—— (in press). Middle Stone Age tools from Klasies River main site, conventions and symbolic cognition. In A. Nowell and I. Davidson (eds), *The Cutting Edge: Stone Tools and the Evolution of Cognition*. Boulder: Colorado University Press.

CHAPTER 27

THE MIDDLE STONE AGE
OF EASTERN AFRICA

LAURA BASELL

INTRODUCTION

THE Middle Stone Age (MSA) covers the evolution, emergence and dispersal of *Homo sapiens*. Increased research interest during recent decades makes a comprehensive site-focused overview difficult, and is related to significant advances in geochronology and integrated geoarchaeological approaches. In addition, a burgeoning body of palaeoenvironmental data, some acquired independently of archaeological investigations, permits clearer understandings of the environments in which MSA hominins lived. Some of the most exciting developments continue to be driven through archaeological fieldwork and discoveries, but additional stimuli now come from disciplines like genetics that have reinvigorated old debates and identified new research questions, particularly concerning hominin dispersals within and outside Africa (Lahr, Ch. 23 above).

The primary focus here is on archaeological data and on published material from key stratified sites with some form of geochronological control from across eastern Africa, a region that encompasses some 3,800,000 km², east (and to some degree south) of the Congo Basin, from Ethiopia in the north to Zambia in the south (Figs 27.1 and 27.2). More detailed information is available from other major reviews (Clark 1982; McBrearty and Brooks 2000; Phillipson 2005; Willoughby 2001; Barham and Mitchell 2008). Reading them and this chapter, however, one must bear in mind that even this part of Africa is under-researched compared to many other regions of the world. Dates for the MSA vary across Africa, but in eastern Africa it is presently considered to begin during the Middle Pleistocene, ~300 kya, at sites such as Gademotta, Ethiopia (Morgan and Renne 2008), and to end at between ~30–40 kya at sites such as Enkapune Ya Muto, Kenya (Ambrose 1998), or a little more recently further south in Zambia. Although the latest MSA sites can be dated by radiocarbon, the limits of which now extend back to ~50 kya using pre-treatment techniques (Brock et al. 2010), most cannot, requiring archaeologists to employ a wide variety of other methods, including optically stimulated luminescence (OSL), thermoluminescence (TL), electron spin resonance (ESR), cosmogenic isotopes, potassium- or argon-argon (K/Ar or Ar/Ar), and obsidian hydration (Brown 2011). That sites have been dated by different techniques and at different stages in the development

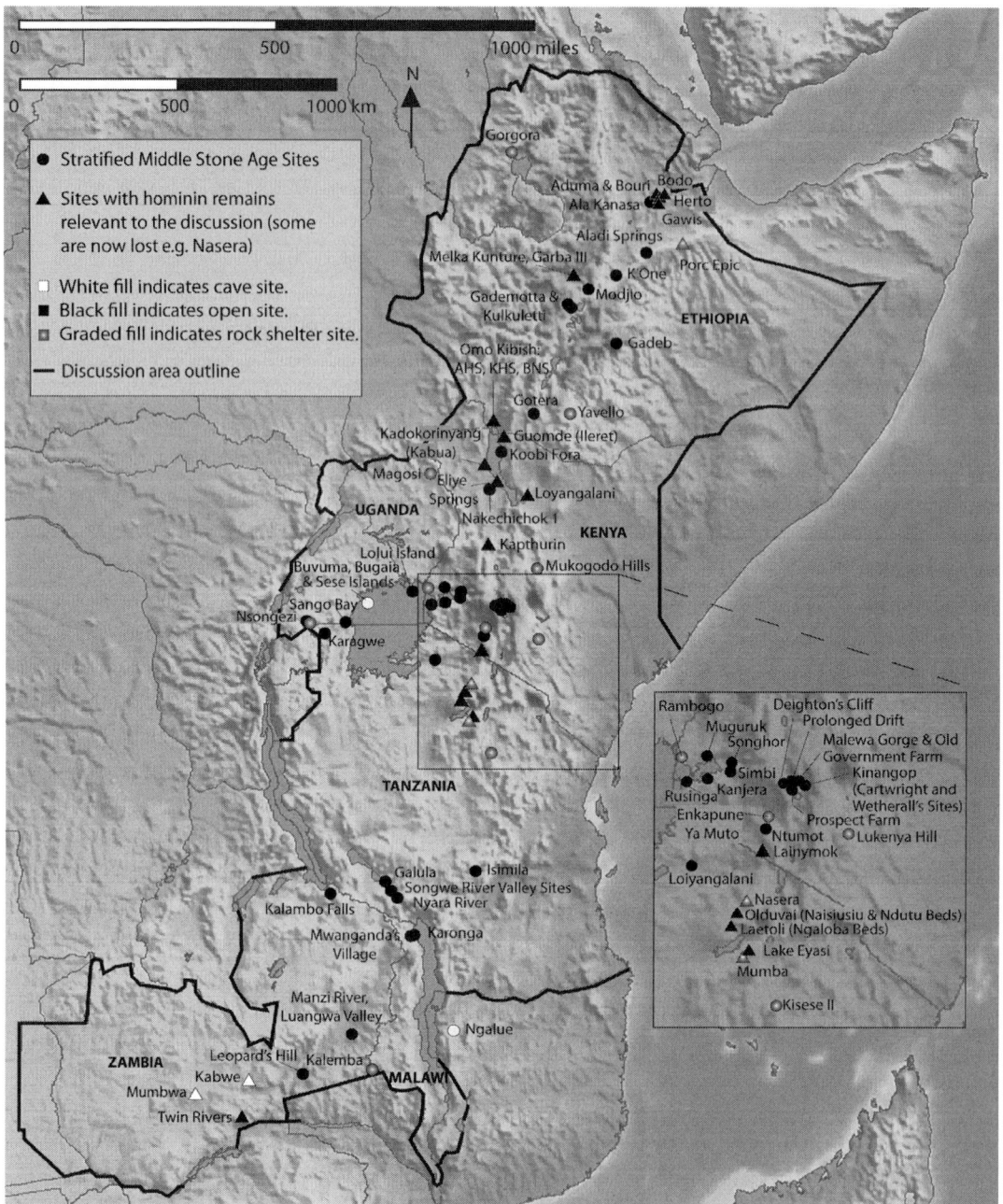

FIG. 27.1 Map of key eastern African Middle Stone Age sites.

Country	Site Name	Possible MIS	Past Site Situation	Hominin?
ZAM	Kalemba, Layers K, H and G	2 or 3	RS	N
ZAM	Leopard's Hill	2 or 3	RS	N
KEN	Rambogo	3	RS	N
KEN	Rusinga: Wasiriya Beds	3	FM/IS?	N
TAN	Nyara River	3	FM	N
KEN	Lukenya Hill	3	RS	Y
KEN	EYM	3	RS	N
TAN	Naisiusiu	3	FM?	N
KEN	Mukogodo Hills (Shurmai)	3	RS	N
KEN	Prospect Farm	3	HS/LM	N
KEN	Prolonged Drift	3 or 4	FM/LM	N
TAN	Nasera	3 or 4	RS	Y (Lost)
ETH	K'One	4	CAL	N
ETH	Gotera	5 to 3	FM	N
ETH	Porc Epic	5 to 2	C	Y
TAN	Mumba Unit V	3 or 4	RS/LM	Y
ETH	Aduma & Bouri	5b to d	FM	Y
KEN	Simbi	3 to 6	FM	N
ZAM	Twin Rivers (G block)	5 to 3	COLL C/HT	
MOZ	Ngalue	5 to 3	C	N
ZAM	Kalambo Falls Sangoan	5 to 3	FM	N
ZAM	Manzi River	5	FM	N
ETH	Omo Hominin III cranial frags (Members III)	5	FM	Y
ETH	Omo BNS (Members II/III Junction)	5	FM	N
TAN	Lake Eyasi *Homo sapiens*	5	LM	Y
TAN	Mumba Unit VI and VII	5 to 6	RS/LM	
ZAM	Mumbwa Units VII	5	C/DAM	N
ZAM	Mumbwa Units IX to XIV	6	C/DAM	Y (Unit XI)
TAN	Lake Eyasi	6	LM	Y
ETH	Herto	6	FM	Y
ETH	PHS. Member I	7	FM	Y
KEN	Muguruk	3 to 6	FM	N
KEN	Kanjera	7	LM?	Y?
KEN	Malewa Gorge	7	FM	N
TAN	Ngaloba	7 to 12	FM?	Y
ZAM	Kalambo Falls Acheulean	7 to 6	FM	N
ETH	Gademotta & Kulkuletti	6 to 8	LM	N
ZAM	Twin Rivers	11 to 6	COLL C/HT	Y?
TAN	Isimila	8	FM/LM	N
KEN	Kapthurin MSA	7 or 8	FM/LM	N
KEN	Deightons Cliff	8	FM?	N
KEN	Guomde (Ileret)	8	LM	Y
MAL	Mwanganda's Village	9	LM/FM	N
ETH	Melka Kunture	9 to 7	FM	N
ZAM	Kabwe	9	COLL C	Y
KEN	Eliye Springs	9 to 7	LM	Y
ETH	Gawis	11	FM	Y
TAN	Ndutu Beds MSA	5 to 13	LM/FM	N
KEN	Kapthurin Ach/MSA	8 to 14	LM/FM	Y
TAN	Lake Ndutu Hominin site	8 to 25	LM	Y
KEN	Kapthurin Group 1	13 to 14	FM	Y
KEN	Kinangop	11 to 15	FM/HS	N
ETH	Bodo	15	FM	Y

FIG. 27.2 Middle Stone Age sites in eastern Africa by country indicating the relative antiquity of sites, past site situation, and associated hominin remains, adapted and updated from Basell (2008: fig. 2). MIS attributions are approximate and are based on published dates. Note that for many of these sites the dates given are thought to be minimum estimates (e.g. Kalambo Falls is likely to be much older). Some hominin sites are included where no dates have yet been published, but a range has been suggested by the excavators (e.g. Gawis). Site situations are abbreviated as follows: C cave; COLL C collapsed cave; C/DAM cave/dambo; FM fluvial margin; HT hill top; IS island; LM lake margin; RS rockshelter; HS hillside.

of those techniques, and the fact that fewer than 80 eastern African MSA sites have any form of radiometric temporal control at all raises additional problems.

One final caution concerns terminology. Despite its many problems, the term 'Middle Stone Age', originally devised by Goodwin and van Riet Lowe (1929) for the southern African record and incorporating several site- or regionally specific subdivisions (Basell 2010), is used here in preference to the 'mode' system of Grahame Clark (1977). Reasons include: the fact that several modes may occur in a single MSA site (Tryon and McBrearty 2002); at any one time or place, modes emphasize the dominant technological mode subsuming innovation; and the use of modes may misleadingly imply that progressive technological evolution took place.

CLIMATES AND ENVIRONMENTS

The MSA occurred in a global climate regime dominated by the 100 kya climatic cycle of northern hemisphere glacials and interglacials within which were smaller fluctuations (stadials and interstadials). Such climatic fluctuations probably influenced the evolution of the genus *Homo*, the distribution and movements of hominin and other faunal populations, and the pace of behavioural innovation and change (Vrba et al. 1995). Although detailed treatment of this topic is beyond the scope of this chapter, several important points should be made.

First, geological rates of global climatic change determined from ocean cores do not easily translate to archaeological timescales, or 'lived time'. Secondly, precisely how climatic shifts affected eastern Africa is a major research topic, for which there are few data before the Last Glacial Maximum. However, it is clear that we can assume neither that glacial phases equate to tropical aridity (and interglacials to wetter periods), nor that the environmental response in terms of vegetation cover or other factors during one global glacial phase was the same in the next (Adams and Faure 1997a, 1997b). Eastern Africa's topographic complexity and its relationship to the Inter-Tropical Convergence Zone make it especially difficult to model the region's responses to climatic change. More positively, the region's rift lakes, Quaternary volcanic history, and ice-capped mountains offer tremendous potential for elucidating environmental responses to climatic change. Fluctuating sea levels periodically offered landscapes and resources now drowned, particularly along the Kenyan and Tanzanian coasts with their shallow coastal shelf and numerous islands. In modelling the impacts of sea-level fluctuations, and of other climate-related changes, it should be emphasized that the extremes of full glacial and interglacial conditions are rare on a Quaternary time-scale, for some 96 per cent of which intermediate, globally cool conditions prevailed.

HOMININ POPULATIONS

Fossil and genetic evidence for hominin evolution in Africa, including eastern Africa (Figs 27.1 and 27.2), is discussed in detail elsewhere in this volume (by Foley and Lahr, respectively: Chs 20 and 23 above). Here, it is sufficient to emphasize just a few concerns, the first of which is the sparse and fragmentary nature of the fossil remains dating to this period and their combination of plesiomorphic *Homo erectus* features and derived later *Homo* traits (Harvati et al. 2010).

('Plesiomorphic' refers to the generalized characteristics that appeared early in the evolution of a taxonomic group and are therefore widespread. They are less helpful in further dividing a group into lower-level taxa.) How this combination of plesiomorphic and derived traits should be understood is debated (McBrearty and Brooks 2000; Marean and Assefa 2005). One approach places the root of *Homo sapiens* at ~600 kya with the site of Bodo, Ethiopia (de Heinzelin et al. 2000), after which a grade-based taxonomy divides fossils into early and late archaic and, finally, anatomically modern *Homo sapiens* (Bräuer 1992). Alternatively, early archaic specimens are assigned to *Homo heidelbergensis* or *Homo rhodesiensis*, of which Bodo is the oldest African representative fossil, with later archaic fossils designated *Homo helmei* (Foley, Ch. 20 above) or archaic *Homo sapiens*, followed by more recent fossils of anatomically modern *Homo sapiens*. Presently, the oldest fossils assigned to *Homo sapiens* come from the Kibish Formation in southern Ethiopia's Omo Valley, and have an inferred age of ~195 kya (McDougall et al. 2005).

As a generalization, hominins in eastern Africa dated to ~600–200 kya are commonly classified as *Homo heidelbergensis* and archaic *Homo sapiens*, with a greater number of remains attributed to *Homo sapiens* after 200 kya and this designation alone used after Marine Isotope Stage (MIS) 5 (~125 kya). While these patterns should not be over-interpreted, given problems with species definition, chronology, and recent studies suggesting that even some late Pleistocene fossils retained archaic features (e.g. Allsworth-Jones et al. 2010), the possibility that more than one species could have produced MSA artefacts is strong. Very little is currently known about how such groups might have interacted, if at all. In terms of brain size at least, most specimens are in the modern range, with that from Kabwe, Zambia, for example, being close to the modern average (Rightmire 2004). Significantly, this individual's enlarged hypoglossal canal also suggests greater tongue control than in previous hominins and a modern speech anatomy (Kay et al. 1998; cf. DeGusta et al. 1999).

Hominin population densities were comparatively low throughout the MSA, although quantifying them remains a major challenge; estimates based on ethnographic parallels, primate group sizes, environmental carrying capacities, or the density of archaeological sites over time are all problematic. The expectation is that population densities fluctuated over time and were influenced by climatic changes. The possibility that climatic factors produced an evolutionary 'bottleneck' has been particularly intensively discussed, as it implies a severe reduction and isolation of hominin populations with genetic repercussions. Precisely when this occurred remains debated, but MIS 6 and 4 have been suggested. Eastern Africa is important in this context as an area that could have maintained populations in refugia during periods of hyper-aridity, i.e. times of particularly low precipitation *and* high evapo-transpiration (Lahr and Foley 1994; Ambrose 1998; Basell 2008). Evolutionary change, including changes in behaviour and technology, often seem to be stimulated during such episodes of stress and population fragmentation.

Hominin behaviour

Lithic technology

Stone artefacts are the most prolific finds at MSA sites and constitute the vast majority of evidence for MSA technology. Because many sites do not have hominin fossil remains, it is frequently impossible to determine which hominin/s produced the artefacts at a particular site, and archaeologists working in eastern Africa have increasingly moved away from discussions centred on 'modern/non-modern' definitions, emphasizing instead the diversity of technological adaptations among middle and late Pleistocene hominins. This replaces an earlier analytical focus on typological definitions of retouched pieces, to permit the identification and change ('evolution') of lithic industries. More attention is now being paid to entire lithic assemblages, including analyses of debitage, which is the most abundant category at nearly every MSA site. This shift has enabled a better appreciation of core reduction strategies and technology (Pleurdeau 2006; Shea 2008; Diez-Martín et al. 2009). Although lithic sequences have been described at many sites, beyond site-specific or occasionally regional analyses, it is presently not possible to identify the relative importance of social, functional, raw material, or other causes of change.

Prepared core techniques are known from Late Acheulean assemblages in eastern Africa, but the earliest sites with stone artefacts described as MSA are the Kapthurin Formation in Kenya and Gademotta in Ethiopia (Table 27.1). At Kapthurin the Acheulean (which includes blades at ~500 kya) was followed by interstratified MSA and Acheulean assemblages dated to MIS 8, ~284 kya (Deino and McBrearty 2002; Tryon and McBrearty 2002; Tryon 2006; Johnson and McBrearty 2010). Incorporated in these assemblages is a Levallois approach (see Tryon, Ch. 8 above; Fig. 27.3) to biface blank production, as well as 'Sangoan' components (Clark 2001; Basell 2010). Further north in Ethiopia, the early MSA at Gademotta underlies a layer now redated to ~276 kya (Morgan and Renne 2008), though here there are no 'heavy duty' Sangoan components to accompany points, blades and the use of the Levallois technique.

Discoidal and Levallois reduction techniques remain common in other MSA assemblages, which were made on a wide range of raw materials; irregular, bipolar, and blade cores (including punch struck blade cores at Gademotta and Kulkuletti; Wendorf and Schild 1974) are less frequent, though well documented at many sites. While unretouched flakes dominate most assemblages, foliate bifaces, varied handaxe forms, including diminutive handaxes, cleavers, and picks also persist. In an elegant study of the artefacts associated with the earliest modern *Homo sapiens* at Omo, Shea (2011) argues that there are few differences (only local variations) between them and other Ethiopian sites, and suggests that the comparative lack of change over the period ~280–80 kya represents cultural continuity, and perhaps demographic stability in the region. Recent research in northern Kenya around Lake Turkana and in the Kapedo Tuffs (Tryon et al. 2008; Shea and Hildebrand 2010) hints at a different technological pattern, perhaps related to differences in raw materials. Generally, sites with 'heavy duty' Sangoan, and subsequent Lupemban, assemblage components occur more frequently south of the Kapthurin Formation. Some are old, but sites with Lupemban components dated to MIS 3 suggest that these artefacts continued in use, or were reinvented, until near the end of the MSA sequence (Basell 2010; Table 27.1).

Levallois, discoidal, blade, and irregular core reduction techniques continued in use in the later MSA, and assemblages remained dominated by unretouched flakes. A general reduction in artefact size is apparent at some sites. Bifacial points, blades, and rare formal tools also continued to be produced on a wide range of raw materials, but handaxes and other large cutting tools are rare after MIS 5. At Porc-Epic, and possibly Gorgora, both in Ethiopia, distinctive backed pieces appear (Leakey 1943; Pleurdeau 2006), but at the former obsidian hydration dates of 61–77 kya conflict with radiocarbon dates of 31–43 kya (Michels and Marean 1984; Assefa 2006). Further south, the appearance of geometric backed microliths is thought to be a significant indicator of the hafting of stone tools (Ambrose 2002), for example

Table 27.1 Simplified characterization of Middle Stone Age lithic technological and typological change in eastern Africa. This is based on the published descriptions of lithic analyses that vary in focus and type and uses commonly found descriptive terms for artefact types. Large circles represent lithic components regularly found and/or emphasized in assemblages of the corresponding attribution ('Terminology' column), while smaller circles indicate artefacts found in lower frequencies, or present at only a limited number of sites, that are less frequently discussed. The absence of a circle does not necessarily mean a lithic category has never been found in an assemblage of that attribution, but does imply that it is less commonly referred to or not known. Additional qualifications of the principal assemblage components are given under each 'Terminology' heading and a few selected key sites are listed on the right. HD after a lithic category indicates that this is a principal component of J. D. Clark's 'heavy duty' tool kit, and LD refers to his 'light duty' (see text). These terms are particularly pertinent in discussions of the Sangoan and Lupemban.

Terminology	CORES	RETOUCHED PIECES ('TOOLS')	DEBITAGE	OTHER LITHICS	Selected African sites mentioned in this chapter, of particular relevance to the definition and age of the terminologies listed

Terminology referred to in the text, broadly following the dominant tripartite system. NB: the order can no longer be considered as a simple 'progression' or behavioural 'development' from one 'stage' to the next. E.g. interstratified ESA and MSA at Kapthurin; different ages for Lupemban occurrences; re-attribution of transitional MSA–LSA Level V at Mumba to LSA. See text for references.

Cores: Unspecialised single platform, Irregular, Multiple platform, Radial/Discoidal, Levallois, Bipolar, Blade, Parallel sided blade, Bladelet and/or Microlithic

Retouched pieces ('Tools'): Choppers (HD), Handaxes, Diminutive handaxes, Cleavers, Picks (HD), Knives (HD), Core-Axes (HD), Lanceolate bifaces, Points (unifacial and bifacial) (Can be HD and LD depending on size), Points with basal thinning (unifacial and bifacial), Scrapers (tend to reduce in size over time. Many forms, HD and LD), Modified flakes, Borers/Awls (LD), Proto-burins, Outils ecaillés, Denticulates, Notches, Burins (LD), Backed blades (LD), Truncated flakes and blades (LD), Geometric Trapezes/'Microliths' (LD)

Debitage: Non-Levallois flakes (small triangular flakes considered LD), Blades (can be LD), Levallois Flakes, Dominance of small flakes and blades, Microlithic Bladelets

Other lithics: Grind stones, Hammer stones, Polyhedrons, Spheroids, Cobbles

Terminology (description)	Selected African sites
Late Acheulean. Large cutting tools (LCT) include handaxes (different forms e.g. ovates, lanceolate, triangular etc.), cleavers and picks. But note that these tools are sometimes entirely lacking. Levallois is sometimes very large.	Kapthurin Formation, Kalambo Falls, Melka Kunture (Garba III), Turkana Basin Sites, Isimila, Herto, Aduma
Sangoan (seen by some as 'transitional' and sometimes grouped with Lupemban). Blade cores are rare. Core-axes are often heavier than Acheulean bifaces. Bifacial picks are large. Core scrapers are also common. Flakes can be both small (Muguruk) and large (Lake Eyasi) with simple platforms.	Kalambo Falls, Muguruk, Kapthurin, Simbi, Sango Bay, Lake Eyasi, Herto
Lupemban (seen by some as 'transitional' and sometimes grouped with Sangoan). Core axes are often smaller than Sangoan core-axes.	Kalambo Falls, Rambogo, Muguruk, Twin Rivers
Early Middle Stone Age. Increasing core preparation. Levallois includes preferential and recurrent methods, and is occasional microlithic. Some points are considered as 'Stillbay-like'. Backed blades are large.	Mumba, Omo Kibish, Melka Kunture (Garba III), Gademotta and Kulkuletti, Aduma and Bouri, Porc Epic, Mumbwa
Later Middle Stone Age. Levallois includes preferential and recurrent methods. Blade cores often use a Levallois-like production method. Large backed 'knives' on flakes. Points increasingly abundant.	Enkapune Ya Muto, Lukenya Hill, Olduvai, Rambogo, Mumba, Prospect Farm, Ndutu Beds at Olduvai, Porc Epic, Mumbwa, Prospect Farm
'Transitional' Middle to Late Stone Age. Double platform cores common, and bipolar cores increase compared to radial methods. Backed blades are large. Points are small. Bipolar (as before) often on quartz. Occasional microlithic debitage.	Ntumot, Kalambo Falls, Mumba, Naisiusiu (Olduvai), Nasera, Kisese II, Kalemba, Leopard's Hill, Mukogodo Hills sites.
Early Late Stone Age. Cores are often prismatic. Geometric microliths are not always present. Knives are partly bifacial and finely worked. Flattened discoids present and core-scrapers. Generally fewer points. Bladelets, blades and flakes are often backed. Microburins also known.	Matupi Cave, Mumba, Lukenya Hill, Kalambo Falls, Enkapune Ya Muto, Ntumot, Prospect Farm, Naisiusiu Beds at Olduvai, Nasera, Loyangalani; Leopard's Hill, Kalemba

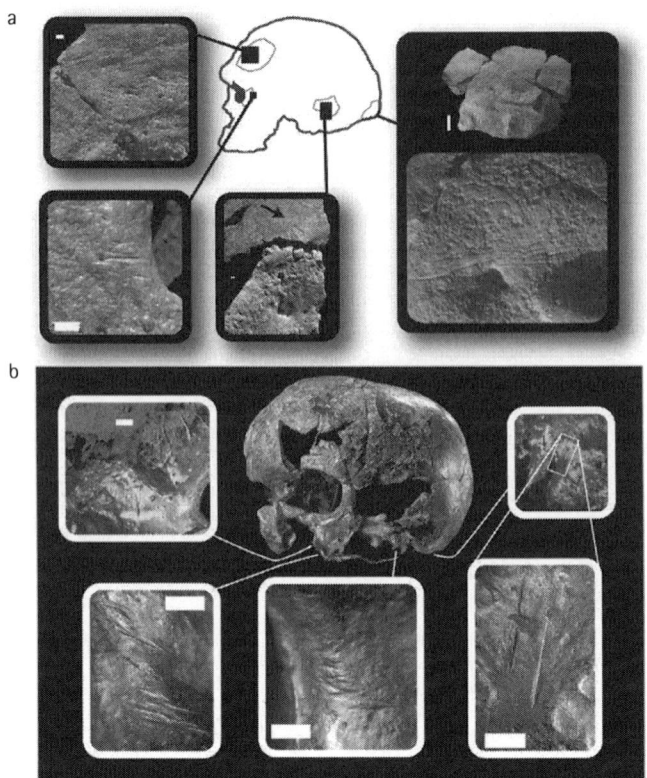

FIG. 27.3 Cultural modification of the Herto adult and child crania from Clark et al. (2003: fig. 2): a, BOU-VP-16/2 adult cranial fragments to show selected defleshing cutmarks on the left zygomatic and parietal asterionic corne and other more superficial artificial scoring above the left temporal line and across the occipital plane; b, BOU-VP-16/5 child's cranium with defleshing cutmarks on the left sphenoid and right and left temporals and post-mortem polish on the parietals. Vertical scale bar, 1cm; horizontal scale bars, 1mm. Reproduced with permission from Nature Publishing Group.

at Twin Rivers, Zambia, where they are bracketed between dates of >400 and 140 kya (Barham 2002) and may closely match the Lower Lupemban at Kalambo Falls (Clark and Brown 2001). Similarly, at Mumbwa rare crescentic backed blades, bifacial and unifacial points, awls, borers, and scrapers occur in association with hearths (~107 to >120 kya) (Barham 2000, 2002; Willoughby 2007).

Other sites are more recent, including two in Kenya, the Naisiusiu Beds (> 42 kya) (Ambrose 1998) and Enkapune ya Muto, where microliths are associated with large backed blades and scrapers in the Nasampolai Industry at ~45 kya (Ambrose 1998, 2002). As with the ESA/MSA, the MSA/LSA transition is not clear-cut, and many of the artefact types and technological adaptations seen in the later MSA are present in the early LSA. The transition to the LSA tends to be marked by an overall reduction in the size of stone artefacts, an increasing use of true blade core techniques, bipolar and microlithic core reduction strategies, and a decrease in Levallois and radial techniques. Backed pieces and geometric microliths become more dominant at many sites, while there is a decrease in the quantity of points and, at some sites, scrapers. However, identifying the transition is complicated by differences in categorization, including debate over the definition 'microlithic', how backing is achieved, the precise definition of 'true' blade reduction strategies, and the behavioural significance of such features (Ambrose 2002; Diez-Martín et al. 2009). For example, Mumba, Bed V in Tanzania (~29–52 kya), originally considered by Mehlman (1991) to be MSA/LSA transitional, has recently been resampled, reanalysed, and reattributed to the early LSA (Diez-Martín et al. 2009).

Subsistence and palaeoenvironments

Bone from MSA sites in eastern Africa is typically highly fragmentary and species definition is frequently impossible. Where bone has been identified, the species represented vary between sites, but frequently include extant taxa such as elephant, bovids, equids, suids, rhinoceros, and hippopotamus. It is nevertheless clear that faunal remains from MSA archaeological contexts demonstrate bone accumulation and carcass processing by people. At Herto, Ethiopia, this included repeated systematic butchery (percussion fractures and cutmarks) of hippopotamus carcasses, including newborns, and those of bovids (Clark et al. 2003). Likewise at Porc-Epic, and despite extensive fragmentation, hominins were probably hunting a wide range of wooded grassland and woodland grazing species, gaining primary access to carcasses, butchering carcasses using stone tools, and breaking the bones to extract marrow (Assefa 2006). Evidence for how animals were procured is scarce, but alcelaphines may have been specifically intercepted at one site at Lukenya Hill, Kenya (Marean 1997). Importantly, basal thinning of MSA stone points is strongly suggestive of hafting, and impact fractures on their tips may indicate hunting (Shea 2006). The plant component of hominin diets is much more poorly understood, with analyses of macroscopic and microscopic plant remains from sites like Mumbwa, Rambogo, Kalambo Falls, and Prolonged Drift emphasizing palaeoenvironmental reconstruction rather than subsistence; Assefa et al.'s (2008) impressive study of faunas at Omo-Kibish has a comparable focus.

Non-lithic technologies

Only at Mumbwa and Enkapune ya Muto is charcoal found in concentrations described as hearths. The Mumbwa hearths, which comprise concentrations of burnt sediment and ash with charcoal within stone surrounds, are the older, as they occur in both Unit V (~39 kya) and Unit VII (~120–100 kya) (Barham 2000). The apparent paucity of sites exhibiting evidence of the controlled use of fire may be taphonomic, as eastern Africa's MSA record includes relatively few deep cave and rockshelter sequences. The only open site with burnt sediments is at Omo (Shea 2008), where reddened patches at the BNS location are associated with ostrich eggshell fragments but without macroscopic charcoal. Wood only rarely preserves, and Kalambo Falls is the only site to have yielded wooden tools. They occur in both Acheulean and Sangoan levels, the latter with U-series dates of 65–85 kya that are probably too young (McKinney 2001). Evidence of bone tools is also scarce: of four pointed bone objects recovered from Mumbwa (Barham 2000), only one is probably humanly modified, while doubts remain over the associations of the three bone points found at Kabwe with the *Homo heidelbergensis* remains from the same site (Barham et al. 2001).

Eastern Africa has yet to produce finds of comparable antiquity to the shell beads and engraved ochre now known from Blombos, Taforalt, and other sites in South and North Africa (Lombard, Garcea, Chs 26 and 29). Ostrich eggshell beads are, however, known from a few sites, including Mumba, where examples are directly dated by AMS to 29–33 kya (Conard 2005), significantly younger than many of the dates on associated bone and shell (Mehlman 1991; Hare et al. 1993). Somewhat older are the beads and preforms associated with the Sakutiek Industry at Enkapune ya Muto, which has been described as early LSA with some MSA elements; one bead is directly dated to ~40 kya (Ambrose 1998). Beads reported from Loiyangalani and Kisese II remain undated (Inskeep 1962; Thompson et al. 2004).

Ochre occurs in both early and later MSA contexts, sometimes with grindstones, as at Kapthurin (Tryon and McBrearty 2002). Of particular interest is the site of Twin Rivers, Zambia, where hominins selected different colours of haematite, not just the closest or most prolific (Barham 2000). Although the haematite could have been used in producing mastic for hafting stone tools (Wadley 2005), the apparent choice of colours suggests that non-utilitarian factors were also involved. Interestingly, the raw materials used to make stone artefacts at Omo may also display a preference for red (Shea 2008). Backed and geometric stone tools from Nasampolai (~46–39 kya) contexts at Enkapune ya Muto bear traces of ochre (Ambrose 1998), while striated ochre is known from other MSA sites such as Porc-Epic, Rambogo, and Mumba. Art is still missing from the regional MSA record, and there is no evidence for burial, although all three hominin crania from Herto, Ethiopia, carry cutmarks, suggestive of some kind of deliberate mortuary practice (Clark et al. 2003) (Fig. 27.3).

CONCLUSIONS

Although the MSA is often characterized by a shift from handaxe production towards discoidal and Levallois techniques, the pattern is not straightforward. There is no simple change over time in the wide range of lithic reduction strategies employed, although the proliferation of points (which is related to the use of prepared core techniques) can be considered one of its 'markers' (Fig. 27.4). Handaxes did not simply disappear, and many other forms and reduction techniques are also present. While there may be differences between northern and southern areas of eastern Africa regarding the dominance of 'heavy duty' artefacts during the early MSA, these components and other large cutting tools, as well as handaxes, do seem to reduce significantly in size from around the MIS 5/6 transition, accompanied by a slight increase in the variability of retouched pieces and raw materials from non-local sources (Basell 2008). The decreasing size of artefacts may be related to a broadening in the range of functions that they fulfilled, with many of the smaller examples most effectively employed if hafted, in some instances at least as parts of composite tools. Not only might this imply greater flexibility and adaptability to fluctuating environments and resources, but smaller artefacts also suggest greater portability, something that could be related to the exploitation of a wider range of ecological niches (Basell 2008). This hypothesis is supported by the presence in some assemblages of non-local raw materials, most strikingly at sites in Kenya and northern Tanzania, where provenancing studies indicate that obsidian was sometimes moved over distances greater than 250 km (Merrick and Brown 1984; Merrick et al. 1994).

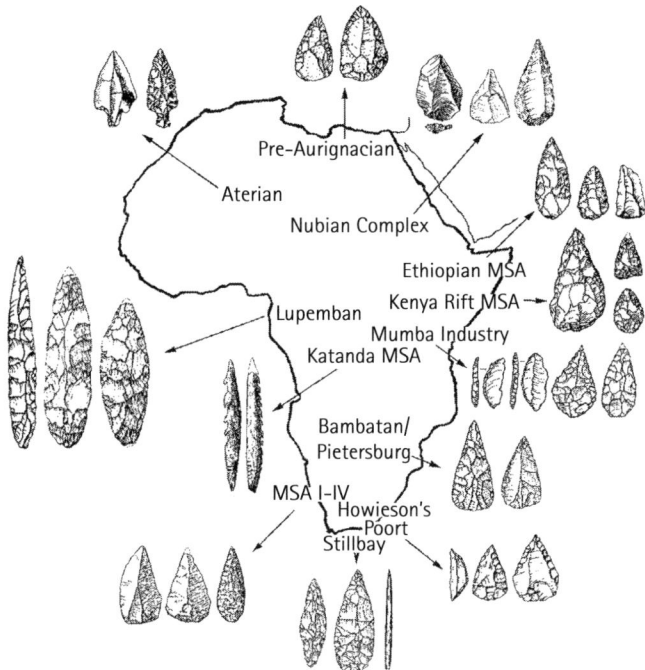

FIG. 27.4 Map of distribution of point styles in the African Middle Stone Age from McBrearty and Brooks (2000: fig. 5) after Clark (1993: fig. 1). Reproduced with permission from Elsevier and Princeton University Press.

Although evidence for the controlled use of fire remains minimal, it seems likely that MSA hominins used it, as well as being highly skilled in working stone and probably bone and wood, plus a wide range of other resources that have not preserved. MSA hominins appear to have exploited a range of different ecozones, and many MSA sites are focused on ecotones, maximizing access to resources. Examples include Gademotta and Kulkuletti, Porc-Epic, and Lukenya Hill. Over time, use of rockshelters and caves also seems to have increased. Beyond this, how different hominin groups and individuals interacted remains unknown, although the pathology of some fossils suggests that some individuals required a higher degree of care and cutmarks on the Herto crania hint at ritualized treatment of dead individuals. That hominins had language during the later MSA seems to be generally accepted and rarely debated, but for the earlier MSA this remains contested (Ambrose 2001; Coolidge and Wynn 2007). Despite all the inadequacies of our chronology and the comparative paucity of stratified sites, our understanding of eastern Africa's MSA has dramatically improved over recent years. The picture emerging is one of complex behaviour, with local variations that may well represent the emergence of regional identities (Clark 1988). What accounts for such differences or for pan-regional changes over time, i.e. the mechanisms of change, remains a major research priority.

Recent improvements in our understanding of the MSA highlight the increasing difficulty in discussing eastern African Stone Age archaeology in terms of the tripartite system (ESA–MSA–LSA and transitions) derived from Goodwin and van Riet Lowe (1929), as the terms now lack any simple behavioural, technological, or typological correlation. Undated sites cannot easily be assigned to a Stone Age period on the basis of technology or typology alone. It is unlikely that the terms will be abandoned, as their application is widespread in the literature and previous attempts to discard them have failed. Increasingly the differentiation between attributions to ESA–MSA–LSA, or indeed specific industries, is based less on the presence or absence of particular lithic types or reduction strategies and more on the relative abundance of particular analytical categories. In the absence of a common framework for lithic analyses in eastern Africa, the challenge for researchers is to analyse stone artefacts in ways that facilitate comparison, enabling them to be clear about why a particular assemblage should be attributed to the ESA, MSA, or LSA. Such research will have to incorporate technological analyses and statistically sound characterizations of assemblage variability, combined with reliable chronological controls, where possible obtaining dates using more than one dating method. Geoarchaeological analyses that inform explanations of site formation, and what might account for the variability in an assemblage, are also essential in assessing the behavioural significance of assemblages. Other key research priorities in advancing our knowledge of the eastern African MSA include improving integration of palaeoenvironmental and palaeolandscape change with geochronological, archaeological, and genetic data, and the continued identification and controlled excavation of long sequences. Although much work remains, the MSA is presently one of the most exciting and dynamic periods in the study of human evolution.

References

ADAMS, A., and FAURE, H. (1997a). *Review and Atlas of Palaeovegetation: Preliminary Land Ecosystem Maps of the World since the Last Glacial Maximum*. Oak Ridge National Laboratory. http://www.esd.ornl/gov/ern/qen/adams1.html. Website accessed 18 Jan. 2011.

—— (1997b). Preliminary vegetation maps of the world since the Last Glacial Maximum: an aid to archaeological understanding. *Journal of Archaeological Science* 24: 623–47.

ALLSWORTH-JONES, P., HARVATI, K., and STRINGERT, C. B. (2010). The archaeological context of the Iwo Eleru cranium from Nigeria and preliminary results of new morphometric studies. In P. Allsworth-Jones (ed.), *West African Archaeology: New Developments, New Perspectives*. Oxford: Archaeopress, 29–42.

AMBROSE, S. H. (1998). Chronology of the Later Stone Age and food production in eastern Africa. *Journal of Archaeological Science* 25: 377–92.

—— (2001). Palaeolithic technology and human evolution. *Science* 291: 1748–53.

—— (2002). Small things remembered: origins of early microlithic industries in sub-Saharan Africa. *Archaeological Papers of the American Anthropological Association* 12: 9–30.

ASSEFA, Z. (2006). Faunal remains from Porc-Epic: paleoecological and zooarchaeological investigations from a Middle Stone Age site in southeastern Ethiopia. *Journal of Human Evolution* 51: 50–75.

—— YIRGA, S., and REED, K. E. (2008). The large-mammal fauna from the Kibish Formation. *Journal of Human Evolution* 55: 501–12.

BARHAM, L. S. (ed.) (2000). *The Middle Stone Age of Zambia, South Central Africa*. Bristol: Western Academic and Specialist Press.

—— (2002). Backed tools in Middle Pleistocene central Africa and their evolutionary significance. *Journal of Human Evolution* 43: 585–603.

—— and MITCHELL, P. J. (2008). *The First Africans: African Archaeology from the Earliest Toolmakers to Most Recent Foragers*. Cambridge: Cambridge University Press.

—— PINTO LLONA, A. C., and STRINGER, C. B. (2001). Bone tools from Broken Hill (Kabwe) Cave, Zambia and their evolutionary significance. *Before Farming* 2: 88–103.

BASELL, L. S. (2008). Middle Stone Age site distributions in eastern Africa and their relationship to Quaternary environmental change, refugia and the evolution of *Homo sapiens*. *Quaternary Science Reviews* 27: 2484–98.

—— (2010). Middle Stone Age Sangoan-Lupemban lithic assemblages of Africa. In P. Allsworth-Jones (ed.), *West African Archaeology: New Developments, New Perspectives*. Oxford: Archaeopress, 15–28.

BRAUER, G. (1992). Africa's place in the evolution of *Homo sapiens*. In G. Bräuer and F. H. Smith (eds), *Continuity or Replacement: Controversies in* Homo sapiens *Evolution*. Rotterdam: Balkema, 83–98.

BROCK, F., HIGHAM, T. F. G., DITCHFIELD, P., and BRONK RAMSEY, C. (2010). Current pretreatment methods for AMS radiocarbon dating at the Oxford Radiocarbon Accelerator Unit (ORAU). *Radiocarbon* 52: 103–12.

BROWN, A. G. (2011). Dating surfaces and sediments. In K. J. Gregory and A. Goudie (eds), *The Sage Handbook of Geomorphology*. London: Sage, 192–209.

CLARK, J. D. (1982). Cultures of the Middle Palaeolithic/Middle Stone Age. In J. D. Clark (ed.), *Cambridge History of Africa*, vol. 1: *From the Earliest Times to c. 500 B.C.* Cambridge: Cambridge University Press.

—— (1988). The Middle Stone Age of Eastern Africa and the beginnings of regional identity. *Journal of World Prehistory* 2: 235–305.

—— (1993). African and Asian perspectives on the origins of modern humans. In M. J. Aitken, C. B. Stringer, and P. A. Mellars (eds), *The Origin of Modern Humans and the Impact of Chronometric Dating*. Princeton, NJ: Princeton University Press, 148–78.

—— (ed.) (2001). *Kalambo Falls Prehistoric Site*, vol. 3: *The Earlier Cultures: Middle and Earlier Stone Age*. Cambridge: Cambridge University Press.

—— BEYENE, Y., WOLDEGABRIEL, G., et al. (2003). Stratigraphic, chronological and behavioural contexts of Pleistocene *Homo sapiens* from Middle Awash, Ethiopia. *Nature* 423: 747–52.

—— and BROWN, K. S. (2001). The Twin Rivers Kopje, Zambia: stratigraphy, fauna, and artefact assemblages from the 1954 and 1956 excavations. *Journal of Archaeological Science* 28: 305–30.

—— (1977). *World Prehistory: A New Outline*. Cambridge: Cambridge University Press.

CONARD, N. J. (2005). An overview of the patterns of behavioural change in Africa and Eurasia during the Middle and Late Pleistocene. In F. d'Errico and L. Backwell (eds), *From Tools to Symbols: From Early Hominins to Modern Humans*. Johannesburg: Witwatersrand University Press, 293–332.

COOLIDGE, F. L., and WYNN, T. (2007). *The Rise of* Homo sapiens: *The Evolution of Modern Thinking*. Oxford: Wiley-Blackwell.

DE HEINZELIN, J., CLARK, J. D., SCHICK, K. D., and GILBERT, W. H. (eds) (2000). *The Acheulean and the Plio-Pleistocene Deposits of the Middle Awash Valley, Ethiopia*. Tervuren: Musée Royal de l'Afrique Centrale.

DEGUSTA, D., GILBERT, W., and TURNER, S. (1999). Hypoglossal canal size and hominid speech. *Proceedings of the National Academy of Sciences (USA)* 96: 1800–1804.

DEINO, A. L., and MCBREARTY, S. (2002). ^{40}Ar/^{39}Ar dating of the Kapthurin Formation, Baringo, Kenya. *Journal of Human Evolution* 42: 185–210.

DIEZ-MARTÍN, F., DOMÍN-GUEZRODRIGO, M., SÁNCHEZ, P., et al. (2009) The Middle to Later Stone Age technological transition in East Africa: new data from Mumba Rockshelter Bed

V (Tanzania) and their implications for the origin of modern human behavior. *Journal of African Archaeology* 7: 147–73.

GOODWIN, A. J. H., and VAN RIET LOWE, C. (1929). The Stone Age cultures of South Africa. *Annals of the South African Museum* 27: 1–289.

HARE, P. E., GOODFRIEND, G. A., BROOKS, A. S., KOKIS, J. E., and VON ENDT, D. W. (1993). *Chemical Clocks and Thermometers: Diagenetic Reactions of Amino Acids in Fossils*. Washington, DC: Carnegie Institution, 80–85.

HARVATI, K., HUBLIN, J.-J., and GUNZ, P. (2010). Evolution of middle–late Pleistocene human cranio-facial form: a 3-D approach. *Journal of Human Evolution* 59: 445–64.

INSKEEP, R. R. (1962). The age of the Kondoa rock paintings in light of recent excavations at Kisese II rock shelter. In *Actes du IVème Congrès Panafricain de Préhistoire et de l'Étude du Quaternaire*, ed. G. Mortelmans and J. Nenquin. Tervuren: Musée Royal de l'Afrique Centrale, 249–56.

JOHNSON, C., and MCBREARTY, S., (2010). 500,000 year old blades from the Kapthurin Formation, Kenya. *Journal of Human Evolution* 58: 193–200.

KAY, R., CARTMILL, M., and BALOW, M. (1998). The hypoglossal canal and the origin of human vocal behavior. *Proceedings of the National Academy of Sciences (USA)* 95: 5417–19.

LAHR, M. M., and FOLEY, R. (1994). Multiple dispersals and modern human origins. *Evolutionary Anthropology* 3: 48–60.

LEAKEY, L. S. B. (1943). The industries of the Gorgora Rockshelter, Lake Tana. *Journal of East African Uganda Natural History Society* 17: 199–230.

MAREAN, C. W. (1992). Implications of Late Quaternary mammalian fauna from Lukenya Hill (south-central Kenya) for palaeoenvironmental change and faunal extinction. *Quaternary Research* 37: 239–55.

—— (1997). Hunter-gatherer foraging strategies in tropical grasslands: model building and testing in the East African Middle and Later Stone Age. *Journal of Anthropological Archaeology* 16: 189–225.

—— and ASSEFA, Z. (2005). The middle and upper Pleistocene African record for the biological and behavioural origins of modern humans. In A. B. Stahl (ed.), *African Archaeology: A Critical Introduction*. Oxford: Blackwell, 93–219.

MCBREARTY, S., and BROOKS, A. S. (2000). The revolution that wasn't: a new interpretation of the origin of modern human behavior. *Journal of Human Evolution* 39: 453–563.

MCDOUGALL, I., BROWN, F. H., and FLEAGLE, J. G. (2005). Stratigraphic placement and age of modern humans from Kibish, Ethiopia. *Nature* 433: 733–6.

MCKINNEY, C. (2001). The uranium-series age of wood from Kalambo Falls. In J. D. Clark (ed.), *Kalambo Falls Prehistoric Site*, vol. 3: *The Earlier Cultures: Middle and Earlier Stone Age*. Cambridge: Cambridge University Press, 665–74.

MEHLMAN, M. J. (1991). Context for the emergence of modern man in eastern Africa: some new Tanzanian evidence. In J. D. Clark (ed.), *Cultural Beginnings*. Bonn: Rudolf Habelt, 177–96.

MERRICK, H. V., and BROWN, F. H. (1984). Obsidian sources and patterns of source utilization in Kenya and northern Tanzania: some initial findings. *African Archaeological Review* 2: 129–52.

—— —— and NASH, W. P. (1994). Use and movement of obsidian in the Early and Middle Stone Ages of Kenya and northern Tanzania. In S. T. Childs (ed.), *Society, Culture and Technology in Africa*. Philadelphia: MASCA, 29–44.

MICHELS, J. W., and MAREAN, C. A. (1984). A Middle Stone Age occupation site at Porc-Epic Cave, Dire Dawa (east-central Ethiopia), Part II. *African Archaeological Review* 2: 64–71.

MORGAN, L. E., and RENNE, P. R. (2008). Diachronous dawn of African's Middle Stone Age: new ^{40}Ar/^{39}Ar ages from the Ethiopian Rift. *Geological Society of America* 36: 967–70.

PHILLIPSON, D. W. (2005). *African Archaeology*. Cambridge: Cambridge University Press.

PLEURDEAU, D. (2006). Human technical behaviour in the African Middle Stone Age: the lithic assemblage of Porc-Epic Cave (Dire Dawa, Ethiopia). *African Archaeological Review* 22: 177–97.

RIGHTMIRE, P. G. (2004). Brain size and encephalization in early to mid-Pleistocene *Homo*. *American Journal of Physical Anthropology* 124: 109–23.

SHEA, J. J. (2006). The origins of lithic projectile point technology: evidence from Africa, the Levant, and Europe. *Journal of Archaeological Science* 33: 823–46.

SHEA, J. J. (2008). The Middle Stone Age archaeology of the Lower Omo Valley Kibish Formation: excavations, lithic assemblages, and inferred patterns of early *Homo sapiens* behavior. *Journal of Human Evolution* 55: 448–85.

——(2011). *Homo sapiens* is as *Homo sapiens* was: behavioral variability versus 'behavioral modernity' in Paleolithic archaeology. *Current Anthropology* 52: 1–35.

——and HILDEBRAND, E. A. (2010). The Middle Stone Age of West Turkana, Kenya. *Journal of Field Archaeology* 35: 355–64.

THOMPSON, J. C., BOWER, J. R. F., FISHER, E. C., et al. (2004). Loiyangalani: behavioural and taphonomic aspects of a Middle Stone Age site in the Serengeti Plain, Tanzania. *PaleoAnthropology* 2004: A56.

TRYON, C. (2006). Early Middle Stone Age lithic technology of the Kapthurin Formation (Kenya). *Current Anthropology* 47: 367–75.

——and MCBREARTY, S. (2002). Tephrostratigraphy and the Acheulian to Middle Stone Age transition in the Kapthurin Formation, Kenya. *Journal of Human Evolution* 42: 211–35.

TRYON, C., ROACH, N. T., and LOGAN, M. A. (2008). The Middle Stone Age of the northern Kenyan Rift: age and context of new archaeological sites from the Kapedo Tuffs. *Journal of Human Evolution* 55: 652–64.

VRBA, E. S., DENTON, G. H., PARTRIDGE, T. C., and BURCKLE, L. H. (eds) (1995). *Paleoclimate and Evolution with Emphasis on Human Origins*. New Haven, Conn.: Yale University Press.

WADLEY, L. (2005). Putting ochre to the test: replication studies of adhesives that may have been used for hafting tools in the Middle Stone Age. *Journal of Human Evolution* 49: 587–601.

WENDORF, F., and SCHILD, R. (1974). *A Middle Stone Age Sequence from the Central Rift Valley, Ethiopia*. Warsaw: Ossolineum.

WILLOUGHBY, P. (2001). Middle and Later Stone Age technology from the Lake Rukwa Rift, southwestern Tanzania. *South African Archaeological Bulletin* 56: 34–45.

——(2007). *The Evolution of Modern Humans in Africa: A Comprehensive Guide*. Walnut Creek, Calif.: AltaMira Press.

CHAPTER 28

HUNTING AND GATHERING IN AFRICA'S TROPICAL FORESTS AT THE END OF THE PLEISTOCENE AND IN THE EARLY HOLOCENE

ELS CORNELISSEN

INTRODUCTION

THE equatorial lowland tropical forest extends in West Africa from Sierra Leone in the west to Ivory Coast in the east, is interrupted by the savannah Dahomey Gap in southern Bénin and Togo, and then continues from southern Nigeria across southern Cameroon, Equatorial Guinea, and Gabon and into the Congo Basin of Congo-Brazzaville and Congo-Kinshasa (Fig. 28.1). Its current distribution, structure, and composition were established within the last two or three millennia. Rainfall and seasonality determine various botanical formations within the forest, ranging from non-seasonal inundated and dense tropical forest to Afromontane forest to seasonal semi-deciduous forest to wet and dry woodland.

Today the presence within and at the borders of these forests of 'Pygmy' hunter-gatherers and farmers, who have different subsistence strategies and phenotypes, has inspired research in various fields. Those living in Atlantic Central Africa's forests have become the focus of genetic studies that may be helpful for reconstructing demographic history in areas poorly documented in the archaeological record. Combining the results of analyses of various genetic parameters (Quintana-Murci et al. 2008; Patin et al. 2009; Verdu et al. 2009; Batini et al. 2011 and references therein), some chronological anchors for the history of Pygmy hunter-gatherer populations can be identified. The most recent common ancestor of Pygmy and farming populations would have lived about 70–60 kya. A period of isolation between the two groups most likely accounts for their phenotypic difference. The subdivision between western and eastern Pygmies would be approximately 20,000 years old with subsequent genetic differentiation occurring among the western Pygmies within the past 2,800 years. Cultural factors and past environmental fluctuations may have affected population growth, contraction, fragmentation, and gene flow (Campbell and Tishkoff 2010).

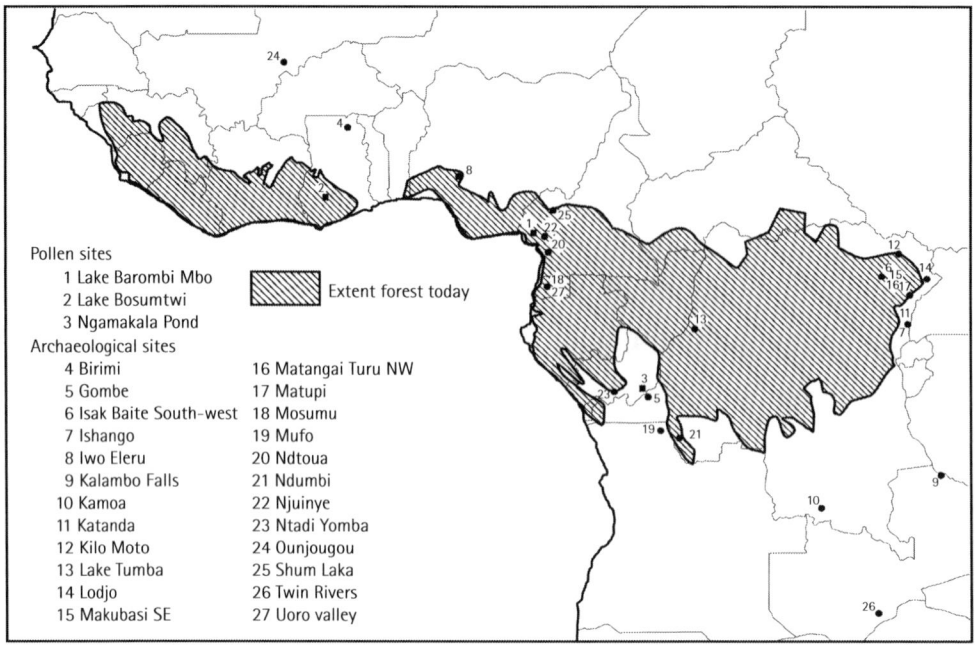

FIG. 28.1 Current distribution of forests in West and Central Africa, archaeological and palaeoenvironmental sites cited in Chapter 28.

Documenting cultural and behavioural aspects remains a challenge for archaeological, palaeoenvironmental, and palaeontological research in the region. At the end of the Pleistocene and in the early Holocene, when genetic evidence suggests a split of Pygmy hunter-gatherers into western and eastern groups, a continuity is observed in technology (Mercader and Brooks 2001; Cornelissen 2002; Mercader and Martí 2002) regardless of changes in environment that resulted in forest fragmentation. In order to assess in which environment hunter-gatherers were precisely operating, reconstructions of the palaeoenvironment are essential.

VEGETATION HISTORY

For reconstructing the history of the rainforest, marine cores offer continuous records over large spans of time, but provide less detailed information on environmental changes in specific areas of the continent (Dupont et al. 2000: 112). Combining marine records that cover long periods of time with more recent terrestrial palynological data that run over briefer periods, Dupont et al. (2000) propose 11 time slices for the last 150,000 years in equatorial West and Central Africa. Important modifications in terms of composition and distribution of lowland rainforest began as a result of climate changes. In this broad regional picture (figs 5 and 9 in Dupont et al. 2000) rainforest was most likely widespread during MIS 1 (since 12 kya) and 5 (130–74 kya), severely reduced during MIS 3 (59–29 kya) and MIS 4 (74–59 kya) and

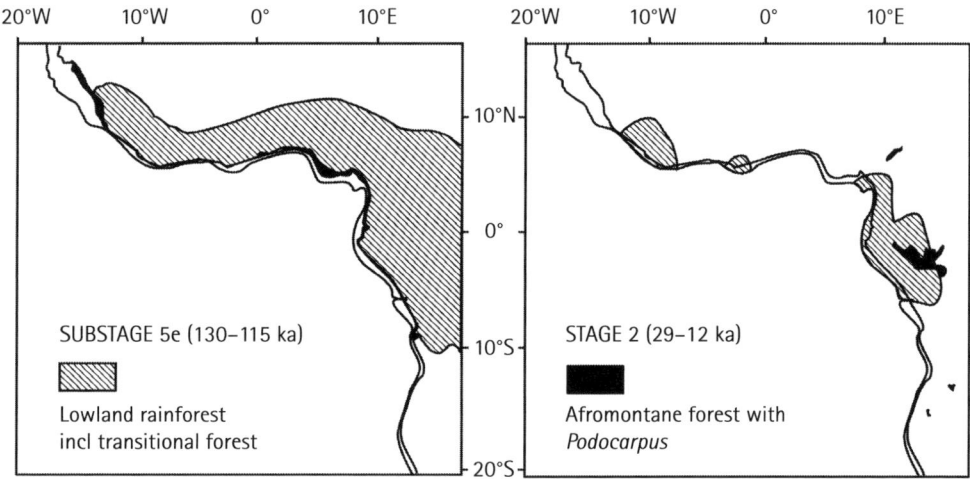

FIG. 28.2 Illustration of hypothetical reconstructions of maximum (left) and minimum (right) extent of forests in response to climate changes based on Dupont et al. (2000: fig. 9 I and B).

even more severely reduced during MIS 2 (29–12 kya) and MIS 6 (150–130 kya). As an illustration, Fig. 28.2 represents the two extremes of hypothetical reconstructions: (1) the maximum extent of forest during warm and humid stages (5e, 130–115 kya); and (2) its minimum extent during cold and dry stages (early MIS 2, 29–12 kya).

An overview of research conducted on the continent itself (Runge 2007) lists several features indicative of sparse vegetation and dry conditions in the area now under forest cover, which proves not to have been an unbroken and stable, immovable mass particularly during the Last Glacial Maximum (LGM) c. 25–16 kya.

Among the terrestrial sites two key data sets are consistently used in reconstructing the history of the African forest and the environmental setting of archaeological sites during the recent Quaternary. They are the pollen records recovered from sediment cores of Lake Bosumtwi in Ghana and Lake Barombi Mbo in the lowland tropical rainforest of western Cameroon (Maley 2004). Both sites span the time interval of the end of the Pleistocene and early Holocene. The Ngamakala Pond in Congo-Brazzaville, situated today in grasslands, also has a record going back to 24 kya (Elenga et al. 2004). At both Lake Barombi Mbo and Ngamakala during the LGM the prevailing vegetation types were semi-deciduous forests and grasslands (Elenga et al. 2004: 184). The LGM dry spell around 20 kya lasted much longer and was cooler than the second, relatively well-documented dry period of around 2.5 kya based on the pollen records of Lakes Barombi Mbo and Bosumtwi (Maley 2004), and from Nyabessan swamp, southern Cameroon (Ngomanda et al. 2009). Modelling and new analyses provide new insights and more fine-tuning, as in the case of the key site of Lake Barombi Mbo (Lebamba et al. 2010). The dramatic and often rapid changes in climatic conditions and consequently in environments, however, make it difficult if not impossible to determine the actual environmental conditions in which people found themselves at a particular moment in time. At archaeological sites, faunal remains that result from hunting or fishing provide both environmental and behavioural information. If firewood was not transported over long distances, charcoal reflects the site's immediate environs. Phytoliths in cave sediments in equatorial regions may be considered primarily of anthropogenic origin and thus shed light on human selection of natural resources. For the northeastern forest refuge in the Ituri (Congo-Kinshasa) they suggest that during the LGM the area consisted of a variety of vegetation formations, including forests, mosaics of forests and grasslands, and perhaps parkland environments rather than a homogeneous forest block (Mercader et al. 2000).

Though the data are flimsy, the palaeoenvironment before, during and after the LGM appears highly dynamic, shifting in composition in response to climatic fluctuations. They also offer a more heterogeneous picture than a simple contraction into forest refuges during dry and cool periods from which forest spread again under warm and humid conditions.

ARCHAEOLOGICAL EVIDENCE

Eastern, Southern, and Western Central Africa

In this variable environmental setting, two broad technological traditions for the period and area under consideration can be identified. They are the Pleistocene Lupemban and its later Holocene successor, the Tshitolian, with an important bifacial component and made from a variety of raw materials, and late Pleistocene and early Holocene microlithic industries, made essentially from quartz. Middle Stone Age industries that have no Lupemban affiliation also exist in the area, but most were collected on the surface and remain undated and without information on their palaeoenvironmental context. A number of regional surveys list relevant archaeological sites and their research history (Van Noten 1982; Lanfranchi and Clist 1991; Clist 1995; Mercader and Brooks 2001; Casey 2002, 2005; Cornelissen 2002; Mercader 2002a, 2002b; Barham and Mitchell 2008; Taylor 2011). There is also broad consensus on the disparate character and lack of chronological, environmental, and behavioural resolution of that archaeological record.

The Lupemban industry has been dated to beyond 230 kya at Twin Rivers, Zambia (Barham and Smart 1996). In Atlantic Central Africa, however, no radiometric evidence is yet available outside the limits of radiocarbon dating. This may be an outcome of methodological constraints (Taylor 2011), but for the time being there are very few stratigraphic grounds for inferring older ages and no dates to close the gap between Twin Rivers and the later Pleistocene Lupemban sites in, for instance, Gabon and Congo. Moreover, if the Lupemban in Zambia is to be correlated with that of the southern belt of Central Africa and Atlantic Central Africa, this implies that its technology remained unchanged for more than 200,000 years irrespective of multiple environmental changes or of changes in human species (from *Homo heidelbergensis* to *H. sapiens*; Foley, Ch. 20 above).

The bifacial Lupemban component includes core-axes and lanceolates next to light duty equipment. Grinding implements are rare. Core-axes, chopping tools, and core scrapers may relate to a woodworking function but could have served to gather vegetable food, strip bark and cut. The finely bifacially retouched lanceolates, in contrast, probably served as throwing or stabbing spears, but could have also been used for cutting and slashing, thus providing a valuable aid in forest zone food collecting (Clark 1963: 192). Rots and Van Peer (2006) make a very convincing case for core-axes having been used as hafted heavy duty implements in subsurface digging activities or subsurface exploitation of lithic raw material, plant foods, or perhaps iron oxides. The interesting

FIG. 28.3 Core-axes and other implements in polymorphic sandstone from lower Congo, Congo-Kinshasa, stored at the Royal Museum for Central Africa (6679–6758), collected on the surface near Mbanza Ngugu. Scale in cm (photograph copyright Royal Museum of Central Africa).

point here is that food tubers in tropical forests have to be dug out. There is nevertheless a difference in morphology and typology between core-axes from Sai Island, Sudan (Rots and Van Peer 2006), and those collected at the surface at various sites in Lower Congo (Fig. 28.3).

Because of the presence of core-axes, the Lupemban technological complex has, ever since Desmond Clark's (1963) initial suggestion, evoked a link with woodworking and hence with more closed vegetation. However, the palaeoenvironmental setting of Lupemban sites to the south of the area covered by rain forest today is indicative of open, and not densely forested, landscapes such as the *Brachystegia*-dominated *miombo* woodland at Kalambo Falls, Zambia (Taylor et al. 2001). Elsewhere, Mufo in northeastern Angola was set in an open woodland and savannah between 34 and 14 kya (Clark 1971: 1220) and the environment at the time of occupation at Twin Rivers was open grassland, to judge from the presence of zebra, wildebeest, hartebeest, and blesbok (Clark and Brown 2001: 313). For Lupemban industries found *in situ* there is, in sum, no direct evidence for a forest setting or exploitation.

Core-axes and lanceolates render Lupemban surface sites extremely visible, and they have been reported practically everywhere in Central and West Africa. In northeastern Congo, mining sites such as Kilo Moto yielded long, fine bifacial lanceolates up to 30cm in length. These were also found at undated sites in the Lodjo Valley (Van Noten 1982: 30–31 and fig. 15). To the south, the older part of the sequence at Kamoa (Katanga, Congo-Kinshasa; Cahen 1975) is also undated. A Late Acheulean industry is overlain by MSA industries that combine Lupemban characteristics such as numerous core-axes with well-developed prepared core techniques of the kind typical of the MSA. The combination of albeit fewer and shorter core-axes with general size reduction continues in the succeeding transitional LSA industry. The most recent industry, dating c. 6000–1800 BP, is microlithic. Quartz and quartzite become more frequent than the polymorphic sandstones that are used throughout the sequence and outcrop only 1.5 km from the site. Geomorphological and pollen evidence situates the occupation at Kamoa in open landscapes for all phases. Though many core-axes have been collected on the surface in Katanga, their association with abundant Levallois debitage does not validate their affiliation with Sangoan or Lupemban industries (Cahen 1982).

Cahen (1976, 1978a, 1978b) also conducted extensive research on the site of Gombe ex-Kalina at Kinshasa (Congo-Kinshasa), which in the 1930s produced the first dated sequence of Sangoan–Lupemban–Tshitolian industries, or, in local terms, Kalinian–Djokocian–Ndolian industries. Exhaustive refitting of artefacts belonging to the different industries revealed post-depositional disturbances resulting in buried 'stone-lines'. These disturbances have been explained as subsurface movements catalysed by biogenic activity and the action of gravity concentrating coarse material such as stones, including artefacts, near the base of a sand mantle, which may still contain diffuse horizons of stone over its entire thickness. Because sites in the southern Congo River basin yielding typologically identical material are located in the same sedimentological context of a homogeneous mantle of redistributed Kalahari sands, this process was probably general and systematic for the entire area (Cahen and Moeyersons 1977). This interpretation of stone-lines implies that all sites are in secondary position, and led Cahen to assemble all previously identified industries into a single post-Acheulean industrial complex.

Stone-lines have other interpretations with less destructive consequences for the associated archaeological material. For the site of Mosumu (Equatorial Guinea; Mercader et al. 2002), cultural deposition and stone-line formation are considered as chronologically, behaviourally and environmentally unrelated events. At Mosumu, the use of quartz as raw material increased from the Middle to the Later Stone Age. The MSA has a restricted presence of bifacial technology with lanceolate points, 'core-axes' (Mercader et al. 2002), and bifacial thinning flakes. The succeeding LSA is microlithic. Occupation started well before 35 kya and continued throughout the late Pleistocene and Holocene. Environmental reconstruction from Lake Barombi Mbo in nearby western Cameroon lends support to the hypothesis that MSA and LSA groups subsisted in a tropical forest context because the pollen record between 28 and 20 kya includes tropical forest families (Mercader and Martí 2002: 86). Lupemban sites are recognized in similar contexts in Gabon (Clist 1995) and Congo-Brazzaville (Lanfranchi and Clist 1991).

The Holocene Tshitolian industry maintains the bifacial trimming of the Lupemban. Compared to its Pleistocene Lupemban predecessor, the Tshitolian has a quite restricted distribution, concentrated in northeastern Angola and the lower Congo River basin (Cahen 1978b: fig. 5). Gradual size reduction through time and backed microliths, including *petits tranchets*, are typical. Tshitolian assemblages come from a variety of open-air sites, but also from more secure rock-shelter contexts such as Ntadi Yomba in Congo-Brazzaville (van Neer and Lanfranchi 1985; Lanfranchi 1991). Geometric microliths appear relatively late, around 7 kya. Amongst the numerous tool types, bifacial pieces in the shape of a *noyau de mangue* (mango kernel) are very characteristic. Those from Ntadi Yomba date to 7 kya and some show traces of polish at the distal end. Fauna from this layer comes from dense and gallery forest and Guinean savanna. Also present were nine human fragmentary bones, four of which belong to children (Van Neer and Lanfranchi 1985: 354).

Central Africa's second technological tradition consists of microlithic industries on quartz that date back to the Late Pleistocene and continue well into the recent Holocene. The small size of quartz nodules has often been invoked to explain the size reduction and to argue against a true technological innovation. However, in a number of cases people chose to use quartz even when other raw materials of 'good' flaking quality were available; examples include Kamoa (Cahen 1975), Shum Laka (Lavachery 2001; Cornelissen 2003), and Ndumbi (Planquaert 1976). Technological microlithic know-how and templates may have rendered quartz an appropriate raw material, but perhaps quartz and its ubiquity also guided choices in technology. If small replicable inserts were the ultimate goal of general size reduction, quartz is highly suitable because it is a very hard material and flakes may not need any backing, secondary trimming, or intentional retouch to serve as small inserts in composite tools.

Compared to the very large number of Lupemban surface sites, sites with quartz microlithic assemblages are few in number, partly because scatters of quartz debitage may appear natural and thus remain unnoticed. Controlled surface collections do, however, reveal the presence of both technological traditions in exactly the same area. An example of this co-occurrence of industries on polymorphic sandstone of Lupemban and Tshitolian affinities and of microlithic industries on quartz is the site of Ndumbi, a tributary of the Kwango (Bandundu, Congo-Kinshasa; Planquaert 1976). On the flood plains northeast of Lake Tumba (Fiedler and Preuss 1985) two assemblages were collected. To the west the assemblage contained, amongst others, small bifacially worked points, on fine and coarse quartzite, reminiscent of the Lupemban or early Tshitolian. To the east a quartz industry was collected with few intentionally retouched pieces. All may date to any time after 25 kya. Another case in point is found in the Uoro Valley (Equatorial Guinea; Mercader and Martí 1999: 17). To the east of the river, quartz industries of unclear affiliation occur, comprising Middle to Later Stone Age debitage. To the west, sites yield Middle Stone Age bifacial artefacts made from various raw materials. Since none of these co-occurrences are from dated and excavated sites, the contemporaneity of the variable exploitation of raw materials and technological choices remains an open question, as do issues of functional interpretation and the identity of the prehistoric artisans.

The late Pleistocene levels of Ishango 11 contain a quartz microlithic assemblage dating back to c. 25–20 kya (de Heinzelin 1957; Brooks and Smith 1987; Brooks and Robertshaw 1990; Boaz et al. 1990; Mercader and Brooks 2001). They succeed the sites of Katanda in the Semliki Valley in the Western Rift (Kivu, Congo-Kinshasa), which date to 80–70 kya (Feathers and Migliorini 2001). At that time, the valley was fringed with relatively dense gallery forest in proximity to open savannahs that offered a wide variety of environments for exploitation, from river and lake shores to dense forest. The stone industry found at Katanda was made on quartz and quartzite, lacks any characteristic tools such as handaxes, core-axes, lanceolates, blades, or microliths, but contains distinctive cores attesting to the use of radial flaking (Fig. 28.4), as well as grindstones. Associated bone tools, which include barbed points, are amongst the oldest on the continent or, indeed, the world (Yellen 1996, 1998: 193; Yellen et al. 1995). No continuous archaeological record documents human occupation for the period between 70 and 25 kya in the Semliki Valley, but the hunter-gatherer-fisher communities of Ishango had developed their technological know-how in bone working to high standards by 25 kya. The three successive late Pleistocene levels at Ishango

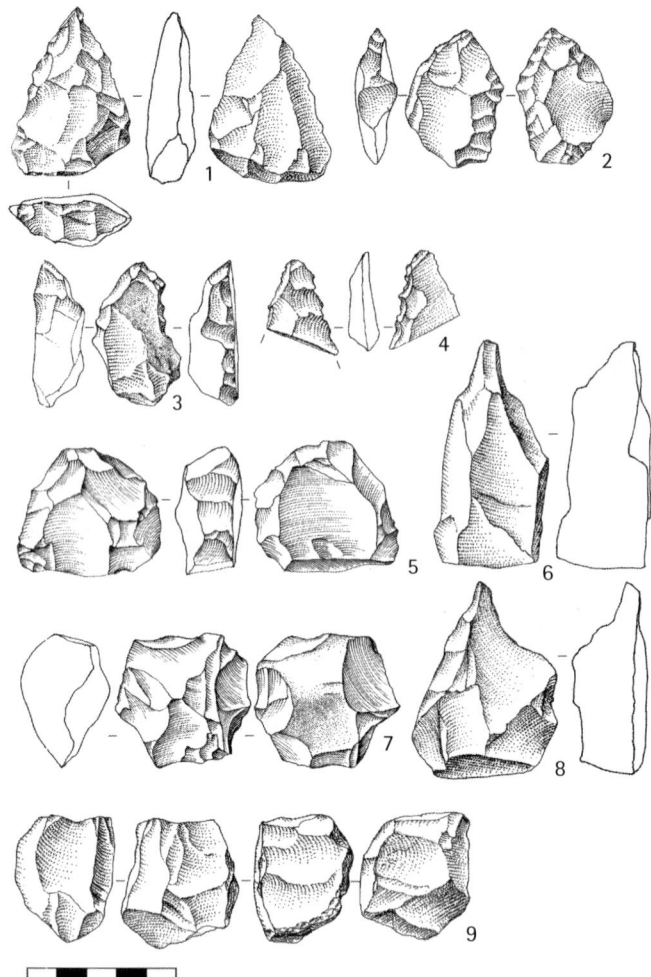

FIG. 28.4 Selection of stone artefacts from the Katanda sites, Semliki Valley, Congo-Kinshasa, all in quartz or quartzite except 5 and 7 in chert. Scale in cm.

11 contain all stages of the manufacturing process of various types of tools such as uniserial and biserial barbed harpoons (Brooks and Smith 1987; Yellen 1996) as well as two engraved bone handles. The original publication (de Heinzelin 1957, 1962) considers the first bone handle as the oldest material expression of mathematical thought. Curiously, the debate on whether this is the case is held, not among archaeologists, but among mathematicians (Huylebrouck 2008, Keller 2010). It is intriguing that the bone handles are part of a sophisticated Late Pleistocene bone industry. Perhaps they were not *per se* mathematical, but expressed for the first time the ideas of symmetry and standardization; Ishango artisans may have needed to materialize certain measurements in order to produce bone tools of similar size and proportions, but this needs further archaeological investigation.

The environmental setting of the 25–20 kya level at Ishango (Peters 1990; Mercader and Brooks 2001) is reconstructed from the fauna and reveals an environment quite similar to that in the older Katanda layers. From the Ishangan levels come the only human remains dated prior to the Holocene in all of Central and West Africa, within and outside the forests. They stand out in their robustness in comparison to modern humans (Twiesselmann 1958; Boaz et al. 1990; Crevecoeur 2008). As observed elsewhere (Crevecoeur et al. 2009), Late Pleistocene modern human variation may differ from that of recent humans (cf. Foley 1991).

Occupation is not documented in the Semliki Valley for a long interval after 20 kya, yet the technology in levels that post-date 7 kya (de Heinzelin 1957; Brooks and Smith 1987) remains a prolific quartz industry, as in the older Ishangan levels, though without the latter's elaborate bone equipment.

Not far from the open air sites of the Semliki Valley are the Matupi cave in Mount Hoyo (Van Noten 1977, 1982), and a further ten rockshelters excavated in the Ituri forest (Mercader et al. 2000; Mercader and Brooks 2001). Matupi yielded a sequence of quartz industries of which the lower part, dated to between 40 and 20 kya, may not be fully microlithic (Van Noten 1982; Mercader and Brooks 2001). Animals were hunted here in an open environment throughout most of the sequence, with access to more wooded and forested areas (Van Neer 1989). Three of the ten Ituri sites span the transition from Pleistocene to Holocene. They are Matangai Turu Northwest, Isak Baite Southwest, and Makubasi Southeast, for which phytolith analysis sets their occupation within the rainforest (Mercader et al. 2000). All the sites yielded microlithic quartz assemblages. In a comparative analysis conducted on them and Ishango, Mercader and Brooks (2001: 213–14) concluded that the inhabitants of both the savannah and forests of northeastern Congo used identical reduction modes and made similar raw material choices from the later Pleistocene onwards.

A comparable pattern is observable at the open-air site of Njuinye and the rock shelter of Shum Laka in Cameroon. As at Matupi, the basal layers at Njuinye are dated to before ± 35 kya and yielded quartz debitage of unclear cultural affiliation (Mercader and Martí 2002: 75). The overlaying level 3, dated to throughout the LGM and into the Holocene, contains industries on quartz and, for the upper part, also on other, exotic raw materials. Tool production is relatively unstandardized and of microlithic affiliation. This continues in the top layer, which contains some pottery sherds. The basal layers at Shum Laka in the northwestern Grassfields of Cameroon are also dated to the latter part of OIS 3 (± 32 kya; Lavachery 2001; Cornelissen 2003). Here again the raw material is quartz, as at Njuinye, until the early Holocene. During most of its more than 30,000-year history, Shum Laka was situated in mixed environments; game was hunted in forest, while firewood (represented archaeologically by charcoal) was collected in the vicinity of the site, not just from forest trees but also from grasses, savannah shrubs, and wooded savannah trees (Lavachery 2001; Cornelissen 2003).

Human bones that might belong to hunter-gatherers were found in the Holocene layers of Shum Laka (Ribot et al. 2001). A first funeral phase is dated around 7 kya, a second to 3 kya. Funerary practices were quite varied and comprise single, double, and multiple inhumations, mostly of children. Dates were obtained from the skeletons themselves; there is no charcoal for these periods in the cave.

Shum Laka differs from all other essentially microlithic quartz sites in Central Africa in that from around 7–6 kya basalts were exploited for a macrolithic industry that includes radial and prepared cores and bifacial axe-hoe-like tools and blades (Lavachery 2001). This industry bears a strong resemblance to Mode 3 MSA-type technologies, but is firmly dated to the mid-Holocene. On this lithic substratum pottery was introduced. The phenomenon of a MSA look-alike basalt industry has also been observed at the Ndtoua rock shelter, today located in forest in southern Cameroon (Lavachery et al.

2005: 182). At the bottom of a 2 m-thick stratigraphic sequence, a quartzite and quartz microlithic assemblage with a significant macrolithic component is dated to *c.* 5500 BP. This is overlain by a microlithic assemblage on quartz and rock crystal. Pottery appears in the next level of abundant microlithic quartz artefacts dated to *c.* 1900 BP. The upper level contains some stone tools. Initially the larger artefacts from the lowest level were identified as late MSA/early LSA and a Late Pleistocene/Early Holocene age was assumed (Lavachery et al. 2005).

The Central Congo Basin

All the sites described so far for Central Africa encircle a large area that is, archaeologically speaking, virtually invisible: the lowland forest and wet forest of the inner Central Congo basin along the Congo River and its tributaries. Except for the previously mentioned surface sites on the floodplains of Lake Tumba, no Stone Age sites have been reported for this region. Archaeological exploration of the riverbanks (Eggert 1993; Wotzka 1995) has nevertheless proved successful, revealing intensive occupation by pottery-producing communities, who settled the inner basin from 2.5 kya onward. None of these sites or pit structures contains stone tools of any kind. Difficult access to raw material may explain the absence of stone tool assemblages, coupled with low visibility of, for instance, quartz assemblages, and recent fluvial and alluvial shifting of shores and floodplains that may constantly rearrange associated materials. The technological capacity of exploiting bone as a raw material is attested since 70 kya to the east of the forest, and may have provided a valuable alternative; however, given the extreme acidity of the waters of Congo River tributaries, finding bone equipment is highly unlikely.

West Africa

As in many parts of Central Africa, Lupemban occurrences are essentially based on undated surface sites in West Africa. The conventional view is that there was scant human occupation prior to the Holocene; at least, there are no securely dated sites in stratigraphic context for the late Pleistocene (Casey 2005: 232). Undated macrolithic assemblages that contain neither pottery nor ground stone might indicate occupation of the area prior to the Holocene (Casey 2002: 51), but the mid-Holocene assemblages from Cameroon invite caution in their interpretation as MSA. To the north of the tropical rainforest in West Africa, radiometric dated sites such as Birimi in northeastern Ghana and Ounjougou in central Mali attest to the variety of human occupation and technology. Though these sites were never in a forested setting, migration from north to south in response to climatic changes is often invoked to explain the appearance of new technological features—for instance, when the Sahel and Sahara became too dry and people presumably moved southwards. At Birimi, a flake industry with a Levallois component is directly associated with OSL dates on the sediments enclosing them, dating these to between ~41 kya and ~24 kya (Quickert et al. 2003), which may lend support to an MSA affiliation of some of the more southern macrolithic sites. Ounjougou is an exceptionally long sequence spanning the last 150,000 years at which Levallois, discoidal, and non-Levallois laminar industries, bifacial foliate pieces, and assemblages of small cores and choppers reminiscent of mode I indus-tries all alternate (Soriano et al. 2010).

The archaeological record in West Africa becomes richer in the early Holocene. Prolific flaked stone assemblages of unmodified, utilized, and retouched flakes, frequently in quartz and sometimes including geometric microliths, occur in the area (today covered by forest) between 13 kya and 5 kya (Casey 2002, 2005). A series of dates reveals continuous use throughout the Holocene of the rock shelter of Iwo Eleru in southeastern Nigeria (Shaw and Daniels 1984). The site now lies in rainforest, and based on the record from Lake Bosumtwi, located 750 km to its west and at the same latitude, might have been so for most of its occupa-tion. From the basal layers to the top, quartz assemblages occur to which pottery and ground tools were added in later stages. The oldest date of 11,200 ± 200 BP (I-1753) was obtained on charcoal associated with a poorly preserved skeleton of a probably male adult found in a contracted burial. Originally Brothwell and Shaw (1971) suggest that this Late Stone Age West African was markedly different from members of succeeding populations. A later mor-phometric study (Allsworth-Jones et al. 2010: 40) reveals important archaic elements that indeed align the overall modern-looking Iwo Eleru skeleton with specimens of early modern and late archaic humans.

Conclusion

Stone artefacts often provide the only means for identifying sites, reconstructing behaviour, and determining cultural affiliation in West and Central Africa. For the period covering the end of the Pleistocene and early Holocene, lithic industries can be grouped into two broad technological traditions: the Lupemban–Tshitolian assemblages and microlithic quartz industries. From the available evidence the Lupemban is older than the microlithic quartz industries in the eastern part of Central Africa, whereas in southwestern Central Africa the bifacial tradition is contemporaneous with the older microlithic quartz industries of eastern and northwestern Central Africa. Neither of the broad technological complexes appears to relate to specific environments, but they allowed their makers to settle in wet, dry, and sea-sonal ecosystems with similar technologies from the Late Pleistocene onwards throughout the environmental changes brought about by the Last Glacial Maximum and throughout the entire Holocene. It may thus be argued that hunter-gatherer communities were sufficiently flexible and capable of exploiting a variety of environments to adapt to environmental changes regardless of stone technology. The longevity of Lupemban industries and quartz microlithic industries in Central Africa from the end of the Pleistocene, and for the latter in West Africa at least from the early Holocene onward, is quite astonishing. It is tempting to see the pattern of two broad technological traditions paralleled in the pattern detected in the genetics of two different human populations at the end of the Pleistocene. Even if different human populations would leave different signatures in their material culture and, more spe-cifically, their stone tools, the current distribution of western and eastern hunter-gatherers in the Central African forest is not reflected in the Pleistocene or Holocene distribution of the two broad technological complexes; microlithic quartz industries, in particular, cover almost the entire northern part of West and Central Africa's currently forested areas. However attractive, due to the poor resolution of the archaeological record, this hypothesis is pure speculation. Human skeletal material to document possible changes or continuity in phenotype of the prehistoric hunter-gatherers is unfortunately limited to one single specimen for the Late Pleistocene, that from Iwo Eleru.

A combination of poor access to and conservation of raw material may explain the absence of evidence in the forests of the central Congo basin. However, secure access to water and a variety of environments made densely forested areas hospitable during periods of environmental stress as a consequence of climatic changes such as those of the Last Glacial Maximum. A clement environment would argue against absence of human occupation in forested environments, and also against forests as a barrier or as inducing genetic separation as such. Other restrictions may have existed, but they were apparently not of an environmental order, nor are they visible in lithic technology.

References

ALLSWORTH-JONES P., HARVATI, K., and STRINGER, C. (2010). The archaeological context of the Iwo Eleru cranium from Nigeria and preliminary results of new morphometric studies. In P. Allsworth-Jones (ed.), *West African Archaeology: New Developments, New Perspectives*. Oxford: Archaeopress, 29–42.

BARHAM, L. S., and MITCHELL, P. J. (2008). *The First Africans: African Archaeology from the Earliest Toolmakers to Most Recent Foragers*. Cambridge: Cambridge University Press.

—— and SMART, P. L.. (1996). An early date for the Middle Stone Age of central Zambia. *Journal of Human Evolution* 30: 587–90.

BATINI, C., LOPES, J., BEHAR, D. M., CALAFELL, F., JORDE, L. B., VAN DER VEEN. L., QUINTANA-MURCI, L., SPENDINI, G., DESTRO-BIOSOL, G., and COMAS, D. (2011). Insights into the demographic history of African Pygmies from complete mitochondrial genomes. *Molecular Biology and Evolution* 28: 1099–1110.

BOAZ, N. T., PAVLAKIS, P. P., and BROOKS, A. S. (1990). Late Pleistocene-Holocene human remains from the Upper Semliki Area, Zaire. In N. T. Boaz (ed.), *Evolution of Environments and Hominidae in the African Western Rift Valley*. Martinsville: Virginia Museum of Natural History, 273–99.

BROOKS, A. S., and ROBERTSHAW, P. (1990). The Glacial Maximum in tropical Africa: 22 000–12 000 BP. In C. S. Gamble and O. Soffer (eds), *The World at 18 000 BP*, vol. 2: *Low Latitudes*. London: Unwin Hyman, 121–67.

—— and SMITH, C. C., (1987). Ishango revisited: new age determinations and cultural interpretations. *African Archaeological Review* 6: 65–78.

BROTHWELL, D., and SHAW, T. (1971). A late Upper Pleistocene proto-West African negro from Nigeria. *Man*, 6: 221–7.

CAHEN, D. (1975). *Le Site Archéologique de la Kamoa (Région du Shaba, République du Zaïre): De l'Âge de la Pierre Ancien a l'Âge du Fer*. Tervuren: Royal Museum for Central Africa.

—— (1976). Nouvelles fouilles à la pointe de la Gombe (ex-pointe de Kalina), Kinshasa, Zaïre. *L'Anthropologie* 80: 573–602.

—— (1978a). New excavations at Gombe (ex-Kalina) point, Kinshasa, Zaire. *Antiquity* 52: 51–6.

—— (1978b). Vers une révision de la nomenclature des industries préhistoriques de l'Afrique Centrale. *L'Anthropologie* 82: 5–36.

—— (1982). The Stone Age in the south and west. In Van Noten (1982: 41–56).

—— and MOEYERSONS, J. (1977). Subsurface movements on stone artefacts and their implications for the prehistory of Central Africa. *Nature* 266: 812–15.

CAMPBELL, M. C., and TISHKOFF, S. A. (2010). The evolution of human genetic and phenotypic variation in Africa. *Current Biology* 20: R166–73.

CASEY, J. (2002). The archaeology of Ghana from the Pleistocene to the mid-Holocene. In J. Mercader (ed.), *Under the Canopy: The Archaeology of Tropical Rainforests*. Piscataway, NJ: Rutgers University Press, 35–63.

—— (2005). Holocene occupations of the forest and savanna. In A. B. Stahl (ed.), *African Archaeology: A Critical Introduction*. Oxford: Blackwell, 225–48.

CLARK, J. D. (1963). *Prehistoric Cultures of Northeast Angola and Their Significance in Tropical Africa*. Lisbon: Diamang Publicacoes Culturais.

—— (1971). Human behavioral differences in southern Africa during the late Pleistocene. *American Anthropologist* 73: 1213–36.

—— and BROWN, K. S. (2001). The Twin Rivers Kopje, Zambia: stratigraphy, fauna, and artefact assemblages from the 1954 and 1956 excavations. *Journal of Archaeological Science* 28: 305–30.

CLIST, B. (1995). *Gabon: 100 000 Ans d'Histoire*. Libreville: Centre Cultural Français Saint-Exupéry.

CORNELISSEN, E. (2002). Human responses to changing environments in Central Africa between 40,000 and 12,000 BP. *Journal of World Prehistory* 16: 197–235.

—— (2003). On microlithic quartz industries at the end of the Pleistocene in Central Africa: the evidence from Shum Laka (NW Cameroon). *African Archaeological Review* 20: 1–24.

CREVECOEUR, I. (2008). Variability of Palaeolithic modern humans in Africa: future prospects of the Ishango human remains (re-)study. In Huylebrouck (2008: 87–97).

—— ROUGIER, H., and GRINE, F., and FROMENT, A. (2009). Modern human cranial diversity in the Late Pleistocene of Africa and Eurasia: evidence from Nazlet Khater, Peştera cu Oase, and Hofmeyr. *American Journal of Physical Anthropology* 140: 347–58.

DE HEINZELIN, J. (1957). *Les Fouilles d'Ishango*. Brussels: Institut des Parcs Nationaux du Congo Belge.

—— (1962). Ishango. *Scientific American* 26: 105–16.

DUPONT, L. M., JAHNS, S., MARRET, F., and NING, S. (2000). Vegetation change in equatorial West Africa: time-slices for the last 150 ka. *Palaeogeography, Palaeoclimatology, Palaeoecology* 155: 95–122.

EGGERT, M. (1993). Central Africa and the archaeology of the equatorial rainforest: reflections on some major topics. In T. Shaw. P. J. J. Sinclair, B. Andah, and A. Okpoko (eds), *The Archaeology of Africa: Food, Metals and Towns*. London: Routledge, 289–329.

ELENGA, H., MALEY, J., VINCENS, A., and FARRERA, I. (2004). Palaeoenvironments, palaeoclimates and landscape development in Atlantic Equatorial Africa: a review of key sites covering the last 25 kyrs. In R. W. Battarbee, F. Gasse, and C. E. Stickley (eds), *Developments in Paleoenvironmental Research: Past Climate Variability through Europe and Africa*. Dordrecht: Kluwer, 181–98.

FEATHERS, J. K., and MIGLIORINI, E. (2001). Luminescence dating at Katanda: a reassessment. *Quaternary Science Reviews* 20: 961–6.

FIEDLER, L., and PREUSS, J. (1985). Stone tools from the Inner Zaïre Basin (Région de l'Équateur, Zaïre). *African Archaeological Review* 3: 179–87.

FOLEY, R. (1991). Hominids, hunters and hunter-gatherers: an evolutionary perspective. In T. Ingold, D. Riches, and J. Woodburn (eds), *Hunters and Gatherers: History, Evolution and Social Change*. Oxford: Berg, 207–21.

HUYLEBROUCK, D. (ed.) (2008). *Ishango, 22000 and 50 years Later: The Cradle of Mathematics?* Brussels: Koninklijke Vlaamse academie van Belgie voor wetenschapppen en kunsten.

KELLER, O. (2010). *Les Fables d'Ishango, ou l'Irrésistible Tentation de la Mathématique-Fiction.* http://www.bibnum.education.fr/files/Ishango-analyse.pdf

LANFRANCHI, R. (1991). Congo. In Lanfranchi and Clist (1991: 110–14).

—— and CLIST, B. (eds) (1991). *Aux Origines de l'Afrique Centrale.* Libreville: Ministère de la Coopération et du Développement.

LAVACHERY, P. (2001). The Holocene archaeological sequence of Shum Laka Rockshelter (Grassfields, Cameroon). *African Archaeological Review* 18: 213–47.

—— MACEACHERN, S., BOUIMON. T., et al. (2005). Komé to Ebomé: archaeological research for the Chad Export Project, 1999–2003. *Journal of African Archaeology* 3: 175–93.

LEBAMBA, J., VINCENS, A., and MALEY, J. (2010). Pollen, biomes, forest successions and climate at Lake Barombi Mbo (Cameroon) during the last *ca.* 33 000 cal yr BP: a numerical approach. *Climate of the Past Discussions* 6: 2703–40.

MALEY, J. (2004). Les variations de la végétation et de paléoenvironnements du domaine forestier africain au cours du Quaternaire récent. In J. Renault-Miskovsky and A. M. Semah (eds), *Guide de la Préhistoire Mondiale.* Paris: Artcom Errance, 143–78.

MERCADER, J. (2002a). Forest people: the role of African rainforests in human evolution and dispersal. *Evolutionary Anthropology* 11: 117–24.

—— (2002b). Foragers of the Congo: the early settlement of the Ituri forest. In J. Mercader (ed.), *Under the Canopy: The Archaeology of Tropical Rainforests.* Piscataway, NJ: Rutgers University Press, 93–116.

—— and BROOKS, A. S. (2001). Across forests and savannas: Later Stone Age assemblages from Ituri and Semliki, Democratic Republic of Congo. *Journal of Anthropological Research* 5: 197–217.

—— and MARTí, R. (1999). Middle Stone Age sites in the tropical forests of Equatorial Guinea. *Nyame Akuma* 51: 14–24.

—— —— (2002). The Middle Stone Age occupation of Atlantic Central Africa: new evidence from Equatorial Guinea and Cameroon. In J. Mercader (ed.), *Under the Canopy: The Archaeology of Tropical Rainforests.* Piscataway, NJ: Rutgers University Press, 64–92.

—— —— MARTíNEZ, J. L., and BROOKS, A. (2002). The nature of 'stone-lines' in the African Quaternary record: archaeological resolution at the rainforest site of Mosumu, Equatorial Guinea. *Quaternary International* 89: 71–96.

—— RUNGE, F., VRYDAGHS, L., DOUTRELEPONT, H., EWANGO, C. E. N., JUAN-TRESSERAS, J., (2000). Phytoliths from archaeological sites in the tropical forest of Ituri, Democratic Republic of Congo. *Quaternary Research* 54: 102–12.

NGOMANDA, A., NEUMANN, K., SCHWEIZER, A., and MALEY, J. (2009). Seasonality change and the third millennium BP rainforest crisis in southern Cameroon (Central Africa). *Quaternary Research* 71: 307–18.

PATIN, E., LAVAL, G., BARREIRO, L. B., SALAS, A, SEMINO, O., SANTACHIARA-BENERECETTI, S., KIDD, K. K., KIDD, J. R., VAN DER VEEN, L., HOMBERT, J.-M., GESSAIN, A., FROMENT, A., BAHUCHET, S., HEYER, E. and QUINTANA-MURCI, L. (2009). Inferring the demographic history of African farmers and Pygmy hunter–gatherers using a multilocus Resequencing Data Set. *PLoS Genetics* 5(4). doi:10.1371/journal.pgen.1000448.

PETERS, J. (1990). Late Pleistocene hunter-gatherers at Ishango (eastern Zaire): the faunal evidence. *Revue de Paléobiologie* 9: 73–112.

PLANQUAERT, M. (1976). Les industries préhistoriques du Moyen-Kwango (République du Zaïre). *Africa-Tervuren* 22: 19–27.

QUICKERT, N. A., GODFREY-SMITH, D. I. and CASEY, J. L. (2003). Optical and thermoluminescence dating of Middle Stone Age and Kintampo bearing sediments at Birimi, a multi-component archaeological site in Ghana. *Quaternary Science Reviews* 22: 1291–7.

QUINTANA-MURCI, L., QUACH, H., HARMANT, C., et al. (2008). Maternal traces of deep common ancestry and asymmetric gene flow between Pygmy hunter-gatherers and Bantu-speaking farmers. *Proceedings of the National Academy of Sciences (USA)* 105: 1596–1601.

RIBOT, I., ORBAN, R., and DE MARET, P. (2001). *The Prehistoric Burials of Shum Laka Rockshelter (North-West Cameroon)*. Tervuren: Royal Museum for Central Africa.

ROTS, V., and VAN PEER, P. (2006). Early evidence of complexity in lithic economy: core-axe production, hafting and use at Late Middle Pleistocene site 8-B-11, Sai Island (Sudan). *Journal of Archaeological Science* 33: 360–71.

RUNGE, F. (2007). Des déserts et des forêts: histoire du paysage et du climat de l'Afrique Centrale au Quaternaire Supérieur/Of deserts and forests: Late Quaternary landscape and climate history of Central Africa. *Geo-Eco-Trop* 31: 1–18.

SHAW, T., and DANIELS, S. G. H. (1984). Excavations at Iwo Eleru, Ondo State, Nigeria. *West African Journal of Archaeology* 14: 1–129.

SORIANO, S., RASSE, M., TRIBOLO, C., and HUYSECOM, E. (2010). Ounjougou (Pays Dogon, Mali): une séquence à haute résolution pour le Paléolithique moyen d'Afrique sahélienne. *Afrique, Archéologie et Arts* 6: 49–66.

TAYLOR, N. (2011). The origins of hunting and gathering in the Congo Basin: a perspective on the Middle Stone Age Lupemban industry. *Before Farming* 2011(1): article 6.

TAYLOR, D. M., MARCHANT, R., and HAMILTON, A. C. (2001). A reanalysis and interpretation of palynological data from the Kalambo Falls prehistoric site. In J. D. Clark (ed.), *Kalambo Falls Prehistoric Site*, vol. 3: *The Earlier Cultures: Middle and Earlier Stone Age*. Cambridge: Cambridge University Press, 66–81.

TWIESSELMAN, F. (1958). *Les Ossements Humains du Gîte Mésolithique d'Ishango*. Brussels: Institut des Parcs Nationaux du Congo Belge.

VAN NEER, W. (1989). *Contribution to the Archaeozoology of Central Africa*. Tervuren: Royal Museum for Central Africa.

—— and LANFRANCHI, R. (1985). Etude de la faune découverte dans l'abri tshitolien de Ntadi Yomba (République Populaire du Congo). *L'Anthropologie* 89: 351–64.

VAN NOTEN, F. (1977). Excavations at Matupi Cave. *Antiquity* 51: 35–40.

—— (ed.) (1982). *The Archaeology of Central Africa*. Graz: Akademische Druck- und Verlaganstalt.

VERDU, P., AUSTERLITZ, F., ESTOUP, A., et al. (2009). Origins and genetic diversity of Pygmy hunter-gatherers from western Central Africa. *Current Biology* 19: 312–18.

—— WOTZKA. H.P. (1995). *Studien zur Archäologie des zentral-afrikanischen Regenwaldes*. Frankfurt: Heinrich Barth Institut.

YELLEN, J. E. (1996). Behavioural and taphonomic patterning at Katanda 9: a Middle Stone Age Site, Kivu Province, Zaire. *Journal of Archaeological Science* 23: 915–32.

—— (1998). Barbed bone points: tradition and continuity in Saharan and sub-Saharan Africa. *African Archaeological Review* 15: 173–98.

—— BROOKS, A. S., CORNELISSEN, E., MEHLMAN, M. J., and STEWART, K. (1995). A Middle Stone Age worked bone industry from Katanda, Upper Semliki Valley, Zaire. *Science* 268: 553–6.

CHAPTER 29

HUNTER-GATHERERS OF THE NILE VALLEY AND THE SAHARA BEFORE 12,000 YEARS AGO

ELENA GARCEA

INTRODUCTION

THE Sahara has not always been a desert, but arid episodes have been recurrent. Consequently, human populations living there must have been able to deal with an unpredictable environment—a task, or rather a complexity of tasks, that not all could perform in all periods. Given this caveat, the immediate questions that may come to mind are 'who' succeeded and 'when' such accomplishments occurred. This chapter focuses on North Africa's crucial role in the development of its regional identities, and the spread of Anatomically Modern Humans out of Africa.

With regards to the first question, 'who?', no human fossils dating to the Middle and Upper Pleistocene have been found in the Sahara, though a few come from the Blue Nile (Singa) and northeastern Libya (Haua Fteah) and others, more numerous, from the Maghreb. The association of similar *Homo sapiens* fossils from Jebel Irhoud, Morocco (Hublin 2002), and Haua Fteah (Hublin 2000), associated with similar Early Middle Stone Age (MSA) industries, suggests that the makers of the Early MSA assemblages found in the Sahara were anatomically modern populations that spread across the Sahara before reaching the African Mediterranean coasts. The second question, 'when?', can be answered with recently dated, or redated, fossil remains and archaeological units that provide consistent chronological frameworks. Modern humans appeared in North Africa around, or slightly after, 200 kya and biological evidence suggests continuity between the makers of the Early MSA and those of the late MSA Aterian complexes (Hublin 2000). Furthermore, human fossils from Jebel Irhoud show morphological similarities with other remains outside Africa, in particular those from Skhul and Qafzeh, Israel (Hublin 2000), supporting the hypothesis that these populations were among the authors of the out-of-Africa dispersal (Lahr, Ch. 23 above). The latest concurring chronological, archaeological, environmental and palaeontological data give North Africa an unprecedented role in scenarios of modern human origins and out-of-Africa dispersals (Hublin and McPherron 2012; Barham, Ch. 24 above).

CLIMATE CHANGE AND ENVIRONMENT EVOLUTION

Humid phases in North Africa were favoured by increased rainfall, supported by a northward shift of the Intertropical Convergence Zone, moving beyond the central Saharan watershed (around 21°N) and bringing summer monsoon and flooding as far as the Mediterranean (Rohling et al. 2002; Smith 2010). The period 420–200 kya was a time with long humid inter-glacials, when very large lakes and river systems developed even in the Sahara. Lake Megafezzan, in southwestern Libya, reached a maximum size of 135,000 km^2 at this time, never attained again even during the moist conditions of Marine Isotope Stage (MIS) 5 (Drake et al. 2008). This very wet period was followed by MIS 6 (186–127 kya), which on the contrary brought extremely cold and dry conditions (Castañeda et al. 2009). The spread of modern humans in North Africa occurred at the onset of MIS 6, or slightly before, but not during the major development of Lake Megafezzan. The newcomers, who originated in East Africa, must have had remarkable skills to expand along the Nile Valley and into the Sahara and adapt to a variable, unreliable environment and survive through MIS 6.

A humid phase at the transition from MIS 6 to MIS 5e is recorded in the Egyptian Western Desert, at Kharga and Kurkur Oases, the Great Sand Sea, Bir Sahara, and Bir Tarfawi (Fig. 29.1).

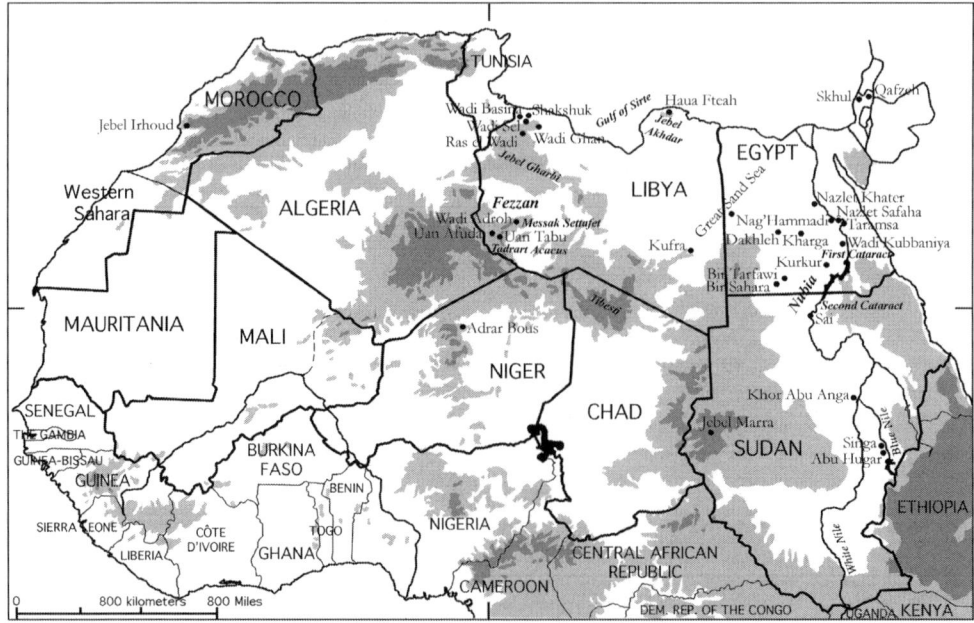

FIG. 29.1 Map of sites mentioned in Chapter 29.

Lacustrine sediments show the existence of active palaeolakes in central and southern Egypt and northern and western Sudan: the Dakhleh lake reached an extent of 1,700 km^2. In Libya, numerous small lakes and a few larger ones (1,000–2,000 km^2) replaced the giant Lake Megafezzan, and others formed in the Gulf of Sirte and the Kufrah basin (Drake et al. 2008). Lake Megafezzan still existed, but was now much smaller (1,400–1,730 km^2; Smith 2010). Marine records show that a presently extinct river system existed in Libya around 124–119 kya, stretching from the southern Sahara to the Mediterranean sea. Enhanced humidity was recorded at c. 124 (MIS 5e), 102 (MIS 5c), and 81 kya (MIS 5a), and, in the Sahara, supported an increase of C3 vegetation, including trees and cool-season grasses and sedges, which are typical of the Mediterranean and tropical rainforests, during MIS 5 (120–110 kya) and MIS 3 (50–45 kya) (Castañeda et al. 2009). In spite of these lacustrine and riverine resources, the climate remained semi-arid during the entire MIS 5. Later, during MIS 4 and 3, semi-desert and desert conditions prevailed, but enclaves of forest survived in a few areas that acted as refugia, particularly during MIS 3.

In northwestern Libya, during the arid phases of MIS 4 and 2, springs were a critical water resource as they could outflow along faults also during hyper-arid periods and thus created locally favourable conditions (Garcea and Giraudi 2006). Groundwater activity continued, even though the Sahara expanded towards the Mediterranean coast (Giraudi 2005). Otherwise, humid episodes were favoured by increases in winter moisture on the Mediterranean littoral (Smith 2010), which could have created corridors and refugia for human populations (Bailey et al. 2008). Only a few other restricted areas remained more humid, including the Jebel Marra, in western Sudan, where high lake levels were dated between 23.5 and 16.0 kya, and the Tibesti mountains, in the southern Sahara, where two lacustrine phases occurred during the Last Glacial Maximum (LGM), at 24.0–18.7 and 18.3–14.6 kya (Williams 2009). In fact, although the LGM was cold and arid, it was not as severely dry as MIS 6 and 4 (Castañeda et al. 2009).

OUT OF NORTH AFRICA

The Out-of-Africa Anatomically Modern Human dispersal into Eurasia is currently the most accredited model (Stringer 2001). It is known as 'Out of Africa 2' because it represents the second major wave of hominin emigration outside Africa, following the first by *Homo erectus*, or *ergaster*, over a million years ago (Out of Africa 1; Foley, Ch. 20 above). Lahr (Ch. 23 above) considers the route(s) and timing of this expansion in more detail, but it is worth noting here that while most scholars tend to search for 'the' route out of Africa, a multiple-dispersal perspective may be a more accurate interpretation of events (Garcea 2010a). This chapter deals with the northern route, but palaeoenvironmental, stratigraphical, and archaeological evidence also support a southern route from the Horn of Africa across the Bab el Mandab Strait into the Arabian peninsula (Armitage et al. 2011).

The second dispersal from North Africa, undertaken by *Homo sapiens*, began around 130 kya when vegetation and drainage networks could sustain potential migratory corridors (Smith 2010). According to Drake et al. (2008), a series of lake basins across the Sahara

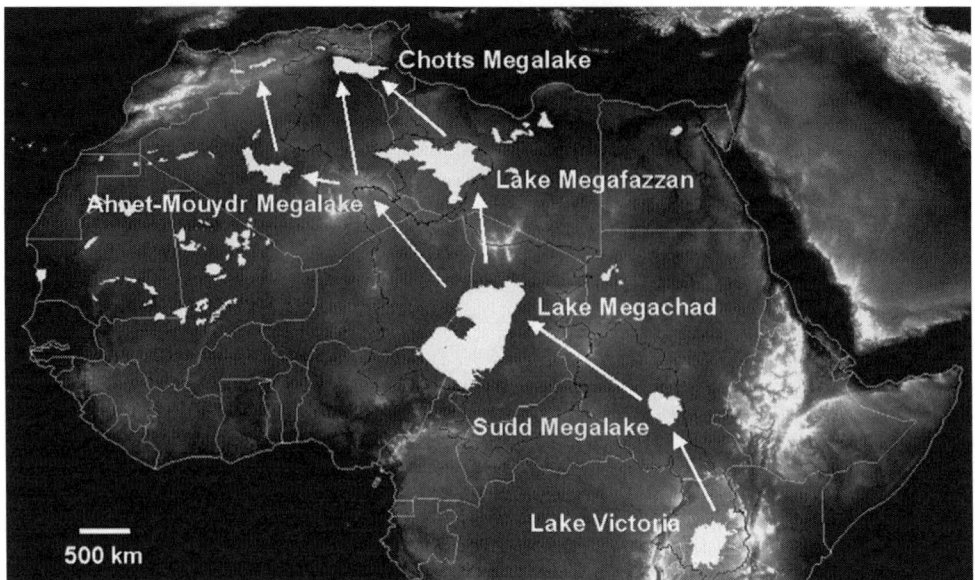

FIG. 29.2 Map of Saharan megalake basins and possible routes out of Africa outlined by Drake et al. (2008: fig. 15) (reproduced with permission of Elsevier).

offered a network of corridors connecting East Africa to the Mediterranean (Fig. 29.2). Furthermore, eastern Libya's Kufrah River was either another corridor towards the Mediterranean (Paillou et al. 2009) or formed an inland delta, comparable to, but larger than, today's Okavango Delta (Drake et al. 2008). Migrations out of Africa were also favoured by the water resources of the Levant, which, after the end of MIS 5, were richer than those of North Africa (Smith 2010).

The Out of Africa 2 movement exhibited two temporally distinct events, one occurring between 130 and 80 kya, the other post-dating 50 kya. This interruption was probably due to both an abrupt, cold and dry climate change that affected the southeastern Mediterranean basin at the onset of MIS 4, and technological improvements that came into play in the second phase. As these two events were significantly different, I suggest distinguishing them as 'Out of Africa 2a' and 'Out of Africa 2b' (Garcea 2010a). The Out of Africa 2a movement failed because the African *H. sapiens* were not adjusted like the Levantine Neanderthals to cope with the cold climate of MIS 4, and became extinct in the Levant around 75 kya (Bailey et al. 2008). Conversely, the Out of Africa 2b migration succeeded thanks to the re-established favourable conditions of MIS 3 and new technologies, including projectile armatures that were more effective than thrusting spears and allowed hunting from greater distances with decreased risk for the hunters. This new equipment, which favoured subsistence diversification, systematic exploitation of small prey, and successful hunting of large game, and had further effects on social organization, may have been a key factor in the ultimately successful expansion of *Homo sapiens* beyond Africa (Shea 2010).

During the Upper Pleistocene, hunter-gatherers changed their means of subsistence and enhanced their adaptive skills. These changes, which were not simply ecological or

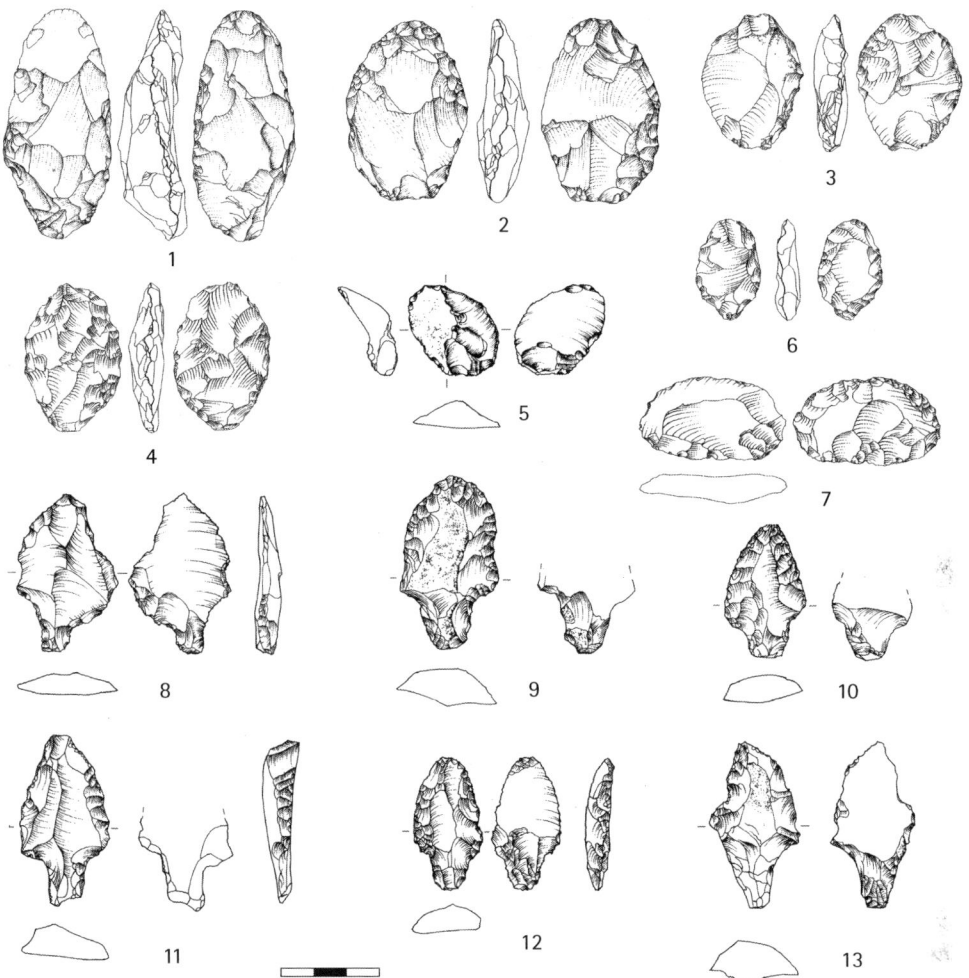

FIG. 29.3 Aterian tools from the Jebel Gharbi, Libya.

technological but primarily social and cultural, foreshadow a distinctive feature of some early and middle Holocene foragers: social and economic intensification. The onset of distinct regional identities seems to be related to increased intensification, and already within the MSA, stone point production displays culturally significant interregional stylistic variability.

One widespread regional unit typifying North Africa is the Aterian, comprising tanged and ventrally retouched points, bulbar basal thinning, and bifacial retouching (Fig. 29.3). Its almost complete absence from the Nile Valley, where other complexes exist (see below), confirms the potential use of different migration routes out of Africa (Osborne et al. 2008). The earliest dates, from Morocco, place the Aterian at the beginning of the Upper Pleistocene, around 122–121 kya (Barton et al. 2009), and a wide time-span (~150 to ~45 kya) is assumed for it at Adrar Bous, Niger (Williams 2008). All the most recently obtained dates concur in the Aterian disappearing by 40 kya at the latest.

The Mediterranean coast and its
surroundings

Africanist archaeologists have often ignored North Africa, whereas Eurocentric scholars annexed it to Europe and the Levant (Garcea 2012). Brooks et al. (2006), McBrearty (2007), and Barham and Mitchell (2008) rightly point out that African MSA toolkits differ from European Middle Palaeolithic ones principally in the insignificance of side-scrapers and the relevance of points. According to them, MSA points, used as projectile armatures of composite tools, express cognitive sophistication, and their regional diversification evidences a structured social organization of their anatomically modern makers. As North Africa's MSA inhabitants also produced points, they shared with their East, Central, and southern African contemporaries comparable technological solutions to resource acquisition and processing. Within this all-African panorama, North Africa expressed its identities with characteristic cultural units.

The prehistory of the African Mediterranean coast is best known from current investigations in and around two mountain ranges in northern Libya: the Jebel Gharbi to the west and the Jebel Akhdar to the east. In the former, sediments at Ras el Wadi with Early MSA material date to 146 kya, and this cultural unit probably appeared in the region even before that date. A gap seems to separate the Early MSA from the Aterian, which is provisionally dated by U/Th at 60 ± 20 kya. Aterian occupations lasted a long time in the Jebel Gharbi, until c. 40 kya, and at Wadi Sel, Site SJ-02–68, they show distinct phases in two overlying layers (Barich et al. 2006).

The Jebel Gharbi offered a particularly favourable habitat because active faults opened outlets of underground aquifers, providing water even during dry periods (Garcea and Giraudi 2006). The period between roughly 40 and 20 kya recorded a demographic contraction in most of North Africa. However, the mountain ranges of northern Libya were not totally abandoned. Soils including Aterian artefacts formed during MIS 3 and are dated to c. 50 kya at Shakshuk West. Another wet episode, < 32–31 kya at Ras el Wadi, and 30–28 kya at Shakshuk East, corresponded to the beginning of the Lower Later Stone Age (LSA). This unit exhibits both continuity with previous Aterian traditions and evidence for cultural change. Continuities are apparent in hafting technique and settlement system, while innovations comprise blade technology, microlithic technology for the production of composite tools, and the use of the soft hammer and the punch techniques.

Subsequent reductions in temperature (including the LGM) that decreased evaporation resulted in positive water balances in local drainage systems at Ras el Wadi and Wadi Basina, with the last humid episode of the Pleistocene recorded in the Wadi Ghan and at Shakshuk West around 13 kya (Garcea and Giraudi 2006). Across North Africa the cultural units associated with these late Pleistocene humid phases have been variously named: Upper LSA, Iberomaurusian or Eastern Oranian in Libya, Late Upper Palaeolithic or Iberomaurusian in Morocco, and Late Palaeolithic in the Nile Valley. In spite of the confusing terminologies, these units shared similar chronologies and technological solutions. In the Jebel Gharbi, the Upper LSA dated from 20 kya at Shakshuk (Site SJ-00–56) lasted until 13 kya in the Wadi Ghan (Site SG-99–41).

In northeastern Libya, the Jebel Akhdar is particularly known for the Haua Fteah cave, first excavated by McBurney (1967) and reinvestigated by Barker (Barker et al. 2009). This cave has yielded the longest (14 m deep) sequence of human occupation in North Africa beginning with the Early MSA and continuing into historic periods. New investigations have confirmed that the Early MSA occupation started during MIS 6 and continued through the temperate last interglacial (MIS 5) and the succeeding cold interval (MIS 4). It is still unclear whether the Aterian is attested at Haua Fteah, or when the MSA ended there, but MSA arte-facts are in any case more common in the desert and peri-desert south of the Jebel Akhdar than in the mountain range. The earliest (Lower) LSA industry, on the other hand, the Dabban, is concentrated in the drainage headwaters of the Jebel Akhdar. New radiocarbon dates for Dabban layers at Haua Fteah place it between 31 and 22 kya. The Upper LSA is then represented by the Eastern Oranian, now redated to between 16 and 13 kya.

THE NILE VALLEY

Numerous Late Acheulean artefacts suggest a considerable hominin presence in the Nile Valley during the late Middle Pleistocene. While in the Egyptian stretch of the valley none is *in situ* (Vermeersch 2010), Site 8-B-11, on Sai Island, Sudanese Nubia, preserves a remarkably long stratigraphic sequence linking North Africa and sub-Saharan Africa, with both Late Acheulean materials and Sangoan, Lupemban, and Early Nubian Complex assemblages that represent different MSA units. The Late Acheulean, dating from 200 kya, appears in levels interstratified with others including Sangoan materials. Comparison with Herto, Ethiopia, suggests a replacement of the local Late Acheulean pre-*sapiens* population by a more behav-iourally modern Sangoan-making *H. sapiens* population practising hafting of core-axes, using non-local raw materials, and manufacturing of grinding stones for the preparation of pig-ments or vegetal material (Van Peer and Vermeersch 2007). Comparable replacements are attested at Khor Abu Anga and Abu Hugar, south of Sai Island, consistent with a southeastern and upstream origin for these Sangoan groups. Also relevant, though sadly unassociated with any artefacts, is the calvaria of an archaic form of *H. sapiens* from Singa on the Blue Nile, near Abu Hugar, dated to 133 kya (McDermott et al. 1996).

In the Egyptian Nile Valley, artefacts at flint and chert quarries document a long period of occupation, beginning with the Lupemban and followed by the Nubian and Lower Nile Valley Complexes, but living sites remain virtually unknown. Like the Aterian, which is absent from the Nile Valley, except at E-78–11 in Wadi Kubbaniya west of Aswan, the Nubian and Lower Nile Valley Complexes represent regional adaptations. The Early Nubian Complex, found in Lower Egypt, Nubia, the Eastern Sahara, and the Red Sea Mountains, used the Levallois and Nubian core reduction methods with a considerable production of points, whereas the Lower Nile Valley Complex, which is common in Upper Egypt and later in date, employed the classical Levallois technique and lacked points (Van Peer 1998). Towards the end of MIS 5, the Nubian Complex evolved into the Late Nubian Complex, which no longer included bifacial foliates, while the Late Lower Nile Valley Complex devel-oped sophisticated quarrying strategies, as shown at the large (3000 m²) site of Nazlet Safaha (Vermeersch 2002).

As in the Maghreb, MIS 4 signalled a phase of demographic reduction in the Nile Valley due to intermittent discharge of the river. Nevertheless, this was a time of major conceptual changes in the handling of raw materials. Core reduction shifted from exploitation of surfaces to exploitation of volumes, suggesting more efficient core management, with blade production, first indicated in the Taramsan technocomplex. At Taramsa 1, a rare burial occurs near a lithic workshop and dates to *c.* 75 kya (Vermeersch 2010). As this individual shows similar features to early anatomically modern humans from the Levant, it can be correlated with the first phase of the Out of Africa 2 movement, i.e. Out of Africa 2a.

In the Lower LSA (Upper Palaeolithic), a highly sophisticated system of chert exploitation is evident at Nazlet Khater 4, where underground mine galleries were built and exploited from about 40 kya. Vermeersch (2010) suggests that at this time sand dunes dammed the Nile River, obstructing its flow and forming lakes, such as Nag'Hammadi in Upper Egypt. Fishing groups settled along the banks of these lakes until the end of the Pleistocene, when Lakes Victoria and Tana started to feed the Nile again, causing a catastrophic dam breach that led to massive depopulation of the valley. While not agreeing on an interruption in the flow of the main Nile, Schild and Wendorf (2010) do admit a highly seasonal drainage with sediment aggradation in rainy episodes and formation of isolated water pools.

During MIS 2, the Nile Valley was the only habitable stretch of land in the hyperarid deserts to either side. A plethora of techno-complexes is distinguished on technological, geographic and chronological criteria, but also because of different research histories. The First Cataract seems to have acted as a cultural border, separating techno-complexes to the south, linked with more southerly regions, from those to the north, which were connected with Mediterranean traditions. Retaining the Levallois technique, the Shuwikhatian (Upper Egypt, *c.* 25 kya) and the Gemaian (Lower Nubia, ≥ 22 kya) represent the earliest Upper LSA units. The Isnan (Upper Egypt, 14–12 kya) and the Arkinian (Lower Nubia, *c.* 12.8–10 kya) are the latest complexes. Perhaps because people were exploiting seasonal (possibly scarce) resources in small, isolated groups, many techno-complexes developed in relatively limited areas (Schild and Wendorf 2010). Similarities between two other industries, the Fakhurian (≥ 24.4–22.5 kya) and the Kubbaniyan (21–19.5 kya) and the Iberomaurusian of the Maghreb (Barton and Bouzouggar, Ch. 30 below) may reflect connections along the Mediterranean coast given the uninhabitable nature of the Sahara from the end of the Aterian until the beginning of the Holocene (Schild and Wendorf 2010).

THE WESTERN DESERT

Caton-Thompson (1946, 1952) was the first to recognize a long cultural sequence at Kharga and Dakhleh Oases in Egypt's Western Desert. People living there shared many traits with Saharan populations and also had access to the Nile Valley (Kleindienst 1998). The Balat Unit at Dakhleh and the Dharb el-Gaga Unit at Kharga belong to the Late Acheulean (> 300 kya), while the Early MSA (220–125 kya) is represented by the Gifata Unit and the succeeding Teneida Unit at Dakhleh and the Refuf (Lower Levalloisian) and the Mata'na Units (Upper Levalloisian) at Kharga (Kleindienst 2006). Thereafter, numerous sites at both oases document the Aterian. Kharga is the easternmost area where it is abundant, while sites at Dakhleh include both workshops and living sites dating to between < 100 and > 40 kya (Hawkins and

Kleindienst 2002). Aterian populations appear to have been present during drier spells than their Early MSA predecessors (Hawkins 2012). Another unit, named Sheikh Mabruk Unit at Dakhleh and Khargan Unit at Kharga, post-dates the Aterian (Wiseman 1999).

Further south at Bir Tarfawi different phases of formation of permanent lakes were identified and mostly date to cold, dry intervals in MIS 6 (140–130 kya) and MIS 5a/4 (84–60 kya). Another minor lake formed during the Last Glacial, although the last substantial humid event ended before 60 kya. The only phase of lake formation that can be related to a humid spell is that of 114 kya. Early MSA sites containing foliate pieces appeared before the earliest lake *c.* 160 kya and persisted in association with the lakes of MIS 5, whereas the Aterian, found in surface sites overlying sediments dated to *c.* 70 kya, was separated from it by a period of hyper-aridity (Wendorf et al. 1993). Bir Tarfawi and another site, Bir Sahara East, confirm that MSA and particularly Aterian populations could survive in semi-arid to arid environments, where water was available. Given limitations to movement under severe conditions, raw material availability was the second important factor: good quality quartzitic sandstone was accessible 3 km east of Tarfawi (Wendorf et al. 1993).

SITES IN THE SAHARA

In addition to the Egyptian oases, Libya's central Sahara has been thoroughly investigated. Systematic surveys show that Early MSA assemblages were more common in open-air contexts than in rockshelters and caves, which were intensively used in later periods. The frequency of ephemeral sites suggests a high-mobility pattern, including plains, mountain ranges, and plateaux. An Early MSA assemblage from Wadi Adroh, in the Messak Settafet plateau, resembles the White Lake phase at Bir Tarfawi dated *c.* 160 kya (Van Peer 2001). Uan Afuda, in the Tadrart Acacus range, is one of the rare sites where a few MSA artefacts occur below a Holocene stratigraphic series; they are dated with TL and OSL around 70 kya (Martini et al. 1998).

Stratified Aterian sites are extremely rare in the Sahara. One exception is the Uan Tabu rockshelter, in the Tadrart Acacus where a rich Aterian assemblage is separated from overlying Holocene deposits by an erosional unconformity surface. Its upper layer is OSL-dated to 61 ± 10 kya. The remarkable thickness (1 m) of this Aterian deposit and the high quantity of its retouched tools suggest that Uan Tabu was a living site where a wide range of activities were performed over a long time (Garcea 2001, 2010b). Numerous other sites throughout the Sahara also indicate low mobility and intensive exploitation of local resources, suggesting, as in Egypt's Western Desert, that Aterian foragers developed strategies to adapt to arid environments by settling near the few available water sources (Garcea 2012).

We do not know when exactly the Aterian occupation ended in the Sahara, but a date of 60 kya for the upper horizon at Uan Tabu is probably not far from the time when people had to leave the desert because it had become too dry for their survival. A long period of abandonment followed, lasting until the early Holocene, when new occupants returned, often at the same sites (Barich, Ch. 31 below). The reappropriation of the Aterian settlement system by Holocene foragers hints that the intensification strategies put in place by their predecessors appeared still successful after many millennia.

REFERENCES

ARMITAGE, S. J., JASIM, S. A., MARKS, A. E., PARKER, A. G., USIK, V. I., and UERPMANN, H.-P. (2011). The southern route 'out of Africa': evidence for an early expansion of modern humans into Arabia. *Science* 331: 453–6.

BAILEY, G., CARRIÓN, J. S., FA, D. A., FINLAYSON, C., FINLAYSON, G., and RODRÍGUEZ-VIDAL, J. (2008). The coastal shelf of the Mediterranean and beyond: corridor and refugium for human populations in the Pleistocene. *Quaternary Science Reviews* 27: 2095–9.

BARHAM, L. S., and MITCHELL, P. J. (2008). *The First Africans: African Archaeology from the Earliest Toolmakers to Most Recent Foragers*. Cambridge: Cambridge University Press.

BARICH, B. E., GARCEA, E. A. A., and GIRAUDI, C. (2006). Between the Mediterranean and the Sahara: geoarchaeological reconnaissance in the Jebel Gharbi, Libya. *Antiquity* 80: 567–82.

BARKER, G., ANTONIADOU, A., BARTON, H., et al. (2009). The Cyrenaican Prehistory Project 2009: the third season of investigations of the Haua Fteah cave and its landscape, and further results from the 2007–2008 fieldwork. *Libyan Studies* 40: 1–41.

BARTON, R. N. E., BOUZOUGGAR, A., COLLCUTT, S., SCHWENNINGER, J.-L., and CLARK-BALZAN, L. (2009). OSL dating of the Aterian levels at Dar es-Soltan I (Rabat, Morocco) and implications for the dispersal of modern *Homo sapiens*. *Quaternary Science Reviews* 28: 1914–31.

BROOKS, A. S., NEVELL, L., YELLEN, J. E., and HARTMAN, G. (2006). Projectile technology of the African MSA: implications for modern human origins. In E. Hovers and S. Kuhn (eds), *Transitions Before the Transition: Evolution and Stability in the Middle Paleolithic and Middle Stone Age*. New York: Springer, 233–56.

CASTAÑEDA, I. S., MULITZA, S., SCHEFUSS, E., et al. (2009). Wet phases in the Sahara/Sahel region and human migration patterns in North Africa. *Proceedings of the National Academy of Sciences (USA)* 106: 20159–63.

CATON-THOMPSON, G. (1946). *The Aterian Industry: Its Place and Significance in the Palaeolithic World*. London: Royal Anthropological Institute of Great Britain and Ireland.

—— (1952). *Kharga Oasis in Prehistory*. London: Athlone Press.

DRAKE, N. A., EL-HAWAT, A. S., TURNER, P., et al. (2008). Palaeohydrology of the Fazzan Basin and surrounding regions: the last 7 million years. *Palaeogeography, Palaeoclimatology, Palaeoecology* 263: 131–45.

GARCEA, E. A. A. (ed.) (2001). *Uan Tabu in the Settlement History of the Libyan Sahara*. Florence: All'Insegna del Giglio.

—— (2010a). Bridging the gap between in and out of Africa. In E. A. A. Garcea (ed.), *South-Eastern Mediterranean Peoples Between 130,000 and 10,000 Years Ago*. Oxford: Oxbow Books, 174–82.

—— (2010b). The spread of Aterian peoples in North Africa. In E. A. A. Garcea (ed.), *South-Eastern Mediterranean Peoples Between 130,000 and 10,000 Years Ago*. Oxford: Oxbow Books, 37–53.

—— (2012). Modern human desert adaptations: a Libyan perspective on the Aterian complex. In J.-J. Hublin and S. P. McPherron (eds), *Modern Origins: A North African Perspective*. New York: Springer, 127–42.

—— and GIRAUDI, C. (2006). Late Quaternary human settlement patterning in the Jebel Gharbi, northwestern Libya. *Journal of Human Evolution* 51: 411–21.

GIRAUDI, C. (2005). Eolian sand in the peridesert North-Western Libya and implications for Late Pleistocene and Holocene Sahara expansion. *Palaeogeography, Palaeoclimatology, Palaeoecology* 218: 161–73.

HAWKINS, A. L. (2012). The Aterian of the oases of the Western Desert of Egypt: adaptation to changing climatic conditions? In Hublin and McPherron (2012: 157–75).

—— and KLEINDIENST, M. R. (2002). Lithic raw material usages during the Middle Stone Age at Dakhleh Oasis, Egypt. *Geoarchaeology* 17: 601–24.

HUBLIN, J.-J. (2000). Modern–nonmodern hominid interactions: a Mediterranean perspective. In O. Bar-Yosef and D. Pilbeam (eds), *The Geography of Neanderthals and Modern Humans in Europe and the Greater Mediterranean*. Cambridge: Peabody Museum, 157–82.

—— (2002). Northwestern African Middle Pleistocene hominids and their bearing on the emergence of *Homo sapiens*. In L. S. Barham and K. Robson-Brown (eds), *Human Roots: Africa and Asia in the Middle Pleistocene*. Bristol: Western Academic & Specialist Press, 99–121.

—— and McPHERRON, S. P. (eds) (2012). *Modern Origins: A North African Perspective*. New York: Springer.

KLEINDIENST, M. R. (1998). What is the Aterian? The view from Dakhleh Oasis and the Western Desert, Egypt. In M. Marlow and A. J. Mills (eds), *The Oasis Paper 1: The Proceedings of the First Conference of the Dakhleh Oasis Project*. Oxford: Oxbow Books, 1–14.

—— (2006). On naming things: behavioral changes in the Later Middle to Earlier Late Pleistocene, viewed from the Eastern Sahara. In E. Hovers and S. Kuhn (eds), *Transitions Before the Transition: Evolution and Stability in the Middle Paleolithic and Middle Stone Age*. New York: Springer, 13–28.

MARTINI, M., SIBILIA, E., ZELASCHI, C., et al. (1998). TL and OSL dating of fossil dune sand in the Uan Afuda and Uan Tabu rockshelters, Tadrart Acacus (Libyan Sahara). In M. Cremaschi and S. Di Lernia (eds), *Wadi Teshuinat: Palaeoenvironment and Prehistory in South-Western Fezzan (Libyan Sahara)*. Florence: All'Insegna del Giglio, 67–72.

McBREARTY, S. (2007). Down with the revolution. In P. Mellars, K. Boyle, O. Bar-Yosef, and C. Stringer (eds), *Rethinking the Human Revolution*. Cambridge: McDonald Institute for Archaeological Research, 133–51.

McBURNEY, C. B. M. (1967). *The Haua Fteah (Cyrenaica) and the Stone Age in the South-East Mediterranean*. Cambridge: Cambridge University Press.

McDERMOTT, F., STRINGER, C. B., GRÜN, R., WILLIAMS, C. T., DIN, V. K., and HAWKESWORTH, C. J. (1996). New Late-Pleistocene uranium-thorium and ESR dates for the Singa hominid (Sudan). *Journal of Human Evolution* 31: 507–16.

OSBORNE, A. H., VANCE, D., ROHLING, E. J., BARTON, N., ROGERSON, M., and FELLO, N. (2008). A humid corridor across the Sahara for the migration of early modern humans out of Africa 120,000 years ago. *Proceedings of the National Academy of Sciences (USA)* 105: 16444–7.

PAILLOU, P., SCHUSTER, M., TOOTH, S., et al. (2009). Mapping of a major paleodrainage system in eastern Libya using orbital imaging radar: the Kufra River. *Earth and Planetary Science Letters* 277: 327–33.

ROHLING, E. J., CANE, T. R., COOKE, S., et al. (2002). African monsoon variability during the previous interglacial maximum. *Earth and Planetary Science Letters* 202: 61–75.

SCHILD, R., and WENDORF, F. (2010). Late Palaeolithic hunter-gatherers in the Nile Valley of Nubia and Upper Egypt. In E. A. A. Garcea (ed.), *South-Eastern Mediterranean Peoples Between 130,000 and 10,000 Years Ago*. Oxford: Oxbow Books, 89–125.

SHEA, J. J. (2010). Neanderthals and early *Homo sapiens* in the Levant. In E. A. A. Garcea (ed.), *South-Eastern Mediterranean Peoples Between 130,000 and 10,000 Years Ago*. Oxford: Oxbow Books, 126–43.

SMITH, J. R. (2010). Palaeoenvironments of eastern North Africa and the Levant in the Late Pleistocene. In E. A. A. Garcea (ed.), *South-Eastern Mediterranean Peoples Between 130,000 and 10,000 Years Ago*. Oxford: Oxbow Books, 6–17.

STRINGER, C. B. (2001). Modern human origins: distinguishing the models. *African Archaeological Review* 18: 67–75.

VAN PEER, P. (1998). The Nile corridor and the Out-of-Africa model: an examination of the archaeological record. *Current Anthropology* 39: S115–49.

——. (2001). Observations on the Palaeolithic of the south-western Fezzan and thoughts on the origin of the Aterian. In Garcea (2001: 51–62).

—— and VERMEERSCH, P. M. (2007). The place of northeast Africa in the early history of modern humans: new data and interpretations on the Middle Stone Age. In P. Mellars, K. Boyle, O. Bar-Yosef, and C. B. Stringer (eds), *Rethinking the Human Revolution*. Cambridge: McDonald Institute for Archaeological Research, 187–98.

VERMEERSCH, P. M. (ed.) (2002). *Palaeolithic Quarrying Sites in Upper and Middle Egypt*. Leuven: Leuven University Press.

—— (2010). Middle and Upper Palaeolithic in the Egyptian Nile Valley. In E. A. A. Garcea (ed.), *South-Eastern Mediterranean Peoples Between 130,000 and 10,000 Years Ago*. Oxford: Oxbow Books, 66–88.

WENDORF, F., CLOSE, A. E., and associates (1993). *Egypt during the Last Interglacial: The Middle Palaeolithic of Bir Tarfawi and Bir Sahara East*. New York: Plenum Press.

WILLIAMS, M. A. J. (2008). Geology, geomorphology and prehistoric environments. In D. Gifford-Gonzalez (ed.), *Adrar Bous: Archaeology of a Central Saharan Granitic Ring Complex in Niger*. Tervuren: Royal Museum for Central Africa, 25–54.

—— (2009). Late Pleistocene and Holocene environments in the Nile basin. *Global and Planetary Change* 69: 1–5.

WISEMAN, M. (1999). Late Pleistocene prehistory in the Dakhleh Oasis. In C. S. Churcher and A. J. Mills (eds), *Reports from the Survey in the Dakhleh Oasis, Western Desert of Egypt, 1977–1987*. Oxford: Oxbow Books, 109–15.

CHAPTER 30

HUNTER-GATHERERS OF THE MAGHREB 25,000–6,000 YEARS AGO

NICK BARTON AND ABDELJALIL BOUZOUGGAR

INTRODUCTION

IN broad terms, in North Africa the period 25–6000 BP encompassed both later Palaeolithic foraging societies and the transition to early farming ways of life. This rather banal description belies the fact that within this time span major changes occurred in climate and environment and shifts in human behaviour were neither gradual nor unilinear. Barker (2006) has proposed, for example, that hunter-gatherer societies in this part of Africa underwent a major transformation from highly mobile to more sedentary economies, and that key changes attributed to the Neolithic were already embedded in foraging systems well before the advent of farming. Some of the assumptions behind these ideas are examined here.

PALAEOENVIRONMENTAL BACKGROUND

The Maghreb is a semi-arid upland area of northwest Africa defined geographically by the high ranges of the Atlas Mountains in the south and the Mediterranean in the north. Although much of the northern Maghreb is characterized by Mediterranean forests, less dense woodland, and scrub, areas in the south support a drier steppic and semi-desert vegetation (Blondel and Aronson 1999). Variability in altitude, temperature and rainfall give the Maghreb a distinctive range of habitats supporting a rich flora and fauna.

Marine cores (e.g. MD95–2043 from the Alboran Sea) record past climatic fluctuations and reveal periods of intense cooling (Heinrich Events) when cold polar surface waters entered the western Mediterranean (Moreno et al. 2004). They can also be correlated with the Greenland ice $\partial^{18}O$ core sequence, which reveals high-frequency, abrupt climatic oscillations

(Dansgaard-Oeschger (D-O) cycles), including a marked cooling during the Last Glacial Maximum (LGM) *c.* 21–19,000 BP. Climate modelling suggests that colder and more vigorous northwesterly winds swept across the Mediterranean in the cooler D-O episodes, producing major aridity in North Africa, especially during the LGM. Pollen trapped in marine cores suggests a link between such cold, dry conditions, and a rise in steppic species (*Artemisia*, Chenopodiaceae, and *Ephedra*), and, conversely increases in deciduous and evergreen oaks when climate improved (Sánchez Goñi et al. 2002).

Much the same pattern is reflected in land pollen records, although they cover shorter periods than the marine cores and are mostly Holocene in age (Reille 1977; Lamb et al. 1989; Lamb and van der Kaars 1995). One notable exception is that from Lake Ifrah in the Middle Atlas, which spans the period 25–5000 BP (Cheddadi et al. 2009). It confirms that LGM temperatures were 15°C cooler than now, with very low average annual precipitation of around 300 mm. Such conditions were even too cold and dry for cedar (*Cedrus atlantica*), which only rose in values between 19,000 and 16,000 BP. Although deciduous type oaks also grew during this period, it was only after the beginning of the Holocene that January temperatures rose to +5°C, allowing a vast expansion of these species and the decline of cedar, which is intolerant of a very warm climate (Cheddadi et al. 2009). A shorter core from Chataigneraie, Algeria, provides a similar picture, indicating a major presence of cedar at 11,000 BP followed by a marked decline as temperatures rose after 9000 BP (Salamani 1993).

Other proxy records come from caves in the form of hearth charcoals and microfauna. For example, at Kehf el Hammar in northern Morocco the presence of juniper, deciduous oak, and pine in levels that also produced gerbils (*Gerbillus* sp.) and jirds (*Meriones* sp.) suggests that climate was semi-arid and cooler *c.* 14,000 BP (Barton et al. 2005). In eastern Morocco, at Grotte des Pigeons (Taforalt), a fine-grained sediment record reveals a noticeable increase in Aleppo pine (*Pinus halepensis*) and evergreen oaks (*Quercus*) from 14,000 BP with a virtual absence of cedar until a resurgence in layers younger than 10,900 BP (Bouzouggar et al. 2008). Generalizing from these observations, the severely arid climate of the LGM was probably followed by gradually rising temperatures after 19,000 BP and a more intense warming with greater humidity from 13,000 BP. Cooler conditions resumed between 11,000 and 9,000 BP, with a subsequent rise in temperatures and moisture that reached a peak sometime before 6500 BP.

EPIPALAEOLITHIC

Age, origins and distribution

The Iberomaurusian represents the earliest epipalaeolithic/Later Stone Age technology in the Maghreb following the Middle Palaeolithic (Lubell 2001; Bouzouggar et al. 2008). Since its initial use by Pallary in 1909 to describe lithic industries dominated by microlithic backed bladelets, different names have been given to it in different areas, such as 'Oranian', 'Mouillian', 'Eastern Iberomaurusian', or 'Eastern Oranian' (Bouzouggar et al. 2008). Nowadays, Iberomaurusian bladelet technology is known from Morocco (10°W) in the west as far east as Cyrenaica (22°E), but apparently excludes parts of western Libya (Lubell 2001). Its southerly extent is not well understood, but it is known from at least 33°N on Morocco's Atlantic

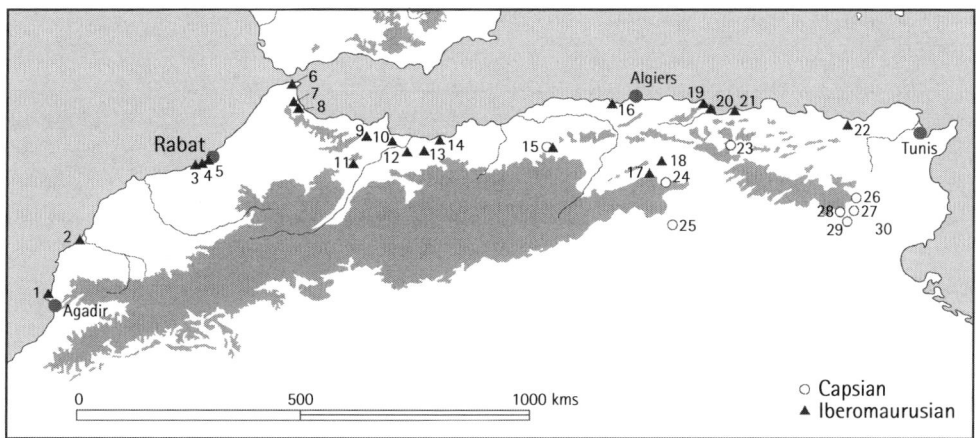

FIG. 30.1 Distribution of major Iberomaurusian and Capsian sites in the Maghreb: 1 Cap Rhir; 2 El Khenzira; 3 Contrebandiers; 4 El Harhoura II; 5 Dar es-Soltan I; 6 Ghar Cahal; 7 Kehf El Hammar; 8 Hattab II; 9 Ifri El Baroud; 10 Ifri n'Ammar; 11 Kifan Bel Ghomari; 12 Taforalt; 13 Le Mouillah; 14 Rachgoun; 15 Columnata; 16 Rassel; 17 El Hamel; 18 El-Onçor; 19 Afalou; 20 Tamar Hat; 21 Taza; 22 Ouchtata; 23 Medjez II; 24 Dakhlat es-Saâdane; 25 Aïn Naga; 26 Khanguet El-Mouhaâd; 27 Aïn Misteheyia; 28 Relilaï; 29 Kef Zoura D; 30 El Mekta.

coast (Grébénart 1975; Fig. 30.1). Sites are often concentrated fairly close to the present coastline (Brahimi 1970), but increasing numbers are also known well inland (Lubell et al. 1984; Close and Wendorf 1990).

Following a recent review, it now seems unlikely that the Iberomaurusian is much older than 18,000 BP in the western Maghreb (Bouzouggar et al. 2008), although a charcoal date (MC-822) of 20,600 ± 500 BP for Layer 84/5 at Tamar Hat, Algeria (Saxon et al. 1974), suggests it may be slightly older further east. The lack of an obvious precursor in the region has led to the view that there must have been a break with preceding Middle Palaeolithic/MSA technologies (Close and Wendorf 1990: 43). At Taforalt the Iberomaurusian replaces a non-Levallois flake industry, but the situation may vary regionally. Blade tools with a minimum age of 21,920 ± 110 BP (OxA-11872) underlie the Iberomaurusian at Kehf el Hammar (Barton et al. 2005), while in Cyrenaica there is implied continuity with the underlying Dabban Later Stone Age blade industry (Barker et al. 2009).

The Iberomaurusian's origins thus remain obscure, although the idea that it was part of the same cultural processes that resulted in the widespread appearance of backed bladelet industries across much of North Africa and the Near East c. 23,000–20,000 BP (Vermeersch 1992; Godfrey-Smith et al. 2003; Goring-Morris and Belfer-Cohen 2003) seems the most logical. In this respect it would offer broad comparisons with parallel developments in southern Africa (Klein 2009). However, whether it originated from the east along the Mediterranean littoral or via a more southerly route is still open to doubt. A more radical proposal for links with Epigravettian industries in Italy (Camps 1974; Ferembach 1985; Debénath 2003) is unlikely because of chronological discrepancies (Zampetti 1989) and the apparent absence of such assemblages in Sicily (Kozlowski 2005: 530).

The dating of the younger end of the Iberomaurusian is also not without controversy, but it appears to have persisted until at least 10,935 ± 40 BP (OxA-13479; Barton et al. 2007) at Taforalt, while continuation into the early Holocene also seems likely given dates from Ifri el-Baroud also in eastern Morocco (9677 ± 60 BP Bln-4755; Moser 2003: 100) and Ghar Cahal in the Tingitane peninsula of northern Morocco (9470 ± 55 BP, OxA-11321; Bouzouggar et al. 2008). More contentious is a single thermoluminescence date of 8900 ± 1100 BP associated with an Iberomaurusian human burial from Hattab II (Barton et al. 2008) and discussed further below.

Human associations

Some of the earliest examples of human cemeteries are found in the epipalaeolithic of the Maghreb, including Afalou-bou-Rhummel (Arambourg et al. 1934; Hachi 1996, 2003) and Columnata (Chamla 1970) in Algeria and Taforalt in Morocco (Ferembach et al. 1962). Though anatomically modern, the people buried in these cemeteries were very robustly built and are grouped together under the term Mechta-Afalou (Camps 1974). Excavations at Taforalt recovered a remarkable assemblage of partial and whole skeletons from a series of burials in horizons towards the rear of the cave with Iberomaurusian bone and lithic artefacts (Ferembach et al. 1962). Although the burials were never fully described, recent work at the site (Humphrey et al. 2012) and on the museum collections (Mariotti et al. 2009, Belcastro et al. 2010) has added considerably more detail. Stratigraphic considerations make a maximum age of 12,675 ± 50 BP (OxA-13477) likely, broadly consistent with dates from Ifri n' Ammar in the Eastern Rif (Moser 2003) and Afalou Bou Rhummel (Hachi et al. 2002).

A most distinctive aspect of these Iberomaurusian burials is the evidence they provide for the practice of dental evulsion, i.e. the deliberate removal of healthy teeth, usually the incisors, during an individual's lifetime (Fig. 30.2). Numerous reasons have been proposed for this custom including group identification, decoration, and rites of passage linked to

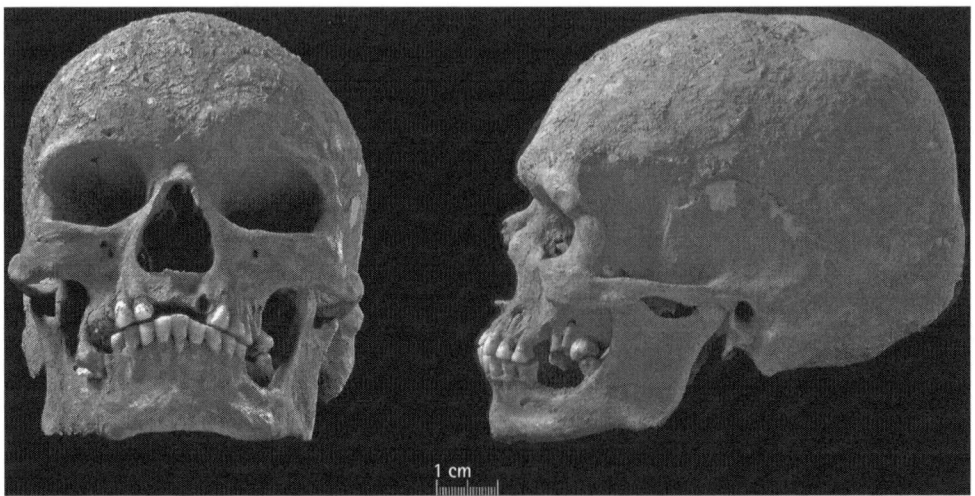

FIG. 30.2 Anterior and left lateral views of the Hattab II skull showing dental evulsion of the upper incisors (photograph, Ian Cartwright, copyright Institute of Archaeology, University of Oxford).

puberty or marriage (Humphrey and Bocaege 2008). Whatever the explanation, the practice must have been visually very striking, leading Close and Wendorf (1990) to suggest that the Maghrebi Iberomaurusians had a strong, socially shared identity that may have lasted over 10,000 years.

Material culture

Iberomaurusian lithic inventories are often dominated by microlithic backed bladelets (Fig. 30.3) that generally make up 40–80% of the total tool assemblage (Camps 1974: 63). Chronological subdivisions are not obvious, though at some eastern Moroccan sites (Ifri n'Ammar and Taforalt) slightly higher numbers of retouched blades and bladelets with fine marginal (Ouchtata) retouch have been observed in the earlier Iberomaurusian layers. Later increases in microlithic backed points are reflected in the appearance of the microburin technique. The only other change, noted at Ifri n' Ammar, is the occurrence of small geometric microliths (mainly crescents) in sediments dating to c. 11,009 ± 144 BP (Erl-4399; Moser 2003). Further studies are ongoing at Taforalt to examine whether there is any consistency in the overall pattern of change.

The Iberomaurusian has a well-developed bone technology with conspicuous evidence for the manufacture of small points, *poinçons*, and *sagaies*, plus examples of decorated bone at a number of sites, including Taforalt and Ghar Cahal (Bouzouggar et al. 2008). Also relatively common are perforated marine shell ornaments. Their presence at sites sometimes >40 km inland suggests contact with the coast throughout this period. Ostrich eggshell is also often abundant, though beads are uncommon so it is likely that such items are food residues or fragments of water containers.

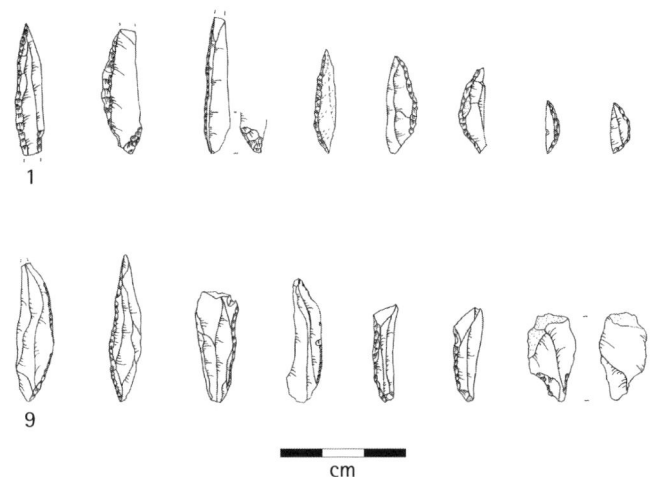

FIG. 30.3 Iberomaurusian lithic microliths, Taforalt Cave, Morocco. Grey Series (upper row) 1–6 pointed and curve-backed bladelets, 7–8 small segments. Yellow Series (lower row) 9–12 curve-backed and marginally backed forms (9, 12 Ouchtata retouch), 13–14 La Mouillah points, 15 large distal microburin (drawn by Joshua Hogue).

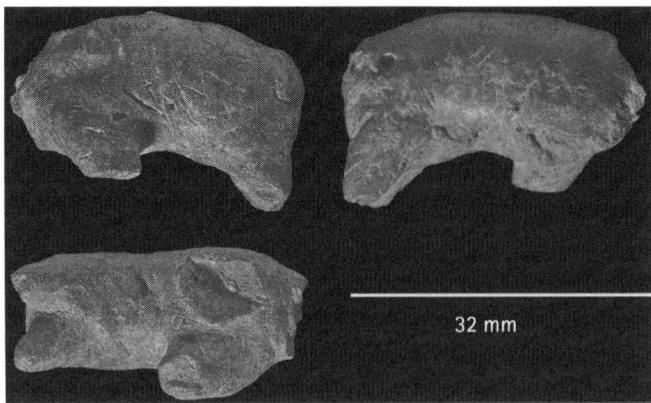

FIG. 30.4 Afalou modelled clay zoomorphic figure, Algeria (Ref. F3 Af89 CII 191 21.08.89). Reproduced with permission from Hachi 2003 (photograph, Ian Cartwright, copyright Institute of Archaeology, University of Oxford).

Besides rare examples of engraved bone, decorated art is represented by engravings on stone, including the famous motif of a Barbary sheep on a small cobble from Taforalt (Roche 1963). Cobbles painted with red pigment have also been reported at Ifri n'Ammar. Other enigmatic and highly distinctive decorated items are made from modelled clay, most spectacularly at Afalou (Fig. 30.4), where anthropomorphic and animal figures were fashioned out of different clays and then intentionally baked at temperatures of 500–800°C (Hachi et al. 2002). Although similar figurative art has only been recognized at Tamar Hat, also in Algeria (Saxon et al. 1974), small balls of modelled clay are known from Ifri n' Ammar (Moser 2003).

Subsistence and behaviour

At many sites Barbary sheep (*Ammotragus lervia*) are a major component of the large vertebrate fauna, with charring, calcining, and cutmarks demonstrating their origin as food refuse. The bones of these animals also sometimes make up a very high proportion of the total ungulate fauna (94 per cent at Tamar Hat), leading to speculation that they were herded rather than hunted (Saxon et al. 1974). Preferential selection of young males and older females at Tamar Hat supposedly supported this conclusion, but later work demonstrated underlying taphonomic problems with this argument (Close and Wendorf 1990). Nevertheless, the presence of such large numbers of a single species certainly suggests specialized forms of hunting, and this seems borne out by other studies.

Similar claims for intensification in the use of plant foods and the gathering of wild grasses (Lubell et al. 1984) have yet to be substantiated. Whether these were early experiments in controlling resources that were later abandoned is unclear, but it is interesting to consider the conditions that may have given rise to such attempts. One theory sees attempts to control wild Barbary sheep as a risk-reducing strategy in response to increased regional aridity (Barker 2006), but one abandoned in favour of earlier foraging practices once wetter conditions had been re-established (cf. di Lernia, Ch. 36 below). However, whether such domestication experiments were widespread or localized, and whether they were specifically driven by climatic change or other factors, remains controversial.

Table 30.1 Iberomaurusian AMS determinations on single charcoals from Ghar Cahal (GC), Kehf el Hammar (KEH), and Taforalt Sector 8 (TAF). All dates are presented in stratigraphic order. Cal BP AMS determinations are corrected using the IntCal04 calibration curve (Reimer et al. 2004) and the OxCal 4.0 calibration software (Bronk Ramsey 2001)

Laboratory code	Layer	Site identifier	Charcoal species	$\partial^{13}C$	AMS date BP (uncalibrated)	AMS cal BP (95.4%)
OxA-11321	10	GC 01/4/10	Phillyrea/Rhamnus	−24.0	9,470 ± 55	11071–10573
OxA-11322	12	GC 01/4/12	Phillyrea/Rhamnus	−25.5	11,180 ± 65	13209–12941
OxA-11323	12	GC 01/4/12	Phillyrea/Rhamnus	−24.9	11,125 ± 65	13159–12909
OxA-11926	3	KEH 5/H8/3	Pinus	−24.1	13,345 ± 50	16232–15480
OxA-11927	4a	KEH 2A/H8/4A	Pinus	−21.9	13,805 ± 55	16832–16081
OxA-11929	5	KEH 59/H8/5	Juniperus/Tetraclinus	−21.0	14,110 ± 60	17194–16391
OxA-11928	6	KEH 56/H8/6	Pinus	−23.4	14,005 ± 55	17054–16298
OxA-11417	6 base	KEH 23/63–72	Leguminosae	−22.9	15,940 ± 80	19335–18954
OxA-13479	G88–200	TAF03/200	Pinus sp.	−23.8	10,935 ± 40	12940–12840
OxA-13480	G89–202	TAF03/202	Pinus sp.	−23.3	10,950 ± 45	12960–12839
OxA-13516	G89–203	TAF03/203	Pinus sp.	−23.9	11,065 ± 45	13083–12899
OxA-13517	G90–204	TAF03/204	Dicotyledon (unidentified)	−26.8	10,990 ± 45	13034–12857
OxA-13477	G97–36	TAF03/36	Conifer	−21.4	12,675 ± 50	15190–14704
OxA-13478	G99–90	TAF03/90	Juniperus/Tetraclinus	−21.2	12,495 ± 50	14945–14240
OxA-16267	SNC/18cm	TAF06/5415	Tetraclinus articulata	−21.1	14,005 ± 60	17058–16294
OxA-16268	SNC/27cm	TAF06/5416	Tetraclinus articulata	−22.5	14,515 ± 60	17879–17022
OxA-16272	SNC/37cm	TAF06/5421	Quercus sp.	−23.3	14,630 ± 60	17995–17219
OxA-16269	SNC/58cm	TAF06/5417	Juniperus sp.	−21.1	15,790 ± 60	19146–18867
OxA-16270	SNC/70cm	TAF06/5418	Pinus sp.	−23.6	16,285 ± 65	19555–19230
OxA-16242	SNC/78cm	TAF06/5419	Dicotyledon (unidentified)	−24.8	16,630 ± 75*	19940–19535
OxA-16273	SNC/86cm	TAF06-5422	Pinus sp.	−23.6	17,515 ± 75	21033–20410

* Low carbon yield.

A related question concerns the apparently synchronous occurrence of large-scale midden deposits in caves across the western Maghreb around 13,000 BP. These horizons, which seem to mark a significant change in subsistence activities and a diversification in resource exploitation, contain large numbers of edible land molluscs, paralleling the slightly later Capsian *escargotières* of Algeria and Tunisia. Lubell (2004) suggests that they formed an important part of the diet and were perhaps even deliberately husbanded. As new dates (especially those from Taforalt; Bouzouggar et al. 2008; Table 30.1) indicate, this was also the period in which large planned cemeteries make an appearance, although it is still uncertain whether these phenomena were connected or even contemporaneous. Further studies currently in progress will help throw light on the nature of the specific changes at 13,000 BP, and on whether these led to reduced mobility and more sedentary behaviour.

THE CAPSIAN

In Algeria and Tunisia, the Capsian industry followed the Iberomaurusian (Lubell 2001). Its lithic assemblages too are based on bladelet production and contain many backed tools. After long debate its two sub-divisions, the Typical Capsian and the Upper Capsian (Vaufrey (1936), are now thought to be chronologically successive (Jackes and Lubell 2008). The main distinction is that the Upper Capsian has more geometric microliths, plus pressure-flaked bladelets (Tixier 1976; Sheppard 1987; Rahmani 2004). Pressure-flaked blades are absent so far in the Iberomaurusian of Morocco, but do occur there in some Neolithic assemblages, as at Kaf Taht el Ghar. However, no Capsian assemblage of either variant has yet been formally recognised in Morocco. The earliest dates for the Typical Capsian fall in the range 9400–9100 BP, with the transition to the Upper Capsian around 8200 BP (Jackes and Lubell 2001). Additional diagnostic attributes include ostrich eggshell and marine shell beads, plus a variety of bone tools and decorated bone and shell artefacts (Lubell 2001). As in the later Iberomaurusian, the Capsian is also characterized by large middens (*escargotières*) made up of tens of thousands of land-snail shells. Unlike any of the earlier middens, however, those of the Capsian often consist of visible mounds at inland, open-air localities. Most of the human remains from Capsian have been excavated from these *escargotières* (Lubell 2001). Dental evulsion is not as prevalent as in the Iberomaurusian and, where present, significantly more common amongst females (Humphrey and Bocaege 2008). This suggests increased regional variability in this practice after about 9500 BP.

THE NEOLITHIC AND ISSUES OF CONTINUITY

Despite claims for the precocious appearance of cereals in aceramic cultural contexts in Morocco (Ballouche and Marinval 2003; Daugas et al. 2008), it now seems clear that the Neolithic was intrusive in much of the Maghreb and followed a complex process of introduction (Linstädter 2003; Manen et al. 2007). According to this view the oldest Neolithic in western Morocco is no earlier than 5600 BP, and its domesticated plants and animals and

Table 30.2 List of dates associated with early Neolithic Cardial Ware in northern Morocco (after Bouzouggar et al. 2008) Cal BP and BC AMS determinations are corrected using the IntCal04 calibration curve (Reimer et al. 2004) and the OxCal 4.0 calibration software (Bronk Ramsey 2001)

Site	Material	TL dates		14C ages BP		Cal ages BP 95.4% probability	Cal ages BC 95.4% probability
Kaf Taht el Ghar	Charcoal			Ly-3821	6050 ± 120	7246–6656	5297–4707
	Charcoal			Ly-7288	6520 ± 80	7568–7290	5619–5341
	Wheat grain			Ly-971	6350 ± 80	7430–7028	5481–5079
	Ceramic	Cle-126	6780 ± 550				
	Ceramic	Cle-127	6350 ± 800				
	Ceramic	Cle-128	5800 ± 750				
	Ceramic	Cle-129	7200 ± 750				
Hassi Ouenzga	Charcoal			Bln-4956	6035 ± 47	7002–6748	5053–4799
	Charcoal			KIA-437	6290 ± 60	7414–7013	5465–5064
	Charcoal			KIA-436	6330 ± 60	7420–7160	5471–5211
	Charcoal			Bln-4957	6611 ± 40	7568–7436	5619–5487
	Charcoal			Bln-4913	6683 ± 48	7654–7464	5705–5515
	Charcoal			KIA-434	6770 ± 60	7722–7510	5773–5561
Achakar Idoles	Charcoal			Gif A-92332	5830 ± 80	6846–6444	4897–4495
	Ceramic	Cle-120	6900 ± 600				
El Khil C	Charcoal			Rabat-119	5720 ± 151	6894–6213	4945–4264
	Ceramic	Cle-118	6400 ± 500				
Wadi Tahadart	Marine shell			UQ-1556	5600 ± 200*	6858–5938	4909–3989
	Ceramic	Cle-122	6490 ± 560				
	Ceramic	Cle-123	5047 ± 580				
	Ceramic	Cle-124	6710 ± 510				
	Ceramic	Cle-125	6850 ± 520				
El Harhoura II	Human bone			Ly-2149	5980 ± 210	7317–6351	5368–4402
	Marine shell			Ly-1601	5800 ± 150*	6966–6296	5017–4347
Contrebandiers	Ceramic	Cle-136	6600 ± 600				

* without marine correction

Cardial impressed wares (Table 30.2) are likely to have been imported from southern Spain (Linstädter 2008); cemeteries as at Rouazi-Skhirat and El Kiffen contain single inhumations, often accompanied by pottery and personal items (Daugas 2002; Bouzouggar 2006). In contrast, in eastern Morocco and Algeria the process seems to have been delayed. Lithic traditions of 'epipalaeolithic type' persist at sites like Hassi Ouenzga with a gradual introduction of ceramics of more diversified and local types, followed later by the appearance of domesticated animals (Linstädter 2008).

Arguments for continuity between the latest forager societies and those of the Neolithic therefore rest on limited evidence. In northern and western Morocco there is a clear break in the cultural sequence. Changes such as the introduction of pressure flaking have only so far been registered in Neolithic Cardial ware assemblages such as Wadi Tahadart and Kaf That el Ghar (Bouzouggar 2006). It is nonetheless interesting that dental evulsion continued into the Neolithic (Camps 1974), albeit in regionally differentiated form: rare in the east of the Maghreb, it affected 71 per cent of individuals in the west, with males and females once more treated equally in this respect (Chamla 1978).

According to currently available evidence, we would therefore agree with those (e.g. Jackes and Lubell 2008) who argue for population and cultural continuity across the Pleistocene/Holocene divide. In the western Maghreb the Iberomaurusian continued well into the Holocene at sites like Hattab II, and hunter-gatherer archaeological signatures remained virtually unchanged from the late Pleistocene. Such epipalaeolithic ways of life, including substantial hunting of Barbary sheep, were only gradually replaced by an intrusive Neolithic economy based on cereal cultivation after 5600 BP.

REFERENCES

ARAMBOURG, C., BOULE, M., VALLOIS, H., and VERNEAU, R. (1934). *Les Grottes Paléolithiques des Beni-Segoual (Algérie)*. Algiers: Archives de l'Institut de Paléontologie Humaine.

BALLOUCHE, A., and MARINVAL, P., (2003). Données palynologiques et carpologiques sur la domestication des plantes et l'agriculture dans le Néolithique ancien du Maroc septentrional: le site de Kaf Taht el-Ghar. *Revue d'Archéométrie* 27: 49–54.

BARKER, G. (2006). *The Agricultural Revolution in Prehistory*. Oxford: Oxford University Press.

——— ANTONIADOU, A., BARTON, H., et al. (2009). The Cyrenaican Prehistory Project 2009: the third season of investigations of the Haua Fteah cave and its landscape, and further results from the 2007–2008 fieldwork. *Libyan Studies* 40: 55–94.

BARTON, R. N. E., BOUZOUGGAR, A., BRONK RAMSEY, C., et al. (2007). Abrupt climatic change and chronology of the Upper Palaeolithic in northern and eastern Morocco. In P. A. Mellars, K. Boyle, O. Bar-Yosef, and C. B. Stringer (eds), *Rethinking the Human Revolution: New Behavioural and Biological Perspectives on the Origins and Dispersal of Modern Humans*. Cambridge: McDonald Institute for Archaeological Research, 177–86.

——— ——— COLLCUTT, S. N., et al. (2005). The late upper Palaeolithic occupation of the Moroccan northwest Maghreb during the last glacial maximum. *African Archaeological Review* 22: 77–100.

——— HUMPHREY, L.T., et al. (2008). Human burial evidence from Hattab II Cave (Oued Laou-Tétuoan, Morocco) and the question of continuity in Late Pleistocene–Holocene mortuary practices in Northwest Africa. *Cambridge Archaeological Journal* 18: 195–214.

BELCASTRO, M. G., CONDEMI, S., and MARIOTTI, V. (2010). Funerary practices of the Iberomaurusian population of Taforalt (Tafoughalt, Morocco, 11–12,000 BP): the case of Grave XII. *Journal of Human Evolution* 58: 522–32.

BLONDEL, J., and ARONSON, J. (1999). *Biology and Wildlife of the Mediterranean Region.* Oxford: Oxford University Press.

BOUZOUGGAR, A. (2006). Le Néolithique de la région de Tanger-Tétouan: contribution de la technologie lithique. In D. Bernal, B. Raissouni, J. Ramos, and A. Bouzouggar (eds), *I Seminario Hispano-Marroqui de Especialización en Arqueología.* Cadiz: Universidad de Cádiz, 133–42.

——— BARTON, R. N. E., BLOCKLEY, S., et al. (2008). Re-evaluating the age of the Iberomaurusian in Morocco. *African Archaeological Review* 25: 3–19.

BRAHIMI, C. (1970). *L'Ibéromaurusian littoral de la région d'Alger.* Paris: Arts et Métiers Graphiques.

BRONK RAMSEY, C. (2001). Development of the radiocarbon calibration program OxCal. *Radiocarbon* 43: 355–63.

CAMPS, G. (1974). *Les Civilisations Préhistoriques de l'Afrique du Nord et du Sahara.* Paris: Doin.

CHAMLA, M. C. (1970). Les hommes epipaléolithiques de Columnata. *Mémoires du Centre de Recherches Anthropologiques Préhistoriques et Ethnographiques* 15: 5–115.

——— (1978). Le peuplement de l'Afrique du Nord de l'Épipaléolithique á l'époque actuelle. *L'Anthropologie* 82: 385–430.

CHEDDADI, R., FADY, B., FRANÇOIS, L., et al. (2009). Putative glacial refugia of *Cedus atlantica* deduced from Quaternary pollen records and modern genetic diversity. *Journal of Biogeography* 36: 1361–71.

CLOSE, A. E., and WENDORF, F. (1990). North Africa at 18 000 BP. In C. S. Gamble and O. Soffer (eds), *The World at 18 000 BP*, vol. 2: *Low Latitudes.* London: Unwin Hyman, 41–57.

DAUGAS, J.-P. (2002). Le Néolithique du Maroc: pour un modèle d'évolution chronologique et culturelle. *Bulletin d'Archéologie Marocaine* 19: 135–75.

——— EL IDRISSI, A., BALLOUCHE, A., MARINVAL, P., and OUCHAOU, B. (2008). Le Néolithique ancien au Maroc septentrional: données documentaires, sériation typochronologique et hypothèses génétiques. *Bulletin de la Société Préhistorique Française* 105: 787–812.

DÉBENATH, A. (2003). Le Paléolithique supérieur de Maghreb. *Praehistoria* 3: 259–80.

FEREMBACH, D. (1985). On the origin of the Iberomaurusians (Upper Palaeolithic: North Africa): a new hypothesis. *Journal of Human Evolution* 14: 393–7.

——— DASTUGUE, J., and POITRAT-TARGOWLA, M. J., (1962). *La Nécropole Épipaléolithique de Taforalt (Maroc oriental): étude des Squelettes Humaines.* Rabat: Edita Casablanca.

GODFREY-SMITH, D. I., VAUGHAN, K. B., GOPHER, A., and BARKAI, R. (2003). Direct luminescence chronology of the Epipalaeolithic Kebaran site of Nahal Hadera V, Israel. *Geoarchaeology* 18: 461–75.

GORING-MORRIS, A. N., and BELFER-COHEN, A. (eds) (2003). *More than Meets the Eye: Studies on Upper Palaeolithic Diversity in the Near East.* Oxford: Oxbow Books.

GRÉBÉNART, D. (1975). Une armature nouvelle de l'epipaléolithique saharien: la pointe de Tarfaya. *Bulletin de la Société Préhistorique Française* 75: 68–9.

HACHI, S. (1996). L'Ibéromaurusien, découverte des fouilles d'Afalou (Bédjaîa, Algérie). *L'Anthropologie* 100: 55–76.

——— (2003). *Les Cultures de l'Homme de Mechta-Afalou.* Algiers: CRAPE.

——— FRÖLICH, F., GENDRON-BADOU, A., DE LUMLEY, H., ROUBET, C., and ABDESSADOK, S., (2002). Figurines du Paléolithique supérieur en matière minérale plastique cuite d'Afalou

Bou Rhummel (Babors, Algérie): premières analyses par spectroscopie d'absorption infrarouge. *L'Anthropologie* 106: 57–97.

HUMPHREY, L. T., and BOCAEGE, E. (2008). Tooth evulsion in the Maghreb: chronological and geographical patterns. *African Archaeological Review* 25: 109–23.

——— BELLO. S., TURNER, E., BOUZOUGGAR, J., and BARTON, R. N.E. (2012). Iberomaurusian funerary behaviour: evidence from new excavations at grotte des pigeons, Taforalt, Morocco. *Journal of Human Evolution* 62: 261–73.

JACKES, M., and LUBELL, D. (2008). Early and middle Holocene environmental and Capsian cultural change: evidence from the Télidjène Basin, eastern Algeria. *African Archaeological Review* 25: 41–55.

KLEIN, R. G. (2009). *The Human Career*. Chicago: University of Chicago Press.

KOZLOWSKI, J. K. (2005). Paléolithique supérieur et Mésolithique en Méditerranée: cadre culturel. *L'Anthropologie* 109: 520–40.

LAMB, H.F., EICHER, U., and SWITSUR, V. R. (1989). An 18,000 year record of vegetation, lake-level and climatic change from Tigalmamine, Middle Atlas, Morocco. *Journal of Biogeography* 16: 65–74.

LAMB, H. F., and VAN DER KAARS, S. (1995). Vegetational response to Holocene climatic change: pollen and palaeolimnological data from the Middle Atlas, Morocco. *The Holocene* 5: 400–8.

LINSTÄDTER, J. (2003). Le site néolithique de l'abri d'Hassi Ouenzga (Rif Oriental, Maroc). *Beiträge zur Allgemeine und Vergleichende Archäologie* 23: 85–138.

——— (2008). The Epipalaeolithic–Neolithic transition in the Mediterranean region of northwest Africa. *Quartär* 55: 41–62.

LUBELL, D. (2001). Late Pleistocene–Early Holocene Maghreb. In P. N. Peregrine and M. Ember (eds), *The Encyclopedia of Prehistory*, vol. 1: *Africa*. New York: Kluwer, 129–49.

——— (2004). Prehistoric edible land snails in the circum-Mediterranean: the archaeological evidence. In J.-J. Brugal and J. Desse (eds), *Petits Animaux et Sociétés Humaines: du Complément Alimentaire aux Ressources Utilitaires*. Antibes: APDCA, 77–98.

——— SHEPPARD, P., and JACKES, M. (1984). Continuity in the epipalaeolithic of northern Africa with an emphasis on the Maghreb. *Advances in World Archaeology* 3: 143–91.

MANEN, C., MARCHAND, G., and CARVALHO, A. F. (2007). Le Néolithique ancient de la péninsule ibérique: vers une nouvelle évaluation du mirage africain? In J. Evin (ed.), *XXVIe Congrès Préhistorique de France*. Paris: Société Préhistorique Française, 133–51.

MARIOTTI, V. M., BONFIGLIOLI, B., FACCHINI, F., CONDEMI, S., and BELCASTRO, M. G. (2009). Funerary practices of the Iberomaurusian population of Taforalt (Tafoughalt; Morocco, 11–12,000 BP): new hypotheses based on a grave by grave skeletal inventory and evidence of deliberate human modification of the remains. *Journal of Human Evolution* 56: 340–54.

MORENO, A., CACHO, I., CANALS, M., GRIMALT, J. O., and SANCHEZVIDAL, A. (2004). Millennial scale variability in the productivity signal from the Alboran Sea record, Western Mediterranean Sea. *Palaeogeography, Palaeoclimatology, Palaeoecology* 211: 205–19.

MOSER, J. (2003). *La Grotte d'Ifri n'Ammar*, vol. 1: *L'Ibéromaurusien*. Cologne: Allgemeine und Vergleichende Archäologie-Forschungen.

RAHMANI, N. (2004). Technological and cultural change among the last hunter-gatherers of the Maghreb: the Capsian (10,000–6000 bp). *Journal of World Prehistory* 18: 57–105.

REILLE, M. (1977). Contribution pollenanalytique à l'histoire holocène de la végétation des montagnes du Rif (Maroc septentrional). *Supplementary Bulletin AFEQ (Association Française pour l'Étude du Quaternaire)* 50: 53–76.

REIMER, P. J., BAILLIE, M. G. L., BARD, E., et al. (2004). IntCal04 terrestrial radiocarbon age calibration, 0–26 cal kyr bp. *Radiocarbon* 46: 1029–58.

ROCHE, J. (1963). *L'Épipaléolithique Marocaine*. Lisbon: Fondation Calouste Gulbenkian.

SALAMANI, M. (1993). Premières données paléophytogéographiques du cèdre de l'Atlas (*Cedrus atlantica*) dans la région de Grande Kabylie (NE Algérie). *Palynosciences* 2: 147–55.

SANCHEZ GOÑI, M. F., CACHO, I., TURON, J. L., et al. (2002). Synchroneity between marine and terrestrial responses to millennial scale climatic variability during the last glacial period on the Mediterranean region. *Climate Dynamics* 19: 95–105.

SAXON, E. C., CLOSE, A., CLUZEL, C., MORSE, V., and SHACKLETON, N. J. (1974). Results of recent excavations at Tamar Hat. *Libyca* 22: 49–91.

SHEPPARD, P. J. (1987). *The Capsian of North Africa: Stylistic Variation in Stone Tool Assemblages*. Oxford: British Archaeological Reports.

TIXIER, J. (1976). L'industrie lithique capsienne de l'Aïn Dokkara (région de Tébessa, Algérie). *Libyca* 24: 21–54.

VAUFREY, R. (1936). Stratigraphie capsienne. *Światowit* 16: 15–34.

VERMEERSCH, P. M. 1992. The Upper and Late Palaeolithic of northern and eastern Africa. In F. Klees and R. Kuper (eds), *New Light on the Northeast African Past: Current Prehistoric Research*. Cologne: Heinrich-Barth-Institut, 100–53.

ZAMPETTI, D. (1989). La question des rapports entre la Sicilie et l'Afrique du Nord pendant le Paléolithique supérieur final. In I. Herschkovitz (ed.), *People and Culture in Change*. Oxford: British Archaeological Reports, 459–76.

CHAPTER 31

HUNTER-GATHERER-FISHERS OF THE SAHARA AND THE SAHEL 12,000–4,000 YEARS AGO

BARBARA E. BARICH

In the final and most arid phases of the Pleistocene, human occupation in the Sahara dramatically decreased and may even have been completely interrupted (Garcea, Ch. 29 above). This means that the groups present from the early Holocene onwards, in areas that are today desert, were immigrants, who reoccupied territories long abandoned as soon as more favourable climatic conditions permitted. The archaeological record documents the adaptations that their way of life underwent through successive episodes of early and mid-Holocene climate change. This chapter first, together with the relevant palaeoclimatic evidence, looks at three themes of general relevance for early/middle Holocene Saharan and Sahelian hunter-gatherer-fishers: microlithic toolkits; the innovation of pottery; and the development, at least in some areas, of a more sedentary pattern of settlement. It then examines the archaeological records of different parts of the Saharan/Sahelian region in more detail (Fig. 31.1).

MICROLITHIC ARTEFACTS

In parallel to the environmental changes, the end of the Pleistocene in northern Africa saw people producing a wider range of stone tools than previously, perhaps in part linked to exploitation of a greater variety of environmental niches caused by increases in population density. Along with retouching blades and microblades using pressure flaking and a greater use of bone tools, one clear technological development was the use of composite hafted tools. These involved hafting microliths (Fig. 31.2) in wooden or bone handles, thus achieving tools of more flexible design that were also easier to repair and involved less wastage of raw material compared to macrolithic implements. These composite artefacts were also very versatile, as

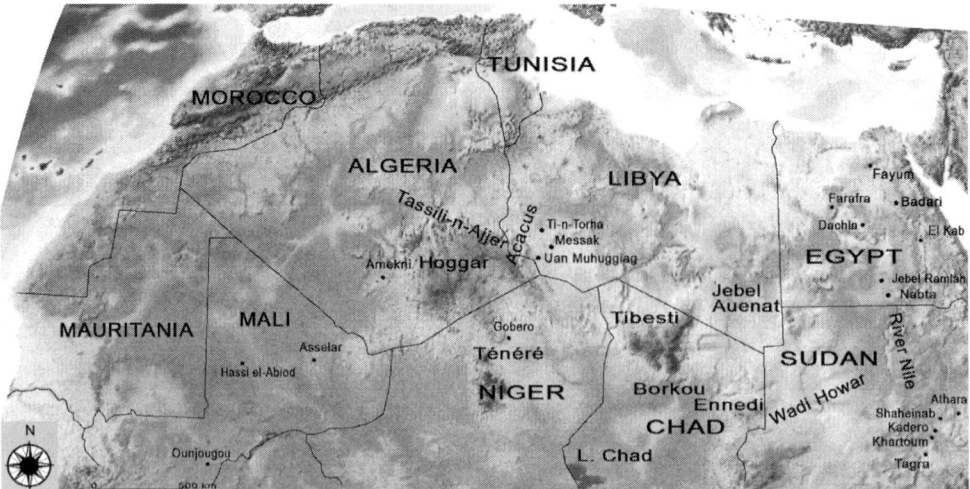

FIG. 31.1 Map of the Sahara and the Nile Valley with sites cited in Chapter 31 (produced by M. Pennacchioni according to the Digital Chart of the World, Elevation Data of Africa, US Geological Survey).

they could be used for a wide range of activities (e.g. a composite tool intended for use as a harpoon could, with modification of its handle, also have been used as a sickle for harvesting wild grasses). These tools could be produced quickly and their greater use was probably also linked to exploitation of more specialized, seasonally available resources, but their social significance should also be examined. The repetition of their production and their very widespread and long-lasting occurrence across the whole of North Africa must reflect quite precise rules. Within these social and technological contexts, the creation and negotiation of individual and group identities must have been a continual phenomenon through both material and immaterial actions. In this way, making backed microliths following precise standards may have been a means of subtle social transformation and affirmation (Close 2002).

POTTERY

If a microlithic technological tradition had already appeared in North Africa before the end of the Pleistocene, the same cannot be said for ceramics, which appear for the first time at the beginning of the Holocene. From the central Saharan massifs to Egypt's Western Desert, and further south to the Khartoum area on the Upper Nile, a largely homogeneous production of pottery was everywhere present in the ninth/tenth millennia BP (Haaland and Haaland, Ch. 37 below). Along with the examples recently discovered at Ounjougou in Mali (Huysecom et al. 2004), these are the oldest ceramics known in Africa and form one of the oldest pottery traditions in the world (Jesse 2010: table 1). From an economic point of view, however, the people making this pottery only exploited wild resources, a fact that has contributed to

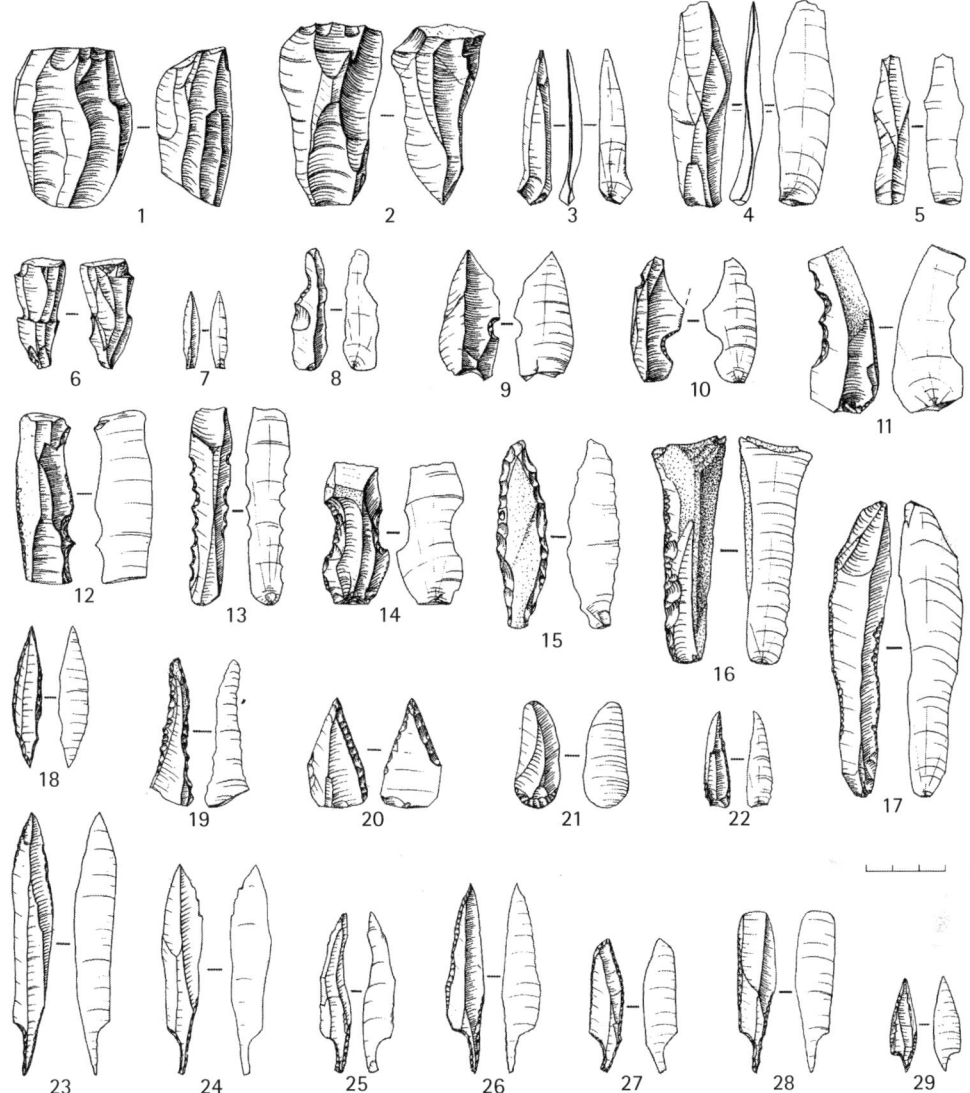

FIG. 31.2 Microlithic industry from Niger (from Barich 1998).

deconstructing a long-standing prejudice: that pottery in itself could indicate the 'Neolithic' status of an archaeological context.

In the first phase of their appearance, and at a time when ostrich eggshell containers had their widest distribution, ceramics were fairly rare. The contrast between the popularity of ostrich eggshells used as water containers and the rarity of pottery would seem to indicate that the former were essential to human groups (for water supply in an arid environment), while ceramics may not have played a practical role and were not related to economic needs (Barich 2010a: 150–51). The limited quantity of these early ceramics also shows that they were not in regular use in everyday activities, but rather suggests that their significance lies primarily in the symbolic and social spheres (see also Livingstone Smith et al. 2005). The exchange of ceramics (a rare and prestige good in those times) may have played an important role in consolidating relationships and solidarity between groups that needed to be able to rely on efficient networks of alliances and information as they moved into new territories, often perhaps for the first time, as climate ameliorated and the Sahara was gradually resettled. Physicochemical analyses suggest as much. At Nabta and Bir Kiseiba in Egypt's Western Desert, for instance, while most vessels were produced within each basin, some fragments demonstrate the movement of pots (or at least sherds) between them (Nelson 2001: 540).

These ceramics, the oldest of which from Niger date to the tenth millennium BP (Roset 2000: 268), were skilfully produced in a way that meant they were diversified both in terms of form, as well as decoration (Fig. 31.3). Large fragments allow the original forms to be reconstructed. There were two types of vessel: one with a round base and an open mouth, the other with a short neck and closed mouth; these are two classic models even among later groups in Niger. All these ancient ceramics are richly decorated, and the almost total absence of non-decorated fragments in the Egyptian and Nigerien collections suggests that the entire surface of the vessels was decorated. This was done before firing, with vessels later being exposed directly to the sun or fired under the sand using rudimentary kilns. In this case the absorption of carbon monoxide given off when near the heat source produced a brown surface colour. In some cases the surface was then burnished, obtaining a brilliant black colour. Decoration consisted of comb impressions, often using a rocker motion, with punched impressions in one or two areas, cord impressions, or more rarely incisions. Most

FIG. 31.3 Dotted wavy line pottery from Ti-n-Torha East, Libya (photograph, Barbara E. Barich).

of the decorative motifs belong to the wavy and, more broadly, the dotted wavy line family (the latter consisting of a series of parallel lines formed of points, which are sometimes wavy) (Jesse 2003).

In the past, the early Holocene pottery sites of the southern Sahara were included in a single broad cultural tradition defined as the 'Neolithic of Sudanese tradition' (Camps 1969: 197), the 'Saharo-Sudanese Neolithic' (Camps 1974), or the 'African aqualithic' (Sutton 1974). More recent evaluations (e.g. Holl 2005) show, however, that they comprise a very complex set of cultures, and that their relationships cannot be understood simply in terms of diffusion from a single source.

Semi-sedentary settlements

A final general theme of relevance for this chapter is the evidence for human exploitation of new environmental resources and the changes that this may have encouraged in people's settlement pattern, specifically the appearance of semi-permanent settlements where storage and selection of resources was practised, as well as incipient forms of food production. This issue has been studied in great detail, and was confirmed by the Egyptian Western Desert contexts (see Barich 2008a; McDonald 2009).

During the early Holocene, both the Saharan area and the Nile Valley provided generalized ecosystems for hunting-fishing-gathering activities for broad-spectrum environmental exploitation. Exploiting a wide diversity of resources near their home bases, people did not need to move much. This reduced nomadism led to residential or semi-residential attitudes in periods of greatest productivity that may have preadapted them for the subsequent adoption of food production (Clark 1976a). Storage, which allowed groups to cope with less favourable seasons, also ultimately limited mobility, as it tied people to the resources that they had put by. Another consequence is likely to have been a reduction in the intervals between births, as women no longer had to carry infants too far. Hunter-gatherer ethnographies (e.g. Lee 1979) suggest that women typically leave a gap of three to five years between births in order adequately to fulfil their dual roles as mother and gatherer. Where storing excess resources allowed women more freedom, the result will also have been more time for their parental role.

Another significant consequence of storage and delayed consumption may have been the creation of socioeconomic inequalities. In fact, sedentism and village life allowed hunter-gatherers to use goods that were not easily transportable, such as grindstones, containers, and storage silos. All these new habits probably helped transform earlier egalitarian ideologies as, among mobile hunter-gatherers, gathering is immediately followed by redistribution among all group members, a practice of food sharing that is the basis for strong sense of social solidarity. In contrast, in more sedentary environments goods can be exchanged through commercial relationships, or, instead of exchanging them for another good, people can use them to gain status and therefore power and prestige. Testart (1982) saw these situations as the basis on which some individuals might take up a position of pre-eminence. The practice of storage and the delayed consumption with which it is associated (Woodburn 1982) probably acted as an important beginning in the transformation of North African hunter-gatherer societies.

THE RE-ESTABLISHMENT OF THE MONSOON CYCLE

Oxygen isotope measurements on foraminifera from marine sediments of Africa's west coast show that the ocean had warmed up by 14 kya, but wind intensity had already begun to lower by 16 kya (Sarnthein et al. 1982). Following a return to more arid conditions during the Younger Dryas stadial, Greenland ice core data indicate a very rapid rise in temperature about 10,000 BP (6°C in 70 years) and temperatures then peaked at values a little higher than those of today around 9000–8500 BP. While ocean temperatures were very similar to today's, insolation was greater by 7 per cent, allowing the monsoon to push into higher latitudes and producing more intensive rainfall across the whole of tropical Africa (Rühlemann et al. 1999).

Pollen analyses from sites in northern Mali, Niger, and southwestern Libya show that savannah reached as far as 20–22°N (about 400–500 km north of its current limit) and extended into the higher regions of the Ahaggar, Aïr, and Tassili mountains (Neumann 1993; Maley 2000; Mercuri 2008) . Further to the east, the Nile probably continued to flow even during the most arid periods, but at the beginning of the Holocene increased dramatically due to the enormous renewal of its sources in Ethiopia and the equatorial region. The river's activity can be compared to that of Lake Turkana, where three significant increases in lake level are recorded over some 7,000 years (9500–7200 BP, 6600–4000 BP, and >3200 BP) (Butzer and Cooke 1982: 59).

Radiocarbon dates from human settlements in the Sahara also track climatic oscillations in the early and middle Holocene. In the central-eastern Sahara (Libya, Chad, and Egypt), for example, an initial reoccupation phase at the beginning of the Holocene (9500–8000 BP) was followed by a period of relatively stable climate (8000–6100 BP) interrupted by an abrupt arid oscillation. This was followed by a return to humid conditions, with occupation moving to the plateaux to exploit the water basins there (6300–4500 BP). Thereafter, however, the area became progressively more arid and was increasingly abandoned (Kuper and Kröpelin 2006: 803). Samples from the West Nubian palaeolake situated between 18 and 19°N near the border between Libya and Chad have provided accurate documentation of these climatic episodes (Hoelzmann et al. 2001). Sediments from the palaeolake have been dated between 9400 and 3800 BP, and it is estimated that in the earliest phase (9400–7500 BP) it reached a maximum extent of about 4,000 km².

THE SAHARAN REGION AT THE BEGINNING
OF THE HOLOCENE: EGYPT, LIBYA, AND NIGER

The re-establishment of the monsoon cycle in the earliest phase of the Holocene was accompanied by a rapid emergence of sites (Barich 2008b), exemplified in Egypt's Western Desert by the Nabta and Bir Kiseiba sequences (Wendorf et al. 2001). The first reoccupation of Bir Kiseiba (known as the El Adam phase, 10,000–8200 BP) is important because of the possibility that it provides evidence for very early domestication of cattle (Gautier 1984). Even though this hypothesis has long been debated (di Lernia, Ch. 36 below), it appears as the most likely to justify the appearance of cattle in the westernmost deposits (like at Uan Muhuggiag in the Libyan Sahara) from the eighth millennium BP (Barich 1987a, 2010b). Furthermore it has been fundamental in encouraging archaeologists to examine the subsistence base of these early Saharan settlers in a new light.

The succeeding El Nabta Neolithic (8100–7900 BP) represents a recolonization of the same region during a new wet phase that followed an oscillation of extreme aridity. More regular rainfall now encouraged more stable settlement and even the appearance of a semi-permanent village: Nabta E-75–6 (Fig. 31.4) with aligned structures—hut bases, hearths, storage pits—and a layout similar to Ti-n-Torha East in the Acacus Mountains of southwestern Libya. The lithic industry from E-75–6 resembles those from other sites in the Western Desert, such as Wadi Bakht in the Gilf Kebir, Abu Ballas and Lobo in the Great Sand Sea, the Masara B horizon at Dakhla, and the early Holocene horizon at Farafra. Domestic cattle bones were still rare at E-75–6 and sheep/goats also appear very late in the overall Nabta sequence, being recorded at E-75–8 and at Hidden Valley in the Farafra Oasis c. 7000 BP. Along with hunting and a perhaps limited role for domestic stock, macroplant remains and numerous grindstones show that wild grains (including sorghum and millet) were clearly an important component of the diet during the El Nabta phase.

Much further west, the Tadrart Acacus in southwestern Libya was one of the central Sahara's main occupation centres. In Wadi Ti-n-Torha, excavations at Ti-n-Torha East Shelter revealed a real proto-village with at least ten hut bases up against the rock wall (Barich 1998) (Fig. 31.5). Radiocarbon dates indicate that occupation, which was associated with a Later Stone Age/Epipaleolithic industry with a high component of blade and microblade tools, began at the end of the tenth millennium BP and probably persisted to c. 7500–7000 BP.

FIG. 31.4 Site E-75–6 at Nabta Playa, Egypt (from Barich 1998).

FIG. 31.5 View of the hut in the Ti-n-Torha East Shelter, Libya (photograph, Barbara Barich).

Throughout this period, people exploited a wide range of animal resources, including Barbary sheep, gazelles, hares, fish (*Clarias* sp.), and birds. The presence of *Bos* remains, still in an initial phase of domestication, is uncertain. However, a large quantity of gathered plants from the millet family (Barich 1992; Wasylikowa 1992) shows that the communities living in the village were engaging in a complex and differentiated use of their environment. These data are confirmed by the nearby site of Two Caves (Fig. 31.6) where a thick deposit indicates that human occupation, at least in certain periods of the year (probably winter), must have been semi-sedentary (Barich 1987b).

Other sites in the Tadrart Acacus provide further evidence of these changes. At Uan Tabu Shelter, for example, excavations revealed a deep stratigraphy divided into four units

FIG. 31.6 View of Ti-n-Torha Two Caves Shelter, Libya (photograph, Barbara Barich).

(Garcea 2001). Units 1–3 date to the early Holocene (8800–8400 BP) and are strongly anthropogenic in origin (ash, charcoal, and a large and diverse quantity of material culture remains—pottery, plant fibres, stone, bone, and wood tools). The rich fauna from Unit 3 include many specimens of Barbary sheep (*Ammotragus lervia*), and the site may have been used specifically for hunting this species at particular times of the year. Not far from Uan Tabu, *Ammotragus* was also strongly present at Uan Afuda Shelter, where sediments include the remains of *Ammotragus* dung together with plant remains interpreted as animal fodder. On the basis of these finds and their location within the shelter, di Lernia (1999) suggests that Barbary sheep were kept in captivity and that the site was an exceptional example of cultural control of a flock of animals during the later pre-pastoralist ('Late Acacus': 8900–7400 BP) occupation of the region (di Lernia and Garcea 1997; di Lernia, Ch. 36 below).

Both Ti-n-Torha East and Uan Tabu produced pottery decorated with impressions using the so-called dotted wavy line motif. Impressions were executed using pointed implements, spatulae, and cords, following a tradition typical of the early Saharan Holocene that can be directly compared to the Tagalagal complex in Niger, which is also dated to the ninth millennium BP (Fig. 31.2). Indeed, in general terms the stratigraphic sequences and chronologies of these Libyan sites correspond in many ways with those of early Holocene sites in Niger, although the latter have not yet provided as much evidence for the subsistence resources that people used.

The first indications of early Holocene hunter-gatherers in Niger came with the work of Desmond Clark (1976b) in the Aïr region, which identified a microlithic Epipalaeolithic industry characterized by microblades, and Ounan and Bou Saada points in the Wadi Greboun and along ancient shorelines in the Adrar Bous area. Roset's (1987) research subsequently provided a stratigraphic basis for an adequate regional reconstruction that showed that sites contemporary to Temet 1 (9650–9450 BP), Tin Ouaffadene (9360–9080 BP), and Adrar Bous 10 (9220–8840 BP) were all tied to lake expansions during a phase of intense rainfall. The associated lithic assemblages are well exemplified by Temet 1, the oldest site (Fig. 31.2), which was similar to the Epipaleolithic industry identified by Clark at Wadi Greboun. Here, however, ceramics were also present, while in the Bagzanes Mountains, immediately south of the Greboun massif, the Tagalagal site also provided a series of early dates (9500–9200 BP) for a layer with pottery. The Tagalagal pottery shows both a variety of forms and well-developed decoration, including the dotted wavy line motif widespread among early Holocene Saharan communities. Faunal remains of wild mammals and fish along with numerous grindstones indicate that these ceramics were made by people practising a hunting-fishing-gathering economy.

Although Roset (1987) tended to rule out a true preceramic Epipaleolithic horizon, palaeoenvironmental data now suggest that wet conditions favourable for human occupation were episodically present in parts of Niger from *c.* 13,000 BP (Roset et al. 1990; Williams 2008). Recent reassessment of the data from Clark's (1976b) mission to the Aïr-Ténéré also suggests that the local LSA sequence in the Adrar Bous region began with the macrolithic Ounanian industry around 12,000–11,000 BP (Smith 2008). A gap in the area's settlement history that corresponds broadly to the Younger Dryas was followed *c.* 9500 BP by a quite different industry known as the Kiffian, characterized by microlithic stone tools and pottery. Smith parallels the Kiffian to the Late Acacus phase in southwestern Libya, as well as to the sites of Temet 1 and Tagalagal. A continued reliance on wild resources seems likely, including hippopotamus, antelope, and fish (obtained using harpoons), complemented by wild grains (inferred from the presence of grindstones). Only from around 7400 BP is an economy centred on cattle herding evident with the appearance of the Ténérean industry (Smith 2008).

THE LAKE AREAS OF THE SAHEL

Further south and southwest, research in the lake and marsh areas of the western edge of Niger and Mali document a dense population of hunter-fishers who intensively exploited aquatic fauna. In Mali important fieldwork has focused on the Taoudenni Basin (Petit-Maire 1991) and the nearby areas of the Erg in-Sakane, Tagnout Chaggeret, and Hassi el Abiod, where re-establishment of the monsoon was associated with a very wet phase with rainfall of up to 400 mm per year. Following sporadic Ounanian occupation in the early Holocene, from 7500 BP large open-air settlements formed along the lake shores for which both ecology and human lifestyles can be reconstructed in detail.

The groups who lived at Hassi el Abiod settled near the large expanses of lake or marsh north of the Inner Niger Delta (Dutour 1997). Unlike early Saharan groups, they placed much greater emphasis on fish, especially large taxa such as Nile perch (*Lates*), along with other aquatic animals, such as hippopotami, turtles, and crocodile (*Crocodylus niloticus*) (de Broin 1983). Freshwater molluscs were also gathered (especially *Melanoides tuberculata*, *Bulinus truncatus*, and *Aspatharia* spp.) and a range of terrestrial mammals hunted, including warthogs, rhinoceros, equids, and antelope. Artefact assemblages include double-pointed fish hooks and unilaterally multi-barbed harpoons with pierced tangs that were undoubtedly used to procure aquatic resources; but the lithic industry, which includes small scrapers, blades, bladelets, and large crescents, is not particularly striking. Ceramics continue the same tradition already seen in the Sahara, and sometimes occur in burials, which were placed directly within settlement sites.

After 4500 BP, groups with a similar toolkit and economy moved further south, pushing down to the Inner Niger Delta, which until then had been almost permanently flooded, and giving rise to the Kobadi culture. This then rapidly spread through the mid-Niger region, from the northwestern Delta, the so-called Méma region, as far as Gao (Raimbault 1986; Raimbault and Commelin 2001–2). Kobadi itself is 15 km northeast of Mampala, in the central Sahel, not far from Mali's border with Mauritania. Partly covered by an ancient dune formation, it has a high concentration of food remains and artefacts distributed over a wide area, 250×25 m. As at Hassi el Abiod and the more easterly site of Gobéro discussed below, inhumation burials, which here numbered more than 100, were mixed in with the occupation remains. Lithic and bone artefacts are quite rare, but pottery is common, both complete vessels found within graves and fragments scattered on the surface. Two ceramic groups have been identified, distinctive in their shape and manufacturing characteristics (Gallin 2001–2). Decoration consists exclusively of impressed designs, but now also includes the use of plant fibres and direct impressions with a roulette, a fashion later widely developed in West Africa and beyond (Haour et al. 2010). The economy again featured intensive exploitation of aquatic resources in the form of fish, crocodile, turtles, and manatee (*Trichecus senegalensis*), while hunting focused on large mammals such as hippopotamus, buffalo, antelope, and warthog (Jousse and Chenal-Velarde 2001–2). An important difference from the Hassi el Abiod groups, however, is the fact that cattle now make up 60 per cent of the faunal remains. Cultural affinities between the Kobadi groups and Malian Saharan populations suggests that they may have moved south from the Sahara as climatic conditions worsened there between 7000 and 5500 BP, and especially from 4000 BP (Raimbault 1996).

FUNERARY BELIEFS AND PRACTICES

Evidence for funerary practices among Saharan hunter-gatherers is rare. Until a few decades ago only isolated graves were known, although Asselar (Mali), Amekni and Ti-n-Hanakaten (Algeria), and Uan Muhuggiag (Libya) all provided clear indications for a precise ritual involving inhumation in a contracted position, with the head oriented in a precise direction and the body accompanied by rare grave goods. At Amekni, three burials were placed in niches in the rock wall against which the settlement was located (Camps 1969). In one a 30-year-old woman lay on her side in a flexed position, accompanied by a ceramic fragment, while the others were of young children also in flexed positions on one side. An infant's grave at Uan Muhuggiag revealed that particular care had been taken to wrap it in leather closed with plant fibres, a choice that favoured a process of natural mummification (Mori and Ascenzi 1959). As people settled, some groups began burying their dead in larger cemeteries. The Hassi el Abiod cemetery in Mali, mentioned above, contained a group of 89 individuals and is one of the largest complexes known (Petit-Maire and Riser 1983). Individuals were placed in crouched positions, on their right or left side, always with the head pointing east. Grave goods were few, generally consisting of simple jewellery and ceramics.

Dutour (1997) has described the Hassi el Abiod population as 'mechtoid', an observation that relates them to populations in the Maghreb. A notable affinity also exists between them and the Kiffian burials from Gobéro in the Agadez region of Niger (Sereno et al. 2008). Gobéro is the largest cemetery yet found in the central Sahara, and saw men, women and children buried in simple shallow ditches without a tumulus, so that in many cases the bodies were later exposed by aeolian deflation. Radiocarbon dating shows that the site was used by at least two different population groups, between 8000 and 7000 BP by hunter-gatherer-fisher groups with a Kiffian-like material culture, and around 5500 BP by pastoral groups of the Ténérian culture. The two different burial series were clearly accompanied by different rituals. Although the dead were placed in a crouched position on one side in both cases, the Kiffian individuals were compressed, almost as if they had been tightly wrapped up, and accompanied by few grave goods, while Ténérian burials included a much larger number of objects, some, such as hippopotamus ivory bracelets and plaques, of excellent craftsmanship.

CONCLUSION

Reoccupation of the Sahara after a long period in the late Upper Pleistocene when it appears to have been abandoned by people (Garcea, Ch. 29 above) was closely tied to the development of more favourable climatic conditions at the beginnings of the Holocene, and this new occupation continued to be linked to climatic variations. While in the central Saharan area

FIG. 31.7 Rock art image in the Roundheads Style, Tassili, Algeria (from Barich 1998).

people exploited a broad spectrum of resources and engaged in some of the first experiments with animal domestication, in the lake environments of the Sahel, tied to the hydrographic system of Niger and Chad, they particularly emphasized fishing resources. These latter societies, in particular, show a strong affinity to those settled on the Upper Nile (Haaland and Haaland, Ch. 37 below)—a similarity that explains their earlier description as 'Neolithic of Sudanese tradition', a designation given by Arkell (1955) on the basis of similarities in the decorative motifs of early pottery from the Sahara and Sudan.

Though not discussed here in detail, Saharan rock art, with hundreds of painted or incised images on rock walls, provides unparalleled evidence of the symbolic world of the Sahara's early Holocene occupants. Although dating remains difficult (Muzzolini 1995; Mori 1998; Smith, Ch. 11 above), the oldest paintings are probably of hunter-gatherer origin. Known in the Tassili, the Acacus, and a small part of Tibesti, this 'Roundhead' art (Fig. 31.7) is very rich in subject matter, whilst the scant characterization of the human figure perhaps indicates a disinterest in individuality. Compared to the bubaline style of engravings that show wild game (including the extinct giant buffalo *Pelorovis (Bubalus) antiquus*) in a highly realistic manner and may be older (Mori 1998), women are nevertheless more frequently depicted in Roundhead paintings. This may reflect their enhanced role in society, consistent with the increased importance of gathered foods in Late Acacus times and their presumed authorship of ceramics (Barich 1998).

REFERENCES

ARKELL, A. J. (1955). The relations of the Nile Valley with the Southern Sahara in Neolithic times. In L. Balout (ed.), *Actes du IIème Congrès Panafricain de Préhistoire d'Alger 1952*. Casablanca: Edita, 345–6.

BARICH, B. E. (1987a). Uan Muhuggiag and the pastoralism in the Central Sahara. In B. E. Barich (ed.), *Archaeology and Environment in the Libyan Sahara: The Excavations in the Tadrart Acacus 1978–1983*. Oxford: British Archaeological Reports, 255–66.

—— (1987b). The Two Caves shelter: an Early Holocene site in the north-eastern Acacus. In B. E. Barich (ed.), *Archaeology and Environment in the Libyan Sahara: The Excavations in the Tadrart Acacus 1978–1983*. Oxford: British Archaeological Reports, 13–61.

——(1992). The botanical collections from Ti-n-Torha/Two Caves and Uan Muhuggiag (Tadrart Acacus, Libya): an archaeological commentary. *Origini* 16: 109–23.

——(1998). *People, Water, and Grain: The Beginnings of Domestication in the Sahara and the Nile Valley*. Rome: L'Erma di Bretschneider.

——(2008a). Living in the oasis: beginning of village life at Farafra and in the Western Desert of Egypt. In Z. Sulgostowska and A. J. Tomaszewski (eds), *Man–Millennia–Environment: Studies in Honour of Romuald Schild*. Warsaw: Polish Academy of Sciences, 145–50.

——(2008b). Africa, Sahara: West and Central Sahara. In D. M. Pearsall (ed.), *Encyclopedia of Archaeology*. New York: Academic Press, 61–5.

——(2010a). *Antica Africa: Alle Origini delle Società*. Rome: L'Erma di Bretschneider.

——(2010b). Muhuggiag (Uan) (Tadrart Acacus, Libye). *Encyclopédie Berbère* 32: 5101–4.

BUTZER, K. W., and COOKE, H. B. S. (1982). The palaeo-ecology of the African continent: the physical environment of Africa from the earliest geological to Later Stone Age times. In J. D. Clark (ed.), *The Cambridge History of Africa*, vol.1: *From the Earliest Times to c. 500 B.C.* Cambridge: Cambridge University Press, 1–69.

CAMPS, G. (1969). *Amekni, Néolithique ancien du Hoggar*. Paris: CRAPE.

——(1974). *Les civilisations préhistoriques de l'Afrique du Nord et du Sahara*. Paris: Doin.

CLARK, J. D. (1976a). The domestication process in sub-Saharan Africa with special reference to Ethiopia. In E. S. Higgs (ed.), *Origine de l'Élevage et de la Domestication*. Nice: UISPP, 56–115.

——(1976b). Epi-palaeolithic aggregates from Greboun Wadi, Air, and Adrar Bous, northwestern Ténéré, Republic of Niger. In B. Abebe, J. Chavaillon, and J. E. G. Sutton (eds), *Proceedings of the Seventh Panafrican Congress of Prehistory and Quaternary Studies, Addis Ababa 1971*. Addis Ababa: Ministry of Culture, 67–78.

CLOSE, A. E. (2002). Backed bladelets are a foreign country. *Archaeological Papers of the American Anthropological Association* 12: 31–44.

DE BROIN, F. (1983). Chéloniens. In N. Petit-Maire and J. Riser (eds), *Sahara ou Sahel? Quaternaire Récent du Bassin de Taoudenni (Mali)*. Marseilles: CNRS, 211–33.

DI LERNIA, S. (ed.) (1999). *The Uan Afuda Cave: Hunter-Gatherer Societies of Central Sahara*. Florence: All'Insegna del Giglio.

——and GARCEA, E. A. A. (1997). Some remarks on Saharan terminology: pre-pastoral archaeology from the Libyan Sahara and the Middle Nile Valley. *Libya Antiqua* 3: 11–23.

DUTOUR, O. (1997). Peuplement du Sahara au Pléistocène Supérieur: le point de vue paléoanthropologique. In T. Tillet (ed.), *Sahara: paléomilieux et peuplement préhistorique au Pléistocène Supérieur*. Paris: L'Harmattan, 409–21.

GALLIN, A. (2001–2). Proposition d'une étude stylistique de la céramique imprimée de Kobadi. *Préhistoire Anthropologie Méditerranéenne* 10–11: 117–44.

GARCEA, E. A. A. (ed.) (2001). *Uan Tabu in the Settlement History of the Libyan Sahara*. Florence: All'Insegna del Giglio.

GAUTIER, A. (1984). Archaeozoology of the Bir Kiseiba region, Eastern Sahara. In A. E. Close (ed.), *Cattle-Keepers of the Eastern Sahara*. Dallas, Tex.: Southern Methodist University Press, 49–72.

HAOUR, A., MANNING, K., ARAZI, N., et al. (2010). *African Pottery Roulettes Past and Present: Techniques, Identification, and Distribution*. Oxford: Oxbow Books.

HOELZMANN, P., KEDING, B., BERKE, H., KRÖPELIN, S., and KRUSE, H. J. (2001). Environmental change and archaeology: lake evolution and human occupation in the Eastern Sahara during the Holocene. *Palaeogeography, Palaeoclimatology, Palaeoecology* 169: 193–217.

HOLL, A. F. C. (2005). Holocene 'aquatic' adaptations in tropical North Africa. In A. B. Stahl (ed.), *African Archaeology: A Critical Introduction*. Oxford: Blackwell, 174–86.

HUYSECOM, E., OZAINNE, S., RAELI, F., BALLOUCHE, A., RASSE, M., and STOKES, S. (2004). Ounjougou (Mali): a history of Holocene settlement at the southern edge of the Sahara. *Antiquity* 78: 579–93.

JESSE, F. (2003). Early ceramics in the Sahara and the Nile Valley. In L. Krzyzaniak, K. Kroeper, and M. Kobusiewicz (eds), *Cultural Markers in the Later Prehistory of Northeastern Africa and Recent Research*. Poznán: Poznán Archaeological Museum, 35–50.

——(2010). Early pottery in Northern Africa: an overview. *Journal of African Archaeology* 8: 219–38.

JOUSSE, H., and CHENAL-VELARDE, I. (2001–2). Nouvelles données sur la faune mammalienne de Kobadi (Mali) au Néolithique: implications paléoéconomiques et paléoenvironnementales. *Préhistoire Anthropologie Méditerranéenne* 10–11: 145–66.

KUPER, R., and KRÖPELIN, S. (2006). Climate-controlled Holocene occupation in the Sahara: motor of Africa's evolution. *Science* 313: 803–7.

LEE, R. B. (1979). *The !Kung San: Men, Women and Work in a Foraging Society*. Cambridge: Cambridge University Press.

LIVINGSTONE SMITH, A., BOSQUET, D., and MARTINEAU, R. (eds) (2005). *Pottery Manufacturing Processes: Reconstitution and Interpretation*. Oxford: Archaeopress.

MALEY, J. (2000). Last Glacial Maximum lacustrine and fluviatile formations in the Tibesti and other Saharan mountains and large-scale climatic teleconnections linked to activity in the subtropical Jet Stream. *Global and Planetary Change* 26: 121–36.

MCDONALD, M. M. A. (2009). Increased sedentism in the central oases of the Egyptian Western Desert in the early to mid-Holocene: evidence from the peripheries. *African Archaeological Review* 26: 3–43.

MERCURI, A. M. (2008). Human influence, plant landscape evolution and climate inferences from the archaeobotanical records of the Wadi Teshuinat area (Libyan Sahara). *Journal of Arid Environments* 72: 1950–67.

MORI, F. (1998). *The Great Civilisations of the Ancient Sahara*. Rome: L'Erma di Bretschneider.

——and ASCENZI, A (1959). La mummia infantile di Uan Muhuggiag: osservazioni antropologiche. *Rivista dell'Istituto di Antropologia* 46: 125–48.

MUZZOLINI, A. (1995). *Les Images Rupestres du Sahara*. Toulouse: Collection Préhistoire du Sahara.

NELSON, K. (2001). The pottery of Nabta Playa: a summary. In Wendorf et al. (2001: 534–43).

NEUMANN, K. (1993). Holocene vegetation of the Eastern Sahara: charcoal from prehistoric sites. In L. Krzyzaniak, M. Kobusiewicz, and J. A. Alexander (eds), *Environmental Change and Human Culture in the Nile Basin and Northern Africa until the Second Millennium B.C.* Poznán: Poznán Archaeological Museum, 153–69.

PETIT-MAIRE, N. (ed.) (1991). *Paléoenvironnements du Sahara: Lacs Holocènes à Taoudenni (Mali)*. Marseilles: CNRS.

—— and RISER, J. (eds) (1983). *Sahara ou Sahel? Quaternaire Récent du Bassin de Taoudenni (Mali)*. Marseilles: CNRS.

RAIMBAULT, M. (1986). Le gisement néolithique de Kobadi (Sahara malien) et ses implications paléohydrologiques. In H. Faure, L. Faure, and E. S. Diop (eds), *Changements globaux en Afrique Durant le Quaternaire: Passé–Présent–Futur*. Paris: ORSTOM, 395–7.

—— (1996). L'impact de la dégradation climatique holocène sur le Néolithique du Sahara malien et les données du faciès sahélien de Kobadi. *Préhistoire Anthropologie Méditerranéenne* 5: 135–46.

—— and COMMELIN, D. (2001–2). La poterie du site néolithique de Kobadi dans le Sahara malien. *Préhistoire Anthropologie Méditerranéenne* 10–11: 107–16.

ROSET, J. P. (1987). Paleoclimatic and cultural conditions of Neolithic development in the early Holocene of northern Niger (Air and Ténéré). In A. E. Close (ed.), *Prehistory of Arid North Africa*. Dallas, Tex.: Southern Methodist University Press, 211–34.

—— (2000). Céramique et néolithisation en Afrique saharienne. In J. Guilaine (ed.), *Premiers Paysans du Monde: Naissances des Agricultures*. Paris: Errance, 263–90.

ROSET, J. P., DE BROIN, F., FAURE, M., GAYET, M., GUÉRIN, C., and MOUCHET, F. (1990). La faune de Tin Ouaffadene et d'Adrar Bous 10, deux gisements archéologiques de l'Holocène ancien au Niger nord-oriental. *Géodynamique* 5: 67–89.

RÜHLEMANN, C., MULITZA, S., MÜLLER, P. J., WEFER, G., and ZAHN, R. (1999).Warming of the tropical Atlantic ocean and slowdown of thermohaline circulation during the last deglaciation. *Nature* 402: 511–14.

SARNTHEIN, M., TETZLAFF, G., KOOPMANN, B., WOLTER, K., and PFLAUMANN, U. (1982). Glacial and interglacial wind regimes over the eastern subtropical Atlantic and north-west Africa. *Nature* 293: 193–6.

SERENO, P. C., GARCEA, E. A., JOUSSE, H., et al. (2008). Lakeside cemeteries in the Sahara: 5.000 years of Holocene population and environmental change. *PLOS One* 3(8): 1–22. (e 2995).

SMITH, A. B. (2008). The Kiffian. In D. Gifford-Gonzalez (ed.), *Adrar Bous: The Archaeology of a Granitic Ring Complex in Central Sahara, Niger*. Tervuren: Royal Africa Museum, 179–99.

SUTTON, J. E. G. (1974). The aquatic civilization of middle Africa. *Journal of African History* 15: 527–46.

TESTART, A. (1982). The significance of food storage among hunter-gatherers: residence patterns, population densities, and social inequalities. *Current Anthropology* 23: 523–37.

WASYLIKOWA, K. (1992). Holocene flora of the Tadrart Acacus area, SW Libya, based on plant macrofossils from Uan Muhuggiag and Ti-n-Torha/Two Caves archaeological sites. *Origini* 16: 125–59.

WENDORF, F., SCHILD, R., and associates (2001). *Holocene Settlement of the Egyptian Sahara*, vol. 1: *The Archaeology of Nabta Playa*. New York: Kluwer Academic/Plenum.

WILLIAMS, M. A. J. (2008). Geology, geomorphology and prehistoric environments in Adrar Bous. In D. Gifford-Gonzalez (ed.), *Adrar Bous: The Archaeology of a Granitic Ring Complex in Central Sahara, Niger*. Tervuren: Royal Africa Museum, 25–54.

WOODBURN, J. (1982). Egalitarian societies. *Man* 17: 431–51.

CHAPTER 32

HUNTER-GATHERER-FISHERS OF EASTERN AND SOUTH-CENTRAL AFRICA SINCE 20,000 YEARS AGO

SIBEL BARUT KUSIMBA

INTRODUCTION

A growing number of sites and sequences are now coming together to paint a more complete picture of East African hunter-gatherers of the last 20,000 years. During this period Mode 5 microlithic technologies became widespread as hunter-gatherers adapted to different environments, ranging from highly mobile hunters of large game to sedentary forest dwellers with broad diets, and semi-sedentary hunter-fisher-gatherers. Other themes that emerge are greater assemblage diversity through time and an elaboration of the skills and technologies required to adapt to particular environments and the resources they could provide, including experiments in resource intensification. Although specific ethnographic examples have limited applicability, greater evidence of symbolic behaviour, long-term traditions, and diverse adaptations make most archaeologists comfortable with using more general analogies to modern hunter-gatherers. Ethnographic and ethnoarchaeological records similarly help us to understand how some foraging societies survived into the more recent past, and the nature of their interactions with both farmers and herders.

East Africa (broadly equated here to Kenya, Uganda, and Tanzania) and south-central Africa (broadly equated with Zambia and Malawi) differ in the environments and resources they offer to foragers. In spite of East Africa's equatorial location, dramatic variations in altitude create a mosaic of different vegetation zones that today include savannah, grassland, thorn scrub, and montane tropical forest. Well-known 'magnets' for the settlement of hunter-gatherers include the basins of Lakes Turkana and Victoria, the Rift Valley, and the rich grasslands of the floor of the Rift extending from northern Kenya into Tanzania. These areas doubtless also reflect the intensity of research activity, as suggested by recent discoveries along the East African coast (Chami and Kwekason 2003). Other areas, such as much of central and southern Tanzania, Malawi, and Uganda, have still seen very little fieldwork.

Unlike equatorial East Africa, south-central Africa lacks the relief and high quality soils of volcanic mountain ranges (although most areas are above 1,000 m in elevation) and experiences a longer and more well-defined dry season of eight months or more. Vegetation includes dry deciduous forest and the well-known *Brachystegia* or miombo woodlands of central and southern Zambia. Places known to have attracted hunter-gatherers were rich in game animals and in fruit and nut trees but, perhaps especially in this region, water. They include the Kafue Valley and its broad floodplain, the Kafue Flats (Derricourt 1985), the Luangwa Valley and Muchinga Escarpment (Gutin and Musonda 1985), and the valleys of the Zambezi River.

LATE PLEISTOCENE HUNTER-GATHERERS

Peaking around 18,000 years ago, the Last Glacial Maximum (LGM) was the most arid period of the last 100,000 years. With the monsoon rains that today bring rainfall to East Africa weak or nonexistent (Zonneveld et al. 1997), grasslands expanded, forests contracted, and lakes reached low stands or dried up all over Africa (Kiage and Liu 2006). Reconstructions of East African environments at this time that model an expansion of dry habitats of thorn scrub and grassland into higher altitudes and around lakes as tropical rainforests and montane forests became smaller are borne out by palaeoclimatic data from lakes and glaciers (Bonnefille et al. 1990; Aucour et al. 1994). Important lakes like Victoria and the Central Rift lakes of Kenya that provide water for surrounding areas through evaporation were dry or nearly dry at this time (Johnson et al. 1996). Nevertheless, given the expansion of desert and scrub north and south of the Equator, tropical Africa probably still offered people some of the period's more mesic (i.e. moderately moist) environments, with potential refugia in highlands, the lowland tropical forests along the eastern edge of the Congo Basin, and around lakes and rivers.

East Africa seems to have been one of the earliest places where a Mode 5 technology has been documented, and it appears contemporaneously or immediately post-dating Mode 3 industries at several sites (Ambrose 1998, 2002) before 40,000 BP. These sites include Enkapune ya Muto (Ambrose 1998), Kisese II rockshelter in Central Tanzania, with a radiocarbon date on ostrich eggshell exceeding 30,000 BP, Matupi Cave (Van Noten 1977), the Naisiusiu Beds at Olduvai Gorge (Skinner et al. 2003), and Mumba and Nasera Rockshelters (Prendergast et al. 2007). These small tool industries occur later in time and are stylistically distinct from the Howeison's Poort microlithic industry of southern Africa. After a prolonged period in which both technologies were in use (Prendergast et al. 2007), microlithic technologies were well established by 20,000 years ago. Re-excavation and re-dating of several key sites, such as Mumba Shelter in northwestern Tanzania (Prendergast et al. 2007), is proving just as critical in understanding the succession of industries involved here as fieldwork at completely new sites.

Given the LGM's aridity it makes sense to hypothesize that foragers were relatively mobile, at least in open grassland settings. One settlement focus seems to have been rockshelter sites on high land that provided views of the surrounding plains, possible locations for mass kills and resources such as small non-migratory animals, firewood, and water. The large number of rockshelter sites such as Mumba (Prendergast et al. 2007), Enkapune ya Muto (Ambrose 1998), and Lukenya Hill (Kusimba 2001) demonstrates that landscape use took advantage of these strategic locations. From these locations, raw materials for stone tools were carried significant distances, up to 100 km in the case of obsidian from Kenya's Central Rift Valley. At GvJm62 at Lukenya Hill, for example, obsidian from the Central Rift was fashioned into large bladelets and segments and is recovered in a presumably exhausted phase of the operational chain as large segments, that were relatively rare in the assemblages. By contrast, small local obsidian bombs were flaked open using a bipolar method (Kusimba 2001). Interestingly, the roughly contemporary Robberg Industry of southernmost Africa (Mitchell, Ch. 33 below) used a broadly similar multi-component microlithic toolkit, favoured rockshelters, and has been thought to have practised a highly mobile adaptation. Such potential comparisons between different regions of Africa that are typically considered separately warrant further investigation.

Faunal exploitation offers an important window into hunter-gatherer subsistence strategies. At Lukenya Hill, Marean (1992) hypothesized that GvJm 46 was a kill site for a now-extinct small alcelaphine that was killed using a drive method. At other sites, a more generalized hunting pattern prevailed, suggesting that drive hunting took place during an annual migration. Lithic assemblages show evidence of both more sedentary occupations, as inferred from the local raw materials used at GvJm 46, and greater mobility, as at another Lukenya Hill site, GvJm 22, where larger proportions of Rift Valley obsidian were made into a variety of microlithic tools. Adaptation to these grassland environments, where large animals were probably locally abundant but unpredictable, must have involved both the use of mobility and the ability to exploit local areas for lower-ranked resources, like plants, using technologies such as the digging stick weights found at GvJm62. Grassland environments were not, however, the only ones to have been occupied around the LGM; Ishango on the shores of Lake Edward, at the extreme eastern edge of the Congo Basin, documents the importance of aquatic resources, especially fish, procured in part using bone harpoons (Stewart 1989; Cornelissen, Ch. 28 above); comparable strategies may have been pursued around other, as yet unresearched lakes elsewhere in the region. South-central Africa is also not as well as understood as East Africa's Central Rift. Mode 3 assemblages are evident late into Marine Isotope Stage 3, with possibly transitional industries then registered at Kalemba, Leopard's Hill, and Mumbwa (Phillipson 1976; Barham 2000) before the appearance of unequivocally microlithic assemblages after the Last Glacial Maximum, the Nachikufan I (Group I in the Lunsemfwa Basin; Musonda 1984).

THE PLEISTOCENE-HOLOCENE TRANSITION

As elsewhere in Africa, a major climatic shift occurred toward the end of the Pleistocene and into the early Holocene. This transition was far from direct and took several thousand years, with periods of oscillation in temperature regimes and between drier and wetter climates. Beginning around 14,500 BP, a variety of paleoclimatic proxy data show increasing temperatures and wetter conditions (Timm et al. 2010). Montane forests began to expand at this time in several regions. Abruptly increased rainfall and wetter conditions then alternated with droughts until a period of colder, drier climate (12,700–11,800 BP)—the local expression of the global Younger Dryas—took conditions back to more or less those of the LGM (Kiage and Liu 2006; Garcin et al. 2009). After this, however, came probably the wettest period of the last 100,000 years. In East Africa, tropical montane forests expanded into lower altitudes, savannah and woodland replaced scrub, Rift Valley lakes reached high stands, and palaeolakes such as Lake Suguta filled now-dry volcanic valleys (Gasse et al. 1980; Garcin et al. 2009).

During this early Holocene wet phase, lakes and rivers were a magnet for humans, and harpoon-assisted fishing of the kind that became well established throughout much of today's Sahara and Sahel (Barich, Ch. 31 above) also appears in East Africa around Lake Turkana and at Nasera near Lake Eyasi, where fishing was combined with the open grassland hunting of large game. Around Lake Turkana at the numerous Galana Boi formation sites, such as Lothagam (Robbins 1974), Lowasera, GaJj11 and FxJj12, fishers of Nile perch (*Lates* spp.) and cichlids, lived on the ancient lakeshore using abundant bone harpoons to fish and to hunt crocodiles, hippopotami, and antelope (Phillipson 1977). At Lothagam excavations discovered more than 200 barbed bone spear/harpoon points, microlithic tools, undecorated pottery, an abundance of fish bones, and fragmentary skeletons of twenty-one individuals, mostly from burials. The Lake Turkana fishers used local obsidian to make backed microliths, and did not have obsidian exchange networks as extensive as those of later pastoralists in the Central Rift Valley (Nash et al. 2011); however, some of their obsidian is from unknown sources, possibly in Ethiopia (Ndiema et al. 2010). Decorated pottery discovered to the west of Lothagam has been dated to 7960 ± 140 BP (Robbins 1972, 2006). While similarities have been noted between their material culture and similar adaptations in North Africa and along the Middle Nile (Haaland and Haaland, Ch. 37 below)—adaptations that were likewise spurred by wetter early Holocene environments (Yellen 1998)—the differences should also be noted. Most importantly, the earliest Lake Turkana sites do not contain pottery before about 7000 BP, perhaps because wild grains—that may have been cooked in pots in northern Africa—were lacking from the early Holocene Lake Turkana diet. Over time, however, the technique of spear-fishing for large fish seems to have declined over time as smaller fish were sought out (Stewart 1989), perhaps with methods such as nets or weirs, which would indicate a strategy of intensification in the collection of smaller but more rapidly reproducing species.

Fishing was probably also undertaken at sites in Kenya's Central Rift around Lake Naivasha/Nakuru, given the single harpoon found at Gamble's Cave, but the evidence is not as strongly developed as further north (Stewart 1989). Following blade- and bladelet-dominated industries of terminal Pleistocene age such as the Kiteko in central Kenya (Bower et al. 1977; Ambrose 2002) and the Ntumot in the southern Rift Valley (Ambrose 2002), around 12,000 years ago a blade-based Mode 4 tradition, known as Eburran, became established among the late Pleistocene/Holocene people of the Central Rift. More hunters then than fishers, the people responsible for the Eburran preferred intermediate altitudes in between forests and grassland lakeshores, and used the abundant local obsidian for their tools at sites like Nderit Drift and Gamble's Cave (Ambrose et al. 1980; Ambrose 1984). A hiatus in these sites around 10500–8500 BP may reflect a relocation of settlement during the period of highest rainfall. Less well known, but documenting occupation beyond Kenya, quartz microlithic assemblages have been excavated at Nsongezi in Uganda (Nelson and Posnansky 1970) and in northern Tanzania (Prendergast et al. 2007).

In south-central Africa, Mode 3 technologies had developed into (or been replaced by) Mode 5 microlithic ones at least by the LGM at sites such as Leopard's Hill Kopje and Kalemba. There and in much of Zambia the first well-described Mode 5 technology is the Nachikufan Industry, characterized by pointed backed bladelets, some backed crescent forms and scrapers, bone points, bored stones, and ground stone axes; broadly similar assemblages occur in the Lunsemfwa Basin (Musonda 1984) and at Mumbwa (Barham 2000) in central areas of Zambia. Being associated with a *Brachystegia* woodland, the faunal remains recovered show an emphasis on smaller woodland species that were probably trapped or snared (Gutin and Musonda 1985), while interpretation of the bored stones as digging stick weights strongly suggests a diet rich in underground plant foods such as tubers. The Nachikufan microlithic tradition persisted in several 'phases' until well after the introduction of farming in the early first millennium AD, differentiating over time into several regional industries—for example that known as Makwe after a site to the east of the Luangwa River (Phillipson 1976; Gutin and Musonda 1985).

MID- AND LATE HOLOCENE HUNTER-GATHERER-FISHERS: THE QUESTION OF INTENSIFICATION

For the Holocene we have a much more refined 'weather report' on which to base our understanding of the changing stage to which human actors adapted. Overall this period began warm and wet with high lake stands and expanded woodlands and forests, but was punctuated by dry periods at 8.2 kya, 4.5 kya, 4.2 kya, and 3.5–2.3 kya (Bonnefille et al. 1990; Street-Perrott and Perrott 1994; Kiage and Liu 2006), which gradually established broad, present-day features of East Africa's environment and climate, such as the bimodal rainfall pattern (Marshall 1990) and particular drought-resistant vegetation zones (Kiage and Liu 2006). In south-central Africa, a dry and hot period between 7.0 and 4.5 kya was likewise followed by a climate broadly similar to that of today. We can also postulate a growing human impact on the environment through activities such as forest clearance and exploitation of firewood, but solid evidence of this is well documented only for the last 2,000 years, thus broadly coinciding with the introduction of farming (Taylor and Marchant 1994/95; Marchant and Taylor 1998).

From about 8500 BP Eburran hunter-gatherers seem to have returned to the Nakuru/Naivasha Basin, again preferring the forest/grassland ecotone at sites like Masai Gorge Rockshelter (Ambrose 1985). By analogy with modern Ogiek foragers and based on faunal data, Ambrose (1984) suggests that they were relatively sedentary and that their diet emphasized trapping and snaring of forest/savannah game (instead of larger plains antelope; Marean 1992), with honey a major source of carbohydrates, given the paucity of plant foods in tropical montane forests. Best known from Enkapune ya Muto, the Eburran's archaeological record exhibits a major gap *c.* 6000–3300 BP, probably because people followed the forest/savannah ecotone upslope as climate dried (Ambrose 1984). Further north, fish continued to be intensively exploited at sites near Lake Turkana, but from at least 7500 BP we also have evidence of coarsely made pottery being part of the local toolkit (Robbins 1974; Phillipson 1977).

The shores of Lake Victoria constitute a third area of sustained hunter-gatherer research, building on earlier observations, such as those of Robertshaw (1991) at Gogo Falls. Key projects include those reported by Dale and Ashley (2010), Dale et al. (2004), Karega-Munene (2002), and Lane et al. (2006, 2007). Several sequences here have produced Kansyore pottery which, as elsewhere in East Africa, is typically associated with quite expedient quartz microlithic assemblages. Around Lake Victoria sites include shell middens (e.g. Usenge 1 and 2) on the lake's former shoreline that may signal intensified exploitation of aquatic resources in the middle millennia of the Holocene (Robertshaw et al. 1983). Early Kansyore lacks ceramics altogether. The evidence from Pundo and Usenge, and some other sites around Lake Victoria suggest that ceramics first appear after c. 2400 cal BC (Dale and Ashley 2010). Open-air sites (e.g. Gogo Falls and Wadh Lang'o) along rivers feeding into the lake have different fish taxa, including *Barbus*, which could have been caught at nearby rapids during spawning runs, tilapia, which prefers shallower waters, and mudfish. Fish were an abundant and important source of protein; for instance, the average mudfish provided 9–11 kg of meat. Seasonal movement, or perhaps semi-permanent living at the riverine sites with the smaller lakeshore sites used in the dry season or as logistical fishing camps, seems likely (Dale et al. 2004; Prendergast 2010). Such strategies, along with the use of pottery in perhaps storing or processing food, provoke thoughts that some Kansyore groups were engaging in more delayed return forms of subsistence behaviour.

In south-central Africa, industries that succeed the Nachikufan are known for their small ground stone axes, possibly used for making bark cloth, hafted microliths, and the ubiquity of bored stones, suggesting exploitation of tubers, and the exploitation of tree nuts (Phillipson 1976). Assemblages can be divided into scraper-rich vs microlith-rich assemblages, probably due to differences in site function (Bisson 1990). In general, Zambian sites show a focus on small game probably related to their woodland Holocene environment. At the waterlogged Kafue Flats site of Gwisho, which dates to around 2800 BP, more than thirty burials were found, along with bedding, wooden structures, and wooden artefacts including bows and arrow shafts; plants with known uses as arrow poison were also preserved; the Gwisho people were significantly taller than modern San, possibly due to a much richer diet; they hunted relatively large, water-loving antelope such as the lechwe (Fagan and Van Noten 1971). Rock art styles that are likely to be associated with these Zambian foragers, as well as with others further north in East Africa, are discussed by Smith (Ch. 11 above). Though rich in paintings (Masao 1979), the Kondoa area of Tanzania has still seen regrettably little archaeological exploration, beyond the pioneering work of Inskeep (1962), which established the presence of microlithic toolkits there >30,000 BP.

Hunter-gatherers, herders, and farmers

Africa has the best-known and richest ethnographic and historical record of foraging societies that survived into the 20th century (Kent 1996). The historical character of the origins of food production in Africa no doubt shaped forager survival into the present. First, Africa's huge size and environmental diversity mean that there were more centres of independent plant and animal domestication, and also more environments quite different from those in which many domesticates were first developed. The spread of food production, particularly cattle pastoralism, was then slowed by the cultural and biological adjustments needed as these new plants and animals were brought from southward (e.g. Gifford-Gonzalez 2000). Other biomes, like the Central African lowlands and parts of East Africa's highlands, were never particularly well suited to African cereals, and instead were truly 'domesticated' with the arrival of the banana, an ultimately Southeast Asian crop (Fuller and Hildebrand, Ch. 35 below). These challenges to domestication, coupled with a relatively low population density in most areas, meant that hunting societies could survive long-term in 'internal frontiers' less amenable to farming such as deserts, forests, and lakeshores (cf. Lane 2004). Finally, many farming communities in Africa practise extensive methods that tread lightly on the landscape and are themselves relatively mobile, thus engendering few conflicts with neighbouring foragers.

In spite of their persistence, no existing hunting societies in Africa are *sui generis* good models of the Stone Age. All have accommodated food producers in one way or another. Based on ethnographic evidence—which can provide a source of testable ideas, but never a telescope to the past—forager–farmer relationships may have been structured in three different ways. The first, symbiosis, involves exchanges of mutual benefit, such as forest food or labour for agricultural produce or secondary products of livestock. In these cases both societies depend on each other, although each may feel they have an upper hand; forager labour can meet chronic shortages of human energy needed for farming, while farmers provide staple carbohydrates. The farmers, however, can shape the scale of this relationship because their labour needs are often the limiting factor. Well-known examples include Central African rainforest groups such as the Efe and Lese (Bailey 1991) and the Mbuti (Turnbull 1966). In East Africa, two other strategies remain more common. The first is the parallelist strategy. Parallelists adopt changes to make themselves more similar to those of neighbouring food producers; the Ogiek of the highlands of the Kenyan Rift have adopted the age sets and patrilines of the neighbouring Maasai, allowing them to form alliances and trade honey and wild animal products to Maa- and Kalenjin-speaking peoples for secondary products like milk. Their social structural parallels the dominant society, allowing them to form alliances and trade while still preserving their foraging identities. Their patrilineal inheritance of territories and associated beehives is a complement to the pastoralists' corporate groups which structure the inheritance of cattle (Kusimba 2003). Peripatetics constitute a second variant. Adopting the most flexible strategy possible, these groups maintain their own society but adopt a variety of exchange relationships with others, often being mobile or flexible generalists. Their role often changes over time as they adapt to new opportunities in surrounding communities, and they often play important roles in regional economies. The Boni and Wataa of the Kenya coast have, for example, maintained their identity through symbiosis with neighbouring Oromo and Swahili people (Kassam 2000, 2004)

The earliest archaeological cases of forager/hunter interaction and exchange are an intriguing exercise in identification, not just of archaeological remains, but also of our own categories like 'forager' or 'herder'. The Lake Victoria Kansyore sites of Wadh Lang'o (Lane et al. 2007) and Gogo Falls (Robertshaw 1991; Karega-Munene 2002) are some of the best-studied examples of forager/farmer interaction in East Africa, mostly indicated by the bones of caprines in sites where there is long-term continuity in both lithic and ceramic assemblages. Caprines appear in varying amounts and are often juveniles, which suggests several possible scenarios, including exchange and the keeping by foragers of small herds (cf. Ikeya 1993; Sadr, Ch. 44 below). In any case, from at least 3300 BP they undoubtedly formed a mixed strategy that included hunting and a clear reliance on fishing (Lane et al. 2007; Prendergast 2010).

It seems likely that in several other parts of East Africa too—for example, the Central Rift Valley (Marean 1992) and around Lake Turkana (Marshall et al. 1984)—the origins of food production were a case of adding sheep/goat to a foraging menu: what Sadr (1998) terms 'foragers with sheep'. As around Lake Victoria, keeping small stock was probably compatible with seasonal changes in the species of game or fish that people sought. Only subsequently do archaeological sequences, such as that from Enkapune ya Muto (Ambrose 1998), register a fuller commitment to a herding economy or show changes in ceramic assemblages that suggest a broader range of social interactions with pastoralists or (in the Usenge 3 case) farming populations. Toward the apparent southern limit of pastoralist expansion in East Africa during the first millennium BC (cf. Lane, Ch. 40 below), small amounts of Pastoral Neolithic and Iron Age ceramics at the site of Mumba in Tanzania's Eyasi Basin, along with small numbers of caprine remains, also hints at such exchanges beginning around 3000 BP (Mabulla 2007; Prendergast et al. 2007). After 1000 BP further south in the Kondoa region of central Tanzania, foragers shared a frontier with Iron Age food producers, incorporating iron tools and Early Iron Age pottery garnered through trade around the same time (Soper and Golden 1969; Masao 1979).

As the record of hunting peoples moves into historical range, archaeology and other records can be linked together (e.g. Mutundu 1999). Like other hunters who supported the growth of cities and complex trade patterns in Southeast Asia (Morrison and Junker 2002), the Waata of southeastern Kenya were foragers of the arid bushland (*nyika*) of the coastal hinterland, who supplied ivory to coast-bound caravans and the East African coast port towns of the Swahili. They were known as clients of the Oromo and gave one of each pair of tusks they procured to their Oromo overlords; like so many other foragers, they were looked down on by farmers and herders, who nonetheless sought their expertise as hunters, like the Kamba, and their ritual expertise, in particular as circumcisers for the Oromo (Kusimba et al. 2005). At Kisio Shelter, about 150 km from the coast, foragers left remains of a diet rich in small bovids, hyrax, hare, birds, and snails, used expedient lithic technologies, and had access to pottery, Indian and European glass beads, and arrowheads hammered from sheet metal. Unlike Pleistocene foragers, Kisio's residents rarely had access to the large bovids of the plains, but focused their diet instead on the local resident fauna of the outcrops around the site (Kusimba et al. 2005), as also documented among the Mukogodo on Kenya's Laikipia Plateau (Mutundu 1999).

Other hunter-gatherer/forager frontiers can link archaeological evidence of foraging with historical and ethnographic information. Around Lake Eyasi, foragers hunted and fished at Mumba Shelter while pastoralists occupied nearby open-air sites (Prendergast et al. 2007). Today's Hadzabe, numbering only 1,000, nevertheless demonstrate a continuity into the archaeological past through their highly distinctive language and genetics and their oral traditions of site and landscape use. Indeed, Mabulla (2007) suggests that forager knowledge of landscapes and resources was at least as valuable to incoming farmer/herders as pottery and goats were to foragers; perhaps proximity to foragers was a real determinant of the initial landscape use and migration of early farmers, and may explain at least some of the contours of the 'Bantu expansion'. Further south in Zambia, sites around the Kafue Flats show that foragers (known to their farming neighbours as BaTwa) continued to inhabit rockshelters after the local introduction of farming (Clark 1950; Phillipson 1976). For northern Zambia, at least, Musonda (1987) argues that foragers maintained clear independence from—and perhaps had very little to do with—farmers for several centuries, until traded ceramics and rare domestic stock begin to appear in forager rockshelter sequences in the second millennium AD (cf. Phillipson 1976).

Even today, East African communities assert their identity as hunters and as legitimate custodians of 'natural' ecosystems that are degrading all over Africa in the shadow of climate change and overexploitation (Lynch 2006). Recently, the Kenyan government initiated a plan to rehabilitate the highland Mau Escarpment, the rivers of which support important grasslands, farmlands, and game parks, as they attempt to mitigate the environmental damage of deforestation. The Ogiek, after many years of being alienated from their land by corrupt government officials (Okwembah 2009), are now asserting themselves as custodians of forest sites deemed crucial to environmental preservation. Time will tell if the promise given to the Ogiek and other hunters like them is fulfilled.

REFERENCES

AMBROSE, S. H. (1984). The introduction of pastoral adaptations to the highlands of East Africa. In J. D. Clark and S. A. Brandt (eds), *From Hunters to Farmers: The Causes and Consequences of Food Production in Africa*. Berkeley: University of California Press, 212–39.

—— (1985). Excavations at Masai Gorge Rockshelter, Naivasha. *Azania* 20: 29–68.

—— (1998). Chronology of the Later Stone Age and food production in East Africa. *Journal of Archaeological Science* 17: 377–92.

—— (2002). Small things remembered: origins of early microlithic technology in sub-Saharan Africa. *Archaeological Papers of the American Anthropological Association* 12: 9–30.

—— HIVERNEL, F., and NELSON, C.M. (1980). The taxonomic status of the Kenya Capsian. In R. Leakey and B. Ogot (eds), *Proceedings of the VIIIth Panafrican Congress of Prehistory and Quaternary Studies*. Nairobi: International Louis Leakey Memorial Institute for African Prehistory, 248–52.

AUCOUR, A.-M., HILLAIRE-MARCEL, C., and BONNEFILLE, R., (1994). Late Quaternary biomass changes from ^{13}C measurements in a highland peatbog from Equatorial Africa (Burundi). *Quaternary Research* 41: 225–33.

BAILEY, R. C. (1991). *The Behavioural Ecology of Efe Pygmy Men in the Ituri Forest, Zaire*. Ann Arbor: University of Michigan Museum of Anthropology.

BARHAM, L. S. (2000). *The Middle Stone Age of Zambia, South Central Africa*. Bristol: Western Academic & Specialist Press.

BISSON, M. S. (1990). Lithic reduction sequences as an aid to the analysis of Late Stone Age quartz assemblages from the Luano Spring, Chingola, Zambia. *African Archaeological Review* 8: 103–38.

BONNEFILLE, R., ROELAND, J., and GUIOT, J. (1990). Temperature and rainfall estimated for the past 40,000 years in equatorial Africa. *Nature* 346: 347–439.

BOWER, J. R, NELSON, C. M., WAIBEL, A. F., and WANDIBBA, S. (1977). The University of Massachusetts Later Stone Age/Pastoral Neolithic sites in Serengeti. *Azania* 21: 129–33.

CHAMI, F., and KWEKASON, A. (2003). Neolithic pottery traditions from the island, the coast and the interior of Africa. *African Archaeological Review* 20: 65–80.

CLARK, J. D. (1950). A note on the pre-Bantu inhabitants of Northern Rhodesia and Nyasaland. *South African Journal of Science* 47: 80–85.

DALE, D., and ASHLEY, C. Z. (2010). Holocene hunter-fisher-gatherer communities: new perspectives on Kansyore-using communities of western Kenya. *Azania* 45: 24–48.

DALE, D., MARSHALL, F., and PILGRAM, T. (2004). Delayed-return hunter-gatherers in Africa? Historic perspectives from the Okiek and archaeological perspectives from the Kansyore. In G. M. Crothers (ed.), *Hunters and Gatherers in Theory and Archaeology*. Carbondale, Ill.: Center for Archaeological Investigations, 340–73.

DERRICOURT, R. (1985). *Man on the Kafue: The Archaeology and History of the Itezhitezhi Area of Zambia*. London: Ethnographica.

FAGAN, B., and VAN NOTEN, F. (1971). *The Hunter-Gatherers of Gwisho*. Tervuren: Musée Royal de l'Afrique Centrale.

GARCIN, Y., JUNGINGER, A., MELNICK, D. OLAGO, D., STRECKER, M., and TRAUGH, M. (2009). Late Pleistocene-Holocene rise and collapse of Lake Suguta, northern Kenya rift. *Quaternary Science Reviews* 28: 911–25.

GASSE, F., ROGNON, R., and STREET, F. (1980). Quaternary history of the Afar and Ethiopian Rift lakes. In M. A. J. Williams and H. Faure (eds), *The Sahara and the Nile*. Rotterdam: Balkema, 361–400.

GIFFORD-GONZALEZ, D. (2000). Animal disease challenges to the emergence of pastoralism in sub-Saharan Africa. *African Archaeological Review* 17: 95–139.

GUTIN, J. A., and MUSONDA, F. (1985). Faunal remains from Mufulwe rock shelter, Zambia, and their implications. *South African Archaeological Bulletin* 40: 11–16.

IKEYA, K. (1993). Goat-raising among the San in the central Kalahari. *African Study Monographs* 14(1): 39–52.

INSKEEP, R. R. (1962). The age of the Kondoa rock paintings in the light of recent excavations at Kisese II rock shelter. In G. Mortelmans and J. Nenquin (eds), *Actes du IV Congres Panafricain de Préhistoire et de l'Étude du Quaternaire*. Tervuren: Musée Royale de l'Afrique Centrale, 249–56.

JOHNSON, T. C., SCHOLZ, C., TALBOT, M., et al. (1996). Late Pleistocene dessication of Lake Victoria and rapid evolution of cichlid fishes. *Science* 273: 1091–3.

KAREGA-MUNENE (2002). *Holocene Foragers, Fishers and Herders of Western Kenya*. Oxford: Archaeopress.

KASSAM, A. (2000). When will we be people as well? Social identity and the politics of cultural performance: the case of the Waata Oromo of East and Northeast Africa. *Social Identities* 6: 189–206.

——(2004). Marginalization of the Waata Oromo hunter-gatherers of Kenya: insider and outsider perspectives. *Africa* 74: 194–216.

KENT, S. (1996). *Cultural Diversity among Twentieth Century Foragers: An African Perspective*. Cambridge: Cambridge University Press.

KIAGE, L. M., and LIU, K. (2006). Late Quaternary paleoenvironmental changes in East Africa: a review of multiproxy evidence from palynology, lake sediments, and associated records. *Progress in Physical Geography* 30: 633–58.

KUSIMBA, S. B. (2001). The Pleistocene Later Stone Age in East Africa: excavations and lithic assemblages from Lukenya Hill. *African Archaeological Review* 18: 77–123.

——(2003). *African Foragers: Environment, Technology, Interactions*. Walnut Creek, Calif.: AltaMira Press.

——KUSIMBA, S., and WRIGHT, D. (2005). The development and collapse of precolonial ethnic mosaics in Tsavo, Kenya. *Journal of African Archaeology* 3: 345–65.

LANE, P. J. (2004). The 'moving frontier' and the transition to food production in Kenya. *Azania* 39: 243–64.

——ASHLEY, C., and OTEYO, G., (2006). New dates for Kansyore and Urewe wares from northern Nyanza, Kenya. *Azania* 41: 123–38.

—— SEITSONEN, O. HARVEY, P., MIRE, S., and ODEDE, F. (2007). The transition to farming in eastern Africa: new faunal and dating evidence from Wadh Lang'o and Usenge, Kenya. *Antiquity* 81: 62–81.

LYNCH, G. (2006). Negotiating ethnicity: identity politics in contemporary Kenya. *Review of African Political Economy* 107: 49–65.

MABULLA, A. (2007). Hunting and foraging in the Eyasi Basin, northern Tanzania: past, present, and future prospects. *African Archaeological Review* 24:15–33.

MARCHANT, R., and TAYLOR, D. (1998). Dynamics of montane forest in central Africa during the late Holocene; a pollen-based record from western Uganda. *The Holocene* 8: 375–81.

MAREAN, C. (1992). Hunter to herder: large mammal remains from the hunter-gatherer occupation at Enkapune ya Muto, rock shelter, Central Rift, Kenya. *African Archaeological Review* 10: 65–128.

MARSHALL, F. (1990). Origins of specialized pastoral production in East Africa. *American Anthropologist* 92: 873–94.

—— STEWART, K., and BARTHELME, J. (1984). Early domestic stock at Dongodien in northern Kenya. *Azania* 19:120–7.

MASAO, F. T. 1979. The Later Stone Age and the rock paintings of central Tanzania. *Studien zur Kulturkunde Wiesbaden* 1: 301–11.

MERRICK, H., and BROWN, F. (1984). Obsidian sources and patterns of source utilization in Kenya and northern Tanzania: some initial findings. *African Archaeological Review* 2: 129–52.

MORRISON, K., and JUNKER, L. (2002). *Forager-Traders of Southeast Asia*. Cambridge: Cambridge University Press.

MUSONDA, F. B. (1984). Late Pleistocene and Holocene microlithic industries from the Lunsemfwa Basin, Zambia. *South African Archaeological Bulletin* 39: 24–36.

—— (1987). The significance of pottery in Zambian Later Stone Age contexts. *African Archaeological Review* 5: 147–58.

MUTUNDU, K. K. 1999. *Ethnohistoric Archaeology of the Mukogodo in North Central Kenya*. Oxford: Archaeopress.

NASH, B., MERRICK, H., and BROWN, F. (2011). Obsidian types from Holocene sites around Lake Turkana, and other localities in northern Kenya. *Journal of Archaeological Science* 38: 1371–6.

NDIEMA, E., DILLIAN, C. D., and BRAUN, D. R. (2010) Interaction and exchange across the transition to pastoralism, Lake Turkana, Kenya. In C. D. Dillian and C. L. White (eds), *Trade and Exchange: Archaeological Studies from History and Prehistory*. New York: Springer, 95–110.

NELSON, C. M., and POSNANSKY, M. (1970). The stone tools from the re-excavation of Nzongezi rock shelter, Uganda. *Azania* 5: 120–72.

OKWEMBAH, D. (2009). How Moi allies acquired land meant for Ogiek. http://www.nation. co.ke/News/-/1056/818058/-/vnkkoe/-/index.html. Accessed 17 Feb. 2010.

PHILLIPSON, D. W. (1976). *The Prehistory of Eastern Zambia*. Nairobi: British Institute in Eastern Africa.

—— (1977). Lowasera. *Azania* 12: 1–32.

PRENDERGAST, M. E. (2010). Kansyore fisher-foragers and transitions to food production in East Africa: the view from Wadh Lang'o, Nyanza Province, Kenya. *Azania* 45: 82–111.

PRENDERGAST, M. E. and LANE, P. J. (2010). Middle Holocene fishing strategies in East Africa: zooarchaeological analysis of Pundo, a Kansyore shell midden in northern Nyanza (Kenya). *International Journal of Osteoarchaeology* 20: 88–112.

—— LUQUE, L., DOMÍNGUEZ-RODRIGO, M., DÍEZ MARTÍN, F., MABULLA, A., and BARBA, R. (2007). New excavations at Mumba rockshelter (Tanzania). *Journal of African Archaeology* 5: 163–89.

ROBBINS, L. H. (1972). Archaeology in the Turkana district, Kenya. *Science* 176: 359–66.

—— (1974). *The Lothagam Site: A Later Stone Age Fishing Settlement in the Lake Rudolf Basin, Kenya*. East Lansing: Michigan State University Museum.

—— (2006). Lake Turkana Archaeology: the Holocene. *Ethnohistory* 53:71–83.

ROBERTSHAW, P. T. (1991). Gogo Falls: excavations at a complex archaeological site east of Lake Victoria. *Azania* 26: 63–195.

—— COLLETT, D. P., GIFFORD, D., and MBAE, N. B. (1983). Shell middens on the shores of Lake Victoria. *Azania* 18: 1–44.

SADR, K. (1998). The first herders at the Cape of Good Hope. *African Archaeological Review* 15: 101–22.

SKINNER, A. R., HAY, R. L., MASAO, F., and BLACKWELL, B. A. B. (2003). Dating the Naisiusiu Beds, Olduvai Gorge, by electron spin resonance. *Quaternary Science Reviews* 22: 1361–6.

SOPER, R., and GOLDEN, B. (1969). An archaeological survey of Mwanza Region, Tanzania. *Azania* 4:15–79.

STEWART, K. M. (1989). *Fishing Sites of North and East Africa in the Late Pleistocene and Holocene: Environmental Change and Human Adaptation*. Oxford: British Archaeological Reports.

STREET-PERROT, F. A. and PERROT, R. (1994). Holocene vegetation, lake levels, and climate of Africa. In H. E. Wright (ed.), *Global Climates since the Last Glacial Maximum*. Minneapolis: University of Minnesota Press, 322–56.

TAYLOR, D., and MARCHANT, R., (1994/5). Human impact in the Interlacustrine Region: long-term pollen records from the Rukiga Highlands. *Azania* 29/30: 283–95.

TIMM, O., KOHLER, P., TIMMERMANN, A., and MENVIEL, L. (2010). Mechanisms for the onset of the African Humid Period and Sahara greening 14.5–11 ka bp. *Journal of Climate* 23: 2612–33.

TURNBULL, C. (1961). *The Forest People*. London: Jonathan Cape.

—— (1966). *Wayward Servants: The Two Worlds of the African Pygmies*. London: Eyre & Spottiswoode.

VAN NOTEN, F. (1977). Excavations at Matupi Cave. *Antiquity* 51: 35–40.

YELLEN, J. E. (1998). Barbed bone points: tradition and continuity in Saharan and sub-Saharan Africa. *African Archaeological Review* 15: 172–98.

ZONNEVELD, K., GANNSEN, G., TROELSTRA, S., VERSTEEGH, G., and VISCHER, H. (1997). Mechanisms forcing abrupt fluctuations of the Indian Ocean summer monsoon during the last deglaciation. *Quaternary Science Reviews* 16: 187–201.

CHAPTER 33

···

SOUTHERN AFRICAN HUNTER-GATHERERS OF THE LAST 25,000 YEARS

···

PETER MITCHELL

INTRODUCTION

··

SOUTHERN AFRICAN hunter-gatherers have long served as archetypes of what Lee (1979) termed the 'forager mode of production', Sahlins (1976) the 'original affluent society', and Binford (1980) simply 'foragers'. As part of broader global debates (Headland and Reid 1989), such characterizations have also been challenged by those emphasizing the supposedly subordinating and transforming impacts on Kalahari San of centuries of interaction with herding and farming societies (Wilmsen and Denbow 1990). Also notable are the influence of San rock art research on studies of Upper Palaeolithic European cave art (Lewis-Williams 2002), and benchmark studies of prehistoric diet and seasonal mobility that pioneered stable isotope analysis of human skeletons (Parkington et al. 1987). Today, southern African hunter-gatherers are central to discussions of the biological origins of *Homo sapiens* and the emergence of complex forms of cognition (Lahr, Wadley, Lombard, Chs 23, 25, 26 above). The wider relevance of their archaeology could not be plainer.

This chapter summarizes the overall trajectories of the region's hunter-gatherer communities over the past 25,000 years, emphasizing themes of greatest importance in contemporary research. More extensive syntheses include both sub-continental (Deacon and Deacon 1999; Mitchell 2002, 2005) and regional (e.g. Parkington 2006; Mitchell and Smith 2009; Campbell et al. 2009) studies.

BACKGROUND

··

As discussed here, southern Africa comprises present-day Botswana, Lesotho, Namibia, South Africa, Swaziland, and Zimbabwe, plus the bulk of Mozambique and southernmost Angola (Fig. 33.1). Biogeographically, it encompasses twelve distinct terrestrial biomes south of the Kunene, Cubango, and Zambezi rivers at ~17°S, including moist woodlands, extensive savannahs of variable grassland and woodland composition, and large stretches of more arid desert and semi-desert (the latter known as Karoo), as well as temperate grasslands and the Mediterranean-like ecology of the Cape's *fynbos* region. Organizing this complexity is the distinction between summer (mostly in the north and east) and winter (in the far southwest) rainfall regimes, and the fact that much of the sub-continent's western half experiences little, and unreliable, precipitation. Today's climate and ecologies have broadly held throughout the Holocene, but fluctuations in rainfall, the most critical variable for biological productivity at these latitudes, have impacted human settlement, especially in more arid areas. Translating such shifts into meaningful statements about resource productivity remains challenging, as does correlating multiple palaeoenvironmental proxies and identifying briefer climatic episodes, especially across the Pleistocene/Holocene transition.

Home to populations speaking click languages of the Tuu (!Ui-Taa), Ju-≠Hoan, and Khoe-Kwadi families (Barnard 1992; Güldemann 2008), southern Africa corresponds to the area within which people of broadly Khoisan physical type are known in the bio-archaeological record (Morris 2003). Although skeletons from Gwisho, southern Zambia, show Khoisan features (Fagan and van Noten 1971) and some connections are discernible between lithic industries either side of the Zambezi, for the most part hunter-gatherer toolkits in southern Africa are distinct from those of south-central or eastern Africa; archaeology provides no justification for imagining a Khoisan presence in the latter region or deriving southern African hunter-gatherers from it (*pace* Ehret 2002). The quite different rock art traditions of southern versus south-central/eastern Africa confirm this, reinforcing the rationale for treating southern Africa as a distinct, if permeable, entity on the map of Africa's past (Smith, Ch. 11 above).

The outlines of southern Africa's hunter-gatherer sequence established by Goodwin and van Riet Lowe (1929) were fleshed out by regional studies in the 1960s to 1980s, mostly undertaken

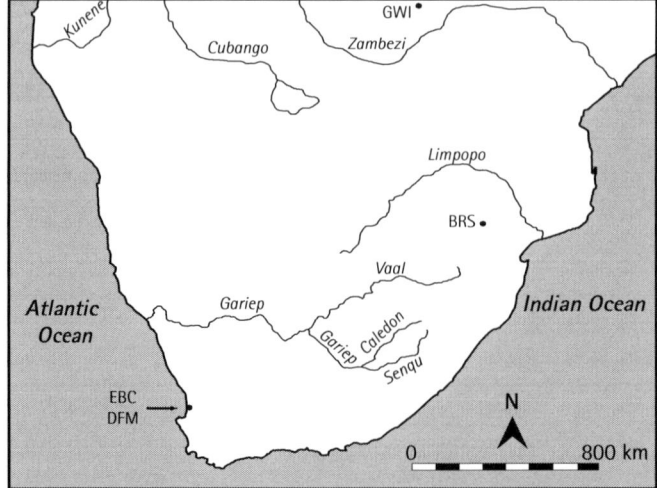

FIG. 33.1 Southern Africa showing the major localities and archaeological sites discussed in Chapter 33. Site names are abbreviated thus: BRS Bushman Rock Shelter; DFM Dunefield Midden; EBC Elands Bay Cave; GWI Gwisho (courtesy Rachel King).

within a paradigm emphasizing subsistence and the links between cultural and environmental change (e.g. Deacon 1976). A partial paradigm shift occurred in the mid-1980s, spurred by recognition that San ethnography provided the key to understanding the meaning and content of San rock art (Vinnicombe 1976; Lewis-Williams 1981). Revolutionizing the latter, this impelled other archaeologists to explore anthropological studies of Kalahari San groups for concepts that could address questions about how people related to people, and not just to nature. Innovative studies of aggregation and dispersal, gift exchange, gender, burial, and the constitution of group identities resulted (e.g. Hall and Binneman 1987; Wadley 1987, 1997; Mazel 1989; Hall 2000a). Although the tightness of linkages between ethnographic practice and excavated materials requires further study (Barham 1992), these projects effected lasting changes in how archaeologists think about the past. Today, researchers seek a more integrated understanding of past hunter-gatherers that builds bridges within archaeology (e.g. between excavated data and those secured from recording rock art) and between it and other disciplines.

LATE PLEISTOCENE HUNTER-GATHERERS

For Goodwin and van Riet Lowe (1929) physical anthropology ('archaic'/'modern' fossils), rock art (absent/present), and stone tools (prepared core technology/microlithic toolkits) justified distinguishing between the Middle and Later Stone Ages. While it is acknowledged that rock art occurs in terminal Middle Stone Age (MSA) contexts, that *H. sapiens* was responsible for MSA lithic assemblages, and that not all Later Stone Age (LSA) ones are microlithic, links to the material culture of ethnographically attested hunter-gatherers (notably bone tools and ostrich eggshell beads) long placed an upper boundary of 40 kya on the transition to the LSA (Deacon 1984). Although their dearth during MIS 3 (60–25 kya) remains unexplained (Lombard and Parsons 2010), art, jewellery and other indicators of complex cognition are now unequivocally decoupled from changes in stone tools (Lombard, Ch. 26 above): if the MSA/LSA transition retains relevance it thus lies squarely in the organization of lithic technology. Available evidence (Mitchell 2002: 112–17) also indicates that southern Africa neither followed a single trajectory nor shared in East Africa's apparently early and more comprehensive (~40 kya) shift to microlithic toolkits (Ambrose 2002), though environmental changes presumably helped define and frame the choices people made.

Large areas of southern Africa may have been very lightly settled, even abandoned, during MIS 2 (25–10 kya), which brought greater (though not unvarying) aridity to much of the summer-rainfall zone. Reduced evapotranspiration and, in the winter-rainfall zone, increased precipitation may explain continued settlement in parts of Botswana (Robbins et al. 1994), Namibia (Vogelsang et al. 2010), and Namaqualand (Orton 2008). Such areas may have constituted stable refugia, along with the Cape (and its now-drowned continental shelf) and topographically diverse areas of eastern and southeastern South Africa able to sustain a diversity of resources because of their more reliable rainfall. All known rockshelter sequences nevertheless show highly punctuated occupation across this period, suggesting that conditions were mostly less clement for human survival than during the Holocene. That survival did not, however, depend on a radically different economy or mobility pattern focused on large, migratory game as once thought (Deacon 1972). Plants almost certainly underpinned late Pleistocene diets (Deacon 1993), with shellfish and other marine resources probably exploited along the coast, contacts with which (judging from rare finds of seashell ornaments) reached 200 km inland. Still longer-distance connections are demonstrated by similarities in toolkit. From Swaziland to Namaqualand, for instance, people invested heavily in producing standardized but generally unmodified bladelets from bipolar or specialized bladelet cores. These bladelets were then used as inserts in composite hunting and process-ing tools (Binneman 1997), effecting economies in raw material use and facilitating tool maintenance and reliability. Such toolkits are generally known as Robberg, although some researchers (e.g. Parkington 1993) eschew such broad, technocomplex-level designations in favour of stressing underlying continuities and smaller-scale adjustments.

Dating to 19–12 kya, Robberg toolkits occur south of the Limpopo and Orange Rivers, with macrolithic assemblages in south-central Namibia, toolkits employing bladelets spo-radically present in northeastern Zimbabwe and northwestern Botswana, and Mode 3 tech-nologies perhaps persisting in Zimbabwe's Matopo Hills (Mitchell 2002: 123–5). Such differences may reflect long-term isolation of human populations in different parts of south-ern Africa across MIS2 and are supported by the geography of the Tuu and Ju-≠Hoan lan-guage families; genetic analyses may be able to establish the time-depth of such divergences between northern and southern hunter-gatherer populations (Mitchell 2010).

THE PLEISTOCENE/HOLOCENE TRANSITION

From broadly 12 to 8 kya, assemblages across South Africa (including semi-arid interior areas with little or no occupation in Robberg times), Lesotho, Swaziland, south-central Namibia, and south-central Zimbabwe share a general preference for larger flakes and scrap-ers and an aversion to bladelet production or microlithic tools. Such Oakhurst or late Pleistocene/early Holocene non-microlithic assemblages include several regional variants, but the overall impression is one of considerable expediency, although end-retouched scrap-ers with adze-like lateral retouch usable for a range of extractive and maintenance tasks are quite widespread after 9.5 kya. Why bladelet technology was so comprehensively abandoned is unknown: existing arguments, though perhaps relevant at more local scales (Deacon 1984; Ambrose and Lorenz 1990), ignore how it may have been used and deployed and fail to engage with the sub-continental scale of the change, which exceeds ecological shifts in any one biome or raw-material availability at single sites.

These questions are of interest because the assemblages in question broadly span the Pleistocene/Holocene transition, a period of immense potential for comparative studies of hunter-gatherer archaeology (Straus et al. 1996). Certainly, resource availability must have altered considerably over this period. Elands Bay Cave on South Africa's Atlantic coast, for example (Fig. 33.2), documents how people successively rescheduled their use of the site and the resources available from it as it shifted, owing to rising sea level, from being inland to being at the coast (Parkington 1988). More generally, from 11 kya evidence of shellfish, fish, rock lobster, and seabird exploitation becomes widely apparent at coastal sites in the Cape (other coastlines are very poorly known), mirrored in many cases by greater use of

FIG. 33.2 Elands Bay Cave, a major source of information for the Pleistocene/Holocene transition, with the Atlantic Ocean in the background (photograph, Peter Mitchell).

smaller-sized terrestrial foods (Parkington 1988; Walker 1995a). Direct evidence of plant food consumption also survives: at Bushman Rock Shelter, for instance, geophytes (edible underground storage organs) alternated with fruits and nuts depending on overall temperature (Wadley 1987), while marula (*Sclerocarya birrea*) was important in the Matopo Hills (Walker 1995a) and *!nara* melon (*Aganthosicyos horrida*) in the Namib Desert (Sandelowsky 1977).

HOLOCENE HUNTER-GATHERERS
AND THEIR ROCK ART

The Oakhurst was succeeded by another microlithic technology, the Wilton, but instead of bladelets as in the Robberg this emphasized small, standardized scrapers and backed microliths, initially segments, subsequently backed bladelets and points of various kinds, with adzes an increasingly common element later on (Wadley 2000). Wilton assemblages show an interesting chronological pattern, with the earliest dates three to four millennia older in Zimbabwe and Namibia than in the Cape Fold Belt, where an east-to-west trend is also evident. Evidence for population movements that might explain this pattern is lacking. Instead, the changes in hafting design, tool standardization, and artefact type subsumed under the Wilton heading were probably adopted for various, local reasons, with risk minimization to cope with adverse climate change a contributory factor (Bousman 2005). Though some of the regional variation found in mid/late Holocene southern African assemblages warrants wholly different designations (e.g. Binneman 2006/7), in broad terms it was this toolkit that persisted until stone tool-making ended in the subcontinent in the 19th century.

Plant foods underwrote mid/late Holocene subsistence strategies across southern Africa. Occupation was sporadic where they were less reliable (e.g. the Karoo), but more intensive where geophytes or nut/fruit-bearing trees served as mainstays, as in the Matopo Hills or the Cape (Deacon 1993). The scarcity of sites in northern South Africa (Limpopo and Mpumalanga) is perplexing in this context, as species such as marula are plentiful here, but perhaps people preferred open-air campsites (Korsman and Plug 1994), though limited fieldwork may also be relevant (cf. van Doornum 2007, 2008).

Orchestrating site occupation histories and subsistence evidence into models of seasonal mobility was long a major research theme. The most detailed such study, focused around Elands Bay Cave, used ecological parameters and excavated faunal and botanical indicators to envisage people spending summers inland and winters on the coast. Initially applied over a broader time-frame, the model was later restricted to the period 4300–2000 BP (Parkington et al. 1987). However, stable isotope analysis of human remains shows that at this time individuals dying at the coast had markedly different diets from those dying inland (Sealy and van der Merwe 1988). While debate continues (Parkington 2001), and coastal dwellers certainly ate terrestrial foods as well (Lee-Thorp et al. 1989), these results are inconsistent with regular seasonal movements between coast and interior. Indeed, on some readings regional settlement may have been overwhelmingly coastal in nature c. 3000–2100 BP, when higher rainfall and cooler seas enhanced terrestrial and marine productivity, encouraging creation of enormous 'megamiddens' that consist mostly of discarded black mussels (*Choromytilus meridionalis*) that Jerardino et al. (2008) interpret as residential camps (cf. Henshilwood et al. 1994, who consider them briefly, if regularly, occupied stations at which shellfish were dried for transport and consumption inland).

In the southern Cape, too, stable isotope analyses suggest that many mid-/late Holocene individuals maintained distinct diets over quite short distances (Sealy 2006), consistent with the packing of groups into smaller sections of the landscape indicated by the development of regionally circumscribed artefact styles and raw-material choices and the emergence of formal burial at particular locations, probably to assert claims to land ownership (Hall 2000a). Bio-anthropological analysis of these burials is producing much new evidence (Pfeiffer 2009), including compelling evidence of interpersonal violence in the southwestern Cape c. 2600–2100 BP. Unlike the recent Kalahari, this involved close-quarter weaponry and attacks on women and children (Pfeiffer and van der Merwe 2004), patterns that fit a context of growing competition for resources within a larger, spatially more confined population during the 'megamidden' period. Strikingly, this region's only two burial clusters date to the end of the same period and again show distinct and quite localized isotopic signatures (Manhire 1993; Dewar 2010). Differences in the timing of these processes require explanation, but occupation may have been less continuously intensive in the southwestern Cape than the southern, though without the mid-Holocene abandonment previously envisaged (e.g. Jerardino and Yates 1996; Orton 2009).

How far such changes can helpfully be understood as 'intensification' (Lourandos 1983) may be debated, although the term has been applied (especially in KwaZulu-Natal's Thukela Basin, a major focus of social approaches to the archaeological record; Mazel 1989). Opportunities to exploit productive *r*-resources (*sensu* Hayden 1990) in ways capable of producing social formations radically different from those attested ethnographically were, however, constrained by the absence of readily domesticable plants and animals (Barham and Mitchell 2008: 395–8), though we should not then expect that mid-/late Holocene foragers were identical to some or all recent San; the patterns just discussed emphasize this.

ROCK ART

Southern Africa's hunter-gatherer rock art (Fig. 33.3) is better understood than that of any other part of the continent (Smith, Ch. 11 above) because of the insights gained from using San concepts and beliefs (Lewis-Williams 2008), especially the ethnographies of contemporary Kalahari San and the now extinct /Xam of the Northern Cape, for whom an extensive archive exists (Skotnes 2007). Much of the art relates to the power of shamans to heal the sick, control animals, make rain, and move between different tiers of the cosmos (Lewis-Williams and Pearce 2004), though other levels of meaning exist (Lewis-Williams 1998) and additional perspectives warrant investigation, including ethology (e.g. Eastwood 2006) and the phenomenology of the body (Blundell 2004). Claims that creation myths or ideas about the spirits of the dead, rather than shamanism, inform key paintings in the Maloti-Drakensberg region (Solomon 1997, 2008) are, however, exaggerated, although references to gender distinctions concerned with hunting, initiation, and control of weather do seem apparent in the mountains of the Western Cape (Parkington 1999, 2003). Eastwood's (2005, 2006) work in the central Limpopo Basin emphasizes another theme, female puberty rites, and draws on a different ethnographic dataset, that of Khoe-speaking San, since one such group, the Hietshware, probably produced the paintings in question. While similarities in belief and practice between ethnolinguistically divergent San groups should not be denied (Lewis-Williams and Biesele 1978), there is still much scope for exploring regional variation (Hampson et al. 2002) and for undertaking more detailed, historically contextualized analyses of the ethnography used to interpret the art (Solomon 2011).

While rock art offers the best possibility for developing that people-centred archaeology for which southern African researchers have striven since the mid-1980s (Smith 2010), to relate it to other components of the archaeological record it must be dated. In rare cases, imagery of Europeans and other comparatively well-dated phenomena allows social change to be explored (Blundell 2004). For the 19th century a major focus concerns how some San participated in the formation of new social groups through processes of creolization that

FIG. 33.3 Painting of a rain animal, Doring Valley, Western Cape Province, South Africa (photograph, Peter Mitchell).

drew upon novel kinds of imagery, such as baboons and horses (Challis 2009). Such studies are exciting because they integrate diverse data sets within shortlived and spatially limited contexts and emphasize the two-way, creative nature of interaction rather than more unidirectional alternatives that stress only how San were influenced by farmers (Jolly 1996). Further progress nevertheless requires much more widespread use of the AMS radiocarbon technique to date paint directly (Mazel 2009), as well as integrating the study of parietal imagery with excavation of the sites at which people painted. Current data—including finds of exfoliated images in excavated contexts—indicate that some surviving paintings are as old as 3500 or 3000 BP in the Western Cape and the Maloti-Drakensberg, and perhaps as much as 6000 BP in Zimbabwe; some open-air engravings may be even older (Barham and Mitchell 2008: 392).

Hunter-gatherers and others:
THE LAST 2,000 YEARS

The juxtaposition of hunter-gatherers, herders, farmers (including indigenous states like Great Zimbabwe), and European settlers over the past 2,000 years makes southern Africa uniquely well placed for exploring the relations between different social formations, including foragers. Much recent work has addressed these themes, though hunter-gatherers remain on its margins (Swanepoel et al. 2008). Across southern Africa's more arid western third, domestic livestock (sheep, and probably also cattle) were available from shortly before 2000 BP (Sadr, Ch. 44 below). Linguistics and genetics (Güldemann 2008; Henn et al. 2008) suggest that both population movement by those keeping livestock and transmission of animals between indigenous foragers were involved in processes that then, or later (Sadr 1998), saw the establishment in the Cape of communities ancestral to the Khoekhoen whom European settlers encountered from 1488. The tendencies toward greater sedentism and resource specialization signalled by stable isotope analyses, mega-midden formation, and—in the northern Kalahari (a key area for onward movement of livestock and the dispersal of Khoe-speakers)—freshwater fishing (Robbins et al. 1994, 1998b) could all suggest that foragers were interested in acquiring new resources (including pottery, useful for both cooking and storage; Sadr and Sampson 2006) for reasons of economic security and prestige. The relations that subsequently prevailed were doubtless complex, with foragers persisting in the interstices of pastoralist settlement and areas unattractive to herders, such as the Cederberg Mountains and much of the Karoo (where the forager/herder frontier in the Seacow Valley is particularly well known; Sampson 2010). However, the dietary diversity evident in well-studied areas like that around Elands Bay makes clear that there was no single or simple response to pastoralist presence (Jerardino 2007). In the same locality, the exceptionally well-preserved, extensively excavated, and short-lived sites at Dunefield Midden offer great scope for resolving person, time, and space to address social questions such as foodsharing (Parkington et al. 2009; Stewart 2011). Combining a predominantly hunted and gathered diet and formal, microlithic toolkit with sheep and traces of ritual behaviour otherwise known only from pastoralists, they also emphasize the difficulty of disentangling hunters from herders in much of the archaeological record and, indeed, perhaps the foolishness of assuming that hard-and-fast distinctions always existed (cf. Parsons 2007).

Across southern Africa's eastern half, foragers interacted principally with farming communities; arguments for ancestral Khoekhoen dispersing from near the Limpopo across the interior to the Cape (Smith and Ouzman 2004) are uncompelling. In Zimbabwe and Mozambique, replacement of hunter-gatherers seems to have been rapid, and genetic analyses attest to population admixture in the latter region (Pereira et al. 2001; Salas et al. 2002). Further south, preliminary studies demonstrate high 'Khoisan' contributions to the mitochondrial DNA of South African Nguni-speakers, fitting linguistic and anthropological evidence for extensive intermarriage between female San and Bantu-speaking men (Hammond-Tooke 1998), a pattern of hypergamy of much wider relevance in situations of farmer–forager contact (Bentley et al. 2009). Unanswered but critical is the timing of this interaction, as Nguni is a second-millennium introduction to southern Africa (Schoeman, Ch. 64) and Mazel (1989) posits much more equal exchange relations in the Thukela Basin before AD 1000. Those ties included the movement of iron, pottery, and even livestock in return for ostrich eggshell beads and probably many 'invisible' plant, animal, and mineral products not only there but across the wider Maloti–Drakensberg region (Mitchell 2009). The same may have happened in the Kalahari, with hunter-gatherers perhaps also producing the specularite that was intensively mined in the Tsodilo Hills (Robbins et al. 1998a), but readings of interaction that imply forager dependency (Wilmsen and Denbow 1990) are contestable both theoretically and empirically (Solway and Lee 1990; Sadr 1997), although there is some evidence for their incorporation into late farming communities (Hall 2000b).

Overall, San peoples undoubtedly survived best in areas unattractive to farmers by reason of aridity or cold. Elsewhere, hypergamy, unequal demographic growth, refocusing of exchange ties toward farmers, and increasing appropriation of the landscape for cultivation and herding undercut the social and biological reproduction of foraging societies (Wadley 1996). Rock art captures some of these changes: in the Caledon Valley, for instance, richly painted sites may have substituted for the 'real' aggregation of increasingly dispersed populations (Wadley and McLaren 1998) and sheep, cattle (Fig. 33.4), and cattle-hide shields were incorporated into paintings as potent images (Loubser and Laurens 1994), not least as hunter-gatherers themselves acquired livestock (Jolly 2007). Such groups may have been best able to withstand, albeit temporarily, what by the 19th century were rapidly expanding and ultimately overwhelming frontiers of European and agropastoralist expansion. Regrettably, except for the Seacow Valley (Sampson 1995) and, on a smaller scale, the Northern Cape (Deacon 1996), excavation has yet to address such changes, partly because sufficiently fine-grained deposits are often lacking (Klatzow 2010).

Archaeologists have also examined foragers in relation to the formation and growth of *indigenous* states. Recent excavations document much earlier forager occupation in the Shashe-Limpopo Basin (van Doornum 2007, 2008), querying suggestions that forager settlement intensified there in the early centuries AD as farmers and their resources appeared on the scene, although arguments that foragers produced skins for trade with Zhizo farmers after 900 still resonate (Hall and Smith 2000). Thereafter, newly arriving K2 communities (see Pikirayi, Ch. 63 below) may have sought ivory (for trading on to the Indian Ocean coast) from foragers, but also drew on the latter's power as aborigines to make rain (Schoeman 2006). However, that power was lost as K2 ancestors proliferated and farmers appropriated former forager sites, overpainting San art and appropriating its potency (cf. Walker 1997), leaving hunter-gatherers spatially displaced or subsumed into the emerging Mapungubwe

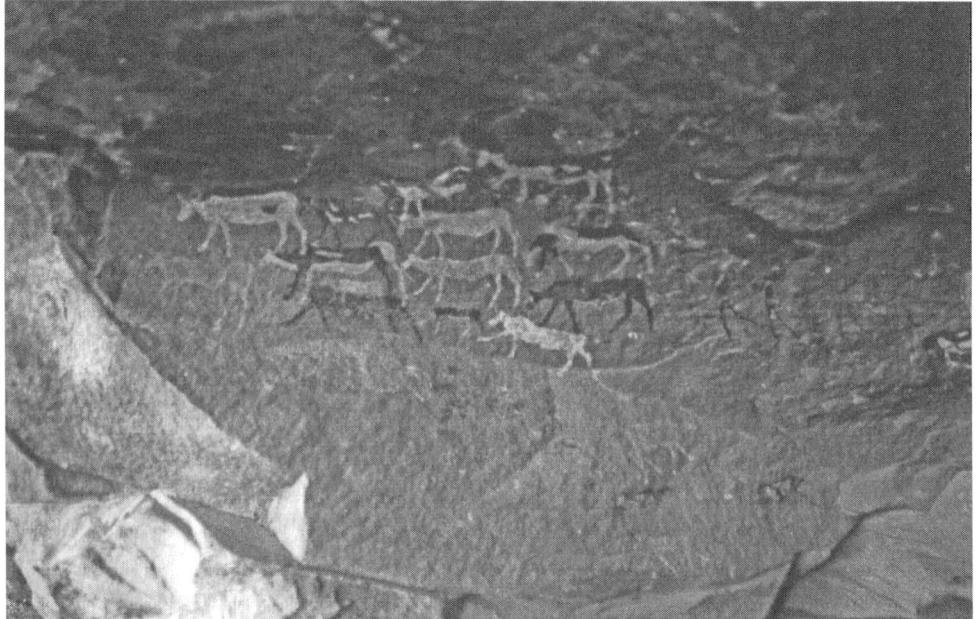

FIG. 33.4 Painting of cattle from the Caledon Valley, South Africa (photograph, Peter Mitchell).

polity by the late 13th century (Hall and Smith 2000). The ramifications of such changes beyond the Shashe-Limpopo area and hunter-gatherer connections—if any—with later states (Great Zimbabwe, Khami etc.) now merit comparable study.

CONCLUDING COMMENTS

For a long time, southern Africa's Later Stone Age has been treated as 'Khoisan history' (Deacon and Deacon 1999), both because it is undoubtedly the past of today's Khoe-, Ju-,≠Hoan-, and Tuu-speaking peoples and because their ethnography guides its interpretation. The first of these points is undeniable, even though in practice most archaeological research into hunter-gatherers has concerned groups who have no clearly identifiable descendants, while those that survive today have seen comparatively little study of their own direct ancestors (Walker 1995b). The second invites debate, for despite the great gains made by drawing on Kalahari and /Xam ethnography to understand both rock art and excavated records, archaeologists persist in emphasizing just a few of over twenty extant San groups, all living in semi-arid environments very different from the subcontinent's other biomes. Moreover, while sometimes recognizing the need to 'de-!Kung' southern African prehistory (Parkington 1984), they have struggled to avoid generalizing ethnographic data across time as well as space. Rock art research, in particular, has suffered for want of an independent chronology. It might thus be wise, while making full use of the riches that San ethnography offers, for future work to place itself within a broader context by using a more explicit body of hunter-gatherer-specific archaeological theory (cf. Kelly 1995; Humphreys 2007), exploring comparisons with other parts of the world (e.g. Hiscock and O'Connor 2005), and tracking the history of ethnographically recognizable patterns (cf. Stahl 2001).

REFERENCES

AMBROSE, S. H. (2002). Small things remembered: origins of early microlithic industries in sub-Saharan Africa. *Archaeological Papers of the American Anthropological Association* 12: 9–30.

—— and LORENZ, K. G. (1990). Social and ecological models for the Middle Stone Age in southern Africa. In P. A. Mellars (ed.), *The Emergence of Modern Humans*. Edinburgh: Edinburgh University Press, 3–33.

BARHAM, L. S. (1992). Let's walk before we run: an appraisal of historical materialist approaches to the Later Stone Age. *South African Archaeological Bulletin* 47: 44–51.

—— and MITCHELL, P. J. (2008). *The First Africans: African Archaeology from the Earliest Toolmakers to Most Recent Foragers*. Cambridge: Cambridge University Press.

BARNARD, A. (1992). *Hunters and Herders of Southern Africa: A Comparative Ethnography of the Khoisan Peoples*. Cambridge: Cambridge University Press.

BENTLEY, R. A., LAYTON, R. H., and TEHRANI, J. (2009). Kinship, marriage and the genetics of past human dispersals. *Human Biology* 81: 159–79.

BINFORD, L. R. (1980). Willow smoke and dogs' tails: hunter-gatherer settlement systems and archaeological site formation. *American Antiquity* 45: 4–20.

BINNEMAN, J. N. F. (1997). Usewear traces on Robberg bladelets from Rose Cottage Cave. *South African Journal of Science* 93: 479–81.

—— (2006/7). Archaeological research along the south-eastern Cape coast part 2: caves and shelters: Kabeljous River Shelter 1 and associated stone tool industries. *Southern African Field Archaeology* 15/16: 57–74.

BLUNDELL, G. (2004). *Nqabayo's Nomansland: San Rock Art and the Somatic Past*. Uppsala: Uppsala University Press.

BOUSMAN, C. B. (2005). Coping with risk: Later Stone Age technological strategies at Blydefontein Rock Shelter, South Africa. *Journal of Anthropological Archaeology* 24: 193–226.

CAMPBELL, A., ROBBINS, L., and TAYLOR, M. (eds) (2009). *Tsodilo Hills: Copper Bracelet of the Kalahari*. Gaborone: Botswana Society.

CHALLIS, S. (2009). Taking the reins: the introduction of the horse in the nineteenth-century Maloti-Drakensberg and the protective medicine of baboons. In Mitchell and Smith (2009: 104–5).

DEACON, H. J. (1972). A review of the post-Pleistocene in South Africa. *South African Archaeological Society Goodwin Series* 1: 26–45.

—— (1976). *Where Hunters Gathered: A Study of Holocene Stone Age People in the Eastern Cape*. Claremont: South African Archaeological Society.

—— (1993). Planting an idea: an archaeology of Stone Age gatherers in South Africa. *South African Archaeological Bulletin* 48: 86–93.

—— and DEACON, J. (1999). *Human Beginnings in South Africa*. Cape Town: David Philip.

DEACON, J. (1984). Later Stone Age people and their descendants in southern Africa. In R. G. Klein (ed.), *Southern African Prehistory and Palaeoenvironments*. Rotterdam: Balkema, 221–328.

DEACON, J. (1996). Archaeology of the Flat and Grass Bushmen. In J. Deacon and T. A. Dowson (eds), *Voices from the Past: /Xam Bushmen and the Bleek and Lloyd Collection*. Johannesburg: Witwatersrand University Press, 245–70.

DEWAR, G. (2010). Late Holocene burial cluster at Diaz Street midden, Saldanha Bay, Western Cape, South Africa. *South African Archaeological Bulletin* 65: 26–34.

EASTWOOD, E. B. (2005). From girls to women: female imagery in the San rock paintings of the Central Limpopo Basin, southern Africa. *Before Farming* 2005(3): article 2.

—— (2006). Animals behaving like people: San rock paintings of kudu in the central Limpopo Basin, southern Africa. *South African Archaeological Bulletin* 61: 26–39.

EHRET, C. (2002). *The Civilizations of Africa: A History to 1800*. Oxford: James Currey.

FAGAN, B. M., and VAN NOTEN, F. L. (1971). *The Hunter-Gatherers of Gwisho*. Tervuren: Musée Royal de l'Afrique Centrale.

GOODWIN, A. J. H., and VAN RIET LOWE, C. (1929). The Stone Age cultures of South Africa. *Annals of the South African Museum* 27: 1–289.

GÜLDEMANN, T. (2008). A linguist's view: Khoe-Kwadi speakers as the earliest food-producers of southern Africa. *Southern African Humanities* 20(1): 93–132.

HALL, S. L. (2000a). Burial sequence in the Later Stone Age of the Eastern Cape Province, South Africa. *South African Archaeological Bulletin* 55: 137–46.

—— (2000b). Forager lithics and Early Moloko homesteads at Madikwe. *Natal Museum Journal of Humanities* 12:33–50.

—— and BINNEMAN, J. N. F. (1987). Later Stone Age burial variability in the Cape: a social interpretation. *South African Archaeological Bulletin* 42: 140–52.

—— and SMITH, B. W. (2000). Empowering places: rock shelters and ritual control in farmer-forager interactions in the Northern Province. *South African Archaeological Society Goodwin Series* 8: 30–46.

HAMMOND-TOOKE, W. D. (1998). Selective borrowing? The possibility of San shamanistic influence on Southern Bantu divination and healing practices. *South African Archaeological Bulletin* 53: 9–15.

HAMPSON, J., CHALLIS, W., BLUNDELL, G., and DE ROSNER, C. (2002). The rock art of Bongani Mountain Lodge and its environs, Mpumalanga Province, South Africa: an introduction to problems of southern African rock-art regions. *South African Archaeological Bulletin* 57: 15–30.

HAYDEN, B. (1990). Nimrods, piscators, pluckers and planters: the emergence of food production. *Journal of Anthropological Archaeology* 9: 31–69.

HEADLAND, T. N., and REID, L. A. (1989). Hunter-gatherers and their neighbours from prehistory to the present. *Current Anthropology* 30: 43–66.

HENN, B. M., GIGNOUX, C., LIN, A. A., et al. (2008). Y-chromosomal evidence of a pastoralist migration through Tanzania to southern Africa. *Proceedings of the National Academy of Sciences (USA)* 105: 10693–8.

HENSHILWOOD, C. S., NILSSEN, P., and PARKINGTON, J. E. (1994). Mussel drying and food storage in the late Holocene, south-west Cape, South Africa. *Journal of Field Archaeology* 21: 103–9.

HISCOCK, P., and O'CONNOR, S. (2005). Arid paradises or dangerous landscapes: a review of explanations for Palaeolithic assemblage change in arid Australia and Africa. In P. Veth, M. Smith, and P. Hiscock (eds), *Desert Peoples: Archaeological Perspectives*. Oxford: Blackwell, 58–77.

HUMPHREYS, A. J. B. (2007). Behavioural ecology and hunter-gatherers: from the Kalahari to the Later Stone Age. *South African Archaeological Bulletin* 62: 98–103.

JERARDINO, A. (2007). Excavations at a hunter-gatherer site known as 'Grootrif G' shell midden, Lamberts Bay, Western Cape Province. *South African Archaeological Bulletin* 62: 162–70.

—— BRANCH, G. M., and NAVARRO, R. (2008). Human impact on precolonial west coast marine environments of South Africa. In J. M. Erlandson and T. C. Rick (eds), *Human Impacts on Marine Environments*. Berkeley: University of California Press, 279–96.

—— and YATES, R. (1996). Preliminary results from excavations at Steenbokfontein Cave: implications for past and future research. *South African Archaeological Bulletin* 51: 7–16.

JOLLY, P. (1996). Symbiotic interactions between Black farmers and south-eastern San: implications for southern African rock art studies, ethnographic analogy and hunter-gatherer cultural identity. *Cultural Anthropology* 37: 277–306.

—— (2007). Before farming? Cattle kept and painted by the south-eastern San. *Before Farming* 2007(4), DC: article 2.

KELLY, R. L. (1995). *The Foraging Spectrum: Diversity in Hunter-Gatherer Lifeways*. Washington, DC: Smithsonian Institution Press.

KLATZOW, S. (2010). Interaction between hunter-gatherers and Bantu-speaking farmers in the eastern Free State: a case study from De Hoop cave. *South African Historical Journal* 62: 229–51.

KORSMAN, S., and PLUG, I. (1994). Two Later Stone Age sites on the farm Honingklip in the eastern Transvaal. *South African Archaeological Bulletin* 49: 24–32.

LEE, R. B. (1979). *The !Kung San: Men, Women and Work in a Foraging Society*. Cambridge: Cambridge University Press.

LEE-THORP, J. A., SEALY, J. C., and VAN DER MERWE, N. J. (1989). Stable carbon isotope ratio differences between bone collagen and bone apatite, and their relationship to diet. *Journal of Archaeological Science* 16: 585–99.

LEWIS-WILLIAMS, J. D. (1981). *Believing and Seeing: Symbolic Meanings in Southern San Rock Paintings*. New York: Academic Press.

—— (1998). *Quanto?*: the issue of many meanings in southern African San rock art research. *South African Archaeological Bulletin* 53: 86–97.

—— (2002). *The Mind in the Cave: Consciousness and the Origins of Art*. London: Thames & Hudson.

—— (2008). The evolution of theory, method and technique in southern African rock art research. *Journal of Archaeological Method and Theory* 13: 343–77.

—— and BIESELE, M. (1978). Eland hunting rituals among northern and southern San groups: striking similarities. *Africa* 48: 117–34.

—— and PEARCE, D. G. (2004). *San Spirituality: Roots, Expression and Social Consequences*. Walnut Creek, Calif.: AltaMira Press.

LOMBARD, M., and PARSONS, I. (2010). Fact or fiction? Behavioural and technological reversal after 60ka in southern Africa. *South African Archaeological Bulletin* 65: 224–8.

LOUBSER, J. N. H., and LAURENS, G. (1994). Depictions of domestic ungulates and shields: hunter/gatherers and agro-pastoralists in the Caledon River Valley area. In T. A. Dowson and J. D. Lewis-Williams (eds), *Contested Images: Diversity in Southern African Rock Art Research*. Johannesburg: Witwatersrand University Press, 83–118.

LOURANDOS, H. (1983). Intensification: a late Pleistocene–Holocene archaeological sequence from southwestern Victoria. *Archaeology in Oceania* 18: 81–94.

MANHIRE, A. H. (1993). A report on the excavations at Faraoskop Rock Shelter in the Graafwater District of the south-western Cape. *Southern African Field Archaeology* 2: 3–23.

MAZEL, A. D. (1989). People making history: the last ten thousand years of hunter-gatherer communities in the Thukela Basin. *Natal Museum Journal of Humanities* 1: 1–168.

MAZEL, A. D. (2009). Images in time: advances in the dating of Maloti-Drakensberg rock art since the 1970s. In Mitchell and Smith (2009: 81–98).

MITCHELL, P. J. (2002). *The Archaeology of Southern Africa*. Cambridge: Cambridge University Press.

—— (2005). Modeling Later Stone Age societies in southern Africa. In A. B. Stahl (ed.), *African Archaeology: A Critical Introduction*. Oxford: Blackwell, 150–73.

—— (2009). Hunter-gatherers and farmers: some implications of 2000 years of interaction in the Maloti-Drakensberg region of southern Africa. *Senri Ethnological Studies* 73: 15–46.

—— (2010). Genetics and southern African prehistory: an archaeological view. *Journal of Anthropological Sciences* 88: 73–92.

—— and SMITH, B. W. (eds) (2009). *The Eland's People: New Perspectives in the Rock Art of the Maloti-Drakensberg Bushmen*. Johannesburg: Wits University Press.

MORRIS, A. G. (2003). The myth of the East African 'Bushmen'. *South African Archaeological Bulletin* 58: 85–90.

ORTON, J. (2008). A late Pleistocene microlithic Later Stone Age assemblage from coastal Namaqualand, South Africa. *Before Farming* 2008(1): article 3.

—— (2009). Rescue excavations at the Diaz Street Midden, Saldanha Bay, South Africa. *Azania* 44: 107–20.

PARKINGTON, J. E. (1984). Changing views of the Later Stone Age of South Africa. *Advances in World Archaeology* 3: 89–142.

—— (1988). The Pleistocene/Holocene transition in the western Cape, South Africa: observations from Verlorenvlei. In J. Bower and D. Lubell (eds), *Prehistoric Cultures and Environments in the Late Quaternary of Africa*. Oxford: British Archaeological Reports, 349–63.

—— (1993). The neglected alternative: historical narrative rather than cultural labelling. *South African Archaeological Bulletin* 48: 94–7.

—— (1999). Western Cape landscapes. *Proceedings of the British Academy* 99: 25–35.

—— (2001). Mobility, seasonality and southern African hunter-gatherers. *South African Archaeological Bulletin* 56: 1–7.

—— (2003). Eland and therianthropes in southern African rock art: when is a person an animal? *African Archaeological Review* 20: 135–48.

—— (2006). *Shorelines, Strandlopers and Shell Middens*. Cape Town: Creda Communications.

—— FISHER, J. W., and TONNER, T. W. W. (2009). 'The fires are constant, the shelters are whims': a feature map of Later Stone Age campsites at the Dunefield Midden site, Western Cape Province, South Africa. *South African Archaeological Bulletin* 64: 104–21.

—— POGGENPOEL, C. A., BUCHANAN, W., ROBEY, T., MANHIRE, A. H., and SEALY, J. C. (1987). Holocene coastal settlement patterns in the western Cape. In G. N. Bailey and J. E. Parkington (eds), *The Archaeology of Prehistoric Coastlines*. Cambridge: Cambridge University Press, 22–41.

PARSONS, I. (2007). Hunter-gatherers or herders? Reconsidering the Swartkops and Doornfontein Industries, Northern Cape Province, South Africa. *Before Farming* 2007(4): article 3.

PEREIRA, L., MACAULAY, V., TORRONI, A., SCOZZARI, R., PRATA, M. J., and AMORIN, A. (2001). Prehistoric and historic traces in the mtDNA of Mozambique: insights into the Bantu expansions and the slave trade. *Annals of Human Genetics* 65: 439–58.

PFEIFFER, S. (2009). The incorporation of bioarchaeology into Khoesan studies. *South African Archaeological Bulletin* 64: 193–4.

—— and VAN DER MERWE, N. J. (2004). Cranial injuries to Later Stone Age children from the Modder River Mouth, Western Cape Province, South Africa. *South African Archaeological Bulletin* 59: 59–65.

ROBBINS, L. H., MURPHY, M. L., CAMPBELL, A. C., and BROOK, G. A. (1998a). Intensive mining of specular haematite in the Kalahari, *ca.* AD 800–1000. *Current Anthropology* 39: 144–50.

—— —— —— —— et al. (1998b). Test excavation and reconnaissance palaeoenvironmental work at Toteng, Botswana. *South African Archaeological Bulletin* 53: 125–32.

—— —— STEWART, K. M., CAMPBELL, A. C., and BROOKS, G. A. (1994). Barbed bone points, paleoenvironment and the antiquity of fish exploitation in the Kalahari Desert, Botswana. *Journal of Field Archaeology* 21: 257–64.

SADR, K. (1997). Kalahari archaeology and the Bushman debate. *Current Anthropology* 38: 104–12.

—— (1998). The first herders at the Cape of Good Hope. *African Archaeological Review* 15: 101–22.

—— and SAMPSON, C. G. (2006). Through thick and thin: early pottery in southern Africa. *Journal of African Archaeology* 7: 235–52.

SAHLINS, M. (1976). *Stone Age Economics*. London: Tavistock.

SALAS, A., RICHARDS, M., DE LA FE, T., et al. (2002). The making of the African mtDNA landscape. *American Journal of Human Genetics* 71: 1082–1111.

SAMPSON, C. G. (1995). Acquisition of European livestock by the Seacow River Bushmen between AD 1770–1890. *Southern African Field Archaeology* 4: 30–6.

—— (2010). Chronology and dynamics of Later Stone Age herders in the Seacow River valley, South Africa. *Journal of Arid Environments* 74: 842–8.

SANDELOWSKY, B. H. (1977). Mirabib: an archaeological study in the Namib. *Madoqua* 10: 221–83.

SCHOEMAN, M. H. (2006). Imagining rain-places: rain-control and changing ritual landscapes in the Shashe-Limpopo Confluence Area, South Africa. *South African Archaeological Bulletin* 61: 152–65.

SEALY, J. C. (2006). Diet, mobility and settlement pattern among Holocene hunter-gatherers in southernmost Africa. *Current Anthropology* 47: 569–95.

—— and VAN DER MERWE, N. J. (1988). Social, spatial and chronological patterning in marine food use as determined by $\partial^{13}C$ measurements of Holocene human skeletal remains from the south-western Cape, South Africa. *World Archaeology* 20: 87–102.

SKOTNES, P. (ed.) (2007). *Claim to the Country*. Johannesburg: Jacana.

SMITH, B. W. (2010). Envisioning San history: problems in the reading of history in the rock art of the Maloti-Drakensberg mountains of South Africa. *African Studies* 69: 345–58.

—— and OUZMAN, S. (2004). Taking stock: identifying Khoekhoen herder rock art in southern Africa. *Current Anthropology* 45: 499–526.

SOLOMON, A. C. (1997). The myth of ritual origins? Ethnography, mythology and interpretation of San rock art. *South African Archaeological Bulletin* 52: 3–13.

—— (2008). Myths, making and consciousness: differences and dynamics in San rock arts. *Current Anthropology* 49: 59–86.

—— (2011). Writing San histories: the /Xam and 'shamanism' revisited. *Journal of Southern African Studies* 37: 99–117.

SOLWAY, J. S., and LEE, R. B. (1990). Foragers, genuine or spurious? Situating the Kalahari San in history. *Current Anthropology* 31: 109–46.

STAHL, A. B. (2001). *Making History in Banda: Anthropological Visions of Africa's Past.* Cambridge: Cambridge University Press.

STEWART, B. A. (2011). 'Residues of parts unchewable': stages two and three of a multivariate taphonomic analysis of the Dunefield Midden bovid bones. *Azania: Archaeological Research in Africa* 46: 141–68.

STRAUS, L. G., ERIKSEN, B. V., ERLANDSON, J. M., and YESNER, D. R. (eds) (1996). *Humans at the End of the Ice Age: The Archaeology of the Pleistocene-Holocene Transition.* New York: Plenum Press.

SWANEPOEL, N., ESTERHUYSEN, A. B., and BONNER, P. (eds) (2008). *Five Hundred Years Rediscovered: Southern African Precedents and Prospects.* Johannesburg: Wits University Press.

VAN DOORNUM, B. (2007). Tshisiku Shelter and the Shashe-Limpopo confluence area hunter-gatherer sequence. *Southern African Humanities* 19: 17–67.

—— (2008). Sheltered from change: hunter-gatherer occupation of Balerno Main Shelter, Shashe-Limpopo confluence area, South Africa. *Southern African Humanities* 20(2): 249–84.

VINNICOMBE, P. V. (1976). *People of the Eland.* Pietermaritzburg: University of Natal Press.

VOGELSANG, R., RICHTER, J., JACOBS, Z., EICHHORN, B., LINSEELE, V., and ROBERTS, R. G. (2010). New excavations of Middle Stone Age deposits at Apollo 11 rockshelter, Namibia: stratigraphy, archaeology, chronology and past environments. *Journal of African Archaeology* 8: 185–218.

WADLEY, L. (1987). *Later Stone Age Hunters and Gatherers of the Southern Transvaal: Social and Ecological Interpretations.* Oxford: British Archaeological Reports.

—— (1996). Changes in the social relations of precolonial hunter-gatherers after agropastoral contact: an example from the Magaliesberg, South Africa. *Journal of Anthropological Archaeology* 15: 205–17.

—— (ed.) (1997). *Our Gendered Past: Archaeological Studies of Gender in Southern Africa.* Johannesburg: Witwatersrand University Press.

—— (2000). The Wilton and pre-ceramic post-classic Wilton industries at Rose Cottage Cave and their context in the South African sequence. *South African Archaeological Bulletin* 55: 90–106.

—— and MCLAREN, G. (1998). Tandjesberg Shelter, eastern Free State, South Africa. *Natal Museum Journal of Humanities* 10: 19–32.

WALKER, N. J. (1995a). *Late Pleistocene and Holocene Hunter-Gatherers of the Matopos.* Uppsala: Societas Archaeologica Upsaliensis.

—— (1995b). The archaeology of the San: the Late Stone Age of Botswana. In A. J. G. M. Sanders (ed.), *Speaking for the Bushmen.* Gaborone: Botswana Society, 54–87.

—— (1997). In the footsteps of the ancestors: the Matsieng creation site in Botswana. *South African Archaeological Bulletin* 52: 95–104.

WILMSEN, E. N., and DENBOW, J. R. (1990). Paradigmatic history of San-speaking peoples and current attempts at revision. *Current Anthropology* 31: 489–524.

PART V

FOOD FOR THOUGHT

*The Archaeology of African Pastoralist
and Farming Communities*

CHAPTER 34

DOMESTICATING ANIMALS IN AFRICA

DIANE GIFFORD-GONZALEZ
AND OLIVIER HANOTTE

INTRODUCTION

THE process of animal domestication has fascinated people for centuries and, since Darwin, a variety of evolutionary paradigms have been applied to thinking about it. While few archaeologists today would view animal domestication as an index of human progress, evolutionist ideas often lurk in implicit assumptions about domestication, including the view of it as an *invention*. Rather, domestication is an ongoing *biological process,* a form of co-evolution, with selection continuing over each generation, as humans, plants, and animals interact with one another in ways that are mutually beneficial in a Darwinian sense. Gene frequencies in humans as well as animals may shift, as exemplified by genetic mutations for lactase persistence among East African populations that enable milk digestion into adulthood (Tishkoff et al. 2007). Such African mutations parallel the better-documented co-evolutionary case of northwestern Europe, where human populations display high rates of another mutation for lactase persistence, geographically coinciding with genes for high milk protein production among cows (Beja-Pereira et al. 2003).

The domestication-as-invention viewpoint also assumes that all animals are equally domesticable 'raw materials,' disregarding their physiological and behavioural variability and how this responds to human manipulation. For example, captive endangered species may tolerate humans and respond to training cues, but nonetheless fail to reproduce. Domesticates descend from species that could breed and thrive under human management. The domestication-as-invention perspective also often produces a profound lack of curiosity about *ongoing* evolutionary changes in domestic species after their documented first appearances. Archaeologists concerned with trade, urbanization, and the emergence of social complexity tend to consider domestic species as a necessary but uninteresting part of the infrastructure, once the Rubicon of initial appearance has been crossed. Ignoring the co-evolution of species in settled and complex societies dismisses a vast amount of relevant historical information that may be especially vital to modern communities dealing with social and environmental changes.

DIAGNOSING DOMESTICATION IN ANIMALS

Animal domestication research has benefited from seeing it as an evolutionary process and from the synergy between zooarchaeology and modern animal genetics. Before modern DNA amplification and sequencing techniques were applied to animal domestication, zooarchaeologists took three approaches to diagnosing it, all based on the study of bone elements, though two are now seen as less reliable. *Morphological analysis* suffers from the fact that animals in incipient phases of domestication will, by definition, exhibit wild phenotypes. *Metrical analysis* rests on the assumption that size reduction is a universal characteristic of mammalian domestication, and this has recently been called into question by thorough comparative studies (Zeder et al. 2006). *Demographic profile analysis* diagnoses domestication from mortality profiles constructed from archaeological samples. Young-dominated age-at-death profiles are common in early farming, diverging from prime-age-dominated ones typical of hunting. This approach is the most dependable for defining early phases of domestication (Zeder et al. 2006).

Modern genomics contributes two additional methods that elucidate the ancestry and relationships of domesticates by allowing studies of the present and past genetic make-up of domesticates. *Modern DNA analysis* compares the degree of similarities or differences in several types of nuclear and/or cytoplasmic genetic markers within and amongst populations. This permits identification of wild ancestral species, subspecies, or populations, geographic centre(s) of origin, evolutionary bottlenecks and expansions, and introgressions (consistent hybridizations) between related species, as well as expansions and migrations (Fig. 34.1).

Different genetic markers provide complementary information. Mitochondrial DNA (mtDNA), nearly exclusively maternally inherited, is the genetic marker of choice for unravelling domestication events, because successful domestication means successful captive breeding (Hanotte 2007). Mitochondrial DNA sequences typically show different depths of variation within domesticates. Each individual sequence is referred to as a haplotype. Closely related haplotypes are grouped within a haplogroup. The presence of distinct haplogroups within the wild ancestors' range may indicate distinct domestication events. This inference is especially compelling when the haplogroups are predominantly found in distinct geographic areas within the wild ancestral range, and when they reflect a divergence from a common ancestor at much earlier times than the estimated age of domestication, as shown for zebu and taurine cattle (Loftus et al. 1994), as well as for European and Asian pigs (Larson et al. 2005).

In mammals, the paternally inherited Y chromosome can be used in a similar way to trace the number of paternal lineages contributing to a domestic species. Y-DNA has been used to address the question of male introgression (domestic or wild) in livestock populations. Nuclear microsatellites, on the other hand, are both paternally and maternally inherited.

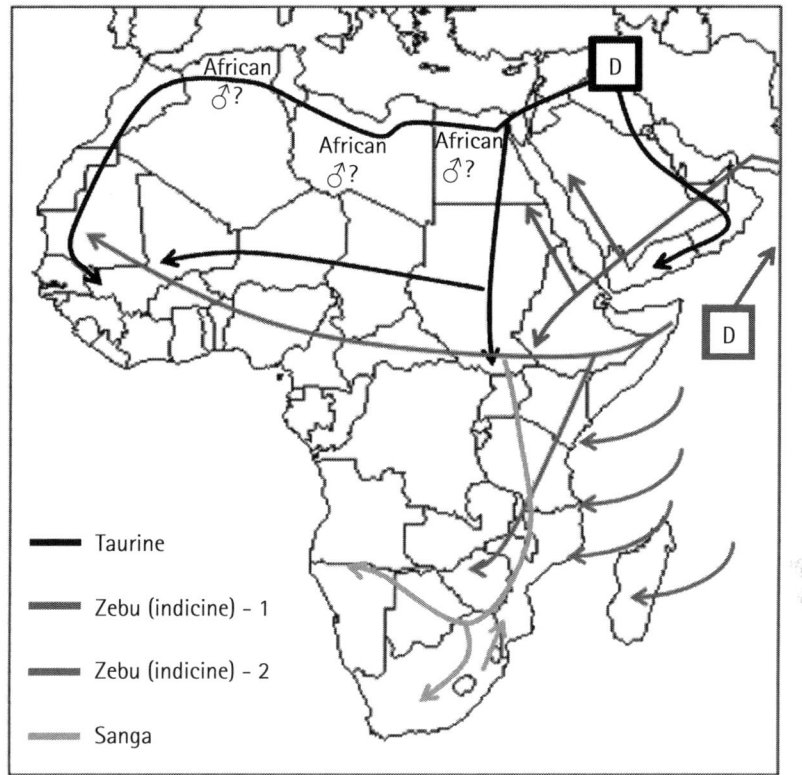

FIG. 34.1 The genetic make-up of African cattle has been intensively studied. The continent's cattle show influences from two major centres of domestication, one in Southwest Asia, the other from the north of the Indian subcontinent. Independent domestication of the African aurochs is now doubtful, though male-mediated introgression from African aurochs remains possible. The earliest domestic African cattle were humpless and of the taurine type, while two distinct zebu influences and times of entry are found in African cattle. Central and southern African Sanga cattle are an ancient, admixed population derived from zebu and taurine cattle.

They are particularly powerful for tracing the movements and history of domesticated populations from their centres of origins.

Modern DNA studies have two drawbacks. First, they only provide information on a species' present day genetic make-up, thus necessarily presenting an incomplete picture of past variability; second, dating domestication processes using modern DNA information alone remains a challenge.

Ancient DNA analysis offsets the drawbacks of modern DNA studies by providing a snapshot of a domesticated species' genetic diversity in the past and allowing study of now-extinct ancestral populations. It entails amplification and analysis of genetic material extracted from bones, teeth, or eggshells. However, ancient DNA research must cope with nucleic acid degradation over time, limiting the quantity and the fragment length (base pairs) of genetic material recoverable. Bacterial and fungal DNA can contaminate genetic material extracted from archaeological specimens, and extreme precautions must be taken in field and laboratory to avoid between-sample or modern DNA contamination. Ancient DNA research is thus a time-consuming and expensive endeavour, limiting the number of samples that can be analysed in a single study. Nevertheless, ancient DNA studies have allowed several important questions to be addressed, such as the possible genetic contribution of extinct wild populations to the modern genetic pool.

Genetic research is less fully developed in Africa than in Europe, but important data on the history of African breeds have been recovered from these approaches. The following section synthesizes zooarchaeological and genetic data on major domesticated species in Africa, focusing especially on breed traits that reflect the co-evolutionary changes they underwent on the continent.

CURRENT GENETIC AND ZOOARCHAEOLOGICAL KNOWLEDGE OF AFRICAN DOMESTICATES

By the fifth millennium BC caprines and cattle are found in association across North Africa, interpreted by some (e.g. Smith 1992) as an invariant 'package' introduced from Southwest Asia. However, archaeological evidence suggests that these taxa entered Africa separately and that each may have a different early history.

Goats

The zooarchaeological practice of placing sheep and goat bones into a single category obscures the respective histories of such skeletally similar species. Whenever possible, the aim should now be to sort the sheep from the goats. Many breeds of goats (*Capra hircus*) live in Africa, all descended from the non-native wild bezoar goat of Southwest Asia, which was domesticated by 10,000 BP (Zeder and Hesse 2000). Globally, goats display at least six distinct mtDNA lines, and, unlike cattle, little geographic patterning in the expression of their mtDNA haplogroups. This lack of such phylogeographic patterning is compatible with a single regional domestication centre, with human management of multiple haplotypes in wild or semi-domesticated goat populations before geographic dispersal (Naderi et al. 2008).

Y-chromosome research suggests a common origin for goat patrilines on the coasts of the Levant, and the Maghreb (Algeria, Tunisia, Morocco), reflecting, according to the authors, a dispersal of male goats from Southwest Asia via early maritime colonization or commerce (Pereira et al. 2009). This supports Hassan's (2000) earlier prediction that caprines were introduced to Africa from Southwest Asia c. 5000 BC by two routes: one along the Mediterranean coast, where they appear in sites earlier than do cattle, and another via the Red Sea Hills of Egyptian Red Sea coast. Caprines, thus far not identified to species, appeared before cattle in the Khartoum region of the Sudanese Nile, where they were integrated into a gathering-intensive way of life by the late sixth/early fifth millennium BC (Haaland and Haaland, Ch. 37 below). Another, overland route across the Sinai from the Levant may account for their appearance in the Nile Delta (di Lernia, Ch. 36 below).

The phenotypes of African goats reflect substantial adaptation to local conditions. The so-called Sahelian and Sudanian breeds are light-coloured, long-limbed, and heat-tolerant, while Somali goats of arid eastern Africa are also predominantly light-coloured, though possessing different ear form and body build. By contrast, breeds associated with more closed habitats in western Africa display dwarfing. The West African Dwarf, or 'forest goat', is widespread in closed habitats, has short legs and a high reproductive rate, and is trypan-otolerant. Dwarf goats dating to the second millennium BC are found at Ntereso and Kintampo, Ghana (Carter and Flight 1972). The Nigerian Dwarf breed may have a distinct origin because it displays overall reduction in body size, rather than only shortened legs. The breed is very prolific, reproducing twice a year, often with more than two offspring per birth. The South African Boer breed is another stocky goat that thrives on poor forage and has a high reproductive rate (Porter and Mason 2002).

In brushy and wooded African habitats, the tsetse fly transmits trypanosomes to hoofed animals. Through their co-evolution with the infection, indigenous wild bovids are trypano-tolerant, but domestic livestock develop acute and often fatal symptoms. Not all infected animals die, but trypanosomes persist in recovered animals and may resurge if parasite infestations, malnutrition, or late stages of pregnancy cause loss of condition. Modern pastoralists use goats as 'shock troops' to clear brushy habitats in tsetse zones, in part because they vigorously defend themselves against tsetse bites, curtailing the number of blood meals by which trypanosomal infection is transmitted. Experiments show that the ratio of tsetse feeding attempts to success-ful blood meals is 63:1 in goats versus 4:1 in cattle (Gifford-Gonzalez 2000).

Sub-Saharan African goats remain poorly studied at the molecular level. Mitochondrial and microsatellite DNA indicate a lack of phylogeographic structure among them (Chenyambuga et al. 2004), while microsatellite loci provide evidence for a Sahelian goat introgression in West African Dwarf goat populations (Hoeven et al. 2007).

Sheep

Sheep (*Ovis aries*) descend from varieties of the Asiatic mouflon (*Ovis orientalis*). Five mtDNA lineages have been identified (Meadows et al. 2007). In Africa, haplogroup A is the most widespread, accounting for all sampled eastern and southern African sheep (Bruford and Townsend 2006), despite a much more diverse representation of haplogroups in the Arabian Peninsula. However, analysis of an archaeological sheep assemblage from the Western Cape identified haplogroup B only (Horsburgh and Rhines 2010). Y-chromosome analysis identifies two separate lineages on the African continent with no clear phylogeo-graphic signal, possibly due to the small number of breeds examined so far.

Modern African sheep breeds are morphologically diverse. Two varieties exist, thin-tailed and fat-tailed or fat-rumped sheep. North African breeds of both types produce coarse wool, whereas sub-Saharan sheep are smooth-coated. Autosomal microsatellite loci analyses sup-port the inference that West African thin-tailed sheep (Fig. 34.2) and eastern and southern African fat-tailed sheep form two distinct genetic groups (Muigai 2002).

Archaeological evidence suggests two geographically distinct entry points of domestic sheep on the African continent: Egypt and the Horn/Red Sea region. Sheep were present at Merimde, Egypt, by 5000 BC, probably entering the Nile Delta from the Levant (Gautier 2002). Thin-tailed sheep are depicted in Old Kingdom tomb paintings (*c.* 2686–2125 BC), whilst fat-tailed sheep are depicted during the Middle Kingdom, *c.* 2055–1650 BC (Clutton-Brock 1993). Fat-tailed or fat-rumped sheep are also shown in rock art from Ethiopia to

FIG. 34.2 Djallonke sheep from Guinea (photograph, Olivier Hanotte).

South Africa, probably reflecting their value to farmer and pastoralist diets low in fats. Sheep are the earliest securely dated domesticate in southern Africa, appearing in the late first millennium BC (Sadr, Ch. 44 below).

Regional adaptations build on these two phenotypes. Sahel-type sheep, distributed in drier regions from Mauritania to Chad, are smooth-coated, thin-tailed, and lop-eared, while males have corkscrew-type horns, resembling those in Dynastic Egyptian art. The West African Dwarf sheep is a thin-tailed, hairy sheep, small and trypanotolerant, occupying humid tropical habitats of West to Central Africa. Males diverge from the Sahel-type, possessing recurved horns and a throat ruff. Compared to the dwarf goats of the same region, this breed displays slower growth rates and higher offspring mortality, possibly resulting from a greater vulnerability to trypanosomiasis.

Cattle

The possible domestication of African cattle (*Bos taurus* × *indicus*) from wild North African ancestors is open to debate (di Lernia, Ch. 36 below). Modern mtDNA and Y-chromosome DNA demonstrate independent domestications of indicine or humped cattle in South Asia and of taurine or straight-backed cattle in Southwest Asia. A distinctive African mtDNA haplogroup (T1) in modern breeds initially led researchers to posit an independent domestication from the wild North African aurochs (Bradley and Loftus 2000; Edwards et al. 2004). However, full genome mitochondrial sequencing has indicated very close relationships among all T haplogroups, arguing against distinct cattle domestication centres in Africa and Southwest Asia (Achilli et al. 2009). Most recently, Pérez-Pardal et al. (2010a, 2010b) have reported that Y-chromosome evidence points to a contribution from indigenous male African aurochs to domesticated cattle in Africa.

A preponderance of zooarchaeologists, including the analyst with first-hand experience with the specimens (Gautier 1987), questions the osteological evidence for 10,000 year-old domestic cattle in Egypt's Western Desert. Uncontroversial dates for domestic *Bos* in the Nabta-Kiseiba area are *c.* 5750–4550 BC, and cattle are not associated with caprines until a few centuries later (Gautier 1984). Two sites south of the Nile's Second Cataract and east of the later Kerma civilization recently reported remains of domestic cattle with associated dates *c.* 7000 BC (Honegger 2005: 247). The proximity of these Nubian occurrences to the Nabta-Kiseiba region suggests that domestic cattle first appeared in the grassy hinterlands of the Nile.

From skeletal evidence, Saharan rock art, and Dynastic Egyptian representations, Africa's oldest cattle were straight-backed and had lyre-shaped horns. Saharan rock art depicts cows with full udders, possibly reflecting incipient dairying. The C-14010 allele for lactase persistence is high in speakers of Nilo-Saharan languages, which span the central Sahara and Lake Chad Basin into eastern Africa. The estimated age of the mutation is 6,000–7,000 years, hinting at the emergence of a co-evolutionary trajectory early in the use of domestic cattle (Tishkoff et al. 2007).

Dates indicate that domestic African cattle dispersed west and south from the eastern Sahara (MacDonald and MacDonald 2000; Brooks et al. 2009). West African Sahelian and trypanotolerant cattle breeds and those of East Africa's Great Lakes region display straight-backed morphology. With the final Saharan desiccation about 2500 BC, pastoralists shifted south with the Sahelian biome, some entering environments similar to those typical of the earlier Sahara. Others entered regions that exposed their herds to new disease challenges (Casey, Ch. 41 below).

Genetic research and modelling based on modern populations of African cattle has clarified the later history of African cattle, including introgressions of South Asian Y-chromosome heritage (Hanotte et al. 2000). Genetic evidence suggests that zebu cattle probably entered Africa in the region of the Horn of Africa. South Asian zebu bulls crossbred with local African taurine cows earliest in East Africa, then north, west, and south of this, producing the so-called Sanga cattle (Epstein 1957). Genetic calibration suggests that this was well under way by the start of the second millennium AD, and that Sanga cattle had reached southern Africa by the late first millennium AD, although cattle are known there archaeologically from the start of that millennium (Sadr, Ch. 44 below). A more recent introgression of male mediated zebu genes recorded in the genetics is probably linked with the devastating late 19th/early 20th century rinderpest epidemics, which decimated earlier cattle stocks from Sudan to South Africa. The earliest non-controversial archaeological evidence for humped zebu cattle in Africa are mid-first millennium AD rock paintings of cattle and camels in the Horn of Africa (Clutton-Brock 2000).

Modern cattle breeds reflect adaptations to regional conditions. In the Sahel, the Fulani-Sudanese breed is straight-backed, with the lyre-shaped horns depicted in ancient Saharan art. Tolerating drier habitats well, these are dairy cattle and beasts of burden. The N'Dama (Fig. 34.3), Baoulé, Somba, and other West African shorthorns are all small, straight-backed breeds renowned for their ability to survive in tsetse-infested zones. Trypanotolerance in cattle reflects complex genetic control involving several genes and gene networks, with parasitaemia and anaemia, major consequences of trypanosomal infection, under distinct genetic controls (Hanotte et al. 2003). Both taurine and zebu genetic factors contribute to trypanotolerance in crossbred populations, suggesting a general mechanism of tolerance to blood parasite infection amongst tropical domestic bovines.

When the size diminution typical of trypanotolerant cattle began, and whether it was initially an adaptation to sleeping sickness, are open questions. Size diminution occurs in wild

FIG. 34.3 N'Dama bull, cow, and calf in Guinea (photograph, Olivier Hanotte).

and domestic animals subject to a variety to stresses, not just trypanosomal infection. Smaller adult size and earlier age of first reproduction may have conferred advantages upon cattle for other reasons.

Tsetse is confined to bushy habitats in West, Central, and East Africa and can therefore be avoided by herders with grazing stock. However, cattle in East African savannahs risk infection with theileriosis or East Coast Fever (ECF), caused by the protozoan parasite *Theileria parva parva* and transmitted from host to host by ticks. Theileriosis still kills nearly half a million cattle yearly, with mortality as high as 90 per cent in herds first exposed to ECF. The original infection route was probably from African buffalo encountered by pastoralists moving their cattle into eastern and Central Africa (Gifford-Gonzalez 2000). *T. p. parva* is one of two sub-species; the other, *T. parva lawrencei*, is the infectious agent for Corridor Disease (CD) in African buffalo. Like ECF, CD is transmitted from host to host by ticks and, as a co-evolved parasite, causes few clinical symptoms in buffalo. However, like ECF, CD infection in cattle manifests as an acute, often fatal disease.

Indigenous African cattle breeds have evolved higher resistance to ECF through both tick resistance and *Theileria* tolerance. Total tick load determines the intensity of ECF infection, so inhibition of tick blood meal episodes behaviourally and immunologically lowers infection rates. Central African Ankole cattle, a straight-backed breed with large horns, have strong resistance to tick infestation and higher productivity in the face of *Theileria* infection. Ankole cattle lack trypanotolerance, indicating this disease was not a risk in the Central African environments in which they evolved. East African Boran cattle, a humped African zebu, display high resistance to heat and ticks and are productive on poorer forage and lower amounts of water compared to exotic breeds. While the Boran varieties generally display poor response to trypanosomal infection, the Orma Boran, herded in tsetse regions near the Indian Ocean coast, do display trypanotolerance (Hanotte et al. 2003), suggesting that selection can situationally favour stronger expression of this trait. The humped Nguni, Tuli, and Afrikander breeds of southern Africa carry as little as one-sixth the tick load of European cattle breeds stocked on the same pasturage, and also show higher calving rates.

Dromedary camels

The dromedary or one-humped camel (*Camelus dromedarius*) descends from Holocene ancestors in the Arabian Peninsula, where no wild representatives survive today (Grigson et al. 1989). Its superior ability to forage in semi-deserts with far-flung water sources and to endure treks across true desert enabled Africans on the margins of such dry zones to exploit them more fully. Radiocarbon dates thus far suggest a very recent emergence of camel-based pastoralism in Africa. Rowley-Conwy (1988) reports camel dung from Qasr Ibrim, Lower Nubia, in the early first millennium BC, but the species is not ubiquitous in the Nile Valley until 1,000 years later. Initially used in Roman North Africa as a draft animal, by cal. AD 400 it had reached as far west as Senegal (MacDonald and MacDonald 2000) and undoubtedly greatly facilitated the expansion of trans-Saharan trade. In the Horn of Africa, by contrast, its representation in rock art at Laga Oda, Ethiopia, may be as recent as AD 1300–1600 (Clark and Williams 1978).

Pigs

Domestic pigs (*Sus scrofa*) were a common domesticate in prehistoric and Dynastic Egypt, though their present use is governed by cultural and religious restrictions. Mitochondrial DNA reflects domestication of multiple lineages across the broad North African and Eurasian range of wild boar, *Sus scrofa*. Some African suid populations were included in a large-scale geographic study of pig mitochondrial, Y-chromosome, and microsatellites (Ramírez et al. 2009). Breeds in Bénin and Nigeria reflect a European origin, possibly resulting from 15th–16th-century Portuguese explorations. A more complex and intriguing picture of pig genetics emerges in western Kenya and Zimbabwe, where European and East Asian mtDNA haplotypes could reflect introduction in colonial times of a European x Asian crossbreed, because 18th-/19th-century British breeds were strongly admixed with Chinese pigs. However, the presence in high frequencies of a Y-chromosome haplotype absent from European-Asian crossbreeds in Kenyan and Zimbabwean Mukota pigs raises the possibility that East and South African domestic pigs might have initially reached the continent following direct pre-European contact with Southeast or East Asia via trans-Indian Ocean trade (Amills et al. 2012). This possibility should caution archaeologists against dismissing pig bones found in precolonial eastern and southern African sites as intrusive, and instead encourage their referral for zooarchaeological and genetic study.

Donkeys

Molecular genetics has largely resolved a long debate over the origins of the domestic donkey (*Equus asinus*). Subspecific forms of its ancestor were distributed across arid zones of Africa and Arabia, but phylogenetic analysis of wild and domestic mtDNA lineages of both it and its close relatives exclude East Asian wild asses and half-asses as maternal contributors to the domestic species. Instead, they identify two ancestral mtDNA haplogroups: one from the Nubian wild ass (*E. africanus africanus*) and another from a subclade resembling, but not identical to, the Somali wild ass (*E. a. somaliensis*) (Beja-Pereira et al. 2004; Kimura et al. 2011). The former clade was undoubtedly domesticated in

Africa, but a centre of domestication in southern Arabia cannot be entirely ruled out for the latter.

The domestic donkey is found in Southwest Asia by 2500 BC, but early Dynastic donkey burials at Abydos in Upper Egypt date closer to 3045 BC, consistent with its representation on some late Predynastic stone palettes (Rossel et al. 2008). Further south, donkeys are reported from cave deposits at Jebel Shaqdud, Sudan, around 1950 BC (Peters 1991), as well as from Bronze Age royal burials at Kerma (cf. Welsby, Ch. 51 below). In recent African societies, donkeys are not considered food animals and their remains are disposed of away from settlements and food debris—something that may account for the rarity of donkey remains in African archaeological sites (Marshall and Weissbrod 2010).

Cats

Because its native range includes Africa and it is ubiquitous in Dynastic Egyptian art and mortuary practices, the domestic cat (*Felis catus*) was long considered to have been domesticated in Egypt. More recent archaeological and genetic evidence indicates an older and geographically different origin. A large-scale mtDNA and microsatellite analysis of cats on three continents (O'Brien et al. 2008) suggests cats underwent domestication in what are now Israel, the United Arab Emirates, and Saudi Arabia around 10,000 years ago, while the fact that domestic cats comprise five mtDNA lineages, each of very considerable antiquity (>100,000 years), indicates at least five distinct ancestral founding populations.

Wild cats were doubtless attracted to rodents and birds parasitizing stored grains in farming settlements, and may have self-domesticated as individuals capable of tolerating proximity to humans and naturally found mates with similar levels of tolerance (Driscoll et al. 2009). The 7500 BC joint burial of a human and a juvenile cat in Shillourokambos, Cyprus, suggests early taming (Vigne et al. 2004).

Dogs

The dog (*Canis familiaris*) is the oldest and most phenotypically diverse of all domesticated animals, with the first archaeological finds dating to 13,000–15,000 BC in Siberia (Sablin and Khopachev 2002). All dogs, including those kept by Aboriginal Australians and Native Americans, descend from the Eurasian wolf, *Canis lupus* (Wayne et al. 2006). A recent large-scale mtDNA study provides convincing evidence for an origin from over 50 female founders in southern China around 16,300 years ago (Pang et al. 2009).

Dogs are documented with foragers, pastoralists, and farmers throughout Africa, and often had considerable economic, and also ritual, importance among groups who hunt (e.g. Mitchell 2009). Boyko et al. (2009) found African village dogs to be little mixed genetically with non-African breeds, Africa-derived Afghan hounds, salukis, and basenjis clustering genetically with village dogs from the same regions of origin, but Rhodesian ridgebacks and pharaoh dogs possess mostly non-African ancestry. Research on the genetics of dogs in Africa is at such an early stage that, unlike cattle, it is not possible to use it to trace their spread in Africa. For similar reasons to donkeys, present-day African dogs are usually disposed of away from settlements, which may account for their rare recovery during excavation.

Chickens

The red jungle fowl (*Gallus gallus*) is the wild ancestor of the domestic chicken (Fig. 34.4), with five subspecies from India to southern China. Compared to domestic ungulates, chickens are more efficient converters of forage into body mass and, if used for their eggs, their energy needs are about a third of that required for meat production. Their rapid adoption into farming systems is thus quite understandable.

Multiple mitochondrial lineages are compatible with multiple domestication events over the geographic range of *G. gallus* subspecies (Liu et al. 2006). Published studies on the genetic diversity of chickens in Africa indicate the presence of Indian and Southeast Asian haplogoups (Muchadeyi et al. 2008; Razafindraibe et al. 2008; Mwacharo et al. 2011). While the timing and entry points of the two lineage remain unverified, results hint at the distribution of diverse chicken lineages into Africa. Patchy textual and archaeological evidence also implies that chickens entered Africa at different points along the continent including northeastern, western, eastern, and southern Africa in the first millennium AD, a time of intense overland and maritime trade. Claims for second or third millennium BC chickens at Machaga Cave, Zanzibar, rest upon a few bones of uncertain identity in poorly dated deposits (*pace* Chami 2001), but chickens had reached Egypt, if in small numbers, as early as the New Kingdom (Bard 1996: 363).

Guinea fowl

The domestic guinea fowl (*Numida meleagris*) is an African domesticate that spread to other continents in historic times, providing eggs and meat and helping to guard farmsteads as any disturbance will set off their loud calls. In the first millennium AD in Sahel, guinea fowl came to share settlements with chickens and in many regions were supplanted by them (MacDonald 1992). Guinea fowl are more likely than chickens to run feral, laying eggs away from human settlements. Wild African guinea fowl eggs may be gathered and placed under sitting chickens, which tend to them once hatched, thereby introducing a constant flow of wild genes into already

FIG. 34.4 Chickens in a portable cage on a bicycle in a market in western Kenya (photograph, Olivier Hanotte).

behaviourally problematic captive populations. Guinea fowls' ability to consume ticks (Grafton 1971) and hunt snakes may have outweighed their frailties as domestic poultry in the eyes of livestock owners.

CONCLUSION

African domesticates, whether or not originally derived from foreign ancestors, have adapted to disease challenges throughout their range, reflecting local selective pressures under human management. Adaptations include dwarfing and associated increases in fecundity, tick resistance, and resistance or tolerance to several mortal infectious diseases. The genetics of these traits are yet to be fully explored, but reflect the animal side of the close co-evolution between humans and domestic animals in Africa. To fixate upon whether or not cattle were independently domesticated from wild African ancestors, or to dismiss chickens' successful spread through Africa because they were introduced from Asia, ignores the more interesting and relevant questions of how domestic species adapted to the demands of African environments and how African people integrated them into their lives, and how entire landscapes also required 'domestication' for these mutual relationships to be sustained (cf. Terrell et al. 2003)

Genetic analysis does not supplant archaeological evidences but rather produces new questions about human agency and cultural contact that can only be investigated through further archaeological research. In turn, animal geneticists benefit from interacting with archaeologists to formulate new research agendas concerning the species they study. If mindful of the mutual benefits reaped by frequent consultation and collaboration, especially in the nascent field of ancient DNA analysis, both sets of practitioners can emulate the mutualism that characterizes the intertwined lives of people and the animals that live with them.

REFERENCES

ACHILLI, A., BONFIGLIO, S., OLIVIERI, A., et al. (2009). The multifaceted origin of taurine cattle reflected by the mitochondrial genome. *PLoS One* 4(6): e5753.

AMILLS, M., RAMÍREZ, O., GALMAN-OMITOGUN. O., and CLOP, A. (2012). Domestic pigs in Africa. *African Archaeological Review* DOI: 10.1007/s10437-012-9111-2.

BARD, K. (ed.) (1996). *Encyclopedia of the Archaeology of Ancient Egypt*. London: Routledge.

BEJA-PEREIRA, A., ENGLAND, P. R., FERRAND, N., et al. (2004). African origins of the domestic donkey. *Science* 304: 1781.

—— LUIKART, G., ENGLAND, P. R., et al. (2003). Gene-culture coevolution between cattle milk protein genes and human lactase genes. *Nature Genetics* 35: 311–13.

BOYKO, A. R., BOYKO, R. H., BOYKO, C. M., et al. (2009). Complex population structure in African village dogs and its implications for inferring dog domestication history. *Proceedings of the National Academy of Science (USA)* 106: 13903–8.

BRADLEY, D. G., and LOFTUS, R. (2000). Two Eves for *taurus*? Bovine mitochondrial DNA and African cattle domestication. In R. M. Blench and K. C. Macdonald (eds), *The Origins and Development of African Livestock. Archaeology, Genetics, Linguistics, and Ethnography*. London: UCL Press, 244–58.

BROOKS, N., CLARKE, J., GARFI, S., and PIRIE, A. (2009). The archaeology of Western Sahara: results of environmental and archaeological reconnaissance. *Antiquity* 83: 918–34.

BRUFORD, M. W., and TOWNSEND, S. J. (2006). Mitochondrial DNA diversity in modern sheep. In M. A. Zeder, D. G. Bradley, E. Emshwiller, and B. D. Smith (eds), *Documenting Domestication: New Genetic and Archaeological Paradigms*. Berkeley: University of California Press, 306–16.

CARTER, P. L., and FLIGHT, C. (1972). Report on the fauna from the sites of Ntereso and Kintampo rock shelter six in Ghana, with evidence for the practice of animal husbandry in the second millennium B.C. *Man* 7: 277–82.

CHAMI, F. A. (2001). Chicken bones from Neolithic limestone cave site, Zanzibar. In F. A. Chami, G. Pwiti, and C. Radimilahy (eds), *People, Contacts and the Environment in the African Past*. Dar es Salaam: DUP Press, 84–97.

CHENYAMBUGA, S. W., HANOTTE, O., HIRBO, J., et al. (2004). Genetic characterization of indigenous goats of sub-Saharan Africa using microsatellite DNA markers. *Asian-Australian Journal of Animal Science* 17: 445–52.

CLARK, J. D., and WILLIAMS, M. A. J. (1978). Recent archaeological research in southwestern Ethiopia (1974–1975). *Annales d'Éthiopie* 11: 19–44.

CLUTTON-BROCK, J. (1993). The spread of domestic animals in Africa. In T. Shaw, P. J. J. Sinclair, B. Andah, and A. Okpoko (eds), *The Archaeology of Africa: Foods, Metals, and Towns*. London: Routledge, 43–60.

—— (2000). Cattle, sheep, and goats. In R. M. Blench and K. C. Macdonald (eds), *The Origins and Development of African Livestock: Archaeology, Genetics, Linguistics, and Ethnography*. London: UCL Press, 30–7.

DRISCOLL, C. A., MACDONALD, D. W., and O'BRIEN, S. J. (2009). From wild animals to domestic pets: an evolutionary view of domestication. *Proceedings of the National Academy of Sciences (USA)* 106: 9971–8.

EDWARDS, C. J., MACHUGH, D. E., DOBNEY, K. M., et al. (2004). Ancient DNA analysis of 101 cattle remains: limits and prospects. *Journal of Archaeological Science* 31: 695–710.

EPSTEIN, H. (1957) The sanga cattle of East Africa. *East African Agricultural Journal* 22: 149–64.

GAUTIER, A. (1984). Archaeozoology of the Bir Kiseiba region, Eastern Sahara. In F. Wendorf, R. Schild, and A. E. Close (eds), *Cattle-Keepers of the Eastern Sahara*. Dallas, Tex.: Southern Methodist University Press, 49–72.

—— (1987). Prehistoric men and cattle in North Africa: a dearth of data and a surfeit of models. In A. E. Close (ed.), *Prehistory of Arid North Africa: Essays in Honor of Fred Wendorf*. Dallas: Southern Methodist University Press, 163–87.

—— (2002). The evidence of the earliest livestock in North Africa: or adventures with large bovids, ovicaprids, dogs and pigs. In F. A. Hassan (ed.), *Droughts, Food, and Culture: Ecological Change and Food Security in Africa's Late Prehistory*. New York: Kluwer, 195–224.

GIFFORD-GONZALEZ, D. (2000). Animal disease challenges to the emergence of pastoralism in sub-Saharan Africa. *African Archaeological Review* 18: 95–139.

GRAFTON, R. N. (1971). Winter food of the helmeted guineafowl in Natal. *Ostrich Supplement* 8: 475–85.

GRIGSON, C., GOWLETT, J. A. J., and ZARINS, J. (1989). The camel in Arabia: a direct radiocarbon date. *Journal of Archaeological Science* 16: 355–62.

HANOTTE, O. (2007). Origin and history of livestock diversity. In B. Richkowsky and D. Pilling (eds), *Section A: The State of the World's Animal Genetic Resources for Food and Agriculture*. Rome: FAO, 5–19.

—— RONIN, Y., AGABA, M., et al. (2003). Mapping of quantitative trait loci controlling trypanotolerance in a cross of tolerant West Africa N'Dama and susceptible East African Boran cattle. *Proceedings of the National Academy of Sciences (USA)* 100: 7443–8.

—— TAWAH, C. L., BRADLEY, D. G., et al. (2000). Geographic distribution and frequency of a taurine *Bos taurus* and an indicine *Bos indicus* gamma specific allele amongst sub-Saharan African cattle breeds. *Molecular Ecology* 9: 387–96.

HASSAN, F. A. (2000). Climate and cattle in North Africa: a first approximation. In R. M. Blench and K. C. MacDonald (eds), *The Origins and Development of African Livestock: Archaeology, Genetics, Linguistics, and Ethnography*. London: UCL Press, 61–86.

HOEVEN, E., FIDALIS, M. N., LEAK, S. G. A., GEERTS, S., HANOTTE, O., and JIANLIN, H. (2007). Introgression of the Sahelian breed into West African dwarf goats. In A. R. Njogu (ed.), *Proceedings of the 28th International Scientific Council for Trypanosomiasis Research and Control Conference*. Nairobi: African Union/IBAR, 622–6.

HONEGGER, M. (2005). Kerma et les débuts du Néolithique africain. *Genava* 53: 239–49.

HORSBURGH, K. A., and RHINES, A. (2010). Genetic characterization of an archaeological sheep assemblage from South Africa's Western Cape. *Journal of Archaeological Science* 37: 2906–10.

KIMURA, B., MARSHALL, F. B., CHEN, S., et al. (2011). Ancient DNA from Nubian and Somali wild ass provides insights into donkey ancestry and domestication. *Proceedings of the Royal Society B: Biological Sciences* 278: 50–57.

LARSON, G., DOBNEY, K., ALBARELLA, U., et al. (2005). Worldwide phylogeography of wild boar reveals multiple centers of pig domestication. *Science* 307: 1618–21.

LIU, Y.-P., WU, G.-S., YAO, Y.-G., et al. (2006). Multiple maternal origins of chickens: out of the Asian jungle. *Molecular Phylogenetics and Evolution* 38: 12–19.

LOFTUS, R. T., MACHUGH, D. E., NGERE, L. O., et al. (1994). Mitochondrial genetic variation in European, African and Indian cattle populations. *Animal Genetics* 25: 265–71.

MACDONALD, K. C. (1992). The domestic chicken (*Gallus gallus*) in sub-Saharan Africa: a background to its introduction and its osteological differentiations from indigenous fowls (Numidinae and *Francolinus* sp.). *Journal of Archaeological Science* 19: 303–18.

—— and MACDONALD, R. H. (2000). The origins and development of domesticated animals in arid West Africa. In R. M. Blench and K. C. Macdonald (eds), *The Origins and Development of African Livestock: Archaeology, Genetics, Linguistics and Ethnography*. London: UCL Press, 127–62.

MARSHALL, F. B., and WEISSBROD, L. (2010). The consequences of women's use of donkeys for pastoral flexibility: Maasai ethnoarchaeology. *Documenta Archaeobiologiae* 7: 55–75.

MEADOWS, J. R. S, CEMAL, I., KARACA, O., GOOTWINE, E., and KIJAS, J. W. (2007). Five ovine mitochondrial lineages identified from sheep breeds of the Near East. *Genetics* 175: 1371–9.

MITCHELL, P. J. (2009). The canine connection: dogs and southern African hunter-gatherers. In S. Badenhorst, P. J. Mitchell, and J. C. Driver (eds), *Animals and People: Archaeozoological Papers in Honour of Ina Plug*. Oxford: Archaeopress, 104–16.

MUCHADEYI, F. C., EDING, H., SIMIANER, H., WOLLNY, C. B. A., GROENEVELD, E., and WEIGEND, S. (2008). Mitochondrial DNA D-loop sequences suggest a Southeast Asian and Indian origin of Zimbabwean village chickens. *Animal Genetics* 39: 615–22.

MUIGAI, A. W. (2002). *Characterisation and Conservation of Indigenous Animal Genetic Resources: Genetic Diversity and Relationships of Fat-Tailed and Thin-Tailed Sheep of Africa*. Juja: Jomo Kenyatta University of Agriculture and Technology.

MWACHARO, J. M., BJØRNSTAD, G., MOBEGI, V., et al. (2011). Mitochondrial DNA reveals multiple introductions of domestic chicken in East Africa. *Molecular Phylogenetics and Evolution* 58: 374–82.

NADERI, S., REZAEI, H. R., POMPANON, F., et al. (2008). The goat domestication process inferred from large-scale mitochondrial DNA analysis of wild and domestic individuals. *Proceedings of the National Academy of Sciences (USA)* 105: 17659–64.

O'BRIEN, S. J., JOHNSON, W., DRISCOLL, C., et al. (2008). State of cat genomics. *Trends in Genetics* 24: 268–79.

PANG, J.-F., KLUETSCH, C., ZOU, X.-J., et al. (2009). mtDNA data indicate a single origin for dogs south of Yangtze River, less than 16,300 years ago, from numerous wolves. *Molecular Biology and Evolution* 26: 2849–64.

PEREIRA, F., QUEIRÓS, S., GUSMÃO, L., et al. (2009). Tracing the history of goat pastoralism: new clues from mitochondrial and Y chromosome DNA in North Africa. *Molecular Biology and Evolution* 26: 2765–73.

PÉREZ-PARDAL, L., ROYO, L. J., BEJA-PEREIRA, A., et al. (2010a). Multiple paternal origins of domestic cattle revealed by Y-specific interspersed multilocus microsatellites. *Heredity* 105: 511–19.

—— —— ——, et al. (2010b). Y-specific microsatellites reveal an African subfamily in taurine (*Bos taurus*) cattle. *Animal Genetics* 41: 232–41.

PETERS, J. (1991). The faunal remains from Shaqadud. In A. E. Marks and A. Mohammed-Ali (eds), *The Late Prehistory of the Eastern Sahel*. Dallas, Tex.: Southern Methodist University Press, 197–235.

PORTER, V. and MASON, I. L. (2002). *Mason's World Dictionary of Livestock Breeds, Types and Varieties*, New York: C.A.B International.

RAMÍREZ, O., OJED, A., TOMÀS, A., et al. (2009). Integrating Y-chromosome, mitochondrial, and autosomal data to analyze the origin of pig breeds. *Molecular Biology and Evolution* 26: 2061–72.

RAZAFINDRAIBE, H., MOBEGI, V. A., OMMEH, S. C., et al. (2008). Mitochondrial DNA origin of indigenous Malagasy chicken. *Annals of the New York Academy of Sciences* 1149: 77–9.

ROSSEL, S., MARSHALL, F., PETERS, J., PILGRAM, T., ADAMAS, M. D., and O'CONNOR, D. (2008). Domestication of the donkey: timing, processes, and indicators. *Proceedings of the National Academy of Sciences (USA)* 105: 3715–20.

ROWLEY-CONWY, P. (1988). The camel in the Nile Valley: new radiocarbon accelerator (AMS) dates from Qasr Ibrim. *Journal of Egyptian Archaeology* 74: 245–8.

SABLIN, M. V., and KHOPACHEV, G. A. (2002). The earliest Ice Age dogs: evidence from Eliseevichi. *Current Anthropology* 43: 795–9.

SMITH, A. B. (1992). Origins and spread of pastoralism in Africa. *Annual Review of Anthropology* 21: 125–41.

TERRELL, J. E., HART, J. P., BARUT, S., et al. (2003). Domesticated landscapes: the subsistence ecology of plant and animal domestication. *Journal of Archaeological Method and Theory* 10: 323–68.

TISHKOFF, S. A., REED, F. A., RANCIARO, A., et al. (2007). Convergent adaptation of human lactase persistence in Africa and Europe. *Nature Genetics* 39: 31–40.

VIGNE, J.-D., GUILAINE, J., DEBUE, K., HYE, L., and GÉRARD, P. (2004). Early taming of the cat in Cyprus. *Science* 304: 259.

WAYNE, R. K., LEONARD, J. A., and VILÀ, C. (2006). Genetic analysis of dog domestication. In M. A. Zeder, D. G. Bradley, E. Emshwiller, and B. D. Smith (eds), *Documenting Domestication: New Genetic and Archaeological Paradigms*. Berkeley: University of California Press, 279–93.

ZEDER, M. A., EMSHWILLER, E., SMITH, B. D., and BRADLEY, D. G. (2006). Documenting domestication: the intersection of genetics and archaeology. *Trends in Genetics* 22: 139–45.

—— and HESSE, B. (2000). The initial domestication of goats (*Capra hircus*) in the Zagros Mountains 10,000 years ago. *Science* 287: 2254–7.

CHAPTER 35

DOMESTICATING PLANTS IN AFRICA

DORIAN FULLER AND ELISABETH HILDEBRAND

INTRODUCTION

DURING the last 10,000 years, cultivation and herding have supplanted hunting and gathering as economic strategies almost everywhere. Africa's sequence of economic change differs from that of most continents in that herding tended to precede crop farming, and domestication of indigenous plants occurred fairly late—during the last 5,000 years (Marshall and Hildebrand 2002). Different innovations in subsistence strategies took place in different parts of Africa: some regions saw animal domestication and the spread of herding, others the domestication of seed crops or the cultivation of perennial plants propagated vegetatively.

These distinct trajectories of change can contribute to global research by showing different causes, consequences, and processes for different transitions to food production in different parts of the world. Although still sparse, hard archaeological evidence for these processes is beginning to accumulate in different parts of Africa. This evidence allows us to trace how the domestication of various indigenous African crops (Fig. 35.1) led to the development of a wide array of agricultural economies within Africa and, eventually, how those economies gave new resources and tastes to other regions of the world.

CULTIVATION, DOMESTICATION, AND AGRICULTURE

A shift from *hunting and gathering*—procuring wild resources that have undergone relatively little interference by humans—to *food production*—human intervention in the life cycles of plants and animals to enhance their productivity, palatability, distribution, predictability, or other traits relevant to human consumption—is perhaps the most fundamental economic change that occurred in prehistory. Different parts of the globe had different pathways to food production, in part due to differences in environments, available

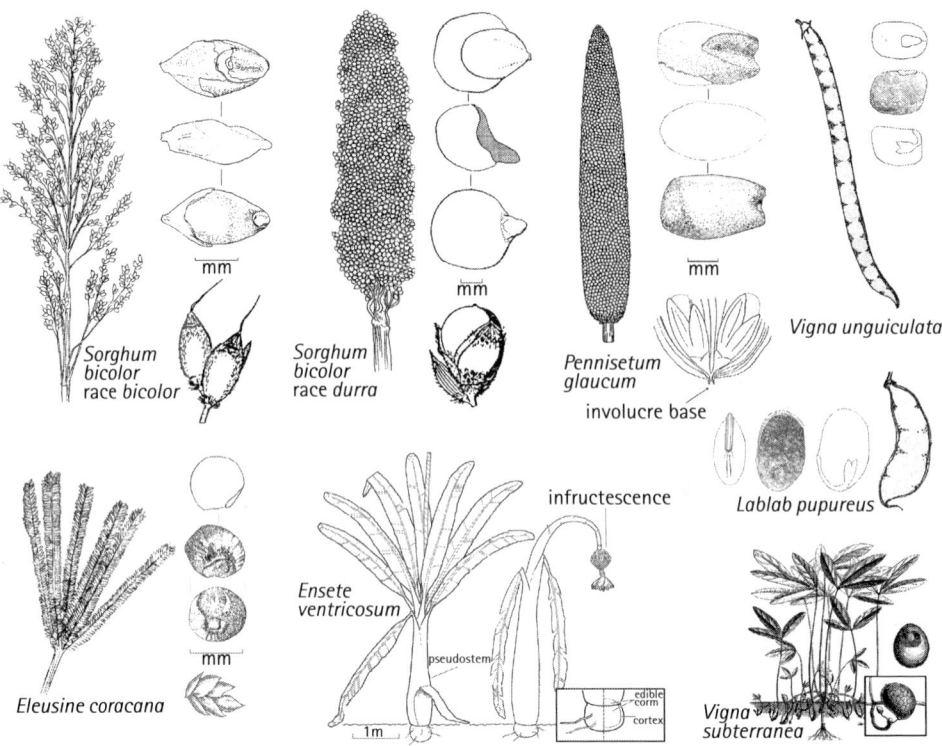

FIG. 35.1 Selected crops of African origin, including cereals, pulses and the tuber crop enset. The cereals illustrated contrast the seed heads of sorghum (*Sorghum bicolor*) races bicolor (hulled) and durra (free-threshing), pearl millet (*Pennisetum glaucum*), and finger millet (*Eleusine coracana*); examples of spikelets and grains are also shown, including drawings of archaeological specimens of *Sorghum* race *bicolor* from Umm Muri Sudan (*c.* 150 BC), *P. glaucum* from Karkarichinkat, Mali (*c.* 2400 BC), and *E. coracana* from Musanze, Rwanda (*c.* AD 1100). Pulse pods and seeds include the cowpea (*Vigna unguiculata*), hyacinth bean (*Lablab purpureus*), and Bambara groundnut (*Vigna subterranea*). Views of the enset (*Ensete ventricosum*) plant include a growing individual (left), a fruiting plant near the end of its life cycle (centre), and a close-up of the edible corm (right). (*Vigna subterranea* is reproduced from Engler 1936; sorghum spikelets are from Snowden 1936; *Ensete* illustration by Hildebrand, other drawings by Fuller).

resources, and human cultures. Food production, in its various forms, laid the foundations for social transformations that shaped the development of complex societies in different parts of the world and that continue to influence patterns of interaction between different cultures and geopolitical units today. Scholars split this major economic change into three different subcategories related to plant food production (Harris 2007) and others related to animal food production (see Gifford-Gonzalez and Hanotte, Ch. 34 above):

> *Cultivation* is a human action that enhances the survival, reproduction or growth of certain plants. It may include preparing soil, planting seeds, seedlings, tubers, or

other plant parts, weeding and tending plants as they mature, and/or protecting them from predators.

Domestication describes genetic and morphological changes on the part of a plant population in response to selective pressures imposed by cultivation. Whereas 'cultivation' denotes a change in human activities, 'domestication' is an ensuing change in plant genotype or morphology. Most seed crops share a clear 'grain domestication' syndrome of morphological change (Fuller 2007), but vegecultural domesticates have diverse biological responses to cultivation (Hildebrand 2007a).

Agriculture is the form of land use that results from cultivation and/or domestication. It is a *change in the landscape*, as people regularly cultivate and focus more attention on domestic plants. Agriculture creates fields for larger scale production of crops; how one distinguishes agriculture from small-scale cultivation varies according to the parameters of particular geographic and cultural contexts. The shift to dependence may or may not be rapid or permanent: some societies have existed for millennia in a state of 'low-level food production' without crossing such a threshold (Smith 2001).

In the case of seed crops, one expects cultivation first, followed by domestication and finally agriculture. Southwest Asia's archaeological record follows this sequence: weeds (indicating cultivation) are present before domesticates (Willcox 2012). However, this sequence need not apply in every instance. Vegetatively propagated plants may be cultivated on a large scale without exhibiting permanent morphological or genetic change, and *décrue* techniques (broadcasting seeds into receding flood-waters) could create optimal environments for wild populations of cereals.

These evolutionary schemes imply several distinct transitions that must be identified and explained. Initial cultivation, a key behavioural change in humans, is difficult to discern. During pre-domestication cultivation, morphological changes begin to occur, some of which may be evident in assemblages of ancient plants. The shift to agriculture may be detected quantitatively via a surge of cultivated species in subsistence remains and via regional landscapes dominated by crops and weeds.

The clearest archaeological indicators of cultivation are 'hard' domestication traits: tough rachises that hold cereal grains securely, reduced germination inhibition—often visible in the seed coat—in many other plants. These traits may gradually rise in frequency in cultivated populations. Their predominance (domestication) marks the end of a process of biological evolution that began with an earlier change in human practices (cultivation). Other traits, such as grain size, evolve gradually under cultivation; diachronic change may be evaluated in large assemblages with an extended temporal range, but isolated specimens are ambiguous (Fuller 2007). Determining wild vs domestic status for vegetatively propagated plants can be even more challenging (Hildebrand 2003a).

Once plant remains are identified conclusively as domestic, archaeobotanists must assess their quantity, contextual integrity, and consistency with other aspects of the archaeological record. Dozens of seeds constitute more robust evidence than a single individual. Rodent burrows and other possible bioturbation agents must be considered, and direct AMS dating of domestic specimens is more rigorous than relying on 'associated' dates. Isolated finds that appear to be millennia earlier than all other instances require extra scrutiny (Harlan and de Wet 1973; Neumann and Hildebrand 2009).

The African archaeological record has not yet yielded much evidence for either initial cultivation or shifts towards morphological domestication in most regions and for most crops of African origin. Our evidence is clearest for the emergence of sedentary village societies already dependent on cultivation, usually of domesticated crops, or for the arrival of herders practising some form of cultivation. To compare and explain different African plant domestication events will require more research in many parts of the continent.

APPROACHES TO THE STUDY OF DOMESTICATION AND AGRICULTURE

Investigations of early crops and agriculture have recourse to two complementary data sources: modern studies (botanical and ethnobotanical) and ancient plant remains recovered from archaeological or palaeoecological sites. Rock art constitutes a third line of evidence for agricultural activities (e.g. Brandt 1984: 178), but it is rare and can be difficult to date so we do not discuss it here.

Modern botanical and genetic studies of crops and their sister taxa can assess what differences have evolved between domesticated and wild plants and identify which processes of natural or human selection might have fostered these changes (Hildebrand 2003a; Zeder et al. 2006: 66–168; Fuller and Allaby 2009). Ecological and geographical research focusing on 'wild progenitors' (populations of wild plants closely related to domestic crops) can provide information on the regions(s) and kinds of habitats where cultivation began (Harlan 1992). Linguistic studies can shed light on the past use of wild and domestic plants by various cultural groups and the pathways by which specific crops probably spread (Rossel 1998; Blench 2006). Ethnographic and ethnobotanical observations of traditional cultivation methods, and the use of 'wild progenitors' and complementary resources, can clarify the economic and social circumstances of prehistoric plant domestication (Hildebrand 2007a, 2009).

Ancient plant remains, and the contexts in which they appear, form a second data source. Archaeobotanical research applies botanical methods and background knowledge to archaeological problems and materials. Identification and analysis of ancient plant materials can show, and explain, changing patterns of human behaviour in past societies and amplify our knowledge of surrounding environments. Archaeobotanists may specialize in the study of preserved seeds and fruits, wood charcoal, phytoliths, and pollen and/or starch grains. Key aspects of archaeobotanical studies pertaining to plant domestication include morphological assessment of a specimen's wild vs domestic status, direct dating of ancient domesticates, and understanding the social, economic, and environmental contexts of early crop use.

Macroremains (seeds, fruits, and other parts like chaff) can furnish concrete evidence for early crops and agriculture (Zohary and Hopf 2000). They are most typically preserved via carbonization (being charred in or near a fire), or less commonly by desiccation, waterlogging, or incorporation into daub, mud-brick, or pottery. Carbonization tends to destroy all but the hardest parts (such as grains) and may also distort shapes and cause shrinkage. Nevertheless, charred seeds of crops such as pearl millet, finger millet, and cowpea allow us to study changes in size and/or shape over time. Preserved chaff can reveal other domestication traits, such as whether seeds were dispersed naturally or were processed by threshing and dependent on human sowing.

Studying plants that are not harvested for their seeds, such as tubers and some tree fruits (like oil palm), requires examining other lines of archaeobotanical evidence. Phytoliths—microscopic silica bodies deposited in plant tissues—may be used to identify enset (native to Africa and Asia, and grown in Ethiopia for its starchy pseudostem and corm) and bananas (native to southeast Asia and later introduced to Africa); these members of the Musaceae family have distinctive volcano-shaped phytoliths. Charred fragments of some roots and tubers may be identified on the basis of their parenchyma tissue (Hather 2000). Recovery and recognition of starch grains found in residues on ancient tools and ceramics may allow identification of yams, other tubers, and other plants processed by ancient peoples (Torrence and Barton 2006). Phytolith, parenchyma, and starch research is just beginning to contribute new perspectives to African archaeobotany.

THE BIOGEOGRAPHY OF AFRICAN CROP ORIGINS

Archaeological and botanical studies have revealed evidence for a growing number of distinct regions of independent domestication around the world. Among the twenty-four possible centres of early cultivation now recognized, at least five are in Africa (Purugganan and Fuller 2009).

Table 35.1 Summary of major indigenous African plant domesticates

Latin name	Common name	Early evidence: summary and comments
West African Sahara/Sahel		
Pennisetum glaucum	Pearl millet	Tilemsi Valley, Mali, from c. 2400 BC; Mauretania and Ghana by c. 1700 BC; India by 1700 BC
Citrullus lanatus	Watermelon	Southwestern Libya back to c. 4000 BC, but could be wild; in Egypt by c. 2000 BC
West African grassy woodlands		
Digitaria exilis	Fonio	Niger River bend from c. AD 400; Senegal before AD 500
Brachiaria deflexa	Black fonio	Brachiaria sp. finds along the Niger River from c. 500 BC and Senegal by AD 500
Oryza glaberrima	African rice	Wild in Nigeria c. 1000 BC; probably cultivated along Niger River bend from c. 500 BC
Vigna unguiculata	Cowpea	Ghana by 1700 BC; probable Indian finds by 1700 BC

Latin name	Common name	Early evidence: summary and comments
West African grassy woodlands		
Vigna subterranea	Bambara groundnut	Nigeria, *c.* 500 BC; Burkino Faso by AD 200
Macrotyloma geocarpum	Kersting's groundnut	
Adansonia digitata	Baobab tree	Burkina Faso, *c.* 1000 BC; in eastern Africa from *c.* AD 500
Hibiscus cannabinus	Kenaf	
Forest margins of West/Central Africa		
Dioscorea cayenensis and related species	Yam	
Plectranthus rotundifolius	Hausa potato	
Plectranthus esculentus	Dazo	
Elaeis guineensis	Oil palm	Used by hunter-gatherers in Ghana >4000 BC; with other crops from *c.* 1700 BC. Pollen evidence for increase and then expansion in West Africa from *c.* 1500 BC
Cola nitida and *C. acuminata*	Kola nut	
East Sudanic grasslands		
Sorghum bicolor	Sorghum	In India by 1700 BC. Wild in Egypt's Western Desert (*c.* 8000 BC) and north Sudan (7000–3000 BC); in Nubia by 500 BC and in Libya by 500 BC
Lablab purpureus	Hyacinth bean	In India by 1700 BC; Nubia and South African finds only from the past ~2,000 years
Hibiscus sabdariffa	Roselle	
Gossypium herbaceum	Short-staple cotton	Nubia for the past 2,000 years; archaeobotanical specimens are not distinct from Asian origin cotton
Citrullus lanatus	Watermelon	Southwestern Libya back to *c.* 4000 BC, but could be wild; Egypt by *c.* 2000 BC
Ethiopian uplands		
Eragrostis tef	T'ef	Northern Ethiopia, Eritrea, Yemen, *c.* 500 BC
Eleusine coracana	Finger millet	Northern Ethiopia and Nigeria by AD 100; widespread in eastern Africa from AD 400; probably in India *c.* 1000 BC
Avena abyssinica	Ethiopian oats	Semi-domesticate from weed
Ensete ventricosum	Enset	
Dioscorea cayenensis and related species	Yam	
Coccinia abyssinica	Anchote	
Pisum abyssinicum	Ethiopian pea	Egypt Red Sea Coast import from *c.* AD 100
Guizotia abyssinica	Noog	Aksum, Ethiopia, *c.* AD 500
Coffea arabica	Coffee	

Botanically, the closest wild relatives of many crops have been identified as native to Africa (Table 35.1). Knowledge of their modern geographic distributions, refined by genetic, systematic, and palaeoenvironmental studies, allows us to outline five regions of initial cultivation (Fig. 35.2). The *West African Sahara/Sahel* has wild pearl millet (*Pennisetum glaucum*) and clear archaeobotanical evidence for its domestication at least 4,500 years ago (Manning et al. 2011); watermelons probably also originate in this zone (Wasylikowa and van der Veen 2004). To the south, the *West African grassy woodlands* are home to fonio cereals, cowpea, Bambara groundnut, African rice (*Oryza glaberrima*), and the baobab tree; it is unclear whether these were domesticated before or after domestic pearl millet spread into the area. Further south, in *forest margin* areas, western African yams, oil palm, and kola were first brought into cultivation. East of Lake Chad, *East Sudanic grasslands* were the likely home of early cultivation of sorghum and perhaps the hyacinth bean. The *Ethiopian uplands* have several domesticates: the tiny-seeded cereal t'ef (possibly originally derived from lower

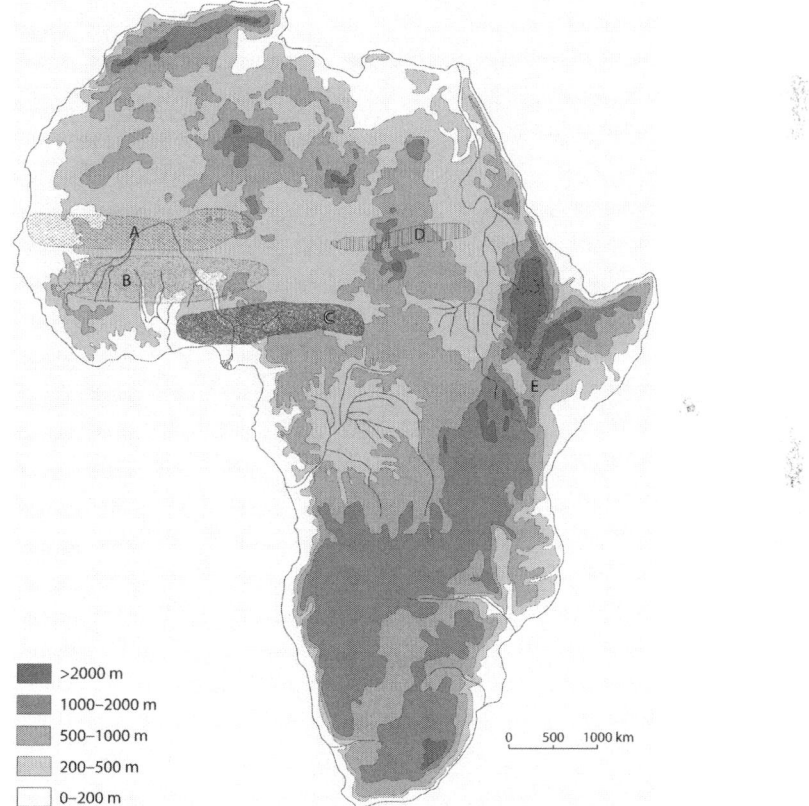

>2000 m
1000–2000 m
500–1000 m
200–500 m
0–200 m

0   500   1000 km

FIG. 35.2 Probable geographic locations of the five centres of indigenous crop domestication in Africa, on a topographic base map. (A) West African Sahara/Sahel: pearl millet (*Pennisetum glaucum)* and possibly watermelon. (B) West African grassy woodlands: fonio cereals, cowpea, Bambara groundnut, African rice (*Oryza glaberrima*), and baobab. (C) Forest margins: West African yams, oil palm and kola. (D) East Sudanic grasslands: sorghum and possibly hyacinth bean. (E) Uplands of Ethiopia (t'ef, enset, noog, coffee, yams, and possibly finger millet) and eastern Africa (an alternative location for finger millet domestication).

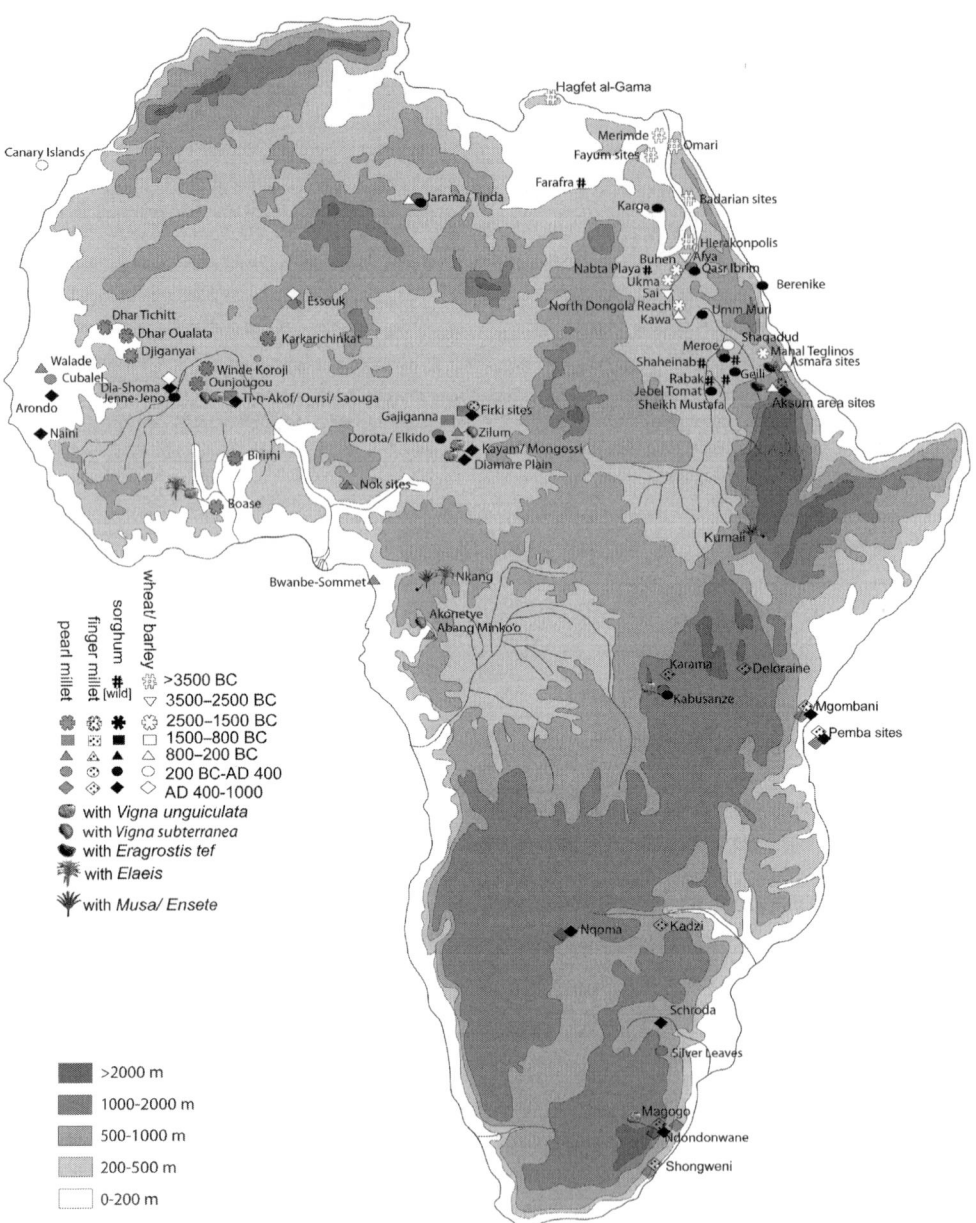

FIG. 35.3 Sites with early archaeobotanical evidence for the spread of major African crops (sorghum, pearl millet, finger millet, wheat, and barley), with indications of early finds of t'ef, cowpea, Bambara groundnut, oil palm, and *Musa/Ensete*.

areas), the oilseed noog, a local pea (*Pisum abyssinicum*) and enset (*Ensete ventricosum*), which provides large quantities of starch and construction/wrapping material. Early cultivation of eastern African yams, coffee, and anchote (which has edible fruits, tubers, and greens) probably took place at slightly lower elevations. Finger millet domestication probably occurred in upland Ethiopia or other highland parts of eastern Africa.

Among Africa's many indigenous crops (Figs 35.1, 35.2), direct archaeobotanical evidence for domestication is only available for pearl millet (Manning et al. 2011) and t'ef (D'Andrea 2008). More indirect forms of evidence point to fairly late, mid-Holocene origins for other taxa (Fig. 35.3), including five major crops (pearl millet, finger millet, sorghum, cowpea, and hyacinth bean) in India, to which they must have been transported after initial cultivation in Africa (Fuller 2003; Boivin and Fuller 2009).

DISSEMINATION OF AFRICAN CROPS
TO ASIA AND BEYOND

Developing this last point, southern India has firm evidence for pearl millet and directly dated hyacinth bean (*Lablab purpureus*) by 1600–1500 BC, sorghum by 1400 BC, and finger millet by *c.* 1000 BC. In northwest India, clear evidence extends earlier to 1700–2000 BC. Early reports of sorghum from Kunal and finger millet from early Rodji await chronological confirmation, but might stretch the South Asian use of African crops back to *c.* 2200/2500 BC (Fuller and Boivin 2009). This Indian evidence poses a challenge to African archaeologists, as these crops must have been cultivated (and were in all likelihood domesticated) in Africa before their arrival in India. These finds also testify to the importance of long-distance contacts around the Indian Ocean (Fuller et al. 2011). Pearl millet is the only African crop found so far earlier on its home continent (Manning et al. 2011), but this is undoubtedly due to more limited archaeobotanical sampling across Africa. Domestic finger millet, in contrast, appears in the Indian archaeological record a full millennium before the earliest African finds (Giblin and Fuller 2011).

Numerous other crops may have been exchanged between India and Africa in prehistory, but have not yet been found archaeologically (Blench 2003; Fuller et al. 2011). In many cases confusion remains as to whether cultivars were originally African or tropical Asian in origin. For example, while the Hausa potato (*Plectranthus rotundifolius*), roselle (*Hibiscus sabdariffa*), and kenaf (*H. cannabinus*) can be regarded as African crops that were introduced to Asia, jute (*Corchorus olitorius*), tree cotton (*Gossypium arboreum*), okra (*Abelmoschus esculentus*), gungo peas (*Cajanus cajan*), and drumstick tree (*Moringa oleifera*) probably originated in India. Others, such as tamarind (*Tamarindus indica*), may have been naturally distributed on both continents. There are also apparent 'trans-domesticates' in which a wild African form may have travelled to South Asia as a weed, and later undergone domestication. This appears to be the case for both winged bean (*Psophocarpus tetragonolobus*) from eastern Africa's upland forests and gaur bean (*Cyamopsis tetragonoloba*) from the Sudanic grasslands.

In the past 500 years, African crops have also spread to low and intermediate latitudes of the New World (Mitchell 2005: 200; Carney and Rosomoff 2009). With the massive transport of African peoples across the Atlantic during the slave trade, West African foods were key sources of sustenance obtained from the same West African ports. These tropical crops were well suited to agriculture in the tropical and sub-tropical lands in the Americas, and the African diaspora brought knowledge of the practices for their cultivation (Carney 2001; Carney and Rosomoff 2009). The first rice cultivation in the Americas (in Brazil and the Carolinas) was carried out by slaves with African *Oryza glaberrima*, only later supplanted by the more productive Asian rices (*O. sativa*) (Carney 2001). Black-eyed peas (*Vigna unguiculata*) and gungo peas (*Cajanus cajan*) are major plant protein sources in cooking of the Caribbean and southern United States. Bananas, which had been established in West Africa in prehistoric times, became important staples in parts of tropical America, while varieties of sorghum with high sugar content in their stems were key in production of molasses, an important locally produced sweetener when sugar transport costs were high. Coffee is now a major agricultural commodity in central and South America. Most recently, t'ef farming has taken hold in Idaho to supply the Ethiopian expatriate community in the United States.

EXTERNAL CONTRIBUTIONS: CROPS INTRODUCED TO AFRICA

Several important crops were introduced from Asia to Africa in the remoter past, while a further set of important cultigens (notably maize (*Zea mays*) and manioc (*Manihot esculenta*)) was introduced from the Americas by the Portuguese during and after the 16th century (cf. Schoeman, Thiaw and Richard, Chs 64 and 68 below; Mitchell 2005: 197–201; Carney and Rosomoff 2009: 54–9). The Asian crops may be divided into three groups in terms of probable entry routes (Table 35.2).

One group came from Southwest Asia. Wheats, barley, and some legumes were the earliest basis of agriculture in the Egyptian Nile Valley from 4500 BC (Wetterstrom 1993) and had reached Sudanese Nubia by 2700 BC (Hildebrand 2007b), though agriculture remained confined to the Nile floodplain. The same crops then appear in pre-Aksumite archaeological contexts in the northern Ethiopian and Eritrean highlands in the first millennium BC (Boardman 1999; D'Andrea et al. 2007), but because this area has yielded few archaeobotanical remains from prior periods, it is unclear when Southwest Asian crops became established, and how: they may have spread upstream along the Nile's tributaries or have arrived via the Red Sea and Yemen, where they were grown *c.* 3000 BC (Boivin and Fuller 2009). Southwest Asian crops have undergone a high degree of varietal differentiation and local adaptation in Ethiopia, where they complement indigenous domesticates such as t'ef and enset and are cultivated almost as far south as the Kenyan border.

A second set of crops came from South Asia via Arabia. Broomcorn millet of Chinese origin arrived in Nubia by the Kerma period (*c.* 1700 BC; cf. Welsby, Ch. 51 below), although sesame and Indian tree cotton arrived much later, perhaps by 100 BC (Boivin and Fuller 2009).

Maritime exchange brought a third set of tropical southeast Asian crops along the margins of the Indian Ocean to eastern Africa's coasts, after which they spread inland and contributed to tropical forest farming economies in Central Africa (Fuller et al. 2011). This group includes the important vegecultural trio of Asian yams, taro, and bananas, as well as coconut, mango, Asian rice, and mung bean on the eastern African coast. Although the tree crops were certainly present by 1,000 years ago on Pemba Island, Tanzania (Walshaw 2010), the arrival in Africa of the others is poorly dated and mostly lacks archaeological evidence. Phytolith finds suggest bananas may have been grown in Cameroon by *c.* 500 BC (Mbida et al. 2006), but are yet to be fully substantiated (Neumann and Hildebrand 2009).

Table 35.2 Major crop plants introduced to Africa from Asia

Common and Latin names	Early evidence in region of origin	Early evidence in Africa/comment
Southwest Asian crops		
Wheats (*Triticum dicoccum, T. durum, T. aestivum*)	Fully domesticated c. 8000 BC	Egypt c. 4500 BC; Nubia c. 3000 BC; Ethiopia c. 1000 BC
Barley (*Hordeum vulgare*)	Fully domesticated c. 8000 BC	Egypt c. 4500 BC; Nubia c. 3000 BC; Ethiopia c. 1000 BC
Pea (*Pisum sativum*)	Fully domesticated c. 8000 BC	Egypt c. 4500 BC; Nubia c. 1000 BC
Lentil (*Lens culinaris*)	Fully domesticated c. 8000 BC	Egypt c. 4500 BC; Nubia and Ethiopia c. 1000 BC
Broad bean (*Vicia faba*)	Fully domesticated c. 8000 BC	Egypt c. 4500 BC; Nubia c. 500 BC
Flax (*Linum usitatissimum*)	Fully domesticated c. 8000 BC	Egypt c. 3500 BC; Nubia and Ethiopia c. 1000 BC
Grape (*Vitis vinifera*)	Cultivated by 5000 BC	Egypt c. 3500 BC; Nubia c. 2000 BC; Ethiopia c. AD 500
South/East Asia via Arabian Sea		
Broomcorn millet (*Panicum miliaceum*)	North China, c. 6000 BC; Pakistan c. 1900 BC	Nubia c. 1700 BC
Foxtail millet (*Setaria italica*)	North China, c. 6000 BC	Unclear. Nubia has a related local species, *S. sphaceleata*, 1000 BC–AD 1500.
Tree cotton	Pakistan, c. 5000 BC	Hard to distinguish from native cotton. Cotton in Nubia by 100 BC, Libya by AD 100, Ethiopia by c. AD 500
Sesame	Pakistan, c. 2500 BC	Egypt 1300 BC; Libya and Nubia c. AD 100
Aubergine (*Solanum melongena*)	India/SE Asia	Egypt, Islamic period (c. AD 700)
Southeast Asia via Indian Ocean		
Taro (*Colocasia esculenta*)	Southeast Asia (multiple ?)	
Asian Greater Yam (*Dioscorea alata*)	Southeast Asia	
Banana (*Musa sapientum*)	New Guinea, c. 4000 BC	? Cameroon c. 500 BC
Drumstick tree (*Moringa oleifera*)	India	
Asian rice (*Oryza sativa*)	Fully domesticated in South China by c. 4500 BC	Pemba (Tanzania) c. AD 1000; imports to Egypt by AD 300

From the foregoing sections, one can see that people domesticated several different crops in different parts of Africa, creating a wealth of indigenous forms of food production. Africa contributed many crops to the global cornucopia, but crops from other continents also enriched African agricultural diversity and cuisines. We now turn to an in-depth consideration of how the domestication of specific African crops may have proceeded, couched in an understanding of the changes in plant morphology and distribution that can occur under manipulation by humans.

DOMESTICATION IN SEED CROPS

Cultivation of seed crops can introduce selective pressures that favour morphological changes leading to more efficient harvest by humans (seed retention) and/or higher yields per plant (larger seed size or more seeds per head). This 'domestication syndrome' includes evolution of non-dispersing seeds that become dependent on humans for dispersal. Appendages involved in wild seed dispersal, such as bristles, may be reduced. In the case of pearl millet, an aerodynamic one-grained involucre is replaced by a larger involucre holding two or more grains. This key shift away from natural seed shedding to seed retention is manifest in cereals in the attachment scars on base of spikelets (the grain in its husk). This process has been demonstrated quantitatively for the Southwest Asian cereals wheat and barley and for Asian rice (Fuller and Allaby 2009; Fuller et al. 2009; Purugganan and Fuller 2009). In the case of African pearl millet, seed retention is manifest in a torn stalk beneath the bristle that surrounds the grains (Fig. 35.1).

Among African cereals, pearl millet has the most robust assemblages, and datasets for tracking morphological changes during domestication with the predominance of non-shattering chaff in ceramic impressions from the Tilemsi Valley, Mali, attest to the development of seed retention before 2000 BC (Manning et al. 2011). Diagnostic attributes of pearl millet (involucre bases) preserve especially well archaeologically, but similar processes should be observable on the spikelet bases of both African rice (given the parallel of Asian rice: Fuller et al. 2009) and sorghum. Sorghum spikelet bases have occasionally been studied in charred material, such as wild examples from early Holocene Nabta Playa, c. 7000 BC (Wasylikowa et al. 1995) and domesticated material from Meroitic Nubia, 200 BC–AD 300 (Rowley-Conwy 1991; Fuller 2004a). However, few archaeobotanical remains have been recovered from the eastern Sahel 3000–500 BC, when sorghum's morphological changes presumably occurred (cf. Haaland 1999), and the oldest known fully domesticated varieties currently appear in Africa only from c. 500 BC (Fuller 2004b; Pelling 2005; Clapham and Rowley-Conwy 2007). For African rice, Murray's (2007) study of the large assemblage from Dia in Mali's Inland Niger Delta, which establishes that it was domesticated before AD 1, provides a baseline for future research.

For other seed crops, the only morphological traits that show change over time in archaeobotanical assemblages are the size and shape of the seeds themselves. Such changes have been important in the study of early cowpea (D'Andrea et al. 2007) and allow us to distinguish wild from domesticated finger millet (Giblin and Fuller 2011). For the Ethiopian domesticate t'ef, however, higher yield in the cultivar may have been achieved mainly through increasing numbers of seeds rather than seed size (D'Andrea 2008). In pearl millet, besides the chaff evidence for non-shattering reviewed above, samples from several sites provide metric data on grain size. Early assemblages of similar date show a subtle change in grain shape, which becomes apically thicker and more club-shaped. However, a major increase in seed size appears delayed (D'Andrea et al. 2001). Selection for larger grain size may have occurred in multiple discrete locations in Africa and also after the plant reached India. The presence of small-grained populations in later periods suggests that some factors may work against larger grains in pearl millet, such as selection for increasing grain numbers per plant (as with t'ef).

Many seed crops have also undergone further selection for enhancements and diversification. Sorghum, pearl millet, and finger millet, for example, have many domesticated landraces are free-threshing and have lost the persistent hulls that require labour for dehusking, which are typically present among the wild forms of these cereals. This free-threshing trait is typical of most modern domesticated finger millet and pearl millet. In sorghum, the widespread race bicolor requires dehusking (as does the *kafir* race grown in southern Africa), whereas more advanced cultivated races such as *durra*, *caudatum*, and *guinea* are free-threshing. The evolution of some free-threshing types had already taken place by 100 BC (Pelling 2005: 402).

DOMESTICATION IN TUBER CROPS

Plants with large, starchy underground storage organs—roots, tubers, corms, and rhizomes—are collectively referred to here as 'tuber crops' or 'tuber plants'. They are distinctive in that an individual plant offers a large package of starch that is easily digestible after minimal processing (e.g. roasting). Tuber crops may follow sequences of cultivation and morphological change that differ markedly from those of seed crops for several reasons (Hildebrand 2007a). First, the useful part of the plant is not the reproductive organ. Therefore, harvesting practices by humans are unlikely to pose strong, direct selective pressures on the next generation. Second, many tuber plants are perennials (a single plant dies back and regrows every year) rather than annuals (individual plants grow and die in a single season). Therefore, even if selective pressures exist, they operate slowly, even in populations seeing regular human use. Third, human cultivation practices may induce the useful part of the plant—the starchy organ—to exhibit *phenotypic* alteration without changes in its genotypic makeup: a wild yam with a thin, tough tuber penetrating deep into hard clay soil may, for example, after repeated harvests that disturb the surrounding soil and leave the perennial crown of the yam intact to regrow, develop a large, tender tuber that grows predominantly in soft soil near the surface.

For all these reasons, tuber crops can be cultivated for long periods and on a large scale (agriculture) without undergoing domestication. Tuber crops differ from seed crops in another important way: the parts of the plant most likely to be deposited in an archaeological site consist of soft tissue vulnerable to swift decay that may or may not exhibit morphological attributes relevant to either phenotypic or genotypic change. All these factors combine to present archaeobotanists with a difficult task: tuber crops are difficult to recover and lack a consistent 'domestication syndrome' that is easily identifiable in archaeobotanical remains.

CHANGES IN AFRICAN TUBER CROPS DUE TO
HUMAN MANIPULATION: ENSET AND YAMS

Despite these challenges, modern observations about plants' life cycle and environmental preferences can show how relations between two African taxa and humans intensified over time in Ethiopia (Hildebrand 2007a, 2009).

Enset (*Ensete ventricosum*) has a large corm that can feed an extended family for several days, plus additional starch and fibre in its pseudostem. It can be harvested at any time of year, but consuming the corm kills the plant. Its leaves provide shelter, wrapping, and construction material. It grows wild in moist uplands that typically have forest as a climax vegetation type, and thrives in disturbed areas. At the end of its life, enset develops a banana-like infructescence (Fig. 35.1); thousands of hard, heavy seeds roll downhill or are carried to distant locations in the digestive tracts of frugivores (Hildebrand 2003a).

During initial stages of cultivation, human dispersal and tending of seeds would have helped enset colonize new habitats, especially those disturbed naturally or through human action. This cultivation may have increased enset's density in upland and mid-altitude areas, perhaps even resulting in an agricultural landscape, but would not help it grow in hot, dry lowlands. The practice of cloning enset, by cutting the pith–corm interface to stimulate shoot production, probably developed later. Over time, cloned enset eventually lost the ability to produce viable seeds and is now considered a domesticate, one fully dependent on humans for propagation and morphologically distinct from its wild relative, with which it has no genetic exchange (Hildebrand 2003a).

Yam plants (*Dioscorea cayenensis* and related species) provide several kilogrammes of starch that is superior to enset corm in taste and texture. Yam tubers must be harvested in the dry season, but careful harvesting can preserve perennial parts of the plant for subsequent regrowth. Yams require less moisture than enset and grow wild in low- and mid-altitude areas. In low grasslands, their foliage twines up onto shrubs or bushes, while in wooded mid-altitudes they twine onto trees to gain access to sunlight. Yams tolerate cool, moist upland conditions, but only if natural or human disturbance breaks up the forest canopy; sunlight is key. Light, winged seeds allow dispersal via wind (Hildebrand 2009).

Through land clearance, humans may have unintentionally created or expanded upland and mid-altitude habitats favourable for natural dispersal of yams. Humans may also have intentionally transplanted yams from lowland settings into disturbed upland areas, contributing to the development of an agricultural landscape. However, human intervention would not have altered the survival, reproduction, or distribution of yams in lowland areas where they naturally thrive. Many yams now under cultivation in Southwest Ethiopia appear to be capable of independent survival and reproduction. Genetic exchange between garden and wild populations appears to be bidirectional, such that cultivated yams may not be fully 'domesticated'. Farmers today still transplant yams from wild environments into their gardens, inducing the phenotypic changes described above (Hildebrand 2003b).

These modern observations illustrate some important points about interactions between humans and tuber plants in Africa. First, the earliest stages of these crops' cultivation in Southwest Ethiopia took place in highland settings, because these are the environments where human interventions would have improved survival and reproduction. Second, biological differences among various tuber plants make them susceptible to different kinds of human manipulation, defeating attempts to generalize about processes of change (Hildebrand 2007a). Third, some tuber plants underwent multiple stages of cultivation before domestication (enset), while others may not be fully domesticated even today (yams); this reinforces the notion that agricultural landscapes may be achieved before full domestication occurs. While gleaned from African taxa, these points apply equally to other regions of tuber plant domestication, such as the Andes and Southeast Asia.

FRUITS, VEGETABLES, AND TREES

Grains, pulses, and tuber crops make up only a small proportion of the plants domesticated in Africa. Others include soft-stemmed fruits (such as melons, gourds), vegetable crops (like anchote), and some trees (e.g. oil palm, coffee, kola, tamarind, and baobab). Because each species has a distinctive anatomy, lifecycle, manner of propagation, and use, it is hard to generalize about morphological changes during the domestication process. Increased fruit size and palatability are recurrent changes, but are not always directly observable in archaeobotanical assemblages. More research is needed, both in comparing modern wild and domestic populations of these plants and in recovering archaeobotanical specimens, though early exploitation and woodland management for oil palm is becoming increasingly well documented (Sowunmi 1999; D'Andrea et al. 2006). Finds of cowpea after *c.* 1700 BC in Ghana (D'Andrea et al. 2007) and Bambara groundnut for the past 2,000 years in Burkina Faso and Cameroon (Kahlheber and Neumann 2007) likewise provide some indication of the history of domestication of some key African pulses.

NON-ALIMENTARY CROPS

Short-staple cotton (*Gossypium herbaceum*) was domesticated from an African wild species. Tree cotton (*G. arboreum*) was introduced from South Asia and became important in Africa. In the past 200 years a third cotton species native to Mesoamerica (*G. barbadense*) supplanted the first two (Wendel 1995). Cotton cultivation is evident from Meroitic Nubia (cf. Welsby, Ch. 51 below) from the last centuries BC, and by the early centuries AD in Libya and Ethiopia (Pelling 2005; Clapham and Rowley-Conway 2009). Cotton production became established in West Africa by the 8th century AD (Nixon et al. 2011: 234).

THE LESSONS OF AFRICA

Although African archaeobotanical data are still limited (Fig. 35.3; Table 35.1), recent results demonstrate the potential of focused sampling for filling geographical and chronological gaps. Current limitations are due to the relatively late incorporation of archaeobotany into

African archaeology, logistical challenges running flotation in remote areas with poor access to water or electricity, and in some cases preservation problems in low latitudes (Young and Thompson 1999). Holocene African archaeobotany is also an underpopulated research field.

The transition from hunting and gathering to farming was not a single event, but a complex, multi-stage phenomenon encompassing many discrete changes in human behaviour, plant morphology, and ecological structure. Archaeobotanical documentation, together with modern biological and ethnobotanical data, hints at the rich diversity of pathways to food production on the continent. The contexts, motives, and processes of domestication for semi-desert pearl millet, lowland forest oil palm, and highland enset must have varied tremendously. Thus, different regions of Africa, with their distinct environments, local resources, and cultures, witnessed different narratives in which people began managing certain plants closely and started processes of change that ultimately transformed subsistence economies, social structures, and landscapes. Filling in these different narratives, and comparing and explaining them, is now one of the most compelling challenges for African archaeobotany.

Amid this diversity of plants, environments, and pathways to food production, Africa's five centres of origin offer intriguing grounds for comparison with more than a dozen centres on other continents (Purugganan and Fuller 2009). In some regions of the world, such as southwestern Asia, permanent settlement and plant cultivation were the first steps away from hunting and gathering, followed by use of pottery and domestic animals (Fuller 2007). Elsewhere—New Guinea, tropical America, and parts of South Asia—the first food production consisted of shifting cultivation and mobile settlement and was not accompanied by pottery (Denham and Haberle 2008).

The African archaeological record shows points of similarity and contrast to prehistoric sequences of economic change on other continents. The Sahara, the Sahel, and the Nile Valley, like eastern Asia but unlike many other regions of the world, witnessed the use of ceramic technology before food production of any kind (cf. Barich, di Lernia, Haaland and Haaland, Chs 31, 36, 37 this volume). Northern portions of Africa are similar to highland South America and parts of Asia, in that animal husbandry was the first form of food production (cf. di Lernia, Ch. 36 below). In many parts of Africa, the mobility required for herding may have prevented humans from exercising steady selection necessary to induce morphological change in plant populations, such that plant domestication occurred later in Africa than in most of the world (Marshall and Hildebrand 2002).

As the African archaeobotanical record continues to grow, it will be possible to undertake more detailed comparisons with other parts of the globe. These comparisons will flesh out the alternative cultural experiences and human motivations for domestication episodes and subsistence changes in the past, and enrich our understanding of the landscapes, crop complexes, and cuisines that prevail in different parts of the world today.

REFERENCES

BLENCH, R. (2003). The movement of cultivated plants between Africa and India in prehistory. In K. Neumann, A. Butler, and S. Kahlheber (eds), *Food, Fuel and Fields: Progress in African Archaeobotany*. Cologne: Heinrich Barth Institut, 273–92.

—— (2006). *Archaeology, Language, and the African Past*. Lanham, Md.: AltaMira Press.

BOARDMAN, S. (1999). The agricultural foundation of the Aksumite empire, Ethiopia. In M. Van Der Veen (ed.), *The Exploitation of Plant Resources in Ancient Africa*. New York: Kluwer, 137–48.

BOIVIN, N. L., and FULLER, D. Q. (2009). Shell middens, ships and seeds: exploring coastal subsistence, maritime trade and the dispersal of domesticates in and around the ancient Arabian Peninsula. *Journal of World Prehistory* 22: 113–80.

BRANDT, S. A. (1984). New perspectives on the origins of food production in Ethiopia. In J. D. Clark and S. A. Brandt (eds), *From Hunters to Farmers: The Causes and Consequences of Food Production in Africa*. Berkeley: University of California Press, 173–90.

CARNEY, J. A. (2001). *Black Rice: The African Origins of Rice Cultivation in the Americas*. Cambridge, Mass.: Harvard University Press.

—— and ROSOMOFF, R. N. (2009). *In the Shadow of Slavery: Africa's Botanical Legacy in the Atlantic World*. Berkeley: University of California Press.

CLAPHAM, A., and ROWLEY-CONWY, P. (2007). New discoveries at Qasr Ibrim, Lower Nubia. In R. Cappers (ed.), *Fields of Change: Progress in African Archaeobotany*. Groningen: Barkhuis, 157–64.

—— —— (2009). The archaeobotany of cotton (*Gossypium* sp. L.) in Egypt and Nubia with special reference to Qasr Ibrim, Egyptian Nubia. In A. Fairbairn and E. Weiss (eds), *From Foragers to Farmers: Papers in Honour of Gordon C. Hillman*. Oxford: Oxbow Books, 244–53.

D'ANDREA, A. C. (2008). T'ef (*Eragrostis tef*) in ancient agricultural systems of highland Ethiopia. *Economic Botany* 62: 547–66.

—— KAHLHEBER, S., LOGAN, A. L., and WATSON, D. J. (2007). Early domesticated cowpea (*Vigna unguiculata*) from central Ghana. *Antiquity* 81: 686–98.

—— KLEE, M., and CASEY, J. (2001). Archaeobotanical evidence for pearl millet (*Pennisetum glaucum*) in sub-Saharan West Africa. *Antiquity* 75: 341–8.

—— LOGAN, A. L., and WATSON, D. J. (2006). Oil palm and prehistoric subsistence in tropical Africa. *Journal of African Archaeology* 4: 195–222.

—— SCHMIDT, P. R., and CURTIS, M. C., (2008). Paleoethnobotanical analysis and agricultural economy in early first millennium bce sites around Asmara. In P. R. Schmidt, M. C. Curtis, and Z. Teka (eds), *The Archaeology of Ancient Eritrea*. Asmara: Red Sea Press, 207–16.

DENHAM, T., and HABERLE, S. (2008). Agricultural emergence and transformation in the upper Wahgi Valley during the Holocene: theory, method and practice. *The Holocene* 18: 481–96.

ENGLER, A. (1936). *Syllabus der Pflanzenfamilien*. Berlin: Borntraeger.

FULLER, D. Q. (2003). African crops in prehistoric South Asia: a critical review. In K. Neumann, A. Butler, and S. Kahlheber (eds), *Food, Fuel and Fields: Progress in African Archaeobotany*. Cologne: Heinrich Barth Institut, 239–71.

—— (2004a). The central Amri to Kirbekan survey: a preliminary report on excavations and survey 2003–04. *Sudan and Nubia* 8: 4–16.

—— (2004b). Early Kushite agriculture: archaeobotanical evidence from Kawa. *Sudan and Nubia* 8: 70–4.

—— (2007). Contrasting patterns in crop domestication and domestication rates: recent archaeobotanical insights from the Old World. *Annals of Botany* 100: 903–24.

—— and ALLABY, R. (2009). Seed dispersal and crop domestication: shattering, germination and seasonality in evolution under cultivation. In L. Ostergaard (ed.), *Fruit Development and Seed Dispersal*. Oxford: Wiley-Blackwell, 238–95.

—— and BOIVIN, N. (2009). Crops, cattle and commensals across the Indian Ocean: current and potential archaeobiological evidence. *Études Océan Indien* 42/43: 13–46.

FULLER, D. Q., BOIVIN, N., HOOGERVORST, T., and ALLABY, R. (2011). Across the Indian Ocean: the prehistoric movement of plants and animals. *Antiquity* 85: 544–58.

—— QIN, L., ZHENG, Y., et al. (2009). The domestication process and domestication rate in rice: spikelet bases from the Lower Yangtze. *Science* 323: 1607–10.

GIBLIN, J., and FULLER, D. Q. (2011). First and second millennium AD agriculture in Rwanda: archaeobotanical finds and radiocarbon dates from seven sites. *Vegetation History and Archaeobotany* 20: 253–65.

HAALAND, R. (1999). The puzzle of the late emergence of domesticated sorghum in the Nile Valley. In C. Gosden and J. Hather (eds), *The Prehistory of Food*. London: Routledge, 397–418.

HARLAN, J. R. (1992). Indigenous African agriculture. In C. W. Cowan and P. J. Watson (eds), *The Origins of Agriculture*. Washington, DC: Smithsonian Institution Press, 59–70.

—— and DE WET, J. M. J. (1973). On the quality of evidence for origin and dispersal of cultivated plants. *Current Anthropology* 14: 51–5.

HARRIS, D. R. (2007). Agriculture, cultivation and domestication: exploring the conceptual framework of early food production. In T. Denham, L. Vrydaghs, and J. Iriarte (eds), *Rethinking Agriculture: Archaeological and Ethnoarchaeological Perspectives*. Walnut Creek, Calif.: Left Coast Press, 16–35

HATHER, J. (2000). *Archaeological Parenchyma*. London: Archetype.

HILDEBRAND, E. A. (2003a). Comparison of domestic vs. forest-growing *Ensete ventricosum* (Welw.) Cheesman, Musaceae in Ethiopia: implications for detecting enset archaeologically, and modeling its domestication. In K. Neumann, A. Butler, and S. Kahlheber (eds), *Food, Fuel and Fields: Progress in African Archaeobotany*. Cologne: Heinrich Barth Institut, 49–70.

—— (2003b). Motives and opportunities for domestication: an ethnoarchaeological study in southwest Ethiopia. *Journal of Anthropological Archaeology* 22: 358–75.

—— (2007a). A tale of two tuber crops: how attributes of enset and yams may have shaped prehistoric human-plant interactions in southwest Ethiopia. In T. Denham, L. Vrydaghs, and J. Iriarte (eds), *Rethinking Agriculture: Archaeological and Ethnoarchaeological Perspectives*. Walnut Creek, Calif.: Left Coast Press, 273–98.

—— (2007b). The significance of Sai Island for early plant food production in Sudan. *CRIPEL* 26: 173–81.

—— (2009). The utility of ethnobiology in agricultural origins research: examples from southwest Ethiopia. *Current Anthropology* 50: 693–7.

KAHLHEBER, S., and NEUMANN, K. (2007). The development of plant cultivation in semi-arid West Africa. In R. Cappers (ed.), *Fields of Change: Progress in African Archaeobotany*. Groningen: Barkhuis, 320–46.

MANNING, K., PELLING, R., HIGHAM, T., SCHWENNINGER, J. L., and FULLER, D. Q., (2011). 4500-year old domesticated pearl millet (*Pennisetum glaucum*) from the Tilemsi Valley, Mali: new insights into an alternative cereal domestication pathway. *Journal of Archaeological Science* 38: 312–22.

MARSHALL, F., and HILDEBRAND, E. A. (2002). Cattle before crops: the beginnings of food production in Africa. *Journal of World Prehistory* 16: 99–143.

MBIDA, C., DE LANGHE, E., VRYDAGHS, L., et al. (2006). Phytolith evidence for the early presence of domesticated banana (*Musa*) in Africa. In M. Zeder, D. Bailer, E. Emshwiller, and B. D. Smith (eds), *Documenting Domestication: New Genetic and Archaeological Paradigms*. Berkeley: University of California Press, 68–81.

MITCHELL, P. J. (2005). *African Connections: Archaeological Perspectives on Africa and the Wider World*. Walnut Creek, Calif.: AltaMira Press.

MURRAY, S. (2007). Identifying African rice domestication in the middle Niger Delta (Mali). In R. Cappers (ed.), *Fields of Change: Progress in African Archaeobotany*. Groningen: Barkhuis, 53–62.

NEUMANN, K., and HILDEBRAND, E. A. (2009). Early bananas in Africa: the state of the art. *Ethnobotany Research and Applications* 7: 353–62.

NIXON, S., MURRAY, M. A., and FULLER, D. Q. (2011). Plant use at an early Islamic merchant town in the West African Sahel: the archaeobotany of Essouk-Tadmakka (Mali). *Vegetation History and Archaeobotany* 20(3): 223–39.

PELLING, R. (2005). Garamantean agriculture and its significance in a wider North Africa context: the evidence of plant remains from the Fazzan Project. *Journal of North African Studies* 10: 397–411.

PURUGGANAN, M. D., and FULLER, D. Q. (2009). The nature of selection during plant domestication. *Nature* 457: 843–8.

ROSSEL, G. (1998). *Taxonomic-Linguistic Study of Plantain in Africa*. Leiden: CNWS.

ROWLEY-CONWY, P. (1991). The sorghum from Qasr Ibrim, Egyptian Nubia, *c*.800 BC–AD 1811. In J. Renfrew (ed.), *New Light on Early Farming*. Edinburgh: University of Edinburgh Press, 191–212.

SMITH, B. D. (2001). Low-level food production. *Journal of Archaeological Research* 9:1–43.

SNOWDEN, J. D. (1936). *The Cultivated Races of Sorghum*. London: Adlard & Son.

SOWUNMI, M. A. (1999). The significance of the oil palm (*Elaeis guineensis* Jacq.) in the late Holocene environments of west and west central Africa: a further consideration. *Vegetation History and Archaeobotany* 8: 199–210.

TORRENCE, R., and BARTON, H. (eds) (2006). *Ancient Starch Research*. Walnut Creek, Calif.: Left Coast Press.

WALSHAW, S. C. (2010). Converting to rice: urbanization, Islamization and crops on Pemba, AD 700–1500. *World Archaeology* 42: 137–54.

WASYLIKOWA, K., and VAN DER VEEN, M. (2004). An archaeobotanical contribution to the history of the watermelon. *Vegetation History and Archaeobotany* 14: 213–17

—— SCHILD, R., WENDORF, F., KROLIK, H., KUBIAKMARTENS, L., and HARLAN, J. R. (1995). Archaeobotany of the early Neolithic site E-75-6 at Nabta Playa, Western Desert, South Egypt (preliminary results). *Acta Palaeobotanica* 35: 133–55.

WENDEL, J. (1995) Cotton. In J. Smatt and N. W. Simmonds (eds), *Evolution of Crop Plants*, 2nd edn. London: Longman, 358–66.

WETTERSTROM, W. (1993). Foraging and farming in Egypt. In T. Shaw, P. J. J. Sinclair, B. Andah, and A. Okpoko (eds), *The Archaeology of Africa: Food, Metals and Towns*. London: Routledge, 165–226.

WILLCOX, G., (2012). Searching for the origins of arable weeds in the Near East. *Vegetation History and Archaeobotany* 21: 163–7.

YOUNG R., and THOMPSON, R. (1999). Missing plant foods? Where is the archaeobotanical evidence for sorghum and finger millet in East Africa? In M. Van Der Veen (ed.), *The Exploitation of Plant Resources in Ancient Africa*. New York: Kluwer, 63–72.

ZEDER, M. A., BRADLEY, D. G., EMSHWILLER, E., and SMITH, B. D. (2006). *Documenting Domestication: New Genetic and Archaeological Paradigms*. Berkeley: University of California Press.

ZOHARY, D., and HOPF, M. (2000). *Domestication of Plants in the Old World*. Oxford: Oxford University Press.

CHAPTER 36

THE EMERGENCE AND SPREAD OF HERDING IN NORTHERN AFRICA

A Critical Reappraisal

SAVINO DI LERNIA

INTRODUCTION

THE causes, origin, and diffusion of pastoralism in Africa have been fervently discussed over the last decades (Clark and Brandt 1984; Blench and MacDonald 2000; Smith 2005). We can assume that there are several reasons for this: (i) an obsession with seeking the earliest thing—whatever this is; (ii) the relevance of pastoralist societies in contemporary Africa; (iii) the quest for an African 'supremacy' or 'primacy', when compared to other geographical areas; (iv) the relations between herding activities and agriculture; (v) the spread of herding-related realities of immense importance to the subsequent history of African societies. Whatever the reason(s), recent syntheses and comments on the origins and spread of animal herding in Africa have clearly revitalized the debate (Gifford-Gonzalez 2000, 2005; Marshall and Hildebrand 2002; Hassan 2002; Mitchell 2005).

Most theoretical models and explanatory inferences remain based, however, on weak foundations. Throughout this chapter, I thus try to assess critically the analytical basis of recent papers. Some themes are constant: the relations between climate change(s) and the origins and spread of herding activities; the role of intensification in resource exploitation; the relevance of ideological aspects, particularly rock art and ritual monuments; the potential of ethnographic analogy. J. Desmond Clark (1967: 15) identified and discussed these issues almost fifty years ago, but when we combine the repeated emphasis on these matters and the objective weakness of the analytical basis of most studies dealing with African pastoralism, we realize that only with a new period of archaeological research can the scenario change.

DEFINITIONS AND ARCHAEOLOGICAL PROBLEMS

No general consensus exists on how to define pastoralism in Africa (or elsewhere), and this issue alone deserves a specific work. Gifford-Gonzalez (2005: 188) recently defined pastoral groups as those 'who depend primarily on the products of their hoofed domestic animals, and who organize their settlement and mobility strategies to suit the dietary needs of their livestock'. Adopting Dyson-Hudson and Dyson-Hudson's (1980) definition, Marshall and Hildebrand (2002: 114) classify pastoralists 'as people who rely heavily on production from domestic herds, and move herds to pasture'. Andrew Smith's (2005) ecological view appears to include aspects other than the economic, such as ideological values and landscape perception. Mobility and relations with cultivation and/or agriculture are also systematically pinpointed (following Khazanov 1984; Holl 1998), even though the complex mechanisms of reciprocal relations between sedentary people and nomads are difficult to decode and hard to identify archaeologically. The problem of pastoral visibility adds further difficulties (di Lernia 2002; Smith 2005) and faunal preservation often represents a dramatic obstacle, especially in surface or slightly buried deposits (as in much of the Sahara).

Research strategies and archaeological explanations depend on theoretical definition(s), and for North African contexts, an approach excessively skewed towards economic aspects would probably be too simplistic. I believe that Ingold's (1980) approach is still the most flexible, for it encompasses not only aspects of economic production but also the various possible degrees of animal management, with an important emphasis on their ideological facets.

EARLIEST DOMESTIC CATTLE: AN AFRICAN(IST) TALE

Despite the many works on the subject, the most recent 'hard' analytical data on earliest cattle domestication in Africa date back, ultimately, to the late 1970s and early 1980s, when Wendorf and associates collected a few, poorly preserved bones of large bovid(s) at Nabta Playa and Bir Kiseiba (Gautier 2001) in the Egyptian Sahara (cf. Gifford-Gonzalez and Hanotte, Ch. 34 above). No other site since has provided fresh, direct evidence of such ancient cattle exploitation, at least in terms of faunal remains (Fig. 36.1). Indeed, the discovery of these bones from Egypt's Western Desert animated one of the hottest, never-ending debates in African archaeology. The first publications (Gautier 1980; Wendorf and Schild 1980) referred to the presence of 'putative' domestic cattle at Nabta dated to around 8800 BP (8840 ± 90 BP; SMU-416), findings later followed by indications of an even earlier record from Site E-79-8 at Bir Kiseiba—a few surface remains dated to c. 9500 BP: not only the earliest African evidence, but the earliest in the world.

Two lines of argument were developed, osteological and ecological (Close and Wendorf 1992; Wendorf and Schild 1994). As far as the former goes, the bones found in the Egyptian oases could belong to Cape buffalo, giant buffalo, or wild or domestic cattle. If we exclude the

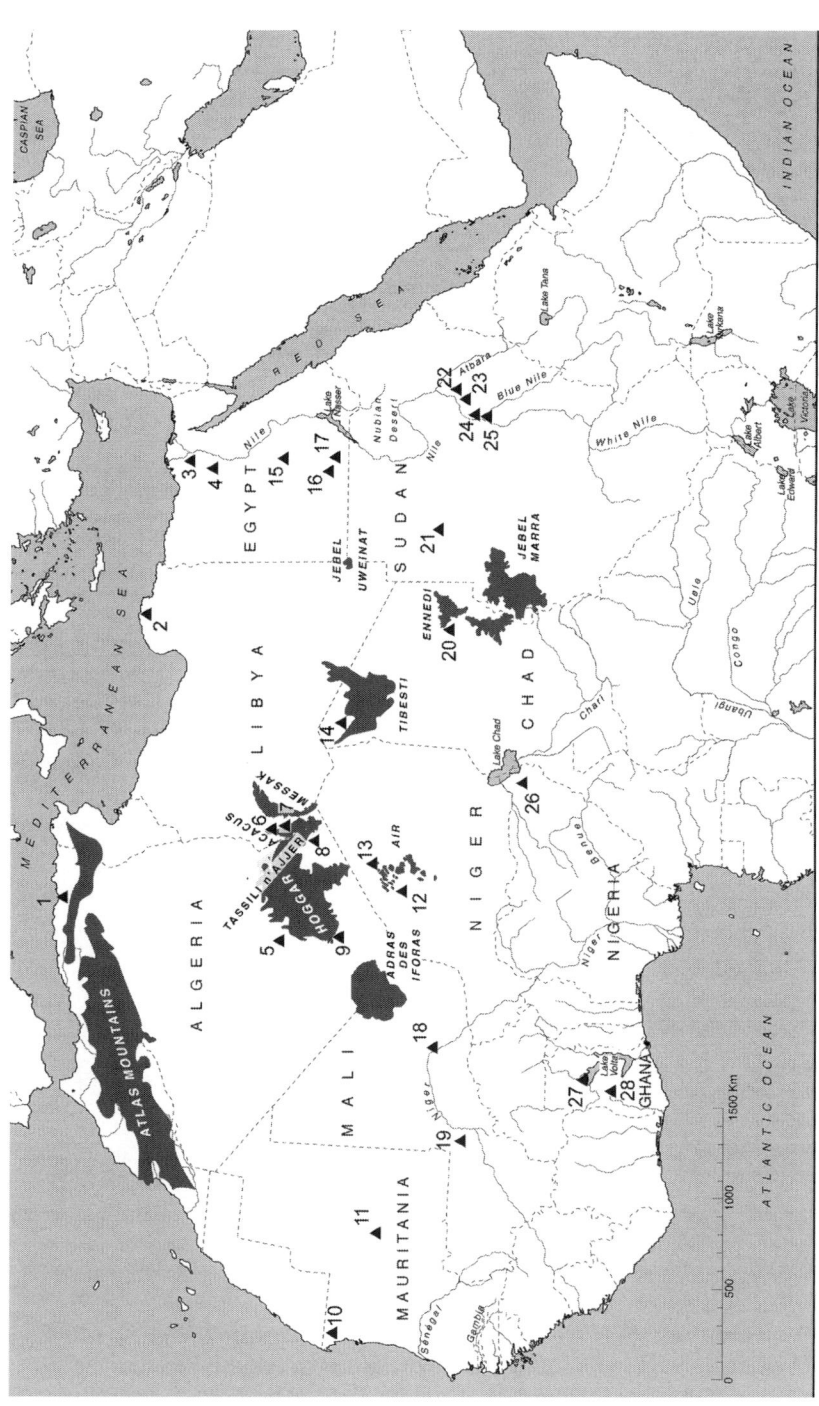

FIG. 36.1 North Africa with location of the sites with the earliest domesticates (modified after Gifford-Gonzalez 2005). All dates are BP. 1 Grotte Capeletti 6530 ± 250; 2 Haua Fteah 7000–6400; 3 Merimde Benisalame 5830 ± 60; 4 Fayum 5860 ± 115; 5 Meniet 5400 ± 150; 6 Ti-n-Torha 7440 ± 220; 7 Uan Muhuggiag 7438 ± 220; 8 Ti-n-Hanakaten mid-8th–6th millennia; 9 Adrar Tiyouine 5420 ± 130; 10 Chami 4200; 11 Dhar Tichitt 3850 ± 250; 12 Arlit 5200 ± 140; 13 Adrar Bous 6325 ± 300; 14 Enneri Bardagué 7455 ± 180; 15 Kharga E-76-7 7890 ± 65; 16 Bir Kiseiba E-79-8 9840 ± 380; 17 Nabta E-75-3 8840 ± 90; 18 Karkarichinkat 4010 ± 160; 19 Kobadi 3335 ± 100; 20 Délébo 7180 ± 300; 21 Wadi Howar 5200; 22 El Kadada 5710 ± 110; 23 Shaheinab 6500; 24 Kadero 5630 ± 70; 25 Um Direwa 6010 ± 90; 26 Gajiganna 3100; 27 Ntereso 3600; 28 Kintampo 6 3600.

first for morphological reasons and the second for metrical ones, the only possible species left is *Bos primigenius*, but definition of its status—wild or domestic—was founded on eco-logical grounds, as the other animals (gazelle, hares, jackals, tortoises) found at Nabta and Kiseiba are typical of a very harsh environment with only 100–200mm of rain per year. In these conditions, Wendorf and colleagues argue that wild cattle could not survive without human intervention, including assistance with the provision of water, i.e. they could not sur-vive without being domesticated.

From the very beginning, criticism was directed at both arguments. Metrical data for the Nabta and Kiseiba bones reinforced the idea of larger, wild animals (Grigson 2000: 48), while the ecological line of explanation was also vehemently disputed, with Smith (1986) claiming that the environment described by Wendorf and colleagues does not exist in nature. The rug-ged landscape surrounding the playas should have been able to sustain other medium- to large-sized animals, such as hartebeest, addax, and consequently wild cattle: the archaeo-zoological assemblages from Nabta and Bir Kiseiba represent a cultural selection, not an ecological one.

The dispute around the status of these cattle bones accelerated with genetic research carried out on modern breeds (Bradley et al. 1996). The distance between African cattle and Asian *Bos taurus* indicates discrete genetic populations, separated around 22,000 years ago, suggesting separate domestication processes and an African origin in the east-ern Sahara (Hanotte et al. 2002). Although the genetic influence of other centres of cattle domestication in modern breeds was underlined (Hanotte et al. 2002: 339), along with the possibility that the geographical relationships and timing of domestication could easily overlap (cf. Beja-Pereira et al. 2006 for Europe), proponents of African origins for African cattle applauded this genetic evidence as an additional proof. Interestingly, other genetic studies on similar issues leading to different results did not receive the same attention (Caramelli 2006).

For a few scholars, the idea of a local, autonomous centre of cattle domestication in north-east Africa was therefore accepted, with subsequent efforts focused on addressing *why* and *how* this happened (in particular, Marshall and Hildebrand 2002) and *why* and *when* early cattle from the Sahara spread to the rest of the continent (in particular, Hassan 2000, 2002; Reimer 2007).

A FEW CONCEPTS: INTENSIFICATION, SEDENTISM, AND DELAYED-RETURN SYSTEMS

Who might these first 'cattle herders' have been? Under what conditions and in what kind of context did domestication occur? Recent work has combined ideas of resource intensi-fication with its temporal organization. Following Woodburn's (1982) theoretical division between immediate and delayed-return systems, Cremaschi et al. (1996), Hassan (2000), di Lernia (2001), and Marshall and Hildebrand (2002) all hypothesized a similar pattern for the Sahara, though expressing differences in their hypothetical evolutionary trajectories. Marshall and Hildebrand (2002) emphasized, in particular, that the need to cope with erratic variations in rainfall (and thus resources) led Saharan hunter-gatherers to increase the predictability of their food security, specifically through cattle, ultimately leading to their domestication.

From a different perspective, the hard evidence of foragers corralling Barbary sheep (*Ammotragus lervia*) between 8500 and 7500 BP at some Libyan sites (di Lernia 2001) led to the suspicion that controlled exploitation of plants and animals should be considered a social response to increasing aridity, one needed in order to maintain a semi-sedentary way of life that repeatedly used the same locations over more than one season, as stable isotope analyses indicate (Tafuri et al. 2006). However, the difficulty of associating the socioeconomic status of these human groups with a delayed-return system of resource exploitation (or these first 'cattle herders') is evident from contrasting the various attempts to define them as 'would-be pastoralists', 'cattle-assisted gatherer-hunters', and 'part-time cattle pastoralists' (Wendorf et al. 2001).

If we look at these contexts without focusing exclusively on cattle domestication, it is clear that many Early Holocene Saharan groups are characterized by small band size, increasing sedentism, and an emphasis on a broad spectrum of resources (MacDonald 2000; di Lernia 2001; Marshall and Hildebrand 2002; Garcea 2004; Reimer 2007). Within this scenario, great variation exists, depending on several factors: local environment, resource availability, social network, group organization, etc. Because their material culture is often restricted and badly preserved, and only occasionally is more than one segment of the archaeological record present at the same site(s), not all groups practised, or are archaeologically visible as practising, delayed-return systems. Nonetheless, recent approaches have shown a propensity to extend a delayed-return system to contexts where hard evidence is lacking or partial. Pottery and intensified use of wild cereals provide evidence in this regard, but do not occur in the same place and at the very same moment. Surface materials have regrettably been associated with other (surface) evidence, creating a picture for which the analytical base is probably weaker than most admit. Ceramic containers, for example, occurred in southern Saharan contexts first, and only later in central and eastern areas (Close 1995: 23).

A review of the published data therefore conveys a murkier picture: not all sites have pottery, nor firm evidence of the delayed use of mammals, nor indications of increasing sedentism, at least not at the very same time. Furthermore, in all the sites considered, the exploitation of wild cattle shows evidence of neither intensive hunting nor taming: all attempts to demonstrate these developments have failed (Barich 1974). Archaeozoological data nevertheless point to a much narrower timing for the presence of cattle bones in firmly dated faunal assemblages (Smith 2005).

We must thus admit that what all Saharan 'complex' hunter-gatherers share is a strong emphasis on wild cereal exploitation, rather than a similar emphasis on animal use—a scenario that has not received the attention it deserves. In this sense, the intensive collection of wild cereals in most (if not all) early Holocene sites should be addressed as the *true* cultural response to the need for maintaining predictable food security. The taming and/or control of wild animals probably had instead a major role in the ideological world, as possibly indicated at the Qadan site of Tushka, where burials with the skulls of wild cattle suggest that they were assigned an important symbolic significance since the end of the Pleistocene, between 14,500 and 12,500 BP (Wendorf 1968).

After cattle, or together? The theoretical implications of introduction of sheep and goat

The debate on cattle domestication has seriously diverted attention away from other animals, some domesticated in Africa (e.g. donkeys and guinea fowl), others imported (sheep and goats) (Gifford-Gonzalez and Hanotte, Ch. 34 above). This has, in turn, hampered a full understanding of the domestication process, while the very large analytical scale has led to the neglect of a micro-evolutionary appreciation of local differences and adaptations (Hassan 2002). In other words, rather than focusing on specific situations, much of the debate on the introduction of sheep and goats has related to the processes surrounding cattle domestication. Scarce attention and a great deal of tortuous reasoning (e.g. MacDonald 2000: 9) have been advanced to explain other intriguing questions, such as the lack of 'Near Eastern' grains in any North African site at the very same time as the introduction of sheep and goats. Moreover, to maintain an early date for cattle domestication (*c.* 9000 BP) forces us to accept a later introduction of sheep/goats, i.e. two distinct, autonomous processes for adopting means of food security based on animal herding, even though these animals—when separated—convey different forms of herding activities, mobility strategies, and settlement pattern. This needs emphasizing, as the scale of investigation and the bone sample size of the earliest contexts ($\geq$7000 BP) seriously limit(ed) in-depth appreciation of ancient pastoral organization.

Sheep and goats: when and how did they enter Africa?

Probably because there is no competition in this case for an African supremacy—sheep and goats have no wild progenitors in Africa—general 'agreement' exists on their provenance (southwest Asia). Differences are instead evident regarding the timing and the route they followed, either with their herders or via exchange. The time-frame considered is quite wide, roughly 7800–7000 BP, and is again bracketed by a few sites with old dates scattered over an immense area: the earliest dates vary from a possible early introduction at 7800 BP during the El Jerar occupation at Nabta Playa (Smith 2005) or, more prudently, in the Middle Neolithic, *c.* 7200 BP (Gautier 2001); more to the east, in the Red Sea Hills, sheep/goats are attested at Sodmein Cave, near Qusseir, *c.* 7100–7000 BP (Vermeersch et al. 1996); in the Western Desert again, *c.* 7000–6900 BP in the Dakhla (McDonald 1998) and Farafra oases (Barich 2002); *c.* 7000/6500 BP at Haua Fteah, Cyrenaica, on the Mediterranean coast (Klein and Scott 1986); around 6500 BP at Grotte Capelletti in northern Algeria's Aurès Mountains (the earliest occupation is dated around 6500 BP: Roubet 1979). The earliest date (7438 ± 220 BP; Mori 1965) for Uan Muhuggiag in the Acacus Mountains is one of the few definitely discarded dates, probably because subsequent excavations failed to find levels older than 6000 years BP (Barich 2002): further soundings, however, demonstrated that basal levels at Una Muhuggiag are actually dated around the end of the eighth millennium BP and slightly later (7200 ± 210 BP, 6900 ± 220

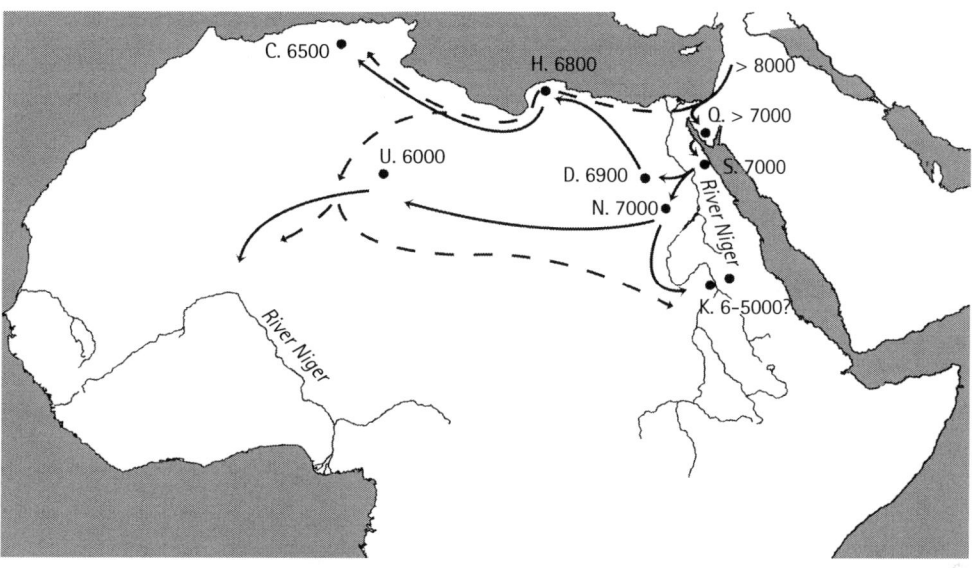

FIG. 36.2 Suggested models for the spread of small livestock in Africa. Key: dotted lines (after Smith 1984: fig. 2); black lines with sites (after Close 2002: fig. 9). C: Grotte Capeletti; D: Dakhla; H: Haua Fteah; K: Kadada and other central Nile sites; N: Nabta; Q: El Qaa; S: Sodmein; U; Uan Muhuggiag, Uan Telocat.

BP and 6690 ± 130 BP; Cremaschi and di Lernia 1998: 313). A parsimonious picture might therefore be that of a diffuse presence of pastoral groups with domestic sheep/goats over a very large area of North Africa clustering around 7200–7000 BP.

There is no unanimous consensus on the path followed by sheep and goats, whether across northern Sinai and the Nile Delta (Smith 1984) or via southern Sinai across the Gulf of Suez (Close 2002). It remains difficult to draw maps—with directions and hypothetical timing—from just a few, badly preserved archaeological sites, and in this sense the two hypotheses have equally fragile datasets (Fig. 36.2). However, given that most of the sites just discussed were excavated decades ago and that excavation size, the number and preservation quality of faunal remains, and their association with radiocarbon dates are all problematic, it would be no surprise if the picture changed rapidly.

Revising data on earliest African domesticates: Occam's razor and the need for fresh information

Information is thus scarce, patchy, and often controversial, and even when this dearth of data is recognized (Gautier 1987), the tendency to underestimate it remains. Hassan (2002: 13) was certainly right to assert that 'the dating of the earliest cattle in Africa depends in some cases on a single age determination ... [but by] eliminating, for the moment, occurrences with a single age determination, and averaging the two or three oldest consistent age measurements, the picture of the dispersal of cattle in Africa becomes much clearer.' It is therefore unexpected that his map shows the nuclear area as being in the region of Nabta and Kiseiba, which, as we have seen, does not exactly fit the very requirements he himself indicates.

Moreover, disputes over the age of the earliest African domesticates should also be placed within a wider context, including northeast Africa's relations with southwest Asia (Krzyzaniak et al. 1996; MacDonald 2000; Garcea 2004; Smith 2005). The nature of the relationships between climate change, resource availability, sedentism, and chronology of introduction of large and small livestock are still poorly understood, and critical areas like the Levant, the Sinai and the western regions of the Arabian Peninsula may well add essential information (Edens and Wilkinson 1998; Kuijt and Goring-Morris 2002).

Given the data available so far, what is therefore striking is the poverty of *recent* field research primarily devoted to the analysis of animal domestication, or perhaps the difficulty of finding new evidence. The emphasis on Nabta and Bir Kiseiba, often based on circular arguments and founded on ephemeral (when not contradictory) elements, is probably best seen in the context of a specific epoch of African archaeology's research history, the late 1970s, when great attention was paid to tracing local pathways within generalized evolutionary models. As noticed by Holl (2005: 182), sometime in African archaeology 'the over-reaction against the excesses of diffusionist theories resulted in an anti-migrations twist'. It is no accident that claims of local domestication were advanced roughly at the same period, especially in the central Sahara (Uan Muhuggiag: Mori 1965), but also in Europe (e.g. Ducos 1976).

The genetic evidence, just like the ecological arguments, has often been misused, often feeding circular reasoning. Furthermore, recent data on the analysis of lineage T1, the most frequent gene marker in modern North African taurine cattle, seem to suggest that this and other T groups were domesticated in the Near East, and then spread to North Africa (Achilli et al. 2008). Early Holocene cattle culling strategies also appear to be dominated by animals of large size, probably male, a pattern that maximizes meat returns and is more typical of hunters than herders (Zeder 2008).

Combining the rejection of the (so far) fragile evidence from the Egyptian oases with: (i) the quasi-contemporaneity of firm radiocarbon dates for (metrically and morphologically) domesticated cattle with the earliest small livestock; (ii) the consistency of radiocarbon dates, with different sites spread across North Africa clustering in the second half of the eighth millennium BP, including the *Steinplatze*—concentration of pebbles and stones with traces of fire activity—which increase significantly after 7500 BP (Gabriel 1987); and (iii) the presence of rock art focusing on cattle and indicating a mature animal management strategy, an introduction of domesticated cattle from outside Africa appears the most parsimonious one. A cut-off date (MacDonald 2000) for *full* adoption of the pastoral economy can then be reasonably placed at around 7500–7000 BP, with subsequent dispersal easily accommodated within the few centuries envisaged by Hassan (2002). Even so, negotiation, successes, and failures will all have been required, as indeed is indicated by the patchy evidence of coexisting groups of hunter-gatherers and first herders across the Sahara until the middle Holocene (Barham and Mitchell 2008: 361).

Reasons for the movement of such herders into northeast Africa have, it must be admitted, yet to be found, but the relation with the abrupt dry spell globally recorded at 8.2 kya (c. 7500–7300 BP) may be significant (Barham and Mitchell 2008: 358). Short but particularly strong in its impact, such major climate deterioration could have triggered rapid, intermittent, and multidirectional movements of shepherds in and between southwest

Asia and northeast Africa. Mobility is, of course, a key strategy for pastoral groups seeking to cope with resource uncertainties and increasing risk perception (Hassan 2002; di Lernia 2006).

THE SPREAD OF AFRICAN HERDERS

General agreement exists that varying climatic regimes were influential in driving the movements of early herders from east to west across the Sahara. Hassan (2002) has defined the timing, duration, and speed of these movements, which are widely and definitively attested over much of North Africa by 6000 BP, matching them against a high-resolution definition of the Holocene arid spells (Kuper and Kröpelin 2006; Kröpelin et al. 2008). Many archaeological elements—pottery decoration, rock art, funerary practices—seem to have quite similar features over enormous areas within a narrow time-span; and even allowing for important differences, this 'homogeneity' has often been placed under a single cultural rubric (e.g. Sutton 1974).

One of the recent and best-tracked phenomena that involves rapid 'leap-frog' movements is the so-called 'cattle cult' (Paris 2000; Applegate et al. 2001; Hassan 2002; di Lernia 2006; Tauveron et al. 2009; di Lernia et al. 2013). Pits or stone monuments containing articulated or disarticulated bones of mostly domestic cattle are one of the few solid proofs of the rapid circulation of ideas, rituals, and possibly people within African pastoral groups. Such behaviour, first attested at Nabta c. 6400 BP (Applegate et al. 2001) and then in the central Sahara (Niger and Libya) by the end of the same millennium, has been related to increasingly arid conditions and interpreted as a social response to a severe environmental deterioration (di Lernia 2006).

The dispersal of pastoral groups from the Sahara southward and westward has been illuminated by several research projects: many elements—including rock art (Muzzolini 1995), funerary practices (Smith 2001), pottery decoration (Garcea 1993), settlement systems (di Lernia 2002), and the statistical analysis of radiocarbon dates (Vernet 2002)—indicate movement(s) of people with cattle and caprines around 5000 BP. This major human dispersal, which probably did not take the form of a true migration wave, displays different timings and intermittent movements. Furthermore, the first appearance of cattle-based economies south of the Sahara was seriously delayed when compared to the appearance there of small stock—a 'lag' due to severe animal diseases typical of more southerly regions such as trypanosomiasis, which is fatal to cattle. For pastoralists, these new unfamiliar environments were a major challenge, if not true barriers, hampering 'smooth' movement east and south (Gifford-Gonzalez 2000).

However, this generally accepted scenario should probably also be revisited with different theoretical bases and new field data. The movement(s) did not empty the 'original homeland' areas: the central Sahara, for example, testifies to an intense and rich cultural life during the same period, as indicated by settlements, funerary monuments, and rock art (Holl 2004). Furthermore, local processes of cultural complexity eventually led to the rise of chiefdom forms of political organization and, eventually, to the Garamantian state (Leone and Moussa, Ch. 53 below). Understanding the reasons for such 'movements' from the central ranges of the Sahara, while usually linked to climate degradation, thus calls for further explanation and new research.

Perspectives and objectives: a future
for the study of African pastoralism

Reviewing the literature on the emergence and dispersal of pastoralists in Africa highlights the patchy and uneven distribution of proxy data, often derived from excavations or survey undertaken (many) decades ago. The imbalance between the Nile Valley and the (central and eastern) Sahara on one side and the rest of North Africa on the other is striking. We still rely on data that have less than satisfactory radiocarbon determinations and stratigraphic associations. Furthermore, much of the debate has been absorbed by discussions of the wild vs domesticated status of cattle bones from the eastern Sahara, leaving little space for other issues, much less a different theoretical approach. If, in principle, one could accept the idea of working with scarce data, the 'animal bone' focus has nevertheless come close to verging on obsession.

As an example, molecular genetic data from modern human populations have barely been considered as a way of tracking possible relations with past dynamics (MacEachern 2000; Smith 2005). Genetics would seem to be useful, however, for testing different hypotheses on the type of diffusion (demic vs cultural) associated with the spread of livestock (cf. Myles et al. 2005). Similarly, scarce attention has been directed to the analysis of the social organization of human groups by studying their mobility patterns or diet (Tafuri et al. 2006; Finucane et al. 2008; Sereno et al. 2008). Another challenge is to use ethnoarchaeological research in new and creative ways, for example in studying the complexity of contemporary pastoral systems (Mayor et al. 2005; Lane 2006) or the relations between hunter-gatherers and livestock keepers (Smith 1998).

The very issue of specialized pastoralism is also still troubled by the quality of data: insights on transhumance/mobility models or herd composition and their links to social organization remain rare. Ethnoarchaeological research could again be useful, not only for driving possible analogical directions but also for informing laboratory-based approaches: it is surprising, then, that scarce attention has been given towards analysing dung deposits (Chang and Koster 1986), particularly those in cave environments (Cremaschi et al. 1996; Rosen et al. 2005). Analyses of pottery aimed at detecting evidence of dairying (Evershed et al. 2008) should also be undertaken, and could add substantial information on how livestock were actually exploited, as recently done in the Middle Pastoral sites of Takarkori in the central Sahara (Dunne et al. 2012). Recent research on the genetic signature of lactose tolerance (−13910T) provides another interesting perspective on the time-depth and geographical distribution of dairying practices (Myles et al. 2005). Finally, information on animal by-products or at least differences in herd composition could usefully be investigated by means of geoarchaeological approaches: for example, the increase of spherulites at Uan Muhuggiag has been interpreted as evidence for herd reorganization with the aim of maintaining a larger component of adult individuals for exploitation of by-products, possibly milk (Cremaschi et al. 1996).

Across the decades, we have seen dozens of maps on a continental scale trying to simplify processes of immense complexity, often based on badly collected bones or poorly published, scanty data. We know nearly nothing of the archaeological contexts used for drawing these maps and yet we keep using them. It is thus no coincidence if the debate in Africa appears rather immobilized and fragile when compared to other areas of research. Reanalysis of museum collections from those over-cited sites scattered across North Africa using the most up-to-date laboratory techniques would certainly be of interest. This could help produce a better understanding of African pastoralism by moving away from 'bone'-oriented obsessions and following new avenues of investigation. But most importantly, I believe, it is time to go back to archaeology and, with new field research, look at the African scenario of herds and people in a different light.

REFERENCES

ACHILLI, A., PELLECCHIA, M., UBOLDI, C., et al. (2008). Mitochondrial genomes of extinct aurochs survive in domestic cattle. *Current Biology* 18: 157–8.

APPLEGATE, A., GAUTHIER, A., and DUNCAN, S. (2001). The North tumuli of the Nabta Late Neolithic ceremonial complex. In F. Wendorf et al. (2001: 468–88).

BARHAM, L. S., and MITCHELL, P. J. (2008). *The First Africans: African Archaeology from the Earliest Toolmakers to Most Recent Foragers*. Cambridge: Cambridge University Press.

BARICH, B. E. (1974). La serie stratigrafica dell'Uadi Ti-n-Torha (Acacus, Libia). *Origini* 8: 7–184.

—— (2002). Cultural responses to climatic changes in North Africa: beginning and spread of pastoralism in the Sahara. In F. A. Hassan (ed.), *Droughts, Food and Culture. Ecological Change and Food Security in Africa's Later Prehistory*. New York: Kluwer Academic/Plenum, 209–23.

BEJA-PEREIRA, A., CARAMELLI, D., LALUEZA-FOX, C., et al. (2006). The origin of European cattle: evidence from modern and ancient DNA. *Proceedings of the National Academy of Sciences (USA)* 103: 8113–18.

BLENCH, R. M. (2006). *Archaeology, Language, and the African Past*. Walnut Creek, Calif.: AltaMira Press.

—— and MACDONALD, K. C. (eds) (2000). *The Origins and Development of African Livestock: Archaeology, Genetics, Linguistics and Ethnography*. London: UCL Press.

BRADLEY, D. G., MACHUGH, D. E., CUNNINGHAM, P., and LOFTUS, R. T. (1996). Mitochondrial diversity and the origins of African and European cattle. *Proceedings of the National Academy of Sciences (USA)* 93: 5131–5.

CARAMELLI, D. (2006). The origins of domesticated cattle. *Human Evolution* 21: 107–22.

CHANG, C., and KOSTER, H. A. (1986). Beyond bones: toward an archaeology of pastoralism. *Advances in Archaeological Method and Theory* 9: 97–148.

CLARK, J. D. (1967). The position of research in African archaeology: future developments and needs. *African Studies Bulletin* 10(2): 10–18.

—— and BRANDT, S. (eds) (1984). *From Hunters to Farmers: The Causes and Consequences of Food Production in Africa*. Berkeley: University of California Press.

CLOSE, A. E. (1995). Few and far between: early ceramics in North Africa. In W. K. Barnett and J. W. Hoopes (eds), *The Emergence of Pottery: Technology and Innovation in Ancient Societies*. Washington, DC: Smithsonian Institution Press, 23–37.

—— (2002). Sinai, Sahara, Sahel: the introduction of domestic caprines to Africa. In Jennerstrasse 8 (eds), *Tides of the Desert*. Cologne: Heinrich Barth Institut, 459–69.

—— and WENDORF, F. (1992). The beginnings of food production in the eastern Sahara. In A. E. Gebauer and T. D. Price (eds), *Transitions to Agriculture in Prehistory*. Madison, Wis.: Prehistory Press, 63–72.

CREMASCHI, M., and DI LERNIA, S. (1998). The geoarchaeological survey in central Acacus and surroundings (Libyan Sahara): environment and cultures. In M. Cremaschi and S. di Lernia (eds), *Wadi Teshuinat: Palaeoenvironment and Prehistory in South-Western Fezzan (Libyan Sahara)*. Florence: All'Insegna del Giglio, 243–96.

—— —— and Trombino, L., (1996). From taming to pastoralism in a drying environment: site formation processes in the shelters of the Tadrart Acacus massif (Libya, central Sahara). In L. Castelletti and M. Cremaschi (eds), *Micromorphology of Deposits of Anthropogenic Origin*. Forlì: ABACO, 87–106.

Di Lernia, S. (2001). Dismantling dung: delayed use of food resources among early Holocene foragers of the Libyan Sahara. *Journal of Anthropological Archaeology* 20: 408–41.

—— (2002). Dry climatic events and cultural trajectories: adjusting Middle Holocene pastoral economy of the Libyan Sahara. In F. A. Hassan (ed.), *Droughts, Food and Culture: Ecological Change and Food Security in Africa's Later Prehistory*. New York: Kluwer Academic/Plenum, 225–50.

—— (2006). Building monuments, creating identity: cattle cult as a social response to rapid environmental changes in the Holocene Sahara. *Quaternary International* 151: 50–62.

—— Tafuri M.A., Gallinaro M., Alhaique F., BalassE M., Cavorsi L., Fullagar P.D., Mercuri A.M., Monaco A., Perego A., Zerboni A. (2013). Inside the 'African Cattle Complex": Animal Burials in the Holocene Central Sahara. PLOS ONE 8 (2): 1–28. doi:10.1371/journal.pone.0056879.

Ducos, P. (1976). Some evidence for the origin of domestication in France. In J. Guilane (ed.), *The Prehistory of France*. Paris: CNRS, 165–77.

Dunne J., Evershed R.P., Salque M., Cramp L., Bruni S., Ryan K., Biagetti S. & di Lernia S. (2012). First dairying in green Saharan Africa in the fifth millennium BC. *Nature* 486: 390–394.

Dyson-Hudson, R., and Dyson-Hudson, N. (1980). Nomadic pastoralism. *Annual Review of Anthropology* 9: 15–61.

Edens, C., and Wilkinson, T. J. (1998). Southwest Arabia during the Holocene: recent archaeological developments. *Journal of World Prehistory* 12: 55–119.

Evershed, R., Payne, S., Sherratt, A. G., et al. (2008). Earliest date for milk use in the Near East and southeastern Europe linked to cattle herding. *Nature* 455: 528–31.

Finucane, B., Manning, K., and Touré, M. (2008). Late Stone Age subsistence in the Tilemsi Valley, Mali: stable isotope analysis of human and animal remains from the site of Karkarichinkat Nord (KN05) and Karkarichinkat Sud (KS05). *Journal of Anthropological Archaeology* 27: 82–92.

Gabriel, B. (1987). Palaeoecological evidence from neolithic fireplaces in the Sahara. *African Archaeological Review* 5: 93–103.

Garcea, E. A. A. (1993). *Cultural Dynamics in Saharo-Sudanese Prehistory*. Rome: GEI.

—— (2004). An alternative way towards food production: the perspective from the Libyan Sahara. *Journal of World Prehistory* 18: 107–54.

Gautier, A. (1980). Contributions to the archaeozoology of Egypt. In Wendorf and Schild (1980: 317–44).

—— (1987). Prehistoric man and cattle in North Africa: a dearth of data and a surfeit of models. In A. E. Close (ed.), *Prehistory of Arid North Africa: Essays in Honor of Fred Wendorf*. Dallas, Tex.: Southern Methodist University Press, 163–87.

—— (2001). The early to late Neolithic archeofaunas from Nabta and Bir Kiseiba. In Wendorf et al. (2001: 609–35).

Gifford-Gonzalez, D. (2000). Animal disease challenges to the emergence of pastoralism in sub-Saharan Africa. *African Archaeological Review* 17: 95–139.

—— (2005). Pastoralism and its consequences. In A. B. Stahl (ed.), *African Archaeology: A Critical Introduction*. Oxford: Blackwell, 187–224.

Grigson, C. (2000). *Bos africanus* (Brehm)? Notes on the archaeozoology of the native cattle of Africa. In Blench and MacDonald (2000: 38–60).

HANOTTE, O., BRADLEY, D. G., OCHIENG, J. W., VERJEE, Y., HILL, E. W., and REGE, J. E. O. (2002). African pastoralism: genetic imprints of origins and migrations. *Science* 296: 336–9.

HASSAN, F. A. (2000). Climate and cattle in North Africa: a first approximation. In Blench and MacDonald (2000: 61–86).

—— (2002). Palaeoclimate, food and cultural change in Africa: an overview. In F. A. Hassan (ed.), *Droughts, Food and Culture: Ecological Change and Food Security in Africa's Later Prehistory*. New York: Kluwer Academic/Plenum, 11–26.

HOLL, A. F. C. (1998). The dawn of African pastoralism: an introductory note. *Journal of Anthropological Archaeology* 17: 81–96.

—— (2004). *Holocene Saharans: An Anthropological Perspective*. London: Continuum.

—— (2005). Holocene 'aquatic' adaptations in North Tropical Africa. In A. B. Stahl (ed.), *African Archaeology: A Critical Introduction*. Oxford: Blackwell, 174–86.

INGOLD, T. (1980). *Hunters, Pastoralists and Ranchers: Reindeer Economies and Their Transformations*. Cambridge: Cambridge University Press.

KHAZANOV, A. (1984). *Nomads and the Outside World*. Cambridge: Cambridge University Press.

KLEIN, R. G., and SCOTT, K. (1986). Re-analysis of faunal assemblages from the Haua Fteah and other late quaternary archaeological sites in Cyrenaican Libya. *Journal of Archaeological Science* 13: 515–42.

KRÖPELIN, S., VERSCHUREN, D., LÉZINE, A.-M., et al. (2008). Climate-driven ecosystem succession in the Sahara: the past 6000 years. *Science* 320: 765–8.

KRZYZANIAK, L., KROEPER, K., and KOBUSIEWICZ, M. (eds) (1996). *Interregional Contacts in the Late Prehistory of Northeastern Africa*. Poznán: Poznán Archaeological Museum.

KUIJT, I., and GORING-MORRIS N. (2002). Foraging, farming, and social complexity in the Pre-Pottery Neolithic of the southern Levant: a review and synthesis. *Journal of World Prehistory* 16: 361–440.

KUPER, R., and KRÖPELIN, S. (2006). Climate-controlled Holocene occupation in the Sahara: motor of Africa's evolution. *Science* 313: 803–7.

LANE, P. J. (2006). Present to past: ethnoarchaeology. In C. Tilley, W. Keane, S. Kuechler, M. Rowlands, and P. Spyer (eds), *Handbook of Material Culture*. London: Sage, 402–24.

MacDONALD, K. C. (2000). The origins of African livestock: indigenous or imported? In Blench and MacDonald (2000: 2–17).

MacEACHERN, S. (2000). Genes, tribes, and African history. *Current Anthropology* 41: 357–84.

MAYOR, A., HUYSECOM, E., GALLAY, A., RASSE, M., and BALLOUCHE, A. (2005). Population dynamics and paleoclimate over the past 3000 years in the Dogon Country, Mali. *Journal of Anthropological Archaeology* 24: 25–61.

MARSHALL, F., and HILDEBRAND, E. (2002). Cattle before crops: the beginning of food production in Africa. *Journal of World Prehistory* 16: 99–143.

McDONALD, M. M. A. (1998). Early African pastoralism: view from Dakhleh Oasis (south central Egypt). *Journal of Anthropological Archaeology* 17: 124–42.

MITCHELL, P. J. (2005). *African Connections: Archaeological Perspectives on Africa and the Wider World*. Walnut Creek, Calif.: AltaMira Press.

MORI, F. (1965). *Tadrart Acacus: Arte Rupestre e Culture del Sahara Preistorico*. Turin: Einaudi.

MUZZOLINI, A. (1995). *Les Images Rupestres du Sahara*. Toulouse: Collection Préhistoire du Sahara.

MYLES, S., BOUZEKRI, N., HAVERFIELD, E., CHERKAOUI, M., DUGOUJON, J.-M., and WARD, R. (2005). Genetic evidence in support of a shared Eurasian–North African dairying origin. *Human Genetics* 117: 34–42.

PARIS, F. (2000). African livestock remains from Saharan mortuary context. In Blench and MacDonald (2000: 111–26).

REIMER, H. (2007). When hunters started hunting: pastro-foragers and the complexity of Holocene economic change in the Western Desert of Egypt. In M. Bollig, O. Bubenzer, R. Vogelsang, and H.-P. Wotzka (eds), *Aridity, Change and Conflict in Africa*. Cologne: Heinrich Barth Institut, 105–44.

ROSEN, S. A., SAVINETSKY, A. B., PLAKHT, Y., et al. (2005). Dung in the desert: preliminary results of the Negev Holocene Ecology Project. *Current Anthropology* 46: 317–28.

ROSSEL, S., MARSHALL, F., PETERS, J., PILGRAM, T., ADAMS, M. D., and O'CONNOR, D. (2008). Domestication of the donkey: timing, processes, and indicators. *Proceedings of the National Academy of Sciences (USA)* 105: 3715–20.

ROUBET, C. (1979). *Économie Pastorale Préagricole en Algérie Orientale: le Néolithique de Tradition Capsienne. Exemple: l'Aurès*. Paris: CNRS.

SERENO, P. C., GARCEA, E. A. A., JOUSSE, H., et al. (2008). Lakeside cemeteries in the Sahara: 5000 years of Holocene population and environmental change. *PLoS ONE* 3(8): e2995.

SMITH, A. B. (1984). Origins of the Neolithic in the Sahara. In Clark and Brandt (1984: 88–92).

—— (1986). Cattle domestication in North Africa. *African Archaeological Review* 4: 197–203.

—— (1998). Keeping people on the periphery: the ideology of social hierarchies between hunters and herders. *Journal of Anthropological Archaeology* 17: 201–15.

—— (2001). Ideas on the later cultural history of the Central Sahara. *Sahara* 12: 101–6.

—— (2005). *African Herders. Emergence of Pastoral Traditions*. Walnut Creek, Calif.: AltaMira Press.

SUTTON, J. E. G. (1974). The aquatic civilizations of Middle Africa. *Journal of African History* 15: 527–46.

TAFURI, M. A., BENTLEY, R. A., MANZI, G., and DI LERNIA, S. (2006). Mobility and kinship in the prehistoric Sahara: strontium isotope analysis of Holocene human skeletons from the Acacus Mts. (southwestern Libya). *Journal of Anthropological Archaeology* 25: 390–402.

TAUVERON, M., STRIEDTER, K. H., and FERHAT, N. (2009). Neolithic domestication and pastoralism in Central Sahara: the cattle necropolis of Mankhor (Tadrart Algérienne). *Palaeoecology of Africa* 29: 179–86.

VERMEERSCH, P. M., VAN PEER, P., MOEYERSONS, J., and VAN NEER, W. (1996). Neolithic occupation of the Sodmein area, Red Sea Mountains, Egypt. In G. Pwiti and R. Soper (eds), *Aspects of African Archaeology*. Harare: University of Zimbabwe Press, 411–19.

VERNET, R. (2002). Climate during the Late Holocene in the Sahara and the Sahel: evolution and consequences on human settlement. In F. A. Hassan (ed.), *Droughts, Food and Culture. Ecological Change and Food Security in Africa's Later Prehistory*. New York: Kluwer Academic/Plenum, 47–64.

WENDORF, F. (ed.) (1968). *The Prehistory of Nubia*. Dallas, Tex.: Southern Methodist University Press.

—— and SCHILD, R. (eds) (1980). *Prehistory of the Eastern Sahara*. New York: Academic Press.

—— —— (1994). Are the early Holocene cattle in the Eastern Sahara domestic or wild? *Evolutionary Anthropology* 3: 118–28.

—— —— and associates (eds) (2001). *Holocene Settlement of the Egyptian Sahara: The Archaeology of Nabta Playa*. New York: Kluwer Academic/Plenum.

WOODBURN, J. (1982). Egalitarian societies. *Man* 17: 431–51.

ZEDER, M. A. (2008). Domestication and early agriculture in the Mediterranean Basin: origins, diffusion, and impact. *Proceedings of the National Academy of Sciences (USA)* 105: 11597–604.

CHAPTER 37

EARLY FARMING SOCIETIES ALONG THE NILE

RANDI HAALAND AND GUNNAR HAALAND

Introduction

THE Biblical story of Joseph catches some important dimensions of the role the Nile played in providing food security for the populations of the Egyptian part of the river valley, as well as for surrounding regions of dryland farmers and pastoralists during Dynastic rule. This role was not only affected by naturally caused fluctuations in floods depositing fertilizing silt, but also by the pivotal role the state played in extracting, storing, and redistributing agricultural surpluses to carry the Egyptian population through years of insufficient food production, investing in water control and redistributing agricultural products to specialized craftsmen.

Farming activities within the Nile valley grew from multiple roots: (a) rich fish resources in the river itself provided a favourable habitat for broad-spectrum forager patterns of resource exploitation, including the gathering of wild sorghum; (b) pastures and water stimulated seasonal migrations of nomadic pastoralists to the river; (c) northern Egypt's Mediterranean climate encouraged settlement by agro-pastoralists from the Near East; and (d) symbiotic and competitive interactions with agro-pastoralists of the lakes and wadis between the Nile and Chad/Libya took place during the mid- and late Holocene. The Nile Valley was thus attractive to people practising different kinds of resource utilization and originating from different cultural backgrounds. Given differences in micro-environments, these relationships connecting the people of the Nile Valley to those of wider regions differed from place to place as well as over time, and were affected by both climatic fluctuations and local technological and politico-economic developments. The Nile's farming systems evolved in contexts that were not just ecological, but also political, economic, and ritual. Bearing in mind the distinction between cultivation, which involves human activities directed towards increasing the yield of preferred species, and domestication, which involves biological changes in species from wild to domesticated varieties, it is the interplay of processes in these different contexts that is considered here.

The rivers and the savannah/Sahel:
different courses in the emergence
of early farming systems

The development of animal husbandry and cultivation in Africa had different roots and took different courses among people living in drier savannah/Sahelian regions and those living close to large rivers. From a common broad-spectrum resource utilization including hunting, gathering, and fishing, differences in natural conditions favoured different courses of intensification of resource utilization in these two areas. In the archaeological record, broad-spectrum adaptations are often associated with the use of pottery. Though initially rare, pottery was a significant technical innovation, as boiling made a much wider range of foods (fish, meat and wild grains) more digestible; the advantages of this for enhancing child survival (and thus eventual population increase) at weaning and in early childhood deserve particular mention (Haaland 1992).

Dating from the tenth to the sixth millennia BC, elaborately decorated pottery types (here considered variations on the Khartoum Wavy Line tradition) has been recovered from a wide area from the Atlantic to the Nile and from Lake Turkana to Upper Egypt (Jesse 2010) Along the Nile, this tradition was first recognized by Arkell (1949) at the Khartoum Hospital site at the junction of the Blue and White Niles (Fig. 37.1). Along with pottery of the so-called wavy/dotted wavy line type, bone harpoons are also characteristic, while faunal remains indicate exploitation of both aquatic (fish, crocodile, hippopotamus) and terrestrial (antelope, elephant) resources. No plant remains survive, but grindstones suggest they were also consumed. Elsewhere along the main Nile, other important sites include Geili (Caneva 1988) and Saqqai (Garcea 1993; Caneva 1994), with many others in Dongola, as well as in the desert regions to the west of the Nile. The work of the ACACIA research group in Wadi Howar, a major (now dry) tributary feeding into the Nile from the west, has documented a vast West Nubian palaeolake stretching from the Nile to Chad and Libya until the second millennium BC (Kuper and Kröpelin 2006; Bubenzer et al. 2007). The drier climate from the third/fourth millennium BC gradually led to the formation of smaller lakes and rivers (Kröpelin 1993). In the archaeological record this environmental change is reflected in increasingly regional cultural diversification (particularly the occurrence of the distinct Leiterband pottery) and ecological adaptations (particularly the increased importance of livestock, as expressed ritually in pots buried in pits with cattle bones (Keding 2000). The drying out of the West Nubian Palaeolake from the late mid-Holocene led not only to the 'Wadi Howar diaspora' of Eastern Sudanic speakers along the Nile from Dongola to East Africa (Dimmendaal 2007), but also to a diversification of adaptive strategies that may have led to increased intergroup exchange and competition for access to resources along the Sudanese Nile, thus stimulating trends towards political centralization and social stratification.

Sutton (1974) coined the term 'aqualithic' (see Holl 2005 for a critique of its over-inclusive use) for broad-spectrum adaptations during the early part of the Holocene, when rainfall was significantly higher than today in the Sahara and the Sahel and savannah-like vegetation stretched 500 km further north than its present distribution (Hassan 1986; Kuper and Kröpelin 2006). Plant remains from Site E-75-6 at Nabta Playa in Egypt's Western Desert, for instance,

FIG. 37.1 Map of the main sites mentioned in Chapter 37.

document harvesting in the late seventh millennium BC of a broad spectrum of grasses that today grow in the summer-rainfall Sahelian zone (Wasylikowa et al. 1997; Wendorf and Schild 2001). Intriguingly, the sorghum present may show morphological changes suggestive of early human manipulation to increase its productivity (Wasylikowa et al. 1997). Comparable evidence of plant gathering comes from sites in Fezzan, southwestern Libya (Garcea 2006; Barich, Ch. 31 above), but the possibility that cattle were present this early at Nabta or elsewhere in the Western Desert at Bir Kiseiba remains controversial (di Lernia, Ch. 36 above).

Built structures representing house foundations are known from both Nabta and the Dakhla Oasis (Wendorf and Schild 1998; McDonald 2009). Sedentism is generally considered a precondition for plant cultivation leading to domestication, but in northeast Africa was apparently interrupted by another development, pastoralism. Under savannah/Sahelian conditions the seasonality of pasture and water availability varies between localities (Marshall and Hildebrand 2002), as does the threat of animal diseases. As reliance on animal husbandry increased, this probably favoured a change to more mobile settlement, which in turn prevented the continuity of local cultivation required for selection for domesticated varieties (Neumann 2005).

While this argument seems plausible for the drier savannah/Sahelian regions, along the major rivers conditions were different. Three large Mesolithic sites in the Atbara region (Abu Darbein, el Damer, Aneibis) date from the eighth to the sixth millennia BC and combine a fauna similar to that from the Khartoum Hospital site with remains of wild grasses (*Sorghum* sp., *Setaria* sp., and *Panicum* sp.), grindstones, and a huge amount of pottery for storing, cooking, and serving (Fig. 37.2; Haaland and Magid 1995). A most important development is evidence for deep river fishing employing both harpoons and disk-shaped pottery pieces probably used as sinkers for fishing nets. Multiple burials indicate a long-term occupation that may have led to increased pressure on cereal resources and, we suggest, increased human concern about their growth.

A great increase in grindstones and larger settlement sites from the fifth millennium BC may signal simple cultivation activities (Haaland 1999). If so, selection for domesticated varieties may have been operative for a long time. This assumption is strengthened by the fact that the greatest genetic diversity of domesticated sorghum (~450 local strains) occurs in Sudan and by the possibility, raised by botanists, that *Sorghum bicolor*, the closest domesticated variety to the wild *S. verticilliflorum*, may have been domesticated there as early as 6000 BC (McGovern 2009). If such an inference is even roughly correct, then it implies that in Sudan incipient cultivation and possible domestication occurred in the period conventionally labelled Khartoum Mesolithic. It is thus surprising that the first archaeological evidence for domesticated sorghum actually comes from India *c.* 2000 BC and significantly

FIG. 37.2 Ceramic vessel probably used for serving from the Mesolithic site of Aneibis, Atbara, Sudan, dated to the seventh millennium BC (photograph courtesy of Anne Marie Olsen).

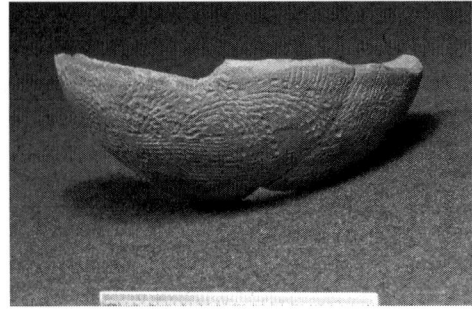

pre-dates any finds from within Africa itself (Fuller 2003; Fuller and Hildebrand, Ch. 35 above). Of course, if wild sorghum had been brought to India this would have served to isolate a sorghum gene pool on which selection pressures could then have operated. Within Africa, such isolation could perhaps have been brought about if the introduction of livestock to the Sudanese Nile led to broad-spectrum-focused seasonal settlements expanding into microenvironments outside the habitat of wild sorghum (Haaland 1999). We return to this after discussing the introduction of farming into the Egyptian Nile valley.

EGYPT AND THE NEAR EASTERN
FARMING COMPLEX

Hardly any Mesolithic sites have been recovered from the Nile Delta, probably because they are covered by silt (Kuper and Kröpelin 2006). Further south, around the Fayum Lake the so-called Qarunian culture does, however, attest to a broad-spectrum adaptation (Wenke 2009). Re-analysis of earlier excavations by Caton-Thompson and Gardener (1934) shows that between 8000 and 6000 BC fishing was of major importance, supplemented by hunting and gathering. The first evidence of farming comes about 5200 BC, when the Fayum was reoccupied after a hiatus in settlement.

Evidence for early farming is first found around 5200 BC, when the Fayum was reoccupied by people whose material culture was radically different from the Qarunian tradition and included pottery, grindstones, and sickle blades. Most importantly, this reoccupation was undertaken by farmers, who cultivated barley and emmer wheat (both undoubtedly of Levantine origin) and kept sheep, goats, cattle, and pigs (Ginter and Kozlowski 1986). The Lower Nile Valley was already part of exchange networks covering not only regions upstream and towards the Sahara but also the Levant, where cereals and livestock had been domesticated several thousand years earlier. The settlement of Cyprus by farmers c. 9000 BC indicates increased competition among farmers in the Near East and it is therefore possible that people expanded from the Levant (and probably also from the Sahara) into the Egyptian Nile much earlier than the evidence from the Fayum currently shows.

The highly productive agricultural complex that then developed in Egypt used a variety of food crops, including wheat, barley, lentils, peas, beans, and various oil plants, as well as flax for textiles (Midant-Reynes 2000; Wenke 2009). The cereals sown after inundation in October on moist riverbanks that, with clearing and weeding, would have been both fertile and easily cultivated (Wenke 2009), were made into bread and beer—both staples of the later Pharaonic diet (Samuel 2000). The importance of beer is manifested by several breweries, of which the fourth-millennium BC Tell el Farkha is probably one of the oldest in the world (Cialowicz 2007). Certain elements of an earlier broad-spectrum economy were also maintained, as seen in the great importance of fish in the diet, the consumption of wild fruits, and the use of papyrus for making items like ropes and mats. Integration of animal husbandry and cultivation enhanced the overall productivity of the system, for example through the use of cattle to thresh grain and (later) to plough. Correspondingly, livestock were fed on grain residue, as well as on *berseem* (Egyptian clover), a nutritional fodder crop that also increased the nitrogen content in the soil (McCown et al. 1979).

The further spread of this agricultural complex is evident during 5000–4100 BC at Merimde Beni Salama (Hendricks and Vermeersch 2000). Interestingly, the early material culture recovered there resembles Levantine traditions, while later material is similar to Saharan traditions, supporting the view that multiple groups of different origins and perhaps practising slightly different adaptations were settling the Egyptian Nile valley. Maadi, near Cairo, where domesticated donkeys are evident shortly after 4000 BC (Midant-Reynes 2000: 215), appears to have played a central role in exchange networks with the Levant (Caneva et al. 1987; Hartung 2003). Buto, one of few sites to have been excavated within the Delta, also demonstrates an important engagement in the flow of goods over a wide area, perhaps including Mesopotamia (von der Way 1997; Wenke 2009). Perhaps significantly, in Pharaonic times Buto was home to the cobra goddess Wadjet, who was strongly associated with the royal crowns, and came to symbolize the political centralization of Lower Egypt.

The Near Eastern agricultural complex spread southward along the Nile into Upper Egypt. Pottery recovered from Nabta Playa from about 5000 BC shows similarities with Near Eastern pottery, while remains of barley indicate that people who were already using wild sorghum had now begun to cultivate crops of Near Eastern origin; domesticated cattle are also certainly present by this time (Wendorf and Schild 1998, 2002). Retraction of the savannah vegetation as climate aridified in the mid-Holocene led eventually, however, to the abandonment of Nabta Playa and many other oasis settlements in the middle Holocene (Hassan 1988). Along the Nile itself, though, occupation persisted and *c.* 4000 BC the site of el-Badari contains barley and wheat, as well as sickles and other objects indicating the importance of fishing, hunting, and possibly pastoralism (Hassan 1988; Midant-Reynes 2000). The Badarian people engaged in far-flung exchange networks that connected them to regions further south, as well as the Near East. More than 100 km south of el-Badari sites like Amra, Naqada, and Hierakonpolis also document the cultivation of wheat and barley, along with the keeping of domesticated cattle, sheep, goats, and pigs (Midant-Reynes 2000). Hierakonpolis clearly underwent some kind of population explosion between 3800 and 3400 BC, by which point the town was divided into different occupational quarters for producing pottery, beer, stone vases, palettes, and other commodities. Many used luxury materials (carnelian, turquoise, gold, silver, obsidian, lapis lazuli, ivory, and crystal) to produce items for consumption by an emerging elite (Wenke 2009). Cobblestone foundations are interpreted as the remains of a fortified palace, temple, and administrative centre (Hoffmann 1982). Paralleling Buto in the north, Hierakonpolis was the home of the vulture goddess Nekhen, who in Pharaonic times symbolized royal power in Upper Egypt.

The Nile environment was rich in resources but difficult to defend, and conflicts with neighbouring villages or raids by desert tribes were realities of life with which farmers had to cope (Wenke 2009). It is in such situations that political centralization and social differentiation emerged. In the Egyptian case, its complex farming system could not have evolved outside a context of political institutionalization of rights in crops and animals. This concern about order is reflected in the Pharaonic conceptual opposition between *Maat* (order, truth, and law) and *Isfet* (chaos, lies, and violence). Belief in the ruler as sustainer of order is a general legitimizing idea in early civilizations all over the world (Trigger 2003), and a rich inventory of myth and ritual practices makes the idea compelling, as Kemp (2006) describes for Pharaonic Egypt and Shaw discusses in Chapter 50 below.

The topography and climate of the Nile Valley limited the establishment of the productive Near Eastern farming system to the area between the Mediterranean Sea and Sudanese Nubia. Further south was the less productive sorghum/millet zone, while savannah/desert regions to the east and west were unsuitable to farming systems productive enough to allow appropriation of surplus food required to maintain the complex division of labour of the emerging Egyptian state(s). The same natural features that restricted that state's long-term spatial expansion also served as a protective barrier against competing polities in the Near East, while desert nomads could be a nuisance but rarely a serious threat. In the late fourth millennium BC Lower Nubia shared in the processes of centralization and elite emergence found downstream of Aswan, but its much more limited arable land restricted state formation possibilities here, which were, in any case, violently curtailed when the new Dynastic state employed force against a potential rival (Wilkinson 1999). Thereafter, Egyptian policy until the end of the Old Kingdom (c. 2150 BC) employed military raids, trading expeditions, and alliances with local chiefdoms to secure precious resources such as gold and ivory from Nubia (Edwards 2004). Such relationships probably had a significant impact in shaping politico-economic and cultural developments along the Sudanese Nile.

THE SUDANESE NILE NEOLITHIC

People associated with the aqualithic traditions discussed earlier were undoubtedly affected by the introduction of farming into Egypt and the political and economic developments connected with it. Arkell's (1953) excavations at Shaheinab, north of Omdurman, the first excavated site of the so-called Khartoum Neolithic, produced, for example, evidence of participation in long-distance exchange networks (amazonite from the Sahara) as well as the creation of new symbols of power (stone mace-heads). Now dated to c. 4700 BC, Shaheinab's material culture includes a wider range of stone and bone tools than found with the Khartoum Mesolithic, including fish hooks and stone 'gouges' that may have been used to till the soil (Haaland 1987). Faunal remains include not only sheep and goat but also domesticated cattle (Tigani 1988), but in contrast to Egypt, animal husbandry was practised with few mutually supporting linkages to cultivation (McCown et al. 1979). This introduction of livestock to central Sudan by the beginning of the fifth millennium BC thus shows a rapid spread of pastoralism, perhaps brought about both by sedentary people adopting livestock as a component in their broad-spectrum economy and by nomads geographically expanding into a previously unoccupied niche. Certainly, after 3000 BC it is highly likely that pastoralists played an important role in exchange networks linking the Nile with the Red Sea (Fattovich 1991). Material from Sai Island (situated between the Second and Third Cataracts) indicates that from this period north–south contact increased, probably reflecting both regional diversification along the Sudanese Nile and in the West Nubian Palaeolake area and the growing politico-economic dominance of early Pharaonic Egypt. This is manifested in the occurrence of Near Eastern crops (wheat and barley) and in pottery types showing influences from A-Group sites in the north and Pre-Kerma sites further south. The Sai people may have acted as middlemen mediating a flow of Nubian products (gold, ivory, ebony, and cattle) to the elites in Pharaonic Egypt (Garcea and Hildebrand 2009).

Sites dating from the early fifth millennium BC to the emergence of the Kerma-based kingdom of Kush in the mid/late third millennium (Welsby, Ch. 51 below) show much greater variation than hitherto with the larger sites generally located along old riverbanks 6–7 km away from the Nile. Different activities appear to have taken place in different types of settlements. Kadero (c. 4850–4250 BC) is particularly relevant for understanding such differentiation. It produced large amount of animal bones (88 percent of them livestock, mainly cattle) (Krzyzaniak 1991, 2004). The burial ground at the outskirts of the site shows differences in grave location related to gender and age, but some graves with a very rich inventory of maceheads, jewellery, pottery, and bucrania indicate the more explicit formation of an elite.

Large amount of cattle bones are rarely found on pastoralist sites (Edwards 2004: 57–8) and their presence at Kadero therefore suggests that the site had a special significance as a ritual centre integrating people occupying other, functionally differentiated task sites. One such site is Zakiab, located closer to the Nile and most probably focused on dry-season fishing and herding, to judge from the artefacts and fauna found there. Conversely, numerous grindstones, plant remains (mainly wild sorghum and millets), and the bones of domesticated animals suggest that a third site, Um Direiwa, probably served as a cultivating/herding settlement. Its lack of items with possible ceremonial functions and the absence of graves there and at Zakiab supports the hypothesis that these smaller sites were ritually, economically, and politically linked to Kadero (Haaland 1987).

Large sites similar to Kadero with rich burial grounds are found further downstream at Geili (Caneva 1988) and al-Ghaba (Reinold 2001), and at a somewhat later site, al-Kadada (Geus 1991). In Dongola, just south of Kerma, several large sites dating from 4500–4000 BC have cemeteries with over 1,000 burials. Kadruka yielded several exceptionally rich graves, including a male buried with two bucrania, nine mace-heads, several ivory bracelets, and a beautifully decorated calciform beaker (Reinold 2001). A strong focus on body decoration is also evident, both along the Sudanese Nile and in Predynastic Egypt (Wengrow 2001). As well as beads, amulets and bracelets made from materials that include semi-precious stones like carnelian or marine shells from the Red Sea, ivory lip-plugs, and palettes used to prepare red ochre and malachite pigments for body painting are also common. Characteristic too of very rich burials at the largest sites, such as Kadero, is the deposit of bucrania as grave goods, something that presages the later prominence of cattle in elite Kerman burials (Welsby, Ch. 51 below). As well as being items of wealth that could be individually accumulated and could serve as a source of social differentiation, cattle could also be used as symbols of power, from associations with motherly nurture and succour to manly political dominance and power to the protection of cosmic stability. Underlining the commonalities between Neolithic populations along the Sudanese Nile and those of Predynastic Egypt that were ancestral to the later Pharaonic state, all these associations are, of course, very much evident in Ancient Egyptian iconography and belief (cf. Wengrow 2001).

Another important aspect of Neolithic material culture, at least after 4500 BC, is the increased occurrence of different types of drinking vessels such as small cups, beakers (Caneva 1994), and elaborately decorated calciform beakers (Reinold 2001; Krzyzaniak 2004) (Fig. 37.3). Dirar (1993) has argued that fermented foods such as sorghum beer have a long time-depth in Sudan, with 30–50 different varieties recognized. They may well have been drunk from vessels of this kind, and it seems likely that it was during the fifth millennium BC, or even earlier, that the

FIG. 37.3 Calciform beaker from the Neolithic site of Kadero (photo, Maciej Jordezka courtesy of Poznan Archaeogical Museum collection).

typical African 'pot and porridge/beer' cuisine emerged (Haaland 2007); residue analyses of pottery from the Blue Nile provide some support for their use in such beer brewing (Fernandez and Tresseras 2000). Beer—and other kinds of alcohol—are now widely recognized to have played important roles in cultural history in many parts of the world (cf. Edwards 1996; Dietler 2001), and the occurrence of both simple and elaborated drinking vessels in the Sudanese Neolithic indicates socially mediated differences in how it was consumed there. Indeed, it is difficult to see that the elaborately shaped ceramic vessels were used for anything else than serving drinks like beer on festive occasions. Occasions for such conspicuous consumption may express differences internal to specific political units, but also relations of competition, as well as alliances, between the leaders of different units in inter-group elite feasting where beer and the material items involved in its consumption served as signs validating rank. Activities that lead to increase and maintenance of a regular supply of grain must have been an important concern for incipient politico-economic elites. On the background of increasing importance of wild sorghum cultivation at Um Direiwa by 4800 BC, it is thus surprising that until recently evidence of domesticated sorghum had still not been found in Sudan before 500 BC (Fuller 2004). A possible solution to this puzzle may be that domestication took place on off-Nile savannah sites where, in the rainy season, the occupants of sites along the Nile Valley were engaged in other activities such as the cultivation of morphologically wild sorghum and cattle rearing (Hoelzmann et al. 2001; Kuper and Kröpelin 2006).

It is in such savannah locations where sown sorghum could survive if subjected to simple cultivation activities after weeding that domestication may have taken place. More intensive settlement of such areas may possibly have been undertaken as one strategy to reduce risks to life and livelihood if people enhanced their dependence on herding, hunting and gathering and abandoned riverbank settlements in the face of increased warfare in the early stages of state formation along the Middle Nile and of raiding expeditions from Egypt (cf. Wenke 2009). Areas such as the Sudd swamps, the Jebel Moya Mountains, and the Rabak, Butana, and Gash localities at some distance from the main Nile may all have been attractive under such conditions. Recently, morphologically domesticated sorghum has indeed been recovered from such an environment at the site of Mehel Teglinos in the Kassala region, dating to 3860 ± 60 BP (Beldados and Constantini 2011).

Beyond the Butana, in eastern Sudan, the Gash Group (3000–1500 BC) has been particularly well studied (Haaland 1989). People here practised a broad-spectrum economy based on aquatic resources, domesticated cattle, sheep, and goats, and plant foods, but more specialized pastoralist groups also occupied the area. Ceramics show close similarities with the pottery used by Pan-Grave and C-Group populations in Upper Egypt and Nubia, suggesting connections among a broad range of pastoralist communities in and west of the Red Sea Hills (Fattovich 1991; Sadr 1991; Hafsaas 2006). Since sedentary people practising a broad-spectrum economy and more specialized pastoral groups occupied overlapping niches, it is reasonable to infer competition and conflicts between them—a competition that may incidentally have increased local scarcities of grain and thus stimulated increased cultivation activities that eventual led to sorghum's domestication. Moving still further afield, long-distance exchange networks connected the Gash region with Yemen across the Red Sea (Fattovich 1991; Hafsaas 2006: 132), whence further dispersal into the Indian subcontinent by 2000 BC might have been possible. It may thus be that it is in the Gash Delta that the earliest evidence of African domesticated sorghum is to be found.

Conclusion

This chapter has inferred some plausible aspects of the life-worlds that people in the Nile Valley created, from the first indication of farming activities until the formation of large-scale political units. In Egypt this process ended with establishment of the first dynasties; in northern Sudan with the kingdom of Kerma; and among Nilotic-speaking peoples in the Sudd it has lasted until the present. The interplay of sociocultural processes in these different natural environments led over time to dramatic differences in social formations, including contrasts between sedentary farmers/fishermen and migratory herdsmen and between centralized states and acephalous communities. However, it may be possible, as Wengrow (2006) has pointed out, to see long-term continuities alongside this in, for example, traditions that emphasized self-representation in body decoration as the primary medium for constructing identity, while simultaneously engaging in collaborative social acts towards the deceased. The importance of this concern is manifested in a variety of forms, from the body decorations of many people in South Sudan today to dismembered skeletons in Neolithic graves, and even to the mummies of Pharaonic times. Different temporal manifestations of this concern must be seen as an outcome of variations in natural and politicoeconomic conditions favouring different trajectories of change (Barth 2002).

References

ARKELL, A. J. (1949). *Early Khartoum*. Oxford: Oxford University Press.

—— (1953). *Esh Shaheinab*. Oxford: Oxford University Press.

BELDADOS, A., and CONSTANTINI, L. (2011). Sorghum exploitation at Kassala and its environs, north eastern Sudan in the second and first millennia BC. *Nyame Akuma* 75: 33–9.

BARTH, F. (2002). An anthropology of knowledge. *Current Anthropology* 43: 1–18.

BUBENZER, O., BOLTON, A., and DARIUS, F. (2007). *Atlas of Cultural and Environmental Change in Arid Africa*. Cologne: Afrika Praehistorica.

CANEVA, I. (ed.) (1988). *El Geili: The History of a Middle Nile Environment 7000 B.C.–A.D. 1500*. Oxford: British Archaeological Reports.

—— (1994). Recipienti per liquidi nelle pastorali dell alto Nilo. In I. Caneva (ed.), *Drinking in Ancient Societies*. Padua: Sargon, 209–26.

——, FRANGIPANE, M., and PALMIERI, A. (1987). Predynastic Egypt: new data from Maadi. *African Archaeological Review* 5: 105–14.

CATON-THOMPSON, G., and GARDENER, E. W. (1934). *The Desert Fayum*. London: Royal Anthropological Institute.

CIALOWICZ, K. M. (2007). From residence to early temple: the case of Tel el-Farkha. In K. Kroeper (ed.), *Archaeology of Early Northeastern Africa*. Poznán: Poznán Archaeological Museum, 916–34.

DIETLER, M. (2001). Driven by drink: the role of drinking in the political economy and the case of early Iron Age France. *Journal of Anthropological Archaeology* 9: 352–406.

DIMMENDAAL, G. J. (2007). Eastern Sudanic and Wasi Howar and Wadib Melik diaspora. *Sprache und Geschichte in Africa* 18: 37–67.

DIRAR, H. A. (1993). *The Indigenous Fermented Food of the Sudan: A Study of African Food and Nutrition*. Wallingford: CAB International.

EDWARDS, D. N. (1996). Sorghum, beer and Kushite society. *Norwegian Archaeological Review* 29: 65–77.

EDWARDS, D. N. (2004). *The Nubian Past: An Archaeology of the Sudan*. London: Routledge.

FATTOVICH, R. (1991). At the periphery of the empire: the Gash Delta (eastern Sudan). In W. V. Davies (ed.), *Egypt and Nubia*. London: British Museum, 40–48.

FERNÁNDEZ, V., and TRESSERAS, J.-J. (2000). New data on intensive plant processing and beer brewing in the Mesolithic and Neolithic periods of central Sudan. *Nyame Akuma* 54: 42.

FULLER, D. Q. (2003). African crops in prehistoric south Asia. In K. Neumann, A. Butler, and S. Kahlheber (eds), *Food, Fuel and Fields*. Cologne: Heinrich Barth Institute, 239–72.

—— (2004). Kawa. *Sudan and Nubia* 6: 70–74.

GARCEA, E. A. A (1993). *Cultural Dynamics in Saharan-Sudanese Prehistory*. Rome: Gruppo Editoriale Internazionale.

—— (2006). Semi-permanent foragers in semi-arid environments of North Africa. *World Archaeology* 38: 197–219.

—— and HILDEBRAND, E. A. (2009). Shifting social networks along the Nile: Middle Holocene ceramic assemblages from Sai island, Sudan. *Journal of Anthropological Archaeology* 28: 304–22.

GEUS, F. (1991). Burial customs in the Upper Main Nile: an overview. In W. V. Davies (ed.), *Egypt and Nubia*. London: British Museum, 57–73.

GINTER, B., and KOZLOWSKI, J. (1986). *Kulturelle und Paleoklimatische Sequenz in der Faiyum-Depression: Eine Zusammensetzende Darstellung der Forschungsarbeiten in den Jahren 1976–81*. Cairo: Mitteilungen des Deutschen Archäologischen Instituts Abteilung.

HAALAND, R. (1987). *Socio-Economic Differentiation in the Neolithic Sudan*. Oxford: British Archaeological Reports.

—— (1992). Fish, pots, and grain. *African Archaeological Review* 10: 43–64.

—— (1995). Sedentism, cultivation, and plant domestication in the Holocene Middle Nile region. *Journal of Field Archaeology* 22: 157–73.

—— (1999). The puzzle of the late domestication of sorghum. In C. Gosden and J. Hather (eds), *The Prehistory of Food*. London: Routledge, 397–418.

—— (2007). Porridge and pot, bread and oven: food ways and symbolism in Africa and the Near East from the Neolithic to the present. *Cambridge Archaeological Journal* 17: 165–82.

—— and MAGID, A. M. (1995). *Aqualithic Sites along the Rivers Atbara and the Nile*. Bergen: Alma Mater.

HAFSAAS, H. (2006). *Cattle Pastoralists in a Multicultural Setting: The C-Group People in Lower Nubia, 2500–1500 BCE*. Ramallah: Birzeit University Press.

HASSAN, F. A. (1986). Desert environment and origins of agriculture in Egypt. *Norwegian Archaeological Review* 19: 63–76.

—— (1988). Predynastic Egypt. *Journal of World Prehistory* 2: 135–85.

HENDRICKS, S., and VERMEERSCH, P. (2000). Prehistory: from the Paleolithic to the Badarian Culture. In I. Shaw (ed.), *The Oxford History of Ancient Egypt*. Oxford: Oxford University Press, 17–43.

HOELZMANN, P., KEDING, B., BERKE, H., KRÖPELIN, S., and KRUSE, H. (2001). Environmental change and archaeology: lake evolution and human occupation in the Eastern Sahara during the Holocene. *Palaeogeographhy, Palaeoclimatology, Palaeoecology* 169: 193–217.

HOFFMANN, M. A. (1982). *The Predynastic of Hierakonpolis: An Interim Report*. Giza: Cairo University Herbarium.

HOLL, A. F. C. (2005). Holocene 'aquatic' adaptations in North tropical Africa. In A. B. Stahl (ed.), *African Archaeology: A Critical Introduction*. Oxford: Blackwell, 174–86.

JESSE, F. (2010). Early pottery in northern Africa: an overview. *Journal of African Archaeology* 8: 219–38.

KEDING, B. (2000). New light on the Holocene occupation of the Wadi Howar region (Eastern Sahara/Sudan). In L. Krzyzaniak and M. Kobusiewicz (eds), *Cultural Markers in the Later Prehistory of Northeastern Africa*. Poznán: Poznán Archaeological Museum, 89–104.

KEMP, B. (2006). *Ancient Egypt: Anatomy of a Civilization*. Routledge. London.

KRÖPELIN, S. (1993). *ZurRekonstruktion der spätquartären Umwelt am unteren Wadi Howar (Südöstliche Sahara/NW-Sudan)*. Berlin: Berliner Geografische Abhandlungen.

KRZYZANIAK, L. (1991). Early farming in the Middle Nile Basin: recent discoveries at Kadero (central Sudan). *Antiquity* 65: 159–72.

—— (2004). Kadero. In D. A. Welsby and J. R. Anderson (eds), *Sudan Ancient Treasures*. London: British Museum, 49–53.

KUPER, R., and KRÖPELIN, S. (2006). Climate-controlled Holocene occupation in the Sahara: motor of Africa's evolution. *Science* 313: 803–7.

MARSHALL, F., and HILDEBRAND, E. (2002). Cattle before crops: the beginnings of food production in Africa. *Journal of World Prehistory* 16: 99–143.

MCCOWN, R., HAALAND, G., and DE HAAN, K. (1979). Interaction between cultivation and livestock production in semi-arid Africa. In A. Hall, G. H. Cannell, and H. W. Lawton (eds), *Agriculture in Semi-Arid Environments*. Berlin: Springer, 297–332.

MCDONALD, M. A. (2009). Increased sedentism in the central oasis of the Western Desert in the early to mid-Holocene: evidence from the peripheries. *African Archaeological Review* 26: 3–43.

MCGOVERN, P. (2009). *Uncorking the Past: The Quest for Wine, Beer and Other Alcoholic Beverages*. Berkeley: University of California Press.

MIDANT-REYNES, B. (2000). *The Prehistory of Egypt*. Oxford: Blackwell.

NEUMANN, K. (2005). The romance of farming: plant domestication and farming in Africa. In A. B. Stahl (ed.), *African Archaeology: A Critical Introduction*. Oxford: Blackwell, 249–76.

REINOLD, J. (2001). Kadruka and the Neolithic of the Northern Dongola Reach. *Sudan and Nubia* 5: 4–10.

SADR, K. (1991). *The Development of Nomadism in Ancient Northeast Africa*. Philadelphia: University of Pennsylvania Press.

SAMUEL, D. (2000). Brewing-baking. In P. Nicholson and I. Shaw (eds), *Ancient Egyptian Materials and Technology*. Cambridge. Cambridge University Press, 537–76.

SUTTON, J. E. G. (1974). The aquatic civilization of Middle Africa. *Journal of African History* 15: 527–46.

TIGANI, A. (1988). *Zooarchaeology in the Middle Nile Valley: A Study of Four Neolithic Sites near Khartoum*. Oxford: British Archaeological Reports.

TRIGGER, B. G. (2003). *Understanding Early Civilizations*. Cambridge: Cambridge University Press.

VON DER WAY, T. (1997). *Tell el-Fara'in Buto 1: Ergebnisse zum Frühen Kontext Kampagnen der Jahre 1983–1989*. Mainz: Phillip von Zabern.

WASYLIKOWA, K., MITKA, J., WENDORF, F., and SCHILD, R. (1997). Exploitation of wild plants by the Early Neolithic hunter-gatherers of the Western Desert, Egypt: Nabta Playa as a case study. *Antiquity* 71: 932–41.

WENKE, R. L. (2009). *The Ancient Egyptian State*. Cambridge: Cambridge University Press.

WENDORF, F., and SCHILD, R. (1998). Nabta Playa and its role in northeastern African prehistory. *Journal of Anthropological Archaeology* 17: 97–123.

—— —— (2001). *Holocene Settlements of the Eastern Sahara*, vol. 1: *The Archaeology of Nabta Playa*. New York: Kluwer.

—— —— (2002). Implications of incipient social complexity in the Late Neolithic in the Egyptian Sahara. In R. Friedman (ed.), *Egypt and Nubia: Gifts of the Desert*. London: British Museum, 13–20.

WENGROW, D. (2001). Rethinking 'cattle cults' in early Egypt: towards a prehistoric perspective on the Narmer Palette. *Cambridge Archaeological Journal* 11: 91–104.

—— (2006). *The Archaeology of Early Egypt: Social Transformations in North-East Africa. 10.000 to 2650 BC*. Cambridge: Cambridge University Press.

WILKINSON, T. A. H. (1999). *Early Dynastic Egypt*. London: Routledge.

CHAPTER 38

PATHWAYS TO FOOD PRODUCTION IN THE SAHEL

PETER BREUNIG

INTRODUCTION

CONSIDERED globally, food production is one of the most important turning points in human history. With it came social and economic changes that paved the way for much more complex political and social systems. Older classifications of the past into rigid stages such as 'Palaeolithic' and 'Neolithic' are now viewed much more critically because linear models of development do not do justice to the complexity and diversity of the partly concurrent, often interrelated ways of life and economies of foragers, herdsmen, fishers, and farmers. Much evidence shows that cultivation does not necessarily lead to the disappearance of alternatives such as hunting and gathering or herding, but should be considered as only one among several economic strategies preference for which may change according to circumstances. For this reason, new chronological surveys use alternative concepts to divide the past into time and space—for example, economic changes or archaeological traditions—rather than the earlier 'ages and stages' (McIntosh 2006). The desirability of doing this is enhanced in Africa because of the terminological confusion over the use of the term 'Neolithic'. While defined by the presence of ceramics and grinding tools in the Francophone tradition, independently of whether or not food was produced from domesticated species (Huysecom et al. 2004: 579), in the Anglophone world the concept is always linked to agriculture and livestock keeping. As the African record shows that single elements of what was once thought in Europe and the Near East to be a single 'Neolithic complex', such as ceramics and food production, appeared (probably independently) over thousands of years, the term retains little utility for the continent's archaeology. This is all the more so as food production itself is not a temporally homogenous phenomenon in Africa, its two basic pillars—plant cultivation and domestic animals—appearing farther apart chronologically in Africa than on any other continent (Marshall and Hildebrand 2002).

THE ORIGIN OF DOMESTIC ANIMALS AND CROPS

While agriculture outside Egypt is little more than 4,000 years old, the first domestic animals go back almost twice as far. Most important in Africa are cattle, followed by sheep and goats in different proportions according to time and place. The last two certainly originated in the Near East, but opinions differ as to the time and place of the domestication of cattle and the beginning of pastoralism as a livelihood in which domestic animals were at the centre of subsistence (Gifford-Gonzalez and Hanotte, Ch. 34 above; di Lernia, Ch. 36 above). It is clear, however, that a pastoral economy in which cattle were critical was widespread over the central and southern areas of the then still Sahel-like Sahara by 5000 BC at the latest (Smith 2005).

Such an economy requires particular ecological conditions. Precipitation must not be too high, in order to keep away the tsetse fly vector that spreads trypanosomiasis, nor too low, because herds need daily access to water. In the late Holocene, suitable regions extended further and further south from the Sahara, as the desert's desiccation advanced (Smith 1980). By 2000 BC at the latest, the inroads of late Holocene aridity brought about the migration of Saharan pastoralists into the savannah south of the Sahara and the beginning of food production in the Sahel (Kuper and Kröpelin 2006).

Diffusionist explanations are now regarded rather sceptically, but population movements in general are not to be rejected out of hand. Thus, along with the seemingly plausible pressures of climate change, various finds point to migration of people from the Sahara into the Sahel. The strongest argument lies in the origin of cattle and ovicaprids. Both lack wild ancestors south of the Sahara, and the temporal patterning of radiocarbon dates associated with the oldest finds of these animals all point to the same trend: the oldest finds come from the central and eastern Sahara, while dates become more recent as they extend further south into the sub-Saharan zone (Shaw 1981; Gautier 1987; Krzyzaniak 1992).

Other arguments are furnished by similarities in the archaeological finds from both regions, including bifacially retouched, winged projectile points (Fig. 38.1). Such points are widely distributed in time and space in the Sahara (Hugot 1957), but appear rather rarely in the Sahel, and only in the context of the postulated immigration of Saharan populations. This indicates that the tradition of projectile points could have been imported into the Sahel with these populations, and at once suggests hunting. Nonetheless, archaeological analysis of the region's inventory of finds shows that hunting of wild mammals, reptiles, and birds did not play a large role in its first agropastoralist societies (Linseele 2007).

Ceramics provide a further argument for close relations between the southern Sahara and the Sahel to its south. Despite the high age of individual finds, ceramics appear in the savannahs of West Africa—in contrast to the Sahara—only from the second millennium BC, i.e. from the time of the drift south of pastoral groups. The argument that the popularity of ceramics is connected to the arrival of migrants from the Sahara is supported by the fact that in both regions the pottery of this time exhibits great similarities in technique and decorative pattern (MacDonald 1996a; Wendt 2007) (Fig. 38.2). More comprehensive large-scale studies that examine pottery assemblages from both ecological zones are, however, still needed.

The southern Sahara and the western Sahel—the region into which the pastoralists affected by the aridification of the Sahara advanced—are the homeland of the wild forms of important African crops such as pearl millet (*Pennisetum glaucum*) and African rice (*Oryza*

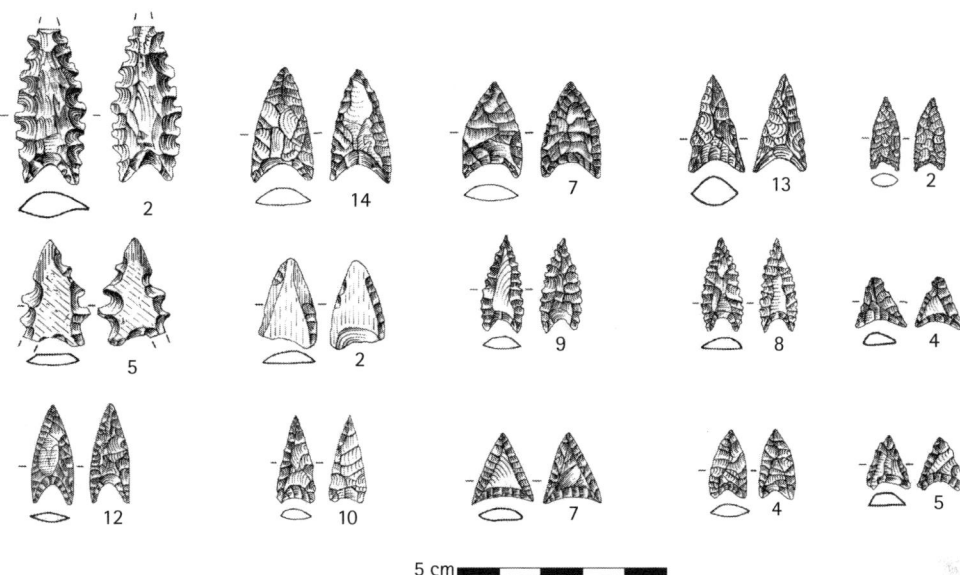

FIG. 38.1 Projectile points retouched on both surfaces from the central Sahel. The pieces come from different phases of the Gajiganna Complex in the Chad Basin of northeastern Nigeria and are dated to the second and early first millennia BC (drawings by Barbara Voss).

FIG. 38.2 Ceramic vessels with geometric decoration from the agropastoral phase (II a/b) of the type-site of the Gajiganna Complex in the Chad Basin of northeastern Nigeria (c. 1500–1000 BC). Similar specimens of contemporaneous ceramics are known from the south-central and eastern Sahara (photograph and drawing by Barbara Voss).

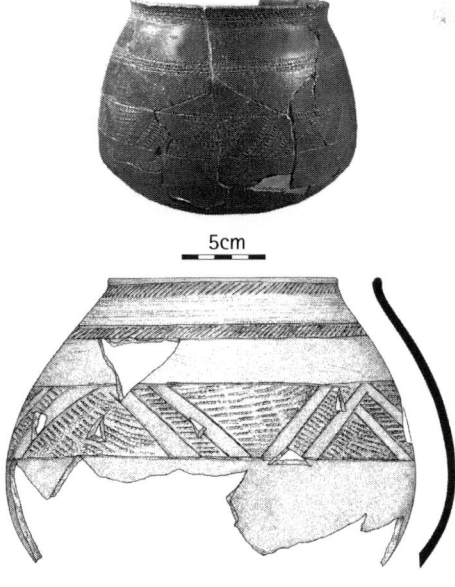

glaberrima). Along with East Africa, these areas have been considered since the 1970s to be one of the hypothetical birthplaces of Africa's crops (Harlan 1971). So far, however, research has been unable to answer certain associated central questions (Neumann 2005). For example, we still do not know to what extent increasing late Holocene aridity influenced or gave rise to the beginnings of agriculture, nor what economic role crops played in view of the savannah's rich natural food resources. It is also unclear where crops were first domesticated—in the Sahara or in the Sahel? Or, from whom the first farmers evolved: pastoralists driven out of the Sahara, local hunter-gatherers, or both?

THE FIRST FARMING COMMUNITIES

The diffusion of the pastoral economy from the Sahara into the Sahel and the nearly contemporary domestication of crops there (according to archaeobotanical evidence) suggest a connection between the two economic innovations. It is conceivable that the Saharan pastoralists were sensitized to the cultivation of certain plants through intensive use of them even before their advance into the Sahel, and that they may even have already begun cultivating them within the present-day Sahara. But until now, only the Sahel and the Sahara/Sahel borderlands have yielded indications of the formation of settled communities dependent for their subsistence on domestic animals and cultivated crops, albeit without ceasing to hunt and gather. The composition and uncertain economic meaning of these individual components, including the role of the native population in the development of the innovations, differs according to the current state of research into the place and time in which they appear. By the end of the second millennium BC, however, it is likely that populations in practically all the large regions of the Sahel had direct or indirect contact with cattle, ovicaprids, and pearl millet to begin with and perhaps other crops as well (Neumann 1999; 2003; 2005; D'Andrea and Casey 2002; Van Neer 2002; Kahlheber and Neumann 2007). Looked at globally, however, these economic innovations in sub-Saharan Africa were a relatively late phenomenon (Neumann 2003).

The evolution of food-producing communities has been better investigated, in several extensive and long-term case studies, in the West African Sahel than in the central and eastern parts of the wider Sahel region. Among the hypotheses that may be deduced from this West African evidence is the presumption that the appearance of settled farming communities in the second millennium BC unleashed an economic flowering and an associated increase in population. This is indicated by the number and size of settlements found and the accumulation of large quantities of cultural goods, for which the known case studies offer no parallels from earlier times. A further presumption is that the rise of settled farming communities was not a region-wide event affecting the whole Sahel. Instead, their early development was restricted to core areas where environmental conditions encouraged the permanent settlement of communities. In particular, the environment had to provide sufficient pasture for domestic animals and suitable fields for the cultivation of pearl millet. Clearly, the presence of adequate water played a decisive role, because the known core regions where the first settled farmers in the West African Sahel appeared all lie in well-watered districts, among them the Inner Niger Delta, the neighbourhood of Lake Chad in northeastern Nigeria, and the then lake-covered foothills of the Tichitt-Oulata-Néma escarpment in Mauritania (Fig. 38.3).

These regions have relatively low precipitation, and therefore no problem with the tsetse fly, but are still adequately and constantly supplied with water. Other regions of the Sahel stand in remarkable contrast, including northeastern Burkina Faso, where long-term field studies of the archaeological record of the second millennium BC have brought to light no evidence of a pastoral economy or the beginnings of an agricultural economy, only traces of hunting and gathering. Only at the end of that millennium do the first indications of food production appear, in the form of isolated finds of pearl millet (Vogelsang et al. 1999). Perhaps it is no accident that some centuries later, precisely in the other, richly watered regions, the beginnings of agropastoralism were followed by the first developments toward complex social systems. Regarded in this light, the second millennium BC saw the formation of the socioeconomic prerequisites for the complex societies that arose in parts of West Africa at the end of the first millennium AD (MacDonald, Ch. 57 below).

The earliest evidence of crops found to date on the Sahara–Sahel border comes from the archaeological remains, known for several decades, in the Karkarichinkat region of the lower Tilemsi Valley in northeastern Mali. Recent field work there has led to the dating of domesticated pearl millet to at least the third millennium BC, pushing back even earlier the presumed beginnings of the farming economy that stands behind it (Manning et al. 2011). Thus, the paradoxical disparity in the African and Indian (early third millennium BC; Fuller 2003) datings of domesticated pearl millet, which is of African origin, is reduced to a much smaller interval than before, and the rise of the first farming economies on the Sahara–Sahel border becomes more likely.

One of the first instances of food-producing communities known to research also lies on the Sahara–Sahel border, specifically in southeastern Mauritania along the escarpment of Dhars Tichitt, Oulata, and Néma. This area has yielded many sites, dated to the second and early/

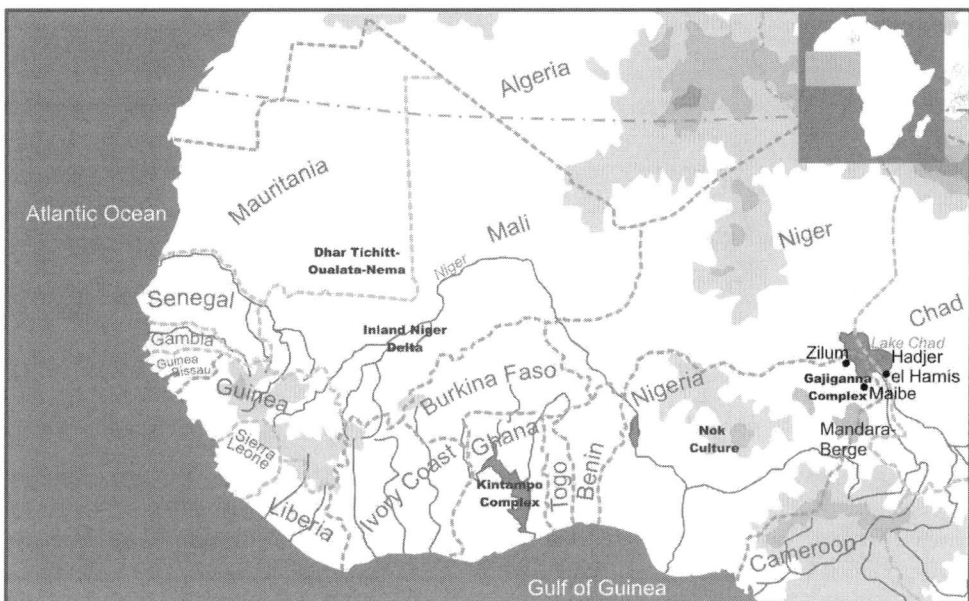

FIG. 38.3 Map of West Africa showing places mentioned in Chapter 38 and archaeological groupings (drawn by Barbara Voss).

middle first millennia BC, of a population that has for decades been associated with the rise of an agropastoral economy (Munson 1976; Amblard 1984; Holl 1986; Amblard-Pison 2006; MacDonald et al. 2009). As there are no known precursors for these sites, this economy may have come about through migration rather than through the further development of a local population. The sites themselves are found either near lakes at the foot of the escarpment or on the edge of the plateau, and there are differing opinions on their relation to each other. The plateau sites consist in part of impressively large house and farm structures built of stone. Up to 90 hectares in area, they are the oldest villages of West Africa and embody a community that must have had a social organization quite different from that of small hunter-gatherer groups (cf. MacDonald, Ch. 57 below). To a not inconsiderable degree, it is probable that the particular environmental conditions along the escarpment, especially the availability of water, made settlement of the region possible (Person et al. 1996; Holl 2009). While a transition from gathering to the cultivation of pearl millet was at first assumed (Munson 1976), more recent studies indicate that pearl millet was cultivated from the beginning of the sequence (c. 1800 BC) (Amblard 1996; Fuller et al. 2007; MacDonald et al. 2009). This may indicate that domestication itself took place elsewhere, perhaps further north, and that the settled community with its agropastoral economy came into the Tichitt–Oualata–Néma region as a complete package.

In the Chad Basin of northeastern Nigeria there arose a central Sahelian counterpart of Tichitt–Oualata–Néma, the Gajiganna Complex, discovered in the 1990s and named after the site where it was first found. This tradition began in the early second millennium BC and lasted about 1,500 years, defined by common artefacts (ceramics and bone and stone tools) and patterns of settlement, burial, and economy (Neumann 1999; Breunig and Neumann 2002a; Breunig 2005; Wendt 2007). Before the Gajiganna Complex, the region was inaccessible because of the high water levels of Lake Chad. Only when the water receded did pastoral communities penetrate the extensive clay plains (Gajiganna I), leaving small campsites with relatively few remains. Faunal remains indicate the economic importance of cattle herding (Linseele 2007). Despite archaeobotanical testing and study of plant impressions in the ceramics of this phase, however, little evidence of crops has been found (Klee et al. 2004). This suggests that the Gajiganna Complex was a prelude to the development, from pastoral forerunners, of the settled farming economy that appeared in the following phase, Gajiganna IIa/b. This picture may be false, since the evidence of crops comes exclusively from plant impressions resulting from the organic tempering of ceramics. The ceramics of phase I, are however, exclusively inorganically tempered. Only in the following phase (Gajiganna IIa/b), from around 1500 BC, do ceramics become progressively more organically tempered. No later than this time, pastoralists settled and lived in small, perhaps family-centred village settlements, mostly beside or near seasonally or continually flooded clay plains. With a settled way of life and the construction of mudbrick huts, low settlement hills arose, most with one to two metres of dense stratigraphy. Henceforth, the economic base consisted in part of cattle, ovicaprids and, to a small degree, hunting and fishing (Linseele 2007). But the great economic innovation was the cultivation of pearl millet, demonstrated by the impressions of grains in potsherds dated to 1200 BC (Klee et al. 2004). The greatest density of settlements extends from c. 1500 to 1000 BC, but then appears to come to an abrupt end (Fig. 38.4).

The Inland Niger Delta is comparable to the Chad Basin in the richness of its aquatic environment and availability of resources. Here, too, Holocene settlement began in the second millennium BC, after the area, just like the Chad Basin, became accessible because of more arid climatic conditions (MacDonald 1996b). One of the colonizing groups, called Kobadi, were fishermen

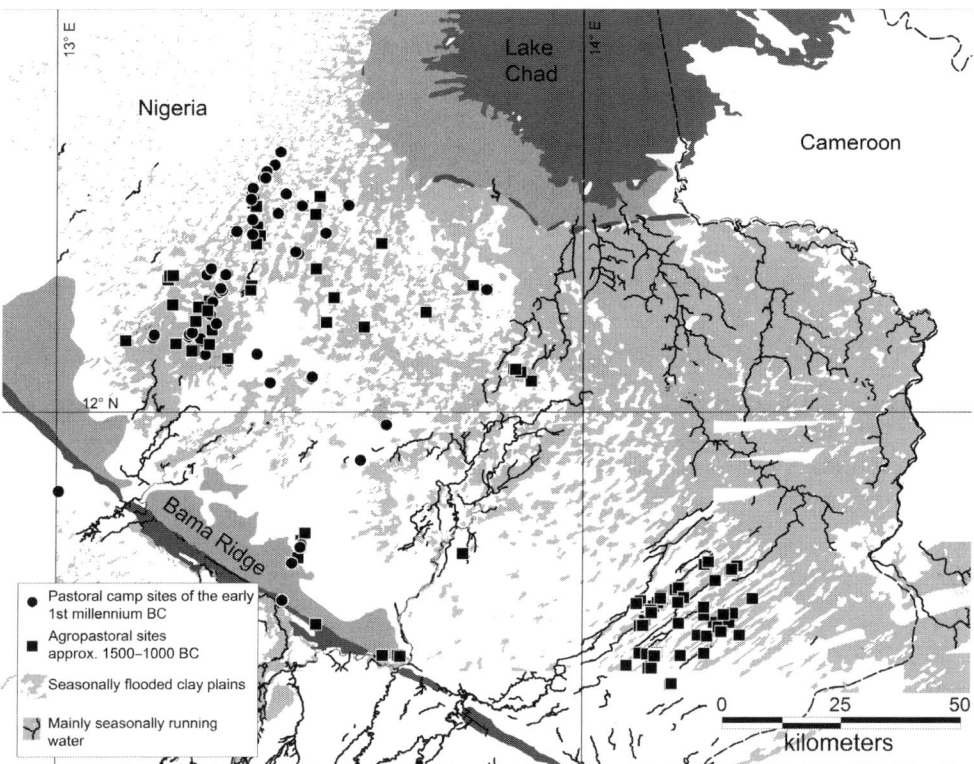

FIG. 38.4 Map of the Chad Basin in northeastern Nigeria with archaeological sites from the pastoral and agropastoral phases of the Gajiganna Complex (second millennium BC). The high density of sites indicates a flowering of the first food-producing communities in the region.

who had neither domestic animals nor crops (Raimbault and Dutour 1989; MacDonald and Van Neer 1994). About the middle of the second millennium BC, agropastoralist communities migrated from the north, including the Tichitt–Oualata–Néma region, among others, into the Inland Delta (Ndondi–Tossokel in the Méma region, Windé Koroji in the Gourma region), interacting with the resident Kobadi population (MacDonald 1996a). The Inland Niger Delta thus provides further evidence of the beginnings of an agropastoralist economy, initiated by populations from the north, in the second millennium BC, but also evidence that communities with different origins and subsistence economies existed simultaneously side by side.

THE ERA AFTER THE FIRST FOOD PRODUCERS

In the broad context of human history, food production in the Sahel, as elsewhere in the world, represents a point of no return. The advantages of domestic animals and crops and the relative independence from less controllable natural resources that they offered were obvious and enticing, unleashing a dynamic process of development. That only about 3,000 years passed between the first farmers and the first great West African states shows how rapidly society evolved there in comparison with other regions of the world. But this was no linear development, despite its swiftness. After the flowering of the second millennium, the first food-producing communities experienced a profound crisis (Breunig and Neumann 2002b). This is indicated by the fact that the traditions of the above-mentioned complexes are interrupted or are scarcely attested by archaeology in the following millennium. Villages and sites rich in finds are succeeded by nothing at all or by sparse remains of human settlement. The Tichitt–Oualata–Néma tradition ended without a comparable successor. In the Gajiganna Complex, the era of settlement mound formation is followed by shallow accumulations of finds that bespeak a new way of life characterized by high mobility. In the Sahel of Burkina Faso, the archaeology of the first millennium BC is almost wholly unknown.

The change or collapse of the first farming communities thus seems to have been a supraregional, zone-encompassing phenomenon, and consequently one with supraregional origins. A first possibility is an irruption of drought in the early first millennium BC (Breunig and Neumann 2002b). Greater dryness would have affected both pastures and crop yields, leaving the wettest regions, such as the Inland Niger Delta or the Lake Chad area, less affected. But it is also conceivable that the great second millennium BC experiment with food production, settled life, and the break with an ancestral way of life dependent on hunting and gathering led, along with the drought, to social, ecological, economic, or health problems. Food production means accumulation of property and thereby creates social divisions and the potential for conflict within, or between, communities. Food production also leads inevitably to ecological changes through overgrazing, loss of woodland, and degradation of the soil. If there is little room for escape into still unaffected areas, a decline in harvests is the result, with the potential for social conflict. For a large community with domestic animals, living at close quarters for a long time also entails medical problems up to the level of epidemics. The widespread disappearance of the first farming traditions from the archaeological picture suggests that they were afflicted by one or more of these problems. One reaction may have been a reversion to greater mobility and intensified grazing, which would explain the decline in finds. Testing these or other explanations of the first-millennium BC crisis requires more detailed ecological and economic analysis of more suitable and extensive archaeological archives—something at which only attempts have been made in the Sahel so far. In the case of the Gajiganna Complex in the Chad Basin of northeastern Nigeria, relevant recent studies have yielded indications that the crisis there unleashed a cultural upheaval beginning around 500 BC (called Gajiganna Phase III, because its ceramics belong to the tradition of the foregoing phases). The upheaval encompassed practically all aspects of the life of that time, and is without parallel for this era in the Sahel (Breunig 2009).

The fundamental change is immediately evident in the new settlements. While the first farmers of the second millennium BC lived in what were probably family-organized villages or hamlets averaging hardly more than 2–3 ha in area, settlements now attain an area of 10 ha and, in some cases, even up to 30 ha, in which a quite differently organized society must have existed. Besides the considerable growth, there is a further novelty in the fact that the settlements in one region are completely surrounded by ditches, discovered by geomagnetic surveys and test pits. This has been most thoroughly studied at the site of Zilum (Magnavita et al. 2006) (Fig. 38.5). There and in other places, ditches that are many hundreds of metres long and several metres broad and deep suggest considerable communal construction work,

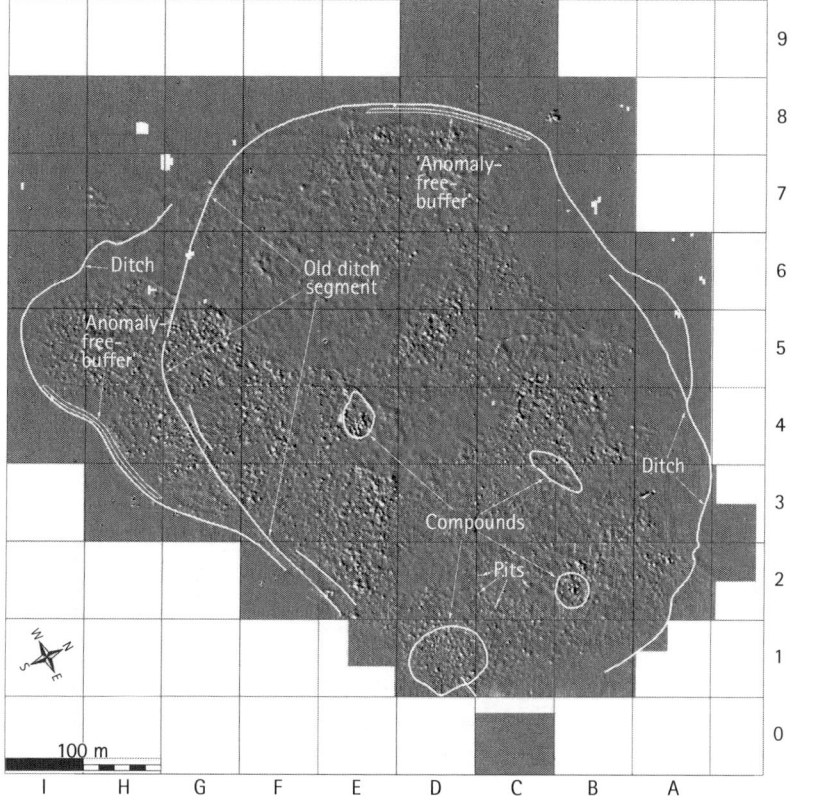

FIG. 38.5 Plan of geomagnetic survey of the mid-first millennium BC settlement of Zilum, Chad Basin, Nigeria (from Magnavita et al. 2006). The plan shows quarries discovered by excavation, round structures that probably mark the boundaries of compounds, and the several construction phases of the ditches that surrounded the settlement. A zone free of finds suggests that a wall may have stood parallel to the ditch. Test trenches prompted by magnetic data uncovered conical anomalies that were underground granaries.

perhaps organized by means of leadership and its attendant social differentiation. Social differentiation is also indicated by the beginnings of specialized handcrafts, such as the mass production of pottery. For example, the quantity of ceramics excavated from test areas at a 10ha site called Maibe, dated to *c.* 500 BC, implies the production of 1,500 tonnes of pottery and some 100,000 vessels. It is hard to imagine such a quantity without the presence of specialized potters, especially as radiocarbon dates suggest the settlement may have existed for little more than a century. The supply of raw material for stone tools also points to specialization. Stone was indispensable for grinding equipment and ground stone axes (a projected 200 kg at Maibe). Since stone is not found in the Chad Basin, it must have been brought from up to 200 km away. In the second and early first millennia BC, there were more or less regional patterns in the geographical distribution of the types of stone in use (e.g. sandstone dominated in the western part of Gajiganna Complex distribution area, granite to the east). The pattern has to do mostly with the corresponding range of the deposits, their accessibility, and their distance from the archaeological sites. Inventories of finds from around 500 BC reveal a

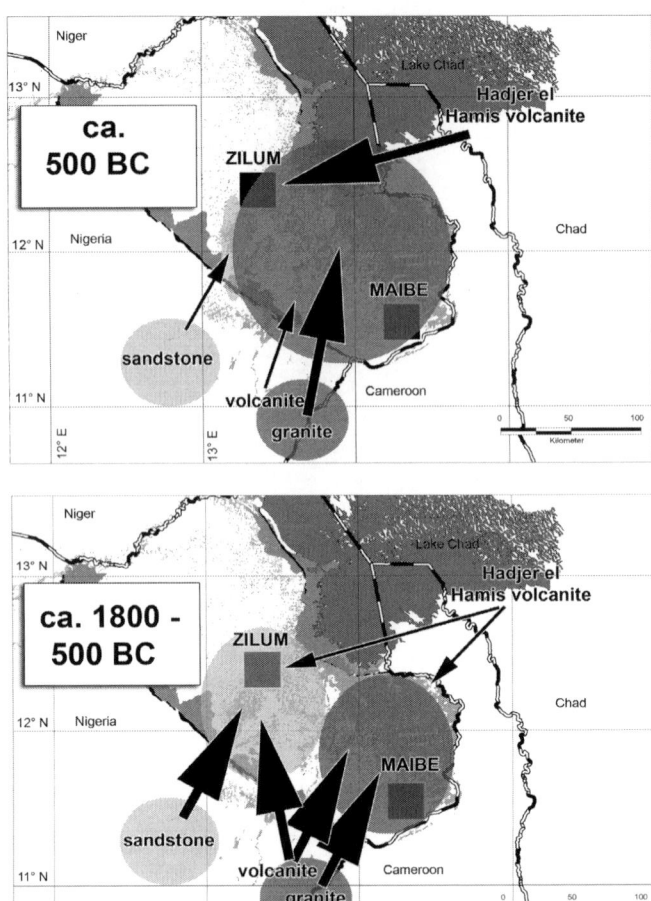

FIG. 38.6 Schematic representation of the supply of lithic raw material for the stoneless Chad Basin during the time of the first food-producing communities of the Gajiganna Complex (redrawn after Rupp 2005).

reorganization of the system (Fig. 38.6). Formerly insignificant sources of volcanic rock, such as Hadjer el Hamis (Chad) to the south of Lake Chad, were opened, replacing or supplementing the vulcanite previously obtained from the Mandara Mountains in the southern Chad Basin. There was also a uniform diffusion of all raw materials without regional preferences. The market was thus homogenized in that all products were available in all areas (Rupp 2005). This organized—and perhaps in case of need forced—procurement of resources may have promoted the emergence of traders as a powerful social group, of the kind that took part in the exchange of goods across the Sahara only a few centuries later.

The dimensions of the changes are also seen in the fact that in the mid-first millennium BC more people lived together in one place than ever before in sub-Saharan Africa. Projections based on house numbers suggest population figures of a few thousand inhabitants. Their communal life rested on a productive economy that, for the first time in the region, no longer depended on the cultivation of pearl millet, but was supplemented by new

FIG. 38.7 Ceramic vessels from the Maibe site, Chad Basin, northeastern Nigeria, c. 500 BC.

crops, such as cowpeas (*Vigna unguiculata*) (Kahlheber and Neumann 2007). Countless granary pits indicate that a surplus was the result (Fig. 38.5). Very large ceramic vessels up to a metre in height, appearing for the first time, probably also served the increased need for stockpiling (Fig. 38.7). The positioning of storage capacity within settlements is an indication of disturbed times, consistent with fortifying measures such as the defence of settlements by ditches. Population growth and a productive economy were followed by the first appearance of iron, a technological innovation with far-reaching consequences for society and the environment alike (McIntosh and McIntosh 1988). In the Chad Basin, however, iron is only one of the many changes at this time and, according to the available chronological evidence, not the first.

No comparable developments effecting such a profound transformation of social, economic, and material life are known in other regions of the Sahel in the first millennium BC. Further south, however, in central Nigeria, the Nok Culture may be an exception. Dating

FIG. 38.8 Almost life-size head of a Nok Culture terracotta, excavated from the Nok site of Kushe, Nigeria, in March 2010 (photographs courtesy of Barbara Voss).

mostly to the first millennium BC, its impressive terracottas, found over an area of 100,000 km² (Fagg 1977) (Fig. 38.8), point to a society with common (and complex) rituals or religious practices. Studies now under way (Breunig and Rupp 2010) indicate that the Nok Culture, like contemporary communities in the Chad Basin, depended principally on the cultivation of pearl millet and cowpeas (Kahlheber et al. 2009). No conceivable forerunners from the second millennium BC have yet been discovered, so Nok represents the beginning of food production in this zone. The Nok sites, located by case studies in the central area of distribution, are mostly several hectares in area and lie closer together than the modern settlements (Rupp 2010). As in the Chad Basin, an abrupt growth in population seems to have accompanied the establishment of economies based on food production.

CONCLUSION

The foregoing archaeological data argue that the origin of food production in the Sahel was the Sahara, at least in its pastoral component. Those from the better studied western Sahel argue further for a subdivision—only partly confirmed for the east—of the beginning of food production into three phases (Fig. 38.9). The first of these comprises the second millennium BC, and saw the massive immigration of pastoral communities from the southern Sahara and the establishment and flowering of settled, food-producing communities in some core regions. One of the biggest unanswered questions is whether the cultivation of pearl millet as the first and only crop was a Sahelian innovation or whether it was imported along with domestic animals by incoming Saharan pastoralists. The answer probably lies north of the Sahel in the Sahara–Sahel border area.

The second phase comprises the crisis into which apparently all the farming communities of the western Sahel fell during the first millennium BC, as indicated by the disappearance or diminution of their remains in the archaeological record. Thereafter, the third phase is characterized by a renewed cultural and economic flowering, to which new crops probably contributed. They were accompanied by new forms of settlement and by social changes, including craft specialization and increased population density. An important technological

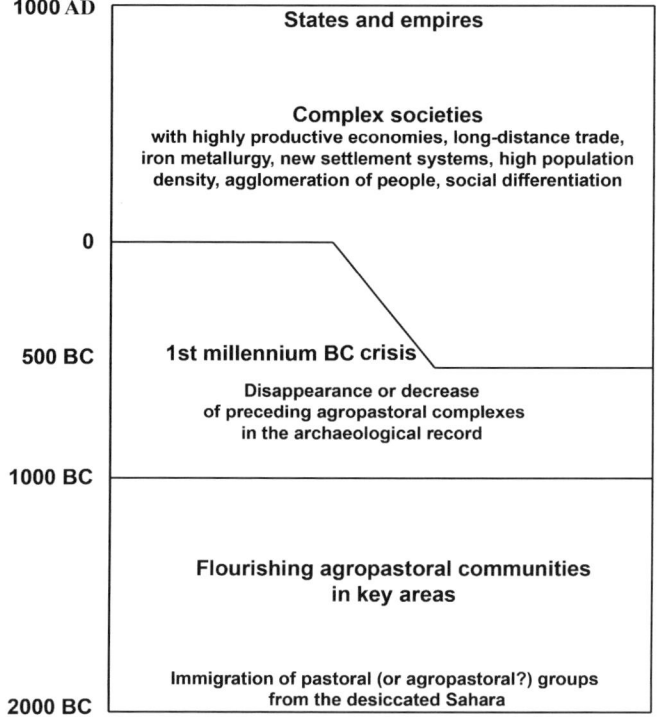

FIG. 38.9 Schematic representation of the development of the early phases of food production in the West African Sahel.

innovation of this phase was the smelting of iron. In some regions, such as the Chad Basin of Nigeria and the area of the central Nigerian Nok Culture, the changes took place around 500 BC, or perhaps even slightly earlier. In other parts of the Sahel, comparable developments are first found in the first millennium AD. The changes of this phase created the economic and social basis for the complex world of the first states at the end of that millennium.

REFERENCES

AMBLARD, S. (1984). *Tichitt-Walata: Civilisation et Industrie Lithique*. Paris: Éditions Recherches sur les Civilisations.

—— (1996). Agricultural evidence and its interpretation on the Dhars Tichitt and Oualata, south-eastern Mauritania. In G. Pwiti and R. Soper (eds), *Aspects of African Archaeology*. Harare: University of Zimbabwe, 421–7.

AMBLARD-PISON, S. (2006). *Communautés Villageoises Néolithiques des Dhars Tichitt et Oualata (Mauritanie)*. Oxford: Archaeopress.

BREUNIG, P. (2005). Groundwork of human occupation in the Chad Basin, Northeast Nigeria, 2000 BC–1000 AD. In A. Ogundiran (ed.), *Precolonial Nigeria: Essays in Honor of Toyin Falola*. Trenton: Africa World Press, 105–31.

—— (2009). Cultural change in the first millennium BC: evidence from Nigeria, West Africa. In S. Magnavita, L. Koté, P. Breunig, and O. A. Idé (eds), *Crossroads/Carrefour Sahel:*

Cultural and Technological Developments in First Millennium BC/AD West Africa. Frankfurt: Africa Magna, 15–26.

BREUNIG and NEUMANN, K. (2002a). From hunters and gatherers to food producers: new archaeological and archaeobotanical evidence from the West African Sahel. In F. A. Hassan (ed.), *Droughts, Food and Culture. Ecological Change and Food Security in Africa's Later Prehistory*. New York: Kluwer Academic/Plenum, 123–55.

—— (2002b). Continuity or discontinuity? The 1st millennium BC-crisis in West African prehistory. In Jennerstrasse 8 (eds), *Tides of the Desert*. Cologne: Heinrich Barth Institut, 491–505.

—— and RUPP, N. (2010). Outline of a new research project on the Nok Culture of central Nigeria, West Africa. *Nyame Akuma* 73: 46–54.

D'ANDREA, A. C., and CASEY, J. (2002). Pearl millet and Kintampo subsistence. *African Archaeological Review* 19: 147–73.

FAGG, B. (1977). *Nok Terracottas*. Lagos: Nigerian Museums.

FULLER, D. Q. (2003). African crops in prehistoric South Asia: a critical review. In K. Neumann, A. Butler, and S. Kahlheber (eds), *Food, Fuel and Fields: Progress in African Archaeobotany*. Cologne: Heinrich Barth Institut, 239–71.

——, MACDONALD, K.C., and VERNET, R. (2007). Early domesticated pearl millet in Dhar Néma (Mauritania): evidence of crop processing waste as ceramic temper. In R. Cappers (ed.), *Fields of Change: Progress in African Archaeobotany*. Groningen: Barkhuis, 71–6.

GAUTIER, A. (1987). Prehistoric men and cattle in North Africa: a dearth of data and a surfeit of models. In A. E. Close (ed.), *Prehistory of Arid North Africa: Essays in Honor of Fred Wendorf*. Dallas: Southern Methodist University Press, 163–87.

HARLAN, J. R. (1971). Agricultural origins: centers and non-centers. *Science* 174: 468–74.

HOLL, A. F. C. (1986). *Economie et société Néolithique du Dhar Tichitt (Mauritanie)*. Paris: Éditions Recherche sur les Civilisations.

—— (2009). Coping with uncertainty: Neolithic life in the Dhar Tichitt-Walata, Maurit (*ca.* 4000–2300 BP). *Comptes Rendus Géoscience* 341: 703–12.

HUGOT, H. J. (1957). Essai sur les armatures de pointes de flèches du Sahara. *Libyca* 5: 89–236.

HUYSECOM, E., OZAINNE, S., RAELI, F., BALLOUCHE, A., RASSE, M., and STOKES, S. (2004). Ounjougou (Mali): a history of Holocene settlement at the southern edge of the Sahara. *Antiquity* 78: 579–93.

KAHLHEBER, S., and NEUMANN, K. (2007). The development of plant cultivation in semi-arid West Africa. In T. Denham, J. Iriarte, and L. Vrydaghs (eds), *Rethinking Agriculture: Archaeological and Ethnoarchaeological Perspectives*. Walnut Creek, Calif.: Left Coast Press, 320–46.

—— HÖHN, A., and RUPP, N. (2009). Archaeobotanical studies at Nok sites: an interim report. *Nyame Akuma* 71: 2–17.

KLEE, M., ZACH, B., and STIKA, H. P. (2004). Four thousand years of plant exploitation in the Lake Chad Basin (Nigeria), part III: plant impressions in potsherds from the Final Stone Age Gajiganna Culture. *Vegetation History and Archaeobotany* 13: 131–42.

KRZYZANIAK, L. (1992). The later prehistory of the upper (main) Nile: comments on the current state of research. In F. Klees and R. Kuper (eds), *New Light on the Northeast African Past: Current Prehistoric Research*. Cologne: Heinrich Barth Institut, 239–48.

KUPER, R., and KRÖPELIN, S. (2006). Climate controlled Holocene occupation in the Sahara: motor of Africa's evolution. *Science* 313: 803–7.

LINSEELE, V. (2007). *Archaeofaunal Remains from the Past 4000 Years in Sahelian West Africa: Domestic Livestock, Subsistence Strategies and Environmental Changes*. Oxford: Archaeopress.

MacDonald, K. C. (1996a). Tichitt-Walata and the Middle Niger: evidence for cultural contact in the second millennium BC. In G. Pwiti and R. Soper (eds), *Aspects of African Archaeology*. Harare: University of Zimbabwe, 429–40.

—— (1996b). The Windé Koroji Complex: evidence for the peopling of the eastern Inland Niger Delta (2100–500 BC). *Préhistoire Anthropologie Méditerranéennes* 5: 147–65.

—— and Van Neer, W. (1994). Specialised fishing peoples in the Later Holocene of the Méma Region (Mali). *Annales du Musée Royal de l'Afrique Centrale, Sciences Zoologiques* 274: 243–51.

—— Vernet, R., Martinón-Torres, M., and Fuller, D. Q. (2009). Dhar Néma: from early agriculture to metallurgy in southeastern Mauritania. *Azania: Archaeological Research in Africa* 44: 3–48.

Magnavita, C., Breunig, P., Ameje, J., and Posselt, M. (2006). Zilum: a mid-first millennium BC fortified settlement near Lake Chad. *Journal of African Archaeology* 4: 153–69.

Manning, K., Pelling, R., Higham, T., Schwenninger, J.-L., and Fuller, D. Q. (2011). 4500-year old domesticated pearl millet (*Pennisetum glaucum*) from the Tilemsi Valley, Mali: new insights into an alternative cereal domestication pathway. *Journal of Archaeological Science* 38: 312–22.

Marshall, F., and Hildebrand, E. (2002). Cattle before crops: the beginnings of food production in Africa. *Journal of World Prehistory* 16: 99–143.

McIntosh, S. K. (2006). The Holocene prehistory of West Africa 10,000–1000 BP. In E. K. Akyeampong (ed.), *Themes in West Africa's History*. Oxford: James Currey, 11–32.

—— and McIntosh, R. J. (1988). From stone to metal: new perspectives on the later prehistory of West Africa. *Journal of World Prehistory* 2: 89–133.

Munson, P. J. (1976). Archaeological data on the origins of cultivation in the southwestern Sahara and their implications for West Africa. In J. R. Harlan, J. M. De Wet, and A. B. L. Stemler (eds), *Origins of African Plant Domestication*. The Hague: Mouton, 187–210.

Neumann, K. (1999). Early plant food production in the West African Sahel: new evidence from the Frankfurt project. In M. Van Der Veen (ed.), *The Exploitation of Plant Resources in Ancient Africa*. New York: Kluwer Academic/Plenum, 73–80.

—— (2003). The late emergence of agriculture in Sub-Saharan Africa: archaeological evidence and ecological considerations. In K. Neumann, A. Butler, and S. Kahlheber (eds), *Food, Fuel and Fields: Progress in African Archaeobotany*. Cologne: Heinrich Barth Institut, 71–92.

—— (2005). The romance of farming: plant cultivation and domestication in Africa. In A. B. Stahl (ed.), *African Archaeology: A Critical Introduction*. Oxford: Blackwell, 249–75.

Person, A., Amblard-Pison, S., Saoudi, N. E., Saliège, J. F., and Gérard, M. (1996). Les Dhars de la Mauritanie sud-orientale: environnements refuges sahariens au Néolithique. *Préhistoire Anthropologie Méditerranéennes*, 5: 119–34.

Raimbault, M., and Dutour, O. (1989). Les nouvelles données du site néolithique de Kobadi dans le Sahel Malien: la mission 1989. *Travaux de LAPMO* 1989: 175–83.

Rupp, N. (2005). Land ohne Steine: die Rohmaterialversorgung in Nordost-Nigeria von der Endsteinzeit bis zur Eisenzeit. Ph.D thesis, Goethe University, Frankfurt-am-Main. http://publikationen.ub.uni-frankfurt.de/volltexte/2005/2355/

—— (2010). Beyond art. Archaeological studies on the Nok Culture, central Nigeria. In P. Allsworth-Jones (ed.), *West African Archaeology: New Developments, New Perspectives*. Oxford: Archaeopress, 67–78.

Shaw, T. (1981). The Late Stone Age in West Africa and the beginnings of African food production. In C. Roubet, H. J. Hugot, and G. Souville (eds), *Préhistoire Africaine: Mélanges Offerts au Doyen Lionel Balout*. Paris: Éditions ADPF, 213–35.

SMITH, A. B. (1980). Domesticated cattle in the Sahara and their introduction into West Africa. In M. A. J. Williams and H. Faure (eds), *The Sahara and the Nile*. Rotterdam: Balkema, 489–501.

—— (2005). *African Herders: Emergence of Pastoral Traditions*. Walnut Creek, Calif.: AltaMira Press.

VAN NEER, W. (2002). Food security in Western and Central Africa during the Late Holocene: the role of domestic stock keeping, hunting and fishing. In F. A. Hassan (ed.), *Droughts, Food and Culture: Ecological Change and Food Security in Africa's Later Prehistory*. New York: Kluwer Academic/Plenum, 251–74.

VOGELSANG, R., ALBERT, K. D., and KAHLHEBER, S. (1999). Le sable savant: les cordons dunaires sahéliens au Burkina Faso comme archive archéologique et paléoécologique du Holocène. *Sahara* 11: 51–68.

WENDT, K. P. (2007). *Gajiganna: Analysis of Stratigraphies and Pottery of a Final Stone Age Culture of Northeast Nigeria*. Frankfurt: Africa Magna.

CHAPTER 39

ARCHAEOLOGICAL EVIDENCE FOR THE EMERGENCE OF FOOD PRODUCTION IN THE HORN OF AFRICA

MATTHEW CURTIS

INTRODUCTION

THE Horn of Africa (Fig. 39.1) is one of Africa's most culturally varied regions and the world's most physiographically diverse areas, possessing an extensive range of climates, topographies, vegetation, and soils, often found vertically stratified over short horizontal distances. Food-producing communities in the Ethiopian and Eritrean highlands, in particular, benefit from extensive montane environments where tropical climates are tempered by altitude and patterns of precipitation and soil conditions are conducive for the cultivation of crops of Western Asian origin, such as wheat and barley, along with a wide range of African tropical vegetables and grains. Western Asian crops require cool season growth, while African cultivars are adapted to shorter day lengths and summer rain. The highlands provide conditions suitable for both, and also contain large plateau environments advantageous for cattle grazing, ample mountain landscapes for caprine (goat and sheep) pasturage, and corridors for seasonal population movement via extensive river and stream valleys that directly link highland and lowland areas and facilitate productive pastoral transhumance patterns.

Food production in the highlands of northern and central Ethiopia and Eritrea is characterized by cultivation of t'ef, wheat, barley, and millet grain crops, as well as a number of legumes, and small-scale keeping of cattle, goat, and sheep. T'ef (*Eragrostis tef*), a highly nutritious grain, is vital to Ethiopian and Eritrean highland food traditions, being the preferred base for the making of *injera*, a fermented griddle bread that is the region's primary staple food. Its fast maturation, ability to grow in a wide range of soil types, and drought- and

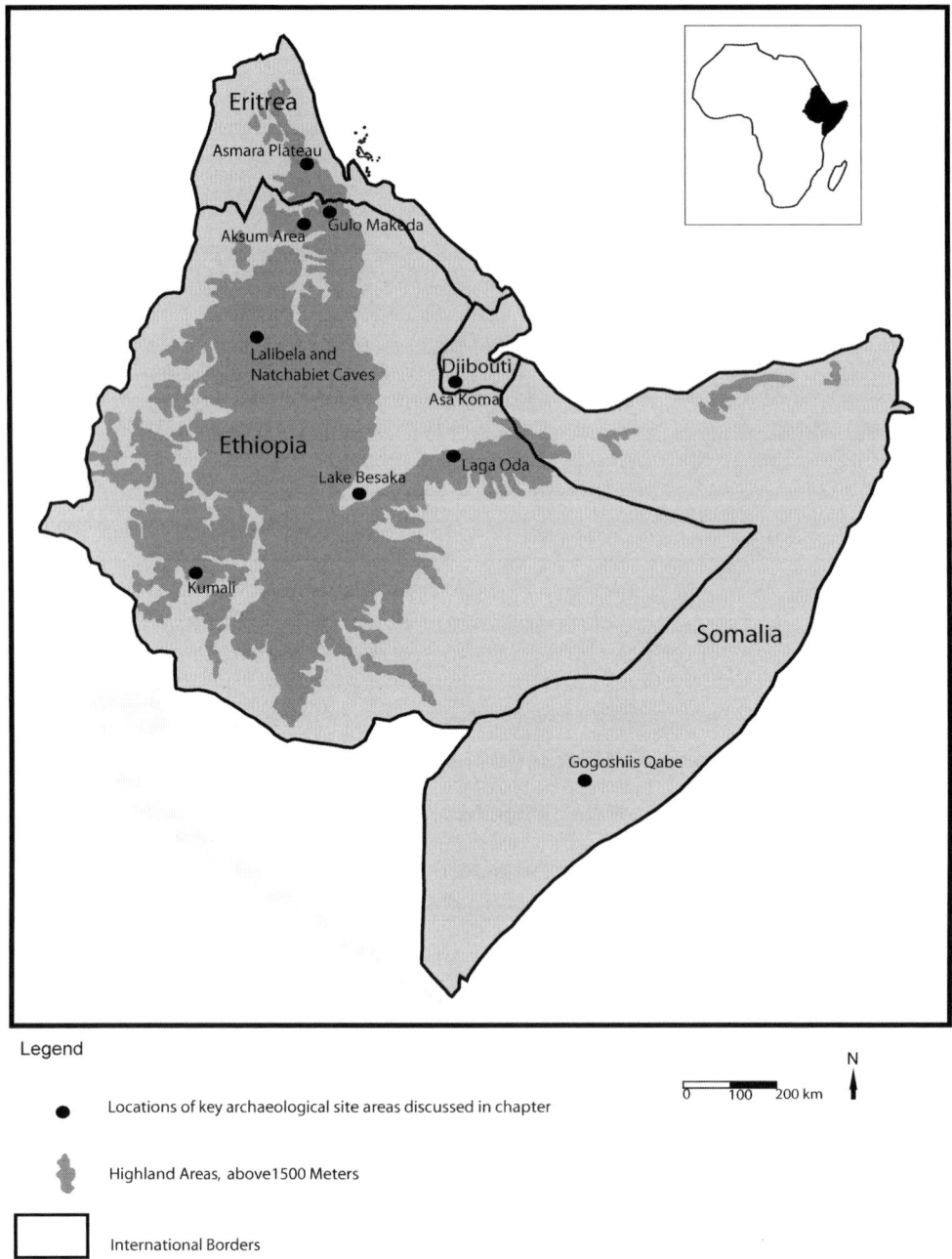

Legend

● Locations of key archaeological site areas discussed in chapter

Highland Areas, above1500 Meters

International Borders

N

0   100   200 km

FIG. 39.1 Map of the Horn of Africa showing archaeological sites and localities mentioned in Chapter 39.

pest-resistance qualities make t'ef the most widespread of crops and central to understanding the origins of food production in the region (Tefera and Ketema 2001; D'Andrea 2008). The adjacent lowlands of western Ethiopia and Eritrea have food-producing traditions centred on sorghum cultivation and cattle and caprine pastoralism. Food production traditions in the eastern lowlands of Eritrea, Djibouti, eastern Ethiopia, and Somalia focus primarily on pastoralism, with a particular emphasis on camels. Highland southwestern Ethiopia and the adjacent south-central Rift Valley region are home to a continuum of food-producing traditions encompassing pastoralism, agropastoralism, horticulture, and more intensive forms of agriculture (Stump, Ch. 46 below). Particularly important are horticultural traditions focusing on the vegetatively propagated tuber crops of enset (*Ensete ventricosum*) and yams (*Dioscorea cayenenis* and related species). Enset, an endemic domesticate of the Horn that provides a nutritious starchy food in small areas without terracing and is both drought- and pest-resistant, has a widespread, and probably very ancient, presence in the food production traditions of southwestern and south-central Ethiopia (Brandt et al. 1997). As it does today, enset cultivation probably supported substantial human population densities (Fig. 39.2) and was part of a vegetative agricultural tradition, including the propagation of other tuber crops such as yams that largely characterized the southern highlands of the Horn of Africa before the arrival of plough-using farmers in the historic period.

In consequence of its diverse climate, physiography, human landscapes, and dynamic food-producing systems the Horn has long been recognized as a major world centre of plant domesticates, possesses diversity in cattle and goat breeds, and provides some of the densest and most varied concentrations of ancient pastoral rock art in Africa (not discussed further here for lack of space, but see Smith, Ch. 11 above). As with two neighbouring regions, the Sahel (Barich, Ch. 31 above) and East Africa (Lane, Ch. 40 below), domesticated cattle entered local economies before the archaeologically visible appearance of domesticated plants in the early/mid-first millennium BC. Archaeological research carried out over the last two decades suggests that the latter period was crucial for changes in settlement, technology, and economies that then helped bring about the appearance of

FIG. 39.2 Barley field (foreground) and enset plants (background) in the Gamo Highlands of southwestern Ethiopia, 2008 (photograph, Matthew Curtis).

complex societies in the region (Finneran 2007; Curtis 2008; Fattovich 2010; Phillipson, Ch. 55 below).

THE MIDDLE TO LATE HOLOCENE TRANSITION AND THE FIRST APPEARANCE OF FOOD PRODUCTION IN THE HORN

A central problem with understanding the transition from early/mid-Holocene foraging economies to mid/late Holocene food-producing economies in the Horn is the relative dearth of archaeological investigation of sites, with deposits spanning the crucial transitional period *c.* 5000–1000 BC that include both kinds of occupation. Evidence for a shift to food production during this period must thus be gleaned from a mere handful of excavated sites, notably Lake Besaka (Clark and Williams 1978; Brandt 1980) and Asa Koma (Gutherz et al. 1996; Lesur 2007). In many areas that have been intensively surveyed, such as Eritrea's Asmara Plateau or that around Aksum, Ethiopia, fairly detailed documentation of both domesticated cattle and caprines and domesticated plants during the first millennium BC remains unmatched by evidence of earlier, non-food producing economies (Curtis and Schmidt 2008; D'Andrea et al. 2008a; Curtis 2009). Compounding this paucity of mid- to late Holocene sites is the general investigative bias toward highland (>1,500 m) areas in the northern Horn (Tigray and Eritrea) and toward sedentary village or proto-urban site types dating to the terminal part of this crucial time frame (i.e. 'pre-Aksumite', 'proto-Aksumite', and 'Aksumite' periods of the first millennium BC to first millennium AD). Only very recently have archaeological studies of food production focused on areas outside the northern Horn, such as southwestern Ethiopia. Here, several rockshelters with substantial archaeological deposits have been located in the Kafa region, but only one (Kumali) spans the middle to later Holocene (Hildebrand and Brandt 2010; Hildebrand et al. 2010). It is not surprising, then, that many interpretations concerning the transition to food production in the Horn draw on analyses of pastoral rock art (e.g. Brandt and Carder 1987), historical linguistics (e.g. Ehret 1979), surface artefacts (e.g. Fattovich 1988), and (more indirectly) excavations in areas outside the Horn proper, such as the Gash Delta of eastern Sudan (Fattovich 1984).

The middle to late Holocene transition nevertheless seems to have been critical for the incorporation of domesticated animals and plants into both highland and lowland economies in the Horn of Africa. Overall, for much of the early and middle Holocene (*c.* 9000–3500 BC), the Eritrean/Ethiopian highlands saw abundant and evenly distributed (less seasonal) rainfall, as evidenced by increased arboreal pollen, high lake and river levels, soil formation, and low river turbidity (Gebru et al. 2009; Marshall et al. 2009). Thereafter, climate became more arid, punctuated by three shorter moist phases (2000–1500 BC; 500 BC–AD 500; AD 1000–1040) and two more arid ones (1500–500 BC; AD 500–1000) (Brancaccio et al. 1997; Berakhi et al. 1998; Machado et al. 1998). The first archaeological evidence for domesticated animals appears *c.* 2500 BC, with domesticated plants following around 800 BC within agropastoral or mixed farming traditions.

Summarizing the archaeological evidence for domesticated animals in the Horn

Cattle

The earliest domestic cattle remains (*Bos taurus*) appear in the regional archaeological record from the third millennium BC, at least 2,000 years after their appearance in the Sudanese Nile Valley and at least 3,000 after their appearance across the Red Sea in Yemen (Harrower et al. 2010). In Djibouti, Asa Koma (Guérin and Faure 1996; Gutherz et al. 1996; Lesur 2007), an open-air site in the Gobaad Plain near Lake Abhé, has produced domesticated cattle bones in deposits dating to *c*. 2000 BC that are suggestive of a community largely reliant on wild animal resources, including a range of semi-arid savannah terrestrial species and large quantities of fish. Freshwater fish (mostly tilapia and catfish) constitute 96 per cent of the total faunal assemblage at Asa Koma, but terrestrial mammals such as hare, side-striped jackal, dik-dik, dorcas gazelle and bushbuck are also present (Lesur 2007).

Further south, excavated cattle remains from Gogoshiis Qabe rockshelter, Somalia, date to somewhere between 2300 and 1000 BC (Brandt and Carder 1987) and, like Asa Koma, suggest cattle pastoralism within a largely foraging economy. In the Ethiopian Rift Valley, cattle teeth fragments occur at the third millennium BC FeJx 3 site at Lake Besaka (Brandt 1986). Unlike Asa Koma, the Lake Besaka finds are associated with low lake levels and an absence of the fish found in older layers of the same deposit. A broader discontinuity in material culture from earlier 'foraging' occupations at Lake Besaka may also be evident, with one component of this an increased number of stone scrapers similar to those used recently in the Horn by hide tanners (Brandt 1996; Weedman 2006). A stone bowl fragment similar in form to stone bowls found at Pastoral Neolithic sites in Kenya and Tanzania (e.g. Bower and Nelson 1978), in the same occupation phase as the cattle remains, points to possible regional connections that warrant further investigation.

Several highland rockshelter sites have also produced cattle remains from datable contexts. At Laga Oda, near Dire Dawa in the foothills of Ethiopia's eastern highlands, fragmentary faunal remains of domestic cattle are associated with microlithic tools, ostrich eggshell beads, ochre, and pottery in contexts thought to date to *c*. 2000 BC (Clark and Williams 1978). Sickle sheen gloss and polish observed on stone tools that implies intensive wild grass (sorghum? millet?) collection suggests that cattle keeping was combined with the use of wild grains (Clark and Prince 1978). Various rockshelters in Tigray (Barnett 1999; Finneran 2000a, 2000b) have also produced cattle, but with only very limited information on the dating of the relevant deposits. Elsewhere, Dombrowski (1970) found cattle associated with caprines and domesticated barley and legumes in a mid-first-millennium BC rockshelter just east of Lake Tana, while in southwestern Ethiopia cattle were kept by people who made pottery and microlithic tools by at least 2000 years ago (Hildebrand and Brandt 2010; Hildebrand et al. 2010).

Domesticated cattle remains are present in significant quantities in early/mid-first-millennium BC Ancient Ona village sites in the greater Asmara area (Shoshani et al. 2008; Schmidt 2009), as well as at Kidane Mehret and Ona Nagast in the Aksum area of Tigray, Ethiopia (Cain 2000; Bard et al. 2000). These sites show a preference for butchering older individuals, suggesting that cattle may have been bred primarily for agricultural and other work-related tasks (ploughing, carrying, etc.) and/or milking (and bleeding?). Along with later proto-urban and urban assemblages from Bieta Giyorgis, Maleke, and the D site at Kidane Mehret (Cain 1999; Bard et al. 2000; Phillipson 2000), they suggest that cattle keeping was no longer undertaken by mobile foraging populations, but was an integrated component of a fully agropastoral economy.

Caprines

Evidence for caprines (*Ovis aries/Capra hircus*) is also fairly scant before the first millennium BC. Caprines are known from Lake Besaka *c.* 1500 BC (Clark and Williams 1978; Brandt 1980), at the end of the second millennium BC at Gogoshiis Qabe, Somalia (Brandt and Carder 1987), and from the 1st century AD at the Kumali rockshelter site in southwestern Ethiopia. They also occur in early/mid-first-millennium BC contexts in the greater Asmara area of Eritrea, where they may have been eaten more commonly than cattle, perhaps because the latter were reserved for milking and use in traction (Shoshani et al. 2008; Schmidt 2009). In the same area, sites situated in rocky uplands of the eastern portion of the Asmara Plateau possess higher frequencies of caprines relative to cattle than in the better-watered, open plains of the central plateau, suggesting subregional variation in subsistence practices (Shoshani et al. 2008; Schmidt 2009). Later sites in both highland Eritrea and northern Ethiopia indicate that caprines continued to be kept alongside cattle through the late first millennium BC and into Aksumite times (Bard et al. 2000; Cain 2000; Phillipson 2000).

Other domesticated animals

We have very little understanding of the history of other domesticated animals in the Horn. Donkeys (*Equus asinus*) were probably first domesticated in northeastern Africa, perhaps from populations centred in or immediately adjacent to the Horn (Beja-Pereira et al. 2004; Marshall 2007; Kimura et al. 2010). Remains of domesticated donkey dating to the first millennium BC are present at the site of Mezber in the Gulo Makeda region of Tigray, Ethiopia (D'Andrea et al. 2010). Camels (*Camelus dromedarius*) are depicted in rock art across the region (e.g. Graziosi 1964; Brandt and Brook 1984; Calegari 1999) and first millennium AD Aksumite inscriptions (Littmann et al. 1913). However, they are only found in archaeological deposits dating to the last 500 years at sites such as Laga Oda (Clark and Williams 1978) and perhaps somewhat earlier at Gobedra Shelter near Aksum (Phillipson 1977). Horses are even more elusive: referenced in Ethiopian texts from the 6th century, but completely missing from ancient archaeological assemblages. Chickens are present from the first millennium BC at Mezber (D'Andrea et al. 2010) and from later dating contexts at Aksum (Cain 2000). Pigs are also almost wholly unknown from archaeological deposits, though possibly present in post-AD 500 contexts near Aksum (Cain 2000).

SUMMARIZING THE ARCHAEOLOGICAL EVIDENCE FOR DOMESTICATED PLANTS IN THE HORN

The northern part of the Horn is the only area of sub-Saharan Africa where a southwestern Asian crop complex was established early and existed contemporaneously with a fully established African crop complex. The antiquity of that complex's presence in highland Ethiopia/Eritrea is indicated by its long-standing recognition as a centre of genetic diversity for both tetraploid wheats, such as emmer (*Triticum dicoccum*) and durum (*Triticum durum*), and barley (*Hordeum vulgare*) (Engels et al. 1991; Harlan 1992). The latter, in particular, has historically been a major food source in the highlands, which boast the greatest diversity in the world of morphological types, genetic races, and disease-resistant lines (Abebe et al. 2008; Backes et al. 2009). Although debated, recent genetic research suggests that barley may have been independently domesticated there (Orabi et al. 2007). The region also seems to be a centre of genetic diversity for sorghum (*Sorghum bicolor*), a tropical African grain with origins in the savannahs south of the Sahara. Possibly cultivated in the Sudanese Nile Valley area as early as 4000 BC (Haaland and Haaland, Ch. 37 above)—though definitive evidence of this is much later (Fuller and Hildebrand, Ch. 35 above)—sorghum, along with other African crops, such as pearl millet, may have found the Horn a key conduit for transmission to South Asia, where it is firmly attested by the mid-second millennium BC (Fuller 2003).

Among the most important plant crops first domesticated in the Horn itself were the cereal t'ef (*Eragrostis tef*), the oil crop noog (*Guizotia abyssinica*), coffee (*Coffea arabica*), and enset (*Ensete ventricosum*). Finger millet (*Eleusine coracana*), the non-shattering Ethiopian oat (*Avena abyssinica*), and Ethiopian pea (*Pisum abyssinicum*) represent other important species, although their position as indigenous domesticates is less secure (e.g. Butler 2003). Plants such as shiny leaf buckthorn (*Rhamnus prinoides*) used in brewing mead, Ethiopian mustard (*Brassica carinata*), the tuber crops Oromo dinch (*Plectranthus edulis*) and anchote (*Coccinia abyssinica*), kosso (*Hagenia abyssinica*), used for its medicinal qualities, hyacinth bean (*Lablab purpureus*), and the mildly narcotic plant khat (*Catha edulis*) are examples of other plants native to the Horn, but less intensively cultivated.

Archaeobotanical evidence for the contemporaneous cultivation of Southwest Asian domesticates such as hulled barley, lentils, and linseed (flax) alongside the indigenous Ethiopian/Eritrean cereal domesticate t'ef is apparent by the second half of the first millennium BC in the Ancient Ona site of Mai Chiot, Eritrea (D'Andrea 2008; D'Andrea et al. 2008b; Schmidt 2009). However, archaeobotanical samples recovered thus far from early/mid-first-millennium BC contexts both in the greater Asmara area and at sites in highland Ethiopia demonstrate a crop repertoire dominated by Southwest Asian crops (Dombrowski 1970; Boardman 1999, 2000; Bard et al. 2000; D'Andrea 2008; D'Andrea et al. 2008b; Schmidt 2009). Only from Aksumite contexts of the early/mid-first millennium AD is there robust evidence for the contemporaneous cultivation of Southwest Asian and African plant crops. Published data come primarily from three locations in the Aksum area: the D site at Kidane Mehret (Boardman 2000), the K site at Maleke Aksum (Boardman 1999, 2000), and Ona Nagast on Bieta Giyorgis hill (Bard 1997; D'Andrea 2008). As well as emmer, barley, linseed (*Linum usitatissimum*), and lentils (*Lens esculentus*), there is evidence of bread wheat (*Triticum aestivum*), chickpeas (*Cicer arietinum*), and fava beans (*Vicia faba*), as well as important African domesticates: t'ef, noog, finger millet, and sorghum. Grapes (*Vitis vinifera*), grass peas (*Lathyrus sativus*), peas (*Pisum sp.*), gourds (*Lagenaria siceraria*), cress (*Lepidium sativum*), and cotton (*Gossypium* sp.) are all attested from the Late Aksumite Maleke Aksum K site.

Emerging trends can be discerned from these first-millennium BC/first-millennium AD archaeobotanical data from the northern Horn. Farming communities of the first millennium BC appear to have relied heavily on barley, linseed, and to a lesser extent wheat (particularly emmer) and lentils. Recent isotopic analyses of human bone from a first-millennium BC burial at the Etchmare East site in Gulo Makeda, Ethiopia, tentatively confirm a heavy reliance on Western Asian domesticates, particularly grains, and indicate that most dietary protein came from plant rather than animal sources (D'Andrea et al. 2010). African grains do not appear with any significant frequency until the Aksumite period, only becoming well represented after AD 550. The archaeobotanical record from the Aksum area demonstrates a shift in crops between the first millennium BC and first millennium AD, with gradually increasing reliance on the two specifically northern Ethiopian domesticates, t'ef and noog, the wider African domesticates, finger millet and sorghum, and Southwest Asian species like lentils, chickpeas, and grass peas; other new crops (cotton, grapes, gourds) were also introduced. Of the crops that appear earliest, only emmer declines in frequency through time, substituted by the free-threshing wheats favoured today (D'Andrea et al. 1999; Lyons and D'Andrea 2003). Although the dearth of t'ef, sorghum, and finger millet in the earlier deposits may at least partly reflect taphonomic biases concerning preservation and identification (Lyons and D'Andrea 2003; D'Andrea 2008), it seems evident that an expansion of an already diverse crop repertoire occurred during the Aksumite period, with tropical African grains playing a larger role.

There is also some evidence for sub-regional variation in crop repertoires during the first millennium BC, especially on the Asmara Plateau area of Eritrea (Fig. 39.3) where small-scale excavations of domestic contexts within large village and small town settlements tentatively suggest that communities situated in the open, better-watered, and more fertile plains west of Asmara relied predominantly on emmer wheat and barley, while evidence for wheat and barley is much reduced in contemporary sites located in the much rockier and steeper eastern portion of the plateau. A similar case of spatial localization is observed for linseed over the same period (D'Andrea et al. 2008b; Schmidt 2009). In such patterns we may observe subregional variation in subsistence practices that were closely associated with soil conditions, access to water, and topographic qualities.

While the overwhelming focus of this discussion and of research to date has been on northern Ethiopia and Eritrea, recent reporting of two partial seeds of coffee and possible leaves of domestic enset from an early first-millennium AD rockshelter context in the Kafa region of southwestern Ethiopia (Hildebrand et al. 2010) hints at the potential of ongoing and future fieldwork for delivering insights into plant domestication beyond the grain- and legume-based traditions of the northern Horn.

FIG. 39.3 Walls of an Ancient Ona Culture early farming household of the first millennium BC, Asmara Plateau, Eritrea (photograph, Matthew Curtis).

CONCLUDING THOUGHTS

Over the last five decades, several explanatory frameworks for the origins of food production in the Horn have been proposed (for reviews see Brandt 1984; Barnett 1999; Finneran 2007). In many of them, the stimulus for change from foraging to food-producing economies comes via the arrival in the highlands of migrants originating from distant locales, such as the Nile Valley or Arabia. Looking increasingly at more localized contexts and processes, more recent investigations have offered multi-causal explanatory frameworks. Particularly important have been ethnoarchaeological approaches that attempt to explore food-producing traditions and strategies and their correlates in the region's living communities to build stronger models for interpreting past cultivation practices and foodways, preservation and archaeological issues, and particular technological attributes of food production (D'Andrea et al. 1999; D'Andrea and Haile 2002; Lyons and D'Andrea 2003; Hildebrand 2007; Lyons 2007). Recently, Harrower et al. (2010) have considered why food production in the Horn occurred relatively late compared to Southwest Asia and the Nile Valley. Available evidence suggests that, as elsewhere in Africa, food production in the Horn first appeared among mobile pastoralists and spread patchily (but cf. Hildebrand et al. 2010). The diversity of ecological settings conditioned by the siting of settlements in proximity to various altitudinal microclimates may have given little incentive for sedentism until the early first millennium BC, when a period of renewed aridity may have compelled populations to concentrate in more favourable highland plateau zones, such as those around Asmara and Aksum (Curtis 2008). It is at this time that we see fully agropastoral economies appearing in the highlands of the northern Horn, characterized by the cultivation of cereals and legumes and the keeping of cattle and caprines. By the mid-first millennium BC these communities lived in sedentary hamlets, villages, and small towns composed of stone architecture, often located in upland areas overlooking watercourses of moderate to high water flow potential and higher-fertility soils. The presence of metal sickles, the high frequencies of milling and hand stones, the caching of ash (perhaps for fertilizer), models of yoked oxen, and the prominent use of large ceramic storage vessels suggest increasing sophistication of agropastoral practices across the region (Phillipson 1998; Phillips 2004; Michels 2005; Finneran 2007; Curtis and Schmidt 2008; D'Andrea et al. 2008a; Curtis 2009; Fattovich 2010).

This period also saw the amplification of interregional interaction linking these communities more closely to neighbouring cultures in Africa and the southern Red Sea world. This seems to have offered some individuals and groups opportunities to form new relationships with both foreign and local communities, forging new identities that subsequently initiated shifts in culturally imbued preferences (Curtis 2004, 2008; Manzo 2009). Such shifts may have proved crucial to the incorporation of domesticates, long known but resisted or ignored, into existing social and economic frameworks. Exploring such issues will be essential in future research concerning the origin of food production in the Horn of Africa. Equally important will be an expansion in temporal and geographic concerns to include archaeological investigations of food systems outside the northern highlands, particularly the origins and development of enset and tuber crops in southern Ethiopia, and the later incorporation of African, Asian, and New World domesticates with their associated social and economic changes in the early modern period.

References

ABEBE, T. D., BAUER, A. M., and LEÓN, J. (2008). Morphological diversity of Ethiopian barleys (*Hordeum vulgare* L.) in relation to geographic regions and altitudes. *Hereditas* 147: 154–64.

BACKES, G., ORABI, J., WOLDAY, A. W., YAHYAOUI, A., and JAHOOR, A. (2009). High genetic diversity revealed in barley (*Hordeum vulgare*) collected from small-scale farmer's fields in Eritrea. *Genetic Resources and Crop Evolution* 56: 85–97.

BARD, K. A. (1997). Environmental history of early Aksum. In K. A. Bard (ed.), *The Environmental History and Human Ecology of Northern Ethiopia in the Late Holocene*. Naples: Istituto Universitario Orientale, 19–25.

—— COLTORTI, M., DRAMIS, F., FATTOVICH, R. (2000). The environmental history of Tigray (Northern Ethiopia) during the Holocene: a preliminary outline. *African Archaeological Review* 17: 65–86.

BARNETT, T. (1999). *The Emergence of Food Production in Ethiopia*. Oxford: Archaeopress.

BEJA-PEREIRA, A., ENGLAND, P. R., FERRAND, N., et al. (2004). African origins of the domestic donkey. *Science* 304: 1781.

BERAKHI, O., BRANCACCIO, L., CALDERONI, G., DRAMIS, F., and UMER, M. (1998). The Mai Maikdem sedimentary sequence: a reference point for the environmental evolution of the highlands of northern Ethiopia. *Geomorphology* 23: 127–38.

BOARDMAN, S. (1999). The agricultural foundation of the Aksumite Empire, Ethiopia: an interim report. In M. Van Der Veen (ed.), *The Exploitation of Plant Resources in Ancient Africa*. New York: Kluwer, 137–48.

—— (2000). Contributions on archaeobotany. In Phillipson (2000: 268–70, 363–8, 412–14).

BOWER, J. R. F., and NELSON, C. M. (1978). Early pottery and pastoral cultures of the Central Rift Valley, Kenya. *Man* 13: 554–66.

BRANCACCIO, L., CALDERONI, G., COLTORTI, M., DRAMIS, F., and OGBAGHEBRIEL, B. (1997). Phases of soil erosion during the Holocene in the highlands of western Tigray (northern Ethiopia): a preliminary report. In K. A. Bard (ed.), *The Environmental History and Human Ecology of Northern Ethiopia in the Late Holocene*. Naples: Istituto Universitario Orientale, 29–44.

BRANDT, S. A. (1980). Archaeological investigations at Lake Besaka. In R. E. Leakey and B. A. Ogot (eds), *Proceedings of the Eighth Panafrican Congress of Prehistory and Quaternary Studies*. Nairobi: International Louis Leakey Memorial Institute for African Prehistory, 239–43.

—— (1984). New perspectives on the origins of food production in Ethiopia. In J .D. Clark and S. A. Brandt (eds), *From Hunters to Farmers: The Causes and Consequences of Early Food Production in Africa*. Berkeley: University of California Press, 173–90.

—— (1986). The Upper Pleistocene and early Holocene prehistory of the Horn of Africa. *African Archaeological Review* 4: 41–82.

—— (1996). The ethnoarchaeology of flaked stone tool use in southern Ethiopia. In G. Pwiti and R. Soper (eds), *Aspects of African Archaeology*. Harare: University of Zimbabwe Press, 733–88.

—— and BROOK, G. A. (1984). Archaeological and paleoenvironmental research in northern Somalia. *Current Anthropology* 25: 119–21.

—— and CARDER, N. (1987). Pastoral rock art in the Horn of Africa: making sense of udder chaos. *World Archaeology* 19: 194–213.

—— SPRING, A., CLIFTON, H., et al. (1997). *The 'Tree Against Hunger': Enset-Based Agricultural Systems in Ethiopia*. Washington, DC: American Association for the Advancement of Science.

BUTLER, A. (2003). The Ethiopian pea: seeking the evidence for separate domestication. In K. Neumann, A. Butler, and S. Kahlheber (eds), *Food, Fuels and Fields*. Cologne: Heinrich Barth Institut, 37–48.

CAIN, C. (1999). Results from zooarchaeological analysis at Axum, Ethiopia. *Archaeozoologia* 10: 27–45.

—— (2000). Archaeozoology. In Phillipson (2000: 369–72, 414–17).

CALEGARI, G. (1999). *L'arte Rupestre dell'Eritrea: Repertorio Ragionato ed Esegesi Iconografica*. Milan: Società di Scienze Naturali.

CLARK, J. D., and PRINCE, G. R. (1978). Use-wear in Later Stone Age microliths from Laga Oda, Haraghi, Ethiopia, and possible functional interpretations. *Azania* 13: 101–10.

—— and WILLIAMS, M. (1978). Recent archaeological research in SE Ethiopia: some preliminary results. *Annales d'Éthiopie* 11: 19–44.

CURTIS, M. C. (2004). Ancient interaction across the southern Red Sea: new suggestions for cultural exchange and complex societies during the first millennium BC. In P. Lunde and A. Porter (eds), *Trade and Travel in the Red Sea Region*. Oxford: Archaeopress, 57–70.

—— (2008). New perspectives for examining change and complexity in the northern Horn of Africa during the first millennium BCE. In P. R. Schmidt, M. C. Curtis, and Z. Teka (eds), *The Archaeology of Ancient Eritrea*. Trenton, NJ: Red Sea Press, 329–48.

—— (2009). Relating the Ancient Ona Culture to the wider northern Horn: discerning patterns and problems in the archaeology of the first millennium BC. *African Archaeological Review* 26: 327–50.

CURTIS, M. C., and SCHMIDT, P. R. (2008). Landscape, people, and places on the ancient Asmara plateau. In P. R. Schmidt, M. C. Curtis, and Z. Teka (eds), *The Archaeology of Ancient Eritrea*. Trenton, NJ: Red Sea Press, 64–108.

D'ANDREA, A. C. (2008). T'ef (*Eragrostis tef*) in ancient agricultural systems of highland Ethiopia. *Economic Botany* 92: 547–66.

—— and HAILE, M. (2002). Traditional emmer processing in highland Ethiopia. *Journal of Ethnobiology* 22: 179–217.

—— LYONS, D. E., HAILE, M., and BUTLER, E. A. (1999). Ethnoarchaeological approaches to the study of prehistoric agriculture in the Ethiopian Highlands. In M. Van Der Veen (ed.), *The Exploitation of Plant Resources in Ancient Africa*. New York: Plenum, 101–22.

—— MANZO, A., HARROWER, M. J., and HAWKINS, A. (2008a). The Pre-Aksumite and Aksumite settlement of northeast Tigrai, Ethiopia. *Journal of Field Archaeology* 33: 151–76.

—— RICHARDS, M. P., PAVLISH, L. A., WOOD, S., MANZO, A., and WOLDE-KIROS, H. S. (2010). Stable isotopic analysis of human and animal diets from two pre-Aksumite/Proto-Aksumite archaeological sites in northern Ethiopia. *Journal of Archaeological Science* 38: 367–74.

—— SCHMIDT, P. R., and CURTIS, M. C. (2008b). Paleoethnobotanical analysis and agricultural economy at early first millennium bce sites around Asmara. In P. R. Schmidt, M. C. Curtis, and Z. Teka (eds), *The Archaeology of Ancient Eritrea*. Trenton, NJ: Red Sea Press, 207–16.

DOMBROWSKI, J. (1970). Preliminary report on excavations in Lalibela and Natchabiet Caves, Begemeder. *Annales d'Éthiopie* 8: 21–9.

EHRET, C. (1979). On the antiquity of agriculture in Ethiopia. *Journal of African History* 20: 161–77.

ENGELS, J. M. M., HAWKES, J. G., and WOREDE, M. (1991). *Plant Genetic Resources of Ethiopia*. Cambridge: Cambridge University Press.

FATTOVICH, R. (1984). Data for the history of the ancient peopling of the northern Ethiopian–Sudanese borderland. In S. Rubenson (ed.), *Proceedings of the 7th International Conference of Ethiopian Studies*. Uppsala: Scandinavian Institute for African Studies, 177–86.

—— (1988). Remarks on the late prehistory and early history of northern Ethiopia. In T. Beyene (ed.), *Proceedings of the Eighth International Conference of Ethiopian Studies*. Addis Ababa: Institute of Ethiopian Studies, 85–104.

—— (2010). The development of ancient states in the northern Horn of Africa, c. 3000 BC–AD 1000: an archaeological outline. *Journal of World Prehistory* 23: 145–75.

FINNERAN, N. (2000a). A new perspective on the Late Stone Age of the northern Ethiopian Highlands: excavations at Anqqer Baahti, Aksum, Ethiopia 1996. *Azania* 35: 21–51.

—— (2000b). Excavations at the Late Stone Age site of Baahti Nebait, Aksum, northern Ethiopia, 1997. *Azania* 35: 53–73.

—— (2007). *The Archaeology of Ethiopia*. New York: Routledge.

FULLER, D. Q. (2003). African crops in prehistoric South Asia: a critical review. In K. Neumann, A. Butler, and S. Kahlheber (eds), *Food, Fuels and Fields*. Cologne: Heinrich Barth Institut, 239–71.

GEBRU, T., ESHETU, Z., HUANG, Y., et al. (2009). Holocene palaeovegetation of the Tigray Plateau in northern Ethiopia from charcoal and stable organic carbon isotopic analyses of gully sediments. *Palaeogeography, Palaeoclimatology, Palaeoecology* 282: 67–80.

GRAU, H. (1981). Handoga: site d'habitat de pasteurs nomades? *Archeologia Paris* 159: 55–9.

GRAZIOSI, P. (1964). New discoveries of rock paintings in Ethiopia. *Antiquity* 138: 91–9, 187–90.

GUÉRIN, C., and FAURE, M. (1996). Chasse au chacal et domestication du boeuf dans le site Néolithique d'Asa-Koma (République de Djibouti). *Journal des Africanistes* 66: 299–311.

GUTHERZ, X., JOUSSAUME, R., AMBLARD, S., MOHAMED, G., BONNEFILLE, R., DUDAY, H., GOURAUD, G., THIÉBAULT, S., and THIAM EL HADJI, I. (1996). Le site d'Asa Koma (République de Djibouti) et les premiers producteurs dans la Corne de l'Afrique. *Journal des Africanistes* 66: 255–97.

HARLAN, J. R. (1992). Indigenous African agriculture. In P. J. Watson and C. W. Cowan (eds), *Agricultural Origins in World Perspective*. Washington, DC: Smithsonian Institution Press, 59–69.

HARROWER, M. J., McCORRISTON, J., and D'ANDREA, C. A. (2010). General/specific, local/ global: comparing the beginnings of agriculture in the Horn of Africa (Ethiopia/Eritrea) and Southwest Arabia (Yemen). *American Antiquity* 75: 452–72.

HILDEBRAND, E. A. (2007). A tale of two tuber crops: how attributes of enset and yams may have shaped prehistoric human–plant interactions in southwest Ethiopia. In T. Denham, L. Vrydaghs, and J. Iriarte (eds), *Rethinking Agriculture: Archaeological and Ethno archaeological Perspectives*. Walnut Creek, Calif.: Left Coast Press, 273–98.

—— and BRANDT, S. A. (2010). An archaeological survey of the tropical highlands of Kafa, SW Ethiopia. *Journal of African Archaeology* 8: 43–63.

—— —— and LESUR-GEBREMARIAM, J. (2010). The Holocene archaeology of southwest Ethiopia: new insights from the Kafa Archaeological Project. *African Archaeological Review* 27: 255–89.

KIMURA, B., MARSHALL, F., CHEN, S., et al. (2010). Ancient DNA provides insights into African wild ass phylogeny and donkey domestication. *Proceedings of the Royal Society B: Biological Sciences* 278: 50–7.

LESUR, J. (2007). *Chasse et Élevage dans la Corne de l'Afrique Entre le Néolithique et les Temps Historiques*. Oxford: Archaeopress.

LITTMANN, E., KRENCKER, D., and VON LÜPKE, T. (1913). *Deutsche Aksum-Expedition*. Berlin: Reimer.

LYONS, D. E. (2007). Integrating African cuisine: rural cuisine and identity in Tigrai, Highland Ethiopia. *Journal of Social Archaeology* 7: 346–71.

—— and D'ANDREA, A. C. (2003). Griddles, ovens, and agricultural origins: an ethnoarchaeological study of bread baking in Highland Ethiopia. *American Anthropologist* 105: 515–30.

MACHADO, M. J., PEREZ-GONZALEZ, A., and BENITO, G. (1998). Paleoenvironmental changes during the last 4000 years in the Tigray, northern Ethiopia. *Quaternary Research* 49: 312–21.

MANZO, A. (2009). *Capra nubiana* in Berbere sauce? Pre-Aksumite art and identity building. *African Archaeological Review* 26: 291–303.

MARSHALL, F. (2007). African pastoral perspectives on domestication of the donkey: a first synthesis. In T. Denham, L. Vrydaghs, and J. Iriarte (eds), *Rethinking Agriculture: Archaeological and Ethnoarchaeological Perspectives*. Walnut Creek, Calif.: Left Coast Press, 371–407.

MARSHALL, M. H., LAMB, H. F., DAVIES, S. J., et al. (2009). Climatic change in northern Ethiopia during the past 17,000 years: a diatom and stable isotope record from Lake Ashenge. *Palaeogeography, Palaeoclimatology, Palaeoecology* 279: 114–27.

MICHELS, J. W. (2005). *Changing Settlement Patterns in the Aksum–Yeha Region of Ethiopia, 700 BC–AD 850*. Oxford: Archaeopress.

ORABI, J., BACKES, G., WOLDAY, A., and YAHYAOUI, A. (2007). The Horn of Africa as a centre of barley diversification and a potential domestication site. *Theoretical and Applied Genetics* 114: 1117–27.

PHILLIPS, J. (2004). Pre-Aksumite Aksum and its neighbours. In P. Lunde and A. Porter (eds), *Trade and Travel in the Red Sea Region*. Oxford: Archaeopress, 79–85.

PHILLIPSON, D. W. (1977). The excavation of Gobedra Rock-Shelter, Axum. *Azania* 12: 53–82.

PHILLIPSON, D. W. (1998). *Ancient Ethiopia: Aksum, its Antecedents and Successors*. London: British Museum Press.

—— (ed.) (2000). *Archaeology at Aksum, Ethiopia, 1993–97*. London: British Institute in Eastern Africa.

SCHMIDT, P. R. (2009). Variability in Eritrea and the archaeology of the northern Horn during the first millennium BC: subsistence, ritual, and gold production. *African Archaeological Review* 26: 305–25.

SHOSHANI, J., GHEBREGIORGIS, M., and SCHMIDT, P. R. (2008). Interpretations of faunal remains from archaeological sites on the Asmara plateau of Eritrea. In P. R. Schmidt, M. C. Curtis, and Z. Teka (eds), *The Archaeology of Ancient Eritrea*. Trenton, NJ: Red Sea Press, 217–33.

TEFERA, H., and KETEMA, S. (2001). Production and importance of tef in Ethiopian agriculture. In H. Tefera, G. Belay, and M. Sorrells (eds), *Narrowing the Rift: Tef Research and Development*. Addis Ababa: Ethiopian Agricultural Research Organization, 3–7.

WEEDMAN, K. (2006). An ethnoarchaeological study of hafting and stone tools among the Gamo of southern Ethiopia. *Journal of Archaeological Method and Theory* 13: 188–237.

CHAPTER 40

THE ARCHAEOLOGY OF PASTORALISM AND STOCK-KEEPING IN EAST AFRICA

PAUL LANE

INTRODUCTION

THE history of pastoralism and stock-keeping in East Africa extends over some 4,500–5,000 years, during which time a diverse range of herd management strategies and settlement systems was followed by an equally diverse range of ethnic groups and pastoralist societies. The historical record documents several examples of mobile stock herders becoming sedentary farmers and agropastoralists, hunter-gatherers acquiring livestock and adopting a pastoralist lifestyle and the cultural traditions of their pastoralist neighbours, and impoverished pastoralists becoming either temporary or longer term foragers. Such evidence, plus numerous examples of ethnic shifting, caution against assuming that pastoralism is a single, unitary mode of subsistence or that a single causal factor or process drove its adoption. Archaeological evidence, especially if coupled with palaeoenvironmental data, and that of population genetics and historical linguistics offer an excellent means of tracking how varied these pastoralist economies and cultures have been and when, where, and why they have changed. Significantly, the adoption of domestic livestock occurred upwards of 1,000 years before crops were grown—one of the few examples in the world where herding preceded cultivation in the transition to food production (Marshall and Hildebrand 2002; Marshall and Weissbrod 2011).

DEFINITIONS

Archaeologists use the term 'Pastoral Neolithic' (PN) to refer to the era in eastern Africa during which domesticated livestock were first integrated into subsistence economies. Bower and Nelson's (1978: 562) definition of PN cultures as those 'which (1) relied substantially on domesticated stock for their livelihood; (2) used pottery, and (3) employed typical Later Stone Age technologies for the manufacture of edged tools' is perhaps the most concise. The term nonetheless masks considerable diversity regarding the relative importance of livestock in subsistence strategies, preferred ceramic styles, the range of formal stone tools and associated manufacturing techniques and debris, site distributions and their placement within the landscape, and associated burial practices and forms. Over the history of the discipline the term has also been employed by different archaeologists to convey rather different meanings (Karega-Mŭnene 2003), and the very use of the word 'Pastoral' has been contested on the grounds that it unduly emphasizes herding relative to other food resources and 'Neolithic' because of its reliance on a few key (supposedly diagnostic) artefact types as both chronological and cultural markers (Karega-Munene 2002; 2003: 19–20). The term 'Pastoral Iron Age' (PIA), used to refer to pastoralist societies after the adoption of iron metallurgy c. 1250 years ago to the last few centuries, is equally problematic, given that stone-tool use and manufacture continued for up to 500 years following the first use of iron. Moreover, iron production was not a major component of these societies and, at least historically, smiths tended to be marginalized and of low social status (Larick 1986). While both terms are still used as shorthand to refer to different time-frames and material traditions, it is important to recognize their limitations. Ultimately, it may be simpler to refer to the societies associated with these complexes as 'early' (or 'pioneer') and 'later' pastoralists. This would certainly facilitate comparison between the different phases and might make it easier to identify the degree of continuity or discontinuity across the spectrum of pastoralist traditions, as well as providing a new analytical focus for studying pastoralist practices.

ORIGINS

Current evidence suggests that the transition to generalized, mixed cattle and sheep/goat pastoralism had occurred in some parts of the northern lowlands bordering Lake Turkana by c. 4500–4200 BP (Barthelme 1985), by c. 4500–4300 BP in central Kenya and parts of the eastern highlands (Ambrose 2003; Lane 2011), by c. 3800–3500 BP in the Tsavo and middle Sabaki River areas of southeastern Kenya (Wright 2005), and by c. 4400–4150 BP in southern and western Kenya and northern Tanzania (Karega-Mŭnene 2002; Prendergast 2011) (Fig. 40.1). All five principal domestic animals (cattle, sheep, goats, camels, and donkeys) were domesticated outside the immediate region, although in the case of the donkey and perhaps the camel this may have happened only marginally further north, in the Horn of Africa (Gifford-Gonzalez and Hanotte, Ch. 34 above). The fact that none of these species was domesticated locally implies that their introduction was either through the southward migration of stock-keeping populations or through various forms of livestock exchange, or, as seems more probable, some combination of these.

Current genetic evidence suggests that the allele associated with lactase persistence and found in today's East African populations developed c. 7,000–3,000 years ago. This early date is consistent with the archaeological evidence for the introduction of livestock, while its rapid spread among different populations supports a model of demic diffusion (Tishkoff et al. 2007). Thus far, however, it has not been possible to establish whether this allele first emerged among Cushitic-speaking Afro-Asiatic populations or Nilotic-speaking Nilo-Saharan ones. The evidence from historical linguistics also points to a southward expansion of small

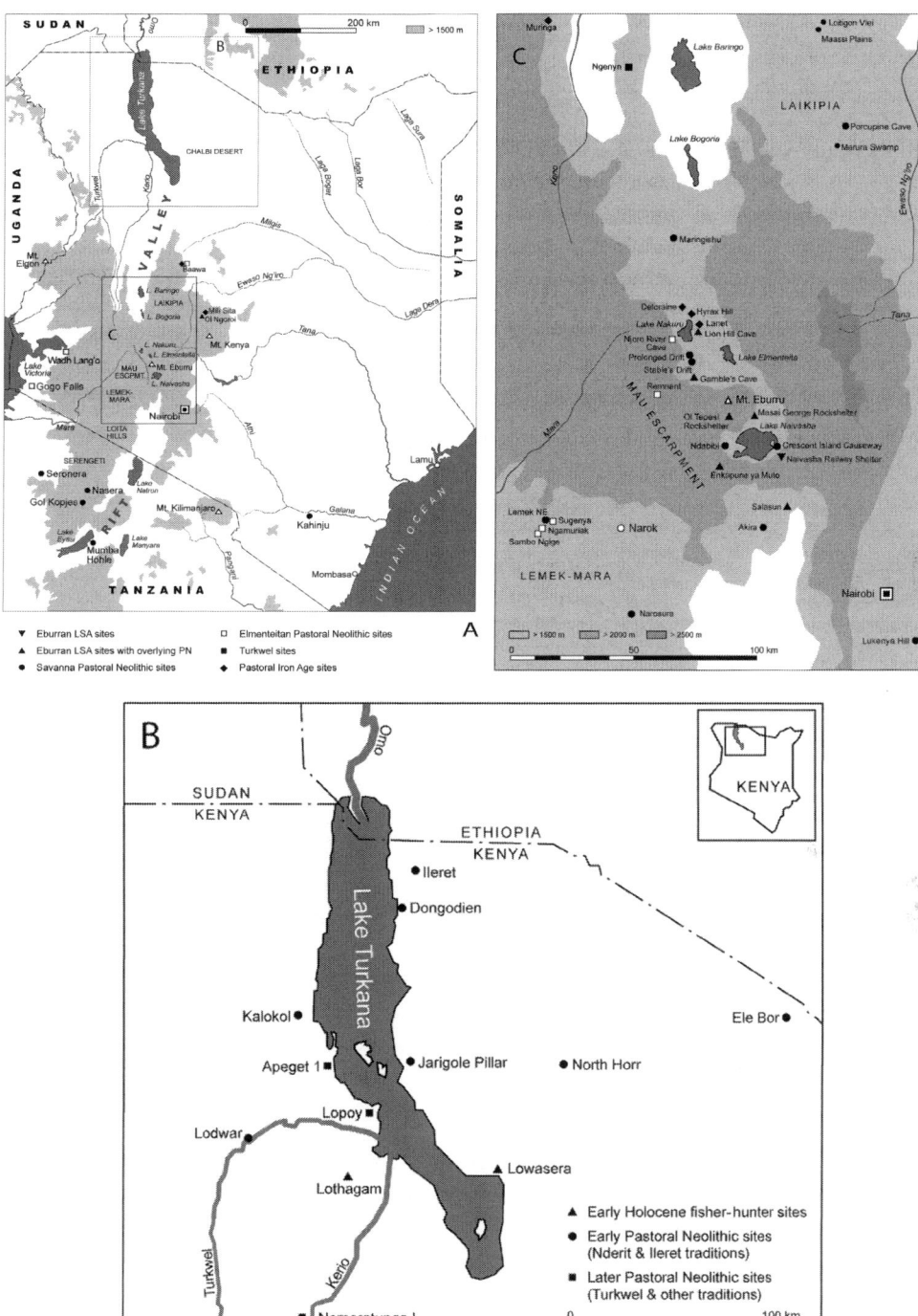

FIG. 40.1 Location of the key sites mentioned in Chapter 40.

groups of herders from South Sudan, Ethiopia and (possibly) Somalia. Critically, the data suggest that these early pastoralists were speakers of proto-Southern Cushitic languages (Ehret 2003). More recently, it has been proposed that the spread of domestic stock and the changes in material culture, settlement strategies, burial practices, and inferred social relations that accompanied this southward movement can be divided into two phases—an initial exploratory period *c.* 5000–3500 BP and a later period of consolidation, settlement, and social fragmentation *c.* 3500–2000 BP (Marshall et al. 2011). During the former, communities with livestock, who were probably already experienced herders, moved into the Lake Turkana Basin in response to the increasing desiccation of the Sahara from the fifth millennium BC (Haaland and Haaland, Ch. 37 above). Supplementary evidence from genetics, physical anthropology, and bioarchaeology (including the use of radiogenic isotopes such as strontium) that might support or refute some of these arguments is largely lacking, however, and there remain considerable conceptual and analytical challenges associated with trying to differentiate 'herders' from 'foragers with livestock' (Prendergast and Mutundu 2009).

Whatever the precise mechanisms, the transition to food production in East Africa was a very uneven process characterized by often quite localized uptake and stretching over several millennia. The available evidence certainly suggests that initially the southward spread of herding economies was more of a 'trickle' than a full-blown 'wave' or 'splash' (Bower 1991), involving alternating moving and static 'frontiers' between herders and foragers (Lane 2004), with the latter possibly obtaining stock for themselves through theft or exchange (Ambrose 1984). The genetic complexity of East African populations (Poloni et al. 2009) and the extended history of gene-flow between Afro-Asiatic and Nilo-Saharan populations historically associated with pastoralism (Campbell and Tishkoff 2010) also indicate considerable interaction between allochthonous and autochthonous populations.

THE LAKE TURKANA REGION

Around 4500–4200 BP at least two new pottery traditions appear for the first time in the archaeological record of the Lake Turkana Basin. Termed 'Nderit' and 'Ileret', these are distinguishable in how they were decorated, the range of decorative motifs employed, and the preferred shape/s of the vessels produced (Table 40.1; Fig. 40.2a–b). The earliest dated remains of domestic ovicaprines and cattle are associated with these new pottery traditions at sites like North Horr, Dongodien, and Ileret. These early herders also exploited fish, as did the basin's Late Stone Age (LSA) inhabitants (Kusimba, Ch. 32 above), but, in contrast to them, early herding communities consumed a wider range of taxa (Stewart 1989). The stone tools used continued to emphasize *outils écaillés* and backed microliths (although in contrast to LSA hunter-fisher camps, geometric forms are absent and crescents much scarcer), with scrapers a more significant component than previously (Barthelme 1985). Obsidian, probably obtained locally (Nash et al. 2011), also became the preferred raw material. This period witnessed the first appearance of stone bowls, made by a combination of pecking and grinding pieces of lava, pumice, and similar 'soft' stones. Taken together, these changes in the archaeological record support the hypothesis of migration into the Lake Turkana Basin and the case for these newcomers bringing with them livestock and new ways of exploiting the landscape. These pioneer communities nonetheless interacted with local hunter-gatherer-fishers.

Further changes in subsistence strategies and ceramic styles are evident from *c*. 1800 BP, as indicated by the appearance of a new pottery tradition. Although its dating and distribution remain poorly defined, it occurs mostly on sites in the Turkwel area southwest of the lake, hence the designation 'Turkwel tradition' (Lynch and Robbins 1979; Fig. 40.2c). Lopoy, some 7 km from the lake's current shoreline and occupied around 1000–950 BP, is one of the key sites (Robbins 1984). Covering a large area, it includes several middens, hearths, butchery areas, and ashy patches that may represent burned livestock enclosures. Domesticated

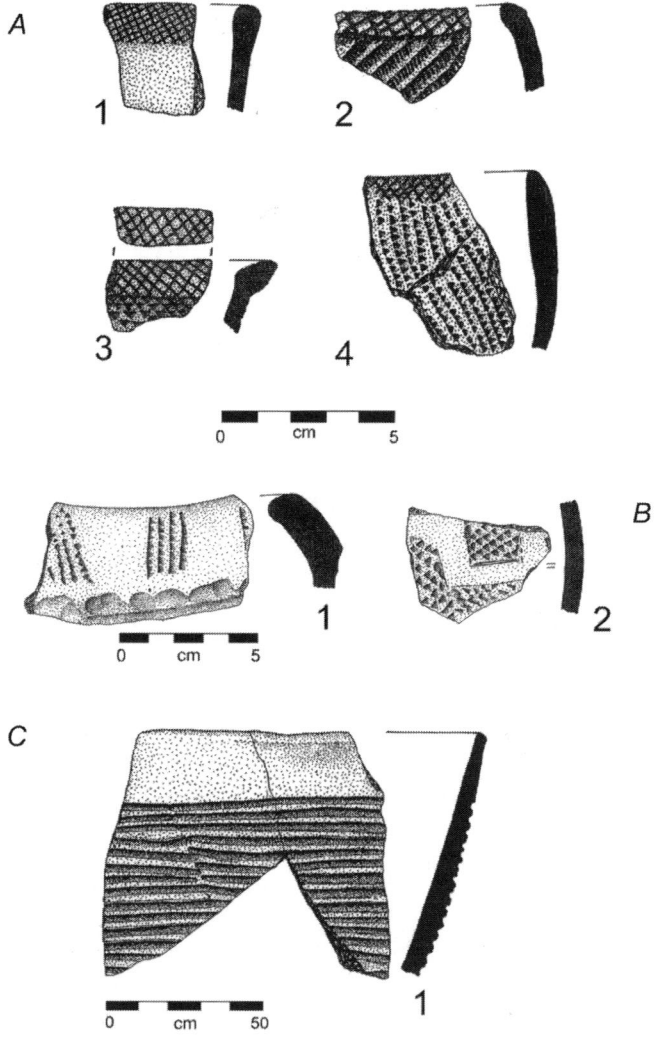

FIG. 40.2 Examples of Pastoral Neolithic pottery: (A) Northern Nderit pottery 1–4: decorated rims (source: Barthelme 1985: 1: 160, fig. 61/d, 2: 158, fig. 59/b, 3: 160, fig. 61/c, and 4: 268, reproduced with kind permission from John Barthelme). (B) Ileret pottery: decorated rim (source: Barthelme 1985: 201, fig. 76/a, reproduced with kind permission from John Barthelme). (C) Turkwel pottery from Lopoy: decorated rim (source: Lynch and Robbins 1979: 326, fig. 3/a, © Cambridge University Press, reproduced with permission).

Table 40.1 Main diagnostic aspects of different Pastoral Neolithic traditions

Tradition	Characteristics	Representative sites
Nderit	Date range: c. 4500–2500 BP *Pottery*: Constricted bowls are the main vessel type; decorated on both the exterior (typically with rows of angular impressions and milling or cross-hatching on the rims) and interior (typically with deeply scored lines) surfaces of the pot. Relatively thin-walled, vessel lips can be incised or milled. *Lithics*: Non-uniform; common tool types include large blades produced using a punch-flaking technology (typically on obsidian), geometric microliths, and a range of scrapers (typically small).	Dongodien, GaJi2, Jarigole, Il Lokeridede (GaJi23), Stable's Drift
Ileret	Date range: c. 4500–2500 BP *Pottery*: Only decorated on the exterior surface (usually just below the rim), with incised or impressed herring-bone motifs being the most characteristic type of decoration. *Lithics:* Heterogeneous, microliths—some double backed, scrapers include side, notched, & composite forms; *outils écaillés*.	Ileret, North Horr
Turkwel	Date range: c. 1800–950 BP *Pottery*: Thin-walled pots and bowls with external, closely spaced horizontal (although occasionally vertical or angled), grooved decoration. Vessel rims sometimes have signs of nicking or pinched decoration. *Lithics*: Fairly unstandardized microlithic industry, chert and chalcedony rather than obsidian being the preferred raw material.	Lopoy, Apeget
Narosura	Date range: c. 2800–1400 BP *Pottery:* Vessel forms include beakers, and open- and narrow-mouthed bowls; some gourd-shaped vessels also occur. Decoration is mostly in the form of triangular-shaped comb stamped panels and incised lines of cross-hatching. *Lithics*: Similar to Nderit.	Narosura, Prolonged Drift, Salasun, Crescent Island Causeway
Maringishu	Date range: ≥1700–? BP *Pottery:* Characteristic form is a straight-sided bowl with a slightly pointed base, sometimes referred to as an 'ovoid beaker' shape. Typical decoration comprises a panel of undulating ridges immediately below the rim.	Maringishu, Hyrax Hill, Kahinju
Akira	Date range: c. 1900–1200 BP *Pottery*: Vessels are highly burnished and have very thin walls, and decoration is typically made up from incised panels. Some similarities with Narosura pottery (such as use of burnishing and hatching and cross-hatching below the rim).	Seronera, GvJM 44

Elmenteitan	Date range: Most sites date to between c. 3300–1200 BP.	Ngamuriak, Sugenya, Sambo
	Pottery: Open-mouthed bowls with slightly everted lips, carinated cups, large cauldron-like bowls, and platters. Lugs (sometimes perforated vertically), handles, spouts often present. Largely undecorated; where present, decoration comprises milling around the rims and/or occasional random panels of impressed punctuations.	Ngige, Maasai Gorge, Oldorotua 1, Gogo Falls, Wadh Lang'o
	Lithics: Long, broad, thin blades produced using punch technique on prepared cores with small, coarsely abraded striking platforms. Blades used whole, some retouched along the edges; also snapped or segmented into rectangular blanks for the manufacture of various tool forms including geometric and non-geometric microliths, scrapers, and burins, all typically larger than SPN equivalents. Outils écaillés also common.	

ovicaprines and bovids are present, but several bone concentrations point to the intensive exploitation of lacustrine resources, such as crocodile and Nile perch (*Lates niloticus*). Whether the site was utilized by a single community practising a mixed pastoral, hunting, and fishing economy or by separate hunting-fishing and pastoral communities is a matter of debate. Other Turkwel sites around Lake Turkana include Apeget 1, dated to c. 1900 BP.

Aside from settlement remains, important burial, commemorative, and rock art complexes around Lake Turkana are attributable to different PN traditions. The Jarigole Pillar site on the east side of the lake comprises a large oval-shaped mound from which at least 28 basalt pillars protrude. The surface is scattered with large quantities of broken pottery (mostly Nderit tradition) and other material, including animal bone, flaked stone tools, and flaking debris, beads made of ostrich eggshell, shell (including some from the Indian Ocean coast), and amazonite, and clay cattle figurines (Nelson 1995). The mound was used repeatedly for interring human burials and bundles containing bones and grave goods. Although not fully excavated and poorly dated, the mound possibly contains several hundred burial pits, and was used over some considerable time as an ossuary and place of commemoration.

In West Turkana, several more pillar sites occur near Lothagam, with others further north at Kalokol and two complexes at Lokori near the Kerio River southwest of the lake (Hildebrand et al. 2011). Known as Namoratung'a by the Turkana, these have similar but not identical characteristics. Those at Lokori consist of circular rings of short, upright stones enclosing single inhumation burials in shallow pits covered by several layers of stone slabs. Of the forty excavated burials most were of adult males, although adult women and children of both sexes were also represented (Lynch and Robbins 1979). Some of the upright kerbstones also have engraved petroglyphs. In all, over 1,000 different engravings and 142 distinct geometric designs have been documented. The latter consist largely of circle, spiral, and line motifs similar to designs used by a variety of recent pastoralist communities as cattle brands and to some of the white, painted motifs found at rock shelters further south on the Laikipia Plateau and in the Rift Valley, which are probably of late PIA date. Recent reappraisal of the Lokori evidence and more extensive ethnographic study of the Turkana practice of marking skin by Russell (2013), cautions against simplistic interpretations of the motifs as indicators of either ethnic or linguistic (e.g. Cushitic, Nilotic) affiliation and has demonstrated that a specific type or style of motif can have multiple authorships. The Lokori burials are dated *c.* 2350–1050 BP, but this estimate must be treated with caution, as the older of the two dates derives from a radiocarbon assay on bone apatite. More recent work on sites near Lothagam and Kalokol has generated new dates on charcoal and ostrich egg shell that are considerably older (*c.* 4900–300 BP), with the possibility that those at Lothagam may pre-date those at Kalokol by as much as *c.* 600 years (Hildebrand et al. 2011: 188, 197).

THE CENTRAL AND SOUTHERN RIFT VALLEY

The Enkapune ya Muto rockshelter has produced some of the earliest dates for the presence of domestic livestock in central Kenya in the form of a few caprine teeth associated with typical LSA Eburran 5 stone artefacts and an overwhelmingly wild fauna dated to *c.* 4520–4310 BP. Pottery, including samples of the Nderit and Ileret traditions, first occurs, also associated with an Eburran 5 stone tool industry, over a millennium earlier, *c.* 4860 BP (*c.* 5650–5500 cal. BP) (Ambrose 1998). Cattle appear after *c.* 3400 BP (*c.* 3700–3480 cal. BP), after which domestic stock become dominant and are now associated with pottery and stone tools more characteristic of the Elmenteitan (Table 40.1). The particular characteristics of the faunal, lithic, and ceramic assemblages at Enkapune ya Muto have been interpreted as indicative of interaction by an autochthonous hunter-gatherer community with neighbouring pastoralist groups over the course of a millennium or more, followed by full-scale adoption of livestock. Other Eburran 5 horizons in rockshelters elsewhere in the Central Rift are similarly overlain by horizons containing Elmenteitan material, such as at Gamble's Cave and Masai Gorge Rockshelter. The long period between the initial occurrence of domesticates and/or small quantities of ceramics associated further north with early pastoralists, and subsequent full-scale adoption of a pastoralist economy and corresponding changes in artefactual assemblages, may point to the existence of a cultural 'frontier' between immigrant and autochthonous groups involving degrees of social interaction but neither complete assimilation nor integration (Lane 2004).

The evidence for a distinct stock-keeping and herding presence in these landscapes after 3000 BP is more extensive. That from the central Kenya Rift and adjacent highlands, as well as the Serengeti and the footslopes of Mt Kilimanjaro, northern Tanzania, is conventionally divided into three broad groupings: the Savannah Pastoral Neolithic (SPN), Elmenteitan, and Eburran 5 (Table 40.1; Ambrose 2003). Within these categories there is considerable diversity and 'fuzziness' in the material traditions of broadly contemporary sites in adjacent areas, especially in terms of the ratio of wild to domesticated fauna, the overall diversity of artefact assemblages, site locations, and evidence for the exploitation and exchange of different obsidian sources. Thus, the Narosura, Prolonged Drift, and Crescent Island Causeway sites have all been assigned to the SPN, yet their faunas show marked differences in the proportion of wild to domesticated species and the relative proportions of cattle to ovicaprines among the domesticated component (Gifford-Gonzalez 1998; Mutundu 2010).

Domestic stock are also attested from sites in the Serengeti Plains and around Lake Eyasi and Mount Kilimanjaro, northern Tanzania, from *c.* 2300–1900 BP. These include open sites such as Seronera, where Akira and Nderit ceramics are reported, as well as several rockshelters, including Nasera and Mumba, where domesticates and PN pottery are often found in association with LSA Kansyore ceramics (Kusimba, Ch. 32 above). With the exception of the more recently obtained dates from Mumba, there are problems associated with some of the dates for the first appearance of domestic stock at these sites (see Prendergast and Mutundu 2009; Prendergast 2011). Nonetheless, all of the more reliable dates do suggest a slowing down of the southward expansion of pastoralism and perhaps the establishment of a stable frontier between pastoralist and herder populations. This, as Prendergast (2011) notes, is interesting, given that domesticated sheep and cattle are well attested at Toteng in northern Botswana by *c.* 2000 BP and on sites in the Western Cape Province of South Africa *c.* 2000–1800 BP (Sadr, Ch. 44 below). More sustained AMS dating of carefully selected samples from relevant contexts from sites in northern Tanzania may clarify this in the future, as might fieldwork in areas between central Tanzania and southern Zambia.

Savannah Pastoral Neolithic

This has the widest spatial distribution and sites are generally found some 1,500–2,050 m above sea level in vegetation zones associated with open habitats, such as along the central Rift Valley floor, the Loita Plains of southwestern Kenya, the Serengeti, and western Kilimanjaro. Settlements are typically large, with a preference for ecological and topographical settings similar to those preferred by modern Maasai, such as gently sloping ridges and hills, and on well-drained soils. While SPN ceramics (Fig. 40.3a) occur at sites with high percentages of wild fauna (e.g. Prolonged Drift), in general terms SPN faunal assemblages tend to have high proportions of cattle and ovicaprines relative to wild game. Inhumation under stone cairns, in rockshelters, and in rock-filled crevices formed the dominant burial tradition. Accompanying grave goods can include stone bowls, pestles, ochre palettes, and large obsidian blades. The obsidian typically comes from sources in the Naivasha and Nakuru–Elmenteita Basins in the central Rift Valley (Merrick and Brown 1984). Stone bowls, various polished stone artefacts, and rubbing stones also occur on settlement sites. Some of the 'axes' may have been used for shaping and straightening the horns of cattle, while others may have been used as hoes. Nonetheless, despite the possibility that some sites were situated in areas that were potentially suitable for cultivation (Robertshaw and Collett 1983), no confirmed botanical evidence for crops or an isotopic signature for cereal consumption has yet been reported. This may well be due to poor sampling for archaeobotanical remains and the lack of bioarchaeological research on pastoralist diets, however, and both topics warrant greater attention in the future.

In terms of ceramics, two SPN macrotraditions have been proposed, one comprising the Nderit and Ileret ceramic traditions, the other the Narosura (Fig. 40.3b), Akira, and Maringishu ceramic traditions (Ambrose 2003; see Table 40.1). The former might represent an exploratory phase, while the latter could be associated with a period of consolidation. Maringishu ceramics are found in the Lake Nakuru Basin and immediately adjacent areas. The only dated site is Maringishu itself, occupied around 1700 BP, where this kind of pottery occurred in association with Narosura pottery and a largely cattle and caprine faunal assemblage. On the Laikipia Plateau, Maringishu ceramics have been found in association with Akira material (Siiriäinen 1984). Pottery assigned to the Akira ceramic tradition was first identified at Seronera in the Serengeti and at GvJM 44, Lukenya Hill, southeast of Nairobi. Examples of this material have also been found in southwestern Kenya's Lemek–Mara region (Robertshaw 1990) where it occurs in the same contexts as Elmenteitan stone tools. Also known from Nasera, Mumba Höhle, and other sites around Lake Eyasi, northern Tanzania, it may well represent the final stage of PN expansion (Bower 1991). As with Nderit pottery, it

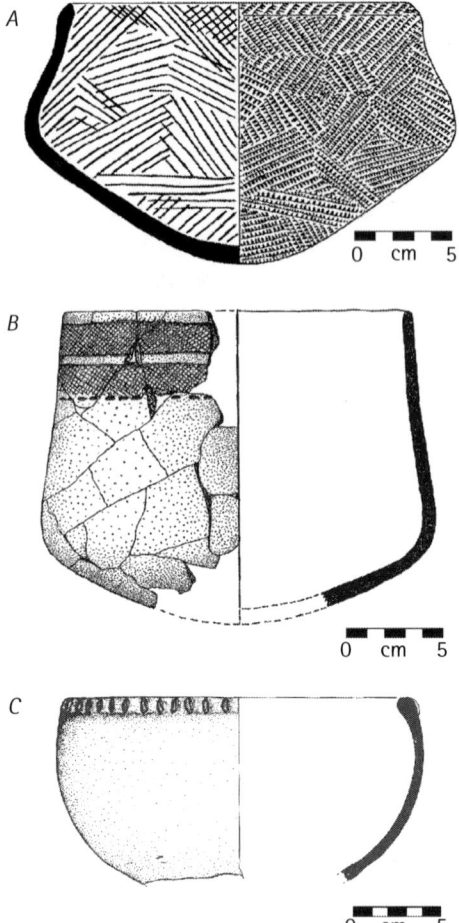

FIG. 40.3 Examples of Savannah Pastoral Neolithic and Elmenteitan pottery from Kenya: (A) Schematic drawing of a decorated Nderit bowl from Stable's Drift (source: Sutton 1964: 29, fig. 3/1, © South African Archaeological Association, reproduced with permission). (B) Narosura pottery—decorated bowl with slightly everted rim (source: Odner 1972: 61, fig. 21/c, © BIEA, reproduced with permission). (C) Elmenteitan pottery—hemispherical bowl with nicked rim from Ngamuriak (source: Robertshaw 1990: 188, fig. 9.2/m, © BIEA, reproduced with permission).

has been found on sites with a predominantly wild fauna (especially in the Serengeti ecosystem) and, in view of its quite wide geographical distribution, may have been a highly valued exchange item that was perhaps made by hunter-gatherers (Robertshaw 1990).

Elmenteitan

Most sites with Elmenteitan material are found in a band stretching from the Naivasha–Nakuru area across the Loita Hills and the Mara Plains as far as the southeastern margins of

Lake Victoria. However, Elmenteitan material has also been reported from the Laikipia Plateau east of the Kenya Rift (Siiriäinen 1984). A range of locations was utilized, including open sites situated in grassland and bushland habitats, and rockshelters. The open sites are often large (in the Lemek–Mara area, for instance, they are significantly bigger than modern Maasai settlements) and are typically single-component sites, suggesting relatively short occupancies. Along the Mau Escarpment, open sites occur at higher elevations, while rockshelters are found at lower altitudes (Robertshaw 1988), whereas around Lake Naivasha they are typically found above 1,900m near the savannah/forest ecotone (Ambrose 1984).

The faunal assemblages from sites in the Central Rift Valley (e.g. Masai Gorge) and especially the neighbouring Loita–Mara region (e.g. Ngamuriak, Sugenya, Sambo Ngige) indicate subsistence economies heavily reliant on the intensive use of livestock, even in areas where wild game was probably abundant (Robertshaw 1988). Assemblages from the lower-elevation rockshelters along the Mau Escarpment (such as Enkapune ya Muto), on the other hand, are dominated by ovicaprines, and their occupation may well have been on a seasonal basis.

Faunal material from Ngamuriak indicates a herd management and culling strategy focusing on adults and young adults. The bones of both cattle and small stock were highly fragmented, suggesting intensive extraction of nutrients. The evidence also indicates an absence of stress, with the inhabitants able to feed surplus animals until they reached full meat weight (Marshall 1990). The large number of mature animals in the assemblage points to considerable dietary reliance on milk. This development may have been related to the evolution of a bimodal rainfall regime, which would have allowed reduced mobility, thus lowering the stress experienced by cattle under more nomadic conditions that prevents them from lactating (Marshall 1990). At Sugenya, there is evidence for comparatively high slaughter rates for juvenile cattle, which could indicate conspicuous consumption on the part of wealthier settlements or individual herders (Simons 2005). One driver of such wealth differences may have been differential access to exchange networks, particularly supplies of obsidian from sources in the Central Rift (Robertshaw 1990).

At sites closer to Lake Victoria, such as Gogo Falls (Karega-Mūnene 2002) and Wadh Lang'o (Lane, Ashley et al. 2007; Prendergast 2011), Elmenteitan levels directly overlie LSA Kansyore horizons and contain more mixed wild and domestic assemblages, as well as evidence for fishing and shellfish collection. This faunal diversity may have been a necessary adaptation to an environment where tsetse fly was locally prevalent (Marshall and Stewart 1995), perhaps arising from competition with other pastoralist groups for grazing (Marshall et al. 2011: 58). Alternatively, the evidence could indicate '"poor" pastoralists in the process of re-establishing their herds after some sort of calamity' (Robertshaw 1990: 300). At both sites the earliest dated remains of domesticated livestock occur in LSA Kansyore horizons (at Wadh Lang'o c. 4400–4150 BP and c. 3960–3560 BP at Gogo Falls), which could imply a process of subsistence change on the part of autochthonous hunter-gatherers as also documented in the Central Rift (Kusimba, Ch. 32 above). The gathering of wild plant foods is also attested at Gogo Falls, and similar practices may well become documented more widely as sampling for botanical remains is practised more regularly.

Compared with SPN pottery, Elmenteitan ceramics (see above, Fig. 40.3c) exhibit far less spatial and temporal diversity. A further difference is the Elmenteitan preference for cremation rather than inhumation. Like SPN inhumations, these burials are sometimes accompanied by stone bowls (typically, these are broken, however), utilized obsidian blades, and stone pestles and grinding stones. Pottery and powdered red ochre have also been recovered from some cremation burials. The richest assemblage, comprising 78 individuals, comes from Njoro River Cave (Leakey and Leakey 1950). The four radiocarbon dates available for the site cluster around 3350–3050 BP (Merrick and Monaghan 1984).

THE PASTORAL IRON AGE

From 2000 BP to 1400 BP, there was yet another shift in the Central Rift and adjacent areas back to more highly mobile settlement strategies and an increased reliance on foraged wild resources, even among groups of previously specialized pastoralists (Bower 1991). Further changes probably occurred around 900–800 years ago following the adoption of iron-manufacturing technologies among pastoralist communities of the Central Rift. Archaeologists term this phase the Pastoral Iron Age. One of the earliest dated occurrences of this transition comes from Deloraine 'main site' (c. AD 620–890), near Rongai on the edge of the Mau Escarpment northwest of Lake Nakuru. This site contains abundant remains of cattle and evidence of cereal cultivation, as well as evidence for the manufacture and use of iron implements, and may well represent a development of earlier PN Elmenteitan traditions (Ambrose et al. 1984), as implied by continuities in the layout of ceramic decoration. The processes by which this technological change occurred remain poorly understood, but it is possible that among other changes it triggered (or accompanied, or even followed) included changes in weaponry, military methods and tactics, settlement design, and even the consolidation of warrior age-sets in at least some pastoralist societies (Sutton 1993). From c. AD 500, there is increasing evidence for the adoption of iron by other PN groups, which seems to have precipitated a marked qualitative decline in stone tool production, especially in the use of obsidian.

Characteristic of PIA sites in the Central Rift Valley, such as Lanet (Posnansky 1967) and Hyrax Hill (Leakey 1945) on the edge of Nakuru, and Muringa and other sites across the Western Highlands (Sutton 1973) is the presence of Lanet ware (Table 40.2, Fig. 40.4a). This pottery type is distributed across most of the areas previously occupied by Elmenteitan and SPN groups. It is also associated with the 'Sirikwa hole' earthwork sites that are especially common along the Elgeyo Escarpment, Uasin Gishu, and in the Nandi area. Sirikwa sites range in date from the 12th to 18th centuries AD (Davies, Ch. 49 below).

Further south, in the northeastern Mara Plains, the transition from the PN Elmenteitan to later cultural traditions is mainly represented by changes in ceramics, a diminishing reliance on stone tools, and changes in obsidian sources and associated exchange networks (Robertshaw 1990). These later sites, dating to c. cal. AD 1100–1400, are tentatively attributed to the 'Oldorotua' tradition (Siiriäinen et al. 2009). Twisted-string roulette (TGR) decorated pottery is also present in low quantities on some of them (Robertshaw 1990: 295). PIA sites on the Laikipia and Leroghi Plateaux on the eastern side of the Rift Valley are associated with a pottery tradition known as 'Kisima Ware' (Fig. 40.4b), which has been tentatively associated with the Laikipiak Maasai, although it was quite possibly made by neighbouring 'forager' communities. Recent surveys and excavations have extended its chronological range back beyond cal. AD 1500 (Siiriäinen 1984), with new evidence derived in particular from two large, open-air pastoralist settlements, Mili Sita and Maasai Plains (Lane 2011). The Maasai Plains site, the older of the two, was occupied c. cal. AD 1400–1480, roughly coinciding with a possible period of increased precipitation (Verschuren et al. 2000) that would have made the

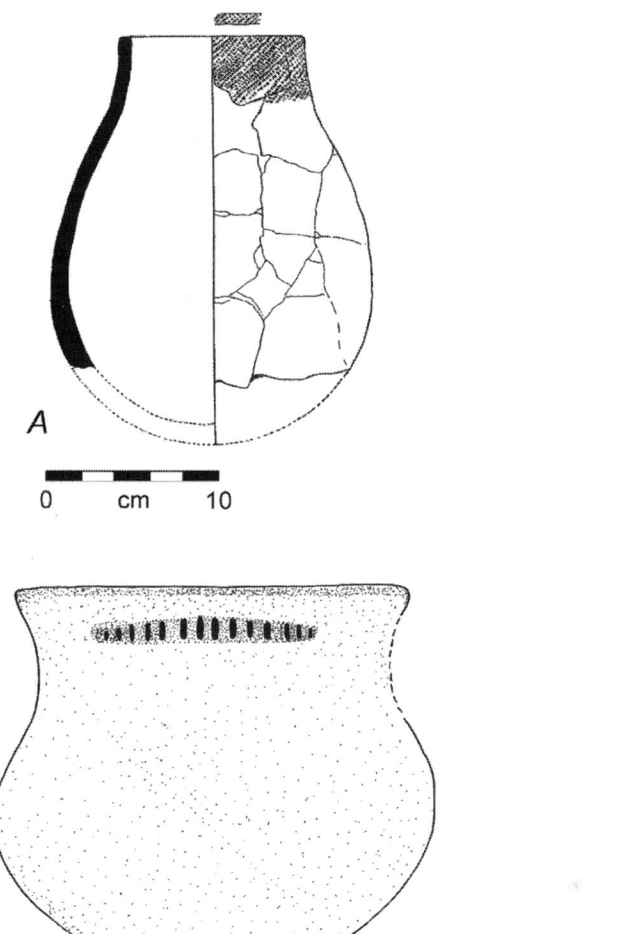

FIG. 40.4 Examples of Pastoral Iron Age pottery from Kenya: (A) Pottery of Lanet tradi-
tion—reconstructed elongated, gourd-shaped pot with cord-roulette decoration from Hut
A (source: Posnansky 1967: 99, fig. 6, © BIEA, reproduced with permission). (B) Kisima
Ware from Laikipia—reconstructed pot from Maasai Plains (source: Causey 2010: 116, fig. 3,
© BIEA, reproduced with permission).

Laikipia Plateau more attractive to pastoralists, especially for seasonal grazing. Mili Sita
appears to have been occupied around cal. AD 1640–1730.

Despite the significance given to iron in the appellation PIA, there has been remarkably
little research on the adoption of this technology among pastoralists or on the technology
itself. The only detailed archaeometallurgical study (Iles and Martinón-Torres 2009) relates
to two clusters of smelting remains associated and coeval with the Mili Sita settlement and a
third contemporary cluster a few kilometres away. In each cluster, furnace shape and the
number and positioning of tuyère ports differed, yet a very similar technical approach was

Table 40.2 Main diagnostic aspects of different Pastoral Iron Age wares

Ware	Characteristics	Representative sites
Lanet	Date range: *c.* 900–1700 cal. AD *Pottery:* Tall jars with simple rims and other gourd-shaped vessels predominate. Decorated with twisted-string roulette motifs around the rim and in horizontal and vertical strips possibly imitating the leather supporting straps of milk gourds.	Lanet, Muringa, Hyrax Hill, Sirikwa sites
Oldorotua	Date range: *c.* 1100–1400 cal. AD *Pottery:* Generally thick-walled and sand-tempered, with a marked absence (or very low proportion) of mica inclusions. Decoration is scarce; tends to be restricted to around the rim in the form of horizontal, vertical, and cross-hatched incisions.	JuJe 32
Twisted-string roulette (TGR)	Date Range: *c.* >1650–1810 cal. AD *Pottery:* Use of TGR in horizontal, vertical, and diagonal bands immediately below the rim.	GuJf 70
Kisima	Date Range: *c.* >1400–1750 cal. AD *Pottery:* Shallow, wide-mouthed, necked vessels and wide-mouthed jars are the most common forms. Largely undecorated; main diagnostic feature is the use of raised, notched appliqué ridges below the rim either for decoration, or in some cases as handles. Notches may also be present around the outer lip.	Maasai Plains, Mili Sita, Porcupine Cave, Baawa

employed at all three. Elsewhere, three eroded furnace- or forge-bases have been recorded adjacent to a settlement with Kisima ware pottery and dated to *c.* AD 1300–1390 (Lane, Straight and Hilton 2007) near Maralal. North of here, Larick (1986) found smelting sites occurred in three topographical settings (mountain bases, mountain ridges, and plains oasis sites), although the causes of these differences remain unclear. The only other reported excavated pastoralist ironworking remains are those from JuJe 32, in the Maasai Mara, Kenya (Siiriäinen et al. 2009). In this case the furnace was roughly triangular, with one bowed side and tuyère ports in each corner.

Single inhumation within stone cairns seems to have been the preferred mode of burial during the PIA, with isolated cairns, groups, and larger cairn-fields common in both highland and lowland areas. There is considerable typological variation and, as at Baawa, northern Kenya, earlier PN burial cairns were sometimes reused for multiple interments (Lane, Straight, and Hilton 2007). Examples have been excavated at various sites along the Eastern Rift including the Ngorongoro Crater and around Lake Eyasi, Tanzania, and at Hyrax Hill, Ilkek near Gilgil, and in the Western Highlands, Kenya. While many cairns, especially those in the Rift, are of PN date and often contain associated stone bowls and Nderit ware pottery, thus probably dating to the late second millennium BC, other excavated examples are more recent. A detailed comparative regional study is needed, however, to clarify the relationships between cairn function, form, chronology, and cultural affiliations.

REFERENCES

AMBROSE, S. H. (1984). The introduction of pastoral adaptations to the highlands of East Africa. In J. D. Clark and S. A. Brandt (eds), *From Hunters to Farmers: The Causes and Consequences of Food Production in Africa*. Berkeley: University of California Press, 212–39.

—— (1998). Chronology of the Later Stone Age and food production in East Africa, *Journal of Archaeological Science* 25: 377–92.

—— (2003). East African Neolithic. In P. N. Peregrine and M. Ember (eds), *Encyclopedia of Prehistory*, vol. 1: *Africa*. London: Kluwer Academic/Plenum, 97–109.

—— MARSHALL, F. B., and COLLETT, D. P. (1984). Excavations at Deloraine, Rongai, 1978. *Azania* 19: 79–104.

BARTHELME, J. (1985). *Fisher-Hunters and Neolithic Pastoralists in East Turkana, Kenya*. Oxford: British Archaeological Reports.

BOWER, J. R. F. (1991). The Pastoral Neolithic of East Africa. *Journal of World Prehistory* 5: 49–82.

—— and NELSON, C. M. (1978). Early pottery and pastoral cultures of the central Rift Valley, Kenya. *Man* 13: 554–66.

CAMPBELL, M. C., and TISHKOFF, S. A. (2010). The evolution of human genetic and phenotypic variation in Africa. *Current Biology* 20: R166–73.

CAUSEY, M. J. (2010). New archaeological discoveries from the Laikipia Plateau, Kenya. *Azania* 45: 112–36.

EHRET, C. (2003). Language family expansions: broadening our understandings of cause from an African perspective. In P. Bellwood and C. Renfrew (eds), *Examining the Farming/Language Dispersal Hypothesis*. Cambridge: McDonald Institute, 163–76.

GIFFORD-GONZALEZ, D. (1998). Early pastoralists in East Africa: ecological and social dimensions. *Journal of Anthropological Archaeology* 17: 166–200.

HILDEBRAND, E., SHEA, J., and GRILLO, K. (2011). Four middle Holocene pillar sites in West Turkana, Kenya. *Journal of Field Archaeology* 36: 181–200.

ILES, L., and M. MARTINÓN-TORRES (2009). Pastoralist iron production on the Laikipia Plateau, Kenya: implications for wider archaeometallurgical studies. *Journal of Archaeological Science* 36: 2314–26.

KAREGA-MŨNENE (2002). *Holocene Foragers, Fishers and Herders of Western Kenya*. Oxford: Archaeopress.

—— (2003). The East African Neolithic: a historical perspective. In C. M. Kusimba and S. B. Kusimba (eds), *East African Archaeology: Foragers, Potters, Smiths and Traders*. Philadelphia: University of Pennsylvania Museum of Archaeology and Anthropology, 17–32.

LANE, P. J. (2004). The 'moving frontier' and the transition to food production in Kenya. *Azania* 39: 243–64.

—— (2011). An outline of the later Holocene archaeology and precolonial history of the Ewaso Basin, Kenya. *Smithsonian Contributions to Zoology* 632: 11–30.

—— ASHLEY, C. Z., SEITSONEN, O., HARVEY, P., MIRE, S., and ODEDE, F. (2007). The transition to farming in eastern Africa: new faunal and dating evidence from Wadh Lang'o and Usenge, Kenya. *Antiquity* 81: 62–81.

—— STRAIGHT, B., and HILTON, C. (2007). Excavations at Baawa, Samburu District, Kenya: preliminary report on the 2006 season. *Nyame Akuma* 68: 34–46.

LARICK, R. (1986). Iron smelting and interethnic conflict among precolonial Maa-speaking pastoralists of north-central Kenya. *African Archaeological Review* 4: 165–76.

LEAKEY, M. D. (1945). Report on the excavations at Hyrax Hill, Nakuru, Kenya Colony. *Transactions of the Royal Society of South Africa* 30: 271–409.

—— and LEAKEY, L. S. B. (1950). *Excavations at Njoro River Cave*. Oxford: Clarendon Press.

LYNCH, B. M., and ROBBINS, L. H. (1979). Cushitic and Nilotic prehistory: new archaeological evidence from north-east Kenya. *Journal of African History* 20: 319–28.

MARSHALL, F. B. (1990). Origins of specialized pastoral production in East Africa. *American Anthropologist* 92: 873–94.

—— GRILLO, K., and ARCO, L. (2011). Prehistoric pastoralists and social responses to climatic risk in East Africa. In N. F. Miller, K. M. Moore, and K. Ryan (eds), *Sustainable Lifeways: Cultural Persistence in an Ever-Changing Environment*. Philadelphia: University of Pennsylvania Museum of Archaeology and Anthropology, 39–74.

—— and HILDEBRAND, E. (2002). Cattle before crops: the beginnings of food production in Africa. *Journal of World Prehistory* 16: 99–143.

—— and STEWART, K. M. (1995). Hunting, fishing and herding pastoralists of western Kenya: the fauna from Gogo Falls. *Archaeozoologia* 7: 7–27.

—— and WEISSBROD, L. (2011). Domestication processes and morphological change through the lens of the donkey and African pastoralism. *Current Anthropology* 52 (supplement 4): S397–413.

MERRICK, H. V., and BROWN, F. H. (1984). Obsidian sources and patterns of source utilization in Kenya and northern Tanzania: some initial findings. *African Archaeological Review* 2: 129–52.

—— and MONAGHAN, M. C. (1984). The date of the cremated burials in Njoro River Cave. *Azania* 19: 7–11.

MUTUNDU, K. K. (2010). An ethnoarchaeological framework for the identification and distinction of Late Holocene archaeological sites in East Africa. *Azania* 45: 6–23.

NASH, B. P., MERRICK, H. V., and BROWN, F. H. (2011). Obsidian types from Holocene sites around Lake Turkana, and other localities in northern Kenya. *Journal of Archaeological Science* 38: 1371–6.

NELSON, C. M. (1995). The work of the Koobi Fora Field School at the Jarigole Pillar site. *Kenya Past and Present* 27: 49–63.

ODNER, K. (1972). Excavations at Narosura, a Stone Bowl site in the southern Kenya Highlands. *Azania* 7: 25–92.

PRENDERGAST, M. E. (2011). Hunters and herders at the periphery: the spread of herding in eastern Africa. In H. Jousse and J. Lesur (eds), *People and Animals in Holocene Africa: Recent Advances in Archaeozoology*. Frankfurt: Africa Magna, 43–58.

—— and MUTUNDU, K. K. (2009). Late Holocene archaeological faunas in East Africa: ethnographic analogues and interpretive challenges. *Documenta Archaeobiologiae* 7: 203–32.

POLONI, E. S., NACIRI, Y., BUCHO, R., et al. (2009). Genetic evidence for complexity in ethnic differentiation and history in East Africa. *Annals of Human Genetics* 73: 582–600.

POSNANSKY, M. (1967). Excavations at Lanet, 1957. *Azania* 2: 89–114.

ROBBINS, L. H. (1984). Late prehistoric aquatic and pastoral adaptations west of Lake Turkana, Kenya. In J. D. Clark and S. A. Brandt (eds), *From Hunters to Farmers: The Causes and Consequences of Food Production in Africa*. Berkeley: University of California Press, 206–12.

ROBERTSHAW, P. T. (1988). The Elmenteitan: an early food-producing culture in East Africa. *World Archaeology* 20: 57–69.

—— (1990). *Early Pastoralists of South-Western Kenya*. Nairobi: British Institute in Eastern Africa.

—— (1991). Gogo Falls: excavations at a complex archaeological site east of Lake Victoria. *Azania* 26: 63–195.

—— and COLLETT, D. (1983). The identification of pastoral peoples in the archaeological record: an example from East Africa. *World Archaeology* 15: 67–78.

RUSSELL, T. (2013). Through the skin: Exploring pastoralist marks and their meanings to understand parts of East African rock art. *Journal of Social Archaeology* 13, 3–30.

SIIRIÄINEN, A. (1984). *Excavations in Laikipia: An Archaeological Study of the Recent Prehistory in the Eastern Highlands of Kenya*. Helsinki: Suomen Muinais-muistoyhdistksen Aikakauskirja Finska Fornminnesförenengens Tidskrift.

—— SEITSONEN, O., and LAURÉN, J. (2009). Pastoralists in the northeastern Mara Plains, Kenya: archaeological investigations of the Pastoral Neolithic and Pastoral Iron Age. *Azania* 44: 163–93.

SIMONS, A. (2005). Exchange networks, socio-political hierarchies and the archaeological evidence for differential wealth amongst pastoralists in southwestern Kenya. *Nyame Akuma* 64: 36–40.

STEWART, K. M. (1989). *Fishing Sites of North and East Africa in the Late Pleistocene and Holocene: Environmental Change and Human Adaptation*. Oxford: British Archaeological Reports.

SUTTON, J. E. G. (1964). A review of pottery from the Kenya Highlands. *South African Archaeological Bulletin* 19: 27–35.

—— (1973). *The Archaeology of the Western Highlands of Kenya*. Nairobi: British Institute in Eastern Africa.

—— (1993). Becoming Maasailand. In T. Spear and R. Waller (eds), *Being Maasai: Ethnicity and Identity in East Africa*. London: James Currey, 38–60.

TISHKOFF, S. A., REED, F. A., RANCIARO, A., et al. (2007). Convergent adaptation of human lactase persistence in Africa and Europe. *Nature Genetics* 39: 31–40.

VERSCHUREN, D., LAIRD, K. R., and CUMMING, B. R. (2000). Rainfall and drought in Equatorial East Africa during the past 1,100 years. *Nature* 403: 410–14.

WRIGHT, D. K. (2005). New perspectives on early regional interaction networks of East African trade: a view from Tsavo National Park, Kenya. *African Archaeological Review* 22: 111–40.

CHAPTER 41

THE STONE TO METAL AGE IN WEST AFRICA

JOANNA CASEY

INTRODUCTION

THE term 'Stone to Metal Age' (SMA) was coined by Pierre de Maret (1994/5: 320) to describe 'a stage without metals but with advanced technical traits such as ceramics and polished stone, and sometimes possible indications of food production' intermediate between the Later Stone Age (LSA) and the Iron Age. A new term was thought necessary because the frequent use of the term 'Neolithic' with reference to ground stone tools and pottery assemblages from this period had proved particularly problematic in Africa (Sinclair et al. 1993). Some definitions of the Neolithic include farming, yet in Africa the defining artefacts appear long before any evidence for plant and animal domestication. Although it has been criticized for being inexact and for perpetuating an 'Ages and Stages' view of African prehistory (Ambrose 1997: 382), the term 'SMA' is thus used here, bearing in mind Lavachery's (2001) caution as to its provisional nature pending further research.

Such research has, as in most of Africa, thus far suffered from too few archaeologists working in a vast area, thereby making it difficult to get an overview of developments. Low ground visibility in the heavily forested regions of southern West Africa, unstable political environments, and variable infrastructure have exacerbated the patchy coverage. From the 1950s until the 1980s much of the archaeological research in West Africa addressed the earlier prehistory and the origins of settlement and agriculture during the SMA. More recently the focus has shifted toward later time periods (Holl 2009), but research currently being conducted on the SMA is producing very interesting and surprising results.

Climate change is thought to have been a significant factor in the SMA. At the end of the Pleistocene around 12,000 years ago, warm, humid conditions brought about a northward shift in the vegetation zones that currently characterize West Africa. Forests and savannahs expanded, the desert contracted, and animals and people spread out over what is now the Sahara. During the mid-Holocene, around 4500 BP, the climate changed abruptly, causing vegetation zones to contract and assume their current locations (Shanahan et al. 2006; Itambi et al. 2010; Le Drézan et al. 2010). People living in the Sahara by hunting, gathering, fishing, and herding responded by locating their settlements closer and closer to the disappearing water sources, increasing their reliance on domestic crops and eventually abandoning the Sahara altogether. It is around this time that substantial evidence appears for human settlement of the southern parts of West Africa.

In West Africa there is very little evidence for people south of the Sahara prior to the mid-Holocene, and such evidence as does exist is primarily of small, scattered groups of mobile hunter-gatherers, some of whom returned frequently, possibly even seasonally, to the same places. These earliest LSA sites date to around 12,000 BP and are dominated by chipped stone assemblages, primarily in quartz and often with geometric microliths. They are generally distinguished from an earlier and even less well-known Middle Stone Age by the small size of their knapping debris, although a macrolithic aspect of the LSA is also known (MacDonald and Allsworth-Jones 1994; Casey 2003). A number of these LSA sites are overlain by SMA assemblages recognizable by the appearance of ground stone tools and pottery and dating to 5000 years or later (Fig. 41.1). The best known are: Iwo Eleru (Shaw and Daniels 1984), Afikpo (Andah and Anozie 1980), Rop (Eyo 1972; David 1993), Dutzen Kongba (Federal Department of Antiquities Nigeria 1974; York 1978), and Mejiro Cave (Willett 1962) in Nigeria; Rim (Andah 1978) and Maadaga (Breunig and Wotzka 1993) in Burkina Faso; Kourounkorokalé (MacDonald 1997) in Mali; and, technically in Central Africa but significant for this discussion, Shum Laka in Cameroon (Lavachery 2001; see also Cornelissen, Ch. 28 above). SMA sites that lack this stratification include Sopie and Kokasu in Liberia (Gabel 1976), Yengema, Yagala, and Kamabai in Sierra Leone (Atherton 1972; Coon 1968), and several Kintampo Complex sites in Ghana (Stahl 1985; Casey 2000; Watson 2005, 2008). Uncountable scatters of lithic debris throughout West Africa also most likely date to the LSA, some accompanied by potsherds and/or ground stone (Chenorkian 1983; MacDonald 1997).

Davies (1967) and Shaw (1978) both argued that before the desiccation of the Sahara, not only were Saharan inhabitants not compelled to move southward, but it was virtually impossible for them to do so. Postulated barriers to human occupation in southern West Africa include the difficulty of making a living in the dense rainforest prior to the advent of iron tools, and potentially lethal diseases such as malaria, onchocerciasis, and trypanosomiasis,

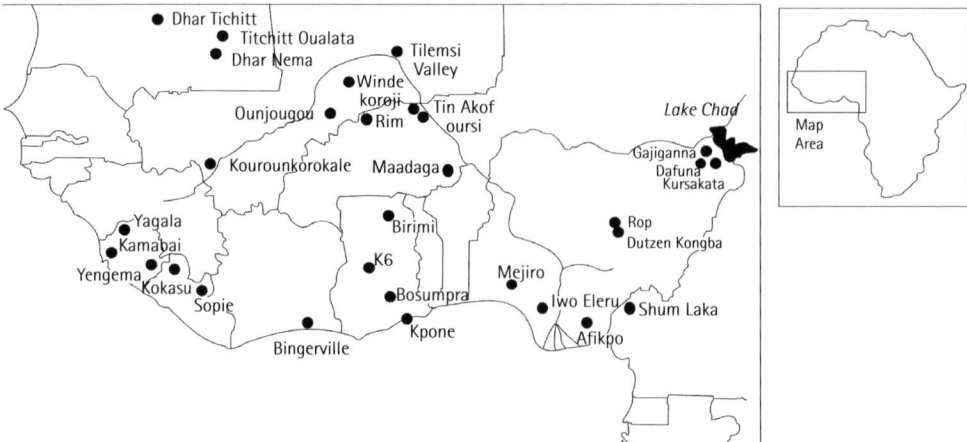

FIG. 41.1 Map of sites mentioned in Chapter 41.

the latter an added problem to herders because it can be devastating to cattle (Smith 1992). Only when climate zones contracted could people, and especially herders, move south.

The artefacts found at many early sites support a northern origin for SMA people in southern West Africa. Projectile points are often in a 'Saharan Style' with concave or convex bases, and pottery often bears comb and roulette impressions very similar to types known from the Sahara and the Nile Valley as early as the tenth millennium BP. Davies's (1967) view that Holocene culture change in southern West Africa was due to successive migrations from the north received little challenge for some decades. However, while the climate change scenario appears neatly to explain the timing and direction of settlement south of the Sahara, the correlation is not perfect, and it is the deviations from this model that require us to consider the meaning of these changes rather than simply to chronicle their occurrences. Notwithstanding supposedly difficult living conditions prior to the mid-Holocene, evidence of human occupation does, in fact, exist long before the final dry period, even in what would then have been heavily forested environments (Casey 2003). Significant examples include an early fourteenth-millennium BP date from Bingerville Highway, southern Ivory Coast (Chenorkian 1983), and the site of Iwo Eleru in southern Nigeria, which was occupied recurrently from the early twelfth millennium BP (Shaw and Daniels 1984); Shum Laka was occupied repeatedly from the early tenth millennium BP (Lavachery 2001); and in central and coastal Ghana the sites of Bosumpra (Shaw 1944; A. Smith 1975), Kpone (Dombrowski 1977; Nygaard and Talbot 1984), and the lower levels of K6 (Stahl 1985) date to the sixth/seventh millennia BP. These Ghanaian sites, along with Shum Laka and Konduga (Nigeria; Breunig et al. 1996), have very early evidence for ceramics, suggesting that the final desiccation of the Sahara was not the only impetus for the population of southern West Africa. Most surprising, however, are recent finds from Ounjougou, Mali, the pottery from which is not only the earliest in southern West Africa but, at 9400 cal. BC, may be the earliest on the continent (Huysecom et al. 2009).

The very early pottery at all these sites, including Ounjougou, is found in small quantities, but is often sufficiently different from overlying ceramics to indicate that it is not intrusive. The idea of an aceramic vs ceramic LSA is challenged by these early dates for pottery, but after c. 4500 BP a significant increase in pottery throughout West Africa does suggest both larger and more settled populations. The earlier dates thus imply that before then people occasionally made pottery for specific purposes, and that the significant factor in the increased occurrence of pottery after 4500 BP is most likely a change in conditions that made it more advantageous to make and use it. These are undoubtedly the same conditions that encouraged population growth, either through the increased fertility that comes with sedentism and a reliable, carbohydrate-rich diet or through immigration. As savannahs spread in West Africa during the mid-Holocene, people probably had the opportunity and the need to rely more heavily on cereal grasses and legumes that required ceramic vessels for their preparation, while as they stayed for longer periods of time in the same place there would also have been an increased need for vessels to store water and foodstuffs. Not only would people have been making more vessels, but the longer duration of their stays would also have increased the amount of broken pottery in their settlements and thus their archaeological visibility.

The sharp, edge-ground stone tools, the other characteristic artefact type of the SMA, are more difficult to track than pottery. Most familiar are the ground, roughly wedge-shaped 'axes', 'adzes', or 'celts', but West Africa has produced a staggering variety of such tools of many sizes and shapes (Fig. 41.2). As a morphological type, they are identifiable by having a working edge formed by grinding acutely from one or both sides. Most are ground all over, but some only on their working edges, while the body of the tool retains the scars of bifacial flaking. They are generally made from heavy, coarse-grained materials, such as metamorphosed volcanics and quartzites, that favour strength and durability over sharpness. Remains of 'axe factories' have been found at sources of good-quality raw materials in several places in West Africa, such as in Ghana at Buroburo (Nunoo 1969) and near Kintampo (Rahtz and Flight 1974). Nearby grinding grooves for finishing axes generally help to identify the sites, but in many cases the materials were quarried and shaped in one place and finished in another. With their large-format flaking debris, and lack of datable materials or diagnostic artefacts, these workshops are easily mistaken for sites from earlier time periods (MacDonald and Allsworth-Jones 1994).

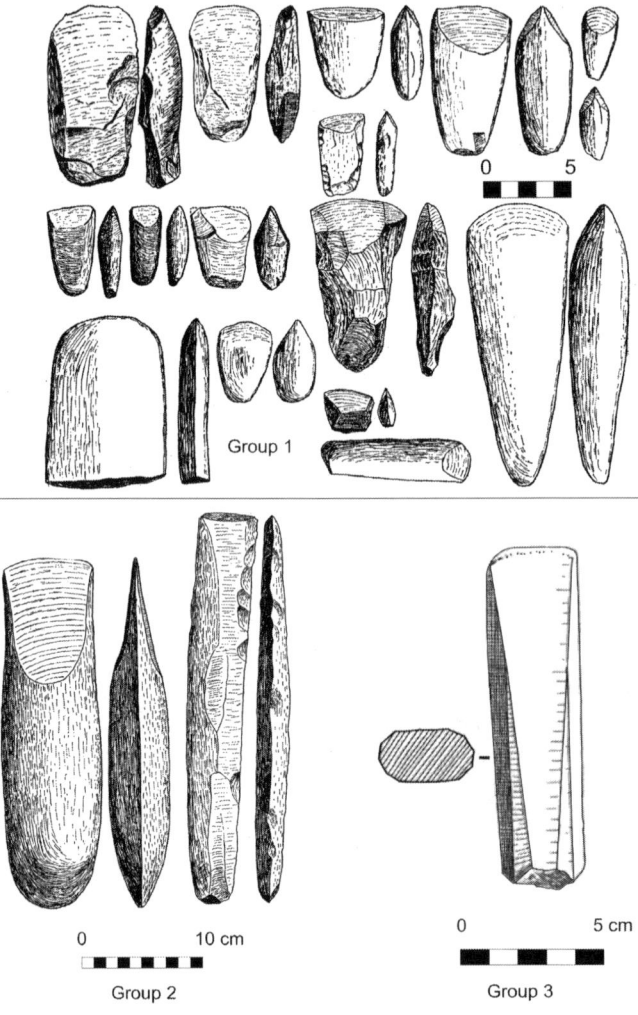

FIG. 41.2 Edge-ground tool types from West Africa. Group 1: tools from Senegal, Ivory Coast, Burkina Faso, Ghana and Bénin (Davies 1967: 194); Group 2: long axes from Ivory Coast (Davies 1967: 202); Group 3: faceted axe from Ghana (Nunoo 1948).

Although ground stone tools were previously thought to be associated with farming, their closer association appears to be with cutting and working wood, as there are many instances worldwide where they occur among peoples who did not farm (Hayden 1981, 1989). A reduction in mobility tends to increase the need to cut trees for fuel and construction materials and to clear land. These needs would have been even more acute as people started to require more fuel to make pottery and to cook dried grains and legumes. It is also likely that ground stone tools had multi-purpose roles as generalized, heavy-duty tools.

The sources of the raw materials used to make stone axes are not spread evenly throughout West Africa, so they were most probably extensively traded. Most appear to have reached their destinations in finished form, because flakes of the raw material are often rare, and those that do occur usually have grinding on their dorsal surfaces, indicating that they became detached from finished axes while they were being used. Many axes were extensively reground and repaired when they became damaged (Casey 2000). Both the rarity of the raw material and the workmanship involved in their production would appear to have made axes valuable, yet they were abandoned with relative frequency on archaeological sites. The chronology of these ground stone tools is not completely certain, as their absence from some sites, especially small lithic scatters, may be due to the types of activities performed there and to curation practices. Another taphonomic problem is raised by the fact that they are still sought and used as offerings and for medicine throughout West Africa, and have often been considered to be 'thunderbolts' of supernatural origin (as in the case of the Yoruba thunder god Shango), featuring in local shrines (Westcott and Morton-Williams 1962; cf. Insoll, Ch. 12 above). Moreover, when they occur in later periods, it is unclear if they were still being manufactured or had been collected from earlier sites. Interestingly, at Shum Laka, flakes with polished dorsal surfaces occur in the earliest ceramic-bearing layers dated to 7000–6000 BP, but whole ground stone tools are not found until 2150–900 BP (Lavachery 2001). At Ounjougou, pottery appears nearly 12,000 years ago, while polished stone axes do not appear until around 4000 BP (Ozainne et al. 2009).

There have been few analyses of the chipped stone component of SMA sites, primarily because quartz, the most common material, is so difficult to analyse. Those that have been undertaken have looked at fine-grained quartz or non-quartz materials. Sites are generally characterized by a profusion of lithic debris with very low numbers of recognizable tools such as geometric microliths, scrapers, bifaces, points, and retouched flakes. Microscopic analysis suggests that, at least in some places, the objective of reduction was to make usable edges for immediate application without retouching (Casey 2000). People applied a variety of reduction techniques suitable to the material at hand, and while small flake size is characteristic of LSA and SMA assemblages, there are also macrolithic assemblages on coarser materials such as basalts and quartzites (MacDonald and Allsworth-Jones 1994; Cornelissen 2003).

From around 4000 BP people in sub-Saharan West Africa increasingly settled down, creating much larger sites with evidence for durable structures and an increasing density of artefacts. The Kintampo Complex (also known as the Kintampo Tradition or Kintampo Culture) is the earliest and best-known settled SMA tradition (Stahl 1985; Casey 2000; Watson 2005). Kintampo has an easily recognized assemblage consisting of comb-stamped, rouletted, and slipped pottery, a prolific flaked stone industry, grinding stones, and ground stone axes. Stone bracelets, beads, ground haematite, clay figurines, bone harpoons, and projectile points are also frequent (Fig. 41.3) The type specimen of the Kintampo Complex is the

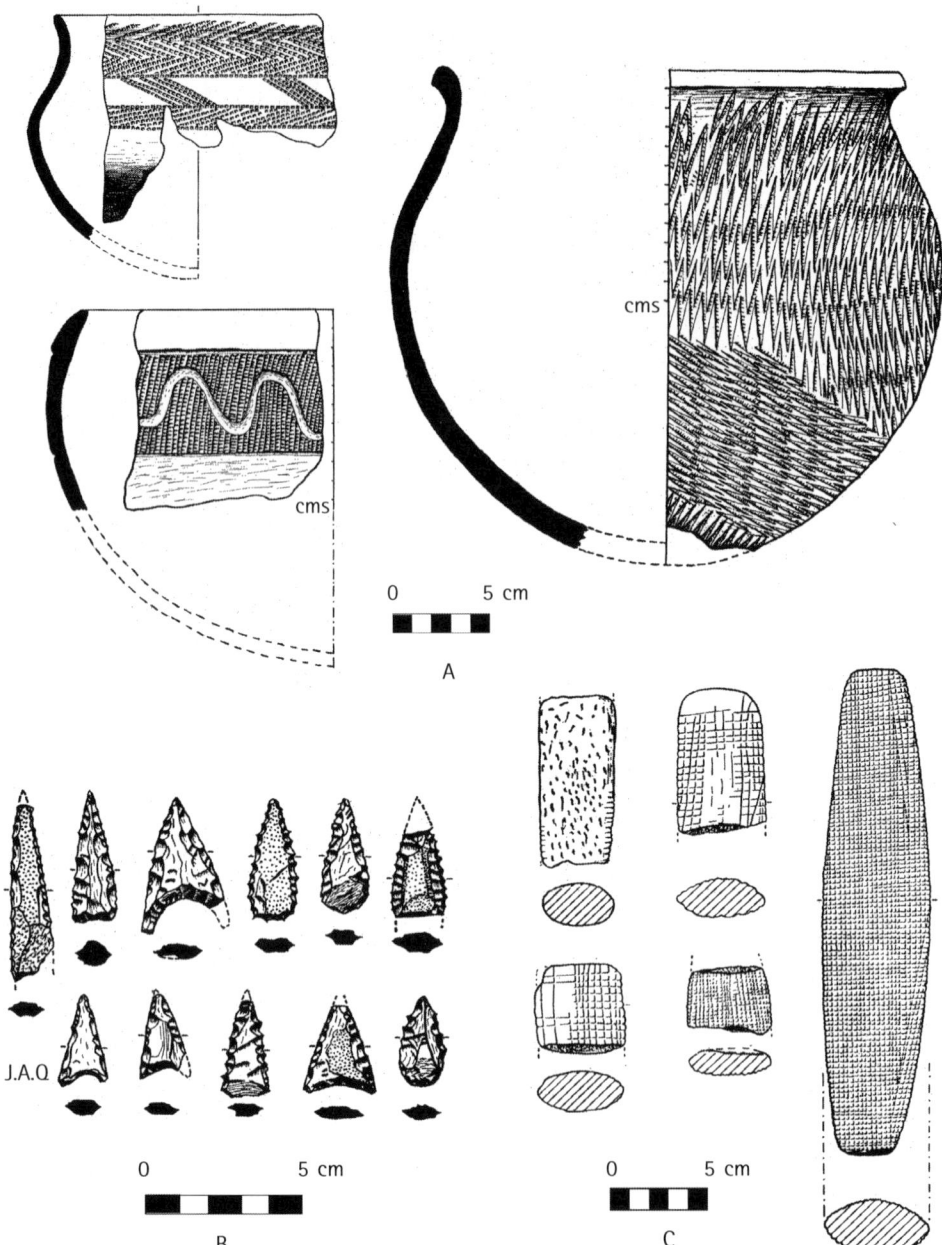

FIG. 41.3 Kintampo LSA artefacts from Ntereso, Ghana: (A) ceramics (Davies 1967: 278, 279); (B) projectile points (Davies 1967: 281); (C) 'terracotta cigars' (Davies 1967: 280).

'terracotta cigar', an elliptical item made of lightweight, fine-grained sandstone that has been scored or pecked all over. Pieces of terracotta cigars bearing evidence of abrasion and, less frequently, secondary shaping, boring, and grooving appear in profusion on many Kintampo sites. Their purpose, however, is unknown. Burned daub bearing impressions of poles indicate wattle and daub construction, and at some sites structures were outlined with circular or rectangular arrangements of stones. Kintampo sites are found throughout Ghana from the northern savannah to the coast, indicating that Kintampo peoples had a very flexible lifestyle that enabled them to occupy many environmental zones, and that they adjusted their subsistence strategies and tool-making techniques to local resources. Terracotta cigars have been found in non-Kintampo contexts in Ivory Coast and Togo, but only Dabakala in Ivory Coast appears to be a true Kintampo site, where surface collections yielded terracotta cigars, stone bracelet fragments, and chipped stone (Chenorkian 1983).

The very few SMA sites to have yielded organic remains indicate a heavy reliance on wild plants and animals and varying relationships to domestic species. The SMA is thus an important time for considering the spread of domestic plants and animals and the incorporation of farming into people's subsistence strategies. Early indications that SMA peoples manipulated their environments and were developing complex relationships with plant and animal resources came from pollen cores in Lake Bosumtwi, Ghana, and off West Africa's coast. These cores showed an increase in open woodlands and oil palm (*Elais guineensis*) pollen coinciding with evidence for SMA settlement, suggesting forest clearing and encouragement, if not actual husbandry, of oil palms (Sowunmi 1981, 1985; Talbot et al. 1984). At Madaaga and Oursi, abrupt changes from forest to Sahel vegetation accompanied by human occupation indicate that climate alone was not responsible for these environmental changes (Breunig et al. 1996), while at K6 in central Ghana, a change from forest species to those that prefer open environments, waste places, and live commensally with humans suggests land-clearing activities and food storage (Stahl 1985). Analysis of Later Stone Age coastal shell middens in Ivory Coast (Chenorkian 1983), Ghana (Nygaard and Talbot 1984), and Nigeria (Derefaka and Anozie 2002) indicates that people used complex lagoonal and estuarial environments and the strands and forests that abut them by exploiting all available resources. Nzewunwa (1980) has suggested that the food remains found in shell middens indicate a highly deficient diet that must have been supplemented with starchy plant foods that are rarely preserved. Domesticated pearl millet (*Pennisetum glaucum*) is now known from Karkarichinkat in Mali's Tilemsi Valley as early as 2500 cal. BC (Manning et al. 2011), although its precise point of origin remains unknown. Finds from second millennium cal. BC sites reaching from southeastern Mauritania in the west to northeastern Nigeria in the east indicate that it spread rapidly across the Sahelian belt (Amblard and Pernès 1989; MacDonald 1996; Klee et al. 2000, 2004; Neumann et al. 2001; D'Andrea and Casey 2002; MacDonald et al. 2009). Millet cultivation appears, however, to have been only one part of diverse subsistence strategies that variously included hunting, gathering, herding, fishing, and the production of a few other domestic and semi-domestic species such as cowpeas and oil palm (D'Andrea et al. 2006, 2007; Kahlheber and Neumann 2007).

Domestic animals long pre-date domestic plants in Africa, and husbandry of cattle and caprines appears right across the Sahara between the eighth and sixth millennia BP (Gifford-Gonzalez 2005; di Lernia, Ch. 36 above). Domestic cattle appear south of the Sahara around 2500 cal. BC in Mali's Tilemsi Valley (Manning et al. 2011), and after 4,000 years ago at Dhar Tichitt, Mauritania (Holl 1985), and around the Lake Chad Basin (Breunig et al. 1996). Below the Sahel, evidence for them is less conclusive. Domestic caprines have, nevertheless, been confirmed in central Ghana at the Kintampo site of K6 (Stahl 1985), but the status of bovid bones found at other Kintampo sites has always been in question, due either to ambiguous specimens or to disturbed contexts. The earliest certain *Bos* south of the Sahel postdates Kintampo at 2640 ± 40 BP (Watson 2005, 2010).

The SMA was very much more complex than would appear from these widely spaced sites and impoverished remains. The older view of refugee populations escaping rapid aridification by heading for uninhabited regions to the south has given way to richer hypotheses about the part that humans may have played in bringing about environmental change, and about relationships between the newcomers and the people already in southern West Africa. Recent research suggests that in the Mid-Holocene the peoples of the southern Sahara and the Sahel had generalized economies that utilized resources across the wild-domestic spectrum (Finucane et al. 2008; Linseele 2010). Trade and communication among far-flung populations was likely to have been a feature of SMA societies. In the Sahara and the Sahel, seasonal movements of nomadic herders probably provided links between communities, and may have contributed to their ability to become sedentary through regular supplies of essential resources such as salt. As vegetation zones shifted southward with aridification, not only could pastoralists bring their herds further south, but communities that relied upon the links and resources they provided could also become established. Some SMA peoples may have developed agropastoral economies, but symbiotic relationships among subsistence specialists in herding, farming, and fishing were likely to have been an important feature of the cultural and economic landscape, as they are today in the Inland Niger Delta and in varying forms throughout West Africa (Casey 1998; Gifford-Gonzalez 2005; Linseele 2010).

Evidence for the importance of trade is seen in the ground stone tools that arrived at their destinations in finished form, and were made from materials with a patchy distribution, and in the presence of terracotta cigars at Kintampo sites that are always made from the same material, though its source remains unknown. Broad similarities in the surface treatment of SMA pottery are thus less likely to indicate the movements of a cohesive culture than a sphere of familiarity, influenced and reinforced by trade, communication, and movement. The discovery in waterlogged sediments at Dufuna, northern Nigeria, of a mahogany canoe dated to nearly 8000 BP (Breunig et al. 1996) that could have been used to exploit local fish stocks and was sufficiently commodious to transport people and goods significant distances along waterways underlines the likely antiquity of such networks of exchange.

REFERENCES

AMBLARD, S., and PERNÈS, J. (1989). The identification of cultivated millet (*Pennisetum*) amongst plant impressions on pottery from Oued Chebbi (Dhar Oualata, Mauritania). *African Archaeological Review* 7: 117–26.

AMBROSE, S. H. (1997). The ceramic Late Stone Age. In J. O. Vogel (ed.), *Encyclopedia of Precolonial Africa*. Walnut Creek, Calif.: AltaMira Press, 381–5.

ANDAH, B. (1978). The Later Stone Age and Neolithic of Upper Volta reviewed in a West African context. *West African Journal of Archaeology* 9: 85–117.

—— and ANOZIE, F. (1980). Preliminary report on the prehistoric site of Afikpo (Nigeria). *West African Journal of Archaeology* 10: 83–102.

ATHERTON, J. H. (1972). Excavations at Kamabai and Yagala Rockshelters, Sierra Leone. *West African Journal of Archaeology* 2: 39–74.

BREUNIG, P., NEUMANN, K., and VAN NEER, W. (1996). New research on the Holocene settlement and environment of the Chad Basin in Nigeria. *African Archaeological Review* 13: 111–45.

—— and WOTZKA, H.-P. (1993). Archäologische Forschungen im Südosten Burkina Fasos 1989/90: Vorbericht über die erste Grabungskampagne des Frankfurter Sonderforschungsbereiches 268 'Westafrikanische Savanne'. *Beiträge zur Allgemeinen und Vergleichenden Archäologie* 11: 145–87.

CASEY, J. (1998). The ecology of food production in West Africa. In G. Connah (ed.), *Transformations in Africa: Essays on Africa's Later Past*. Leicester: Leicester University Press, 46–70.

—— (2000). *The Kintampo Complex: The Late Stone Age on the Gambaga Escarpment, Northern Ghana*. Oxford: Archaeopress.

—— (2003). The archaeology of West Africa from the Pleistocene to the Holocene. In J. Mercader (ed.), *Under the Canopy: The Archaeology of Tropical Rain Forests*. New Brunswick, NJ: Rutgers University Press, 35–63.

CHENORKIAN, R. (1983). Ivory Coast prehistory: recent developments. *African Archaeological Review* 1: 127–42.

COON, C. S. (1968). *Yengema Cave Report*. Philadelphia: University of Pennsylvania Museum.

CORNELISSEN, E. (2003). On microlithic quartz industries at the end of the Pleistocene in Central Africa: the evidence from Shum Laka (NW Cameroon). *African Archaeological Review* 20: 1–24.

D'ANDREA, A. C., and CASEY, J. (2002). Pearl millet and Kintampo subsistence. *African Archaeological Review* 19: 147–73.

——, and KAHLHEBER, S., LOGAN, A. L., and WATSON, D. J. (2007). Early domesticated cowpea (*Vigna unguiculata*) from central Ghana. *Antiquity* 81: 686–98.

—— LOGAN, A. L., and WATSON, D. J. (2006). Oil palm and prehistoric subsistence in tropical West Africa. *Journal of African Archaeology* 4: 195–222.

DAVID, N. (1993). Rop Rock Shelter: re-excavation and reassessment. In B. Andah, P. de Maret, and R. C. Soper (eds), *Proceedings of the 9th Congress of the Pan-African Association of Prehistory and Related Studies, Jos, Nigeria 1983*. Ibadan: Rex Charles, 146–52.

DAVIES, O. (1967). *West Africa Before the Europeans*. London: Methuen.

DE MARET, P. (1994/5). Pits, pots and the far west stream. *Azania* 29/30: 318–23.

DEREFAKA, A. A., and ANOZIE, F. N. (2002). Economic and cultural prehistory of the Niger Delta. *African Arts* 35: 78–83, 96.

DOMBROWSKI, J. C. (1977). Preliminary note on excavations at a small midden near Tema, Ghana. *Nyame Akuma* 10: 31–4.

EYO, E. (1972). Rop Rock Shelter excavations 1964. *West African Journal of Archaeology* 2: 13–16.

FEDERAL DEPARTMENT OF ANTIQUITIES NIGERIA (1974). Excavations at Dutzen Kongba near Jos, Nigeria (preliminary notice). *Nyame Akuma* 4: 7–20.

FINUCANE, B., MANNING, K., and TOURÉ, M. (2008). Late Stone Age subsistence in the Tilemsi Valley, Mali: stable isotope analysis of human and animal remains from the site of Karkarichinkat Nord (KN05) and Karkarichinkat Sud (KS05). *Journal of Anthropological Archaeology* 27: 82–92.

GABEL, C. (1976). Microlithic occurrences in the Republic of Liberia. *West African Journal of Archaeology* 6: 21–35.

GIFFORD-GONZALEZ, D. (2005). Pastoralism and its consequences. In A. B. Stahl (ed.), *African Archaeology: A Critical Introduction*. Oxford: Blackwell, 187–224.

HAYDEN, B. (1981). Research and development in the Stone Age: technological transitions among hunter-gatherers. *Current Anthropology* 22: 519–48.

—— (1989). From chopper to celt: the evolution of resharpening. In R. Torrence (ed.), *Time, Energy and Stone Tools*. Cambridge: Cambridge University Press, 519–48.

HOLL, A. F. C. (1985). Subsistence patterns of the Dhar Tichitt Neolithic, Mauritania. *African Archaeological Review* 3: 151–62.

—— (2009). World views, mind-sets and trajectories in West African archaeology In P. R. Schmidt (ed.), *Postcolonial Archaeologies in Africa*. Santa Fe, NM: SAR Press, 129–48.

HUYSECOM, E., RASSE, M., LESPEZ, L., et al. (2009). The emergence of pottery in Africa during the tenth millennium cal. BC: new evidence from Ounjougou (Mali). *Antiquity* 83: 905–17.

ITAMBI, A. C., VON DOBENECK, T., and ADEGBIE, A. T. (2010). Millennial-scale precipitation changes over Central Africa during the late Quaternary and Holocene: evidence in the sediments from the Gulf of Guinea. *Journal of Quaternary Science* 25: 267–79.

KAHLHEBER, S., and NEUMANN, K. (2007). The development of plant cultivation in semi-arid West Africa. In T. Denham, J. Iriarte, and L. Vrydaghs (eds), *Rethinking Agriculture: Archaeological and Ethnoarchaeological Perspectives*. Walnut Creek, Calif.: Left Coast Press, 320–46.

KLEE, M., ZACH, B., and SITKA, H. P. (2000). Four thousand years of plant exploitation in the Chad Basin of northeast Nigeria I: the archaeobotany of Kursakata. *Vegetation History and Archaeobotany* 9: 223–37.

—— —— —— (2004). Four thousand years of plant exploitation in the Lake Chad Basin (Nigeria), part 3: plant impressions in potsherds from the Final Stone Age Gajiganna culture. *Vegetation History and Archaeobotany* 13: 131–42.

LAVACHERY, P. (2001). The Holocene archaeological sequence of Shum Laka Rock Shelter (Grassfields, Western Cameroon). *African Archaeological Review* 18: 213–47.

LE DRÉZAN, Y., LESPEZ, L., RASSE, M., et al. (2010). Hydrosedimentary records and Holocene environmental dynamics in the Yamé Valley (Mali, Sudano-Sahelian West Africa). *Comptes rendus géoscience* 342: 244–52.

LINSEELE, V. (2010). Did specialized pastoralism develop differently in Africa than in the Near East? An example from the West African Sahel. *Journal of World Prehistory* 23: 43–77.

MACDONALD, K. C. (1996). The Windé Koroji Complex: evidence for the peopling of the eastern inland Niger Delta (2500–500 BC). *Préhistoire et Anthropologie Méditerranéennes*, 5: 147–65.

—— (1997). Kourounkorokalé revisited: the Pays Mande and the West African microlithic technocomplex. *African Archaeological Review* 14: 161–200.

—— and ALLSWORTH-JONES, P. (1994). A reconsideration of the West African macrolithic conundrum: new factory sites and an associated settlement in the Vallée du Serpent, Mali. *African Archaeological Review* 12: 73–104.

—— VERNET, R., MARTINON-TORRES, M., and FULLER, D. Q. (2009). Dhar Néma: from early agriculture to metallurgy in southeastern Mauritania. *Azania* 44: 3–48.

MANNING, K., PELLING, R., HIGHAM, T., SCHWENNINGER, J.-L., and FULLER, D. Q. (2011). 4500-year old domesticated pearl millet (*Pennisetum glaucum*) from the Tilemsi Valley, Mali: new insights into an alternative cereal domestication pathway. *Journal of Archaeological Science* 38: 312–22.

Morton-Williams, P. (1962). The symbolism and ritual context of the Yoruba Laba Shango. *Journal of the Royal Anthropological Institute* 92: 23–37.

Neumann, K., Breunig, P., and Kahlheber, S. (2001). Early food production in the Sahel of Burkina Faso. *Berichte des Sonderforschungsbereichs* 268: 327–34.

Nunoo, R. B. (1948). A report on excavations at Nsuta Hill, Gold Coast. *Man* 90: 73–6.

——(1969). Buroburo factory excavations. *Actes du Premier Colloque International d'Archéologie Africaine.* Fort Lamy: Institut National Tchadien pour les Sciences Humaines, 321–33.

Nygaard, S., and Talbot, M. (1984). Stone Age archaeology and environment on the southern Accra Plains, Ghana. *Norwegian Archaeological Review* 17: 19–38.

Nzewunwa, N. (1980). *The Niger Delta: Aspects of its Prehistoric Economy and Culture.* Oxford: British Archaeological Reports.

Ozainne, S., Huysecom, E., Mayor, A., Robion-Brunner, C., and Soriano, S. (2009). Une chronologie pour le peuplement et le climat du pays dogon: la séquence culturelle et environnementale du gisement d'Ounjougou (Mali). *Antropos* 18: 37–46.

Rahtz, P. A., and Flight, C. (1974). A quern factory near Kintampo, Ghana. *West African Journal of Archaeology* 4: 1–31.

Shanahan, T. M., Overpeck, J. T., Wheeler, C. W., et al. (2006). Palaeoclimatic variations in West Africa from a record of late Pleistocene and Holocene lake level stands of Lake Bosumtwi, Ghana. *Palaeogeography, Palaeoclimatology, Palaeoecology* 242: 287–302.

Shaw, C. T. (1944). Report on investigations carried out in the cave known as 'Bosumpra' at Abetifi, Kwahu, Gold Coast Colony. *Proceedings of the Prehistoric Society* 10: 1–67.

Shaw, T. (1978). *Nigeria: Its Archaeology and Early History.* London: Thames & Hudson.

——(1984). Archaeological evidence and effects of food producing in Nigeria. In J. D. Clark and S. A. Brandt (eds), *From Hunters to Farmers.* Berkeley: University of California Press, 152–7.

——and Daniels, S.G.H. (1984). Excavations at Iwo Eleru, Ondo State, Nigeria. *West African Journal of Archaeology* 14: 1–269.

Sinclair, P., Shaw, T., and Andah, B. (1993). Introduction. In T. Shaw, P. J. J. Sinclair, B. Andah, and A. Okpoko (eds), *The Archaeology of Africa: Food, Metals and Towns.* London: Routledge, 1–31.

Smith, A. B. (1975). Radiocarbon dates from Bosumpra Cave, Abetifi, Ghana. *Proceedings of the Prehistoric Society* 41: 179–82.

——(1992). *Pastoralism in Africa.* London: Hurst.

Sowunmi, M. A. (1981). Late Quaternary environmental changes in Nigeria. *Pollen et spores* 23: 125–48.

——(1985). The beginnings of agriculture in West Africa: botanical evidence. *Current Anthropology* 26: 127–9.

Stahl, A. B. (1985). Reinvestigation of Kintampo 6 Rockshelter, Ghana: implications for the nature of culture change. *African Archaeological Review* 3: 117–50.

Talbot, M., Livingstone, D. A., Parker, P. G., et al. (1984). Preliminary results from sediment cores from Lake Bosumtwi, Ghana. *Paleoecology of Africa* 16: 176–92.

Watson, D. J. (2005). Under the rocks: reconsidering the origin of the Kintampo Tradition and the development of food production in the savanna-forest/forest of West Africa. *Journal of African Archaeology* 3: 3–55.

——(2008). The Late Stone Age in Ghana: the re-excavation of Bosumpra Cave in context. In T. Insoll (ed.), *Current Archaeological Research in Ghana.* Oxford: Archaeopress, 137–49.

WATSON, D. J. (2010). Within savanna and forest: a review of the Late Stone Age Kintampo Tradition, Ghana. *Azania* 45:141–74.

WILLETT, F. (1962). The microlithic industry from Old Oyo, eastern Nigeria. In G. Mortelmans and J. Nenquin (eds), *Actes du Vème Congrès Panafricain de Préhistoire et de l'Étude du Quaternaire*. Tervuren: Musée Royale de l'Afrique Centrale, 261–71.

YORK, R. N. (1978). Excavations at Dutsen Kongba, Plateau State, Nigeria. *West African Journal of Archaeology* 8: 139–63.

CHAPTER 42

THE APPEARANCE AND DEVELOPMENT OF METALLURGY SOUTH OF THE SAHARA

BERTRAM B. B. MAPUNDA

INTRODUCTION

AFRICANIST archaeometallurgists have conveniently divided Africa into two subregions when discussing the continent's metallurgical history: (1) north of the Sahara Desert, including the Mediterranean littoral, the Lower Nile Valley and the Red Sea coast; and (2) south of the Sahara (sub-Saharan Africa), including West, East, Central and southern Africa (Kense 1985; Miller and van der Merwe 1994; Mapunda 2002, 2010; Childs and Herbert 2005). This division reflects the fact that the metallurgical history of the two subregions differs. For example, the north, especially Egypt, along with the Nubian part of the Nile Valley and the Red Sea coast, experienced an elaborate bronze technology, whereas, with the exception of parts of Nigeria such as at Igbo Ukwu and Benin and, on a very limited scale, the Zimbabwe Tradition of southern Africa (Miller 2001), the south did not (Kense 1985). Moreover, in Egypt (and the Middle East for that matter), some two to four millennia intervened between the first performance of iron smelting (c. 5000 BC) and its becoming a regularly used metal (c. 1000 BC) (Waldbaum 1980). In sub-Saharan Africa, where iron was the dominant metal, with copper following far behind, metallurgy seems to have begun and to have developed spatially, as well as in complexity, almost instantaneously, without a prolonged delay (Tylecote 1975; Holl 2000). Finally, during the Bronze and Early Iron Ages, approximately 3000 BC–AD 500, the north was more closely linked with the rest of the Mediterranean world in culture and technology than with sub-Saharan Africa (Snodgrass 1980; Noble et al. 1994).

This metallurgical history justifies treating sub-Saharan Africa separately from northern Africa as approached here. This chapter therefore begins with a theoretical review of the origins of metallurgy as a background upon which the sub-Saharan case discussed subsequently is anchored. Its main body is further split in two: the appearance of metallurgy in the region and its

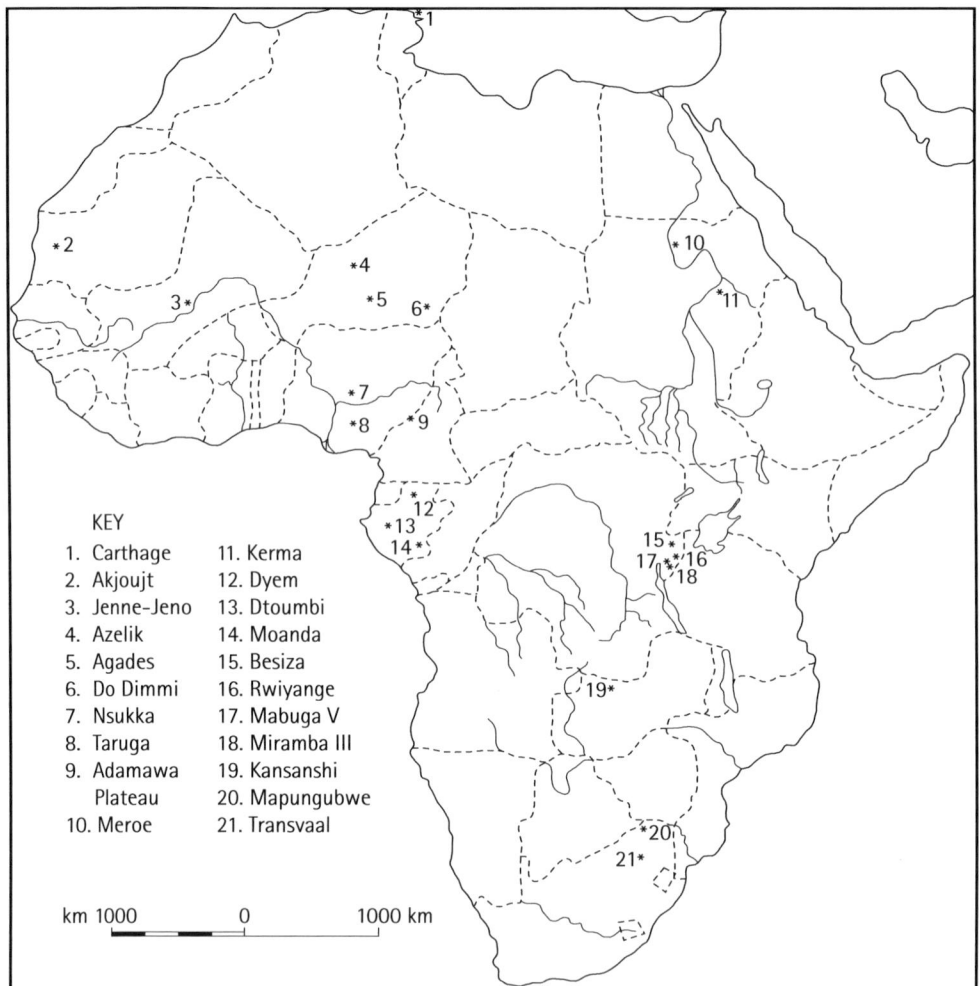

FIG. 42.1. Map of Africa showing sites mentioned in Chapter 42, and other important iron smelting localities.

subsequent development. The former section considers the *how* debate, which is basically theoretical, as well as the *when* question, whereas the latter section focuses upon space (*where*) (Fig. 42.1) and evaluates the available evidence in terms of its scientific validity as well as its sociopolitical matrix. A concluding summary suggests some ways forward for future research.

THE APPEARANCE OF METALLURGY:
THEORETICAL FRAMEWORK

Archaeometallurgists apply two main theories when explaining the origins of metallurgy at any given place: serendipity and adoption. The first holds that the first ever process of metal production must have come about by chance or as an accident rather than as a deliberate, intentional, or premeditated undertaking. This line of thinking hinges upon the fact that technological inventions—including contemporary technologies such as computers, telephones, and radios—are cumulative, with 'new' inventions in essence founded upon some primitive traits of themselves. We observe this in archaeology as well, for example through the development of stone tools from the Mode 1 technologies characteristic of the Oldowan to the Mode 5 microlithic toolkits of many more recent hunter-gatherers (Clark 1969).

However, metallurgy differs from stone tool production in the sense that it is transformative and thermal; the ore is transformed from solid to liquid and back to solid, at which stage it changes its physical and chemical properties, whereas stone tool production involves modifying size and morphology while generally leaving the original stone (core) and the product (stone tool) chemically the same. The question is, therefore: how did the first metallurgists know that through heat treatment native gold or copper becomes soft and malleable? Or, more intriguingly, how did they know that after malachite is heated to a certain temperature it melts and copper separates from other materials (impurities)? Because these processes are completely different from those used to produce stone tools, we can comfortably argue that their initial discovery was accidental. Adoption, on the other hand, explains situations where one society acquires knowledge from serendipitous inventors—something likely to be true of the majority of cases with any given invention. Archaeological research has, it should be noted, unambiguously demonstrated that metallurgy itself was invented more than once, most compellingly in the case of the Americas, where metallurgical studies confirm that the techniques employed, the preference for copper (and to some degree bronze) and precious metals, and the complete absence of iron smelting followed very different trajectories from those taken by Old World metallurgists (Lechtman 1980).

A third factor must also be considered with reference to ironworking in particular, and that is pyrotechnology. The point here is that it is frequently stated that ironworking could not have been invented independently by any given people unless they had been practising other fireborne technologies that required high temperatures, such as kiln-fired pottery, glass beads, and clay figurines, but especially the smelting of copper or lead (Wertime 1968, 1980). It is argued that these technologies would have provided potential iron smelters with the basic skills and experience that could then have been improved with little effort to reach the temperatures and complexities required for iron smelting (Tylecote 1975; Wertime 1980; Craddock 2010). Proponents of this view thus reject the possibility of serendipitous discovery of iron technology except where this might have come about through smelting of copper using haematite, an iron ore, as a flux in copper smelting that became overheated, resulting in the unintentional production of an iron bloom (Tylecote 1975). With these ideas in mind we can now examine the appearance of metallurgy in sub-Saharan Africa and its subsequent development.

THE APPEARANCE OF METALLURGY SOUTH OF THE SAHARA: HOW, WHEN, AND WHERE DID IT HAPPEN?

How did it happen?

When compared with the rest of the Old World, including Mediterranean Africa, sub-Saharan Africa has a unique history of metallurgical development. While Mediterranean

Africa, Asia, and Europe went through all three metallurgical ages, Copper, Bronze and Iron, the available evidence indicates that sub-Saharan Africa did not experience the first two, at least at any elaborate level. Instead, it moved into iron production straight away and almost exclusively, with only limited copper and bronze working. By the mid/late first millennium BC, several areas of sub-Saharan Africa were in full mastery of ironworking technology—skills that continued until they were interrupted by colonial intrusion in the late 19th/early 20th centuries. On the other hand, evidence for copper working is quite scanty, though its origins go back to the first millennium BC in West Africa and the first millennium AD in central and southern Africa and it intensified and expanded in both regions during the second millennium AD (Herbert 1984; Childs and Killick 1993; Bisson 2000; Childs and Herbert 2005). Early copper-working sites include Agadez and Azelik in central Niger (900–300 cal. BC), Akjoujt in western Mauritania (800–200 cal. BC), and Kansanshi in northern Zambia (4th century cal. AD) (Herbert 1984; Bisson 2000; Alpern 2005), but despite this evidence 'one can hardly speak of a Copper Age on the basis of present evidence' (Alpern 2005: 60), as early copper working was quite localized.

Evidence for working in and use of other metals such as gold, lead, and silver is even scarcer and appears much later. The earliest archaeological finds of gold, for example, in sub-Saharan Africa date to the 7th/8th centuries AD at Jenné-Jeno (Mali) and the 13th century at Mapungubwe (South Africa) (Childs and Herbert 2005).

The relatively late appearance of metallurgy in sub-Saharan Africa and the apparent absence there of Chalcolithic and Bronze Ages have made the question of how the region acquired the knowledge of metal production in the first place difficult and complex. As already indicated, two schools of thought exist, one advocating an external origin (adoption), the other subscribing to local invention (serendipity).

The external origins school is premissed upon the assumption that sub-Saharan Africa acquired the knowledge of metallurgy at a late date when compared to neighbouring regions of Asia and Europe. During the third millennium BC, bronze was already in regular use in the Near East and the eastern Mediterranean, and a millennium later iron took over from it as a regular, utilitarian metal there, whereas sub-Saharan Africa became a regular producer and user of copper and iron only several centuries after that. Despite the likelihood that copper working in Mauritania and Niger reaches back to the first half of the first millennium BC, this has not altered the external origin viewpoint since at least some of the artefacts at Akjoujt resemble others from Iberia and North Africa (Lambert 1971). Linked to this is the assumption that ironworking started almost simultaneously with that of copper, thus precluding the possibility that the latter helped spur the development of the former.

Different routes have been proposed for the introduction of iron working into sub-Saharan Africa. A trans-Saharan route or routes tracing back to the early/mid-first millennium BC Phoenician settlement at Carthage in modern Tunisia has attracted considerable interest (e.g. Miller and van der Merwe 1994; Phillipson 2005), but efforts to uncover direct evidence to support this continue to meet with little or no success. For example, while Carthage was founded in the late 9th century BC, iron did not gain regular usage there until the 3rd century BC (Alpern 2005), several centuries after it had become common in some parts of western Africa.

Given this, Sudan, and specifically the civilizations that developed there along the Middle Nile in the third to first millennia BC (Welsby, Ch. 51 below), has also been canvassed as a possible source (Childs and Herbert 2005). Craddock (2010: 34), for example, has wondered if iron smelting might have been developed independently there, though acknowledging that currently there is no evidence for this—a conclusion independently reached by Abdu and Gordon (2004) in their recent reassessment of ironworking in the Meroitic state. Other possibilities include a point of inception in Ethiopia (from across the Red Sea) and thence south into East Africa, or a direct transmission over the Indian Ocean to the East African coast (cf. Mapunda 1997).

Although there is no evidence for any of these routes having been used, an external source for sub-Saharan metallurgy continues to be strongly advocated, not least because of the continued absence of evidence within sub-Saharan Africa for iron smelting (which involves a relatively complex pyrotechnology) having been preceded by less complex, low-temperature pyrotechnologies such as those required to produce copper, lead, tin, glass, and/or kiln-fired pottery and terracotta (Wertime 1980; Kense 1985; Kense and Okoro 1993; Craddock 2010). Nonetheless, despite the possible use of haematite as a flux in putatively earlier copper smelting having been raised by some (e.g. Woodhouse 1998), as Craddock (2010: 34) has argued, 'to postulate the invention of iron smelting without knowledge of copper smelting is akin to claiming the invention of the movie camera but with no knowledge of photography.'

The alternative possibility, local invention, nevertheless retains its advocates, partly because of the lack of evidence for an external source and partly because of the distinctiveness of sub-Saharan smelting technologies, notably slag-tapping furnace pits, compared to those used in Europe or the Middle East (Andah 1979; Schmidt 1983; Craddock 2010). The technological dexterity and variability of metallurgical production demonstrated both ethnographically and archaeologically in sub-Saharan Africa (Chirikure, Ch. 10 above) have also led many archaeologists to believe that African ironworkers must have been the proprietors, rather than mere copiers, of the technology (Schmidt 1981, 1983; Okpoko 1987; David et al. 1989; Mapunda 2002, 2010). Thirdly, the universality of the pyrotechnology hypothesis has also been questioned on the grounds that it represents the importation of western models that are often held not to work because the cultural and ecological background upon which they rest differ from those of sub-Saharan Africa (Andah 1979). In this particular case, the thesis that iron technology is likely to have been preceded by copper technology is based largely on ethnographic and experimental research undertaken in Iran in the 1960s (Wertime 1968); but even if valid there, does the same pattern have to hold true everywhere else? Might the abundance and recognizability of iron ores relative to copper or tin south of the Sahara have facilitated independent discovery, perhaps using different methods in different regions (Andah 1979)? Fourthly and finally, while proponents of an external origin emphasize that metallurgy south of the Sahara is significantly younger than in the eastern Mediterranean and Near East, advocates of an independent emergence of iron smelting south of the Sahara make reference to examples where dates preceding the mid-first millennium BC have emerged. A well-known instance concerns the work of van Grunderbeek et al. (2001) in the Great Lakes region of East Africa, where iron smelting at Gesiza, Rwanda has been dated to the 9th century cal. BC and at Mubuga V and Rwiyange I in Burundi to between the mid-15th and 8th centuries cal. BC. More recently, Zangato and Holl (2010) have published dates ranging between 2300 and 1900 cal. BC from the Adamawa Plateau of northeastern Cameroon and the western part of the Central African Republic.

When did it happen?

As these examples show, the questions of *how* and *when* metallurgy appeared in sub-Saharan Africa are inextricably intertwined. Currently, students of African archaeometallurgy tend to emphasize prudence when estimating the timing of the origins of metallurgy in sub-Saharan Africa, although the history of science demonstrates the possible errors entailed by overemphasizing consensus within an established paradigm (Kuhn 1962). Accordingly, the oldest widely recognized evidence for both ironworking (e.g. at Taruga, Nigeria) and copperworking (e.g. at Agadez in central Niger) is dated to the middle first millennium cal. BC (Killick et al. 1988; Killick 2004; Alpern 2005; Childs and Herbert 2005; Pringle 2009).

Earlier dates for copper working in Grébénart's (1988) so-called Copper I phase in the Agadez region are now widely discounted (Killick et al. 1988), but debate continues to surround radiocarbon dates said to be associated with evidence of iron smelting that are 'anomalous' in the sense that they are significantly earlier than the consensus view. Those reported by van Grunderbeek (1992; van Grunderbeek et al. 2001) from Rwanda and Burundi and by Zangato and Holl (2010) from the Central African Republic and Cameroon are pre-eminent in this respect. Their evaluation takes place, however, in what has become an 'irrevocably political context' (MacEachern 2010: 39), with concerns of 'manipulation' having been raised by some (Chami 2009).

The critical issues here are twofold. First, claims for iron smelting before the middle of the first millennium BC, like all other chronological assessments, depend upon the unambiguous association of the material dated with the activity for which a date is sought. In other words, we need to be absolutely sure that, if radiocarbon dates have been obtained on charcoal, the charcoal in question is definitely associated with the evidence of iron smelting or iron working that is the object of our enquiry and, moreover, that the charcoal in question accurately dates the activity, i.e. it is neither contaminated nor subject to the 'old wood effect' where charcoal from a long-lived tree species may return a date much older than the activity being investigated. Moreover, to be useful, the standard deviations associated with the radiocarbon dates obtained must be sufficiently small and the radiocarbon calibration curve sufficiently clear-cut to allow conversion of individual radiocarbon determinations into precise, calibrated dates. In both the Rwandan and the Central African/Cameroonian cases just mentioned (Killick 2004; Chirikure 2010), as well as with dates of the third to early first millennia BC from Niger and Nigeria (Calvacoressi and David 1979; Grébénart 1987; Eze-Uzomoka 2010), these conditions have not yet been met. Until and unless they are, the only sound conclusion to draw is that they should be treated as tentative dates.

Where did it start?

Turning to our third question, the simple, and probably correct, answer to this question would be: 'metallurgy in sub-Saharan Africa started where we get the oldest date.' But the answer to this is, of course, dependent on resolving the difficulties just raised.

The best thing the existing data can do is to guide us toward identifying clusters of uncontested early dates as opposed to specific location(s). For West Africa, the earliest such dates for iron smelting come from Nigeria in the 6th century BC (Tylecote 1975), while small-scale copper smelting is attested in the Agadez and Azelik areas of central Niger and at Akjoujt in western Mauritania in the mid-first millennium BC (Bisson 2000; Alpern 2005). In Central Africa, sites in Gabon, Cameroon, and Congo-Brazzaville have evidence of iron production and working between the 7th and 2nd centuries BC (Schmidt et al. 1985; Clist 1989; Oslisly 1993). In northeast Africa, bronze working was clearly established in the Kerma kingdom in the late third millennium BC, with iron production under way further south at Meroë beginning in the mid-first millennium BC, but largely concentrated in the period in and after the first century BC (Haaland and Haaland 2007; Welsby, Ch. 51 below). Finally, in East Africa's Interlacustrine region we have a series of widely accepted dates for iron smelting from the mid-first millennium BC from northwestern Tanzania (Schmidt 1983, 1997; Schmidt and Childs 1985).

Whether all or some of these clusters represent centres of independent invention in sub-Saharan Africa or whether they are merely concentrations of an adopted technology is difficult to tell from the available data. What we can suggest, however, is that, *if* claims for early dates are accepted, then West Africa and Central Africa stand a better chance for independent invention (Andah 1979; Schmidt 1983, 1997), while northeastern Africa, considering its proximity to both Egypt and the Arabian Peninsula, may conform better to the adoption model (Childs and Herbert 2005; Craddock 2010). Eastern Africa has often been said to have adopted iron metallurgy from West Africa as part of a broader package associated with the spread of Bantu languages and farming (Schmidt 1983; de Maret, Ch. 43 below). As indicated earlier, however, claims for iron smelting in West and Central Africa older than the mid-first millennium BC remain highly controversial, while attempts to pinpoint dates within the latter period are severely handicapped by a plateau in the radiocarbon calibration curve at this crucial time (Killick 2004)—something that inevitably makes it even more difficult to assess the case for independent invention rather than acquisition of the necessary skills from elsewhere. To overcome this difficulty, not only must archaeologists be much more rigorous and careful in their use of radiocarbon dating and citation of radiocarbon dates (making due allowance for the fact that these are, in the end, no more than statistical probabilities), but they must also employ alternative dating strategies. Two, in particular, may be of help. First, at least the relative ages of sites—especially for those falling during the aforementioned plateau—could be defined through recourse to carefully defined regional ceramic sequences, something gradually being developed in areas such as the Inland Niger Delta and northern Nigeria. Second, there is scope for applying optically stimulated luminescence (OSL) and thermoluminescence (TL) dating techniques to the remains of furnaces. Although precision may not always be better than for radiocarbon in the first/second millennia BC (Godfrey-Smith and Casey 2003), at least if furnaces have been correctly identified as such the result would be an unimpeachable set of dates for metallurgical activity, something possible with iron only if iron objects themselves are dated, rather than assumptions being made about the associations between charcoal—often of taxonomically unknown origin—and metallurgical residues (Killick 2004). For a much more recent period, Ohinata's (2001) extensive use of OSL to date iron-smelting furnaces in Swaziland provides an excellent demonstration of the technique's potential.

The development of metallurgy
in sub-Saharan Africa

By the late 19th century, when European imperial rule had expanded across most of sub-Saharan Africa, almost every local community had knowledge of metals, and a good number knew how to produce them. Although iron and copper were the leading metals in sub-Saharan Africa at this time, knowledge of gold, as well as of copper's alloys with tin and zinc (bronze and brass), was also evident in some areas. However, intentional production of these alloys appeared much later than that of either iron or copper. Bronze is known to have been produced in South Africa by the 15th century AD, whereas brass, a common alloy in West Africa, started to be locally produced as late as the 19th century (Bisson 2000). Also worth noting is the variation in the technology of metal production not only between but also within communities (Chirikure, Ch. 8 above).

As for spatial expansion, archaeologists, historians, historical linguists, and archaeo-metallurgists have emphasized diffusionist models to explain the spread of metallurgy within sub-Saharan Africa. Popular starting points have been West Africa and northeastern Africa, not only because they have the oldest, generally accepted dates but also because they more conveniently conform to models of external origin for sub-Saharan metallurgy as a whole. In addition, the West African centre has been used to explain the origin and spread of Bantu speakers, who have also been assumed to have been the carriers of ironworking tech-nology to the rest of sub-Saharan Africa (Collett 1982; Ehret 1998, 2002; Phillipson 2005). As discussed by de Maret (Ch. 43 below), the general agreement between linguists and archaeo-logists that Bantu speakers originated in the borderlands of Nigeria and Cameroon fits this suggestion well, and also matches relatively closely with the location of Taruga, one of the earliest widely accepted iron-smelting sites in West Africa (Schmidt 1981). Difficulties remain, however, not least the chronological ambiguities already considered. The lack of 'linking evidence' between West Africa and northeast Africa and between centres north of the Equator and the sub-Equatorial region is also a major concern. If some of the strongest evidence for a model of diffusion is the presence of 'footprint technology' along the proposed route, then we must admit that thus far the limited investigations possible in or west of Sudan have failed to show any direct connection between the Nile and Niger-Chad Basins (Holl 1993). Likewise, archaeological evidence along the alleged Bantu migration route in what is today Cameroon, Equatorial Guinea, Gabon, the Central African Republic and Congo-Kinshasa is patchy, to say the least. As Eggert (2005: 315) notes, 'we do not possess any firm material (i.e., ceramic) link between these regions themselves, for instance, between the inner Congo basin on the one hand and northwestern Central Africa on the other.'

CONCLUSION

'To say that the history of metallurgy in sub-Saharan Africa is complicated is perhaps an understatement.' This is how Chirikure (2010: 25) opens his review of recent claims for early (second/third millennia cal. BC) iron smelting in the Central African Republic and Cam-eroon by Zangato and Holl (2010). The present review not only underlines the acceptability of this observation, but also aims to explain some of the reasons why the situation is as it is. That it provides a largely theoretical version of the history of metallurgy in sub-Saharan Africa is because of the continued lack of conclusive data (though for detail on the sociocul-tural context of copper and iron metallurgies, see Herbert 1984, 1993). This is frustrating, especially to non-archaeometallurgists (fellow archaeologists, historians, historical linguists, and anthropologists), who would like to make sense of their own findings as well as testing some of their hypotheses.

In such a situation we have no alternative but to stick to the same advice we have been hearing for decades: to await but, more importantly, also to search for more data (Okafor 1993; Mapunda 2002, 2010; Childs and Herbert 2005). As we do so, archaeometallurgists need to strategize their own research approaches. Resonating with Craddock's (2010) recent suggestion to undertake further investigations of metallurgy at Kerma, Childs and Herbert (2005: 281), for example, have urged archaeologists to shift their attention to northeast Africa and Arabia during the crucial centuries of the first millennium BC. In both cases this is so because it is here, rather than at Carthage, where the potential for transmitting metallurgy from the Lower Nile or across the Red Sea lies. But this will only solve part of the problem, as it still leaves unexplained the appearance of metallurgy in the western and probably the sub-Equatorial regions of sub-Saharan Africa. Here, it is the continued difficulty in identifying technological similarities between North Africa and sub-Saharan Africa and the mid-first millennium BC dates from sites in Nigeria (let alone controversial claims for anything older) that continues to give support to autochthonous invention as a valid hypothesis. Clearly essential here is the wider employment of the strategies outlined above for improving our chronological frameworks (OSL and TL dating of furnaces, ceramic typologies, and an application and citation of radiocarbon dates that consistently pays due attention to questions of association, sample lifespan, and calibration, as well as recognition that radiocarbon determinations are, in the end, no more than statements of probability).

Yet a concern for chronology, however important, must not lead to neglect of the cultural and ecological factors that made the adoption and spread of new technologies possible (Okpoko 1987). This, then, calls for a multidisciplinary approach that will deploy a diversity of techniques and methodologies to examine such matters as internal demands for metals, the cultural and technological interactions people had with metal ores that might have led to their thermal processing of the same, and the availability of and access to ores. Studying the origins of other technologies such as basketry, textiles, and pottery may also help shed light on those of metallurgy itself.

REFERENCES

ABDU, B., and GORDON, R. (2004). Iron artefacts from the land of Kush. *Journal of Archaeological Science* 31: 979–98.

ALPERN, S. B. (2005). Did they or didn't they invent it? Iron in sub-Saharan Africa. *History in Africa* 32: 41–94.

ANDAH, B. (1979). Iron Age beginnings on West Africa: reflections and suggestions. *West African Journal of Archaeology* 9: 135–50.

BISSON, M. S. (2000). Precolonial copper metallurgy: sociopolitical context. In J. O. Vogel (ed.) *Ancient African Metallurgy*. Walnut Creek, Calif.: AltaMira Press, 83–145.

CALVACORESSI, D., and DAVID, N. (1979). A new survey of radiocarbon and thermoluminescence dates for West Africa. *Journal of African History* 20: 1–29.

CHAMI, F. (2009). The atomic model view of society: application in studies of the African past. In P. R. Schmidt (ed.), *Postcolonial Archaeologies in Africa*. Santa Fe, NM: SAR Press, 39–56.

CHILDS, S. T., and HERBERT, E. (2005). Metallurgy and its consequences. In A. B. Stahl (ed.), *African Archaeology: A Critical Introduction*. Oxford: Blackwell, 276–300.

CHILDS, S. T., and KILLICK, D. J. (1993). Indigenous African metallurgy: nature and culture. *Annual Review of Anthropology* 22: 317–37.

CHIRIKURE, S. (2010). On evidence, ideas and fantasy, the origins of iron in sub-Saharan Africa: thoughts on É. Zangato and A. F. C. Holl's 'On the iron front'. *Journal of African Archaeology* 8: 25–8.

CLARK, J. G. D. (1969). *World Prehistory: A New Outline*. Cambridge: Cambridge University Press.

CLIST, B. (1989). Archaeology in Gabon, 1886–1988. *African Archaeological Review* 7: 59–95.

COLLETT, D. P. (1982). Models of the spread of the Early Iron Age. In C. Ehret and M. Posnansky (eds), *The Archaeological and Linguistic Reconstruction of African History*. Berkeley: University of California Press, 182–98.

CRADDOCK, P. (2010). New paradigms for old iron: thoughts on É. Zangato and A. F. C. Holl's 'On the iron front'. *Journal of African Archaeology* 8: 29–36.

DAVID, N., HEIMANN, R., KILLICK, D. J., and WAYMAN, M. (1989). Between bloomery and blast furnace: Mafa iron-smelting technology in north Cameroon. *African Archaeological Review* 7: 183–208.

EGGERT, M. K. H. (2005). The Bantu problem. In A. B. Stahl (ed.), *African Archaeology: A Critical Introduction*. Oxford: Blackwell, 301–26.

EHRET, C. (1998). *An African Classical Age: Eastern and Southern Africa in World History 1000 B.C. to A.D. 400*. Oxford: James Currey.

—— (2002). *The Civilization of Africa: A History to 1800*. Oxford: James Currey.

EZE-UZOMAKA, P. (2010). Excavation of Amaovoko: a further study of the Lejja iron smelting culture. In F. Chami and C. Radimilahy (eds), *Studies in the African Past*. Dar es Salaam: E&D Vision, 178–91.

GODFREY-SMITH, D. I., and CASEY, J. L. (2003). Direct thermoluminescence chronology for Early Iron Age smelting technology on the Gambaga Escarpment. *Journal of Archaeological Science* 30: 1037–50.

GRÉBÉNART, D. N. (1987). Characteristics of the final Neolithic and Metal Ages in the region of Agades (Niger). In A. E. Close (ed.), *Prehistory of Arid North Africa: Essays in Honour of Fred Wendorf*. Dallas, Tex.: Southern Methodist University Press, 287–316.

—— (1988). *Les Premiers Métallurgistes en Afrique Occidentale*. Abidjan: Nouvelles Éditions Africaines.

HAALAND, G., and HAALAND, R. (2007). God of war, worldly ruler and craft specialists in the Meroitic kingdom of Sudan: inferring social identity from material remains. *Journal of Social Archaeology* 7: 372–392.

HALLO, W. W., and SIMPSON, W. K. (1998). *The Ancient Near East: A History*. New York: Harcourt.

HERBERT, E. (1984). *Red Gold of Africa: Copper in Pre-Colonial History and Culture*. Madison: University of Wisconsin Press.

—— (1993). *Iron, Gender, and Power: Rituals of Transformation in African Societies*. Bloomington: Indiana University Press.

HOLL, A. F. C. (1993). Transition from Late Stone Age to Iron Age in the Sudano-Sahelian zone: a case study from the Perichadian Plain. In T. Shaw, P. J. J. Sinclair, B. Andah, and A. Okpoko (eds), *The Archaeology of Africa: Food, Metals, and Towns*. London: Routledge, 330–43.

—— (2000). Metals and pre-colonial African society. In J. O. Vogel (ed.), *Ancient African Metallurgy: The Socio-Cultural Context*. Walnut Creek, Calif.: AltaMira Press, 1–82.

KENSE, F. (1985). The initial diffusion of iron to Africa. In R. Haaland and P. Shinnie (eds), *African Iron Working: Ancient and Traditional*. New York: Norwegian University Press, 11–27.

—— and OKORO, J. A. (1993). Changing perspective in traditional iron production in West Africa. In T. Shaw, P. J. J. Sinclair, B. Andah, and A. Okpoko (eds), *The Archaeology of Africa: Food, Metals, and Towns*. London: Routledge, 449–58.

KILLICK, D. J. (2004). What do we know about African iron working? *Journal of African Archaeology* 2: 97–112.

—— VAN DER MERWE, N. J., GORDON, R., and GRÉBÉNART, D. (1988). Reassessment of the evidence for early metallurgy in Niger, West Africa. *Journal of Archaeological Science* 15: 367–94.

KUHN, T. (1962). *The Structure of Scientific Revolutions*. Chicago: University of Chicago Press.

LAMBERT, N. (1971). Les industries sur cuivre dans l'Ouest Saharien. *West African Journal of Archaeology* 1: 9–21.

LECHTMAN, H. (1980). The Central Andes: metallurgy without iron. In T. Wertime and J. Muhly (eds), *The Coming of the Age of Iron*. New Haven, Conn.: Yale University Press, 267–334.

MACEACHERN, S. (2010). Thoughts on E. Zangato and A. F. C. Holl's 'On the iron front'. *Journal of African Archaeology* 8: 39–41.

MAPUNDA, B. (1997). Patching up evidence for ironworking in the Horn. *African Archaeological Review* 14: 107–24.

—— (2002). *Ufundichuma Asilia Afrika Mashariki: Chimbuko, Kukua na Kukoma Kwake* [Indigenous Ironworking in East Africa: Origins, Development, and Termination]. Peramiho: Peramiho Printing Press

—— (2010). *Contemplating the Fipa Iron Working*. Kampala: Foundation Publications.

MILLER, D. (2001). Metal assemblages from Greefswald areas K2, Mapungubwe Hill and Mapungubwe Southern Terrace. *South African Archaeological Bulletin* 56: 83–103.

—— and VAN DER MERWE, N. J. (1994). Early metal working in sub-Saharan Africa: a review of recent research. *Journal of African History* 35: 1–36.

NOBLE, T. F. X., STRAUSS, B. S., OSHEIM, D. J., NEUSCHEL, K. B., COHEN, W. B., and ROBERTS, D. D. (1994). *Western Civilization: The Continuing Experiment*. Boston, Mass.: Houghton Mifflin.

OHINATA, F. (2001). Archaeology of iron-using farming communities in Swaziland: pots, people and life during the first and second millennia AD. DPhil. thesis, University of Oxford.

OKAFOR, E. E. (1993). New evidence on early iron-smelting from southeastern Nigeria. In T. Shaw, P. J. J. Sinclair, B. Andah, and A. Okpoko (eds), *The Archaeology of Africa: Food, Metals, and Towns*. London: Routledge, 432–48.

OKPOKO, A. I. (1987). Early metal using communities in West Africa. *West African Journal of Archaeology* 17: 205–27.

OSLISLY, R. (1993). The Neolithic/Iron Age transition in the middle reaches of the Ogooué Valley in Gabon: chronology and cultural change. *Nyame Akuma* 40: 17–21.

PHILLIPSON, D. W. (2005). *African Archaeology*. Cambridge: Cambridge University Press.

PRINGLE, H. (2009). Seeking Africa's first iron men. *Science* 323: 200–2.

SCHMIDT, P. R. (1981). *The Origins of Iron Smelting in Africa: A Complex Technology in Tanzania*. Providence, RI: Brown University.

SCHMIDT P. R., (1983). Further evidence for an advanced prehistoric iron technology in Africa. *Journal of Field Archaeology* 10: 421–34.

SCHMIDT, P. R. (1997). *Iron Technology in East Africa.* Oxford: James Currey.

—— and CHILDS, T. S. (1985). Innovation and industry during the Early Iron Age in East Africa: the KM2 and KM3 sites of northern Tanzania. *African Archaeological Review* 3: 53–94.

—— DIGOMBE, L., LOCKO, M., and MOULEINGUI, B., (1985). Newly dated Iron Age sites in Gabon. *Nyame Akuma* 26: 16–18.

SNODGRASS, A. (1980). Iron and early metallurgy in the Mediterranean. In T. Wertime and J. Muhly (eds), *The Coming of the Age of Iron.* New Haven, Conn.: Yale University Press, 335–74.

TYLECOTE, R. F. (1975). The origin of iron smelting in Africa. *West African Journal of Archaeology* 5: 1–10.

VAN GRUNDERBEEK, M.-C. (1992). Essai de délimitation chronologique de l'Âge du Fer Ancien au Burundi, au Rwanda et dans la région des Grands Lacs. *Azania* 26: 53–80.

—— ROCHE, E., and DOUTRELEPONT, H. (2001). Un type de fourneau de fonte de fer associé à la culture Urewe (Âge de Fer Ancien) au Rwanda et au Burundi. *Mediterranean Archaeology* 14: 271–97.

WALDBAUM, J. (1980). The first archaeological appearance of iron and the transition to the Iron Age. In T. Wertime and J. Muhly (eds), *The Coming of the Age of Iron.* New Haven, Conn.: Yale University Press, 69–98.

WERTIME, T. (1968). A metallurgical expedition through the Persian Desert. *Science* 159: 927–35.

—— (1980). The pyrotechnological background. In T. Wertime and J. Muhly (eds), *The Coming of the Age of Iron.* New Haven, Conn.: Yale University Press, 1–24.

WOODHOUSE, J. (1998). Iron in Africa: metal from nowhere. In G. Connah (ed.), *Transformations in Africa: Essays on Africa's Later Past.* London: Leicester University Press, 160–85.

ZANGATO, E., and HOLL, A. F. C. (2010). On the iron front: new evidence from North-Central Africa. *Journal of African Archaeology* 8: 7–23.

CHAPTER 43

ARCHAEOLOGIES OF THE BANTU EXPANSION

PIERRE DE MARET

THE BANTU LANGUAGES

THE close similarities between most of the languages spoken in the southern half of Africa attracted attention as early as 1498, when one of Vasco da Gama's shipmates, who spoke several languages from the continent's west coast, realized that he could communicate with inhabitants of the Limpopo estuary on its east coast (Vansina 1979). The term 'Bantu' (from *ba-ntu*, plural of *mu-ntu*, human being) was coined in 1885 by Wilhelm Bleek (1862, 1869) to refer to those languages that had obviously a common origin. From its original linguistic meaning, the term was soon used in a cultural sense, and then gradually also to designate an archaeological occurrence or even a race.

Today, over 300 million Africans speak approximately 500 Bantu languages—depending on how one differentiates languages from dialects—almost one third of the continent's total population (Fig. 43.1). They constitute by far Africa's largest language group, their distribution over a large part of sub-Saharan Africa is striking, and their origin, history and interconnections have generated considerable discussion (e.g. Phillipson 1976; Eggert 1992, 2005; Vansina 1995; Robertson and Bradley 2000; Ehret 2001; Bostoen and Grégoire 2007). Considering their close distribution over an area of more than 11 million km^2 and their many similarities, these languages must have spread fairly rapidly and rather recently. How did they spread? When, from where, and why did this expansion take place? How do we reconcile the current widespread distribution of the Bantu languages with the narrow timeframe of their dispersal? These are some of the questions debated by linguists, historians, archaeologists, and more recently molecular anthropologists. Moreover, because of its recent date and massive extent, the expansion of Bantu is of far more than purely African relevance (e.g. Cavalli-Sforza et al. 1994; Diamond and Bellwood 2003). Understanding it is thus of the greatest interest not only for all the people concerned with the past, but also for scholars in a large array of disciplines, from both a theoretical and methodological viewpoint.

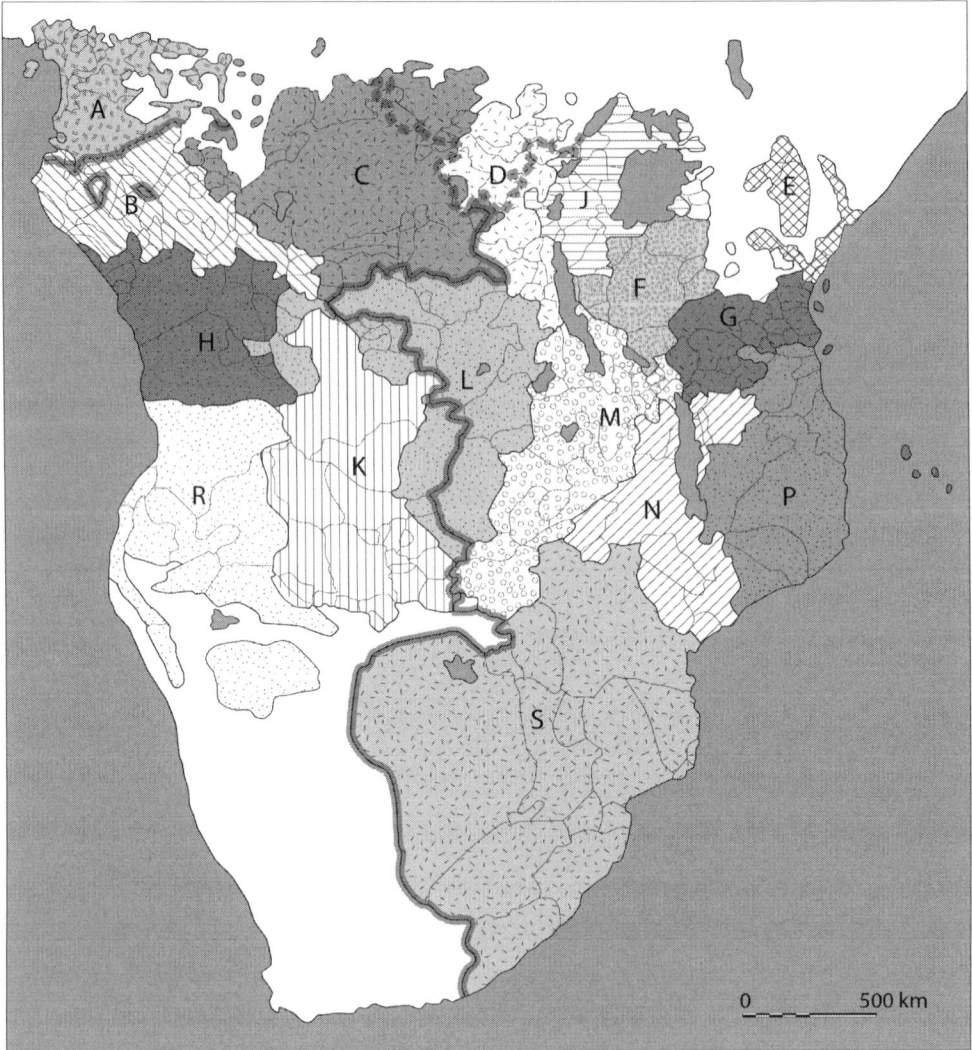

FIG. 43.1 Present-day distribution of Bantu languages (letters refer to their grouping in 15 language zones based on their similarities). The bold lines separate the upper northwest corner from the rest and the West/Central Bantu languages from the Eastern/Southern Bantu languages, suggesting major steps in their dispersal.

CLASSIFICATION OF BANTU LANGUAGES

Scholarly interest in Bantu started in the 19th century, about the same time as Indo-European studies, and was often influenced by concepts devised in that field of research. For a century, linguistics provided the data that led to the first explanatory grand scheme. First, Johnston (1886) postulated that the spread resulted from a large-scale migration probably two millennia ago from an ancestral tongue located in northwest Cameroon, and then Meinhof (1899) successfully reconstructed several aspects of that proto-language. Half a century later, Greenberg (1949a, 1949b) showed that all the Bantu languages belong to a subgroup of a much larger 'Niger-Congo' family, with Bantu likely originating in the Grassfields region of Cameroon, as this was where the greatest number of closely related non-Bantu languages occur (Greenberg 1955). This conclusion has been generally accepted and today the Bantu languages are considered a subset of the Benue-Congo branch of the broader Niger-Congo phylum (Bostoen and Grégoire 2007). Although further work is needed to clarify their exact status within Benue-Congo—crucial to understanding how and when the Bantu languages dispersed—glottochronological estimates suggest that this took place in the second (Vansina 1995; Klieman 2003) or first millennium BC (Nurse and Philippson 2003).

In contrast to the classical comparative study devised for Indo-European languages, the historical classification of Bantu languages is complicated by the lack of ancient written records, a huge linguistic diversity, the sheer amount of languages and dialects, lack of data in several regions and the poor quality of some ancient linguistic descriptions (Bostoen and Grégoire 2007). Most attempts at classifying their relationships with one another thus rely on lexicostatistics, a statistical comparison of a list of basic words from the different languages. Though not undisputed (Blench, Ch. 4 above), this at least allows a general classification to be drawn up even for areas where data are sparse or not very reliable. Establishing the relationship between languages allows their relative chronological position to be inferred and a genealogical tree to be outlined showing the various subgroups split progressively from the original 'mother' tongue. The most recent general lexicostatistical study (Bastin et al. 1999) distinguishes four main groups, two limited to the upper northwest corner of the distribution area (where languages are most diverse amongst each other and distinct from the rest) and two enjoying a much larger distribution: West/Central Bantu and Eastern/Southern Bantu (Fig. 43.1). The border between these last two groups runs north–south from the Equator to South Africa and separates a quite coherent East Bantu group from a much more fragmented West Bantu one, within which several subgroups may exist (Bastin and Piron 1999).

How the initial split between East and West Bantu occurred is still debated, one major issue being how the language that was at the origin of East Bantu languages reached the Great Lakes region from the Proto-Bantu homeland in Cameroon. Both models postulate a 'Western Stream', i.e. a movement southward from the homeland, along the Atlantic coast or inland through the forest, to its southern margins, around the Congo River estuary (e.g. Henrici 1973; Vansina 1984; Ehret 2001) (Fig. 43.2). Fragmentation would have occurred in the process, with one branch reaching the Great Lakes region by following the river system upstream or moving eastward around the southern edge of the rainforest. Alternatively, the region of secondary dispersal near the Great Lakes could have been reached from the homeland by following the northern limit of the rainforest eastward, followed by movement south along the Indian Ocean coast, and also further inland, as far as South Africa, the so-called 'Eastern Stream' (Bastin et al. 1999; Bostoen and Grégoire 2007).

Thus far, it is impossible to choose between these two models, both because we lack linguistic data in some key areas at the northern edge of the rainforest and, more generally, because lexicostatistics and the 'family tree' that it produces cannot account for all the historical dynamics that take place as languages evolve, including borrowing and convergence. Languages trees are, indeed, misleading as they leave no room for a language to have multiple origins, and give the impression that branching off reflects a radical change rather than

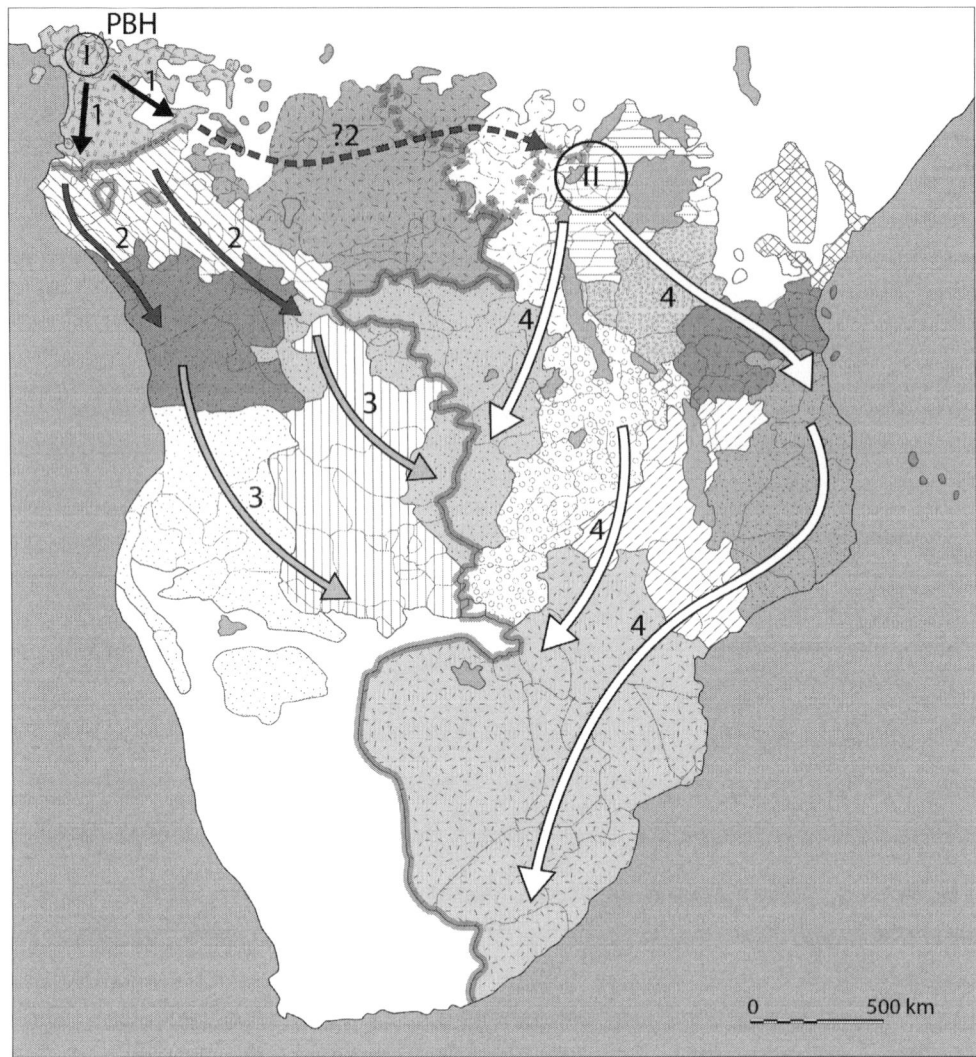

FIG. 43.2 Hypothetical dispersion routes of Bantu languages from I (Proto-Bantu Home-land) and II (region of secondary dispersal).

slower processes of language differentiation (Vansina 1995; Nurse 1997). Too rigid and too sequential from both temporal and spatial standpoints, wave (Vansina 1995) or rhizome-like models (de Maret 1994/5) may better represent the simultaneity of some stages, the multi-plicity of language origins and the many mixtures that must have taken place.

Recognizing these points demands that the sociolinguistics of Bantu must also be investi-gated. Reconstruction of the cultural vocabulary of early forms of the Bantu languages has thus attracted much attention, with the languages and geographical areas in which they occur potentially informing us about not only migration and language shifts, but also the histories of particular cultural items and social, political, and ideological structures other-wise difficult to ascertain. Examples include the reconstruction to Proto-Bantu of words for pottery (Bostoen 2005a, 2006), goats, dogs, and guinea fowl (Klieman 2003), palm oil (Bostoen 2005b), yam (Maniacky 2005), and plantain (Guthrie 1970), but not for cereals. A mixed subsistence strategy in the Grassfields homeland of Proto-Bantu is thus likely (Vansina 1994/5). Later, early speakers of Eastern Bantu languages probably acquired cereals and cattle from speakers of other language families in or close to the Great Lakes region (Ehret 1998). Vocabulary reconstruction can, however, be misleading, as Guthrie's (1970) reconstruction of terms for iron tools and weapons to Proto-Bantu shows. Far from supporting a causal link and correlation between the spread of ironworking and that of Bantu (e.g. Oliver 1966), there is no sound linguistic evidence for knowledge of metallurgy at the initial stages of the Bantu dispersal (de Maret and Nsuka 1977; Vansina 2006)

ARCHAEOLOGICAL BACKGROUND

To avoid the kind of circular reasoning and lack of critical assessment of concepts and methods that have often characterized previous explanations of the Bantu migration (Gramly 1978; Vansina 1980; Möhlig 1989; Robertson and Bradley 2000; Eggert 2005; see also Blench; Ashley; Gosselain and Livingstone Smith, Chs 4, 6, 9 above), only the linguistic aspects of the phenomenon have been considered thus far. It is now the turn of archaeology.

West-Central Africa

A useful starting point is the likelihood that Niger-Congo's diversity is such that its own dispersal probably began even before food production started to be incorporated into the subsistence strategies of West African populations; but regrettably little archaeological evidence exists for the Niger-Benue confluence of Nigeria, where the centre of expansion of the Benue-Congo languages is probably located (Blench 2006). Nearby, the terracotta sculptures of the Nok Culture remind us of the degree of sophistication achieved by some cultures with pottery and polished stone tools in the vicinity of the Bantu homeland around 3000 BP (Rupp et al. 2005).

In the homeland in northwest Cameroon, two major rockshelters have been excavated, Shum Laka (de Maret 1989, 1996; Lavachery 2001; Cornelissen 2003) and Mbi Crater (Asombang 1988, 1998) (Fig. 43.3). At Shum Laka, a quartz microlithic industry starting around 32,000 BP continued almost unchanged until the period 7000–6000 BP, when a macrolithic component of basalt and tuffs, polished stones tools, and most probably pottery appeared. Four burials in Shum Laka and one in Mbi belong broadly to the same period, and testify to elaborate burial practices. Another change took place around 5000–4000 BP with the increasing production of large blades and bifacial tools of basalt and a new pottery tradition. Six other funerary structures were dated to this later phase between 3300 and 2940 BP in Shum Laka. One of the best-preserved adult skeletons shows morphological similarities with modern Central Africans (Ribot et al. 2001).

Immediately south of the Bantu homeland, in the northern fringe of Cameroon's Equatorial rainforest, several large sites have been investigated (e.g. de Maret 1989; Essomba 1992; Mbida 1998; Eggert et al. 2006; Oslisly 2006; Meister 2007). Featuring large pits and dating to 2600–1500

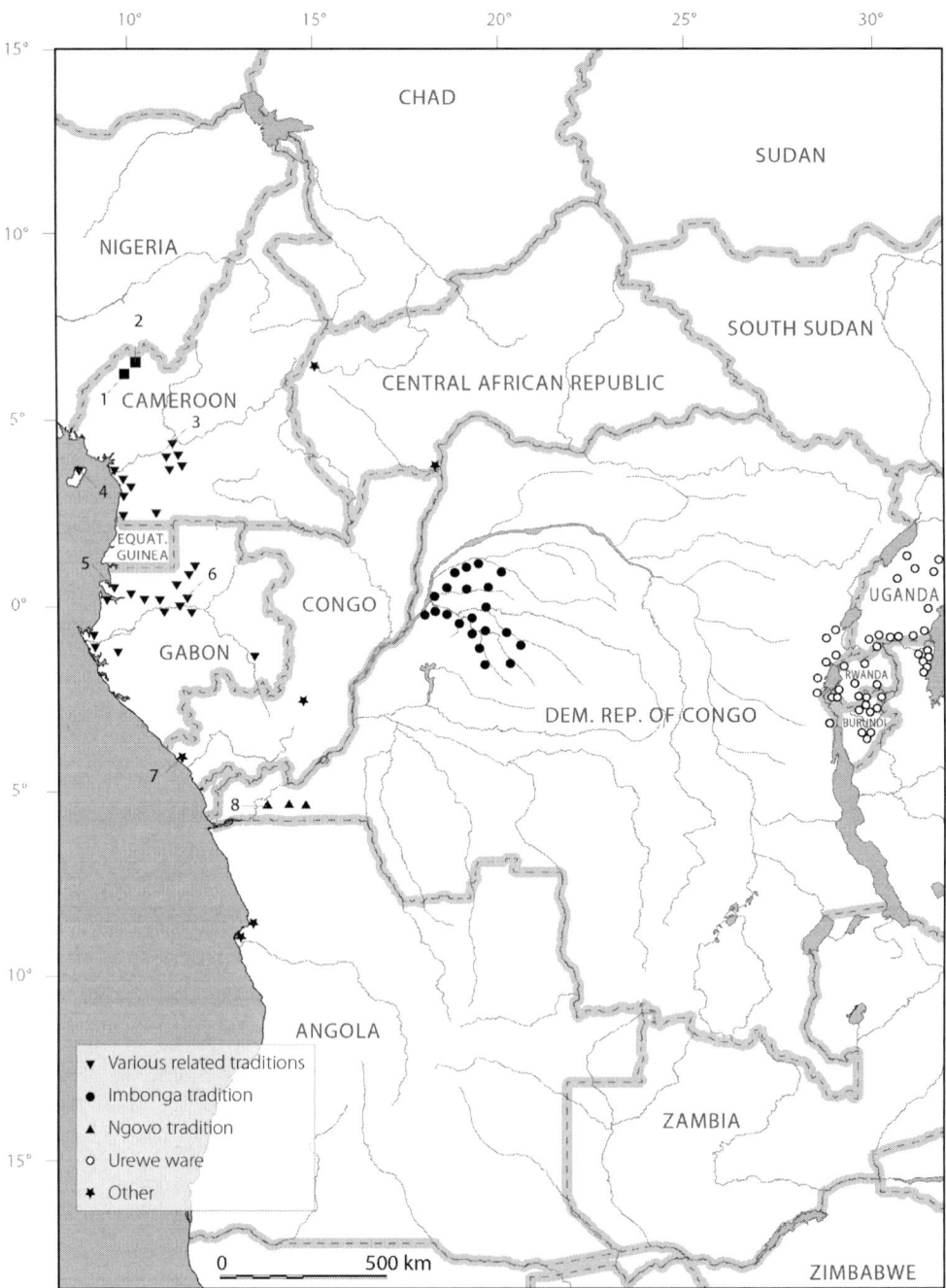

FIG. 43.3 Map of Central Africa showing sites of the 'Stone to Metal Age' and their main traditions. **1** Shum Laka; **2** Mbi; **3** Nkang; **4** Bioko; **5** Libreville; **6** Lopé; **7** Tchissanga; **8** Sakuzi.

BP, they have produced pottery, often extensively decorated by comb stamping (Fig. 43.4), charred remains of palm and *Canarium* nuts, and a few ground and polished stone axes/ hoes. The progressive disappearance of flaked lithic technology is puzzling, but may reflect its replacement by iron tools, evidence for the production of which is certainly present by 2300 BP (Lavachery et al. 1996; Clist 2006). Much older dates claimed to be associated with iron metallurgy just to the north and beyond the Bantu area in the Central African Republic (Zangato and Holl 2010) remain controversial (Pringle 2009; and see Mapunda, Ch. 42 above).

Subsistence information is sparse at most sites, with bone usually destroyed by acidic soils, though faunal remains confirm hunting, fishing and keeping of caprines (Mbida et al. 2000). Yams must have played a significant role, but leave no detectable traces so far in the archaeological record (Neumann 2005). Intriguingly, the earliest direct archaeobotanical evidence for cultivation consists of banana phytoliths at Nkang, north of Yaoundé (Mbida et al. 2000). As domesticated bananas originated in Southeast Asia, their presence in Cameroon's rainforest as early as 2500 BP is unexpected and requires substantiation by additional evidence

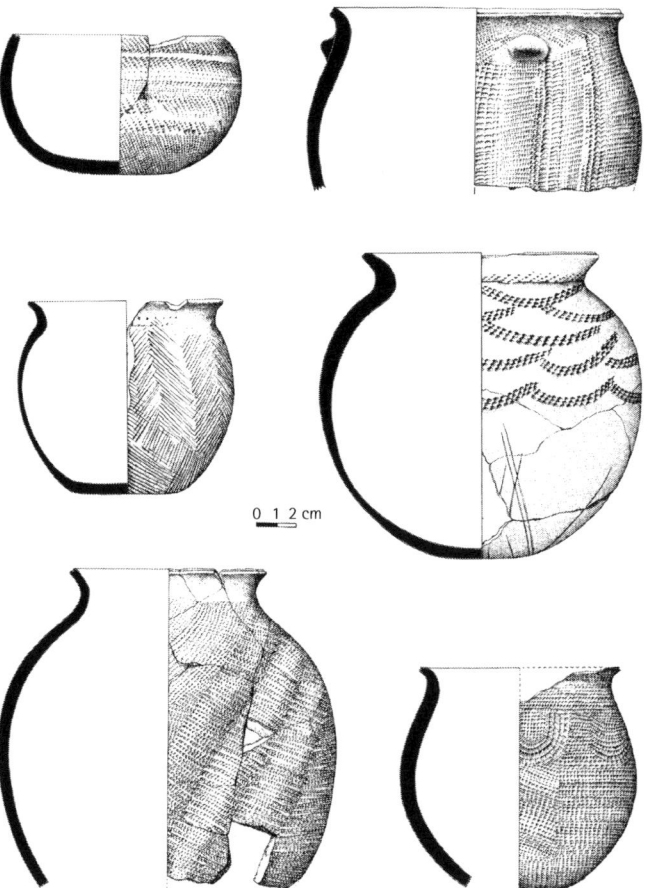

0 1 2 cm

FIG. 43.4 Examples of Stone to Metal Age pottery from Obobogo, near Yaounde, Cameroon.

(Vansina 2003; Mbida et al. 2005). However, even if they only reached the area several centuries later, their adoption must have had major consequences in providing a staple crop much better adapted than yams for rainforest cultivation (Vansina 1990: 61).

Also of interest is the presence of pearl millet (*Pennisetum glaucum*) in contexts dating to 2350–2100 BP (de Maret 1992; Eggert et al. 2006). Though also unexpected, as it is a savannah crop not cultivated in the rainforest in recent times (Eggert et al. 2006), the word for pearl millet has been reconstructed in Narrow West Bantu (Kahlheber et al. 2009). Another cultigen typical of the savannah, the Bambara groundnut (*Vigna subterranea*), is also attested, but rather later, *c.* 1750 BP (Eggert et al. 2006). The presence of these species points to a link with agricultural practices further north, in the Sahelian zone (Meister 2007), and fits with other archaeobotanical evidence of a drier climate ~2800–2300 BP. Retreat of rainforest in favour of patches of savannah (Schwartz 1992; Maley and Brenac 1998; Maley 2004) could have facilitated the penetration of immigrant agriculturalists from the north in some areas (Eggert et al. 2006).

Archaeological sites associated with similar ceramic and subsistence signatures, plus ground and polished stone axes/hoes, are known further south in the Libreville and Lopé areas of Gabon (Fig. 43.3) from 2600 BP (Clist 1995; Assoko Ndong 2002), again coinciding with the onset of a drier episode that opened up the rainforest and created patches of savannah in the centre of Gabon (Schwartz 1992). The spread of iron metallurgy, probably after 2400 BP, appears to have had little impact on either subsistence practices or social organization, though it did not reach the offshore island of Bioko, where stone tools remained in use into the 18th century; archaeologically little known, an earlier occupation became much more substantial sometime before 1400 BP (de Maret 1982; Martin del Molino 1989; Clist 1991).

East of the Atlantic coastal forest, in the area where the major rivers of the Congo Basin converge, systematic surveys along waterways have uncovered another major archaeological sequence, starting with the Imbonga tradition (2440–2160 BP; Eggert 1987). The flat bases, shape, and elaborate decoration of its pottery resemble contemporary ceramics in Gabon and Cameroon (Wotzka 1995). Subsequently, a series of other pottery traditions emerged as populations fanned out progressively along the river systems and moved upstream (Eggert 1987, 1992; Wotzka 1995), but the appearance of iron metallurgy in these areas remains undated.

South of Gabon, Djambala and Tchissanga date the first pottery in Congo-Brazzaville to 2500–2300 BP (Lanfranchi and Pinçon 1988; Denbow 1990), while on the other side of the Congo River and outside the rainforest in Congo-Kinshasa, pottery may be much earlier (*c.* 3500 BP) at Sakuzi, though this needs confirmation (de Maret 1982). So far, only the Ngovo group, with large, thick, roughly decorated pots and polished stone tools, has been consistently dated between 2300 and 2000 BP (de Maret 1986) and neither in Lower Congo nor the central Congo Basin has iron metallurgy yet been dated before 2000 BP (Eggert 1992, 1993).

Due to the many different archaeological contexts explored and uncertainties related to the radiocarbon calibration curve in the first millennium BC, no precise sequence for the appearance of pottery, food production (including caprines), villages, and metallurgy can yet be proposed for these western parts of Central Africa. Speculatively, however, changes do seem to spread from north to south, following the coast and going upstream to the interior, usually in more or less a couple of centuries. Innovations do not, however, seem to have happened all at once, and their full scale and significance are debatable. A few potsherds, for instance, do not prove the practice of pottery, while large sites could result from a long occupation or repeated small-scale ones rather than an extensive settlement. Concluding that either foraging *or* farming was the dominant subsistence strategy is also premature, and today's practices show a wide continuum, with considerable seasonal and local variation and significant inputs from riverine, lacustrine, and coastal resources (de Maret 1994/5; Vansina 1994/5). Changes in subsistence were probably gradual and reversible (Oslisly and White 2007), but while contrasting farming to foraging is not very relevant, farming did have a major impact: villagers became more sedentary. Taken literally or implying food production, the term 'Neolithic' is inappropriate in such a betwixt-and-between context. Thus, this complex transition period is better referred to as 'Stone to Metal Age' (de Maret 1982, 1994/5).

This schematic archaeological sequence may well provide us with the material backdrop of the colonization of the rainforest by the first Bantu speakers. The time-frame and processes involved and reconstructions of Proto-Bantu vocabulary broadly coincide with archaeological evidence, but just because linguistic data and archaeological data do not contradict each other, they do not yet explain the Bantu phenomenon. More data are needed from both disciplines to understand what triggered the various movements and processes and when.

Great Lakes Africa

The same is true for the Great Lakes region, where the secondary point of dispersal of all the ensuing East Bantu languages is generally located. Archaeological research has focused on second-millennium AD major population centres in western Uganda (Reid, Ch. 61 below) and on early metallurgy in Rwanda, Burundi, and northwestern Tanzania (Mapunda, Ch. 42 above). It is in that area, west of Lake Victoria, that a relationship between the appearance of a Dimple-Based ware (Leakey et al. 1948) characteristic of the beginning of the Iron Age and the spread of Bantu speakers was first proposed (Posnansky 1961; Hiernaux 1962). Renamed Urewe ware (Posnansky 1967), this pottery was soon seen as the parent style of similar ceramic traditions diffusing rapidly through eastern and southern Africa (Huffman 1970; Soper 1971; Phillipson 1976; cf. Ashley 2010).

West of Lake Victoria, little is known about what preceded Urewe and there is no evidence of polished tools or of stone industries with pottery (Nenquin 1967). The Early Iron Age thus gives the impression of starting there rather abruptly with elaborate ironworking technologies, mostly concentrations of cylindrical shaft furnaces, built using decorated clay bricks, associated with Urewe ceramics. New evidence regarding Urewe ceramics suggests a significant degree of inter-assemblage variability in relation with localized adaptation and non-domestic contexts (Ashley 2010). An Urewe burial dated to *c.* AD 400 also provides evidence of long-distance exchange, probably in connection with wealth accumulation, but also childhood malnutrition, suggesting agricultural insecurities (Giblin et al. 2010). Dates remain controversial, going back to ≥2500 BP and continuing until around 1500 BP, with settlements starting on rather poor soil before favouring fertile regions, well suited for incipient agriculture (Schmidt 1978, 1997; MacLean 1994/5; Van Grunderbeek et al. 2001), though direct evidence for agriculture is so far limited to pollen of finger millet and sorghum in Rwanda (Van Grunderbeek et al. 1992). Direct archaeological evidence of animal husbandry is equally minimal and controversial. On purely archaeological grounds, it is thus difficult to identify the subsistence strategies practised in this secondary dispersal area, and the generally accepted model of pioneer small-scale communities of sedentary agriculturalists needs to be substantiated by more archaeological research. Fortunately this is not the case on the eastern shore of Lake Victoria, where recent work on Kansyore sides provides a richer picture of the transition to food production (Lane et al. 2007; Prendergast 2010) and of the fluid switches between foraging, fishing, herding, and agriculture (Barut Kusimba, Ch. 32 above).

Linguistic research, on the other hand, indicates that Proto-Great Lakes Bantu speakers grew yams and raised caprines before entering the area, after which encounters with pre-existing Sudanic speakers (themselves archaeologically invisible as yet!) would have introduced them to cattle, millet, and sorghum (Ehret 1998; Schoenbrun 1998). Once again, linguistics and archaeology do not contradict each other, but given the still very patchy archaeological coverage of the Great Lakes area, this is hardly a confirmation of the underlying general hypothesis. Moreover, key areas to the north, east, and south of the Congo Basin remain even more poorly known.

A GENETIC PERSPECTIVE

In the last two decades molecular anthropologists have also become increasingly interested in the Bantu question. Unfortunately, however, the Bantu expansion model is once again used uncritically as an archetypal example of the concurrent dispersion of human genes, language, and agriculture (Diamond and Bellwood 2003). Since it is far from being fully understood linguistically or archaeologically, the risk is high of again lapsing into reinforcing previous hypotheses rather than testing them. The alleged connection between language and genes is also controversial (MacEachern, Ch. 5 above), and there remains a shortage of genetic data for some key areas. It is thus premature to use the results of molecular anthropology to test the various scenarios proposed to explain the present distribution of Bantu languages. However, and importantly, genetic markers do seem to indicate that their 'expansion' may have resulted from the actual movement of people, rather than just a linguistic and a cultural diffusion (Cruciani et al. 2002; Salas et al. 2002; Wood et al. 2005; Pakendorf et al. 2011). If an increasingly consistent database and future genetic research confirm this conclusion, it will be a major step in elucidating the processes at work. For the moment, several studies appear also to demonstrate cultural and physical contact between immigrant Bantu populations and resident hunter-gatherers, both in Central and in southern Africa, with migrating males from Bantu-speaking groups commonly interbreeding with local women (Destro-Bisol et al. 2004; Quintana-Murci et al. 2008; Berniell-Lee et al. 2009; Tishkoff et al. 2007, 2009; Verdu et al. 2009; Schuster et al. 2010; Pakendorf et al. 2011).

CONCLUSION

Encompassing a series of changes and movements that took place during several millennia over one of the largest continental masses on earth, the Bantu phenomenon cannot be accounted for by a single and simplistic paradigm. Connected with, if not triggered by, major climatic changes, complex population movements starting north of Central Africa resulted in the progressive colonization of a vast area further south and multiple interactions and admixture with its previous inhabitants. While they did not come as a single 'Bantu package', over time several parallel and interacting changes took place with the development of food production, the diffusion of iron metallurgy, and the spread of various crops. These inter-related processes expanded over multiple ecological systems resulting in a mosaic of inter-connected situations that kept evolving.

Despite large lacunae in geographical and temporal coverage, the scale, speed, chron-ology, and general direction of these changes are significant. Wotzka's (2006) compila-tion and calibration of over 1,200 late Holocene radiocarbon dates from sites located between 5°N and 5°S is extremely telling, and shows 'a basic chronological west to east succession of settlement intensity peaks as well as a general chronological north–south gradient of early settlement' (Wotzka 2006: 281). This does, of course, concur with the broad linguistic models of diffusion. Moreover, in addition to the coincidence between the major intensification of human settlement of Central Africa *c.* 2500–1500 BP, equiva-lent to *c.* 800 cal. BC–cal. AD 700, and the driest phase of the last 12,000 years (Elenga et al. 2004), briefer cycles of growth, contraction, and recovery appears to have struc-tured settlement across the continent, from the Atlantic to the Indian Oceans. Migra-tion, climate, disease (Wotzka 2006), and, we may add, new subsistence patterns may help explain this.

To go further, in addition to expanded archaeological fieldwork and the contributions now emerging from genetics, other fields should also be considered more fully than in the recent past. Physical anthropology is one, long overlooked because of the rejection of racial modelling (but see Hiernaux 1968; Gramly 1978). Demography is another: did population spread continuously, in waves, or by a more jump-like process? how large were initial popu-lations and how fast did they grow? Relations with autochthonous hunter-gatherers are obvi-ously critical here and, as Klieman (2003) shows for tropical forest foragers, undoubtedly complex, as languages, technologies, rituals, and genes came to be shared. Comparative studies of myths and rituals that may reveal symbolic connections through today's Bantu area (de Heusch 1972, 1982) and of material culture also have a role to play, while the lengthy and complex training required for making particular kinds of ceramics as well as the distri-bution of decoration techniques (Gosselain 2000) offer another strong argument in favour of actual population movement rather than merely a diffusion of languages, agriculture and cultural items. Whether, as such research continues, the Bantu phenomenon is best under-stood as a colonization, migration, expansion, dispersal, or diffusion is (at least in part) of purely ideological and semantic importance. Terming it simply 'Bantuization' may prove to be sufficient recognition of the complexity, dynamism, and adaptability that the Bantu odys-sey implies.

References

ASHLEY, C. Z. (2010). Towards a socialised archaeology of ceramics in Great Lakes Africa. *African Archaeological Review* 27: 135–63.

ASOMBANG, R. (1988). Bamenda in Prehistory: the Evidence from Fiye Nkwi, Mbi Crater and Shum Laka Rockshelters. Ph.D, University College London.

ASOMBANG, R. (1998). Ten years of archaeological research in the Bamenda Grassfields. In M. Delneuf, J.-M. Essomba, and A. Froment (eds), *Paléoanthropologie en Afrique Centrale: un bilan de l'archéologie au Cameroun*. Paris: L'Harmattan, 193–202.

ASSOKO NDONG, A. (2002). Synthèse des données archéologiques récentes sur le peuplement à l'Holocène de la réserve de faune de la Lopé, Gabon. *L'Anthropologie* 106: 135–58.

BASTIN, Y., COUPEZ, A., and MANN, M. (1999). *Continuity and Divergence in the Bantu Languages: Perspectives from a Lexicostatistic Study*. Tervuren: Musée Royal de l'Afrique Centrale.

——– and PIRON, P. (1999). Classifications lexicostatistiques: bantou, bantou et bantoïde. De l'intérêt des 'groupes flottants'. In J.-M. Hombert and L. M. Hyman (eds), *Bantu Historical Linguistics: Theoretical and Empirical Perspectives*. Stanford, Calif.: CSLI, 149–64.

BERNIELL-LEE, G., CALAFELL, F., BOSCH, E., et al. (2009). Genetic and demographic implications of the Bantu expansion: insight from human paternal lineages. *Molecular Biology and Evolution* 26: 1581–9.

BLEEK, W. (1862, 1869). *A Comparative Grammar of South African Languages*, parts 1 and 2. London: Trübner.

BLENCH, R. (2006). *Archaeology, Language and the African Past*. Lanham, Md.: AltaMira Press.

BOSTOEN, K. (2005a). *Des Mots et des Pots en Bantou: une Approche Linguistique de l'Histoire de la Céramique en Afrique*. Frankfurt: Peter Lang.

—— (2005b). A diachronic onomasiological approach to early Bantu oil palm vocabulary. *Studies in African Linguistics* 34: 143–88.

—— (2006). What comparative Bantu pottery vocabulary may tell us about early human settlement in the Inner Congo Basin. *Afrique & Histoire* 5: 221–63.

—— and GRÉGOIRE, C. (2007). La question bantoue: bilan et perspectives. *Mémoires de la Société de Linguistique de Paris*, nouvelle série 15: 73–91.

CAVALLIS-FORZA, L. L., MENOZZI P., and PIAZZA, A. (1994). *The History and Geography of Human Genes*. Princeton, NJ: Princeton University Press.

CLIST, B.-O. (1987). A critical reappraisal of the chronological framework of the early Urewe Iron Age industry. *Muntu* 6: 35–62.

—— (1991). Guinée Équatoriale. In R. Lanfranchi and B.-O. Clist (eds), *Aux Origines de l'Afrique Centrale*. Libreville: Sépia.

—— (1995). *Gabon: 100.000 Ans d'Histoire*. Libreville: Sépia.

—— (2006). Mais où se sont taillées nos pierres en Afrique Centrale entre 7.000 et 2.000 BP? In H.-P. Wotzka (ed.), *Grundlegungen: Beiträge zur europäischen und afrikanischen Archäologie für Manfred K. H. Eggert*. Tübingen: Francke, 291–302.

CORNELISSEN, E. (2003). On microlithic quartz industries and the end of the Pleistocene in Central Africa: the evidence from Shum Laka (NW Cameroon). *African Archaeological Review* 20: 1–24.

CRUCIANI, F., SANTOLAMAZZA, P., SHEN, P., et al. (2002). A back migration from Asia to sub-Saharan Africa is supported by high-resolution analysis of human Y-chromosome haplotypes. *American Journal of Human Genetics* 70: 1197–1214.

DE HEUSCH, L. (1972). *Le Roi Ivre ou l'Origine de l'État*. Paris: Gallimard.

—— (1982). *Rois Nés d'un Coeur de Vache*. Paris: Gallimard.

DE MARET, P. (1982). From the Stone Age to the Iron Age. In F. Van Noten (ed.), *The Archaeology of Central Africa*. Graz: Akademische Druck-und Verlagsanstalt, 57, 59–65.

DE MARET, P. (1986). The Ngovo Group: an industry with polished stone tools and pottery in Lower-Zaire. *African Archaeological Review* 4: 103–33.

—— (1989). Le contexte archéologique de l'expansion bantu en Afrique centrale. In T. Obenga (ed.), *Les Peuples Bantu: Migration, Expansion et Identité Culturelle*. Paris: L'Harmattan, 118–38.

—— (1992). Sédentarisation, agriculture et métallurgie du Sud-Cameroun: synthèse des recherches depuis 1978. In Essomba (1992: 247–62).

—— (1994/5). Pits, pots and the Far-West Streams. *Azania* 29/30: 318–23.

—— (1996). Shum Laka (Cameroon): general perspectives. In G. Pwiti and R. Soper (eds), *Aspects of African Archaeology*. Harare: University of Zimbabwe, 275–80.

—— and NSUKA, F. (1977). History of Bantu metallurgy: some linguistic aspects. *History in Africa* 4: 43–65.

DENBOW, J. (1990). Congo to Kalahari: data and hypothesis about the political economy of the western stream of the Early Iron Age. *African Archaeological Review* 8: 139–75.

DESTRO-BISOL, G., COIA, V., BOSCHI, I., et al. (2004). The analysis of variation of mtDNA hypervariable region 1 suggests that eastern and western Pygmies diverged before the Bantu expansion. *American Naturalist* 163: 212–26.

DIAMOND, J., and BELLWOOD, P. (2003). Farmers and their languages: the first expansions. *Science* 300: 597–603.

EGGERT, M. K. H. (1987). Imbonga and Batalimo: ceramic evidence for early settlement of the Equatorial rainforest. *African Archaeological Review* 5: 129–45.

—— (1992). The Central African rain forest: historical speculation and archaeological facts. *World Archaeology* 24: 1–24.

—— (1993). Central Africa and the archaeology of the Equatorial rainforest: reflections on some major topics. In T. Shaw, P. J. J. Sinclair, B. Andah, and A. Okpogo (eds), *The Archaeology of Africa: Food, Metals and Towns*. London: Routledge, 289–329.

—— (2005). The Bantu problem and African archaeology. In A. B. Stahl (ed.), *African Archaeology: A Critical Introduction*. Oxford: Blackwell, 301–26.

—— HÖHN, A., KAHLHEBER, S., MEISTER, C., NEUMANN, K., and SCHWEIZER, A. (2006). Pits, graves and grains: archaeological and archaeobotanical research in southern Cameroon. *Journal of African Archaeology* 4: 273–98.

EHRET, C. (1998). *An African Classical Age: Eastern and Southern Africa in World History 1000 B.C. to A.D. 400*. Charlottesville: University of Virginia Press.

—— (2001). Bantu expansions: re-envisioning a central problem of early African history. *International Journal of African Historical Studies* 34: 5–41.

—— (2002). Language family expansion: broadening our understanding of cause from an African perspective. In P. Bellwood and C. Renfrew (eds), *Examining the Farming/Language Dispersal Hypothesis*. Cambridge: McDonald Institute for Archaeological Research.

ELENGA, H., MALEY J., VINCENS, A., and FARRERA, I. (2004). Paleoenvironments, paleoclimates and landscape development in Atlantic Equatorial Africa: a review of key sites covering the last 25 years. In R. W. Battarbee, F. Gasse, and C. E. Stickey (eds), *Past Climate Variability through Europe and Africa*. Dordrecht: Springer, 181–98.

ESSOMBA, J.-M. (ed.) (1992). *L'Archéologie au Cameroun: Actes du Premier Colloque International de Yaoundé (6–9 janvier 1986)*. Paris: Karthala.

GIBLIN, J., CLEMENT, A., and HUMPHRIS, J. (2010). An Urewe burial in Rwanda: exchange, health, wealth and violence *c.* AD 400. *Azania* 45: 276–97.

GOSSELAIN, O. (2000). Materializing identities: an African perspective. *Journal of Archaeological Method and Theory* 7: 187–217.

GRAMLY, R. M. (1978). Expansion on Bantu-speakers versus development of Bantu language *in situ*: an archaeologist's perspective. *South African Archaeological Bulletin* 33: 107–12.

GREENBERG, J. H. (1949a). Studies in African linguistic classification, I: The Niger-Congo Family. *Southwestern Journal of Anthropology* 5: 79–100.

—— (1949b). Studies in African linguistic classification, III: The position of Bantu. *Southwestern Journal of Anthropology* 5: 309–17.

—— (1955). *Studies in African Linguistic Classification*. New Haven, Conn.: Compass.

GUTHRIE, M. (1970). *Comparative Bantu: An Introduction to the Comparative Linguistics and Prehistory of the Bantu Languages*, vol. 3. Farnborough: Gregg.

HENRICI, A. (1973). Numerical classification of Bantu languages. *African Language Studies* 14: 82–104.

HIERNAUX, J. (1962). Les débuts de l'âge des métaux dans la région des grands lacs africains. In G. Mortelmans and J. Nenquin (eds), *Actes du IVe Congrès Panafricain de Préhistoire et de l'Etude du Quarternaire*, III: *Préhistoire et Protohistoire*. Tervuren: Musée Royal de l'Afrique Centrale, 381–9.

—— (1968). Bantu expansion: the evidence from physical anthropology confronted with linguistic and archaeological evidence. *Journal of African History* 9: 505–15.

HUFFMAN, T. N. (1970). The Early Iron Age and the spread of the Bantu. *South African Archaeological Bulletin* 25: 3–21.

JOHNSTON, H. H. (1886). *The Kilima-Njaro Expedition: A Record of Scientific Exploration in Eastern Equatorial Africa*. London: Kegan Paul & Trench.

KAHLHEBER, S., BOSTOEN, K., and NEUMANN, K. (2009). Early plant cultivation in the Central African rain forest: first millennium BC pearl millet from South Cameroon. *Journal of African Archaeology* 7: 252–72.

KLIEMAN, K. A. (2003). *The Pygmies Were Our Compass: Bantu and Batwa in the History of West Central Africa, Early Times to c. 1900 C.E.* Portsmouth, NH: Heinemann.

LANE, P., ASHLEY, C. Z., SEITSONEN, O., HARVEY, P., MIRE, S., and ODEDE, F. (2007). The transition to farming in eastern Africa: new faunal and dating evidence from Wadh Lang'o and Usenge, Kenya. *Antiquity* 81: 62–81.

LANFRANCHI, R., and PINÇON, B. (1988). Résultats préliminaires des prospections archéologiques récentes sur les plateaux et collines Teke en République populaire du Congo (1984–1987). *Nsi* 3: 24–31.

LAVACHERY, P. (2001). The Holocene archaeological sequence of Shum Laka Rock Shelter (Grasslands, Western Cameroon). *African Archaeological Review* 18: 213–47.

—— CORNELISSEN, E., MOEYERSONS, J., and DE MARET, P. (1996). 30,000 ans d'occupation, 6 mois de fouilles: Shum Laka, un site exceptionnel en Afrique centrale. *Anthropologie et Préhistoire* 107: 197–211.

LEAKEY, M. D., OWEN, W. E., and LEAKEY, L. S. B. (1948). *Dimple-Based Pottery from Central Kavirondo, Kenya Colony*. Nairobi: Coryndon Memorial Museum.

MACLEAN, M. R. (1994/95). Late Stone Age and Early Iron Age settlement in the Interlacustrine Region: a distinct case study. *Azania* 29/30: 296–302.

MALEY, J. (2004). Les variations de la végétation et des paléo-environnements du domaine forestier africain au cours du Quaternaire récent. In A.-M. Sémah and J. Renault-Miskovsky (eds), *L'Évolution de la Végétation depuis deux Millions d'Années*. Paris: Artcom/Errance, 143–78.

—— and BRENAC, P. (1998). Vegetation dynamics, palaeoenvironments and climatic change in the forests of Western Cameroon during the last 28,000 years bp. *Review of Palaeobotany and Palynology* 99: 157–87.

MANIACKY, J. (2005). Quelques thèmes pour 'igname' en bantou. In K. Bostoen and J. Maniacky (eds), *Studies in African Comparative Linguistics with Special Focus on Bantu and Mande: Essays in Honour of Y. Bastin and C. Grégoire*. Tervuren: Musée Royal de l'Afrique Centrale, 165–87.

MARTIN DEL MOLINO, A. (1989). Prehistoria de Guinea Equatorial. *Africa 2000* 4(10–11): 4–21.

MBIDA, C. (1988). Premières communautés villageoises au sud du Cameroun. Synthèses et données nouvelles. In M. Delneuf, J.-M. Essomba and A. Froment (eds), *Paléoanthropologie en Afrique Centrale. Un Bilan de l'Archéologie au Cameroun*. Paris: L' Harmattan, 203–11.

—— DOUTRELEPONT, H., VRYDAGHS, L., et al. (2005). The initial history of bananas in Africa: a reply to Jan Vansina, *Azania* 2003. *Azania* 40: 128–35.

—— VAN NEER, W., DOUTRELEPONT, H., and VRYDAGHS, L. (2000). Evidence for banana cultivation and animal husbandry during the first millennium BC in the forest of southern Cameroon. *Journal of Archaeological Science* 27:151–62.

MEINHOF, C. (1899). *Grundriss einer Lautlehre der Bantu Sprachen*. Leipzig: F. A. Brockhaus.

MEISTER, C. (2007). Recent archaeological investigations in the tropical rain forest of southwest Cameroon. In J. Runge (ed.), *Dynamics of Forest Ecosystems in Central Africa during the Holocene: Past–Present–Future*. London: Taylor & Francis, 43–57.

MÖHLIG, W. J. G. (1989). Sprachgeschichte, Kulturgeschichte und Archäologie: die Kongruenz der Forschungsergebnisse als methodologisches Problem. *Paideuma* 35: 189–96.

NENQUIN, J. (1967). *Contributions to the Study of Prehistoric Cultures of Rwanda and Burundi*. Tervuren: Musée Royal de l'Afrique Centrale.

NEUMANN, K. (2005). The romance of farming: plant cultivation and domestication in Africa. In A. B. Stahl (ed.), *African Archaeology: A Critical Introduction*. Oxford: Blackwell, 249–75.

NURSE, D. (1997). The contributions of linguistics to the study of history in Africa. *Journal of African History* 38: 359–91.

—— and PHILIPPSON, G. (2003). Towards a historical classification of the Bantu languages. In D. Nurse and G. Philippson (eds), *The Bantu Languages*. London: Routledge, 164–81.

OLIVER, R. (1966). The problem of the Bantu expansion. *Journal of African History* 7: 361–76.

OSLISLY, R. (2006). Les traditions culturelles de l'Holocène sur le littoral du Cameroun entre Kribi et Campo. In H.-P. Wotzka (ed.), *Grundlegungen: Beiträge zur europäischen und afrikanischen Archäologie für Manfred K.H. Eggert*. Tübingen: Francke, 303–17.

—— and WHITE, T. (2007). Human impact and environmental exploitation in Gabon during the Holocene. In T. Denham, J. Iriarte, and L. Vrydaghs (eds), *Rethinking Agriculture: Agricultural and Ethnoarchaeological Perspectives*. Walnut Creek, Calif.: Left Coast Press, 347–60.

PAKENDORF, B., BOSTOEN, K., and DE FILIPPO, C. (2011). Molecular perspectives on the Bantu expansion: a synthesis. *Language Dynamics and Changes* 1: 50–88.

PHILLIPSON, D. W. (1976). Archaeology and Bantu linguistics. *World Archaeology* 8: 65–82.

POSNANSKY, M. (1961). Pottery types from archaeological sites in East Africa. *Journal of African History* 2:177–98.

—— (1967). The Iron Age in East Africa. In W. Bishop and J. D. Clark (eds), *Background to Evolution in Africa*. Chicago: University of Chigaco Press, 629–49.

PRENDERGAST, M. (2010). Kansyore fisher-foragers and transitions to food production in East Africa: the view from Wadh Lang'o, Nyanza Province, Western Kenya. *Azania* 45: 83–111.

PRINGLE, H. (2009). Seeking Africa's First Iron Men. *Science* 323: 200–2.

QUINTANA-MURCI, L., QUACH, H., HARMANT, C., et al. (2008). Maternal traces of deep common ancestry and asymmetric gene flow between Pygmy hunter-gatherers and Bantu-speaking farmers. *Proceedings of the National Academy of Sciences (USA)* 105: 1596–1601.

RIBOT, I., ORBAN R., and DE MARET, P. (2001). *The Prehistoric Burials of Shum Laka Rockshelter (North-West Cameroon)*. Tervuren: Musée Royal de l'Afrique Centrale.

ROBERTSON, J. H., and BRADLEY, R. (2000). A new paradigm: the African Early Iron Age without Bantu migrations. *History in Africa* 27: 287–323.

RUPP, N., AMEJE, J., and BREUNIG, P. (2005). New studies on the Nok Culture of Central Nigeria. *Journal of African Archaeology* 3: 283–90.

SALAS, A, RICHARD, M., DE LA FE, T., et al. (2002). The making of the African mtDNA landscape. *American Journal of Human Genetics* 171: 1082–111.

SCHMIDT, P. (1978). *Historical Archaeology: A Structural Approach in an African Culture*. Westport, Conn.: Greenwood Press.

—— (1997). Archaeological views on a history of landscape change in East Africa. *Journal of African History* 38: 393–421.

SCHOENBRUN, D. L. (1998). *A Green Place, A Good Place: Agrarian Change, Gender and Social Identity in the Great Lakes Region to the 15th Century*. Portsmouth, NH: Heinemann.

SCHUSTER, S. C., MILLER, W., RATAN, A., et al. (2010). Complete Khoisan and Bantu genomes from Southern Africa. *Nature* 463: 943–7.

SCHWARTZ, D. (1992). Assèchement climatique vers 3.000BP et expansion Bantu en Afrique centrale atlantique: quelques réflexions. *Bulletin de la Société Géologique de France* 163: 353–61.

SOPER, R. (1971). A general review of the Early Iron Age of the southern half of Africa. *Azania* 6: 5–38.

TISHKOFF, S. A., REED, F. A., FRIEDLAENDER, F. R., et al. (2007). History of click-speaking populations of Africa inferred from mtDNA and Y chromosome genetic variations. *Molecular Biology and Evolution* 24: 2180–95.

—— —— ——, et al. (2009). The genetic structure and history of Africans and African Americans. *Science* 324: 1035–44.

VAN GRUNDERBEEK, M. C. (1992). Essai de délimitation chronologique de l'Âge du Fer Ancien au Burundi, au Rwanda et dans la région des Grands Lacs. *Azania* 27: 53–80.

—— ROCHE, E., DOUTRELEPONT, H. (1982). L'Âge du Fer Ancien au Rwanda et au Burundi: archéologie et environnement. *Journal de la Société des Africanistes* 52: 5–58.

—— —— —— (2001). Un type de fourneau de fonte de fer associé à la culture Urewe (Âge du Fer Ancien) au Rwanda et au Burundi. *Mediterranean Archaeology* 14: 271–97.

VANSINA, J. (1979). Bantu in the crystal ball, I. *History in Africa* 6: 287–333.

—— (1980). Bantu in the crystal ball, II. *History in Africa* 7: 293–325.

—— (1984). Western Bantu expansion. *Journal of African History* 25: 129–45.

—— (1990). *Paths in the Rainforests: Towards a History of Political Tradition in Equatorial Africa*. Madison: University of Wisconsin Press.

—— (1994/5). A slow revolution: farming in subequatorial Africa. *Azania* 29/30: 15–26.

—— (1995). New linguistic evidence and 'the Bantu expansion'. *Journal of African History* 36: 173–95.

—— (2003). Bananas in Cameroon c.500 BCE? Not proven. *Azania* 38: 174–716.

—— (2006). Linguistic evidence for the introduction of ironworking into Bantu-speaking Africa. *History in Africa* 33: 321–61.

VERDU, P., AUSTERLITZ, F., ESTOUP, A., et al. (2009). Origins and genetic diversity of Pygmy hunter-gatherers from western Central Africa. *Current Biology* 19: 1–7.

WOOD, E. T., STOVER, D. A., EHRET, C., et al. (2005). Contrasting patterns of Y chromosome and mtDNA variation in Africa: evidence for sex-biased demographic processes. *European Journal of Human Genetics* 13: 867–76.

Wotzka, H.-P. (1995). *Studien zur Archäologie des zentralafrikanischen Regenwaldes: Die Keramik des inneren Zaïre-Beckens und ihre Stellung im Kontext der Bantu-Expansion.* Cologne: Heinrich Barth Institut.

—— (2006). Records of activity: radiocarbon and the structure of Iron Age settlement in Central Africa. In H.-P. Wotzka (ed.), *Grundlegungen: Beiträge zur europäischen und afrikanischen Archäologie für Manfred K. H. Eggert.* Tübingen: Francke, 271–89.

Zangato, E., and Holl, A. F. C. (2010). On the iron front: new evidence from North-Central Africa. *Journal of African Archaeology* 8: 7–23.

CHAPTER 44

THE ARCHAEOLOGY OF HERDING IN SOUTHERNMOST AFRICA

KARIM SADR

INTRODUCTION

DURING the last fifty years or more the conventional view has been that livestock and pottery first reached the frontiers of southern Africa with immigrant, Bantu-speaking farmers. The herding way of life then spread southwards with the Khoekhoe-speaking branch of the indigenous 'Khoesan' populations (Walker 1983; Elphick 1985; Parkington et al. 1986; A. Smith 1990, 1992; Boonzaier et al. 1996). Archaeologically, the Bantu migrations are well documented (Huffman 2007; de Maret, Ch. 43 above; Mitchell, Ch. 45 below), but the evidence for Khoekhoen migration is meagre. Indeed, linguistic and chronological evidence refutes the conventional view. In many southeastern Bantu languages the words for livestock are of Khoe origin (Ehret 2008), and southern African pottery pre-dates the arrival of the first farmers (Sadr and Sampson 2006). Two alternatives present themselves: either the earliest livestock and pottery reached southernmost Africa by a process of diffusion and without the help of any migrating herder-potters (Deacon 1984; Klein 1986; Kinahan 1996a; Sadr 2004, 2008a) or a migration of *non*-Bantu-speaking herders brought livestock to the subcontinent before the arrival of Bantu farmers (Ehret 2008; Fauvelle-Aymar 2008; Güldemann 2008; Blench 2009). The remainder of this chapter discusses the archaeological evidence from these two perspectives.

CERAMICS

The earliest Later Stone Age (LSA) pottery from the western parts of South Africa, northern Namibia, and northern Botswana/western Zimbabwe is all thin-walled and well-fired (Sadr and Sampson 2006). Vessels are generally small. Before about AD 300, in the South African coastal areas and the Orange River Basin, thin ware was undecorated (Sadr 2008b). To the north, in the Limpopo Basin, the Kalahari, and northwestern Namibia, thin ware was decorated with incised lines, comb stamped impressions, and an effect referred to as rippling. Spouted vessels were not uncommon here, but absent in the south. A ceramic-free zone separates these early northern decorated thin wares from the southern plain ones, but this gap could reflect insufficient research. Further north, in the upper Zambezi and Congo Basins and along Angola's coast, the earliest thick-walled ceramic pots (later clearly associated with Iron Age, farming villages) are known from Benfica in Angola and Situmpa in western Zambia (Clark and Fagan 1965; Dos Santos and Ervedosa 1970). Further south, thick ware first appeared in the late 3rd century AD at the farming village of Matola near Maputo in Mozambique (Morais 1988; Maggs and Whitelaw 1991). Given the much earlier dates of southern thin-walled pots and the absence of thin ware in Central and East Africa, there is little reason to think that the first southern African potters were influenced by immigrant farmers from further north.

From AD 600 to 1000, farmer ceramics spread rapidly at the expense of thin ware (Sadr 2008b). In the north, many of the early first-millennium AD sites that contained northern, decorated thin ware were abandoned by the 6th century. Where occupation continued, the stone tool-using inhabitants of these sites switched to using farmer thick ware (e.g. Hall and Smith 2000; van Doornum 2007). A similar and contemporary ceramic replacement took place in the southeastern part of South Africa in rockshelters in the Thukela Basin of KwaZulu-Natal, where farmer-made thick-walled pots replaced earlier undecorated thin ware (Mazel 1986).

Possibly as a result of the advancing farmer frontier, decorated thin-walled pots with spouts, which were characteristic of the northern thin wares in the first half of the first millennium AD, now appeared in the south, previously the province of undecorated thin ware. The appearance of the northern decoration techniques and spouted vessels (but not the decoration tools, design layouts, and vessel shapes) in the southern assemblages just after their disappearance in the north might suggest an infiltration of people who brought some ideas regarding pottery style and perhaps other cultural traits, but who assimilated into local cultures to such an extent that their arrival is not marked in the archaeological record as a rupture.

Faunal remains

Bones of domesticated livestock have been dated to the 1st centuries BC and AD in northern Botswana, as well as on the west and south coasts of South Africa (Sealy and Yates 1994; Henshilwood 1996; Vogel et al. 1997; Robbins et al. 2005). All are in LSA contexts. There is little reason to doubt the validity of these AMS radiocarbon dates obtained directly from the livestock bones, although as most samples were from post-cranial remains (mostly sheep, some cattle, but no definite goats), some residual doubt lingers around their correct identification as domestic animals. Assuming that at least some of these early dates come from sheep and cattle, one can conclude that the earliest domesticated livestock in southern Africa are about two or three centuries older than the earliest securely dated villages of iron-using farmers and herders south of the Zambezi (Morais 1988; Sadr and Sampson 2006). Bantu-speaking farmers, in other words, could not have been the agents responsible for introducing livestock into the LSA economies of southernmost Africa.

Although the first millennium AD LSA sites with livestock remains can certainly be called herder sites, the proportion of livestock is much lower than one might expect from pastoralists' sites. Published reports of 102 LSA site components include 88 with less than 10 per cent livestock bones (Sadr 2008a). As a comparison, southern African iron-using, village-dwelling agropastoralists, who revered their stock and gave a central position to cattle in their daily lives, and who rarely consumed them except on special occasions, have left behind kitchen middens where livestock bones regularly account for more than 40 per cent of the mammalian fauna (Huffman 2007; Sadr 2008a). Indeed, throughout Africa, archaeological sites of pastoralists are commonly identified by a predominance of livestock bones in the mammalian faunal remains (e.g. Garcea 2003). Usually, however, the pastoral phase in any given African region is preceded by a period of casual herding, where a few livestock bones are found among a predominantly wild faunal assemblage (Cremaschi and di Lernia 1998; Kuper and Kröpelin 2006).

If not due to specific cultural practices that removed livestock bones from LSA sites, the dearth of LSA livestock may suggest a casual herding strategy of the kind recorded among mid- to late 20th-century Kalahari foragers who kept small flocks of goats (Ikeya 1993; Kent 1993). This may represent a transitional stage to 'true' pastoralism, or a distinct 'pastro-foraging' subsistence strategy that is no longer common. Either way, the low proportion of livestock bones on the sites of modern Kalahari goat-herders (Kent 1993) falls within the range seen on most LSA sites in southern Africa. Isotopic evidence from human skeletons in southernmost Africa's LSA sites suggests that consumption of domesticated livestock may have become more important in the early second millennium AD (Sealy 2010), but the faunal remains do not reflect this.

Could the first livestock have reached LSA sites in southernmost Africa without the protection of skilled herders? Certainly, defenceless livestock could not have wandered freely for long, but one can imagine that an initial group of pastoralists might have introduced both livestock and herding skills to a neighbouring group of hunter-gatherers, who then passed these skills on down the line. The spread of horses among Native Americans in the 17th and 18th centuries provides an analogy for such transfer of domestic animals (Forbes 1959). Alternatively, livestock may have spread with scattered herders who assimilated into local cultures as they moved on, thus archaeologically remaining invisible.

STONE TOOLS

Around 2,000 years ago, in some parts of southern Africa scraping tools became more common in LSA assemblages, while backed elements such as segments (perhaps used as arrowheads) became rarer. Some see this change as marking the arrival of immigrant Khoekhoe pastoralists (Beaumont and Vogel 1984; A. Smith et al. 1991; Beaumont et al. 1995; cf. Parsons 2007). Results of archaeological survey in the landscape around Kasteelberg on the Vredenburg Peninsula north of Cape Town tend to refute this interpretation (Sadr and Gribble 2010). Sixty-three dated assemblages among 129 surveyed sites suggest that finer-grained raw materials such as silcrete did indeed give way to coarser assemblages, and the numbers of different types of formally retouched tools did in fact drop through time, with backed elements and bladelets becoming numerically less important. But these changes were gradual, went through several stages, and began long before livestock reached southern Africa. As Janette Deacon (1984: 323) remarked almost thirty years ago, 'sites where both pre- and post-pottery/domestic stock assemblages occur show no significant difference in the stone artefacts through this sequence'. If there was infiltration of herders from north to south, their traces may be detectable in lithics, but technological studies rather than the traditional typological classification may be the way to document this.

Ostrich eggshell beads

A. Smith et al. (1991) suggested that the diameters of ostrich eggshell beads at Witklip and Kasteelberg, both on the Vredenburg Peninsula, indicated separate bead-making traditions of, respectively, local hunter-gatherers and immigrant Khoekhoe pastoralists in the first fifteen centuries AD. The issue became a heated debate (Kinahan 1996b; A. Smith et al. 1996), but later re-examination of a small sample of beads from six sites on Kasteelberg suggested that the difference in average diameter, as Kinahan (1996b) had also noted, may simply reflect changing fashions, with average bead size increasing from 5 mm to more than 6 mm around 2000 BP (Sadr et al. 2003). Alas, a large-scale comparative study of bead sizes in the southern African LSA was abandoned some years ago, and until such time as its results come to light or the work is started afresh bead diameters cannot be considered a definite marker for distinguishing herders from hunters. The matter is complicated by the fact that, ethnographically, bead diameter (a function of how much time and effort has been spent grinding) can differ depending on whether the beads were made for export or a community's own use (Tapela 2001).

Discussion

The pace of new fieldwork on early herder sites has diminished. Among other factors, retirements and a shift in interest towards the study of the Middle Stone Age and the last 500 years seem to have taken their toll. The gaps on the archaeological map of early herders in southern Africa thus promise to remain blank for some time. A brief tour of the horizon highlights these gaps in research coverage (Fig. 44.1).

In Zimbabwe, research on early herder sites has focused on the Matopo Hills (Walker 1995; Burrett 2007), where Bambata Cave remains the best documented early herder site, having produced decorated, thin-walled potsherds (Bambata ware) and a few, as yet undated, bones of domesticated sheep. Other Zimbabwean sites have produced weaker signals of LSA herders and ceramics, but it will take many more excavations to unravel the history of the earliest herders in this landscape. Likewise, only one site in the Kalahari, Toteng, has provided the key evidence of directly dated livestock bones and decorated thin-walled ceramics (Robbins et al. 2005, 2008). Güldemann (2008), nevertheless makes a convincing case that the wetter Kalahari in the last few centuries BC was the staging post for the dispersal of the first

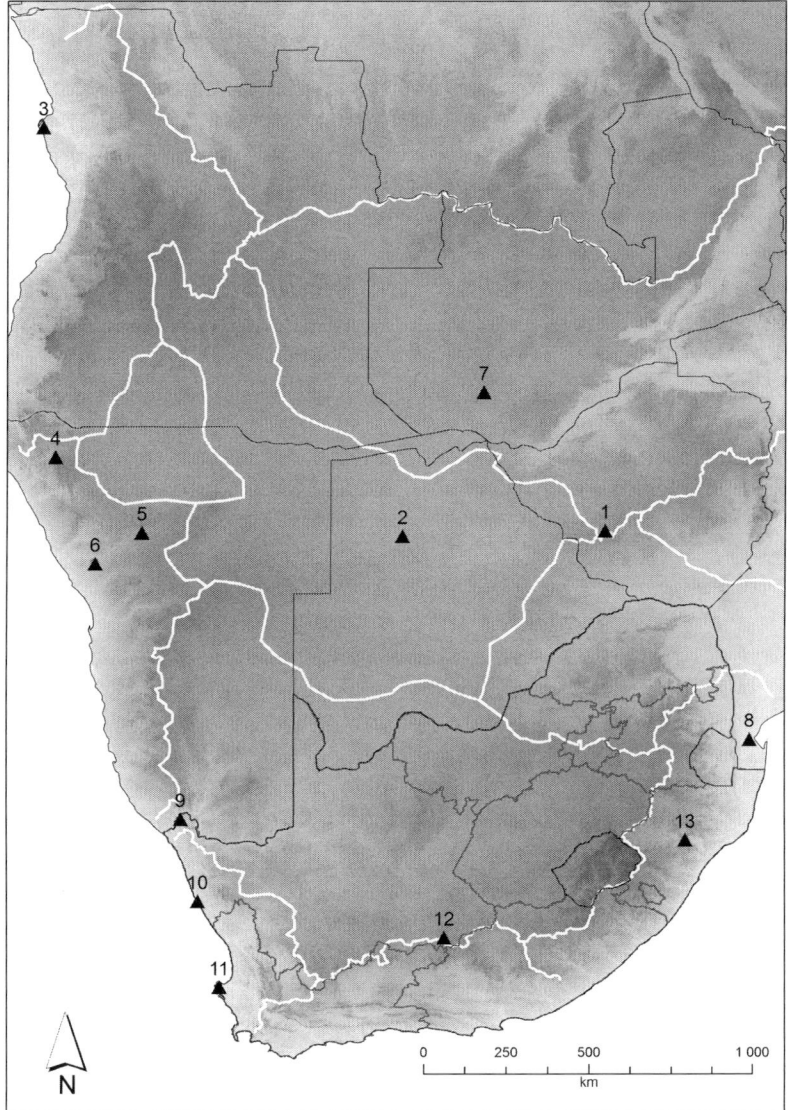

FIG. 44.1 Map of central and southern Africa showing sites and boundaries mentioned in the text. White lines show major basins; grey lines show province boundaries in South Africa; black lines show national boundaries. (1) Bambata is in Zimbabwe on the boundary of the Kalahari, Zambezi, and Limpopo basins. (2) Toteng is in Botswana and the Kalahari basin. (3) Benfica is in the Angolan coastal basin. (4,5,6) Oruwanje, Geduld and the Brandberg sites are in the Namibian coastal basin. (7) Situmpa is in Zambia and the Zambezi basin. (8) Matola is in Mozambique. (9) The Richtersveld sites are in South Africa, near the mouth of the Orange River. (10) Spoegrivier is in the Northern Cape Province of South Africa and in the west coastal basin. (11) The Vredenburg Peninsula is in the west coast basin of the Western Cape Province of South Africa. (12) The Seacow valley sites are in the Orange River basin on the boundary between the Northern, Western, and Eastern Cape Provinces. (13) The Thukela River valley sites are in the eastern coastal basin of South Africa, in KwaZulu-Natal Province.

Khoe-speaking herders into southern Africa; and geomorphological research in the Makgadikgadi Pans (Burrough et al. 2009) has identified land surfaces from that period that now require the attention of archaeologists able to deal with low-density, barely visible early herder sites. Even without such fresh surveys, however, several known LSA sites with Bambata sherds along the Boteti River would no doubt repay excavation. As elsewhere in the subcontinent, no one site will shed all the necessary light, but quantity can compensate for lack of quality deposits in the Kalahari sands, as it can in many other parts of the subcontinent. In northern Namibia, active research on traces of the earliest herders also ceased some years ago, but important excavations by Ralf Vogelsang and his colleagues from the University of Cologne are now being published (Vogelsang and Eichhorn 2011). Here, the site of Oruwanje with potsherds and undatable sheep bones in LSA layers of 3,000 years ago illustrates well the frustrations associated with trying to recreate the earliest history of herding in the subcontinent (Albrecht et al. 2001). Stratigraphic associations can deceive, and direct dating of potsherds and bones remains a challenge. Further south, important sites in the Brandberg/Dâures massif (Kinahan 2001) and at Geduld (A. Smith and Jacobson 1995) include early thin-walled ceramics and indications of livestock herding, but no directly dated bones. Pastoralism seems to be restricted to the second millennium AD (Kinahan 1996a).

South of the Orange River, excavations by Lita Webley at Spoegrivier Cave and in the Richtersveld produced excellent evidence for early sheep and ceramics (Webley 1997; Vogel et al. 1997). The University of Cape Town's Archaeology Contracts Office has carried out many contract archaeology projects in coastal Namaqualand, publication of which should provide further information regarding early herders in this landscape. On the Western Cape coast, field reports from completed surveys and excavations of early herder sites continue to be published (e.g. Jerardino and Maggs 2007; Sadr and Gribble 2010). The Eastern Cape coast, potentially the source of the earliest pottery in the subcontinent (Sadr and Sampson 2006), long ago produced tantalizing hints of early herder sites that still need to be followed up (Derricourt 1977). Further inland, the history of LSA herders and hunters in the Upper Karoo has been intensively investigated (Sampson 1984, 1985; Sadr and Sampson 1999), and publications on this subject continue to appear (e.g. Sampson 2010).

The Orange River Basin beyond the Seacow Valley and as far as southern Botswana has been surprisingly unproductive for evidence of early herders (Sadr 2002). Despite tantalizing clues, past work at sites in the Northern Cape Province has not produced clear signs of early first-millennium AD thin-walled pottery and sheep (Humphreys and Thackeray 1983; Sealy and Yates 1994; A. Smith 1995; Couzens and Sadr 2010). The absence of such evidence for herders in the early first millennium AD seems to confirm the spatial gap noted between the decorated thin-walled first-millennium ceramics in the north and the undecorated thin ware of the south (Sadr 2008b). This paucity of evidence for early herders in the central part of the subcontinent has obvious implications for the hypothesis of early herder arrival by coastal routes. In KwaZulu-Natal, the issue of early LSA herders has not been addressed at all, even though several sites have produced distinct undecorated, black, thin-walled ceramics (Sadr 2008b). Further north and east, in Swaziland and Mozambique, there has been no substantial research on the question of early LSA herders, and to the west, in Lesotho, the available evidence suggests a relatively late (and perhaps short-lived or intermittent) take-up of livestock by hunter-gatherers (Mitchell et al. 2008).

It used to be thought that the paucity of evidence for LSA herders had to do with the invisibility of their sites. Now that this myth has been laid to rest (Fauvelle-Aymar et al. 2006;

Arthur 2008), the door is open for new fieldwork using appropriate methods to document the details of how and when herding spread through southern Africa.

Summary and conclusion

To date, there is no archaeological evidence to show that a coherent folk (demic) migration abruptly brought livestock and ceramic technology to southernmost Africa around 2,000 years ago. Archaeologists are able to detect such migrations (Ashley, Ch. 6 above), and in southern Africa the sites of early farming communities stand out as an example of such a cultural and economic intrusion into a landscape of indigenous hunters-gatherers-fishers-herders. The LSA archaeology of the last few millennia shows no comparable evidence. After searching for several decades, it seems unlikely that archaeologists have missed the relevant finds. It is more probable that herding spread through southern Africa in a process other than folk migration. Several key bits of evidence suggest infiltration and subsequent hybridization may have been the main processes at play in this history.

African oral traditions amply demonstrate that groups of people are constantly on the move. Comparative linguistic studies show the same (Ehret 2008; Güldemann 2008), as do the latest genetic studies (Tishkoff et al. 2009). The apparent fact that in southernmost Africa cattle seem to have spread later than sheep (Klein 1986) might be an example of such multiple infiltrations. The isotopic signatures noted by Sealy (2010) might indicate the same. Other indications of a constant ebb and flow of people and new techniques and ideas can be seen in distribution maps of isolated traits such as geometric rock art (B. Smith and Ouzman 2004; Eastwood and Smith 2005) and, as discussed above, in spouted and decorated thin wares (Sadr 2008b), as well as later lugged wares (Sadr 1998).

All indications are that herding in southern Africa probably began with infiltrations of individuals and small groups with livestock sometime in the last five centuries BC from a source most probably to the northeast (Ehret 2008; Güldemann 2008). Genetic work eventually may identify the source of these newcomers more accurately (Mitchell 2010). Ceramic technology may have spread about the same time and probably through similar processes of infiltration, but possibly from south to north (Sadr and Sampson 2006). Local hunter-gatherer-fisher-foragers in the paths of these infiltrations adopted the new skills and techniques, but not to the extent of transforming their own local cultures and life-ways. The lack of osteological evidence for immigrant herders (Stynder 2009) and continuity of various practices at the LSA sites from before to after the introduction of livestock and ceramics has been noted more than once. Hunters did not become pastoralists, but simply added a new resource with its required managerial skills into their existing palette of economic and social practices, assimilating without replacing older traditions. In some parts of the sub-continent, such as along the upper Vaal River, livestock and thin-ware ceramics seem not to have filtered into hunter-gatherer LSA communities until much later. In others, such as on the west coast, local hunter-fisher-forager-herders may have exploited their newly acquired livestock and ceramics as a means of acquiring social capital through feasts (Sadr 2004), although even here they may have been building upon ideas of delayed returns that were already practised in other forms in the last millennium BC (Henshilwood et al. 1994; Jerardino 2010).

The substantial gaps in this big picture should remind us that there still is much room for basic archaeological research on the spread of herding practices and communities in southernmost Africa.

REFERENCES

ALBRECHT, M., BERKE, H., EICHHORN, B., et al. (2001). Oruwanje 95/1: a late Holocene stratigraphy in northwestern Namibia. *Cimbebasia* 17: 1–22.

ARTHUR, C. (2008). The archaeology of indigenous herders in the Western Cape of southern Africa. *Southern African Humanities* 20: 205–20.

BARNARD, A. (2008). Ethnographic analogy and the reconstruction of early Khoekhoe society. *Southern African Humanities* 20(1): 61–75.

BEAUMONT, P. B., SMITH, A. B., and VOGEL, J. C. (1995). Before the Einiqua: the archaeology of the frontier zone. In A. B. Smith (ed.), *Einiqualand: Studies of the Orange River Frontier.* Cape Town: UCT Press, 236–64.

—— and VOGEL, J. C. (1984). Spatial patterning of the Ceramic Later Stone Age in the Northern Cape, South Africa. In M. Hall, G. Avery, D. M. Avery, M. L. Wilson, and A. J. B. Humphreys (eds), *Frontiers: Southern African Archaeology Today.* Oxford: British Archaeological Reports, 80–95.

BLENCH, R. (2009). Was there an interchange between Cushitic pastoralists and Khoisan speakers in the prehistory of Southern Africa and how can this be detected? *Sprache und Geschichte in Afrika* 20: 31–49.

BOONZAIER, E., MALHERBE, C., SMITH, A. B., and BERENS, P. (1996). *The Cape Herders: A History of the Khoikhoi of Southern Africa.* Cape Town: David Philip.

BURRETT, R. S. (2007). Beyond the pots and bones: subtle changes in the archaeological record of Bambata Cave. *Zimbabwean Prehistory* 27: 31–9.

BURROUGH, S. L., THOMAS, D. S. G., and BAILEY, R. M. (2009). Mega-lake in the Kalahari: a late Pleistocene record of the Palaeolake Makgadikgadi system. *Quaternary Science Reviews* 28: 1392–411.

CLARK, J. D., and FAGAN, B. M. (1965). Charcoals, sands, and channel decorated pottery from Northern Rhodesia. *American Anthropologist* 67: 354–71.

COUZENS, R., and SADR, K. (2010). Rippled ware at Blinkklipkop, Northern Cape. *South African Archaeological Bulletin* 65: 196–203.

CREMASCHI, M., and DI LERNIA, S. (1998). The geoarchaeological survey in central Tadrart Acacus and surroundings (Libyan Sahara): environment and cultures. In M. Cremaschi and S. Di Lernia (eds), *Wadi Teshuinat Palaeoenvironment and Prehistory in South-Western Fezzan (Libyan Sahara).* Florence: All'Insegna del Giglio, 243–96.

DEACON, J. (1984). Later Stone Age people and their descendants in southern Africa. In R. G. Klein (ed.), *Southern African Prehistory and Palaeoenvironments.* Rotterdam: Balkema, 221–329.

DERRICOURT, R. (1977). *Prehistoric Man in the Ciskei and Transkei.* Cape Town: Struik.

DOS SANTOS, J. R., and ERVEDOSA, C. M. N. (1970). A estação arqueológica de Benfica, Luanda–Angola. *Ciencias Biológicas* (Luanda) 1: 31–51.

EASTWOOD, E. B., and SMITH, B. W. (2005). Fingerprints of the Khoekhoen: geometric and handprinted rock art in the central Limpopo Basin, South Africa. *South African Archaeological Society Goodwin Series* 9: 63–76.

EHRET, C. (2008). The early livestock raisers of southern Africa. *Southern African Humanities* 20(1): 7–35.

ELPHICK, R. (1985). *Khoikhoi and the Founding of White South Africa*. Johannesburg: Ravan Press.

FAUVELLE-AYMAR, F.-X. (2004). Between the first herders and the last herders: are the Khoekhoe descendants of the Neolithic 'hunters-with-sheep'? *Before Farming* 3: 271–81.

—— (2008). Against the 'Khoisan paradigm' in the interpretation of Khoekhoe origins and history: re-evaluation of Khoekhoe pastoral traditions. *Southern African Humanities* 20(1): 77–92.

—— SADR, K., BON, F., and GRONENBORN, D. (2006). The visibility and invisibility of herders' kraals in South Africa, with reference to a possible early contact period Khoekhoe kraal at KFS 5 (Western Cape). *Journal of African Archaeology* 4: 253–71.

FORBES, J. D. (1959). The appearance of the mounted Indian in northern Mexico and the Southwest, to 1680. *Southwestern Journal of Anthropology* 15: 189–212.

GARCEA, E. A. A. (2003). Animal exploitation and pottery technology during Pastoral times: the evidence from Uan Telocat, Libyan Sahara. *Journal of African Archaeology* 1: 111–26.

GÜLDEMANN, T. (2008). A linguist's view: Khoe-Kwadi speakers as the earliest food-producers of southern Africa. *Southern African Humanities* 20(1): 93–132.

HALL, S. L., and SMITH, B. W. (2000). Empowering places: rock shelters and ritual control in farmer-forager interactions in the Northern Province. *South African Archaeological Society Goodwin Series* 8: 30–46.

HENSHILWOOD, C. (1996). A revised chronology for pastoralism in southernmost Africa: new evidence of sheep at *c.* 2000 B.P. from Blombos Cave, South Africa. *Antiquity* 70: 945–9.

—— NILSSEN, P., and PARKINGTON, J. E. (1994). Mussel drying and food storage in the late Holocene, SW Cape, South Africa. *Journal of Field Archaeology* 21: 103–9.

HUFFMAN, T. N. (2007). *Handbook of the Iron Age: The Archaeology of Pre-Colonial Farming Societies in Southern Africa*. Pietermaritzburg: University of KwaZulu-Natal Press.

HUMPHREYS, A. J. B., and THACKERAY, A. I. (1983). *Ghaap and Gariep: Later Stone Age Studies in the Northern Cape*. Cape Town: South African Archaeological Society.

IKEYA, K. (1993). Goat raising among the San in the central Kalahari. *African Studies Monographs* 14: 39–52.

JERARDINO, A. (2010). Large shell middens in Lamberts Bay, South Africa: a case of hunter-gatherer resource intensification. *Journal of Archaeological Science* 37: 2291–2302.

—— and MAGGS, T. M. O'C. (2007). Simon se Klip at Steenbokfontein: the settlement pattern of a built pastoralist encampment on the west coast of South Africa. *South African Archaeological Bulletin* 62: 104–14.

KENT, S. (1993). Sharing in an egalitarian Kalahari community. *Man* 28: 479–514.

KINAHAN, J. (1996a). A new archaeological perspective on nomadic pastoralist expansion in south-western Africa. *Azania* 34/35: 211–26.

—— (1996b). Alternative views on the acquisition of livestock by hunter-gatherers in southern Africa. *South African Archaeological Bulletin* 51: 106–8.

—— (2001). *Pastoral Nomads of the Namib Desert: The People History Forgot*. Windhoek: Namibia Archaeological Trust.

KLEIN, R. G. (1986). The prehistory of Stone Age herders in the Cape Province of South Africa. *South African Archaeological Society Goodwin Series* 5: 5–12.

KUPER, R., and KRÖPELIN, S. (2006). Climate-controlled Holocene occupation in the Sahara: motor of Africa's evolution. *Science* 313: 803–7.

MAGGS, T. M. O'C., and WARD, V. (1980). Driel Shelter: rescue at a Late Stone Age site on the Tugela River. *Annals of the Natal Museum* 24(1): 35–70.

—— and WHITELAW, G. (1991). A review of recent archaeological research on food producing communities in southern Africa. *Journal of African History* 32: 3–24.

MAZEL, A. D. (1986). Mbabane Shelter and eSinhlonhlweni Shelter: the last two thousand years of hunter-gatherer settlement in the central Thukela Basin, Natal, South Africa. *Annals of the Natal Museum* 27: 389–453.

MITCHELL, P. J. (2010). Genetics and southern African prehistory: an archaeological view. *Journal of Anthropological Sciences* 88: 73–92.

—— PLUG, I., BAILEY, G. N., and WOODBORNE, S. (2008). Bringing the Kalahari debate to the mountains: late first millennium AD hunter-gatherer/farmer interaction in highland Lesotho. *Before Farming* 2008/2: article 4.

MORAIS, J. M. (1988). *The Early Farming Communities of Southern Mozambique*. Uppsala: Uppsala University Press.

PARKINGTON J., YATES, R., MANHIRE, A., and HALKETT, D. (1986). The social impact of pastoralism in the southwestern Cape. *Journal of Anthropological Archaeology* 5: 313–29.

PARSONS, I. (2007). Hunter-gatherers or herders? Reconsidering the Swartkops and Doornfontein Industries, Northern Cape Province, South Africa. *Before Farming* 2007: 123–32.

ROBBINS, L. H., CAMPBELL, A. C., MURPHY, M. L., et al. (2005). The advent of herding in southern Africa: early AMS dates on domestic livestock from the Kalahari Desert. *Current Anthropology* 46: 671–7.

—— —— et al. (2008). Recent archaeological and palaeoenvironmental research at Toteng, Botswana: early domesticated livestock in the Kalahari. *Journal of African Archaeology* 6: 131–49.

SADR, K. (1998). The first herders at the Cape of Good Hope. *African Archaeological Review* 15: 101–32.

—— (2002). Encapsulated Bushmen in the archaeology of Thamaga. In S. Kent (ed.) *Ethnicity, Hunter-Gatherers, and the 'Other': Association or Assimilation in Africa*. Washington, DC: Smithsonian Institution Press, 28–47.

—— (2004). Feasting on Kasteelberg? Early herders on the west coast of South Africa. *Before Farming* 3: 167–83.

—— (2008a). Invisible herders? The archaeology of Khoekhoe pastoralists. *Southern African Humanities* 20(1): 179–203.

—— (2008b). An ageless view of first millennium AD southern African ceramics. *Journal of African Archaeology* 6: 103–30.

—— and GRIBBLE, J. (2010). The stone artefacts from the Vredenburg Peninsula archaeological survey, west coast of South Africa. *Southern African Humanities* 22: 19–88.

—— and SAMPSON, C. G. (1999). Khoekhoe ceramics of the upper Seacow River valley. *South African Archaeological Bulletin* 54: 3–15.

—— —— (2006). Through thick and thin: early pottery in southern Africa. *Journal of African Archaeology* 4: 235–52.

—— SMITH, A., PLUG, I., ORTON, J., and MÜTTI, B. (2003). Herders and foragers on Kasteelberg: interim report of excavations 1999–2002. *South African Archaeological Bulletin* 58: 27–32.

SAMPSON, C. G (1984). A prehistoric pastoralist frontier in the upper Zeekoe valley, South Africa. In M. Hall, G. Avery, D. M. Avery, M. L. Wilson, and A. J. B. Humphreys (eds), *Frontiers: South African Archaeology Today*. Oxford: British Archaeological Reports, 96–110.

—— (1985). *Atlas of Stone Age Settlement in the Central and Upper Seacow Valley. Memoirs of the National Museum (Bloemfontein)* 20: 1–116.

—— (2010). Chronology and dynamics of Later Stone Age herders in the upper Seacow River valley, South Africa. *Journal of Arid Environments* 74: 842–48.

SEALY, J. C. (2010). Isotopic evidence for the antiquity of cattle-based pastoralism in southern-most Africa. *Journal of African Archaeology* 8: 66–81.

—— and YATES, R. (1994). The chronology of the introduction of pastoralism to the Cape, South Africa. *Antiquity* 68: 58–67.

SMITH, A. B. (1990). On becoming herders: Khoikhoi and San ethnicity in southern Africa. *African Studies* 49: 51–73.

—— (1992). *Pastoralism in Africa*. Johannesburg: Witwatersrand University Press.

—— (1995). Archaeological observations along the Orange River and its hinterland. In A. B. Smith (ed.), *Einiqualand: Studies of the Orange River Frontier*. Cape Town: UCT Press, 263–300.

—— and JACOBSON, L. (1995). Excavations at Geduld and the appearance of early domestic stock in Namibia. *South African Archaeological Bulletin* 50: 3–14.

—— SADR, K., GRIBBLE, J., and YATES, R. (1991). Excavations in the south-western Cape, South Africa, and the archaeological identity of prehistoric hunter-gatherers within the last 2000 years. *South African Archaeological Bulletin* 46: 71–91.

—— YATES, R., and JACOBSON, L. (1996). Geduld *contra* Kinahan. *South African Archaeological Bulletin* 51: 36–9.

SMITH, B. W., and OUZMAN, S. (2004). Taking stock: identifying Khoekhoen herder rock art in southern Africa. *Current Anthropology* 45: 499–526.

STYNDER, D. D. (2009). Craniometric evidence for South African Later Stone Age herders and hunter-gatherers being a single biological population. *Journal of Archaeological Science* 36: 798–806.

TAPELA, M. (2001). An archaeological examination of ostrich eggshell beads in Botswana. *Pula* 15: 60–74.

TISHKOFF, S. A., REED, F. A., FRIEDLAENDER, F. R., et al. (2009). The genetic structure and history of Africans and African Americans. *Science* 324: 1035–44.

VAN DOORNUM, B. (2007). Tshisiku Shelter and the Shashe–Limpopo Confluence Area hunter-gatherer sequence. *Southern African Humanities* 19: 17–67.

VOGEL, J., PLUG, I., and WEBLEY, L. (1997). New dates for the introduction of sheep into South Africa: the evidence from Spoegrivier Cave in Namaqualand. *South African Journal of Science* 93: 246–8.

VOGELSANG, R., and EICHHORN, B. (2011). *Under the Mopane Tree: Holocene Settlement in Northern Namibia*. Cologne: Heinrich Barth Institut.

WALKER, N. J. (1983). The significance of an early date for pottery and sheep in Zimbabwe. *South African Archaeological Bulletin* 38: 88–92.

—— (1995). *Late Pleistocene and Holocene Hunter-Gatherers of the Matopos: An Archaeological Study of Change and Continuity in Zimbabwe*. Uppsala: Societas Archaeologica Upsaliensis.

WEBLEY, L. (1997). Jakkalsberg A and B: the cultural material from two pastoralist sites in the Richtersveld, Northern Cape. *Southern African Field Archaeology* 6: 3–20.

CHAPTER 45

EARLY FARMING COMMUNITIES OF SOUTHERN AND SOUTH-CENTRAL AFRICA

PETER MITCHELL

INTRODUCTION

THE first millennium AD saw much of south-central and southern Africa transformed by the expansion and consolidation of communities that combined cultivation with herding and smelted and forged iron. Speakers of Bantu languages, they assimilated, displaced, or traded with aboriginal hunter-gatherers and were ancestral to the second-millennium farmers discussed by Pikirayi and Schoeman (Chs 63 and 64 below). Following Pwiti (1996) and recognizing the importance of food production as a way of life, I refer to them as 'Early Farming Communities', using 'agropastoralists' as an alternative. Borrowed from European prehistory, the term 'Early Iron Age' holds decreasing appeal: it overemphasizes iron at the expense of other technologies and creates an impression of societies as static blocks rather than complex, dynamic entities.

Ceramics provide the principal basis for ordering the archaeological record left by these populations and tracing connections between them. Their discussion thus precedes that of subsistence, settlement pattern and worldview, and trade and sociopolitical organization. The chapter ends by considering the emergence of greater political complexity in the late first millennium, the relations between the populations discussed here and their successors, and the processes by which Early Farming Communities themselves expanded. As with other parts of the continent, research coverage of these issues is uneven: South Africa is best served, with important work also undertaken in Botswana (Segobye 1998), Zambia (Phillipson 1977), and Zimbabwe (Pikirayi 1997); conversely, Namibia has seen little concerted fieldwork (Kose 2009), Angola none, Swaziland a single doctoral thesis (Ohinata 2001). Recent reviews include Mitchell (2002), Mitchell and Whitelaw (2005), and Parkington and Hall (2010).

A REGIONAL OVERVIEW: SPACE, TIME, AND CERAMICS

Bantu-speaking populations mostly dependent on domesticated plants and animals for their subsistence expanded through central and eastern Africa during the first millennium BC (de Maret, Ch. 43 above). However, south of the Great Lakes and the Congo Basin evidence of their presence is tenuous before the early centuries AD; late first-millennium BC/first-century AD dates and associations with livestock for Situmpa ware in southern Zambia are unreliable (Sadr and Sampson 2006). Similarities in ceramic design help link sites together. The most widely used approach (Huffman 2007) employs multidimensional analysis of vessel profile, decoration layout, and motif to reconstruct different ceramic types, and reliably separates the ceramics of contemporary southern African populations, showing substantial overlap with designs in other media, such as beadwork. In the absence of significant trade in pottery, it may thus identify groups of people among whom such codes were shared, learned, and transmitted. Significant overlap may exist with ethnolinguistic differences because language is the primary means through which people think about and reflect upon the world—an overlap that permits us to use ceramic style to recognize and trace the movements of people. However, no necessary correlation exists between the ceramic styles identified by archaeologists and any particular social, political, or 'tribal' entity (cf. Hall 1983). Moreover, styles can spread in ways other than migration (Huffman 2007), although studies emphasizing the agency of individual potters or communities in selecting and modifying particular pots or their designs (cf. Hodder 1982) have yet to make their mark in southern or south-central Africa (but cf. Fredriksen 2009). Another concern lies in the emphasis accorded decoration at the expense of undecorated pottery; physico-chemical studies and experimental work (Pikirayi 1997), as well as *chaîne opératoire* approaches (Gosselain and Livingstone Smith, Ch. 9 above), explore production, use, and exchange and can offer alternative classificatory frameworks (Sinclair 1987).

Most of the pottery made by Early Farming Communities in south-central and southern Africa (the 'thick' wares of Sadr and Sampson 2006) shares a common style with the Urewe ceramics of Great Lakes Africa, similarities that led David Phillipson (1977) to group them together within the Chifumbaze Complex. This comprises two traditions, Kalundu and Urewe, the latter divided into Nkope and Kwale branches (Huffman 2007). The pottery made by contemporary Shona speakers can be traced phase by phase backwards to Happy Rest, the earliest Kalundu ceramics in southern Africa, while modern Swahili pottery derives from the Tana facies of the Kwale branch of Urewe. As both Shona and Swahili are Eastern Bantu languages (cf. de Maret, Ch. 43 above), the links posited above between material culture and language suggest that the makers of all Kalundu and Urewe Tradition ceramics spoke Eastern Bantu languages (Huffman 2007). Conversely, quite different ceramics are found along the southern fringes of the equatorial forests. Geography and similarities with pottery still made today suggest that this Naviundu Tradition was made by speakers of Western Bantu languages. It includes the ceramics from Nqoma and Divuyu in Botswana's Tsodilo Hills (Denbow 1990), others in northern Namibia (Sandelowsky 1979), and facies ancestral to the Luangwa pottery still made in Zambia and Malawi (Huffman 1989). Insofar as these groups practised cultivation they seem to have acquired cereals, and also cattle, from an Eastern

Bantu source, probably replacing earlier root/tree crops that could not be grown this far south (Vansina 1994/95).

Returning to the Urewe Tradition, two dispersal routes from East Africa seem likely (Fig. 45.1). One, represented by the Mwabulambo and Nkope facies of the Nkope branch, reached Malawi by the 4th century, subsequently entering northern Zimbabwe (Pwiti 1996). Derived jointly from it and Bambata pottery (see below), Gokomere ceramics then attest to the expansion of farming populations across the rest of Zimbabwe and central Mozambique (Sinclair et al. 1993); Dambwa represents another mid-first-millennium expansion, in this case toward the Victoria Falls area of western Zambia (Vogel 1984). Later facies of the Nkope branch include the Zhizo, Leokwe, and Toutswe pottery associated with the beginnings of social complexity in the Shashe-Limpopo Basin from the 10th century (Pikirayi, Ch. 63

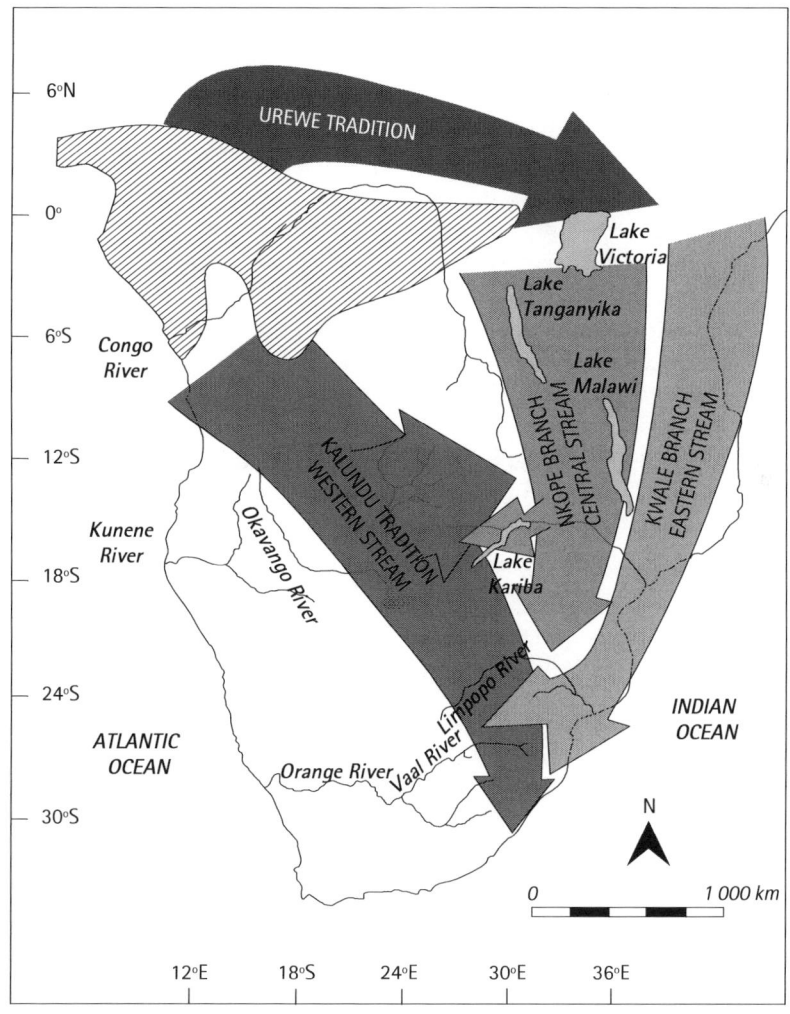

FIG. 45.1 Likely dispersal routes of Early Farming Communities across sub-Equatorial Africa (redrawn after Huffman 2007, courtesy Rachel King).

below). A second dispersal route originating among makers of Kwale pottery in eastern Kenya lay closer to Africa's Indian Ocean coast. Dating to the 4th/early 5th centuries and thus broadly contemporary with the expansion of Nkope, Silver Leaves is its earliest southern African expression, chiefly from southern Mozambique, Swaziland and South Africa's Limpopo Province. It was followed by Mzonjani (*c.* AD 450–750), best known from Limpopo, Mpumalanga, and KwaZulu-Natal, but also Broederstroom near Johannesburg, and then by Garonga in South Africa's far northeast (Huffman 2007).

While people making Urewe Tradition ceramics settled the eastern parts of south-central and southeastern Africa, and wares linked with Naviundu signal the arrival of Bantu speakers further west in northern Namibia, Botswana, and western Zambia, makers of Kalundu Tradition pottery were the earliest farmers in the rest of the region discussed here, taking advantage, in South Africa at least, of agriculturally more favourable wetter conditions (Parkington and Hall 2010). In Zambia, the principal groups, all formerly assigned to the 'western stream' of the Early Iron Age, are Kalundu and Kapwirimbwe in the south, Chondwe in the Copperbelt, and Kalambo in the northeast (Phillipson 1977). Further south, several related subdivisions are discernible, one of the oldest being Happy Rest in 6th-/8th-century Limpopo and southeastern Botswana. Huffman's (2007) analyses indicate that Happy Rest was 'ancestral' to the Gumanye, Great Zimbabwe, and Khami pottery of second millennium Zimbabwe (Pikirayi, Ch. 63 below), the Doornkop facies made in Mpumalanga and southern Limpopo in the late first millennium (which then evolved into the K2, Mapungubwe, and related ceramics of southern Africa's first states; Pikirayi, Ch. 63 below) and the Msuluzi/Ndondonwane/Ntshekane succession known from KwaZulu-Natal and the Eastern Cape *c.* AD 650–1050. Completing this picture, the late first millennium Diamant facies of northwestern Limpopo and adjacent parts of Botswana gave rise to a series of facies (Baratani, Eiland, Broadhurst) that continued as late as the 15th century.

The Kalundu Tradition's origins probably lie in early first-millennium AD central Angola, where pottery from Benfica near Luanda provides a possible source (Huffman 2007). Connections with further south will become clearer once fieldwork fills the current void over most of Angola and the far west of Zambia. In the meantime, debate continues over the associations between Benfica—and the remainder of the Kalundu Tradition—and the Bambata pottery of early/mid-first-millennium Botswana, Zimbabwe, and northern South Africa. Its thinness, association with stone tools, and frequent occurrence in rockshelters (Toteng, northern Botswana, is an exception: Robbins et al. 2008) have traditionally seen it attributed to hunter-gatherers or herders (Sadr 2008, Ch. 44 above). However, Huffman (2005) identifies Bambata as the earliest southern African manifestation of Kalundu on the basis of profile, design layout, and motif, noting that thinner Bambata A pottery may have been made for trade with foragers and/or herders, spreading south ahead of farmers themselves.

SUBSISTENCE AND ECOLOGY

While ceramics rightly attract archaeological attention, it is the lifeways of the people who made them that hold greater interest. As far as subsistence is concerned we know most about livestock, though the role of particular species is debated; cultigens and wild plant foods are less well understood because of taphonomic biases and a still insufficiently wide deployment of flotation (Jonsson 1998). Pearl millet (*Pennisetum americanum*), sorghum (*Sorghum bicolor*), and finger millet (*Eleusine coracana*) were the principal crops, attested by grindstones where seeds themselves have not survived; pulses (groundnuts—*Voandzeia subterranea*—and cowpeas—*Vigna unguiculata*) and cucurbits were also grown. Cultivation was probably garden-based, with villages often found in low-lying locations close to rivers and soils suitable for hoes (cf. Vogel 1984). The unusually well-studied Thukela Basin demonstrates such points especially well, revealing a dynamic intensification of settlement as population grew and became more differentiated between a few large and many smaller sites in Ndondondwane times before eventually collapsing in the 11th century (Greenfield and van Schalkwyk 2008). More generally, the requirements of cereal agriculture (≥350 mm of rain during the summer growing season and ≥500mm during the year, with nocturnal temperatures of ≥15°C; Huffman 1996) restricted agropastoralist settlement to miombo and savannah biomes and saw it gradually attenuate along South Africa's east coast until finally stopping about 33.5°S (Maggs 1994/5). Another constraint, aridity, curtailed settlement of the Kalahari, though occupation at Divuyu and Nqoma (Fig. 45.2) demonstrate that wetter conditions must have prevailed in its north during the late first/early second millennia (Denbow 1990).

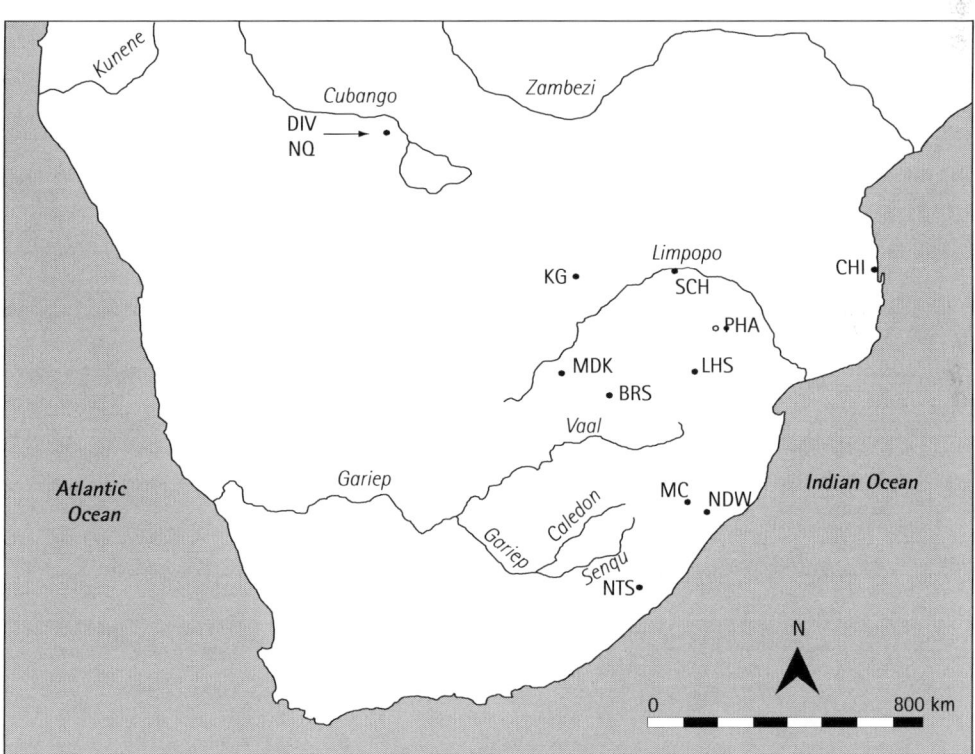

FIG. 45.2 Southern Africa showing the major localities and archaeological sites discussed in Chapter 45. Site names are abbreviated thus: BRS Broederstroom; CHI Chibuene; DIV (Divuyu); KG Kgaswe; LHS Lydenburg Heads Site; MC Msuluzi Confluence; MDK Madikwe; NDW Ndondonwane NQ (Nqoma); NTS Ntsitsana; PHA Phalaborwa; SCH Schroda (courtesy Rachel King).

For variety, and as insurance against crop failure, people collected wild plants, including marula (*Sclerocarya birrea*: Jonsson 1998). Along the Indian Ocean coast they also gathered shellfish, perhaps on seasonal visits from further inland (Horwitz et al. 1991), but neither freshwater nor marine fish were regularly exploited (Whitelaw 2009; cf. Denbow 1999). Hunting, on the other hand, was important where livestock keeping was hampered by diseases like trypanosomiasis, such as in northern Zimbabwe and Kruger National Park (Plug 1987, 1997); game may have been particularly helpful as a protein source during the earliest stages of farming settlement (Badenhorst 2008).

Along with cereals and pulses, domestic animals (principally cattle, sheep, and goats, though chickens and dogs are also attested) underpinned Early Farming Communities' subsistence strategies. Caprines (sheep rather than goats) were generally more numerous, ceding primacy from the 8th century to cattle (Arnold 2008; Badenhorst 2008), but this is not invariable; cattle are more common on some Zambian sites, for example (Plug 1981). Moreover, differential slaughtering and disposal practices and preservation biases mean that eating patterns reconstructed from faunal assemblages may not equate directly to stockholding patterns. Thus, Huffman (2007) argues that phytolith analysis of byres and dung-lined pits indicates a much stronger presence of cattle at Broederstroom than is evident from a skeletally estimated cattle:sheep ratio of 1:42; the same approach has identified the presence of cattle from the (Mzonjani phase) beginnings of agropastoralist settlement in South Africa (Huffman 1998), contrary to arguments that they—and the social relations they imply—only became important toward the end of the first millennium (Hall 1986). Phytolith signatures nevertheless require interrogation, since cattle produce much more dung, and more slowly decomposing dung, than caprines (Badenhorst 2009a). The numbers of cattle required to maintain a viable herd—and thus implied by recovery of just a few individuals—are also disputed (Huffman 1998; cf. Badenhorst 2008).

The introduction of farming, including livestock keeping, the establishment of larger, more permanent settlements, and the consumption of wood for building, fuel, and charcoal for smelting iron presumably impacted on the ecology of southern and south-central Africa. Such impacts may have been particularly pronounced where, as in KwaZulu-Natal's Thukela Valley, some villages were occupied for several generations. The absence there today of nyala (*Tragelaphus angasii*) may reflect progressive clearance of originally dense riverine woodlands (Maggs 1994/5). By way of another example, in southwestern Zambia declining soil fertility was accommodated by shifting settlements in cycles of slash-and-burn cultivation (Vogel 1984).

SETTLEMENT ORGANIZATION AND WORLDVIEW

Pits, middens, and grainbin foundations are the major features surviving at most early farming settlements, the houses of which were typically built using *daga* (clay-and-dung) plaster on a pole framework (Huffman 2007). Fundamental to understanding the structure of these villages and the worldview of their inhabitants in much of the region is a model of settlement organization known as the Central Cattle Pattern (CCP) (Fig. 45.3). This recognizes the centrality of cattle in integrating communities through their use in bridewealth payments, sacrifice to ancestors, and political relations between individuals. Settlements are organized

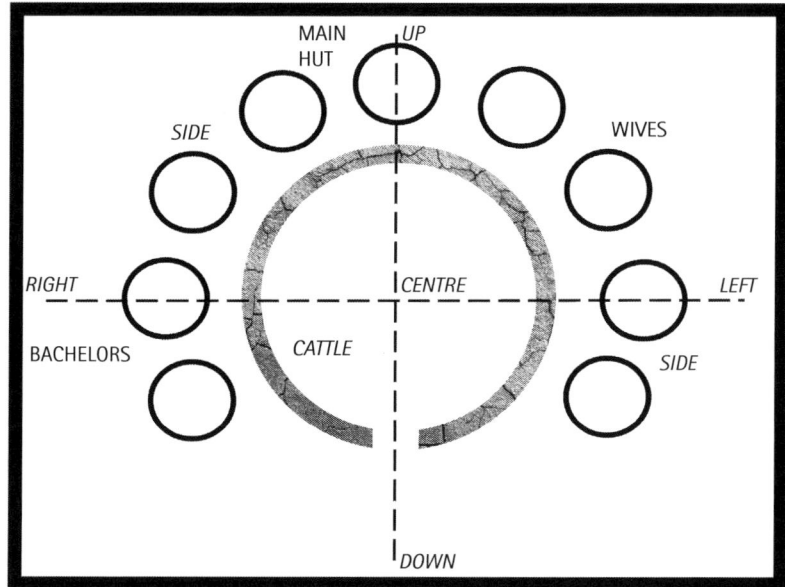

FIG. 45.3 The Central Cattle Pattern (redrawn after Kuper 1980, courtesy Chris Wingfield).

around one or more central byres, with the leading man living at their apex, his wives and juniors lower down and further away to left and right. Important people, mostly men, are buried in or close to the byre, where grain may be stored under ancestral protection, and men congregate in a nearby court area to work and settle disputes. Characteristic of southern Africa's patrilineal Eastern Bantu-speaking inhabitants today (Kuper 1980), the CCP can be traced back through the second millennium into the first at sites like Kgaswe and Broederstroom, but perhaps also to the very start of agropastoralist settlement in South Africa if the links between language, worldview, and ceramic design are as tight as they seem (Huffman 2001). It is not, however, without its critics.

One concern is that relatively few early farming settlements combine comprehensive excavation with single-phase occupation (Ndondonwane, KwaZulu-Natal, is an exception; Greenfield and van Schalkwyk 2003; Fowler and Greenfield 2009; cf. Whitelaw 2005). Inferring overall settlement organization must thus often depend upon only partial knowledge of what survives. Moreover, the normative emphasis of the CCP risks ignoring variation in settlement organization, such as the apparently peripheral location of the cattle byre at Ntsitsana (Prins and Grainger 1993). Returning to a point raised earlier, whether the numbers of cattle identifiable in the archaeological record can sustain the model has also been debated, with Martin Hall (1986) proposing that for much of the first millennium cattle were too few to be used in bridewealth and political transactions, and that social relations were much more egalitarian than those recorded ethnographically. Badenhorst (2008, 2009b) repeats this objection, argues that central byres may not have been exclusively used to keep cattle, and suggests that function, rather than worldview, dictated the location of livestock enclosures and storage pits, producing a situation of equifinality in the archaeological record that cannot then be used to identify the CCP. Specific ethnographic data and the consistency with which the CCP ties together disparate data about subsistence, settlement, and ideology tend to refute these claims (Huffman 2007), but the historical contexts of the ethnographies used to generate both the CCP and the alternative Forest Pattern described for Western Bantu speakers (Huffman 2007), which is hinted at in the Tsodilo Hills (Denbow 1990), certainly require interrogation (Lane 1994/5).

Worldview can also be approached from other data. Ceramic figurines and mask fragments (most spectacularly at the Lydenburg Heads Site: Whitelaw 1996) are, for example, not produced in South Africa today except by the Venda and northeast Sotho, who use them in initiation ceremonies undertaken near chiefs' cattle byres and courts. Strikingly, this is precisely their location at Ndondonwane, where their incorporation of snake and crocodile symbolism suggests the tapping of ideas of seniority, gender, and security comparable to those found in later Shona and Venda culture (Fowler 2008). Among other parallels, the Lydenburg heads demonstrate dental modification that resembles the filing and/or removal of incisors known from several first-millennium burials (e.g. Morris 1993), something no longer practised by Eastern Bantu speakers in southern Africa, but associated with Western Bantu speakers who reckon descent matrilineally, or bilaterally, rather than patrilineally. Matching this, cross-cultural generalizations regarding the kinship systems of African societies that emphasize hoe-based horticulture and caprines over cattle suggest that many first-millennium southern African farming communities were matrilineal (Badenhorst 2010), though this necessitates rejecting the CCP and its patrilineal associations. Another ritual practice involved placing of bottomless pots, grindstones, and other material in pits, frequently in residential areas, something that Whitelaw (1994/5) links, through ethnographic parallels, with the disposal of items used in girls' puberty rituals so that they could not be used by witches or cause pollution. Burials, a further source of rich insight, are not uncommon, but have not yet been comprehensively studied; in South Africa, at least, location and treatment do however conform to the expectations raised by the CCP (Huffman 2007).

TECHNOLOGY, TRADE, AND THE EMERGENCE OF COMPLEXITY

Paradoxically, iron objects are rare in first-millennium 'Iron Age' contexts, furnace fragments, tuyères, and slag being commoner. Best preserved are the iron and copper items from Divuyu and Nqoma (Miller 1996), most of which are items of jewellery, though tools and weapons are also known. Several examples of furnaces have been excavated (e.g. Swan 2007), most of simple bowl type. Intriguingly, while in the ethnographic record smelting took place away from settlements because of the supernatural threats posed by its associations with human reproduction, it may have been undertaken within some villages during the first millennium (Mitchell and Whitelaw 2005). Positive identification and association with other features can, however, be problematic, and in some cases smelting debris clearly post-dates occupation (Greenfield and Miller 2004).

Some sites produced more iron than others: in KwaZulu-Natal this may have been to exchange with hunter-gatherers at Msuluzi Confluence (Maggs 1980), but at Mamba I (van Schalkwyk 1994/5) it forms part of a pattern whereby many settlements ceased producing their own iron in the late first millennium. The implication here is one of trade—and perhaps political dependency—between sites, further evidence for which comes from considering other resources. Thus copper, more restricted in distribution than iron, moved as beads over 600 km from Phalaborwa in the 8th century (Miller and Whitelaw 1994) and was likewise worked and exchanged on a small scale in Zambia and Zimbabwe (Phillipson 1977). Salt extracted from springs and saline ash (Phillipson 1970; Evers 1975) was also traded, and we can assume that other resources too were widely exchanged; certainly, ostrich eggshell beads at villages in KwaZulu-Natal form part of a broader regional set of exotica moving between farmers and foragers (Mitchell 2009), while Denbow (1999) describes a complex exchange network across the northern Kalahari, concretely signalled by movements of copper, iron, specularite, fish, seashells, and other items. Here and in KwaZulu-Natal some larger sites probably developed into local political centres, identified in part by specializations in working high-status (ivory) or otherwise unusual (talc schist ornaments and cosmetics) materials (van Schalkwyk 1994/5; Whitelaw 1994/5). Overall, the pattern is one of increasing production of items suitable for exchange across much of the region by the late first millennium.

Such exchanges engaged with emerging networks in the wider Indian Ocean world (Pwiti 2005). Evidence includes marine shells and glass beads from a variety of mid/late first-millennium contexts, including the Tsodilo Hills, where shells of both Atlantic and Indian Ocean origin document connections of ultimately transcontinental scope. Rare instances of Middle Eastern pottery are also known, perhaps earlier than AD 500 at Chibuene, southern Mozambique (Sinclair et al. 1993), and from the 9th century near Durban (Whitelaw 1994). By way of return, ivory and skins were exported from southeastern Africa by the 10th century (Freeman-Grenville 1962), something confirmed archaeologically by the ivory-working debris, carnivore bones, glass beads, and cowrie shells from Schroda, the largest Zhizo site in the Shashe-Limpopo Basin (van Schalkwyk and Hanisch 2002); iron from eastern Botswana is another possible export (Kiyaga-Mulindwa 1993). While control over livestock and agricultural land was also important, manipulation of long-distance trade and use of imports as prestige goods to reward followers and signal status were critical in the development of sociopolitical complexity in these areas from the 10th century (Pikirayi, Ch. 63 below). In contrast, glass beads are extremely rare in first-millennium Zambia and Malawi, though cowries at Chundu Farm and a glass fragment at Kumadzulo indicate that contacts reached the Victoria Falls region (Vogel 1984).

CHANGE AND CONTINUITY: EARLY AND LATER FARMING COMMUNITIES

Little has been said thus far about how Early Farming Communities dispersed or about their relationships with their agropastoralist successors or hunter-gatherer contemporaries. Genetics, in particular, is opening up new avenues here. In both Mozambique (Salas et al. 2002) and southern Angola/northern Namibia (Coelho et al. 2009) some assimilation of indigenous 'Khoisan' hunter-gatherers is evident, perhaps of the kind evident much later and rather further south at Madikwe, South Africa, where a 'client' forager presence seems evident within a Later Farming Community Moloko homestead (Hall 2000). Although comparably detailed DNA studies have yet to be reported or undertaken elsewhere, the language and culture of modern Nguni speakers (Hammond-Tooke 1998) suggest that intermarriage was probably significantly more frequent in southeastern South Africa. Further north, foragers seem to have been rapidly displaced or assimilated across much of Zimbabwe (Walker and Thorp 1997), while in Zambia they persisted longer in relationships of avoidance (Musonda 1987) or exchange (Phillipson 1976).

In general terms (and the topic would benefit from greater theoretical attention and comparative examination), farming almost certainly spread through a combination of demographic increase and forager assimilation (Vansina 1995), spurred on by drought, declining soil fertility, and community fission at the level of individual settlements (Jones 1984); forager uptake without migration fits neither the scale nor the rapidity of expansion (*pace* Robertson 2000). However, farming's spread was not universal, and in many instances probably proceeded by 'hopping' from one favourable location to another (cf. Whitelaw and Moon 1996), only later infilling the areas between. In northeastern Namibia, for example, no evidence of cereal cultivation or herding has yet been found before the 19th century, even though iron production and ceramics similar to Kalundu and Naviundu Traditions occur from the mid-first millennium AD (Kose 2009). The Dama of north-central Namibia and 'River Bushmen' of northern Botswana, both physically negroid but speaking Khoe languages, may represent further instances, ones where people of 'farmer descent' were assimilated by indigenous groups (Barnard 1992).

Connections between Early Farming Communities and their successors also warrant greater attention. In southernmost Africa, ceramic design and other data (Maggs 1994/5; Huffman 2007) indicate that they were replaced early in the second millennium by later arrivals from eastern Africa who introduced the Nguni and Sotho/Tswana languages (Schoeman, Ch. 64 below). The precise relationships between these immigrants and older agropastoralist communities are, however, significantly under-researched, although material culture (with linguistic backing in some cases) indicates that Shona and Venda speakers have much stronger connections to first-millennium farmers, and that others (makers of Eiland and Broadhurst ceramics) survived well after AD 1000. North of the Zambezi, another major disjunction is obvious, with Kalundu Tradition ceramics replaced by others derived from the Naviundu Tradition. This 11th-century Luangwa expansion reflects the spread of matrilineal, Western Bantu-speaking societies in which men, not women, make pottery across much of south-central Africa (Phillipson 1977; Huffman 1989). The historical connections between this movement and that of ancestral Nguni and Sotho/Tswana speakers, as well as the broader ecological and cultural contexts of both, merit sustained, collaborative research by southern, south-central, and East African specialists alike.

References

Arnold, E. R. (2008). A consideration of livestock exploitation during the Early Iron Age in the Thukela Valley, KwaZulu-Natal. In S. Badenhorst, P. J. Mitchell, and J. C. Driver (eds), *Animals and People: Archaeozoological Papers in Honour of Ina Plug*. Oxford: Archaeopress, 152–68.

Badenhorst, S. (2008). Subsistence change among farming communities in southern Africa during the last two millennia: a search for potential causes. In S. Badenhorst, P. J. Mitchell, and J. C. Driver (eds), *Animals and People: Archaeozoological Papers in Honour of Ina Plug*. Oxford: Archaeopress, 215–28.

—— (2009a). Phytoliths and livestock dung at Early Iron Age sites in southern Africa. *South African Archaeological Bulletin* 64: 45–50.

—— (2009b). The Central Cattle Pattern during the Iron Age of southern Africa: a critique of its spatial features. *South African Archaeological Bulletin* 64: 148–55.

—— (2010). Descent of Iron Age farmers in southern Africa during the last 2000 years. *African Archaeological Review* 27: 87–106.

BARNARD, A. (1992). *Hunters and Herders of Southern Africa: A Comparative Ethnography of the Khoisan Peoples.* Cambridge: Cambridge University Press.

COELHO, M., SEQUEIRA, F., LUISELLI, D., BELAZA, S., and ROCHA, J. (2009). On the edge of Bantu expansions: mtDNA, Y chromosome and lactase persistence genetic variation in southwestern Angola. *BMC Evolutionary Biology* 9: 80.

DENBOW, J. R. (1990). Congo to Kalahari: data and hypotheses about the political economy of the western stream of the Early Iron Age. *African Archaeological Review* 8: 139–75.

—— (1999). Material culture and the dialectics of identity in the Kalahari: AD 700–1700. In S. K. Mcintosh (ed.), *Beyond Chiefdoms: Pathways to Complexity in Africa.* Cambridge: Cambridge University Press, 110–23.

EVERS, T. M. (1975). Recent Iron Age research in the eastern Transvaal, South Africa. *South African Archaeological Bulletin* 30: 71–83.

FOWLER, K. D. (2008). Social memory and the antiquity of snake and crocodile symbolism in southern Africa. In S. Badenhorst, P. J. Mitchell, and J. C. Driver (eds), *Animals and People: Archaeozoological Papers in Honour of Ina Plug.* Oxford: Archaeopress, 169–85.

—— and GREENFIELD, H. J. (2009). Unravelling settlement history at Ndondonwane, South Africa: a micro-chronological analysis. *Southern African Humanities* 21: 345–93.

FREDRIKSEN, P.-D. (2009). Kvifor sprakk karet? Keramisk handverk som strategiar for problemløysing innan ein termodynamisk filosofi i det sørlege Afrika. *Oslo Arkeologiske Serie/ Oslo Archaeological Series* 12: 85–110.

FREEMAN-GRENVILLE, G. P. S. (1962). *The East African Coast: Select Documents from the First to the Earlier Nineteenth Century.* Oxford: Clarendon Press.

GREENFIELD, H. J., and MILLER, D. E. (2004). Spatial patterning of Early Iron Age metal production at Ndondonwane, South Africa: a question of cultural continuity between the Early and Late Iron Ages. *Journal of Archaeological Science* 31: 1511–32.

—— and VAN SCHALKWYK, L. O. (2003). Intra-settlement social and economic organization of Early Iron Age farming communities in southern Africa: a view from Ndondonwane. *Azania* 38: 121–38.

—— (2008). Early Iron Age regional settlement and demographic patterns along the eastern seaboard of South Africa: a view from the lower Thukela River Valley. In S. Badenhorst, P. J. Mitchell, and J. C. Driver (eds), *Animals and People: Archaeozoological Papers in Honour of Ina Plug.* Oxford: Archaeopress, 131–51.

HALL, M. (1983). Tribes, traditions and numbers: the American model in southern African Iron Age studies. *South African Archaeological Bulletin* 38: 51–61.

—— (1986). The role of cattle in southern African agropastoral societies: more than bones alone can tell. *South African Archaeological Society Goodwin Series* 5: 83–7.

HALL, S. L. (2000). Forager lithics and early Moloko homesteads at Madikwe. *Natal Museum Journal of Humanities* 12: 33–50.

HAMMOND-TOOKE, W. D. (1998). Selective borrowing? The possibility of San shamanistic influence on Southern Bantu divination and healing practices. *South African Archaeological Bulletin* 53: 9–15.

HODDER, I. (1982). *Symbols in Action*. Cambridge: Cambridge University Press.

HORWITZ, L., MAGGS, T. M. O'C., and WARD, V. (1991). Two shell middens as indicators of shellfish exploitation patterns during the first millennium AD on the Natal North Coast. *Natal Museum Journal of Humanities* 3: 1–28.

HUFFMAN, T. N. (1989). Ceramics, settlements and late Iron Age migrations. *African Archaeological Review* 7: 155–82.

—— (1996). Archaeological evidence for climatic change during the last 2000 years in southern Africa. *Quaternary International* 33: 55–60.

—— (1998). The antiquity of *lobola*. *South African Archaeological Bulletin* 53: 57–62.

—— (2001). The Central Cattle Pattern and interpreting the past. *Southern African Humanities* 13: 19–35.

—— (2005). The stylistic origin of Bambata and the spread of mixed farming in southern Africa. *Southern African Humanities* 17: 52–79.

—— (2007). *Handbook to the Iron Age: The Archaeology of Pre-Colonial Farming Societies in Southern Africa*. Pietermaritzburg: University of KwaZulu-Natal Press.

JONES, P. (1984). Mobility and migration in traditional African farming and Iron Age models. In M. Hall, G. Avery, D. M. Avery, M. L. Wilson, and A. J. B. Humphreys (eds), *Frontiers: Southern African Archaeology Today*. Oxford: British Archaeological Reports, 289–96.

JONSSON, J. (1998). *Early Plant Economy in Zimbabwe*. Uppsala: Uppsala University Press.

KIYAGA-MULINDWA, D. (1993). The Iron Age peoples of east-central Botswana. In T. Shaw, P. J. J. Sinclair, B. W. Andah, and A. Okpoko (eds), *The Archaeology of Africa: Food, Metals and Towns*. London: Routledge, 386–90.

KOSE, E. (2009). New light on ironworking groups along the Middle Kavango in northern Namibia. *South African Archaeological Bulletin* 64: 130–47.

KUPER, A. (1980). Symbolic dimensions of the southern Bantu homestead. *Africa* 1: 8–23.

LANE, P. J. (1994/95). The use and abuse of ethnography in Iron Age studies of southern Africa. *Azania* 29/30: 51–64.

MAGGS, T. M. O'C. (1980). Msuluzi Confluence: a seventh century Early Iron Age site on the Tugela River. *Annals of the Natal Museum* 24: 111–45.

—— (1994/5). The Early Iron Age in the extreme south: some patterns and problems. *Azania* 29/30: 171–8.

MILLER, D. E. (1996). *The Tsodilo Jewellery: Metal Work from Northern Botswana*. Cape Town: University of Cape Town Press.

—— and WHITELAW, G. (1994). Early Iron Age metal working from the site of KwaGandaganda, Natal, South Africa. *South African Archaeological Bulletin* 49: 79–89.

MITCHELL, P. J. (2002). *The Archaeology of Southern Africa*. Cambridge: Cambridge University Press.

—— (2009). Hunter-gatherers and farmers: some implications of 2000 years of interaction in the Maloti-Drakensberg region of southern Africa. *Senri Ethnological Studies* 73: 15–46.

—— and WHITELAW, G. (2005). The archaeology of southernmost Africa *c*. 2000 BP to the early 1800s: a review of recent research. *Journal of African History* 46: 209–41.

MORRIS, A. G. (1993). Human remains from the Early Iron Age sites of Nanda and kwaGandaganda, Mngeni Valley, Natal, South Africa. *Natal Museum Journal of Humanities* 5: 83–98.

MUSONDA, F. B. (1987). The significance of pottery in Zambian Later Stone Age contexts. *African Archaeological Review* 5: 147–58.

OHINATA, F. (2001). Archaeology of iron-using farming communities in Swaziland: pots, people and life during the first and second millennia AD. DPhil. thesis, University of Oxford.

PARKINGTON, J. E., and HALL, S. L. (2010). The appearance of food production in southern Africa 1,000 to 2,000 years ago. In C. Hamilton, B. K. Mbenga, and R. Ross (eds), *The Cambridge History of South Africa*, vol. 1: *From Early Times to 1885*. Cambridge: Cambridge University Press, 63–111.

PHILLIPSON, D. W. (1970). Excavations at Twickenham Road, Lusaka. *Azania* 5: 77–118.

—— (1976). *The Prehistory of Eastern Zambia*. Nairobi: British Institute in Eastern Africa.

—— (1977). *The Later Prehistory of Eastern and Southern Africa*. London: Heinemann.

PIKIRAYI, I. (1997). Pots, people and culture: an overview of ceramic studies in Zimbabwe. In G. Pwiti (ed.), *Caves, Monuments and Texts: Zimbabwean Archaeology Today*. Uppsala: Societas Archaeologica Upsaliensis, 69–87.

PLUG, I. (1981). Upper Zambezi Iron Age projects: specialist reports. *Archaeologica Zambiana* 20: 17–22.

—— (1987). Iron Age subsistence strategies in the Kruger National Park, South Africa. *Archaeozoologia* 1: 117–25.

—— (1997). Early Iron Age buffalo hunters on the Kadzi River, Zimbabwe. *African Archaeological Review* 14: 85–106.

PRINS, F. E., and GRAINGER, J. E. (1993). Early farming communities in northern Transkei: the evidence from Ntsitsana and adjacent areas. *Natal Museum Journal of Humanities* 5: 153–74.

PWITI, G. (1996). Settlement and subsistence of prehistoric farming communities in the mid-Zambezi Valley, northern Zimbabwe. *South African Archaeological Bulletin* 51: 3–6.

—— (2005). Southern Africa and the East African coast. In A. B. Stahl (ed.), *African Archaeology: A Critical Introduction*. Oxford: Blackwell, 378–91.

ROBBINS, L. H., CAMPBELL, A. C., MURPHY, M. L., et al. (2008). Recent archaeological research at Toteng, Botswana: early domesticated livestock in the Kalahari. *Journal of African Archaeology* 6:131–50.

ROBERTSON, J. H. (2000). A new paradigm: the African Early Iron Age without Bantu migrations. *History in Africa* 27: 282–323.

SADR, K. (2008). An ageless view of first millennium AD southern African ceramics. *Journal of African Archaeology* 6: 103–30.

—— and SAMPSON, C. G. (2006). Through thick and thin: early pottery in southern Africa. *Journal of African Archaeology* 4: 235–52.

SALAS, A., RICHARDS, M., DE LA FE, T., et al. (2002). The making of the African mtDNA landscape. *American Journal of Human Genetics* 71: 1082–1111.

SANDELOWSKY, B. H. (1979). Kapako and Vungu Vungu: Iron Age sites on the Kavango River. *South African Archaeological Society Goodwin Series* 3: 52–61.

SEGOBYE, A. (1998). Early Farming Communities. In P. J. Lane, A. Reid, and A. Segobye (eds), *Ditswa Mmung: The Archaeology of Botswana*. Gaborone: Pula Press, 101–14.

SINCLAIR, P. J. J. (1987). *Space, Time and Social Formation: A Territorial Approach to the Archaeology and Anthropology of Zimbabwe and Mozambique, c. 0–1700 AD*. Uppsala: Societas Archaeologica Upsaliensis.

—— PIKIRAYI, I., PWITI, G., and SOPER, R. (1993). Urban trajectories on the Zimbabwean plateau. In T. Shaw, P. J. J. Sinclair, B. Andah, and A. Okpoko (eds), *The Archaeology of Africa: Food, Metals and Towns*. London: Routledge, 705–31.

SWAN, L. M. (2007). Early iron manufacturing industries in semi-arid south-eastern Zimbabwe. *Journal of African Archaeology* 5: 315–38.

VAN SCHALKWYK, J. A., and HANISCH, E. O. M. (2002). *Sculptured in Clay: Iron Age Figurines from Schroda, Limpopo Province, South Africa*. Pretoria: National Cultural History Museum.

VAN SCHALKWYK, L. O. (1994/95). Settlement shifts and socio-economic transformations in early agriculturist communities in the lower Thukela Basin. *Azania* 29/30: 187–98.

VANSINA, J. (1994/5). A slow revolution: farming in subequatorial Africa. *Azania* 29/30: 1–14.

—— (1995). New linguistic evidence and 'the Bantu expansion'. *Journal of African History* 36: 173–95.

VOGEL, J. O. (1984). An Early Iron Age settlement system in southern Zambia. *Azania* 19: 61–78.

WALKER, N. J., and THORP, C. R. (1997). Stone Age archaeology in Zimbabwe. In G. Pwiti (ed.), *Caves, Monuments and Texts: Zimbabwean Archaeology Today*. Uppsala: Societas Archaeologica Upsaliensis, 9–32.

WHITELAW, G. (1994). KwaGandaganda: settlement patterns in the Natal Early Iron Age. *Natal Museum Journal of Humanities* 6: 1–64.

—— (1994/5). Towards an Early Iron Age worldview: some ideas from KwaZulu-Natal. *Azania* 29/30: 37–50.

—— (1996). Lydenburg revisited: another look at the Mpumalanga Early Iron Age sequence. *South African Archaeological Bulletin* 51: 75–83.

—— (2005). Comment on Greenfield and van Schalkwyk's article on Ndondonwane, *Azania*, 2003. *Azania* 40: 122–7.

—— (2009). An Iron Age fishing tale. *Southern African Humanities* 21: 195–212.

—— and MOON, M. (1996). The distribution and ceramics of pioneer agriculturists in KwaZulu-Natal. *Natal Museum Journal of Humanities* 8: 53–79.

CHAPTER 46

....

THE ARCHAEOLOGY OF AGRICULTURAL INTENSIFICATION IN AFRICA

....

DARYL STUMP

INTRODUCTION: THEMES IN THE STUDY OF AFRICAN INTENSIVE AGRICULTURE

BOTH agricultural intensification and the study of the processes that prompt intensification have a long history in Africa, perhaps most famously through a series of related arguments that saw state formation in Ancient Egypt as resulting from a need to manage complex irrigation systems. As briefly outlined here, such arguments have subsequently been challenged, both by research in Egypt itself and by studies from elsewhere in Africa and other parts of the world. Taken together, this work demonstrates that there are multiple reasons why a community might choose to increase its inputs of labour to establish, maintain, or expand an agricultural system. This point is illustrated here through reference to societies throughout sub-Saharan Africa that have undergone periods of intensification and dis-intensification over the last 500 years or so, and through a summary of the far older processes of agricultural change undertaken in north and northeastern Africa.

The focus here is primarily archaeological, but research from a variety of disciplinary backgrounds informs our understanding of intensification in Africa. Indeed, with an ever greater number of case studies and a more nuanced understanding of the range of possible trajectories of change, it becomes increasingly clear that intensification defies a single over-arching definition. Increased inputs of labour are perhaps the preferred criterion, but there are problems with defining intensification in terms of labour, particularly from an archaeological perspective. Not least of these is a potential bias towards sites where labour-intensive features are preserved: 'permanent' stone-built terraces being more archaeologically visible than the annual construction of earthen bunds, for example. Similarly, in the absence of data on maintenance requirements, it may not be clear that particular agricultural features or strategies are necessarily labour-intensive. It might also be objected that evidence of attempts to intensify production does not mean that such attempts were successful. Equally, without information on yields (archaeologically only discernible indirectly via evidence for the trade or storage of surpluses, or through ethnographic or experimental data) it may be difficult to distinguish attempts to increase production from what Geertz (1963) termed 'agricultural involution': the need to increase labour per unit of land merely in order to maintain current production levels, perhaps as a result of falling soil fertility. The term 'intensification' is thus used here in its broadest possible sense to encompass a variety of processes that might be better described as specialization, diversification, innovation, or risk mitigation.

Related to this last point, a review of existing summaries reveals a change in emphasis over the last twenty years or so. Where earlier gazetteers tended to treat instances of agricultural intensification as isolated and insular responses to local historical and environmental condi- tions (Grove and Sutton 1989; Critchley et al. 1994), more recent overviews note the existence (and perhaps the necessity) of relationships between intensive cultivators and neighbouring groups, with these neighbours acting as either trading partners, consumers, or sources of reciprocal support (e.g. Widgren 2010). This different perspective reflects a more critical view of generalized models of agricultural change, because such models have typically explained intensification as a response to local forcing factors, including a need to feed a growing population, and/or counteract resource degradation, and/or support a community that is prevented by environmental or political restrictions from expanding, migrating, or fragmenting (the so-called 'siege hypothesis'). By demonstrating a range of trajectories of agricultural change, historical and archaeological case studies from across Africa challenge the validity of such schemes in specific instances, and warn against employing potentially teleological models as aids to historical or archaeological interpretation.

Examples of African intensive
agricultural systems

Saharan northeast Africa: Egypt and Sudan

Although there is insufficient space here to discuss it in any detail, it is clearly impossible to consider agricultural intensification in Africa without mention of irrigation along the Nile in Ancient Egypt (cf. Shaw, Ch. 50 below). Indeed, the perceived need to develop social mechanisms to oversee the construction, maintenance, and management of irrigation sys- tems in Egypt was famously seen by Wittfogel (1957) as integral to the formation of a central- ized state during the late fourth millennium BC, while in a related argument Carneiro (1970) saw the impossibility of sustaining agricultural settlements away from the Nile as leading to increases in population density and intensification of agriculture, ultimately prompting state formation (Hassan 1997). Both contentions have been challenged, however, on the grounds that the vast majority of irrigation appears to have been managed locally without centralized or regional bureaucratic intervention from the time of its inception during the Early Dynas- tic period (c. 3100–2700 BC), remaining primarily a local concern until at least the Graeco- Roman period (Hassan 1997). Moreover, despite the economic importance of barley and emmer wheat from the Predynastic period onwards, the husbandry of small and large stock remained important throughout Egyptian history. It has thus been argued that irrigation originated as a risk mitigation measure designed to cope with fluctuations in the level of the annual Nile flood, only being truly intensively exploited when perennial irrigation was adopted in the 19th century AD (Hassan 1997).

The *shaduf* manual water-lifting lever was also a feature of irrigation in this area, apparently having been developed in Egypt during the New Kingdom (1550–1070 BC), before spreading south along the Nile into Sudan. Indeed, Trigger (1965) suggested that the type of irrigation employed can be used to characterize arable areas adjacent to the Nile as either *seluka* land (periodically inundated), *shaduf* land (irrigated by mechanically lifting water up to three metres), or *saqia* land (requiring water to be lifted up to eight metres by the use of animal-powered water wheels). Within Sudan the main stretch of *seluka* land lies either side of the Dongola Reach between the Fourth and Third Cataracts, an area that includes the Kerma Basin which, together with the wide floodplain to the south of the Third Cataract, acted as the arable resource base for the Bronze Age Kerma polity in the early second millennium BC (Welsby, Ch. 51 below). Further south, but still within the Dongola Reach, a similar case can be made for the development of a power base for the kingdom of Kush at Napata during the 9th century BC (Welsby, Ch. 51). Meroë, Napata's successor as the political centre of Kush between the 4th century BC and the 4th century AD, is also located in an area with potential for irrigated farming of fertile alluvial soils, although in this period the economy appears to have also placed considerable emphasis on animal keeping. Nevertheless, the prevalence within archaeological assemblages of *qudas* pottery vessels attests to the importance of the *saqia* water wheel, and the *saqia* has even been credited as significant in the reoccupation of Lower Nubia by the Meroitic state in the 2nd/3rd centuries AD, since it made it possible to irrigate more land than had been achievable using the human operated *shaduf* (Connah 1987: 30, 46, 53). Edwards (2004: 165) notes, however, that evidence for use of the *saqia* is limited in Lower Nubia, and suggests that even irrigated agriculture in this area could hardly be described as intensive at this time.

The construction of large areas of agricultural terracing in Sudan appears to be a much later development. Extensive terraced agriculture is observable in the Darfur hills, particularly around Jebel Marra, where large areas continue to be cultivated, in places incorporating artificial irrigation (Sutton 1985; Grove and Sutton 1989). Using archaeological data and a survey of settlement types through aerial photography, Häser (2000, cited by Widgren 2010: 331–2) suggests that settlements associated with terracing predate AD 1650. Traces of field systems and their associated settlements are also evident in hilly locations east of Darfur in Kordofan, including extensive areas of stone-built terraces in the Nuba Hills (Sutton 1985; Grove and Sutton 1989). As in Jebel Marra, currently cultivated examples can be reasonably described as labour-intensive since they are often combined with the stall-feeding of cattle for manure accumulation. The date of the system's inception remains uncertain, but terraces may have been in place from at least the 18th century (Ewald 1990; Widgren 2010: 332).

Ethiopia

Dates for the inception of intensive agricultural systems are not known in the majority of Ethiopian cases, and there is also a noteworthy discrepancy between currently available linguistic and archaeological data. A study of inscriptions and historical sources relating to

FIG. 46.1 Dry-stone agricultural terracing at Konso, Ethiopia. Left: uncultivated hillside terraces. Right: in-field terracing immediately outside Dera town wall (photographs, Daryl Stump 2010).

Aksum in Ethiopia's northern highlands, for example, suggests that terraces, irrigation, and ox-drawn ploughs were in use between the 1st and 4th centuries AD (Kobishchanov 1979), although this conclusion has not been confirmed archaeologically and, indeed, a recent review of historical and palaeoenvironmental data combined with geoarchaeological and palaeobotanical research concluded that Aksumite agriculture was entirely rain-fed (Sulas et al. 2009). A marked difference between the available historical and linguistic data also occurs for the southern Ethiopian highlands, with Ehret (2002: 131) arguing that Highland East Cushitic linguistic influences in the modern languages of this area indicate that furrow irrigation was in use by 2000 BC, and that 'probably well before 1000 BCE the irrigation farmers of the southern Ethiopian Highlands increasingly turned to building stone-walled terraces'. Direct archaeological data for the origins of such practices is lacking, but oral historical and genealogical work centred on the intensively cultivated terraced landscape around Konso (Fig. 46.1) in southwestern Ethiopia indicates that these practices were in place by the 16th century AD (Amborn 1989). These two sources of data need not be contradictory, therefore, but at present there is no archaeological evidence to confirm the long chronology suggested by Ehret.

Eastern Africa

No doubt in part the result of being the focus of more research than elsewhere on the continent, eastern Africa offers examples of all the issues raised above and thus helps highlight the variety of trajectories that communities might take towards agricultural intensification (Fig. 46.2). These include instances of non-intensive irrigation undertaken for subsistence, as risk mitigation, or as opportunism within primarily pastoral economies, as among the Turkana in northern Kenya (Adams 1989); examples of intensification in order to exploit commercial opportunities, such as the expansion of irrigation and terracing to supply long distance 19th-century trade caravans at Baringo, Kenya (Adams and Anderson 1988); and examples that contradict Boserup's (1965) view that intensification is likely to result from a need to feed a rising population, with the history of Iraqw, Tanzania, demonstrating that intensification can prompt population increases through in-migration (Börjeson 2007).

Similarly, one might look to the development of the complex irrigation system on the slopes of Mount Kilimanjaro, Tanzania, as an example of how a technology developed prior to 19th-century European contact might adapt to the demands of a modern cash economy. In this case, a pre-existing irrigation system apparently developed to support the cultivation of bananas and finger millet was converted and extended to support the commercial production of coffee. This said, although the origins of the Kilimanjaro irrigation system probably date to at least the 16th century, there is little agreement on the original impetus for the construction of the channel network. Indeed, observers have forwarded a range of hypotheses, including: attempts to feed a growing population; to support communities forced to retreat from raids by Maasai pastoralists; to avoid the danger of attacks by animals or hostile neighbours when collecting domestic water; to produce agricultural surpluses that could be traded

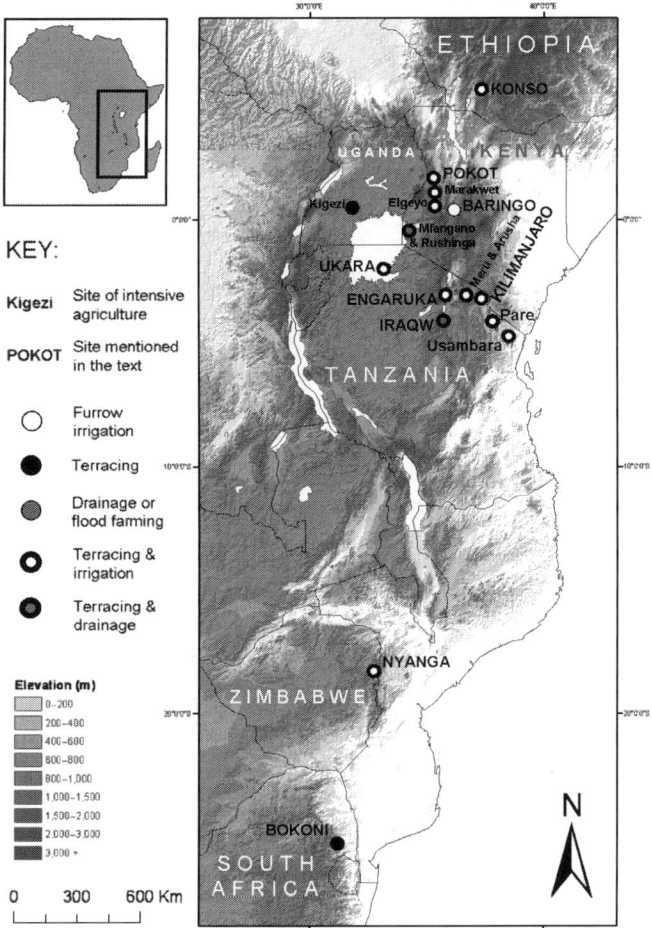

FIG. 46.2 Map showing the location of areas of precolonial intensive agriculture in eastern and southern Africa.

for cattle; and efforts by local chiefs to increase the supply of finger millet and its ritually important beer derivative (Stump and Tagseth 2009: 107–8). While it is possible that all of these factors played a role in different areas and at different times, it is nevertheless significant that these alternative hypotheses posit very different trajectories of change, on the one hand apparently confirming the suggestion that communities will only commit to increased labour when land shortage or rising population force them to do so, while on the other asserting that the construction of irrigation features was motivated solely by the political and economic advantages afforded by the production of tradable surpluses.

Choosing between these alternative models would require detailed historical or archaeological data or, more probably, a combined interdisciplinary approach. Davies' (2010b) study of the history of the irrigation-using Pokot society of Kenya, for example, combined oral historical work on the age sets associated with particular irrigation furrows with test excavations and surveys of abandoned and extant furrows and house platforms. The results suggest that a relatively stable population had progressively migrated upslope over the last 300 years, building or extending small-scale irrigation systems in the process. This study demonstrates that Wittfogel (1957) was misguided in citing Pokot as an example of centralized irrigation management, and that a Boserupian correlation between population density and intensification cannot be accepted for this location without considerable caveats. Just as significantly, Davies further argues that local systems of land tenure would have played an important role in household decisions as to whether to intensify production or to move to a new plot, thus emphasizing the potential importance of archaeologically invisible institutions, while simultaneously highlighting the role played by ethnographic (or ethnoarchaeological) analogies in interpreting such systems.

In the Pokot case it can be plausibly argued that the relationship between the archaeological subject community and their modern successors allows the use of such ethnographic analogies whilst minimizing the risk of simply projecting the observable present into the past. With an entirely abandoned site like that of Engaruka in northeastern Tanzania this is much more problematic, not least because the site's desertion sometime in the late 17th to mid-18th centuries after an occupation of some 300 years makes it difficult to identify the most appropriate source of analogies (Sutton 2004). There are nevertheless also advantages to studying abandoned agricultural sites, since they afford the opportunity to examine features and soils undisturbed by subsequent maintenance or cultivation. Indeed, archaeological fieldwork at Engaruka (Figs 46.3 and 46.4) since the early 1960s challenges the simplistic assumption that abandoned sites necessarily represent evidence of failed economies, or result from local resource degradation, or constitute examples of communities unable to adapt to changing environmental and economic conditions (Sutton 2004; Stump 2006; Widgren 2010). Thus, although the importance of ethnographic, historic, and modern sources has been stressed here, it is also clear that archaeological data are necessary to assess fully the efficacy and sustainability of intensive agronomies. Farrington's (1985: 5) warning that abandoned sites may be unrepresentative on the grounds that they generally occupy land that is 'too wet, too dry or too steep' to have prompted later populations to rework or destroy earlier field systems should be borne in mind, but Engaruka nevertheless acts as an example of an abandoned intensive agronomy that may not have been as marginal as Farrington's comments imply: 'too dry' for rain-fed agriculture, perhaps, but apparently capable of supporting a comparatively high population density through the watering of some 2,000 ha of low terraces and stone-bounded fields via a complex network of stone-lined irrigation furrows (Sutton 2004; Stump 2006).

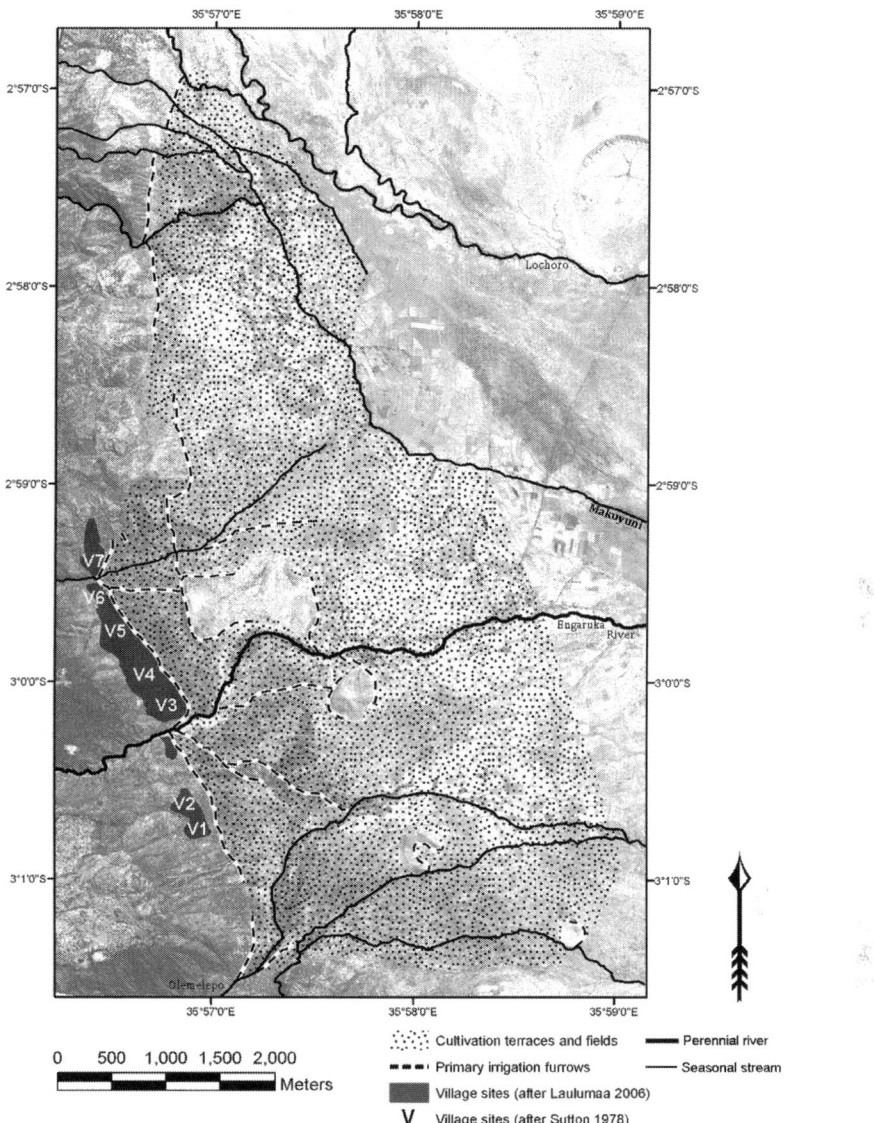

FIG. 46.3 Extent of cultivated fields, settlement sites, and primary irrigation furrows, Engaruka, Tanzania.

As with any archaeological site, discerning past population levels requires a detailed chronology of settlement areas, but this is particularly significant for discussions of agricultural intensification given that population density has been seen as a direct proxy for the level of intensification. Netting (1993: 269) cites a figure of 60 people per km² as the point at which a community might start to feel the pressure to intensify production, and considers that sustaining 200 people/km² in the absence of any technological innovation would require continuous cropping without fallowing. With ground and aerial photographic surveys recording some 1,750 habitation platforms covering 37 ha on the lower slopes

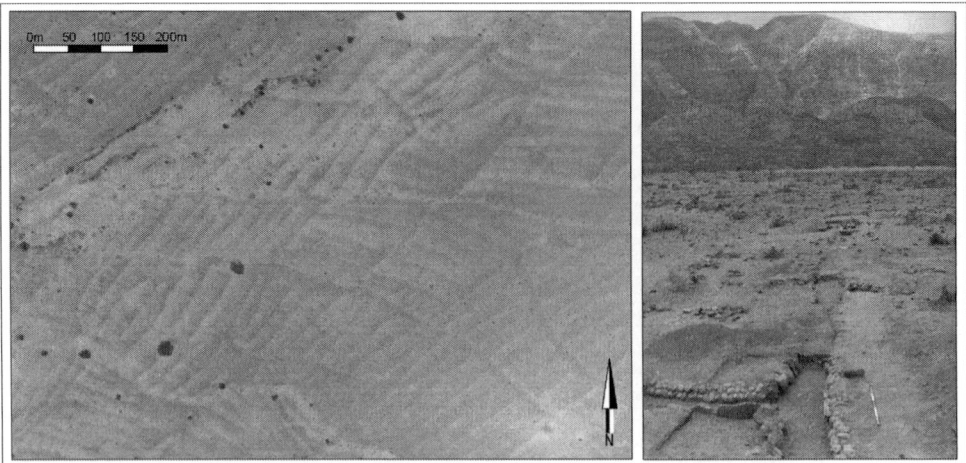

FIG. 46.4 Irrigated dry-stone terracing within the Northern Fields, Engaruka, Tanzania. Left: vertical aerial photograph of terracing (Tanzania Survey 1964; Engaruka No. 55) centred approximately on the excavated area shown to right. Right: excavated sections through irrigation furrows (photograph, Daryl Stump 2003).

overlooking the former cultivation area, Engaruka's population has been estimated as being 4,000–5,000, i.e. 250 people/km^2 if it is assumed that the visible field remains formed the sole support for this community (Laulumaa 2006; Davies 2010b). If Netting's (1993) figures correlating population density with intensification are accepted, therefore, sustaining a population at this level would certainly have required intensive cultivation. Nevertheless, the current lack of information regarding the development of the habitation areas at Engaruka means that such estimates remain speculative, since it is still unclear how many terraces were occupied at any one time or, for that matter, whether individual terraces were occupied for extended periods. However, excavation results go some way towards addressing the latter issue, demonstrating that deep anthropogenic layers beneath habitation platforms are levelling deposits rather than evidence of extended occupation as previously thought.

Details of population changes through time are also unavailable for the extant examples of East African intensive agriculture, but population figures from the late 19th/early 20th centuries are available for some systems. As already noted, they show an apparent correlation with the level of intensification in some instances (e.g. at Ukara; Netting 1993: 52–3) but not others (e.g. at Iraqw; Börjeson 2007). Predictably, there is also variation in the relationship between population densities and the use of labour-intensive cultivation techniques even within neighbouring or related systems, as can be seen on Kilimanjaro (Stump and Tagseth 2009: 107).

Southern Africa

With the exception of the two large archaeological complexes of Nyanga, Zimbabwe, and Bokoni, South Africa, there are comparatively few accounts of the use of irrigation, terracing, or other intensive agricultural techniques in southern Africa. Adams' (1989: 25) brief gazetteer mentions only the floodwater farming employed in the Okavango Delta, Botswana, and South Africa's Pongolo floodplain, though Soper (2002: 27–8) notes that seasonally flooded stream headwaters may have formed an important element of local agriculture prior to their suppression by colonial authorities who saw them as limiting dry season stream flows. He also considers that the use of raised beds to farm waterlogged areas was more common in Zimbabwe in the recent past (Soper 2002: 55). Nevertheless, Nyanga and Bokoni (Figs 46.5 and 46.6) constitute remarkable exceptions: the former consists of stone-built settlements, approximately 22,000 ha of dry-stone terracing and a comparable area of raised beds or cultivation ridges (Soper 2002), whilst the latter comprises a chain of settlements, cattle kraals, terracing, and possible irrigation features that together extend some 150 km along the highveld escarpment in Mpumalanga (Maggs 2008).

The subject of several small-scale excavation and survey projects from the late 1960s onwards (see Maggs 2008 and references therein), the Bokoni sites are currently under combined historical and archaeological investigation. From what is currently known, they appear to represent the remains of a mixed economy based on the keeping of small and large stock and on the cultivation of crops (including sorghum and cowpeas) within terraced fields. Historical work indicates that the Bakoni constructed them perhaps as much as 500 years ago, and abandoned them when this group was subjugated and subsumed by the Pedi in the early 19th century (Delius and Schoeman 2008).

At present little is known about the relative chronological development of Bokoni sites, but the importance of this information for assessing the degree of agricultural intensification is clearly illustrated by previous work at Nyanga, where a series of apparently short-lived settlements suggest that a relatively small population built, farmed, and then abandoned sections of the terraced landscape (Soper 2002). The large area of terraces visible today were thus built cumulatively, apparently primarily as a result of stone clearance from fields, and would never have been all farmed contemporaneously. This suggests that the system was not as labour-intensive as might be assumed from a superficial view of the landscape, although the presence of numerous sunken stock enclosures nevertheless point to the accumulation of manure for maintaining soil fertility, the spreading of which may well have represented a

FIG. 46.5 Dry-stone agricultural terracing at Nyanga, Zimbabwe. Left: near Nyautare. Right: Maristvale (both reproduced from Soper 2002, plates 1 and 5)

FIG. 46.6 Bokoni dry-stone terracing, Verlorenkloof, South Africa. Top: shallow dry-stone hillside terraces probably formed by slope deposits accumulating behind low stone walls (M. Widgren, pers comm.). Bottom: buttressed terrace and/or channel revetment (photographs, Daryl Stump 2009).

laborious task, especially if this necessitated the collection and transportation of cattle fodder.

Dating of the areas of terraces and cultivation ridges at Nyanga has largely been surmised from radiocarbon dates from associated settlements, and indicate construction began in the mid- to late 17th century and terminated in the 19th century, with the cultivation ridges perhaps employed for slightly longer. Some of the settlements high above the terraced zone are considerably older, however, and may have been occupied from as early as the 14th century (Soper 2002).

West Africa

In a recent review of historic intensive and terraced agriculture in West Africa, Widgren (2010) considers such practices to be more common here than in East Africa, but notes that the area has attracted less historical research, exceptions being historical, archaeological, palaeoenvironmental, and ethnoarchaeological studies of the Dogon of Mali (e.g. Mayor et al. 2005); Netting's (1993) study of the process of intensification and subsequent dis-intensification among the Koyfar of Nigeria (including collaboration with the archaeologist G. D. Stone); and an archaeological and linguistic examination of the Mandara Mountains of Cameroon (MacEachern 2003). Incidences of localized terracing are also noted in Houndé (Burkina Faso), among the Kassena of southern Burkina Faso and northern Ghana, at Atakora (on the border of Togo and Bénin), at Kamuka, Nsukka, Maku and Tangale Waja (Nigeria), and at Guere (Chad) (Grove and Sutton 1989; Widgren 2010).

To this list of terraced sites should be added the widespread use of mechanical water lifting devices (Adams 1989), as well as examples of flood recession farming such as in the Inland Niger Delta (Adams 1989) and the Firki plains to the west of Lake Chad (Connah 1985). Indeed, these last two examples illustrate a bias within summaries of African intensive agriculture (including that presented here), since both are potentially of considerable antiquity but are difficult to study archaeologically, as they rely upon the annual construction of channels and/or earthen bunds. Nevertheless, on the basis of evidence recovered from associated settlements, Connah (1985) considers that the cultivation of sorghum through flood recession techniques in Firki may have a history extending back to the early first millennium AD.

Widgren (2010: 333–5), however, also notes multiple instances of labour-intensive practices employed in a series of locations in the semi-arid plains stretching from Senegal to Nigeria; describing these economies as intensive due to their use of combinations of manuring, mulching, intercropping, soil ridging, and irrigation. This, it is argued, refutes the suggestion that intensive agriculture in West Africa is primarily associated with communities that were forced to retreat into isolated highland locations to avoid slave raiding, particularly over the last 500–600 years. However, from an archaeological perspective Widgren's observation reinforces concerns regarding the archaeological visibility of such activities: archaeobotanical evidence may reveal crop repertoires, but will not discern intercropping practices, fallowing regimes, or the function of apparent 'weed' species. Likewise the presence of channels, reservoirs, or certain features discemible through soil micromorphology may demonstrate irrigation, but say nothing of irrigation schedules, while chemical signatures or botanical remains may indicate manuring, but cannot demonstrate frequency of fertilization. Archaeological studies may therefore struggle to identify abandoned sites of this type. As importantly, these same factors make it very difficult to estimate yields even on sites where the presence of stone-built agricultural features strongly suggest intensification.

North Africa

With its links to the Mediterranean world, it is perhaps unsurprising that North Africa provides the clearest archaeological examples of intensification prompted by interactions with economies centred outside Africa, as with the introduction and subsequent local adoption of floodwater harvesting to feed wadi floor fields by Roman (or 'Romano-Libyan') farmers in northwest Libya between the late 1st and 7th centuries AD (Barker 2002). Further south in

FIG. 46.7 View west over a foggara at Taglit (Taqallit), near Ubari in Fezzan, southwest Libya (photograph courtesy of David Edwards, 2000).

Libya one might also look to the introduction of subterranean channels (known locally as *foggara* and in the Middle East as *qanat* or *falaj*) during the Garamantian period (*c.* 500 BC–AD 500) as an example of the role played by a technology developed outside Africa in the intensification of a pre-existing farming system, in this case the construction of many hundreds of *foggaras* often several kilometres long and up to 20 m deep in order to draw water from aquifers and supplement irrigation around oases (Mattingly 2000; Leone and Moussa, Ch. 53 below; Fig. 46.7).

Qanats, wadi-floor agriculture, and other forms of water and soil conservation are by no means limited to these comparatively early examples, as abandoned and maintained incidences of such practices from across northern Africa attest (Critchley et al. 1994). It is interesting to note, however, that these archaeological case studies from Libya present contrasting conclusions regarding the efficacy and sustainability of these two systems, with Barker (2002) arguing that palaeoenvironmental evidence indicates that Romano-Libyan farmers were able to produce and even export crops in a very low rainfall environment that is essentially the same as that today, whilst Mattingly (2000: 175) tentatively suggests that the decline of the Garamantian civilization may have been linked to over-exploitation of the non-renewing water supply contained in aquifers.

CONCLUDING REMARKS

Although organized geographically, the examples briefly introduced above are included primarily to illustrate the diversity in agricultural strategies across Africa and as a means to further explore themes common to the study of historic intensive agronomies both in Africa and elsewhere. This summary should in no way be seen as exhaustive; indeed, far more thorough gazetteers of African intensive archaeology are available. Some of these are aimed predominantly at an archaeological or historical audience (e.g. Sutton 1985; Grove and Sutton 1989; Widgren 2010), while others are targeted towards those interested in the developmental potential of apparently long-lived and sustainable 'traditional' practices (e.g. Adams and Anderson 1988; Adams 1989; Critchley et al. 1994). That this latter group remain interested in the possible extension or rehabilitation of such systems itself points to the potential relevance of archaeological data, but it should also be clear that much still needs to be done in order to refine our understanding of what drives and sustains individual examples of agricultural intensification across the continent (Stump 2010). It should be clear, too, that the range of trajectories displayed in the archaeological and historical record points to the significance of political, economic, and environmental contingencies, all of which are subject to changes through time.

REFERENCES

ADAMS, W. M. (1989). Definition and development in African indigenous irrigation. *Azania* 24: 21–7.

—— and ANDERSON, D.M. (1988). Irrigation before development: indigenous and induced change in agricultural water management in east Africa. *African Affairs* 87: 519–35.

AMBORN, H. (1989). Agricultural intensification in the Burji-Konso cluster of south western Ethiopia. *Azania* 24: 71–83.

BARKER, G. (2002). A tale of two deserts: contrasting desertification histories on Rome's desert frontiers. *World Archaeology* 33: 488–507.

BOSERUP, E. (1965). *The Conditions of Agricultural Growth: The Economics of Agrarian Change under Population Pressure*. London: Allen & Unwin.

BÖRJESON, L. (2007). Boserup backwards? Agricultural intensification as 'its own driving force' in the Mbulu Highlands, Tanzania. *Geografiska Annaler*, series B, *Human Geography* 89: 203–17.

CARNEIRO, R. L. (1970). A theory of the origin of the state. *Science* 169: 733–8.

CLARK, J. D. (1962). Africa, south of the Sahara. In R. Braidwood and G. Willey (eds), *Courses Towards Urban Life*. New York: Wenner Gren Foundation, 1–33.

CONNAH, G. (1985). Agricultural intensification and sedentism in the *firki* of N.E. Nigeria. In I. S. Farrington (ed.), *Prehistoric Intensive Agriculture in the Tropics*, pt 2. Oxford: British Archaeological Reports, 765–86.

—— (1987). *African Civilizations: Precolonial Cities and States in Tropical Africa: An Archaeological Perspective*. Cambridge: Cambridge University Press.

—— (1987). *African Civilisations: An Archaeological Perspective*, 2nd edn. Cambridge: Cambridge University Press.

CRITCHLEY, W. R. S., REIJ, C., and WILLCOCKS, T. J. (1994). Indigenous soil and water conservation: a review of the state of knowledge and prospects for building on traditions. *Land Degradation and Rehabilitation* 5: 293–314.

DAVIES, M. I. J. (2010a). A view from the east: an interdisciplinary 'historical ecology' approach to a contemporary agricultural landscape in northwest Kenya. *African Studies* 69: 323–43.

—— (2010b). From platforms to people: rethinking population estimates for the abandoned agricultural settlement at Engaruka, northern Tanzania. *Azania* 45: 203–13.

DELIUS, P., and SCHOEMAN, M. H. (2008). Revisiting Bokoni: populating the stone ruins of the Mpumalanga escarpment. In N. J. Swanepoel, A. Esterhuysen, and P. Bonner (eds) *Five Hundred Years Rediscovered: Southern African Precedents and Prospects*. Johannesburg: Wits University Press, 135–68.

EDWARDS, D. J. (2004). *The Nubian Past*. London: Routledge.

EHRET, C. (2002). *The Civilisations of Africa: A History to 1800*. Oxford: James Currey.

EWALD, J. (1990). *Soldiers, Traders, and Slaves: State Formation and Economic Transformation in the Greater Nile Valley, 1700–1885*. Madison: University of Wisconsin Press.

FARRINGTON, I. S. (1985). The wet, the dry and the steep: archaeological imperatives and the study of agricultural intensification. In I. S. Farrington (ed.), *Prehistoric Intensive Agriculture in the Tropics*. Oxford: British Archaeological Reports, 1–9.

GEERTZ, C. (1963). *Agricultural Involution: The Process of Ecological Change in Indonesia*. Berkeley: University of California Press.

GROVE, A. T., and SUTTON, J. E. G. (1989). Agricultural terracing south of the Sahara. *Azania* 24: 114–22.

HÄSER, J. (2000). *Siedlungsarchäologie in der Jebel Marra-Region Darfur/Sudan: Archaologischer Einsatz von Fernerkundungsdaten im Sahelgebiet*. Rahden: Marie Leidorf.

HASSAN, F. (1997). The dynamics of a riverine civilization: a geoarchaeological perspective on the Nile Valley, Egypt. *World Archaeology* 29: 51–74.

KOBISHCHANOV, Y. M. (1979). *Axum*. London: Pennsylvania State University Press

LAULUMAA, V. (2006). Estimates of the population of ancient Engaruka: a new approach. *Azania* 41: 95–102.

MACEACHERN, A. S. (2003). Du Kunde: processes of Montagnard ethnogenesis in the northern Mandara Mountains of Cameroon. http://www.mandaras.info/MandarasPublishing/MacEachern_DuKunde_PhD.pdf Website accessed 1 Feb. 2011.

MAGGS, T. M. O'C. (2008). The Mpumalanga Escarpment settlements: some answers, many questions. In N. J. Swanepoel, A. Esterhuysen, and P. Bonner (eds), *Five Hundred Years Rediscovered: Southern African Precedents and Prospects*. Johannesburg: Wits University Press, 169–81.

MAYOR, A., HUYSECOM, E., GALLAY, A., RASSE, M., and BALLOUCHE, A. (2005). Population dynamics and paleoclimate over the past 3000 years in the Dogon Country, Mali. *Journal of Anthropological Archaeology* 24: 25–61.

MATTINGLY, D. (2000). Twelve thousand years of human adaptation in Fezzan (Libyan Sahara). In G. Barker and D. Gilbertson (eds), *The Archaeology of Drylands: Living at the Margin*. London: Routledge, 156–73.

NETTING, R. (1993). *Smallholders, Householders: Farm Families and the Ecology of Intensive, Sustainable Development*. Stanford, Calif.: Stanford University Press.

SOPER, R. (2002). *Nyanga: Ancient Fields, Settlements and Agricultural History in Zimbabwe*. Nairobi: British Institute in Eastern Africa.

STUMP, D. (2006). The development and expansion of the field and irrigation system at Engaruka, Tanzania. *Azania* 41: 69–94.

—— (2010). Ancient and backward or long-lived and sustainable: the role of the past in debates concerning rural livelihoods and resource conservation in eastern Africa. *World Development* 38: 1251–62.

—— and TAGSETH, M. (2009). The history of precolonial and early colonial agriculture on Kilimanjaro: a review. In T. Clack (ed.), *Culture, History and Identity: Landscapes of Inhabitations in the Mount Kilimanjaro Area, Tanzania*. Oxford: Archaeopress, 107–24.

SULAS, F., MADELLA, M., and FRENCH, C. (2009). State formation and water resources management in the Horn of Africa: the Aksumite Kingdom of the Northern Ethiopian Highlands. *World Archaeology* 41: 2–15.

SUTTON, J. E. G. (1985). Irrigation and terracing in Africa. In I. S. Farrington (ed.), *Prehistoric Intensive Agriculture in the Tropics*. Oxford: British Archaeological Reports, 737–63.

—— (2004). Engaruka: the success and abandonment of an integrated irrigation system in an arid part of the Rift Valley, *c.* 15th to 17th centuries. In M. Widgren and J. E. G. Sutton (eds). *Islands of Intensive Agriculture in Eastern Africa.* Oxford: James Currey, 114–32.

TRIGGER, B. (1965). *History and Settlement in Lower Nubia.* New Haven, Conn.: Yale University Publications in Archaeology.

WIDGREN, M. (2010). Besieged palaeonegritics or innovative farmers: historical political ecology of intensive and terraced agriculture in West Africa and Sudan. *African Studies* 69: 323–43.

WITTFOGEL, K. (1957). *Oriental Despotism: A Comparative Study of Total Power.* New Haven, Conn.: Yale University Press.

PART VI

POWER, PRESTIGE, AND CONSUMPTION AFRICAN TOWNS AND STATES AND THEIR NEIGHBOURS

CHAPTER 47

THE ARCHAEOLOGY OF AFRICAN URBANISM

PAUL SINCLAIR

ARCHAEOLOGICAL APPROACHES TO AFRICAN URBANISM

URBANISM, and especially the origins and forms of cities and the links between urban origins and the emergence of political complexity, have fascinated archaeologists since the earliest days of the discipline. Africanists have often treated urbanism on the basis of generalizations from local and subregional studies (e.g. Hull 1976; Winters 1983; Shaw et al. 1993; Anderson and Rathbone 2000), and with reference to developments in other parts of the world. Uncritical application of trait lists developed elsewhere (especially the Near East), nonetheless, gave predictably few 'jackpot' examples of urban settlements in the early years of African archaeology, leading to derogatory comparisons from an evolutionist perspective between Africa and other continents, notwithstanding the more balanced appreciations developed by early archaeological explorations of southern Africa's Zimbabwe Culture (Pikirayi, Ch. 63 below) and confirmed by more recent fieldwork establishing the indigenous African origins of towns in areas as distant as Mali (McIntosh and McIntosh 1980) and East Africa's Swahili coast (La Violette, Ch. 62 below). Rather more rarely, but perhaps appropriately given the patchiness of available data and the complexity of the topic, has African urbanism been the subject of synthesis (but see Connah 2001, 2005; Coquery-Vidrovitch 2005).

Of particular importance in recent decades has been the work of Roland Fletcher (1995, 1998), who has provided the most sophisticated intra-site analytical frame so far for understanding the transition from mobile to sedentary societies and from agricultural settlements to urban agglomerations. Based upon extensive empirical comparisons from Africa and elsewhere, his works aim ultimately at cross-cultural insights. Fletcher identifies key intra-site variables (population size and settlement density) that are constrained in both mobile and sedentary cases by interaction and communication indices. Important transition constraints from mobile camps to sedentary settlements occur in relation to settlements of 1–2 ha in size, between agricultural settlements and urban sites at 100 ha, and from agricultural towns to large-scale urban agglomerations at 10,000 ha (100 km²). These are upper limits, however, and Africa's archaeological record has many examples of (for instance) agricultural towns that were less than 100 ha in extent.

Two other key developments have been the application of inter-site spatial analyses in countries as diverse as Mali (McIntosh and McIntosh 1980) and Zimbabwe (Sinclair 1987) and the initiation by the Urban Origins Project in Eastern Africa of 19 concurrent field projects focused on urbanism in nine eastern and southern African countries (Sinclair 1989). Many of these projects emphasized new investigative techniques such as geochemical analysis of soil phosphates, coring, and magnetometry, especially in those parts of urban sites lacking stone buildings (e.g. Radimilahy 1998).

Further developments in archaeological field survey, excavation, and analysis and the integration of documentary and oral evidence continue to transform the image of African urbanity. We now have available a battery of techniques to accomplish multi-scalar analysis of settlement systems, including satellite imagery, systematic and random sampling strategies for field survey and on-site surface collections, non-invasive geophysical mapping, larger-scale area excavations, and the more regular use of wet sieving and flotation to retrieve organic remains. They are matched by further developments on the theoretical front and new definitions of urbanism that now guide research in different regions. In West Africa, for instance, Andah (1999; Table 47.1) developed a more culturally specific set of urban criteria suitable for the Sudan, Sahel, and Guinea regions of West Africa, while in northeast Africa Fattovich (1999) stressed the importance of size (a quite large and dense population), diversity of function (craft, commercial, administrative, and cultural, together pointing to a complex social organization), and monumental buildings and/or an intended plan (stressing the authority of a central power). Similarly, in west-central Africa de Heusch (1982) and de Maret (1999) identified the central role of kingship and ritual in attracting large numbers of people.

More recently, questioning the ontological base of African archaeology, and linear evolutionism in particular, has led to recognition of the limitations of top-down/bottom-up dichotomies in framing social complexity and increasingly sophisticated treatments of hierarchical and lateral (heterarchical) forms of organization, especially in Mali's Inland Niger Delta (McIntosh 1999). Current work includes studies of how societies there responded to

Table 47.1 Characteristic criteria of urbanized sites in the Sudan, Sahel, and Guinea regions of West Africa (after Andah 1999)

One or several shrines located in the centre (later one of several mosques)

One palace in most cases fortified

A large centrally located market

A transportation depot or transit station

A military depot—sometimes centrally located (conquest or military centre)

A defensive (rather than a conquest) outpost

Predominance of a building style

A centrally located palace and market

A palace market and fortification

environmental change and even more sophisticated treatment of self-organizing systems (McIntosh 2005). This approach, which has great potential, owes much to the earlier work of Tainter (1988) and Crumley (1995; see also McIntosh et al. 2000; Allen et al. 2003), and is echoed by Curtis (2009) in regard to the settlement systems of the Eritrean coastal plain.

After this summary of different archaeological approaches to urbanism in Africa, some key themes are apparent, among them the need for inter- and intra-site analyses and an integrated view of socio-environmental interactions including energy regimes, economy, politics, and ideological organizing principles, all treated diachronically. This mirrors development of the concepts of eco-dynamics (McGlade 1995) and resilience theory (Walker et al. 2006). Archaeological applications on urbanism in Western Asia that consider several slow-moving variables operating on the macroscale also hold interest for modelling African urban systems (Redman and Kinzig 2003), though with the exception of a landscape-oriented application in south western Zimbabwe (Manyanga 2006) applications of resilience theory are still few. One particular limitation is the difficulty of integrating cultural and symbolic values and learned behaviour into the modelling process.

Historical contributions

Historians and other social scientists have also contributed to discussion and analysis of African urbanism. A notable example is the overview by Hull (1976), who from a mainly architectural and town planning standpoint distinguished 'spiritual', 'ceremonial', 'governance', 'refuge', and 'visionary' cities in pre-colonial Africa, explaining the expansion of urban complexes through a strong focus on governance and the physical and ideological projection of the power needed to appropriate surplus and control labour. The decline and disappearance of African cities, on the other hand, was attributed to such factors as environmental degradation, collapse of political superstructure, the succession of neighbouring cities, and external attack.

Hull's approach was criticized by Winters (1983), who provides a wide-ranging discussion on urban definitions and downplays the role of commerce, at least for early 'Black African' (*sic*) urbanism, to focus on political cities characterized by 'religiously sanctioned kingship'. Two other categories—'Islamic' and 'Post-Industrial'—are more strongly characterized by economic and commercial interests. This division between Black African, Islamic, and European categories underlies many treatments of urbanism (see below). While hardly doing justice to Africa's cultural and linguistic complexity, it finds echoes in the sixfold classification of O'Connor (1983), a geographer, whose analysis focused on Anglophone West Africa and the shift of population from rural to urban areas.

Despite the substantial historical systems theory contribution to the study of the Kongo kingdom by Ekholm (1972), sub-Saharan Africa was largely neglected by early contributions to World Systems theory (Benjamin 2006). More recent work has, however, emphasized the importance of considering Africa within this kind of perspective. Analyses by Beaujard (2005) of the western Indian Ocean and Kea (2004) of the western Sahel exemplify this, as does Chase Dunn and Willard's (1994) situation of the development of Cairo in relation to cities in western Asia.

Another approach that has stimulated discussion between historians and archaeologists is the concept of the 'city-state' as a small-scale, territorially based political unit suitable for interpreting African examples. First aired in African archaeology by Vérin (1992), the concept was more recently reintroduced by Abungu (1998), as well as in African contributions to Hansen (2003). More recently still, Coquery-Vidrovitch's (2005: 25) defined cities 'as a centre of dense human population and cultural diffusion and the conditions of its existence the inseparable economic and political means by which production and exchange are organised'. While merging her longstanding position on the importance of long-distance trade for the African mode of production and consequently urban formation with a newer focus on production, politics, and cultural form, this still misses out the roles of craft specialization and non-productive elites, as well as any assessment of the importance of ideological factors as centralizing tendencies in processes of urbanisation. As it stands, her definition remains insufficient for an integrated, cross-disciplinary treatment of African urbanism. The work of the *Annales* school of historians (Braudel 1972), with its interest in geographical and cultural perspectives including *mentalité*, does however provide a multi-scalar frame of reference more suited to integrating diachronic (*longue durée*) and synchronic archaeological and historical perspectives (*événements*). Developed in a landscape context for Roman North Africa by Johansson de Château (2009), this approach probably has considerable untapped potential elsewhere in the continent.

Towards an operational concept of urbanism

Drawing upon the concepts outlined above, the approach taken to urbanism here is inevitably tentative, as the necessary operational concepts have not yet been fully developed. We can, however, identify some that are desirable, including a multiscalar spatiotemporal framework, the importance of not restricting analytical perspectives to the confines of Africa alone, the necessity of integrating nature and society in ways that not only take the 'external' forcing mechanisms of climate change and constraints into account but also consider the effects of human action in inducing those changes. Moreover, while recognizing the value of synchronic comparisons and long-term diachronic perspectives, such general enquiries must not blind us to the rich mosaic of cultural variability manifested in urban settlement systems throughout Africa, and the critical input of decisions by individual social actors in bringing them about. Finally, cities cannot be understood in isolation (countrysides, ecosystems, networks of settlement, and trade networks are all essential components of successful analyses), nor should they necessarily be understood in (familiar?) hierarchical terms; lateral, heterarchical organizational forms also warrant consideration. With these thoughts in mind, let us now survey the variety of African urban experience.

The Nile Valley

The Nile Valley saw the earliest development of urbanism in Africa (Shaw, Ch. 50 below). Given the doubts expressed by Sjöberg (1960) on the existence of urbanism in Ancient Egypt, the past 50 years have seen remarkable developments in the field of urban studies that gainsay earlier suggestions that evidence had been destroyed, or rendered inaccessible, by centuries of flooding and silt deposition. Kemp (2006) and O'Connor (1993) provide excellent overviews, with fundamental contributions including those of Butzer (1976), Kemp (1977a, 1977b), Bietak (1979), and Hassan (1993), the latter integrating a detailed assessment of Nile flood levels and climate change with his analysis of the development of urban systems. Troy (1999) provides an overview of urbanism in the Nile valley and broader regional issues concerning environmental and cultural dynamics are discussed by Pedersen et al. (2010).

Predynastic towns include the serially hegemonic capitals of Naqada, Hierakonpolis, and Thinis in Upper Egypt (Hoffman et al. 1986), while contemporaries like Buto in the Delta were associated with early trade to the Near East. The typical spatial layout of these settlements and of later Early Dynastic/Old Kingdom ones shows a walled, relatively densely settled core with functionally differentiated ritual, administrative, and production sectors (Hassan 1993). Subsequently, some Middle Kingdom towns like Kahun were planned on a grid system, while fortress towns such as Dabba in the eastern Delta or Buhen in Lower Nubia were also established. Later, some New Kingdom towns expanded significantly in size and complexity, dominated by the twin themes of kingship and ritual cults. The short-lived royal capital of Akhenaten at Amarna provides especially detailed insights into urban layout. Examples include Thebes, Heliopolis, and Memphis, the latter founded, according to tradition, by the founder of the First Dynasty as an administrative centre at the juncture between Upper and Lower Egypt.

O'Connor's (1993) southward extension of the analytical frame of early Nile Valley urbanism brings into sharp focus the now largely submerged urban history of Lower Nubia, though post-flooding excavations at Qasr Ibrim have established the incredibly long duration of its urban history from the first millennium BC into the modern period (Alexander 1988). The major contribution of recent decades must, however, be the excavations at Kerma, which have provided significant new detail on sub-Saharan Africa's first urban settlement (Bonnet 1990). Subsequent to this Bronze Age instance and Egypt's New Kingdom annexation of most of Nubia, a gradual southward shift of urban development is apparent, first to Napata and then to Meroe, both capitals of the kingdom of Kush (Welsby, Ch. 51 below). The possibility that this was encouraged by the vulnerability of urban centres to climatic change compounded by human actions, such as over-grazing, salinization affecting agriculture, and/or depletion of firewood, especially through metalworking, merits investigation.

THE MAGHREB

Urbanism along the North African coast has long been perceived as directly linked to the expansion of Phoenician, Greek, and Punic trade settlements during the first millennium BC and the subsequent conquest of the whole littoral by Rome (Krings 1995; Peyras and Tirologos 1999), though much remains to be done to elucidate the early transformations of farming communities into urban societies (Leone and Moussa, Ch. 53). Carthage itself became one of the Roman Empire's largest cities, on a par with Alexandria to its east, though precisely how it maintained itself from the resources of the surrounding landscape warrants further attention (Merrills 2004; cf. Johansson de Château 2009). Excellent preservation, of course, makes North Africa one of the most informative areas for studying Roman urbanism as a whole (e.g. Sorel 1973/4). That most of today's major urban centres have been continuously occupied since soon after North Africa's conquest by the Arabs in the 7th/early 8th centuries, if not before, renders extensive archaeological investigation less than easy, but the work of Redman (1986) at the coastal town of Qasr es Seghir, Morocco, illustrates what is possible under favourable circumstances.

THE SAHEL

In his overview of African civilizations Connah (2001) points to the African savannahs as being highly favourable for the development of complex societies. Bivar and Shinnie's (1962) pioneering contribution to the study of urbanism in the central Sahel was followed by Connah (1981) and Breunig (Breunig et al. 1996) in the Lake Chad Basin and by Effah-Gyamfi (1985) and Haour (2003) in Hausaland. Further west, some of the earliest aggregated sedentary settlements come from the Dhar Tichitt region of southeastern Mauritania in the late second millennium BC (MacDonald, Ch. 57 below), while the transformational work of McIntosh and McIntosh (1980) established that towns like Jenné-jeno in Mali's Inland Niger Delta not only significantly pre-date the establishment of trade with Muslim North Africa, but may also have been organized in non-hierarchical ways that undermine traditional evolutionist trajectories and classifications (McIntosh 1999). Their work was later expanded to the Senegal Valley (McIntosh and McIntosh 1992) and was built on by others elsewhere along the Middle Niger (e.g. Bedaux et al. 2005). Such towns were involved in long-distance trade, including increasingly trade across the Sahara, and much effort has also been expended on investigating settlements particularly associated with that commerce, notably at Tegdaoust (the ancient Awdaghost; summarized by Holl 2006) and Koumbi Saleh (Berthier 1997) in Mauritania and, more recently, Essouk (the ancient Tadmakka) in northern Mali (Nixon 2009).

THE GUINEAN ZONE

Forests, with their restrictions on site visibility, are difficult places for archaeologists to work in, and West Africa is no exception. This region nevertheless saw significant precolonial urban development, especially in southern Nigeria and Ghana (Andah 1976, 1999; Ogundiran, Ch. 59 below). The extensive earthwork complexes surrounding sites such as Benin (Connah 1975) and Old Oyo (Agbaje-Williams 1983) merit particular mention, as do those of Igbomina (Usman 2004) and the principal Yoruba city, Ife (Willet 1970; Ogundiran 2003). Given the previous lack of detailed intra-site surveys, new initiatives applying methods such as phosphate testing to investigate this aspect of West African urbanism are particularly welcome (e.g. Folorunso et al. 2008). Indigenous processes of synoecism and population growth were probably important factors in driving urban development here, but some towns, notably Begho (Anquandah 1993) and Bono Manso

(Effah-Gyamfi 1985) at the forest–savannah ecotone in Ghana, thrived through their role in long-distance trade networks linking north to the Middle Niger and beyond. Shared characteristics of these towns include walling, nucleated markets, and division into ethnically defined neighbourhoods.

THE ETHIOPIAN HIGHLANDS

The Ethiopian Highlands and their nearby coastal lowlands are justly famous for the massive stone stelae of Aksum and the rock-cut churches of Lalibela, strong symbols of African civilization (Munro-Hay 1991; Phillipson, Ch. 55 below). Aksum itself has been relatively extensively explored, but other Aksumite towns less so—a bias in focus seen in early archaeological efforts in eastern and southern Africa as well. A particular characteristic of Ethiopian kingship in medieval times was the emphasis on large, mobile settlements associated with the imperial court (Horvath 1969) that provided the stimulus for analyses of mobile kingship in early medieval Europe (Peyer 1964). Little or nothing has been excavated at contemporary Islamic towns in Ethiopia or Eritrea, though the plan and architecture of Harar in the east of Ethiopia have received attention (Hecht 1982; Ahmed 1990).

THE GREAT LAKES REGION AND THE CENTRAL AFRICAN INTERIOR

In both these areas of Africa, large settlements associated with precolonial kingdoms arose largely, if not wholly, independently of long-distance, transcontinental trade. In Uganda, Ntusi had reached 100 ha by the 15th century, in part using cattle as a reservoir of wealth and patronage for emerging elites (Sutton 1998; Reid, Ch. 61 below). More recent, mid-19th-century capitals, such as Rubaga and Mutesa, seem to have been highly structured, but were occupied only briefly. In Buganda, for instance, oral traditions indicate that the capital was moved ten times in little more than a generation. Significantly, too, when considering communication and transport constraints, many inhabitants seem to have been only part-time residents (Reid 1999).

In both the Great Lakes region and Central Africa buildings were made from perishable materials such as timber, grass, and daub. In the latter region, the kingdom of Kongo, centred in northwestern Angola, has received most attention (e.g. Ekholm 1972), including discussion of the stone buildings (mostly churches and other religious foundations) constructed after contact with the Portuguese in the late 1400s (Thornton 2000). Sadly, Kongo's capital, Mbanza Kongo (modern São Salvador), remains almost wholly unexplored archaeologically (de Maret 1982), but throughout Central Africa most towns had a central royal area surrounded by extensive settlement areas in which individual households maintained gardens and fields for their own subsistence (de Maret 1999). Royal prestige, ideology, and ritual were key attractors of population aggregation.

THE EAST AFRICAN COAST AND
WESTERN INDIAN OCEAN

Studies of urbanism in these regions are inextricably connected with the archaeology of the Swahili (La Violette, Ch. 62 below), beginning with the pioneering contributions of Kirkman (1954, 1963) at Gedi and Chittick (1974, 1984) at Kilwa and Manda, and also at Mogadishu (Chittick 1982), plus the comparative architectural studies of Garlake (1966). Subsequent work (e.g. Horton 1996) has dispelled the conclusions of these early studies that Swahili urbanism was some form of colonial implant from the Middle East, but until recently urban archaeology was undoubtedly focused too narrowly on the stone-built quarters of more elite sections of the community and major public buildings (mosques, palaces) to the exclusion of residential zones where poorer people constructed homes in perishable materials (Kusimba 1999). Several projects have now begun redressing this imbalance (La Violette, Ch. 62 below). In another development, Wilson's (1982) detailed spatial analysis, which demonstrated the presence of settlement hierarchies in some regions of the coast, is now being complemented by research focused on the rural hinterlands of key urban sites, such as Kilwa (Wynne-Jones 2007) and the island settlement complexes of e.g. Pemba (La Violette and Fleisher 2009; Fleisher 2010). Participation in trading networks that spanned the western Indian Ocean (Beaujard 2005) was important in driving urbanization, but La Violette and Fleisher (2009) also note from their work on Pemba that village aggregation into towns may also have been influenced by the attractive and binding capacity of Islam.

The Swahili world extended beyond the African mainland to the Comores, where small, walled towns were established in the late first millennium AD. Research suggests that settlements cycled between coastal and more inland locations in response to shifts in local land use dynamics (including soil erosion) and long-distance trade (Allibert et al. 1983; Wright 1984). On the northwest coast of the much larger island of Madagascar, Radimilahy (1998, Ch. 65 below) has continued earlier studies by Vérin (1996), with a particular focus on the walled town of Mahilaka. Inland, on Madagascar's central plateau other important studies have focused on detailed mapping of evolving settlement patterns around Antananarivo, capital of both the modern state and the 19th-century precolonial Merina kingdom (Wright 2007). One interesting long-term trend is that towards a decreasing use of timber and increasing use of mudbrick through the second millennium AD, perhaps linked to gradual deforestation for land clearance, firewood, building, and iron smelting (Rakotovololona 1990).

SOUTHERN AFRICA

In the forest woodland of Zambia's copperbelt, settlement systems seem to have been heterarchical more than centralized, with chiefly settlements large but short-lived (Bisson 1992; Fletcher 1998). Further south, on and around the Zimbabwe Plateau, however, elites came during the second millennium AD to reside within stone-walled enclosures that served to delineate them from the rest of the population. Great Zimbabwe is but the largest and most impressive of several hundred such sites found in Zimbabwe and adjacent areas of Botswana,

Mozambique, and South Africa (Huffman 1996; Pikirayi 2001, Ch. 63 below). Inter-site spatial analyses support arguments that Great Zimbabwe, together with its Mapungubwe predecessor and Torwa and Mutapa successors (the former focused first at Khami and then at Danangombe) were politically organized at a state level of complexity (Huffman 1986; Sinclair 1987; Sinclair et al. 1993; Pikirayi et al. 2010). Particularly interesting historical archaeological insights into issues of urbanism are provided by recent work at Tswana towns (Schoeman, Ch. 64 below), for instance Kaditshwene (Boeyens 2003) and Marothodi (Anderson 2009) and their possible predecessors Lose and Bosutswe (Denbow et al. 2008). Mirroring earlier concerns on the Swahili coast, however, comparatively little work has yet been undertaken, or published, on non-elite sectors of the major settlements, making population estimates imprecise (Sinclair 1987). Moreover, bearing in mind the arguments of Fletcher (1995, 1998), it is possible that not all areas of these sites were occupied at the same time and that not all residents were present throughout the year.

REFERENCES

ABUNGU, G. (1998). City States of the East African coast and their maritime contacts. In G. Connah (ed.), *Transformations in Africa: Essays on Africa's Later Past*. London: Leicester University Press, 204–18.

AGBAJE-WILLIAMS, B. (1983). A contribution to the archaeology of Old Oyo. Ph.D thesis, University of Ibadan.

AHMED, A. M. (1990). A survey of the Harar Djugel (wall) and its gates. *Journal of Ethiopian Studies* 23: 321–34.

ALEXANDER, J. A. (1988). The Saharan divide in the Nile Valley: the evidence from Qasr Ibrim. *African Archaeological Review* 6: 73–90.

ALLIBERT, C., ARGANT, A., and ARGANT, J. (1983). Le site de Bagamoyo (Mayotte, archipel des Comores). *Études Océan Indien* 2: 5–40.

ALLEN T. F. H., TAINTER, J. A., and HOEKSTRA, T. A. (1999). Systems supply-side sustainability research and behavioral science. *Systems Research* 16: 403–27.

—— —— —— (2003). *Supply-Side Sustainability*. New York: Columbia University Press.

ANDAH, B. (1976). An archaeological view of the urbanisation process in the earliest West African states. *Journal of the Historical Society of Nigeria* 8: 1–20.

—— (1995). Early urban societies and settlements of the Guinea and savannah regions of West Africa. *West African Journal of Archaeology* 25: 103–52.

ANDAH, B. (1999). Genesis and development of settlements in the Guinea and savanna regions. In Sinclair (1999).

ANDERSON, D., and RATHBONE, R. (eds) (2000). *Africa's Urban Past*. Oxford: James Currey.

ANDERSON, M. S. (2009). *Marothodi: The Historical Archaeology of an African Capital*. Woodford: Atikan Media.

ANQUANDAH, J. (1993). Urbanisation and state formation in Ghana during the Iron Age. In Shaw et al. (1993: 642–51).

BEAUJARD, P. (2005). The Indian Ocean in Eurasian and African world-systems before the sixteenth century. *Journal of World History* 16: 411–65.

BEDAUX, R., POLET, J., SANOGO, K., and SCHMIDT, A. (eds) (2005). *Recherches Archéologiques à Dia dans le Delta Intérieur du Niger (Mali): Bilan des Saisons de Fouilles 1998–2003*. Leiden: CNWS.

BENJAMIN, J. (2006). The world and Africa: World Systems theories and the erasure of East Africa from world history. *World History Bulletin* 22: 20–7.

BERTHIER, S. (1997). *Recherches Archéologiques sur la Capitale de l'Émpire de Ghana*. Oxford: Archaeopress.

BIETAK, M. (1979). Urban archaeology and the 'town problem'. In K. Weeks (ed.), *Egyptology and the Social Sciences*. Cairo: American University in Cairo Press, 95–144.

BISSON, M. (1992). A survey of Late Stone Age and Iron Age sites at Luano, Zambi. *World Archaeology* 24: 234–48.

BIVAR, A. D. H., and SHINNIE, P. L. (1962). Ancient Kanuri capitals. *Journal of African History* 3: 1–10.

BOEYENS, J. (2003). The Iron Age sequence in the Marico and early Tswana history. *South African Archaeological Bulletin* 58: 63–78.

BONNET, C. (ed.) (1990). *Kerma, Royaume de Nubie*. Geneva: Musée d'Art et Histoire.

BRAUDEL, F. (1972). *The Mediterranean and the Mediterranean World in the Age of Philip II*. London: Collins.

BREUNIG, P., NEUMANN, K., and VAN NEER, W. (1996). New research on the Holocene settlement and environment of the Chad Basin in Nigeria. *African Archaeological Review* 13: 111–45.

BUTZER, K. W. (1976). *Early Hydraulic Civilization in Egypt: A Study in Cultural Ecology*. Chicago: University of Chicago Press.

CHASE DUNN, C., and WILLARD, A. (1994). Cities in the central political/military network since CE 1200: size hierarchy and domination. *Comparative Civilizations Review* 30: 104–32.

CHITTICK, H. N. (1974). *Kilwa: An Islamic Trading City on the East African Coast*. Nairobi: British Institute in Eastern Africa.

—— (1982). Medieval Mogadish. *Paideuma* 28: 44–6.

—— (1984). *Manda: Excavations At An Island Port On The Kenya Coast*. Nairobi: British Institute In Eastern Africa.

CONNAH, G. (1975). *The Archaeology of Benin: Excavations and other Researches in and around Benin City, Nigeria*. Oxford: Oxford University Press.

—— (1981). *Three Thousand Years in Africa: Man and his Environment in the Lake Chad Region of Nigeria*. Cambridge: Cambridge University Press.

—— (2001). *African Civilizations*. Cambridge: Cambridge University Press.

—— (2005). Holocene Africa. In C. Scarre (ed.), *The Human Past*. London: Thames & Hudson, 350–91.

COQUERY-VIDROVITCH, C. (2005). *The History of African Cities South of the Sahara*. Princeton, NJ: Markus Weiner.

CRUMLEY, C. (1995). Heterarchy and the analysis of complex societies. *Archaeological Papers of the American Anthropological Association* 6: 1–5.

CURTIS, M. (2009). Relating the Ancient Ona culture to the wider northern Horn: discerning pattern and problems in the archaeology of the first millennium BC. *African Archaeological Review* 26: 327–250.

DE HEUSCH, L. (1982). *The Drunken King or the Origin of the State*. Bloomington: Indiana University Press.

DE MARET, P. (1982). The Iron Age in the west and south. In F. Van Noten (ed.), *The Archaeology of Central Africa*. Graz: Akademische Druck- und Verlagsanstalt, 77–96.

—— (1999). Urban origins in central Africa: the case of Congo. In Sinclair (1999). Website accessed 12 Jan. 2010.

DENBOW, J., SMITH, J., NDOBOCHANI, N.M., ATWOOD, K., and MILLER, D. (2008). Archaeological excavations at Bosutswe, cultural chronology, paleoecology and economy. *Journal of Archaeological Science* 35: 459–80.

EFFAH-GYAMFI, K. (1985). *Bono Manso: An Archaeological Investigation into Early Akan Urbanism*. Calgary: University of Calgary Press.

—— (1986). Ancient urban sites in Hausaland: a preliminary report. *West African Journal of Archaeology* 16: 117–34.

EKHOLM, K. (1972). *Power and Prestige: The Rise and Fall of the Kongo Kingdom*. Uppsala: Skriv Service.

FATTOVICH, R. (1999). The development of urbanism in the northern Horn of Africa in ancient and medieval times. In Sinclair (1999).

FLEISHER, J. (2010). Swahili synoecism: rural settlements and town formation on the central East African coast, AD 750–1500. Journal of Field Archaeology 35: 265–82.

FLETCHER, R. J. (1995). *Limits of Settlement Growth: Theoretical Outline*. Cambridge: Cambridge University Press.

—— (1998). African urbanism: scale, mobility and transformations. In G. Connah (ed.), *Transformations in Africa: Essays on Africa's Later Past*. London: Leicester University Press, 104–38.

FOLORUNSO, C. A., OYELARAN, P. A., TUBOSUN, B. J., and AJEKIGBE, P. G. (2008). Revisiting old Oyo: report on an interdisciplinary field study. http://cohesion.rice.edu/CentersAndInst/SAFA/emplibrary/Folorunsoetal,C.SAfA2006.pdf; website accessed 12 Jan. 2010.

GARLAKE, P. S. (1966). *The Early Islamic Architecture of the East African Coast*. Nairobi: British Institute in Eastern Africa.

HANSEN, M. H. (ed.) (2003). *A Comparative Study of Thirty City-State Cultures*. Copenhagen: Royal Danish Academy of Sciences and Letters.

HAOUR, A. (2003). *Ethnoarchaeology in the Zinder Region, Republic of Niger: The Site of Kufan Kanawa*. Oxford: Archaeopress.

HASSAN, F. (1993). Town and village in Ancient Egypt: ecology, society and urbanization. In Shaw et al. (1993: 551–86).

HECHT, E.-D. (1982). The city of Harar and the traditional Harar house. *Journal of Ethiopian Studies* 15: 56–78.

HOFFMAN, M. A., HAMROUSH, H. A., and ALLEN, R. O. (1986). A model of urban development for the Hierakonpolis region from Predynastic through Old Kingdom times. *Journal of the American Research Center in Egypt* 23: 175–87.

HOLL, A. F. C. (2006). *West African Early Towns: Archaeology of Households in Urban Landscapes*. Ann Arbor: University of Michigan Museum of Anthropology.

HORTON, M. (1996). *Shanga: The Archaeology of a Muslim Trading Community on the Coast of East Africa*. Nairobi: British Institute in Eastern Africa.

HORVATH, R. (1969). The wandering capitals of Ethiopia. *Journal of African History* 10: 205–19.

HUFFMAN, T. N. (1986). Iron Age settlement patterns and the origins of class distinction in southern Africa. *Advances in World Archaeology* 5: 291–338.

—— (1996). *Snakes and Crocodiles: Power and Symbolism in Ancient Zimbabwe*. Johannesburg: Witwatersrand University Press.

HULL, R. W. (1976). *African Cities and Towns before the European Conquest*. New York: W. W. Norton.

JOHANSSON DE CHÂTEAU, L. (2009). *Roman and Native Colonialism and the Archaeology of Rural Water Management in the Maghreb*. Uppsala: Uppsala University Press.

KEA, R. A. (2004). Expansions and contractions, world historical change and the western Sudan world-system *c.* 1200/1000 BC–1200/1250 AD. *Journal of World Systems Research* 3: 723–816.

KEMP, B. (1977a). The city of el-Amarna as a source for the study of urban society in Ancient Egypt. *World Archaeology* 9: 124–39.

—— (1977b). The early development of towns in Egypt. *Antiquity* 51: 185–200.

—— (2006). *Ancient Egypt: Anatomy of a Civilization.* London: Routledge.

—— and STEVENS, A. (2011). *Busy Lives at Amarna: Excavations in the Main City (Grid 12 and the house of Ranefer, N49.18)*, vol. 1: *The Excavations, Architecture and Environmental Remains.* London: Egyptian Exploration Society.

KIRKMAN, J. (1954). *The Arab City of Gedi: Excavations at the Great Mosque, Architecture and Finds.* Oxford: Oxford University Press.

—— (1963). *Gedi: The Palace.* The Hague: Mouton.

KRINGS, V. (ed.) (1995). *La Civilisation Phénicienne et Punique.* Leiden: E. J. Brill.

KUSIMBA, C. (1999). *The Rise and Fall of Swahili States.* Walnut Creek, Calif.: AltaMira Press.

LA VIOLETTE, A., and FLEISHER, J. (2009). The urban history of a rural place: Swahili archaeology on Pemba Island, Tanzania, 700–1500 AD. *International Journal of African Historical Studies* 42: 433–55.

MAGGS, T. M. O'C. (1976). *Iron Age Communities of the Southern Highveld.* Pietermaritzburg: Natal Museum.

MANYANGA, M. (2006). *Resilient Landscapes: Socio-Environmental Dynamics in the Shashi-Limpopo Basin, Southern Zimbabwe c. AD 800 to the Present.* Uppsala: Uppsala University Press.

McGLADE, J. (1995). Archaeology and the ecodynamics of human-modified landscapes. *Antiquity* 69: 113–32.

McINTOSH, R. J. (2005). *Ancient Middle Niger Urbanism and the Self-Organising Landscape.* Cambridge: Cambridge University Press.

—— TAINTER, J., and McINTOSH, S. K. (eds) (2000). *The Way the Wind Blows: Climate, History and Human Action.* New York: Columbia University Press.

McINTOSH, S. K. (1995). *Excavations at Jenné-Jeno, Hambarketolo, and Kaniana (Inland Niger Delta, Mali): The 1981 Season.* Berkeley: University of California Press.

—— (1999). Modeling political organization in large-scale settlement clusters: a case study from the Inland Niger Delta. In S. K. Mcintosh (ed.), *Beyond Chiefdoms: Pathways to Complexity in Africa.* Cambridge: Cambridge University Press, 66–79.

—— and McINTOSH, R. J. (1980). *Prehistoric Investigations in the Region of Jenné, Mali: A Study in the Development of Urbanism in the Sahel.* Oxford: British Archaeological Reports.

—— —— (1992). Cities without citadels: understanding urban origins along the middle Niger. In T. Shaw, P. J. J. Sinclair, B. Andah, and A. Okpoko (eds), *The Archaeology of Africa: Food, Metals and Towns.* London: Routledge, 622–41.

MERRILLS, A. H. (2004). *Vandals, Romans and Berbers: New Perspectives on Late Antique North Africa.* Aldershot: Ashgate.

MUNRO-HAY, S. (1991). *Aksum: An African Civilization of Late Antiquity.* Edinburgh: Edinburgh University Press.

NIXON, S. (2009). Excavating Essouk-Tadmakka (Mali): new archaeological investigations of early trans-Saharan trade. *Azania: Archaeological Research in Africa* 44: 217–55.

O'CONNOR, A. (1983). *The African City.* London: Hutchinson.

O'CONNOR, D. (1993). Urbanism in Bronze Age Egypt and northeast Africa. In Shaw et al. (1993: 570–86).

OGUNDIRAN, A. (2003). Chronology, material culture and pathways to the cultural history of Yoruba–Edo region, 500 B.C.–A.D., 1899. In T. Falola and C. Jennings (eds), *Sources and Methods in African History: Spoken, Written and Unearthed*. Rochester, NY: University of Rochester Press.

PEDERSÉN, O., SINCLAIR, P. J. J., HEINE, I., and ANDERSSON, J. (2010). Cities and urban landscapes in the Ancient Near East and Egypt, with special focus on the city of Babylon. In P. J. J. Sinclair, G. Nordquist, F. Herschend, and C. Isendahl (eds), *The Urban Mind: Cultural and Environmental Dynamics*. Uppsala: Department of Archaeology and Ancient History, 113–47.

PEYER, H. C. (1964). Das Reisekönigtum des Mittelalters. *Vierteljahrschrift für Sozial- und Witschaftgeschichte* 51: 1–21.

PEYRAS, J., and TIROLOGOS, G. (eds) (1999). *L'Afrique du Nord Antique: cultures et paysages*. Besançon: Presses Universitaires de Franche-Comté.

PIKIRAYI, I. (2001). *The Zimbabwe Culture*. Walnut Creek, Calif.: AltaMira Press.

—— MANYANGA, M., and CHIRIKURE, S. (2010). Conceptualizing the urban mind in pre-European southern Africa: rethinking Mapungubwe and Great Zimbabwe. In P. J. J. Sinclair, G. Nordquist, F. Herschend, and C. Isendahl (eds), *The Urban Mind: Cultural and Environmental Dynamics*. Uppsala: Department of Archaeology and Ancient History, 573–90.

RADIMILAHY, C. (1998). *Mahilaka: An Archaeological Investigation of an Early Town in Northwestern Madagascar*. Uppsala: Uppsala University Press.

RAKOTOVOLOLONA, S. (1990). Premiers résultats de la fouille d'Ankadivory. In P. J. J. Sinclair and J. A. Rakotoarisoa (eds), *Urban Origins in Eastern Africa: Proceedings of the 1989 Madagascar Workshop*. Stockholm: Swedish Central Board of National Antiquities, 85–90.

REDMAN, C. L. (1986). *Qsar es Seghir: An Archaeological View of Medieval Life*. New York: Academic Press.

—— and KINZIG, A. P. (2003). Resilience of past landscapes: resilience theory, society and the *longue durée. Conservation Ecology* 7(1): 14. http://www.consecol.org/vol7/iss1/art14/

REID, A. (1999). The character of urbanism in inter-lacustrine eastern Africa. In Sinclair (1999).

SHAW, T., SINCLAIR, P. J. J., ANDAH, B., and OKPOKO, B. (eds) (1993). *The Archaeology of Africa: Food, Metals and Towns*. London: Routledge.

SINCLAIR, P. J. J. (1987). *Space, Time and Social Formation: A Territorial View of Archaeology and Anthropology in Zimbabwe and Mozambique 0–1700 AD*. Uppsala: Societas Archaeologica Upsaliensis.

—— (1989). Urban origins in eastern Africa: a regional cooperation project. *World Archaeological Bulletin* 3: 3–51.

—— (ed.) (1999). *The Development of Urbanism from a Global Perspective: Proceedings of the Second World Archaeological Congress Intercongress, Mombasa*. http://www.arkeologi.uu.se/afr/projects/BOOK/default.htm. Website accessed 12 Jan. 2010.

—— PIKIRAYI, I., PWITI, G., and SOPER, R. (1993). Urban trajectories on the Zimbabwean plateau. In Shaw et al. (1993: 705–31).

SJÖBERG, G. (1960). *The Pre-Industrial City, Past and Present*. Glencoe, Ill.: Free Press.

SOREL, D. (1973/4). La pénétration romaine en Afrique du Nord dans l'Antiquité. Un exemple: Timgad jusqu'à la mort de l'Empereur Trajan. *Options Méditerranéennes* 18: 35–9.

SUTTON, J. E. G. (1998). Ntusi and Bigo: farmers, cattle-herders and rulers in western Uganda, AD 1000–1500. *Azania* 33: 39–72.

TAINTER, J. (1988). *The Collapse of Complex Societies*. Cambridge: Cambridge University Press.

THORNTON, J. R. (2000). Mbaanza Kongo/São Salvador: Kongo's holy city. In D. Anderson and R. Rathbone (eds), *Africa's Urban Past*. Oxford: James Currey, 67–84.

TROY, L. (1999). Resource management and ideological manifestation: the towns and cities of ancient Egypt. In Sinclair (1999).

USMAN, A. (2004). On the frontier of Empire: understanding the enclosed walls in Northern Yoruba, Nigeria. *Journal of Anthropological Archaeology* 23: 119–32.

VÉRIN, P. (1992). États ou cités-états dans le nord de Madagascar. *Taloha* 11: 65–71.

—— (1996). *The History of Civilisation in North Madagascar*. Rotterdam: A. A. Balkema.

WALKER, B. H., KINZIG, A. P., ANDERIES, J. M., and RYAN, P. (eds) (2006). Exploring resilience in social ecological systems: comparative studies and theory development. *Ecology and Society* 11: guest editorial.

WHEATLEY, P. (1970). The significance of traditional Yoruba urbanism. *Comparative Studies in Social History* 12: 393–423.

WILLET, F. (1970). Ife and its archaeology. In J. D. Fage and R. Oliver (eds), *Papers in African Prehistory*. Cambridge: Cambridge University Press, 303–26.

WILSON, T. H. (1982). Spatial analysis and settlement patterns on the East African Coast. *Paideuma* 28: 201–19.

WINTERS, C. (1983). The classification of traditional African cities. *Journal of Urban History* 10: 3–31.

WRIGHT, H. T. (1984). Early seafarers of the Comoro Islands: the Dembeni phase of the IX–Xth centuries AD. *Azania* 19: 13–60.

—— (ed.) (2007). *Early State Formation in Central Madagascar: An Archaeological Survey of Western Avaradrano*. Ann Arbor: University of Michigan Museum of Anthropology.

WYNNE-JONES, S. (2007). Creating urban communities at Kilwa Kisiwani, Tanzania, AD 800–1300. *Antiquity* 81: 363–80.

CHAPTER 48

....

THE ARCHAEOLOGY OF THE PRECOLONIAL STATE IN AFRICA

....

J. CAMERON MONROE

INTRODUCTION

....

THE study of the early state holds a central place in global archaeology, and Africa is no exception. For much of the 20th century scholars commonly argued that precolonial African states were the product of Mediterranean, Near Eastern, or European intervention and were thus of little analytical value to scholars seeking to identify the processes of cultural evolution unobstructed by outside influences. This argument is now correctly viewed as the product of an explicitly racist colonial ideology that sought historical precedent for colonial 'civilizing' projects. As archaeologists have moved from focusing on pristine origins to issues of political processes, and from outlining universal evolutionary trajectories to variable pathways towards social complexity, the histories of state formation in Africa emerge as ideal contexts in which to explore the dynamics of social complexity and political centralization in comparative perspective. This chapter outlines how archaeologists have examined and could examine the precolonial state in Africa. It begins by sketching colonial-era discourse on the nature of state and civilization in Africa, and then discusses how a comparative approach focusing on the nature of power has much to offer our understanding of political process in precolonial African contexts. It also examines major 'hotbeds' of state formation within four broadly defined subregions of the continent: northeast, southeast, central and western Africa (Fig. 48.1). By necessity, this discussion glosses much of the detail provided in subsequent chapters of this Handbook, and some important centres are excluded for lack of space. Throughout, the emphasis is on how indigenous political entrepreneurs articulated both local and exotic sources of power, a process that shaped the political contours of early states in Africa dramatically.

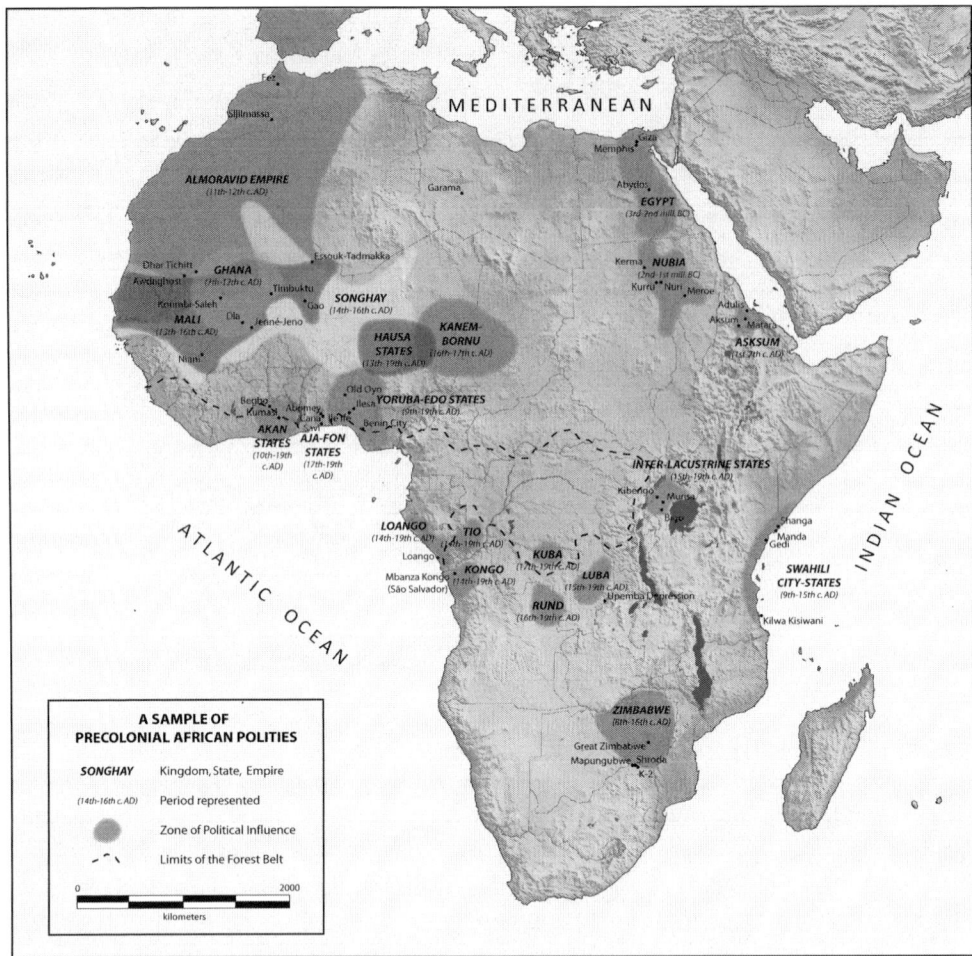

FIG. 48.1 Precolonial African states and sites mentioned in the text. The map presents only a sample of the total number of such polities that emerged in Africa in the precolonial era. Additionally, shaded areas represent our current understanding of maximal zones of political influence, rather than clear territorial boundaries, which rarely existed in precolonial polities.

COLONIAL MYTHS OF THE AFRICAN STATE

African archaeology emerged in the late 19th and early 20th centuries alongside European colonial expansion across the continent (Stahl 1999; Robertshaw 1990)—a legacy with enduring implications for the study of precolonial African states. European expansion was marked by numerous encounters with African polities, both ancient and modern, that brought African states to world attention. Many such polities did not fit then-accepted models of civilization, defined in terms of a set of achievements associated with literacy and civic life (Morgan 1985). In the absence of clear evidence for 'civilization' so defined, the study of the precolonial African state became enmeshed in colonial ideologies that cast Africa as a recipient of cultural progress developed elsewhere. Political institutions, irrigation, metallurgy, monumental art and architecture—indeed, all the then-recognized trappings of civilization (Childe 1936)—were attributed to Mediterranean or Near Eastern influences. African culture was thus defined by stagnation and inertia, flowering only when stimulated by racially superior foreign conquerors. This interpretation not only supported the imperialist logic of European colonial enterprises in Africa (Fagan 1981; Schrire et al. 1986) but also contributed to recent ethnic strife and genocide (Eltringham 2006). However, little corroborating evidence could be marshalled for actual contact between northern cultures and those of Africa south of the Sahara in antiquity, rendering their long-term influence on scholarship short-lived (Posnansky 1966, 1982).

The same was not the case, however, for societies of the Swahili Coast and of the central and western Sahel, for which historical and material evidence for contact with the medieval Islamic world was clear. Near Eastern chroniclers documented networks of expansive cities and states ruled by powerful kings, which flourished across these regions during the late first and early second millennia AD (Bovill 1958; Levtzion 1973). Archaeological excavation in such cities has, furthermore, revealed the presence of both large quantities of Near Eastern trade goods and evidence for Islamic religious practices. Such evidence led many to conclude that the cities and their rulers identified in these zones of contact were the product of expanding trade routes across the Sahara, the Persian Gulf, and the Indian Ocean (Levtzion 1973: 10). The medieval state in Africa was thus viewed as 'a superstructure erected over village communities of peasant cultivators rather than a society which has grown naturally out of them' (Oliver and Fage 1962: 47). These diffusionist arguments clearly denied Africans a history of cultural creativity and dynamism, again justifying the 'civilizing' mission of European colonialism across the continent (Stahl 2001).

Despite some continued interest in exogenous explanations for the origins of sub-Saharan African civilisations among scholars (Diop 1987), as well as the inversion of such arguments to explain African influences elsewhere (Diop 1974; Bernal 1987), archaeologists of the postcolonial era have generally rejected external explanations for African cultural achievements and have questioned the validity of the cultural yardstick with which earlier generations of scholars measured African 'progress' (Connah 2001; Stahl 2001). This intellectual turn resulted in a proliferation of surveys and excavations at precolonial sites, focused on understanding the chronology and regional extent of particular cultural formations in precolonial Africa (e.g. Shaw et al. 1993). Archaeology has recovered evidence for the autochthonous development of iron technology, urbanism, farming, and other classic indices of civilization. As African archaeology reached maturity, how long-distance interactions actually articulated within African sociopolitical and cultural systems was increasingly emphasized (Connah 2001; Mitchell 2005). However, the nature of this articulation and its role in the emergence of African civilization remain poorly understood, largely because the continued focus on origins and indices has handicapped our ability to adequately account for the *processes* of state formation. A comparative approach to state formation, drawing upon long-standing anthropological discussions on the nature of power in complex societies, has the potential to shed substantial and necessary light on this issue.

ARCHAEOLOGIES OF SOCIAL COMPLEXITY AND THE STATE

Archaeologists have long sought the factors leading to the rise of the earliest states. In crafting explanatory models, they have drawn from anthropological frameworks to define the nature of early states in comparative perspective. Building on Weber's (1968) classic definition of the state as a bureaucratic entity that possesses a monopoly on the legitimate use of physical force, a generation of anthropologists applied the concept of the state to a range of African societies (Fortes and Evans-Pritchard 1940). Anthropological debates about the nature of states and non-states largely moved away from Africa after the Second World War, resulting in what Susan McIntosh (1999a) has referred to as an 'Oceanic hegemony' in models for sociopolitical complexity. However, anthropologists continued to define states in similar ways, as societies marked by the presence of centralizing government institutions, notably kingship and bureaucracy, in which access to power is largely class-based.

Explaining how decentralized political systems transformed into centralized states has been the focus of sustained research for more than half a century. A number of seminal studies (Eisenstadt 1964; Flannery 1972) identified two general processes implicit to state formation in the past: *specialization*, the amount of internal differentiation into discrete information processing subsystems, and *centralization*, the degree of linkage between subsystems and their highest-order controls (Flannery 1972: 409). This model assumes that any number of different systemic processes can interact to stimulate expansions in political scale, complexity, and integration (Flannery 1983). The state, as a highly centralized and specialized set of political institutions, emerges in an adaptive response to scalar stress and production risk resulting from population growth and competition for resources (Johnson and Earle 2000). States thus vary along a sliding scale of size, complexity, and degree of integration (Earle 1987; Johnson and Earle 2000), leading some archaeologists to propose the catch-all-term 'complex societies', defined broadly as societies with institutionalized subsystems charged with performing diverse yet specialized functions (Shils 1975; Smith 2003).

Africa is playing an increasingly important role in this discussion. In particular, it has contributed examples in which social hierarchy is only one potential resolution to the related problems of scalar stress and production risk. Susan McIntosh, for example, has suggested that we conceptualize social complexity 'as the degree of internal differentiation (*horizontal* as well as *vertical*) and the intricacy of relations within a system' (McIntosh 1999a: 11, emphasis added; cf. Paynter 1989). This perspective has illuminated an alternative pathway to social complexity, referred to as *heterarchy* (McIntosh 1999a). Whereas hierarchies are characterized by ruling elites and centralized government, heterarchies are defined by the presence of overlapping and decentralized political institutions (Crumley 1995; McIntosh 1999a). Hierarchical and heterarchical political structures are not mutually exclusive; rather, they exist along independent sliding scales of horizontal and vertical complexity, a point with significant implications for our broader understanding of the nature of social complexity. The realization that states are not the natural outcome of evolutionary development, but rather one possible response to the demands of scalar stress, renders their study even more crucial for understanding the African past. Indeed, in the face of a clear alternative to the state, archaeologists must account for what factors encouraged social hierarchy rather than heterarchy to emerge. The answer lies in the central issue of *power* and the processes of political centralization.

In opposition to the foregoing view of the state, political centralization is increasingly examined in terms of the complex of strategies employed by elites and drawn from a broad range of military, ritual, political, and economic sources of power (Brumfiel 1992; Yoffee 1993; Earle 1997; Stein 1998). Rather than a hard-and-fast category defined by measurable thresholds and clearly defined boundaries, the state emerges as an eclectic set of potentially overlapping and mutually reinforcing power strategies and political practices designed to centralize control over labour, ritual practice, the production and flow of wealth and resources, and political decision-making in the hands of an elite class. Power, and the means of achieving power, thus stand centre stage in archaeological discussions of the emergence of social complexity and the state worldwide (Earle 1997; Stein 1998; Smith 2003; Yoffee 2005). A primary objective for studying African social complexity must therefore be to examine how political entrepreneurs were able to acquire enough political, economic, ideological, and/or coercive power to tip the balance towards forms of social hierarchy that resulted in states. In this respect, the archaeological evidence strongly suggests African entrepreneurs drew from a diverse set of local and exotic cultural and material resources in crafting political power strategies, resulting in an equally diverse array of state forms across the continent in the precolonial era.

SIGNS OF THE STATE IN PRECOLONIAL AFRICA

The political strategies deployed by African elites in their quest for power are invisible to the archaeologist, but the material remains of the political practices engendered by such strategies are readily available for archaeological analysis. Indeed, signs of the state are hard to overlook. Archaeological research has identified a diverse host of material manifestations of state formation processes across the continent (Fig. 48.1). Although the timing and nature of state formation was anything but uniform, each case was characterized by evidence for social hierarchy, territorial expansion and integration, economic specialization, control over labour, long-distance exchange, and the promulgation of state ideologies. In all cases, agriculturally productive environments, opportunities for local and interregional trade, and the cunning and initiative of indigenous leaders resulted in the florescence of complex societies in the precolonial period. In most cases, cultural and material gains from long-distance trade provided particularly valuable opportunities for emerging elites to manifest greater levels of political centralization. Four broadly defined geographic zones have been particularly important for archaeological analyses of state formation on African soil: northeast, southeast, central, and western Africa.

Northeast Africa

The earliest examples of the state in Africa took root in its northeast, along the Nile Valley and in the Ethiopian highlands (Fig. 48.1). Here, environmental productivity encouraged population growth, local and interregional exchange, and the florescence of three of the most impressive civilizations of the ancient world: Egypt, Nubia, and Aksum. These societies, which interacted in complex ways, emerged between the fourth millennium BC and the first millennium AD due to the complex interaction between local and long-distance processes that integrated northeast Africa with the Mediterranean and Near Eastern worlds in antiquity.

The Egyptian Nile Valley provided the context for one of the clearest examples of state formation in Africa. As the Sahara desiccated over the course of the fourth millennium BC, settled agriculturalists and mobile pastoralists were attracted to the Nile Valley in high numbers (Shaw, Ch. 50 below). These communities profited from marked agricultural fertility, the result of annual Nile flooding, as well as opportunities for long-distance trade with the Mediterranean and Near Eastern worlds. These factors allowed for rapid population expansion, settled town life, and the production of agricultural surpluses in the Predynastic period (Wenke 1989). Over time, emerging elites sponsored long-distance trade, vast engineering projects, interregional conquest, and a state bureaucracy as early as the first half of the third millennium BC. During the Early Dynastic period (3000–2686 BC), mortuary data from the royal site of Abydos attest to clear status differences, with kings buried with accompanying wealth goods in elaborate underground complexes (Dreyer 1992). During the Old Kingdom (2686–2181 BC), clear evidence for a well-established state emerges. This period was marked by the emergence of divine kingship, bureaucratic expansion, and the florescence of royal art and architectural projects, including the construction of the royal pyramids of Giza and their associated pyramid towns (Lehner 2008; Kemp 1992). Twice during both the Middle (2055–1800 BC) and the New Kingdom (1550–1069 BC) periods, Egypt expanded into Nubia to the south (as well as into the Levant to the north). Egypt's southern expansion left clear material traces in the form of twelve military garrisons across Lower Nubia, seven temple towns and smaller administrative settlements across Upper Nubia, as well as the influx of vast quantities of material wealth from sub-Saharan Africa into Egypt itself. Ancient Egypt, marked by an extensive state bureaucracy and regional administration, serves, therefore, as a classic African example of political centralization in the ancient world.

In parts of Nubia to the south, however, the gifts of the Nile were also coupled with extensive pasturage and direct access to the natural riches of eastern Africa. Between the mid-fourth and mid-second millennia BC, village communities of agropastoralists began to organize into a handful of small-scale polities (O'Connor 1991). These communities, particularly those in Lower Nubia, were undoubtedly influenced by intermittent Egyptian colonial interests. Upper Nubia's position as an intermediary between the Mediterranean and sub-Saharan African worlds, however, provided opportunities for elites there to intensify the process of political centralization in the civilizations of Kerma (first half of the second millennium BC), Napata (9th–4th centuries BC) and Meroë (4th century BC–4th century AD). The earliest clear archaeological evidence for the state in this region comes from the city of Kerma (Welsby, Ch. 51 below). This urban community was marked by a palace complex, a public audience hall, a massive mud-brick temple structure, centres for craft production, a city wall, and elaborate royal tumulus burials containing both local and imported Egyptian wealth items, as well as both cattle and human sacrificial offerings (Bonnet 1992; Reisner 1923), clear statements of both the extensive wealth and relative coercive authority of Kerman elite (Fig. 48.2). Kerma's power extended into the north as well, taking control of Egyptian garrisons occupied centuries earlier. Kerma itself would fall in the wake of Egyptian imperial expansion in the New Kingdom, yet later examples of state formation along the Nubian Nile were no less impressive. Pyramid complexes at Kurru, Nuri, and Meroë, for example, attest to the creative ways with which Egyptian iconography was reinterpreted in terms of a local Nubian political ideology (Smith 2003). The urban complex of Meroë, furthermore, was characterized by palaces, temples, and domestic quarters, and was a centre of major iron production throughout its history (Shinnie and Bradley 1980). More than simply Egypt's southern neighbour, Nubia provides a clear example of local elites strategically balancing local and exotic sources of wealth and power in the process of state formation.

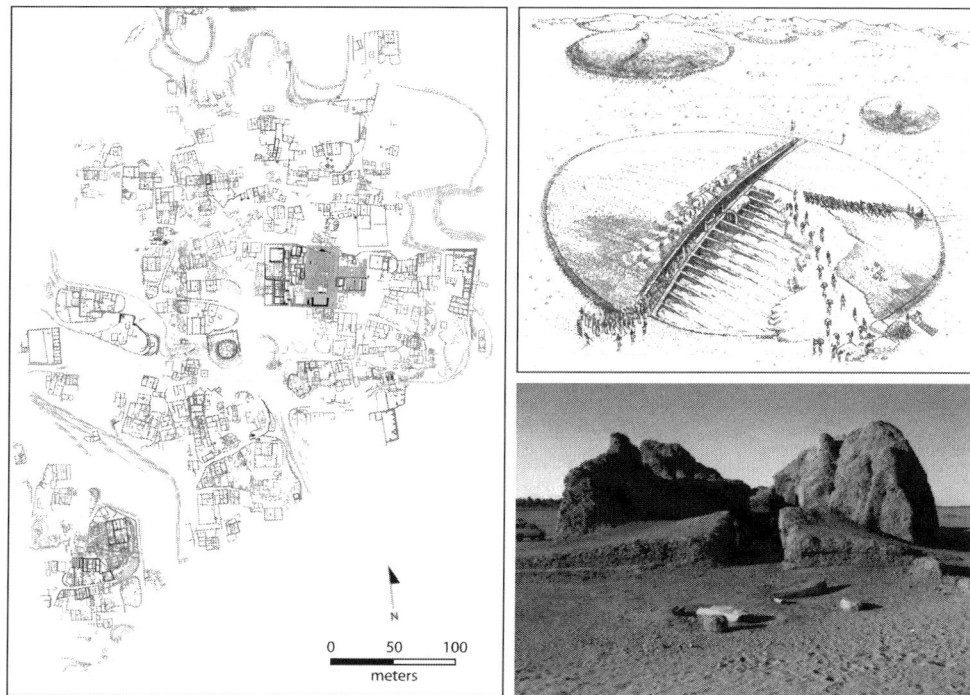

FIG. 48.2 Plan and monuments of Kerma, Sudan. Left: Kerma city plan (after Bonnet et al. 2003). Top right: royal tumulus grave (after O'Connor 1993: 52, illustration by Michael Graham). Bottom right: temple structure located in the Kerma Necropolis (photograph J. Cameron Monroe).

Subsequent state development in the Ethiopian highlands was also clearly the result of the complex relationship between local factors and the shifting tides of long-distance trade in antiquity (Phillipson, Ch. 55 below). Good soils, seasonal rainfall, and extensive pasturage provided the natural setting for the earliest experiment in state formation in the Horn of Africa. Archaeological research on Eritrean and Ethiopian sites, such as Asmara and Yeha, has collectively documented the emergence of social complexity in the first millennium BC in the form of urbanism, monumental ritual architecture, and evidence for long-distance contact with Nubian civilization to the northwest (Fattovich 1990; Phillipson and Schmidt 2009; Schmidt and Curtis 2001). The clearest archaeological evidence for the state, however, comes from the Aksum and its immediate hinterlands in northern Ethiopia. Aksumitic civilization thrived from the 1st to 7th centuries AD, and early in the 4th century the royal dynasty adopted Christianity as a unifying religious ideology. Aksum's rapid rise was clearly tied to global patterns in trade. Artefacts of Roman and Byzantine origin, for example, are not uncommon at Aksumite sites during its period of growth, and Aksum's rise and the demise of Meroe in the 4th century can be attributed in no small way to the relative expansion of commerce along the coast of the Red Sea, rendering the Upper Nile somewhat obsolete as an artery of international trade in this period. Aksum itself flourished into an expansive city into this period, marked by stone royal palaces rendered in the distinctive Aksumitic style, as well as monumental pre-Christian royal tombs marked by extravagant monolithic stelae (Munro-Hay 1980; Phillipson 1998, 2000). Similar structures at Adulis on the Eritrean coast and further inland at Matara indicate a settlement hierarchy suggestive of some form of regional political integration (Anfray 1974). Aksum's decline by the 8th century, undoubtedly due in part to the expansion of Islam and the rise of Near Eastern control over maritime trade routes, marked the end of a notable experiment in precolonial African state formation.

Southeast Africa

Whereas the emergence of states in antiquity was limited to northeast Africa, between the late 9th and 15th centuries AD a series of centralized polities sprang up across eastern and southern Africa in response to both local and interregional processes. These forces resulted in a complex network of states across the Swahili Coast and the Zimbabwe Plateau (Fig. 48.1).

Along the coast of East Africa (Somalia through Mozambique) settled agricultural communities transformed into major centres of long-distance trade with the Indian Ocean world over the course of the period just defined (Kusimba 1999; La Violette, Ch. 62 below). Swahili cities or 'stone towns' such as Gedi (Kenya), Kilwa Kisiwani (Tanzania), Manda (Kenya), and Shanga (Kenya) were characterized by elite cores, marked by elaborate mosques and palace structures (Kirkman 1954; Garlake, 1966; Chittick 1974, 1984; Horton 1996), and surrounded by extensive wattle and daub structures inhabited by commoners (Horton 1996: 23–4; LaViolette and Fleisher 2005). The Indian Ocean trade introduced a host of new luxury goods to the East African littoral, and coastal elites went to great lengths to control access to them. Chinese porcelain, Near Eastern vessels, and associated exotic finds within Swahili cities attest to the degree to which they were able to centralize control over such long-distance trade networks. These Swahili communities also blended Near Eastern and Bantu cultural practices in dynamic ways. The adoption of Islam, evidenced by the ubiquity of mosque construction at Swahili cities (Insoll, Ch. 12 above), provided a common cultural language with which to facilitate maritime exchange over long distances and engender a sense of social distinction from rural agriculturalists (Robertshaw 2003). Despite the fact that the international style materialized by the residents of these urban communities appears never to have penetrated into the countryside to any significant degree, Swahili communities were interconnected with their rural hinterlands in complex economic mosaics involving hunter-gatherers, mobile pastoralists, settled farmers, and urban residents (Kusimba and Kusimba 2005). The result was a series of powerful yet geographically restricted city-states, ruled by a Muslim merchant elite class, who were able to dominate the Indian Ocean trade until the advent of the Portuguese at the end of the 15th century.

In the interior, the Zimbabwe Plateau and adjacent areas provided cool, well-watered, and lightly wooded environment ideal for agriculture and widespread pastoralism, as well as proximity to interior products (especially gold and ivory) in demand on the coast. The earliest experiments with social complexity are archaeologically visible in the Shashe–Limpopo confluence to the south of the plateau itself. From the 8th to the 13th centuries AD the sites of Schroda, K-2, and Mapungubwe provide an archaeological sequence marked by the rise of a rain-making cult at chiefly centres, deepening regional settlement hierarchies, the expanding use of material goods to mark social status, and intensifying levels of trade with the Swahili coast (Pikirayi, Ch. 63 below; Huffman 2000). Between the 13th and 16th centuries, however, indigenous Shona societies on the Zimbabwe plateau itself developed

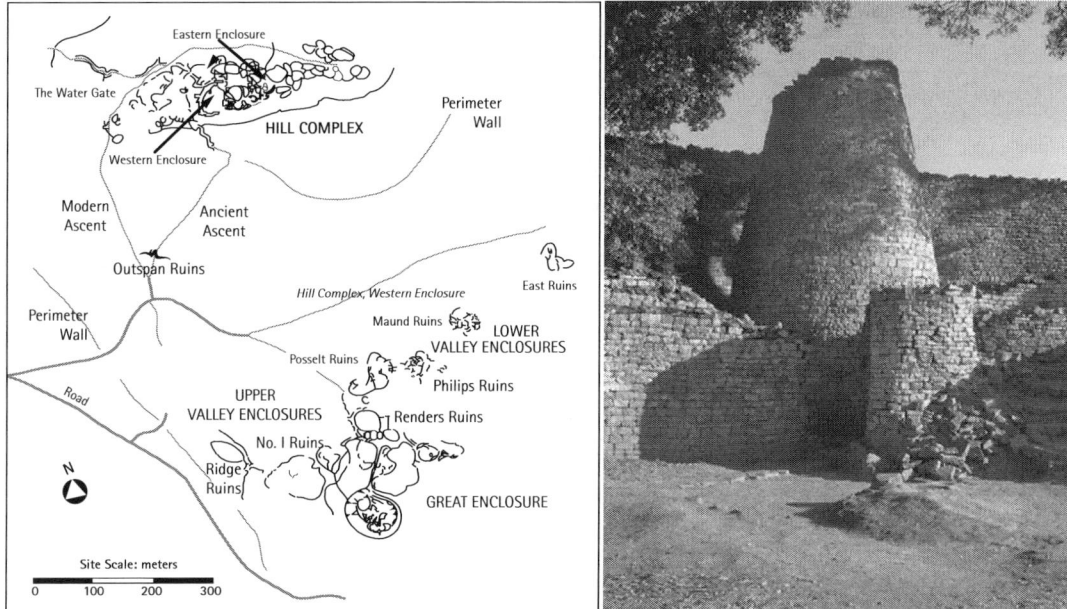

FIG. 48.3 Great Zimbabwe, Zimbabwe. Left: site plan (after Chirikure and Pikirayi 2008: 978; illustration by Neil Rusch). Right: the conical tower in the Great Enclosure (photograph courtesy of Innocent Pikirayi).

the clearest evidence of the state in the region. This polity, centred at Great Zimbabwe, was characterized by system of kingship supported by large population densities, long-distance trade, the continued importance of the rain-making cult, and control of extensive wealth in cattle (Reid 1996). A monumental stone architectural complex at Great Zimbabwe served as the royal core of a sprawling settlement (Huffman 1996) (Fig. 48.3). Additionally, the widespread distribution of smaller 'zimbabwe' sites across the plateau suggests that Great Zimbabwe sat at the apex of a multi-tiered settlement hierarchy, a regional pattern consistent with our understanding of how states emerged (Sinclair and Lundmark 1984; Sinclair et al. 1993). Near Eastern and East Asian ceramics, Syrian glass, and iron implements from Central Africa recovered at Great Zimbabwe attest to its role as a key node in the trade of resources from the interior (principally gold, copper, tin, and ivory) to Swahili merchants along the coast (Garlake 1973). The rise of centralized political authority on the Zimbabwe plateau was thus undeniably connected to the ability of elites to control ritual rain-making powers, extensive wealth in cattle, and trading connections with coastal Swahili states.

Central Africa

Central Africa, extending along the Equatorial belt from the Atlantic coast to the Great Lakes region, provides some of the clearest historical examples of centralized states in sub-Saharan Africa. These are best known from historical and linguistic studies of early settlement and state formation, and archaeology has provided tantalizing glimpses of political processes in the deeper past. Linguistic evidence suggests that political authority across this region varied

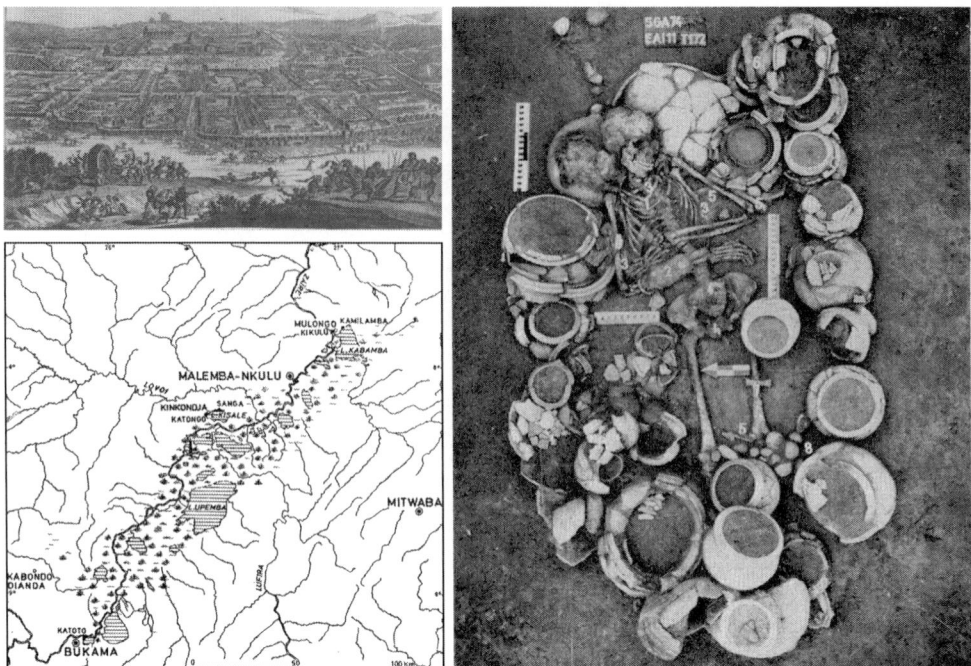

FIG. 48.4 View of Loango, Congo-Brazzaville, and sites in the Upemba Depression, Congo-Kinshasa. Top left: The city of Loango in the seventeenth century (Dapper 1686: 320–1). Bottom left: Archaeological sites in the Upemba Depression (after de Maret 1977). Right: Kisalian grave from Shanga, Congo-Kinshasa.

between two ideological poles, the first accentuating the powers of kings and royal dynasties, and the second seeking to diminish the aggrandizing tendencies of elites in favour of the corporate body as a whole (Vansina 1990; see also Blanton et al. 1998 for a New World comparison). The result was a series of political traditions that hold significant potential for archaeological analysis (de Maret, Ch. 43 above).

Polities in and around the Congo Basin are well documented in the historical period. Along the Atlantic Coast, the kingdoms of Kongo, Loango, and Tio served as major political players in the era of the Atlantic slave trade. Although there are almost no archaeological data relating to these polities, oral traditions and king-lists indicate that they emerged out of settled communities engaged in farming, iron production, and long-distance trade (in copper luxuries and coastal resources in particular) some time in the 14th century AD (Thornton 2001; Vansina 1990). Historical sources from subsequent periods suggest that Tio, Loango, and Kongo were expansive urban polities, ruled by sacred kings and a network of officials distributed across provinces (Martin 1972; Thornton 1983; Vansina 1973) (Fig. 48.4). Kongo in particular may have ruled over a territory of 150,000 km², and its capital, Mbanza Kongo (São Salvador), was home to as many as 40,000 inhabitants (Thornton 1983). Rural capitals such as Mbanza Mbata (Congo-Kinshasa) and Mbanza Soyo (Angola) served as nodes of political control across its territories, and limited archaeological evidence has revealed elite burials at such sites marked by large quantities of imported European and local goods (de Maret 1982).

On the eastern reaches of the Congo Basin, contemporary polities such as the Kuba, Luba, and Rund kingdoms are known from ethnohistorical and ethnographic sources. Although

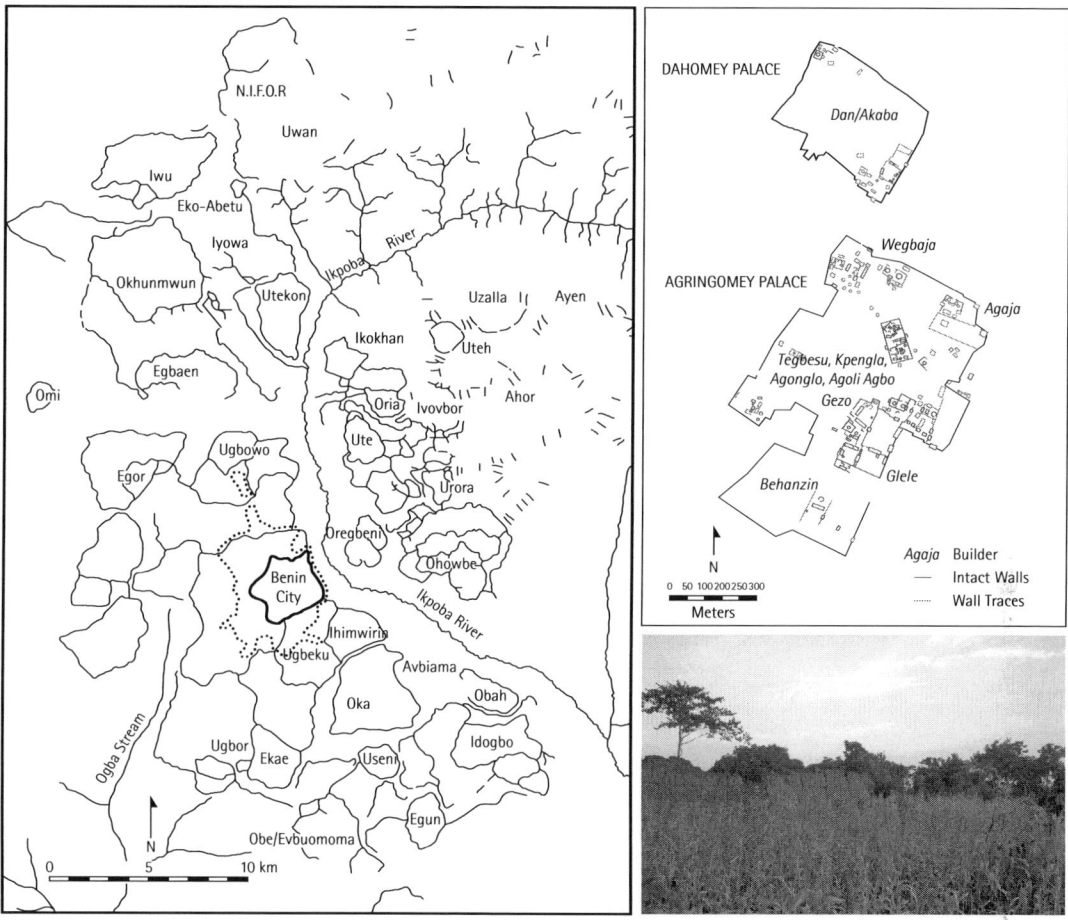

FIG. 48.5 Earthworks and monuments of the kingdoms of Benin, Nigeria, and Dahomey, Bénin. Left: earthworks of the kingdom of Benin, Benin City, Nigeria (after Connah 2000: 163; original illustration by Patrick Darling). Top right: the royal palace of Dahomey, Abomey, Bénin. Bottom right: Dahomean palace wall, Cana-Mignonhi, Bénin (photograph, J. Cameron Monroe).

their origins are unclear, archaeological evidence from the Upemba Depression illuminates aspects of the origins of the Luba kingdom in particular (Fig. 48.4). Archaeologists identified more than 50 sites, including over 300 burials, which document an uninterrupted Iron Age sequence from the 5th to the 19th century AD. Excavated burials from five sites in particular (Kamilamba, Katonga, Kikulu, Malemba Nkulu, and Sanga) document the emergence of social hierarchy by the end of the first millennium, and demonstrate clear cultural-historical connections with the Luba people of today (de Maret 1977, 1979, 1992). By the 8th century AD some burials were associated with copper luxuries, and two were marked by elaborate ceremonial iron axes, symbols of political power among the Luba in later periods. In one such axe grave an iron anvil was placed next to the skull, recalling latter traditions that identify blacksmiths as the founders of kingdoms across the region (de Maret 1985). By the 10th century AD, grave goods in select graves became both more abundant and elaborate; some of the wealthiest graves were those of children (de Maret 1979, 1982), indicating the shift from *achieved* to *ascribed* social status. Power and kinship became intertwined, laying the groundwork for accentuated levels of status distinction and political centralization in later centuries. Importantly, there is little material evidence for the Indian Ocean trade in this region, suggesting that incipient social hierarchy was a 'home-grown' phenomenon (de Maret 1979).

On the eastern reaches of Central Africa, the Great Lakes region provides a valuable comparison with developments to the west. Here, a cool and dry climate, coupled with environmental diversity, provided fertile ground for the emergence of centralized states in the precolonial period. At the time of European contact in the 19th century, the kingdoms of Buganda, Ankole, and Bunyoro contained urban communities with populations in the tens of thousands of people ruled by kings with extensive bureaucratic institutions (Beattie 1960). Archaeological evidence for the precursors to such polities comes from the Bunyoro-Kitara region of western Uganda (Reid, Ch. 61 below). Whereas little evidence for intensive settlement is visible during the first millennium AD, during the early second millennium communities of ironworking cattle pastoralists and sorghum farmers emerged across this region (Robertshaw 1994, 1999). From the 15th century onwards, the sites of Bigo, Munsa, and Kibengo emerged as regional royal capitals, surrounded by extensive ditch systems requiring thousands of man-hours to build (Sutton 1998). These features probably served as either cattle pens or ways of demarcating agricultural land, rather than as defensive city walls, suggesting that agricultural resources were an important target of elite attention in this period (Robertshaw 2003). Indeed, similar to evidence from the Upemba Depression to the West, long-distance trade played a relatively minor role in underwriting political authority in the Bunyoro–Kitara region. However, here there is little overall evidence for elite status differentiation at settlements in this region, suggesting alternative forms of elite power that may have depended on popular consensus rather than coercion (Robertshaw 2003).

Western Africa

Across West Africa, including the Saharan, savannah, and forest zones, metalworking agricultural and pastoral communities organized in complex ways over the course of the fourth millennium BC through to the first millennium AD, resulting in clear evidence for experiments in social complexity. The advent of Islam and the explosion of trans-Saharan trade towards the end of the first millennium AD nevertheless provided new opportunities for elites to advance their political agendas, tipping the political balance in favour of some of the clearest examples of centralized states in sub-Saharan Africa (Fig. 48.1).

Nowhere did such forces play a more formative role in the formation of centralized states than in the western reaches of the Sahara, where trading empires emerged as a direct result of emerging global commerce in the late first/early second millennia AD. From Morocco to Mali, nomadic pastoral peoples plied the Sahara from the fourth millennium BC, leaving clear evidence for incipient social hierarchy in the form of tumulus burials and differential access to luxury goods (polished stone axes, hachettes, bracelets, and beads) (MacDonald 1998). Between the early second and late first millennia BC, some of these 'mobile elites' experimented with forms of political integration, demonstrated by multi-tiered settlement hierarchies at sites such as Dhar Tichitt (southern Mauritania) (Holl 1985), as well as the large settlements and elaborate underground water-extraction system of the Garamantes (southwest Libya) (Mattingly 2003). Although some degree of trade across the Sahara is documented as early as the 3rd century AD, by the end of the first millennium AD Islamicized pastoralists began to centralize control over a rapidly expanding trans-Saharan trade. In the 11th and 12th centuries, Berber Almoravids expanded across the region as far south as southern Mauritania and as far north as the Iberian Peninsula. They and subsequent polities thereby established networks of Islamic trading entrepôts across the Sahara (Tadmakka, Sijilmassa, Fez, Awdaghost, etc.). Archaeological research at such sites has revealed elite quarters and craftsmen's workshops, the presence of exotic luxury goods, and extensive storage facilities (Holl 2006). These towns, and their respective governors, were clearly focused on the trans-shipment of sub-Saharan products northwards, and vice versa, as early as the mid-8th century AD (Nixon 2009).

The West African savannah, an arid landscape broken by the Senegal and Niger Rivers, provided a wealth of opportunities for African states to emerge in the pre-Islamic period (MacDonald, Ch. 57 below). Excavations at the tell sites of Dia and Jenné-jeno in the inland Niger region of Mali suggest that significant settlement nucleation began during the first millennium BC, and that by the mid-first millennium AD such sites had been transformed into urban centres with populations in the tens of thousands. Such cities were locked into complex interregional exchange networks, linking adjacent regions economically. However, the lack of archaeological evidence for differential access to wealth and resources at such sites has led scholars to suggest that communities such as Jenné-jeno resisted social hierarchy for centuries, depending instead on heterarchical forms of political and social integration (McIntosh 2005; McIntosh and McIntosh 1993; McIntosh 1999b). With the advent of Islam and the rapid expansion of demand for sub-Saharan resources in North Africa and the Near East in the late first millennium, however, heterarchical cities were rapidly incorporated into decidedly hierarchical militaristic empires, linking Near Eastern, Sahelian, and forest belt communities in complex ways (Sutton 1997). By the early second millenium AD, archaeological evidence from mortuary sites such as El Oualadji in the Middle Niger region points towards the emergence of monumental burial tumuli, associated with elaborate luxury goods (Raimbault and Sanogo 1991). Additionally the period is marked by a terracotta tradition depicting warriors, in the form of men on horseback. Such data suggest the emergence of hierarchical social institutions in the early first millenium AD, an era of intensifying trans-Saharan commerce.

Historical sources provide valuable insights into the nature of political centralization across this region in the second millennium AD. The Soninke kingdom of Ghana (focused in southeast Mauritania and adjacent parts of Mali) developed centralized kingship sometime in the mid-first millennium, yet the expansion of trans-Saharan trading networks clearly contributed to its rapid expansion such that it dominated the region from the 10th to the 12th centuries. Furthermore, the fall of Ghana and the subsequent rise of Mali (13th–15th centuries) and Songhay (14th–16th centuries), as well as the Sayfawa state of Kanem-Bornu (16th–17th centuries) and the Hausa states of northern Nigeria (13th–19th centuries), reflect the shifting dynamics of trans-Saharan trade over the course of the second millennium. Archaeology has yet to contribute to our understanding of the nature of regional integration in these polities, yet long-distance trade was clearly an important factor in their development (Haour 2007). High quantities of Near Eastern pottery and glass, as well as forest products such as ivory found at sites such as Gao (Mali), Essouk-Tadmakka (Mali), and Koumbi-Saleh (Mauritania), all attest to the importance of long-distance trade throughout the histories of these settlements (Berthier 1997; Insoll 1997; Nixon 2009). As on the Swahili Coast, the adoption of Islam played an important role in the emergence of these polities, providing a common cultural language for establishing long-distance economic contacts.

Further to the south, agricultural communities distributed widely across the West African forest belt and Dahomey Gap began to reap the benefits of a well-developed iron industry during the first millennium AD (Gronenborn, Ogundiran, Chs 58 and 59 below). Iron production allowed these communities to transform virgin forest into a network of urban polities, providing the framework for the emergence of expansionist states and empires in subsequent centuries. Over the course of the late first and early second millennia large towns formed along the northern forest fringe of modern Ghana, and by the 15th century the political landscape was dominated by centralized Akan polities that had coalesced around opportunities yielded by trans-Saharan demand for forest products, notably gold, ivory, and kola nut (Posnansky 1976; Sutton 1997). Further to the east, in Nigeria's forest zone, similar patterns held. The kingdom of Ife (9th–14th centuries) emerged along the northern fringe of the forest zone and likewise tapped into opportunities for trade provided by the expansion of Sahelian polities to the north (Sutton 1997). Dozens of additional Yoruba polities influenced by the model of kingship established at Ife proliferated across the Nigerian forest over the course of the 15th and 16th centuries. Some, such as Oyo and Ilesa, weakened the dominant power of Ife as these newcomers jockeyed for commercial position (Smith 1969; Ogundiran 2003). Oyo itself expanded dramatically during the 17th and 18th centuries, establishing colonial enclaves on its political frontiers (Usman 2000; Ogundiran 2002). Towards the coast, similar factors encouraged the rise of the Edo kingdom of Benin, a likely source of forest resources for the northern trade. To the west, in the Aja-Fon region of the Dahomey Gap, the rise of the Atlantic slave trade provided opportunities for elites to establish palace-centric polities, such as Allada, Hueda, and Dahomey, which integrated European material culture into state ritual practices and experimented with forms of centralized regional integration over time (Kelly 1997; Monroe 2007; Norman, 2009).

States across this region were characterized by the florescence of impressive artistic traditions, such as the production of sophisticated brass and terracotta heads at Ile-Ife, possible representations of 13th/14th-century Yoruba kings, as well as brass castings from the Edo city of Benin, which were clearly made by specialists (Willett 1967; Ben-Amos, 1980). Additionally, political centres and their secondary centres and colonial enclaves across this region were marked by enormous palace complexes and/or expansive earthwork systems, representing centralized control over vast quantities of labour (Ozanne 1969; Connah 1975; Soper and Darling 1980; Darling 1984; Norman and Kelly 2006; Monroe 2010).

CONCLUSIONS

African archaeology today has clearly established a safe distance from the problematic arguments of the colonial era. Whereas African states were once universally described in terms of exotic influences, we now recognize the clear indigenous origins of social complexity and the state. A generation of archaeological research across the continent has identified the autochthonous development of classic indices of civilization (urbanism, farming, metallurgy, etc.), requiring archaeologists to rethink the relationship between local and long-distance factors in the emergence of states. In each of the cases examined above, the emergence of social complexity and the state was presupposed by patterns of political and economic integration prior to intrusion from outside. State formation in the examples outlined above was marked by clear evidence for social hierarchy, territorial expansion and integration, economic specialization, control over labour, long-distance exchange, and the promulgation of state ideologies. Also in each case, however, archaeology has revealed the dynamic ways that elites made creative use of both local and exotic sources of power in this process. From antiquity through the medieval and early modern eras, 'global' forces have clearly shaped the historical contours of this process. In particular, long-distance trade provided new sources of both economic and ideological power with which local elites across sub-Saharan Africa advanced their own political agendas. Indeed, across the four broad sub-regions examined above, ongoing archaeological research illuminates how elites managed to centralize coercive, economic, ideological, and political power in a variety of ways, tipping the balance towards a variety of forms of political organization. Further research in each of these geographic zones, integrating systematic survey and excavation at a range of archaeological site types, has great potential to clarify our understanding of these issues.

REFERENCES

ANFRAY, F. (1974). Deux villes Axoumites: Adoulis et Matara. *IV Congresso Internazionale de Studi Etiopici (Roma, 10–15 aprile 1972)*. Rome: Accademia Nazionale dei Lincei.

BEATTIE, J. (1960). *Bunyoro, an African Kingdom*. New York: Holt.

BEN-AMOS, P. (1980). *The Art of Benin*. London: Thames & Hudson.

BERNAL, M. (1987). *Black Athena: The Afroasiatic Roots of Classical Civilization*. New Brunswick, NJ: Rutgers University Press.

BERTHIER, S. (1997). *Recherches Archéologiques sur la Capitale de l'Empire de Ghana: Étude d'un Secteur d'Habitat à Koumbi Saleh, Mauritanie: Campagnes II–III–IV–V (1975–1976)–(1980–1981)*. Oxford: Archaeopress.

BONNET, C. (1992). Excavations at the Nubian royal town of Kerma. *Antiquity* 66: 611–25.

—— (2003). Kerma : rapport préliminaire sur les campagnes de 2001–2002 et 2002–2003. *Genava* 51: 257–300.

BOVILL, E. W. (1958). *The Golden Trade of the Moors*. London: Oxford University Press.

BRUMFIEL, E. M. (1992). Breaking and entering the ecosystem: gender, class, and faction steal the show. *American Anthropologist* 94: 551–67.

CHILDE, V. G. (1936). *Man Makes Himself*. London: Watts.

CHIRIKURE, S., and PIKIRAYI, I. (2008). Inside and outside the dry stone walls: revisiting the material culture of Great Zimbabwe. *Antiquity* 82: 976–93.

CHITTICK, H. N. (1974). *Kilwa: An Islamic Trading City on the East African Coast*. Nairobi: British Institute in Eastern Africa.

—— (1984). *Manda: Excavations at an Island Port on the Kenya Coast*. Nairobi: British Institute in Eastern Africa.

CONNAH, G. (1975). *The Archaeology of Benin: Excavations and Other Researches in and around Benin City, Nigeria*. Oxford: Clarendon Press.

—— (2001). *African Civilizations: An Archaeological Perspective*. Cambridge: Cambridge University Press.

CRUMLEY, C. L. (1995). Heterarchy and the analysis of complex societies. *Archaeological Papers of the American Anthropological Association* 6: 1–6.

DARLING, P. J. (1984). *Archaeology and History in Southern Nigeria: The Ancient Linear Earthworks of Benin and Ishan*. Oxford: British Archaeological Reports.

DE MARET, P. (1977). Sanga: new excavations, more data, and some related problems. *Journal of African History* 18: 321–37.

—— (1979). Luba roots: a first complete Iron Age sequence in Zaire. *Current Anthropology* 20: 233–5.

—— (1982). The Iron Age in the west and the south. In F. Van Noten (ed.), *The Archaeology of Central Africa*. Graz: Akademische Druck- und Verlagsanstalt, 77–96.

—— (1985). The smith's myth and the origin of leadership in Central Africa. In R. Haaland and P. Shinnie (eds), *African Iron Working*. Bergen: Norwegian University Press, 73–87.

—— (1992). *Fouilles Archéologiques dans la Vallée du Haut-Lualaba, Zaïre, II: Kamilamba, Kikulu et Malemba-Nkulu, 1975*. Tervuren: Musée Royal de l'Afrique Centrale.

DIOP, C. A. (1974). *The African Origin of Civilization: Myth or Reality*. Chicago: L. Hill.

—— (1987). *Precolonial Black Africa: A Comparative Study of the Political and Social Systems of Europe and Black Africa, from Antiquity to the Formation of Modern States*. Westport, Conn.: L. Hill.

DREYER, G. (1992). Recent discoveries in the U-cemetery at Abydos. In E. C. M. Van Den Brink (ed.), *The Nile Delta in Transition: 4th–3rd Millennium B.C.* Jerusalem: Israel Exploration Society, 293–300.

EARLE, T. K. (1987). Specialization and the production of wealth: Hawaiian chiefdoms and the Inka Empire. In T. K. Earle and E. M. Brumfiel (eds), *Specialization, Exchange and Complex Societies*. Cambridge: Cambridge University Press, 64–75.

—— (1997). *How Chiefs Come to Power: The Political Economy in Prehistory*. Stanford, Calif.: Stanford University Press.

EISENSTADT, S. N. (1964). Social change, differentiation and evolution. *American Sociological Review* 29: 375–86.

ELTRINGHAM, N. (2006). 'Invaders who have stolen the country': the Hamitic hypothesis, race and the Rwandan genocide. *Social Identities* 12: 425–46.

FAGAN, B. (1981). Two hundred and four years of African archaeology. In J. D. Evans, B. W. Cunliffe, and A. C. Renfrew (eds), *Antiquity and Man: Essays in Honour of Glyn Daniel*. London: Thames & Hudson, 396–421.

FATTOVICH, R. (1990). Remarks on the Pre-Aksumite period in northern Ethiopia. *Journal of Ethiopian Studies* 23: 1–33.

FLANNERY, K. V. (1972). The cultural evolution of civilizations. *Annual Review of Ecology and Systematics* 3: 399–426.

—— (1983). Archaeology and ethnology in the context of divergent evolution. In K. V. Flannery and J. Marcus (eds), *The Cloud People: Divergent Evolution of the Zapotec and Mixtec Civilizations*. New York: Academic Press, 361–2.

FORTES, M., and EVANS-PRITCHARD, E. E. (1940). *African Political Systems*. London: Oxford University Press.

GARLAKE, P. S. (1966). *The Early Islamic Architecture of the East African Coast*. Nairobi: Oxford University Press.

—— (1973). *Great Zimbabwe*. London: Thames & Hudson.

HAOUR, A. (2007). *Rulers, Warriors, Traders, Clerics: The Central Sahel and the North Sea, 800–1500*. New York: Oxford University Press.

HOLL, A. F. C. (1985). Background to the Ghana empire: archaeological investigations on the transition to statehood in the Dhar Tichitt Region (Mauritania). *Journal of Anthropological Archaeology* 4: 73–115.

——— (2006). *West African Early Towns: Archaeology of Households in Urban Landscapes*. Ann Arbor: University of Michigan Press.

HORTON, M. (ed.) (1996). *Shanga: The Archaeology of a Muslim Trading Community on the Coast of East Africa*. Nairobi: British Institute in Eastern Africa.

HUFFMAN, T. N. (1996). *Snakes and Crocodiles: Power and Symbolism in Ancient Zimbabwe*. Johannesburg: Witwatersrand University Press.

——— (2000). Mapungubwe and the origins of the Zimbabwe Culture. *South African Archaeological Society Goodwin Series* 8: 14–29.

INSOLL, T. (1997). Iron Age Gao: an archaeological contribution. *Journal of African History* 38: 1–30.

JOHNSON, A. W., and EARLE, T. K. (2000). *The Evolution of Human Societies: From Foraging Group to Agrarian State*. Stanford, Calif.: Stanford University Press.

KELLY, K. G. (1997). The archaeology of African-European interaction: investigating the social roles of trade, traders, and the use of space in the seventeenth- and eighteenth-century Hueda kingdom, Republic of Benin. *World Archaeology* 28: 351–69.

KEMP, B. J. (2006). *Ancient Egypt: Anatomy of a Civilization*. New York: Routledge.

KIRKMAN, J. S. (1954). *The Arab City of Gedi: Excavations at the Great Mosque, Architecture and Finds*. London: Oxford University Press.

KUSIMBA, C. M. (1999). *The Rise and Fall of Swahili States*. Walnut Creek, Calif.: AltaMira Press.

——— and KUSIMBA, S. B. (2005). Mosaics and interactions: East Africa, 2000 B.P. to the present. In A. B. Stahl (ed.), *African Archaeology: A Critical Introduction*. Oxford: Blackwell, 392–419.

LA VIOLETTE, A., and FLEISHER, J. (2005). The archaeology of sub-Saharan urbanism: cities and their countrysides. In A. B. Stahl (ed.), *African Archaeology: A Critical Introduction*. Oxford: Blackwell, 327–52.

LEHNER, M. (2008). *The Complete Pyramids*. London: Thames & Hudson.

LEVTZION, N. (1973). *Ancient Ghana and Mali*. London: Methuen.

MACDONALD, K. C. (1998). Before the Empire of Ghana: pastoralism and the origins of cultural complexity in the Sahel. In G. Connah (ed.), *Transformations in Africa: Essays on Africa's Later Past*. London: Leicester University Press, 71–103.

MARTIN, P. (1972). *The External Trade of the Loango Coast, 1576–1870*. Oxford: Clarendon Press.

MATTINGLY, D. J. (2003). *The Archaeology of Fazzān*. London: Society for Libyan Studies.

MCINTOSH, R. J. (2005). *Ancient Middle Niger: Urbanism and the Self-Organizing Landscape*. Cambridge: Cambridge University Press.

——— and MCINTOSH, S. K. (1993). Cities without citadels: understanding urban origins along the Middle Niger. In T. Shaw, P. J. J. Sinclair, B. Andah, and A. Okpoko (eds), *The Archaeology of Africa: Foods, Metals and Towns*. London: Routledge, 622–41.

MCINTOSH, S. K. (1999a). Pathways to complexity: an African perspective. In S. K. Mcintosh (ed.), *Beyond Chiefdoms: Pathways to Complexity in Africa*. Cambridge: Cambridge University Press, 1–30.

——— (1999b). Modeling political organization in large-scale settlement clusters: a case from the Inland Niger Delta. In S. K. Mcintosh (ed.), *Beyond Chiefdoms: Pathways to Complexity in Africa*. Cambridge: Cambridge University Press, 66–79.

MITCHELL, P. J. (2005). *African Connections: An Archaeological Perspective on Africa and the Wider World,* Walnut Creek, Calif.: AltaMira Press.

MONROE, J. C. (2007). Continuity, revolution, or evolution on the Slave Coast of West Africa: royal architecture and political order in precolonial Dahomey. *Journal of African History* 48: 349–73.

—— (2010). Power by design: architecture and politics in precolonial Dahomey. *Journal of Social Archaeology* 10: 477–507.

MORGAN, L. H. (1985). *Ancient Society*. Tucson: University of Arizona Press.

MUNRO-HAY, S. (1980). *Excavations at Aksum: An Account of Research at the Ancient Ethiopian Capital Directed in 1972–74 by the Late Dr Neville Chittick*. Nairobi: British Institute in Eastern Africa.

NIXON, S. (2009). Excavating Essouk-Tadmakka (Mali): new archaeological investigations of early Islamic trans-Saharan trade. *Azania: Archaeological Research in Africa* 44: 217–55.

NORMAN, N. L. (2009). Hueda (Whydah) country and town: archaeological perspectives on the rise and collapse of an Atlantic countryside and entrepôt. *International Journal of African Historical Studies* 42: 387–410.

—— and KELLY, K. G. (2006). Landscape politics: the serpent ditch and the rainbow in West Africa. *American Anthropologist* 104: 98–110.

O'CONNOR, D. (1991). Early states along the Nubian Nile. In W. V. Davies (ed.), *Egypt and Africa: Nubia from Prehistory to Islam*. London: British Museum Press, 145–65.

—— (1993). *Ancient Nubia: Egypt's Rival in Africa*. Philadelphia: University Museum, University of Pennsylvania.

OGUNDIRAN, A. O. (2003). Chronology, material culture, and pathways to the cultural history of Yoruba-Edo region, Nigeria, 500 B.C.–A.D. 180. In T. Falola and C. Jennings (eds), *Sources and Methods in African History: Spoken, Written, Unearthed*. Rochester, NY: University of Rochester Press, 33–79.

—— (2002). *Archaeology and History in Ìlàrè District (Central Yorubaland, Nigeria) 1200–1900 A.D.* Oxford: Archaopress.

OLIVER, R. A., and FAGE, J. D. (1962). *A Short History of Africa*. Harmondsworth: Penguin.

OZANNE, P. (1969). A new archaeological survey of Ife. *Odu* 1: 28–45.

PAYNTER, R. (1989). The archaeology of equality and inequality. *Annual Review of Anthropology* 18: 369–99.

PHILLIPSON, D. W. (1998). *Ancient Ethiopia. Aksum: Its Antecedents and Successors*. London: British Museum Press.

—— (ed.) (2000). *Archaeology at Aksum, Ethiopia, 1993–7*. London: British Institute in Eastern Africa.

—— and SCHMIDT, P. R. (eds) (2009). *Re-evaluating the Archaeology of the First Millennium BC in the Northern Horn*. *African Archaeological Review* 26(4) (special issue): 255–350.

POSNANSKY, M. (1966). Kingship, archaeology, and historical myth. *Uganda Journal* 30: 1–12.

—— (1976). Archaeology and the origins of the Akan society in Ghana. In G. Sieveking, D. G. Longworth, I. H. Wilson, and G. Clark (eds), *Problems in Economic and Social Archaeology*. London: Duckworth, 49–58.

—— (1982). African archaeology comes of age. *World Archaeology* 13: 345–58.

RAIMBAULT, M., and SANOGO, K. (eds) (1991). *Recherches Archéologiques au Mali: les Sites Protohistoriques de la Zone Lacustre*. Paris: ACCT-Karthala.

REID, D. A. M. (1996). Cattle herds and the redistribution of cattle resources. *World Archaeology* 28: 43–57.

REISNER, G. A. (1923). *Excavations at Kerma*. Cambridge, Mass.: Peabody Museum of Harvard University.

ROBERTSHAW, P. (1990). *A History of African Archaeology*. London: James Currey.

—— (1994). Archaeological survey, ceramic analysis and state formation in western Uganda. *African Archaeological Review* 12: 105–31.

—— (1999). Seeing and keeping power in Bunyoro-Kitara, Uganda. In S. K. Mcintosh (ed.), *Beyond Chiefdoms: Pathways to Complexity in Africa*. Cambridge: Cambridge University Press, 49–58.

—— (2003). The origins of the state in East Africa. In C. M. Kusimba and S. B. Kusimba (eds), *East African Archaeology: Foragers, Potters, Smiths, and Traders*. Philadelphia: University of Pennsylvania Museum of Archaeology and Anthropology.

SCHMIDT, P. R., and CURTIS, M. (2001). Urban precursors in the Horn: early 1st-millennium BC communities in Eritrea. *Antiquity* 38: 393–421.

SCHRIRE, C., DEACON, J., HALL, M., and LEWIS-WILLIAMS, J. D. (1986). Burkitt's milestone. *Antiquity* 60: 123–31.

SHAW, T., SINCLAIR, P. J. J., ANDAH, B., and OKPOKO, A. (eds) (1993). *The Archaeology of Africa: Foods, Metals and Towns*. London: Routledge.

SHILS, E. (1975). *Center and Periphery: Essays in Macrosociology*. Chicago: University of Chicago Press.

SHINNIE, P. L., and BRADLEY, R. J. (1980). *The Capital of Kush: Meroe Excavations, 1965–1972*. Berlin: Akademie.

SINCLAIR, P. J. J., and LUNDMARK, H. (1984). A spatial analysis of archaeological sites from Zimbabwe. In M. Hall, G. Avery, D. M. Avery, M. L. Wilson, and A. J. B. Humphreys (eds), *Frontiers: Southern African Archaeology Today*. Oxford: British Archaeological Reports, 277–88.

—— PIKIRAYI, I., PWITI, G., and SOPER, R. (1993). Urban trajectories on the Zimbabwean plateau. In Shaw et al. (1993: 705–31).

SMITH, A. (2003). *The Political Landscape: Constellations of Authority in Early Complex Polities*. Los Angeles: University of California Press.

SMITH, R. S. (1969). *Kingdoms of the Yoruba*. London: Methuen.

SMITH, S. T. (2003). *Wretched Kush: Ethnic Identities and Boundaries in Egypt's Nubian Empire*. London: Routledge.

SOPER, R. C., and DARLING, P. (1980). The walls of Oyo-Ile. *West African Journal of Archaeology* 10: 61–81.

STAHL, A. B. (1999). Perceiving variability in time and space: the evolutionary mapping of African societies. In S. K. Mcintosh (ed.), *Beyond Chiefdoms: Pathways to Complexity in Africa*. Cambridge: Cambridge University Press, 39–55.

—— (2001). *Making History in Banda: Anthropological Visions of Africa's Past*. Cambridge: Cambridge University Press.

STEIN, G. (1998). Heterogeneity, power, and political economy: some current research issues in the archaeology of Old World complex societies. *Journal of Archaeological Research* 6: 1–44.

SUTTON, J. E. G. (1997). The African lords of the intercontinental gold trade before the Black Death: al-Hasan bin Sulaiman of Kilwa and Mansa Musa of Mali. *Antiquaries Journal* 77: 221–42.

—— (1998). Farmers, cattler-herders and rulers in western Uganda, AD 1000–1500. *Azania* 33: 39–72.

THORNTON, J. K. (1983). *The Kingdom of Kongo: Civil War and Transition, 1641–1718*. Madison: University of Wisconsin Press.

—— (2001). The origins and early history of the Kingdom of Kongo, c.1350–1500. *International Journal of African Historical Studies* 34: 89–120.

USMAN, A. (2000). A view from the periphery: northern Yoruba villages during the Old Oyo Empire, Nigeria. *Journal of Field Archaeology* 27: 43–61.

VANSINA, J. (1973). *The Tio Kingdom of the Middle Congo, 1880–1892*. Oxford: Oxford University Press.

—— (1990). *Paths in the Rainforests: Towards a History of Political Tradition in Equatorial Africa*. Madison: University of Wisconsin Press.

WEBER, M. (1968). *Economy and Society: An Outline of Interpretive Sociology*. New York: Bedminster Press.

WENKE, R. (1989). Egypt: origins of complex societies. *Annual Review of Anthropology* 19: 129–55.

WILLETT, F. (1967). *Ife in the History of West African Sculpture*. New York: McGraw-Hill.

CHAPTER 49

···

THE ARCHAEOLOGY OF CLAN- AND LINEAGE-BASED SOCIETIES IN AFRICA

···

MATTHEW DAVIES

INTRODUCTION: THE COMPLEXITY OF SOCIAL FORMS IN AFRICA

MUCH archaeology in Africa, and indeed the rest of the world, has focused on hierarchically and centrally organized 'state' and 'chiefdom'-level societies (based on Polynesian and western models) and has had less to say about alternative forms of complex social organization. There are many reasons for this bias—not least the fact that strongly centralized societies often leave the most visible archaeological remains—but it is increasingly clear that alternative forms of social organization were much more common in the past. Moreover, the universality of widely used categories such as 'chiefdom' and 'state' and the pathways between them have been challenged, leading to significant critiques of older concepts of social complexity and alternative approaches (Crumley 1995; Yoffee 1993; Stein 1998; McIntosh 1999a). There is also growing recognition that archaeologists, particularly in Africa, may be fundamentally misreading the archaeological record because they subconsciously look only for archaeological traditions and sites that fit into predefined frameworks based on western ideals (David and Sterner 1999; Stahl 1999).

To the credit of Africanist archaeologists, many of these global critiques have drawn on African case material—something perhaps explained by the great diversity of African social and political forms and the inability of generations of archaeologists and anthropologists to fit them into more globally accepted frameworks. Wide variation in the nature of social forms across Africa has long been recognized in anthropological research, and was given particular notoriety by Fortes and Evans-Pritchard's (1940) simplistic classification of

African societies as either headed or 'acephalous' (lacking a head; cf. Southall 1956). However, perhaps because of this entrenched dichotomy, African archaeologists, until recently, have failed to fully engage with the complexity of societies that organize themselves through diverse principles of kinship (clans and lineages), as well as age-sets, civil societies, sodalities, title-taking societies, and a variety of situational and semi-political specialists. Commonly subsumed under categories such as egalitarian, segmentary, or kin-based, such societies are often assumed to fit into evolutionary schemes at the level of 'tribe'. However, their specific social structures have not always been considered in detail, and variations between them, as well as diachronic processes of social change within them, have rarely been explored.

This chapter briefly explores some examples of the archaeology of broadly 'kin-based' societies, and considers the potential that such archaeology holds for our understanding of human action or practice through time. In doing so it emphasizes some of the ways in which the African archaeological record has been neglected and discusses how and why this imbalance might be addressed.

SOCIAL COMPLEXITY: HIERARCHY
VS HETERARCHY

It has become increasingly clear that archaeology has tended to equate social complexity with the process of hierarchical political centralization, and the existence of an established vertical control order with a single seat of authority headed by a single ruler or ruling elite (Crumley 1995; McIntosh 1999a). Such hierarchically dominated political structures have been seen as a stage in the idealized historical trajectory of the West, which traces its ancestry from the Orient, through the Classical Greeks and Romans (Blanton 1998). Such notions have greatly influenced anthropology, to the extent that it has often been argued that social complexity progresses (some might say 'inevitably') by a series of evolutionary stages, through the 'band' and 'tribe' to the 'chiefdom' and the 'state', each encompassing a higher degree of political centralization (Fried 1967; Cohen and Service 1978; Friedman and Rowlands 1978).

In Africa, evolutionary models have been invoked to explain increasing centralization in a number of regions, most notably the Nile Valley (Kemp 2006), but also Ethiopia (Munro-Hay 1993), West Africa (MacDonald 1998), and southern Africa (Huffman 2000; Mitchell 2002; Kim and Kusimba 2008). However, there are also regions of Africa where this neo-evolutionary trajectory clearly does not hold or is inapplicable, such as wide regions of West Africa, where a number of large urban polities seem to have lacked any clear, centralized control hierarchy (McIntosh 1999b) or where hierarchies were more variable (David and Sterner 1999), and broad regions of eastern Africa (see below).

It is increasingly clear that hierarchical political centralization cannot be taken alone as synonymous with 'complexity', and the neo-evolutionary framework with its increasing scales of hierarchical centralization can therefore no longer remain an effective paradigm for describing the development and nature of many (if not most) societies. In contrast, the terminology used to describe non-hierarchical complexity has revolved around the concept of 'heterarchy', which implies principles of organization in which decision-making loci may be arranged in various ways, with some structurally above others, but also with multiple loci interacting at the same level or alternating their position with respects to context (Crumley 1995). In Mali's Inland Niger Delta, such heterarchical societies have been termed 'horizontally' structured, where various short vertical control hierarchies represented by civil institutions, such as title-taking societies, interact with each other (both cooperatively and antagonistically) in the operation of governance, with no single group able to obtain a privileged or monopolistic position (McIntosh 2005). Blanton (1998) has considered heterarchical principles in a wider range of societies, arguing that most archaic states fluctuated between centralizing (hierarchical) and decentralizing (heterarchical) forces, encompassing multiple loci of power/authority. In another influential paper, Blanton and colleagues' (Blanton et al. 1996) use of 'dual processual theory' implies that many societies are in flux between the extremes of corporate power (egalitarianism) and networking or exclusionary power (autocracy).

Extending such thinking to Africa and the archaeology of broadly kin-based clan and lineage societies, we need a much more dynamic, non-hierarchically based model if we are to understand the nature of social organization, interaction, and change. As demonstrated below, superficially simple clan- and lineage-based societies are actually very complex with regard to specialized social roles and social institutions as well as the number and extent of social relations found within them. They further display complexity in their dealings with the more centralized societies with which they interact, and in their potential to become more centralized themselves.

The nature of clan- and lineage-based
societies in Africa

In the broadest terms, clan- and lineage-based societies in Africa are structured around the general principles of segmentary organization outlined by Evans-Pritchard (1940) in his seminal work on the Nuer people of South Sudan (cf. Fortes and Evans-Pritchard 1940). In segmentary systems, descent is traced linearly from a founding ancestor such that society may be divided into a series of branching lineages based on kinship. At any point in this system lineage branches may be contrasted with branches of a similar scale or level, and it is these scalar relationships between lineage 'segments' that bring order to the system. In any dispute, social units of a similar size and scale become structurally opposed to one another, and the system therefore ensures that parties in a dispute are relatively well 'matched', encouraging resolution rather than all-out conflict.

While basic segmentary principles hold true for a wide range of societies throughout Africa, their operation varies considerably according to the size of the society in question, its territorial extent, and the degree to which descent is remembered or calculated. More importantly, Evans-Pritchard sought to promote the segmentary concept as an aspect of social organization that might be applied to a very wide range of human societies, and because of this he tended to downplay alternative, yet often coexisting, organizational principles and social institutions (see also Fortes 1940 and Bohannan and Bohannan 1969 for similar

West African examples; see Southall 1956 for critique of the segmentary concept). Perhaps the most widespread alternative structuring principle is that of an age- or generation-set system, whereby all members of the society are initiated into a named group of their age/ generational peers with whom they pass through a sequence of life stages. Such ties act somewhat in antithesis to ties of descent, in that they cut across boundaries of kinship and unite individuals irrespective of their clan and lineage affiliation (Simonse and Kurimoto 1998: 1). While they vary greatly in purpose, function, range, composition, and associated ceremony, it is common for sets to organize themselves so as to act, on occasion, as a corporate group independently of corporate groups formed on principles of kinship. An inherent tension between sets is also common, such that succeeding sets act as a check on the monopoly of power, wealth, and force by other sets (Simonse and Kurimoto 1998).

Territorial or residential corporate units are also very common, and decision-making within them often involves the operation of local councils or discussion groups. For example, although subject to basic segmentary principles and the operation of an age-set system, among most Kalenjin peoples in Kenya the primary means of community-based decision-making on a day-to-day basis revolves around the council or *kokwa*, a formal discussion group comprising all circumcised adult men. The *kokwa* and similar councils are highly effective and flexible social institutions that lend themselves well to decision-making in a variety of socioeconomic situations, including the management of land and resources (including irrigation) and conflict resolution (Davies 2009). Similarly, in many areas of West Africa various residential corporate groups form the basis of decentralized political systems. Good examples include the Tallensi as described by Fortes (1940) and the Tiv as described by Bohannan and Bohannan (1969). The Tiv, for example, have a light hierarchy of lineage head at each increasing level of lineage aggregation. Within residential units, the senior lineage heads takes on a leadership role but does so through group consensus. Lineage heads do not possess a monopoly on authority, and only have direct influence over their immediate kin.

Formal or institutional roles centred on the individual also occasionally appear—the most famous perhaps being the position of leopard-skin chief/priest among the Nuer (Evans-Pritchard 1940)—although it is now becoming increasingly clear that strong charismatic individual leaders, generally referred to as 'prophets', have been historically found in a wide range of East African communities, where they seem to particularly prosper during times of social stress and conflict (Anderson and Johnson 1995). The positions of such individuals are *situational* in the sense that they only apply in very specific contexts; beyond such contexts they find it more difficult to use their position to influence other members of society. In a similar vein, a number of groups recognize 'symbolic' or 'ritual' heads (often referred to as kings) who possess little executive authority. The divine kings of the Shilluk of South Sudan (Evans-Pritchard 1948) are perhaps the most enigmatic example, though they exemplify broader traditions of situational or contextual leadership which, given the existence of related shrines and other structures, may have an archaeological signature (Kleppe 1991; Mawson 1991; Schnepel 1991).

This brief discussion shows that in the ethnographic literature African clan- and lineage-based communities are somewhat less easily dismissed as 'egalitarian' and are more 'complex' in their social and political structures than previously assumed in most archaeological literature. Political life in such societies is complex in a way that empha-sizes the decentralization of power/authority by means of dividing it between a wide range of political institutions and actors, each of which may be more or less dominant in certain circumstances or situations. Such societies represent very good examples of complex het-erarchical organization and, although rarely (if ever) developing into centralized chief-doms or states, and only occasionally leaving substantial archaeological remains, they nevertheless have a great deal to contribute our understanding of human society, in both past and present.

Clan- and lineage-based societies
in the archaeological record

As suggested above, clan- and lineage-based societies have largely been overlooked in Afri-can archaeology. This is predicated on at least two presumptions: first, that as such societies are assumed to lack social 'complexity', it is also assumed that they lack complex material forms and therefore that the archaeological evidence for such societies is unlikely to be forth-coming; second, that such societies only represent stagnant phases in a general evolutionary scheme.

The first assumption holds true only inasmuch as the material traces of such societies may be more ephemeral and less easily recognized by archaeologists with a predilection for the structural architecture typified by Eurasian 'civilizations'. However, as noted above, numer-ous 'non-centralized' societies create shrines and other features which may be identified archaeologically (Insoll, Ch. 12 above). Equally informative are the settlement structures and settlement patterns left by non-centralized communities, which may offer a wealth of infor-mation about their nature and dynamics through time. As will be demonstrated below, sig-nificant potential for such studies may be found in eastern Africa, while similar attempts have been made also in West Africa, particularly among the Tiv (Folorunso and Ogundele 1993; Ogundele 2005).

The second assumption is, however, by far the more damning, for it implies that African societies are only interesting and/or only change when engaged in some 'significant' event predefined by western standards, such as being the first farmers, the first metalworkers, or the first builders of states or urban settlements. As such, early clan- and lineage-based socie-ties have largely been considered in detail only when associated with the spread of food pro-duction or metals into a region. Moreover, this is despite the fact that throughout much of sub-Saharan African prehistory it is precisely such 'interstadial' people who formed the bulk of the African population (Stahl 1999: 47). The contrast between the study of the first live-stock keepers in eastern Africa during the 'Pastoral Neolithic' (PN) associated with the spread of domesticates and the study of the later 'Pastoral Iron Age' (PIA) with no such asso-ciations is particularly illustrative of this situation. The former are the subjects of numerous high-profile studies, papers, and overviews (Lane, Ch. 40 above), while the latter have been the subject of only a handful of studies (Posnansky 1957; Ambrose 1984; Sutton 1987, 1993b; Lane 2011).

CASE STUDY: THE ARCHAEOLOGY OF THE
SIRIKWA AND RELATED COMMUNITIES

The archaeology of some of eastern Africa's best-known clan- and lineage-based societies exemplifies the points just made. The region and period in question is that of the Central Rift Valley of Kenya and northern Tanzania during the Pastoral (PIA) and Later Iron Age (LIA), approximately AD 1000 to the present (Fig. 49.1). The early PIA, some 1100 years ago, is poorly understood, with very few sites known in any detail, the best being Deloraine on Kenya's Mau Escarpment (Sutton 1993b). It is clearer that by AD 1200, the Central Rift and Western Highlands of Kenya were relatively densely inhabited by a group (or groups) of people who practised both cereal cultivation and pastoralism, used metals occasionally, and created distinctive roulette-decorated pottery (Lane, Ch. 40 above). These people are principally known from their characteristic settlement sites, known as 'Sirikwa' holes or hollows, which comprise a central shallow depression, often reinforced at the edges by stone revetment, around which a series of habitation structures is normally found (Figs 49.1 and 49.2). The central depression appears to have been a semi-fortified cattle kraal, with people living in connected huts around the exterior (Fig. 49.3). Large dung middens commonly flank the entrance to the hollow and display postholes for substantial gate posts (Sutton 1973, 1987).

This Sirikwa tradition represents a distinct new way of life that seems to have been something of a break from the preceding early PIA; moreover, it is an exceedingly long-lived tradition, extending into the 18th century in some places (Sutton 1987, 1993a). Sirikwa settlements are numerous, with more than 200 located in a variety of environmental zones and altitudes. Sutton (1973) initially suggested that Sirikwa settlements represent small communities of mixed agropastoralists, perhaps clustered into small lineage-based units, living in a political climate where small-scale cattle raiding was not uncommon, hence the requirement for minor defensive structures. However, a closer examination of the Sirikwa economy from a number of sites distributed widely in space and time suggests that there was greater social variation and economic specialization within the Sirikwa tradition than originally thought. Reinterpretations of the early Central Rift sites at Hyrax Hill near Nakuru, Kenya, suggest that at times the Sirikwa economy was much more pastoral in nature, with domestic animals kept in quantities and proportions akin to modern specialized pastoral communities, and with more ephemeral surrounding settlements. Similarly, some sites, such as Chemagel in Kenya's Western Highlands, may have had a more agricultural economy, with fewer livestock and more permanent structures and settlement (Sutton 1987, 1993a; Kyule 1997). It also seems likely that at this time other communities began forming around the Sirikwa, communities who practised various economic specializations and probably interacted with their Sirikwa neighbours. Most notable among these is the specialized irrigation farming community of Engaruka in northern Tanzania that, while a little outside the core Sirikwa region, nonetheless represents the gradual intensification and specialization of economies and socioeconomic interaction at the time (Stump, Ch. 46 above; Sutton 2004).

There is little evidence for socioeconomic differentiation within Sirikwa or surrounding communities: all sites are relatively standardized in the levels and qualities of artefacts found,

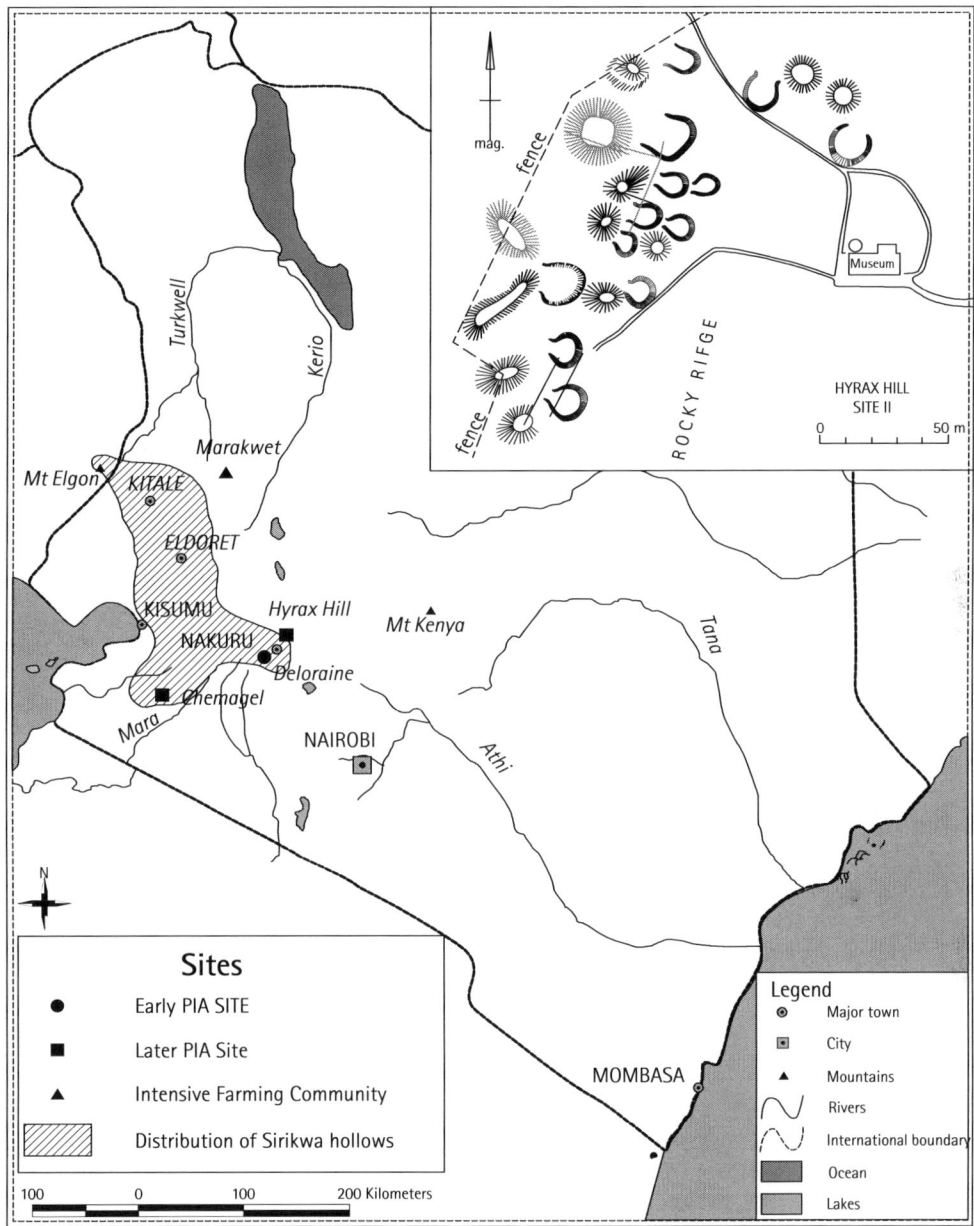

FIG. 49.1 Major Pastoral Iron Age (PIA) sites in central Kenya and the distribution of Sirikwa hollows. *Inset*: cluster of thirteen Sirikwa hollows and associated mounds at Hyrax Hill near Nakuru, Kenya (reproduced from Sutton 1987 with kind permission of John Sutton and the British Institute in Eastern Africa).

FIG. 49.2 Sirikwa hollow at Chemagel, Kenya (reproduced from Sutton 1973 with kind permission of John Sutton and the British Institute in Eastern Africa).

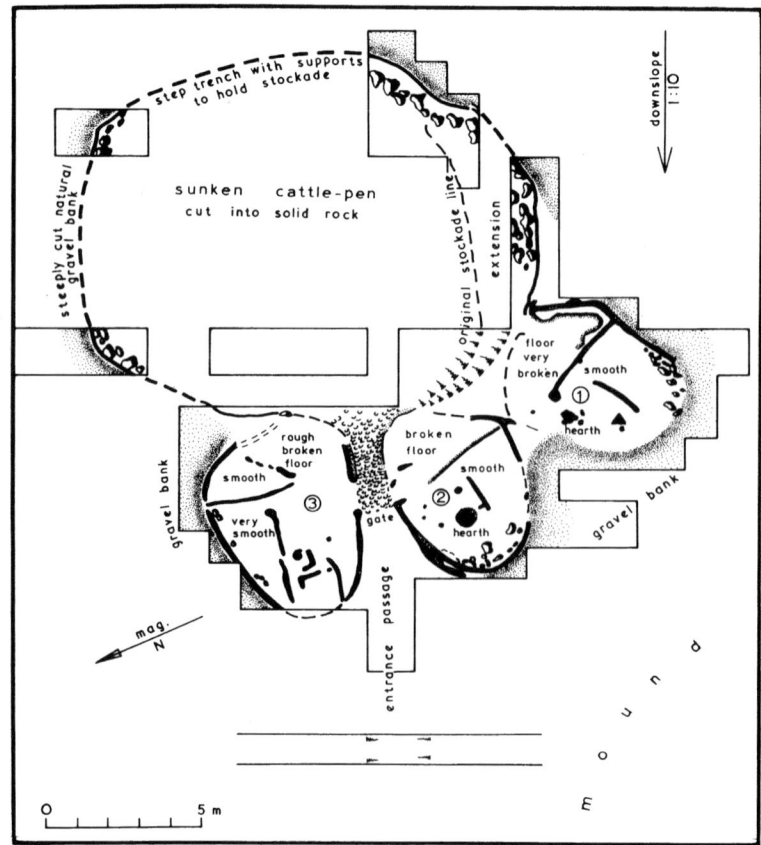

FIG. 49.3 Plan of Sirikwa hollow and adjacent huts at Hyrax Hill, Kenya (reproduced from Sutton 1987 with kind permission of John Sutton and the British Institute in Eastern Africa).

and structures and faunal remains seem to vary in relation to moderate specialization and familial size rather than formal social differentiation. Despite this lack of stratification, the basic Sirikwa pattern seems to have been an extensive and highly dominant way of life that almost certainly encompassed a degree of regional specialization, exchange, and interaction, and exercised a degree of hegemony over a vast area for more than 500 years. Unfortunately, we know little about Sirikwa social organization, despite there being a large number of Sirikwa sites available for investigation. For example, more detailed analysis of the spatial layout of the domestic areas around Sirikwa hollows, especially the number and size of house floors and associated artefacts, would give a much clearer idea of the number of people living around each hollow, potential variation in activity areas, and important variations in such structures across the spatial and temporal range of the Sirikwa phenomenon (see Fig. 49.3.). Similarly, analysis of distinct clusters of Sirikwa hollows, the number and scale of hollows in each cluster, and the distribution between clusters would probably shed significant light on broader aspects of Sirikwa social life, including the social and economic interactions between different groups and settlement clusters.

Also important would be the further analysis of the communities that arose around the core Sirikwa areas, particularly intensive agricultural settlements within and around the Rift Valley. To date, in-depth research has only concentrated on the interrelated Pokot, Marakwet, and Elgeyo farming regions of northwest Kenya (Sutton 1973; Soper 1983; Davies 2008, 2010a), and the abandoned agricultural settlement of Engaruka, where a total population of more than 3,000 people lived at densities that should rightly be referred to as 'urban' (Stump, Ch. 46 above; Davies 2010b). Despite this, Engaruka resembles the Sirikwa in displaying very little in the way of social stratification or wealth disparity. Indeed, while its settlement pattern is very different from that of the Sirikwa, the social structure may have been similar, i.e. non-hierarchical, organized around heterarchical principles based on kinship and with crosscutting social institutions and governance by small local councils and occasionally charismatic situational leaders. As with the Sirikwa phenomenon, closer examination of interconnected domestic areas at Engaruka would probably shed more information on the site's social structure; the distribution of features such as 'communal hearth' areas and grindstones might be particularly informative.

Although Engaruka may be the most extreme example, settlements like it seem to have arisen very widely throughout the Rift Valley region over the last 500 years, with many persisting into historic times. In particular, on the basis of historic patterns, Håkansson (1994) and others (Börjeson 2005; Davies 2010a) have argued that such communities were part of regional economic exchange dynamics that linked specialized farmers with specialized herders. In many ethnohistoric cases, such as in Pokot/Marakwet, Baringo, and Arusha, these farming and pastoral communities, while radically different in terms of economy and settlement pattern, were nevertheless similar in terms of social structure and concepts of governance. This is particularly true among the Pokot and Marakwet of Northwest Kenya, where the local councils (*kokwa*) that govern rights to irrigation water among farmers in the hills may be employed to very different ends among pastoral sections of the community (Davies 2009). Also important are shared age-set systems, as well as formal ties of kinship and reciprocal exchange that tend to operate beyond the boundaries of single groups and unite ethnically and economically diverse communities on the basis of shared values. Such heterarchical principles of organization thus seem to be adaptable to a wide range of economic and environmental situations and to work across and between societies. If archaeologists can build on such ethnohistorical data and examine social structures within archaeological phenomena like the Sirikwa or Engaruka, they may be able to expand upon current understandings of the organization of such communities. This may also allow us to learn more about the social processes leading to spatial or temporal variations/changes within archaeological traditions, as well as about broad principles of social structure, community interaction, and change in human societies generally.

BROADER ANALYSES OF CLAN- AND
LINEAGE-BASED COMMUNITIES

While the Sirikwa and related communities form one particularly useful dataset for the analysis of non-centralized clan- and lineage-based societies through time, a number of other archaeological/historical traditions offer significant potential. In West Africa I have already noted the work carried out on Tiv settlement patterns (Folorunso and Ogundele 1993; Ogundele 2005). In eastern Africa a particularly informative sociocultural transition that might gain much from a more detailed archaeological analysis is the shift from the Sirikwa-dominated lifestyle to that of the Maasai way of life, which began some 500 years ago and came to the fore in the 18th century. The development of the Maasai community had radical effect on its neighbours, including the Sirikwa, and revolved not merely around technical advantages but also around important social changes, including the reorganization of Maasai age-sets and the development of what Sutton (1993a) calls Maasai ideology (cf. Galaty 1993). Archaeologically, the shift in settlement patterns and lifestyles that accompanied the Maasai expansion would be particularly informative, and some tentative steps have already been taken in this direction (Larick 1986; Lamprey and Waller 1990; Mbae 1990).

Other informative historical traditions, albeit as yet poorly studied from an archaeological perspective, might include those relating to various societies in the Lake Victoria region from the EIA and into the LIA (Ashley 2010). Such examples include the *ohinga* stone-walled enclosure (Lofgren 1967; Onjala 2003) and the *gunda-buche* earth-and-bank enclosure (Odede 2008) traditions of the Luo of western Kenya; the various 'fort' structures known from the Bungoma and Bukusu region of western Kenya (Scully 1979); and mosaic economies of the Tsavo region of southern Kenya as studied by Kusimba and Kusimba (2005). The embryonic work conducted on each of these traditions encourages an attempt to move beyond common neo-evolutionary frameworks and towards understandings of novel social structures and process of social action. The research by Kusimba and Kusimba has been particularly pioneering in this regard, demonstrating significant complexity in the economic interaction of groups with various social structures and identities. Most importantly, Kusimba and Kusimba (2005) argue that both economy and identity are fluid and adaptable, and this points towards innovation, original agency, and complexity of a different kind. The Kusimbas' model has much in common with the above discussion, and might be well applied more broadly to other communities.

Conclusion

Much research into 'complex' societies is built upon the identification of specialization and stratification within single settlements (or related complexes of them) with clear markers of unified cultural traditions. However, complexity in terms of specialization and stratification among African clan- and lineage-based societies seems to have operated at the level of ethnic group, whereby a distinct way of life was a marker of relative ideological status and wealth—although this was probably valued differently by individuals occupying different social positions or with different identities (such as craft caste or gender). Within such communities, overt personal accumulation and the attempt to wield overt personal authority were checked by decentralizing tendencies, such that at the community level the society might be thought of as relatively egalitarian and governed by a variety of horizontally arranged social institutions. However, when viewed at the level of interacting communities and kin groups, social distinction of a sort may be seen in competition between groups, the interconnected specialization of societies, and the relative ideologies and values attached to them. Archaeology is only just beginning to understand the complexity of such relations and their temporal dynamics. They are likely to have formed a cornerstone of much of Africa's past, but represent lifeways radically different from those found elsewhere in time and space.

Clan- and-lineage based communities in Africa, and the nature of governance within them as well as the regional interactions between them, were certainly complex, but they operated in ways that archaeology has rarely understood and thus they have been largely overlooked because they do not fit predefined concepts. Thus, for instance, the archaeology of the Sirikwa, Maasai, and others in eastern Africa offers significant potential to produce novel approaches to the study of 'acephalous' societies more generally. If successful, such approaches offer the potential for testing some of the more recent models concerning the variety of African social forms and the nature of complexity, authority, and social change in African prehistory.

References

Ambrose, S. H. (1984). Excavations at Deloraine, Rongai, 1978. *Azania* 19: 79–104.

Anderson, D., and Johnson, D. (eds) (1995). *Revealing Prophets: Prophecy in Eastern African History*. Oxford: James Currey.

Ashley, C. (2010). Towards a socialised archaeology of ceramics in the Great Lakes Africa. *African Archaeological Review* 27: 135–63.

Bohannan, L., and Bohannan, P. (1969). *The Tiv of Central Nigeria*. London: International African Institute.

Blanton, R. E. (1998). Beyond centralisation: steps toward a theory of egalitarian behaviour in archaic states. In G. M. Feinman and J. Marcus (eds), *Archaic States*. Santa Fe, NM: SAR Press, 135–72.

—— Feinman, G. M., Kowalewski, S. A., and Peregrine, P. N. (1996). A dual-processual theory for the evolution of Mesoamerican civilisation. *Current Anthropology* 37: 1–14.

Börjeson, L. (2005). *A History under Siege: Intensive Agriculture in the Mbulu Highlands, Tanzania, 19th Century to the Present*. Stockholm: Stockholm University.

COHEN, R., and SERVICE, E. (eds) (1978). *Origins of the State: The Anthropology of Political Evolution*. Philadelphia: Institute for the Study of Human Issues.

CRUMLEY, C. L. (1995). Heterarchy and the analysis of complex societies. *Archaeological Papers of the American Anthropological Association* 6: 1–6.

DAVID, N., and STERNER, J. (1999). Wonderful society: the Burgess Shale creatures, Mandara polities, and the nature of prehistory. In S. K. Mcintosh (ed.), *Beyond Chiefdoms: Pathways to Complexity in Africa*. Cambridge: Cambridge University Press, 97–109.

DAVIES, M. I. J. (2008). The irrigation system of the Pokot, northwest Kenya. *Azania* 43: 50–76

—— (2009). Wittfogel's dilemma: heterarchy and ethnographic approaches to irrigation management in Eastern Africa and Mesopotamia. *World Archaeology* 41: 16–35.

—— (2010a). A view from the East: an interdisciplinary 'historical ecology' approach to a contemporary agricultural landscape in northwest Kenya. *African Studies* 69: 279–97.

—— (2010b). From platforms to people: rethinking population estimates for the abandoned agricultural settlement of Engaruka, northern Tanzania. *Azania* 45: 203–13.

EVANS-PRITCHARD, E. E. (1940). *The Nuer: A Description of the Modes of Livelihood and Political Institutions of a Nilotic People*. Oxford: Oxford University Press.

—— (1948). *The Divine Kingship of the Shilluk of the Nilotic Sudan*. Cambridge: Cambridge University Press.

FOLORUNSO, C. A., and OGUNDELE, S. O. (1993). Agriculture and settlement among the Tiv of Nigeria: some ethnoarchaeological observations. In T. Shaw, P. Sinclair, B. Andah, and A. Okpoko (eds), *The Archaeology of Africa: Food, Metals and Towns*. London: Routledge, 274–88.

FORTES, M. (1940). The political system of the Tallensi of the Northern Territories of the Gold Coast. In Fortes and Evans-Pritchard (1940: 239–71).

—— and EVANS-PRITCHARD, E. E. (eds) (1940). *African Political Systems*. London: Oxford University Press.

FRIED, M. H. (1967). *The Evolution of Political Society: An Essay in Political Anthropology*. New York: Random House.

FRIEDMAN, J., and ROWLANDS, M. (1978). Notes towards an epigenetic model of the evolution of 'civilisation'. In J. Friedman and M. Rowlands (eds), *The Evolution of Social Systems*. London: Duckworth, 201–76.

GALATY, J. G. (1993). Maasai expansion and the new East African pastoralism. In T. Spear and R. Waller (eds), *Being Maasai: Ethnicity and Identity in East Africa*. London: James Currey, 61–86.

HÅKANSSON, N. T. (1994). Grain, cattle and power: social processes of intensive cultivation and exchange in precolonial western Kenya. *Journal of Anthropological Research* 50: 249–76.

HUFFMAN, T. N. (2000). Mapungubwe and the origins of the Zimbabwe culture. *South African Archaeological Society Goodwin Series* 8: 14–29.

KEMP, B. (2006). *Ancient Egypt: Anatomy of a Civilisation*. London: Routledge.

KIM, N. C., and KUSIMBA, C. M. (2008). Pathways to complexity and state formation in the Southern Zambezian region. *African Archaeological Review* 25: 131–52.

KLEPPE, E. J. (1991). Divine kingdoms in northern Africa: material manifestations. In I. Hodder (ed.), *The Meanings of Things: Material Culture and Symbolic Expression*. London: Taylor & Francis, 195–201.

KUSIMBA, C. M., and KUSIMBA, S. B. (2005). Mosaics and interactions: East Africa, 2000 BP to present. In A. Stahl (ed.), *African Archaeology: A Critical Introduction*. Oxford: Blackwell, 392–419.

KYULE, M. D. (1997). The Sirikwa economy: further work at site II on Hyrax Hill. *Azania* 32: 21–30.

LAMPREY, R., and WALLER, R. (1990). The Loita-Mara region in historical times: patterns of subsistence, settlement and ecological change. In P. Robertshaw (ed.), *Early Pastoralists of South-Western Kenya*. Nairobi: British Institute in Eastern Africa, 16–35.

LANE, P. J. (2011). An outline of the later Holocene archaeology and precolonial history of the Ewaso Basin, Kenya. *Smithsonian Contributions to Zoology* 632: 11–30.

LARICK, R. (1986). Iron smelting and interethnic conflict among precolonial Maa-speaking pastoralists of north-central Kenya. *African Archaeological Review* 4: 165–76.

LOFGREN, L. (1967). Stone structures of South Nyanza. *Azania* 2: 75–88.

MACDONALD, K. C. (1998). Before the Empire of Ghana: pastoralism and the origins of complexity in the Sahel. In G. Connah (ed.), *Transformations in Africa: Essays on Africa's Later Past*. London: Leicester University Press, 71–103.

MAWSON, A. N. M. (1991). Bringing what people want: shrine politics among the Agar Dinka. *Africa* 61: 354–69.

MBAE, N. B. (1990). The ethnoarchaeology of Maasai settlements and refuse disposal patterns in the Lemek area. In P. Robertshaw (ed.), *Early Pastoralists of South-Western Kenya*. Nairobi: British Institute in Eastern Africa, 279–92.

MCINTOSH, R. J. (2005). *Ancient Middle Niger: Urbanism and the Self-Organizing Landscape*. Cambridge: Cambridge University Press.

MCINTOSH, S. K. (1999a). Pathways to complexity: an African perspective. In S. K. Mcintosh (ed.), *Beyond Chiefdoms: Pathways to Complexity in Africa*. Cambridge: Cambridge University Press, 1–30.

—— (1999b). Modelling political organisation in large-scale settlement clusters: a case study from the inland Niger Delta. In S. K. Mcintosh (ed.), *Beyond Chiefdoms: Pathways to Complexity in Africa*. Cambridge: Cambridge University Press, 66–79.

MITCHELL, P. J. (2002). *The Archaeology of Southern Africa*. Cambridge: Cambridge University Press.

MUNRO-HAY, S. (1993). State development and urbanism in northern Ethiopia. In T. Shaw, P. J. J. Sinclair, B. Andah, and A. Okpoko (eds), *The Archaeology of Africa: Foods, Metals and Towns*. London: Routledge, 609–19.

ODEDE, F. (2008). *Gunda-buche*: the bank-and-ditch fortified settlement enclosures of western Kenya, Lake Victoria Basin. *Azania* 43: 36–49.

OGUNDELE, S. O. (2005). Ethnoarchaeology of domestic space and spatial behaviour among the Tiv and Ungwai of Central Nigeria. *African Archaeological Review* 22: 25–52.

ONJALA, I. O. (2003). Spatial distribution and settlement system of the stone structures of south-western Kenya. *Azania* 38: 99–120.

POSNANSKY, M. (1957). Excavations at Lanet, Kenya, 1957. *Azania* 2: 89–114.

SCHNEPEL, B. (1991). Continuity despite and through death: regicide and royal shrines among the Shilluk of the Southern Sudan. *Africa* 61:40–70.

SCULLY, R. T. K. (1979). Nineteenth century settlement sites and related oral traditions from the Bungoma area, Western Kenya. *Azania* 14: 81–96.

SIMONSE, S., and KURIMOTO, E. (1998). Introduction. In E. Kurimoto and S. Simonse (eds), *Conflict, Age and Power in North East Africa: Age Systems in Transition*. Oxford: James Currey, 1–28.

SOPER, R. C. (1983). A survey of the irrigation system of the Marakwet. In B. E. Kipkorir, R. C. Soper, and J. W. Ssenyonga (eds), *Kerio Valley: Past, Present and Future*. Nairobi: University of Nairobi Institute of African Studies, 75–94.

SOUTHALL, A. (1956). *Alur Society: A Study in Processes and Types of Domination*. Cambridge: Heffer.

STAHL, A. B. (1999). Perceiving variability in time and space: the evolutionary mapping of African societies. In S. K. Mcintosh (ed.), *Beyond Chiefdoms: Pathways to Complexity in Africa*. Cambridge: Cambridge University Press, 39–55.

STEIN, G. (1998). Heterogeneity, power and political economy: some current research issues in the archaeology of Old World complex societies. *Journal of Archaeological Research* 6: 1–44.

SUTTON, J. E. G. (1973). *The Archaeology of the Western Highlands of Kenya*. Nairobi: British Institute in Eastern Africa.

—— (1987). Hyrax Hill and the Sirikwa: new excavations on Site II. *Azania* 22: 1–36.

—— (1993a). Becoming Maasailand. In T. Spear and R. Waller (eds), *Being Maasai: Ethnicity and Identity in East Africa*. London: James Currey, 38–60.

—— (1993b). Deloraine and the Iron Age of the Central Rift. *Azania* 28: 103–25.

—— (2004). Engaruka: the success and abandonment of an integrated irrigation system in an arid part of the Rift Valley, c.15th to 17th centuries. In M. Widgren and J. E. G. Sutton (eds), *Islands of Intensive Agriculture in Eastern Africa*. Oxford: James Currey, 114–32.

YOFFEE, N. (1993). Too many chiefs? (or, safe texts for the '90s). In N. Yoffee and A. G. Sherratt (eds), *Archaeological Theory: Who Sets the Agenda?* Cambridge: Cambridge University Press, 60–78.

CHAPTER 50

PHARAONIC EGYPT

IAN SHAW

INTRODUCTION

PERHAPS the most distinctive aspect of Egyptian archaeology is the existence of a very large corpus of ancient written material (comprising texts in the hieroglyphic, hieratic, and demotic scripts), which allows the surviving material culture of the Pharaonic period (*c.* 3100–332 BC) to be considered within a rich and diverse cognitive context that is not available for most other regions of Africa until comparatively recent times. The beginning of Egyptian archaeology as a complete historical discipline, comprising the study of both texts and archaeology, was thus made possible by Jean-François Champollion's decipherment of Egyptian hieroglyphs in 1822, closely followed by Thomas Young's decipherment of the demotic script in the late 1820s (Parkinson 1999; Ray 2007). Together, they transformed the archaeology of ancient Egypt from prehistory into history, and the translation of a whole range of documents soon enabled Egyptology to take its place alongside the study of the Classical civilizations. The decipherment of the texts meant, however, that the study of Pharaonic Egypt as a whole required both linguistic and anthropological skills, and Egyptian material culture—temples, tombs, cities, artefacts, and organic remains—would always have to be discussed and interpreted in the context of a richly detailed corpus of texts written on stone, papyrus, and potsherds. The documents themselves relate primarily to religious, ritualistic, and funerary aspects of ancient Egypt, although some specific bodies of material, such as the Abusir papyri (Posener-Kriéger 1976) and Lahun papyri (Quirke 2005; Collier and Quirke 2002–6), and the ostraca and papyri from Deir el-Medina (McDowell 1999), also convey some sense of economic and social activities.

Although the linguistic achievements of Champollion and Young in the 1820s represent a very definite watershed in the emergence of Egyptian archaeology, it is more difficult to determine at what point a simple antiquarian interest in Egyptian antiquities can be said to have changed into the scientific archaeological discipline of Egyptology. The early 19th century was primarily characterized by systematic plundering on behalf of rich patrons, something only curtailed by Auguste Mariette's institution of the Egyptian Antiquities Service (now the Supreme Council of Antiquities) and the first national collection of antiquities, now the core of Cairo's Egyptian Museum, in the second half of the 1800s (Reid 2002; El-Saddik 2005). A truly scientific archaeology, however, only emerged through the work of

Flinders Petrie (Drower 1985), which paid attention to every detail of the archaeological deposits, rather than simply concentrating on exposing the large monumental features of sites, and emphasized selective excavation over wholesale stripping, as at the late Eighteenth-Dynasty capital of Tell el-Amarna (Petrie 1894). Ordering of Egyptian prehistory by 'sequence dating', a relative chronology grounded on gradual changes in the composition of individual funerary assemblages, was another of his major contributions (Petrie 1891), and has been broadly confirmed by later stratigraphic excavations and radiocarbon dating (Kemp 1982; Hassan 1985; Hendrickx 1996; Savage 2001).

These advances were developed by the slightly later fieldwork of George Reisner, who pioneered multidisciplinary investigations and was the first to recognize the need to provide sufficiently detailed records of his surveys or excavations so that future researchers could use them to reconstruct both the site and the process by which it was originally examined. As the pursuit of treasures for private and foreign collections came to an end from the 1920s, the funding and motivation of archaeological work began to be increasingly dictated by universities and cultural institutes, leading ultimately to a healthier situation in which sites and monuments are now largely studied to seek answers to research questions. It should be noted, however, that the Egyptian Supreme Council of Antiquities still tends to operate a system whereby specific individuals or institutions (and, more generally, specific nations) are allowed to work continuously at particular major sites, such as the temple of Hatshepsut on the west bank at Thebes (modern Luxor), restored and analysed by a Polish expedition since 1961 (Szafranski 2007), and the necropolis at Abusir, excavated by a Czech expedition since 1960 (Verner and Benešovská 2008; see Fig. 50.1). This allocation of annually renewable site concessions can sometimes have the effect of encouraging a culture whereby fieldwork is

FIG. 50.1 The mastaba of Ptahshepses at Abusir, Egypt, as restored by the Czech expedition that has been excavating and reconstructing the site of Abusir since 1960 (photograph, Ian Shaw).

simply a continuous process of slightly unfocused data collection, although at its best it can also allow archaeologists to build up minutely detailed pictures of the interactions between human populations and specific landscapes. Barry Kemp's work at Amarna since 1977 (Kemp and Stevens 2010) and Mark Lehner's work at an Old Kingdom settlement associated with the Giza necropolis (Lehner and Wetterstrom 2006) exemplify this well.

Building on the results of these and other workers, the remainder of this chapter tackles four issues of contemporary concern in the archaeology of Pharaonic Egypt: chronology; state formation; regime change; and race and ethnicity. As space does not permit detailed discussion of the history or the archaeology of the Pharaonic state, readers should consult recent syntheses such as Shaw (2000), Kemp (2006), and David (2007).

Egyptian archaeological data: issues of material culture and chronology

One of the foremost problems in the archaeology of Pharaonic Egypt is the recurrent bias towards data from Upper (i.e. southern) Egypt. Despite the work undertaken at Delta sites both in the late 19th century and since the 1980s, the prevailing view of Egyptian society and history continues to be heavily biased towards Upper Egypt, and in particular, the rich remains of the Theban region (see Fig. 50.2). This situation stems partly from the survival of more

FIG. 50.2 Map of Egypt showing the sites mentioned in Chapter 50 (Ian Shaw).

impressive standing architectural remains in Upper Egypt, but also from the relatively poor conditions of preservation in the Delta, where high population, the submergence of archaeological deposits below the ground-water level, and the agricultural use of tell sites for fertilizer have all tended to reduce the attraction (and indeed the visibility) of Lower Egyptian archaeological sites. Although the initiation of a number of new projects at Delta sites since the 1980s has begun to redress this balance, it will be many years before the weight of evidence from all periods can be said to be spread equally across southern, northern, and middle Egypt.

As well as this geographical bias, a further significant problem is the increasing dislocation between the processes of change in material culture and the traditional politically based chronological system of dynasties, kingdoms, and 'intermediate periods', which may now be approaching the end of its usefulness. Ancient Egyptian political history from *c.* 3000 BC to AD 395 is traditionally divided into three periods: the Pharaonic, Ptolemaic, and Roman. By far the longest of the three was the Pharaonic period (*c.* 3000–332 BC), which is made up of a sequence of thirty dynasties, conventionally grouped into the Early Dynastic period, the Old Kingdom, the First Intermediate Period, the Middle Kingdom, the Second Intermediate Period, the New Kingdom, the Third Intermediate Period, and the Late Period (Table 50.1).

Table 50.1 Pharaonic Egypt: chronological chart

PREHISTORY

Badarian Period	*c.* 4500–3800 BC
Amratian (Naqada I) Period	*c.* 4000–3500 BC
Gerzean (Naqada II) Period	*c.* 3500–3200 BC
Naqada III/'Dynasty 0'	*c.* 3200–3000 BC
PHARAONIC/DYNASTIC PERIOD (*c.* 3000–332 BC)	
Early Dynastic Period	3000–2686 BC
1st Dynasty	3000–2890 BC
2nd Dynasty	2890–2686 BC
Old Kingdom	2686–2181 BC
3rd Dynasty	2686–2613 BC
4th Dynasty	2613–2494 BC
5th Dynasty	2494–2345 BC
6th Dynasty	2345–2181 BC
First Intermediate Period	2181–2055 BC
7th and 8th Dynasties	2181–2125 BC
9th and 10th Dynasties	2160–2025 BC
11th Dynasty (Thebes only)	2125–2055 BC
Middle Kingdom	2055–1650 BC
11th Dynasty (all Egypt)	2055–1985 BC
12th Dynasty	1985–1795 BC
13th Dynasty	1795–after 1650 BC
14th Dynasty	1750–1650 BC

PREHISTORY	
Second Intermediate Period	1650–1550 BC
15th Dynasty (Hyksos)	1650–1550 BC
16th Dynasty (minor Hyksos)	1650–1550 BC
17th Dynasty (Theban)	1650–1550 BC
New Kingdom	1550–1069 BC
18th Dynasty	1550–1295 BC
Ramessid period	1295–1069 BC
19th Dynasty	1295–1186 BC
20th Dynasty	1186–1069 BC
Third Intermediate Period	1069–664 BC
21st Dynasty	1069–945 BC
22nd Dynasty	945–715 BC
23rd Dynasty	818–715 BC
24th Dynasty	727–715 BC
25th Dynasty (Kushite period)	747–656 BC
Late Period	664–332 BC
26th Dynasty (Saite Period)	664–525 BC
27th Dynasty (1st Persian Period)	525–404 BC
28th Dynasty	404–399 BC
29th Dynasty	399–380 BC
30th Dynasty	380–343 BC
2nd Persian Period	343–332 BC
PTOLEMAIC PERIOD	332–30 BC
Macedonian Dynasty	332–305 BC
ROMAN PERIOD	30 BC–AD 311

The names and relative dates of the various rulers and dynasties in the Pharaonic period derive from a number of textual sources. These sources include the *Aegyptiaca*, a history compiled by an Egyptian priest called Manetho in the early 3rd century BC (Wadell 1940), and much earlier 'king-lists' that give the names and sequences of rulers as recorded on the walls of tombs and temples, but also in papyri (such as the Nineteenth Dynasty document known as the Royal Turin Canon) and elsewhere, such as the list in the Wadi Hammamat greywacke quarries; Redford (1986). It is usually presumed that Manetho himself used king-lists of these types as his sources.

Egypt's 'traditional' absolute chronology tends to rely on complex webs of textual references, combining such elements as names, dates, and genealogical information into an overall historical framework that is more reliable in some periods than in others (e.g. Kitchen 1991). The two most important documents for assigning absolute dates to the traditional Egyptian chronological framework are two records of the 'heliacal rising' of the dog-star Sirius, one dating to the late Twelfth Dynasty, the other to the early Eighteenth (Krauss 1985). By assigning absolute dates to these documents, Egyptologists have been able to extrapolate a set of absolute dates for the whole of the Pharaonic period, on the basis of records of the lengths of reign of the other kings of the Middle and New Kingdoms (e.g. Hornung et al. 2006). Because of its well-respected traditional chronological framework, Egyptology was one of the first archaeological disciplines to benefit from radiocarbon dating, since, in the late 1940s, a series of well-dated Egyptian artefacts were used as benchmarks to assess the reliability of the newly invented radiocarbon technique (Libby 1955). The subsequent recognition of the necessity of calibrating radiocarbon years in order to anchor them in actual time (Shaw 1985; Hassan and Robinson 1987) still left concerns that the available radiocarbon dates for Egypt and Nubia sometimes appear to differ significantly from the conventional chronology (Bonani et al. 2001). However, a recent systematic attempt to radiocarbon date samples of known age (through either their archaeological context or associated textual data) has been largely successful in demonstrating good synchronization between radiocarbon dates and the conventional chronology (Dee et al. 2010).

Although the traditional division of Pharaonic history into dynasties has become firmly embedded in the literature, many modern scholars would now question the historical validity of distinguishing between Sixth or Seventh Dynasties, for example, or between the 'Third Intermediate Period' and the 'Late Period' (e.g. Malek 1989, 1997). The three 'intermediate periods' have proved to be particularly awkward phases, partly because at these times there was often more than one ruler or dynasty reigning simultaneously in different parts of the country. Excavations since the 1960s have gradually produced a rival—and archaeologically more relevant—chronological system, based simply on changes in material culture and supported by a framework of stratigraphic analysis and radiometric dates (O'Connor 1974; Trigger et al. 1983). Future chronologies of the Pharaonic period will need to integrate political change with the socioeconomic and art-historical fluctuations observable in the archaeological record.

CURRENT ISSUES AND PROBLEMS IN THE ARCHAEOLOGY AND ANTHROPOLOGY OF PHARAONIC EGYPT

In recent years, Egyptian archaeology has encountered some problems that are entirely specific to northeast Africa, the Nile region, and Near Eastern studies, but has also had to deal with other challenges experienced across archaeology as a whole. In 1990 O'Connor (1990: 244) attempted to summarize the situation that Egyptian archaeology found itself in towards the end of the 20th century: 'Intellectual change within Egyptology is essential if society and culture are to receive the attention their importance in prehistoric and Pharaonic Egypt [deserves].' He went on to discuss the importance of making greater use of archaeological data to answer questions about Egyptian culture, particularly those many aspects of society not really addressed by the surviving ancient texts, and also stressed the need to develop a more self-conscious and explicit history of Egyptology, so that the biases and preoccupations of key scholars could be better understood. Twenty years later some of the same issues apply, but clearly new debates have emerged, both with the discovery of new data and with

the development of new archaeological and analytical techniques. Three issues merit particular attention here: state formation, regime change, and the contemporary politics of race
and ethnicity in Ancient Egypt.

State formation

As in other areas of archaeology, Egyptologists have tended to debate a number of issues
relating both to the emergence of the initial Egyptian state and to the processes by which that
state was subsequently transformed, occasionally quite dramatically.

In the last few centuries of the prehistoric period, Egypt began to change from a very
fragmented collection of farms and villages into a highly centralized and sophisticated
state (Wengrow 2006: 151–217). This period, spanning the late Predynastic period and the
beginning of the Early Dynastic period, is sometimes described as the 'Protodynastic', lasting from about 3200 to 2900 BC. It is possible, given the survival of depictions of battles on
late Predynastic mobiliary art, such as the Battlefield Palette (c. 3100 BC; British Museum
EA20971), that this was a time of growing conflict within Egypt, as more and more local
chiefs and their villages grew stronger, expanded, and competed with one another. Eventually three main areas—Naqada, Hierakonpolis, and This—seem to have been struggling
for power (Wilkinson 1999: 44–52; Kemp 2006: 73–8). All three were in Upper Egypt, and
it is possible that the earlier emergence of kingdoms in Upper (southern) Egypt, as
opposed to Lower Egypt, was determined at least partly by physical geography. In Upper
Egypt the relatively narrow confines of the Nile Valley may have created the kind of political and demographic 'pressure cooker' needed to encourage the growth of city-states,
whereas settlements in the north of Egypt (the Delta) were scattered over a much wider
area of fertile land and were therefore perhaps less prone to military conflict and resultant
political unification. It is also possible that the strength and precocity of Upper Egyptian
states was tied in with their exploitation of goldmines and trade routes in the Eastern
Desert.

With each local victory the political geography of Upper Egypt was gradually altered until,
on the brink of unification, it must have consisted of a series of large regions, rather like the
provinces or nomes of the Pharaonic period, each struggling for supremacy. It was around
this time that a whole set of votive maceheads and palettes were produced that served as
vivid symbols of power. These artefacts, particularly the Narmer Palette (Fig. 50.3), Narmer
Macehead, and Scorpion Macehead, are among the most important pieces of evidence for
understanding the beginnings of the Egyptian state (Trigger 1979; Davis 1992; Stevenson
2009).

When the first real attempt to summarize the nature of Early Dynastic Egypt was published 50 years ago (Emery 1961), a great deal of the primary evidence was freshly excavated,
although the study of Egyptian prehistory, like many other aspects of the modern discipline,
was very much in its infancy. This lack of data saw Emery constantly looking forward into
the Pharaonic period for comparisons and analogies that could anchor his subject as a specific stage of the Egyptians' cultural development. The prevailing 'culture history' approach
in archaeology as a whole also encouraged him to attribute changes in archaeological cultures to what Trigger (1979: 206) succinctly terms 'external factors, that were subsumed
under the general headings of migration and diffusion'.

FIG. 50.3 The Narmer Palette (Cairo JE32169): a greywacke votive palette from Hierakonpolis dating to the beginning of the historical period in Egypt, *c.* 3100 BC (drawing courtesy of A. Jones).

In contrast, Wilkinson's (1999) more recent monograph on the emergence and nature of Early Dynastic Egypt benefits considerably from the more anthropological approaches to state formation that have come to dominate our views of early complex societies. Emery was keen to promote the idea that the emergence of Egyptian civilization at the end of the fourth millennium BC was the result of the invasion or immigration of the so-called Dynastic Race from Mesopotamia. Now, however, the massive advances in our knowledge of prehistory (Midant-Reynes 2000) and recent excavations of the early royal necropolis at Abydos (Dreyer 1992; O'Connor 2009) and the city and cemetery at Hierakonpolis (Friedman and Adams 1992), both in Upper Egypt, have convincingly demonstrated that the development and inauguration of the Pharaonic age was largely an indigenous Egyptian phenomenon, arising steadily, and almost inevitably, out of processes of late Predynastic social, economic, and political change within the Nile Valley (Wilkinson 1999: 44; Wengrow 2006).

Regime change in Pharaonic Egypt

As in the modern Middle East, regime change seems to have been a constant feature of Pharaonic Egypt (Crawford 2007), despite the stress usually placed on the continuity and conservatism of government and culture in the Nile Valley. The apparently abrupt and calamitous end of the Old Kingdom (*c.* 2686–2181 BC) provides a much-debated example. How did the great pyramid-building elite of the Old Kingdom eventually find themselves so reduced in political and economic power that they were seemingly incapable of constructing even the puniest of stone tombs for their rulers? Two factors above all have inspired Egyptologists to regard the period of about 130 years (2181–2055 BC) following the end of the Sixth Dynasty as a kind of dark age. The first is the almost total absence of monumental architecture, including a conspicuous dearth of royal funerary structures; the second the survival of a number of texts, most admittedly dating no earlier than the Middle Kingdom (2055–1786 BC), that suggest the occurrence of some great political (and perhaps environmental) cataclysm, whereby the accepted social order was turned on its head: foremost among these are *The Prophecy of Neferti* and *The Admonitions of Ipuwer* (Enmarch 2009). The various hypotheses and explanations concerning the end of the Old Kingdom can be divided into three basic types: environmental, political, and socioeconomic.

Hassan (1997) and others have argued that the late Old Kingdom may have been characterized by an increasingly arid or unpredictable climate, and that texts such as *The Admonitions of Ipuwer* describe social disorder resulting from demographic pressure and famine. Bell (1971) has also argued that, like African rainmakers, many of the pharaohs of the early First Intermediate Period may have been put to death by their own subjects for their failure to produce good agricultural conditions. More recently, however, several flaws in this mixture of environmental and textual arguments have been pointed out. First, the link sometimes made between low rainfall and the Nile inundation is highly suspect, given that the Nile flood is much more influenced by the El Niño Southern Oscillation (ENSO) phenomenon over the Indian Ocean than by the aridity of the Sahara (Vercoutter 1993). Second, *The Admonitions of Ipuwer* is not a very reliable text, given that it survives only in New Kingdom versions. Although clearly Twelfth-Dynasty in style, there is no guarantee that it relates directly to events in the First Intermediate Period. Moreover, while it belongs with various other Middle Kingdom misanthropic or pessimistic texts in a genre possibly inspired by environmental or social problems following the end of the Old Kingdom, it would be dangerous to treat any of these texts as if they were factual historical documents (Seidlmayer 2000: 145–6).

In point of fact, several factors seem to have brought about the fall of the Old Kingdom, including climatic change, the increased power of provincial rulers (whose posts became hereditary), the granting of too many tax exemptions to high officials and temples, a consequent decrease in royal wealth and authority, and a possible loss of prestige by the last Memphite pharaohs. The gradual decline in the size and quality of royal pyramid complexes may have been a result or symptom of the above factors, but proving that the construction of royal pyramid complexes and (in the Fifth Dynasty) sun temples gradually bled the economy dry is difficult, as most of our economic evidence derives from funerary contexts. This makes it difficult to assess the nature of the entire Old Kingdom economy, and the extent to which it was dominated by state-organized royal funerary or religious expenditure.

Furthermore, the First Intermediate Period itself was not quite the chaotic 'dark age' that excessively literal interpretations of Middle Kingdom 'pessimistic' texts suggest. Certainly, there was some political decentralization, and wealth was probably channelled into producing funerary equipment for local rulers and their officials rather than being absorbed by royal pyramid-building. There are good grounds to believe, however, that the demise of the highly centralized elite culture of the Old Kingdom actually brought with it significant benefits, such as the development of greater cultural diversity in the regions and a greater propensity for technological innovation. The production of wheel-made pottery, for instance, had been introduced in the Old Kingdom (Fig. 50.4), but only became the standard method of production as a result of provincial experimentation during the First Intermediate Period (Seidlmayer 2000: 121–5). A wide range of new types of funerary object also became popular in provincial burials after the end of the Old Kingdom. Previously, the grave goods in burials belonging to poorer individuals had been selected entirely from among the kinds of objects used in daily life, but in the First Intermediate Period many objects made purely for funerary use began to appear.

FIG. 50.4 Scene from the Fifth-Dynasty tomb of Ty at Saqqara, Egypt, showing a potter using a wheel to fashion a vessel (Ian Shaw).

The end of the great pyramid-building epoch is thus only a total calamity if we look at it through the eyes of the pharaohs themselves. Seen from the point of view of those who had been excluded from the favoured royal entourage during the Third to Sixth Dynasties, the Old Kingdom's demise almost certainly represented an opportunity for social advancement and economic improvement, as power and wealth became less centralized and slightly more evenly distributed through the country. Political power nevertheless remained in the hands of a small elite group, now simply spread throughout the country in the form of powerful local rulers rather than clustered around the king at Memphis. In other words, the end of the Old Kingdom was probably more about devolution than revolution.

Race and ethnicity in the Nile region and the Afrocentrist position

Since Egypt is undoubtedly part of Africa, its inhabitants—both ancient and modern—are, in a strict geographical sense, certainly 'African'. The question of whether the ancient Egyptians were 'black', however, is much more complicated. To many modern writers—particularly those who seek to define Egypt as a purely 'black African' civilization—its geographical location is sufficient proof that its people were fundamentally 'black' (see Diop 1974 for such an 'Afrocentrist' interpretation of the emergence of Egyptian civilization, and see also Bernal 1987 for detailed arguments that Egypt was an essentially African culture and that it had a significant influence on ancient Greece). Over the years, increasing numbers of Egyptian skeletons of many different periods have been studied, and the conclusions reached have often had significant effects on Egyptologists' ideas concerning population movements in and out of Egypt and Nubia. For instance, as already noted, Emery (1961: 39) claimed, on the basis of skull measurements, that the late Predynastic Egyptians were effectively conquered by a New Race from the east, while Flinders Petrie at one stage suggested, on similar grounds, that the pyramid builders of the Old Kingdom were invaders from Asia (Derry 1956: 81). However, as the methodology of biological anthropologists has improved, such simplistic assertions have become less common, and it is now widely recognized that the slippery idea of 'racial types' cannot readily be assessed on the basis of skeletal remains. More recent analyses of Egyptian skeletal material suggest that the people of ancient Egypt had strong racial and ethnic links with the peoples of Europe and south Asia as well as with the occupants of sub-Saharan Africa (e.g. Brace et al. 1993).

How, then, did the Egyptians view themselves? As in many other cultures, they seem to have gained a sense of their own identity primarily by contrasting themselves with the peoples of the world outside Egypt. The iconography of the Egyptians' depictions of themselves and foreigners suggests that for most of their history they saw themselves as midway between black, woolly-haired Africans and pale, bearded Asiatics. The tombs of the New Kingdom pharaohs Seti I (1294–1279 BC) and Ramesses III (1184–1153 BC) in the Valley of the Kings include scenes specifically depicting figures representing the various human types in the universe over which the sun god Ra presided. These types included reddish-brown Egyptians, whose skin colour contrasts equally starkly both with the black-skinned Kushites (Nubians) and the paler-skinned Libyans and Asiatics. Although partly based on skin colour and other physical characteristics, these ancient ethnic types were also based on varieties in hair styles and costume, and their function was clearly to allow the Egyptians to define themselves as a national group, relative to the rest of the world (Kemp 2006: 19–59). Such depictions, however, would presumably have been recognized by the Egyptians themselves as simplified stereotypes, given that the thousands of portrayals of individual Egyptians show that the population as a whole ranged across a wide spectrum of complexions, from light to dark brown.

Egypt was not only part of the African continent, but also well positioned to establish close contacts with the Near East and the Mediterranean. The language spoken by the Egyptians is an autonomous branch of the Afroasiatic/Hamito-Semitic phylum, and seems to have been primarily African in origin. It was, however, increasingly influenced by Semitic tongues (especially from the New Kingdom onwards). The concept of 'black' people, on the other hand, is a modern construct that only confuses the situation when attempts are made to apply it to ancient contexts. The ancient Egyptians themselves would not have understood the modern racial concept of 'blackness', and clearly never defined their 'Egyptian-ness' in purely racial terms. Instead, the culture and archaeological record of ancient Egypt was the product of the interaction of many racial groups.

FUTURE DIRECTIONS

Over the last 40 years, since the full-scale resumption of Egyptian field archaeology (following the conclusion of the Nubian rescue campaign of the 1960s, see Säve-Söderbergh 1987), scientific methods of survey and analysis have been increasingly applied to archaeological projects in the Nile Valley, resulting in a wave of fresh insights into such things as Egyptian economics, ethnicity, politics, and processes of social and technological change. Simultaneously, in the more traditional areas of Egyptology, many new ideas have been assimilated from linguistics, literary criticism, and art history. Like other areas of 21st-century archaeology and anthropology, Egyptology has become a highly diverse discipline, embracing aspects of philology, sociology, bio-anthropology, geophysics, and many other areas of study (for a more detailed discussion of the growth of science in Egyptology, and the innovative directions in which it is taking the discipline, see Shaw 2001). Although Egyptologists occasionally have difficulty in shaking off their traditional somewhat isolationist image, especially in terms of the way they are regarded by archaeologists working in other geographical and historical areas, the increasingly multidisciplinary nature of the subject appears to be slowly breaking down such barriers and preconceptions.

REFERENCES

BEDNARSKI, A. (2005). *Holding Egypt: Tracing the Reception of the 'Description de l'Égypte' in Nineteenth-Century Great Britain*. London: Golden House.

BERNAL, M. (1987). *Black Athena: The Afroasiatic Roots of Classical Civilization*. New Brunswick, NJ: Rutgers University Press.

BONANI, G., HAAS, H., HAWASS, Z., et al. (2001). Radiocarbon dates of Old and Middle Kingdom monuments in Egypt. *Radiocarbon* 43: 1297–1320.

BRACE, C. L., TRACER, D. P., YAROCH, L. A., ROBB, J., BRANDT, K., and RUSSELL NELSON, A. (1993). Clines and clusters versus 'Race:' a test in ancient Egypt and the case of a death on the Nile. *American Journal of Physical Anthropology* 36(S17): 1–31.

COLLIER, M., and QUIRKE, S. (2002–6). *The UCL Lahun Papyri*. Oxford: British Archaeological Reports.

CRAWFORD, H. (ed.) (2007). *Regime Change in the Ancient Near East and Egypt: From Sargon of Agade to Saddam Hussein*. Oxford: British Academy.

DAVID, R. (ed.) (2007). *Oxford Handbook to Life in Ancient Egypt*. Oxford: Oxford University Press.

DAVIS, W. (1992). *Masking the Blow: The Scene of Representation in Late Prehistoric Egyptian Art*. Berkeley: University of California Press.

DEE, M. W., BROCK, F., HARRIS, S. A., et al. (2010). Investigating the likelihood of a reservoir offset in the radiocarbon record for ancient Egypt. *Journal of Archaeological Science* 37: 687–93.

DERRY, D. E. (1956). The dynastic race in Egypt. *Journal of Egyptian Archaeology* 42: 80–85.

DIOP, C. A. (1974). *The African Origin of Civilization: Myth or Reality*. New York: L. Hill.

DREYER, G. (1992). Recent discoveries at Abydos Cemetery U. In E. C. M. Van Den Brink (ed.), *The Nile Delta in Transition: 4th–3rd Millennium BC*. Tel Aviv: van den Brink, 293–9.

DROWER, M. (1985). *Flinders Petrie: A Life in Archaeology*. London: Victor Gollancz.

EL-SADDIK, W. (2005). The Egyptian Museum. *Museum International* 57: 31–5.

EMERY, W. B. (1961). *Archaic Egypt*. Harmondsworth: Penguin.

ENMARCH, R. (2009). *A World Upturned: Commentary on and Analysis of The Dialogue of Ipuwer and the Lord of All*. London: British Academy.

FRIEDMAN, R. (ed.) (2002). *Egypt and Nubia: Gifts of the Desert*. London: British Museum Press.

—— and ADAMS, B. (eds), (1992). *The Followers of Horus: Studies Dedicated to Michael Hoffman*. Oxford: Oxbow.

HASSAN, F. A. (1985). Radiocarbon chronology of Neolithic and Predynastic sites in Upper Egypt and the Delta. *African Archaeological Review* 3: 95–116.

—— (1997). The dynamics of a riverine civilization: a geoarchaeological perspective on the Nile Valley, Egypt. *World Archaeology* 29: 51–74.

—— and ROBINSON, S.W. (1987). High-precision radiocarbon chronometry of ancient Egypt, and comparisons with Nubia, Palestine and Mesopotamia. *Antiquity* 61: 119–35.

HENDRICKX, S. (1996). The relative chronology of the Naqada culture: Problems and possibilities. In A. J. Spencer (ed.), *Aspects of Early Egypt*. London: British Museum Press, 36–69.

HORNUNG, E., KRAUSS, R., and WARBURTON, D. (2006). *Ancient Egyptian Chronology*. Leiden: Brill.

KEMP, B. J. (1982). Automatic analysis of Predynastic cemeteries: a new method for an old problem. *Journal of Egyptian Archaeology* 68: 5–15.

—— (2006). *Ancient Egypt: Anatomy of a Civilisation*. London: Routledge.

—— and STEVENS, A. (2010). *Busy Lives at Amarna: Excavations in the Main City (Grid 12 and the House of Ranefer, N49.18)*. London: Egypt Exploration Society.

KITCHEN, K. (1991). The chronology of ancient Egypt. *World Archaeology* 23: 201–8.

KRAUSS, R. (1985). *Sothis- und Monddaten: Studien zur astronomischen und technischen Chronologie Altägypten*. Hildesheim: Gerstenberg.

LEHNER, M., and WETTERSTROM, W. (2006). *Giza Reports I*. Brighton: AERA.

LIBBY, F. W. (1955). *Radiocarbon Dating*. Chicago: University of Chicago Press.

MALEK, J. (1989). A chronological scheme and terminology for the early part of Egyptian history: a contribution to a discussion. *Discussions in Egyptology* 15: 37–55.

—— (1997). La division de l'histoire d'Égypte et l'égyptologie moderne. *Bulletin de la Société Française d'Égyptologie* 138: 6–17.

MCDOWELL, A.G. (1999). *Village Life in Ancient Egypt: Laundry Lists and Love Songs*. Oxford: Oxford University Press.

MIDANT-REYNES, B. (2000). *The Prehistory of Egypt: From the First Egyptians to the First Pharaohs*. Oxford: Blackwell.

O'CONNOR, D. (1974). Political systems and archaeological data in Egypt: 2600–1780 BC. *World Archaeology* 6: 15–38.

—— (1990). Egyptology and archaeology: an African perspective. In P. Robertshaw (ed.), *A History of African Archaeology*. London: Routledge: 236–521.

—— (2009). *Abydos: Egypt's First Pharaohs and the Cult of Osiris*. London: Thames & Hudson.

PARKINSON, R. (1999). *Cracking Codes: The Rosetta Stone and Decipherment*. London: British Museum Press.

PETRIE, W. M. F. (1891). Tell el Hesy *(Lachish)*. London: Palestine Exploration Fund.

—— (1894). *Tell el Amarna*. London: Methuen.

PODZORSKI, P. V. (1990). *Their Bones Shall Not Perish: An Examination of Predynastic Human Skeletal Remains from Naga-ed-Dêr in Egypt*. New Malden: SIA.

POSENER-KRIEGER, P. (1976). *Les Archives du Temple Funéraire de Neferirkare (les Papyrus d'Abousir)*. Cairo: IFAO.

QUIRKE, S. (2005). *Lahun: A Town in Egypt 1800 BC, and the History of its Landscape*. London: Golden House.

RAY, J. D. (2007). *The Rosetta Stone and the Rebirth of Ancient Egypt*. London: Profile.

REDFORD, D. (1986). *Pharaonic King-Lists, Annals, and Day-Books: A Contribution to the Study of the Egyptian Sense of History*. Indiana: Benben.

REID, D. M. (2002). *Whose Pharaohs? Archaeology, Museums, and Egyptian National Identity from Napoleon to World War I*. Berkeley: University of California Press.

SAVAGE, S. H. (2001). Towards an AMS radiocarbon chronology of Predynastic Egyptian ceramics. *Radiocarbon* 43: 1255–77.

SÄVE-SÖDERBERGH, T. (ed.) (1987). *Temples and Tombs of Ancient Nubia: The International Rescue Campaign at Abu Simbel, Philae and Other Sites*. London: Thames & Hudson.

SEIDLMAYER, S. (2000). The First Intermediate Period. In Shaw (2000: 118–47).

SHAW, I. (1985). Egyptian chronology and the Irish oak calibration. *Journal of Near Eastern Studies* 44: 295–317.

—— (ed.) (2000). *Oxford History of Ancient Egypt*. Oxford: Oxford University Press.

—— (2001). Egypt: Dynastic. In T. Murray (ed.), *Encyclopedia of Archaeology: History and Discoveries*, vol. 2. New York: ABC Clio, 440–55.

STEVENSON, A. (2009). Palettes. In W. Wendrich (ed.), *UCLA Encyclopedia of Egyptology*. Los Angeles: UCLA. Available at: http://digital2.library.ucla.edu/viewItem.do?ark=21198/zz001nf6c0

SZAFRANSKI, Z. E. (2007). Deir el-Bahari: Temple of Hatshepsut. In E. Laskowska-Kusztal (ed.), *Seventy Years of Polish Archaeology in Egypt*. Warsaw: Polish Centre of Mediterranean Archaeology, 91–104.

TRIGGER, B. (1979). The Narmer palette in cross-cultural perspective. In M. Görg and E. Pusch (eds), *Festschrift Elmar Edel*. Bamberg: M. Görg, 409–19.

—— KEMP, B. J., O'CONNOR, D., and LLOYD, A. B. (1983). *Ancient Egypt: A Social History*. Cambridge: Cambridge University Press.

VERCOUTTER, J. (1993). La fin de l'Ancien Empire: un nouvel examen. *Atti di VI Congresso di Egittologia*. Turin: International Association of Egyptologists, 557–62.

VERNER, M., and BENEŠOVSKÁ, H. (2008). *Unearthing Ancient Egypt: Fifty Years of the Czech Archaeological Exploration in Egypt*. Prague: Charles University.

WADELL, W. G. (1940). *Manetho*. Cambridge: Harvard University Press.

WENGROW, D. (2006). *The Archaeology of Early Egypt: Social Transformations in North-East Africa*. Cambridge: Cambridge University Press.

WILKINSON, T. (1999). *Early Dynastic Egypt*. London: Routledge.

CHAPTER 51

KERMA AND KUSH AND THEIR NEIGHBOURS

DEREK WELSBY

THIS chapter considers two of Africa's great civilizations which developed in the Nile Valley on the southern margins of the Sahara. The first, with its capital at Kerma, was the earliest urban civilization in sub-Saharan Africa, and rose to rival Pharaonic Egypt. The second, the kingdom of Kush, lasted for over 1,000 years and for a time controlled a vast swathe of territory from Central Sudan to the shores of the Mediterranean.

THE RISE OF KERMA

The first urban societies to develop in sub-Saharan Africa emerged during the middle Holocene along the northern Dongola reach of the Nile immediately south of the Third Cataract (Fig. 51.1). This area was especially favourable for animal husbandry and agriculture, and food production had developed here by the fifth millennium BC, possibly earlier (Haaland and Haaland, Ch. 37 above).

Beginning around 3000 BC, we have evidence in the Kerma region for a large settlement, still imperfectly known, provided with massive earth and timber defences protecting circular huts, along with a number of rectilinear buildings, stock enclosures and storage areas (Honegger 2004). By about 2400 BC the settlement had shifted 4 km to the west, presumably in response to the Nile's shifting channels. On the new site developed the metropolis of what the Ancient Egyptians called the kingdom of Kush, its distinctive cultural assemblage being recognized by archaeologists as the Kerma Culture. Detailed studies divide this into three main phases: *Kerma Ancien* (2400–2050 BC), *Kerma Moyen* (2050–1750 BC), and *Kerma Classique* (1750–1450 BC) (Gratien 1978).

The kingdom appears to have expanded rapidly; *Kerma Ancien* material is now known from as far upstream as Abu Hamed, and typical graves of this period have been recorded at the Fourth Cataract. To the north, contemporary material is found on Sai Island. Under the Middle Kingdom pharaohs Senusret I (1956–1911 BC) and III (1870–1831 BC)

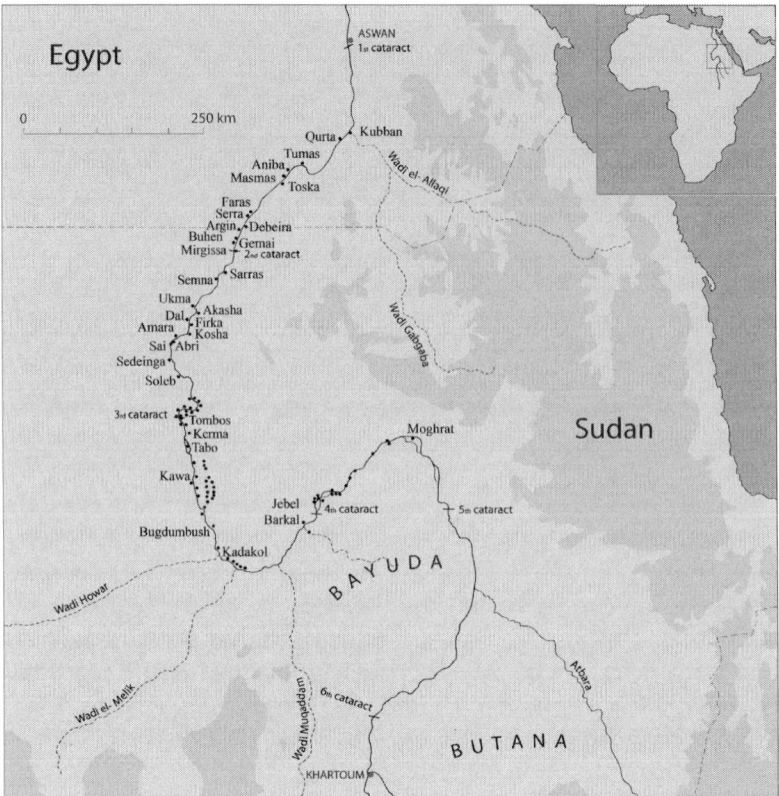

FIG. 51.1 Sites of the Kerma period between the First and the Fifth Cataracts of the Nile.

Egypt expanded upstream to at least the Semna Cataract, if not to Sai. Relations between the two states fluctuated over the centuries, involving trade but also at least the threat of military confrontation, as indicated by the massive fortresses built by the Egyptians to guard their southern frontier.

With the Egyptian withdrawal back to the First Cataract at the end of the Middle Kingdom around 1750 BC, the Kushites filled the power vacuum, taking over Egyptian military installations and recruiting/retaining a number of Egyptian officials in the process (Säve-Söderbergh 1949: 55). Later, during the 17th century BC, Kush was the major power along the Nile. Directly controlling the valley from above the Fourth to as far as the First Cataracts, a distance of approximately 1,300 km, it was allied with the Hyksos in the Delta, as made explicit in a letter from the Hyksos king Aaweserra Apepy (c. 1583–1550 BC) to a king of Kush, newly in office, intercepted by the army of the Egyptian pharaoh Kamose (1555–1550 BC). The letter invites the Kushite king to invade Kamose's kingdom from the south (Habachi 1972). Archaeological evidence, including a recently published inscription from Elkab in Upper Egypt (Davies 2003), confirms that at some point the Kushites did indeed raid with impunity deep into Egypt, carrying off loot that included statues of Egyptian officials weighing well over a tonne.

URBANISM AT KERMA

Like its pre-Kerma predecessor, the earliest phase of the settlement at Kerma (Fig. 51.2) featured timber huts, but these were rapidly followed by buildings using both *jalous* (mud formed into roughly shaped blocks) and mud-brick construction techniques. Over its 1,000-year history the town changed dramatically, although archaeology has generally only revealed the latest phases of occupation. During *Kerma Moyen* times its defences consisted of a mud-brick wall strengthened on the exterior with closely spaced projecting D-shaped towers delimiting a rectangular area (Bonnet 1999). Subsequently, the town was surrounded by massive earth and timber defences fronted by an immense ditch up to 50 m wide, which enclosed a sub-circular area with the ditches intruding into the central space from the cardinal points. Entry was through strongly fortified gateways protected by powerful projecting towers.

The town's central area was devoted to religious activities, and housed the main religious monument. In this area occupation was so intensive that over a period of a millennium approximately 12 m of deposits built up. The extant structure is the latest in a long line of monumental buildings on the site (Bonnet 2004). Still standing 19 m high, the western *deff-ufa*, as it is known today, superficially reflects Egyptian architectural forms and its timber-laced mud-brick construction may have been influenced by its northern neighbour. However, in detail it is very different. The main entrance is from the side, where a staircase leads to a small room, presumably the sanctuary, in the structure's heart from which runs a narrow blind-ended corridor. Another staircase then leads up onto the roof.

FIG. 51.2 Kerma's main religious monument still dominates the town.

Elsewhere were administrative quarters connected with the regulation of goods passing through the city gates, and industrial complexes that document on-site production of pottery, glazed composition, and copper-alloy objects. During the *Kerma Classique* period the ditch to the west of the town was partly infilled and a new royal palace constructed over it, along with an associated magazine. Immediately southwest of the town a secondary settlement developed, the initial earthen bank/ditch fortifications of which were later partly strengthened by a stone revetment and rectangular tower. The area within was occupied by a complex of shrines, perhaps dedicated to the funerary cults of the Kerma kings, along with bakeries, dwellings, and workshops (Bonnet 1995).

FUNERARY PRACTICES

Graves dating to the *Kerma Ancien* period are usually deep circular to oval pits with only sufficient space at the bottom to place the tightly crouched inhumation laid on its right side, aligned east–west, facing north, with the hands before the face (Fig. 51.3). Bodies were often laid on a hide covered in red ochre with another hide over them. Grave goods were rare, although copper-alloy mirrors have been found in some graves. The pit was then filled and sealed by a small tumulus, often with concentric rings of small stones set on edge, while the pots used in the funerary feast were placed on the ground close by. During *Kerma Moyen* times grave pits increased greatly in size, and the deceased was accompanied by a range of grave goods including pottery and sacrificed sheep, goats, dogs, and humans. Meat cuts were also included on occasion. The orientation and burial attitude remained the same, but tumuli now had steep sides revetted with small black-stone fragments and a shallow-domed top covered with white quartzite pebbles. Small rectilinear tomb chapels stood to one side, while around the south side a crescent of bucrania, mainly of cattle, was placed, well over 4,000 in number by one tumulus that presumably covered a royal burial (Bonnet 1999). Subsequently, in the *Kerma Classique* period grave pits were often rectangular, while the royal tombs were highly complex structures consisting of a mud-brick skeleton of varying form and a vaulted and painted burial chamber covered by a tumulus up to 90 m in diameter. Accompanying some rulers to their deaths were up to 400 sacrificed humans—family members, retainers, and perhaps prisoners of war (cf. Buzon and Judd 2008).

AGRICULTURE AND ANIMAL HUSBANDRY

The Kerma Basin and, to its south, the Seleim Basin extend over a distance of about 60 km and are watered during the annual inundation by a rise in the water table. This allows the planting of crops without recourse to irrigation, and also supports rich pasturage for animals. During the Kerma period conditions were probably even more favourable, as the climate was somewhat wetter than today and the Nile ran in several channels spaced across the valley floor, significantly increasing the amount of arable land. A little to the south of Kerma,

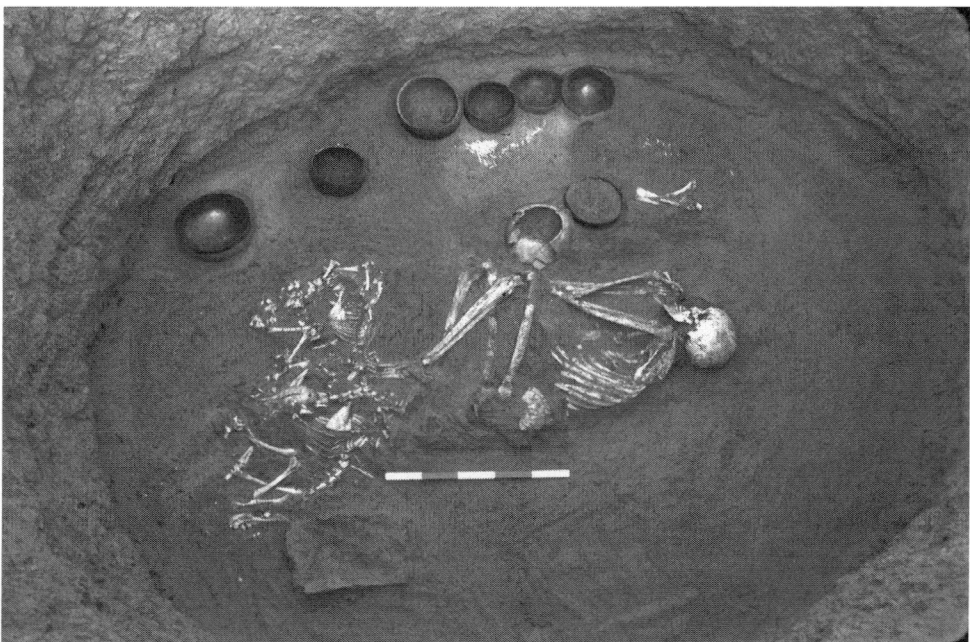

FIG. 51.3 A typical burial of the *Kerma Moyen* at site P37 in the Northern Dongola Reach. The deceased is accompanied with sacrificed sheep/goats, joints of meat, and pottery vessels.

three of these channels have been studied in detail (Welsby 2001). The two eastern ones are lined with closely spaced settlements, some of considerable size. Other settlements are found, although in smaller numbers, on the banks of today's river and along the margins of the Kerma/Seleim Basin. Within most of these settlements distinctive buildings constructed with a wooden frame set on stone post pads and with a raised wooden floor are presumed to have been granaries (Welsby 1997, 2001; Gratien 1999). The region's wealth is also clearly demonstrated by the profligate slaughtering of cattle at some elite funerals (Bonnet 1999).

TRADE

Although agriculture and animal husbandry were the mainstays of Kerma's economy, trade was a major wealth-generating activity for its elite. Some private enterprise probably also occurred on a small scale, as hinted at by the Semna Dispatches (from the Middle Kingdom Egyptian fortress at Semna) which mention, among other things, women trading goods brought on two asses (Smith 1998: 227). Sitting athwart the Nile corridor from Egypt to the African interior, Kerma was ideally situated to dominate trade at a time when long distance trans-Saharan routes, in the absence of the camel, were not a viable option. Egypt had, from early in the Dynastic period, looked south of the First Cataract for a wide range of commodities, among them hard stone, gold, animal products (skins, ivory, ostrich eggs, etc), timber, and slaves. Kerma grew rich as the middleman in this trade, and the relationship between it and Egypt was at most periods much more that of trading partners than protagonists. Documenting this trade on the ground is nevertheless far from easy, although Egyptian reliefs depicting goods from the south demonstrate the produce involved, if not the detailed mechanisms of its movement. Egypt's Middle Kingdom fortresses in Lower Nubia undoubtedly played a key part in her trade with Kush (Gratien 2004: 80), their pivotal role clearly enunciated on the boundary stela of Senusret III that designates Mirgissa as the frontier's official trading post (Emery 1965: 157). Kerma's wide-ranging contacts, which may have been associated with trading activities, are highlighted further south by the discovery of Kerma material at Mahal Teglinos near Kassala, immediately adjacent to Sudan's Eritrean border (Fattovich 1993, 1996; Manzo 1999). While most of the trade goods from Kerma to Egypt have left little trace in the archaeological record, the large amounts of Egyptian goods on Kerma-period sites, particularly pottery (Lacovara 1987), illustrate how these goods may have been paid for, though the pots themselves are invariably containers; residue analyses might help identify their contents.

CONQUEST AND CONTINUITY

With the resurgence of Egyptian power in the late Seventeenth/early Eighteenth Dynasties following the destruction of Hyksos power in the Delta, the Egyptians turned towards Kush and gradually advanced up the Nile. Ahmose I (1550–1525 BC) appears to have established his forward base at Sai, although his cartouche has been discovered near the Kajbar Rapids well to the south (Edwards 2006: 59). The decisive battle of the first round of this conflict took place near the Third Cataract, during which Thutmose I (1504–1492 BC) supposedly personally slew the Kushite king (Emery 1965: 174). Evidence for fire damage at Kerma, particularly in the western *deffufa*, may be attributed to destruction at the hands of Thutmose's army, although a single radiocarbon date of 1380 ± 80 BC suggests that it may have occurred later (Bonnet 1980). It is clear, however, that Thutmose advanced right through the Kushite realm, setting up his boundary inscription at Kurgus a little to the north of the Fifth Cataract (Davies 2001) and establishing a new town (with at least one temple) at Dokki Gel about 1 km north of Kerma. Egyptian control, however, does not appear to have been secure for some time, and the Egyptian remains at Dokki Gel are overlain by another Kushite stratum before it was re-established. Thereafter, the Egyptians dominated the territory of the old Kushite state until the end of the New Kingdom *c.* 1070 BC (Trigger 1976), although Kushite culture survived beneath the veneer of Egyptian civilization (Welsby and Welsby Sjöström 2007).

THE RISE OF THE KUSHITE STATE

Egyptian control of the Middle Nile valley lapsed in the early 11th century BC, and by the 10th century the power vacuum was being filled by the rise of a new polity initially based a little downstream of Jebel Barkal. The earliest evidence for this resurgent Kushite state (Fig. 51.4)

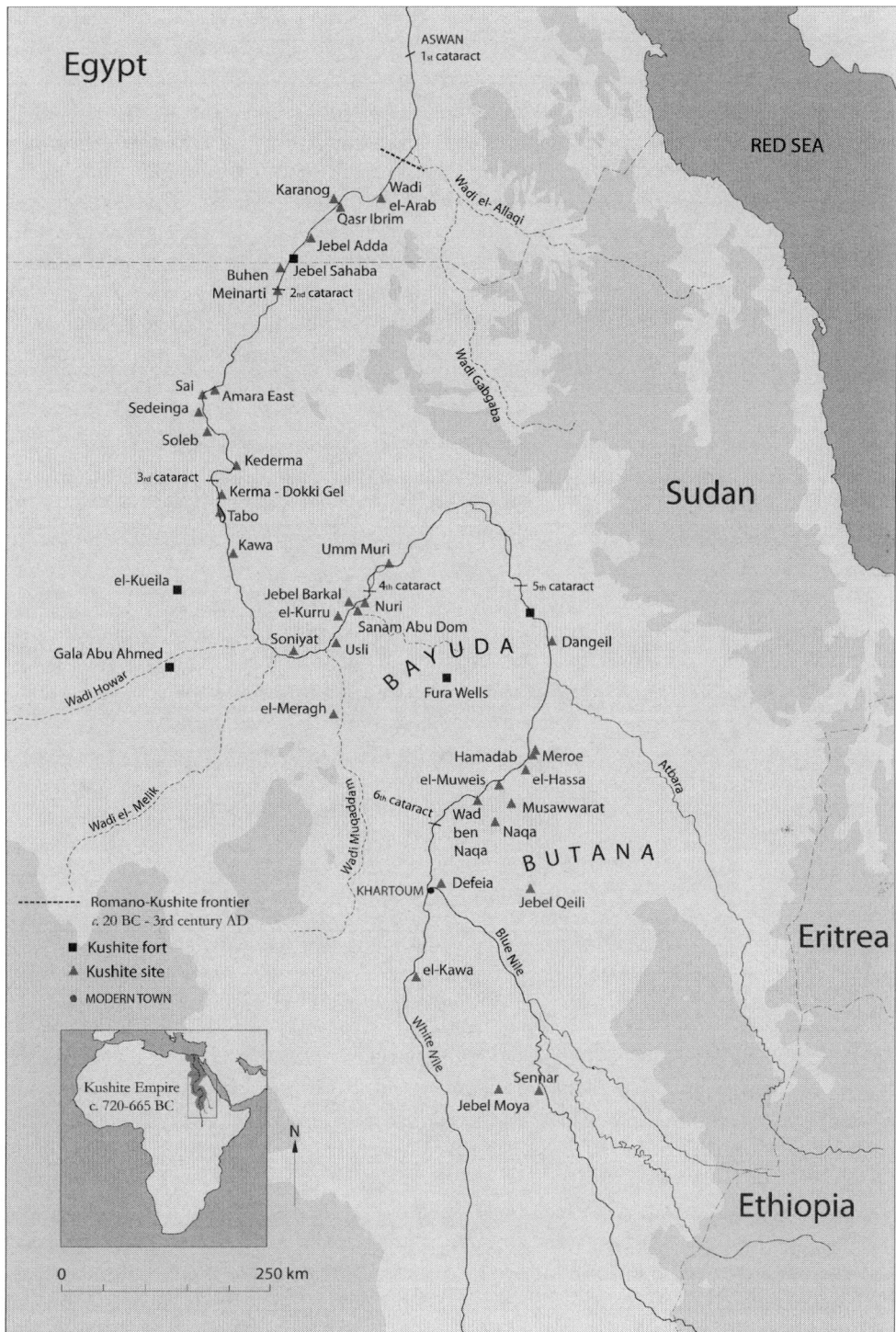

FIG. 51.4 The kingdom of Kush in the aftermath of its expulsion from Egypt in the 7th century BC.

comes from el-Kurru, where George Reisner excavated the ancestral burial ground of the Kushite kings (Dunham 1950). The earliest rulers and their families were buried in a crouched position beneath a tumulus, a custom that clearly harks back to the first (Kerman) kingdom of Kush and beyond. Following this, however, came a very rapid assimilation of Egyptian funerary culture and architectural practices, with a move towards extended burials within graves and the replacement of tumuli first by square mastabas and, finally, by pyramids.

These are but physical manifestations of the adoption of many aspects of Egyptian funerary culture that went hand in hand with the assimilation of Pharaonic religious practices and beliefs. The Kushites adopted Jebel Barkal as their religious centre, and rebuilt, restored and extended the New Kingdom temples there. They also bought into the Egyptian mythology of the site, accepting it as the southern home of the Egyptian, and now their own, state god Amun, who dwelt within the mountain. These ideas were noted on the stelae and inscriptions within the temples and perhaps also by visual representations of the god within the mountain; the famous example dating to the reign of Taharqo (690–664 BC) within Temple B300 may be a copy of a pre-existing image within the temple built by Rameses II (1279–1213 BC) on the same site.

In the mid-8th century BC the Kushites expanded northwards into Egypt not as foreign conquerors but as the champions of Amun (Morkot 2000). Kashta was active at Thebes, but his successor, Piye (747–716 BC), conquered the whole of Egypt, establishing an empire on the Nile the territorial extent of which was not surpassed until the 1820s. His successors became embroiled in the Levant and, faced with the expanding military might of Assyria, fought a long but ultimately unsuccessful series of campaigns that resulted in the loss of Thebes in 663 BC and their expulsion from Egypt. Forced south of Egypt's traditional frontier at the First Cataract, the Kushite state nevertheless prospered along the Middle Nile for another 1,000 years, despite short-lived invasions by Psamtek II (595–589 BC) in 593 BC and Roman armies in 25 BC, both of which may have penetrated as far south as Jebel Barkal.

Urbanism and settlement

Kush was a highly organized state with a strong urban component. The main urban centre developed at Meroe (Fig. 51.5) and, at least by the 5th century BC, this was the main royal residence, while Jebel Barkal (known to the Kushites as Napata) remained the religious centre. Many other settlements were occupied along the Nile, with important towns approaching 20 ha in size each dominated by a large temple at intervals of approximately 10 km near Meroe itself (Baud 2008). In the north, many important New Kingdom towns, such as Kawa, Tabo, Dokki Gel, Soleb, Sedeinga, and Sai, were reoccupied, if indeed they had ever been abandoned. Smaller settlements with rectilinear buildings constructed of mud-brick dotted the banks of the Nile and its islands, even in the cataract zones, as at Meinarti at the Second Cataract (Adams 2000) and Umm Muri at the Fourth Cataract (Payne 2005). In the southern part of the kingdom greater rainfall allowed occupation away from the river, and in the Keraba and Butana regions a Kushite presence established control over transhuming and nomadic populations ranging far from the Nile. Kushite settlements were on the whole very small, Meroe's own population being estimated at between 8,800 and 13,800 people (Grzymski 1981).

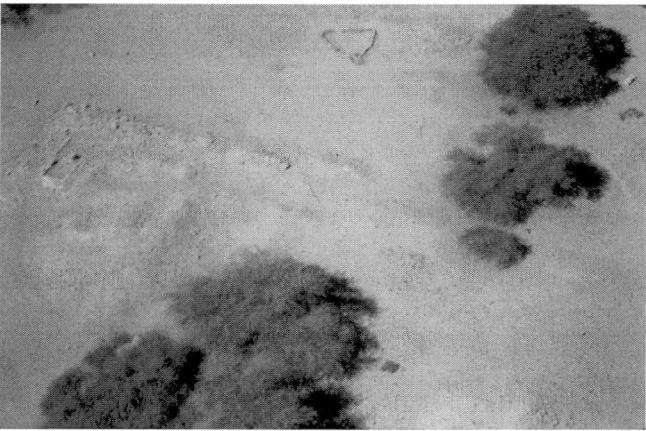

FIG. 51.5 Aerial view of the northern part of the 'Royal City' at Meroe, Sudan.

Population estimates for other sites, particularly in the north, have been derived from studies of associated cemeteries, but are almost certainly too low, as many components of the population may not have been given formal burial and not all cemeteries have been discovered.

Kushite settlements are rare away from the Nile. The northernmost non-riverine settlement is that at el-Meragh in the Wadi Muqaddam, over 60 km south of the Nile. Several well-built houses reflect the official nature of the occupation and date to the early Kushite period (Kendall 2007). Presumably this was an administrative centre; whether it was set along a trade route or was a focus for nomadic populations is unclear, but occupation appears to have been short-lived. In Meroe's hinterland are many more sites, most very little explored, though frequently featuring a complex of buildings that includes a temple and an associated *hafir*, as at Basa (Crowfoot 1911), Duanib (Hintze 1959), and Alim (Hinkel 1985). Naqa is the exception, being both extensive and much studied. While it has large temples and important high-status buildings, little in the way of housing for an urban population is evident (Wildung 1999; Wildung and Kroeper 2006), suggesting that it was not really a town but had a special ritual and ceremonial function. The nearby site at Musawwarat is certainly of this type.

Kushite military installations are rare but strongly defended forts are known at Fura Wells along the 'Royal Road' between Meroe and Napata (Crawford 1953) and at Gala Abu Ahmed in the Wadi Howar, athwart a likely trade and/or invasion route from the west (Jesse and Kuper 2006). Others may exist at the Second and Fifth Cataracts (Welsby 2005). The absence of defences around Kushite towns implies that the army was a significant deterrent against low-level raiding from tribes east and west of the Nile, although several such raids are mentioned and at least one led to the sacking of Kawa (Eide et al. 1996: 492–3).

ECONOMY

The Kushite economy was principally based on the land, and it was the land's carrying capacity that determined the location of both large and small population centres. In the far north the amount of available farmland was limited, and we see a chain of small settlements along the valley. Further south, however, low-lying basins greatly increased the farming land available, notably between Kerma and Kawa, near Jebel Barkal and Sanam Abu Dom at Nuri, and in the Shendi region. Apart from basin cultivation that relied on a very high water table at least during the inundation, the most favoured land was the *seluka*, between the level of the high and low Niles, which could be farmed without resorting to irrigation. Where required, irrigation was provided by the primitive *shaduf*, a counterweighted pole that offered very limited opportunities. The date of introduction of the much more efficient *saqia* is disputed; though arriving in Egypt from Mesopotamia during the Ptolemaic period, it may only have been introduced to Kush in the early centuries AD (Edwards 1996: 88). Animal husbandry was also important and there is considerable evidence for livestock, cattle in particular at Kawa in an early Kushite context, and later for cattle, sheep, and goats at Meroe (Carter and Foley 1980). In the southern part of the kingdom the major *wadis* may have been farmed by transhumers, while a large nomadic population presumably existed in the Keraba and Butana hinterland of Meroe. This is confirmed by the presence of *hafirs*, reservoirs designed to store rainwater run-off that were essential to the nomads for watering their flocks well into the dry season. Apparently constructed by the state (as indicated by large lion statues, temples and other (administrative?) buildings), they offered opportunities for exerting control over and taxing the region's nomads (Welsby 2003).

Ironworking was also important at Meroe (Haaland and Haaland 2007), and a number of other Kushite towns have evidence for ironworking on a substantial scale along with other industrial activities, particularly pottery-making (Edwards 2004: 173–4, and references therein). However, the role of Meroe in the context of the spread of this technology through sub-Saharan Africa has been overstated (Mapunda, Ch. 42 above).

In the early Kushite period vast amounts of wealth may have been accumulated as a result of the conquest of Egypt, and at least some of this loot was found stored within the so-called Treasury at Sanam Abu Dom, at 250 × 64 m by far the largest Kushite building known (Vincentelli 2003: 82, fig. 8.4). Also found here were hard woods and elephant tusks (Griffith 1922: 117, pl. LIIIb), which, along with gold, animal skins, and slaves, would have been the main international trade items. The level of more local trade is difficult to establish, but may have included pottery and foodstuffs. Around the main administrative centres the presence of elite individuals undoubtedly also supported a wide range of specialist craftsmen, architects, and builders.

LANGUAGE

In the early Kushite period we have very limited evidence for the indigenous language. At that time texts were invariably composed in Egyptian and written in Egyptian hieroglyphs. Studies of personal names suggest, however, that the native spoken language was a form of what we know as Meroitic. On present evidence a script was invented to allow this language to be written around the early 2nd century BC. Consisting of both hieroglyphic and so-called cursive forms, it was very different from Egyptian, being alphabetic and consisting of four vowels, fifteen consonants, and four syllabic signs, along with word dividers. The origins of both the script and the language are uncertain, and they vanish after the early 5th century AD. Attempts at decipherment are seriously hampered by the absence of long bilingual inscriptions and by the failure to find closely related and (to us) intelligible languages (Rilly 2007).

The collapse

The discovery of a stone lion at Qasr Ibrim (Plumley 1966) and of a stela at Meroe (Eide et al. 1998: no. 277), both bearing the name of king Yesbokheamani (*c.* 283–300), shows that as late as the early 4th century AD Kush still controlled a vast territory that may actually have expanded to incorporate the region between el-Maharraqa and the First Cataract on the withdrawal of Roman garrisons under Diocletian (285–305) (Török 1997). However, by the mid-4th century royal burials under pyramids at Meroe had ceased. The power of the Kushite kings may partly have derived from the deployment of wealth derived from trade to maintain the support of the Kushite elite through patronage (Edwards 1994). At Meroe, tomb and tomb monuments indicate a diminution in royal wealth in the 3rd and 4th centuries that eroded disparities in wealth and status between the king and the elite buried in the city's Western Cemetery. Problems may have resulted from reduced trade between Kush and the Roman Empire, a reflection of the latter's increasing military and economic problems and a situation exacerbated by the opening of a major rival trade route along the Red Sea control-led by Aksum (Phillipson, Ch. 55 below). Whatever the exact mechanisms of collapse, it is clear that control of Kushite territory fragmented, and several major power centres emerged along the Nile between el-Hobagi in the south and Ballana in the north (Emery 1938; Lenoble 1997). The role of foreign invaders remains unclear, with the possibility of an attack from Aksum far from certain (Behrens 1986; Török 1997). People with names such as Nubae, Nobades, Red Noba, and Annoubades do, however, appear to have entered the Nile Valley at this time, unless they were already there as subjects of Kush. They maintained many Kushite traditions, but abandoned others, including, significantly, the use of Meroitic. The final death knell of Kushite culture came when Christianity, introduced in the 6th century, wiped away the worship of the Egyptian and Kushite gods, ending a tradition at least 3,500 years old.

Between them the two Kushite kingdoms of Kerma and Napata/Meroe dominated the Middle Nile valley for over two millennia. Separated by several centuries of Egyptian rule dur-ing the New Kingdom, they shared a common African heritage heavily influenced at all times by Egypt. When the Egyptian veneer was stripped off, however, there is evidence for continuity particularly in funerary culture and very probably in language (Rilly 2004). The southward trend in the main centre of political power along the Middle Nile (from Kerma to Napata to Meroe) continued under Kush's medieval Nubian successor states, the most powerful of which, Alwa, developed in central Sudan with its capital at Soba East (Edwards, Ch. 54 below).

References

ADAMS, W. Y. (2000). *Meinarti I: The Late Meroitic, Ballaña and Transitional Occupation.* London: Sudan Archaeological Research Society.

BAUD, M. (2008). The Meroitic royal city of Muweis: first steps into an urban settlement of riverine Upper Nubia. *Sudan & Nubia* 12: 52–63.

BEHRENS, P. (1986). The 'Noba' of Nubia and the 'Noba' of the Aezanes Inscription: a matter of confusion. *Afrikanistische Arbeitspapiere* 8: 117–26.

BONNET, C. (1980). Les fouilles archéologiques de Kerma (Soudan). *Genava* 28: 31–72.

—— (1995). Les fouilles archéologiques de Kerma (Soudan): rapport préliminaire sur les campagnes de 1993–1994 et de 1994–1995. *Genava* 43: 33–52, I–VI.

—— (1999). Kerma: rapport préliminaire sur les campagnes de 1997–1998 et 1998–1999. *Genava* 47: 57–76.

—— (2004). *Le Temple Principal de la Ville de Kerma et son Quartier Religieux*. Paris: Éditions Errance.

BUZON, M. R., and JUDD, M. A. (2008). Investigating health at Kerma: sacrificial versus non-sacrificial individuals. *American Journal of Physical Anthropology* 136: 93–9.

CARTER, P. L., and FOLEY, R. (1980). A report on the fauna from excavations at Meroe 1967–72. In P. L. Shinnie and R. J. Bradley (eds), *The Capital of Kush 1*. Berlin: Akademie-Verlag, 298–311.

CRAWFORD, O. G. S. (1953). *Castles and Churches in the Middle Nile Region*. Khartoum: Sudan Antiquities Service.

CROWFOOT, J. W. (1911). *The Island of Meroe*. London: Egypt Exploration Fund.

DAVIES, W. V. (2001). Kurgus 2000: the Egyptian inscriptions. *Sudan & Nubia* 5: 46–58.

—— (2003). Kush in Egypt: a new historical inscription. *Sudan & Nubia* 7: 52–4.

DUNHAM, D. (1950). *The Royal Cemeteries of Kush*, I: *El Kurru*. Cambridge, Mass.: Harvard University Press.

EDWARDS, D. N. (1994). Power and the state in the Middle Nile: Meroe in context. An example for the study of state development in Sudanic Africa. *Cambridge Archaeological Review* 13(1): 5–19.

—— (1996). *The Archaeology of the Meroitic State: New Perspectives on its Social And Political Organisation*. Oxford: British Archaeological Reports.

—— (2004). *The Nubian Past: An Archaeology of the Sudan*. London: Routledge.

—— (2006). Drawings on rocks: the most enduring monuments of Middle Nubia. *Sudan & Nubia* 10: 55–63.

EIDE, T., HÄGG, T., PIERCE, R. H., and TÖRÖK, L. (1996). *Fontes Historiae Nubiorum: Textual Sources for the History of the Middle Nile Region Between the Eighth Century BC and the Sixth Century AD. Vol. 2: From the Mid-Fifth to the First Century BC*. Bergen: University of Bergen.

—— —— —— —— (1998). *Fontes Historiae Nubiorum: Textual Sources for the History of the Middle Nile Region between the Eighth Century BC and the Sixth Century AD. Vol. 3: From the First to the Sixth Century AD*. Bergen: University of Bergen.

EMERY, W. B. (1938). *The Royal Tombs of Ballana and Qustul*. Cairo: Government Press.

—— (1965). *Egypt in Nubia*. London: Hutchinson.

FATTOVICH, R. (1993). The Gash Group of the eastern Sudan: an outline. In L. Krzyzaniak, M. Kobusiewicz, and J. A. Alexander (eds), *Environmental Change and Human Culture in the Nile Basin and Northern Africa until the Second Millennium B.C.* Poznán: Poznán Archaeological Museum, 439–48.

—— (1996). Punt: the archaeological perspective. *Beitrage zur Sudanforschung* 6: 15–30.

GRATIEN, B. (1978). *Les Cultures Kerma: Essai de Classification*. Lille: Université de Lille III.

—— (1999). Some rural settlements at Gism El-Arba in the Northern Dongola Reach. *Sudan & Nubia* 3: 10–12.

—— (2004). From Egypt to Kush: administrative practices and movements of goods during the Middle Kingdom and Second Intermediate Period. In T. Kendall (ed.), *Nubian Studies 1998: Proceedings of the Ninth Conference of the International Society of Nubian Studies.* Boston: Department of Afro-American Studies, Northeastern University, Boston, 74–82.

GRIFFITH, F. L. (1922). Oxford excavations in Nubia. *Liverpool Annals of Archaeology and Anthropology* 9: 67–124.

GRZYMSKI, K. A. (1981). The population size of the Meroitic Kingdom: an estimation. In C. Fyfe and D. Mcmaster (eds), *African Historical Demography* 2. Edinburgh: Centre for African Studies, University of Edinburgh, 259–73.

HAALAND, G., and HAALAND, R. (2007). God of war, worldly ruler, and craft specialists in the Meroitic Kingdom of Sudan: inferring social identity from material remains. *Journal of Social Archaeology* 7: 372–92.

HABACHI, L. (1972). *The Second Stela of Kamose and His Struggle against the Hyksos Ruler and His Capital.* Glückstadt: Kairo Ägyptologische Reihe.

HINKEL, F. W. (1985). Alim–El Hosh–Shaq El Ahmar. In F. Geus and F. Thill (eds), *Mélanges Offerts à Jean Vercoutter.* Paris: Éditions Recherche sur les Civilisations, 163–80.

HINTZE, F. (1959). Preliminary report of the Butana Expedition 1958. *Kush* 7: 171–96.

HONEGGER, M. (2004). The Pre-Kerma: a cultural group from Upper Nubia prior to the Kerma civilisation. *Sudan & Nubia* 7: 38–46.

JESSE, F., and KUPER, R. (2006). Napata in the west? The Gala Abu Ahmed fortress in the Lower Wadi Howar (NW-Sudan). *Archéologie du Nil Moyen* 10: 135–60.

KENDALL, T. (2007). Evidence for a Napatan occupation of the Wadi Muqaddam: excavations at Al-Meragh in the Bayuda Desert (1999–2000). *Cahiers de Recherches de l'Institut de Papyrologie et d'Égyptologie de Lille* 26: 197–204.

LACOVARA, P. (1987). The internal chronology of Kerma. *Beitrage zur Sudanforschung* 2: 51–74.

LENOBLE, P. (1997). From pyramids at Meroe to tumulus at El Hobagi: imperial graves of the Late Meroitic culture. *Kush* 17: 289–308.

MANZO, A. (1999). *Échanges et Contacts le Long du Nil et de la Mer Rouge dans l'Époque proto-Historique (IIIe et IIe Millénaires avant J.-C.): une synthèse préliminaire.* Oxford: British Archaeological Reports Int. Ser. 782.

MORKOT, R. G. (2000). *The Black Pharaohs: Egypt's Nubian Rulers.* London: Rubicon Press.

PAYNE, J. (2005). Excavations of the late Kushite and Medieval settlement on Umm Muri. *Sudan & Nubia* 9: 9–13.

PLUMLEY, J. M. (1966). Qasr Ibrim 1966. *Journal of Egyptian Archaeology* 52: 9–12.

RILLY, C. (2004). The linguistic position of Meroitic. *ARKAMANI Sudan Journal of Archaeology and Anthropology.* http://www.ddl.ish-lyon.cnrs.fr/projets/clhass/PageWeb/ressources/Isolats/Meroitic%20Rilly%202004.pdf

—— (2007). *La Langue du Royaume de Méroé: un Panorama de la plus Ancienne Culture Écrite d'Afrique Subsaharienne.* Paris: Librairie Honoré Champion.

SÄVE-SÖDERBERGH, T. (1949). A Buhen stela from the Second Intermediate Period (Khartoum No. 18). *Journal of Egyptian Archaeology* 35: 50–58.

SMITH, S. T. (1998). The transmission of an administrative sealing system from Lower Nubia to Kerma. *Cahiers de Recherches de l'Institut de Papyrologie et d'Égyptologie de Lille* 17: 219–30.

TRIGGER, B. G. (1976). *Nubia under the Pharaohs.* Boulder, Colo.: Westview Press.

Török, L. (1997). *The Kingdom of Kush: Handbook of the Napatan-Meroitic Civilization*. Leiden: Brill.

Vincentelli, I. (2003). Trade and caravan routes in Meroitic times. In M. Liverani (ed.), *Arid Lands in Roman Times*. Firenze: All'Insegna del Giglio, 79–86.

Welsby, D. A. (1997). The Northern Dongola Reach Survey: the 1996/7 season excavations at sites O16, P1, P4 and P37. *Sudan & Nubia* 1: 4–8.

—— (2001). *Life on the Desert Edge: 7000 Years of Settlement in the Northern Dongola Reach, Sudan*. London: Sudan Archaeological Research Society.

—— (2003). The kingdom of Kush: Rome's neighbour on the Nile. In M. Liverani (ed.), *Arid Lands in Roman Times*. Firenze: All'Insegno del Giglio, 65–78.

—— (2005). The kingdom of Kush: urban defences and military installations. In N. Crummy (ed.), *Image, Craft and the Classical World. Essays in Honour of Donald Bailey and Catherine Johns*. Montagnac: Monique Mergoil, 39–54.

—— and Welsby Sjöström, I. (2007). The Dongola Reach and the Fourth Cataract: continuity and change during the 2nd and 1st millennia bc. *Cahiers de Recherches de l'Institut de Papyrologie et d'Égyptologie de Lille*, 26: 379–98.

Wildung, D. (1999). *Die Stadt in Der Steppe: Grabungen des Ägyptischen Museums Berlin in Naga (Sudan)*. Berlin: Stiftung Preußischer Kulturbesitz.

—— and Kroeper, K. (2006). *Naga: Royal City of Ancient Sudan*. Berlin: Stiftung Preußischer Kulturbesitz.

CHAPTER 52

BERBER, PHOENICIO-PUNIC, AND GREEK NORTH AFRICA

FARÈS K. MOUSSA

INTRODUCTION

LIMITED archaeological knowledge of pre-Roman North Africa belies the significant diversity of peoples who inhabited the region and facilitated contact between it and other areas of the Mediterranean and Africa in the first millennium BC. The reasons for our limited knowledge are various, but do not reflect a lack of interest in its past. Leaving to another chapter (Leone and Moussa, Ch. 53 below) consideration of French and Italian interests in the region's Roman past as justification of their own colonial activities, we can note here the more recent nationalist agendas in the post independence era. In Algeria, the Arabist state appropriated Berber heritage as a part of national identity, in spite of ongoing dissident Berber movements (Hannoum 1997; McDougall 2006; Fenwick 2008; Ghambou 2010). Before the 2011 Revolution in Tunisia, the Ben-Ali regime adopted Punic identity to its own ends through state sponsored propaganda (e.g. Chaâbane 2005), reserving research on Punic heritage for Tunisian archaeologists. Given these historical circumstances, although more scientific archaeological information has begun to emerge in recent years, our archaeological knowledge—particularly concerning Berber and 'Phoenicio-Punic' civilizations—is still limited and remains substantially reliant upon historical sources of Greek and Roman origin.

'BERBER' NORTH AFRICA

As the Sahara dried out in the mid-Holocene, North Africa's more coastal regions also saw conditions become increasingly arid, albeit with some fluctuations (Rognon 1987). Indigenous populations had to adapt to these changes, probably shifting from hunting and gathering toward subsistence strategies that, depending upon location, increasingly employed and depended upon domesticated resources, both livestock and plants. It remains true, however, that direct evidence for this process is still extremely scanty, leading some to suggest that until well into the first millennium BC 'extractive techniques and modes of social organization in the Maghreb were predicated on lithic tool technologies (and crude ceramics) and on economic relations that were rudimentary in nature' (Shaw 2003: 101). One likely exception to this generalization is Cyrenaica in northeastern Libya. Here, limited evidence of Aegean, Egyptian, and Syro-Palestinian pottery at Marsa Matruh indicates that this was probably a stopping-off place for traders voyaging between these areas (White 2002) and perhaps also interested in obtaining goods from Cyrenaica itself: ivory (Hayward 1990), gum, *silphion* (a now extinct medicinal plant), and ostrich eggshell and feathers (Richardson 2000). More extensive coastal surveys have yet to locate significant signs of Bronze Age settlement (White and White 1996), but New Kingdom Egyptian records refer to metal-working populations who lived in 'towns' and kept large numbers of livestock to the west of Egypt itself. The comparatively well-watered mountains of Cyrenaica's Jebel Akhdar are the only plausible location, and the sheer numbers of such 'Libyans' who later infiltrated Egypt imply that they must also have grown cereals and other crops (O'Connor 1990, 1993). The massive Nineteenth-Dynasty fortresses of Zawiyet Umm el-Rakham and Kom el-Abqa'in some 300 km west of Alexandria, which date to just before the first major 'Libyan' invasion recorded in New Kingdom texts (*c.* 1210 BC), underline this point (Snape 2003, 2004).

Further west, archaeological evidence remains similarly scanty, and historical information is of course totally lacking before the mid-first millennium BC. While rock engravings in the Moroccan High Atlas depict daggers similar to those known in the Bronze Age Argaric culture of the Iberian Peninsula, perhaps indicating a second-millennium BC introduction of metallurgy into Morocco (Souville 1986; Alaoui and Searight 1997), the earliest firm evidence of non-nilotic metallurgical activity comes from 7th-century BC Phoenician iron smelting on the island of Mogador, near Essaouira (Aranegui Gascó et al. 2000: 35). Classical authors mention many tribes, including the Numidians from the Aurès steppe (eastern Algeria and western Tunisia), the Mauri from west of the river Moulouya (Morocco), and the Nasamones to the west of the Jebel Akhdar in Libya (Desanges 1962). Archaeological knowledge of them remains relatively limited, however, except for the Garamantes in the Fazzan (southwestern Libya), (Mattingly 2003; Leone and Moussa, Ch. 53 below). These indigenous populations have collectively come to be known as 'Berbers' (Brett and Fentress 1996: 3–8).

Found across much of this area and extending into the Sahara, the ancient Berber script known as Proto-Tifinagh or Libyco-Berber supports the argument for a broadly based ethnolinguistic unity among these groups, with the earliest known examples perhaps dating to between the 7th and 5th centuries BC (Camps 1977). Proto-Tifinagh can be broadly split into eastern and western variants, although various dialects are thought to have existed. The former was deciphered from a bilingual 'key' inscription on the Libyco-Punic mausoleum of Ateban at Dougga (Chabot 1940), whilst the latter has not yet been completely deciphered (Galand 2002). In the north, examples are typically found on funerary monuments, whilst most southern examples are rock engravings, often difficult to date. Debate continues as to the precise origin and affiliation of the language that the script records (Hachid 2000; Galand 2002; Aït Kaci 2007; Pichler 2007).

Within North Africa the best surviving and easily identifiable forms of Berber material culture are funerary structures, particularly ashlar stone-built mausolea, derived from earlier

Neolithic traditions of stone tombs (Camps 1962). Dating from the 3rd/4th centuries BC into the 4th century AD and beyond, these mausolea correspond to a period of increasing prosperity through the participation of those for whom they were built within wider Phoenicio-Punic and Roman trading networks and economies. The result was the adoption of composite Berber, Punicizing, Romanizing, and Hellenizing architectural traditions (Rakob 1979; Coarelli and Thébert 1988). Tomb types include pyramid-topped tower structures, such as the mausolea at Dougga in Tunisia (Poinssot and Salomonson 1959) and El Khroub in Algeria '(Rakob 1979: 158–66)', large drum mausolea such as the Medracen (Camps 1974) (Fig. 52.1) and 'Royal Mausoleum' (Christofle 1951), both in Algeria, and temple mausolea with porticos such as at Simitthus (Chemtou) in Tunisia (Rakob 1979: 119–29) and Ghirza in Libya (Brogan and Smith 1984). The Djedar near Tiaret (Khadra 1974) and the 'Tuareg' tomb of Tin Hanan at Abalessa (Reygasse 1950: 88–108; Rüger 1979), both in Algeria, show the continuity of this tradition into late Antiquity. The burial practices reflected by these monuments appear to be closely related to cults of ancestral worship involving practices of divination and incubation (Camps 1986).

What is largely lacking from the long-standing focus on such monuments as expressions of architecture (Fig. 52.2) or artistic influence is any systematic consideration of them in the context of indigenous state formation (but cf. Camps 1994). Yet we know that during, if not

FIG. 52.1 Numidian mausoleum at Medracen, Algeria, c. 3rd century BC, an architectural composite of local drum 'basina' style with a coursed substructure, Doric capitals, and Egyptianized cornice (photograph, Farès Moussa).

before the 3rd to 1st centuries BC, powerful kingdoms formed within North Africa. Of these, Numidia centred in northeastern Algeria/northwestern Tunisia, played a major role as a Roman ally in the Second and Third Punic Wars, and then became a Roman client state before finally being incorporated into the Roman provincial system in 25 BC. Further west, Mauritania (centred in northern Morocco) gave help to Rome in its war of 112–106 BC against the Numidian king Jugurtha and was later involved in the civil wars that ended the Roman Republic, surviving as a client state under Juba II and his son Ptolemy until annexed in AD 40. Political centralization and the promotion of urban life are, according to historical sources, particularly associated with Juba II (reigned 25 BC–AD 23) in Mauritania and with Massinissa (reigned 204–149 BC) in Numidia. How precisely this was achieved is archaeologically mainly unknown, although large settlements are known at Ichoukane in Algeria (Brett and Fentress 1996: 32) and Garama in southern Libya (Mattingly 2003; Leone and Moussa, Ch. 53 below), (Fig. 52.2) and evidence of urban planning is apparent at pre-Roman Volubilis in northern Morocco (Jodin 1977) and at Dougga in western Tunisia (Khanoussi 2003). Trade with first Carthage and then Rome in North Africa's grain, ivory, metals, cedar, and skins, as well as the provision of slaves and enrichment from providing military contingents are likely to have underpinned these sociopolitical changes, which would bear comparison with developments of roughly the same age north of the Alps, especially in pre-Roman Gaul and Austria (Cunliffe 1997).

FIG. 52.2 Garama, southern Libya, *c.* 1st century BC. A possible 'temple' structure can be seen in the foreground and the mud-brick levels of continued occupation are in the background (photograph, Farès Moussa).

'PHOENICIO-PUNIC' NORTH AFRICA

Given the many references already made to Phoenician and Punic (Carthaginian) presence in North Africa, it is now appropriate to discuss this and the archaeological evidence for it in some detail. Classical literary sources indicate that a Phoenician sanctuary to Heracles (the Phoenician Melqart) was established at Lixus (near Larache, Morocco) on the Atlantic coast before the foundation of Cadiz, an event traditionally placed around 1110 BC (Pliny, *Natural History* XIX: 63). If correct, this would be the earliest Phoenician trading colony or 'emporium' from the Levant anywhere west of Greece. Pliny and others record that Utica in northern Tunisia was supposedly founded a few years later, followed in 814 BC by Elissa's ('Queen Dido's') legendary foundation of Carthage. Debate continues concerning the possible extent and antiquity of such early Phoenician emporia in the western Mediterranean, and there is so far no archaeological evidence at any of these sites before the 7th century BC except at Carthage, where ceramic wares and radiocarbon dates for the earliest phases of the so-called 'Tophet' (see below) do indicate a 9th-century BC presence (Docter et al. 2005), correlating with the foundation narrative dates. Finds at the Spanish port of Huelva also suggest Phoenician trading in the far western Mediterranean in the 9th century (González de Canales et al. 2006) and on Portugal's Atlantic seaboard by the 8th century, perhaps earlier (Arruda 2009); while Rusaddir (modern Melilla) on Morocco's Mediterranean coast and Mogador (modern Essaouira) on its Atlantic coast both date to the 7th century (Jodin 1966; Aranegui Gascó et al. 2000). Other coastal cities are recorded as having been founded by colonists from Phoenician Tyre and Sidon, both now in Lebanon, but many, including Lepcis Magna in Tripolitania, may only have seen permanent settlement as a result of Carthaginian initiative (Markoe 2000: 182).

The circumstances of Carthage's foundation and its name (*Qart-hadasht* 'New Town') suggest that from the outset it was a different type of settlement, a permanent colony rather than an emporium (Aubet 2001: 214–16). Its links with Tyre nevertheless remained strong, as it continued to dispatch tribute there right up to the 2nd century BC. Tyre's fall to the Babylonians in 573 BC nevertheless probably allowed Carthage to establish her own colonies, particularly along the North African coast and in the central Mediterranean. Alliances with Etruscan cities to squeeze the Greek presence in the Tyrrhenian Sea, and trade treaties with Rome indicate a substantial Carthaginian presence in western Sicily and Sardinia from at least the 6th century BC. Changes in cultural practices in the central Mediterranean colonies during the 6th century, such as the transition from cremation to inhumation in Sardinia and Ibiza, akin to practices known in Carthage, also hint at the increased influence of Carthage (Gómez Bellard et al. 1990; Bartolini 2000). The breach of Carthage's final trade treaty with Rome and competition for influence in Sicily was, however, the cause of the first of three Punic Wars between Rome and Carthage (264–241 BC), leading to Carthage's attempts to extend its control of resources and territories to Spain in the late 3rd century and Hannibal's subsequent invasion of Italy. At the end of the Third Punic War (149–146 BC), Carthage itself was besieged and destroyed (Miles 2010).

Despite these military events, Carthage's actions should probably be understood primarily as mercantile interests in controlling trading activities and securing the loyalty of trading allies, rather than expansionist ambitions of occupation (Whittaker 1978). Notably, very few small rural settlements are known outside the principal cities. While perhaps partially due to

FIG. 52.3 View across remains at Kerkouane, Tunisia, *c.* 4th century BC. A red *pavimenta punica* and part of a private bath can be seen in the foreground (photograph, Farès Moussa).

limited systematic rural surveys recording Punic material, this probably reflects the tendency of Carthaginian coastal colonies to trade with rural Berber inland communities for surplus agricultural products, at least until the 2nd or 3rd centuries BC, when there is evidence for more organized intensive agricultural activity (Fentress and Docter 2008). Within Carthage itself few examples of urban monumental edifices or domestic architecture survive or have been excavated, presumably because they were either destroyed in Roman and later periods or remain buried under Roman layers (Docter 2007). Isolated exceptions include the Punic harbours (Hurst 1994) and remains found buried under the later Augustan forum on the east side of Byrsa Hill (Lancel 1983). Further afield, there is the fortified settlement of Kerkouane (Fig. 52.3) at the tip of Cap Bon (Fantar 1986).

Sepulchral monuments and associated small-finds thus dominate the Punic archaeological record. Burial types include Libyco-Punic tower mausolea such as Dougga in western Tunisia (Poinssot and Salomonson 1959) and Sabratha in northwest Libya (Di Vita 1976); *haouanet* (rock-cut) tombs such as at Jebel el Mangoub and Latrech in northeast Tunisia (Ghaki 1999; Stone 2007); shaft tombs such as at Carthage, Cap Bon, and Gigthis in Tunisia (Bénichou-Safar 1982; 71–94; Ben Younes 2007); and the controversial infant cemeteries at Carthage and other locations in North Africa, Sicily and Sardinia (Stager 1980; Brown 1991; Bénichou-Safar 2004). These infant cemeteries have come to be known as 'Tophet', based on a conflation between Roman historical accounts of the Carthaginian immolation of infants and Biblical references to similar practices by the Canaanites at places known by that name. The cemeteries themselves contain the cremated remains of infants and young animals in urns accompanied with inscribed votive stelae dedicated to the god Ba'al Hammon (Roman Saturn) and his consort Tanit (Roman Caelestis), but their reading as proof of infant sacrifices has been questioned by some scholars (e.g. Moscati 1987) and debate has continued ever since. Although methods based on age distribution of cremated remains have been used to either confirm (Smith et al. 2011) or refute (Schwartz et al. 2010) the case for sacrifice, both remain scientifically inconclusive, whilst associated epigraphy and iconography remains largely enigmatic.

Independently of debates about Carthaginian religious practice, recent research has also used the rich iconographic and epigraphic sources from the so-called Tophet at Carthage to examine Phoenicio-Punic identity (e.g. Quinn 2011). Interestingly, few inscriptions from Carthage or any other 'Punic' settlements attest to anyone referring to themselves as such (Prag 2006), and as late as the early 5th century AD St Augustine mentions North Africans referring to themselves as Canaanites (Augustine, *Patrologia Latina* XXXV, 2096). Additionally, there is some evidence that Carthaginians may have referred to themselves as Tyrians (Aubet 2001: 227). Regardless of the degree of genetic or ethnic admixture with indigenous Berber communities, however, it is clear that the lingua franca of most city dwellers along the North African littoral well into the Roman period was the Phoenician dialect that we call 'Punic'.

GREEK NORTH AFRICA

Phoenicians were, of course, not the only eastern Mediterranean population to settle further west during the first millennium BC: large Greek communities established themselves in Sicily and parts of the southern Italian mainland, as well as more ephemerally on the coasts of southern France and northeastern Spain. Other Greek colonists, however, established themselves in Cyrenaica (northeast Libya). According to Herodotus (*Histories*, IV, 150–51, 153, 156–9), settlers from the Aegean island of Thera (modern Santorini) began arriving on the fertile Cyrenaican coast in the late 7th century BC, founding the town of Cyrene in 631 BC. Subsequently, other colonies were established at Apollonia, Tocra, Ptolemais, and Euesperides in the late 6th century BC, dates more or less corroborated by ceramics from the surviving sites (James 2005). Unusually for Classical Greece, Cyrene was ruled by kings, who remained in power until the late 5th century BC. Subsequently, the region passed under the control of the Ptolemaic dynasty of Egypt, a scion of which (Ptolemy Apion) bequeathed to Rome in 96 BC.

Archaeological work relevant to these Greek-founded settlements and their interactions with indigenous populations has recently focused most intensively on Euesperides, founded from Cyrene in the 6th century BC. Located on a lagoon near the sea and close to modern Benghazi, excavations have uncovered much of the site, helped by the fact that the town was abandoned *c.* 250 BC as the lagoon silted up. It was thus not built on by later Roman or Islamic occupations. Domestic architecture, the city's defences, and some of its public buildings have all been investigated, with evidence recovered of intensive production of purple murex dye and trade with both Greek and Punic parts of the Mediterranean (Wilson 2005, 2006). Elsewhere in Cyrenaica, another major project has centred on the extramural sanctuary of Demeter and Persephone at Cyrene itself (White 1981), followed up by further work within the ancient city and its environs (Cyrenaica Archaeological Project 2006) (Fig. 52.4).

FIG. 52.4 Temple of Zeus at Cyrene, Libya, *c.* 5th century BC (photograph, Farès Moussa).

Since the 2011 revolutions much archaeological research in Libya and the rest of North Africa has understandably been put on hold. It is hoped, however, that in due course, new work by archaeologists in North Africa and elsewhere can further explore the relationships between Greek, Phoenician, Carthaginian, and Berber populations during the first millennium BC.

REFERENCES

AÏT KACI, A. (2007). Recherche sur l'ancêtre des alphabets libyco-berbères. *Libyan Studies* 38: 13–38.

ALAOUI, F.-Z. S., and SEARIGHT, S. (1997). Rock art in Morocco. *Proceedings of the Prehistoric Society* 63: 87–102.

ARANEGUI-GASCÓ, C., GÓMEZ BELLARD, C., and JODIN, S. (2000). Los fenicios en Atlántico: perspectivas de nuevas excavaciones en Marruecos. *Revista de Arqueologia* 223: 26–35.

ARRUDA, A. M. (2009). Phoenician colonization on the Atlantic coast of the Iberian Peninsula. In M. Dietler and C. López-Ruiz (eds), *Colonial Encounters in Ancient Iberia: Phoenician, Greek and Indigenous Relations*. Chicago: University of Chicago Press, 113–30.

AUBET, M. E. (2001). *The Phoenicians and the West: Politics, Colonies and Trade*, 2nd edn. Cambridge: Cambridge University Press.

BARTOLINI, P. (2000). *La Necropolis di Monte Sirai,* 1. Rome: Consiglio Nazionale delle Ricerche.

BÉNICHOU-SAFAR, H. (1982). *Les Tombes Puniques de Carthage: Topographie, Structures, Inscriptions et Rites Funéraires.* Paris: CNRS.

——(2004). *Le Tophet de Salammbô à Carthage: Essai de Reconstitution.* Rome: École Française de Rome.

BEN YOUNES, H. (2007). Interculturality and the Punic funerary world. In D. L. Stone and L. M. Stirling (eds), *Mortuary Landscapes of North Africa.* Toronto: University of Toronto Press, 32–42.

BRETT, M., and FENTRESS, E. (1996). *The Berbers.* Oxford: Blackwell.

BROGAN, O., and SMITH, D. J. (1984). *Ghirza: A Libyan Settlement in the Roman Period.* Tripoli: Department of Antiquities.

BROWN, S. (1991). *Late Carthaginian Child Sacrifice and Sacrificial Monuments in their Mediterranean Context.* Sheffield: Sheffield Academic Press.

CAMPS, G. (1962). *Aux Origines de la Berbérie: Monuments et Rites Funéraires Protohistoriques.* Paris: Arts et Métiers Graphiques.

——(1974). Nouvelles observations sur l'architecture et l'âge du medracen, mausolée royal de Numidie. *Comptes Rendus des Séances de l'Académie des Inscriptions et Belles-Lettres* 117(3): 470–517.

——(1977). Recherches sur les plus anciennes inscriptions libyques de l'Afrique du Nord et du Sahara. *Bulletin Archéologique du CTHS* 10–11b: 143–66.

——(1986). Funerary monuments with attached chapels from the northern Sahara. *African Archaeological Review* 4: 151–64.

——(1994). Afrique du Nord: les mausolées princiers de Numidie et de Maurétanie. *Archeologia* 298: 50–9

CHAÂBANE, S. (2005). *Le Retour d'Hannibal ou La Résurgence d'une Époque.* Tunis: Maison Arabe du Livre.

CHABOT, J.-B. (1940). *Recueil des Inscriptions Libyques.* Paris: Imprimerie Nationale.

CHRISTOFLE, M. 1951. *Le tombeau de la Chrètienne.* (Gouvernement Général de l'Algérie, Missions Archéologiques). Paris: Arts et mètiers graphiques.

COARELLI, F., and THÉBERT, Y. (1988). Architecture funéraire et pouvoir: reflections sur l'Hellénisme numide. *Mélanges de l'École Française de Rome: Antiquité* 100: 761–818.

CUNLIFFE, B. W. (1997). *The Ancient Celts.* Oxford: Oxford University Press.

CYRENAICA ARCHAEOLOGICAL PROJECT (2006). http://www.cyrenaica.org/. Website accessed 8 Dec. 2011.

DESANGES, J. (1962). *Catalogue des Tribus Africaines de l'Antiquité Classique a l'Ouest du Nil.* Dakar: Université de Dakar, section d'histoire.

DI VITA, A. (1976). Il mausoleo punico-ellenistico B di Sabratha. *Römische Mitteilungen* 83: 273–85.

DOCTER, R. F. (2007). Published settlement contexts of Punic Carthage. *Carthage Studies* 1: 37–76.

——NIEMEYER, H. G., NIJBOER, A. J., and VAN DER PLICHT, J. (2005). Radiocarbon dates of animal bones in the earliest levels of Carthage. In G. Bartolini, F. Delpino, R. De Marinis, and P. Gastaldi (eds), *Oriente e Occidente: Metodi e Discipline a Confronto. Riflessioni Sulla Cronologia dell'Età del Ferro Italiana.* Pisa: Istituti Editoriali e Poligrafici Internazionali, 557–77.

FANTAR, M. (1986). *Kerkouane: Cité Punique du Cap Bon, Tunisie.* Tunis: Maison Tunisienne de l'Édition.

FENWICK, C. (2008). Archaeology and the search for authenticity: colonialist, nationalist, and Berberist visions of an Algerian past. In C. Fenwick, M. Wiggins, and D. Wythe (eds), *TRAC 2007: Proceedings of the 17th Annual Theoretical Roman Archaeology Conference*. Oxford: Oxbow Press, 75–88.

FENTRESS, E., and DOCTER, R. F. (2008). North Africa: rural settlement and agricultural production. In P. Van Dommelen and C. Gómez Bellard (eds), *Rural Landscapes of the Punic World*. Sheffield: Equinox, 101–28.

GALAND, L. (2002). *Études de Linguistique Berbère*. Louvain: Peeters.

GHAKI, M. (1999). *Les Haouanet de Sidi Mohamed Latrech*. Tunis: Institut National du Patrimoine.

GHAMBOU, M. (2010). The 'Numidian' origins of North Africa. In K. E. Hoffmann and S. G. Miller (eds), *Berbers and Others: Beyond Tribe and Nation in the Maghreb*. Indiana: Indiana University Press, 153–70.

GÓMEZ BELLARD, C., COSTA, B., GÓMEZ BELLARD, F., GURREA, R., GRAU, E., and MARTÍNEZ VALLE, R. (1990). La Colonización Fenicia de la Isla de Ibiza. Madrid: Ministerio de Cultura.

GONZÁLEZ DE CANALES, F., SERRANO, L., and LLOMPART, J. (2006). The precolonial Phoenician emporium of Huelva *ca.* 900–770 BC. *Bulletin Antieke Beschaving* 81: 13–29.

HACHID, M. (2000). *Les Premiers Berbères*. Aix-en-Provence: Ina-yas/Edisud.

HANNOUM, A. (1997). Historiography, mythology and memory in modern North Africa: the story of the Kahina. *Studia Islamica* 85: 85–130.

HAYWARD, L. G. (1990). The origin of the raw elephant ivory used in Greece and the Aegean during the Late Bronze Age. *Antiquity* 64: 103–9.

HURST, H. (1994). *Excavations at Carthage: The British Mission 2*. Oxford: Oxford University Press.

JAMES, P. (2005). Archaic Greek colonies in Libya: historical vs. archaeological chronologies? *Libyan Studies* 36: 1–20.

JODIN, A. (1966). *Mogador, Comptoir Phénicien du Maroc Atlantique*. Tangier: Ministère de l'Éducation Nationale et des Beaux-Arts.

——(1977). Volubilis avant les Romains: dix années de recherches dans la cité punique. *Archeologia* 102: 6–19.

KHADRA, F. (1974). *Les Djedars: Monuments Funéraires Berbères de la Région de Frenda*. Algiers: Office des Publications Universitaires.

KHANOUSSI, M. (2003). L'évolution urbaine de Thugga (Dougga) en Afrique proconsulaire: de l'agglomération numide à la ville africo-romaine. *Comptes-Rendus des Séances de l'Académie des Inscriptions et Belles-Lettres* 147: 131–55.

LANCEL, S. (1983). *La Colline de Byrsa à l'Époque Punique*. Paris: Recherche sur les Civilisations.

MARKOE, G. E. (2000). *Phoenicians*. London: Thames & Hudson.

MCDOUGALL, J. (2006). *History and the Culture of Nationalism in Algeria*: Cambridge: Cambridge University Press.

MATTINGLY, D. J., DANIELS, C. M., DORE, J. N., EDWARDS, D., and HAWTHORNE, J. (eds.) 2003. *The Archaeology of Fazzān: Volume 1, Synthesis*. (princ. ed. D. J. Mattingly). Tripoli and London: Socialist People's Libyan Arab Jamahariya, Department of Antiquities and The Society for Libyan Studies.

MILES, R. (2010). *Carthage Must Be Destroyed: The Rise and Fall of an Ancient Civilization*. London: Allen Lane.

MOSCATI, S. (1987). Il sacrificio punico dei fanciulli: realtà o invenzione? *Accademia Nazionale dei Lincei Quaderno* 261: 3–15.

O'CONNOR, D. (1990). The nature of Tjemhu (Libyan) society in the later New Kingdom. In A. Leahy (ed.), *Libya and Egypt c. 1300–750 BC*. London: School of Oriental and African Studies, 29–113.

——(1993). Urbanism in Bronze Age Egypt and northeast Africa. In T. Shaw, P. J. J. Sinclair, B. W. Andah, and A. Okpoko (eds), *Archaeology of Africa: Food, Metals and Towns*. London: Routledge, 570–86.

PICHLER, W. (2007). *Origin and Development of the Libyco-Berber Script*. Cologne: Rüdiger Köppe.

POINSSOT, C., and J. W. SALOMONSON (1959). Le mausolée libyco-punique de Dougga et les papiers du comte Borgia. *Comptes Rendus de l'Académie des Inscriptions et Belles-Letters*: 141–7.

PRAG, J. R. W. (2006). *Poenus plane est*—but who were the 'Punickes'? *Papers of the British School at Rome* 74: 1–37.

QUINN, J. C. (2011). The cultures of the Tophet: identification and identity in the Phoenician Diaspora. In E. S. Gruen (ed.), *Cultural Identity in the Ancient Mediterranean*. Los Angeles, Calif.: Getty Research Institute, 388–413.

RAKOB, F. (1979). Numidische Königsarchitektur on Nordafrika. In H. G. Horn and Rüger (eds), *Die Numider: Reiter und Könige Nördlich der Sahara*. Cologne: Rudolf Habelt, 119–71.

REYGASSE, M. (1950). *Monuments Funéraires Préislamiques de l'Afrique du Nord*. Paris: Arts et Métiers Graphiques.

RICHARDSON, S. (2000). Libya domestica: Libyan trade and society on the eve of the invasions of Egypt. *Journal of the American Research Centre in Egypt* 36: 149–64.

ROGNON, P. (1987). Late Quaternary climatic reconstruction for the Maghreb (North Africa). *Palaeogeography Palaeoclimatology Palaeoecology* 58: 11–34.

RÜGER, C. B. (1979). Das Garb der Tin Hinan bei Ablessa/Algerien. In H. G. Horn and Rüger (eds), *Die Numider: Reiter und Könige Nördlich der Sahara*. Cologne: Rudolf Habelt, 251–61.

SHAW, B. D. (2003). A peculiar island: Maghrib and Mediterranean. *Mediterranean Historical Review* 18: 93–125.

SCHWARTZ, J. H., HOUGHTON, F., MACCHIARELLI, R., and BONDIOLI, L. (2010). Skeletal remains from Punic Carthage do not support systematic sacrifice of infants. *PLoS One* 5, 2: e9177. doi:10.1371/journal.pone.0009177.

SOUVILLE, G. (1986). Témoignages sur l'âge du bronze au Maghreb occidental. *Comptes-Rendus des Séances de l'Académie des Inscriptions et Belles-Lettres* 130: 97–114.

SMITH, P., AVISHAI, G., GREENE, J. A., and STAGER, L. E. (2011). Aging cremated infants: the problem of sacrifice at the Tophet of Carthage. *Antiquity* 85: 859–74.

SNAPE, S. (2003). The emergence of Libya on the horizon of Egypt. In D. O'Connor and S. Quirke (eds), *Mysterious Lands*. London: UCL Press, 93–106.

——(2004). The excavations of the Liverpool University Mission to Zawiyet Umm el-Rakham 1994–2001. *Annales du Service des Antiquités de l'Egypte* 78: 149–60.

STAGER, L. E. (1980). The rite of child sacrifice at Carthage. In J. G. Pedley (ed.), *New Light on Ancient Carthage*. Ann Arbor: University of Michigan Press, 1–11.

STONE, D. L. (2007). Monuments on the margin: Interpreting the first millennium B.C.E. rock-cut tombs (Haouanet) of North Africa. In D. L. Stone and L. M. Stirling (eds), *Mortuary Landscapes of North Africa*. Toronto: University of Toronto Press, 43–74.

WHITE, A. P., and WHITE, D. (1996). Coastal sites of northeast Africa: the case against Bronze Age ports. *Journal of the American Research Center in Egypt* 33: 11–31.

WHITE, D. (1981). Cyrene's sanctuary of Demeter and Persephone: a summary of a decade of excavation. *American Journal of Archaeology* 85: 13–30.

——(2002). *Marsa Matruh*. Oxford: INSTAP Academic Press.

WHITTAKER, C. (1978). Carthaginian imperialism in the fifth and fourth centuries. In P. Garnsey and C. Whittaker (eds), *Imperialism in the Ancient World*. Cambridge: Cambridge University Press, 59–90.

WILSON, A. I. (2005). Une cité grecque de Libye: fouilles d'Euhésperidès (Benghazi). *Comptes Rendus de l'Académie des Inscriptions et Belles-Lettres, Novembre–Décembre 2003*, 1648–75.

——(2006). New light on a Greek city: archaeology and history at Euesperides. In E. Fabbricotti and O. Menozzi (eds), *Cirenaica: Studi, Scavi e Scoperte. Atti del X Convegno di Archeologia Cirenaica*. Oxford: British Archaeological Reports, 141–52.

CHAPTER 53

ROMAN AFRICA AND THE SAHARA

ANNA LEONE AND FARÈS K. MOUSSA

THIS chapter considers urban and rural organization and economy during the Roman period in North Africa, between the 1st century BC (after the creation of the first African Roman province) and the beginning of the 5th century AD (until the Vandal conquest), highlighting the interactions, connections and exchanges that characterized Romans and local populations, particularly in the Sahara.

COLONIALISM AND ROMAN ARCHAEOLOGY IN NORTH AFRICA

From the second half of the 19th century, in pursuit of their respective colonial interests, France and Italy became the standard-bearers of the Roman 'reconquest' of North Africa (Guilhaume 1992; Lorcin 1995: 21–2; Mattingly 1996; Munzi 2001, 2004; Silverstein 2004: 60–63). The French army excavated and reconstructed Roman archaeological sites, particularly garrison sites of the Roman legionary army in the province (Legio III Augusta), such as Lambaesis in Algeria, and triumphant arches, which became symbolic of the reconquest of North Africa (Dondin-Payre 1991, 1998; see also Oulebsir 2004: 284–7). Intensive non-stratigraphic excavations and reconstructions of monuments were also carried out by the Italians during the Fascist occupation of Libya (Munzi 2001).

The first White Father Christian missions in Africa, established by Cardinal Lavigerie in Algiers in 1868 (O'Donnell 1979), also made notable contributions to early North African archaeology. Early Christian and Jewish cemeteries and the burial places of Christian martyrs such as Perpetua, Felicitas (at Carthage, Tunisia), and Salsa (Tipasa, Algeria) were located and excavated, often under the direction of Père Delattre (Frend 1997: 69–72). Modern churches were built on key sites, such as the basilicas of St Louis at Carthage and St Augustine at Hippone (contemporary Annaba, Algeria), the latter's home town (see Frend 1997; Lancel 2002).

The traditional domination of Classical archaeology in North Africa can be partly attributed to well-preserved and easily recognized Roman material culture and monuments. However, combined with 'colonial' narratives of 'Romanization', which assumed Roman cultural hegemony in North Africa, this has led to a relatively limited knowledge about the pre- and post- Roman phases. These were countered by 'postcolonial' models arguing for indigenous resistance, now increasingly displaced by models of 'hybridism'. Related to these developments, much archaeological research and discovery in the Maghreb, as in other parts of the world, has taken place in the context of nuanced, often contradictory colonialist and nationalist agendas which have unfolded in North Africa particularly since the mid-19th century (on Romanization see Mattingly 1997, 2002; Woolf 1997, 1998; in North Africa, see Benabou 1976; Fentress 2006; on colonial and post-colonial archaeology, see Trigger 1984, 1989; Van Dommelen 1997, 2006, 2011; Gosden 2001, 2004; in North Africa, see Mattingly 1996, 1997; on nationalism in North Africa, see Moussa, Ch. 52 above).

Historical background

The creation of the first Roman province of Africa (Vetus) followed the end of the Punic Wars and the destruction of the Punic city of Carthage in 146 BC. In 46 BC Julius Caesar founded the province of Africa Nova, which included part of the Numidian Kingdom (Moussa, Ch. 52 above). The original province more or less corresponded to the ancient territory of Carthage (Briand-Ponsart and Hugoniot 2006), as delimited by the treaty that ended the Second Punic War in 201 BC, which extended over the northeast of modern Tunisia. Initially, Carthage's former territory was subdivided, subsequently, under Augustus (30 BC–AD 14), Roman control was consolidated. The province of Africa Proconsularis was created through the unification of the two existing provinces, refounding Carthage itself and establishing a series of other colonies, including Thuburbo Minus (Tebourba), Simitthus (Chemtou), Thuburnica, Sicca Veneria (Le Kef), Assuras (Zanfour), and Maxula (Briand-Ponsart and Hugoniot 2006) (Fig. 53.1).

To the west, in Numidia, Cirta (contemporary Constantine, Algeria) became a colony between 36 and 26 BC, and new settlements were founded in Mauritania, although this was still a client kingdom, and became only a Roman province after the death of King Juba II in AD 40. Almost two centuries later, under Septimius Severus (AD 193–211), Numidia was separated from Africa Proconsularis. The whole region was then entirely reorganized at the end of the 3rd century under Diocletian (284–305): Africa Proconsularis was split into Africa Proconsularis Zeugitana, Africa Valeria Byzacena and Africa Tripolitana, Numidia into Numidia Militiana and Cirtensis, and Mauritania into Caesariensis, Tingitana and Sitifiensis (Briand-Ponsart and Hugoniot 2006).

The boundaries in the Vandal period (439–533) are difficult to trace due to limited information. The main question is how far the Vandals extended into Tripolitania. Christian Courtois suggested that the Vandals respected the territorial organization of Roman Africa, keeping control of the region formerly known as Africa Proconsularis and Byzacena, and that the Vandal presence in Tripolitana was limited up to Oea (modern

FIG. 53.1 North Africa showing sites mentioned in Chapter 53. Key to sites: 1. Aghram Nadharif; 2. Assuras; 3. Bulla Regia; 4. Carthage; 5. Cirta; 6. Garama; 7. Ghirza; 8. Kasserine; 9. Lepcis Magna; 10. Maxula; 11. Oea; 12. Sabratha; 13. Sicca Veneria; 14. Simitthu; 15. Theveste; 16. Thuburnica; 17. Thuburbo Minus; 18. Uchi Maius.

Tripoli, Libya) (Courtois 1955: 256–9; see also Modéran 2002: 107–10). However, the suggestion that Lepcis Magna (contemporary Khoms, Libya) remained outside the Vandal kingdom is principally connected to the misinterpretation of a text by Procopius, the 6th-century historian. Procopius in fact refers to the Vandal kingdom as being extended to Tripoli, identified by Courtois with Oea. However, Oea only took this name in the Arab period; Procopius is therefore probably referring to the region of Tripolitana. The Vandals probably controlled the coastal areas, but the extension inland is still unclear (Modéran 1999: 248–9; for a recent synthesis on the Vandal period see Merrills and Miles 2010). In the Byzantine period (534–698) the provinces maintained their structure until they were reorganized, Africa became an exarchate (a military province) under the Emperor Mauritius, at the end of the 6th century. The principal province continued to be Carthage (Zeugi Carthago), with its capital, Carthago Iustiniana. Byzacena and Numidia retained the same administrative borders as in the 4th century before the Vandal conquest (Lepelley 1999: 18–19). Although Tripolitana extended from the Gulf of Sirtes to Tacapes, it was probably only controlled on the coast, while the territory inland was in the hands of local tribes. By the end of the 6th century Tripolitana was attached to the exarchate of Egypt (Pringle 1981: 64), and in AD 647 it was the first to be taken in the Arab conquest. A second Islamic campaign in which Kairouan (in Tunisia) became the new capital of the province of Ifriqya took place around 670–75. This was followed by a third campaign, which concluded the conquest in AD 698 of Carthage. North Africa came under Muslim domination (Pentz 2002: 17–28).

THE GARAMANTES AND LOCAL POPULATIONS

References to local populations in the historical records between the 2nd and the 3rd century were very limited, re-emerging from the 3rd century onwards. Classical writers such as Herodotus, Strabo, Pliny, and Diodorus describe hundreds of Berber tribes and sub-tribes inhabiting the Maghreb at different periods. Some tribes we know had a significant influence through the Roman period, such as the Numidians, the Mauri, and the Garamantes (for a synthesis see Mattingly 1995; on the Mauri, see Modéran 2002; on the Berbers see Brett and Fentress 1996; see also Moussa, Ch. 52 above). In recent years considerable effort has been devoted to the study of the Garamantes (e.g. Mattingly 2003; 2007; 2010, after Pace et al. 1951; Ayoub 1967; Daniels 1975). Thought to be a meeting point of localized late pastoral traditions, movements of people from the Libyan Desert and the Nile in the east, sub-Saharan Africa in the south, and Berbers from the north (Camps 1980; Hachid 2000; Mattingly 2003: 342–7), the Garamantian territories are located principally along the valley of the Wadi al-Ajal in southwest contemporary Libya. 'Early Garamantian' settlements, dating from *c.* 1000 BC are characterized by hill forts and fortified settlements, such as Zinkekra, built on the top edge of the escarpment lining the southern side of the Wadi-al-Ajal (Daniels 1968; Mattingly 2010: 19–84). A transitional 'proto-urban' phase in the second half of the 1st century BC sees the gradual shift of settlements from the top of the escarpment to the valley and the first evidence of occupation in mud-brick and stone-footed constructions at the main Garamantian urban centre of Garama. The 'late Garamantian phase' continues to *c.* AD 700 with more defensive structures. The site of Garama was continuously occupied until modern times, affording recent excavations at Garama a unique stratigraphic sequence (Mattingly 2003, 2007).

ROMAN URBANISM AND BEYOND

The creation of the provinces of Africa Proconsularis, Numidia, Mauritania, and Tripolitana saw the progressive transformation of the North African landscape. Many new towns were founded, which often adopted axial grid town planning such as the regular network of roads (insulae) at Augustan Carthage. In other cases, such as Bulla Regia (ancient) and Dougga (ancient) in western Tunisia or Tiddis (ancient Castellum Tidditanorum) in eastern Algeria, pre-Roman towns did not permit such regular plans, but were often extended.

Many existing cities were monumentalized with the creation of fora, baths, theatres, temples and circuses. A second phase of public development occurred during and immediately after the Emperor Hadrian's visits to North Africa in AD 128 and 132, at which time many cities were refurbished. Much of the building activity carried out in these towns, especially in the 1st to 2nd centuries, relied heavily on the munificence of the local elite. These individuals were probably rich merchants and landowners who, as elsewhere, were integrated into the hierarchical organization of the Roman Empire. Annobal Tapapius Rufus, for example, at the beginning of the 1st century AD paid for the construction of the theatre at Lepcis Magna, commemorating his patronage with a bilingual inscription in Punic and Latin (Mattingly 1995). Finally, monumentality in funerary architecture continued from the Punic period, as exemplified by the mid-2nd-century AD mausoleum of Flavius Secundus in Kasserine (central Tunisia) (Bodel 2001: 39). A final phase of major monumentalization is connected with the Severan period (193–235), and is visible in particular in the new arch, colonnaded street, and forum at Lepcis Magna, from where Septimius Severus himself originated (Ward-Perkins 1993).

Even if a common trend in the monumentalization of these cities is identifiable, the extent and development of this phenomenon varied from province to province. Africa Proconsularis was highly urbanized, especially along the River Bagradas (Medjerda). Cities here were often no more than 10–13 km from one another, with a continuous network of towns from Carthage to Theveste (Tebessa, Algeria) along the main connecting road (Salama 1951). However, in other provinces, such as Tripolitana, urbanization was limited mainly to Sabratha (north-west Libya), Oea, and Lepcis Magna along the c. 900km coast, where cities developed around harbour settlements or *emporia.*

Equally, indigenous populations developed their own urbanism, although ultimately this was influenced by the Roman presence, at least in its architectural form. Recent excavations have uncovered the presence of various Garamantian settlements, located in both central and more peripheral areas of their territory. Excavations at Aghram Nadharif, on the fringes of Garamantian territory in the Barkat Oasis (Liverani 2003, 2005), revealed a stone-built citadel, with a 3 m-wide city wall, at least two towers, and an entrance lined with ramps for animals. This particular settlement, which was abandoned at the end of the 4th century, was strategically located in front of the Wadi Tanezzuft, in a position that Liverani (2005) suggests was central to Saharan trade (Fig. 53.2). There is evidence that at the Garamantian urban centre of Garama, stone-footed structures were constructed that included some architectural elements of Greco-Roman style, as for instance a probable stone-built temple and bath complex, furnished with a heating system (Mattingly 2007: 116–21). Roman influences can be also seen in the monument of Watwat (Fig. 53.3), which recalls the Roman mausoleum of Flavius Secundus at Kasserine in central Tunisia (Mattingly 2007: 106).

ROMAN ECONOMY AND TRADE IN THE MAGHREB AND SAHARA

Many surveys since the 1960s have sought to investigate the various phases of occupation and exploitation of the rural landscape in North Africa (Mattingly and Hitchner 1995; Ørsted et al. 2000; Leone and Mattingly 2004). The archaeological evidence varies considerably from region to region, as well as the relationships between Rome and the indigenous populations of Africa. Although a common trend recorded across the territory is the presence of rural villas and farms, changes to the countryside occurred over time in the way land was managed and exploited (Mattingly 1997; Garnsey 1978; Whittaker 1995; Leone and Mattingly 2004). Sites associated with complex irrigation works and multiple presses suggests that they produced grain, olive oil, and to a lesser extent wine (Mattingly and Hitchner 1995; Ørsted et al. 2000).

Olive oil production was a major industry during the Roman period, and has been extensively studied in Africa Proconsularis and Tripolitana. Calculations on the level of production have been based on archaeological evidence from the size of olive presses and amphorae recorded in surveys (Mattingly 1988). Ceramic containers have been recorded in large

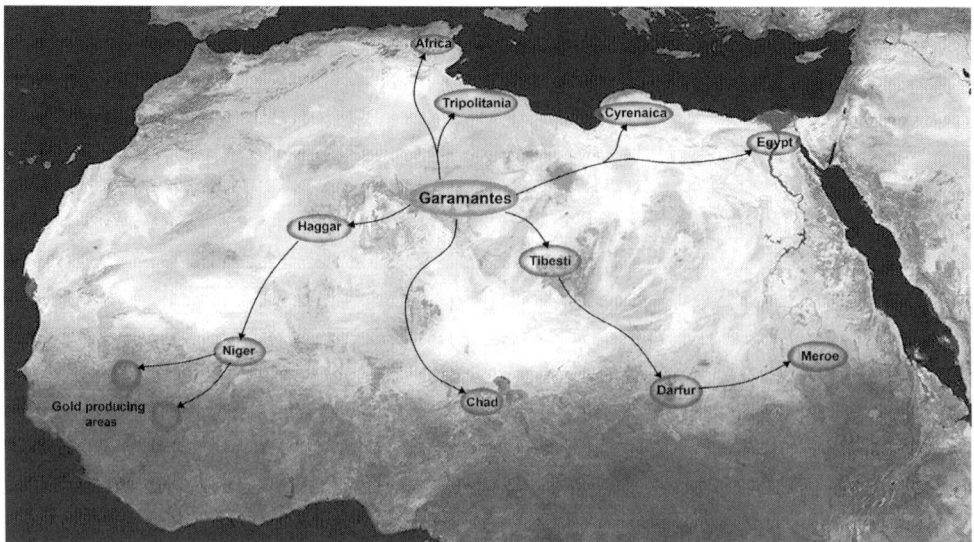

FIG. 53.2 Trade routes of the Garamantes (adapted from Liverani 2000a, reproduced with permission).

FIG. 53.3 The so-called Garamantian 'mausoleum' at Watwat near Garama, Libya. Although known as a 'mausoleum', no chamber or burials directly associated with this structure have been found (photo courtesy of D. J. Mattingly).

quantities up to the 4th century and beyond, attesting to the long-term continuity of the olive oil trade all over the Mediterranean. Evidence of industrial-scale olive oil production is known, such as on the fertile Tarhuna plateau of the Tripolitanian hinterland, where fortified olive farms and rural villas are recorded (and have been rediscovered in recent surveys) (Cowper 1897; Goodchild 1950). Similar evidence is also attested for wine production (Brun 2003), although our knowledge of this production and export in this region is less advanced than in the case of olive oil. Likewise, grain was certainly produced from at least the Punic period; despite various sources which have suggested that grain and wheat were produced on a very large scale for supplying Rome, indicating the region as 'the granary of Rome', this is difficult to confirm archaeologically (for a recent critical review of ancient sources on grain production in North Africa see Davis 2007).

Roman North Africa also exploited abundant fish stocks from the Mediterranean, partly continuing some Punic traditions. From the 1st century BC until at least the 3rd century, evidence of the manufacture of salted fish and fish sauce—*garum*—has been recorded at several coastal sites, including Neapolis near contemporary Nabeul in Tunisia (Sternberg 2000), Sabratha in Libya (Wilson 2007), and Cotta, near modern Tangier (Ponsich and Tarradell 1965; Ponsich 1988: 150–59). The capture of tuna was certainly a significant activity, exploiting the massive seasonal migrations between the Mediterranean and the Atlantic in the summer. These activities are substantiated by the discovery of lead anchors possibly used for anchoring fixed nets (Erbati and Trakadas 2008) and by depiction in mosaics. Perpetuating a Phoenicio-Punic tradition, the production of the distinctive purple dye from murex sea snails used for the robes worn by the senatorial class also continued (see e.g. Fentress et al. 2009).

Pottery such as amphorae were produced for transporting oil, wine, and fish products, in both coastal and rural workshops attached to agricultural estates. Fineware, known as African Red Slip Ware, was extensively produced in North Africa (especially in modern Tunisia) and exported all over the Mediterranean, as were cooking wares, which were widely distributed (Bonifay 2004). Surveys carried out in Tunisia have uncovered a number of pottery workshops that remained active until the 7th century (Bonifay 2004). Evidence for trade into the Sahara can be seen through African Red Slip pottery recorded in the funerary complexes around the Garamantian centre of Germa (Fontana 1990; Dore et al. 2007), as well as the Italian sigillata and African (produced in Tunisia) and Tripolitanian amphorae. More recent surveys have confirmed this trend, highlighting the intensive trading activities of the Romans with the Garamantes and beyond until the 4th century and probably later (Mattingly 2010).

The sourcing of raw materials and crafts production constituted significant activities, supplying export economies and increasingly populated and monumentalized cities. Marble quarried at Chemtou (ancient Simitthu, northern Tunisia) was popular in Rome for its distinctive yellow/brown marble. According to Pliny, the marble was quarried from 78 BC and quarrying was thought to have continued until at least the 3rd century (Ward Perkins 1951; Rakob et al. 1994). A large number of local workshops throughout North Africa produced capitals and architectural decoration in local stones, with a distinctive regional architectural style developing from the 3rd century (Pensabene 1986).

Partial reuse of existing roads but also the development of new systems enabled wider and more intensive trading between the Mediterranean and the Sahara (Salama 1951), which relied heavily on the presence of ports in coastal areas. Road networks continued beyond the frontiers of the Roman Empire and extended to the caravan routes that led to sub-Saharan Africa (see Fig. 53.2). The Roman southern frontier (*limes*) at the southern extent of its territories, lined with a series of castles, citadels, and mountain passes and located in strategic positions along the caravan route (Liverani 2000b), may have been primarily set up to boost economic exchange, rather than to control and protect the territory (see Mattingly 1995).

The early development of trans-Saharan trade, dated at least to the first millennium BC, may be linked to the emergence of the Garamantes as an independent and powerful polity. Located along caravan routes that probably linked Wadi-al-Ajal to the Fayyum and the Nile Delta in northern Egypt, the Tripolitanian coast, and the Niger Bend of West Africa (Liverani 2000a, 2000b), controlling trade routes from the strategic location of Garama is certainly thought to have become a key Garamantian economic activity (see Fig. 53.2). References to 'Garamantian carbuncles' or 'Carthaginian stones' (probably referring to the semi-precious stone carnelian), salt, horse breeding, date cultivation, ivory, ebony, the hunting of 'Ethiopians', perhaps for slaves, and the supply of wild beasts for the Roman amphitheatres hint at the range of African goods traded to the Mediterranean via the Garamantes (see e.g. Herodotus 4.183; Strabo 17.3.19; Pliny 13.111; 37.92; 37.104; Ptolemy 1.8; Claudian *Minor poems* 28.20.23). Evidence of the production of some of these commodities and other local industries in Garama and environs is coming to light in recent excavations, including bead production, ferrous and copper alloy metallurgy, glass making, and pottery production (Mattingly 2003: 355–62). Archaeological evidence from the Sahara also reveals large quantities of amphorae, glass, faience, fine ceramics, and statuary from the Punic and Roman Mediterranean coastal regions. At the same time, evidence of irrigated cultivation (using *foggaras*) including date palm, wheat, barley, grapes, figs, sorghum, watermelon/bitter apple, gourd, olives, and almonds corresponds with the 'Classical Garamantian phase' in the first half of the 1st century (van der Veen 1992; Daniels 1989; Mattingly et al. 2002; Mattingly and Wilson 2003: 39; Pelling 2008). The development of irrigated cultivation including date palm (using *foggaras*: a series of subterranean channels connected trough wells: see Stump, Ch. 46 above) allowed the inhabitants to overcome the aridity of the region. Foggaras were probably introduced to the Fazzan in the later first millennium BC, and remained in use until sometime in the second half of the first millennium AD (Wilson 2006). From the Fezzan area it was exported to the north through the trade routes, and its presence is recorded in various parts of North Africa (Wilson 2006, 2009).

LATE ANTIQUITY IN THE MAGHREB

This picture of exchange and trade between local populations and Roman settlements started to vacillate from the 3rd century. Local populations began to threaten the Roman settlements and their inhabitants (Modéran 1991), a process that contributed to the ultimate contraction and abandonment of these cities in the 9th–10th centuries. Lepcis Magna was one of the first cities to lose control of the territory and come under threat from local populations (Mattingly 1995). From the 4th century, Roman cities, especially those located in the highly urbanized valley of the Bagradas, started to decay. This is for instance the case of Uchi Maius, where in the Vandal period, olive presses had already been installed in the forum (for a discussion on olive presses in North Africa and further bibliography, see Vismara 2008; for a synthesis on the transformation of cities in North Africa from Late Antiquity, see Leone 2007).

From the 3rd century we witness the increased appearance of new independent and structured local communities. On the fringes of the Sahara, at Ghirza (north central Libya), for example, a complex community developed, probably organized into two chiefdoms. Large fortified houses and funerary monuments were constructed that appear to imitate the shapes and decorations characteristic of Roman temples (Brogan and Smith 1984; Mattingly 1999). This period was the beginning of a progressive transformation that ended only in the 10th century, when almost all ancient cities were abandoned and a new landscape organization developed (Leone 2007).

REFERENCES

AYOUB, M. S. (1967). *Excavations in Germa between 1962 and 1966*. Tripoli: Ministry of Education.

BENABOU, M. (1976). *La Résistance Africaine à la Romanisation*. Paris: François Maspéro.

BODEL, J. P. (ed.) (2001). *Epigraphic Evidence: Ancient History from Inscriptions*. London: Routledge.

BONIFAY, M. (2004). *Études sur la Céramique Romaine Tardive d'Afrique*. Oxford: British Archaeological Reports.

BRETT, M., and FENTRESS, E. (1996). *The Berbers*. Oxford: Oxford University Press.

BRIAND-PONSART, C., and HUGONIOT, C. (2006). *L'Afrique Romaine de l'Atlantique à la Tripolitaine (146 av. J.C.–533 ap. J.C.)*. Paris: Armand Colin.

BROGAN, O., and SMITH, D. J. (1984). *Ghirza: A Libyan Settlement in the Roman Period*. Tripoli: Department of Antiquities.

BRUN, J.-P. (2003). Les pressoirs à vin d'Afrique et de Maurétanie à l'époque romaine. *Africa*, n.s. 1: 7–30.

CAMPS, G. (1980). *Berbères: Aux Marges de l'Histoire*. Toulouse: Hesperides.

COURTOIS, C. (1955). *Les Vandales et l'Afrique*. Alger: Gouvernement Général de l'Algérie.

COWPER, H. S. (1897). *The Hill of Graces: A Record of Investigation Among the Trilithons and Megalithic Sites of Tripoli*. London: Methuen.

DANIELS, C. M. (1968). Garamantian excavations: Zinchecra 1965–1967. *Libya Antiqua* 5: 113–94.

—— (1975). An ancient people of the Libyan Sahara. In J. Bynon and T. Bynon (eds), *Hamito-Semitica: Proceedings of a Colloquium held by the Historical Section of the Linguistics Association (Great Britain) at the School of Oriental and African Studies, University of London*. Mouton: The Hague, 249–65.

—— (1989). Excavation and fieldwork amongst the Garamantes. *Libyan Studies* 20: 45–61.

DAVIS, D. K. (2007). *Resurrecting the Granary of Rome: Environmental History and French Colonial Expansion in North Africa*. Athens: Ohio University Press.

DONDIN-PAYRE, M. (1991). L'exercitus Africae inspiration de l'armée française: ense et aratro. *Antiquité Africaine* 27: 141–9.

—— (1998). L'utilisation symbolique des monuments archéologiques d'Algérie: l'arc de Caracalla à Cuicul; le cippe de Nonius Datus. *Africa Romana* 12: 1067–99.

DORE, J. N., LEONE, A., and HAWTHORNE, J. (2007). The Fazzan Project: the pottery type series. In Mattingly (2007: 305–425).

ERBATI, E., and TRAKADAS, A. (2008). *The Morocco Maritime Survey*. Oxford: British Archaeological Reports.

FENTRESS, E. (2006). Romanizing the Berbers. *Past and Present* 190: 3–33.

—— DRINE, A., and HOLOD, R. (2009). *An Island Through Time. Jerba Studies, I: The Punic and Roman Periods*. Portsmouth: *Journal of Roman Archaeology*, Supplement 71.

FONTANA, S. (1990). I manufatti romani nei corredi funerari del Fezzan: testimonianza dei commerci e della cultura dei Garamanti (I–III sec.d.C.). In *L'Afrique du Nord Antique et Médiévale, VI Colloque International. Productions et Exportations Africaines. Actualités Archéologiques*. Aix en Provence: CTHS, 405–20.

FREND, W. H. C. (1997). *The Archaeology of Early Christianity: A History*. London: Geoffrey Chapman.

GARNSEY, P. (1978). Rome's African empire under the Principate. In P. Garnsey and C. R. Whittaker (eds), *Imperialism in the Ancient World*. Cambridge: Cambridge University Press, 223–54.

GOODCHILD, R. G. (1950). Roman Tripolitania: reconnaissance in the desert frontier zone. *Geographical Journal* 115: 161–71.

GOSDEN, C. (2001). Postcolonial archaeology: issues of culture, identity, and knowledge. *In* I. Hodder (ed.), *Archaeological Theory Today*. Oxford: Polity Press, 241–61.

—— (2004). *Archaeology and Colonialism*. Cambridge: Cambridge University Press.

GUILHAUME, J.-F. (1992). *Les Mythes Fondateurs de l'Algérie Française*. Paris: Harmattan.

HACHID, M. (2000). *Les Premiers Berbères: Entre Méditerranée, Tassili et Nil*. Aix en Provence: Edisud.

LANCEL, S. (2002). *Saint Augustine*. London: SCM Press.

LEONE, A. (2007). *Changing Townscapes in North Africa from Late Antiquity to the Arab Conquest*. Bari: Edipuglia.

—— and MATTINGLY, D. J. (2004). Vandal, Byzantine and Arab rural landscapes in North Africa. In N. Christie (ed.), *Landscapes of Change*. Aldershot: Ashgate, 135–62.

LEPELLEY, C. (1999). De la carte de Pierre Salama aux études récents sur la frontière de la Byzacena. In C. Lepelley and X. Dupuis, *Frontières et Limites Géographiques de l'Afrique du Nord Antique: Hommage à Pierre Salama*. Paris: Publications de la Sorbonne, 11–20.

LIVERANI, M. (2000a). The Garamantes: a fresh approach. *Libyan Studies* 31: 17–28.

—— (2000b). The Libyan caravan road in Herodotus IV.181–184. *Journal of the Economic and Social History of the Orient* 43(4): 496–520.

—— (2003). Aghram Nadharif and the southern border of the Garamantian kingdom. In Mario Liverani (ed.), *Arid Lands in Roman Times: Papers from the International Conference (Rome, July 9th–10th, 2001)*. Florence: All'Insegna del Giglio, 23–36.

—— (ed.) (2005). *Aghram Nadharif: The Barkat Oasis (Sha Abiya of Ghat, Libyan Sahara) in Garamantian Times*. Florence: All'Insegna del Giglio.

LORCIN, P. M. E. (1995). *Imperial Identities: Stereotyping, Prejudice and Race in Colonial Algeria*. London: I. B. Tauris.

MATTINGLY, D. J. (1988). Oil for export? A comparison of Libyan, Spanish and Tunisian olive oil production in the Roman empire. *Journal of Roman Archaeology* 1: 33–56.

—— (1995). *Tripolitania*. London: Batsford.

—— (1996). From one imperialism to another: imperialism and the Maghreb. In J. Webster and N. Cooper (eds), *Roman Imperialism: Post-colonial Perspectives*. Leicester: School of Archaeological Studies, University of Leicester, 49–69.

—— (1997). Imperialism and territory: Africa, a landscape of opportunity? In D. J. Mattingly (ed.), *Dialogues in Roman Imperialism. Journal of Roman Archaeology*, Supplementary Series no. 23, 115–38.

—— (1999). The art of the unexpected: Ghirza in the Libyan pre-desert. In S. Lancel (ed.), *Afrique du Nord Antique et Mediévale: Numismatique, Langues, Écritures et Arts du Livre, Specificité des art Figures.* Paris: CTHS, 383–405.

—— (2002). Vulgar and weak 'Romanisation', or time for a paradigm shift? *Journal of Roman Archaeology* 15: 541–6.

—— (ed.) (2003). *The Archaeology of Fazzan*, vol. 1: *Synthesis.* London: Society for Libyan Studies and Socialist People's Libyan Arab Jamahariya Department of Antiquities.

—— (ed.) (2007). *The Archaeology of Fazzan*, vol. 2: *Site Gazetteer, Pottery and Other Survey Finds.* London: Society for Libyan Studies and Socialist People's Libyan Arab Jamahariya Department of Antiquities.

—— (ed.) (2010). *The Archaeology of Fazzan*, vol. 3: *Excavations of C. M. Daniels.* London: Society for Libyan Studies and Socialist People's Libyan Arab Jamahariya Department of Antiquities.

—— EDWARDS, D., and DORE, J. N. (2002), Radiocarbon dates from Fazzan, southern Libya. *Libyan Studies* 32: 9–19.

—— and HITCHNER, R. B., (1995). Roman Africa: an archaeological review. *Journal of Roman Studies* 85: 165–213.

—— and WILSON, A. I. (2003). Farming the Sahara: the Garamantian contribution in southern Libya. In M. Liverani (ed.), *Arid Lands in Roman Times: Papers from the International Conference (Rome, July 9th–10th 2001).* Florence: All'Insegna del Giglio, 37–50.

MERRILLS, A. H., and MILES, R. (2010). *The Vandals.* Oxford: Wiley-Blackwell.

MODÉRAN, Y. (1991). Les premiers raids des tribus sahariennes et la Johannide de Corippus. In *Actes du IVe Colloque International d'Histoire et d'Archéologie de l'Afrique du Nord, 2: L'armée et les Affaires Militaires.* Paris: CTHS, 479–90.

—— (1999). Les frontierès mouvante du Royaume Vandal. In C. Lepelley and X. Dupuis (eds), *Frontières et limites géographiques de l'Afrique du Nord Antique: hommage à Pierre Salama.* Paris: Publications de la Sorbonne, 241–63.

—— (2002). L'établissement territorial des Vandales en Afrique. *Antiquité Tardive* 10: 87–122.

MUNZI, M. (2001). *L'epica del Ritorno: Archeologia e Politica nella Tripolitania Italiana.* Rome: L'erma di Bretschneider.

—— (2004). *La decolonizzazione del passato: archeologia e politica in Libia dall'amministrazione alleata al regno di Idris.* Rome: L'erma di Bretschneider.

O'DONNELL, J. D. (1979). *Lavigerie in Tunisia: The Interplay of Imperialist and Missionary.* Athens: University of Georgia Press.

ØRSTED, P., CARLSEN, J., LADJIMI SEBAJ, L., and BEN HASSEN, H. (eds), (2000). *Africa Proconsularis. Regional Studies in the Segermes valley of Northern Tunisia 3: Historical Conclusions.* Copenhagen: Aarhus University Press.

OULEBSIR, N. (2004). *Les Usages du Patrimoine: Monuments, Musées et Politique Coloniale en Algérie (1830–1930).* Paris: Maison des Sciences de l'Homme.

PACE, B., SERGI, S., and CAPUTO, G. (1951). Scavi sahariani: ricerche nell'Uadi el-Agial e nel'Oasi di Gat. *Monumenti Antichi* 41: 150–551.

PELLING, R. (2008). Garamantian agriculture: the plant remains from Jarma, Fazzan. *Libyan Studies* 39: 41–71.

PENSABENE, P. (1986). La decorazione architettonica, l'impiego del marmo e l'importazione dei manufatti orientali a Roma, in Italia e in Africa (II–VI D.C.). In A. Giardina (ed.), *Società Romana e Impero Tardoantico: le Merci, Gli Insediamenti.* Bari: Laterza, 285–429.

PENTZ, P. (2002). *From Roman Proconsularis to Islamic Ifrīqiyah.* Gylling: Göteborg University- Nationalmuseet.

PONSICH, M. (1988). Aceite de oliva y salazones de pescado: factores geo-económicos de Bética y Tingitana. Madrid: Universidad Complutense.

—— and TARRADELL, M. (1965). *Garum et Industries Antiques de Salaison dans la Mediterranée Occidental*. Paris: Presses Universitaires de France.

PRINGLE, D. (1981). *The Defence of Byzantine Africa from Justinian to the Arab Conquest* (2 vols). Oxford: British Archaeological Reports.

RAKOB, F., KHANOUSSI, M., KRAUS, T., and VEGAS, M. (1994). *Simitthus II: Der Tempelberg und das Römische Lager*. Mainz am Rhein: Philipp von Zabern.

SALAMA, P. (1951). *Les Voies Romaines de l'Afrique du Nord*. Alger: Imprimerie officielle.

SILVERSTEIN, P. A. (2004). *Algeria in France: Transpolitics, Race and Nation*. Indianapolis: Indiana University Press.

STERNBERG, M. (2000). Données sur les produits fabriqués dans une officine de Neapolis (Nabeul, Tunisie). *Antiquité* 112: 135–53.

TRIGGER, B. G. (1984). Alternative archaeologies: nationalist, colonialist, imperialist. *Man*, n.s. 19: 355–70.

—— (1989). *A History of Archaeological Thought*. Cambridge: Cambridge University Press.

VAN DER VEEN, M. (1992). Garamantian agriculture: the plant remains from Zinchecra, Fezzan. *Libyan Studies* 23: 7–39.

VAN DOMMELEN, P. (1997). Colonial constructs: colonialism and archaeology in the Mediterranean. *World Archaeology* 28: 305–23.

—— (2006). Colonial matters: material culture and postcolonial theory in colonial situations. In C. Tilley, W. Keane, S. Kuechler, M. Rowlands, and P. Spyer (eds), *Handbook of Material Culture*. London: Sage, 104–24.

—— (2011). Postcolonial archaeologies: between discourse and practice. *World Archaeology* 43: 1–6.

VISMARA, C. (ed.) (2008). *Uchi Maius 3. I Frantoi. Miscellanea*. Sassari: EDES.

WARD PERKINS, J. (1951). Tripolitania and the marble trade. *Journal of Roman Studies* 41: 89–104.

—— (1993). *The Severan Buildings of Leptis Magna: An Architectural Survey*. London: Society for Libyan Studies.

WHITTAKER, C. R. (1995). Integration of the early Roman west: the example of Africa. In J. Metzler, M. Millett, N. Roymans, and J. Slofstra (eds), *Integration in the Early Roman West: The role of Culture and Ideology*. Luxembourg: Dossiers d'Archéologie du Musée National d'Histoire et d'Art 4, 19–32.

WILSON, A. I. (2006). The spread of foggara-based irrigation in the ancient Sahara. In D. J. Mattingly, S. Mclaren, E. Savage, Y. Al-Fasatwi, and K. Gadgood (eds), *The Libyan Desert: Natural Resources and Cultural Heritage*. London: Society for Libyan Studies, 205–16.

—— (2007). Fish-salting workshops in Sabratha. In L. Lagóstena, D. Bernal, and A. Aréval (eds), *Cetariae 2005: Salsas y Salazones de Pescado en Occidente Durante la Antigüedad*. Oxford: British Archaeological Reports, 173–81.

—— (2009). Foggaras in ancient North Africa: or how to marry a Berber princess. In V. Bridoux (ed.), *Contrôle et Distribution de l'Eau dans le Maghreb Antique et Médiévale*. Rome: École française de Rome, 19–39.

WOOLF, G. (1997). Beyond Romans and natives. *World Archaeology* 28: 339–50.

—— (1998). *Becoming Roman: The Origins of Provincial Civilization in Gaul*. Cambridge: Cambridge University Press.

CHAPTER 54

....

MEDIEVAL AND POST-MEDIEVAL STATES OF THE NILE VALLEY

....

DAVID N. EDWARDS

THE END OF MEROE AND THE ORIGINS OF THE 'NUBIAN' KINGDOMS

....

THE Meroitic kingdom which dominated large parts of the Middle Nile region during the early first millennium AD appears to have disintegrated sometime around AD 300–350 for reasons that still remain unclear. An 'ethnic' explanation, in the form of 'Nubian' invasions/ migrations, has long been assumed (echoing familiar narratives of barbarians and the 'fall of Rome'), while Ethiopian/Axumite military adventures may also have played a role. However, the evidential base for such explanations remains slight, and both Roman and Ethiopian sources are unreliable. How political collapse related to observed cultural changes in the archaeological record in the late and post-Meroitic centuries has also been debated (Lenoble and Sharif 1992; Edwards 2004). The authenticity of significant population changes is questionable, and they are certainly unnecessary to explain the cultural, political, or linguistic developments under way in this period. As such, the origins of the medieval 'Nubian' kingdoms of the Middle Nile region may be sought within the local political dynamics of the larger region following the disintegration of the Meroitic state, rather than in relation to long-established assumptions of intrusive new 'Nubian' ('Noba', 'Nobatai', 'Noubades') populations.

Archaeologically, what seems clear is that by the 4th century a political collapse was accompanied by a swift decline and ultimate abandonment of Meroe and other urban settlements, no longer centres of population and political and religious power. None seems to have survived into the medieval period. Whatever the origins of this collapse, the archaeological evidence suggests that with the disappearance of a central authority and the unifying imperial culture it had generated, new regional cultures developed, albeit grounded in pre-existing cultural traditions within the Meroitic kingdom (Lenoble 1997). New regional cultural forms in turn show some correspondence with an emerging series of successor states,

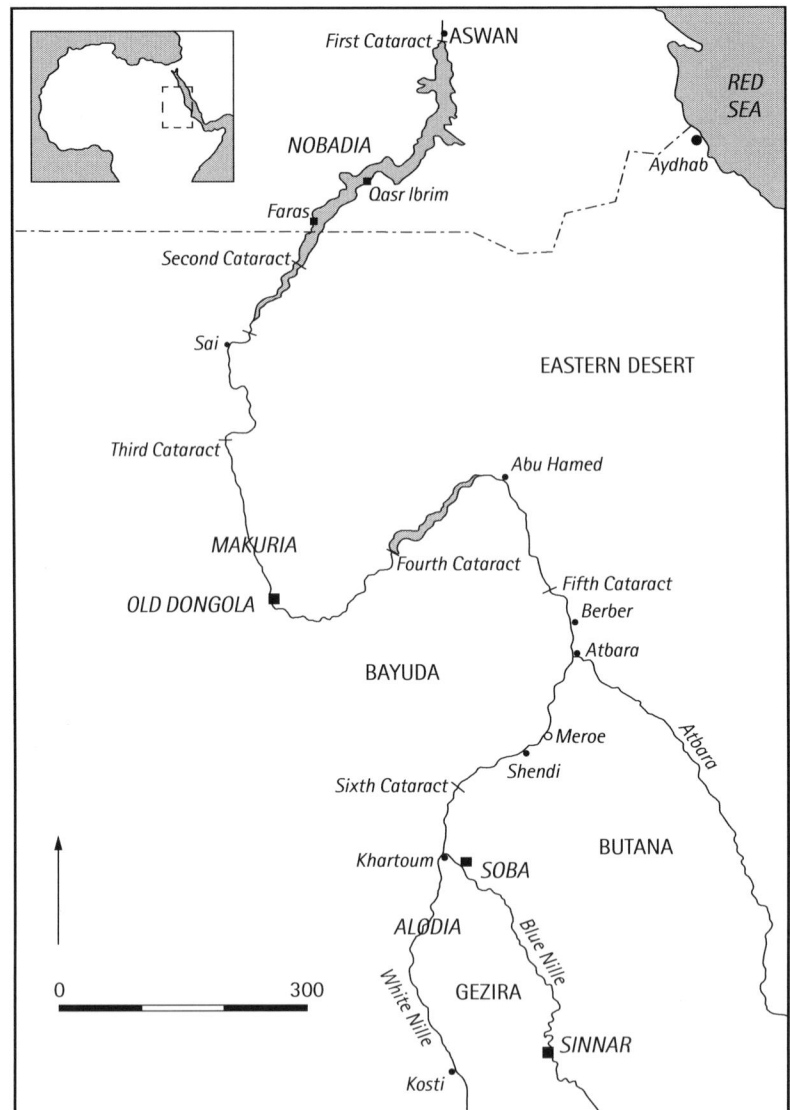

FIG. 54.1 The Middle Nile Valley showing the location of major sites and regions.

identified in external textual sources from the 6th century. Of these, three develop as regional powers during the early medieval period: Nobadia/Noubadia in Lower Nubia, Makuria in the Dongola Reach, and Alodia in central Sudan (Fig. 54.1). Makuria seems to have absorbed Nobadia during the 7th century, while tantalizing historical references in royal titularies suggest some later political unification between Makuria and Alodia, but whether real or aspirational remains unclear.

The formative period of these kingdoms is best understood in Nobadia, on the Romano-Egyptian frontier, where close contacts with late Roman/Byzantine Egypt remain evident during this period, most visibly in the many imported objects buried in the spectacular royal and elite tumulus cemeteries at Ballana and Qustul (Emery 1938; Farid 1963; Williams 1991). Early Nobadian kings may well have enjoyed some form of federate status in relation to the Byzantine government, establishing their own regional dominance by the late 5th century. Very little is known of the early development of new elites and centres of power in Makuria and Alodia, although several cemeteries with impressive tumulus burials of this period (e.g. Ez-Zuma and El-Hobaji) seem likely to relate to their emergence, if not directly with new royal centres of (Old) Dongola and Soba, the origins of which may lie in the 5th or 6th centuries. Further south, material evidence for contacts with Egypt is increasingly sparse during this period and remains so throughout the medieval period.

This new political order was soon closely linked with Christianity, with 'official' (if doubtless incomplete) accounts pointing to the conversion of all three kingdoms during the 6th century (Adams 1977; Kirwan 1987), but almost certainly following a period of more informal contacts with the new religion both from Egypt (Dijkstra 2008) and perhaps Ethiopia. Christianity's arrival also encouraged and facilitated new cultural links with the north, and remained the defining cultural development of the medieval period within riverine Nubia, bringing it within the realm of eastern Christendom. With very little in the way of indigenous historical documentation, the doubtless complex political histories of the Nubian kingdoms are poorly known and at times consist of barely more than king-lists. However, external (largely Arabic) accounts (Vantini 1975) do allow the construction of the outlines of a political history, as well as identifying something of the often dynamic relations between the Nubian kingdoms and their Egyptian neighbours, and the caliphate, more generally.

The early medieval period also saw new settlement landscapes emerging. The potential for riverine farming in the arid north was greatly increased during the early first millennium AD with the spread of new crops (e.g. sorghum, millets, wheat) and cropping regimes, with both winter and summer harvests, integrated with new forms of water-wheel irrigation. Medieval settlements, both in the form of villages and more dispersed farms, are commonly quite visible archaeologically, especially in largely rainless northern Nubia, where mud-brick architecture was widely used (Fig. 54.2). However, settlements that might be termed 'urban' remained few in number. Within more southerly regions, especially in Alodia, pastoral opportunities will have been more significant, practised alongside rain-fed agriculture, and the still poorly documented spread of the camel (Gifford-Gonzalez and Hanotte, Ch. 34 above), present in both Nobadia and Makuria by the mid-first millennium AD, had the potential to transform the exploitation of the more arid landscapes further north through the development of a more specialized form of camel pastoralism.

Much of northern Nubia (Nobadia) has now largely disappeared, inundated by the reservoir created by the Aswan dams. Twentieth-century surveys and salvage excavation programmes nevertheless recovered a vast body of knowledge before this took place, including some hundreds of medieval sites (Adams 1977, 1996, 2005). The results of this work remain incompletely published, but their archives represent a considerable resource for future research, with the potential for diachronic studies of medieval settlement for most of northern Nubia between the Third and First Cataracts. Excavated settlements there commonly display complex histories spanning several centuries, and the same is also apparent in studies of Nubian churches (Adams 1965, 2009; Gartkiewicz 1982).

Further south, the settlement landscapes of the Makurian heartlands are rather less well understood. Until recently, most work focused on the Makurian capital of (Old) Dongola and its monuments (Jakobielski and Scholz 2001), although recent survey work has begun to

FIG. 54.2 A mud-brick palatial structure (adjoining three churches) at Soba, capital of the kingdom of Alodia, Sudan.

establish a wider knowledge base in some areas (e.g. Zurawski 2003). The recently complete Merowe Dam Salvage Programme up-river of the Fourth Cataract has also generated a significant body of new data on medieval settlement in this previously unexplored and rather inhospitable stretch of the Nile Valley (Näser and Lange 2007; Welsby 2008). Areas further up-river have as yet seen little archaeological exploration since pioneering survey work in the 1950s (Crawford 1953). Traces of medieval settlements have also only rarely been identified as yet in the one-time heartlands of the old Meroitic kingdom, although Christian burials are quite widely encountered.

The southernmost kingdom of Alodia seems to have been centred further south, at Soba, a little upstream of Khartoum (Welsby and Daniels 1991; Welsby 1998). Relatively little is known of the kingdom outside its capital, and survey or excavation data for this potentially quite extensive kingdom are few. Alongside a vernacular architecture maintaining Sudanic roundhouse traditions using wood and thatch, only its public buildings (mainly churches) seem to have been constructed in brick (Fig. 54.2), both mud-brick and more durable fired brick. Its territory is likely to have extended southwards a substantial, if still uncertain, distance up both the Blue and White Niles, while its kings probably exercised a significant (if still poorly defined) influence in the open plains to the west and east of the Nile.

External contacts took on a new dimension with the introduction of the institutions of the Church, most obviously represented by its churches and monasteries. Their architecture, monuments, and associated arts (notably wall paintings) remain a major focus of research. More than 130 churches have been identified in Nobadia (Adams 2009), some of which have seen quite extensive excavations and publication. The episcopal centre of Faras is particularly notable for an extraordinary collection of wall paintings recovered from its cathedral during salvage excavations in the 1960s (Michalowski 1967; Jakobielski 1972; Godlewski 2006). Several churches and monasteries, as well as the originally fortified citadel at the Makurian capital of (Old) Dongola, have also been extensively studied (Gartkiewicz 1990; Jakobielski and Scholz 2001), while the recent discovery of a royal mausoleum church

(Zurawski 2008) demonstrates that the potential for spectacular discoveries is by no means exhausted.

How Christianity shaped and transformed medieval Nubian societies is, however, an issue still little addressed (Edwards 2004), while the distinctiveness of much medieval Nubian material culture (for the ceramics see Adams 1986) also suggests the need to consider indigenous Nubian reception of, and responses to, Christianity more carefully. While recent research has shown a greater awareness of the distinctively 'Nubian' idioms of medieval culture in the different parts of the Middle Nile, the much less obvious impact of Byzantine/Egyptian cultural forms in Alodian material culture, when compared with the other kingdoms, clearly invites more systematic investigation. So too does the 'Christianization' (Edwards 1999, 2001), and indeed later 'Islamicization' (Edwards 2006) of Nubia's landscapes.

The rise of literate practices, and their significance, has yet to be systematically explored, although archaeological fieldwork has recovered a significant and varied body of medieval 'Nubian' texts in a range of languages (Lajtar 2003, 2008; van der Vliet 2003; Lajtar and van der Vliet 2010; Ruffini 2012). Greek was already in use as an official language, at least in the north (Burstein 2008), and Coptic too came to be quite widely used in the Church, which was formally linked to the Coptic Alexandrian patriarchate. A written vernacular ('Old Nubian') was also developed by the late 8th/9th centuries for various forms of Nile Nubian languages that had become the primary communal languages of central riverine Sudan (Browne 2002).

The scale of external trading contacts of the medieval kingdoms remains poorly defined. Material evidence for such contacts may be gauged in finds of imported materials ranging from utilitarian pottery (Adams 1986) to (more rarely) fine cloth, glass, and glazed pottery, from Egypt, Syria and beyond. As in earlier periods, such traces are most common in the extended frontier zone between Aswan and the Second Cataract—a region that Arabic sources also identify as being open to commercial activities, which were strictly controlled further south. The relatively small quantities of imported materials found archaeologically in the heartlands of Makuria and Alodia should perhaps not be overemphasized (Edwards 2011). Most such finds relate to low-volume prestigious imports accessed by the religious and secular elites, and in themselves can tell us little of the scale or character of more general trading contacts. Most current portrayals of the scale and nature of Nubian long-distance trade rest on a series of assumptions that there existed an active trade in slaves to the Islamic world, and that this underpinned more general exchanges. Assertions that, for example, the kingdom of Alodia could be characterized as 'primarily a slave-trading state' (Adams 1977: 471) are now regularly cited, despite an absence of more specific evidence for such a trade, or how it might have been organized. That slavery was a normal condition within Nubia cannot be doubted, while it seems clear that some slaves originating in the Middle Nile were reaching external markets throughout the medieval period. The relative invisibility of a Nubian trade in Egypt, in contrast to a flourishing medieval commerce through the Red Sea to India and East Africa (Goitein and Friedman 2007), might suggest that the scale and nature of medieval trading links between Nubia and its northern neighbours merit more critical investigation. An alternative perspective might, however, argue that Nubian trade remained quite modest in scale (e.g. Kapteijns and Spaulding 2005: 22–3) and that, notwithstanding the familiar trope of the 'Nubian slave', the Middle Nile was not a major source of slaves for the Islamic world as is commonly imagined (Edwards 2011).

Historical sources suggest that by the later medieval period, other kingdoms were developing in Darfur, as they were elsewhere in Sudanic Africa during this period (O'Fahey and Spaulding 1974). Although archaeological research has as yet been able to add little to our knowledge of them, some claims of material evidence for links between the Nubian kingdoms and those of Darfur now seem unfounded (McGregor 2001). Links between the riverine kingdoms and the Red Sea region, which had a rather distinct history during this period, also remain unclear. Along the Red Sea coast, several important ports, notably Suakin, ar-Rih/Badi, and Aydhab (Peacock and Peacock 2008), developed during this period, operating within Islamic trading networks linking Egypt and the Near East with Arabia and the Indian Ocean. They also served as hubs for Muslim pilgrims heading eastward, especially to Jeddah, the main port of the Holy Places of Islam. While again, little archaeology has as yet been done on such sites, their distinctive cultural character with strong links to Arabia seems clear. Islamic tombstones commemorate the presence of Arabian merchant families on the Red Sea coast, while also indicating an early incorporation into the Islamic world (Kawatoko 1993), several centuries earlier than in the Sudanese Nile Valley.

The power and influence of Nubian kings may at times have extended into parts of eastern Sudan, but most of this area seems to have remained in the hands of the largely pastoral Beja peoples. While little is known of the medieval archaeology of the Red Sea hinterlands, traces of eastern populations may perhaps be identifiable in some riverine areas, probably relating to a seasonal presence of pastoralists on the Nile that is also suggested by Arabic medieval sources. These may be seen as part of an enduring cultural tradition rooted in cultural traditions of the early to mid-first millennium (Barnard 2008) associated with populations then known as the 'Blemmyes'.

THE END OF THE MEDIEVAL KINGDOMS
AND POST-MEDIEVAL SUDAN

Arab sources suggest that dynastic struggles within Makuria, during which the first Muslim king of Dongola was installed in the early 13th century, contributed to a weakening of its political structures (Welsby 2002). The Black Death, which devastated both Egypt and Ethiopia (Borsch 2005), might also have had an impact on the region, but whether it penetrated beyond Aswan into the Nubian Middle Nile remains unrecorded in contemporary accounts. After the 13th century, however, archaeological evidence becomes increasingly elusive, and for those areas of riverine Nubia for which we have significant survey data, a contraction of settlement in the later medieval period can be suggested. In more northerly areas, the construction of tower houses (Fig. 54.3) seems to be a feature of later medieval settlements, but from the 14th century it is difficult to identify new building works and many settlements appear to have declined, with some probably being abandoned by 1400. The church at Banganarti, for example, seems to have fallen out of use as a pilgrimage centre in the later 14th century (Lajtar 2008), while the cathedral at Qasr Ibrim appears to have been much decayed when perhaps its last bishop was buried there in the 1370s. Increasing political instability may have been accompanied by a pastoralist resurgence, especially in more southerly

FIG. 54.3 A late medieval tower-house in the Third Cataract region of the Nile, Sudan.

regions—something understood, probably mistakenly, in traditional narratives mainly in terms of the immigration of 'Arab' populations (Kapteijns and Spaulding 2005).

The archaeology of the post-medieval period in the Middle Nile has, until recently, been framed largely in terms of an 'Islamic' archaeology, in succession to a 'Christian' medieval archaeology (Adams 1987; El Zein 2004). From the 16th century, the political focus of the region again shifted southwards, centred on the post-medieval Funj kingdom at Sinnar on the Blue Nile (Crawford 1951; Adams 1977). With limited historical evidence (e.g. Holt 1999) it remains unclear how it related to its medieval predecessor in the region, while its archaeology has yet to be significantly researched (Kleppe 2000). The 16th century also saw the northern Nubian regions drawn into a very different world with the entry of the Ottomans into the Middle Nile following the conquest of Egypt. By the later 16th century a broad frontier zone was established downstream of the Third Cataract, beyond which a series of Ottoman frontier garrisons were implanted. Their presence, and the wider vagaries of Ottoman frontier policy (Alexander 1995, 1997, 2009; Elzein, Ch. 66 below), played a significant role in the development of the culturally quite distinctive Nubian-speaking societies that survived in Lower and Middle Nubia into modern times.

Further south, within the Funj kingdom and peripheral territories, the post-medieval period was marked by the development of new dominant communal identities in which Islam was increasingly important. A core theme of this period concerns the growing dominance of groups claiming Islamic identities, something that has continued in the historical development of most of northern Sudan into modern times. Understanding the spread of Islam and the new 'Arab' identities that have become so closely linked with it may be one focus for future research, while recognizing that the impact of such forces remained uneven, and commonly destructive for populations preyed on by forces of the central riverine state(s). While there is very little archaeological information concerning Sinnar or other new

FIG. 54.4 Post-medieval *qubba* tombs at Debba al-Fuqara, Sudan.

settlements founded within the Funj kingdom, new Islamic identities are increasingly evident in the distinctive domed *qubba* tombs (Fig. 54.4) built for Islamic holymen who were commonly foci for the development of new settlements. In more northerly areas, fortified residences and castles housing local elites are quite common landscape features.

While Sinnar remained the dominant political force in the Middle Nile Valley until its seizure by Muhammed Ali's Ottoman Egyptian army in 1821, historical sources suggest that it maintained an uneasy and commonly predatory relationship with populations in the neighbouring savannah plains of Kordofan (Stiansen and Kevane 1998), as well as further south. Raiding on its peripheries seems to have increasingly supported an active slave trade, well documented by the 18th century, that fed markets in Ottoman Egypt (Lane and Johnson 2009). In the west, archaeology (McGregor 2001) has as yet added relatively little to what the historical records can tell us of the Sultanate of Darfur (O'Fahey 1980), which is also known to have been trading with Egypt by the early post-medieval period (Walz 1979).

REFERENCES

ADAMS, W. Y. (1961). The Christian potteries at Faras. *Kush* 9: 30–43.

—— (1965). Architectural evolution of the Nubian church, 500–1400 A.D. *Journal of the American Research Center in Egypt* 4: 87–139.

—— (1977). *Nubia: Corridor to Africa*. London: Allen Lane.

—— (1986). *Ceramic Industries of Medieval Nubia*. Lexington: University of Kentucky Press.

—— (1987). Islamic archaeology in Nubia: an introductory survey. In T. Hägg (ed.), *Nubian Culture Past and Present*. Stockholm: Almqvist & Wiksell, 327–61.

—— (1996). *Qasr Ibrim. The Late Medieval Period*. London: Egypt Exploration Society.

—— (2005). *The West Bank Survey from Faras to Gemai: Sites of Christian Age*. London: Sudan Archaeological Research Society.

—— (2009). *The Churches of Nobadia*. London: Sudan Archaeological Research Society.

ALEXANDER, J. (1995). The Turks on the Middle Nile. *Archéologie du Nil Moyen* 7: 15–35.

—— (1997). Qalat Sai, the most southerly Ottoman Fortress in Africa. *Sudan & Nubia* 1: 16–20.

—— (2009). Ottoman frontier policies in north-east Africa 1517–1914. In A. C. S. Peacock (ed.), *The Frontiers of the Ottoman World*. Oxford: British Academy, 225–34.

BARNARD, H. (2008). *Eastern Desert Ware: Traces of the Inhabitants of the Eastern Deserts in Egypt and Sudan during the 4th to 6th Centuries*. Oxford: Archaeopress.

BORSCH, S. (2005). *The Black Death in Egypt and England: A Comparative Study*. Austin: University of Texas Press.

BROWNE, G. M. (2002). *A Grammar of Old Nubian*. Munich: Lincom.

BURSTEIN, S. (2008). When Greek was an African language: the role of Greek culture in ancient and medieval Nubia. *Journal of World History* 19: 41–61.

CRAWFORD, O. G. S. (1951). *The Fung Kingdom of Sennar*. Gloucester: John Bellows.

—— (1953). *Castles and Churches in the Middle Nile Region*. Khartoum: Sudan Antiquities Service.

DIJKSTRA, J. (2008). *Philae and the End of Ancient Egyptian Religion*. Leuven: Peeters.

EDWARDS, D. (1999). Christianity and Islam in the Middle Nile: towards a study of religion and social change. In T. Insoll (ed.), *Case Studies in Archaeology and World Religion*. Oxford: Tempus Reparatum, 94–104.

—— (2001). The Christianisation of Nubia: some archaeological pointers. *Sudan & Nubia* 5: 89–96.

—— (2004). *The Nubian Past: An Archaeology of the Sudan*. London: Routledge.

—— (2006). Drawing on rocks, the most enduring monuments of Middle Nubia. *Sudan & Nubia* 10: 55–63.

—— (2011). Slavery and slaving in the medieval and post-medieval kingdoms of the Middle Nile. In P. J. Lane and K. C. Macdonald (eds), *Slavery in Africa: Archaeology and Memory*. London: Oxford University Press, 79–108.

EL ZEIN, I. S. (2004). *Islamic Archaeology in the Sudan*. Oxford: Archaeopress.

EMERY, W. B. (1938). *The Royal Tombs of Ballana and Qustul*. Cairo: Government Press.

FARID, S. (1963). *Excavations at Ballana 1958–1959*. Cairo: Government Printing Offices.

GARTKIEWICZ, P. M. (1982). An introduction to the history of Nubian church architecture. *Nubia Christiana* 1: 43–133.

—— (1990). *The Cathedral in Old Dongola and its Antecedents*. Warsaw: Warsaw University Press.

GODLEWSKI, W. (2006). *Pachoras: The Cathedrals of Aetios, Paulos and Petros*. Warsaw: Warsaw University Press.

GOITEIN, S., and FRIEDMAN, M. A. (2007). *India Traders of the Middle Ages: Documents from the Cairo Geniza*. Leiden: Brill.

HOLT, P. M. (1999). *The Sudan of the Three Niles: The Funj Chronicle, 910–1288/1504–1871*. Leiden: Brill.

JAKOBIELSKI, S. (1972). *Faras III: A History of the Bishopric of Pachoras on the basis of the Coptic Inscriptions*. Warsaw: PWN.

—— and SCHOLZ, P. (eds) (2001). *Dongola-Studien*. Warsaw: ZAS.

KAPTEIJNS, L., and SPAULDING, J. (2005). The conceptualisation of land tenure in the precolonial Sudan: evidence and interpretation. In D. Crummey (ed.), *Land, Literacy and the State in Sudanic Africa*. Trenton, NJ: Red Sea Press, 21–41.

KAWATOKO, M. (1993). On the tombstones found at the Bādi' site, the Al-Rīh island. *Kush* 16: 186–203.

KLEPPE, E. J. (2000). The Funj problem in archaeological perspective. In J. Spaulding and S. Beswick (eds), *White Nile, Black Blood: War, Leadership, and Ethnicity from Khartoum to Kampala*. Lawrenceville, NJ: Red Sea Press, 237–61.

KIRWAN, L. (1987). The birth of Christian Nubia: some archaeological problems. *Rivista Degli Studi Orientali* 63: 119–34.

LAJTAR, A. (2003). *Catalogue of the Greek Inscriptions in the Sudan National Museum at Khartoum*. Leuven: Peeters.

—— (2008). Late Christian Nubia through visitors' inscriptions from the Upper Church in Banganarti. In W. Godlewski and A. Lajtar (eds), *Between the Cataracts*. Warsaw: Warsaw University Press, 321–31.

—— and VAN DER VLIET, J. (2010). *Qasr Ibrim: The Greek and Coptic Inscriptions Published on Behalf of the Egypt Exploration Society*. Warsaw: University of Warsaw.

LANE, P. J., and JOHNSON, D. (2009). The archaeology and history of slavery in South Sudan in the 19th century. In A. C. A. Peacock (ed.), *The Frontiers of the Ottoman World*. Oxford: Oxford University Press, 509–37.

LENOBLE, P. (1997). From pyramids at Meroe to tumulus at El Hobagi: imperial graves of the Late Meroitic culture. Franco-Sudanese surveys and excavations between 1983 and 1990. *Kush* 17: 289–308.

—— and SHARIF, N. M. (1992). Barbarians at the gates? The royal mounds of El Hobagi and the end of Meroe. *Antiquity* 66: 626–35.

MCGREGOR, A. J. (2001). *Darfur (Sudan) in the Age of Stone Architecture c. AD 1000–1750*. Oxford: Archaeopress.

MICHALOWSKI, K. (1967). *Faras: Die Kathedrale aus dem Wüstensand*. Einsiedeln: Benziger.

NÄSER, C., and LANGE, M. (eds) (2007). *Proceedings of the Second International Conference on the Archaeology of the Fourth Nile Cataract*. Wiesbaden: Harrassowitz.

O'FAHEY, R. (1980). *State and Society in Darfur*. London: Hurst.

—— and SPAULDING, J. (1974). *Kingdoms of the Sudan*. London: Methuen.

PEACOCK, D., and PEACOCK, A. (2008). The enigma of 'Aydhab: a medieval Islamic port on the Red Sea Coast. *International Journal of Nautical Archaeology* 37: 32–48.

RUFFINI, G. R. (2012). *Medieval Nubia. A Social and Economic History*. Oxford: Oxford University Press.

STIANSEN, E., and KEVANE, M. (eds) (1998). *Kordofan Invaded: Peripheral Incorporation and Social Transformation in Islamic Africa*. Leiden: Brill.

VAN DER VLIET, J. (2003). *Catalogue of the Coptic Inscriptions in the Sudan National Museum at Khartoum*. Leuven: Peeters.

VANTINI, G. (1975). *Oriental Sources Concerning Nubia*. Warsaw: Polish Academy of Sciences.

WALZ, T. (1979). Trading into the Sudan in the sixteenth xentury. *Annales Islamologiques* 15: 211–33.

WELSBY, D. (1998). *Soba II*. London: British Museum Press.

WELSBY, D. (2002). *The Medieval Kingdoms of Nubia*. London: British Museum Press.

—— (2008). The Merowe Dam Archaeological Salvage Project. In W. Godlewski and A. Lajtar (eds), *Between the Cataracts*. Warsaw: Warsaw University Press, 33–47.

—— and DANIELS, C. M. (1991). *Soba: Archaeological Research at a Medieval Capital on the Blue Nile*. Nairobi: British Institute in Eastern Africa.

WILLIAMS, B. B. (1991). *The Noubadian X-Group Remains*. Chicago: Oriental Institute of the University of Chicago.

ZURAWSKI, B. (ed.) (2003). *Survey and Excavations Between Old Dongola and Ez-Zuma*. Warsaw: Neriton.

—— (2008). The churches of Banganarti, 2002–2006. In W. Godlewski and A. Lajtar (eds), *Between the Cataracts*. Warsaw: Warsaw University Press, 303–20.

CHAPTER 55

··

COMPLEX SOCIETIES OF THE ERITREAN/ETHIOPIAN HIGHLANDS AND THEIR NEIGHBOURS

··

DAVID W. PHILLIPSON

INTRODUCTION

THIS chapter[1] focuses on the period between the early last millennium BC and the mid-second millennium AD in the Horn of Africa, roughly comprising the modern states of Eritrea, Ethiopia, Djibouti, and all components of the former Somalia. The region's physical geography is extremely diverse, and it is unwise to propose detailed interregional correlations. The problems are exacerbated by the fact that research coverage is nowhere comprehensive. Indeed, in many areas, it is totally nonexistent, and many chronological uncertainties remain.

Between 3,000 and 2,000 years ago, the highlands of the northern Horn—currently divided between Ethiopia and Eritrea (Fig. 55.1)—saw economic and sociopolitical developments that reflect an unusual degree of contact and interaction between local communities and those of distant regions. Recent studies have revised our understanding of these contacts: not only was their geographical penetration closely circumscribed, but different sections of the indigenous African communities were affected to markedly varying extents. Investigation of these complex situations has involved linking archaeological evidence with that derived from other disciplines; the emerging outcomes include both a multi-stranded historical understanding without parallel in sub-Saharan Africa at this time-depth, and improved appreciation of archaeology's potential contribution to knowledge about periods for which other sources of information are also available.

---

[1] The treatment here offered is based on lectures presented in 2008–9 in Addis Ababa, Berlin, and Oxford. Parts of the text follow (by kind permission of the Editor) a version published in *Mitteilungen der Sudanarchäologischen Gesellschaft zu Berlin* 20: 75–91 (D. W. Phillipson 2009c).

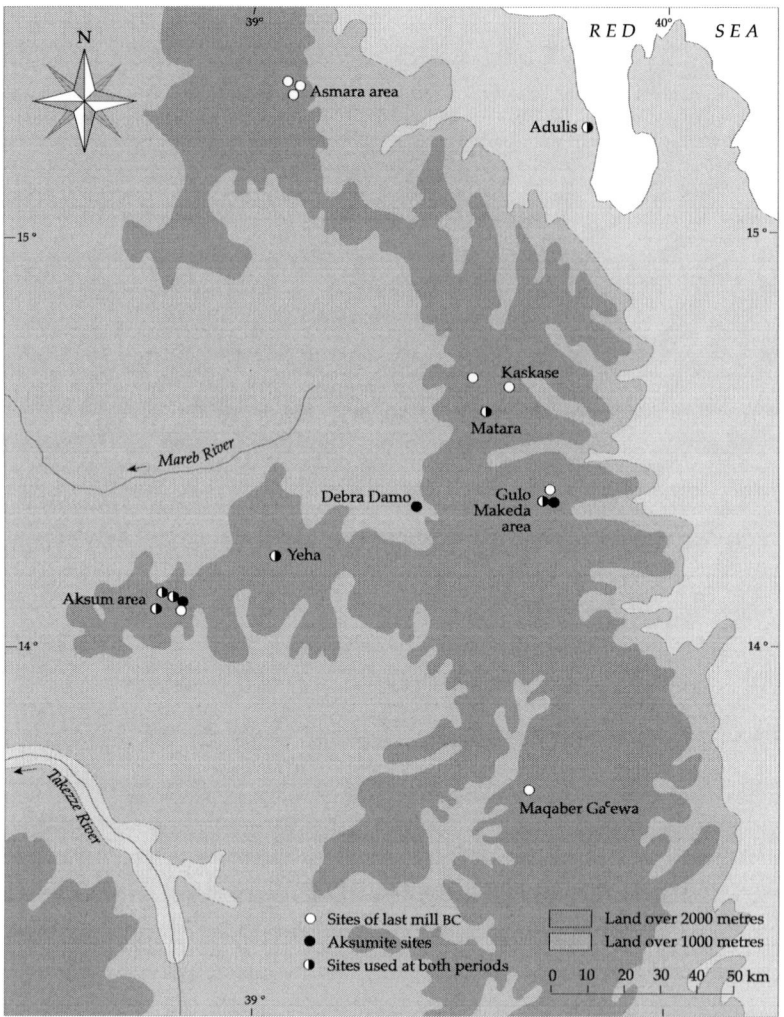

FIG. 55.1 Locations of first-millennium BC and Aksumite sites mentioned in Chapter 55. Please note that this map does not indicate the overall distribution of such sites.

That said, a number of general points may usefully be taken into account. Although detail and precision remain elusive, there is increasing evidence for the substantial antiquity of both cultivation and herding in some regions of the Horn (Curtis, Ch. 39 above) by at least the second millennium BC and probably long before. The plants and animals exploited included species that were initially domesticated locally, as well as others originating in more distant areas of both Africa and Asia; it is not yet possible to ascertain whether the indigenous or allochthonous ones had priority.

There can be little doubt that, at least in most environmentally suitable areas, cultivation and herding were initially adopted by stone-tool-using hunter-gatherers who lacked metallurgical capabilities. Such populations are archaeologically attested and dated in only a few areas of the Horn—notably the Aksum and Temben regions of the northern Ethiopian plateau, the highlands around Harar, the Awash and Southern Ethiopian Rift Valleys, and the low-lying more easterly regions of Djibouti and parts of Somalia—their lithic technology being predominantly of a Mode 5 (microlithic) kind. In several locations, pottery was in use—perhaps as early as the fourth or third millennia BC in northern Ethiopia (Finneran 2007: 59–64)—but the contemporaneity of this innovation with the beginnings of cultivation and/or herding cannot be demonstrated or assumed. The relevance of linguistics for investigating these processes has not yet been adequately shown, although there is general consensus that Semitic languages were spoken in parts of the Horn significantly earlier than the last-millennium BC date formerly postulated (Hudson 2000).

FARMING COMMUNITIES OF THE NORTHERN HORN DURING THE LAST MILLENNIUM BC

It is against this backdrop that we must view the development in the northern highlands, during the first half of the last millennium BC, of the varied societies that were—until recently (see D. W. Phillipson and Schmidt 2009)—conventionally lumped together under the label 'pre-Aksumite'. The idea (e.g. de Contenson 1981) that these societies could be defined collectively by the presence of cultural traits originating in southern Arabia is no longer tenable. Despite the acknowledged difficulties of establishing chronological precision from radiocarbon determinations at this time-depth, it is now apparent that the prevalence of Arabian elements was far from general and varied greatly in intensity, as explained below.

Recent archaeological investigations in both Eritrea and Ethiopia have revealed settlement sites where elements of Arabian derivation are poorly represented, if not totally absent. This essentially indigenous occupation is best represented at sites attributed to the 'ancient Ona' culture around Asmara (Schmidt et al. 2008) and at Kidane Mehret and Ona Negast near Aksum (D. W. Phillipson et al. 2000: 267–379; D'Andrea 2008). In both, predominantly microlithic stone industries of apparently local 'Late Stone Age' affinity were accompanied by rare items of copper alloy, although iron was apparently absent, at least initially. Both the lithic industries and the pottery show significant regional variation but remain poorly known overall due to the uneven coverage of research and publication. Domestic animals and cultivated crops are well attested; the subsistence economy was evidently based on cattle, sheep and goats, wheat, barley, and—less certainly—t'ef. Although draught cattle were employed, use of camels and donkeys is not yet conclusively demonstrated. Here, as in other areas of the Horn, rock art is widely distributed (Calegari 1999; Tekle 2011) but has so far provided little reliable archaeological information because of the difficulty of establishing its age. Houses were rectangular, of undressed dry-stone construction; ashlar masonry and monumental sculpture were apparently not employed in these domestic structures. On the other hand, many parallels are evident with the contemporary inhabitants of southern Arabia; the early developmental stages of certain elements—notably writing and monumental architecture—are so far attested only in the latter region, where the differentiation of elite sectors may have taken place significantly earlier.

Two sites in Tigray provide exceptionally clear evidence for the erection of temples that share so many features with southern Arabia that they may safely be described as Sabaean in style. That at Yeha, near Adwa, comprises a well-preserved rectangular structure, 18.6 × 15.0 m, built of finely dressed sandstone blocks. Detailed examination (Robin and de Maigret 1998;

Japp et al. 2011) indicates the former presence of a massive portico and the strong resemblance of the original structure to Sabaean temples of the early 7th century BC, notably at Baraqish and Marib. Fragments of finely inscribed stonework found reused in later contexts at Yeha demonstrate its dedication to Almaqah, the Sabaean moon god. This stonework was formerly believed to have formed part of the temple structure, but the recent discovery of a remarkably similar inscription at Mekaber Ga'ewa, some 120 km southeast of Yeha, indicates that it had belonged to a central altar (Fig. 55.2; Wolf and Nowotnick 2010). While broadly analogous in overall plan, the Mekaber Ga'ewa temple lacked the finely dressed masonry of Yeha and its southern Arabian comparanda; in this respect it more closely resembled the contemporaneous indigenous domestic architecture of the northern Ethiopian highlands. Other religious sites, more numerous, more widely distributed, and probably later in date, retain massive porticos but are less dominantly Sabaean in character.

Until recently, interpretation of the archaeological record of northern Ethiopia during the last millennium BC depended heavily on epigraphic evidence (see Bernand et al. 1991–2000). However, this evidence is slight, and several of the conclusions previously based on it are untenable (D. W. Phillipson 2009a). In particular, the extent of Sabaean influence has been greatly exaggerated, and the concept of a single 'pre-Aksumite' state (whether or not called 'D'mt') now appears doubtful. The region's population at this time appears to have been diverse, with some elements—particularly the non-elite—showing much stronger continuity with their local predecessors than formerly believed.

FIG. 55.2 The central altar of the Almaqah Temple at Mekaber Ga'ewa near Wukro, Tigray, Ethiopia. It measures approximately 0.9 m square × 0.7 m high (photograph, David W. Phillipson, reproduced by kind permission of Dr P. Wolf).

By at least the late 8th century BC, monumental stone architecture and inscriptions were thus being produced in the northern Horn, in both cases in styles very close to those used in southern Arabia, although the language of most—but not all—of the inscriptions showed significant local differences. These elements were probably the prerogative of elite sectors, whose distinctiveness and prestige they served to emphasize. At this time or shortly afterwards, small numbers of immigrants from southern Arabia may have arrived in Tigray. Their separate identity as a distinct population element may have been short-lived, raising the possibility that individual specialists, such as masons, rather than family groups were involved.

From this time onwards, cultural elements originating in southern Arabia seem to have been adopted by sections of the indigenous population to a very varying extent. Indeed, long-distance influences may be detected with other regions too, notably the Nile Valley (Edwards, Ch. 54 above). At Yeha, a scattered population seems to have been drawn together by the establishment of an elite centre. Local rulers are indicated, owing no demonstrable allegiance to contemporaries in southern Arabia. Elsewhere, as in the Asmara region, there is little evidence for foreign cultural elements or for the presence of local elites. Stimulating suggestions by Curtis (2002) notwithstanding, the reasons for these developments remain poorly understood.

'Proto-Aksumite' developments in regional perspective

By the 4th century BC, connections with southern Arabia had become weaker, but there is evidence for a number of local elite centres in several regions of both Tigray and Eritrea. Particularly in the west, contacts with the Nile Valley were intensified. One of these elite groups, apparently centred on Beta Giyorgis hill, northwest of Aksum, has been more intensively investigated than the others. Beta Giyorgis at this time was, at least in part, an elite settlement whose inhabitants may have exercised authority over a territory which, although restricted in extent, was rich in natural resources and enjoyed access to trade with other regions, both nearby and far distant (Fattovich and Bard 2001; Michels 2005: xiii, 103–21; Fattovich 2010). Broadly parallel developments probably took place in other regions of the northern Horn, but their archaeology has not yet been investigated in detail. Although much of the research so far undertaken in Tigray emphasizes the elite and their long-distance connections, strong indigenous continuity is also attested and extended through the period of Aksumite civilization, to which discussion now turns.

Aksumite civilisation

The ancient kingdom of Aksum flourished during the first seven centuries AD, but its formative processes may be traced significantly earlier and its cultural influence extended very much later; it is thus not the isolated phenomenon implied by previous studies, but one firmly rooted in the overall development processes of Ethiopian civilization. There is little doubt that the kingdom originated as the direct successor to that previously established on Beta Giyorgis and that, following the transfer of its centre to the adjacent plain, its territorial influence greatly increased (see Fattovich 2010). The scant archaeological evidence for these processes remains poorly understood but, supplemented by a number of inscriptions, probably indicates the incorporation of surrounding polities within the hegemony of that centred successively at Beta Giyorgis and at Aksum. For much of its history, the boundaries of the territory subject at any one time to Aksumite control and/or influence remained ill-defined. At their maximum extent they probably included the Massawa area of the Red Sea coast where Adulis—the Aksumite port—was located, together with the highlands of south/central Eritrea and the greater part of Ethiopia's Tigray region. The extent of such influence further to the north and west remains to be determined, although a 4th-century incursion into the Sudanese Nile Valley seems likely. Aksumite influence in the areas west and south of the Takezze River was probably slight. For part of the 6th century, and perhaps on earlier occasions as well, Aksumite rule was also exercised, directly or indirectly, over parts of southern Arabia.

The Aksumite kingdom established far-reaching international trade links in which the export of ivory played a major part, adopted Christianity in the second quarter of the 4th century, and declined some 300 years later. Our knowledge comes from diverse sources: archaeology, epigraphy, numismatics, references in Greco-Roman written sources, and Ethiopian traditions—some of them committed to writing in later times. Interpretation of all these sources is, however, subject to distinct and particular problems (D. W. Phillipson 2009b: 1–3). Some elements of the Aksumite population were literate in Greek and in the local Semitic language, Ge'ez. There has been a tendency in the past to stress overseas connections and to minimize evidence for local continuity and development. Thus, it is now recognized that, although the Aksumite kingdom brought together many influences of diverse origin, numerous aspects of its basic economy and technology were directly descended from local developments during the last millennium BC. These elements prevailed with remarkably little modification throughout the period when Aksumite civilization arose, flourished, and declined.

As with many ancient societies, much of our knowledge about the Aksumites comes from the burials of the dead, those of the elite having received disproportionate archaeological attention. While such tombs, insofar as they have escaped subsequent robbing, reveal much information about funerary customs and material culture, their evidence should not be taken as indicative of conditions prevailing through Aksumite society as a whole. The most elaborate Aksumite tombs are those dated to the 3rd/4th centuries AD in the so-called Stelae Park at Aksum itself, marked by standing monoliths—stelae—each carved in representation of a multi-storey building and originally bearing one or more metal plaques at the apex (Fig. 55.3). It is reasonable to assume, although definitive proof is lacking, that these tombs were those of kings; in any event, they date to the period immediately preceding the conversion of the Aksumite rulers to Christianity. They indicate enormous concentration of resources: the largest stela weighed 517 tonnes and—had it been successfully erected—would have been 33 m high. Later elite tombs retained some of these architectural features, but the use of stelae was apparently discontinued; the tombs traditionally attributed to the 6th-century kings Kaleb and Gabra Masqal lay beneath funerary chapels of clearly Christian form, and had less room for grave goods than had been the case in earlier times. Although the closest known parallels for the technology employed in the quarries where the large stelae were extracted are from Roman Egypt, the architecture in which they were incorporated shows only very general affinity with that of the latter region. Non-elite burials were, of course, much less elaborate, sometimes consisting of a simple pit in which the deceased was interred with few if any artefacts as grave goods, but marked by a small stela of undressed stone. Such burials were sometimes concentrated in separate areas peripheral to the main conurbations. They probably continued in use throughout the first five centuries AD (D. W. Phillipson 2000: 227–8, 427–31, 476–82).

The architecture of the living also varied in accordance with the wealth and status of its users. Buildings were invariably rectangular and, except for roofs, stone was the preferred material although, particularly initially and for the more prestigious structures, the stone walls incorporated horizontal beams held together by transverse wooden ties with rounded ends called 'monkey-heads'. The largest and most elaborate structures—other than tombs and churches—included square central components, with a two- or three-storey tower at each corner, entered by means of monumental stairs central to one or more sides, and standing in a courtyard surrounded by suites of rooms (Fig. 55.4). Such buildings show considerable variation in overall size and elaboration; few, however, have been excavated with a view

FIG. 55.3 The upper section of Aksum Stela 3, showing carving to represent a multi-storey building and pins for fixture of a metal plaque at the apex. The height of the section shown is approximately 5 m (photograph, David W. Phillipson).

to ascertaining their chronology or the uses to which they and their component parts were put. Until this regrettable situation is rectified, the designation of such structures as 'palaces' or 'châteaux' cannot be justified, and the less specific term 'elite structure' remains preferable. Lower strata of Aksumite society used buildings in which ashlar masonry was rarely, if ever, employed, and in which timber was incorporated more sparingly. Most were rectangular, apparently of one storey; as in earlier times, courtyards were often incorporated. The simplest houses are so far known only from clay models; they were likewise of one storey, rectangular, with flat or ridged roofs, the latter apparently thatched.

Buildings of all these types, except perhaps the simplest, occurred in both urban and rural situations. This observation leads to a consideration of the overall nature of settlement in Aksumite times. Although reference is sometimes made to Aksum itself as a city, the term and its connotations may be inappropriate. Aksum, it appears, was—during the first seven centuries AD—a loose concentration of buildings and burial areas. It was not clearly demarcated and, like other places within the Aksumite hegemony, lacked a surrounding wall or other structural means of defence. The very incomplete information available suggests that there may have been some differential between 'town' and 'country' in the activities that were conducted: food production, for example, being for obvious reasons concentrated in the rural areas, while some craft activities the products of which were an elite prerogative were mainly carried out in more urban areas, but the division was rarely rigid.

The subsistence economy remained based on that which had been locally practised during the previous millennium, but as economic and political contacts widened, elements of more

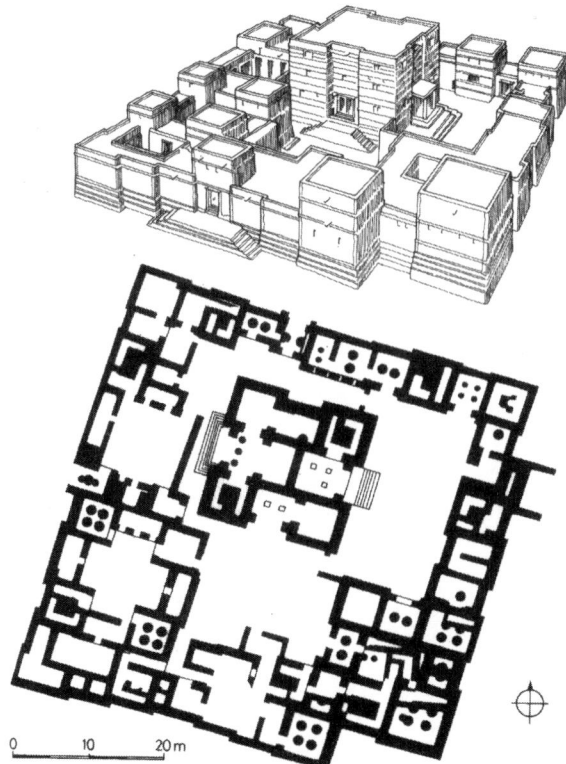

FIG. 55.4 Plan and proposed reconstruction of the Dungur elite structure, Aksum, Ethiopia (after F. Anfray).

distant origin were gradually incorporated. For example, crops such as sorghum and finger mil-let—originally cultivated at lower altitudes—began to be cultivated alongside those exploited in the highlands during earlier times. Cotton is also represented in later archaeological levels at Aksum, although it cannot be determined whether it was grown locally or whether the unproc-essed fibre was imported from elsewhere (Bard et al. 2000; D. W. Phillipson 2000: 468–70).

The material culture and technology of the Aksumite kingdom shared the diversity noted above. Much attention has been paid to high-value items—or their containers—that were imported from the Mediterranean world. Imported commodities included wine in amphorae from areas border-ing the eastern Mediterranean and the northern Red Sea, pottery and glassware from Egypt and North Africa (both also copied by Aksumite craftsmen), and occasional prestige objects such as fine metalwork and engraved gemstones. A 6th-century shipwreck off the Eritrean coast (Pedersen 2008) provides hard evidence for this trade. Overall, it is important neither to exaggerate the scale of Aksumite overseas commerce nor to ignore the elements that are difficult to recognize in the archaeological record. This last point is particularly relevant in connection with Aksumite exports, which apparently consisted primarily of ivory and other raw materials. Most of this long-distance trade was probably conducted by way of the Red Sea and the Aksumite port at Adulis (see Peacock and Blue 2007; Fauvelle-Aymar 2009: 136, 147–9); the associated land journey across the plateau and escarpment must have added considerably to transport costs. Movement of commodities and personnel within the Aksumite realm is demonstrated both by commemorative inscriptions and by distributions of artefacts, notably pottery. This discussion of trade should not, however, obscure the fact that the kingdom was largely self-sufficient and that it developed substantial local expertise in metallurgy, ivory carving, and the manufacture of glass vessels and other items, while retaining other technological traditions—including potting and stone knapping—that derived directly from the practices of local forebears (L. Phillipson 2002, 2009).

The second half of the 3rd century witnessed a rapid increase in material prosperity, concentra-tion of wealth at the political centre, and long-distance trade. Significantly, this was also the time when the issue of Aksumite coinage began. This currency, with denominations in gold, silver, and copper, initially bore inscriptions in Greek—a feature retained for the internationally circulating gold coins until minting was discontinued in the 7th century, although those in silver and copper, which saw mostly local use, were latterly in Ge'ez (Hahn 2000; D. W. Phillipson 2012: 189).

Text-based research on Aksumite history places much emphasis on religion, particularly on the king's adoption of Christianity in the mid-4th century. Previously, a form (or forms) of the polytheistic belief-system of southern Arabia seems to have prevailed in the northern Horn. Neither the recorded details of the conversion of the Aksumite rulers nor the accom-panying controversies need concern us here (see D. W. Phillipson 2009b: 29–32; 2012: 91–105). Two aspects, however, require emphasis. One is that this was a tentative process, probably politically motivated, presented to the king's diverse subjects with skill and selec-tivity. Secondly, it was no isolated phenomenon, but part of a wider 4th-century trend to monotheism that is also attested in southern Arabia (Gajda 2009). A further point to note is that it was at least 100 years, and probably nearer to 150, before the new religion was widely adopted by the populace at large and spread into rural areas distant from the capital. Buildings have been recognized as churches at several Aksumite archaeological sites (e.g. Tekle 2008) and, as discussed in greater detail below, a few churches still in use in Tigray may trace their origins back to Aksumite times. Furthermore, the Ethiopian tradition of manu-script illumination extends back into late Aksumite times (Mercier 2000), and studies of Ethiopian ecclesiastical literature suggest that certain elements have a similar antiquity. Early Muslim historians likewise record the magnificence of the church of Mary at Aksum and the paintings with which it was then adorned. The period between the mid-4th and the early 7th centuries thus seems to have been pivotal in the development of Ethiopian Christianity.

Recognition of this broader picture permits a more meaningful view of events in the early 6th century, when an Aksumite invasion of southern Arabia was led by King Kaleb, apparently with Byzantine connivence and support. Byzantine motives were both economic and political, aimed at securing a trade route to the east that was not subject to Persian control. Elsewhere, notably in Ethiopia, the campaign was presented in religious terms, as avenging a persecuted Christian community and liberating it from domination by non-Christian monotheists recalled—probably misleadingly—as Jews. In neither guise was long-term success achieved. This period saw increased church-building activity in regions under Aksumite rule. In several cases Byzantine influence may be discerned, although local architectural elements predominate. Particularly significant are churches at the Aksumite port of Adulis on the western Red Sea coast; these were fitted with marble sanctuary screens of a type widespread around the central and eastern Mediterranean that were prefabricated in the vicinity of Constantinople; a later section of this chapter will note their specifically Ethiopian significance.

In conclusion, Aksumite civilization may be attributed to a population that erected some of the largest and most elaborate monoliths the world has ever seen, issued a unique coinage in copper, silver, and gold, and practised sophisticated metallurgy, ivory carving, and manuscript illumination. They established their rule over extensive surrounding territory including part of the Arabian peninsula, developed trade links extending from the western Mediterranean in one direction to Sri Lanka in the other, and their Christian rulers were sought as political as well as religious allies by successive Roman and Byzantine emperors. They also maintained the subsistence farming, domestic architecture, and stone-knapping technology of their local forebears.

Contemporary developments in neighbouring regions

It is likely that other regions of the Horn, far beyond those under the direct control of the Aksumite kingdom, were subject to its influence, direct or indirect, long-term or transitory. Although parts of the coastlands of Somalia apparently experienced contact with the Red Sea maritime trade between the Roman Empire and India, notably Ras Hafun, south of Cape Gardafui, and Heis, east of Berbera, there is no evidence that such involvement penetrated inland (Tomber 2008). Elsewhere, it is likely that markedly different conditions prevailed, perhaps sometimes continuing from those of the earlier cultivating and herding peoples, or ancestral to those of the later peoples discussed below. Hard data to replace these suppositions are not yet available.

Decline of Aksum and its effects

Events at Aksum during the late 6th and early 7th centuries had far-reaching implications. Following the Aksumite state's over-extension under Kaleb and his immediate successors, economic strains became apparent. The Aksum area may have suffered environmental deterioration at this time as a result of prolonged population pressure and over-exploitation, although the scale and significance of this has recently been questioned (Sulas et al. 2009). Whatever the ultimate cause of this decline, the coinage was increasingly debased, although the distinction was maintained between Greek-inscribed, internationally circulating gold and Geʿez-inscribed base-metal issues for local use, the latter employing types that emphasized both Christian faith and deteriorating circumstances.

Soon afterwards, major changes took place. Aksum, following the trends described above, ceased to be the capital. Major buildings and monuments were abandoned or put to different, lower-status, uses. For some time, the focus of the state's economy and development had been shifting to the eastern highlands of Tigray. Now, the political centre seems to have followed, although the precise location of the new capital cannot yet be identified. Issue of Aksumite coinage ceased: first the internationally circulating gold, followed by the silver and copper denominations. Significantly, there was a marked reduction in the quantity of elephant ivory reaching the Mediterranean world at this time. These changes may be linked to external events: with growing Arab control of the Red Sea, Christian Ethiopia's principal external trade routes rapidly became inoperable. The state fell back on the exploitation of its own resources, which were now concentrated in the more densely populated eastern part of its territory.

'Medieval' Ethiopia/Eritrea and its Aksumite roots

Subsequent developments, best known in the Tigray eastern highlands, show strong continuity with ancient Aksum. Very little archaeological research has yet been undertaken on sites of this period, and what we know is largely based on the substantial number of ancient churches—both built and rock-hewn—that survive there (Lepage 2006; D. W. Phillipson 2009b). One of the most important is that of Za Mikaʾel Aregawi at the mountain-top monastery of Debra Damo, close to Ethiopia's frontier with Eritrea. Tradition states that it was founded by the Aksumite King Gabra Masqal, son of Kaleb, in the 6th century. Its original plan very strongly resembles those of the churches at Aksum built over the subterranean tombs of Kaleb and Gabra Masqal, noted above. Despite the fact that these Aksum churches were funerary, whereas that at Debra Damo initially was not, it seems highly probable that they are contemporaneous. The traditions that independently link the origins of both buildings with the same 6th-century monarch are thus strengthened. In the Hawzien Plain, some distance to the south of Debra Damo, three low rocky outcrops contain rock-cut churches of a very distinctive type. It seems that they were first created to serve a funerary and/or reliquary purpose, following a tradition traceable back to the 4th–7th centuries; indeed, these monuments, notably those at Degum, may themselves be of late Aksumite origin.

A second, somewhat later group of three much larger and more elaborate rock-hewn churches occurs immediately east of the Hawzien Plain. All have their western parts carved free of the surrounding rock; the eastern parts extend into the rock of the mountain (Fig. 55.5). In each case, one of the easternmost chambers served as a burial place. The decoration on the vaults of these 'Tigray cross-in-square' churches is highly characteristic, and suggests parallels with Coptic designs of late first-millennium Egypt.

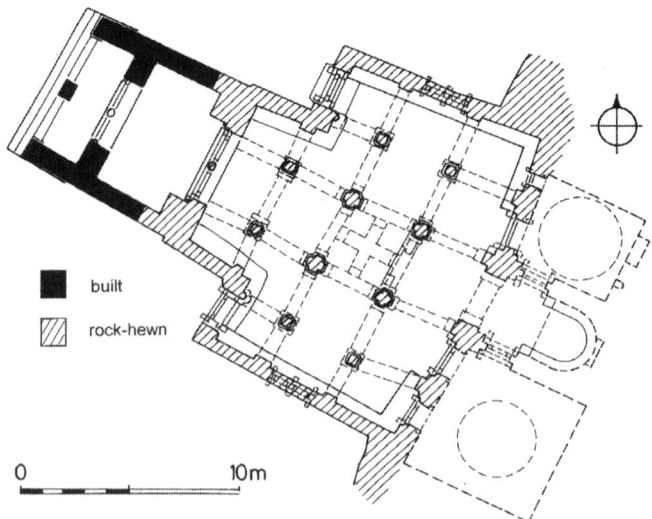

FIG. 55.5 Plan of the 'Tigray cross-in-square' church of Abraha-wa-Atsbaha, Tigray, Ethiopia (after J. Gire).

Several other early churches, both built and rock-hewn, occur in the mountains surrounding the Hawzien Plain. With one possible exception, they seem not to have been funerary. The built ones are exceptionally small and retain architectural features reminiscent of Aksum and Debra Damo. They range greatly in sophistication and richness of decoration, presumably having served communities of varied prosperity. Some retain wooden sanctuary screens that clearly derive from the Byzantine marble ones imported to Adulis several centuries earlier.

Despite their variety, the Tigray rock-hewn churches share several common characteristics. All were excavated from hard sandstone so that, despite their age, they are still in most cases well preserved. Door- and window-frames were not carved, but constructed from timber in the Aksumite style and set into the rock. These particular wooden features are likewise seen in the ancient Tigray built churches, the walls of which are also Aksumite in style, with wooden 'monkey-heads' and horizontal beams.

All the Tigray churches described above appear to be older than the late 10th century. Indeed, between about 1000 and 1100 there seems to have been a virtual hiatus in that region, during which few if any churches were carved or constructed. From the 12th century onwards, the process was resumed, but with major differences: churches were now mostly rock-hewn and set in high—generally mountain-top—locations as befitted their often monastic status. Unlike their predecessors, most were also elaborately decorated with mural paintings.

Further south, in what is now Amhara Region, the earliest churches differ in significant respects from those in Tigray. Both built and rock-hewn examples are known, the latter being carved, not from hard sandstone, but from soft volcanic rock. As a result, it was much easier to show fine detail, but the churches have been more readily susceptible to weathering, wear, and other damage. The picture is dominated by the two tightly interconnecting groups of rock-hewn churches at Lalibela, where a relative chronology is demonstrable on other than purely stylistic grounds. Ecclesiastical tradition unequivocally attributes all the Lalibela churches to the reign of the late 12th/early 13th century king whose name the place now bears. It seems highly probable, however, that the churches' creation spanned a much longer period—a conclusion compatible with the ecclesiastical tradition because it was during Lalibela's reign that the Lalibela church complex as a whole was completed and took the symbolism as a pilgrimage centre that it retains to this day.

Five successive developmental stages can be recognized at Lalibela (D. W. Phillipson 2009b: 123–81; see also Fauvelle-Aymar et al. 2010). The most ancient features did not begin as churches at all, but as defensive features of some sort, protected by massive aboveground stone-built walls, entered by an elaborately protected route and linked by an underground tunnel. Architectural features in the Aksumite style are markedly absent. Although these earliest features may readily be discerned, they have been significantly modified on several subsequent occasions, one of which involved the excavation of extensions—stylistically very different—that now serve as the sanctuaries and presumably mark their conversion to ecclesiastical use. It is only at this third stage that Aksumite-style features may first be recognized.

In the fourth stage, a major and very striking change took place. This is the stage to which belong the great 'monolithic' basilican churches for which Lalibela is justly famous, as well as their built counterparts. Architectural features of Aksumite origin now predominate but, in contrast with the practice in Tigray, door- and window-frames were not wooden inserts but carved integrally from the rock, while horizontal wooden beams—but not 'monkey-heads'— are represented on their walls. To the final stage at Lalibela may be attributed the remarkable sub-complex incorporating the churches where King Lalibela himself is traditionally believed to have been buried. These churches were excavated below features associated with one of the 'monolithic' basilicas and, being so deep in the rock, necessitated major alterations to the drainage system, traces of which may be recognized in many places.

It seems clear that this most recent stage should belong to the period of—or immediately after—King Lalibela's reign in the late 12th and early 13th centuries. It follows that the first four stages must be earlier than this. With the 'monolithic' basilicas attributed to the 11th and possibly early 12th centuries, the non-ecclesiastical defensive features are pushed back well before that, perhaps as far as the 8th century.

The overall picture that emerges from study of the ancient built and rock-hewn churches of Amhara Region indicates that the earliest rock-hewn features there—created at Lalibela in about the 8th century—were not initially churches, being only subsequently converted to that use. There is some evidence, which requires further investigation, for the creation of churches in Amhara Region between 800 and 1000, but their great florescence came in the 11th and early 12th centuries, when the 'monolithic' basilicas at Lalibela were excavated. Rather later, the church complexes at the latter place were extended, including the creation of the burial place for King Lalibela himself, and the site took on the aspect and symbolism that has ensured its eminence as a place of pilgrimage ever since. This picture offers a major contrast with that proposed for eastern Tigray, where churches were being created for hundreds of years before they are attested in Amhara. The architecture of the two regions may only be paralleled in very general ways. In Tigray, Aksumite elements were noticeable throughout, but in Amhara they were initially absent. In the 11th century, there was a marked hiatus in church creation in Tigray, but a major florescence in Amhara Region, with Aksumite features being strongly—even self-consciously—emphasized.

An explanation is thus available for two features emphasized in the above discussion: the 11th-century hiatus in the eastern Tigray sequence of church creation, coinciding with its first major florescence in Amhara Region; and the pronounced emphasis on Aksumite style that marked this period in the latter area. It makes excellent sense if these features are viewed in the context of the transfer of political authority to a more southerly centre, and the strong desire by the new rulers to emphasize their Aksumite antecedents as a prop to their legitimacy. The rulers responsible for this southward expansion of Christian rule are traditionally ascribed to the Zagwe dynasty. The date of the Zagwe ascendancy has often been attributed to the early 12th century, but recent research strongly suggests that it took place significantly earlier (see Tekeste 2006; D. W. Phillipson 2009b: 196–8; Finneran 2009).

The sparse archaeological evidence for early Islam in the Horn

Around the beginning of the 7th century, Aksum apparently received visits by refugees from southern Arabia; these are mainly recorded in Arabic writings of significantly later date, and the details should be interpreted accordingly. Despite this proviso, it is noteworthy that the records praise the reception that Aksum and its ruler accorded these refugees, who included a daughter and two future wives of the Prophet Mohammed. The claim that the Aksumite king in the mid-7th century became a convert to Islam is more problematic, since there is no evidence for this in local non-Muslim tradition or in the Aksumite coinage. The township called Negash is linked in tradition with early Muslim settlement in the eastern highlands of Tigray. It was probably, however, via the Dahlak islands and in the adjacent lowlands that Islam became more firmly established, penetrating the eastern plateau from—perhaps—the 10th century onwards (Insoll 2003: 45–85; Fauvelle-Aymar and Hirsch 2008). In the latter area, ruins of ancient settlements with clear Islamic trading connections have long been recognized, although their detailed archaeological investigation is only now beginning.

The southern and eastern Horn c. AD 1–1500

The regions to the south and east of those discussed above have seen very little archaeological exploration. Christianity was adopted in the Lake Tana region and in some areas further south by the 14th century, churches being of the characteristic circular shape which is now firmly established. Elsewhere, most of the sparse available data relate to funerary monuments in and adjacent to the Rift Valley in southern Ethiopia (Fig. 55.6). There was much local variation, both geographical and chronological, most clearly seen at Tiya and Tuto Fela in the Rift Valley region (Joussaume 2007); no clear patterns or connections with distinct population groups may, however, yet be recognized. These monuments may represent funerary traditions in some way allied to that represented at Aksum, perhaps by parallel descent from a remote common ancestor. Indeed, comparable burials have continued into recent times in parts of Somalia, eastern Ethiopia, and northern Kenya. Otherwise, past events and developments are illustrated mainly through studies of oral history, linguistics, and social anthropology, little attempt having yet been made to link these investigations with the few archaeological discoveries that have been recorded. It is hoped that this will be a major research field in future, casting light on such major events as the Oromo settlement of large areas in southern and central Ethiopia from the late 15th century onwards (Hassen 1990).

Concluding overview

The emphasis given here to developments in the northern highlands of Ethiopia/Eritrea, where archaeological investigation has been concentrated, may give the false impression that these developments were characteristic of the entire region. It is, however, becoming increasingly apparent that the physical and environmental diversity of the Horn has been reflected in its past human settlement well into the second millennium AD. From at least the 17th century BC, and probably long before, the peoples of the northern Ethiopian highlands have received visitors and cultural influences from overseas; these have sometimes proved short-lived, but on other occasions they have been absorbed and become an integral part of local culture and tradition. Innovations have ranged from the commercial and the technological to the literary and the religious, which last saw Christianity and, latterly, Islam adopted from overseas during times when Ethiopia was part of an international community held together by commercial, political, and religious links. Other areas of the Horn were not directly exposed to these influences until more recent times, through processes that still continue.

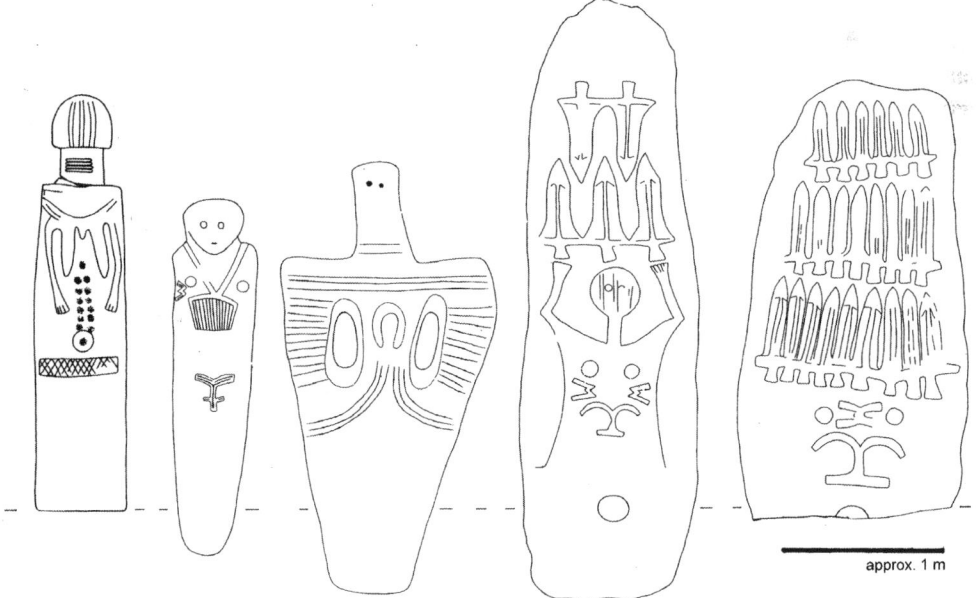

approx. 1 m

FIG. 55.6 Styles of stelae in southern Ethiopia (after F. Anfray).

REFERENCES

BARD, K. A., COLTORTI, M., DIBLASI, M. C., DRAMIS, F., and FATTOVICH, R. (2000). The environmental history of Tigray (northern Ethiopia) in the middle and late Holocene: a preliminary outline. *African Archaeological Review* 17: 65–86.

BERNAND, E., DREWES, A. J., and SCHNEIDER, R. (1991–2000). *Receuil des Inscriptions de l'Éthiopie des Périodes Pré-Axoumite et Axoumite*. Paris: Académie des Inscriptions et Belles Lettres.

CALEGARI, G. (1999). *L'arte Rupestre dell'Eritrea: Repertorio Ragionato ed Esegesi Iconografica*. Milan: Società di Scienze Naturali e Museo Civico di Storia Naturale di Milano.

CURTIS, M. (2002). Ancient interaction across the southern Red Sea: new suggestions for investigating cultural exchange and complex societies during the first millennium BC. In P. Lunde and A. Porter (eds), *Trade and Travel in the Red Sea Region*. Oxford: British Archaeological Reports, 57–70.

D'ANDREA, A. C. (2008). T'ef (*Eragrostis tef*) in ancient agricultural systems of highland Ethiopia. *Economic Botany* 92: 547–66.

DE CONTENSON, H. (1981). Pre-Aksumite culture. In G. Mokhtar (ed.), *General History of Africa*, vol. 2. Paris: UNESCO, 341–61.

FATTOVICH, R. (2010). The development of ancient states in the northern Horn of Africa, c. 3000 BC–AD 1000: an archaeological outline. *Journal of World Prehistory* 23: 145–75.

—— and BARD, K. A. (2001). The Proto-Aksumite period: an overview. *Annales d'Éthiopie* 17: 3–24.

FAUVELLE-AYMAR, F.-X. (2009). Les inscriptions d'Adoulis (Erythrée): fragments d'un royaume d'influence hellénistique et gréco-romaine sur la côte africaine de la Mer Rouge. *Bulletin de l'Institut Français d'Archéologie Orientale* 109: 135–60.

—— BRUXELLES, L., MENSAN, R., BOSC-TIESSE, C., DERAT, M.-L., and FRITSCH, E. (2010). Rock-cut stratigraphy: sequencing the Lalibela churches. *Antiquity* 84: 1135–50.

—— and HIRSCH, B. (2008). Établissements et formations politiques musulmans en Éthiopie et de la corne de l'Afrique au Moyen Âge: vers une reconstruction. *Annales Islamiques* 42: 339–75.

FINNERAN, N. (2007). *The Archaeology of Ethiopia*. London: Routledge.

—— (2009). Settlement archaeology and oral history in Lasta, Ethiopia: some preliminary observations from a landscape study of Lalibela. *Azania: Archaeological Research in Africa* 44: 281–91.

GAJDA, I. (2009). *Le Royaume de Himyar à l'Époque Monothéiste*. Paris: de Boccard.

HAHN, W. (2000). Aksumite numismatics: a critical survey of recent research. *Revue numismatique* 155: 281–311.

HASSEN, M. (1990). *The Oromo of Ethiopia: A History*. Cambridge: Cambridge University Press.

HUDSON, G. (2000). Ethiopian Semitic overview. *Journal of Ethiopian Studies* 33(2): 75–86.

INSOLL, T. (2003). *The Archaeology of Islam in Sub-Saharan Africa*. Cambridge: Cambridge University Press.

JAPP, S., GERLACH, I., HITGEN, H., and SCHNELLE, M. (2011). Yeha and Hawelti: cultural contacts between Saba and D'mt. *Proceedings of the Seminar for Arabian Studies* 41: 145–60.

JOUSSAUME, R. (2007). *Tuto Fela et les Steles du Sud de l'Éthiopie*. Paris: Recherches sur les Civilisations.

LEPAGE, C. (2006). Entre Aksum et Lalibela: les églises du sud-est du Tigray (ix–xii s.) en Éthiopie. *Comptes-Rendus des Séances de l'Académie des Inscriptions et Belles Lettres* 2006: 9–39.

MERCIER, J. (2000). La peinture éthiopienne à l'époque axoumite et au xviii siècle. *Comptes-Rendus des Séances de l'Académie des Inscriptions et Belles Lettres* 2000: 35–71.

MICHELS, J. W. (2005). *Changing Settlement Patterns in the Aksum–Yeha Region of Ethiopia: 700 BC–AD 850.* Oxford: British Archaeological Reports.

PEACOCK, D., and BLUE, L. (eds) (2007). *The Ancient Red Sea Port of Adulis, Eritrea.* Oxford: Oxbow.

PEDERSEN, R. K. (2008). The Byzantine–Aksumite period shipwreck at Black Assarca Island, Eritrea. *Azania* 43: 77–94.

PHILLIPSON, D. W. (2000). *Archaeology at Aksum, Ethiopia, 1993–97.* London: British Institute in Eastern Africa.

—— (2009a). The first millennium BC in the highlands of northern Ethiopia and south-central Eritrea: a reassessment of cultural and political development. *African Archaeological Review* 26: 257–74.

—— (2009b). *Ancient Churches of Ethiopia, Fourth–Fourteenth Centuries.* New Haven, Conn.: Yale University Press.

—— (2009c). Aksumite civilisation, its connections and descendants. *Mitteilungen der Sudanarchäologischen Gesellschaft zu Berlin* 20: 75–91.

—— (2012). *Foundations of an African Civilisation: Aksum and the Northern Horn, 1000 BC–AD 1300.* Woodbridge: James Currey.

—— and SCHMIDT, P. R. (eds) (2009). Re-evaluating the archaeology of the first millennium BC in the northern Horn. *African Archaeological Review* 26: 254–350.

PHILLIPSON, L. (2002). New evidence for the autochthonous foundations of Aksumite material culture. In Baye Yimam, R. Pankhurst, D. Chapple, Yonas Admassu, A. Pankhurst, and Birhanu Teferra (eds), *Ethiopian Studies at the End of the Second Millennium.* Addis Ababa: Institute of Ethiopian Studies, Addis Ababa University, 42–57.

—— (2009). Lithic artefacts as a source of cultural, social and economic information: the evidence from Aksum, Ethiopia. *African Archaeological Review* 26: 45–58.

ROBIN, C., and DE MAIGRET, A. (1998). Le grand temple de Yeha (Tigray, Ethiopie) après la première campagne de fouilles de la mission française (1998). *Comptes-Rendus des Séances de l'Académie des Inscriptions et Belles Lettres* 1998: 737–98.

SCHMIDT, P. R., CURTIS, M. C., and ZELALEM TEKA (eds) (2008). *The Archaeology of Ancient Eritrea.* Trenton, NJ: Red Sea Press.

SULAS, F., MADELLA, M. and FRENCH, C. (2009). State formation and water resources management in the Horn of Africa. *World Archaeology* 41: 2–15.

TEKLE HAGOS (2008). *Archaeological Rescue Excavations at Aksum, 2005–2007.* Addis Ababa: Ethiopian Cultural Heritage Project.

—— (2011). *The Ethiopian Rock Arts: The Fragile Resources.* Addis Abba: Authority for Research and Conservation of Cultural Heritage.

TEKESTE NEGASH (2006). The Zagwe period and the zenith of urban culture in Ethiopia, ca. 930–1270 AD. *Africa* (Rome) 61: 120–37.

TOMBER, R. (2008). *Indo-Roman Trade.* London: Duckworth.

WOLF, P., and NOWOTNICK, U. (2010). The Almaqah temple of Mekaber Ga'ewa near Wuqro (Tigray/Ethiopia). *Proceedings of the Seminar for Arabian Studies* 40: 367–80.

CHAPTER 56

STATES, TRADE, AND ETHNICITIES IN THE MAGHREB

SAID ENNAHID

INTRODUCTION: THE EARLY ISLAMIC PERIOD

THE *Maghreb* is the name the first Arab settlers gave to the newly conquered territories while on the move westward of the seat of the Muslim Caliphate in Damascus in the late 7th century AD. The term 'Maghreb' is used here to refer to the geographic areas covered today by modern North African countries of Morocco (medieval *Maghreb Aqsa*[1] or Farther Maghreb), Algeria (medieval *Maghreb Awsat* or Central Maghreb), and Tunisia (medieval *Ifriqiya*). Abun-Nasr's use of the term Maghreb includes also Libya (Abun-Nasr, 1987: 1). The *futuh* (literally, 'opening', Arabic for 'conquest') of the Maghreb marked a turning point in the history of the region for many centuries to come. In his *Ahsan al-Taqasim fi Ma'rifat al-Aqalim* (The Best Divisions for Knowledge of the Regions), written in 985, the medieval Arab geographer al-Muqaddasi made the first recorded distinction between the terms *Maghreb* (Land of the Setting Sun) and *Gharb* (Muslim territories west of Baghdad, the seat of the empire at the time). The former was used to describe today's Morocco, Algeria, Tunisia, Libya, southern Spain (*al-Andalus* or Muslim Spain), and Sicily, while the latter referred to a broader region including, in addition to the province of the *Maghreb*, the two provinces of Egypt and *al-Sham* (Syria) (al-Muqaddasi 1994: 7, see also Ennahid 2002: 7–8, 33–36). Al-Muqaddasi's description of the Maghreb was accompanied by a map (al-Muqaddasi 1994:199) but it is not as detailed as the one provided by Ibn Hawqal in his *Kitab surat al-ard* (The Picture of the Earth) completed in 988 (Fig. 56.1). Cornu has built a detailed toponymic inventory for the Maghreb in the 9th–10th centuries (Cornu 1985: 109–20, map XII).

[1.] The transliteration system of Arabic words used in the text has been adapted from the *Encyclopedia of Islam*, with the exception of the Arabic letter ق (pronounced 'qaf'), transliterated using the letter *q*.

The *futuh* of the Maghreb brought about slow but long-lasting transformations of the political, economic, sociocultural, and demographic structures of North African societies. The political history of the region in the Islamic period is fairly well covered by several seminal texts (Laroui 1977; Abun-Nasr 1987; El Fasi 1988; Marçais 1991; Julien 1994). At first, the Arab conquest took the form of raids against important Byzantine settlements; in 647 a first military expedition was launched against Ifriqiya (modern day Tunisia) on the eastern border of the Maghreb. Several others followed, and the *futuh* of the Maghreb ended in 710. The Arab conquest proved a long and costly enterprise for the Caliphate in Damascus (see map in Kennedy 2002: 53a). The *futuh* encountered two main resistance movements, the first led by a local Berber chief named Kusalya and the second by a Berber local chieftainess named al-Kahina (Arabic for 'the sorceress' or 'the priestess'). Kusalya's movement, made of a coalition of Berber and Byzantine forces, put a serious halt to the advance of Arab troops in the Maghreb led by Uqba Ibn Nafi, who was killed in an ambush in Tahudha in 683. To put an end to Berber resistance, the caliphate in Damascus appointed a new Arab general, Hassan Ibn al-Nu'man, and provided him with the necessary resources. Hassan Ibn al-Nu'man's biggest challenge was to crush a new Berber tribal coalition led by al-Kahina after the death of Kusalya. The *futuh* of the Maghreb took a new turn with the defeat of al-Kahina's coalition in

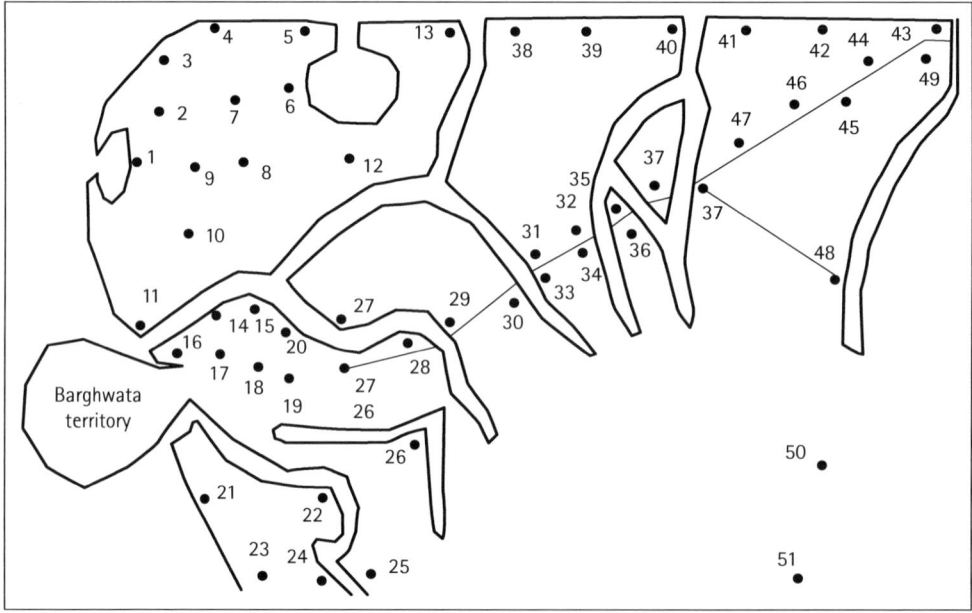

FIG. 56.1 Digitized version of the map of the Maghreb by Ibn Hawqal (AD 988). Source: Ennahid (2002). *Key*: 1 Rîgha Lake; 2 Tâwârt; 3 Djarmâna; 4 Azîla; 5 Tandja; 6 Zallûl; 7 al-Hadjar; 8 al-Basra; 9 al-Aklâm; 10 Kurt; 11 Barbât (Ribât); 12 Marsa Mûsa; 13 Sabta; 14 Malîla; 15 Hadjna; 16 Madâla (Salâ); 17 Banî Sadâl; 18 al-Habash; 19 Banî Radjîk; 20 Dakhla; 21 Ribât Mâsa; 22 Aghmât; 23 Tamaddâlt; 24 al-Sûs; 25 Awdaghust; 26 Sidjilmâsa; 27 Fâs; 28 Namâlta; 29 Karanta; 30 Karmâta; 31 Mazâwurwâ; 32 Sâ'; 33 Tâbrîda; 34 Djarâwa; 35 Tarfâna; 36 Tinimsân; 37 Afkân; 38 Nakûr; 39 Malîla; 40 Ardjakûk; 41 Wâslan; 42 Wahrân; 43 Tanas; 44 Tadjanna; 45 Ghazza; 46 Shalaf; 47 Yalal; 48 Tâhart; 49 Al-Khadrâ'; 50 Sâma; 51 Ghâna.

700; defeated Berber troops merged into Arab ranks to form a new military power to push the now Muslim conquest westward towards the rest of the Maghreb and, soon afterwards, into the Iberian peninsula and southern France. It was a Berber commander and a Berber contingent who, in 711, brought the *futuh* to southern Spain.

Qayrawan: metropolis of the Maghreb

To consolidate their rule over the newly conquered territories, the Arabs declared the Maghreb a new province (*wilaya* of Ifriqiya), depending directly to the caliph in Damascus (i.e. independent of the governor of Fustat, Egypt) by 740–41. The garrison town of Qayrawan, founded in 670 by Uqba Ibn Nafi, became the metropolis (*misr*) of the province of the Maghreb and the seat of *dar al-imara* (governorate headquarters) (see Djaït 1967, 1968 and 2004; Talbi 2010). The governor (*wali*) represented the caliph in all his prerogatives as Commander of the Faithful (*amir al-mu'minin*), i.e. in all matters of religion and conduct within the province. The provincial government was made of a number of *diwans* (registers or offices). At the head of each *diwan* there was an *amil* or provincial officer; the most important *diwans* include *diwan al-jund* (in charge of the military), *diwan al-kharaj* (in charge of tax collection), *bayt al-mal* (the treasury), *dar al-darb* (the mint), *diwan al-rasa'il* (in charge of state correspondence), and *diwan al-barid* (in charge of the post and intelligence services). At first, the provincial government relied on pre-existing Byzantine institutions, personnel, and language (Latin); the process of Arabization of the central administration in the *wilaya* of Ifriqiya was completed between 718–19 and 747–8 (Djaït 2004:142).

During the early Islamic period, Ifriqiyan society was made up essentially of the native Berbers (the majority) and the new and powerful Arab aristocracy (an urban minority with its own sub-hierarchies), in addition to Byzantine elements (*al-rum*), Romanized-Christianized Berbers (*al-afariq*), and Jews. All these diverse population groups moved within a carefully defined set of religious solidarities, material common interests, political power relations, and ethnic affinities. Islam and the Arabic language came to play an important role in the bringing together of these groups (see Brett 1978: 544–55 for details on Islamization and Arabization in the Maghreb).

In addition to its political role within the *wilaya* of Ifriqiya, Qayrawan grew to become an important regional hub of long-distance trade (al-Janhani 2005: 91–116). By the 3rd/9th and 4th/10th centuries a local exchange network had formed between Qayrawan and the nearby cities of al-Abbasiyya, Raqqada, and Sabra (al-Janhani 2005: 93). In the early Islamic period, slave trading was a highly profitable and specialized enterprise at Qayrawan; it had its own markets. Berber slave girls (*jariyya*) were particularly prized, highly priced, and often sent to markets in Syria and Iraq along the coastal route via Tripoli and Fustat. At first, the main source of this trade was through the capture (*saby*) of female prisoners during Arab raids against Berber and Byzantine territories. With the end of the *futuh* period and the conversion to Islam of Berber populations, new sources of slave labour had to be found farther south across the desert, in sub-Saharan Africa. The development of a slave trade with sub-Saharan Africa brought a new element to the already diverse ethnic make-up of Maghrebi society (Brett 1978: 528–9, 550; Haour 2011).

SIJILMASA: GATEWAY TO SUB-SAHARAN AFRICA'S GOLD

The birth of medieval Sijilmasa on the southeastern fringes of Moroccan desert (near modern town of Risani) marked an important moment in the interaction between Maghrebi and sub-Saharan African societies, economies, and cultures. For nearly 650 years, from the founding of the city by Kharijite Berbers in 757–8 until its abandonment in 1393, Sijilmasa was a vibrant meeting place for traders, scholars, and pilgrims from Morocco (Fez, the Sus, and Aghmat), al-Andalus, southern Mauritania (Awdaghust), Ifriqiya, and Iraq (Basra, Kufa, and Baghdad) (Lightfoot and Miller 1996; Messier 1995, 1997, 2001; Miller 2001, 2010; Love 2010; Messier and Fili 2011).

Using a multidisciplinary approach, the joint Moroccan–American Sijilmasa project (1988–98) has achieved important results in understanding the extent and layout of the city and its hinterland, uncovering several structures at the site, and understanding the role of the city as a major hub for the exchange of goods, services, and ideas (Fig. 56.2). The project methodology was based on combining several lines of evidence: textual, oral, remote sensing (aerial photography, Landsat satellite imagery), field reconnaissance, and archaeological fieldwork (Lightfoot and Miller 1996: 86–8). Archaeological evidence from over 60 trenches show that major transformations occurred at the city and its hinterland after it was conquered by the Almoravids in 1055–56 (Messier 2001). These transformations consisted mainly of more efficient management of the city's water resources by harnessing the Wadi Ziz, one of the two main perennial streams in the oasis; the building of a wall, complete with a tower complex, along the course of the wadi; and the building (or reuse) of the city's Great Mosque (*Jami*), the largest standing structure at the site, which remained in service until the early 1900s (Miller 2010).

In the case of Sijilmasa, textual evidence corroborates the archaeological record and provides us with valuable insight on the city's population and economy. The following excerpts from the *Kitab surat al-ard* (The Picture of the Earth), completed in 988 by Ibn Hawqal and the *Kitab al-istibsar* written in the 12th century AD by an anonymous Moroccan chronicler (Anonymous 1985), are particularly revealing. Ibn Hawqal's description shows clearly the economic prominence of Sijilmasa and its people as he witnessed first hand while on a visit to the city in 951:

> I saw at Awdaghust a warrant in which was the statement of a debt owed to one of them [the people of Sijilmasa] by one of the merchants of Awdaghust, who was [himself] one of the people of Sijilmasa, in the sum of 42,000 dinars. (Levtzion and Hopkins 2000:47)

The author of the *Kitab al-istibsar* points to a form of craft specialization based on religious affiliation among the people of the city:

> They (*the inhabitants of Sijilmasa*) call the scavengers 'wrongdoers' (*mujrimun*) and their masons are Jews, whom they restrict to this trade alone (…). The reason why the people of Sijilmasa forced the Jews to practise these two base occupations (*masonry and gutter cleaning and maintenance*) is that the Jews [in former times] liked to inhabit their country to amass wealth because they knew that gold there is

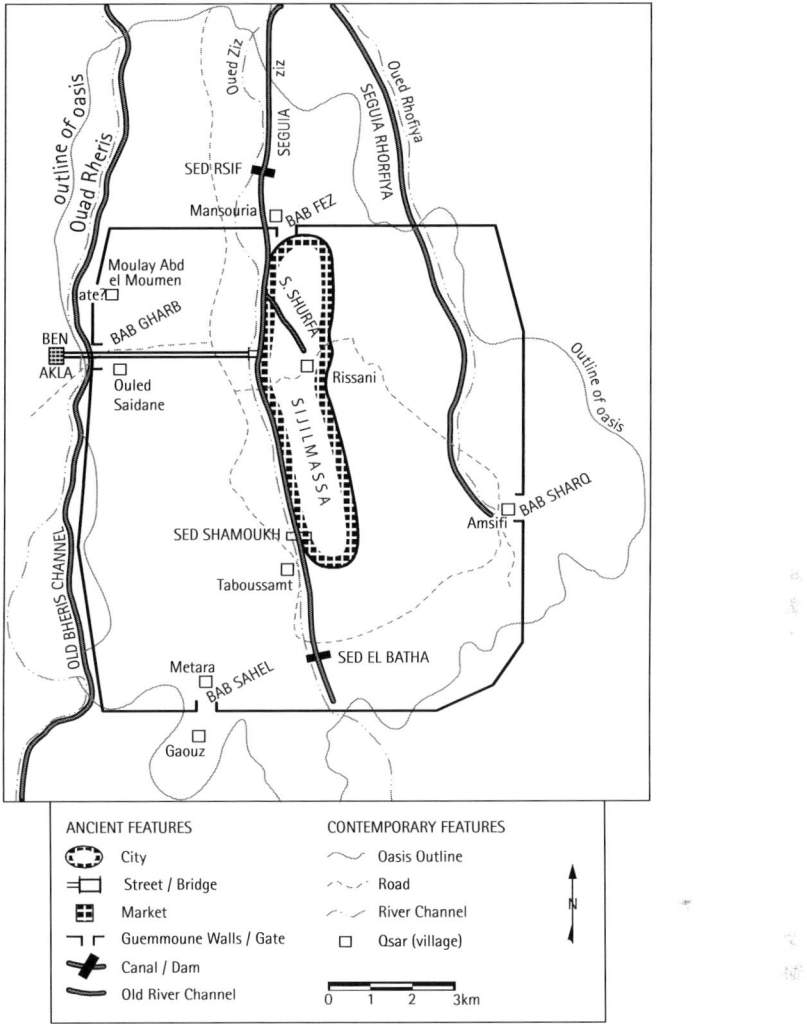

FIG. 56.2 Map of the Sijilmasa landscape, Morocco (copyright Lightfoot and Miller 1996: fig. 7; reproduced with kind permission from the publishers and authors).

more readily available (*amkan*) than it is in other regions of the Maghreb since Sijilmasa is a gateway to its mines [...]. Whomever from other categories of people entered the ranks of the scavengers they called 'wrongdoers' because they did wrong to an occupation reserved for the Jews. They restricted building specially to them for they were perpetually afraid that one of them might kill a Muslim treacherously. (Levtzion and Hopkins 2000: 140; emphasis added)

While there is supporting evidence of the Jews specializing in construction in other Moroccan cities (Zafrani 2000:154), there is no reference to gutter cleaning and maintenance as being an exclusively Jewish occupation. Le Tourneau, in his seminal work on Fez, has made no reference to *qawadsiya*, gutter cleaners (from *qadus*, Moroccan for drain or gutter), as being drawn exclusively from the Jewish community in the city; they were mostly expatriates from the Rif mountains and the Moroccan Saharan desert (Le Tourneau 1987: 238).

Political economy of the Maghreb

Research on political economy of the Maghreb has benefited a great deal from a theoretical model formulated by Boone et al. (1990) that studied state formation and urban growth in the four major dynastic states in medieval Morocco: the Idrisids (789–974), the Almoravids (1073–1147), the Almohads (1130–1276), and the Marinids (1258–1420). Boone et al.'s model was based on previous work by Boone and Redman (1982) (see also Boone and Benco 1999: 53–5).

The model points to a shift from a predominantly agrarian-based economy (i.e. control of surplus generated through food production) under the Idrisids to one based on the expropriation of proceeds from the sub-Saharan gold trade (i.e. control of exchange networks) during subsequent dynastic periods. Anthropological literature refers to these two finance systems as 'staple finance' and 'wealth finance', respectively, based on the works of D'Altroy and Earle (1985) and Earle (1994) on the political economy of the Inka Empire in Andean South America. More importantly, the model links each finance system to a particular pattern of urban growth. One pattern that was multi-tiered and hierarchical, under the Idrisids, comprised a large dynastic state capital, Fez, and a series of second-ranking provincial capitals (e.g. al-Basra, Morocco). To facilitate and service long-distance trade between the Maghreb and sub-Saharan West Africa, Boone et al. (1990: 631–2) predicted a pattern of urban growth marked by the rise of large inland dynastic capitals in which Fez and Marrakech became the most dominant nodes. Data by Godinho (1947: 134–5) demonstrates that both capitals show population sizes substantially larger (over 100,000 inhabitants) than those of second-ranking urban centres in Morocco. A detailed discussion of this model is provided elsewhere (Ennahid 2002: 2–3, 23–7), along with an in-depth analysis of the finance institutions and fiscal resources (in terms of collection, storage, and disbursement) of all four important Maghrebi dynasties: the Idrisids, the Almoravids, the Almohads, and the Marinids. Notably, of sixteen post-Idrisid dynastic mints, those of Fez and Marrakech with Sijilmasa and Aghmat between them contributed nearly 70 per cent of the total gold currency issued in Morocco (Ennahid 2002: 46–7; for numismatic data on the rest of the Maghreb and al-Andalus, see Hazard 1952: 328–44).

The Idrisid agrarian-based economy

Upon the death of Idris II in 829, the territories of the Idrisid state were divided among his eldest sons. Each principality corresponded to a major agricultural or mining region of Morocco. The city of al-Basra was the provincial capital of an important Idrisid principality in northern Morocco (For the Idrisids, see Eustache 1986; for al-Basra, see Eustache 1955; Benco 1987, 2004, 2011). Textual evidence points to al-Basra as the capital of a rich agricultural province (al-Bakri 1965: 216–17). The archaeological site of al-Basra has revealed substantial architectural remains including a cistern, a number of well-preserved house complexes, and a water canalization system. Recent chemical characterization of ceramics by instrumental neutron activation analysis (INAA) (Ennahid 2002: 51–68; Benco et al. 2009) has provided fresh insights into the patterns of local exchange and community interaction between al-Basra and its hinterland. The analysis of faunal remains shows the dominance of sheep, goats, and cattle (Loyet 2004). Studies of al-Basra's ethnobotanical remains point to the dominance of domesticated wheat (primarily *Triticum aestivum* or *Tricum durum*) and barley (Mahoney 2004). Evidence for cotton production, although well-documented textually (Ibn Hawqal 1967: 80), has not yet been found in the archaeological record. It is clear however that al-Basra played a key role in generating agricultural surplus for the Idrisid staple finance system, especially with dairy products and cereals.

Sub-Saharan gold trade: the basis of post-Idrisid dynastic political economy

Prior to the Almoravid period, the Saharan nomads offered *khafara* services (protection and escort) to Maghrebi caravans crossing the desert. They had no knowledge of agriculture and subsisted solely on the meat and dairy products of their herds (Ibn Hawqal 1967: 101–2). In 1054–5, a coalition of these Saharan nomads, the Almoravids, emerged as a regional power that was able to control the two end links of gold traffic between Awdaghust and Sijilmasa (for more details on the Almoravid empire, see Devisse and Hrbek 1988; Levtzion 1978; Messier 1974 and 2001). The Almoravids, however, did not control the sources of African gold (Fig. 56.3). With the Almohads, the Maghreb served as an intermediary zone between sub-Saharan Africa and Europe; several Maghrebi coastal entrepôts (e.g. Tunis and Sabta) were visited by increasing numbers of merchants from Italy, France, and Spain. In 1274, the Marinids conquered Sijilmasa to secure the flow of gold towards their dynastic capital, Fez (Devisse 1972b; Ennahid 2002: 27–31).

Archaeological evidence shows an active exchange network between the Maghreb and sub-Saharan Africa; 'northern luxuries' include manuscripts (Krätli and Lydon 2011), metalwork, copper jewellery, brass, coral beads, glassware, and glass beads (Mitchell 2005: 152–8; for Essouk-Tadmakka in Mali, see Nixon 2009: 246–52). Maghrebi glazed ware has been documented at several sub-Saharan African sites (e.g. Azelik-Takadda in Niger and Tegdaoust, medieval Awdaghust in Mauritania) (Cressier and Picon 1995; Devisse and Picon 1995; El Hraiki et al. 1986, 1995; Louhichi and Picon 1983). Ceramic analysis (using chemical and mineralogical methods) of glazed ware found in sub-Saharan Africa has shed more light on medieval north–south long-distance exchange networks. These analyses indicate that more than half (55 per cent) of the glazed ware found at Tegdaoust was produced in Sijilmasa (Cressier and Picon 1995: 392; Devisse and Picon 1995: 236; El Hraiki et al. 1995: 119). The Azelik-Takadda glazed ware shows chemical compositional similarities with glazed ware produced in medieval Egyptian and Tunisian workshops (Cressier and Picon 1995: 392–3). The glazed ware found in sub-Saharan Africa may have been destined for Maghrebi expatriates rather than for sub-Saharan African markets (Cressier and Picon 1995: 391). Most of the glazed potsherds found at Tegdaoust are associated with a non-local occupation at the site (Devisse 1972a: 52; Devisse

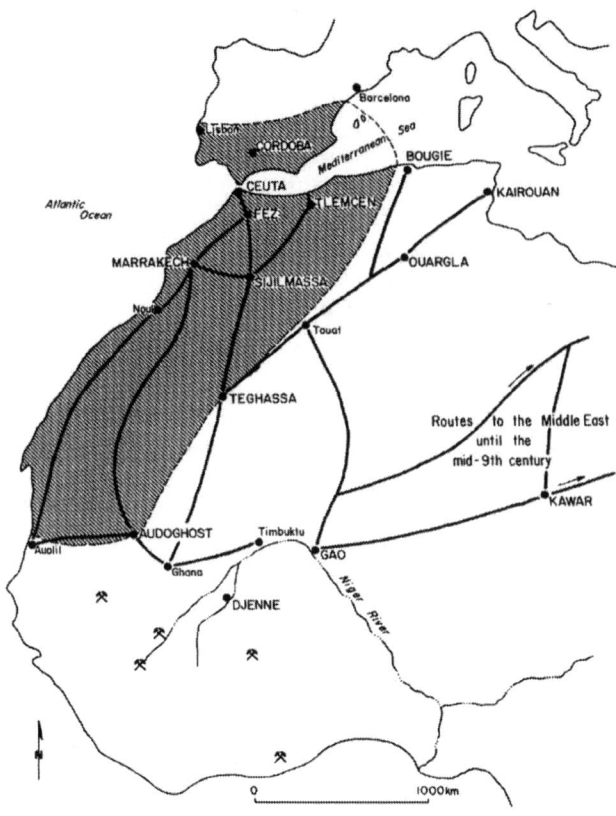

FIG. 56.3 Map of northwest Africa during the Almoravid period. Dark lines indicate gold trade networks. Mining symbols indicate West African gold sources (copyright: Boone et al. 1990: fig. 2, reproduced with kind permission from the publishers and authors).

and Picon 1995: 235–6). Along the same lines, a nearly intact plate with decoration using Qur'anic epigraphy was discovered in Sijilmasa during the 1992 field season and traced to early 11th-century Qal'at of Banu Hammad in eastern Algeria (Lightfoot and Miller 1996: 88). Earlier excavations at the site (in 1988) have uncovered two pottery specimen suspected to be from the Middle Niger, possibly from Jenné-Jeno or Gao (Miller 2001: 49). Chemical, morphological, and technological analyses of glass beads found at al-Basra (Morocco) have revealed interesting similarities to glass and bead production in factories in the Middle East, al-Andalus, and North and sub-Saharan Africa (Robertshaw et al. 2010: 375–376).

CONCLUSION

The results discussed above suggest that one promising direction for future research in North African archaeology is to expand the application of Boone et al.'s (1990) model to the entire region of North Africa. Building on the archaeological, documentary, and numismatic evidence at hand for the Maghreb, archaeologists will be able to test the model on a more regional scale. The objective would be to establish whether the model's main premises concerning state formation and urban growth in the Islamic states of medieval Morocco are applicable to the rest of medieval North Africa. The outcomes of such research would make a welcome contribution by North African archaeology to broader anthropological debates on state formation and urban growth in complex societies.

REFERENCES

ABUN-NASR, J. M. (1987). *A History of the Maghrib in the Islamic Period.* Cambridge: Cambridge University Press.

Anonymous (1985). *Kitab al-Istibsar fi 'aja'ib al-amsar.* Arabic text annotated by Saad Zaghloul Abdel-Hamid. Casablanca: Les Éditions Maghrébines.

AL-BAKRI (1965). *Description de l'Afrique Septentrionale.* Translated by M. De Slane. Paris: Adrien-Maisonneuve.

AL-JANHANI, A.-H. (2005). *al-Mujtama' al-'arabi al-Islami: al-hayat al-iqtisadiyya wal ijtima'iyya.* al-Safat: al-Majlis al-watani li al-thaqafa wal funun wal adab.

AL-MUQADDASI (1994). *The Best Divisions for Knowledge of the Regions: A Translation of Ahsan al-Taqasim fi Marifat al-Aqalim.* Translated by B. A. Collins. Reading: Garnet.

BENCO, N. (1987). *The Early Medieval Pottery Industry at al-Basra, Morocco.* Oxford: Archaeopress.

—— (ed.) (2004). *Anatomy of a Medieval Islamic Town: Al-Basra, Morocco.* Oxford: Archaeopress.

—— (2011). Pottery production at al-Basra, Morocco. In P. Cressier and E. Fentress (eds), *La Céramique Maghrébine du Haut Moyen Âge (VIIIe–Xe siècle): État des Recherches, Problèmes et Perspectives.* Rome: École Française de Rome, 49–62.

—— ENNAHID, S., BLACKMAN, M. J., GLASCOCK, M. D., NEFF, H., and SPEAKMAN, R. J. (2009). Chemical analyses of pottery and clays from the Islamic city of al-Basra and its hinterland in northern Morocco. In J. Z. Stabel-Hansen, M. R. Velasco, M. A. H. Herrera, and A. De Juan Garcia (eds), *Actas del VIII Congreso Internacional de Cerámica Medieval en el Mediterráneo.* Ciudad Real: Asociación Española de Arqueología Medieval, 673–84.

BOONE, J. L., and BENCO, N. (1999). Islamic settlement in North Africa and the Iberian Peninsula. *Annual Review of Anthropology* 28: 51–71.

—— MYERS, E., and REDMAN, C. L. (1990). Archaeological and historical approaches to complex societies: the Islamic states of medieval Morocco. *American Anthropologist* 92: 630–46.

—— and REDMAN, C. L. (1982). Alternate pathways to urbanism in the medieval Maghreb. *Comparative Urban Research* 9: 28–38.

BRETT, M. (1978). The Arab Conquest and the rise of Islam in North Africa. In J. D. Fage (ed.), *The Cambridge History of Africa,* vol. 2. Cambridge: Cambridge University Press, 490–555.

CORNU, G. (1985). *Atlas du Monde Arabo-Islamique à l'Époque Classique IX–Xe Siècles: Répertoires des Toponymes.* Leiden: E. J. Brill.

CRESSIER, P., and PICON, M. (1995). Céramique médiévale d'importation à Azelik-Takadda (République du Niger). In R. El Hraiki and E. Erbati (eds), *Actes du 5ème Colloque International: La Céramique Médiévale en Méditerranée Occidentale.* Rabat: Institut National des Sciences de l'Archéologie et du Patrimoine, 390–99.

D'ALTROY, T. N., and EARLE, T. K. (1985). Staple finance, wealth finance, and storage in the Inka political economy. *Current Anthropology* 26:187–206.

DEVISSE, J. (1972a). Routes de commerce et échanges en Afrique occidentale en relation avec la Méditerranée: un essai sur le commerce africain médiéval du XIe au XVIe siècle, part 1. *Revue d'Histoire Économique et Sociale* 50: 42–73.

—— (1972b). Routes de commerce et échanges en Afrique occidentale en relation avec la Méditerranée: un essai sur le commerce africain médiéval du XIe au XVIe siècle, part 2. *Revue d'Histoire Économique et Sociale* 50: 357–97.

—— and HRBEK, I. (1988). The Almoravids. In M. El Fassi (ed.), *UNESCO General History of Africa: Africa from the Seventh to the Eleventh Century*. Berkeley: University of California Press, 336–66.

—— and PICON, M. (1995). Questions de pots: à propos des céramiques de Tegdaoust (Maurétanie). In R. El Hraiki and E. Erbati (eds), *Actes du 5ème Colloque International: La Céramique Médiévale en Méditerranée Occidentale*. Rabat: Institut National des Sciences de l'Archéologie et du Patrimoine, 235–40.

DJAÏT, H. (1967). La Wilaya d'Ifriqiya au II–VIIIe siècle: étude institutionnelle. *Studia Islamica* 27: 77–121.

—— (1968). La Wilaya d'Ifriqiya au II–VIIIe siècle: étude institutionnelle. *Studia Islamica* 28: 79–107

—— (2004). *Ta'sis al-gharb al-islami: al-qarn al-'awwal wal thani lil hijra—al-sabi' wal thamin lil milad*. Beirut: Dar al-tali'a.

EARLE, T. K. (1994). Wealth finance in the Inka Empire: evidence from the Calchaqui Valley, Argentina. *American Antiquity* 59: 443–60.

EL FASI, M. (ed.) (1988). *UNESCO General History of Africa: Africa from the Seventh to the Eleventh Century*. Berkeley: University of California Press.

EL-HRAIKI, R., ROBERT, D., and PICON, M. (1986). Ateliers producteurs et commerce trans-saharien à l'époque médiévale. *In La Ceramica Medievale nel Mediterraneo Occidentale*. Florence: all'Insegna del Giglio, 51–4.

—— SCHMITT, A. and PICON, M. (1995). Trans-Saharan commerce in the medieval and post-medieval eras: results from the laboratory study of ceramics. *Occasional Papers of the British Museum* 109: 117–22.

ENNAHID, S. (2002). *Political Economy and Settlement Systems of Medieval Northern Morocco: An Archaeological-Historical Approach*. Oxford: Archaeopress.

EUSTACHE, D. (1955). El-Basra, capitale idrissite et son port. *Hésperis* (Rabat) 42: 218–38.

—— (1986). Idrisids. *In* B. Lewis, V. L. Ménage, C. Pellat, and J. Schacht (eds), *Encyclopaedia of Islam*, vol. 2, new edn. Leiden: E. J. Brill, 1035–7.

GODINHO, V. M. (1947). *História Económica e Social da Expansão Portuguesa*. Lisbon: Terra Editora.

HAOUR, A. (2011). The early medieval slave trade of the central Sahel: archaeological and historical considerations. In P. J. Lane and K. C. Macdonald (eds), *Slavery in Africa: Archaeology and Memory*. Oxford: Oxford University Press, 61–78.

HAZARD, H. W. (1952). *The Numismatic History of Late Medieval North Africa*. New York: American Numismatic Society.

IBN HAWQAL (1967). *Kitab surat al-ard (Opus Geographicum)*. Ed. J. H. Kramers. Leiden: E. J. Brill.

JULIEN, C.-A. (1994). *Histoire de l'Afrique du Nord: des Origines à 1830*. Paris: Payot & Rivages.

KENNEDY, H. (ed.) (2002). *An Historical Atlas of Islam*. Leiden: E. J. Brill.

KRÄTLI, G., and LYDON, G. (2011). *The Trans-Saharan Book Trade: Manuscript Culture, Arabic Literacy and Intellectual History in Muslim Africa*. Leiden: E. J. Brill.

LAROUI, A. (1977). *The History of the Maghrib: An Interpretive Essay*. Princeton, NJ: Princeton University Press.

LE TOURNEAU, R. (1987). *Fès avant le Protectorat: Étude Économique et Sociale d'une Ville de l'Occident Musulman*. Rabat: Éditions La Porte.

LEVTZION, N. (1978). The Sahara and Sudan from the Arab conquest of the Maghrib to the rise of the Almoravids. In J. D. Fage (ed.), *The Cambridge History of Africa*, vol. 2. Cambridge: Cambridge University Press, 637–80.

—— and HOPKINS, J. F. P. (eds) (2000). *Corpus of Early Arabic Sources for West African History*. Princeton, NJ: Markus Wiener.

LIGHTFOOT, D., and MILLER, J. (1996). Sijilmassa: the rise and fall of a walled oasis in medieval Morocco. *Annals of the Association of American Geographers* 86:78–101.

LOUHICHI, A., and PICON, M. (1983). Importation de matériel ifriqiyen en Mauritanie. *Revue d'archéometrie* 7:45–58.

LOVE, P. M. (2010). The Sufris of Sijilmasa: toward a history of the Midrarids. *Journal of North African Studies* 15:173–88.

LOYET, M. (2004), Food, fuel, and raw material: faunal remains from al-Basra. In Benco (2004: 21–9).

MAHONEY, N. (2004), Agriculture, industry, and the environment: ethnobotanical evidence from al-Basra. In Benco (2004: 31–42).

MARÇAIS, G. (1991). *La Berbérie musulmane et l'Orient au Moyen Âge*. Casablanca: Éditions Afrique Orient.

MESSIER, R. A. (1974). The Almoravids: West Africa and the gold currency of the Mediterranean Basin. *Journal of Economic and Social History of the Orient* 17: 31–47.

—— (1995). Sijilmassa: intermédiaire entre la Méditerranée et l'Ouest de l'Afrique. In M. Hammam (ed.), *L'Occident musulman et l'Occident chrétien au Moyen Âge*. Rabat: Faculté des lettres et des sciences humaines, 181–96.

—— (1997). Sijilmassa: five seasons of archaeological inquiry by a joint Moroccan-American mission. *Archéologie Islamique* 7: 61–92.

—— (2001). Re-thinking the Almoravids, re-thinking Ibn Khaldun. *Journal of North African Studies* 6:59–80.

—— and FILI, A. (2011). The earliest ceramics of Sigilmasa. In P. Cressier and E. Fentress (eds), *La Céramique Maghrébine du Haut Moyen Âge (VIIIe–Xe siècle): État des Recherches, Problèmes et Perspectives*. Rome: École Française de Rome, 129–46.

MILLER, J. A. (2001). Trading through Islam: the interconnections of Sijilmasa, Ghana and the Almoravid movement. *Journal of North African Studies* 6:29–58.

—— (2010). Revealing north–south relations in the eleventh century. In A. Arbeiter, C. Kothe, and B. Marten (eds), *Hispaniens Norden im 11. Jahrhundert: Christliche Kunst im Umbrach*. Petersberg: Imhof, 73–84.

MITCHELL, P. J. (2005). *African Connections: Archaeological Perspectives on Africa and the Wider World*. Walnut Creek, Calif.: Altamira Press.

NIXON, S. (2009). Excavating Essouk-Tadmakka (Mali): new archaeological investigations of early Islamic trans-Saharan trade. *Azania: Archaeological Research in Africa* 44: 217–55.

ROBERTSHAW, P., BENCO, N., WOOD, M., DUSSUBIEUX, L., MELCHIORRE, E., and ETTAHIRI, A. (2010). Chemical analysis of glass beads from medieval al-Basra (Morocco). *Archaeometry* 52: 355–79.

TALBI, M. (2010). 'al-Kayrawan'. In *Encyclopaedia of Islam*, 2nd edn. Accessed 30 Aug. 2010: http://www.brillonline.nl/subscriber/entry?entry=islam_COM-0473

ZAFRANI, H. (2000). *Deux Mille Ans de Vie Juive au Maroc*. Casablanca: Eddif.

CHAPTER 57

COMPLEX SOCIETIES, URBANISM, AND TRADE IN THE WESTERN SAHEL

KEVIN MACDONALD

INTRODUCTION

SOME of the earliest manifestations of social complexity in sub-Saharan Africa are found in the western Sahel and the central Sahara. Recent decades have significantly improved our understanding of them, although large gaps remain. This chapter considers early evidence for social inequality in the Sahara before examining West Africa's first major polity: Tichitt (1900–400 BC). It then critically evaluates the western Sahel's 'age of empire', its capitals and great trading cities, from the early first millennium AD onwards (Fig. 57.1)

EARLY MANIFESTATIONS OF HIERARCHY AND CONFLICT: TUMULI AND ENCLOSURES

With the advent of pastoralism in arid West Africa during the sixth millennium BC, new potentials for social complexity and economic inequality came into being (MacDonald 1998). Initially, traces of communal ritual events focused on the herds themselves: dating to c. 5500–4800 BC (Paris 2000; di Lernia 2006), small stone tumuli covering articulated cattle remains in the Central Sahara may have reaffirmed herd group alliances via the sacrifice of bulls and subsequent feasting, or have been a form of fertility rite.

A shift in the Saharan pastoral landscape appears in the fifth millennium BC with the advent of monumental tumuli (up to 20 m across) containing individual human burials. The earliest examples, at Emi Lulu in the Tafassasset, date to c. 4700–4200 BC; all those excavated covered male adults, with grave goods virtually absent (Paris 1996). Given the emphasis on construc-

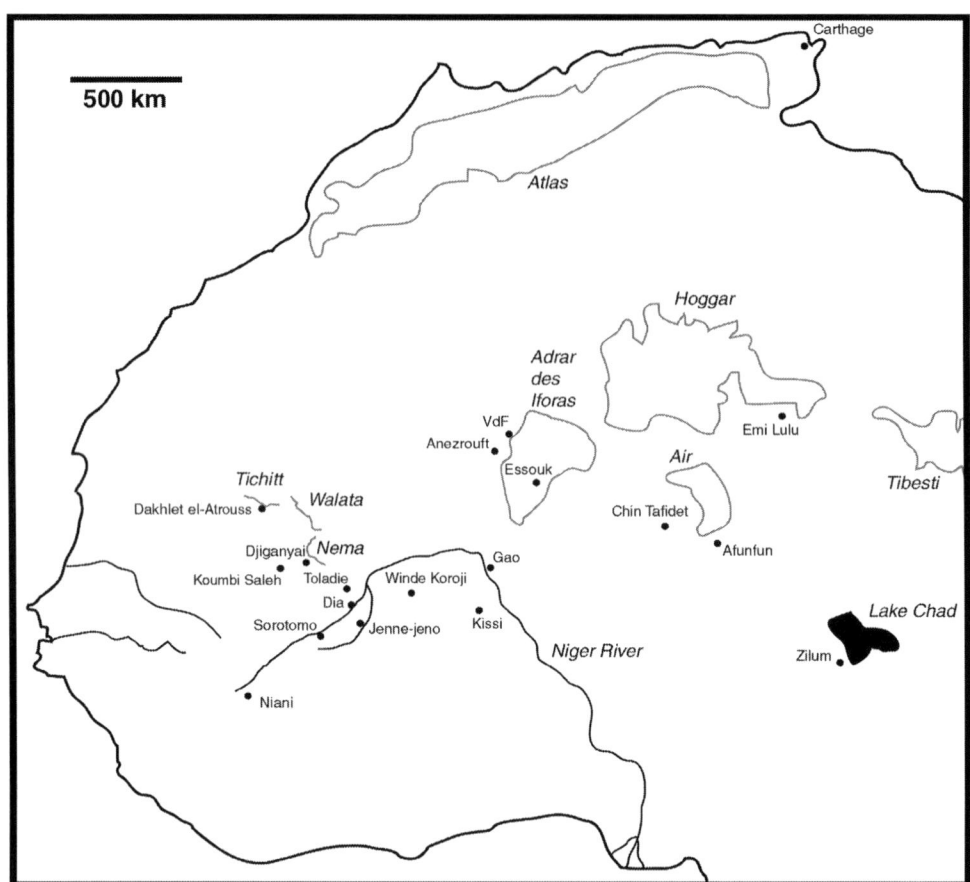

FIG. 57.1 Map showing the locations of sites mentioned in Chapter 57.

tion over material culture, these structures may have been the graves of men of achieved status who had aided herd survival in the face of adversity, building up transitory spikes of livestock wealth, subsequently—as is the case with acephalous pastoral societies today—redistributed through largesse (MacDonald 1998). Later Saharan tumuli (*c.* 2900–1200 BC) include a fuller spectrum of age and gender classes, incorporating adult females, as well as adolescents of both sexes and infants (Paris 1996). The coexistence of such monumental tumuli, each containing single burials, with large open-air cemeteries, strongly suggests an emergence of enduring social differentiation based upon hereditary wealth in herds and grazing territories.

Further west in Mali, especially in the Tessalit region, tumuli formed the focus of larger (≤1.5 ha) oval stone enclosures that perhaps housed entire communities for part of the year or were the venue for ceremonial gatherings. Excavations at one such 'walled village', Anezrouft, date the phenomenon to 3300–2200 BC (Raimbault 1995). Tumuli are incorporated into the enclosure walls, with larger burial monuments inside the enclosure itself, along with scattered quantities of lithic debitage, stone tools, potsherds, ash, and faunal remains (primarily cattle) that attest to domestic activities. The surrounding walls may have been reinforced with acacia *abatis* (Raimbault 1995), or ring ditches such as at the first-millennium BC settlement of Zilum near Lake Chad (Magnavita et al. 2006). While these enclosures may have

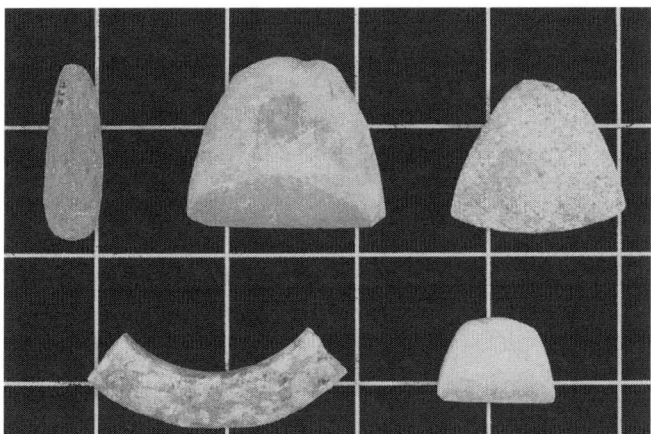

FIG. 57.2 Hachettes and a stone ring fragment from the Windé Koroji Complex, Mali dating to the second and third millennia BC. Scale grid is in inches (1 in. = 2.54 cm) (photograph, Kevin MacDonald).

protected populations and/or herds, the prominence of burial monuments suggests they were also a means of territorial legitimation or a focus for mortuary ceremonies. A few tumuli, like the mid-fourth-millennium BC example at Village de la Frontière (Gaussen and Gaussen 1998), include grave goods, as do third millennium BC open-air cemeteries such as Chin Tafidet and Afunfun, Niger. Burial inventories include stone arm rings, hachettes, pots and small livestock sacrifices. Durable and portable polished stone items, like hachettes and stone arm rings, may have served as early forms of currency or as a tangible means of cementing alliances between groups (Fig. 57.2; Gaussen 1990; MacDonald 1998). They certainly merit further investigation as indicators of social complexity in the early pastoral societies of arid West Africa.

THE TICHITT TRADITION

The occasional sparks of status differentials and territoriality witnessed amongst the mobile pastoralists of the Sahara yielded an enduring blaze of social complexity in the highlands of southeastern Mauritania, which range from west to east in a broad semi-circle around the Hodh depression: Dhar Tagant, Dhar Tichitt, Dhar Walata, and Dhar Néma. The depression was filled with lakes during the Holocene optimum, but after 4000 BC there was a gradual regression, with permanent surface waters fading around 1000 BC (Vernet 1993). It was during this time of climatic degradation that the Tichitt Tradition (c. 1900–400 BC) arose, an early agropastoral economy with domestic pearl millet (Munson 1976; Amblard 1996; Fuller et al. 2007), stone architecture, and a hierarchical settlement landscape (Munson 1980; Holl 1985, 1993). Tichitt's socioeconomic trajectory has been researched and debated for decades, with Munson's work at Dhar Tichitt during the late 1960s followed by that of new researchers there and at the other escarpments (Munson 1976, Holl 1986; Vernet 1993; Ould Khattar 1995; MacDonald et al. 2009; Amblard-Pison 2006; Person et al. 2006). Chronology has, however, been a perennial problem, partly because the deflated nature of many key sites yields only occasional 'cuts' or sediment traps with datable organics, though chaff tempering of the majority of Tichitt ceramics facilitates direct AMS dating of pottery. Munson's (1976) initial eight-phase sequence has now been reduced to three or four developmental phases (Vernet 1993; MacDonald et al. 2009; MacDonald 2011a), although Amblard-Pison (2006) prefers to opt out of chronological ordering in the current state of the evidence. Here, it is argued that the Tichitt ceramic and architectural chronology adequately supports a four-phase developmental sequence.

Pre-Tichitt: Phase 1 (Akreijit Phase), *c.* 2600–1900 BC

Pre-Tichitt sites are small, relatively superficial localities resembling temporary campsites. Once thought to represent dispersed hunter-gatherer populations separated from Tichitt by a brief hiatus (Munson 1976), they are now understood, on the basis of new faunal data from Dhar Néma, to derive from an economy that combined pastoralism with hunting and fishing. While no evidence of domestic cereals has yet been recovered, the notion of an occupation hiatus may be gainsaid by a continuous occupational sequence from Djiganyai, a settlement mound in the Dhar Néma region (MacDonald et al. 2009).

Early Tichitt: Phases 2 and 3 (Khimiya/Goungou Phases),
c. 1900–1600 BC

Munson (1976) originally viewed these phases as a mobile, pre-agricultural period for Tichitt pastoralists. We now know from directly dated cereal samples that domesticated pearl millet (*Pennisetum glaucum*) was farmed during this period (Amblard 1996; MacDonald et al. 2009). However, a degree of continued mobility is still implied by the fact that most well-stratified dates for Tichitt's distinctive dry-stone architecture fall in subsequent periods. Indeed, Amblard-Pison (2006) musters only five 'architectural dates' for Early Tichitt, as defined here, four from surface-collected sherds. It is still unknown whether millet was domesticated locally, but rapidly, during the Pre-Tichitt or Early Tichitt period, or whether a fully formed agropastoral economic package arrived from elsewhere.

Classic Tichitt: Phases 4 to 6 (Nkahl/Naghez/Chebka Phases)
c. 1600–1000 BC

Classic Tichitt represents a major socioeconomic transformation during which most of Tichitt's main population centres developed. As well as the expansion of vast settlements of conjoined stone-walled compounds across Dhars Tichitt and Walata, and as far afield as Dhar Tagant (Ould Khattar 1995), this period also saw the Tichitt Tradition enter the Méma region of the Middle Niger, initially only as dry-season pastoral visitors, but ultimately as permanent settlers (MacDonald 2011a). For Dhar Tichitt itself, a four-tier settlement hierarchy is proposed (Holl 1993), ranging from hamlets (~2 ha), through villages (≤ 10 ha) and district centres (~15 ha) to regional centres (~80 ha). Each district centre may have administered between three and twenty villages and hamlets, while the regional centre of Dakhlet el Atrouss I features 540 stone-walled compounds, most of them containing several dwellings and granaries made of perishable materials (straw, mats, wattle and daub, etc.). This massive settlement is

FIG. 57.3 Plan of Dakhlet el Atrouss I, Mauritania (redrawn after Vernet 1993).

arranged in twenty-six compound clusters, perhaps relating to lineage quarters, with some large outlying walled areas, either for keeping livestock or to protect the soil of garden areas (Fig. 57.3). Surrounding and within the site are well over 100 unexcavated tumuli.

Late Tichitt: Phases 7 and 8 (Arriane/Akjinjeir Phases), *c.* 1000–400 BC

Tichitt's final years are as mysterious as its beginnings. Tichitt Tradition settlements now dwindled within the core Tichitt–Walata region as the Dhars and the Hodh Basin were 'emptied out' (Ould Khattar 1995; MacDonald 2011a; MacDonald et al. 2009). Munson (1980) saw this happening as a result of environmental collapse and Berber incursions aided by iron weaponry. These ideas receive some support from recent studies of early North African trade which reveal an increasing number of Central Saharan Berber agricultural and entrepôt sites from the 5th century BC onwards and mounting evidence for a limited slave trade (Dowler and Galvin 2011). Stylistic affinities in Late Tichitt pottery assemblages and the local advent of iron metallurgy may also indicate syncretism with incoming Berber groups during this period (MacDonald et al. 2009).

Tichitt: political definition, trade, and territory

Several authors have identified Tichitt as the political antecedent of the Empire of Ghana, and therefore West Africa's first large-scale complex society, using terms such as 'chiefdom' (Holl 1985) or even 'incipient state' (Munson 1980). Today, neither term sits well with a growing Africanist scepticism towards the utility of such contrived and imported social categories (S. McIntosh 1999). Instead, let us simply consider Tichitt's characteristics at its apogee (*c.* 1600–1000 BC).

As noted above, a number of settlements from Tichitt and Walata were massive, exceeding the area of many later Middle Niger urban sites, but lacking evidence for socioeconomic diversity or craft specialization. Evidence for active participation in long-distance trade is equivocal, with beads of semi-precious stone (carnelian and amazonite) recovered in limited volumes from Tichitt sites (MacDonald 2011b). Holl (1993) suggests that such items moved as tribute or prestige goods up and down Tichitt's hierarchy of settlements. Yet, at our present state of knowledge, the most striking aspect of Tichitt is the strong settlement hierarchy along the Tichitt and Walata escarpments, coupled with the spread of distinctive settlements and/or ceramics across Dhar Tagant, Dhar Néma, and ultimately into the Middle Niger (Holl 1993; MacDonald 2011a). Unlike sites of the first millennium BC, Tichitt's mid/late second-millennium BC stone walled settlements do not seem designed for defence, but rather to demarcate space, most probably lineage space, with some inequalities visible between the catchments of settlements and groupings of compounds within settlements (Holl 1985, 1993). Tichitt settlements also often feature large enclosures without internal features—probably the base of cattle corrals. Taken together, these indicate a society with internal competition for cattle wealth and territory, perhaps gradually expanding due to seasonal needs for pasture. However, aspects of ritual are also evident, notably the concentration of hundreds of tumuli in the Dhar Tichitt escarpment, compared to barely a dozen in the extensively surveyed and prehistorically well-populated Dhar Walata (Amblard-Pison 2006). Is this a regional difference in mortuary practice or part of a larger ideological phenomenon marking out Dhar Tichitt as an ideological centre of gravity, perhaps an ancestral locality that made it an indispensable dwelling place for elites? Resolving such speculation will require the systematic investigation of Tichitt's tumuli.

THE PRE-ISLAMIC ADVENT OF
TRANS-SAHARAN TRADE

There are good reasons to consider the importance of a pre-Islamic trans-Saharan trade, foremost among them a seminal article by Garrard (1982) which noted that Roman mints at both Carthage and Alexandria suddenly started to strike gold coins at the end of the 3rd century AD. At Carthage this production remained extensive until its conquest by the Arabs in 695, only to be replaced almost immediately by gold dinars at similar levels of production, implying that the Arab gold trade merely took up where the Byzantine trade had left off. These assertions have been surprisingly unreferenced by many sub-Saharan scholars, including those working to finger-print the Byzantine and early Islamic gold of Carthage (Guerra et al. 1999). Their preliminary findings indicate a common gold source for late Byzantine and early Islamic gold workers, although they attribute this—and a subsequent change in gold supply—to a later advent of the Trans-Saharan gold trade. In the light of growing evidence for a 4th-century onset of trans-Saharan commerce, it is clear that alternative hypotheses require systematic testing. Indeed extensive indices of Trans-Saharan commerce from Garamantian sites in southern Libya (Mattingly 2011) and accumulating sub-Saharan evidence, including camel and donkey remains pre-dating AD 400 from the Middle Senegal, articulate well with Garrard's research (MacDonald 2011b: MacDonald and MacDonald 2000).

The most remarkable new evidence comes from Kissi in Burkina Faso, an otherwise inconspicuous series of small settlements and cemeteries, located directly north of the Sirba goldfields (Devisse 1993). Imported finds include hundreds of glass beads, almost all of South Asian origin, as well as copper/brass objects apparently imported from Roman Carthage (Magnavita et al. 2002; Magnavita 2009; Fenn et al. 2009; Robertshaw et al. 2009). Most of these finds come from contexts dated to between AD 400 and 600 and they are complemented by remains of woollen textiles, directly dated to the 6th/7th centuries, and understood, in the absence of evidence for spindle whorls or loom weights, to also be imports (Magnavita 2008).

Why should there be such an elaborate concentration of import finds at Kissi at this date? Its situation near the Sirba goldfields and its proximity to the Niger Bend water corridor provide compelling explanations, and the frequency of imports may also suggest that the Niger Bend was initially more engaged in trans-Saharan trade than the Middle Niger. However, the rarity of archaeological excavations in early first-millennium AD mortuary contexts elsewhere along the Niger may conceal comparable cases.

EARLY TOWNS AND CITIES OF THE MIDDLE NIGER

In the first millennium BC, as the Tichitt Tradition faded, large settlements began to prosper for the first time in the Middle Niger and its floodplain. The earliest and largest was at Dia Shoma, north of the Niger's main channel in the Macina region. The principal settlement during Horizon I (800–400 BC) was at least 19 ha in area, with some smaller satellite sites beyond this. There are traces of earthen architecture, rice agriculture, and livestock keeping, and strong evidence for ironworking during this period, but few indicators of long-distance commerce apart from a couple of glass and faience beads (Bedaux et al. 2005). The earliest ceramics derive largely from the Tichitt Tradition (Bedaux et al. 2001; MacDonald 2011a). Sites of similar dimensions and characteristics north of Dia in the Méma region include Kolima Sud-Est, a single-phase 11 ha settlement dated to 900–400 BC (Takezawa and Cisse 2004). Comparable in size to Tichitt 'district centres', these sites are perhaps most interesting in suggesting the continuation and economic adaptation of the Tichitt Tradition, conceivably including aspects of its sociopolitical structure. However, Dia did not reach its apogee until around AD 1000 (Horizon IV), when the central settlement covered some 34 ha, plus its many satellites, and bone chemistry data suggest multiple populations and dietary groups (Fig. 57.4; Bedaux et al. 2005). For earlier and more substantive evidence of urbanism we must move south into the Inland Delta.

In the 1970s West African archaeology still confronted the view that urbanization and statehood only came with the development of the Arabo-Berber trans-Saharan trade in the 9th century. Roderick and Susan McIntosh's 1977–81 excavations at the Inland Niger Delta site of Jenné-jeno revolutionized perspectives on the origins of African urbanism by showing that by AD 400–900 its tell complex could be defined as fully urban (McIntosh and McIntosh 1980; S. McIntosh 1995). This definition relied partly on concepts co-opted from the 'New Geography', including the 'Rank Size Rule' and 'Central Place Theory', yet Jenné-jeno's role as a regional hub of commerce and interaction, together with the size of its core mound (33 ha), and evidence for the presence of many satellite specialist communities (totalling some further 36 ha), have all become part of defining what constitutes an early African city (McIntosh and McIntosh 1993). Indeed, sites such as Dia and Jenné-jeno are really only the tip of the iceberg: many large tell sites in the Méma, the Macina, and the Inland Delta

FIG. 57.4 Excavations at Dia Shoma, Mali, 1998 (photograph, Kevin MacDonald).

have yet to be investigated with comparable rigour, if at all. For the present, let us examine Jenne-jeno's developmental sequence in greater detail.

Jenné-jeno Phase I/II, 250 BC–AD 400

Jenné-jeno's initial settlement was a 7 ha village within a cluster of other settlements where the subsistence economy combined elements of pastoralism, fishing, and cereal agriculture (especially rice, but also sorghum). Ceramics, highly burnished and with very fine paste (termed 'fineware' or 'deltaware'), resemble those from the same period at Dia Shoma, where elements Jenné-jeno's population are believed to have originated (S. McIntosh 1995; MacDonald 2011a). The presence of iron working in this initial occupation already demonstrates interaction with areas bordering the Inland Delta, since iron ore is absent in its floodplain (McIntosh and McIntosh 1993).

Jenné-jeno Phase III, AD 400–900

Jenné-jeno's location, near the confluence of the Niger and Bani rivers, and at a nexus of natural resources (grains, fish, and grasslands for cattle grazing), led to the site's growth as a locale for trade such that by the end of Phase III it covered 33 ha, with up to 26,000 people estimated to have lived within 1 km of it (S. McIntosh 1995). In the latter portion of this period curvilinear earthen architecture became prevalent, employing distinctive cylindrical bricks, and a city wall was built, perhaps as a communally built bastion against flooding rather than a defensive citadel (McIntosh and McIntosh 1993). In addition to increasing specialization in ironworking activities, with specific smithing settlements, long-distance trade for copper is documented by AD 500, as is trade in gold by 850–950. Ceramics shift to coarser but carefully decorated painted wares, a trend documented elsewhere in the Middle Niger at this time (S. McIntosh 1995). In the absence of elite burials or other clear status indicators, it has been suggested that this was a heterarchical society, with power shared between specialist groups having only a nominal leader (R. McIntosh 1998; S. McIntosh 1999). Regardless, it is clear that Jenné-jeno was a site of interregional commerce centuries before the Arab–Berber trans-Saharan Trade, though ironically lacking the *quantities*—if not the categories (i.e. glass beads and copper alloys)—of long-distance imports documented at non-urban Kissi (MacDonald 2011b).

Jenné-jeno Phase IV: AD 900–1400

During this period Jenné-jeno's material culture diverges significantly from that seen at Dia, perhaps indicating greater cultural autonomy for the Jenné region (S. McIntosh 1995: 369). The Jenné terracotta tradition, which emerges during this phase, exemplifies this: terracotta statuettes are comparatively rare at Dia (Bedaux et al. 2005). Jenné terracottas, while facilitating international recognition of the Middle Niger's artistic achievements, have also attracted unwanted and damaging attention by looters in the employ of the global art market (R. McIntosh et al. 1995; Kusimba and Klehm, Ch. 17 above).

Phase IV also witnesses increasing influence from the Islamic world, with the advent of rectilinear structures and a wave of iconoclasm late in this period. The principal mound appears to have been abandoned in favour of a new Muslim city—modern Jenné—around 1400 (R. McIntosh et al. 1996).

Recently, Roderick McIntosh (2005) has emphasized the 'self-generated'—rather than state- or hierarchically generated—nature of Middle Niger urbanism. In a derivation from his earlier 'Pulse Model' for the genesis of economic specialization and symbiosis in the West African Late Stone Age (McIntosh 1993), he proposes that Middle Niger urban centres were generated organically and gradually from localized networks of subsistence and occupational specialists who found means of maintaining diversified communities through heterarchical political organization. However, multidisciplinary research in Mali's Segou region suggests that there were in fact two different types of urban development, in the Middle Niger (MacDonald and Camara 2012), known there as *Fadugu* (settlements of state power) and *Markadugu* (towns of commercial and/or spiritual foundation). Generated by the sovereign will of a political power, the former were usually transitory—with a lifespan of a few centuries at the most—while the latter, like Dia and Jenné-jeno/Jenné, may well endure for thousands of years, existing outside the state in a semi-autonomous fashion. The archaeology of the former type of settlements in Mali is really only just beginning.

THE EMPIRES: GHANA, GAO, AND MALI

Written sources for arid West Africa effectively begin with the *Tarīkh* of Al-Yaqūbī written in 872/873, which describes a number of kingdoms from Zaghāwa in the east (Kanem; see Gronenborn, Ch. 58 below) to Kawkaw (Gao) and Ghāna in the west (Levtzion and

Hopkins 2000). With this and subsequent written accounts, the difficulty has been bridging a fundamental misalignment between archaeological data and historical texts, with the danger always being that the archaeology is forced into a false alignment. This is particularly the case with the capitals of the western Sudan's great historical empires, which recent research has, for the most part, shown to be highly suspect. Without entering into too much historical background, let us consider the current archaeological evidence for these polities.

Ghana/Wagadu

Ghana, or Wagadu as it is known by Mande oral tradition, was probably West Africa's first empire—or multi-ethnic alliance of 'kingdoms'. First mentioned in passing as a territory and a 'land of gold' by al-Fazri *c.* 825 (Levtzion and Hopkins 2000: 30), the 17th-century *Tarikh es-Soudan* claims that twenty-two kings reigned there both before and after the Hegira, which, even allowing for fanciful exercises in symmetry, suggests origins by at least AD 500 (Houdas 1964). Ghana's capital is usually placed at Koumbi Saleh (a large ruined town in southern Mauritania), but historic sources are by no means unanimous as to its location.

Nevertheless, over a long and complex historiography (Masonen 2000), Koumbi Saleh has evolved as the putative centre of Ghana, whose state territory has been drawn with more attention to natural boundaries such as rivers than to zones of interaction (e.g. Levtzion 1981 places Dia within its territory, but not Jenné-jeno). The problem is that territories traditionally favoured by historians appear to archaeologists to be largely devoid of significant settlements or resources. The highest settlement densities of first-millennium AD Mali are in the Méma (Togola 2008), the Macina (Bedaux et al. 2001), the Inland Delta (McIntosh and McIntosh 1980), and the Lakes Region (Raimbault and Sanogo 1991). Predictably these are areas proximate to waterways with productive soil. Koumbi Saleh, on the other hand, has a relatively sparse archaeological hinterland in an arid landscape, appearing to archaeological eyes as more of an Arab–Berber trade entrepôt than an indigenous capital. Indeed, Berthier's (1997) excavations failed to locate 'urbanized' remains (i.e. earthen or stone buildings) dating before the late 11th century or, in other words, from the apogee of Ghana.

We are thus left with what Roderick McIntosh (1998: 257) described as a 'persistent (but still minority view)... [that Ghana's] heartland was in fact within one of the western basins of the Middle Niger'. Unlike Koumbi Saleh, the Middle Niger was densely settled during the first millennium. The Méma's settlement apogee begins around 700, with the foundation of tell complexes like Akumbu going back to the first few centuries AD and the Méma's largest settlement—76 ha Toladié—dated to at least *c.* 430–670 (Fig. 57.5; Togola and Raimbault 1991; Togola 2008). Likewise, the Lakes Region features the 9 m-high tell of KNT2, with a sequence spanning *c.* AD 250–800, and burial monuments like El Ouladji of 11th/12th-century age fitting al-Bakri's description of Ghana's royal tombs (Raimbault and Sanogo 1991). Combining these data with the urban sequences of the western Sudan's Inland Niger breadbasket (see above), it is remarkable that Koumbi Saleh is still doggedly advanced as the imperial capital. At best, it may represent a late capital, but the archaeology of Ghana's origins and growth remain to be explored across the Middle Niger.

FIG. 57.5 A portion of the settlement mounds of Toladie, Méma region, Mali. Here, up to 15 m of stratified deposits cover an area of 76 ha (photograph, Kevin MacDonald).

Gao

Just as Ghana finds an antecedent in Tichitt, so too Gao does not emerge *ex nihilo*. Along with the newly excavated evidence from Kissi that suggests that the Niger Bend was a major corridor of trade from the 5th century AD, there are also signs of early social complexity from the Songhay homeland in the cemeteries of Asinda-Sikka and Kareygorou and their anthropomorphic/zoomorphic terracotta traditions, and in the appearance of fine, highly fired clay trade beads (of unknown origin) across the region just below the Bend (Gado 1993). A range of dates place these phenomena between AD 450 and 900.

The most important archaeological sites at Gao itself are Gao-Sané (a tell north of the modern town) and Gao Ancien (beneath it) (Insoll 1997, 2000). One or both probably formed the centre of the 'kingdom of Kawkaw' referred to by Al-Yaqūbī in 872/3. Unfortunately, extensive looting at Gao-Sané has precluded its further dating beyond estimates obtained by the Malian Mission Inventaire of the 1980s (Raimbault and Sanogo 1991). Early occupation layers at Gao Ancien date to the middle centuries of the first millennium AD (Insoll 1998, 2000), allowing ample time for the development of the substantial polity noted by Al-Yaqūbī.

Evidence for trans-Saharan trade at Gao is extensive, and far outweighs comparable evidence from Middle Niger sites and Koumbi Saleh. Many hundreds of glass beads and fragments of North African glazed pottery and glasswork have been recovered (Insoll 1998), as well as Gao-Sané's celebrated marble gravestones in Kuffic script, likely to have been imported from Spain in the 11th century (Flight 1975). Recent excavations at the Saharan trade entrepôt of Essouk-Tadmakka, northeast of Gao, also show strong evidence for trans-Saharan commerce from 750 onwards, corresponding with Gao's rise in prosperity (Nixon 2009). Yet the indigenous social basis for this trade, both regionally, and within Gao itself, must be investigated if we are to understand the nature and extent of Gao's *political* power.

Mali (and Sosso)

After Ghana's 11th-century collapse, its constituent territorial elements struggled for power, with Sosso emerging as a dominant player before a southerly Malinke polity rose up against it under the rule of Sundiata Keita *c.* 1240, incorporating its territory and creating an imperial hegemony that eventually stretched from Gao to the Atlantic Ocean (Levtzion 1981). Unfortunately, archaeological attempts to document the settlements of Sosso and Mali have been sparse and frequently unsuccessful.

Sosso's territorial situation is vague, but it probably existed somewhere north of the Niger between Koulikoro and Niono. However, recent oral historical and anthropological surveys have now decisively rejected the notion that it should be equated with the modern village there of the same name (Diarra and Sissoko 2007; Sow et al. 2007). The frequent claim in modern history textbooks that Niani, in northern Guinea, was Sundiata Keita's capital is also suspect. Filipowiak's (1979) excavations attempted to support its historical reputation, but produced radiocarbon dates that entirely missed the epoch of Mali's hegemony. Niani nevertheless remains a large (~50 ha) and important site that may well have served as a Malinke political centre, either before the epoch of Sundiata or subsequent to Mali's collapse. Instead, the capitals of both Mali and other Mande states may have been relatively mobile, shifting location at ruptures between dynasties, or even between rulers (Conrad 1994). Current research near Segou, which has located a major settlement landscape dating to the time of Mali, restores some credit to the notion of its imperial centre being just west of the Inland Delta (Hunwick 1973). Work at Sorotomo, 23 km west of Segou, has revealed a 72 ha settlement first occupied in the 13th century and abandoned amid violence in the 15th (MacDonald et al. 2011). While it is not claimed that Sorotomo was *the* capital of the Mali Empire, it was undoubtedly a major centre of political power at some phase of the empire's development. In the 15th century Mali was to lose territory to Songhay—a descendent of Gao's political tradition—and fade to a core remnant in the Upper Niger Valley.

Overall, the archaeology of the West African empires has been largely limited to attempts at locating capitals and gauging the degree and timing of their participation in trans-Saharan commerce. True archaeologies of the economies and settlement structures of such entities are only just beginning.

REFERENCES

AMBLARD, S. (1996). Agricultural evidence and its interpretation on the Dhars Tichitt and Oualata, south-eastern Mauritania. In G. Pwiti and R. Soper (eds), *Aspects of African Archaeology*. Harare: University of Zimbabwe, 421–7.

AMBLARD-PISON, S. (2006). *Communautés Villageoises Néolithiques des Dhars Tichitt et Oulata (Mauritanie)*. Oxford: British Archaeological Reports.

BEDAUX, R., MACDONALD, K. C., PERSON, A., et al. (2001). The Dia Archaeological Project: rescuing cultural heritage in the Inland Niger Delta (Mali). *Antiquity* 75: 837–48.

—— POLET, J., SANOGO, K., and SCHMIDT, A. (eds) (2005). *Recherches Archéologiques à Dia dans le Delta Intérieur du Niger (Mali): Bilan des Saisons de Fouilles 1998–2003*. Leiden: CNWS.

BERTHIER, S. (1997). *Recherches Archéologiques sur la Capitale de l'Empire de Ghana*. Oxford: Archaeopress.

CONRAD, D. C. (1994). A town called Dakalajan: the Sunjata tradition and the question of ancient Mali's capital. *Journal of African History* 35: 355–77.

DEVISSE, J. (1993). L'or. In J. Devisse (ed.), *Vallées du Niger*. Paris: Réunion des Musées Nationaux, 344–57.

DIARRA, F., and SISSOKO, F. (2007). Les sites archéologiques autour du village de Soso. *Études Maliennes* 66: 4–18.

DI LERNIA, S. (2006). Building monuments, creating identity: cattle cult as a social response to rapid environmental changes in the Holocene Sahara. *Quaternary International* 151: 50–62.

DOWLER, A., and GALVIN, E. R. (eds) (2011). *Money, Trade and Trade Routes in Pre-Islamic North Africa*. London: British Museum Press.

FENN, T. R., KILLICK, D. J., CHESLEY, J., MAGNAVITA, S., and RUIZ, J. (2009). Contacts between West Africa and Roman North Africa: archaeometallurgical results from Kissi, northeastern Burkina Faso. In S. Magnavita, L. Koté, P. Breunig, and O. A. Idé (eds), *Crossroads: Cultural and Technological Developments in First Millennium BC/AD West Africa*. Frankfurt: Magna, 119–46.

FILIPOWIAK, W. (1979). *Etudes Archéologiques sur la Capitale Médiévale du Mali*. Szczecin: Muzeum Nardowe.

FLIGHT, C. (1975) Gao, 1972: First interim report: a preliminary investigation of the cemetery at Sané. *West African Journal of Archaeology* 5: 81–90.

FULLER, D. Q., MACDONALD, K. C., and VERNET, R. (2007). Early domesticated pearl millet in Dhar Néma (Mauritania): evidence of crop-processing waste as ceramic temper. In R. T. J. Cappers (ed.), *Fields of Change: Progress in African Archaeobotany*. Groningen: Barkhuis, 71–6.

GARRARD, T. (1982). Myth and metrology: the early trans-Saharan gold trade. *Journal of African History* 23: 443–61.

GADO, B. (1993). Un 'village des morts' à Bura en République du Niger: un site méthodiquement fouillé fournit d'irremplaçables informations. In J. Devisse (ed.), *Vallées du Niger*. Paris: Réunion des Musées Nationaux, 365–74.

GAUSSEN, J., and GAUSSEN, M. (1998). Vestiges préhistoriques dans le sud Tanezrouft. *Paléo* 1: 7–71.

GAUSSEN, M. (1990). Petits instruments en pierre polie du Sahara méridional (Oued Tilemsi et ses abords). *L'Anthropologie* 94: 559–68.

GUERRA, M. F., SARTHRE, C-O., GONDONNEAU, A., and BARRANDON, J-N. (1999). Precious metals and provenance enquiries using LA-ICP-MS. *Journal of Archaeological Science* 26: 1101–10.

HOLL, A. F. C. (1985). Background to the Ghana Empire: archaeological investigations on the transition to statehood in the Dhar Tichitt region (Mauritania). *Journal of Anthropological Archaeology* 4: 73–115.

—— (1986). *Economie et Société Néolithique du Dhar Tichitt (Mauritanie)*. Paris: Recherches sur les Civilisations.

—— (1993). Late Neolithic cultural landscape in southeastern Mauritania: an essay in spatio-metrics. In A. F. C. Holl and T. E. Levy (eds), *Spatial Boundaries and Social Dynamics: Case*

Studies from Food-Producing Societies. Ann Arbor: International Monographs in Prehistory, 95–133.

HOUDAS, O. (1964). *Tarikh Es-Soudan (par Abderrahman Ben Abdallah Ben 'Imran Ben 'Amir Es-Sa'di).* Paris: Adrien-Maisonneuve.

HUNWICK, J. O. (1973). The mid-fourteenth century capital of Mali. *Journal of African History* 14: 195–206.

INSOLL, T. (1997). Iron Age Gao: an archaeological contribution. *Journal of African History* 38: 1–30.

—— (1998). Islamic glass from Gao, Mali. *Journal of Glass Studies* 40: 77–88.

—— (2000). *Urbanism, Archaeology and Trade: Further Observations on the Gao Region (Mali)—The 1996 Fieldseason.* Oxford: British Archaeological Reports.

LEVTZION, N. (1981). The early states of the western Sudan to 1500. In J. F. Ade Ajayi and M. Crowder (eds), *History of West Africa*, vol. 1, 3rd edn. Harlow: Longman, 129–66.

—— and HOPKINS, J. F. P. (eds) (2000). *Corpus of Early Arabic Sources for West African History.* Princeton, NJ: Markus Wiener.

MACDONALD, K. C. (1998). Before the Empire of Ghana: pastoralism and the origins of cultural complexity in the Sahel. In G. Connah (ed.), *Transformations in Africa: Essays on Africa's Later Past.* London: Leicester University Press, 71–103.

—— (2011a). Betwixt Tichitt and the IND: the pottery of the Faïta Facies, Tichitt Tradition. *Azania: Archaeological Research in Africa* 46: 49–69.

—— (2011b). A view from the south: sub-Saharan evidence for contacts between North Africa, Mauritania and the Niger, 1000 BC–AD 700. In A. Dowler and E. R. Galvin (eds), Money, Trade and Trade Routes in Pre-Islamic North Africa. London: British Museum Press, 72–82.

—— and CAMARA, S. (2012). Segou, slavery, and *Sifinso*. In J. C. Monroe and A. Ogundiran (eds), *Power and Landscape in Atlantic West Africa: Archaeological Perspectives.* Cambridge: Cambridge University Press, 169–90.

—— —— CANOS DONNAY, S., GESTRICH, N., and KEITA, D. (2011). Sorotomo: an ancient Malian capital? *Archaeology International* 13: 52–64.

—— and MACDONALD, R. H. (2000). The origins and development of domesticated animals in arid West Africa. In R. M. Blench and K. C. Macdonald (eds), *The Origins and Development of African Livestock: Archaeology, Genetics, Linguistics and Ethnography.* London: UCL Press, 127–62.

—— VERNET, R., MARTINON-TORRES, M., and FULLER, D. Q. (2009). Dhar Néma: from early agriculture to metallurgy in southeastern Mauritania. *Azania: Archaeological Research in Africa* 44: 3–48.

MAGNAVITA, C., BREUNIG, P., AMEJE, J., and POSSELT, M. (2006). Zilum: a mid-first millennium BC fortified settlement near Lake Chad. *Journal of African Archaeology* 4: 153–70.

MAGNAVITA, S. (2008). The oldest textiles from sub-Saharan West Africa: woolen facts from Kissi, Burkina Faso. *Journal of African Archaeology* 6: 243–57.

—— (2009). Sahelian crossroads: some aspects on the Iron Age sites of Kissi, Burkina Faso. In S. Magnavita, L. Koté, P. Breunig, and O. A. Idé (eds), *Crossroads: Cultural and Technological Developments in First Millennium BC/AD West Africa.* Frankfurt: Magna, 79–104.

—— HALLIER, M., PELZER, C., KAHLHEBER, S., and LINSEELE, V. (2002). Nobles, guerriers, paysans: une nécropole de l'Âge de Fer et son emplacement dans l'Oudalan pré- et proto-historique. *Beiträge zur Allgemeinen und Vergleichenden Archäologie* 22: 21–64.

MASONEN, P. (2000). *The Negroland Revisited: Discovery and Invention of the Sudanese Middle Ages.* Helsinki: Finnish Academy of Science and Letters.

MATTINGLY, D. (2011) The Garamantes of Fezzan: an early Libyan state with trans-Saharan connections. In A. Dowler and E. R. Galvin (eds), *Money, Trade and Trade Routes in Pre-Islamic North Africa*. London: British Museum Press, 49–60.

MCINTOSH, R. J. (1993). The Pulse Model: genesis and accommodation of specialization in the Middle Niger. *Journal of African History* 34: 181–220.

—— (1998). *The Peoples of the Middle Niger*. Oxford: Blackwell Publishers.

—— (2005). *Ancient Middle Niger: Urbanism and the Self-Organizing Landscape*. Cambridge: Cambridge University Press.

—— SINCLAIR, P. J. J., TOGOLA, T., PETRÈN, M., and MCINTOSH, S. K. (1996). Exploratory archaeology at Jenné and Jenné-jeno (Mali). *Sahara* 8: 19–28.

—— TOGOLA, T., and MCINTOSH, S. K. (1995). The good collector and the premise of mutual respect among nations. *African Arts* 28: 60–9.

MCINTOSH, S. K. (ed.) (1995). *Excavations at Jenné-Jeno, Hambarketolo, and Kaniana (Inland Niger Delta Mali): The 1981 Season*. Berkeley: University of California Press.

—— (ed.) (1999). *Beyond Chiefdoms: Pathways to Complexity in Africa*. Cambridge: Cambridge University Press.

—— and MCINTOSH, R. J. (1980). *Prehistoric Investigations in the Region of Jenné, Mali*, part 1. Oxford: British Archaeological Reports

—— —— (1993). Cities without citadels: understanding urban origins along the Middle Niger. In T. Shaw, P. J. J. Sinclair, B. Andah, and A. Okpoko (eds), *The Archaeology of Africa: Food, Metals and Towns*. London: Routledge, 622–41.

MUNSON, P. J. (1976). Archaeological data on the origins of cultivation in the southwestern Sahara and their implications for West Africa. In J. R. Harlan, J. M. J. De Wet, and A. B. Stemler (eds), *Origins of African Plant Domestication*. The Hague: Mouton, 187–209.

—— (1980). Archaeology and the prehistoric origins of the Ghana Empire. *Journal of African History* 21: 457–66.

NIXON, S. (2009). Excavating Essouk-Tadmakka (Mali): new archaeological investigations of early trans-Saharan trade. *Azania: Archaeological Research in Africa* 44: 217–55.

OULD KHATTAR, M. (1995). Les sites Gangara, la fin de la culture de Tichitt et l'origine de Ghana. *Journal des Africanistes* 65: 31–41.

PARIS, F. (1996). *Les Sépultures du Sahara Nigérien du Néolithique à l'Islamisation*. Paris: ORSTOM.

—— (2000). African livestock remains from Saharan mortuary contexts. In R. M. Blench and K. C. Macdonald (eds), *The Origins and Development of African Livestock: Archaeology, Genetics, Linguistics and Ethnography*. London: UCL Press, 111–26.

PERSON, A., JOUSSE, H., MAURER, A. F., and VALLETTE, T. (2006). Les sites du Néolithique final du Dhar Néma (Mauritanie): relations peuplement–environnement. In C. Descamps and A. Camara (eds), *Senegalia: Études sur le Patrimoine Ouest-Africain: Hommage à Guy Thilmans*. Saint-Maur: Sépia, 297–307.

RAIMBAULT, M. (1995). La culture néolithique des 'villages à enceinte' dans la region de Tessalit, au nord-est du Sahara malien. In R. Chenorkian (ed.), *L'Homme Méditerranéen: Mélanges Offerts à Gabriel Camps*. Aix en Provence: Université de Provence, 113–25.

—— and SANOGO, K. (eds) (1991). *Recherches Archéologiques au Mali: les Sites Protohistoriques de la Zone Lacustre*. Paris: ACCT-Karthala.

ROBERTSHAW, P., MAGNAVITA, S., WOOD, M., MELCHIORRE, E., POPELKA-FILCOFF, and GLASSCOCK, M. D. (2009). Glass beads from Kissi (Burkina Faso): chemical analysis and archaeological interpretation. In S. Magnavita, L. Koté, P. Breunig, and O.A. Idé (eds),

Crossroads: Cultural and Technological Developments in first millennium BC/AD *West Africa.* Frankfurt: Magna, 105–18.

Sow, M., Diarra, F., and Kone, S. (2007). La dernière refondation du village Soso ou l'épopée de Soso Baba Keyita. *Études Maliennes* 66: 53–62.

Takezawa, S., and Cisse, M. (2004). Domestication des céreales au Méma, Mali. In K. Sanogo and T. Togola (eds), *XIth Congress of the PanAfrican Association Prehistory and Related Fields, Bamako, February 07–12/2001 ACTS.* Bamako: Soro Print Color, 105–21.

Togola, T. (2008). *Archaeological Investigations of Iron Age Sites in the Méma Region, Mali (West Africa).* Oxford: British Archaeological Reports.

—— and Raimbault, M. (1991). Les missions d'inventaire dans le Méma, Karéri et Farimaké (1984–1985). In Raimbault and Sanogo (1991: 81–98).

Vernet, R. (1993). *Préhistoire de la Mauritanie.* Nouakchott: Centre Culturel Français A. de Saint Exupéry–Sépia.

CHAPTER 58

STATES AND TRADE IN THE CENTRAL SAHEL

DETLEF GRONENBORN

THE CENTRAL SAHEL

THE Central Sahel (from the Arabic for 'shore') is a vast region stretching from the eastern shores of the River Niger to the eastern shoreline of Lake Chad. Its northern border is marked by the Sahara, while to the south it stretches to the mountainous regions of present-day Nigeria and Cameroon, where the environment changes from grassland into more wooded savannah (Fig. 58.1). Inhabited by farmers and cattle herders, powerful empires emerged here during the medieval period, empires that persist today within the political structures of modern Niger, Nigeria, Cameroon, and Chad. The region's main geographical entity is Lake Chad, an enormous body of open water, but only the remnant of a much bigger early Holocene lake (Breunig, Ch. 38 above). Lacking a natural outlet, its waters evaporate during the October–June dry season. To its south the Shari and Logone tributaries cross an enormous flat landscape of clayey soils, remains of the former lake-bed that are today inundated during the rainy season, while to its north today's desert edge was more fertile even up until the 19th century.

THE LATE IRON AGE: THE EMERGENCE OF POLITICAL COMPLEXITY IN THE CHAD BASIN

When exactly political complexity emerged in the central Sahel is uncertain. The first complex settlement systems evolved west of Lake Chad during the mid-first millennium BC (Magnavita et al. 2006), when extensive nuclear sites suddenly appeared in the course of a possible lake transgression during which other sites in the southern Chad Basin were abandoned. Possibly, the rising water table led to a scarcity of resources and a congestion of living

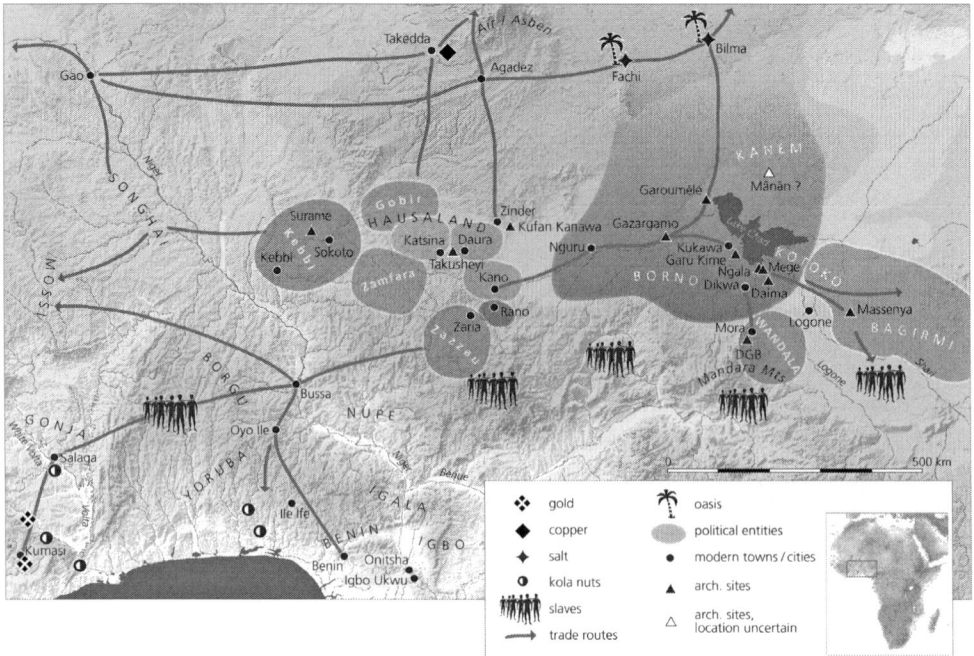

FIG. 58.1 Map of the Central Sahel showing the sites mentioned in Chapter 58.

space, at least in regions around Lake Chad. Although gaps in occupation are also known in other parts of the Sahel (Breunig and Neumann 2002), complexity equally emerges at this time in central Nigeria with the Nok Culture (Breunig, Ch. 38 above). For the following millennium, archaeological indications for political centralization remain scarce, but a succession of burials at Mege and Kursakata in the southern Chad Basin show some kind of continuity in site use (Gronenborn 1998). At the latter, permanent villages supported by a mixed economy of pastoralism and horticulture existed by around AD 800 (Gronenborn 1998; cf. Connah 1981).

In the following centuries, Arabic written sources set in. The earliest reliable such source is al-Bakri, who in the mid-11th century describes the inhabitants of the region of Kanem as black pagans (Levtzion and Hopkins 1981: 64). Almost a century later, al-Idrisi describes the Chad Basin as being extensively settled by people who depended on growing sorghum (Levtzion and Hopkins 1981: 114). The later (1229) account of Yaqut also used earlier works, some perhaps as old as the 10th century, and describes rulers who were held to be sacred and were supported by wealth in livestock and slaves (Levtzion and Hopkins 1981: 171). State formation is thus documented for the central *bilād al-sūdān*, at a time when oral traditions indicate that the Sayfuwa dynasty, which governed the Chad Basin until 1846, was already in place (Lange 1977; Barkindo 1985). Following the introduction of Islam during the 11th century (Last 1985), their rulers, known by the title *mai* ('lord'; Smith 1987: 84), expanded from a core zone in the region of Kanem (see Fig. 58.1) to influence an area from Fezzan in the north to Hausaland in the west.

THE KANEM-BORNO EMPIRE

During the 13th century Kanem was a powerful political player in West Africa and beyond: Ibn Khaldun mentions a caravan with gifts from its king arriving at Tunis in 1257 (Levtzion and Hopkins 1981: 337). Borno, the landscape west of Lake Chad, gradually became the empire's focal point since in the latter 13th century the Sayfuwa were driven out of Kanem through political struggles that may have been compounded by a deteriorating

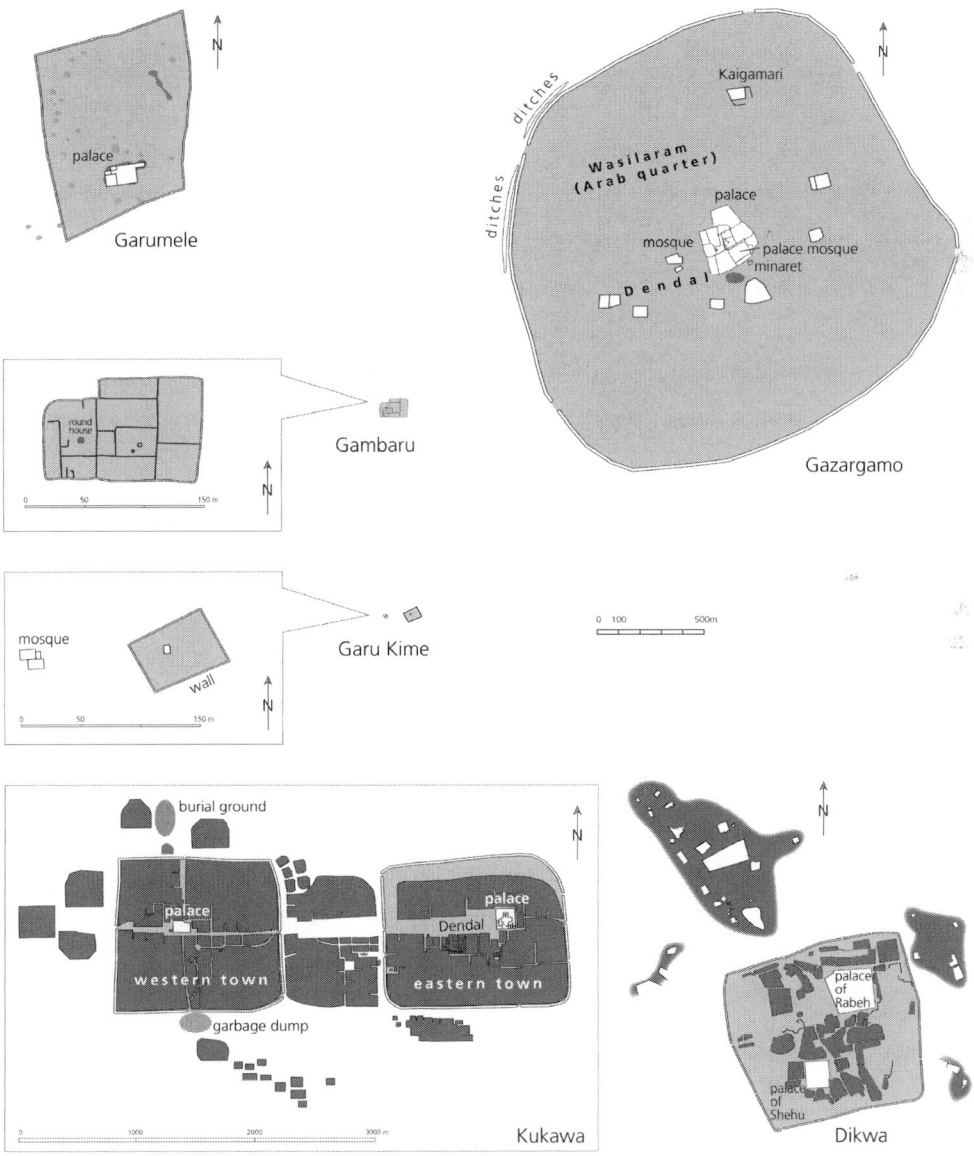

FIG. 58.2 Sites of the Kanem-Borno Empire (13th–early 20th centuries).

climate (Brunk and Gronenborn 2004). A century of unstable conditions followed, during which the seat of government shifted location, settling at one point at Jaja (Levtzion and Hopkins 1981: 187), modern Garoumélé in eastern Niger (Fig. 58.2) (Gronenborn 2001). Excavations confirm its occupation in the 13th/14th centuries cal. AD, while the pottery assemblage fits well into the Late Iron Age style of the wider region (Haour 2008). Typical is a so-called *sgraffito*-decorated ware that archaeologically typifies the expanding Kanem-Borno sphere of influence in the southern Chad Basin (Gronenborn and Magnavita 2000).

Around 1472 the settlement that became Kanem-Borno's focus for the next 300 years was founded in the fertile Komadugu Valley. Birni (Hausa for 'town') Gazargamo was also favourably located at the terminus of the trans-Saharan trade routes reaching from Tripolis through Murzuk to the central Sahel. The site was surrounded by an enormous rampart (see Fig. 58.2) with a circumference of 6.7 km constructed of sand and interrupted by gates, of which all traces have disappeared. Interior structures were constructed from burnt bricks, forming compound walls and house foundations (Connah 1981). The site was destroyed in the course of the Fulani *jihad* in 1808 and pillaged thereafter so that today virtually nothing is visible. However, Connah's (1981) excavations and textual sources emphasize the scale of its walls, palaces, and mosques, as well as the quarters of Arab traders (Gronenborn 2001). Recently, Magnavita (2011) conducted a magnetometer survey of the central palace structures where he identified a possible mosque (see Fig. 58.2). At the nearby palace site of Gambaru (see Fig. 58.2), Hambolu (1996) excavated burnt-brick walls and *sgraffito*-decorated ware. Given the area's importance for the medieval central Sahel, it is surprising that so little archaeological work has been undertaken over the past thirty years.

Much better researched is Garu Kime (Magnavita et al. 2009), south of the 19th-century capital of Kukawa (Fig. 58.2). A rectangular structure of fired-brick walls, rather than a settlement, its date of origin is uncertain, although radiocarbon dates indicate an occupation during the 17th, 18th, and possibly 19th centuries. Its pottery resembles that from Birni Gazargamo, so a general contemporaneity may be inferred, and it may have been a temporary residence for the Borno *mais* ('lords': see above) when they travelled to the region south of Lake Chad that gradually became incorporated into the empire during the 15th and 16th centuries (Gronenborn 2001, 2005; Magnavita et al. 2009).

Kotoko polities of the plains in southeastern Borno

This region is characterized by vast clay plains, locally called *firgi*, remnants of the former more extensive Lake Chad. Sand dunes protruding through these clays and riverbanks were settled after a major retreat of the lake around 1000 cal. BC. Archaeological interest in this area has been notable, because of its many extensive and deeply stratified settlement mounds. Following early work by Lebeuf (1969), Connah (1981) surveyed the Nigerian part of the southern Chad Basin, excavating most notably at Daima. Holl (2002) then worked on the Cameroonian side, while Gronenborn (1998, 2001, 2005) and Wiesmüller (2001) later followed Connah in the west. This long-term archaeological engagement has produced a detailed chronology and pottery typology reaching from around 1000 cal. BC to the present. The past several hundred years are particularly interesting, as they allow study of the expanding influence of the empire of Borno into the lands south of Lake Chad. Before the 14th century this area seems to have been unattractive, even hostile, to the rulers of Kanem and Borno, serving only as a source of slaves. However, climatic deterioration in the north during the latter 13th century shifted the ruling elite's attention south, and raids were undertaken to establish more permanent control. Archaeologically this is visible in the appearance of non-local goods in the upper parts of the mounds, notably carnelian beads of Saharan provenance (Insoll et al. 2004). This increasing external pressure also had the effect of sociopolitical intensification on the societies south of Lake Chad, and a detailed Italian source by Giovanni Anania from 1573 describes powerful independent polities and a flourishing trade in iron with the southern Mandara Mountains (Lange and Berthoud 1972). These societies resisted Islamic expansion until the military campaigns of Mai Idris Alauma during the later 16th century (Lange 1987a), at which point local dynasties were overthrown and replaced by Bornoan elites and colonies. The few native polities to maintain a degree of independence are listed as Kotoko (a Chadic language) city-states or principalities in 19th-century sources.

Archaeologically these 16th-century raids and ethnic cleansings are visible in hiatuses and disruptions in the mound stratigraphies, as at Daima, where occupation was discontinued until the site's resettlement during the 19th century (Connah 1981; Gronenborn 2005). The upper layers of the settlement mounds also show an increasing percentage of *sgraffito*-style pottery as the archaeological indicator of a northwestern influence. During the 19th century the Bornoan influence intensified again when the empire's northern regions were attacked by Tuareg and new colonies were established in the more secure southern regions. This finally resulted in an ethnic change as the local Chadic-speaking population gradually took up a Bornoan identity, adopting the Saharan Kanuri predominantly spoken in Borno (Gronenborn 2001, 2005).

The nineteenth century

Back in the Borno heartland, Gazargamo was destroyed by the invading Fulani in 1808. Their attacks were countered by Muhammad al-Kanemi, a religious scholar who was able to regather the Borno troops and who kept the empire from becoming entangled by the rising Sokoto caliphate (Cohen and Brenner 1984). Now, however, its power base was relocated to a newly chosen site, Kukawa, built in 1814 (Gronenborn 2001). Visited by numerous 19th-century European travellers (see Fig. 58.2), our knowledge of Kukawa is extensive and detailed (e.g. Barth 1857–8; Rohlfs 1868/72; Nachtigal 1971–87; Monteil 1895; Johnston and Muffet 1973), but archaeological research has hardly been undertaken with the exception of a few visits, for instance by Connah (1981: 242).

After the destruction of Kukawa in the course of Rabeh's subjugation of the Kanem-Borno empire in 1893, the capital was shifted to Dikwa, where the usurper established himself and had a fort built. In the earlier 19th century Dikwa (see Fig. 58.2) had enjoyed a certain political independence as a major economic and political centre south of Lake Chad (Gronenborn 2001). Survey of Rabeh's palace and test excavation planned the surviving (but decaying) clay structures and yielded a ceramic assemblage dating to the decade around the turn from the 19th to the 20th century, when Dikwa was first occupied by French troops (1900–02) and then by German ones (1902–15) (Gronenborn and Magnavita 2000; Gronenborn 2001).

Trade and commerce in the Kanem-Borno Empire

Although Kanem-Borno constituted the major economic focus of the central Sahel for over 1,000 years, surprisingly little is known about its trade archaeologically, something due to the limited number of archaeological excavations in settlement sites and the lack of archaeologically investigated burials. Only beads, iron, or copper may be cited as imports from outside, but most archaeological data come from sites in the southern Chad Basin (MacEachern 1993; Gronenborn 1998, 2005). The paucity of data is also explained by the fact that most of the region's commodities were perishable in nature. Nachtigal's (1971–87) description of the markets at Kukawa, for instance, emphasizes calabash bowls and bottles, wooden dishes, mats, and leather products (cushions, bags, and horse-gear), most of the better of which were brought from Kano. Livestock included camels, cattle, goats, chickens, and horses of both North African and local stock. Iron was worked into various tools and weapons, the raw material being obtained locally or imported from the Mandara Mountains to the south (MacEachern 1993). Nachtigal lists as produce grains (sorghum and millet), fruits, groundnuts, sesame, onions, melons, and also occasionally tomatoes, with dates imported from Kawar and Kanem. Exports to the north included ostrich feathers, leather, and textiles (Lovejoy and Baier 1975), while salt brought from the desert oases of Bilma, Kawar, and Fachi was a major trade good both within the Chad Basin and in networks further south between the Volta, the Congo Basin, and the desert oases (Lovejoy 1986). However, the Chad Basin's main trade good was slaves.

Borno's economy was fundamentally based on internal and external slavery. Slaves appear in the earliest historic sources, and Borno's rulers are said to have obtained them with ease. This thorough reliance on human capital as a basis for the internal economy as well as export goods persisted throughout the 19th century until the final abolition of slavery under British colonial rule. Slave raids (Arab *ghazwa*) were documented, for instance, by Nachtigal (1971–87), who gives a horrifying account of the ruthlessness with which non-Muslim small farming settlements in the southern Chad Basin were destroyed and their inhabitants taken into captivity. Most slaves were either sold to Mediterranean North Africa in exchange for weapons and horses or employed in households or on farming estates, with eunuchs a particularly valued export. At least during the well-documented 19th century, rural production was based on slave settlements (Kanuri *kaliari*, from *kalia*, male slave) scattered across the landscape and belonging to the capital's urban elite. Apart from manual labour, slaves could also take up powerful administrative positions, commanding slave troops themselves on further raids to obtain more slaves (Gronenborn 2001; MacEachern 2001).

Summing up, one may state that the archaeology of the Kanem-Borno empire is still very much in a descriptive state. On a more general basis a southward movement of the capitals may be observed, which should be linked with the continuous desiccation of the Sahel. This southward expansion was accompanied by the spread of both Islam and a slave-based economy (Gronenborn 2001; Brunk and Gronenborn 2004).

HAUSALAND

A general southward shift of sites is also visible further west in Hausaland. Today, this is not a politically unified territory but stretches from the river Niger across southern Niger and northern Nigeria to Borno. However, even far beyond this region Hausa serves as the lingua

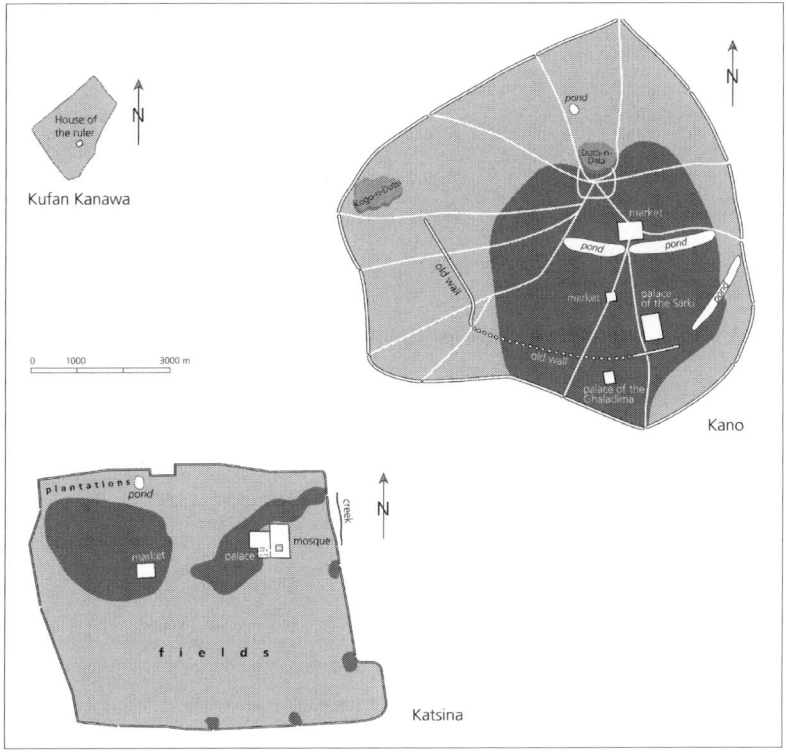

FIG. 58.3 Sites in Hausaland (15th–19th centuries).

franca (Haour and Rossi 2010). When first mapped in the early 19th century, Katsina (Fig. 58.3) was the predominant trading power among the Hausa city-states, with Gobeir (Guber), Zamfara, Daura, and Kano surrounding it (Hornemann 1802).

A Hausa founding tradition, the Bayajidda legend, mentions seven original city-states (*Hausa bakwai*) which emerged from a female dynasty from Daura, the alleged location of the origin of the Hausa identity (Haour 2003: 6–7). Important in this corpus, as well as in another founding tradition—the Kano Chronicle (Palmer 1908), a king list compiled in either the 17th (Sutton 1979; Last 1980) or 19th century (Hunwick 1994)—is the role of a mythical stranger of Near Eastern background, who arrived in early Hausaland to take over political leadership. In some versions of the Bayajidda legend a connection to Borno is stressed, while others relate directly to the Near East (Lange 1987b). Archaeologically, however, the early years of Hausa identity are currently only documented from excavations at Kufan Kanawa (Haour 2003; Haour and Rossi 2010) and at a burial site, Durbi Takusheyi, between Katsina and Daura in Nigeria (Liesegang 2009).

Kufan Kanawa (see Figs 58.1 and 58.3), dating to the 15th century AD and earlier, is regarded as the possible predecessor to Kano, now the major metropolis of northern Nigeria and one of the focal points of Hausaland (Haour 2003, 2005). The site possesses a 6 km, almost rectangular wall within which is a central rectangular stone structure. The few finds recovered from survey and excavation consist mostly of pottery, while the walls were constructed of stone slabs and possibly also an earthen embankment. Some research has also been undertaken within Kano itself and its surroundings (see Fig. 58.3); the inselbergs around which it, like many early Hausa towns, was built show traces of Iron Age occupation, and the city walls have also received attention (Moody 1967; Nast 1996).

While Islam was established in Kanem-Borno—at least among the elite—by the 11th century, in Kano it did not become widely accepted until the late 15th century, when it was ruled by Mohammadu Rumfa (1463–99) (Hunwick 1994). This comparatively late acceptance of Islam in Hausaland is also reflected in the succession of burials at Durbi Takusheyi, which comprise eight burial mounds, each apparently containing one central

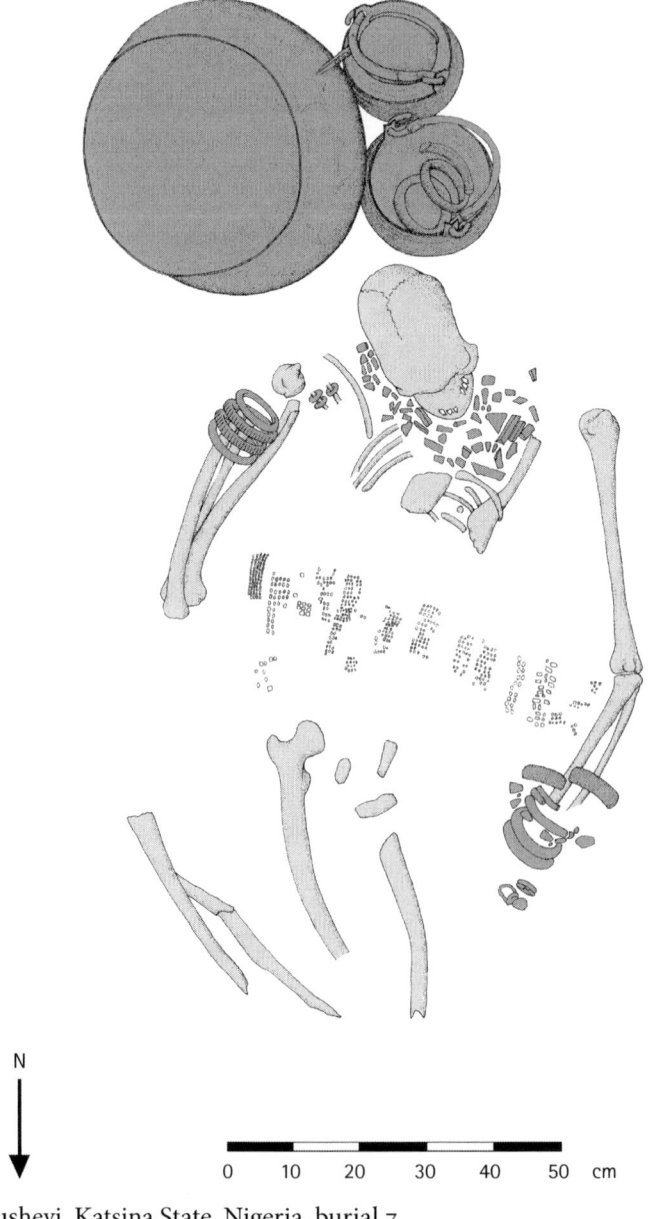

N

0   10   20   30   40   50   cm

FIG. 58.4 Takusheyi, Katsina State, Nigeria, burial 7.

individual interment, spanning some 200 years (Liesegang 2009; Gronenborn et al. 2012). Imported goods in burial 7 (Fig. 58.4), including a bowl of Near Eastern provenance (Haase 2011), date to the late 15th/early 16th centuries and attest to growing international and Islamic influence in Hausaland at this time (Sutton 1979).

Other sites in Hausaland have also been surveyed, but mostly with a focus on their walls (Haour 2003: 53–68). Among them are Zaria and its predecessor, Turunku (Liesegang 2009). Specific interest has been devoted to Surame, an early capital of the state of Kebbi in the west of Hausaland and neighbouring urban sites (Liesegang 2009). Surame is an extensive archaeo-logical site, with still visible walls and evidence of wards and gates. It seems to have been founded towards the end of the 15th century and to have been abandoned during the 17th/early 18th centuries. On the basis of this and other evidence from the neighbouring sites of Gungu and Male, Liesegang (2009) proposed a rapid formation of states and cities towards the 15th/16th centuries without any long-term, gradual local evolution. Sule (2010) undertook sur-veys to understand a past landscape in the Bauchi region at the margins of the present Hausa identity area. He was able to identify various settlement locations including hilltop sites, iron-producing sites, and dyeing pits, and reconstructed past landscape use and conception.

Hausaland remained more or less independent, with one or the other city-state dominating over time, and some occasionally dominated by Borno, until the Fulani *jihad* by Usuman dan Fodio between 1804 and 1809. Starting out from Sokoto dan Fodio launched a series of attacks against the Hausa states, Gobir fell in 1808, Kano, Zaria, and Katsina in 1809. Hausaland was now dominated by the *shehu* (sheikh) residing in Sokoto, and became part of the caliphate.

Trade and commerce in Hausaland

As European traveller descriptions make clear (Olaniyi 2005), during the 19th century Kano was the most important trading city in the central Sudan. Before, however, Katsina (see Fig. 58.3) was an almost equally powerful mercantile centre. In general, Hausaland is more advantageously positioned for long-distance trade compared to Kanem-Borno because of its location midway between the Niger and the Chad Basin and its proximity to Agadez. Major trading goods were gold, kola, and slaves, but also locally produced leather, textiles, and iron. Gold and kola was brought from areas to the west and southwest through connections estab-lished in the 14th century with the advent of merchants and clerics from Mali and Songhay, the *wangara* (Lovejoy 1978). Within Hausa towns these 'diaspora' communities were Muslim and practised as brokers, or craftsmen. Living in separate wards and internationally oriented, they took up a position of a privileged stratum within the emerging Hausa city states. Trade with Borno and other regions in the eastern central Sahel encompassed textiles going east and salt, natron, slaves, horses, and camels returning.

Contacts and exchanges towards the north increased after Islam became established in Hausaland from the late 15th century. Slaves, hides, leather goods, and textiles went north, with steel weapons and chainmail armour coats from Europe, glass beads from the Mediterranean, silk, and semi-precious stone beads and cowries from the Indian Ocean trade network making their way south. As well as being exported, slaves were also embedded in the agricultural settlements around the large Hausa centres. Kano, for instance, was surrounded by a belt of farmsteads, smaller walled settlements, and plantations where slaves were settled by the Kano-based nobility and wealthy merchants, but individual slaves also lived and worked within the households of independent farmers (Lovejoy 1982). Slaves were also embedded in the state structure and the immediate household of the head, the emir. This was reflected in the architecture of the palace in Kano, presumably built around 1500 (Nast 1996).

Even more than Kanem and Borno, Hausaland still lacks any intensive or broader archaeological research. Investigations so far have been selective and have focused on some highly visible remains, but large parts of both Hausaland and Kanem-Bonro remain *terra incognita*. This is all the more regrettable as Hausaland constitutes a core region of an identity that today comprises many million individuals living in an area stretching between Cameroon and the Niger for whom many traditional institutions and offices are still in place.

BAGIRMI AND WANDALA

Apart from the major empires and city states in the northern section of the central Sahel, other, smaller entities emerged in the south: Bagirmi in present-day Chad, and Wandala, north and east of the Mandara Mountains in northern Cameroon and Nigeria.

Bagirmi was presumably founded during the 15th century, as it is depicted on the Fra Mauro map of 1459 (Gronenborn 2001) and was located between the Kotoko city-states and hence the Bornoan sphere of influence and Wadai to the east. Islam became influential in Bagirmi during the 16th century, and the governing system was as despotic as elsewhere in the region (Reyna 1990). Its economy was almost solely based on slave raiding and slave exports, among whom eunuchs featured prominently. Except for a survey of its capital, Massenia (Lebeuf 1967), Bagirmi has so far received little archaeological attention.

More attention has been devoted to the Mandara Mountains and the state of Wandala, which is first mentioned on the Fra Mauro map and also by Anania, who describes the trade in iron from the nearby mountain ranges. Slaves constituted the other major export. Iron was produced by non-Muslim, non-centralized groups in the mountains and then sold as a raw material to the plains, while at the same time montagnards were also the major source of slaves for the Wandala state, a peculiar relationship discussed by MacEachern (1993). Archaeological attention has recently focused on stone structures (platforms and terraces, sometimes enclosed by free-standing walls) concentrated on the northern fringes of the mountains that date to the 13th–17th centuries (David 2008). One site has produced not only domestic deposits but also non-local materials such as copper alloy artefacts and glass beads that indicate external contacts during the 15th–17th centuries, when Borno expanded southward into the *firgi*-plains (MacEachern et al. 2010). The exact function of the stone structures remains uncertain, but they must be seen in the context of the southward pressure of Borno and the emergence of the Wandala state (David 2008).

CONCLUSIONS

Traditional historiography and archaeology would see the central Sahel as having emerged into a landscape of statehood in the course of the southbound expansion of Islam and associated trade and contacts (Bovill 1970). While the effects of external influences cannot be neglected, internal developments are increasingly regarded as equally significant (Haour 2003; David 2008; Haour and Rossi 2010). The relatively recent discovery of extensive walled settlements at the transition from the Neolithic to the Early Iron Age in the Chad Basin (Magnavita et al. 2006) indicates what enormous sites and processes may still await recognition. Hierarchical structures may well already have existed during the first millennium cal. BC, continuing into the early first millennium AD (Gronenborn 1998). Later in that millennium the region must have been a patchwork of independent developments, as proposed by Sutton (1979). Furthermore, genetics point to an East African mid-Holocene origin for the Chad Basin's Chadic-speaking population (Cerný et al. 2009), which indicates entirely different, deeply buried routes not yet explored by archaeology.

The central Sahel came under the sway of the Fulani *jihad* during the early 19th century and about 100 years later was divided between the European colonial powers of Britain, Germany and France. Although these conquests constituted major political disruptions, they could not greatly change long and deep-rooted traditions that continue up to the present day. Within the fast-changing political, social, and economic landscape of the modern states of Nigeria, Niger, and Cameroon, the central Sahel constitutes a landscape in which traditional structures persist.

REFERENCES

BARKINDO, B. (1985). Early states of the Central Sudan: Kanem, Borno and some of their neighbours to *c.* 1500 A.D. In J. F. A. Ajayi and M. Crowder (eds), *History of West Africa*, vol. 1. New York: Longman, 225–54.

BARTH, H. (1857–8). *Travels and Discoveries in North and Central Africa: Being a Journal of an Expedition Undertaken under the Auspices of H.B.M.'s Government, in the Years 1849–1855.* London: Longmans.

BOVILLE, E. W. (1970). *The Golden Trade of the Moors.* London: Oxford University Press.

BREUNIG, P., and NEUMANN, K. (2002). From hunters and gatherers to food producers: new archaeological and archaeobotanical evidence from the West African Sahel. In F. A. Hassan (ed.), *Droughts, Food and Culture: Ecological Change and Food Security in Africa's Later Prehistory.* New York: Kluwer Academic/Plenum, 123–55.

BRUNK, K., and GRONENBORN, D. (2004). Floods, droughts, and migrations: the effects of Late Holocene lake level oscillations and climate fluctuations on the settlement and political history in the Chad Basin. In M. Krings and E. Platte (eds), *Living with the Lake.* Cologne: Rüdiger Köppe, 101–32.

ČERNÝ, V., FERNANDES, V., COSTA, M. D., HÁJEK, M., MULLIGAN, C. J., and PEREIRA, L. (2009). Migration of Chadic speaking pastoralists within Africa based on population structure of Chad Basin and phylogeography of mitochondrial L3f haplogroup. *BMC Evolutionary Biology* 2009, 9:63; doi:10.1186/1471-2148-9-63.

COHEN, R., and BRENNER, L. (1984). Bornu in the nineteenth century. In J. F. A. Ajaji and M. Crowder (eds), *History of West Africa*, vol. 2. Harlow: Longman, 93–128.

CONNAH, G. (1981). *Three Thousand Years in Africa: Man and His Environment in the Lake Chad Region of Nigeria.* Cambridge: Cambridge University Press.

DAVID, N. (2008). *Performance and Agency: The DGB Sites of Northern Cameroon.* Oxford: Archaeopress.

GRONENBORN, D. (1998). Archaeological and ethnohistorical investigations along the southern fringes of Lake Chad, 1993–1996. *African Archaeological Review* 15: 225–60.

—— (2001). Kanem-Borno: a brief summary of the history and archaeology of an empire in the central 'bîlad el-sudan'. In C. DeCorse (ed.), *West Africa During the Atlantic Slave Trade: Archaeological Perspectives*. London: Leicester University Press, 101–30.

—— (2005). The incorporation of southern Chad Basin princedoms into Borno. In C. Baroin, G. Seidensticker-Brikay, and K. Tijani (eds), *Man and the Lake: Proceedings of the 12th Mega Chad Conference, Maiduguri 2nd–9th December 2003*. Maiduguri: Centre for Trans-Saharan Studies, 249–60.

—— and ADDERLEY, P., AMEJE, J., BANERJEE, A., FENN, T., LIESEGANG, G., HAASE, C.-P., USMAN, Y. A., and PATSCHER, S. (2012). Durbi Takusheyi: a high-status burials site in the westen Central bilād al sūdān. *Azania* 47: 256–72.

—— and MAGNAVITA, C. (2000). Imperial expansion, ethnic change, and ceramic traditions in the southern Chad Basin: a terminal nineteenth-century pottery assemblage from Dikwa, Borno State, Nigeria. *International Journal of Historical Archaeology* 4: 35–70.

HAASE, C.-P. (2011). The metal bowl from tumulus 7. In D. Gronenborn (ed.), *Gold, Slaves and Ivory: Medieval Empires in Northern Nigeria*. Mainz: Römisch-Germanisches Zentralmuseum, 102–3.

HAMBOLU, M. O. (1996). Recent excavations along the Yobe valley. In G. Nagel (ed.), *Proceedings, International Symposium SFB 268, Frankfurt/Main 13.12.–16.12.1995*. Frankfurt: Berichte des Sonderforschungsbereichs, 215–29.

HAOUR, A. (2003). *Ethnoarchaeology in the Zinder Region, Republic of Niger: The Site of Kufan Kanawa*. Oxford: British Archaeological Reports.

—— (2005). Power and permanence in precolonial Africa: a case study from the central Sahel. *World Archaeology* 37: 552–65.

—— (2008). The pottery sequence from Garumele (Niger): a former Kanem-Borno capital? *Journal of African Archaeology* 6: 3–20.

—— and ROSSI, B. (2010). Language, history and religion. In A. Haour and B. Rossi (eds), *Being and Becoming Hausa*. Leiden: Brill, 1–34.

HORNEMANN, F. (1802). *Tagebuch seiner Reise von Cairo nach Murzuck der Hauptstadt des Königreichs Fessan in Afrika in den Jahren 1797 und 1798, aus der Teutschen Handschrift desselben herausgegeben von Carl König*. Weimar: Landes-Industrie-Comptoir.

HOLL, A. F. C. (2002). *The Land of Houlouf: Genesis of a Chadic Polity, 1900 B.C.–A.D. 1800*. Ann Arbor: University of Michigan.

HUNWICK, J. (1994). A historical whodunit: the so-called 'Kano Chronicle' and its place in the historiography of Kano. *History in Africa* 21: 127–46.

INSOLL, T., POLYA, D. A., BHAN, K., IRVING, D., and JARVIS, K. (2004). Towards an understanding of the carnelian bead trade from western India to sub-Saharan Africa: the application of UV-LA-ICP-MS to carnelian from Gujarat, India, and West Africa. *Journal of Archaeological Science* 31: 1161–73.

JOHNSTON, H. A. S., and MUFFETT, D. J. M. (1973). *Denham in Bornu*. Pittsburgh: Duquesne University Press.

LANGE, D. (1977). *Chronologie et Histoire d'un Royaume Africain (de la Fin du Xe Siècle Jusqu'à 1808)*. Wiesbaden: Franz Steiner.

—— (1987a). *A Sudanic Chronicle: The Borno Expeditions of Idris Alauma (1564–1576) according to the account of Ahmad b. Fūrtū*. Wiesbaden: Studien zur Kulturkunde.

—— (1987b). The evolution of the Hausa story: from Bawo to Bayajidda. *Afrika und Übersee* 70: 195–209.

—— and BERTHOUD, S. (1972). L'intérieur de l'Afrique occidentale d'après Giovanni Lorenzo Anania (XVIe siècle). *Cahiers d'Histoire Mondiale* 14: 299–351.

LAST, M. (1980). Historical metaphors in the Kano Chronicle. *History in Africa* 7: 161–78.

—— (1985). The early kingdoms of the Nigerian savanna. In J. F. A. Ajayi and M. Crowder (eds), *History of West Africa*, vol. 1. New York: Longman, 167–224.

LEBEUF, A. M. D. (1967). Boum Massénia, capitale de l'ancien royaume du Baguirmi. *Journal de la Société des Africanistes* 27: 214–44.

—— (1969). *Les Principautés Kotoko: Essai sur le Caractère Sacré de l'Autorité*. Paris: CNRS.

LEVTZION, N., and HOPKINS, J. F. P. (eds) (1981). *Corpus of Early Arabic Sources for West African History*. Translated by J. F. P. Hopkins. Cambridge: Cambridge University Press.

LIESEGANG, G. (2009). Selma (8th century BC), Takusheyi (13th/14th century AD) and Surame (16th/17th century AD): research on the rise of the Iron Age, the states of Katsina, Gobir and Kebbi, 'fossilized' urbanism in northern Nigeria 1990–1994 and the impact of paradigms. In A. Dohrmann, D. Bustorf, and N. Poissonnier (eds), *Schweifgebiete. Festschrift für Ulrich Braukämper*. Münster: Lit, 317–40.

LOVEJOY, P. E. (1978). The role of the wangara in the economic transformation of the Central Sudan in the fifteenth and sixteenth centuries. *Journal of African History* 19(2): 173–93.

—— (1982). Polanyi's 'ports of trade': Salaga and Kano in the nineteenth century. *Canadian Journal of African Studies* 16: 245–77.

—— (1986). *Salt of the Desert Sun: A History of Salt Production and Trade in the Central Sudan*. Cambridge: Cambridge University Press.

—— and BAIER, S. (1975). The desert-side economy of the central Sudan. *International Journal of African Historical Studies* 8: 551–81.

MACEACHERN, S. (1993). Selling the iron for their shackles: Wandala–Montagnard interactions in Northern-Cameroon. *Journal of African History* 34: 247–70.

—— (2001). State formation and enslavement in the Southern Lake Chad Basin. In C. DeCorse (ed.), *West Africa during the Atlantic Slave Trade: Archaeological Perspectives*. London: Leicester University Press, 131–51.

—— DATOUANG DJOUSSOU, J.-M., and JANSON, R. (2010). Research at DGB-1, Northern Cameroon, 2008. *Nyame Akuma* 73: 37–45.

MAGNAVITA, C. (2011). Birni Gazargamo: the early capital of Kanem-Borno. In D. Gronenborn (ed.), *Gold, Slaves and Ivory: Medieval Empires in Northern Nigeria*. Mainz: Römisch-Germanisches Zentralmuseum, 58–61.

—— ADEBAYO, O., HAHN, A., et al. (2009). Garu Kime: a late Borno fired-brick site at Monguno, NE Nigeria. *African Archaeological Review* 26: 219–46.

—— BREUNIG, P., AMEJE, J., and POSSELT, M. (2006). Zilum: a mid-first millennium BC fortified settlement near Lake Chad. *Journal of African Archaeology* 4: 153–69.

MONTEIL, P.-L. (1895). *De Saint-Louis à Tripoli par le Lac Tchad*. Paris: Germer Baillière.

MOODY, H. B. L. (1967). Ganuwa: the walls of Kano City. *Nigeria Magazine* 92: 19–38.

NACHTIGAL, G. (1971–87). *Sahara and Sudan*. Translated from the original German with new introduction and notes by A. G. B. Fisher and H. J. Fisher. London: Hurst.

NAST, H. J. (1996). Islam, gender, and slavery in West Africa circa 1500: a spatial archaeology of the Kano Palace, Northern Nigeria. *Annals of the Association of American Geographers* 86: 44–77.

OLANIYI, R. (2005). Kano: the development of a trading city in Central Sudan. In A. Ogundiran (ed.), *Precolonial Nigeria. Essays in Honor of Toyin Falola*. Trenton, NJ: Africa World Press, 301–18.

PALMER, H. R. (1908). The Kano Chronicle. *Journal of the Royal Anthropological Institute of Great Britain and Ireland* 38, 58–98.

REYNA, S. P. (1990). *Wars Without End: The Political Economy of a Precolonial African State.* Hanover, NH: University Press of New England.

ROHLFS, G. (1868/72). *Reise durch Nord-Afrika vom Mittelländischen Meere bis zum Busen von Guinea 1865 bis 1867.* Gotha: Ergänzungsheft No. 25 and 34 zu Petermann's 'Geographischen Mitteilungen'.

SULE, A. S. (2010). Kirfi, Bauchi: an archaeological investigation of the Hausa landscape. In A. Haour and B. Rossi (eds), *Being and Becoming Hausa.* Leiden: Brill, 165–86.

SMITH, A. (1987). The early states of the central Sudan. In A. Smith (ed.), *A Little New Light: Selected Historical Writings of Professor Abdullahi Smith*, vol. 1. Zaria: Gaskia Corporation, 80–130.

SUTTON, J. E. G. (1979). Towards a less orthodox history of Hausland. *Journal of African History* 20: 179–201.

WIESMÜLLER, B. (2001). *Die Entwicklung der Keramik von 3000 BP bis zur Gegenwart in den Tonebenen südlich des Tschadsees.* Frankfurt am Main: Johann Wolfgang Goethe-Universität. Accessed 9 Mar. 2011 at: http://publikationen.stub.uni-frankfurt.de/volltexte/2003/337/index.html

CHAPTER 59

TOWNS AND STATES OF THE WEST AFRICAN FOREST BELT

AKINWUMI OGUNDIRAN

INTRODUCTION

THREE historical processes shaped the origins, development, and proliferation of towns, as well as the ideas, practices, and institutions of social complexity, in West Africa's rainforest belt. First were the millennium-long population increases, the growth of farming communities, and the quest for agricultural land. Second were the towns that developed on major trading routes taking advantage of external commercial relations; and third was the convergence of sociopolitical expansion and external economic opportunities. This chapter emphasizes the importance of towns in the cultural history of the region, as well as the impacts of rainforest ecology on the character of these towns and states, but for reasons of space only those polities and settlements that have received considerable archaeological attention are discussed. Given the theme of this chapter, countries and regions that traverse the rainforest but where we currently have only tentative evidence of indigenous urbanization and state formation before the 19th century are left out of our discussion. These include Guinea-Bissau, Liberia, Sierra Leone, and Ivory Coast. However, we anticipate that future archaeological research may redress this gap.

The archaeological map of urbanization and social complexity in the rainforest belt and its fringes is very spotty (Fig. 59.1) because systematic regional-scale archaeological exploration is made difficult by poor surface visibility and difficult accessibility (see Connah 2008), unlike in the more open Sahel and savannah areas to the north, where most archaeological efforts on the subject of urbanization and state formation in West Africa have concentrated (Gronenborn, Ch. 58 above; MacDonald, Ch. 57 above).

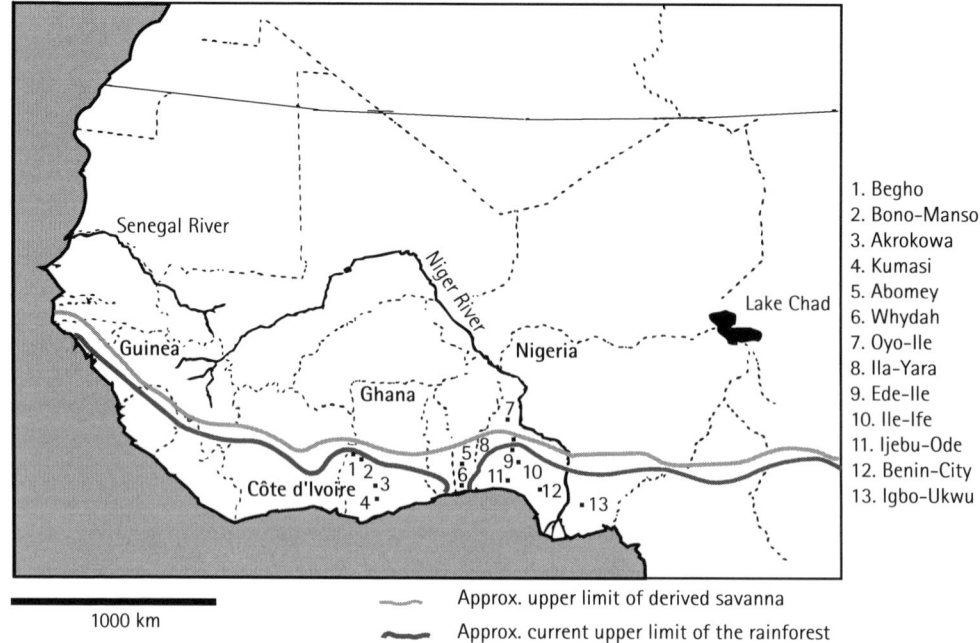

FIG. 59.1 Map of West Africa showing sites mentioned in Chapter 59 (Akinwumi Ogundiran).

EARLY EVIDENCE OF URBAN CENTRES
AND SOCIAL COMPLEXITY

The cultural foundations of the towns and polities of West Africa's rainforest were laid with the development of food production in the first millennium BC (Casey, Ch. 41 above). The fragile rainforest soils and the enormous energy needed for forest clearing seem to have delayed the concentration of populations large enough to form the first towns and complex societies until the late first millennium AD. The rainforest clearing also expanded the habitat for malaria-carrying mosquitoes, thereby increasing the exposure of the settler-farmers to malaria and other debilitating mosquito-borne ailments. The consequence would have been a high mortality rate and low life expectancy in the early farming phases—especially between the second millennium BC and the mid-first millennium AD. This no doubt slowed population growth. These difficulties were overcome, or at least mitigated, through the evolution of partial genetic resistance (i.e. selection for sickle haemoglobin genes) and successful experimentations with herbal remedies (Livingstone 1989).

By the end of the first millennium AD, when urbanism and institutionalized political hierarchies began ossifying into the embodied sociopolitical practices that survive in many parts of the rainforest belt today, the region's ecological landscape was already a mosaic (Vincens et al. 1999). Secondary forest was interspersed with remnants of primary forest, more open bush fallows, farmlands, and settlements. Since the rainforest belt's northern boundaries probably shifted south by at least 50 km during the past 2,000 years, creating an expanding band of derived savannah vegetation in the transitional zone between what is now mostly secondary forest in the south and savannah proper in the north, this chapter covers urban phenomena in both the rainforest and its fringes (cf. Connah 2001).

The increasing scale of social organization that swept across the rainforest and its fringes during the late first/early second millennia AD was imprinted on parts of the rainforest belt by several settlement embankments. This is currently most noticeable in southwestern Nigeria and southern Ghana (e.g. Chouin 2009; Chouin and DeCorse 2010; Darling 1984). There are indications that between the Birim and Pra Valleys, in modern Ghana, farming communities constructed ditch-and-embankments around their settlements during the late first millennium AD (Chouin and DeCorse 2010; also see Kiyaga-Mulindwa 1982). These earthwork settlements generally seem to have been below 400 m in diameter, and rarely exceeded one kilometre in circumference. However, they were densely populated until the mid-14th century, when they were suddenly abandoned over a short period of time. Patrick Darling's path-breaking archaeological survey in the Edo-Esan area of southwestern Nigeria has uncovered over 16,000 km of concentric earthworks forming boundaries around more than 500 interconnected settlements, enclosing a total area of 6,500 km^2 (Darling 1984). His work showed how agricultural communities, who combined yam, oil palm, and vegetable cultivation with hunting and gathering, gradually built up their landscape over time beginning from about AD 500. The largest early enclosures are 3–5 km in diameter and appear to demarcate residential units with their adjoining farmlands, including fallows (Fig. 59.2). Several were enlarged as residential units increased in population size and the adjoining land became available. Between AD 800 and 1000, a large number of these walled villages coalesced (perhaps through voluntary alliances as well as conquest) into larger polities with institutionalized hierarchies, social differentiation, and socioeconomic specializations. As population increased, and the prime area for frontier expansion narrowed, ideologies of unilineal descent based on walled settlements as the preferred units of social organization were probably elaborated in order to access farmland and provide for defence.

It is not clear whether any of the southern Ghanaian earthwork settlements ever evolved into a formal township with diversified economic base, multi-lineage identities, political centralization, and institutionalized social hierarchies. The relationship between these early earthwork settlements and the later centralized political centres such as Kumasi is not known. In contrast, it is fairly certain that it was from the long processes of agricultural expansion and construction of earthwork settlements in the Edo-Esan region that the city of Benin emerged in southwestern Nigeria between the late 12th and mid-13th centuries (Connah 1975; Darling 1998a).

The scale and size of Benin's earthworks reveal something of the dynamics of early urbanism and state formation in the rainforest belt. The main and innermost wall system consisted of a bank and ditch, the embankment having an average height of 17.4 m and a circumference of about 11.6 km. Radiocarbon dates suggest that these core walls were constructed in the late 12th/early 13th centuries (Connah 1975), and it seems likely that they refer to the mature stage of Benin's existence as a city-state or urban kingdom. Earlier phases still await discovery. Benin's rise as an urban centre was probably a political solution to the power struggle between it and other polities in the area for land and for control of trading routes that linked the emerging polities of the rainforest belt. From a strictly archaeological perspective, however, we know little of what Benin City looked like until its invasion by the British in 1897 (see Andah 1982 for a critique). It was, however, undoubtedly occupied by farmers, artisans,

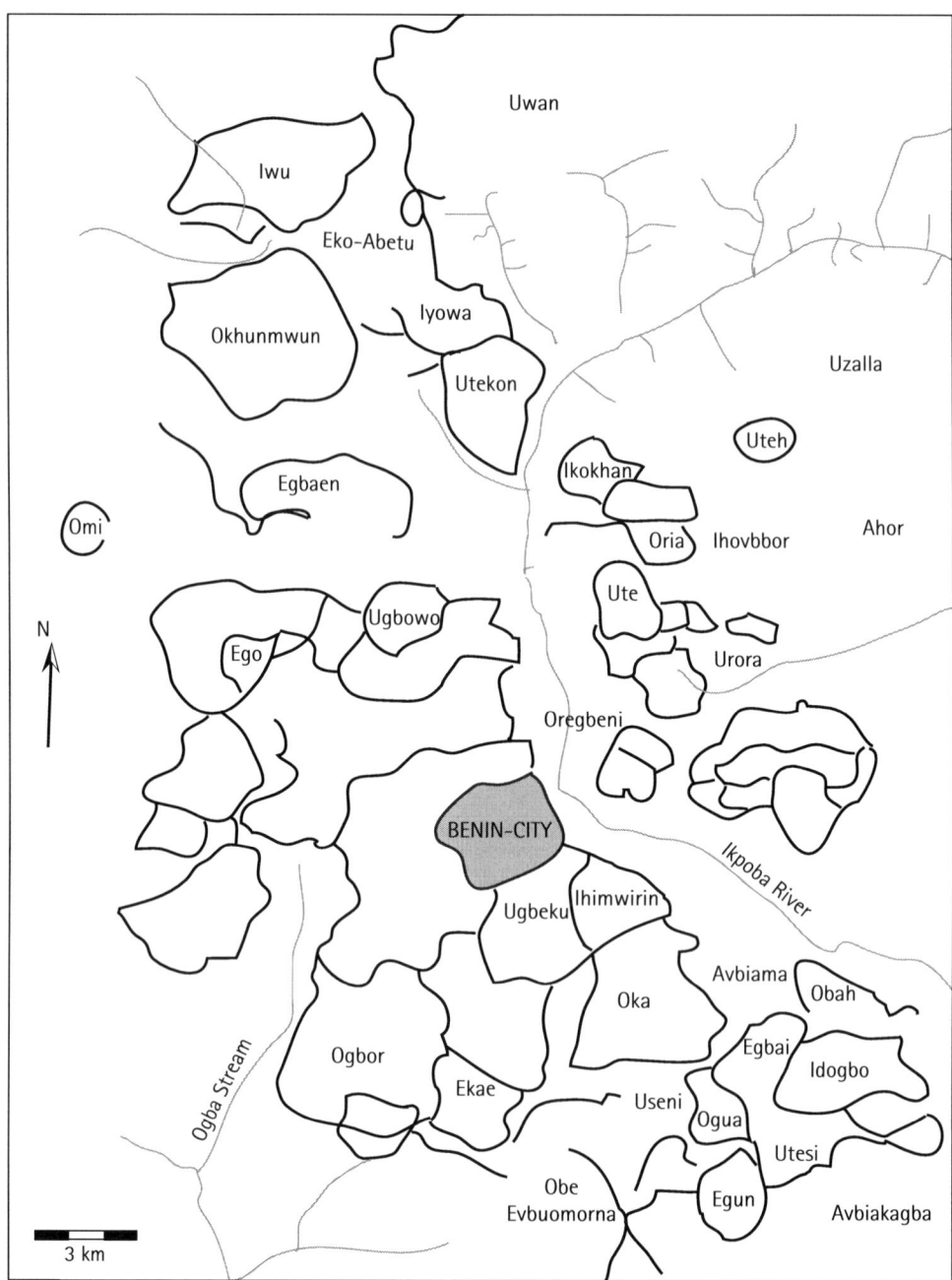

FIG. 59.2 Layout of the Esan-Edo wall complex, Nigeria (Akinwumi Ogundiran, redrawn from Darling 1984).

administrators, and members of the political 'class', especially the king and the leaders of corporate groups. The presence of ivory ornaments, copper and bronze bracelets, elephant tusks, iron finger rings, and carnelian beads in a 12.5 m-deep cistern in the old palace ground indicates the existence of a diverse specialized craft production.

The elaborate specialized craft for which Benin is justly famous seems to have been concomitant with the establishment and consolidation of centralized political authority and institutions that focused primarily on the king. Both archaeological evidence and oral traditions point to the 13th century as the starting point of this development (Egharevba 1968; Connah 1975). Of all the numerous media of Benin arts, three were intimately associated with royalty: coral beads, ivory, and brass/bronze artworks. The kings of Benin monopolized the use of coral beads as their ultimate insignia of authority, and retained the rights to grant a few chiefs the authority to use ivory as badges of office. The crafted brass/bronze objects are, however, the most numerous, and give us the best insights into the development of kingship institution and the rise of Benin political centralization. It appears that until the 15th century, copper/bronze smithing was minimal in Benin and the raw materials probably came primarily from Ile-Ife and from the Nupe territory in the Lower Middle Niger. The sources of the copper-alloy materials, however, shifted after the 15th century, with European traders becoming the primary suppliers of brass (alloy of copper and zinc) to Benin in unprecedented quantities. Hence, successive Benin kings throughout the 17th and 18th centuries used brass sculptures—commemorative heads and plaques—to communicate their authority, power, legitimacy, ideology, and interpretations of events to the public (Ben-Amos 1995).

Benin was not the oldest known urban centre in the rainforest belt. Ile-Ife, in central Yorubaland, so far occupies this position. Ile-Ife also appears to be a product of the nucleation of several agricultural villages (Akintoye 2010). Since most archaeological investigations have been rescue operations, driven by the accidental discovery of sculptures, the broad settlement history and sociopolitical development of this early urban centre are not yet delineated. The corpus and scope of archaeological data from Ile-Ife nevertheless surpass those available for any contemporary urban centre in West Africa's rainforest belt. Recent efforts have focused on interpreting the cultural, economic, and sociopolitical aspects of these archaeological evidence and the regional contexts in which they functioned during the city's Classical period (AD 1000–1500) (Ogundiran 2003). This period witnessed the construction of concentric walls that defined the new urban landscape—an inner wall about 7 km in circumference and a much bigger outer wall some 15 km in length (Ozanne 1969; Fig. 59.3). The paving of several roads and the floors of elite houses and religious sites with potsherds, often laid on edge in herringbone patterns, is a distinctive material characteristic of Ife's urban space (Garlake 1974). Some elite houses also had their walls decorated with ceramic discs—more than 13,000 at the Woye Asiri site alone (Garlake 1977).

The spatial continuity of archaeological finds within and immediately beyond the city walls indicates that Ile-Ife was a densely nucleated settlement, with 70,000–105,000 people probably living there at its 14th/15th-century peak (Kusimba et al. 2006). The process of nucleation was accompanied by a major transformation in political organization, ideology of power and worldview. Central to all these was the ideology of divine kingship, perhaps the most significant of all the institutions developed at Ile-Ife.

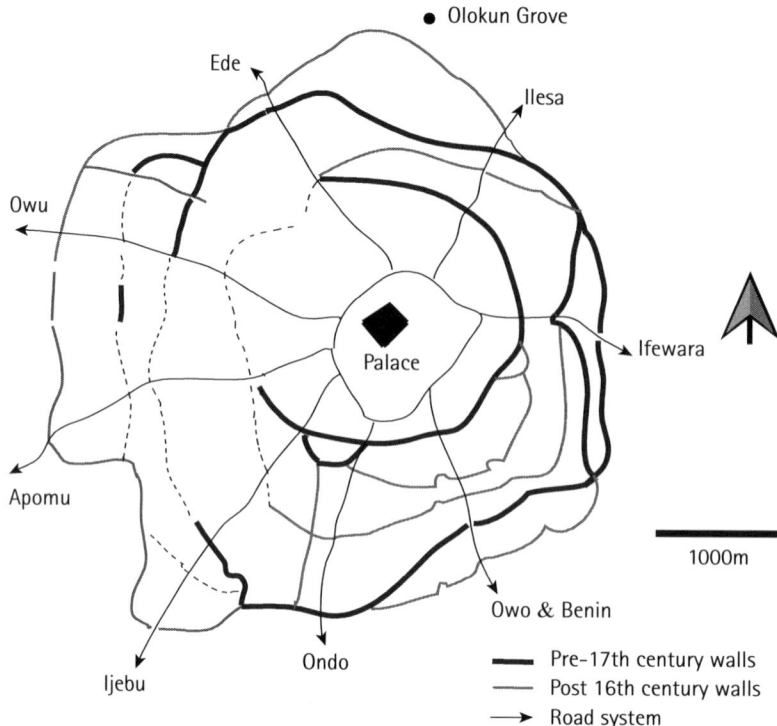

FIG. 59.3 Layout of the Ile-Ife wall complex, Nigeria (Akinwumi Ogundiran, redrawn from Ozanne 1969).

Mortuary evidence indicates that social differentiation intensified throughout the Classical period. Glass and carnelian beads, terracotta, granite, and copper alloy sculptures and occasional human sacrifices accompanied the burials of the elite (Garlake 1974). Life-size naturalistic sculptures (Fig. 59.4) of deceased members of the elite indicate that their cults and shrines were the focus of intensive religious activity and provided a key source of legitimacy for the exercise of political power, authority, inheritance, and group identity (Drewal and Schildkrout 2009).

Brass and bronze casting using the lost-wax method and glass bead manufacture were at least partly controlled by the elite, especially the royalty. It is generally assumed that copper, bronze, and brass sheets were imports into Ile-Ife from the Sahara via the Niger Bend. The production of crafts was very extensive in Ile-Ife after the 10th century AD, and archaeologists have identified an 'industrial' site where the manufacture of glass beads, iron, and perhaps brass/bronze sculptures took place. This is the Olokun grove, less than 2 km from the palace area (see Fig. 59.3). The site has yielded artefacts such as beads, cullet, ceramic crucibles, tuyère fragments, furnaces, and dimpled stones (used for bead grinding and polishing). It is particularly famous for its large-scale glass beads production (Eluyemi 1987; Babalola 2013). With glass beads serving as the most important paraphernalia of Yoruba kingship and social ranking, the evidence of primary glass production in Olokun grove (Lankton et al. 2006) shows the centrality of Ile-Ife to the institutionalization of kingship ideology in the Yoruba-Edo region (Horton 1992: 132; Ogundiran 2003, 2009a).

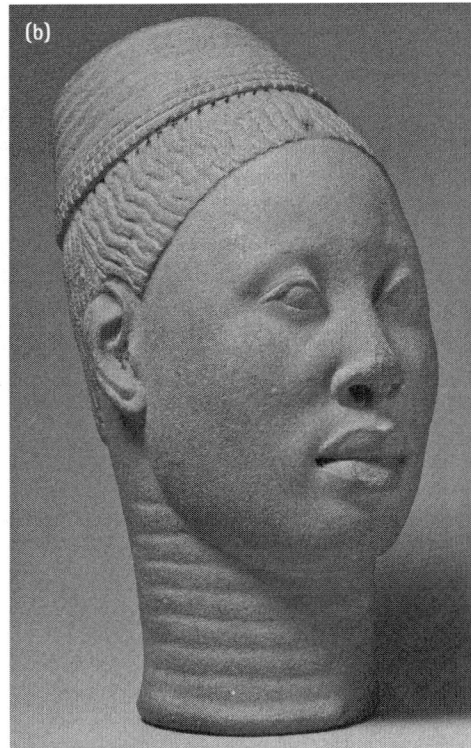

FIG. 59.4 Copper-alloy bust of a king of Ife, early 16th century (height 37 cm) and a terracotta head of a prominent palace official, Lajuwa, 13th–14th centuries (height 32 cm) (National Commission for Museum and Monuments, Nigeria).

The political centralization and material culture elaboration associated with Ife took place in a milieu of region-wide political, economic, social, and cultural networks that reached as far as Benin in the east (Egharevba 1968) and the Sabe territory in the west in the present-day Bénin Republic (Akintoye 2010). The model of divine kingship instituted at Ife came to be seen as the natural order of sociopolitical organization at the regional level, and the elaboration of systems of political centralization and kingship stimulated the further embellishment of the elite material culture, drawing on exotic prestige goods acquired through sustained, if intermittent, socioeconomic relations with communities elsewhere in the rainforest and further north in the savannah and Sahel, especially the Upper Middle Niger. Ile-Ife thus served not only as a political centre but also as a trade entrepôt where forest products, ivory, pepper, and kola nuts were exchanged for Saharan and Sudanese salt, cloth, and copper alloys (Horton 1992). Since gold-bearing deposits exist just 10 km north of the city near a 14th-century town (Itagunmodi) with potsherd pavements (Agbaje-Williams 1995), Ile-Ife may itself have been a supplier of gold to the Mali Empire.

Dates associated with other earthwork complexes in the rainforest belt, such as Sungbo Eredo (Darling 1998b), suggest that large-scale political units developed simultaneously across the Yoruba region at the very end of the first millennium AD. Urbanization and social complexity seem to have reached maturity at about the same time—13th century—in both the rainforest and savannah belts of the Yoruba region. The key town of the Yoruba savannah, Oyo-Ile, appears to have evolved *c.* 1200–1400, perhaps through the forceful merger of several smaller earlier polities (Akintoye 2010). By 1600, however, it was a major urban centre with multiple defensive walls enclosing a high density of residential structures. At its mid-18th century peak as the capital of the Oyo Empire it covered more than 5000 ha and, like Benin and Ile-Ife, was focused both politically and spatially around the institution of divine kingship and the palace that housed it (Agbaje-Williams 1983). Through aggressive military campaigns that were based on cavalry, with the purpose of controlling the trade routes linking the savannah to the coast (Ogundiran 2009b), Oyo-Ile served as a major catalyst for the establishment of new towns and the centralization of authority in northern Yorubaland between the 16th and 18th centuries (Usman 2004).

Westward, the Akan territory of Ghana has also produced early instances of towns and kingdoms. A prominent archaeological example is Begho, located in the rainforest–savannah ecotone (see Fig. 59.1). Already occupied by an internally differentiated agricultural community in the 12th century, it was not until the early 1400s that Begho became a major transit market town for exporting gold from the Akan goldfields and kola nuts from the rainforest hinterlands to the Upper Middle Niger (Posnansky 1973). Identifying about 1,500 mounds, including middens and the deflated walls of houses and workshops, that collectively cover a total area of about 375 ha, archaeological survey has shown that the site grew exponentially from the 14th to 17th centuries. As Posnansky (1973) and Anquandah (1993) have noted, Begho was a multi-ethnic and cosmopolitan town divided into non-contiguous quarters that followed the ethnic, occupational, and religious identities of its residents: the Akan-speaking Brong; the Kramo (Muslims from Mali); the Dwinfuor (artisanal quarter); and the Nyarko (a mixed group). Each quarter retained considerable autonomy though placed under a common centralized authority (Fig. 59.5).

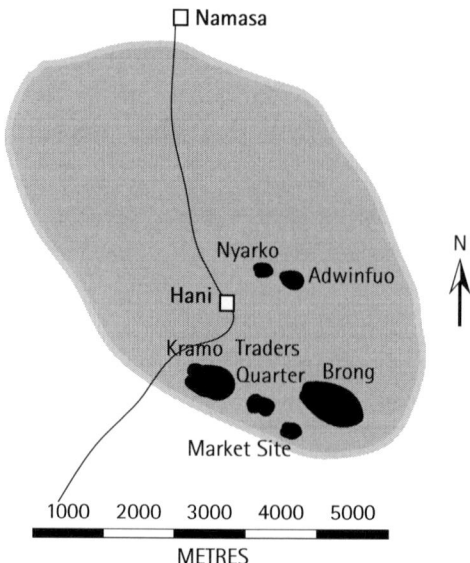

FIG. 59.5 Greater Begho, Ghana, showing the adjoining quarters (Akinwumi Ogundiran, redrawn from Anquandah 1993).

More than an importing and transit market town, Begho fostered local industries and served as a centrifugal force for increased and diversified production, consumption, and circulation of goods in the Akan region until the 17th century. Ivory wasters, spindle whorls, dye pits, and clay crucibles for copper smelting demonstrate the diversity of crafts practised in addition to pottery production. Recent archaeological investigations also show that Begho's hinterland extended up to 30 km in all directions, with villages such as Dapaa and Kulo Kataa consuming Begho's pottery and cloth in exchange for iron and ivory ornaments respectively (Stahl 2001; Stahl and Stahl 2004).

Located in the same region and ecotonal situation as Begho, Bono Manso was ethnically a more homogenous settlement. Founded in the 13th century, it became increasingly more compact and house units became larger as its population grew from the mid-1400s until its abandonment in the 18th century (Effah-Gyamfi 1985). This residential change correlates with Bono Manso's increasing integration into long-distance trade networks linking it with both the Sahel and the coast, but also seems to imply a transformation toward a more centralized form of political organization.

Not all cases of social complexity in the rainforest were accompanied by urbanization. Unique in the archaeology of social complexity in West Africa's rainforest belt is Igbo-Ukwu. Here, we have evidence of institutionalized sociopolitical hierarchies but without the support of an urban centre (Shaw 1970; also see Anozie 1992). Evidence comes from three adjacent sites—Igbo Richard (a grave), Igbo Isaiah (a shrine), and Igbo Jonah (a storage pit). The grave consisted of the remains of a high-ranking man buried in a sitting position in a timber chamber with five other individuals above him. Considering all three sites together, finds included 165,000 (mostly glass) beads, ivory tusks, and ornately decorated bronze sculptures and ceramic vessels (Shaw 1970). They attest to the concentration of wealth in the hands of one or a few individual(s), who possibly held vital political power, including the power over life and death. Seven radiocarbon dates place the sites between the 8th and 11th centuries AD (Shaw 1995: 43).

The political institution that supported the position of the elite individual buried at Igbo Richard is unknown, though Shaw (1970) suggested that it might represent a figure akin to the *Eze Nri*, a titled office-holder with religious and judicial functions in the Oreri and Aguku areas only a few kilometres from Igbo-Ukwu (Onwujeogwu 1981). Keith Ray (1987: 77) has argued that the 'pervasive ritual' icons in the Igbo-Ukwu material served 'to project aspects of the pivotal role of the priest-king within . . . Igbo life and thought'. His interpretations are suggestive of how political rituals and belief systems shaped the ideology and power of the *Nze Nri* authority in Igboland between the 10th and 14th centuries. The existing data give us only glimpses on how successive leaders and their coterie acquired the wealth in imported beads, copper, labour, and knowledge/skills which they evidently controlled to advance the materialization of their power and authority. Goods and labour obtained in return for their local ritual/political activities and privileges may have helped to support specialist craftsmen and to mobilize exports such as ivory, kola nuts, and perhaps metal to exchange for the huge numbers of glass beads and perhaps other imports, such as textiles and horses, found in the excavations. Without doubt, the Igbo-Ukwu finds indicate that segments of Igboland participated in the transcontinental trading networks that passed through the Niger-Benue Valley and from there onward to North Africa, either through the Niger Bend and the Sahara (especially via Gao; Insoll and Shaw 1997) or through the Lake Chad Basin to Nubia and the Nile Valley (Sutton 1991).

TOWNS AND SOCIAL COMPLEXITY AFTER C. 1500

As pioneers in the cultural efflorescence of the rainforest and its fringes, Begho, Benin, Bono Manso, Ile-Ife, Igbo-Ukwu, and Oyo-Ile are canonical in the archaeology of social complexity and urbanization in West Africa's rainforest belt (Connah 2001). Towns seem to have exploded in number and diversity across the Bight of Benin and the Gold Coast and their hinterlands after the 16th century in the middle phase of the commercial relations between Europeans and Africans (c. 1600–1800). This proliferation was part of a major shift in settlement pattern away from the villages and small-scale societies that had straddled the coastal area for over 1,000 years (DeCorse 2005; see Thiaw and Richard, Ch. 68 below) and towards larger and cosmopolitan settlements both on the coast and in the trading corridors that connected the rainforest and savannah hinterlands to the Atlantic coast. Most of these towns flourished as a result of the expanding transatlantic commercial life in which craft specialization in the manufacture of everyday objects (e.g. tobacco pipes and cloth) boomed. Urbanization also intensified as part of the rise of militaristic hegemonic states, such as Oyo, Benin, Dahomey, and Asante. Unlike earlier patrimonial kingdoms and city-states (such as Ile-Ife) which only weakly integrated outlying territories into their metropolises, the hegemonic states built integrated and hierarchical political economic landscapes, with provinces that functioned firmly within the orbit of the state capitals (e.g. Monroe 2007). This new vision of political control involved population resettlement, the establishment of trading towns, colonization, and the construction of public structures. The net result was the transformation of the Bight of Benin and the Gold Coast hinterlands into the most urbanized landscape in Africa during the 18th century.

One good example of this Atlantic Age phenomenon is the Hueda kingdom in modern Bénin (e.g. Norman 2012). Extensive systematic regional survey suggests a three-tier political landscape for Hueda with the capital of Savi at the top, followed by semi-autonomous provincial towns in the middle and villages and hamlets at the base. Savi served the surrounding countryside as a centre for religious, political, economic, and judicial processes. The distribution patterns of artefacts and architectural features show that the countryside was densely populated, and that provincial towns and their outlying countryside were economically integrated in the production and distribution of domestic products. However, the goods germane to forging sociopolitical capital were retained primarily in Savi, and the monarchy had a minimal presence in the provinces, underlining how weakly provincial elites and their followers were integrated into the kingdom's political economy. In contrast, the Dahomean monarchy, which conquered Hueda in 1727, built palaces and established towns across its territories, especially along the major trading highways through which the state delivered human captives to the European traders on the coast and through which it received imported goods in return. This widespread distribution of palace complexes and towns facilitated the much fuller integration of conquered people and lands into the political and economic structures of the Dahomean state (Monroe 2007).

A little over a century before the Dahomean exploit, the savannah city-state of Oyo launched its imperial project by establishing military/administrative/trading colonies in the heart of the rainforest belt, often in areas of major flow of commerce and itinerant traders. The first of these colonies was probably at Ede-Ile, a densely populated walled settlement in central Yorubaland, about 150 km from Oyo itself. The colonists modified the local landscape by planting baobab trees, a savannah species, mostly used Oyo ceramics, and also obtained horses from the capital for transportation and warfare (Ogundiran 2009b). In Yorubaland as a whole, the combination of increasing population as well as the increasing scale of production specialization and commercial activities (in part linked to the imperatives of the Atlantic coast) stimulated the proliferation of towns across the region between 1550 and 1800. Most of these evolved independently of the large, expansionist polities, and tended to be smaller, with populations in the range of 2,000–3,000 (e.g. Ogundiran 2003).

The advent of the Atlantic slave trade did not, however, always produce increasing nucleation. It also led to the decimation of pre-existing polities and towns, especially those built on heterarchical, decentralized political principles. In pre-Atlantic Eguafo, Ghana, for example, traders, ritual specialists, corporate/lineage leaders, and other elites shared power and resources with the paramount ruler at the centre (Spiers 2012).

Discussion and conclusion

The urban centres examined here functioned as political centres, but were also centres of commercial activity, technological innovation, craft specialization, and the high-volume production of consumable commodities. Their political prominence was also often woven into religious and ritual prominence and a few, such as Ile-Ife, articulated a distinct ideology that centred on divine kingship. They were also nodes of economic redistribution, consuming goods of both distant and local origins, and recycling them to maintain patron–client relationships.

The evidence we have so far in the rainforest belt, especially in the Esan–Benin region, strongly indicates that the expansion of agricultural communities culminated in the emergence of the first towns during the third quarter of the first millennium AD. By then the frontiers of population expansion were becoming narrower, necessitating the enlargement of existing settlements. Through processes of synoecism, natural population increase by birth, migration of displaced families, and conquest, such large settlements came to house diverse lineages of different origins and with diverse specializations in medicine, ritual activities, ironworking, and other knowledge-based skills. Ile-Ife and Benin are good examples of the mature city-states that arose in this way. Such early developments may also have taken place not just in the upper reaches of the rainforest but also in the southern frontiers of Yorubaland, possibly during the 10th century in the Ijebu area (Darling 1998b). The maturation of these early towns as bastions of agricultural communities and diversified crafts specialization coincided with transcontinental and regional commercial expansions. In some cases, as at Ile-Ife and perhaps also Igbo-Ukwu, elites tapped into these networks to acquire and redistribute wealth goods that helped them naturalize their political pre-eminence. However, this was not universally so: in central Ghana, for example, although the pull of external trade played a direct role in promoting settlement nucleation, political institutions seem to have retained heterarchical character until the 15th century.

The role of ideology and worldview in the formation and proliferation of urban culture is still insufficiently acknowledged, but both were probably particularly important in the development of urbanization and kingship in the Yoruba–Edo area, extending between present-day southern Bénin and southwestern Nigeria, relative to elsewhere in West Africa's rainforest. The concept of 'town' as the political centre of a polity ruled by a divine king seems to have developed simultaneously between AD 800 and 1000 among several agricultural communities in the Yoruba–Edo region, attaining its most elaborate materialization at Ile-Ife beginning in the 11th century. By then embodied facts of life, the town and divine kingship, as both idea and practice, were replicated at hastened pace between the 13th and 15th centuries across the Yoruba region (Ogundiran 2003). Having assumed ideological existentialist status, the urban centre was more than a seat of power or commerce. It had become a seat of culture and the embodiment of a supra-corporate identity, the polity ruled by a divine king.

The foregoing implies that two major goals defined the character of towns in West Africa's rainforest belt, one community-building, the other authority-building. The early towns of central Ghana and parts of Nigeria's Yoruba–Edo region tend to typify community-building processes, in which corporate groups such as lineages, trading diasporas, and migrants formed governing associations that produced an expanded settlement space—the town. Aspects of these processes perhaps worked in favour of creating the priest-king institution in Igboland, but without creating towns. Later urban centres, on the other hand, especially those established by the militaristic states and empires of the 17th and 18th centuries, were the products of authority-building processes.

Contrary to the popular imagery, the ancestral West Africa's rainforest peoples were intensely mobile, worldly in material goods, and cosmopolitan in their worldview. The demography was very uneven, with the areas encompassing the present-day Ghana, Bénin, and Nigeria being far more densely populated at the end of the first millennium AD than the western axis of the region. It was in the former where we currently have evidence of early and indigenous towns and large-scale polities. Social hierarchies, based on political power, technological skills, age, and religious/spiritual knowledge, characterized the sociopolitical formations, but these hierarchies were permeable and never ossified into rigid class structures. Political power was also very diffuse. Even in states with elaborate kingship institution, power was shared between the royalty and the chieftains of the different lineages that made up the town or city. Although farming was the basis of the economy, domestic craft specialization took roots in the second half of the first millennium AD, laying the groundwork for the itinerant trading and market fairs that generally defined the landscape of the region.

Despite the quickened pace of systematic archaeological research in recent years, critical gaps remain in the study of urbanization and complex society in West Africa. Urbanism and state formation have too often been treated in abstract terms that exclude them from the exegesis of everyday lives, including those at the level of individual households. We need to balance our emphasis on the institutions of towns as gleaned from walls/ditches and sculptures of power with the study of society, i.e. of the people who populated the urban centres. Moreover, our emphasis on the urban space itself has not been matched by proper investigations of the relationship between towns and their rural hinterlands. This is where regional research designs would be useful, despite all the challenges likely to arise from the forest's dense vegetation. Determining the relationship between urban centres and their countryside would allow us to understand towns and cities as part of larger political entities, for the political economy that sustained them can only be grasped when they are investigated in relation to contemporaneous cultural processes at the regional level, properly emphasizing how corporate and individual members used the circulation of goods, ideas, and skills in power negotiations to form and sustain both urban centres and their own political agendas.

REFERENCES

AKINTOYE, S. A. (2010). *A History of the Yoruba People*. Dakar: Amalion.

AGBAJE-WILLIAMS, B. (1983). A contribution to the archaeology of Old Oyo. Ph.D dissertation, University of Ibadan.

—— (1995). *Archaeological Investigation of Itagunmodi Potsherd Pavement Site, Ijesaland, Osun State, Nigeria, 1991/92*. Ibadan: Institute of African Studies.

ALAGOA, E. J., ANOZIE, F. N., and NZEWUNWA, N. (eds) (1989). *The Early History of the Niger Delta*. Hamburg and Port Harcourt: Helmut Buske and University of Port Harcourt Press.

ANDAH, B. W. (1982). Urban 'origins' in the Guinea Forest with special reference to Benin. *West African Journal of Archaeology* 12: 63–71.

ANOZIE, F. N. (1992). Igbo-Ukwu after Thurstan Shaw. *West African Journal of Archaeology* 22: 40–46.

ANQUANDAH, J. (1993). Urbanization and state formation in Ghana during the Iron Age. In T. Shaw, P. J. J. Sinclair, B. Andah, and A. Okpoko (eds), *The Archaeology of Africa: Food, Metals and Towns*. London: Routledge, 642–51.

BABALOLA, A. B. (2013). Emerging perspectives on the archaeology of Ile-Ife, Southwest Nigeria: glass and glass beads production. In A. S. Ajala (ed.), *Orality, Myth and Archaeological Practice*. Cologne: Rudiger Koeppe Verlag, 56–77.

BEN-AMOS, P. G. (1995). *The Art of Benin*. Washington, DC: Smithsonian Institution Press.

CONNAH, G. (1975). *The Archaeology of Benin: Excavations and Other Researches in and Around Benin City, Nigeria*. Oxford: Clarendon Press.

—— (2001). *African Civilizations: An Archaeological Perspective*. Cambridge: Cambridge University Press.

—— (2008). Urbanism and the archaeological visibility of African complex societies. *Journal of African Archaeology* 6: 233–41.

CHOUIN, G. L. (2009). Forests of power and memory: an archaeology of sacred groves in the Eguafo polity, southern Ghana (*c.* 500–1900 A.D.). Ph.D dissertation, Syracuse University.

—— and DECORSE, C. R. (2010). Prelude to the Atlantic trade: new perspectives on southern Ghana's pre-Atlantic history (800–1500). *Journal of African History* 51: 123–45.

DARLING, P. (1984). *Archaeology and History in Southern Nigeria*. Oxford: British Archaeological Reports.

—— (1998a). A legacy in earth: ancient Benin and Ishan, southern Nigeria. In K. W. Wesler (ed.), *Historical Archaeology in Nigeria*. Trenton, NJ: Africa World Press, 143–97.

—— (1998b). Sungbo's Eredo, southern Nigeria. *Nyame Akuma* 49: 55–61.

DECORSE, C. R. (2005). Coastal Ghana in the first and second millennia AD: change in settlement patterns, subsistence and technology. *Journal des Africanistes* 75: 43–54.

DREWAL, H. J., and SCHILDKROUT, E. (2009). *Dynasty and Divinity: Ife Art in Ancient Nigeria*. New York: Museum for African Art.

EFFAH-GYAMFI, K. (1985). *Bono Manso: An Archaeological Investigation into Early Akan Urbanism*. Calgary: University of Calgary Press.

EGHAREVBA, J. U. (1968 [1934]). *A Short History of Benin*, 4th edn. Ibadan: University of Ibadan Press.

ELUYEMI, O. (1987). The technology of the Ife glass beads: evidence from the Igbo-Olokun. *Odu* 32: 200–216.

GARLAKE, P. S. (1974). Excavations at Obalara's land, Ife, Nigeria. *West African Journal of Archaeology* 4: 111–48.

—— (1977). Excavations on the Woye Asiri family land in Ife, western Nigeria. *West African Journal of Archaeology* 7: 57–95.

HORTON, R. (1992). The economy of Ife from *c.* A.D. 900–1700. In A. Akinjogbin (ed.), *The Cradle of a Race: Ife from the Beginning to 1980.* Port Harcourt: Sunray Publications, 122–47.

INSOLL, T., and SHAW, T. (1997). Gao and Igbo-Ukwu: beads, interregional trade and beyond. *African Archaeological Review* 14: 9–24.

KIYAGA-MULINDWA, D. (1982). Social and demographic changes in the Birim Valley, southern Ghana, *c.* 1450 to *c.* 1800. *Journal of African History* 23: 63–82.

KUSIMBA, C., BARUT-KUSIMBA, S., and AGBAJE-WILLIAMS, B. (2006). Precolonial African cities: size and density. In G. Storey (ed.), *Urbanism in the Preindustrial World: Cross-Cultural Approaches.* Tuscaloosa: University of Alabama Press, 145–60.

LANKTON, J. W., IGE, O. A., and REHREN, T. (2006). Early primary glass production in southern Nigeria. *Journal of African Archaeology* 4: 111–38.

LIVINGSTONE, F. B. (1989). Who gave whom hemoglobin S? The use of restriction site haplotype variation for the interpretation of the evolution of the BS-globin gene. *American Journal of Human Biology* 1: 289–302.

MONROE, C. (2007). Dahomey and the Atlantic slave trade: archaeology and political order on the Bight of Benin. In A. Ogundiran and T. Falola (eds), *The Archaeology of Atlantic Africa and the African Diaspora.* Bloomington: Indiana University Press, 100–121.

NORMAN, N. (2012). From the shadow of an Atlantic citadel: an archaeology of the Huedan countryside. In J. C. Monroe and A. Ogundiran (eds), *Power and Landscape in Atlantic West Africa: Archaeological Perspectives.* Cambridge: Cambridge University Press.

OGUNDIRAN, A. (2003). Chronology, material culture, and pathways to the cultural history of Yoruba-Edo Region, Nigeria, 500 B.C.–A.D. 1800. In T. Falola and C. Jennings (eds), *Sources and Methods in African History: Spoken, Written, Unearthed.* Rochester, NY: University of Rochester Press, 33–79.

—— (2009a). Frontier migrations and cultural transformations in Yoruba hinterland, ca. 1575–1700: the case of Upper Osun. In T. Falola and A. Usman (eds), *Movements, Border and Identities Formation in Africa.* Rochester, NY: University of Rochester Press, 37–52.

—— (2009b). Material life and domestic economy in the frontier of the Oyo Empire during the Mid-Atlantic Age. *International Journal of African Historical Studies* 42: 351–85.

ONWUJEOGWU, M. A. (1981). *An Igbo Civilization: Nri Kingdom and Hegemony.* London: Ethnographica.

OZANNE, P. (1969). A new archaeological survey of Ife. *Odu* 1: 28–45.

POSNANSKY, M. (1973). Aspects of early West African trade. *World Archaeology* 5: 149–62.

RAY, K. (1987). Material metaphor, social interaction and historical reconstructions: exploring patterns of association and symbolism in the Igbo Ukwu corpus. In I. Hodder (ed.), *The Archaeology of Contextual Meanings.* Cambridge: Cambridge University Press, 66–77.

SHAW, T. (1970). *Igbo-Ukwu: An Account of Archaeological Discoveries in Eastern Nigeria.* London: Faber & Faber.

—— (1995). Those Igbo-Ukwu dates again. *Nyame Akuma* 44: 43.

SPIERS, S. (2012). The Eguafo polity: between the traders and the raiders. In J. C. Monroe and A. Ogundiran (eds), *Landscapes of Power: Regional Perspectives on West African Polities in the Atlantic Era.* Cambridge: Cambridge University Press.

STAHL, A. B. (2001). *Making History in Banda: Anthropological Visions of Africa's Past*. Cambridge: Cambridge University Press.

—— and STAHL, P. W. (2004). Ivory production and consumption in Ghana in the early second millennium AD. *Antiquity* 78: 86–101.

SUTTON, J. E. G. (1991). The international factor at Igbo-Ukwu. *African Archaeological Review* 9: 145–60.

USMAN, A. (2004). On the frontier of empire: understanding the enclosed walls in northern Yoruba, Nigeria. *Journal of Anthropological Archaeology* 23: 119–32.

VINCENS, A., SCHWARTZ, D., ELENGA, H., et al. (1999). Forest response to climate changes in Atlantic Equatorial Africa during the last 4000 years bp and inheritance on the modern landscape. *Journal of Biogeography* 26: 879–85.

CHAPTER 60

RECENT FARMING COMMUNITIES AND STATES IN THE CONGO BASIN AND ITS ENVIRONS

PIERRE DE MARET

INTRODUCTION

OVER 500 different ethnolinguistic groups live today in the Congo Basin and its periphery. Almost all are farmers and, except in the northeast, all speak Bantu languages. Their origin thus goes back to the gradual colonization of the area by Bantu speakers, a process that began on the forest's northwestern fringe over 2,000 years ago (de Maret, Ch. 43 above).

Using historical linguistics and comparative ethnography in a 'words and things' technique that considers the histories of words with the careful study of the objects, institutions, concepts and customs they designate, Vansina (1990, 1999) outlines the existence of a single ancestral western Bantu tradition the political organization of which was based on two opposed ideological principles: one asserting the supernatural power of leaders, the other the equality of all. Despite the ongoing tensions these twin contradictory ideologies generate between the desire for local autonomy and the need for security, and thus centralization, this tradition proved extremely stable because it achieved equilibrium between competition and cooperation among leaders of equivalent strength (Vansina 1990: 251–4; 1999: 167). In the southern savannahs and the Great Lakes Region, the first ideology prevailed in a few instances, developing into forms of sacred kingship that nevertheless often exercised limited state control over people who continued to prize autonomy. Elsewhere, less centralized forms of political authority were the norm (Vansina 1990).

The very centre of the Congo Basin is one of the few areas in this vast region to have received systematic archaeological research (Fig. 60.1). There, in the middle of the rainforest, thorough survey of the Congo River and its tributaries has identified more than 190 localities with six pottery traditions recognized over a 2,500-year sequence. The first settlers appear to have entered from where the Congo River crosses the Equator, moving

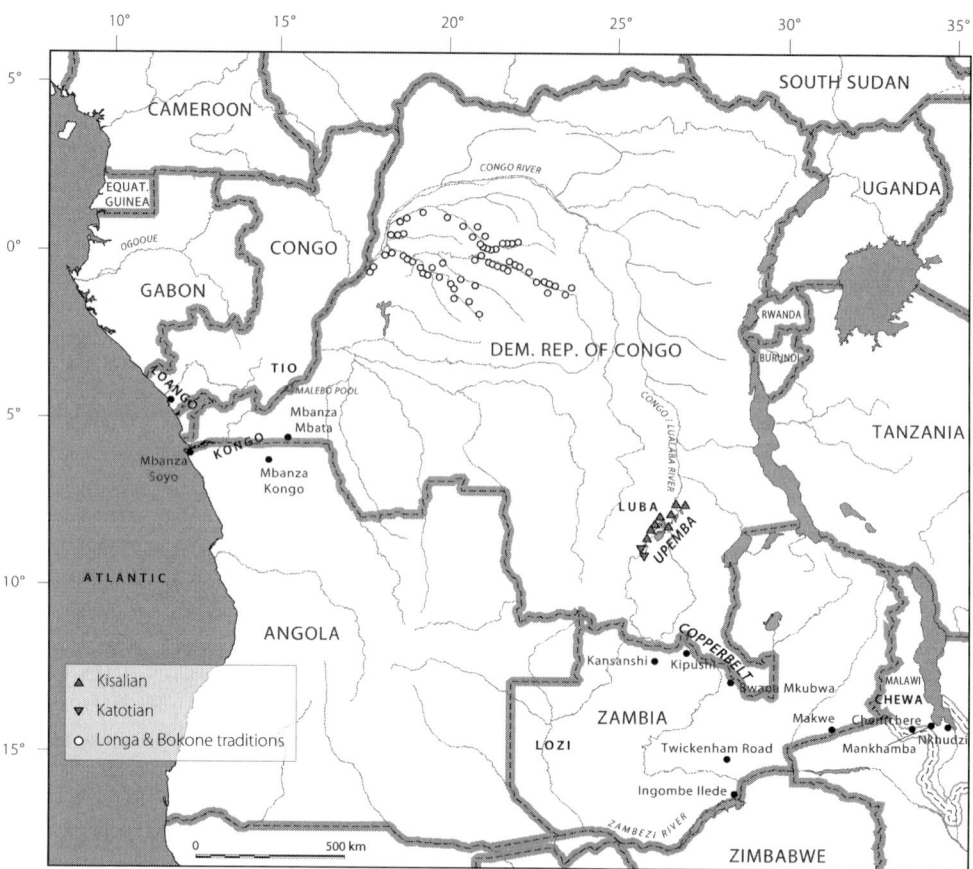

FIG. 60.1 Map of the Congo Basin showing major polities, archaeological sites, and areas mentioned in the text.

slowly upstream later on. The pottery traditions corresponding to the later phases are Longa (AD 500–1000) and Bokone (post-1600) (Eggert 1993; Wotzka 1995). However, besides their basic chronology and general distribution, we know little about the populations that produced them.

THE ATLANTIC COAST AND LOWER CONGO RIVER

Further downstream, the area just outside the forest, along the Atlantic coast and around the lower Congo River was one of the few places where processes of increasing centralization resulted in the emergence of kingdoms. Three are particularly well known: Tio, Loango, and Kongo (Vansina 1990: 146–58). Oral traditions and king-lists place their origin no earlier than the 14th century. Tio probably originated on the dry plateau north of the Malebo Pool, with Loango and Kongo taking shape north of the lower Congo River, possibly in connection with copper deposits there. Although none has received systematic archaeological research, surveys and small-scale excavations illuminate some aspects of the evolution of the area during the last millennium.

Along the banks of the Congo and the Malebo Pool, several sites testify to the development of a major riverside culture from the 11th century (Pinçon 1991). Most probably corresponding to the Tio, this culture controlled the trade network from the Pool to the main waterways further upstream. Major marketplaces arose there, and the structuration of economic space probably went together with the development of the kingdom (Vansina 1973, 1990). In turn, this must have increased the demand for luxuries, like copper items such as the large necklace worn as a symbol of power by the Tio. It is no coincidence that evidence of copper smelting is abundant in the southern part of their territory at the same time. Around the 15th century, however, the centre of power appears to have moved inland (Vansina 1973), producing a noticeable decrease in archaeological remains along the Congo River during the 16th and 17th centuries, perhaps to avoid sleeping sickness or because better profits could be made around the Pool (Pinçon 1991: 248–249).

Due to the formidable rapids at its outlet, the Malebo Pool is the end of the huge navigable network constituted by the Congo River and its tributaries. It has thus acted for centuries as a major commercial hub for goods coming downstream from across the Congo Basin and moving upstream from the Atlantic coast and the area in between. This process culminated in the 19th century under the control of the Tio (Vansina 1973: 247–81), but 17th/18th-century ceramics made by various groups on either side of the Pool from several sites around Kinshasa and Brazzaville, such as Kingabwa, illustrate the antiquity of those exchanges (de Maret 1982; de Maret and Stainier 1999).

In connection with this trade network and the sphere of influence of the various kingdoms, specific currencies were used over large areas. Small shells known as *nzimbu* (*Olivancillaria nana*), for example, collected on the coast near Luanda, were employed throughout the Kongo kingdom and far away along the river north of the Pool (Vansina 1990: 206). A hoard of about 20,000 *nzimbu* discovered in a pot near Kinshasa pre-dates the 16th century because of the absence of other shells resembling *Olivancillaria nana* that were used as fake money after the king's control over the gathering of *nzimbu* weakened with the arrival of the Portuguese (Dartevelle 1953: 154–7). Later, around the 18th century, the *nzimbu* were replaced with the *ngele*, a copper rod in use among the Tio that became the standard of value for slaves and ivory in much of the inner Basin (Vansina 1990: 206).

As with the Tio, most of what we know about Loango and Kongo comes from non-archaeological sources, including accounts from those Europeans who came into contact with them from the late 1400s. Loango, founded by the Vili people, was the first involved in the Atlantic trade, originally exporting ivory and copper, then, by the 17th century, increasingly slaves (Martin 1972). It arose from the fusion of several principalities, probably as a result of increasing local trade in relation to the copper deposits to the south and an inland demand for fish, sea salt, and palm products (Vansina 1990). Politically, Loango was ruled by a matrilineally descended sacred king whose legitimacy was connected to the control of shrines and who governed via a network of officials in the capital and the kingdom's seven provinces (Martin 1972; Hagenbucher-Sacripanti 1973). Loango's institutions influenced its northern neighbours along the coast as far as the Ogooué Estuary (Vansina 1990). Archaeologically, however, all results from the Loango area relate to the Early Iron Age (e.g. Denbow et al. 1988; Denbow 1990; Schwartz and Dechamps 1991) and thus shed no light on the kingdom's history.

Similarly little is known about the origins and the development of the Kongo kingdom before European arrival. Although oral traditions place its emergence around 1400 (Thornton 2001), social stratification and political organization could have developed much earlier, though there are virtually no relevant archaeological data with which to explore this possibility. On the other hand, for the last 500 years a unique body of historical, ethnographic, art-historical, and linguistic sources provides a detailed description of Kongo's history, organization, and daily life, and in particular its unique position as an early trading partner of the Portuguese that adopted and developed its own form of Catholicism (Balandier 1965; MacGaffey 1974, 2000; Thornton 1977, 1982, 1983; Hilton 1985; Fromont 2011).

Divided into several provinces and ruling at its peak over some 150,000 km², Kongo was highly centralized with regard to tribute collection and from judiciary, commercial, and military perspectives. Its capital, Mbanza Kongo (São Salvador, today in northern Angola), was in the 17th century home to perhaps 40,000 inhabitants, but has so far received very limited archaeological study (Esteves 1989; de Maret 2006). At two provincial capitals, Mbanza Mbata (Congo-Kinshasa) and Mbanza Soyo (Angola), however, elite burials were accompanied by a mixture of grave goods of European (crosses and religious medals, glass bottles, decorated nail heads, iron weapons) and local (pottery, stone pipes) origin (de Maret 1982: 82; Abranches 1991). Interestingly, the pipes are frequently carved with motifs that also occur on the Group II ceramics recovered throughout lower Congo up to the Malebo Pool and radiocarbon-dated to the 15th–18th centuries. Several other pottery groups have been recognized across the area, and seem to reflect the exchanges taking place inside the Kongo kingdom during the same period (Mortelmans 1962; de Maret 1982; Clist 1991).

THE UPEMBA DEPRESSION

Archaeological knowledge of state formation is much better 1,500 km to the east in Katanga, where the Luba kingdom emerged near where the Congo River (known locally as the Lualaba) flows through the Upemba Depression, a 200 km-long fertile floodplain dotted with lakes and marshes teeming with wildlife and fish. This has favoured a dense human occupation over the centuries, with people settling on the high ground along the banks. Over fifty such sites have been recorded, occupied for centuries and used alternatively as villages, cemeteries, and fields. Six have been excavated (Nenquin 1963; Hiernaux et al. 1971; de Maret 1977, 1979, 1985a, 1992, 1999). The deposits have been deeply disturbed by successive human activities, and so far it has proved impossible to strip large enough areas to recognize any significant patterns or structures. Nevertheless, the stratigraphies, the ceramic sequence and, above all, the study of over 300 graves establish a complete, well-dated sequence from the 7th century AD to the present that sheds light on the social, economic, technological, and political background to the Luba Kingdom.

Initial Iron Age occupation around the 7th century featured Kamilambian pottery, which resembles rather older Early Iron Age ceramic traditions from the Copperbelt, about 300 km to the south. Population density may have been relatively low at this time and grave goods were restricted to iron weapons and tools. From the 8th century, however, by which point the pottery is known as Early Kisalian, the presence of a few copper ornaments indicates access to the resources of the Copperbelt. Moreover, two elaborate

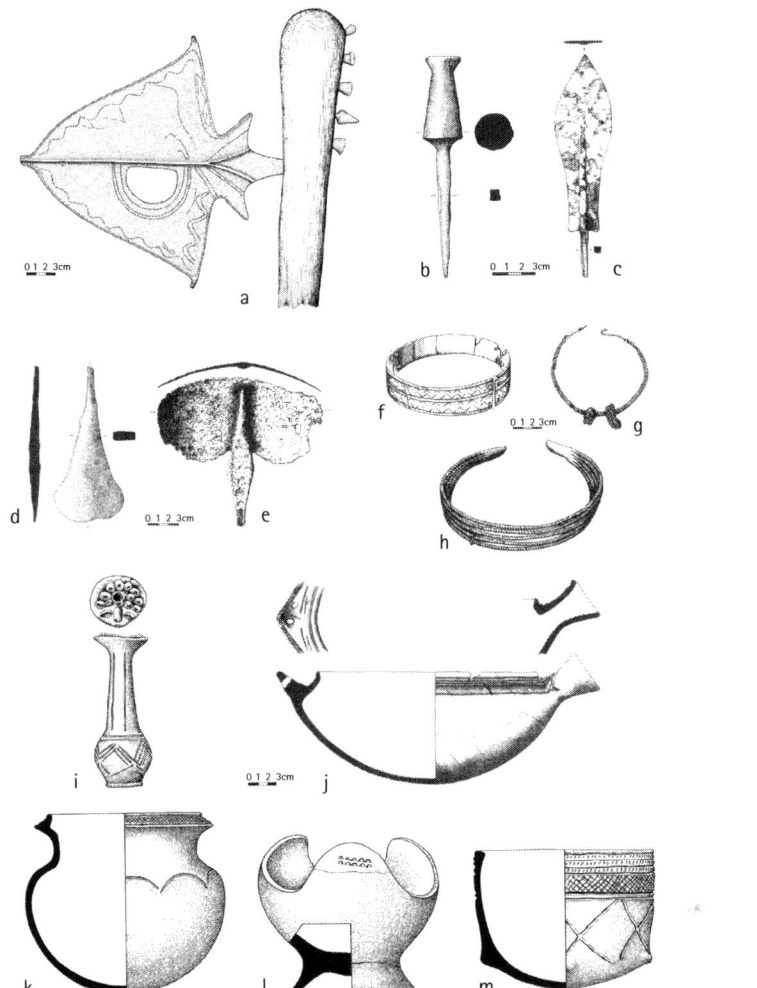

FIG. 60.2 Selection of 8th–13th-century AD Kisalian artefacts: (a) ceremonial iron axe with wooden handle pieced back together; (b) iron anvil; (c) iron spear head; (d) iron axe; (e) iron hoe ; (f) ivory necklace; (g) copper necklace; (h) iron necklace with copper ring; (i) ceramic anthropomorphic bottle; (j) ceramic bowl with spout; (k) ceramic pot; (l) ceramic trilobate brazier; (m) ceramic vessel in the shape of a basket.

ceremonial iron axes, finely engraved and with their wooden handles decorated with iron nails in the shape of miniature anvils, strongly resemble the ceremonial axes used until recently as symbols of power among many Central African populations, including the Luba, who referred to the iron and copper nails used to adorn their axe shafts as 'anvils' (Dewey and Childs 1996).

It is also very telling, however, that only two such ceremonial axes were found in only two graves out of almost 200 Kisalian graves excavated, and that one of those graves also contained, next to the skull, the only functional iron anvil discovered so far (Fig. 60.2). Throughout Central Africa, anvils have often been used as an authority symbol, as many symbolic ties link chiefs and kings to blacksmiths. Often the first king is said to have been a blacksmith, and in many places, like among the Luba themselves, an anvil could be used as regalia, while striking two anvils against each other was a crucial moment in the enthronement of a new ruler (de Maret 1980, 1985b, 1999). The discovery of two anvils in exactly the same position against the skull in the grave of a 17th-century Rwandan king (Van Noten 1972: Fig. 8) further proves their use as a major status symbol. We thus have evidence that by the end of the first millennium AD with the Early Kisalian, a certain amount of hierarchization was taking place, that this was not due to external factors (i.e. involvement with the developing Indian Ocean trade), for which there is no evidence, and that it already involved the manipulation of the same symbols of power that are documented by the Luba in the recent past, over a millennium later.

By the 10th century, the Kisalian was flourishing across the northern part of the Upemba Depression and in its vicinity, while the southern part was occupied by another, but similar, culture, the Katotian (Hiernaux et al. 1972). The number of sites and their size point to a much higher population density during this Classic Kisalian phase. The grave goods are often abundant, elaborate, and diversified, displaying a level of craftsmanship in pottery, basketry, and metallurgy that could have only been achieved by professional artisans (see Fig. 60.2). Basket weaving was also practised, and the shape of some of the baskets is also very similar to the one still used by the Luba in the area. The large amount of copper in circulation—used not just for jewellery but also for fishhooks, small knives, and spearheads—indicates intensive exchange with the Copperbelt to the south, but cowrie shells also point to connections to the east. Those graves with the most grave goods also contained the most unusual and the imported objects; as some of the wealthiest belonged to children, it is likely that status was transmitted between generations. Supporting these developments, artefacts and plant and animal remains indicate that subsistence combined fishing with food production (minimally oil palm, finger millet, and gourds, along with goats and chickens) and some hunting (antelope, hippopotamus, elephant, and crocodile).

Around the 13th century, pottery shapes and decoration and funerary rituals underwent significant change, corresponding to the appearance of Kabambian pottery, though we have no indication what these transformations imply at the sociopolitical level. There is, however, more local variation in pottery and burial rituals, a general decline in grave goods, and perhaps a greater contrast between the wealthiest graves and the others. Also noteworthy is the appearance in Kabambian graves of cast-copper cross-shaped ingots similar to those discovered on the Copperbelt (Bisson 2000). These ingots became more standardized and smaller over time, until in Phase B of the Kabambian, they were also more numerous and their position within the grave shifted from the chest toward the hands and the hips of the deceased. These changes may reflect their use first as a special-purpose currency circulating in the social and ritual sphere and later their evolution into a more versatile currency used also commercially (de Maret 1981). By this time too, around the 16th century, further changes are evident in interment practices, and ceramics use shapes transitional to those of recent Luba pottery. That transition is completed around the 18th century, when both pottery and ritual practices become similar to those documented ethnographically for the Luba, precisely at the time when the Luba state became a major kingdom, its prestige extending far to the south and east, where distant leaders claimed Luba filiation (Reefe 1981).

ZAMBIA AND MALAWI

Within modern Zambia and Malawi, several Late Iron Age pottery traditions have been distinguished that appear to be related to some of today's major ethnic groups. To the west, the Lungwebungu tradition shows greater continuity from the first millennium AD than does the Luangwa tradition, which makes a sudden appearance in central and eastern Zambia around the 11th century (Phillipson 1974), something well seen at Twickenham Road (Phillipson 1970). It seems likely that the Luangwa tradition's expansion reflects that of matrilineal, Western Bantu-speaking populations who moved into much of Zambia, displacing or assimilating communities that spoke Eastern Bantu languages and made Kalundu-type ceramics (Huffman 1989). The subsequent differentiation of Luangwa-making societies into Bemba, Chewa, Nsenga, and elsewhere was probably closely tied to the arrival of chiefly dynasties from southern Congo-Kinshasa in the 15th and 16th centuries (Phillipson 1974). The broadly contemporary expansion of the rich copper deposits in the Copperbelt area, as at Kansanshi, Kipushi, and Bwana Mkubwa (Bisson 2000), is likely to have been linked in some fashion to these developments, and specifically to control of the trade in the cross-shaped copper ingots that were now circulating as currency and status items over a wide area of south-central Africa—north into the Upemba Depression, as we have already seen, but also south into Zimbabwe (Bisson 1975; de Maret 1995; Swan 2007).

Such ingots are well represented in the cemetery marking the late 14th/early 15th-century occupation of the site of Ingombe Ilede, located in the Zambian section of the Zambezi Valley just upstream of the latter's confluence with the Kafue River. As well as cross-shaped copper ingots of 2.3–4.5 kg in weight, grave goods included numerous other metal items: copper wire, copper bars, iron hammers, hoes, and tongs, and iron drawing plates for the production of copper wire. Examples of iron gongs were also found (Fagan 1969). Remarkably, corrosion of copper bangles had, in places, preserved cloth, both of cotton and of bark and both probably of local manufacture, although at least one cotton textile may have been imported from India. *Conus* seashells from the East African coast, gold beads, and many thousands of glass ones further attest to the site's participation in trade with communities accessing goods moving across the Indian Ocean. The associated ceramics, though recalling those of the Luangwa tradition, also resemble pottery from the Urungwe area of northern Zimbabwe, suggesting, like the gold, connections with the Zimbabwe culture south of the Zambezi (see further Pikirayi, Ch. 63 below). Certainly, by the early 1500s Portuguese records attest to trade between the Copperbelt on the one hand and gold-producing areas of the Zimbabwe Plateau on the other (Garlake 1970) for which Ingombe Ilede may have been an important conduit.

For its size, Malawi has probably seen more intensive research than Zambia, and certainly than the other countries discussed here. In the southern half of Malawi, Luangwa-related ceramics appeared shortly after AD 1000 in the form of Kapeni ware (Cole-King 1973), which subsequently evolved into what is termed Mawudzu ware, while ceramics named after the sites of Mwamasapa and Mbande Hill provide a northern counterpart (Phillipson 1977: 175–7). Oral traditions indicate that the rulers of the precolonial Maravi kingdom, the Phiri, originated in the Luba area of Congo-Kinshasa, but were preceded by yet other Chewa speakers some 600–700 years ago (Schoffeleers 1973). These earlier arrivals retained importance as rainmakers under the rule of the Maravi king, the *kalonga*, which by the early 1600s was focused at Mankhamba in central Malawi, with two other Maravi states further south. Excavations at Mankhamba suggest it was first occupied in the 13th century, but while it housed a major rain shrine, a more secular basis for the *kalonga's* power came via involvement with Indian Ocean coast-directed trade. This is reflected in imported glass beads, Chinese porcelain, and other glazed ceramics, and in considerable evidence for the manufacture of ivory bangles and iron implements, both of which are known to have been significant exports (Juwayeyi 2010); spindle whorls substantiate historical evidence that cotton cloth was also valued by coastal traders (cf. Alpers 1975: 25). Connecting Mankhamba with the interior is evidence for local copper smelting, presumably using metal derived from the Copperbelt (Juwayeyi 2010).

The extent to which individuals could access such trade is indicated by the many thousand glass beads found with burials at Nkhudzi Bay and Mtemankhokwe I, cemeteries at the southern end of Lake Malawi of late 18th/early 19th-century date (Juwayeyi 2008). Pottery and a wide variety of iron tools and weapons were also found, along with evidence for the use of salt, for the production of which the local Nyanja people were renowned in the 19th century. Analysis of some of the skeletal remains identified variants of tooth modification/removal focused on the incisors reminiscent of broader Central African patterns, and suggested a diet combining cereals (sorghum, pearl millet, and maize are all plausible: Juwayeyi 2008) with meat (Morris 1993).

Both the Chewa and the Nyanja are associated with traditions of rock paintings found in central Malawi and eastern Zambia (Smith 1997). One tradition consists mainly of often quite large (≥1 m long) spread-eagled designs that resemble stretched animal hides viewed from above, accompanied by snakes and circles. The other comprises highly stylised zoomorphic animal designs accompanied by stick-like human figures. This spread-eagled tradition is almost entirely in white, though a few sites, like Makwe, retain figures outlined in red, and the paint was normally applied very thickly, while the zoomorphic tradition was finger-painted, again almost wholly in white, though sometimes using charcoal. Ethnographic data explain the associations and some of the meanings of each tradition. The white spread-eagled figures and their associated imagery is the work of Chewa women, and the art was produced as part of the *Chinamwali* ceremonies at a girl's coming of age; its symbolism relates particularly to water and fertility, as explored in detail by Zubieta (2006) for the Mwana wa Chentcherere II rockshelter in Malawi. The zoomorphic tradition, on the other hand, belongs to Chewa men, and depicts masked men and animal figures from the ceremonies performed by the *Nyau* association at rites of passage, including *Chinamwali* and funerals. Given the secrecy pertaining to *Nyau*, the production of the rock art, which is no longer undertaken, is difficult to understand, but it seems likely that it may have been made when *Nyau* was banned and forced underground first by the invading Ngoni in the mid-19th century and later during colonial rule (Smith 2001).

As already indicated, western Zambia during the second millennium AD was markedly different from that of areas further east, characterized by the production of ceramics belonging not to the Luangwa but to the Lungwebungu tradition, which extends far into Angola (Phillipson 1977: 179). Angola, however, has seen virtually no archaeological work because of decades of civil war and logistical problems, though the savannah states that developed there in precolonial times may reach back to the 13th century (Miller 1976). Similarly, while the ecological productivity of Upemba's wetlands clearly supported presumably interrelated processes of population growth, exchange, transport, and hierarchy formation (de Maret 1999), the relative merits of ecology, ideology, and other variables have not even begun to be explored in the case of the tightly structured Lozi polity of the Upper Zambezi, which combined cattle herding with intensive recessional cultivation and seasonal movement between dry-season and flood-season settlements (Gluckman 1951). What we do know is that when the Kololo conquered the Lozi state in the 19th century they introduced both a new language (SiLozi, which is cognate with Sotho/Tswana in southern Africa) and a new ceramic tradition, the Linyanti, a highly relevant association for broader considerations of archaeological migration (cf. Ashley, Ch. 6 above).

REFERENCES

ABRANCHES, H. (1991). *Sobre os Basolongo: Arqueologia da Tradição Oral*. Gent: Fina Petrolleos de Angola.

ALPERS, E. A. (1975). *Ivory and Slaves: Changing Patterns of International Trade in East and Central Africa to the Later Nineteenth Century*. Berkeley: University of California Press.

BALANDIER, G. (1965). *La Vie Quotidienne au Royaume de Kongo du XVIe au XVIIIe Siècle*. Paris: Hachette.

BISSON, M. S. (1975). Copper currency in Central Africa: the archaeological evidence. *World Archaeology* 6: 272–92.

—— (2000). Precolonial copper metallurgy: sociopolitical context. In J. Vogel (ed.), *Ancient African Metallurgy: The Sociocultural Context*. Walnut Creek, Calif.: AltaMira Press, 83–145.

CLIST, B. (1991). *L'Archéologie du Royaume Kongo*. In R. Lanfranchi and B. Clist (eds), *Aux Origines de l'Afrique Centrale*. Libreville: Centres Culturels Français d'Afrique Centrale, 253–6.

COLE-KING, P. (1973). *Kukumba Mbiri my Malawi: A Summary of Archaeological Research to 1973*. Zomba: Malawi Government Printer.

DARTEVELLE, E. (1953). *Les N'Zimbu: Monnaie du Royaume de Congo*. Brussels: Mémoires de la Société Royale Belge d'Anthropologie et de Préhistoire.

DE MARET, P. (1977). Sanga: new excavations, more data, and some related problems. *Journal of African History* 18: 321–37.

—— (1979). Luba roots: a first complete Iron Age sequence in Zaire. *Current Anthropology* 20: 233–5.

—— (1980). Ceux qui jouent avec le feu: la place du forgeron en Afrique centrale. *Africa* 50: 263–79.

—— (1981). L'évolution monétaire du Shaba central entre le 7ᵉ et le 18ᵉ siècle. *African Economic History* 10: 117–49.

—— (1982). The Iron Age in the west and the south. In F. Van Noten (ed.), *The Archaeology of Central Africa*. Graz: Akademische Druck-und Verlagsanstalt, 77–96.

—— (1985a). *Fouilles Archéologiques dans la Vallée du Haut-Lualaba, Zaïre: II Sanga et Katongo, 1974*. Tervuren: Musée Royal de l'Afrique Centrale.

—— (1985b). The smith's myth and the origin of leadership in Central Africa. In R. Haaland and P. Shinnie (eds), *African Iron Working*. Bergen: Norwegian University Press, 73–87.

—— (1992). *Fouilles Archéologiques dans la Vallée du Haut-Lualaba, Zaïre: II Kamilamba, Kikulu et Malemba-Nkulu, 1975*. Tervuren: Musée Royal de l'Afrique Centrale.

DE MARET, P. (1995). Croisettes histories. In L. de Heusch (ed.), *Objects: Signs of Africa*. Tervuren: Musée Royal de l'Afrique Centrale, 133–45.

—— (1999). The power of symbols and the symbols of power through time: probing the Luba past. In S. K. McIntosh (ed.), *Beyond Chiefdoms: Pathways to Complexity in Africa*. Cambridge: Cambridge University Press, 151–65.

—— (2006). What to expect in excavating the Kongo Kingdom capital. In H.-P. Wotzka (ed.), *Grundlegungen: Beiträge zur Europäischen und Afrikanischen Archäologie für Manfred K. H. Eggert*. Tübingen: Francke, 319–28.

—— and STAINIER, X. (1999). Excavations in the upper levels at Gombe and the early ceramic industries in the Kinshasa area (Zaïre). In G. Smolla, F.-R. Herrmann, I. Schmidt, and F. Verse (eds), *Festschrift für Günter Smolla*. Wiesbaden: Selbstverlag des Landesamtes für Denkmalpflege Hessen, 477–86.

DENBOW, J. (1990). Rapport préliminaire sur l'archéologie du littoral congolais: prospections et fouilles de la région du Bas-Kouilou effectuées en 1988. *Nsi* 7: 4–9.

—— MANIMA MOUBOUHA, A., and SANVITI, N. (1988). Archaeological excavations along the Loango Coast, Congo. *Nsi* 3: 37–42.

DEWEY, W. J., and CHILDS, S. T. (1996). Forging memory. In M. N. Roberts and A. F. Roberts (eds), *Memory: Luba Art and the Making of History*. New York: Museum of African Art, 61–83.

EGGERT, M. K. H. (1993). Central Africa and the archaeology of the Equatorial rainforest: reflections on some major topics. In T. Shaw, P. J. J. Sinclair, B. Andah, and A. Okpoko (eds), *The Archaeology of Africa: Food, Metals and Towns*. London: Routledge, 289–329.

ESTEVES, E. (1989). Mbanza Kongo, ville archéologique. *Nsi* 6: 159–64.

FAGAN, B. M. (1969). Excavations at Ingombe Ilede 1960–2. In B. M. Fagan, D. W. Phillipson, and S. G. H. Daniels (eds), *Iron Age Cultures in Zambia*, 2. London: Chatto & Windus, 55–161.

FROMONT, C. (2011). Dance, image, myth and conversion in the kingdom of Kongo, 1500–1800. *African Arts* 44: 52–63.

GARLAKE, P. S. (1970). Iron Age sites in the Urungwe District of Rhodesia. *South African Archaeological Bulletin* 25: 25–44.

GLUCKMAN, M. (1951). The Lozi of Barotseland in North-Western Rhodesia. In E. Colson and M. Gluckman (eds), *Seven Tribes of British Central Africa*. Manchester: Manchester University Press, 1–93.

HAGENBUCHER-SACRIPANTI, F. (1973). *Les Fondements Spirituels du Pouvoir au Royaume de Loango*. Paris: ORSTOM.

HIERNAUX, J., DE LONGRÉE, E., and DE BUYST, J. (1971). *Fouilles Archéologiques dans la Vallée du Haut-Lualaba I: Sanga 1958*. Tervuren: Musée Royal de l'Afrique Centrale.

—— MAQUET E., and DE BUYST, J. (1972). Le cimetière protohistorique de Katoto. In H. Hugot (ed.), *Sixième Congrès Panafricain de Préhistoire, Dakar 1967*. Chambéry: Imprimeries Réunies, 148–58.

HILTON, A. (1985). *The Kingdom of Kongo*. Oxford: Clarendon Press.

HUFFMAN, T. N. (1989). Ceramics, settlements and late Iron Age migrations. *African Archaeological Review* 7: 155–82.

JUWAYEYI, Y. M. (2008). Wealth and affluence in southern Malawi during the proto-historic period: the evidence from archaeology, oral traditions and history. *South African Archaeological Bulletin* 63: 102–15.

—— (2010). Archaeological excavations at Mankhamba, Malawi: an early settlement site of the Maravi. *Azania* 45: 175–202.

MACGAFFEY, W. (1974). *An Anthology of Kongo Religion: Primary Texts from Lower Zaïre.* Lawrence: University of Kansas.

—— (2000). *Kongo Political Culture: The Conceptual Challenge of the Particular.* Bloomington: Indiana University Press.

MARTIN, P. (1972). *The External Trade of the Loango Coast, 1576–1870.* Oxford: Clarendon Press.

MILLER, J. C. (1976). *Kings and Kinsmen.* Oxford: Clarendon Press.

MORRIS, A. G. (1993). Mtemankhokwe: human skeletal remains from a Late Iron Age cemetery in the Mangochi District of southern Malawi. *Southern African Field Archaeology* 2: 74–84.

MORTELMANS, G. (1962). Archéologie des grottes Dimba et Ngovo (région de Thysville, Bas-Congo). In G. Mortelmans and J. Nenquin (eds), *Actes du IVe Congrès Panafricain de Préhistoire et de l'Étude du Quaternaire.* Tervuren: Musée Royal de l'Afrique Centrale, 407–25.

NENQUIN, J. (1963). *Excavations at Sanga 1957: The Protohistoric Necropolis.* Tervuren: Musée Royal de l'Afrique Centrale.

PHILLIPSON, D. W. (1970). Excavations at Twickenham Road, Lusaka. *Azania* 5: 77–118.

—— (1974). Iron Age history and archaeology in Zambia. *Journal of African History* 15: 1–25.

—— (1977). *The Later Prehistory of Eastern and Southern Africa.* London: Heinemann.

PINÇON, B. (1991). L'archéologie du royaume teke. In R. Lanfranchi and B. Clist (eds), *Aux Origines de l'Afrique Centrale.* Libreville: Centres Culturels Français d'Afrique Centrale, 253–6.

REEFE, T. Q. (1981). *The Rainbow and the Kings: A History of the Luba Empire to 1981.* Berkeley: University of California Press.

SCHOFFELEERS, J. M. (1973). Toward the identification of a proto-Chewa culture. *Malawi Journal of Social Science* 2: 48–56.

SCHWARTZ, D., and DECHAMPS, R. (1991). Nouvelles céramiques découvertes à Pointe-Noire au Congo (1600 bp) lors d'une fouille de sauvetage. *Nsi* 8/9: 16–23.

SMITH, B. W. (1997). *Zambia's Ancient Rock Art.* Livingstone: National Heritage Conservation Commission of Zambia.

—— (2001). Forbidden images: rock paintings and the *Nyau* secret society of central Malawi and eastern Zambia. *African Archaeological Review* 18: 187–212.

SWAN, L. (2007). Economic and ideological roles of copper ingots in prehistoric Zimbabwe. *Antiquity* 81: 999–1012.

THORNTON, J. K. (1977). Demography and history in the kingdom of Kongo, 1550–1750. *Journal of African History* 18: 507–30.

—— (1982). The kingdom of Kongo *ca.* 1390–1678: the development of an African social formation. *Cahiers d'études africaines* 22: 325–42.

—— (1983). *The Kingdom of Kongo: Civil War and Transition, 1641–1718.* Madison: University of Wisconsin Press.

—— (2001). The origins and early history of the Kingdom of Kongo, *c.* 1350–1500. *International Journal of African Historical Studies* 34: 89–120.

VAN NOTEN, F. (1972). *Les Tombes du Roi Cyirima Rujugira et de la Reine Mère Nyirayushi Kanjogera: Description Archéologique.* Tervuren: Musée Royal de l'Afrique Centrale.

VANSINA, J. (1973). *The Tio Kingdom of the Middle Congo, 1880–1892.* Oxford: Oxford University Press.

—— (1990). *Paths in the Rainforests: Towards a History of Political Tradition in Equatorial Africa.* Madison: University of Wisconsin Press.

VANSINA, J. (1999). Pathways of political development in Equatorial Africa and neo-evolutionary theory. In S. K. Mcintosh (ed.), *Beyond Chiefdoms: Pathways to Complexity in Africa*. Cambridge: Cambridge University Press, 166–72.

WOTZKA, H.-P. (1995). *Studien zur Archäologie des zentralafrikanischen Regenwaldes: Die Keramik des inneren Zaïre-Beckens und ihre Stellung im Kontext der Bantu-Expansion*. Cologne: Heinrich Barth Institut.

ZUBIETA, L. F. (2006). *The Rock Art of Mwana wa Chentcherere II Rock Shelter, Malawi*. Leiden: African Studies Centre.

CHAPTER 61

THE EMERGENCE OF STATES IN GREAT LAKES AFRICA

ANDREW REID

INTRODUCTION

THE states that emerged in the Great Lakes region, which include Buganda, Bunyoro, Nkore, Karagwe, Rwanda, and Burundi (Fig. 61.1), are important on a continental, and even a global, scale because they form the one region of incipient African state formation for which no impact from potential external influences has been credibly proposed. Put simply, the Great Lakes region demonstrates, if demonstration is needed, that African political systems can and did evolve without external stimulus, and confirms the need to look for internal processes of political change in other parts of the continent. Given this significance, it is therefore somewhat surprising that the states of the Great Lakes region remain among the least investigated archaeologically of all the areas of incipient state formation on the continent. Several factors help to explain this. Most important of all is that for countries like Uganda, Rwanda, and Burundi, which featured the promotion of seemingly indigenous political institutions under policies of indirect rule, the pasts that were focused on in colonial times overwhelmingly construed the 19th-century kingdoms as timeless, stable, and unchanging. Ruling elites had to reconfirm their right to political authority in a world substantively changed by the presence of Europeans. Whilst there was no obvious presence of non-Africans to explain the states that had emerged, an imagined non-African population, Hamites, were alleged to have given Africans 'all the civilisation that he possessed before the coming of the white man' (Johnston 1902: 486). Importantly, the idea of Hamites not only served European interests, but was also used by African elites to help confirm their privileged position (Reid 2003a).

This discussion of Great Lakes states will not return to this theme, but it is essential to recognize that in colonial times discussions of history began and largely ended with the polities that were dominant in the late 19th century and had little interest in replacing such historical constructs. Moreover, these constructs are still current in popular discourse today: the notion of Hamites was a major theme used by the perpetrators of the genocide in Rwanda in 1994; in a more positive manner, it is still a major theme voiced by the current ruling elite in Uganda. On the theme of the states themselves, three kingdoms were restored in Uganda in the 1990s (having been abolished in 1967), and this has led to contestations over their status, with riots in Kampala

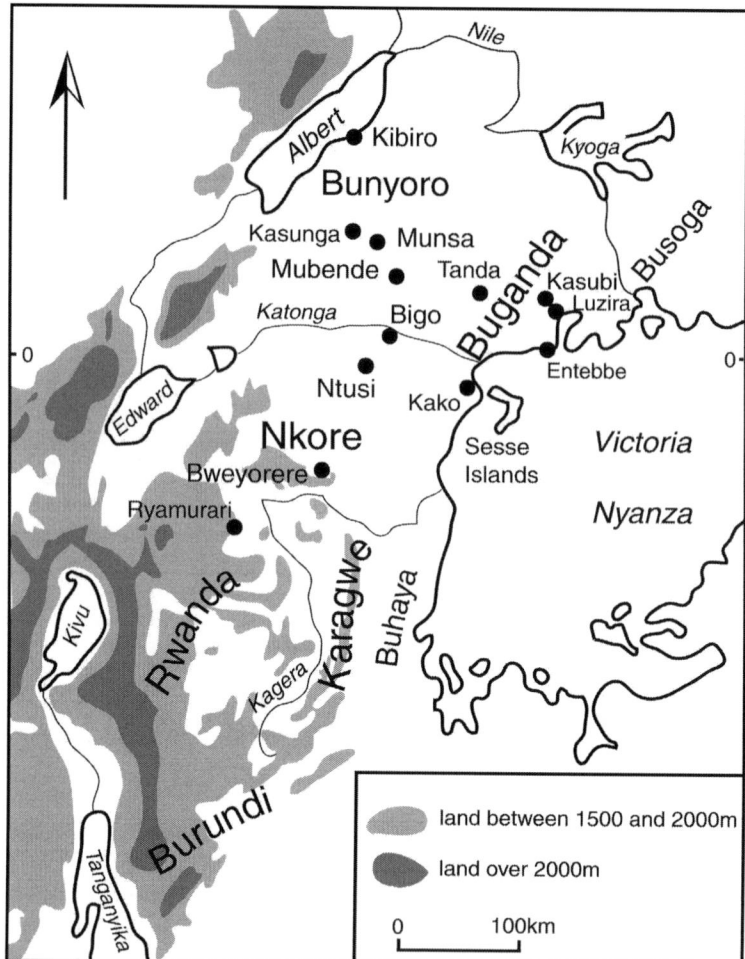

FIG. 61.1 States and sites of the Great Lakes region.

in 2009 and 2010 directly related to the status of the king of Buganda. Concurrently, populations in the country that did not historically have kingship (such as Acholi) are now seeking to create such historical institutions because of the perceived benefits and status that they will bring. This focus on centralized political systems has very much been to the detriment of other localized historical presences, such as clans, which have been almost entirely overlooked.

Historically, therefore, there was no great appetite for archaeological investigations that did anything other than support the dominant political institutions of colonial times. Hence, Schmidt (1990) describes Posnansky's (at the time) innovatory attempts to explore links between oral traditions and archaeology as little more than 'the archaeology of verification'. Schmidt's (1978) own work took place in Buhaya, northwestern Tanzania, where, importantly, indigenous political leadership was weakened by German and then British rule before being entirely replaced at independence by President Julius Nyerere. Schmidt's work was part of a broader re-evaluation of Cwezi traditions, which had been seen as pivotal in colonial histories because they conveyed a historical legitimacy to political institutions and to colonial authority. Largely overshadowed by his subsequent focus on iron smelting (Mapunda,

Ch. 42 above), this early work used a structural approach to these traditions (Schmidt, Ch. 3 above) to help construct a nuanced landscape archaeology that was well ahead of its time and remains essentially unequalled on the African continent. One of the major by-products of this and other historical works was to emphasize that traditions recorded in the 20th century are essentially the product of those times and of the historical circumstances, usually closely associated with the royal courts, in which they were recorded. There may be a kernel of historical truth behind such traditions, but this merely serves to emphasize that archaeology needs to be conducted independently from historical work rather than being led by it. Of more recent relevance is the work of Schoenbrun (1998) and his students in generating histories from their studies of comparative linguistics. These studies work particularly well in the Great Lakes region because it is relatively small and has a great deal of language diversity combined with relatively low levels of population mobility. This work is referred to later in conjunction with the archaeological data discussed below.

Besides these difficult historical circumstances, the development of understanding of the states of the Great Lakes is further constrained by the limitations of the archaeological record itself. There is no tradition of building in permanent materials, with the nearest such tradition being the *ohingini* of western Kenya (Onjala 2003), closely associated with post-first millennium AD settlement of that area. In the Great Lakes, capitals and the individual structures within them were undoubtedly impressive (e.g. Kigongo and Reid 2007), but they were short-lived, frequently occupied for less than five years, and built entirely from non-durable materials; to date, even 19th-century capitals, the locations of which are known, remain archaeologically invisible. Settlement in the region, royal or otherwise, seems generally to have been relatively short-term and dispersed, leaving isolated scatters of archaeological debris across the inhabited landscape. Animal bone only preserves archaeologically where soils have been artificially built up and modified, such as through the deposition of ash and dung, and plant remains are rare because of soil conditions and the general absence of crop-processing techniques that carry a risk of carbonization (Young and Thompson 1999). Indeed, the damp, warm soils, frequently located in forests, lead to very poor conditions of preservation. The vast majority of sites are therefore only identifiable through the presence of pottery or more occasionally slag from iron smelting, which in some instances occurs in huge concentrations. Given these difficult conditions, it is perhaps not surprising that much early attention focused on the earthworks found in parts of western Uganda, although they have revealed little about past society. These earthworks are a part of the story, but by no means the only element, as will be seen below.

CERAMIC TRADITIONS

As has been intimated, colonial histories in the Great Lakes emphasized disjuncture and population replacement as a central theme, serving to separate elites from commoners. In looking for possible indicators of internal processes of change, encouragement is provided by Schoenbrun's historical reconstructions. These suggest that no incursions by distinct language groups occurred during the last 2,000 years. However, a key stumbling block in attempting to argue for cultural continuity in the region has been provided by ceramics. It has long been recognized that there is a major disjuncture in the regional ceramic sequence, shifting from the ornate and accomplished Early Iron Age Urewe ceramics (de Maret, Ch. 60

FIG. 61.2 The ceramic succession in the Great Lakes region.

above) to seemingly much more functional and utilitarian pottery decorated with roulettes. Without necessarily falling back on old 'pots = peoples' arguments of material culture, this radical and seemingly instant transformation did appear to suggest population replacement, but two recent findings appear to change this. First, recent work in Rwanda (Giblin and Fuller 2011) demonstrates that the single very early and high-margin-of-error date for roulette decorated pottery at the cave site of Akameru is most probably too early (now suggested to be *c.* AD 1200) and therefore the earliest secure evidence for roulette decorated pottery in the region comes instead from Ntusi in southern Uganda, dating to the 11th century. More significantly, Ashley's (2010) work on ceramics around the northern shores of the Victoria Nyanza has demonstrated that there is a process of transition in the ceramics, with a less accomplished version of Urewe ceramics produced from around the 8th century and this in turn being replaced by several further non-roulette decorated variants at the turn of the millennium (Fig. 61.2). A final lake-related ceramic, Entebbe pottery, featuring twisted string roulette and broad incision, is used in the first half of the second millennium before eventually being replaced by the typical range of roulette decorated ceramics.

This focus on ceramics may appear to borrow from long-discarded ideas relating to population and material culture, but is unfortunately necessary, as poor preservation means that it is largely the sole source of information at present. The nature of the archaeology around the forested shores of the lake is particularly poor, featuring small scatters of pottery and very little else, only visible in occasional disturbances of the thick vegetation (Reid 2003b). Nevertheless, sites with these post-Urewe ceramic variants are only found on the islands and margins of the lake and never in the mainland interior. This is clearly a lake-based phenomenon, relying on the easier movement and communication across the lake rather than around its forest and swamp-ridden margins. A re-examination of existing pottery assemblages has further demonstrated that figurative art objects made of fired clay were being used at this time. The Luzira figures, originally found in 1929, include a head and two torsos (Fig. 61.3), whilst the Entebbe figurine, recovered in 1964, is a phallic column that includes both male and female genitalia (Reid and Ashley 2007; Ashley and Reid 2008). Unfortunately, these two collections resulted from disturbance during construction work and there is no possibility of further work at either site to explore their contextual relationships. It has to be hoped that future research will locate and explore how such items were being used by society. Nevertheless, with their focus on elements of the human body not seen in earlier times, the various figures may suggest a new focus on individuals and the use of the body. This

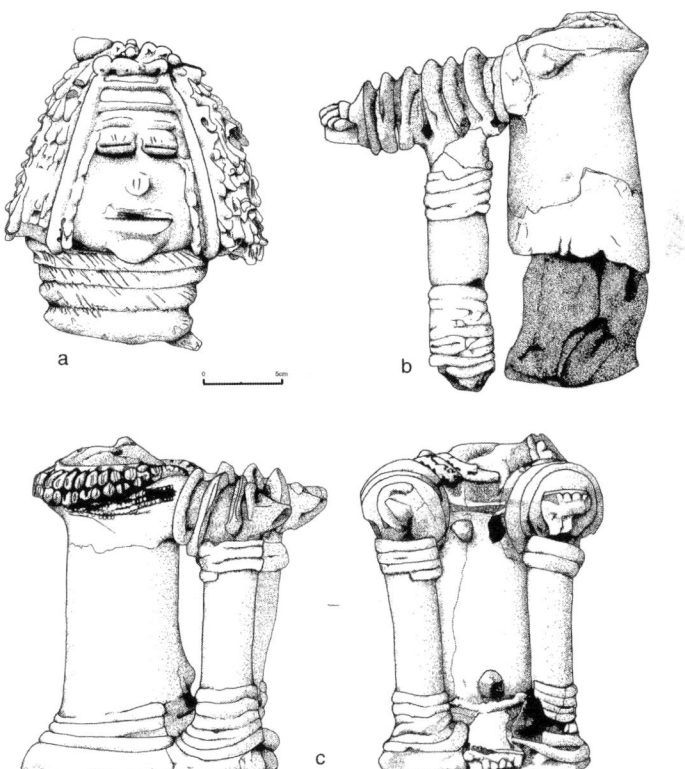

FIG. 61.3 The Luzira figures, Uganda.

might replace the significance placed on Urewe ceramics in earlier times in which ornate vessels were placed occasionally at the base of furnaces and in burials.

Settlement dynamics and economy

This emphasis on activities on the Victoria Nyanza begs a number of questions relating to the economic activities that may have been undertaken at these sites. Fishing is more than likely to have been an important factor, but future research will also have to consider the potential role of bananas. Plantation production of bananas was the mainstay of the agricultural economy in Buganda and neighbouring polities, yet there is currently no archaeological evidence, apart from an exceptionally early occurrence of banana phytoliths from a swamp core taken near Munsa (Lejju et al. 2006). Intriguingly, some Ganda traditions suggest that plantation cultivation originated on the Ssese Islands and rapidly spread across the lake. Schoenbrun (1998) describes a linguistic 'explosion' of terms relating to bananas and banana cultivation at around this time, as well as the appearance of new forms of more personalized and centralized leadership. He also highlights a similar 'explosion' of terms relating to pastoralism and herding at around the beginning of the second millennium AD; importantly, all appear to have been innovated within Great Lakes Bantu languages.

The archaeological evidence for cattle pastoralism is rather better than that for bananas. This evidence derives from the site of Ntusi, which was occupied throughout the first half of the second millennium (Reid 1996). Survey has revealed no evidence for settlement of the area by earlier farmers. From the earliest levels the animal bone assemblages are dominated by cattle, and mortality profiles indicate that the vast majority of animals being slaughtered were extremely young (Fig. 61.4). Such offtake could only have been sustained by having very high numbers of cattle present in the area. In addition, survey in the Mawogola landscape surrounding Ntusi demonstrated that there were a large number of essentially contemporary, small enclosures, situated so as to make best use of the landscape for the purposes of herding. This hinterland presumably provided the political support for the centre at Ntusi. It has also been possible to demonstrate that an increase in size of cattle occurred during the occupation of the site, suggesting that pastoral mores and ideals were being followed. However, it is also important to note that while these pastoralist developments were taking place the site's economy had a strong basis in grain production. Grinding stones are frequently found across the site, and excavations revealed grain storage pits, reaping knives, and two small clusters of carbonized sorghum. A consideration of abrasion on ceramics suggests that a significant proportion of the pottery recovered from the site was used in the preparation of grains (Reid and Young 2000). The importance of this joint evidence for herding and cultivation, in some instances taking place within the same households, is that the distinct economic classes that dominated southwestern Uganda in recent centuries had not yet emerged.

Besides the activity on the lake and the rise of cattle-herding, there is another example of economic specialization in the early second millennium AD at Kibiro (Connah 1996). This site, perched on the eastern shores of Lake Albert, has throughout its history been a centre of salt production harnessing the natural occurrence of a salt-rich stream and increasing the

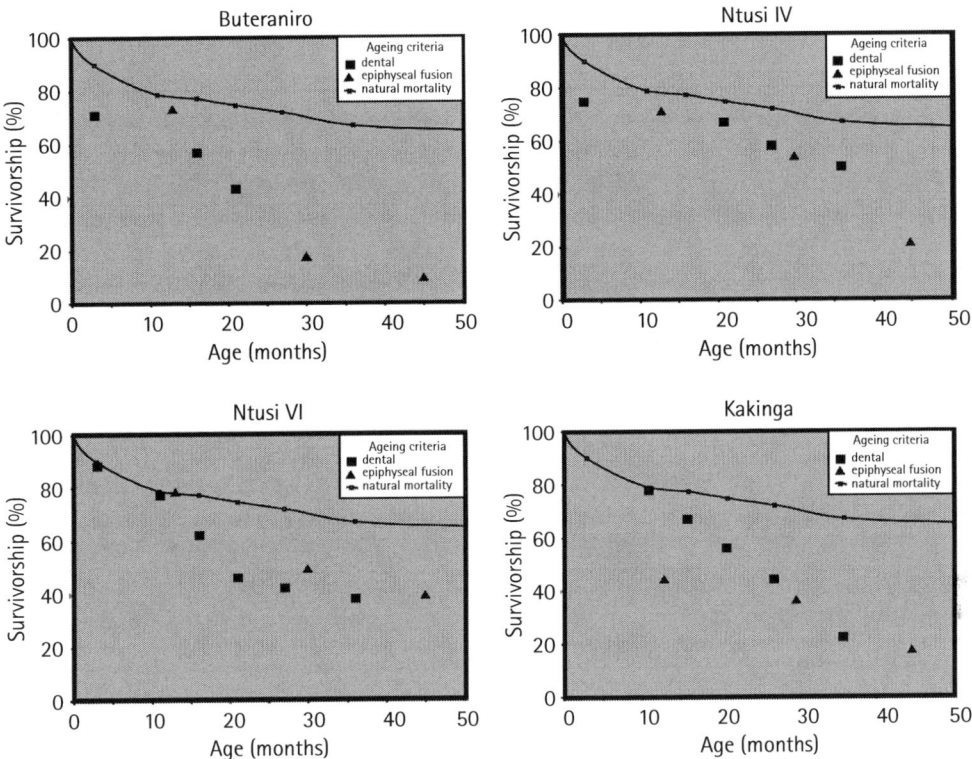

FIG. 61.4 Cattle mortality profiles from select sites around Ntusi, Uganda.

efficiency of salt production through the use of salt 'gardens'. The scale and extent of production in early times is unknown, but this production underwent massive expansion at the height of the Bunyoro state. There are also further suggestions of increased economic specialization and diversification in the region at around this time, including shifts in settlement pattern in Bunyoro, seemingly to control access to the more productive agricultural land (Robertshaw 1994).

The excellent nature of preservation and the recovery of house remains enabling reconstructions of the use of space mark Ntusi as an exceptional site that promises to reveal more of the organization of society at that time. However, because of current habitation it is unlikely that archaeologists will ever be able to excavate locations which would probably have been the main focus of political power at the site. At Munsa, however, this has been possible. Situated to the north of Ntusi in a significantly wetter and more forested landscape, the hilltop centre of this site remains free of human activities, in part because of its current ritual associations. Excavations in this central area encountered an iron-smelting location, a number of pits, including one of huge dimensions, and a significant number of burials dating from the 12th century onwards (Robertshaw 1997). As at Ntusi, cattle dominated the animal bone, although there is extensive evidence across the main part of the site for agricultural activity. In the 15th century a network of ditches was dug focusing on the hilltop centre of the site. These ditches are cut to a depth of four or five metres and the outer line surrounds an area more than a kilometre across. The contention is that these ditches were a final component of the layering of associations of power at the site, through its use in ritual transformations and its association with spirits and with the seat of political authority.

This perspective on the earthworks—as a later act in the construction of power in the landscape—is rather different from the colonial view of the earthworks as defensive capitals akin to British Iron Age hillforts of the first millennium BC (e.g. Wayland 1934). Most attention was devoted to Bigo bya Mugenyi, situated only 13 km to the north of Ntusi. Excavations there in the late 1950s (Shinnie 1960; Posnansky 1969) were driven by the idea that the site was some form of capital of a putative Cwezi Empire, an idea now generally disregarded by academics although still current in popular versions of the past. Bigo's ditch network is more extensive than that at Munsa, but only a very small area at the centre of the site suggests archaeological habitation. Early dating attempts suggest that the ditches may date from the 14th century, which means that they overlap with the later habitation at Ntusi. As yet, there is no clear indication of what the relationship between the two settlements may have been. Furthermore, there is a lack of understanding of the differences between the different ditch networks: those at Munsa and also at Kibengo enclose large areas given over to extensive habitation, whereas at Bigo there is very little habitation and at Kasonko nearby there is no evidence of habitation at all (Sutton 1998). Hence, these ditches remain enigmatic and problematic and currently serve as a distraction from some of the more sound archaeological results that have been produced. At present these ditch networks seem to mark an end to the political developments evidenced at the above sites. Thereafter, there is no evidence for longevity of settlement apart from at ritual centres.

These ritual centres represent a final strand that needs to be added to this consideration of the archaeology of emergent states in the Great Lakes. Guided by the original work of Lanning (1966), Robertshaw (1999) undertook excavation at Mubende and subsequently at Kasunga, both known to have been important shrines in recent times. The earliest deposits at both sites date to the 14th century and both suggest that they were occupied constantly into the 20th century and that they had always fulfilled a ritual role. Hence, some shrines were able to sustain their significance independently both during the time of the emergent states and into the kingdoms themselves. The priestess at Mubende, for instance, was consulted by the rulers of both Bunyoro and Buganda.

LATER KINGDOMS AND THEIR CAPITALS

Nineteenth-century explorers appear to have been struck by the scale and organization of capitals, particularly Buganda, and this does not appear to have simply been a manifestation of the need to impress western audiences with the sophistication of remote African states. A detailed plan of a Ganda capital was produced by Ganda elders thirty years after the capital's abandonment (Roscoe 1911). While this does provide us with an insight into the complexity of the organization of the capital, it is regrettable that there is no physical archaeological evidence for the capital's existence at its location in the present day suburbs of northwestern Kampala. This is in part due to the use of building materials that are not permanent, and the rapid decay of plant remains characteristic of these humid tropics, but most significant of all factors was that the capital was only occupied for two years. Indeed, this short-lived nature of capitals seems to be consistent across the entire region. Elsewhere in the region the capitals tend to have been much smaller, being the residences of the king and the immediate elite of the state. There are only two instances of capitals with substantive archaeological remains, the 18th-century Nkore capital of Bweyorere and the much less well-known 18th-century Mpororo capital of Ryamurari. On a hill beneath the Isingiro escarpment, Bweyorere features a series of low banks that form into a collection of circular enclosures (Posnansky 1968). These appear to replicate the dung middens that encircle the lower reaches of cattle enclosures. While a number of kings are associated with the site, the coherent layout of the banks suggests that these features relate to a single occupation, although Posnansky believed that there was an earlier phase of habitation deposits capped by these banks. This is clearly an exceptional site, both in the sense that there is excellent definition of features and in the sense that other capital sites are not like this at all. It is therefore quite likely that Bweyorere should *not* be considered typical of capitals in the region, and that explanations are needed to define why such an exceptional site exists.

Fortunately, the evidence for iron smelting is significantly better due to the huge amounts of slag waste produced by operations which in places can correctly be described as industrial. Awareness of these iron-smelting operations was first highlighted by the work of Schmidt (1978, 1997). Although Schmidt's focus was primarily ethnoarchaeological, focusing on our understanding of technology, his principal data concern production in the 19th century relating to the Buhaya states. Besides this work, further studies have been undertaken on smelting societies in Biharamulo and Karagwe, and on several different communities in each of Rwanda, Burundi, Bunyoro, and Buganda. By no means should this coverage be taken to have exhausted the areas that specialized in iron production within the Great Lakes region, and recent work has demonstrated that detailed study within each area is an important requirement because of the potential significance of variation in technique. In Buganda, smelting episodes taking place in proximity to one another employed markedly different techniques, including slag tapping and the use of tuyères formed from kaolinite (Humphris et al. 2009). Kaolinite was mined extensively at Tanda and Kako on the western margins of Buganda, as well as being more casually mined throughout much of southwestern Uganda.

Not surprisingly, given the close chronological proximity of these societies to the present as well as in some cases their continued political prominence, it has not been appropriate to excavate burials of past kings, despite the fact that many tombs have been identified and known since early colonial times. The most significant example of these tombs is at Kasubi on the outskirts of Kampala (Fig. 61.5), originally built to house the body of Mutesa I, who died in 1874, but then subsequently converted into a royal mausoleum in colonial times (Kigongo and Reid 2007). The riot which followed the destruction of Kasubi in March 2010, and which prevented Uganda's President Museveni from visiting, demonstrates the degree of sensitivity concerning such sites, and this in turn makes it impossible to countenance excavation. However, one example of an excavated royal burial does exist from Rwanda, where, after the abolition of the kings, archaeologists were led to the secret grave of an 18th-century ruler whose body had been interred in the 1930s. The cured body of Cyrima Rujigira was buried along with a number of items of ornamentation and regalia, including items of perishable materials such as wood and leather (Van Noten 1983). Of particular note are the two hammer anvils that were placed behind his head—an identification of iron smithing with political power that has also been recognized in graves in the Upemba Depression of

FIG. 61.5 The Muzibu-Azaala-Mpanga, the main tomb building, at Kasubi, Uganda, before its destruction in 2010.

Congo-Kinshasa dating back to the 13th century (de Maret 1999). It is highly unlikely that it will be possible to undertake any other excavation of royal burials, so Cyrima Rujigira's tomb provides us with a unique insight that is unlikely to be matched, both for reasons of accessibility and because of the very poor preservation of materials in the region.

In this discussion of royal regalia one further study is worth noting. As a result of work undertaken for the Tanzanian Department of Antiquities, Sassoon (1983) was able to compile an inventory of the regalia of the king of Karagwe, most of which was used in the celebration of the New Moon rituals. Of particular note were the iron cows and the *mpiima*, a hammer anvil with welded cows' horns, both of which symbolize the dual power of cattle and of iron (Reid and MacLean 1995). Regrettably there has been no attempt to investigate how the unique iron cows found their way from the ethnography section of the National Museum in Dar es Salaam onto the international art market.

SUMMARY AND CONCLUSION

This review demonstrates a thin and partial archaeological record that makes attempts at more complex analysis problematic. Enough fieldwork has been undertaken to indicate that preservation of features and materials is a real problem, as are the short-term occupation of sites and the rapid processes of post-depositional decay and transformation. Hence, basic structures such as houses are as yet almost entirely absent, as are overt demonstrations of political centralization such as royal precincts or burials. This makes theorizing about the emergence of states remarkably difficult, as can be seen in a number of papers produced by Robertshaw, largely focusing on Bunyoro-Kitara, in which he attempts to explore possible theoretical leads explaining centralization (e.g. Robertshaw 1999; 2010; Robertshaw and Taylor 2000). On account of the lack of substantive data with which to explore such societies these are, by Robertshaw's own admission, largely speculative. This criticism is not to deny the need to attempt explanation, which should lie at the heart of all our work, but rather to point out the difficulty of undertaking such attempts when armed with data that are simply not robust enough for the purpose.

Perhaps a broader, longer-term, more generalized perspective is needed that recognizes that there are broad processes of transformation taking place across the region from the end of the first millennium AD onwards. These changes are not society-specific, and suggest that there were broadly shared values recognized across the region, notwithstanding the different nature of those societies. From around AD 1000 there are a series of indications of economic diversification into the production of cattle, salt, iron, lake products, new lands for cultivation, and the growing influence of bananas. There will also have been transformations in political leadership, suggested by comparative linguistics (Schoenbrun 1998), that provide the necessary foundation for the emergence of the kingdoms themselves. During the time of the kingdoms the archaeological record becomes still thinner, but nevertheless demonstrates its importance as a primary source to be used in conjunction with more conventional historical resources. In particular, archaeology helps to provide detail on elements situated at a distance from the political centres. This latter progress should serve to reinvigorate archaeological research in the region, demonstrating that it has an important contribution to make, notwithstanding the problems relating to archaeological sites. Future work needs to continue to expand away from the political centres of the 19th century to focus on earlier transformations happening elsewhere in the region, as well as on the nature of society in the smaller polities that still survived on the margins of the 19th-century world. Slowly, and making the most of fortuitous archaeological occurrences, a more substantive and coherent picture will emerge.

REFERENCES

ASHLEY, C. Z. (2010). Towards a socialised archaeology of Great Lakes ceramics. *African Archaeological Review* 27: 135–63.

—— and REID, A. (2008). A reconsideration of the figures from Luzira. *Azania* 43: 95–123.

CONNAH, G. (1996). *Kibiro: The Salt of Bunyoro, Past and Present*. London: British Institute in Eastern Africa.

DE MARET, P. (1999). The power of symbols and the symbols of power through time: probing the Luba past. In S. K. Mcintosh (ed.), *Beyond Chiefdoms: Pathways to Complexity in Africa*. Cambridge: Cambridge University Press, 151–65.

GIBLIN, J. D. and FULLER, D. Q. (2011). First and second millennium A.D. agriculture in Rwanda: archaeobotanical finds and radiocarbon dates from seven sites. *Vegetation History and Archaeobotany* 20: 253–65.

HUMPHRIS, J., MARTINON-TORRES, M., REHREN, T. H., and REID, A. (2009). Variability in single smelting episodes: a pilot study using iron slag from Uganda. *Journal of Archaeological Science* 36: 359–69.

JOHNSTON, H. H. (1902). *The Uganda Protectorate.* London: Hutchinson.

KIGONGO, R., and REID, A. (2007). Local communities, politics and the management of the Kasubi tombs, Uganda. *World Archaeology* 39: 371–84.

LANNING, E. C. (1966). Excavations at Mubende Hill. *Uganda Journal* 30: 153–63.

LEJJU, B. J., ROBERTSHAW, P. T., and TAYLOR, D. (2006). Africa's earliest bananas? *Journal of Archaeological Science* 33: 102–13.

ONJALA, I. (2003). Spatial distribution and settlement system of the stone structures of south-western Kenya. *Azania* 38: 99–120.

POSNANSKY, M. (1968). The excavation of an Ankole capital site at Bweyorere. *Uganda Journal* 32: 165–82.

—— (1969). Bigo bya Mugenyi. *Uganda Journal* 33: 125–50.

REID, A. (1996). Ntusi and the development of social complexity in southern Uganda. In G. Pwiti and R. Soper (eds), *Aspects of African Archaeology.* Harare: University of Zimbabwe Press, 621–8.

—— (2003a). Ancient Egypt and the source of the Nile. In D. C. O'Connor and A. Reid (eds), *Ancient Egypt in Africa.* London: UCL Press, 55–76.

—— (2003b). Recent research on the archaeology of Buganda. In P. J. Mitchell, A. Haour, and J. H. Hobart (eds), *Researching Africa's Past: New Contributions from British Archaeologists.* Oxford: Oxbow, 110–17.

—— and ASHLEY, C. Z. (2007). A context for the Luzira Head. *Antiquity* 82: 99–112.

—— and MACLEAN R. (1995). Symbolism and the social contexts of iron production in Karagwe. *World Archaeology* 27: 144–61.

—— and YOUNG, R. (2000). Pottery abrasion and the preparation of African grains. *Antiquity* 74: 101–11.

ROBERTSHAW, P. T. (1994). Archaeological survey, ceramic analysis and state formation in western Uganda. *African Archaeological Review* 12: 105–31.

—— (1997). Munsa earthworks: a preliminary report. *Azania* 32: 1–20.

—— (1999). Seeking and keeping power in Bunyoro-Kitara, Uganda. In S. K. McIntosh (ed.), *Beyond Chiefdoms: Pathways to Complexity in Africa.* Cambridge: Cambridge University Press, 124–35.

—— (2010). Beyond the segmentary state: creative and instrumental power in western Uganda. *Journal of World Prehistory* 23: 255–69.

—— and TAYLOR, D. (2000). Climate change and the rise of political complexity in western Uganda. *Journal of African History* 41: 1–28.

ROSCOE, J. (1911). *The Baganda: An Account of Their Native Customs and Beliefs.* Cambridge: Cambridge University Press.

SASSOON, H. (1983). Kings, cattle and blacksmiths: royal insignia and religious symbolism in the Interlacustrine states. *Azania* 18: 93–106.

SCHMIDT, P. (1978). *Historical Archaeology: A Structural Approach in an African Culture.* Westport, Conn.: Greenwood Press.

—— (1990). Oral traditions, archaeology, and history: a short reflective history. In P. T. Robertshaw (ed.), *A History of African Archaeology.* London: James Currey, 252–70.

—— (1997). *Iron Technology in East Africa: Symbolism, Science and Archaeology.* Bloomington: Indiana University Press.

SCHOENBRUN, D. L. (1998). *A Green Place, A Good Place: Agrarian Change, Gender, and Social Identity in the Great Lakes Region to the 15th Century.* Oxford: James Currey.

SHINNIE, P. L. (1960). Excavations at Bigo 1957. *Uganda Journal* 24: 16–29.

SUTTON, J. E. G. (1998). Ntusi and Bigo: farmers, cattle herders and rulers in western Uganda 1000–1500. *Azania* 33: 39–72.

VAN NOTEN, F. (ed.) (1983). *Histoire Archéologique du Rwanda*. Tervuren: Musée Royale de l'Afrique Centrale.

WAYLAND, E. J. (1934). Notes on the Biggo bya Mugenyi: some ancient earthworks in northern Buddu. *Uganda Journal* 2: 21–32.

YOUNG, R., and THOMPSON, G. (1999). Missing plant foods? Where is the archaeobotanical evidence for sorghum and finger millet in East Africa? In M. Van Der Veen (ed.), *The Exploitation of Plant Resources in Ancient Africa*. New York: Plenum, 63–72.

CHAPTER 62

THE SWAHILI WORLD

ADRIA LAVIOLETTE

INTRODUCTION

IN the first millennium AD a distinctive mixed farming and fishing society, increasingly engaged with contacts made by way of the Indian Ocean trading system, emerged along East Africa's coast, drawing much of its population, as well as its cultural and economic practices, from the peoples of the near African interior. As this society matured, it forged a unique identity through a combination of factors including: exploitation of the littoral environment, Islamic practice, cosmopolitan urban polities with a mix of stone-built and earth-and-thatch towns and villages, a shared material culture with regional distinctions, including a characteristic mix of locally made and imported goods, and the regionally specific ways in which merchants and others linked domestic economies into large-scale networks extending into the interior of Africa and the Indian Ocean. This entire phenomenon, which has persisted through a range of stages and formations over the past 1,500 years, constitutes what is known as the Swahili world. This chapter summarizes the current state of knowledge about Swahili society as known primarily through archaeology, including broad commonalities that tie the coast together as a culture zone and current directions in archaeological research.

The word 'Swahili' derives from the Arabic for 'coastal-dwelling'. Debate exists as to when the term should be applied, depending on the timing of factors such as the spread of the Swahili language, town formation, and conversion to Islam, all of which become central to later notions of Swahili life but did not appear simultaneously. The spread of Tana Tradition/ Triangular Incised Ware ceramics (see below) signals Swahili origins for many, beginning AD 500–600, while others use the term only after about AD 1000. For our purposes Swahili is used for material dating from the 6th century onward; it can be argued that the spread of settlements along the Eastern African littoral, with the Tana/TIW ceramic signature often in combination with local manufacturing evidence and certain imported material, marks the beginning of a distinctive coastal lifeway. Linguistic studies suggest that it might be later, the 10th or 11th centuries, when the Swahili language emerged from Northeast Coast Bantu languages, a time when we also see a considerable amount of town building on the coast that may be related to another phase of intracoastal migrations. Coastal dwellers who would be called Swahili by outsiders called, and still call, themselves by many names often invoking specific urban or regional affiliations, such as WaAmu and WaVita (the peoples of Lamu and Mombasa respectively). One of the most widely used names has been WaShirazi, which carries the claim of origins in distant parts of the Islamic world but has been argued to relate more probably to origins in the African interior (Allen 1993); the issue of foreign origins became of great political importance in the 20th century. The nomenclature issue reminds us that the lived experience of coastal dwellers in the first millennium—those who founded or joined new settlements as they migrated from other coastal villages, or moved to the coast from inland or even foreign locales—was probably a more gradual transition into a complicated social milieu than archaeological typologies would currently suggest (Chami 1994, 2000). Many attempts have been made to qualify the complexities of Swahili identity, which remains contested (Prins 1961, 1965; Mazrui and Shariff 1994; Mazrui 2007).

Despite the grey areas in our understanding of Swahili origins, there is broad consensus that Swahili society was an indigenous African development. Before the 1980s most scholarship, rooted in racialized British and Arab assumptions about their colonial subjects as well as the impact of colonialism on coastal identities, cast the Swahili as originating from economically motivated Arab and/or Persian colonization and the resulting intermarriage between colonizers and African women. The great impact of 19th-century Omani Arab migration to the Swahili coast led to assumptions that heavy migration had also characterized the coast in much earlier centuries (e.g. Kirkman 1964). Archaeological and linguistic evidence has been used to recast this narrative, arguing convincingly for the African origins of Swahili society and culture, while still acknowledging that some immigration and an openness to select foreign influences were fundamental to Swahili life (Nurse and Spear 1985; Allen 1993; Horton 1996).

Historical evidence and Swahili
archaeology

Historical sources have played an important role in Swahili archaeology from its outset, as the following summary outlines. First- and early second-millennium external documents are evocative, incomplete, and sometimes even fanciful; using them in dialogue with archaeological data has only sometimes been productive (Horton 1997). The earliest known written documentation, the remarkable *Periplus of the Erythraean Sea* (Casson 1989), dates to the 1st century AD and was written by an unnamed, Alexandria-based Greek sailor making a sea voyage from Roman Egypt to East African, southern Arabian, and Indian ports, which he described in inconsistent detail. For scholars of East African coastal archaeology, a compelling reference has been to Rhapta, the Romans' southernmost port of trade, thought to have been on the Tanzanian coast. Rhapta was described as under the authority of Muza in the southwestern Arabian Peninsula. Although such a settlement has not yet been identified, as is the case for many in the *Periplus*, Chami (1999) links it to 1st-century AD horizons in the Rufiji Delta that yielded Roman beads. Exports listed as coming from East Africa include ivory and rhinoceros horn from the interior and nautilus and turtle shell from the coast, while imports included metal implements (despite indigenous iron production), glass, and some foods. A slightly later source, Ptolemy's *Geography*, a Greco-Roman compendium containing sailing coordinates for coastal locations including some on the eastern African littoral, also mentions Rhapta (Freeman-Grenville 1962). Both documents are consistent with archaeological evidence that, before the emergence of Swahili society, some coastal populations engaged in trade and social relations with Mediterranean and Indian Ocean societies during the Early Iron Age, and perhaps even earlier (Chami 2001a).

A gap in known written sources follows, until Chinese accounts begin in the 7th century (Duyvendak 1949; Snow 1988; Shen 1995); Chinese travel to the coast was intermittent at best, but occurred by at least the 15th century, and underwater archaeological research on the topic continues. The documentary record is then largely silent until the late first millennium, when Arab and other accounts begin. An important 10th-century first-hand account is that of al-Mas'udi (Freeman-Grenville 1962), who, in his only report from the coast, describes a place called Qanbalu with a Muslim ruling family; this document inspired Kirkman's (1964) excavations at Ras Mkumbuu on Pemba, with perhaps unnecessarily disappointing results for him (LaViolette 2004). Archaeologists have also made fruitful use of Ibn-Battuta's account of his 14th-century visit to Mogadishu and Kilwa (Fleisher 2004).

Recorded oral traditions and histories, usually linked to specific towns and known as the Swahili chronicles, are another category of sources used in connection with coastal archaeology. Such histories were passed down through generations verbally, and ultimately formalized as written chronicles. They feature sociopolitical relationships through specific events, such as the ties and conflicts between Swahili and interior peoples or between Swahili settlements, marriage alliances with Indian Ocean families, or local leaders' acts of generosity. Most were recorded and published by colonial officers and scholars during the 19th and 20th centuries. A few are lengthy and have been used extensively by historians, such as those from Pate and Kilwa (Pouwels 1993; Tolmacheva 1993). Some twenty more—shorter, less well known, and related to smaller coastal polities—may have under-explored archaeological potential.

OVERVIEW OF SWAHILI ARCHAEOLOGY

Archaeologically, the Swahili world extends some 2,500 km north/south from Mogadishu in Somalia through Kenya and Tanzania to Sofala in Mozambique (Duarte 1993). Included in this expanse are Kenya's Lamu archipelago, Tanzania's Pemba, Unguja (Zanzibar) and Mafia islands, the Comoros archipelago, and northwestern Madagascar (Wright 1994; Radimilahy 1998) (Fig. 62.1). Coastal dwellers sailed extensively for fishing and short-distance travel north and south. Importantly, the outline of the Swahili region corresponds closely with the western edge of the Indian Ocean monsoonal wind system, which facilitated regular long-distance travel among ports around the vast Indian Ocean rim (Mitchell 2005). The environmental niche occupied by the Swahili offered not just rich mangrove and ocean resources *per se* but the ability to develop and engage in long-distance trading relationships, evidence for which is found in the earliest Swahili contexts. These relationships brought exotic goods to coastal towns and villages and also spurred ongoing relationships with peoples in the interior, whose own goods were moved to the coast in exchange for coastal and imported goods.

FIG. 62.1 Major archaeological sites on the Swahili coast (prepared by Jeffrey Fleisher).

While Swahili life beyond its famous mercantilism is becoming better known through new directions in coastal archaeology, there is little doubt that the socioeconomic networks integral to trade had a dramatic impact on Swahili life.

In the late first millennium BC and until the founding of Swahili settlements, the coast was home to a mosaic of smaller-scale societies with economies based on cattle pastoralism and mixed farming and fishing. Early Iron Age Urewe and Kwale ceramics (de Maret, this volume) were used throughout both coastal and more interior regions, suggesting little cultural or economic separation of the coast. What precisely sparked the differences that grew up between coast and the near interior continues to be debated, but by at least the 6th century AD there was a rapid expansion of new earth-and-thatch settlements, mostly on or within short distances of the shore, the residents of which were making a new suite of ceramics called the Tana Tradition (Horton 1996) in reference to the Tana River basin in Kenya (Fig. 62.2). The most recognizable type of these new ceramics has also been called Triangular

FIG. 62.2 Tana Tradition/Triangular Incised Ware rims from 7th–10th-century contexts, Tumbe, Pemba Island, Tanzania; the one at lower right shows use as a grinder, consistent with shell bead production (photograph courtesy of Jeffrey Fleisher).

Incised Ware (TIW) in an effort to be more geographically neutral (Chami 1994). Tana/TIW ceramics are found at nearly all coastal sites from the 6th to 10th centuries, but also at a significant number of inland sites, such that we must see the coastal expansion of Tana/TIW-using people as part of a phenomenon still linked strongly to interior societies (Soper 1971; Chami 2000; Haaland and Msuya 2000; Helm 2000; Walz 2005). Tana/TIW thus joined Kwale and Urewe wares in being pan-regional and remained dominant on the coast until about AD 1000, when more localized ceramic styles replaced them (Chami 2000).

Over the 6th–10th centuries, therefore, a new pattern of coastal life emerged that was linked to interior regions but increasingly differentiated itself. Iron smelting and smithing, boat construction, and shell bead making (Fig. 62.2; Flexner et al. 2008) were part of the local economy. Subsistence was based on mixed agriculture, animal husbandry, fishing, and wild plant and animal resources (Horton and Mudida 1993; Walshaw 2010). Imported goods included a wide variety of glazed ceramics, glassware, copper alloy and other metal jewellery, and stone and glass beads, especially from the Persian Gulf; long-distance trading relationships continued to increase in range over time, eventually including many locations in Southwest and Southeast Asia, the Indian subcontinent, the Maldives, and Indonesia. Although many exports may have been raw materials without lasting archaeological signatures, objects of East African origin have been found in a variety of locations in the Indian Ocean world (Horton and Middleton 2000). After the 7th century, many of the merchants with whom coastal people traded were Muslims, and through this exposure coastal people began conversion to Islam (Insoll 2003). Archaeological evidence for Islamic practice on the coast dates from the mid-8th century, in the form of a timber mosque at Shanga in the Lamu Archipelago, at the base of a superimposed centuries-long series of mosques of increasing size and formality (Horton 1996).

By the 9th century, economic connections between East Africa and the Middle East had grown in scale to include the export of thousands of enslaved people from the interior.

Although direct evidence for trade in captives is scarce, especially in its earliest purported centuries, the practice deserves greater attention as a force tying coastal and interior economies together (Kusimba 2004). Captives were transported through coastal centres, including Unguja and Pemba, to destinations in what is now Iraq, where they laboured on drainage projects at the head of the Gulf of Basra. In 868, a historic uprising known as the Zanj Revolt weakened the caliphate based in Basra, and led to a downturn in Arab interest in slaves from Swahili sources (Popović 1999).

By AD 1000, larger settlements had developed amidst the coast's numerous villages; however, three sites at least—Unguja Ukuu, Tumbe, and Manda—experienced significant scale several centuries earlier (Chittick 1984; Juma 2004; LaViolette and Fleisher 2009). Towns with cosmopolitan urbanity came to characterize coastal culture from early in the second millennium (LaViolette 2008). While the leading edge of Swahili culture may have been in these towns, the majority of Swahili people were undoubtedly villagers. Town and village economies continued to be based on mixed farming, fishing, craft production, and long-distance trade in the centuries after 1000.

The wealth and power of Swahili towns reached their greatest extent in the 11th–14th centuries, as measured by the number and scale of settlements and their material culture (Kusimba 1999; Horton and Middleton 2000). Building in coral (often called stone) became an important medium of Swahili cultural expression and the hallmark of elite dwellings and public and ritual structures within settlements (Allen 1979). In the 9th century Swahili elites adopted a transformative method of mortared coral construction with mangrove pole ceilings and roofs (Garlake 1966). In its earliest manifestation, divers cut *porites* coral from reefs, forming the soft material into blocks that then hardened. The technology included detailing the buildings with finely carved arches, niches and geometric elements. After all was assembled and mortared, builders applied lime plaster, making building surfaces smooth and white. Eventually this system was transformed, such that fossilized coral, called coral rag, was quarried on land, with the *porites* retained for detailing.

In both cases, the resulting architecture—solid but delicate, often multi-storeyed, more permanent than structures of earth and thatch—may have been critical to anchoring the relationships of certain Swahili lineages with important foreign traders. Ethnohistorically, such houses acted as 'customs houses', providing lodging for visiting merchants, helping to establish their elite owners' credibility as business partners, and contributing to the prosperity of the towns and regions. This relationship can also be suggested for pre-1000 dates, but not all settlements with coral houses can be assumed to have had direct ties with international merchants (Horton and Middleton 2000; Fleisher 2010a).

Although far from the dominant housing type on the coast, stone houses, often found in clusters in the towns, became the most identifiable and symbolically laden of Swahili artefacts (Donley-Reid 1987; Fleisher and LaViolette 2007). Excavation of stone architecture, though central to understanding Swahili urban life, was long the sole basis for archaeologists' early reconstructions of Swahili society. This is no longer the case, as the earth-and-thatch structures in towns and villages are now under archaeological study (Fleisher and LaViolette 1999; LaViolette and Fleisher 2009; Pawlowicz 2009; Fleisher 2010b).

Many of the largest Swahili settlements are considered urban, called 'city-states' or 'states' by some (e.g. Kusimba 1999; Sinclair and Håkansson 2000), and marked by complex relations with rural settlements in their local countrysides. Such centres differed in their internal class structures and political styles. Ethnohistoric evidence from later towns suggests two main types: one that emphasized a single leader and elevated him or her far above the majority of the town dwellers, predominantly on the southern coast, and another that emphasized a larger class of elites with less distance between social tiers, more typical of the northern coast (Horton and Middleton 2000). Versions of these types may be represented in earlier centuries, indicated in part by different proportions of coral to earthen architecture in towns. Coastal regions became more distinct from one another after AD 1000, with localized historical trajectories influenced heavily by life and leadership in the larger towns, and also by the diverse characters of relationships between the towns and the non-Swahili rural peoples living beyond them (Horton 1994).

Centuries of mercantile success by coastal elites should not blind us to other aspects of life on the coast, including the probably small proportion of people directly engaged with international trade relative to those numbers participating in activities such as food production, craft production (Fig. 62.3), and ritual specialization. In towns, excavations in earthen houses and their middens have shown the significant level of material consumption of locally made and imported goods by a wide range of urban dwellers. There is evidence for interaction among Swahili settlements themselves (Abungu and Mutoro 1993), including the exchange of goods and architectural idioms. Local and regional production of goods and services were linked to long-distance networks in ways that are still being explored. Exports to foreign locales differed in their destinations depending on shifting regional relationships and possibilities for transhipment; an early dependence on ties to the Persian Gulf expanded to a much vaster region over time, eventually ranging from Europe to Arabia and Oman, India and China (Horton 1987; Kusimba 1999; Horton and Middleton 2000; Fleisher 2010a). Gold obtained through trade with Zimbabwe Plateau societies (Pikirayi, Ch. 63 below) came to be one of the coast's most important exports, along with ivory, iron, animal products, and mangrove poles. Imports continued to feature glazed and unglazed ceramics from far afield, some transporting foods; a wide range of personal items such as beads, metal jewellery, glass

FIG. 62.3 Spindle whorls (12th–15th centuries) made on sherds of imported ceramics, Chwaka, Pemba Island, Tanzania (photograph, Adria LaViolette).

FIG. 62.4 Kilwa-type copper coins from a 15th-century context at Songo Mnara, Tanzania (photograph courtesy of Jeffrey Fleisher).

vessels holding perfumes and ointments, cotton and silk thread and cloth, and Koranic and other religious texts. Copper and silver coins were minted in some of the largest centres (Fig. 62.4); rock crystal and other stones were worked into beads and traded; and iron continued in importance while copper alloys were added to local production (Chittick 1977; Horton and Middleton 2000). Whereas colonial models for early Swahili history assumed foreign dominance of Swahili trade relations, current views have shifted, underscoring Swahili agency in the Indian Ocean world (Horton and Middleton 2000; Connah 2001; Mitchell 2005; Fleisher 2010a).

The active practice of Islam and the presence of religious specialists and elaborate mosques and cemeteries cannot be underestimated in terms of the importance of towns within Swahili society (Pouwels 1987; Wright 1993; Insoll 2003; Horton 2004; LaViolette and Fleisher 2009). While coral architecture is best known from houses, coral mosques and above-ground tombs (including a distinct class of 'pillar tombs') became important constructions throughout the coast (Fig. 62.5). Many settlements with earth-and-thatch domestic architecture featured a coral mosque and tombs; many of these constructions had imported ceramic bowls mortared into them. Mosque and tomb architecture has been the subject of considerable study, as well as other material culture, features and changing foodways that can be linked with Islamic practice and with different sects of Swahili Islam (Garlake 1966; Allen 1993; Horton 1996, 2004; Insoll 2003; Walshaw 2010). As mentioned above, scholarship on Swahili origins has considered numerous scenarios in the emergence of the Swahili world as distinct from more inland societies; the practice of Islam is surely one of the prime movers in their distinction.

Although the late 15th century begins a long-term transformation on the coast, with the advent of Portuguese and, later, renewed Arab interest and intrusion, there is no sharp historical break in the dynamics of Swahili urban and rural life, but rather a series of more gradual transformations. Portuguese ships sailed around the Cape of Good Hope to reach the East African coast for the first time in 1498. The earliest Portuguese activity in the region has not been the focus of archaeological study to date, although their 16th-century presence is known from documentary sources and in some cases from architecture at Malindi, Zanzibar town, elsewhere on Unguja and Pemba islands, and Kilwa (Pearson 1998). Fort Jesus, built by

FIG. 62.5 Pillar tombs with impressions from inset imported ceramics and niches evoking those in houses (foreground), and mosque (background), 10th–16th-century site of Ras Mkumbuu, Pemba Island, Tanzania (photograph, Adria LaViolette).

the Portuguese in 1593 (Kirkman 1974), and the 1697 shipwreck of the *São Antonio de Tanna* in Mombasa have both been the subject of study (Sassoon 1981). The Portuguese were evicted from Mombasa in 1697 after a long siege, which ended the first phase of their colonization efforts on the Swahili coast. Sections of the coast came under immediate attack from Omani Arabs, however, such that from the 16th century onward the Swahili struggled against unwanted incursions of various scales and levels of success. Swahili society prevailed throughout, despite transformations, although disruptions in long-distance trade and losses of regional autonomy weakened the strength of the entire coastal economic system and its ties to both the interior and the Indian Ocean. Historical research has been more significant than archaeological for this later period, although important excavations have laid the foundation for future study at sites such as Gedi/Gede, Ungwana and Vumba Kuu (Kirkman 1954, 1966; Wynne-Jones 2010). The coast was never politically unified before the Omani Sultanate colonized the region in the early 19th century and shifted its capital from Muscat to Zanzibar.

EMERGING QUESTIONS AND DIRECTIONS IN ARCHAEOLOGICAL RESEARCH

The first decades of archaeological research on the Swahili focused exclusively on the ruined stone architecture in the larger towns on the coast; although guided by the now over-turned assumption that the towns were colonial outposts, these early, large-scale excavations provided a foundation still referenced in coastal archaeology since (e.g. Chittick 1974, 1984). However, artefacts considered to be of local manufacture, and therefore not of interest to understanding the 'colony', were largely understudied until the 1980s. Village settlements and the remains of earth-and-thatch structures, or even entire neighbourhoods underlying or situated among stone structures in towns, were mostly ignored. The shift during the 1980s toward viewing the Swahili coast as an African phenomenon triggered new overlapping approaches in archaeological research. These include close examinations of Swahili subsistence, the nature of Islamic practice, functional approaches to Swahili urbanism, interactions between the coast and the near and deep African interiors, Swahili identity and gender dynamics, the relationship between the religious, merchant, and political elites and commoners, and Swahili relationships with their environments.

Urban or 'stonetown' settlements have hardly been abandoned in this new research, but approaches to studying them have changed. The complexity of town histories, including the cultures and practices present in their founding levels, the changing nature of their communities over time, the unfolding of Islamic practice within the towns, and detailed studies of the local economies have been investigated at a number of polities. The former emphasis on international trade left details of the domestic economy obscure, but Horton and Mudida's (1993) extensive faunal analysis at Shanga allowed them to argue for the presence of distinct foodways in different quarters of the town. Attention to the performances around food can be seen in Walshaw's (2010) archaeobotanical analyses at the adjacent sites of Tumbe and Chwaka, Pemba Island, where she traced the early dependence on millet there and a switch to favouring rice and the use of a wide range of wild plants. In a similar vein, Fleisher (2010c) has argued for public feasting, based on changing ceramic forms, as part of a new performance of Islamic ritual life. At a larger scale of analysis, Pawlowicz (2009), surveying the Mikindani region of the southern Tanzanian coast, identified five microenvironments with settlements and explored changing land use through botanical and isotopic analysis. Breen and Lane (2003), and Christie (2011), among others (Breen, Ch. 15 above), have also explored Swahili exploitation of marine environments. Indeed, interest is growing in human/land (and sea) relationships on both the Swahili coast and elsewhere in Africa (Chami et al. 2001). For example, Pollard's (2008) maritime archaeological research at Kilwa shows the massive stone architectural investments Kilwa made to its port in the 13th–16th centuries.

Surveys have also been successful in identifying meaningful regions of rural/urban interaction around larger settlements by locating, through sub-surface testing, numerous earthen village settlements, many of which have been tested or more comprehensively excavated (Kwekason 2007; Wynne-Jones 2007; Pawlowicz 2009; Fleisher 2010b). The archaeology of the rural Swahili and the relationship between town and countryside complicates earlier, exclusively town-based depictions of Swahili life, heavily influenced by 19th- and 20th-century ethnohistoric accounts. Such research has moved the understanding of Swahili urbanism forward by contextualizing town-based studies in their larger rural contexts, as well as by contributing to region-specific understandings of the coast (LaViolette and Fleisher 2005), and the role of materiality in creating urban and rural identities (Wynne-Jones 2007b). Other projects have sought to understand corridors of interaction, including caravan routes, between urban coastal polities and smaller-scale polities to the interior (Helm 2000; Chami 2001b; Walz 2005; Wynne-Jones and Croucher 2007). Among these studies, Kusimba (2004) and Kusimba et al. (2005) have explored interior regions of Kenya through survey, identifying both the presence of ethnic mosaics and the breakdown of such patterns when tensions between coast and interior, related to the slave trade, became increasingly virulent after Omani colonial penetration of coastal regions.

Interest in Swahili archaeology of the last two centuries has also recently blossomed. Focusing on 19th-century plantations, Croucher (2007) has addressed the clove economy on Zanzibar, as well as questions of Swahili identity, gender, and sexuality, while Marshall (2009) has studied fugitive slaves from Swahili and Omani coastal plantations in Kenya, with an emphasis on the creation of new identities and communities in the near hinterland (see also Rhodes 2010). These studies engage cognitive and structural questions, as does ongoing work at Songo Mnara on Swahili urban planning (Fleisher and LaViolette 2007; Wynne-Jones and Fleisher 2010; see also Kusimba 1996).

Some six decades of research on the East African coast has established the region as one of the most compelling for understanding indigenous large-scale African societies. Ongoing research will only complicate the picture, as it continues to go deeper into local Swahili experience at the same time that it increasingly links the Swahili to other peoples and regions.

REFERENCES

ABUNGU, G. H. O., and MUTORO, H. W. (1993). Coast-interior settlements and social relations in the Kenya coastal hinterland. In T. Shaw, P. J. J. Sinclair, B. Andah, and A. Okpoko (eds), *The Archaeology of Africa: Food, Metals and Towns*. London: Routledge, 694–704.

ALLEN, J. V. (1993). *Swahili Origins*. London: Heinemann.

BREEN, C., and LANE, P. J. (2003). Archaeological approaches to East Africa's changing seascapes. *World Archaeology* 35: 467–89.

CASSON, L. (ed.) (1989). *The Periplus Maris Erythraei*. Princeton, NJ: Princeton University Press.

CHAMI, F. A. (1994). *The Tanzanian Coast in the First Millennium AD: An Archaeology of the Iron-Working, Farming Communities*. Uppsala: Societas Archaeologica Upsaliensis.

—— (1999). Roman beads from the Rufiji Delta, Tanzania: first incontrovertible archaeological link with the *Periplus*. *Current Anthropology* 40: 237–41.

—— (2000). A review of Swahili archaeology. *African Archaeological Review* 15: 199–218.

—— (2001a). Chicken bones from Neolithic limestone cave site, Zanzibar. In Chami et al. (2001: 84–97).

—— (2001b). The archaeology of the Rufiji region since 1987 to 2000: coastal and interior dynamics from AD 00–500. In Chami et al. (2001: 7–20).

—— PWITI, G., and RADIMILAHY, C. (eds) (2001). *People, Contacts and the Environment in the African Past*. Dar es Salaam: Dar es Salaam University Press.

CHITTICK, H. N. (1974). *Kilwa: An Islamic Trading City on the East African Coast*. Nairobi: British Institute in Eastern Africa.

—— (1977). The East Coast, Madagascar and the Indian Ocean. In R. Oliver (ed.), *The Cambridge History of Africa*, vol. 3. Cambridge: Cambridge University Press, 183–231.

—— (1984). *Manda: Excavations at an Island Port on the Kenya Coast*. Nairobi: British Institute in Eastern Africa.

CHRISTIE, A. C. (2011). Exploring the social context of maritime exploitation in the Mafia Archipelago, Tanzania: an archaeological perspetive. Unpublished PhD Thesis, University of York.

CONNAH, G. (2001). *African Civilizations*. Cambridge: Cambridge University Press.

CROUCHER, S. K. (2007). Clove plantations on 19th-century Zanzibar: possibilities for gender archaeology in Africa. *Journal of Social Archaeology* 7: 302–24.

DONLEY-REID, L. W. (1987). Life in the Swahili town house reveals the symbolic meaning of spaces and artefact assemblages. *African Archaeological Review* 5: 181–92.

DUARTE, R. T. (1993). *Northern Mozambique in the Swahili World: An Archaeological Approach*. Uppsala: Societas Archaeologica Upsaliensis.

DUYVENDAK, J. L. L. (1949). *China's Discovery of Africa*. London: Probsthain.

FLEISHER, J. B. (2004). Behind the sultan of Kilwa's 'rebellious conduct': local perspectives on an international East African town. In A. M. Reid and P. J. Lane (eds), *African Historical Archaeologies*. New York: Kluwer Academic/Plenum, 91–123.

——(2010a). Housing the market: Swahili merchants and regional marketing on the East African coast, seventh to sixteenth centuries AD. In C. Garraty and B. Stark (eds), *Archaeological Approaches to Market Exchange in Ancient Societies*. Boulder: University Press of Colorado, 141–59.

——(2010b). Swahili synoecism: rural settlements and town formation on the central East African coast, AD 750–1500. *Journal of Field Archaeology* 35: 265–82.

——(2010c). Rituals of consumption and the politics of feasting on the eastern African coast, AD 700–1500. *Journal of World Prehistory* 23:195–217.

——and LAVIOLETTE, A. (1999). Elusive wattle-and-daub: finding the hidden majority in the archaeology of the Swahili. *Azania* 34: 87–108.

————(2007). The changing power of Swahili houses, fourteenth to nineteenth centuries A.D. In R. A. Beck (ed.), *The Durable House: House Society Models in Archaeology*. Carbondale, Ill.: Center for Archaeological Investigations, 175–97.

FLEXNER, J. L., FLEISHER, J. B., and LAVIOLETTE, A. (2008). Bead grinders and early Swahili household economy: analysis of an assemblage from Tumbe, Pemba Island, Tanzania, 7th–10th centuries AD. *Journal of African Archaeology* 6: 161–81.

FREEMAN-GRENVILLE, G. S. P. (1962). *The East African Coast: Select Documents from the First Century to the Early Nineteenth Century*. Oxford: Clarendon Press.

GARLAKE, P. S. (1966). *The Early Islamic Architecture on the East African Coast*. Nairobi: British Institute in Eastern Africa.

HAALAND, R., and MSUYA, C. S. (2000). Pottery production, iron working, and trade in the Early Iron Age: the case of Dakawa, east-central Tanzania. *Azania* 35: 75–106.

HELM, R. M. (2000). Recent archaeological research on the iron-working, farming communities of coastal Kenya. *Azania* 35: 183–9.

HORTON, M. (1987). The Swahili corridor. *Scientific American* 257: 76–84.

——(1994). Closing the corridor: archaeological and architectural evidence for emerging Swahili regional autonomy. In D. Parkin (ed.), *Continuity and Autonomy in Swahili Communities: Inland Influences and Strategies of Self-Determination*. London: School of Oriental and African Studies, 15–21.

——(1996). *Shanga: The Archaeology of a Muslim Trading Settlement on the Coast of East Africa*. London: British Institute in Eastern Africa.

——(1997). Eastern African historical archaeology. In J. O. Vogel (ed.), *Encyclopedia of Precolonial Africa*. Walnut Creek, Calif.: AltaMira Press, 549–54.

——(2004). Islam, archaeology, and Swahili identity. In D. Whitcomb (ed.), *Changing Social Identity with the Spread of Islam: Archaeological Perspectives*. Chicago: Oriental Institute, 67–88.

——and MIDDLETON, J. (2000). *The Swahili*. Oxford: Blackwell.

—— and MUDIDA, N. (1993). Exploitation of marine resources: evidence for the origins of the Swahili communities of East Africa. In T. Shaw, P. J. J. Sinclair, B. Andah, and A. Okpoko (eds), *The Archaeology of Africa: Food, Metals and Towns*. London: Routledge, 673–93.

INSOLL, T. (2003). *The Archaeology of Islam in Sub-Saharan Africa*. Cambridge: Cambridge University Press.

JUMA, A. (2004). *Unguja Ukuu on Zanzibar: An Archaeological Study of Early Urbanism*. Uppsala: Societas Archaeologica Upsaliensis.

KIRKMAN, J. S. (1954). *The Arab City of Gedi: Excavations at the Great Mosque, Architecture, and Finds*. The Hague: Mouton.

—— (1964). *Men and Monuments on the East African Coast*. London: Lutterworth.

—— (1966). *Ungwana on the Tana*. The Hague: Mouton.

—— (1974). *Fort Jesus: a Portuguese Fortress on the East African Coast*. Oxford: Clarendon Press.

KUSIMBA, C. M. (1996). Spatial organization at Swahili archaeological sites in Kenya. In G. Pwiti and R. Soper (eds), *Aspects of African Archaeology*. Harare: University of Zimbabwe, 703–14.

—— (1999). *The Rise and Fall of Swahili States*. Walnut Creek, Calif.: AltaMira Press.

—— (2004). Archaeology of slavery in East Africa. *African Archaeological Review* 21: 59–88.

—— KUSIMBA, S. B., and WRIGHT, D. K. (2005). The development and collapse of precolonial ethnic mosaics in Tsavo, Kenya. *Journal of African Archaeology* 3: 243–65.

KWEKASON, A. (2007). Pre-early iron working sedentary communities on the southern coast of Tanzania. In F. Chami, G. Pwiti, and M. Radimilahy (eds), *Settlements, Economies and Technology in the African Past*. Dar es Salaam: African Archaeological Network, 20–40.

LAVIOLETTE, A. (2004). Swahili archaeology and history on Pemba, Tanzania: a critique and case study of the use of written and oral sources in archaeology. In D. A. M. Reid and P. J. Lane (eds), *African Historical Archaeologies*. New York: Kluwer Academic/Plenum, 125–62.

—— (2008). Swahili cosmopolitanism in Africa and the Indian Ocean world, A.D. 600–1500. *Archaeologies* 4: 24–49.

—— and FLEISHER, J. B. (2005). The archaeology of sub-Saharan urbanism: cities and their countrysides. In A. B. Stahl, (ed.), *African Archaeology: A Critical Introduction*. Oxford: Blackwell, 327–52.

—— —— (2009). The urban history of a rural place: Swahili archaeology on Pemba Island, Tanzania, a.d. 700–1500. *International Journal of African Historical Studies* 42: 433–55.

MARSHALL, L. W. (2009). Fugitive slave communities in 19th-century Kenya: a preliminary report on recent archaeological and historical research. *Nyame Akuma* 72: 21–9.

MAZRUI, A. M. (2007). *Swahili Beyond the Boundaries: Literature, Language, and Identity*. Athens: Ohio University Press.

—— and SHARIFF, I. N. (1994). *The Swahili: Idiom and Identity of an African People*. Trenton, NJ: Africa World Press.

MITCHELL, P. J. (2005). *African Connections: Archaeological Perspectives on Africa and the Wider World*. Walnut Creek, Calif.: AltaMira.

MUTORO, H. W. (1998). Precolonial trading systems of the East African interior. In G. Connah (ed.), *Transformations in Africa: Essays on Africa's Later Past*. London: Leicester University Press, 186–203.

NURSE, D., and SPEAR, T. (1985). *Reconstructing the History and Language of an African Society, 800–1500*. Philadelphia: University of Pennsylvania Press.

PAWLOWICZ, M. (2009). Archaeological exploration of the Mikindani region of the southern Tanzanian coast. *Nyame Akuma* 72: 41–51.

POLLARD, E. (2008). Inter-tidal causeways and platforms of the 13th- to 16th-century city-state of Kilwa Kisiwani, Tanzania. *International Journal of Nautical Archaeology* 37: 98–114.

POPOVIĆ, A. (1999). *The Revolt of African Slaves in Iraq in the 3rd/9th Century.* Princeton, NJ: Markus Wiener.

POUWELS, R. L. (1987). *Horn and Crescent: Cultural Change and Traditional Islam on the East African Coast, 800–1900.* Cambridge: Cambridge University Press.

—— (1993). Reflections on historiography and pre-nineteenth-century history from the Pate 'Chronicles'. *History in Africa* 20: 263–96.

PRADINES, S. (2005). Archéologie et préservation du patrimoine: le projet franco-tanzanien de Kilwa, 2002–2005. *Nyame Akuma* 63: 20–6.

PRINS, A. H. J. (1961). *The Swahili-Speaking Peoples of Zanzibar and the East African Coast.* London: International African Institute.

—— (1965). *Sailing from Lamu: A Study of a Maritime Culture in Islamic East Africa.* Assen: Van Gorcum.

RADIMILAHY, C. (1998). *Mahilaka: An Archaeological Investigation of an Early Town in Northwestern Madagascar.* Uppsala: Uppsala University Press.

RHODES, D. (2010). *Historical Archaeologies of Nineteenth-Century Colonial Tanzania: A Comparative Study.* Cambridge Monographs in African Archaeology 79, BAR International Series 2075. Oxford: Archaeopress.

SASSOON, H. (1981). Ceramics from the wreck of a Portuguese ship at Mombasa. *Azania* 16: 98–130.

SHEN, J. (1995). New thoughts on the use of Chinese documents in the reconstruction of early Swahili history. *History in Africa* 22: 349–58.

SINCLAIR, P. J. J., and HÅKANSSON, T. (2000). The Swahili city-state culture. In M. H. Hansen (ed.), *A Comparative Study of Thirty City-State Cultures.* Copenhagen: Royal Danish Academy of Sciences and Letters, 463–82.

SNOW, P. (1988). *The Star Raft: China's Encounter with Africa.* New York: Weidenfeld & Nicolson.

SOPER, R. C. (1971). Early Iron Age pottery types from East Africa: comparative analysis. *Azania* 6: 39–52.

TOLMACHEVA, M. (1993). *The Pate Chronicle.* East Lansing: Michigan State University Press.

WALSHAW, S. C. (2010). Converting to rice: urbanization, Islamization and crops on Pemba Island, Tanzania AD 700–1500. *World Archaeology* 42: 137–53.

WALZ, J. R. (2005). Mombo and the Mkomazi corridor: preliminary archaeological finds from lowland northeastern Tanzania. In B. B. B. Mapunda and P. Msemwa (eds), *Salvaging Tanzania's Cultural Heritage.* Dar es Salaam: Dar es Salaam University Press, 198–213.

WRIGHT, H. T. (1993). Trade and politics on the eastern littoral of Africa, AD 800–1300. In T. Shaw, P. J. J. Sinclair, B. Andah, and A. Okpoko (eds), *The Archaeology of Africa: Food, Metals and Towns.* London: Routledge, 658–72.

—— (1994). Early seafarers of the Comoro Islands: the Dembeni Phase of the IXth–Xth centuries AD. *Azania* 19: 13–59.

WYNNE-JONES, S. (2007a). Creating urban communities at Kilwa Kisiwani, Tanzania, AD 800–1300. *Antiquity* 81: 368–80.

—— (2007b). It's what you do with it that counts: performed identities in the East African coastal landscape. *Journal of Social Archaeology* 7: 325–45.

—— (2010). Remembering and reworking the Swahili Diwanate: the role of objects and places at Vumba Kuu. *International Journal of African Historical Studies* 43: 407–27.

—— and CROUCHER, S. K. (2007). The central caravan route of Tanzania: a preliminary archaeological reconnaissance. *Nyame Akuma* 67: 91–5.

—— and FLEISHER, J. B. (2010). Archaeological investigations at Songo Mnara, Tanzania, 2009. *Nyame Akuma* 73: 2–9.

CHAPTER 63

....

THE ZIMBABWE CULTURE AND ITS NEIGHBOURS

Origins, Development, and Consequences of Social Complexity in Southern Africa

....

INNOCENT PIKIRAYI

INTRODUCTION

....

IN this chapter, 'social complexity' refers to the development of social formations synonymous with ranked forms of organization that appeared south of the Zambezi from the late first millennium AD. As this happened, some societies were mobilized under political leadership in order to build public works and produce surplus food for people living in urban centres. Political leaders were also able to levy taxes from trade goods to generate surplus wealth that was used to finance public projects such as stone-walled monumental buildings. These southern Zambezian societies were part of a regional network tied to global commerce involving eastern Africa and Asia, and were organized in the form of chiefdoms and states displaying different levels of sociopolitical stratification. Population aggregations resulted in some settlements attracting up to 5,000 people or more, especially from the 10th century AD. The population in these towns displayed an array of specializations, producing goods and services, supported by a hinterland involving farmers, miners, hunters, metalworkers, and other specialists. The bigger settlements were the residences of chiefs or kings. The largest of these sites were probably capital centres, where central authority or government was based, supported by an administrative authority and in some cases an army. Archaeologists have used stone-walled architecture to define the territorial limits of some of these political formations.

This chapter discusses chiefdom and states in southern Zambezia, from Toutswe (700–1300) and Mapungubwe (1200–1300) in the Shashe–Limpopo Basin, through Great Zimbabwe (1300–1550) and then Torwa-Changamire (1400–1830) and Mutapa (1450–1900)

(Fig. 63.1). States are ultimately political and socioeconomic experiments that to a large measure are highly authoritative and consumptive. As such, they are bound to fail, disbanding, collapsing, or declining because of the strain that they exert on their subjects. Hence, greater cultural complexity is not the ideal, but rather an exceptional attainment. Importantly, the southern Zambezian region also saw the development of lesser societies that were impacted upon or spawned by these centralized societies, such as in Nyanga (see Stump, Ch. 46 above).

EARLY CHIEFDOM AND STATE SOCIETIES IN THE SHASHE–LIMPOPO BASIN

The Shashe–Limpopo Basin covers some 415,000 km² of eastern Botswana, northern South Africa, southern Zimbabwe, and southern Mozambique. The Limpopo River roughly flows though its middle as part of a total journey of about 1,800 km before discharging into the Indian Ocean. Where the Shashe River, which drains much of eastern Botswana, joins the Limpopo it forms a spectacular confluence and an extensive floodplain. Political centralization occurred here among agropastoralist societies in a broad area covering western Zimbabwe's plateau, the middle Limpopo Valley, and the eastern fringes of the Kalahari

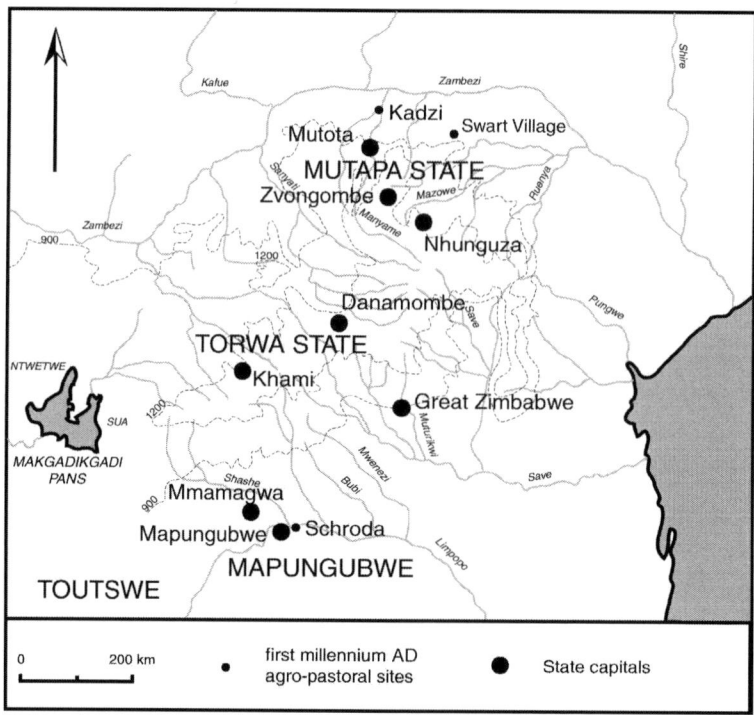

FIG. 63.1 Map showing some of the archaeological sites, chiefdoms, and state societies discussed in Chapter 63.

Desert. Currently, this environment is arid to semi-arid—an observation that underlines the importance of understanding how this region was transformed into productive farmland and what encouraged populations to aggregate here in major centres. We know from studies of past climates that the region experienced increasingly wet conditions from the onset of the second millennium to about AD 1300, a change that undoubtedly attracted farming communities to the Shashe–Limpopo floodplain (Tyson and Lindesay 1992; Tyson et al. 2000, 2002; Holmgren and Oberg 2006; Huffman 2007, 2008; Smith et al. 2007). Manyanga (2007) argues that the societies that lived in this region had capacities to withstand perturbations from instances of climate or economic shocks and to rebuild and renew themselves continuously.

From about AD 900 the middle Limpopo Valley, farming communities who made Zhizo-type pottery inhabited southwestern Zimbabwe and eastern Botswana. These communities lived in sizeable homesteads and villages, some possibly small towns, such as Schroda, Ratho Farm, Leokwe Hill, and Pont Drift in the Limpopo Valley and Mothudi and Mmamgwa (Fig. 63.2) in the upper and lower Motloutse Valleys respectively of eastern Botswana. Some of these centres, such as Schroda, have considerable evidence of ritual activity as exemplified by ceramic figurines, and also received glass beads from the Indian Ocean coast (Wood 2000, 2011), possibly in exchange for animal skins and ivory, as part of regional networks of trade, resource exploitation, and redistribution of goods that also included iron ore mining in the Tswapong Hills of eastern Botswana. Not only was the Basin's broader landscape suitable for cereal cultivation, but its mopane trees and grasslands also encouraged the raising of live-stock—something that developed particularly strongly further west in the Lotsani and Motloutse Valleys and the Tswapong, Tshwerong, Shoshong, Serowe, and Toutswemogala Hills of eastern Botswana. From Schroda and Ratho Farm in the middle Limpopo Valley and extending further west towards the Kalahari margins, lineages established ranked societies, minimally chiefdoms, especially at Toutswemogala, Taukome, and Bosutswe, where sites with Zhizo type pottery attest to increased population and considerable social transformation. It is highly likely that the first chiefdoms and state societies in southern Africa developed around these sites.

FIG. 63.2 An extensive Zhizo settlement in the valley west of Mmamgwa Hill, eastern Botswana (photograph, Innocent Pikirayi).

Around AD 1000, when eastern Botswana was already witnessing considerable social and possibly political transformation, new polities of the same rank and extent developed in south-western Zimbabwe and the middle Limpopo Valley—events associated by archaeologists with the presence of Leopard's Kopje pottery (Huffman 2005, 2007, 2008). Bambandyanalo (K2), Den Staat, Leokwe Hill, Mmamagwa Hill, and Ratho Farm all show clustering of sizeable settlements that can be called towns and, judging from the number of pens and depth of cow dung present at them, also housed sizeable cattle herds. This process of urbanization provided competition for resources among later Zhizo type settlements in eastern Botswana, as Leopard's Kopje sites in the middle Limpopo Valley seem to have had better access to foreign goods whose transhipment into the interior they controlled by virtue of their position along the river and relative proximity to the coast (Manyanga et al 2010).

Leopard's Kopje sites surveyed in the middle Limpopo Valley display a hierarchical spatial pattern of town centres at the helm of numerous villages clustered as well as scattered in the floodplain (Manyanga 2007, Huffman 2007). This suggests a level of political organization synonymous with chiefdoms who were exploiting and competing for resources found in the area. Like their Zhizo counterparts further west, they were now rearing large herds of cattle. One of the largest settlements, Bambandyanalo, grew in size (to over 8 ha) and shows social and economic specialization, as attested by evidence for ivory working. However, while informative as to the lifestyle, demography, and health of the site's inhabitants (Meyer 1998), the quite extensive available skeletal sample does not provide much evidence for social stratification, although ethnographic data suggest that some of the people buried in the cattle pen were probably of high status. Social stratification, however, becomes clear at nearby (1km distant) Mapungubwe Hill, which was inhabited from c. 1220 to 1300.

On and around Mapungubwe Hill—situated, like Bambandyanalo, near the confluence of the Shashe and Limpopo Rivers—archaeologists have identified a pattern synonymous with the emergence of 'sacred leadership' (Huffman 2005, 2007) and the emergence of a ruling elite. The central part of the hilltop housed a palace demarcated by stone walling, which was also used to define entrances to elite housing areas at the foot of the hill (Fig. 63.3). Here, houses were less clustered, with a lot of space between homesteads. The area below also housed what has been identified as a court area (Huffman 2007). A perimeter enclosed commoner housing further down the hill bottom to the west. The inhabitants of this town, who probably numbered more than 5,000, traded in copper, iron, ivory, glass beads, and gold, which is the reason why their rulers were so wealthy. The burial evidence from the hilltop shows considerable social stratification. Twenty-three graves were found here, of which three were associated with gold objects (Tiley 2004). One burial, that of a woman in a sitting position wearing gold bangles around her ankles, had over 12,000 gold beads. A second was that of a man, also in a sitting position, wearing a necklace of gold beads and cowrie shells and accompanied by some objects covered in gold foil. The third burial was also that of a man, buried with a wooden headrest and objects made of gold foil tacked onto a wooden core, which included a bowl, a sceptre, and a rhinoceros.

Archaeological surveys attest to the presence of Mapungubwe-type sites on both the Limpopo River floodplain and adjacent plateau areas (Manyanga 2007). Most homesteads were located on the floodplain and may have exploited this rich, silty environment for cereal cultivation and livestock rearing, attracting people into this region of southern Africa. Grain bin foundations found at both Leopard's Kopje and Mapungubwe type sites attest to the intensification of cereal agriculture during the early second millennium AD. From the distri-

FIG. 63.3 Mapungubwe hilltop, South Africa, showing the palace area (photograph, Innocent Pikirayi).

bution of Iron Age sites in the middle Limpopo Valley and from observations of some communities currently living in the Basin, it seems likely that exploitation of floodplains and adjacent drylands took advantage of the opportunities each of the respective ecologies provided. It was also a mechanism designed to limit the constraints imposed by flooding as well as dryness.

The Limpopo floodplain attracted farming populations when conditions became wetter. According to the archaeological evidence, agriculture intensified in the middle Limpopo floodplain during the K2 period (*c.* 1000–1220) (Huffman 2005). Palaeoclimate proxy data show that rainfall had increased to 500 mm, slightly higher than today's level (Smith et al. 2007), encouraging the planting of sorghum, millet, beans, and cowpeas due to increased moisture conditions in the valley. Archaeological evidence also attests to an expanding population during this time, which may have affected agricultural production (Huffman 2005).

Water management in the Shashe–Limpopo Basin was also regulated by ritual and ceremony. An important feature of this arid environment is rain control (Huffman 2008, Schoeman 2006), i.e. the use of ritual to manage nature and stimulate rain. Archaeological research has identified a number of steep-sided hills in the Basin, with dolly holes, cupules, natural cisterns, and rock tanks, associated with sorghum remains and pottery. It appears that these were used to brew beer and that K2 people were behind some of these rituals, as they were in control of farming activities in the basin, although hunter-gatherers, as 'first people' of the land, could have officiated at them (Schoeman 2006), comparable perhaps to the territorial cults discussed by Ranger (1973) for more northerly areas of southern Africa. Despite the demise of Mapungubwe as a centre of political power in the area around AD 1300, communities in the middle Limpopo Valley may have continued to cope with an unpredictable environment through a combination of forecast and ritual. Elsewhere, on the Zimbabwe Plateau, a new centre of power emerged in the Mutirikwi Valley, which is part of the Save–Runde catchment. Why the state society based at Mapungubwe disintegrated after AD

1300 is not easy to answer at this juncture, but available palaeoclimatic data do not suggest that this was due to environmental deterioration (Smith et al. 2007).

The rise, development, and demise of Great Zimbabwe

With the demise of Mapungubwe, Iron Age farmers akin to early Karanga speakers developed chiefdom-level societies at Chivowa and Gumanye Hills in south-central Zimbabwe (Sinclair 1987; Pikirayi 2001), transforming themselves from simple kin-warranted domestic corporations relying mainly on land and cattle to long-distance traders. With this newly acquired wealth, they financed the building of stone walling. By about 1270 a wealthy elite had emerged at Great Zimbabwe, which laid the foundations of an elaborate urban complex and the centre of a state, constructing stone buildings of unparalleled scale and magnitude from about 1300 (Garlake 1973). For the next 150 years, Great Zimbabwe became the dominant political authority south of the Zambezi (Huffman 1996, 2007).

Great Zimbabwe reached its peak during the 14th and 15th centuries, when elaborate stone walling that symbolized wealth, power, and status was extended towards outlying areas (Fig. 63.4). With an estimated population of nearly 20,000, Great Zimbabwe was the largest metropolis in southern Africa. Composed of elite residences, ritual centres, and houses of commoners and artisans, it covered more than 700 ha. The first stone-wall complex (the Hill Complex) was raised on a whaleback hill at the centre of the site. Here, two large enclosures and intervening smaller enclosures abut from the natural granite boulders and defined the living spaces for royalty. A ritual spearhead, iron gongs, and soapstone bird effigies attest to the presence of elite individuals. Commoner settlements within a perimeter wall at the base of the hill soon became overcrowded, triggering further expansion beyond. Royalty also

FIG. 63.4 A view of Great Zimbabwe showing the Great Enclosure, and some Valley Enclosures (photograph, Innocent Pikirayi).

moved downhill to the more elaborate elliptical enclosure (the Great Enclosure). The largest single stone-built structure in southern Africa, it has a girdle wall 244 m long, 5 m wide, and 10 m high. It encloses sub-enclosures and parallel passages, with a conical tower marking the focus of the settlement. This massive structure represents the peak of development of Great Zimbabwe. Five enclosure complexes to the northeast and east were built in the valley this time (Valley Enclosures), but rose to prominence towards the terminal phases of the settlement. A second peripheral wall on the western precincts attests to the continuously growing city. Stone enclosures in the periphery either housed members of the ruling family or catered for increased administrative functions of the metropolis.

The success of Great Zimbabwe is seen in the fact that it presided over a regional and international economy that exported gold, ivory, and other valuables in return for Persian and Far Eastern stoneware, earthenware, and porcelain, Indian glass beads, and cloth (Wood 2011). The site wielded enormous influence over much of southern Zimbabwe plateau, reaching the Save–Runde confluence and possibly beyond into the Mozambican coastal plains, where Zimbabwe-type capitals exist. This influence could only have happened through management of the local agricultural economy, which, though largely dependent on seasonal rainfall, should also have taken advantage of the unique moisture patterns associated with the semi-arid region in which the site and other capitals were located.

But then, how did such a complex society come to an end? Explanations of Great Zimbabwe's demise remain speculative (Garlake 1978; Pikirayi 2006; Huffman 2007). A simple climatic hypothesis (such as the supposed impact of the Little Ice Age) is certainly incorrect (Huffman 1996); yet Great Zimbabwe's size does suggest that, over time, its significant population could have impacted on its water supply and hydrological budget and thus on agricultural production (Holmgren and Oberg 2006). The long-term impacts of cutting down trees for construction and for use as firewood in cooking, heating, and metallurgy (especially iron smelting and forging) may also have been substantial, as suggested by the absence of *Brachystegia speciformis*—an important source of firewood for domestic cooking, iron smelting and stone quarrying, house construction, and roofing material—from the site's immediate surroundings (Pikirayi 2001: 67). Alternatively, or additionally, political disruption may have been the principal reason behind Great Zimbabwe's decline, particularly competition in its hinterland for resources such as grain, gold, and ivory following the rise of the Torwa state to the southwest (Huffman 2007).

Social organization and spatial symbolism

According to Huffman (1981, 1982, 1985, 2008), it is possible to understand the spatial correlates of Great Zimbabwe's social structure using a binary-coded cognitive framework supported by ethnography. Huffman argues that the kings at Great Zimbabwe resided in the Western Enclosure of the Hill Complex, while the Eastern Enclosure served as a ritual centre. The Great Enclosure in the valley is interpreted as a centre for initiation (see Huffman 1985, 2010, 2011). Huffman argues that it was used for circumcision and acted as a premarital school for boys and girls (known in Venda as *Domba*), citing the existence of symbols for different age groups from the young to the old and ritual objects that supported an initiation centre hypothesis. The Valley Enclosures are interpreted as residences of the royal wives, who occupied this area for the duration of the site's florescence (Huffman 1996, 2010, 2011), under the authority of the most senior or 'first' wife (Huffman 2007).

Huffman's model presents a picture of a society in stasis for 200 years. Beach (1998) made recourse to Shona ethnography and history of political succession to argue that the ruler's residences changed during Great Zimbabwe's 200-year florescence. From this perspective (see also Pikirayi and Chirikure 2011), the Great Enclosure was not an initiation centre, nor were the valley enclosures residences for royal wives. Instead, they were centres adopted by successive rulers. This endorses the idea of a shifting focus during the Great Zimbabwe development, placing serious doubts on the structuralist hypothesis. The combined archaeological sequence and architectural chronology is consistent with an expanding and shrinking settlement (Chirikure and Pikirayi 2008; Collett et al. 1992), and is supported by the distribution of material culture found inside the stone walls of Great Zimbabwe. In particular, the presence of metalworking slag and iron blooms, all falling within the domain of male activities, shows that there was a sizeable male presence in the lower valley enclosures. The *Domba* ceremony—a ceremony introduced among the Venda through centuries of interaction with the Lemba and Sotho–Tswana societies—was not held regularly because it was dependent on the number of young people ready to participate and the nature of the harvest, and initiation centres thus tended to be impermanent structures built of perishable materials. Such an institution is unlikely to have left significant archaeological signatures. By contrast, the Great Enclosure is a permanent building whose construction took place over a long time. It had a broad-based material culture that included local pottery, spindle whorls, symbolic objects, metalworking evidence, and lavish imports. This assemblage is similar to that found on the Hill Complex and in the valley enclosures (Chirikure and Pikirayi 2008).

LATER ZIMBABWE CULTURE STATES IN THE NORTHERN AND WESTERN ZIMBABWE PLATEAU

During the 15th century Great Zimbabwe lost some of its influence to developments in both the northern and western parts of the Zimbabwe Plateau. In the southwest, Khami emerged as a powerful centre of the Torwa state focused on southwestern Zimbabwe and eastern Botswana, while in the north the appearance of other centres constructed along similar lines to Great Zimbabwe suggests a movement of people from the south coinciding with the foundation of the Mutapa state (Beach 1980; Pikirayi 1993).

The Mutapa state

The Mutapa state (*c.* 1450–1900) in northern Zimbabwe is extensively covered in Portuguese written sources (Mudenge 1988; Beach 1994) that refer to it as lying within a region referred to as the 'Rivers of Gold'. Early Portuguese explorers into the interior reported stone-building activity in the Mutapa state, identifying these structures, known as 'Symbaoe' (*zimbabwe*), as the residences of the ruling elite. Using archaeological data, Portuguese written accounts can shed light on the decline of Great Zimbabwe, triggered by changing patterns in the trade in eastern Africa. Archaeology can also enlighten the introduction of merchant capitalism in northern Zimbabwe, evidenced by imported artefacts dating from the 16th century, and assist in the identification of local material culture, such as pottery associated with these imports.

Such associations are crucial in relating local pottery to known ethnic groups such as the Karanga, mentioned in Portuguese written sources as the people of the Mutapa state.

Archaeological research in northern Zimbabwe has revealed the nature of contact between the Zimbabwe Plateau and the Indian Ocean, as well as the nature of settlements associated with this contact since the 16th century, with one focus the African–Portuguese site of Baranda near Mt Fura, a known source of gold, and other sites in the middle Ruya—Mazowe Valley (Pikirayi 1993, 2009). Whereas previous research in northern Zimbabwe could not positively identify local populations represented by the ceramic evidence recovered from sites associated with African–Portuguese trading settlements such as Luanze, Dambarare, Rimuka, and Angwa, at Baranda traded items such as imported ceramics and glass beads dating from the 16th century were associated with local pottery attributable to the Zimbabwe Culture. This discovery provides a new insight into the relationship between the Mutapa state and the Zimbabwe Culture, as Baranda, which is synonymous with the Portuguese trading settlement of Massapa, represents the emergence of non-stone-walled royal courts in northern Zimbabwe at a time after the cessation of stone-building activity at the beginning of the 16th century.

The decline of the Mutapa state was apparently triggered by the highly exploitative nature of the Portuguese merchants and conquistadores in northern Zimbabwe, as attested by their direct interference in royal succession and the destructive nature of goldmining. The appearance of fortifications may indicate decreasing sociopolitical complexity during the late 16th and 17th centuries, when crudely built stone defences were erected on hilltops in the Ruya–Mazowe Basin (Fig. 63.5), the heartland of the Mutapa state (Pikirayi 2009). Detailed Portuguese accounts of fortifications refer, however, to the Lower Zambezi, where people built wooden stockades, and provide only vague references to stone-walled fortifications in northern Zimbabwe. Ceramic evidence from the hillforts nevertheless points to the Budya or related Tonga groups from the Lower Zambezi as their builders, following their movement into the area in response to the turmoil generated by the expansion of Portuguese estate holders further downstream and the southward expansion of the Marave and the Zimba (Pikirayi 2001, 2009).

FIG. 63.5 Some of the fortified settlements on Mt Fura, northern Zimbabwe (photograph, Innocent Pikirayi).

The Torwa–Rozvi states

Broadly contemporary with the emergence of the Mutapa state on the north of the Zimbabwe Plateau, the Torwa state (*c.* 1490–1650) developed in southwestern Zimbabwe and adjacent areas of eastern Botswana (Beach 1980). With its control of these areas, Khami, its capital, may have played a considerable part in undercutting Great Zimbabwe's major gold resource base and diverting its trade to the Indian Ocean coast, mostly via the southern plateau (Pikirayi 2006; Huffman 2007). Important sites here continued, but developed, the traditions of stonewalling seen earlier at Great Zimbabwe, including a proliferation of decoration in chord, check, and herringbone patterns and the construction of solid daub houses on tiered platform surfaces. Although Khami principally dates to the period covered by Portuguese documents, it is never directly mentioned in them. The same sources do, however, suggest that it was founded by rebels or outsiders (*vatorwa*) from the Mutapa state during the second half of the 15th century, such that by about 1494 a dynasty called Torwa had successfully established itself in an area referred to as Guruuswa. Later Portuguese sources report the destruction of Torwa's capital, presumably Khami, in the mid-17th century during a civil war, after which a defeated Torwa ruler appealed to the Portuguese based in the trading station of Manyika for help. The small Portuguese army sent in response was, however, soon driven out of the Torwa kingdom, the centre of which then shifted to Danangombe in central Zimbabwe (Beach 1980: 200–201; 1984: 82). There, the Rozvi dynasty was firmly established by 1680, and stone-walled centres of the Khami type appear in this area, from which the Rozvi dominated much of the Zimbabwe Plateau (Beach 1980; Mudenge 1988).

Disruption and disintegration

Until the 15th century, archaeological evidence seems to suggest that large social formations in the form of chiefdoms and states took over social and economic management of most subsistence-based village societies in southern Zambezia. In this way, they exercised a managerial role over society in social experiments that facilitated wealth creation, ensured loyalties, enhanced networks of interaction and provided protection against hostile neighbours. Aggregating to the size of chiefdoms and states was an exercise that was ultimately resource-consumptive and entailed sharper social and political hierarchies, which in turn required considerable resources to sustain them. The arrival of European merchant capital in the early 16th century presented southern Zambezian social formations with considerable challenges, as it favoured and encouraged individual participation in trade and wealth accumulation. Social disruption became commonplace.

The disintegration of the Mutapa state in the late 16th and 17th centuries was largely a result of competition for resources around the gold and ivory trade, and certainly involved the Portuguese conquistadores. This resulted in rapid loss of political power, corresponding loss of territorial control and influence, and challenges from the periphery (Pikirayi 1993). The polities of Budya in northeastern Zimbabwe, Barwe in the Zambezian lowlands, Manyika in the eastern highlands of Zimbabwe, Teve in the Mozambican plains, Duma in south-central Zimbabwe and Nambya, and Shangwe and Makonde on the northwestern plateau all reflect these challenges to the sociopolitical authority associated with the Zimbabwe Culture. The last vestiges of those states (especially the Rozvi) were then effectively destroyed on the arrival in the region of Nguni predatory and mobile states such as those of the Ngoni (led by Zvangendaba) and Ndebele (led by Mzilikazi) in the early 19th century, following which (in 1890) Zimbabwe itself was colonized by the British.

Concluding remarks

Southern Zambezian states were spheres of cultural interaction and influence, with people sharing roughly the same culture and displaying their identities in material culture forms. Stone architecture was used for this purpose and, along with pottery, was used to negotiate some of these identities. Southern Zambezian states were also tributary in character, extracting surplus production from economically relatively independent producers by political or military coercion. This is how they exercised their hegemony and power. Their ideologies were created and maintained for the specific purposes of supporting the ruling elite, their power, and their achievements and imposing on society as a whole an 'official' understanding or perception of the world around and beyond. This facilitated the continued dominance of the elite's structures of governance, and justified coercion or persuasion in the collection of tribute, taxes, and other essential resources, as well as conquest in the drive for territorial expansion.

The Zimbabwe Plateau and adjacent regions were also environmentally sustainable landscapes (*sensu* Selman 2008) that were largely resilient for much of the period in which these social formations existed. In this regard, the perception of social complexity as the scale of practices characterizing human society measured in terms of differentiation and centralization, stratification and diversity, inequality, and heterogeneity seems to be both practical and workable. Future research may need to focus on how we should understand decline or collapse in this context, and on how societies and leaders made important and impacting decisions in this regard and others.

References

BEACH, D. N. (1980). *The Shona and Zimbabwe, 900–1850*. Gweru: Mambo Press.
—— (1994). *The Shona and Their Neighbours*. Oxford: Blackwell.
—— (1998). Cognitive archaeology and imaginary history at Great Zimbabwe. *Current Anthropology* 1: 47–72.
CHIRIKURE, S., and PIKIRAYI, I. (2008). Inside and outside the dry stone walls: revisiting the material culture of Great Zimbabwe. *Antiquity* 82: 976–93.
GARLAKE, P. S. (1973). *Great Zimbabwe*. London: Thames & Hudson.
—— (1978). Pastoralism and Zimbabwe. *Journal of African History* 19: 479–93.
HALL, M. (1987). *The Changing Past: Farmers, Kings and Traders in Southern Africa*, 200–1860. Cape Town: David Philip.
HOLMGREN, K., and OBERG, H. (2006). Climate change in southern Africa during the past millennium and its implications for societal development. *Environmental Development and Sustainability* 8: 155–95.
HUFFMAN, T. N. (1981). Snakes and birds: expressive space at Great Zimbabwe. *African Studies* 40: 131–50.

HUFFMAN, T. N. (1982). Archaeology and ethnohistory of the African Iron Age. *Annual Review of Anthropology* 11: 133–50.

—— (1985). The Great Enclosure and *domba*. *Man* 20: 543–5.

—— (1996). Archaeological evidence for climate change during the last 2000 years in southern Africa. *Quarterly International* 33: 55–60.

—— (2005). *Mapungubwe: Ancient African Civilization on the Limpopo*. Johannesburg: Wits University Press.

—— (2007). *Handbook to the Iron Age: The Archaeology of Pre-Colonial Farming Societies in Southern Africa*. Scottsville: University of KwaZulu-Natal Press.

—— (2008). Mapungubwe and Great Zimbabwe: the origin and spread of social complexity in southern Africa. *Journal of Anthropological Archaeology* 28: 37–54.

—— (2010). Revisiting Great Zimbabwe. *Azania: Archaeological Research in Africa* 45: 321–8.

—— (2011). Debating Great Zimbabwe. *South African Archaeological Bulletin* 66: 27–40.

MANYANGA, M. (2007). *Resilient Landscapes: Socio-environmental Dynamics in the Shashi-Limpopo Basin, Southern Zimbabwe, c. AD 800 to the Present*. Uppsala: Uppsala University Press.

—— PIKIRAYI, I., and CHIRIKURE, S. (2010). Conceptualising the urban mind in pre-European southern Africa: rethinking Mapungubwe and Great Zimbabwe. In P. J. J. Sinclair, G. Nordquist, F. Herschend, and C. Isendahl (eds), *The Urban Mind: Cultural and Environmental Dynamics*. Uppsala University: Department of Archaeology and Ancient History, 573–90.

MEYER, A. (1998). *The Archaeological Sites of Greefswald*. Pretoria: University of Pretoria Press.

MUDENGE, S. I. G. (1988). *A Political History of Munhumutapa*. Harare: Zimbabwe Publishing House.

PIKIRAYI, I. (1993). *The Archaeological Identity of the Mutapa State: Towards an Historical Archaeology of Northern Zimbabwe*. Uppsala: Societas Archaeologica Upsaliensis.

—— (2001). *The Zimbabwe Culture: Origins and Decline in Southern Zambezian States*. Walnut Creek, Calif.: AltaMira Press.

—— (2006). The demise of Great Zimbabwe, AD 1420–1550: an environmental re-appraisal. In A. Green and R. Leech (eds), *Cities in the World, 1500–2000*. Leeds: Maney Publishing, 31–47.

—— (2009). Palaces, *feiras* and *prazos*: an historical archaeological perspective of African–Portuguese contact in northern Zimbabwe. *African Archaeological Review* 26: 163–85.

—— and CHIRIKURE, S. (2011). Debating Great Zimbabwe. *Azania: Archaeological Research in Africa* 46: 221–31.

RANGER, T. O. (1973). Territorial cults in the history of Central Africa. *Journal of African History* 14: 581–97.

SCHOEMAN, M. H. (2006). Imagining rain places: rain-control and changing ritual landscapes in the Shashe–Limpopo Confluence Area, South Africa. *South African Archaeological Bulletin* 61: 152–65.

SELMAN, P. (2008). What do we mean by sustainable landscape? *Sustainability: Science, Practice and Policy* 4: 23–8.

SMITH, J., LEE THORP, J. A., and HALL, S. L. (2007). Climate change and agropastoralist settlement in the Shashe–Limpopo River Basin, southern Africa. *South African Archaeological Bulletin* 62: 115–25.

TILEY, S. (2004). *Mapungubwe: South Africa's Crown Jewels*. Cape Town: Sunbird Publishing.

TYSON, P. D., KARLEN, W., HOLMGREN, K., and HEISS, G. (2000). The Little Ice Age and medieval warming in South Africa. *South African Journal of Science* 96: 121–6.

——Lee Thorp, J. A., Holmgren, K., and Thackeray, J. F. (2002). Changing gradients of climate change in southern Africa during the past millennium: implications for population movements. *Climate Change* 52: 29–135.

——and Lindesay, J. A. (1992). The climate of the last 2000 years in southern Africa. *The Holocene* 2: 271–8.

Wood, M. (2000). Making connections: relationships between international trade and glass beads from the Shashe–Limpopo area. In M. Lesley and T. M. Maggs (eds), *African Naissance: The Limpopo Valley 1 000 Years Ago*. South African Archaeological Society Goodwin Series 8: 78–90.

——(2011). A glass bead sequence for southern Africa from the 8th to the 16th century AD. *Journal of African Archaeology* 9: 67–84.

CHAPTER 64

SOUTHERN AFRICAN LATE FARMING COMMUNITIES

ALEX SCHOEMAN

INTRODUCTION

SOUTHERN AFRICAN Late Farming Communities were ancestral, or related, to the majority of contemporary southern Africans. These agropastoralists formed part of a broader pre-colonial southern African complex during the second millennium AD that also included hunter-gatherers and pastoralists. European colonial expansion in the 18th and 19th centuries dramatically disrupted these communities and the networks between them while recasting the pre-colonial African past in 'tribal' terms (Hall 1984a). In the 1950s, before the impact of colonialism was fully understood, archaeologists termed the period during which Late Farming Communities lived in southern Africa the 'Late Iron Age', drawing here on the analogy of older stadial terms in European archaeology (Maggs 1992; Mitchell 2002). However, more recently the term 'Iron Age' has become emblematic of older approaches to material culture and group identity. In the postcolonial and post-Apartheid period research has started to transcend older colonial narratives and uncover the complex processes that shaped southern Africa, hence the shift in terminology. Although this chapter is unable to give a full account of this research, it uses a few of the key insights of this research to discuss the archaeology of southern African Late Farming Communities. More detailed accounts include Mitchell (2002), Mitchell and Whitelaw (2005), Huffman (2007), and Swanepoel et al. (2008).

EXCAVATING POTS AND FINDING PEOPLE

A connection between groups and ceramics has been central to the archaeology of southern African farming communities. One of the earliest of these studies was Schofield's (1937) sequencing of the ceramics from Mapungubwe (Fig. 64.1), capital of southern Africa's earliest state (Pikirayi, Ch. 63 above). This was framed in a colonial 'tribal' mindset and linked

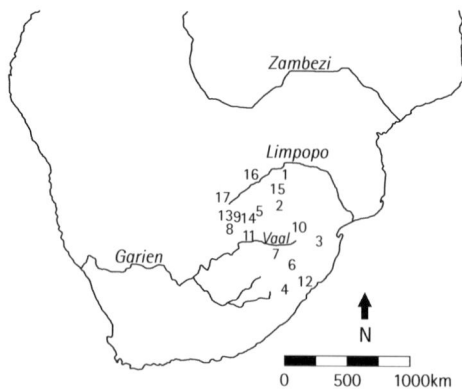

FIG. 64.1 Location of the archaeological sites discussed in Chapter 64. 1 Mapungubwe;
2 Historic Cave; 3 Simunye; 4 Moor Park; 5 Rooiberg; 6 Nqabeni; 7 Ntsuanatsatsi;
8 Mmakgame; 9 Madikwe; 10 Bokoni; 11 Lepalong; 12 Mgungundlovu; 13 Kaditshwene;
14 Marathodi; 15 Makgabeng; 16 Ntsweng; 17 Phalatswe.

comb-stamped Zhizo pottery to Sotho-Tswana speakers, who were then displaced by Shona-
speakers making incised Leopard's Kopje ware. The assumptions about population displacements that underlay this scenario have been shown to be wrong (Calabrese 2007), but the
theoretical underpinnings linking ceramics to bounded groups are still fundamental to the
archaeology of Late Farming Communities. For example, Huffman (2002, 2004) has traced
the movement of Nguni and Sotho–Tswana ancestors through ceramics. This approach is
based on the understanding that culture is a system of meaning that is expressed in ceramics,
among other forms of material culture.

Martin Hall (1984a) opposed an approach to archaeology that assumed that language or
culture were the only identities expressed in ceramics. Not all archaeologists shared his concerns, however, and an identity-centred approach remained dominant until Simon Hall
(1997, 1998) initiated a shift away from these types of ceramic analyses through use of concepts developed in ceramic sociology to link Tswana pots to people's bodies—an approach
also adopted by Paul Lane (1998) with reference to changes in household space. Sociological
approaches such as these form part of a broader trend in African archaeology that is now
moving beyond narrow identification of ceramics and related material culture variation with
ethnic or language groups (Pikirayi 2007; Gosselain and Livingstone Smith, Ch. 9 above;
Wynne-Jones, Ch. 13 above).

Using these insights, ceramics can assist in the identification of local and regional networks, as evident in the presence of Marateng ceramics at sites associated with the Pedi
polity, the Ndzundza capitals, and neighbouring Bokoni towns (see below). This distribution suggests that Marateng is a regional, non-ethnic ceramic style used to signal social
and economic networks (Delius and Schoeman 2008). Ceramic alliances are also visible
at Historic Cave in the Makapan's Valley of South Africa's Limpopo Province, where
comb-stamped ceramics, resembling pottery produced in Bafokeng and Koena chiefdoms from which key Kekana royal wives hailed, were found on a house floor associated
with higher-status individuals. In the fluid political landscape between the 16th and 19th
centuries marriage alliances formed an important political tool. Consequently, the comb-

stamped pottery was used to represent key marriage and associated political alliances (Esterhuysen 2008).

This does not mean that at times ceramic style does not indicate group identity. For example, Ohinata (2002) linked the style of ceramics at Simunye in northeastern Swaziland to ancestors of the Tsonga speakers of present-day southern Mozambique and northern KwaZulu-Natal, South Africa. The discrete distribution of this ceramic style and continuity in material culture to the present suggest that Tsonga speakers existed as a distinct group, who chose to signal an independent identity. A distinct Tsonga identity is also echoed by genetic research on co-ancestry coefficients that found that the closest genetic affinities of Tsonga speakers are with Venda speakers, not with their Swazi- and Zulu-speaking neighbours (Lane et al. 2002).

Overall, the limits of ceramic based approaches have encouraged a number of scholars to approach the pasts of Late Farming Communities through methodologies developed in historical archaeology (Reid and Lane 2004; Pikirayi 2006). This does not mean that periods for which additional historical sources do not exist are ignored, but rather that continuities are followed into deeper time (Behrens and Swanepoel 2008).

THE COMPLEXITY OF LATE FARMER COMMUNITY GROUP MEMBERSHIP

The earliest evidence for Late Farming Communities in southern Africa—Blackburn ceramics—date to the 11th century AD (Huffman 2004). Regrettably, little is known about this period, because only a few, limited excavations have been conducted on Blackburn sites (Mitchell 2002: 345). As sites were not stone-walled, they are difficult to locate and excavate thoroughly.

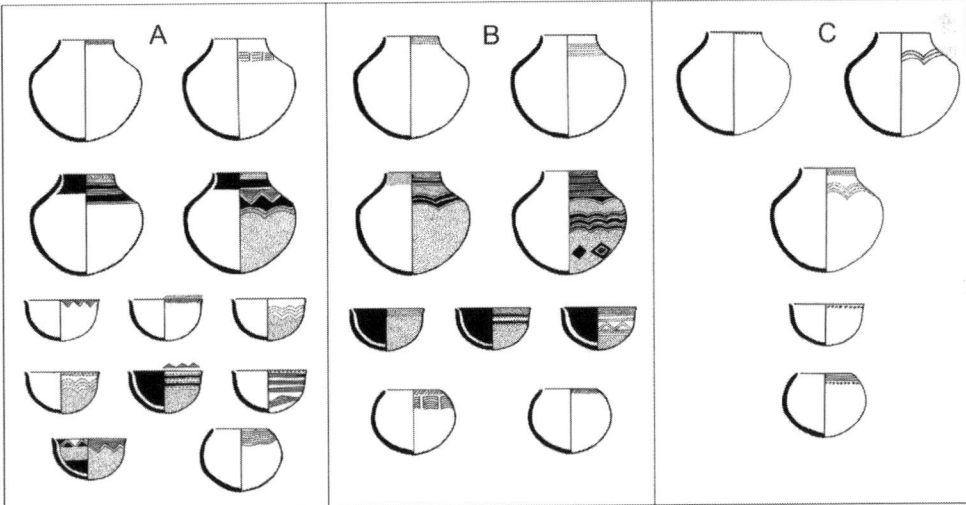

FIG. 64.2 Phase I (A), Phase II (B), and Phase III(C) Moloko ceramics (redrawn after Hall 1998).

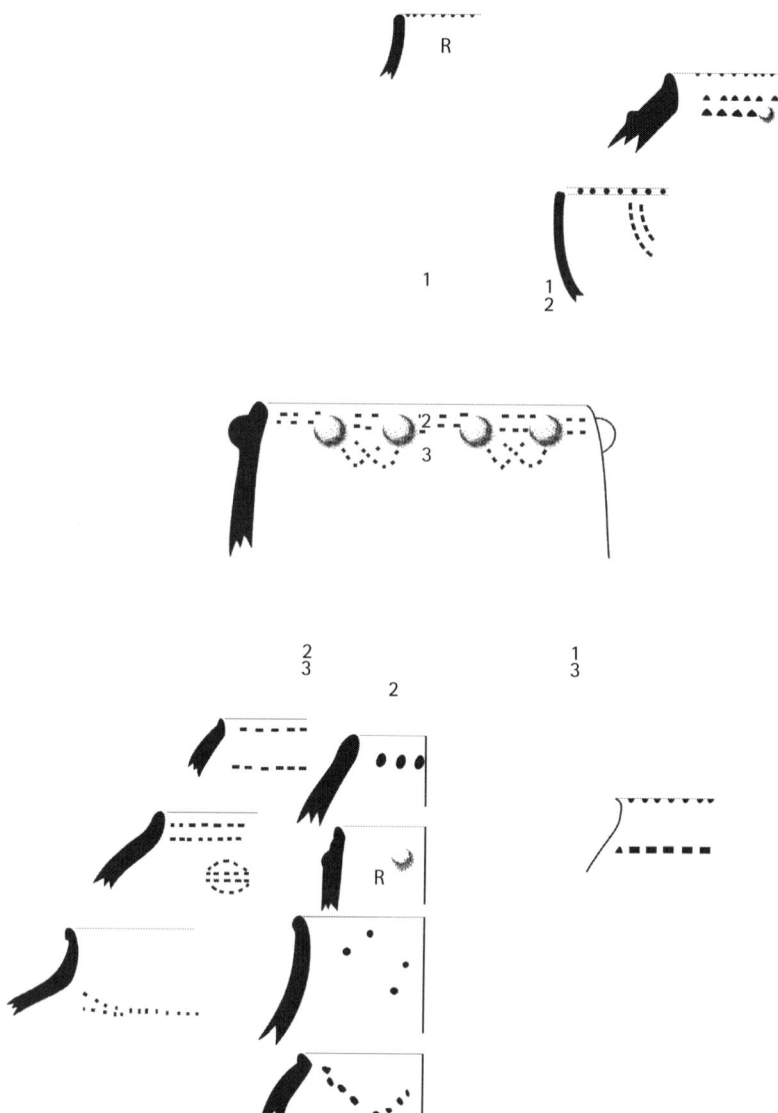

FIG. 64.3 Moor Park ceramics after Huffman (2004: fig. 7a, courtesy of Tom Huffman).

The relationship of Blackburn ceramics to the subsequent ceramic styles—Moloko (Fig. 64.2) and Moor Park (Fig. 64.3)—is not clear. These two styles appear in the archaeological record from the 13th and 14th centuries respectively, and while they are contemporaneous, they cluster in different areas. Moloko sites occur in central and western South Africa and were occupied by the ancestors of Sotho-Tswana speakers, but they pre-date the appearance of stone walling in these areas (Maggs 1976; Mason 1968, 1983; Hall 1998). In contrast, Moor Park ceramics are found on sites marked by very low stone walls (Davies 1974) in areas stretching from KwaZulu-Natal to the Eastern Cape (where the ceramics are known as Umgazana). Because of this distribution, archaeologists associate Moor Park sites with the ancestors of Nguni language speakers, and Huffman (2004) suggests that Moor Park continued into the 19th century in the Eastern Cape, as part of the Cape Nguni ceramic repertoire. Derricourt (1977) found Umgazana ware on the Transkei coast, but the archaeological context in which these ceramics occur in the rest of Eastern Cape is largely unknown because very few relevant archaeological excavations have been conducted in the region.

All three of these ceramic styles differed markedly from the ceramics produced by Early Farming Communities in southern Africa (Mitchell, Ch. 45 above). The simple decoration motifs of the largely undecorated Blackburn and Moorpark assemblages stand in stark contrast to the latter's elaborate designs (Huffman 2004). The vessel shapes, banded design fields, and intensive use of graphite and ochre that characterize Moloko pottery also point to discontinuity (Evers 1983). Similarities in decoration technique nevertheless led Mason (1983) to argue that Moloko ceramics developed out of those made by Early Farming Communities. In KwaZulu-Natal, one of the most intensively researched areas of South Africa for the periods in question, settlement locations also shifted substantially, in tandem with changes in ceramic style during the transition from Early to Late Farming Communities. Sites attributed to the latter are located further upslope, at the base of hills, unlike those of the former, which were established on riverbanks (Maggs 1994/5).

Because ceramic style has been viewed as representing group identity, the prevailing explanation for these changes invokes the arrival of new migrants who spoke languages ancestral to some of those spoken in the southern African region today. In addition, Huffman (2004) harnesses linguistic data relating to the 'Nguni' use of the -ini suffix that developed in East Africa, as well as kinship terminologies similar to those in East Africa such as the use of derivatives of *mazala* to refer to cross-cousins, to argue that ancestral 'Nguni speakers, like Sotho-Tswana, had to have lived in East Africa before they came south'. Parsons (2008) invokes other linguistic sources to suggest that Late Farming Communities moved to South Africa from Mozambique due to the social and demographic changes resulting from intensification of the Indian Ocean trade network at the beginning of the second millennium AD (cf. La Violette, Ch. 62 above; Pikirayi, Ch. 63 above). Debates regarding Late Farming Community origins can only be resolved when more Mozambican and East African archaeological data become available.

Even though archaeological data on origins are scarce, there is an increasing body of evidence that incoming Late Farming Communities did not completely displace earlier people. Older Sala words (a language related to proto-Shona) continued to be used in some of the Nguni languages, for example, pointing to interaction with, or incorporation of, Early Farming Community populations into later Nguni societies (Mitchell 2002: 347–8). The Nguni languages spoken today in KwaZulu-Natal and the Eastern Cape also show evidence of a substantial Khoekhoe/San linguistic contribution (Herbert 1990; cf. Mitchell, Ch. 45 above).

In areas where detailed surveys have been undertaken the archaeological record too reflects continuities, interaction or incorporation of earlier people. The best-known examples are the continuities in the Zimbabwe Culture area (Pikirayi, Ch. 63 above), but links are also visible in the incorporation of Eiland-Broadhurst herringbone designs into Moloko ceramics in the Marico and Rooiberg areas of northwestern South Africa (Boeyens 2003), and in similarities in the spatial distribution of Early and Late Farming Community sites in southeastern Botswana (Denbow 1986). The endurance of older practices is also reflected in ritual, with San religious practices, for example, having a fundamental impact on Cape Nguni divination and healing (Hammond-Tooke 2002).

While there are no clear genetic chronologies, and it is perilous to link language, culture, and biology—for example, languages have been adopted without genetic transfer (Wood et al. 2005)—genetic research has the potential to help explore the complex dynamics that shaped people in southern Africa (Mitchell 2010). The pattern emerging currently suggests the arrival of new people, as well as continuity of older populations. One example concerns sex-biased patterns of gene flow and differentiation manifest in mitochondrial DNA and Y chromosome data from Bantu-speaking populations (see also MacEachern, Ch. 5 above). These patterns represent population movements and expansions in which men were the majority and moved further, or in which males were more effective at transmitting their DNA to children in the areas into which men moved (Wood et al. 2005). In addition, haplogroup Lod (a haplogroup associated with KhoeSan populations) is found at a frequency of 29 per cent among Southeastern Bantu-speakers, which is much higher than its 5 per cent frequency in Mozambique (Schlebusch et al. 2009). This difference begs explanation, which in turn requires more intensive archaeological research in Mozambique.

ARCHAEOLOGY BEYOND 'TRIBES'

In spite of their historical fluidity (Delius 1983), the idea of primordial language-based ethnic groups or 'tribes' was deeply entrenched in the southern African colonial and Apartheid-era psyche and embedded in South African racial discourse (Dubow 1994). In this paradigm cultural identity was seen as paramount: for example, differences between Nguni and Tswana political processes and leadership styles were assumed to be cultural, rather than the product of different socioeconomic or political processes (Kuper 1995).

This approach is reflected in archaeological research based on the uncritical use of ethnographic accounts (Hall 1984a). Researchers have, for example, sometimes inappropriately projected information from ethnographic texts onto historically specific periods, areas, and material culture expressions with which they are not clearly linked (Lane 1994/5). The applicability of ethnography, however, can be limited even when presumed historical and linguistic links exist, as shown by excavations at Nqabeni, KwaZulu-Natal (Hall and Maggs 1979). This is one of a cluster of stone-walled sites dating to shortly before the rise of the Zulu kingdom in the 18th or early 19th centuries and located in the core of Zululand. The central area of Nqabeni comprises a cluster of linked cattle enclosures, and differs markedly from the classic concentric circles described in ethnographic accounts of Zulu homesteads (Hall 1984b). What this means is that the classic Zulu homestead does *not* persist through time and has a limited spatial distribution. Such observations necessarily raise further concerns about the widespread use of ethnographic models by South African archaeologists (Hall 1984b).

Research on Sotho–Tswana archaeological material has also provoked questions about the assumed divisions between Nguni and Sotho–Tswana speakers that underlie most ethnographic accounts. Sotho–Tswana speakers have traditionally been associated with Moloko ceramics. Huffman (2002), however, has suggested that the Fokeng, the earliest Sotho-Tswana group that established Type N settlements such as that at Ntsuanatsatsi (Maggs 1976), are descended from a 15th-century incursion into South Africa's highveld of Mbo

Nguni speakers. Type N sites are associated with Uitkomst pottery, and the subsequent spread of these ceramics across the Vaal River show that the Fokeng introduced stonewalling to the North West Province after merging with the Kwena in the mid-17th century (Huffman 2002).

Hall et al. (2008) suggested that there are flaws in Huffman's (2002) interpretation of the stratigraphic context and the radiocarbon date (1645 ± 10 BP, GrN-5137) for Uitkomst ceramics at Mmakgame (erroneously referred to as Kaditshwene: see Boeyens 2000 for a more thorough explanation) on which Huffman based his sequence. This date in fact calibrates to cal. AD 1734 ± 44 (Hall et al. 2008), and a mid-18th-century date for the earliest Uitkomst ceramics in the Northwest Province of South Africa does not support Huffman's assertion that the Fokeng introduced stone-walling to the area. In spite of these concerns, the possible contribution of Nguni speakers to the creation of 'Tswana' groups highlights the complexity that is masked by seemingly simple linguistic clusters. The hunter-gatherer presence manifest in stone tool manufacturing debris in a back courtyard at Madikwe, a Moloko site in North West Province, adds yet another dimension to the multifaceted nature of Tswana society (Hall 2000).

Complex processes also shaped group formation in northern South Africa. Venda oral traditions recount that their ancestors came from a place of abundant water, interpreted to mean the Great Lakes region in East Africa. However, while this is the narrative told by Venda royals (Singo), smaller, less powerful Venda-speaking groups contest this account and claim local origins (Loubser 1991). The archaeological evidence supports this. Venda-style stone-walled sites pre-date the arrival of the Singo in the late 17th century. In addition, the inclusion of Khami and Moloko stylistic elements in Tavhatshena (ancestral Venda) ceramics suggest that Venda identity actually arose from interaction between Shona and Sotho speakers in the mid-16th century. Venda identity thus *pre-dates* the political consolidation that resulted from the arrival of the Singo (Loubser 1991).

THE RISE AND FALL OF STONE-WALLED TOWNS AND THE MAKING OF COLONIAL SOUTHERN AFRICA

The bulk of archaeological studies on Late Farming Community sites had explored the roots of existing groups, but not all archaeological remains can be traced to contemporary language groups or communities. The complex terraced and stone-walled towns, some up to 4 km in length, in Mpumalanga are an example (Fig. 64.4). Initially, these sites were linked to the Pedi, a North Sotho-speaking group (Collett 1982), but a combination of historical and archaeological sources shows that they formed part of an area known as Bokoni, which had already been established when the Pedi moved into the area in the 1600s (Delius and Schoeman 2008). Investigation of this occupational sequence has allowed archaeologists to start exploring political processes and agricultural intensification (Maggs 2008) for a hitherto long-neglected part of South Africa.

In the mid-1700s regional strife in southern Mpumalanga and Swaziland resulted in a shift of the Bokoni capitals northwards (Delius and Schoeman 2008). In spite of this shift, Bokoni remained in the centre of an area adversely affected by 18th-century state formation

FIG. 64.4 Aerial photograph of one of the Bokoni towns, South Africa (photograph courtesy of G. Williams).

processes that reshaped the political landscape of KwaZulu-Natal (Wright 2008), Mpumalanga (Delius 1983), Swaziland (Bonner 1983) and Mozambique (Harries 1974). Even though open air terraced sites were abandoned in favour of mountain and ravine strongholds, Bokoni did not survive these changes intact (Delius and Schoeman 2008).

Bokoni was not the only area directly affected by the *Mfecane,* or 'time of troubles' between the 1790s and 1830s during which southern Africa experienced major social and economic upheaval, as well as substantial population displacements. Instability related to this period is visible in the archaeological record of the two destroyed Ndzundza capitals in northern Mpumalanga (Schoeman 1998a, 1998b), in people moving into underground caverns at Lepalong in the northwestern Free State (Hall 1995), and in the establishment of the defensive Sotho capital of Thabo Bosiu in Lesotho (Dreyer 1996). Defensive sites such as Thaba Bosiu, however, formed part of a longer trajectory in which people in unstable regions slowly moved into areas that were perceived to be safer. Such moves brought Sotho-speaking communities into closer contact with independent San communities, who commented on the arrival of the newcomers as well as the *Mfecane* violence in their art (Dowson 1995).

The effects of the *Mfecane* also extended north of the Limpopo River, and often the conflict was the result of the arrival of people fleeing the chaos in the south. The migrations from South Africa and Lesotho of the Makololo and the Ngoni are prime examples. The Makololo eventually settled in northern Botswana and colonized parts of western and southern Zambia, while the Ngoni took control over parts of Zambia and Malawi (Kanduza 2008). Several defensive or 'refuge' sites in Zimbabwe date to this period; furthermore, in southwestern Zimbabwe Tswana raids followed by successive incursions of Nguni speakers destroyed the Rozvi state (Pikirayi 2001).

The *Mfecane* was initially attributed to the Zulu king Shaka kaSenzangakhona and the formation of the historic Zulu state. The use of space at Mgungundlovu, capital of Shaka's brother and successor, such as the large central parade ground and housing for the large number of warriors, articulated the militarist ideology at the core of this state (Parkington and Cronin 1979; Roodt 1992). The Zulu state, however, was a symptom of the *Mfecane*, not the cause. Instead, the *Mfecane* was the result of the advancing European colonial frontier from the Cape, increasing inequalities of wealth within and between societies, coupled with droughts at the beginning of the 19th century that transformed longstanding competition over resources and trade into violent chaos (Eldredge 1995).

The widespread cultivation of maize, introduced to southern Africa by the Portuguese, may also have aggravated the impact of droughts on vulnerable communities. Maize is less drought-resistant than traditional cereals (sorghum and pearl millet), and yields would have decreased drastically during droughts at the beginning of the 19th century, resulting in food scarcity and instability that contributed to the *Mfecane* troubles (Hall 1976).

Huffman (1996) has argued that the cultivation of maize and the impact of droughts also resulted in the rise and fall of large stone-walled Tswana towns, such as Kaditshwene, that housed between 16,000 and 20,000 people (Fig. 64.5). This linkage has not, however, been proved, as no remains of maize or grindstones specific to its processing have been found at Kaditshwene and none of the eyewitness accounts of the town mentions maize as a food crop (Boeyens 2000, 2003).

Rather than being a direct result of the switch to maize cultivation, the stone-walled towns of South Africa and Botswana were established in response to a range of factors, including conflict between groups, population growth, increasing sociopolitical complexity, and the centralization of power by chiefs, as well as escalating competition over land and livestock aggravated by an expanding colonial frontier and climatic instability (Van Waarden 1998; Boeyens 2003; Lane 2004). Their increasing spatial complexity was also related to internal dynamics, including gender relations as male and female activities became progressively more segregated and gender roles more differentiated. Changing gender roles are, in turn, linked to improved agricultural production, combined with growing male anxieties over the control of female labour and the security of agricultural production (Hall 1998; Lane 1998).

FIG. 64.5 An illustration of the 'king's district' (*kgosing*) of a Tswana town, originally published in Campbell (1822: opp. p. 233).

Anxieties about regional stability were materialized in the hilltop location of most stone-walled sites dating to the late 17th and early 18th centuries. A key exception was Marathodi, the Rustenburg Tlokwa capital, which was established around AD 1780 on the flats west of the Pilanesberg (Boeyens and Hall 2009). The location of Marathodi was informed by the agricultural potential of the area and its proximity to nickel-copper sulphide pipes. The presence of these pipes is significant because copper production was a central activity at Marathodi, and archaeological evidence indicates that a substantial surplus was produced before the town was destroyed during the *Mfecane* (Hall et al. 2006).

Marathodi was one of the few towns to be destroyed during the *Mfecane*; rather more of the large Tswana towns in South Africa, including Kaditshwene, were abandoned due to internal Tswana wars in the early 1800s, before Mzilikazi's Ndebele moved through the area (Boeyens 2003), whilst the abandonment of others in Botswana has been linked to climatic change and site degradation (Lane 2004). Pinning responsibility for all early 19th-century settlement shifts onto the *Mfecane* is therefore inappropriate.

In the post-*Mfecane* period, white Afrikaans-speaking settler communities gained control over the central and northern parts of South Africa, while British rule was extended over the Eastern Cape and KwaZulu-Natal. One response of Late Farming Communities was to move further away from the reach of the Afrikaner-controlled South African Republic and onto hilltop locations such as Mabotse in the Waterberg (Hall 1997). However, even these defensive locations could not protect people from the advancing colonial frontier, and communities lost their independence and land in a succession of wars. Rock art was used by the affected communities to comment on some of these wars, such as the 1894 Maleboho War between the South African Republic and the Hananwa in the Makgabeng area of South Africa's Limpopo Province (Van Schalkwyk and Smith 2004).

In Botswana, where different dynamics were at play and colonial control was more theory than practice, large towns continued to exist in open areas. Key examples are Ntsweng and Phalatswe, capitals respectively of the Bakwena and Bangwato chiefdoms. The architecture and spatial layouts of the two sites reflect both internal dynamics, such as the role of chiefs, and their different responses to colonialism and the activities of non-conformist missions (Reid et al. 1997). The insights gained from historical archaeology in Botswana highlight the potential profitability of further research into the archaeology of the colonial period in the southern African interior, which has remained under-researched.

Over the last two decades our knowledge about the archaeology of southern African Late Farming Communities has increased dramatically. This is partly due to the shift to the recursive use of archaeological and historical sources. The increase in knowledge, combined with better insights into the impact of colonialism and racism on society and ethnography, has facilitated an archaeology that is no longer limited to tracking 'tribes'. Instead the focus has shifted productively to understanding the very complex processes of group formation and internal dynamics within groups.

REFERENCES

Behrens, J., and Swanepoel, N. (2008). Historical archaeologies of southern Africa: precedents and prospects. In Swanepoel et al. (2008: 23–39).

Boeyens, J. C. A. (2000). In search of Kaditshwene. *South African Archaeological Bulletin* 55: 3–17.

——(2003). The Late Iron Age sequence in the Marico and Early Tswana. *South African Archaeological Bulletin* 58: 63–78.

——and HALL, S. (2009). Tlokwa oral traditions and the interface between history and archaeology at Marothodi. *South African Historical Journal* 61: 457–81.

BONNER, P. (1983). *Kings, Commoners and Concessionaries: The Evolution and Dissolution of the Nineteenth-Century Swazi State*. Cambridge: Cambridge University Press.

CALABRESE, J. A. (2007). *The Emergence of Social and Political Complexity in the Shashi-Limpopo Valley of Southern Africa, AD 900 to 1300: Ethnicity, Class, and Polity*. Oxford: British Archaeological Reports.

CAMPBELL, J. (1822). *Travels in South Africa Under-taken at the Request of the London Missionary Society; Being a Narrative of a Second Journey in the Interior of that Country (1820)*. 2 vols. London: Westley.

COLLETT, D. P. (1982). Excavations of stone-walled ruin types in the Badfontein valley, Eastern Transvaal, South Africa. *South African Archaeological Bulletin* 37: 34–43.

DAVIES, O. (1974). Excavations at the walled early Iron Age site in Moor Park near Estcourt. *Annals of the Natal Museum* 22: 289–323.

DELIUS, P. (1983). *The Land Belongs to Us: The Pedi Polity, the Boers and the British in the Nineteenth-Century Transvaal*. Johannesburg: Ravan Press.

——and SCHOEMAN, M. H. (2008). Revisiting Bokoni: populating the stone ruins of the Mpumalanga escarpment. In Swanepoel et al. (2008: 135–68).

DENBOW, J. (1986). A new look at the later prehistory of the Kalahari. *Journal of African History* 27: 3–28.

DERRICOURT, R. M. (1977). *Prehistoric Man in the Ciskei and Transkei*. Cape Town: Struik.

DOWSON, T. A. (1995). Hunter-gatherers, traders and slaves: the '*Mfecane*' impact on Bushmen, their ritual and their art. In C. Hamilton (ed.), *The Mfecane Aftermath: Reconstructive Debates in Southern African History*. Johannesburg: Wits University Press, 51–70.

DREYER, J. J. B. (1996). Thaba-Bosiu, mountain fortress of Lesotho. In J. J. B. Dreyer, J. S. Brink, Z. L. Henderson, and S. Ouzman (eds), *Guide to Archaeological sites in the Free State and Lesotho*. Bloemfontein: National Museum, 37–46.

DUBOW, S. (1994). Ethnic euphemisms and racial echoes. *Journal of African Studies* 20: 355–70.

ELDREDGE, E. A. (1995). Sources of conflict in Southern Africa c. 1800–1830: the '*Mfecane*' reconsidered. In C. Hamilton (ed), *The Mfecane Aftermath: Reconstructive Debates in Southern African History*. Johannesburg: Wits University Press, 123–62.

ESTERHUYSEN, A. B. (2008). Ceramic alliances: pottery and the history of the Kekana Ndebele in the old Transvaal. In Swanepoel et al. (2008: 135–68).

EVERS, T. M. (1983). 'Oori' or 'Moloko': the origins of the Sotho-Tswana on the evidence of the Iron Age of the Transvaal: reply to R. J. Mason. *South African Journal of Science* 79: 261–4.

HALL, M. (1976). Dendroclimatology, rainfall and human adaptation in the later Iron Age of Natal and Zululand. *Annals of the Natal Museum* 22: 693–703.

——(1984a). The burden of tribalism: the social context of southern African Iron Age studies. *American Antiquity* 49: 455–67.

——(1984b). The myth of the Zulu homestead: archaeology and ethnography. *Africa* 54: 65–79.

——and MAGGS, T. M. O'C. (1979). Nqabeni, a late Iron Age site in Zululand. *South African Archaeological Society Goodwin Series* 3: 159–76.

HALL, S. L. (1995). Archaeological indicators for stress in the Western Transvaal region between the seventeenth and nineteenth centuries. In C. Hamilton (ed.), *The Mfecane Aftermath:*

Reconstructive Debates in Southern African History. Johannesburg: Wits University Press, 307–21.

—— (1997). Material culture and gender correlation: the view from Mabotse in the late nineteenth century. In L. Wadley (ed.), *Our Gendered Past: Archaeological Studies of Gender in Southern Africa*. Johannesburg: Wits University Press, 209–19.

—— (1998). A consideration of gender relations in the Late Iron Age 'Sotho' sequence of the western highveld, South Africa. In S. Kent (ed.), *Gender in African Prehistory*. Walnut Creek, Calif.: AltaMira Press, 235–58.

—— (2000). Forager lithics and early Moloko homesteads at Madikwe. *Natal Museum Journal of Humanities* 12: 33–50.

—— ANDERSON, M., BOEYENS, J., and COETZEE, F. (2008). Towards an outline of the oral geography, historical identity and political economy of the late precolonial Tswana in the Rustenburg region. In Swanepoel et al. (2008: 55–86).

—— MILLER, D., ANDERSON, M., and BOEYENS, J. (2006). An exploratory study of copper and iron production at Marathodi, and early 19th century Tswana town, Rustenburg district, South Africa. *Journal of African Archaeology* 4: 3–35.

HAMMOND-TOOKE, W.D. (2002). The uniqueness of Nguni mediumistic divination in Southern Africa. *Africa* 72: 275–92.

HARRIES, P. (1981). Slavery, social incorporation and surplus extraction: the nature of free and unfree labour in South-East Africa. *Journal of African History* 22: 309–30.

HERBERT, R. K. (1990). The sociohistory of clicks in Southern Bantu. *Anthropological Linguistics* 32: 295–315.

HUFFMAN, T. N. (1996). Archaeological evidence for climatic change during the last 2000 years in southern Africa. *Quaternary International* 33: 55–60.

—— (2002). Regionality in the Iron Age: the case of the Sotho-Tswana. *Southern African Humanities* 14: 1–22.

—— (2004). The archaeology of the Nguni past. *Southern African Humanities* 16: 79–111.

—— (2007). *Handbook to the Iron Age: The Archaeology of Pre-colonial Farming Societies in Southern Africa*. Pietermaritzburg: University of KwaZulu-Natal Press.

KANDUZA, A. M. (2008). Mfecane mutation in Central Africa: a comparison of the Makololo and the Ngoni in Zambia, 1830s–1998. In Swanepoel et al. (2008: 257–72).

KUPER, A. (1995). Machiavelli in precolonial Southern Africa. *Social Anthropology* 3: 1–13.

LANE, A. B., SOODYALL, S., ARNDT, M. E., et al. (2002). Genetic substructure in South African Bantu-speakers: evidence from autosomal DNA and Y-chromosome studies. *American Journal of Physical Anthropology* 119: 175–85.

LANE, P. J. (1994/5). The use and abuse of ethnography in Iron Age studies of southern Africa. *Azania* 29/30: 51–64.

—— (1998). Engendered spaces bodily practices in the Iron Age of southern Africa. In S. Kent (ed.), *Gender in African Prehistory*. Walnut Creek, Calif.: AltaMira Press, 179–204.

—— (2004). Re-constructing Tswana townscapes: toward a critical historical archaeology. In Reid and Lane (2004: 243–67).

LOUBSER, J. H. N. (1991). The ethnoarchaeology of the Venda-speakers in Southern Africa. *Navorsinge van die Nasionale Museum, Bloemfontein* 7: 146–64.

MAGGS, T. M. O'C. (1976). *Iron Age Communities of the Southern Highveld*. Pietermaritzburg: Natal Museum.

—— (1992). Name calling in the Iron Age. *South African Archaeological Bulletin* 47: 131.

—— (1994/5). The Early Iron Age in the extreme south: some patterns and problems. *Azania* 29/30: 171–8.

—— (2008). The Mpumalanga Escarpment settlements: some answers, many questions. In Swanepoel et al. (2008: 169–81).

MASON, R. J. (1968). Transvaal and Natal Iron Age settlement revealed by aerial photography and excavation. *African Studies* 27: 1–14.

—— (1983). 'Oori' or 'Moloko'? The origins of the Sotho-Tswana on the evidence of the Iron Age of the Transvaal. *South African Journal of Science* 79: 261.

MITCHELL, P. J. (2002). *The Archaeology of Southern Africa*. Cambridge: Cambridge University Press.

—— (2010). Genetics and southern African prehistory: an archaeological view. *Journal of Anthropological Sciences* 88: 73–92.

—— and WHITELAW, G. (2005). The archaeology of southernmost Africa *c.* 2000 bp to the early 1800s: a review of recent research. *Journal of African History* 46: 209–41.

OHINATA, F. (2002). The beginning of 'Tsonga' archaeology: excavations at Simunye, northeastern Swaziland. *Southern African Humanities* 14: 23–50.

PARKINGTON, J., and CRONIN, M. (1979). The size and layout of Mgungundlovu 1829–1838. *South African Archaeological Society Goodwin Series* 3: 133–48.

PARSONS, N. (2008). South Africa in Africa more than five hundred years ago: some questions. In Swanepoel et al. (2008: 41–54).

PIKIRAYI, I. (2001). *The Zimbabwe Culture: Origins and Decline of Southern Zambezian States*. Walnut Creek, Calif.: Altamira.

—— (2006). Gold, black ivory, and houses of stone: historical archaeology in Africa. In M. Hall and S.W. Silliman (eds), *Historical Archaeology*. Oxford: Blackwell, 230–50.

—— (2007). Ceramics and group identities. *Journal of Social Archaeology* 7: 286–301.

REID, A. M., and LANE, P. J. (eds) (2004). *African Historical Archaeologies*. London: Kluwer Academic/Plenum.

—— —— SEGOBYE, A. K., BÖRJESON, L. MATHIBIDI, N., and SEKGARAMETSO, P. (1997). Tswana architecture and responses to colonialism. *World Archaeology* 28: 370–92.

ROODT, F. (1992). Evidence for girls' initiation rites in the Bheje umuzi at eMgungundlovu. *South African Journal of Ethnology* 15: 9–14.

SCHLEBUSCH, C. M., NAIDOO, T., and SOODYALL, H. (2009). SNaPshot minisequencing to resolve mitochondrial macro-haplogroups found in Africa. *Electrophoresis* 30: 3657–64.

SCHOEMAN, M. H. (1998a). Excavating Ndzundza Ndebele identity at KwaMaza. *Southern African Field Archaeology* 7: 42–52.

—— (1998b). Material culture 'under the animal skin': excavations at Esikhunjini, a *Mfecane* period Ndzundza Ndebele site. *Southern African Field Archaeology* 7: 72–81.

SCHOFIELD, J. F. (1937). The pottery of the Mapungubwe district. In L. Fouché (ed.), *Mapungubwe: Ancient Bantu Civilization on the Limpopo*. Cambridge: Cambridge University Press, 32–61.

SWANEPOEL, N., ESTERHUYSEN, A. B., and BONNER, P. (eds) (2008). *Five Hundred Years Rediscovered: Southern African Precedents and Prospects*. Johannesburg: Wits University Press.

VAN SCHALKWYK, J. A., and SMITH, B. W. (2004). Insiders and outsiders: sources for reinterpreting a historical event. In Reid and Lane (2004: 325–46).

VAN WAARDEN, C. (1998). The Late Iron Age. In P. J. Lane, A. M. Reid, and A. Segobye (eds), *Ditswa Mmung: The Archaeology of Botswana*. Gaborone: Pula Press, 115–60.

WOOD, E. T., STOVER, D. A., EHRET, C., et al. (2005). Contrasting patterns of Y chromosome and mtDNA variation in Africa: evidence for sex biased demographic processes. *European Journal of Human Genetics* 13: 867–76.

WRIGHT, J. (2008). Rediscovering the Ndwandwe kingdom. In Swanepoel et al. (2008: 217–38).

CHAPTER 65

MADAGASCAR

From Initial Settlement to the Growth of Kingdoms

CHANTAL RADIMILAHY

INTRODUCTION

THE archaeology of Madagascar, the world's third largest island, falls entirely within the most recent periods covered by this volume. However, it also concerns many themes of global interest: colonization, human impacts on the environment, participation in long-distance trade networks, urbanization, state formation and colonialism. This chapter reviews and assesses the evidence currently available from archaeology and other disciplines for tracing the history of Madagascar's inhabitants (Fig. 65.1).

FIRST SETTLEMENT

Linguistic, ethnological, bioanthropological, historical, and, increasingly, genetic studies all insist upon Madagascar's preponderant links with Southeast Asia and Eastern Africa (Deschamps 1972; Vérin 1990). The Malagasy language, which is spoken throughout the island today, is 90 per cent Austronesian in origin, its closest Indonesian relatives being in Borneo (Dahl 1977). A variety of cultural parallels (irrigated rice cultivation, outrigger canoes, musical instruments) reinforce the historical connection to Indonesia. Bioanthropological studies (Rakoto-Ratsimamanga 1940; Chamla 1958) and more recent genetic studies (Soodyall et al. 1995; Hurles et al. 2005; Regueiro et al. 2008; Tofanelli et al. 2009) do the same. The latter also confirm an important influence from Bantu-speaking populations in Africa, especially in the south and southwest of Madagascar—an influence apparent too in language, as Malagasy contains a substratum of Bantu phonological features and vocabulary explicable by an initial settlement of Indonesians on the East African coast followed by colonization of Madagascar itself (Dahl 1988); new genetic work offers some support for this view (Msaidie et al. 2010).

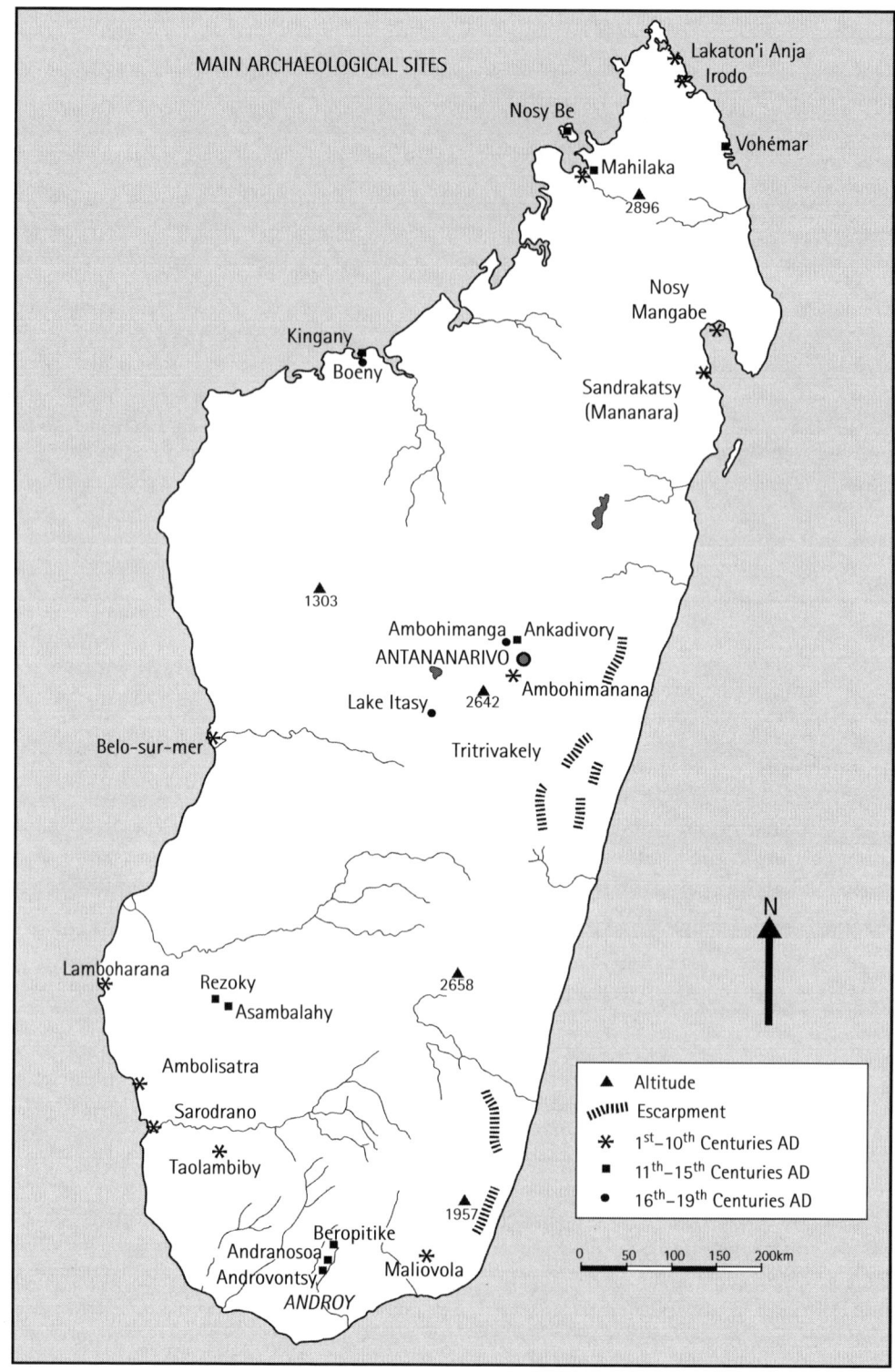

FIG. 65.1 Main archaeological sites in Madagascar (photograph, Antananarivo University Museum, reproduced with permission).

The possibility that Africans were settled on Madagascar even before the arrival of Austronesian speakers has recently been revived by Blench (2007), who emphasizes the importance of hunter-gatherer groups known as Mikea or Vazimba. The latter term is frequently cited in Malagasy traditions (Grandidier 1901), where it refers to indigenous communities encountered in the Central Highlands by mid-second-millennium migrants from Southeast Asia who subsequently absorbed them (Vérin 1981). Following Birkeli (1936), Blench suggests that these Vazimba, and the people known by this name today, could have descended from East African hunter-gatherers who crossed the Mozambique Channel. However, 'there is no archaeological evidence for [such] early settlement' (Blench 2007: 77), and other anthropologists (e.g. Yount et al. 2001) interpret today's Mikea/Vazimba as fugitive or forest specialist groups derived from later populations. Claims for the presence on Madagascar of stone tools that might perhaps derive from very early (pre-Indonesian) settlement (Bloch and Vérin 1966; Kellum-Ottino 1972) are also tenuous or lack secure archaeological contexts (Chami 2011; Radimilahy 2011).

At present, then, palaeontological and palaeoenvironmental data provide the earliest firm evidence for human presence on Madagascar. In the southwest of the island, at Taolambiby, bones of several sub-fossil lemur species (some now extinct) bear butchery marks, including a *Palaeopropithecus ingens* radius directly dated to the 5th/4th centuries BC (2325 ± 43 BP, AA-45960) (Perez et al. 2005). Also in the southwest, similar traces have been observed on directly dated (1st–4th centuries AD) bones of dwarf hippopotamus (*Hippopotamus lemerlei*) from the palaeontological sites of Ambolisatra and Lamboharana (MacPhee and Burney 1991). Pollen cores at Tritrivakely in the central highlands provide another line of evidence, as they register exotic *Cannabis/Humulus* pollen at a date that may be as early as 200 BC (Gasse and Van Campo 1998). Subsequently, early first-millennium AD sediments record drastic decreases in the spores of *Sporormiella* spp., fungi that digest animal faeces, a change read as evidence for a decline in Madagascar's indigenous megafauna; large increases in charcoal particle frequency followed, starting in the southwest and spreading to other coasts and, eventually, the interior. Burney et al. (2004) interpret these data as indicating humanly induced transformations of the Madagascar landscape. Subfossil faunal remains show, however, that many pygmy hippopotami, elephant birds, giant tortoises, and large lemurs survived until at least the end of the first millennium AD and in some cases into the second. Their disappearance was probably the result of several interacting factors, including changes in fire regime, competition from introduced livestock, transformation of vegetation to less productive systems, and hunting (Burney et al. 2004).

Although people appear to have visited Madagascar from the late first millennium BC, such visits may not have amounted to actual settlement. Currently the oldest evidence of this dates to no earlier than the 5th century AD at the rockshelter of Lakaton'i Anja at the island's northern tip. Here, the bones of subfossil fauna consumed by humans are associated with the remains of fish and shellfish and locally made ceramics, different from those deposited at the same site during the second millennium AD (Dewar and Rakotovololona 1992; Dewar 1996). Other sites date to around the 8th century and are located on the coasts. In the northeast they include Irodo (1200 ± 40 BP, GaK-380; Battistini and Vérin 1966), Nosy Mangabe (1250 ± 60 BP, SMU-2501), and Sandrakatsy (1140 ± 60 BP, SMU-2076, and 1240 ± 50 BP, SMU-2359; Wright and Fanony 1992). Elsewhere, there is Sarodrano (1460 ± 90 BP, GaK-928; Battistini and Vérin 1971) in the southwest of the island and Maliovola (1140 ± 30 BP, SMU-2078; Rakotoarisoa 1998) in the southeast. Agricultural communities that supported themselves in large part by slash-and-burn agriculture probably created such sites; iron slag confirms their use of metal tools. The later (12th century or younger) date of sites in the interior and the far south, particularly Androvontsy (Heurtebize and Vérin 1974), Andranosoa and Beropitike (Radimilahy 1981), and Ambohimanana and Ankadivory (Rakotovololona 1994) seems to confirm that the island was peopled from the coasts, and especially the mouths of large rivers.

Before concluding this discussion of Madagascar's early settlement, one further enigma requires attention: the presence of phytoliths of plantain/banana (*Musa* sp.) from mid-first-millennium BC village contexts in Cameroon, on the west side of Africa (Mbida et al. 2000). As *Musa* is of Southeast Asian origin, their discovery, if correct (cf. Vansina 2003), demands trans-Indian Ocean connections even older than those hinted at by palaeonto-logical and palaeoenvironmental data on Madagascar itself. Should claims of banana phy-toliths in much older (third-millennium BC) contexts in Uganda be confirmed (Lejju et al. 2006; cf. however Neumann and Hildebrand 2009), such connections would necessarily be much older still. To explore these possibilities, further work is required by both archaeo-botanists sampling sites in Africa and geneticists studying the ancestry not just of bananas/plantains but also of other Southeast Asian cultigens now grown in Africa, such as taro and species of yam.

SETTLEMENT AND TRADE IN THE LATE FIRST/EARLY SECOND MILLENNIA AD

Archaeological research places Madagascar within a network of maritime and terrestrial exchange in the western Indian Ocean from at least the first millennium AD (Beaujard 2009). One important aspect of these connections concerns how parts of the island formed an inte-gral part of the Islamicized Swahili culture that developed in the wider western Indian Ocean region in the late first/early second millennia. Traces of the arrival of Islamicized settlers, known in Malagasy by the term *Antalaotse* (from the Austronesian *laut*, 'sea'), are found in the presence of Triangular Incised Ware (TIW), a kind of pottery characteristic of the Swahili coast between the 6th and 10th centuries; a derivative tradition using zigzag designs survived until an even later date in southern Madagascar (Rakotoarisoa and Radimilahy 2004). They are also spectacularly evident at Mahilaka, a large (70 ha) stone-walled town (Fig. 65.2) on Ampasindava Bay on the northwest coast (Vérin 1986; Radimilahy 1998).

Mahilaka, Madagascar's first major port and urban centre, arose in the 10th century and flourished until the 15th, broadly paralleling the development of Swahili cities on the East African coast (La Violette, Ch. 62 above). Within its walls were mosques, elite residential areas built using stone masonry, and other areas occupied by more perishable forms of hous-ing. Craft production included iron smelting, manufacture of glass beads and glass vessels, and the working of chlorite schist, which was mined at various places along the east coast (Fig. 65.3). Ceramics resemble those found elsewhere across northern Madagascar and also in the Comores (Wright 1993). The site's inhabitants had access to imported glass beads, brass, Near Eastern *sgraffiato* pottery, and Chinese glazed wares (Radimilahy 1998). Possible exports include chlorite schist bowls, quartz crystal, gold, iron, gum, and timber.

FIG. 65.2 Mahilaka on the northwestern coast of Madagascar: remains of standing walls (photograph, Chantal Radimilahy).

Field surveys have identified numerous contemporary villages close to Mahilaka, on the offshore island of Nosy Be and in northeastern Madagascar, but at these sites evidence of participation in long-distance trade is much more limited. Their inhabitants ate shellfish, fish, turtles, domestic livestock, and at least one endemic terrestrial mammal, the tenrec. Much more detailed information is available for Mahilaka, where the diet included domestic cattle and chickens, as well as fish, turtles, wild mammals, and the earliest evidence yet found for rice (Radimilahy 1998).

Further evidence of a rapid emergence of diverse, complex settlement systems in the 11th/12th centuries comes from scattered finds of pottery similar to that of Mahilaka from

FIG. 65.3 Open-air chlorite schist quarry in northern Madagascar: remains of preliminary rough dressed chlorite schist pot (photograph, Chantal Radimilahy).

along the west coast (Wright et al. 1996) and Androy in the far south. There, large centres surrounded by earthworks include Andranosoa, which also produced imported pottery of Chinese and Persian Gulf origin. Direct links may also have existed with the emerging Zimbabwe Culture of southern Africa (Pikirayi, Ch. 63 above; Radimilahy 1981; Parker Pearson 2010). Andranosoa's inhabitants obtained meat from both wild and domesticated species (Rasamuel 1985), and small communities with similar ceramics and technology existed elsewhere in the southeast of the island (Rakotoarisoa 1998). Additional political entities and kingdoms emerged in the 12th and 13th centuries with the arrival of new, Islamicized immigrants (the Zafiraminia and Zafikazimambo), who brought with them new political ideologies to better control the occupied territories (Ottino 1986; De Flacourt 2007). City-states developed in the northwest, the northeast, the southeast, and the south. In other regions, principally the Central Highlands, the thinness of fertile soils and the high density of a population confined to fortified sites favoured the formation of micro-states (Wright 2007), yet it was only in the 16th century that attempts to unify these diverse polities began.

Mahilaka, and the population of the surrounding area, shrank considerably in size about 1400, but growth continued elsewhere along the coast, including the northeastern port of Vohémar, where over 600 tombs were investigated during the colonial period, their contents suggesting a degree of social differentiation but a common Muslim faith (Vérin 1986); the site's wealth, evident from imported glass and ceramics, was partly founded on the manufacture of chlorite schist vessels exported to East Africa (Dewar and Wright 1993). Other new coastal towns engaged in long-distance trade included Kingany, which had at least one mosque and also imported Chinese celadon and other glazed wares (Wright et al. 1996). Islam, foreign trade, and the social differentiation apparent in how the Kingany community was organized spatially are absent, however, further down the west coast near Belo-sur-Mer (Wright and Rakotoarisoa 2003). Imported ceramics do, on the other hand, occur in small numbers in the southwest, where a more complex settlement pattern of larger and smaller fortified sites and unfortified hamlets, perhaps founded on wet rice agriculture, emerged in the 15th century (Rakotoarisoa 1998). By then herder/hunters had spread more widely into the southern interior, as at Rezoky and Asambalahy (Vérin 1971). In the west, the zone of the *tsingy* in the limestone massif seems to have been the domain of the Vazimba (Fig. 65.4), whose rock paintings (Fig. 65.5) and engravings are now under investigation (Radimilahy 2010; Rasolondrainy 2012).

FIG. 65.4 Structure said to be a Vazimba house in western Madagascar (photograph, Chantal Radimilahy).

FIG. 65.5 Rockshelter with paintings under investigation in limestone massif in southern Madagascar (photograph courtesy of Rasolondrainy T. Reinaldo, reproduced with permission).

Although Lake Itasy, west of Antananarivo, shows a steady increase in charcoal from the 5th century AD (Burney 1987), no archaeological sites of first-millennium age have yet been found in the central highlands. If of human origin, such fires may have been left by a low-density, nomadic population of hunters and herders that may prove difficult to identify archaeologically. From the 1100s, however, pollen cores confirm much more widespread disturbance, almost certainly the result of land clearance and cultivation (Burney 1987), and from the 13th century there is good evidence of village settlement throughout the region (Dewar and Wright 1993). These early (Fiekena) sites, such as Ankadivory (Rakotovololona 1994), are surrounded by defensive ditches and banks but are of generally similar size, suggesting little differentiation. Their inhabitants kept cattle, cultivated rice, and had access to chlorite schist and imported pottery and glass beads (Wright and Rakotoarisoa 2003). In the 14th and 15th centuries, when pollen diagrams record even more intensive land clearance and farming (Burney 1987), settlement clusters emerged, focused on fortified hilltop sites enclosing stone tombs; only these larger sites now had access to Far Eastern ceramics, perhaps accessed from ports such as Kingany (Kus and Wright 1986).

THE DEVELOPMENT OF MORE COMPLEX POLITIES

From the 16th century, population numbers and political centralization accelerated across Madagascar. Research has emphasized four areas: the west and east coasts, the central highlands, and Androy.

Islamicized trading ports controlled only limited areas of Madagascar's west coast. Best known is Boeny, which succeeded Kingany and occupied the whole 20ha extent of the island of that name; spatial segregation of the community's elite (including massive masonry tombs) and commoners is evident (Vérin 1986). Villages on the adjacent mainland were probably dependent on Boeny, which historical sources indicate mainly exported cattle and slaves (Wright et al. 1996). Larger and more powerful kingdoms arose in the 16th/17th centuries, including those of the Sakalava, and are well attested historically (Goedefroit 1998). Sakalava finely combed pottery is well known, but there has been little survey or excavation of relevant sites, although pollen evidence for increased burning may relate to expanding production of cattle for export (Matsumoto and Burney 1994). They are said to have raided various towns on the East African coast, however, most famously Kua on Mafia Island, Tanzania (Piggott 1941).

On the east coast, settlements remained small into the 17th century, funnelling local products into the port of Vohémar. After its demise at the end of the 1600s, close relations developed with European traders, who exchanged guns for slaves (Deschamps 1972). The disappearance of cooking pots may reflect growing access to iron pots as another import, while settlements close to the coast were almost wholly abandoned in favour of others up to 20km inland, presumably for reasons of security (Wright and Fanony 1992). In the mid-1700s the powerful Betsimisaraka confederation extended its occupation over a large part of the region (Berg 1985), but its rapid collapse probably forestalled the creation of any archaeologically identifiable material infrastructure (Wright and Rakotoarisoa 2003).

The central highlands followed a very different trajectory. First, the hierarchical settlement clusters of the 15th century were replaced by more scattered, small villages associated with a quite different ceramic tradition in which craft activities (such as potting and ironworking) were reorganized into distinct areas and from which little evidence of long-distance trade has been recovered. After proliferating in the late 16th/17th centuries with little sign of further changes in technology or production, by the early 1700s sites were much more densely packed into hierarchically organized clusters of major centres and villages (Kus and Wright 1986). By this time deforestation was effectively complete, and the landscape dominated by pasture and rice paddies. Larger (≥ 20 ha), massively fortified capitals such as Ambohimanga emerged in the mid-/late 18th century, dominating smaller settlements. Further population growth (partly fuelled by the adoption of manioc alongside intensification of rice growing) seems likely, and linear frontiers of fortified sites were constructed, as on the southern and western borders of the Ambohimanga polity (Kus and Wright 1986; Wright 2007). Historical sources (both Malagasy and European) record that this period directly preceded King Andrianampoinimerina's formation of the Merina state, which eventually ruled almost all of Madagascar before French colonization in 1895. Because of its recent date and the wealth of archaeological and historical data available, this process of state formation has been comparatively well studied, with one emphasis on how space was symbolically organized to express and give effect to new political structures at the Merina capital, Ambohimanga (Kus 1988/9; Wright 2007). Another dimension of state formation, the conquest of peripheral areas, was explored by Crossland (2001) in Andrantsay. Here, although material culture continued unchanged after Merina conquest in 1808/9, village numbers declined sharply, perhaps partly because of Merina demand for slaves (Campbell 1981) but also because of a deliberate strategy of disrupting ancestral ties to the landscape to create new forms of political legitimacy.

Europeans began visiting Madagascar from the early 1500s, though 17th-century English and French attempts at colonization were repeatedly unsuccessful (Parker Pearson 1997). Nevertheless, trade with Europeans was important in several parts of the island. Following earlier patterns where exotic pottery and glass were used as prestige goods by leaders, elite burials in areas such as Boeny (Vérin 1986) and Androy (Parker Pearson 1997) now used imported items such as silk and guns. Though useful in warfare, which aimed partly at acquiring slaves for trade, guns also held important ritual value (Berg 1985). The development of new power relationships whose economic base was consolidated through exporting slaves, owning cattle, and possessing high-status foreign goods is one of several topics in Malagasy archaeology that merit further archaeological investigation.

REFERENCES

BATTISTINI, R., and VÉRIN, P. (1966). Irodo et la tradition vohémarienne. *Revue de Madagascar* 34: 16–18.

—— —— (1971). Témoignages archéologiques sur la côte Vezo de l'embouchure de l'Onilahy à la Baie des Assassins. *Taloha* 4: 19–27.

BEAUJARD, P. (2009). Un seul système-monde avant le XVIᵉ siècle? L'océan indien au cœur de l'intégration de l'hémisphère afro-eurasien. In P. Beaujard, L. Berger, and P. Norel (eds), *Histoire Globale, Mondialisations et Capitalisme*. Paris: La Découverte Recherches, 82–148.

BERG, G. M. (1985). The sacred musket: tactics, technology and power in eighteenth-century Madagascar. *Comparative Studies in Society and History* 27: 261–79.

BIRKELI, E. (1936). Les Vazimba de la côte ouest de Madagascar: notes d'ethnologie. *Mémoires de l'Académie Malgache* 22: 1–67.

BLENCH, R. M. (2007). New palaeozoogeographical evidence for the settlement of Madagascar. *Azania* 42: 69–82.

BLOCH, M., and VÉRIN, P. (1966). Discovery of an apparently Neolithic artefact in Madagascar. *Man* 1: 240.

BURNEY, D. A. (1987). Pre-settlement vegetation changes at Lake Tritrivakely, Madagascar. *Palaeoecology of Africa* 18: 357–81.

—— BURNEY, L. P., GODFREY, L. R., et al. (2004). A chronology for late prehistoric Madagascar. *Journal of Human Evolution* 47: 25–63.

CAMPBELL, G. (1981). Madagascar and the slave trade, 1810–1895. *Journal of African History* 22: 203–27.

CHAMI, F. (2011). Archaeological research in Comores between 2007 to 2009. In C. Radimilahy and N. Rajaonarimanana (eds), *Civilisations des Mondes Insulaires (Madagascar, Îles du Canal de Mozambique, Mascareignes, Polynésie, Guyanes). Mélanges en l'Honneur du Professeur Claude Allibert*. Paris: Karthala, 811–23.

CHAMLA, M.-C. (1958). *Recherches Anthropologiques sur l'Origine des Malgaches*. Mémoires du Musée National d'Histoire Naturelle, Série A, Zoologie, 19/1.

CROSSLAND, Z. (2001). Time and the ancestors: landscape survey in the Andrantsay region of Madagascar. *Antiquity* 75: 825–35.

DAHL, O. C. (1977). La subdivision de la famille Barito et la place du Malgache. *Acta Orientalia* 38: 77–134.

—— (1988). Bantu substratum in Malagasy. *Études Océan Indien* 9: 91–132.

DE FLACOURT, E. (2007). *Histoire de la Grande Isle Madagascar*, nouvelle édition annotée, augmentée et présentée par Claude Allibert. Paris: Inalco/Karthala.

DESCHAMPS, H. (1972). *Histoire de Madagascar*. Paris: Berger-Levrault.

DEWAR, R. E. (1996). The archaeology of the early colonization of Madagascar. In J. Reade (ed.), *The Indian Ocean in Antiquity*. London: Kegan Paul, 471–86.

—— RADIMILAHY, C., RASOLOFOMAMPIANINA, L. D., and WRIGHT, H. T. (2011). Early settlement in the region of Fenoarivo Atsinanana. In C. Radimilahy and N. Rajaonarimanana (eds), *Civilisations des Mondes Insulaires (Madagascar, Îles du Canal de Mozambique, Mascareignes, Polynésie, Guyanes). Mélanges en l'Honneur du Professeur Claude Allibert.* Paris: Karthala, 677–740.

—— and RAKOTOVOLOLONA, S. (1992). La chasse aux subfossiles: les preuves du XIe au XIIIe siècle. *Taloha* 11: 4–15.

—— and WRIGHT, H. T. (1993). The culture history of Madagascar. *Journal of World Prehistory* 7: 417–66.

GASSE, F., and VAN CAMPO, E. (1998). A 40,000-yr pollen and diatom record from Lake Tritrivakely, Madagascar, in the southern tropics. *Quaternary Research* 46: 299–311.

GOEDEFROIT, S. (1998). *A l'Ouest de Madagascar: les Sakalava de Menabe*. Paris: Karthala.

GRANDIDIER, A. (1901). *L'Origine des Malgaches*. Paris: Imprimerie Nationale.

HEURTEBIZE, G., and VÉRIN, P. (1974). Premières découvertes sur l'ancienne culture de l'intérieur de l'Androy (Madagascar): archéologie de la vallée du Lambomaty sur la Haute Manambovo. *Journal de la Société des Africanistes* 44(2): 113–21.

HURLES, M. E., SYKES, B. C., JOBLING, M. A., and FORSTER, P. (2005). The dual origin of the Malagasy in Island Southeast Asia and East Africa: evidence from maternal and paternal lineages. *American Journal of Human Genetics* 76: 894–901.

KELLUM-OTTINO, M. (1972). Discovery of a Neolithic adze in Madagascar. *Asian Perspectives* 15: 83–6.

KUS, S. (1988/9). Ambohimanga: state formation and the symbolic organization of space. *Omaly Sy Anio* 29/32: 43–53.

—— and WRIGHT, H. T. (1986). Survey archéologique de la région de l'Avaradrano. *Taloha* 10: 49–72.

LEJJU, B. J., ROBERTSHAW, P. T., and TAYLOR, D. (2006). Africa's earliest bananas? *Journal of Archaeological Science* 33: 102–13.

MACPHEE, R. D., and BURNEY, D. (1991). Dating of modified femora of extinct dwarf hippopotamus from southern Madagascar: implications for constraining human colonization and vertebrate extinction events. *Journal of Archaeological Science* 18: 695–706.

MATSUMOTO, K., and BURNEY, D. A. (1994). Late Holocene environmental changes at Lake Mitsinjo, northwestern Madagascar. *The Holocene* 4: 16–24.

MBIDA, C., VAN NEER, W., DOUTRELEPONT, H., and VRYDAGHS, L. (2000). Evidence for banana cultivation and animal husbandry during the first millennium BC in the forest of southern Cameroon. *Journal of Archaeological Science* 27: 152–62.

MSAIDIE, S., DUCOURNEAU, A., BOETSCH, G., et al. (2010). Genetic diversity on the Comoros Islands shows early seafaring as major determinant of human biocultural evolution in the Western Indian Ocean. *European Journal of Human Genetics* 19: 89–94.

NEUMANN, K., and HILDEBRANDT, E. (2009). Early bananas in Africa: the state of the art. *Ethnobotany Research and Applications* 7: 353–62.

OTTINO, P. (1986). *L'Étrangère Intime: Essai d'Anthropologie de la Civilisation de l'Ancien Madagascar*. Paris: Karthala/ORSTOM.

PARKER PEARSON, M. (1997). Close encounters of the worst kind: Malagasy resistance and colonial disasters in southern Madagascar. *World Archaeology* 28: 393–417.

——(ed.) (2010). *Pastoralists, Warriors and Colonists: The Archaeology of Southern Madagascar*. Oxford: British Archaeological Reports.

PEREZ, V. R., GODFREY, L. R., NOWAK-KEMP, M., BURNEY, D. A., RATSIMBAZAFY, J., and VASEY, N. (2005). Evidence of early butchery of giant lemurs in Madagascar. *Journal of Human Evolution* 49: 722–42.

PIGGOTT, D. W. I. (1941). Mafia: history and traditions (collected by Kadhi Amur Omar Saadi). *Tanganyika Notes and Records* 11: 35–40.

RADIMILAHY, C. (1981). Archéologie de l'Androy: sud de Madagascar. *Recherche, Pédagogie et Culture* 9: 55: 62–5.

——(1998). *Mahilaka: An Archaeological Investigation of an Early Town in Northwestern Madagascar*. Uppsala: Uppsala University Press.

——(2010). Un art rupestre malgache ancien? In M. Garlinski and E. Hopkins (eds), *À Madagascar: Photographies de Jacques Faublée, 1938–1941*. Geneva: Musée d'Ethnographie de Genève, 28–9

——(2011). Contribution à l'archéologie du Sud-Ouest de Madagascar. In C. Radimilahy and N. Rajaonarimanana (eds), *Civilisations des Mondes Insulaires (Madagascar, Îles du Canal de Mozambique, Mascareignes, Polynésie, Guyanes). Mélanges en l'Honneur du Professeur Claude Allibert*. Paris: Karthala, 825–53.

RAKOTOARISOA, J.-A. (1998). *Mille ans d'Occupation Humaine dans le Sud-Est de Madagascar: Anosy, une Île au Milieu des Terres*. Paris: L'Harmattan.

——and RADIMILAHY, C. (2004). Impacts on the environment in southern Madagascar: an archaeological perspective. In F. Chami, G. Pwiti, and C. Radimilahy (eds), *Studies in the African Past IV*. Dar es Salaam: Dar es Salaam University Press, 131–51.

RAKOTO-RATSIMAMANGA, A. (1940). Tache pigmentaire héréditaire et origine des Malgaches. *Revue Anthropologique* 50: 5–128.

RAKOTOVOLOLONA, S. (1994). Ankadivory: témoin d'une culture de l'Imerina ancien. *Taloha* 12: 7–24.

RASAMUEL, D. (1985). Alimentation et techniques anciennes dans le Sud Malgache à travers une fosse à ordure du XIème siècle. *Tsiokantimo* 4: 81–109.

RASOLONDRAINY, T. V. R. (2012). Discovery of rock paintings and Libyco-Berber inscription from the upper Onilahy, Isalo Region, Southwestern Madagascar. *Studies in the African Past* 10: 173–93.

REGUEIRO, M., MIRABAI, S., LACAU, H., CAEIRO, J. L., GARCIA-BERTRAND, R. L., and HERRERA, R. J. (2008). Austronesian genetic signature in East Africa, Madagascar and Polynesia. *Journal of Human Genetics* 53: 106–20.

SOODYALL, H., JENKINS, T., and STONEKING, M. (1995). Polynesian mtDNA in the Malagasy. *Nature Genetics* 10: 377–8.

TOFANELLI, S., BERTONCINI, S., CASTRI, L., et al. (2009). On the origins and admixture of Malagasy: new evidence from high-resolution analyses of paternal and maternal lineages. *Molecular and Biological Evolution* 26: 2109–24.

VANSINA, J. (2003). Bananas in Cameroon *c.* 500 BCE? Not proven. *Azania* 38: 174–6.

VÉRIN, P. (1971). Les anciens habitats de Rezoky et d'Asambalahy. *Taloha* 4: 29–45.

——(1981). Madagascar. In G. Mokhtar (ed.), *UNESCO General History of Africa*, vol. 2. Paris: UNESCO, 751–77.

——(1986). *The History of Civilization in North Madagascar*. Rotterdam: Balkema.

Vérin, P. (1990). *Madagascar*. Paris: Karthala.

Wright, H. T. (1993). Trade and politics on the eastern littoral of Africa, AD 800–1300. In T. Shaw, P. J. J. Sinclair, B. Andah, and A. Okpoko (eds), *The Archaeology of Africa: Food, Metals and Towns*. London: Routledge, 658–72.

—— (ed.) (2007). *Early State Formation in Central Madagascar: An Archaeological Survey of Western Avaradrano*. Ann Arbor: University of Michigan, Museum of Anthropology.

—— and Fanony, F. (1992). L'évolution des systèmes d'occupation des sols dans la vallée de la rivière Mananara au nord-est de Madagascar. *Taloha* 11: 16–64.

—— and Rakotoarisoa, J. A. (2003). The rise of Malagasy societies: new developments in the archaeology of Madagascar. In S. M. Goodman and J.P. Benstead (eds), *The Natural History of Madagascar*. Chicago: University of Chicago Press, 112–19.

—— Vérin, P., Ramilisonina, Burney, D. A., Burney, L. P., and Matsumoto, K. (1996). The evolution of settlement systems in the Bay of Boeny and the Mahavavy River valley. *Azania* 31: 37–73.

Yount, J. W., Tsiazonera, and Tucker, B. (2001). Constructing Mikea identity: past or present links to forest and foraging. *Ethnohistory* 48: 257–91.

PART VII

AFRICAN SOCIETIES AND THE MODERN WORLD SYSTEM

CHAPTER 66

THE ARCHAEOLOGY OF THE OTTOMAN EMPIRE IN NORTHERN AND NORTHEASTERN AFRICA

INTISAR SOGHAYROUN EL-ZEIN

HISTORICAL BACKGROUND

ORIGINATING as a small state in northwestern Anatolia under Sultan Osman I (died *c.* 1326), and consolidated during the rule of Süleyman I, 1520–66 (commonly referred to as Süleyman the Magnificent), the Ottoman Empire expanded during the 15th and 16th centuries to include the Levant, Iraq, Arabia, the Balkans, Egypt, and the western North African littoral (Finkel 2005). Whereas the Empire's westward expansion declined following a decisive sea battle in the Gulf of Lepanto (western Greece) in 1571, and in the Balkan territories following defeat by the Holy League at the Battle of Vienna (1683), Ottoman influence remained a significant factor in coastal North Africa, Egypt, the Sudan, and parts of Ethiopia well into the 19th century (Faroqhi 2007). As elsewhere in the Empire, the methods of conquest, the resultant political systems established, and their associated administrative structures and relationships with the Ottoman court in Istanbul, varied considerably across these different Ottoman African territories. These differences inevitably helped shape the material manifestations of an Ottoman presence in virtually all spheres of life, from domestic buildings and marketplaces to frontier forts and mosques, and from systems of land tenure and tax regimes to local craft production and the range of imported and exported commodities.

The presence of the Ottomans in Africa (Fig. 66.1) was motivated by several factors, including a general colonial interest in the continent for its geographical location, its natural and human resources, and its valuable exports (Alexander 2009). As an Islamic empire, territorial expansion was often justified in religious terms, even if more practical motives were the prime movers (Peacock 2009: 14). Ottoman interest in the North Africa littoral, for example, was more due to the need to protect its shipping in the western Mediterranean from the activities of Christian corsairs and defend the empire against Spanish attacks than to any religious imperative, and conquest of these lands was largely the result of action taken

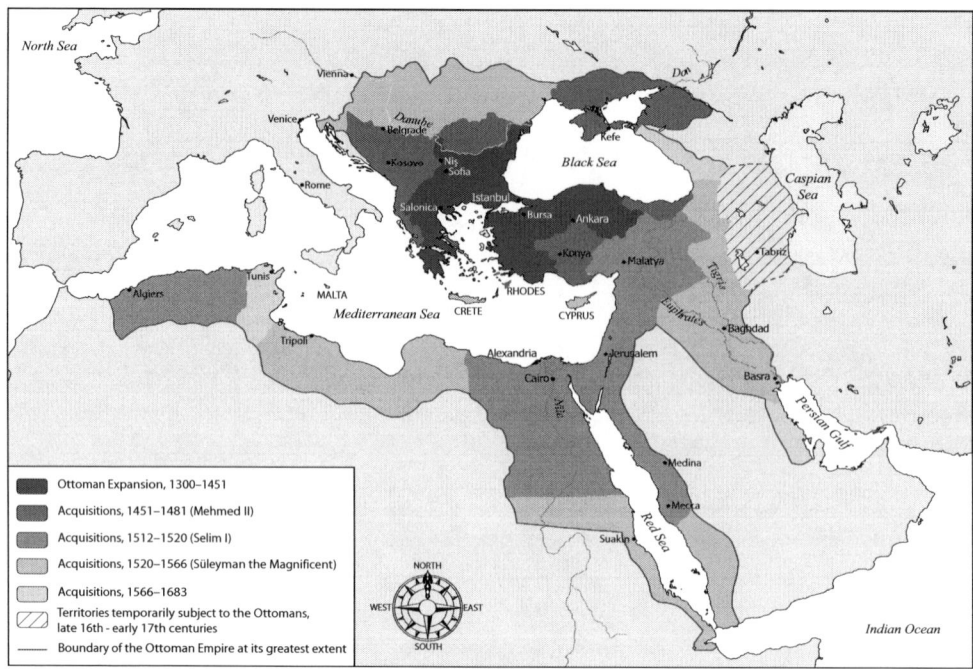

FIG. 66.1 'Map of the expansion of the Ottoman Empire' in *The Frontiers of the Ottoman World*, edited by A C S Peacock, *Proceedings of the British Academy*, volume 156. Oxford: Oxford University Press, p. 6. © The British Academy, 2009.

by individual naval commanders (Heywood 2009; Gürkan 2010). Nonetheless, in some contexts religious concerns were more significant, such as in northeast Africa, where proximity to the pilgrimage (*Hajj*) routes to Mecca seem to have been an important consideration, especially following expansion of the Portuguese into the Indian Ocean and Red Sea during the 16th century and the threat this posed (Özbaran 1994; Alexander 2009). To achieve these different goals, initial expansion began during Selim I's rule with the conquest of Egypt in 1517, which became a fully integrated province, although administered locally by the semi-autonomous Mamluk military class recruited as slaves from Christian populations elsewhere within, or beyond, the Empire. From the 16th to 18th centuries, rural land in the province was legally owned by the Ottoman state, and managed as tax farms by the local elite. This system generated enormous wealth for the Empire, and the province became a major source of grain and supplier of military manpower to other provinces, and consistently paid an annual tribute to Istanbul that was in excess of those paid by any other Ottoman province (Shaw 1962). Aside from its economic importance, Egypt was also the gateway to the Red Sea and Indian Ocean and the rest of North Africa, as well as an important hub in the *Hajj* routes to Mecca and Medina (Winter 2005). Direct control from Istanbul gradually weakened over the centuries, however, and shortly after a brief French occupation at the very end of the 18th century (1798–1801), Egypt passed under the control of Mehmet Ali. An Ottoman general of Albanian origin, Mehmet Ali (1805–49) destroyed the Mamluk elite, reorganized the Egyptian army along European lines, and promoted the country's economic development (Fahmy 2002). Having established himself as the de facto ruler of an independent state (the *khedivate*), Mehmet Ali and his descendants not only ruled Egypt but also sought control over neighbouring regions, notably Sudan, much of which was conquered in 1820–21 (Hill 1959).

At broadly the same time as they conquered Egypt, the Ottomans ended the Portuguese threat to their control of the Red Sea by occupying the major ports on both coasts: on the African side Suakin in Sudan (which in 1555 became the capital of the Ottoman *eyalet* of Habesh) (Pankhurst 1997), and Massawa, Arkiko (Argigo), and Zayla in Eritrea (Abir 1980). However, following unsuccessful attempts to gain a foothold on the Ethiopian plateau, the Ottomans abandoned their wider expansionist ambitions in the region, leaving a small garrison of soldiers in Massawa, which became the most prominent port along the lower reaches of the Red Sea coast, replacing Dahlak Kebir (Insoll 2001). Subsequently, around the middle of the 17th century, they delegated power to locally powerful chiefs from the Arkiko Belew family, but in the 19th century struggles over the control of Massawa and its hinterland between the Ottomans, the increasingly independent Egyptian *khedivate*, and the Christian kingdom of Ethiopia led to a transition to a more involved and direct mode of Ottoman control.

West of Egypt in the Maghreb, Algeria was the first country to become part of the Ottoman Empire, with Algiers being occupied by Khair ad-Din Barbarossa in 1516 (Gürkan 2010). It was administered at first by governors sent from Istanbul, but in 1689 the troops stationed there rebelled against the Ottoman governor, installing one of their officers as ruler with the title of *dey*. Thereafter, the *deys* governed Algeria independently from the central Ottoman government but retained religious ties to the Ottoman sultan, recognizing him as caliph and following the Hanafi school of Islamic law, the official school of the Ottoman Empire. Piracy provided the ruling class of Algiers with its main source of revenue until the middle of the 18th century, when the balance of power in the Mediterranean started to turn in favour of the European powers (McCluskey 2008). As a result, the heavy taxes subsequently imposed on the local population led to conflicts with tribal communities. Led by Sufi leaders, these ultimately weakened the regime of the *deys* on the eve of the French invasion of Algeria in 1830.

Further east, the Ottomans first occupied Tunis in 1534 but were forced out by Spanish troops the following year, leaving Tunisia to the indigenous Hafsid dynasty, which ruled the country under Spanish protection until the Ottomans reconquered it in 1574 (Hess 1978). As in Algeria, but almost a century earlier, in 1591 the Ottoman troops stationed in Tunis resisted the governor sent from Istanbul and established a regime headed by *deys* chosen by the troops. In 1705 the *bey* (provincial governor), Husain ibn Ali, effectively usurped the power of the *deys*, establishing a dynasty that ruled (latterly under French control) until the monarchy was abolished in 1957 (Çelik 1997). Both the earlier *deys* and the Husyanids continued to recognize the religious authority of the Ottoman sultan as caliph.

The northern coast of Libya came under Ottoman control in 1551 with the conquest of Tripoli (Hess 1978), but in 1711 the province underwent a change similar to that already experienced by Tunisia and Algeria when the commander of the local Ottoman cavalry, Ahmed Qaramanli, seized power and launched his own dynasty. The Qaramanlis ruled Libya until 1835, when, in the wake of a tribal rebellion supported by the British, direct Ottoman rule was reimposed. From the mid-16th century Libya became active in the profitable trans-Saharan trade that crossed its territory, becoming another important centre of piracy during the Qaramanli period. Libya remained part of the Ottoman Empire until its conquest by Italy in 1912.

Sudan constitutes the final country to be discussed. Ottoman authority was initially established along the Middle Nile in the later 16th century, following the advance of the frontier from Aswan to Qasr Ibrim in Lower Nubia in 1570 (Hill 1959; Udal 1998). Thereafter, an inconclusive battle in 1582 or 1583 between the Funj sultanate and the Ottomans at Hannek by the Third Cataract stalled further Ottoman expansion upstream along the Nile, leaving the fortress of Sai as the final Ottoman outpost. Although by the 17th century the Mahas of Upper Nubia was ruled by vassals of the Funj, the *meks* (kings) of Mahas, there is at least some evidence for continuing Ottoman influence there at that time (el-Zein 2009: 376; Peacock 2012). Much more direct foreign influence came with the invasion of Sudan by the forces of Mehmet Ali of Egypt in 1820–21, an event that marks the beginning of the period known as the Turkkiya, or Turkish regime. Motivated by the desire to open up new markets and gain more direct access to the resources of equatorial Africa, including slaves and ivory, Egyptian-led forces penetrated ever further upstream into what is now South Sudan, while obtaining the Red Sea coast of Sudan from the Ottomans in 1865 and annexing the sultanate of Darfur in 1874, all before the outbreak of the Mahdist revolution in 1881.

THE ARCHAEOLOGICAL RECORD

Despite over 400 years of an Ottoman presence in some parts of northern and northeastern Africa, archaeological research on the material manifestations of this and the consequences of Ottoman over-rule has been extremely limited. Most specifically archaeological studies have been conducted in the last two decades, often as part of more general surveys, such as the recently documented traces of Ottoman archaeology in the Mahas region of the Sudan (el-Zein 2004, 2009; Edwards and el-Zein 2012) or following chance discoveries, such as the excavation of an Ottoman shipwreck off Sadana Island in the Red Sea (Ward 2001). With the exception of Alexander's (1996, 1997, 2000, 2001, 2009) sustained interest in the Ottoman presence in Nubia and northeast Africa more generally, and emerging studies in the Sudan (see below), there has been no focused research on the archaeology of the Ottoman period in any of the African states mentioned above, or on the archaeological expressions of Ottoman influence beyond the Empire's southern frontiers. This is regrettable, given the scope for such studies.

More specifically, some of the most obvious legacies of Ottoman rule are the many examples of Ottoman architecture that remain across North Africa. As one might expect, given the diverse cultural heritage of the Ottoman Empire as a whole, influences are discernible from Persian, Byzantine, and Greek traditions, as well as previous Islamic styles (Petersen 1996). Besides mosques, they are reflected in theological schools (*madrassas*), hospitals, caravanserais and khans that provided accommodation for merchants and their caravans and stores, market *souqs*, baths (*hammams*), elite houses and palaces, the lodgings of mystical dervish sects (*khangah* and *tekke*), and mausolea. These buildings are complemented by many surviving examples of Ottoman art in materials as varied as pottery, metalwork, ceramic tiles, textiles, glass, and stucco.

Examples are numerous, with Cairo, Algiers, and Tunis in particular retaining many Ottoman-era monuments (Golvin 1985). They include the mosque of Suleiman Pasha al-Khadim at the Citadel in Cairo (1528), which introduced the pencil-shaped Ottoman minaret and the central-domed plan, a design later followed by other mosques, such as that of al Malika Safiya (1610) (Petersen 1996). In Tunis, in contrast, the standard mosque form comprised aisles running perpendicular to the *qibla* wall and a further raised aisle running parallel to it, forming a T-shaped layout, a plan that drew on pre-Ottoman practice, although purely Ottoman designs can also be found, as in the Sidi Mehrez mosque of the later 17th century (Petersen 1996: 289). Mosques in Algiers were also more typically Ottoman in character, inspired by the Sulamaniye mosque in Istanbul and serving as the focus of complexes of schools, libraries, hospitals, and markets around them, as with the El Djedid mosque built in 1660 and the rebuilding of the El Kebir mosque in 1774 (Golvin 1985; Petersen 1996). Further east, in Tripoli, the 1736 Qaramanli mosque located in the middle of a square complex that includes a *madrassa*, a graveyard, and Qaramanli's own tomb, is one of the best examples of Islamic architecture, and combines the thin minarets and domes typical of Ottoman architecture with a fine collection of mosaics and wood carvings (Micara 2008).

Tombs are an important architectural feature of these Ottoman landscapes—in cities these are often associated with holy men (as in Tripoli), particular leaders, or other members of the elite, while those of commoners typically lay in cemeteries outside the city walls. The burial of more important individuals such as leaders and holy men often became shrines, and so were protected from later damage. No systematic comparative study of their different forms or of regional stylistic traditions has been carried out, however, in marked contrast to the time and energy invested in classifying the mortuary architecture of the Classical period found in the same landscapes (e.g. Stone and Stirling 2007). One cemetery where tombs of probably Ottoman date have been the focus of detailed recording and in one case excavation, is that at Jebel Adda, in Egyptian Nubia, possibly associated with the garrison settlements at Sai and Qasr Ibrim (see below). Made of mudbrick, these have a distinctive double-domed superstructure (Fig. 66.2). Around 50 survive at the Jebel Adda cemetery, which also contains a variety of earlier burial types, including 130 'X-Group' tumuli and 30 early Christian graves (Huber and Edwards 2010: 83). As Huber and Edwards note (2010: 88–9), these double-domed tombs are a distinctive regional burial form, and differ from more generic Islamic forms of the post-medieval period in Nubia. One example excavated in the 1960s—Islamic Tomb no. 136—provides additional information concerning their design and construction. The tomb consisted of a mudbrick rectangular burial, with barrel vaulting, excavated into a pre-existing, robbed tumulus. The burial chamber included a single extended inhumation lying roughly north–south with the head facing southwest toward Mecca. The chamber had been blocked off with mudbricks, and brick pavement had been laid above it to support a double domed superstructure over the tomb entrance (Huber and Edwards 2010: 84–6).

Of more private nature are the numerous surviving Ottoman houses which in Cairo were focused around a courtyard, in contrast to earlier Mamluk residences in the city. The Suheimi House (1648 and 1796) is the largest and best preserved of these, along with the late 18th-century house of Sinnarie (1798), which was confiscated by Napoleon and turned into the French Institute. Typical of these houses, and reaching back at least to the Zahabi House, begun in 1638 in the then commercial centre of the city, is their division of the *haramlak* (*harem*—female area) from the *salamlak* (male area) (Salama 2006). Tunis, Algiers, and Tripoli also all retain excellent examples of Ottoman elite private homes, as does Benghazi,

FIG. 66.2 Ottoman tombs at Jebel Adda, Egyptian Nubia, *c.* 1960 (photograph courtesy of Reinhard Huber).

in northeastern Libya, where the house of Omar Pasha Mansour El Kikhia, an Ottoman pasha (governor) from a prominent Benghazi family, includes several balconies and stone archways, as well as an open courtyard containing a fountain. While this building has been restored, remodelled, and converted into the Bait-al Medina al-Thaqafi museum, the same plan was also applied to *fundugs* (hotels for merchants), in which the lower floor was used for storage and the upper for shop units and sleeping rooms. The ancient medinas (old Arab quarters) of both Tunis and Algiers also retain a selection of more everyday housing, interspersed with *hammans, madrassas, zawyias* (small mosques), *souqs*, covered streets (*sabats*), hotels (*foudouks*), cafés, and fountains all built during the Ottoman era (Golvin 1985).

In the Algiers medina at least four different Ottoman house forms are known (Mazouz and Benhsain 2009; see also Salama 2006 for comparisons with Cairo). The most common layout comprises a central courtyard, sometimes with a covering lattice *chbek*, with surrounding ground-floor and first-floor rooms, and roof terrace, accessed via a stairway, with additional rooms. The grander, larger houses are a development of this layout with more rooms added onto the main structure, at times including a personal *hammam* and even a private oven/bakery (which also provided heat for the baths) around the entrance way. By contrast, the simplest and smallest type, known as *aali*, lacks a courtyard, and the ground-floor rooms are often used as boutiques. A recent analysis of the spatial syntax of these house layouts nonetheless indicates that, with the exception of the *aali* form, despite varying in the number of rooms and in apparent complexity, all the other types share the same level of 'spatial depth' (Mazouz and Benhsain 2009).

Archaeological study of Ottoman period houses has been limited, whether in urban settings such as Algiers and Cairo or in smaller towns or rural settlements. One recently documented example is that at the post-medieval fortified village of Jebel Nauri in the Mahas region of northern Sudan near the Third Nile Cataract. Nauri is mentioned by the Turkish traveller Evilya Çelebi, who visited Nubia in 1671–2 and described the settlement as having a rectangular, fortified perimeter and containing three mosques, a bathhouse, and some 600 reed-built houses (Dankoff 2006). Archaeological survey in the area in 2002 documented the surviving remains of the village, including a two-storeyed, multi-roomed house with an associated but physically separate rectangular tower. Both were built of locally produced mudbrick and palm logs for the roofing. The house included a reception room with *mastabas* (mud-plastered stone seats/beds), bedrooms, kitchen, and storage areas (el-Zein 2004).

Fortifications, more generally, are another common element of the built heritage of the Ottoman Empire. Algiers is a prime example, as it did not become a capital until the Ottoman conquest of the 16th century, after which the old town was enclosed by a wall on all sides, including the sea front, with five gates allowing access to the city and the roads leading from them meeting in front of the Ketchaoua mosque (1794). To consolidate these defences, a citadel was constructed at the highest point in the wall. The surviving city walls of Tripoli are likewise of Ottoman age (Petersen 1996: 286), while other fortifications are known from Libya (Fig. 66.3), Tunisia and Egypt, and the Sudan, where Ottoman presence was largely

FIG. 66.3 Ottoman fortress at Wadi Shati, Libya—now used as a regional museum (photograph courtesy of Stefania Merlo).

FIG. 66.4 The Ottoman fortress of Qasr Ibrim, Egypt, about forty years after its abandonment (detail of calotype by Felix Teynard, *c.* 1852; copy kindly provided by Dave Edwards).

confined to a narrow strip along the Nile (el-Zein 2004, 2009), though nevertheless of long standing from the 16th into the 19th centuries (Alexander 1996). Fortresses were a quintessential aspect of 'the Ottoman frontier', and those at Qasr Ibrim in Egyptian Nubia (Fig. 66.4) and on Sai Island (Fig. 66.5), northern Sudan, have been the focus of recent study (el-Zein 2009). The construction of both is associated with the consolidation of Ottoman control over southern Egypt and Nubia during the reign of Süleyman I under the governorship of Ibrahim

FIG. 66.5 Sai Fort, Sudan, viewed from the west (photograph, Intisar Soghayroun el-Zein).

Pasha (Edwards and el-Zein 2012). As part of this expansion, the southern frontier had been extended to the Second Nile Cataract by *c.* 1560, and a new Sanjak (Provincial prefecture)—the 'Sanjak of Ibrim', had been established. This was probably based at El-Diwan/El-Dirr with a garrison at Qasr Ibrim, and possible outposts further south at Jebel Adda and Faras (Alexander 2000; Edwards and el-Zein 2012: 173). Further southward expansion took place in the 1580s, and a garrison was installed on Sai island and a new 'Sanjak of the Mahas' established, albeit briefly (Edwards and el-Zein 2012: 173). Aside from the physical remains of fortifications at the larger sites such as Sai and Qasr Ibrim, several smaller fortified villages like Nauri and Tombos have now been identified through critical analysis of the wealth of toponymic information available in Çelebi's text (Edwards and el-Zein 2012: 174–7).

In contrast to the Nile Valley, coral was widely used for the construction of buildings at Ottoman towns along the Red Sea, most famously at Suakin (Greenlaw 1976; Hinkel 1992). Insoll (2003) has described the situation at Massawa, where the principal building was the Turkish governor's palace, the ground floor of which was occupied by the customs office and a warehouse. Several mosques and tombs were also recorded by contemporary visitors, including Evliya Çelebi (Dankoff 2006: 451). The remains of an Ottoman settlement at Hergigo near Massawa and of the fort established at Debarwa (Eritrea) in the mid-16th century as a strategic point on the coastal–interior trade routes also survive (Insoll 2003: 84; cf. Pankhurst 1982). Debarawa in the late 18th century was divided into two parts constituting a higher and lower town, with Muslims inhabiting the upper sections and the Christians the lower parts. This pattern of dual settlement was replicated in the Ethiopian highlands at Gondar, with Muslims frequently being tolerated in Christian towns where they controlled foreign trade—a profession which in Christian eyes carried a social stigma, as was often the case in other parts of Africa (Insoll 2003: 84).

However, it is Suakin, situated further north on an island site on the coast of Sudan, that has been most extensively investigated. Perhaps best known from the pioneering architectural studies by Greenlaw (1976) when much of the town was still standing, Suakin served as an important Red Sea port for the Christian kingdoms in the 10th–12th centuries, linked by overland trade routes to the Nile Valley and Ethiopia (Mallinson et al. 2009: 471; Breen et al. 2011). The prosperity of the port grew in subsequent centuries, and it was brought under Egyptian Mamluk control in the late 15th century before being surrendered to Ottoman forces in 1517. From then on up to the 19th century, an Ottoman garrison was based on the island, and two forts are recorded as having been built on the adjacent mainland in the 17th century—these are now obscured by recent development. After the Turkish-Egyptian invasion of northern Sudan in 1820–21, Suakin came under Egyptian control, and prospered following the opening of the Suez Canal in 1869. However, following the establishment of the Anglo-Egyptian condominium in 1899 and the decision to construct a new port to the north at Shaykh al-Barghuth (Port Sudan), by 1922 much of the town had been abandoned.

A programme of archaeological and architectural research at Suakin between 2002 and 2007 has clarified several aspects of the early history of Suakin (see Mallinson et al. 2009; Breen et al. 2011). Of the Ottoman remains, investigations were focused on three major structures: Bayt al-Mufti, Bayt Khurshid Efendi, and Bayt al-Basha. Additionally, landscape and underwater surveys in the vicinity of the island and surrounding mainland have helped place the town and its suitability as a port into clearer focus. Of the three building complexes, Greenlaw (1976) considered Khurshid Efendi's house, at the eastern end of the island, to have been the oldest standing building at the time of his survey, and dating to the 16th century. The house is well known from its two-storey *diwan* with lavish plasterwork, illustrated by Greenlaw (1976: 28). As it has now largely collapsed, recent research has concentrated on clearing rubble to recover as much

FIG. 66.6 Excavations in progress at the late 16th-century structure known as the Beit al-Basha, Suakin, 2006 (photograph courtesy of Colin Breen).

as possibie of the surviving decorated stonework and fragments of a wooden oriel window (*rawshan*), as well as recording the plan of the building and its architectural history. Trial excavations at the 'House of the Mufti' produced rather inconclusive results. Those at Bayt al-Basha near the centre of the island, on the other hand, suggest that its construction in the mid-16th century triggered a more general shift to the use of stone for house construction (previously wood and reeds were the preferred raw materials), and that the house itself probably served as the central administrative building for the Ottoman elite (Breen et al. 2011: 217).

Regrettably, the poor conservation status of the Ottoman era buildings at Suakin (Fig. 66.6) can be only too readily paralleled elsewhere in North Africa, partly because of weathering in the face of the elements (e.g. the inscriptions on the Ghar al-Milh complex in Tunis; Heywood 2009: 500), partly because of damage sustained under colonial rule or from more recent developments, and partly because of changes of use, such as the Red Fort in Tripoli which was successively the residence of the Ottoman rulers, the headquarters of the antiquities service, and (briefly) a military store, before becoming the national museum (Fuller 2000).

SUMMARY AND CONCLUSION

The Ottoman occupation of parts of Africa lasted for upward of three centuries, but several areas were always provinces of secondary importance, where Turkish control was largely limited to the control of ports—in Sudan's case the Red Sea area and military forts along the Sudan Nile Valley. Revenues from such regions were typically low and largely grounded on the customs duties collected on goods flowing through the ports and the slave trade (el-Zein 2004: 50–57). Even along the North African littoral and in the Maghreb, the Ottomans had no effective long-term control outside the ports, where there was both a direct Ottoman presence and garrison troops. After some decades, effective control passed to others (among them the Mamluks in Egypt, the Kashifs in the Sudanese Nile Valley, the Beja and Hadendawa at Suakin, and local dynasties in Algeria, Tunisia, and Libya). In all these cases, however, and despite substantial autonomy, local rulers continued to recognize the religious authority of the Ottoman sultan as caliph, and further acknowledged his suzerainty by receiving recruits for their armies from the Ottoman Empire. Indeed, as far south as Old Dongola the Funj ruler's name was followed in the Friday prayers by a mention of the Ottoman sultan in his capacity as the guardian of Mecca and Medina. Even where, as in Tunisia, a different school of Islamic law (the Maliki school) was influential, with Maliki scholars allowed to manage the religious and legal affairs of their communities, the Ottoman preference for the Hanafi school was still adopted officially.

Much of the surviving Ottoman material record in North Africa, or at least academic research relating to it, concerns the built environment. Important as this is, over-concentration in this area has been—and continues to be—at the expense of other fields of research. One of these, still largely undeveloped, is maritime archaeology, a necessity for the study of Ottoman coastal towns, including some of the largest, such as Algiers, Tunis, Tripoli, Suakin, and Massawa (Heywood 2009; Mallinson et al. 2009). Complementing archaeological—including underwater—investigations of the maritime dimension of Ottoman life, contemporary documentary sources would undoubtedly repay serious exploration. We should note also that the activities of the Ottoman navy extended well beyond the official frontiers, including as far south as Mombasa where two raids under the command of Mirale Beque in 1585 and 1588–9 helped destabilize Portuguese control over the Swahili coast (Strandes 1961: 128–43). As well as travellers' accounts, such as that of Çelebi, whose visit to Massawa was noted above, there are also numerous administrative and financial records of Ottoman date, both in North Africa and in Istanbul, not all of them as yet published or translated, which may provide further information about this maritime activity.

Another concern has to be to develop strategies for investigating the daily life of ordinary people, both within the Empire and on its frontiers, as has been attempted for other parts of the Empire (e.g. LaBianca 2000). The evidence recovered from the Ottoman-period wreck (c. AD 1756) off Sadana Island in the Red Sea (Ward 2001), for instance, included the remains of a large cargo of Chinese porcelain coffee cups, ceramic water jars, and *bakdounis* (peony scroll dishes), as well as coffee beans and spices. Control over the trade in coffee, probably exported from the Yemen, was of considerable economic importance to the Ottomans, especially after European powers had captured the lucrative spice trade. Equally importantly, the integration of coffee drinking as a social activity had significant consequences for patterns of consumption and cultural life more generally in the Ottoman world.

Finally, mention must also be made of the need to expand research on the nature, extent, and physical traces of slavery, slave raiding (especially beyond the frontiers of formal Ottoman authority), and the trans-Sahara and transoceanic trades in slaves. Alexander's (2000) general review of the possible archaeological manifestations of slavery provides an important starting point, and especially his clarification of the likely impacts of slave raiding on the residents of the Dar al Harb as opposed to those residing in the Dar al Islam. Indeed, recent research is starting to demonstrate that physical traces of the later manifestations of the slave trade associated with the Turco-Egyptian period survive in both South Sudan (Lane and Johnson 2009) and Ethiopia (González-Ruibal 2011). Additionally, more general historical studies of these areas (e.g. Pankhurst 1997; Collins 1999; Spaulding 1982) as well as within the wider Ottoman Empire (e.g. Toledano 1998), provide an indication of their antiquity, extent, and changing nature, as well as the diverse forms of slavery and unfree labour that existed. However, much more sustained, collaborative research is urgently needed on the earlier manifestations of slavery in the region, and on the links between the Islamic territories in the north and the African states and acephalous societies to the south.

REFERENCES

ABIR, M. (1980). *Ethiopia and the Red Sea*. Totowa, NJ: Frank Cass.

ALEXANDER, J. A. (1988). The Saharan divide in the Nile Valley: the evidence from Qasr Ibrim. *African Archaeological Review* 6: 73–90.

—— (1996). The Turks on the Middle Nile. *Archéologie du Nil Moyen* 7: 15–35.

—— (1997). Qalat Sai, the most southerly Ottoman fortress in Africa. *Sudan & Nubia* 1: 16–20.

—— (2000). The archaeology and history of the Ottoman frontier in the Middle Nile Valley 910–1233/1504–1820 AD. *Adumatu* 1: 47–61.

—— (2001). Islam, archaeology and slavery in Africa. *World Archaeology* 33: 44–60.

—— (2009). Ottoman frontier policies in North East Africa. In Peacock (2009: 225–34).

BARAM, U., and CARROLL, L. (eds) (2000). *A Historical Archaeology of the Ottoman Empire: Breaking New Ground*. New York: Plenum.

BECHHOEFER, W., and IRELAND, S. (1996). *The Ottoman House*. Ankara: British Institute in Anatolia.

BREEN, C., FORSYTHE, W., SMITH, L., and MALLINSON, M. (2011). Excavations at the medieval Red Sea port of Suakin, Sudan. *Azania* 46: 205–20.

ÇELIK, Z. (1997). *Urban Forms and Colonial Confrontation: Algiers under French Rule*. Berkeley: University of California Press.

COLLINS, R. O. (1999). Slavery in the Sudan in history. *Slavery and Abolition* 20: 69–95.

DANKOFF, R. (2006). *An Ottoman Mentality: The World of Evliya Çelebi*, 2nd edn. Leiden: Brill.

EDWARDS, D. N., and EL-ZEIN, I. S. (2012). Post-medieval settlement. In D. N. Edwards (ed.), *The Archaeology of a Nubian Frontier*. Leicester: Mauhaus, 173–207.

EL-ZEIN, I. (2004). The Ottomans and the Mahas in the Third Cataract region. *Azania* 39: 50–57.

—— (2009). Ottoman archaeology of the Middle Nile Valley in the Sudan. In Peacock (2009: 371–84).

FAHMY, K. (2002). *All the Pasha's Men: Mehmed Ali, His Army, and the Making of Modern Egypt*. Cairo: The American University in Cairo Press.

FAROQHI, S. (2007). *The Ottoman Empire and the World Around It*. London: I. B. Tauris.

FINKEL, C. (2005). *Osman's Dream: The Story of the Ottoman Empire 1300–1923*. London: John Murray.

FULLER, M. (2000). Preservation and self-absorption: Italian colonisation and the walled city of Tripoli, Libya. *Journal of North African Studies* 5: 121–54.

GOLVIN, L. (1985). Le legs des Ottomans dans le domaine artistique en Afrique du Nord. *Revue de l'Occident Musulman et de la Méditerranée* 39: 201–26.

GONZÁLEZ-RUIBAL, A. (2011). Monuments of predation: Turco-Egyptian forts in western Ethiopia. In P. J. Lane and K. C. Macdonald (eds), *Slavery in Africa: Archaeology and Memory*. Oxford: Oxford University Press, 251–79.

GREENLAW, J. (1976). *The Coral Buildings of Suakin: Islamic Architecture, Planning, Design and Domestic Arrangements in a Red Sea Port*. Stocksfield: John Wiley & Sons.

GÜRKAN, E. S. (2010). The centre and the frontier: Ottoman cooperation with the North African corsairs in the sixteenth century. *Turkish Historical Review* 1: 125–63.

HATHAWAY, J. (with contributions by K. K. Barbir) (2008). *The Arab Lands under Ottoman Rule, 1516–1800*. Harlow: Pearson Longman.

HESS, A. C. (1978). *The Forgotten Frontier: A History of the Sixteenth-Century Ibero-African Frontier*. London: Chicago University Press.

HEYWOOOD, C. (2009). A frontier without archaeology? The Ottoman maritime frontier in the western Mediterranean 1600–1700. In Peacock (2009: 493–508).

HILL, R. L. (1959). *Egypt in the Sudan 1820–1881*. London: Oxford University Press.

HINKEL, F. W. (1992). *The Archaeological Map of the Sudan*, fascicle 6: *The Area of the Red Sea Coast and Northern Ethiopan Frontiers*. Berlin: Wiley VCH.

HUBER, R., and EDWARDS, D. N. (2010). Gebel Adda Cemetery One, 1963: post-medieval reuse of X-Group tumuli. *Sudan & Nubia* 14: 83–90.

INSOLL, T. (2001). Dahlak Kebir, Eritrea from Aksumite to Ottoman. *Adumatu* 2: 39–50.

——(2003). *The Archaeology of Islam in Sub-Saharan Africa*. Cambridge: Cambridge University Press.

LABIANCA, O. S. (2000). Daily life in the shadow of empire: a food systems approach to the archaeology of the Ottoman Empire. In Baram and Carroll (2000: 203–18).

LANE, P. J., and JOHNSON, D. (2009). The archaeology and history of slavery in South Sudan in the 19th century. In Peacock (2009: 509–37).

MALLINSON, M., SMITH, L., BREEN, C., FORSYTHE, W., and PHILLIPS, J. (2009). Ottoman Suakin 1541–1865: lost and found. In Peacock (2009: 469–92).

MAZOUZ, S., and BENHSAIN, N. (2009). Handling architectural complexity by combining genetic and syntactic approaches: the case of traditional settlements in North Africa. In D. Koch, L. Marcus, and J. Steen (eds), *Proceedings of the 7th International Space Syntax Symposium*. Stockholm: KTH, 1–13.

MCCLUSKEY, P. (2008). Commerce before crusade? France, the Ottoman Empire and the Barbary pirates (1661–1669). *French History* 23: 1–21.

MICARA, L. (2008). The Ottoman Tripoli: a Mediterranean medina. In S. K. Jayyusi, R. Holod, A. Petruccioli, and A. Raymond (eds), *The City in the Islamic World*, vol. 2. Leiden: Brill, 383–408.

PANKHURST, R. (1982). *History of the Ethiopian Towns*. Wiesbaden: Coronet.

——(1997). *The Ethiopian Borderlands*. Lawrenceville, NJ: Red Sea Press.

PEACOCK, A. C. S. (ed.) (2009). *The Frontiers of the Ottoman World*. Oxford: Oxford University Press.

——(2012). The Ottomans and the Funj sultanate in the sixteenth and seventeenth centuries. *Bulletin of the School of Oriental and African Studies* 75: 87–111.

PETERSON, A. (1996). *Dictionary of Islamic Architecture*. London: Routledge

ÖZBARAN, S. (1994). *The Ottoman Response to European Expansion: Studies on Ottoman–Portuguese Relations in the Indian Ocean and Ottoman Administration in the Arab Lands during the Sixteenth Century*. Istanbul: Isis Press.

SALAMA, A. (2006). A typological perspective: the impact of cultural paradigmatic shifts on the evolution of courtyard houses in Cairo. *METU Journal of the Faculty of Architecture* 23: 41–58.

SHAW, S. J. (1962). *The Financial and Administrative Organization and Development of Ottoman Egypt, 1517–1798*. Princeton, NJ: Princeton University Press.

SPAULDING, J. L. (1982). Slavery, land tenure and social class in the Northern Turkish Sudan. *International Journal of African Historical Studies* 15: 1–20.

STONE, D. L., and STIRLING, L. M. (eds) (2007). *Mortuary Landscapes of North Africa*. Toronto: University of Toronto Press.

STRANDES, J. (1961). *The Portuguese Period in East Africa*. Nairobi: Kenya Literature Bureau. (First published as *Die Portugiesenzeit von Deutsch- und English-Ostafrika*, Berlin, 1899.)

TOLEDANO, E. R. (1998). *Slavery and Abolition in the Ottoman Middle East*. Seattle: University of Washington Press.

UDAL, J. O. (ed.) (1998). *The Nile in Darkness: Conquest and Exploration, 1504–1862*. Norwich: Michael Russell.

WARD, C. (2001). The Sadana Island shipwreck: an eighteenth-century AD merchantman off the Red Sea coast of Egypt. *World Archaeology* 32: 368–82.

WINTER, M. (2005). *Egyptian Society Under Ottoman Rule, 1517–1798*. London: Routledge.

CHAPTER 67

CONTEXTS OF INTERACTION

The Archaeology of European Exploration and Expansion in Western and Southern Africa in Comparative Perspective

NATALIE SWANEPOEL

INTRODUCTION

IN a historical context already abundant in documentary, oral, and pictographic sources, why do archaeology? The answer is that, through studying mundane material realities, archaeology has the potential to illuminate how conquest and colonization occurred not as a smooth process but as a series of negotiated encounters. Much of our understanding of the encounter between Europe and Africa has been shaped by a colonialist trope that sees Africa as a historical *terra nullius*, only engaging fully with 'history' at the time of that encounter (Richard 2009), or as falling squarely within a predetermined evolutionary sequence (Stahl 1999). With hindsight, the colonial advance in Africa until almost the entire continent was carved up by European powers at the end of the 19th century may seem inevitable. But, as with all grand narratives, these certainties vanish when the African–European encounter is examined under a microscopic lens such as that provided by archaeology (Hauser 2008).

This chapter examines some of the colonial encounters in western and southern Africa from a comparative standpoint (Fig. 67.1). The time is long past, however, when any short review could hope to do thorough justice to the full scope of this archaeology (but see DeCorse 1997; Mitchell 2002; Pikirayi 2006). It therefore specifically addresses only a limited range of topics: the establishment of European outposts on the coast; the range of interactions that occurred between Europeans and Africans; and the heterogeneous nature of the new societies created in the process. Archaeological research on the expansion of Europe in Africa typically draws on archaeological remains, oral sources, documentary archives, and pictorial resources, including rock art (*inter alia* Hall 2000; Stahl 2001; van Schalkwyk and Smith 2004; Fig. 67.2) and this diversity of sources often requires scholars to work across disciplinary boundaries (Falola and Jennings 2003; Swanepoel et al. 2008).

EUROPE IN AFRICA: ESTABLISHING A PRESENCE

From the 15th century Africa's west coast was the scene of fierce competition between several European nations. Looking first for gold and then for slaves, the Portuguese, and later the Dutch, English, and other European nations, established numerous trading lodges, forts, and castles along the coast, up to 80 in Ghana alone, all built over some 300 years (van Dantzig 1980; Anquandah 1999; Fig. 67.3). Where natural harbours were lacking and in order to facilitate trade, trading stations or factories were also built slightly inland along riverbanks (Wood 1967; Gijanto 2011). Because of their monumental nature, much archaeological

FIG. 67.1 The location of archaeological sites discussed in Chapter 67 (map drawn by C. Bruwer).

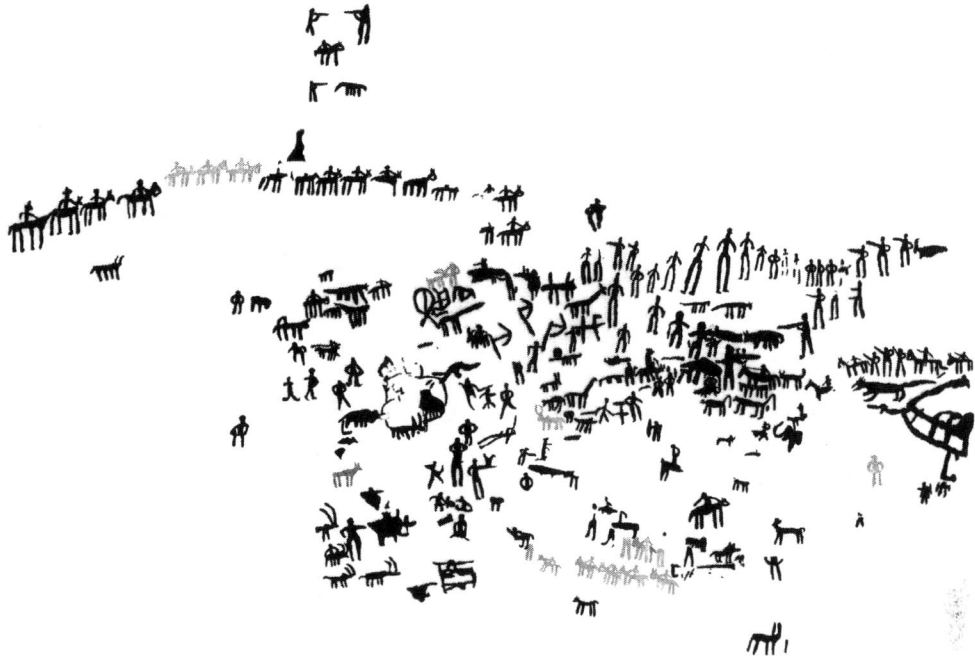

FIG. 67.2 Rock art can be an important source of information about the more recent past. This image depicts a conflict between troops of the South African Republic and the Hananwa, a local polity in Limpopo Province, South Africa (image courtesy of Benjamin Smith).

investigation of these European outposts has focused on their status as architectural monuments (Lawrence 1963; Wood 1967; van Dantzig 1980; Anquandah 1999).

Lacking gold and a population other than foragers and pastoralists, the southern part of Africa's coast proved less attractive to Portuguese traders. Thus, while its bays and natural harbours provided safe anchorage, no trading forts were established at the Cape of Good Hope, though further north, the goldfields of Zimbabwe proved attractive (Pikirayi 2006). By the mid-17th century, however, the Cape's strategic location helped the Dutch East India Company (VOC) solve the problem of resupplying their ships on the way to Indonesia. The remains of this initial occupation and the city and colony that eventually grew up around it have been the subjects of sustained archaeological investigation since the 1980s. We now have a plethora of archaeological studies that speak to everyday life at the Cape during the 17th, 18th, and 19th centuries (Hall et al. 1990a, 1990b, 1993; Jordan 2000; Klose and Malan 2000; Brink 2008).

Since the European exploration and conquest of the African continent was accomplished by means of ship-borne personnel and goods, shipwrecks constitute an important source of information about the kinds of goods desired by African consumers and of the overall process of European colonization (Hall 1993; Breen, Ch. 15 above). Most of the underwater survey and excavation that has taken place thus far has been off the South African coast (Werz 1999), but work is now also under way off the coast of Ghana (Cook and Spiers 2004; DeCorse et al. 2009).

FIG. 67.3 Fort St Sebastian, Ghana (image courtesy of Samuel Spiers).

CONTEXTS OF INTERACTION

As should already be obvious, West and southern Africa differed enormously, most notably in the fact that while the Cape saw the establishment of a settler colony, European settlement in West Africa was initially confined to the coast because of the latter's more unhealthy climate (for Europeans) and the presence there of well-established agricultural societies and polities (Wood 1967). This changed later, however, as European settlement in South Africa expanded, eventually incorporating new territories occupied by indigenous agropastoralists (Mitchell 2002). Even within similar frontier situations, however, the way in which these encounters were expressed materially varied tremendously (Kelly 2002).

The Europeans housed in the trading forts and castles of the West and Central African coast interacted in various ways with the local inhabitants in the vicinity of their outposts, and with societies in the hinterland. Their presence encouraged much of the focus of trade to shift from the interior towards the coast, thus helping to realign previous political and economic axes (van Dantzig 1980). Polities able to manipulate the trade often grew in size and consequence, but were now prey to increased competition from other states (DeCorse and Spiers 2009). While the European presence meant the influx of new goods, new ideas, and new alliances, it should by no means be assumed that it resulted in a total upheaval of existing social and cultural practices. DeCorse's (2001) work at the town of Elmina, which grew up adjacent to Elmina Castle on the Ghanaian coast, has documented that while there were changes in the kinds of goods used, craft production, and building materials and architecture, there was also a great deal of continuity in how the town's inhabitants used space, their foodways, and their ritual behaviour.

At Elmina, as at many of the forts and castles on the coast, Europeans could not dictate terms to the local population, but at least held sway over their own fortified settlements. This was not the case throughout West Africa, however. A case in point is Savi in Bénin, the capital of the Hueda state (*c.* 1660–1727) and one of the primary trading ports in the Atlantic slave trade. This is one of the few instances in which European traders were not allowed to establish separate trading posts, but were forced to occupy lodges (of indigenous materials and design) within the capital itself, adjacent to the palace and each other. Kelly (1997, 2002) documents how the spatial arrangement of Savi worked to separate both the elite and traders from the rest of the population, thus no doubt reinforcing the former's association with European goods and any political or social power derived from associating with those who brought them.

That European 'guests' should be subjected to such stringent rules about where they could stay, and presumably with whom they could interact, is by no means unusual in contact settings in Africa. In late 19th- and early 20th-century Botswana, for example, the leader of the Bangwato, Khama III, insisted that any new buildings in his capital, Phalatswe, should be round, rather than in the rectangular style associated with Europeans. Even Europeans could only build rectangular houses with his express permission, and they were expected to live in a separate ward from others in the town. While Khama III welcomed missionaries as a political resource and allowed them to build their church in the centre of his capital, his Bakwena counterpart, Sechele I, required missionaries to locate themselves some distance from his capital, Ntsweng (Reid et al. 1997).

The situation was substantially different at the Cape. When Europeans first started making landfall on the South African coast they came into contact with non-sedentary San foragers and Khoe herders. Interactions with these local populations thus differed markedly from those with the local kingdoms and states of the West and Central African coastline. Initially Europeans relied on the indigenous Khoe herders to supply them with meat, in return for a range of trade goods, including liquor, tobacco, pipes, copper objects, and beads (Karklins and Schrire 1991). In some cases, such as in the !Khuiseb Delta area on the Namibian coast, such trade may have helped stimulate local economies as European goods penetrated local exchange networks, but ultimately this proved unsustainable, as pastoralists could not translate their newly acquired goods back into cattle when necessity demanded it (Kinahan 2000).

A similar story is revealed at the site of Oudepost, a small VOC outpost north of Cape Town occupied *c.* 1669–1673 and again *c.* 1684–1732. Drawing on the archaeological evidence of faunal and other remains that speak to the interactions between VOC soldiers at the outpost and local Khoekhoe populations, Schrire (1995) argues that pastoralists in this region also fell victim to the inroads that colonists made into their economic base, forcing many of them into servitude on colonial farms (Ross 2010). The record of such incorporation and/or resistance to it by southern Africa's pastoralist and hunter-gatherer populations lies partly in the scattering of European imports and faunal remains found in rockshelters (e.g. Moir and Sampson 1993; Plug and Sampson 1996), but also in the rock art produced during this period (Yates et al. 1993; Ouzman 2005). However, such evidence still needs to be adequately theorized and incorporated into the larger picture of colonial South Africa.

Considering difference: the development of heterogeneous societies

One of the consequences of European expansion was the creation of new societies that were neither wholly European nor wholly African. Again, this differed markedly between regions. Before 1900 in West and Central Africa, the European presence tended to bolster the position of African elites who capitalized on their economic and political relationship, but also led to the emergence of creolized populations, the result of some intermarriage and the widespread adoption of European goods, practices, and religion by some, though not all (Mark 2002). In southern Africa, in contrast, heterogeneous settler societies emerged in several contexts, often marked by highly structured racialized, ethnicized class and gender relations.

Cape colonial life

This is amply demonstrated by the archaeology of South Africa's Western Cape Province. When the VOC established a supply station at the Cape, it had no intention of allowing it to become a settler colony, but before long it became economically expedient to grant land to previous employees of the company (Malan 1997). From these foundations sprang a complex settler colony composed of a motley collection of company officials and other employees, soldiers and sailors, Free Burghers (farmers), slaves (drawn primarily from Madagascar, Mozambique, and the East Indies), manumitted slaves, traders and retailers, servants, and individuals of Khoe or San descent who had been incorporated into Cape society (Ross 2010).

The historical archaeology that developed at the University of Cape Town under the auspices of Martin Hall in the 1980s took as its focus the delineation of this complex colonial society (Lucas 2006). Important themes included the emergence of Free Burgher identity, most signally studied through the evolution of a distinctive 'Cape Dutch' architecture epitomized by the gabled, symmetrical façades found on houses of the region's wine estates (Fig. 67.4). The Free Burghers were often in conflict with VOC officials about their economic and political rights, and their right to challenge the Company was often curtailed. Their architecture, reinforced through social practices such as visiting, thus operated as an alternative discourse to the official one of the VOC (Hall et al. 1988; Brink 2008).

A second theme was the role and positions of slaves and the underclass more generally in Cape society. This has often been a frustrating process as, unlike North America, most slaves at the Cape were not housed in separate quarters (M. Hall et al. 1993). Living in kitchens, lofts, cellars, and outbuildings of their owners' houses, they did not leave a distinct material signature (Brink 2008). The late 17th/early 18th-century site of Vergelegen, with its slave lodge, is a rare exception (Markell 1993; Markell et al. 1995). Even there, however, the artefactual record was not as informative as the isotopic studies of the skeletal remains of a woman who had been buried under the floor. Dietary analysis showed that she had most probably arrived at the Cape when already an adult from a tropical or sub-tropical locality such as Indonesia, the Malay Peninsula, or East Africa, all sources of enslaved labour (Sealy et al. 1993). In another study, Lucas (2004) has used a landscape approach to understand how slaves might have perceived the landscape that they inhabited, and has traced the fate of emancipated slaves in the Dwars River valley after slavery was abolished in 1834.

FIG. 67.4 Rhone, Groot Drakenstein, South Africa (1795) (image courtesy of Yvonne Brink).

It should be remembered, however, that the majority of slaves at the Cape were probably urban inhabitants, though they are no easier to find archaeologically in the city than they are in the countryside. Jordan (2005) has tackled this issue with investigations in one place where it is known that slave women frequently went in the course of their daily work—the washing pools on the slopes of Table Mountain. Excavations at these pools have uncovered a range of artefacts relating to the clothing that the women were laundering, as well as those attesting to their daily lives at the pools.

Slavery indelibly shaped the social, economic, and political culture of the Western Cape and of South Africa as a whole. While domestic slavery was also a feature of life in European outposts in West and Central Africa, it is difficult to discern it archaeologically because of the way in which slaves were integrated into household/fort life. Exceptions occur when, for example, the plantation system was transplanted to the West African coast, as was attempted by the Danes on the Gold Coast in the late 18th and early 19th centuries. Using local slave labour, they hoped to skip the expensive step of transporting slaves overseas, and excavations at one plantation—Frederiksgave—have revealed how Danish planters attempted to control their enslaved workers through the spatial organization of the plantation. This control was, however, imperfect, and the enslaved populations used every means possible to resist their enslavement and make a life for themselves, as shown by archaeological and documentary evidence for not only small-scale acts of sabotage but also the degree to which slaves carved out their own community through subsistence, ritual, and social practices (Bredwa-Mensah 2008).

Eastern Cape landscapes

It was not only the Western Cape that had a heterogeneous population in South Africa. In the 19th century, a new frontier of interaction opened up as the British government, which had permanently taken over the Cape of Good Hope in 1814, settled British immigrants along the Eastern Cape frontier in the 1820s, primarily to act as a buffer between the Xhosa polities in the vicinity of the Fish River and British possessions to the south (Legassick and Ross 2010).

The British takeover resulted in many changes in the material culture inventory of South African sites. In Cape Town there were changes in architecture, as well as the range and styles of goods consumed (Hall 1993), a sometimes gradual shift that is clearly illustrated in colonial probate records (Malan 1997). Similar changes appear in the Eastern Cape. While the situation was often fraught with conflict, a thriving trade was carried on for cattle in return for imported ceramics, beads, alcohol, and other items. The British government tried to exert as much control over this trade as possible, briefly (1824–30) funnelling it through Fort Wiltshire, which drew both Xhosa and European traders. As with earlier sites in West Africa such as Elmina, local chiefs competed to gain control over the new trade resources that were flooding into the area (Bugarin 2002: 1).

The presence of British settlers on the Eastern Cape frontier also gave rise to a new and distinctive society with its own amalgam of different groups—settlers, local and European traders, servants, local Xhosa, manumitted slaves, and relocated Khoekhoen. As with the Free Burghers, British settlers too used architecture and other material culture to signal their new place in the world (Winer and Deetz 1990). Jeppson's work on four Eastern Cape collections excavated from a rural homestead, a town dump, a fort, and a mission station illustrates that diverse populations on the frontier consumed the array of available goods differently. She ascribes this in part to boundary maintenance, but also argues that, over time the 'reciprocal influence [of the colonizers and colonized] ... produce[d] a distinctive Eastern Cape ceramic pattern complexity' (Jeppson 2005: 269).

FUTURE TRENDS

As delineated here, the last three decades have seen significant research accomplished on the nature and extent of the impact of European contact, conquest, and colonization in West and southern Africa. It is perhaps fair to say, though, that this archaeology has not yet fulfilled its transformative potential, although the seeds are there. Going forward, new research is likely to build on existing work on the economic, sociopolitical, and cultural implications of the continuing encounter between Africa and Europe. While much previous work in West Africa may have focused on the Atlantic aspects of that trade, increasingly these interactions are coming to be seen as one of only a number of local, regional, and intercontinental networks of which African societies were and are a part (Stahl 2008). In southern Africa, meanwhile, these regional and intercontinental networks incorporated linkages both inland and across the Atlantic and Indian Oceans. More attention should perhaps be paid to how these networks intersected and overlapped.

While some work on colonial urban contexts in Cape Town and elsewhere in southern Africa continues, there has also been a definite shift towards studying the expanding colonial frontier and how indigenous societies were transformed by, and impacted on, that frontier (Swanepoel et al. 2008). This coincides with an accompanying move away from grand narrative history towards the interplay of documentary, oral, and archaeological sources at a smaller scale that more readily enables archaeologists to examine the agency of individual actors in localized processes of power, knowledge, appropriation, and control (Rowlands 1998).

One theme that is likely to see more in-depth archaeological attention is the impact of colonialism, and more specifically imperialism, at the end of the 19th and beginning of the 20th centuries. This research has implications for much historical ethnography, as the imposition of full-fledged colonialim in the last quarter of the 19th century resulted in many widespread changes to African social, religious, and political life, including material culture. Such changes include the imposition of new settlement patterns, sanitation, and mortuary practices, as well as the introduction of new monetary units and the inclusion of local diverse societies in new colonial 'states' (Rowlands 1998). These states were then further embedded in larger empires, their belonging often attested through the production and consumption of goods (Stahl and Cruz 1998; Stahl 2001).

In South Africa, the impact of industrialization is still under-researched, despite a few projects that have focused on the ethnic and class complexity of agricultural, industrial, and mining landscapes (Behrens 2004, 2005; Lucas 2004) and how they prefigured the landscape of segregation in the 20th century (Weiss 2007). We can expect this work to expand in the future as archaeological sites in these areas are documented ahead of further economic and social development.

Precisely because many of the archaeological remains associated with the expansion of European powers in the world speak to the rise of a modern world system beset by inequality and a colonial history of dispossession and degradation of local cultures, there are contemporary sensitivities around how they are excavated, interpreted, and presented for public consumption. This is clearly demonstrated both in the ongoing debate around the reuse of so-called 'slave forts and castles' as tourist attractions along the West African coast (Osei-Tutu 2007) and in controversies over the excavation of several burial sites in Cape Town (Malan 2004/5; Patrick 2004/5). Archaeologists are often caught squarely in the midst of these political and social negotiations, and need to be sensitive to the larger ramifications of their work.

Lastly, archaeologists are likely to develop more nuanced ways of navigating between different scales of analysis. While Africa was incorporated within a globalizing world, the ways in which this occurred were highly variable across space and time, and the ways in which this process played out will thus have to be interrogated at local, regional, and global scales in order for these differences to be fully recorded and properly understood (Hall 2000; Hauser 2009; Richard 2009).

References

ANQUANDAH, K. J. (1999). *Castles and Forts of Ghana*. Accra: Ghana Museums and Monuments Board.

BEHRENS, J. (2004). Navigating the liminal: an archaeological perspective on South African industrialisation. In A. M. Reid and P. J. Lane (eds), *African Historical Archaeologies*. New York: Kluwer, 347–74.

—— (2005). The dynamite factory: an industrial landscape in late-nineteenth-century South Africa. *Historical Archaeology* 39: 61–74.

BREDWA-MENSAH, Y. (2008). Slavery and resistance on nineteenth century Danish plantations in southeastern Gold Coast, Ghana. *African Study Monographs* 29: 133–45.

BRINK, Y. (2008). *They Came to Stay: Discovering Meaning in the 18th Century Cape Country Dwelling*. Stellenbosch: Sun Press.

BUGARIN, F. (2002). Trade and interaction on the Eastern Cape Frontier: an historical archae-
ological study of the Xhosa and the British during the early nineteenth century. Ph.D thesis,
University of Florida. UMI Microform # 3065909. Ann Arbor: Proquest Information and
Learning Company.

COOK, G., and SPIERS, S. (2004). Central Region Project: ongoing research on early contact,
trade and politics in coastal Ghana, A.D. 500–2000. *Nyame Akuma* 61: 17–28.

DECORSE, C. (1997). Western African historical archaeology. In J. O. Vogel (ed.), *Encyclopedia of Precolonial Africa: Archaeology, History, Language, Cultures, and Environments*. Walnut
Creek, Calif.: AltaMira Press, 545–9.

——(2001). *An Archaeology of Elmina: Africans and Europeans on the Gold Coast, 1400–1900*.
Washington, DC: Smithsonian Institution Press.

——COOK, G., HORLINGS, R., PIETRUSZKA, A., and SPIERS, S. (2009). Transformation in the
era of the Atlantic world: the Central Region Project, coastal Ghana, 2007–2008. *Nyame Akuma* 72: 85–94.

——and SPIERS, S. (2009). A tale of two polities: socio-political transformation on the Gold
Coast in the Atlantic World. *Australasian Historical Archaeology* 27: 29–42.

FALOLA, T., and JENNINGS, C. (eds) (2003). *Sources and Methods in African History: Spoken,
Written, Unearthed*. Rochester, NY: University of Rochester Press.

GIJANTO, L. (2011). Exchange, interaction and trade in local ceramic production in the Niumi
commercial center on the Gambia River. *Journal of Social Archaeology* 11: 21–48.

HALL, M. (1993). The archaeology of colonial settlement in southern Africa. *Annual Review of
Anthropology* 22: 177–200.

——(2000). *Archaeology and the Modern World: Colonial Transcripts in South Africa and the
Chesapeake*. London: Routledge.

——BRINK, Y., and MALAN, A. (1988). Onrust 87/1: an early colonial farm complex in the
western Cape. *South African Archaeological Bulletin* 43: 91–9.

——HALKETT, D., HUIGEN VAN BEEK, P., and KLOSE, J. (1990a). 'A stone wall out of the earth
that thundering cannon cannot destroy'? Bastion and moat at the Castle, Cape Town. *Social
Dynamics* 16: 22–37.

—— —— KLOSE, J., and RITCHIE, G. (1990b). The Barrack Street well: images of a Cape Town
household in the nineteenth century. *South African Archaeological Bulletin* 45: 73–92.

——MALAN, A., AMANN, S., HONEYMAN, L., KISER, T., and RITCHIE, G. (1993). The archaeology of Paradise. *South African Archaeological Society Goodwin Series* 7: 40–58.

HAUSER, M. (2008). *An Archaeology of Black Markets: Local Ceramics and Economies in
Eighteenth-Century Jamaica*. Gainesville: University Press of Florida.

——(2009). Scale locality and Caribbean historical archaeology. *International Journal of
Historical Archaeology* 13: 3–11.

JEPPSON, P. (2005). Material and mythical perspectives on ethnicity: an historical archaeology
study of cultural identity, national historiography and the Eastern Cape frontier of South
Africa, 1820–1860. Ph.D thesis, University of Pennsylvania. UMI Microform # 3197689.
Ann Arbor: Proquest Information and Learning Company.

JORDAN, E. (2005). 'Unrelenting toil': expanding archaeological interpretations of the female
slave experience. *Slavery and Abolition* 26: 217–32.

JORDAN, S. (2000). Coarse earthenware at the Dutch colonial Cape of Good Hope, South Africa: a history of local production and typology of products. *International Journal of Historical Archaeology* 4: 113–43.

KARKLINS, K., and SCHRIRE, C. (1991). The beads from Oudepost 1, a Dutch East India Company outpost, Cape, South Africa. *Beads* 3: 61–72.

KELLY, K. (1997). The archaeology of African–European interaction: investigating the social role of trade, traders, and the use of space in the seventeenth-and eighteenth-century *Hueda* kingdom, Republic of Bénin. *World Archaeology* 28: 351–69.

——(2002). Indigenous responses to colonial encounters on the West African coast: Hueda and Dahomey from the seventeenth through nineteenth century. In C. Lyons and J. Papadopoulos (eds), *The Archaeology of Colonialism*. Los Angeles, Calif.: Getty Research Institute, 96–120.

KINAHAN, J. (2000). *Cattle for Beads: The Archaeology of Historical Contact and Trade on the Namib Coast*. Uppsala: Uppsala University Press.

KLOSE, J., and MALAN, A. (2000). The ceramic signature of the Cape in the nineteenth century, with particular reference to the Tennant Street site, Cape Town. *South African Archaeological Bulletin* 55: 49–59.

LAWRENCE, A. (1963). *Trade Castles and Forts of West Africa*. London: Jonathan Cape.

LEGASSICK, M., and ROSS, R. (2010). From slave economy to settler capitalism: the Cape Colony and its extensions, 1800–1854. In C. Hamilton, B. Mbenga, and R. Ross (eds), *The Cambridge History of South Africa*, vol. 1: *From Early Times to 1885*. Cambridge: Cambridge University Press, 253–318.

LUCAS, G. (2004). *An Archaeology of Colonial Identity: Power and Material Culture in the Dwars Valley, South Africa*. New York: Kluwer.

——(2006). Archaeology at the edge: an archaeological dialogue with Martin Hall. *Archaeological Dialogues* 13: 55–67.

MALAN, A. (1997). The material world of family and household: the Van Sitterts in eighteenth century Cape Town, 1748–1796. In L. Wadley (ed.), *Our Gendered Past: Archaeological Studies of Gender in Southern Africa*. Johannesburg: University of the Witwatersrand Press 273–302.

——(2004/5). Contested sites: negotiating new heritage practice in Cape Town. *Journal for Islamic Studies* 24/25: 15–52.

MARK, P. (2002). *'Portuguese' Style and Luso-African Identity: Precolonial Senegambia, Sixteenth-Nineteenth Centuries*. Bloomington: Indiana University Press.

MARKELL, A. (1993). Building on the past: the architecture and archaeology of Vergelegen. *South African Archaeological Society Goodwin Series* 7: 71–83.

——HALL, M., and SCHRIRE, C. (1995). The historical archaeology of Vergelegen, an early farmstead at the Cape of Good Hope. *Historical Archaeology* 29: 10–34.

MITCHELL, P.J. (2002). *The Archaeology of Southern Africa*. Cambridge: Cambridge University Press.

MOIR, R., and SAMPSON, C. G. (1993). European and Oriental ceramics from rock shelters in the Upper Seacow River Valley. *Southern African Field Archaeology* 2: 35–43.

OSEI-TUTU, B. (2007). Ghana's 'slave castles', tourism, and the social memory of the Atlantic slave trade. In A. Ogundiran and T. Falola (eds), *Archaeology of Atlantic Africa and the African Diaspora*. Bloomington: Indiana University Press, 185–95.

OUZMAN, S. (2005). The magical arts of a raider nation: central South Africa's Korana rock art. *South African Archaeological Society Goodwin Series* 9: 101–13.

PATRICK, M. (2004/5). Down in the woods: reflections on a process. *Journal for Islamic Studies* 24/25: 106–25.

PIKIRAYI, I. (2006). Gold, black ivory and houses of stone: historical archaeology in Africa. In M. Hall and S. Silliman (eds), *Historical Archaeology*. Oxford: Blackwell, 230–50.

PLUG, I., and SAMPSON, C. G. (1996). European and Bushmen impacts on Karoo fauna in the nineteenth century: an archaeological perspective. *South African Archaeological Bulletin* 51: 26–31.

REID, A., LANE, P. J., SEGOBYE, A., BÖRJESON, L., MATHIBIDI, N., and SEKGARAMETSO, P. (1997). Tswana architecture and responses to colonialism. *World Archaeology* 28: 370–92.

RICHARD, F. (2009). Historical and dialectical perspectives on the archaeology of complexity in the Siin-Saluum (Senegal): back to the future? *African Archaeological Review* 26: 75–135.

ROSS, R. (2010). Khoesan and immigrants: the emergence of colonial society in the Cape, 1500–1830s. In C. Hamilton, B. Mbenga, and R. Ross (eds), *The Cambridge History of South Africa*, vol. 1: *From Early Times to 1885*. Cambridge: Cambridge University Press, 168–210.

ROWLANDS, M. (1998). The archaeology of colonialism. In K. Kristiansen and M. Rowlands (eds), *Social Transformations in Archaeology: Global and Local Perspectives*. London: Routledge, 327–33.

SCHRIRE, C. (1995). *Digging Through Darkness: Chronicles of an Archaeologist*. Charlottesville: University Press of Virginia.

SEALY, J. C., MORRIS, A., ARMSTRONG, R., MARKELL, A., and SCHRIRE, C. (1993). An historical skeleton from the slave lodge at Vergelegen. *South African Archaeological Society Goodwin Series* 7: 84–91.

STAHL, A. B. (1999). Perceiving variability in time and space: the evolutionary mapping of African societies. In S. K. Mcintosh (ed), *Beyond Chiefdoms: Pathways to Complexity in Africa*. Cambridge: Cambridge University Press, 39–55.

——(2001). *Making History in Banda: Anthropological Visions of Africa's Past*. Cambridge: Cambridge University Press.

——(2008). The archaeology of African history. *International Journal of African Historical Studies* 42: 241–55.

——and CRUZ, M. (1998). Men and women in a market economy: gender and craft production in west central Ghana *c.* 1775–1995. In S. Kent (ed.), *Gender in African Prehistory*. Walnut Creek, Calif.: AltaMira Press, 205–26.

SWANEPOEL, N., ESTERHUYSEN, A., and BONNER, P. (eds). (2008). *Five Hundred Years Rediscovered: Southern African Precedents and Prospects*. Johannesburg: University of Witwatersrand Press.

VAN DANTZIG, A. (1980). *Forts and Castles of Ghana*. Accra: Sedco.

VAN SCHALKWYK, J. A., and SMITH, B. W. (2004). Insiders and outsiders: sources for reinterpreting a historical event. In A. M. Reid and P. J. Lane (eds), *African Historical Archaeologies*. New York: Kluwer, 325–46.

WEISS, L. (2007). Heritage-making and political identity. *Journal of Social Archaeology* 7: 413–31.

WERZ, B. E. J. S. (1999). *Diving up the Human Past: Perspectives on Maritime Archaeology with Special Reference to Developments in South Africa until 1996*. Oxford: British Archaeological Reports.

WINER, M., and DEETZ, J. (1990). The transformation of British culture in the Eastern Cape, 1820–1860. *Social Dynamics* 16: 55–75.

WOOD, R. (1967). An archaeological appraisal of early European settlements in the Senegambia. *Journal of African History* 8: 39–64.

YATES, R., MANHIRE, A. H., and PARKINGTON, J. E. (1993). Colonial-era paintings in the rock art of the south-western Cape. *South African Archaeological Society Goodwin Series* 7: 59–70.

CHAPTER 68

AN ARCHAEOLOGICAL PERSPECTIVE ON WEST AFRICA AND THE POST-1500 ATLANTIC WORLD

IBRAHIMA THIAW AND FRANÇOIS RICHARD

INTRODUCTION

AFRICA's engagement with the post-AD 1500 Atlantic World has captivated archaeological attention over the past twenty years (e.g. DeCorse 2001a). Building on archaeology's success in investigating the lives of subaltern groups worldwide (e.g. Ferguson 1992), and charting the foundations of capitalism, colonialism, and modernity (Orser 1996), archaeologists have sought to construct 'alternative histories' of the African Atlantic from the ground up. The goals have been to illuminate the lives of African communities that are frequently overlooked or silenced in documentary records, and to re-examine conventional narratives of the 'Atlantic moment' and its effects on the continent.

However, to focus on the archaeology of the 'Atlantic era' *sui generis* is artificial, because Atlantic commerce often articulated with existing political and economic spheres in dynamic and creative ways (Stahl 2004). Thus, one cannot understand Atlantic processes in isolation from different levels of local exchange circuits (Brooks 1993), trans-Saharan networks that connected African communities to the Mediterranean (Austen 2010), and other trading spheres operating on the other side of the continent (Larson 1999; Prestholdt 2008; Alpers 2009). Sadly, few archaeological studies have explored the nature of these interactions (but see Mitchell 2005).

Focusing on West Africa (for southern Africa, see Swanepoel, Ch. 67 above) (Fig. 68.1), the aim here is to give a sense of the themes and questions that have driven archaeological work on Atlantic processes, review some of the trends and insights generated by this research, and explore future directions in this field. The discussion begins by situating historical archaeology in the historiography of the African Atlantic, and then considers archaeological contributions to broader debates about the emergence, dynamics, impacts, and long-term

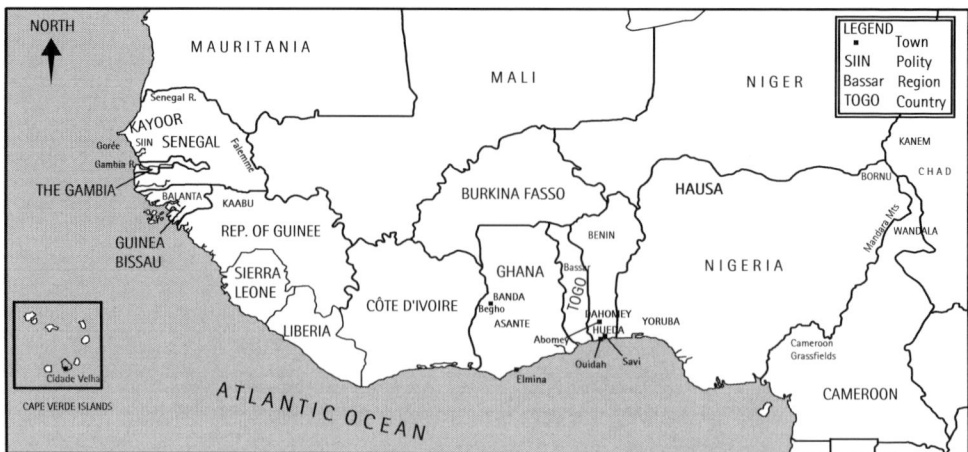

FIG. 68.1 Atlantic West Africa showing the towns, regions, and polities mentioned in Chapter 68.

consequences of the Atlantic economy on African societies. It then proceeds to examine five domains of archaeological research on social transformations: political landscapes, cultural life between the coast and interior, urban dynamics, cultural economies, and technological change. Each is illustrated by synoptic case studies, comparing contexts across the continent to gain insights on the variety of Atlantic experiences. The chapter concludes with a few thoughts on what might lie ahead for the archaeology of the 'African experience'. Opening a dialogue with current archaeological work on the African diaspora, we anticipate that the new frontier of research will not simply *compare* people of African descent on both sides of the Atlantic, but will take trans-oceanic transfers and disjunctures of cultural ideas, practices and identities as its objects of study.

HISTORY AND ARCHAEOLOGY OF
THE ATLANTIC SLAVE TRADE

The Atlantic slave trade is a defining landmark in both African historiography and world history. A structuring element of the Atlantic commerce that entwined the histories of Europe, the Americas, and Africa, it mediated African experiences with the outside world and its long-term effects have shaped international affairs over the past 500 years. Dominated until recently by historians, discussions of the effects of the Atlantic slave trade have often been framed in terms of 'gainers' and 'losers', hinging on assessments of demographic loss (through the export of captives overseas) and its impacts on African societies (Curtin 1969; Lovejoy 1982, 1989; Inikori and Engerman 1992; Eltis 2001). Some scenarios have equated Atlantic exchanges with a process of underdevelopment that relegated the continent to the margins of the world economy and chained its societies to a disruptive architecture of dependency on metropolitan production centres and exterior markets (Wallerstein 1974;

Rodney 1982). Rodney (1966), for instance, raised doubt about the existence of slavery on the Upper Guinean Coast prior to the Atlantic era, arguing that its institutionalization in the region was a direct outcome of European contact. Others, by contrast, have insisted that the Atlantic economy created political opportunities in certain regions, fostering the development of well-organized, thriving polities like the Akan, Benin, and Yoruba states (Fage 1969). Despite their differences, accounts of various stripes have often accorded a preponderant role to Atlantic factors in the making of African histories, and thus unwittingly diminished the roles of African actors in this process (cf. Wolf 1998). Moreover, their panoramic scale of analysis misses much of the nuanced and contradictory ways in which African societies responded to Atlantic processes. Beyond disagreements over the meaning of quantitative measures, these debates owe their acrimony in large part to the fact that Atlantic slavery is bundled with issues of deep moral and political significance, such as the development of racist ideologies and the inhumanity of human bondage, which are inextricably tied to 'modernity' and continue to haunt the postcolonial world. Indeed, while the role of Europeans in the operations of the Atlantic system is rarely contested, the question of African agency and responsibility has been as sensitive and controversial as that of numbers (Curtin 1975; Thornton 1992).

In assessing how far the Atlantic period represents a rupture with what preceded it, elucidating the nature, magnitude, and trajectories of change in pre-Atlantic African societies is essential. By extension, understanding pre-Atlantic landscapes can break down the 'Atlantic packet' into strands of continuity and transformation, posing the issue of its impact as a question rather than a pre-ordained certitude. Recent studies (e.g. Baum 1999; Shaw 2002; Hawthorne 2003; Law 2004), in particular, that employ oral traditions and historical records to transcend the 'either/or' tendencies of earlier debates do indeed give due credit to the dynamism of African cultural institutions. While acknowledging that slaves often constituted the primary imports of a given region, they also underline the wide variety of commercial exchanges, social relations, and material engagements through which Africans negotiated changing times and their position in a gradually globalizing political economy. Archaeological research increasingly adds its weight to both themes.

POLITICAL LANDSCAPES

The political landscapes of the Atlantic either built on old networks or created new ones. The dynamics between various social communities (including agriculturalists, pastoralists, traders, craft specialists, religious groups, and political elites), and the strategies they used to control Atlantic opportunities, have uneven archaeological visibility, but the landscapes these multiple actors produced reflect how the various social and cultural constellations created by the Atlantic were inscribed in space, interacted with one another, and changed through time (Kelly and Norman 2007). In most coastal regions, including Gorée (Senegal) and Elmina (Ghana), Europeans built fortifications that became symbols of foreign might and trade, yet before the imposition of colonial rule in the mid-19th century Europeans exerted limited military and commercial influence beyond their forts. Outside European fortifications, then, it was either local elites and commoners or Afro-Europeans who contributed more lasting signatures to local landscapes.

Only a handful of these coastal trading posts have been investigated archaeologically. While both African and Afro-European residents developed sophisticated tastes, the consumption of new goods and ideas largely answered to African aesthetics and worldviews (DeCorse 2001b). At Gorée Island, for instance, Afro-European women known as *signares* owned most of the stone masonry houses, while ordinary residents were confined to perishable thatch-and-clay architecture (Thiaw 2008). Elsewhere along the Senegalese Petite Côte all way to the Upper Guinea Coast, Luso-Africans and some free African elites and traders developed a unique architecture (often palisaded, whitewashed earth or mudbrick structures) that communicated multiple messages of identity, security, hospitality, and trade to both residents and their foreign trading partners (Mark 2002; Brooks 2003).

Beyond the establishment of coastal commercial enclaves, historians generally agree that the Atlantic economy assisted the development of centralized, predatory kingdoms that dramatically reconfigured West African political fields (Fig. 68.2). In Senegambia, Europeans' divisive diplomacy and strict trade monopolies encouraged political dissent within and between local polities, leading to the intensification of royal authority, state violence, and social instability between the 17th and 19th centuries (Klein 1992; Barry 1998). Although in its infancy, Richard's (2012) work in the Siin region appears to complicate conventional understandings of Senegambian politics, suggesting the emergence of overlapping and competing *local* spheres of power in the wake of the Atlantic expansion. While short-term settle-

FIG. 68.2 The king of Kayoor negotiating with a European merchant (from O. Dapper, *Description de l'Afrique* [1686]). http://gallica.bnf.fr/ark:/12148/btvlb2300087h.item.f44

ments proliferated with the rise of political insecurity, there was also a dramatic increase in site numbers in the 18th century. In lieu of the massive dislocations imagined in some scholarly accounts, survey evidence speaks to the resilience of local social habitats in the face of disruption. Other archaeological signatures indicate that local kings may have been constrained in their capacity to manipulate the spatial environment and consistently enforce acquiescence to their rule. Down the coast, in Upper Guinea, recent research has questioned the tendency to paint non-state societies as the hapless victims of centralized polities (Klein 2001). The Balanta of Guinea-Bissau, for instance, were able to negotiate outside forces and actively engage markets to ensure their survival (Baum 1999; Hawthorne 2003). In their search for protection and social reproduction, coastal communities often participated in enslavement and the sale of captives, and crafted complex partnerships with traders, to obtain the iron needed to repel foreign armies.

Further inland, Europeans, local elites, and traders competed for control of high topographic elevations along the Senegal and Falemme Rivers, major commercial waterways where they established their strongholds (Thiaw 2000). By contrast, the most vulnerable segments of the population, including peasants and slaves, were forced to settle either on the lowlands near the rivers or in uplands further away from major centres of trade and at the mercy of slave hunters.

Unlike Senegambia, the Hueda elite in 17th/18th-century Benin prevented Europeans from establishing trade monopolies by confining them to unfortified trading lodges in their capital at Savi, about 10 km inland (Kelly 1997) (Fig. 68.3). This endowed the palace complex's

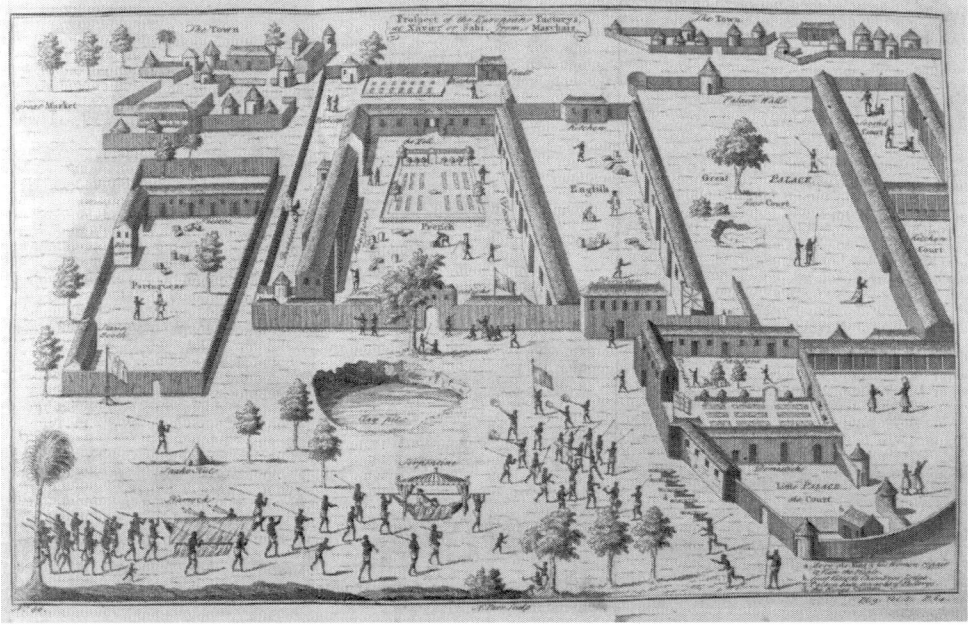

FIG. 68.3 'Prospect of the European factorys at Xavier or Sabi' (1731) (J.-B. Labat, *Voyage du Chevalier des Marchais en Guinée . . . fait en 1725, 1726, & 1727*, in Thomas Astley (ed.), *A New General Collection of Voyages and Travels*, London [1745–47]). http://hitchcock.itc.virginia. edu/Slavery/details.php?categorynum=4&categoryName=European%20Forts%20and%20 Trading20%Posts20%in20%Africa&theRecord=5&recordCount=56

precincts with prestigious status, while keeping the foreigners under surveillance (Kelly and Norman 2007). These restrictions persisted after 1727, when Hueda was conquered by Dahomey, but Europeans were relocated to the town of Ouidah, 3 km inland, near a military garrison and the Dahomean governor overseeing the trade. Archaeological research has also demonstrated the importance of the built landscape in Huedan politics. In the Savi area, a vast system of ditches appears to have defined physical and symbolic boundaries that possibly mediated inter- and intra-polity conflict in a time of heightened tensions (Norman and Kelly 2004; Norman 2009). If the Dahomean conquest introduced changes in local modes of government, material landscapes continued to operate as a critical political resource. After uneven attempts at regional integration during the tumultuous 18th century, Dahomean kings drew strategically on the built environment to expand state authority during the 1800s (Monroe 2007, 2010) (Fig. 68.4). The growth of secondary palaces on the Abomey Plateau from the 17th to 19th centuries, and increasing spatial segregation within them, reflect the development of a centralized political order, aiming to control subordinates and reorganize state bureaucracy to secure the countryside.

Beyond the coast: hinterland dynamics

The coastal regions discussed thus far were undoubtedly the sites of intense interactions between Europeans and Africans that resulted in the emergence of new multicultural elites and traders, new lifeways, and new appetites for exotics. However, hinterland regions were no less affected by Atlantic entanglements, though the dearth of documentary sources in these areas encourages greater use of ethnography and oral histories to supplement archaeological evidence (MacEachern 2001; Stahl 2001). Although direct face-to-face contact with Europeans did not take place in some inland regions until the 19th century, most areas experienced to some degree the ramifications of the Atlantic slave trade.

FIG. 68.4 'The Kingdom of Dahomey's levee' (from A. Dalzel, *The History of Dahomey: An Inland Kingdom of Africa*, London [1793]). http://hitchcock.itc.virginia.edu/Slavery/details. php?categorynum=2&categoryName=Pre-Colonial Africa:Society, Polity, Culture&theRec ord=48&recordCount=261

Stahl's (2001) work in the Banda area of west-central Ghana has shown that this chief-taincy experienced significant changes between its capture by the expanding Asante state in the late 1700s and the imposition of British rule in the late 19th century. Settlement dynamics and exchange relations were affected by the instability resulting from the intensified slave trade and state expansion. Village life in the 16th and 17th centuries indicates the presence of large, durable settlements enmeshed in long-distance trade largely focused on Saharan net-works. After this stable habitat broke off into smaller settlements around the 1650s, signs of steady occupation did not resurface until the late 18th century. By then, the pattern is one of several decades of village existence in the face of episodic turbulence and local production supplemented by regional exchange, of which the most visible traces are New World crops such as maize and tobacco. Material evidence of foreign exotics is limited. This relatively quiet period was followed by abrupt abandonment in the 1820s, and the establishment of a new settlement in the late 1800s bearing the imprints of chronic conflict and colonial dislo-cation. Daily life was reshaped by disruptions in labour, craft production, and trade, evi-denced archaeologically by reconfigurations in pottery making and supply (Stahl and Cruz 1998; Stahl et al. 2008). Ubiquitous imports also attest to the growing effects of commoditi-zation and monetization on local lifeways.

Prior to the Atlantic era, the southern Lake Chad Basin had already experienced signifi-cant changes associated with the expansion of Islam, increased external contact, and the growth of the Kanem-Bornu state and other, smaller polities (Gronenborn, Ch. 58 above). Conflicts and internal political struggles were important sources of slaves, particularly in the plains surrounding the Mandara Mountains and the Biu Plateau. In the face of slaving states like Wandala, agrarian communities frequently assimilated, which resulted in the cultural homogenization of the plains landscape. Other plains-dwelling people retreated to periph-eral areas endowed with natural defences, occasioning vast population movements, espe-cially to the Mandara massif (MacEachern 2001). Processes of enslavement were by no means simple, and rested on ambiguous relations of economic interdependency between raiding polities and their non-state targets, the former desiring the iron and slaves available in the mountains, the latter depending on the outside for some basic resources (MacEachern 1993). If most captives fed regional reservoirs, the Lake Chad area articulated with more dis-tant markets through Bornu and the Hausa states, and many of its slaves probably reached the Atlantic coast in the late 18th century. There are parallels here with central Togo, where de Barros (2001) notes a similar desertion from inhabited plains and relocation to rugged, hilly areas around Mount Bassar following the intensification of slave raids from the nearby Dagomba and Tyokossi polities in the late 1700s.

TOWN AND COUNTRY: URBAN COMMUNITIES AND VILLAGE LIFE

Over the past thirty years, tangible archaeological evidence has demonstrated the antiquity of urban settlements throughout sub-Saharan Africa and intercontinental connections prior to the Atlantic expansion (La Violette and Fleisher 2005; Mitchell 2005). Many more grew during this later era and were shaped by global entanglements with implications of variable intensity on production, consumption, demography, and sociopolitical configurations. It is important, however, not to treat these urban communities *in vacuo*, but rather to examine the nature of their functional and political integration with countrysides (Stahl 2004).

Like modern cities, the population of the Afro-European Atlantic settlements was generally mixed in terms of class, race, gender, and ethnic identity. In addition to enslaved and free Africans, European elite and underclass, some of these towns were also home to a large rural population generally living in distinct neighbourhoods in the outskirts of the European fort, as at Ouidah (Kelly 2009). Closer to the Hueda heartland, recent survey work around Savi has painted a dense and differentiated settlement landscape composed of evenly spaced regional centres, with villages and agricultural zones in between. Artefact distributions suggest a hierarchy of material affluence and access to imported products between these different social spaces (Norman 2009).

Further west, archaeological investigations of the African town adjacent to the fort of Elmina, Ghana, have revealed patterns of interactions that dismantled many prior assumptions about African responses to global economic expansion. Instead of acculturation and assimilation into European ways, DeCorse (2001b) shows significant African continuities in foodways, house layout, and burial practices, despite the rise of an African economic elite.

On Gorée Island, Senegal, on the other hand, Africans and Europeans lived side by side, often in the same houses (Fig. 68.5). Opportunities for spatial growth were limited, and initial experiments with spatial segregation along the lines of race, class, status or religion depicted in early 18th-century maps faded by the middle of the 1700s as the island's popula-

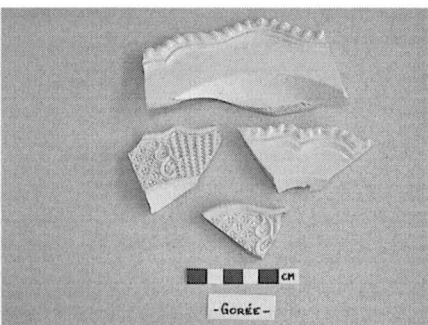

FIG. 68.5 Excavated artefacts from Atlantic-period contexts, Gorée Island, Senegal: upper left, locally produced ceramics, post-1600; bottom left, white stoneware plate rims (1740–70); right, English wine bottles, late 18th/early 19th centuries.

tion grew substantially (Knight-Baylac 1977). By 1750, these constraints imposed new logics of social organization that undermined separation, blurring social distance and encouraging greater population admixture (Thiaw 2008). The material signatures of slavery nevertheless remain archaeologically opaque, perhaps obscured by the coexistence both of slaves destined for export, who were treated like chattels in European forts, and of domestic slaves, who included specialized artisans like masons, carpenters, soldiers, sailors, and domestics (Thiaw 2011). Realignments in Senegambia's export economy resulted in the dramatic increase of domestic slaves after the 1720s (Searing 1993). As Klein (1998) observes, these individuals may literally have worked alongside and eaten from the same bowl as their masters. Ongoing archaeological research in Cape Verde will provide valuable comparative materials on processes of identity-making, cultural construction, and experiences of captivity in the rare context of an uninhabited landmass colonized by a diverse population of merchants, political elites, and slaves (Sørensen et al. 2011). Preliminary results from Citade Velha on the island of Santiago already suggest considerable cultural hybridity in burial and ceramic assemblages.

CULTURAL ECONOMIES: TRADE, CONSUMPTION, AND REGIMES OF VALUE

One of the most fertile arenas of archaeological research on Atlantic Africa has targeted the nature of local societies' entanglements with broader worlds of goods and transformations in local consumption practices and forms of value. This turn to 'cultural economies' emerged in response to the tendency to study Atlantic impacts in simple terms of supply/demand calculations and as 'packages' affecting all aspects of African societies in relatively comparable ways (Richard 2010). More productively, different classes of artefacts can document different trajectories of social and economic practice over time to complicate our sense of 'Atlantic impacts'. Rather than wholesale trends, Atlantic encounters must be viewed as complex interplays of change and continuity. They enveloped compartments and segments of African societies unevenly, as Africans retained the capacity for action and translation under conditions they did not fully control. Changing understandings of wealth and taste were expressed in decidedly local fashion, rather than reflecting the diktat of market forces or outside agendas.

In a seminal paper, Ogundiran (2002) discussed the importance of pre-Atlantic imaginations of status, wealth, and power for understanding the use of Atlantic objects in Yorubaland. Before 1500, beads originating from trans-Saharan trade termini were incorporated into the Yoruba cultural economy as indexes of prestige, a framework that continued to orient the reception of beads later obtained from Atlantic circuits. These practices of valuation, however, also formed the cultural milieu in which cowrie shells came to be interpreted after the 16th century, when they emerged as the undisputed currency in regional markets. While cowries remained associated with status and power, their sheer proliferation eluded sumptuary conventions, and, in slipping past elite control, cowrie circulation combined with new ideas of wealth, personhood, self-realization, and cosmological significance in Yoruba society as whole. Conversely, in the Cameroon Grassfields, Europe's growing economic intrusion and meddlesome diplomacy in the 19th century reconfigured trading zones, favouring the mercantile strategies of central chiefdoms, and granting monopolies over exotic items to those powerful enough to trade in slaves (Rowlands 1989).

As in Nigeria, research in central Ghana shows that African systems of preference informed the repertoire of consumption choices, and mediated the relationship between local crafts and imported products during the Atlantic era. Stahl (2002) has presented a pre-liminary 'cartography of taste', outlining how extant dispositions differently shaped the 'biographies' of pipes, beads, and cloth in Banda. For instance, we see that imported beads were first grafted onto existing traditions of bead use in the 17th century, and differentiated from local manufactures by their incorporation into puberty rituals. By the late 19th century the taste for beads had expanded, probably as a result of the massive influx of monochro-matic, industrially produced beads into the region. Local cloth, by contrast, may have been an emblem of status in the 17th century, possibly obtained from craft specialists in Begho, a pivotal entrepôt 30 km to the south. Over time, cotton-cloth production seems to have shifted downward to the household level, thus affecting its capacity to mark status. In the meantime, imported textiles, due to their connection with long-distance commerce, fash-ioned new registers of value, as they gradually became imbued with powers of social distinc-tion and restricted to elite consumption.

In Senegambia, object trajectories confirm that Africans were discriminating consumers, while telling their own material stories (Richard 2010). In Siin, imported beads were enthu-siastically adopted into local modes of practice from the 17th century, and even appear to have sparked a local manufacturing tradition. Traded tobacco pipes and ceramics, however, never quite managed to infiltrate regional cultural repertoires. By contrast, if liquor bottles enjoyed popularity during the 18th and 19th centuries, material evidence suggests that elites may have sought to patrol social boundaries by regulating the circulation of wine as opposed to more available alcohols like gin or brandy (cf. Gijanto 2011 on ceramics and politics of elite consumption in The Gambia). A subtext here is that Atlantic processes did not always feed the personal indulgence of elites, but contributed to a democratization of consumption, as peasants became integrated into broader worlds of exchange unrestricted by sumptuary rules. More generally, archaeological data caution us against overplaying the material impact of Atlantic commodities, given that trade goods make a very late appearance in local archae-ological assemblages, roughly 250 years after the onset of contact.

TECHNOLOGY

The enslavement and forced migrations of Africans did not only result in demographic changes on both sides of the Atlantic. They also involved the transfer of African technologies and systems of thoughts (Kelly, Ch. 69 below). Although affected by the Atlantic expansion and Europe's Industrial Revolution, African technologies were not swept away; instead, they were appropriated, incorporated, and sometimes readapted to new economic, social, and political situations. In the Bassar region of Togo, for instance, induced-draft furnaces replaced forced-draft techniques for iron smelting. As bellows were no longer needed, this innovation caused reduced production and labour costs, a positive response to population loss resulting from slave raiding in the hinterland, and to competition from European metal imports (de Barros 2001; also Rowlands 1989, for Cameroon). In effect, despite increases in slave raiding and population movements, Bassar iron production intensified over time, reaching its peak between 1890 and 1918, under the German Protectorate.

Besides supplying human cargo, Africa's other contributions to the circulation of material goods, ideas, and people during the Atlantic period have long been overlooked. Diffusion of African crops, agricultural savoir-faire, and foodways was particularly pivotal to the operations of the Atlantic system. Slave cargos relied heavily on African foodstuffs during transit in coastal entrepôts and during the middle passage across the Atlantic, with African rice (*Oryza glaberrima*), for instance, figuring among the staples that provisioned European slave ships in Senegambia and the Guinea Coast (Carney 2001). Indeed, drawing on centuries of rice cultivation in many parts of the region between the Niger and the Senegal River basins, the development of rice as an export crop in late 17th-century South Carolina can be attributed to the arrival of enslaved Africans from these regions, who continued to grow the African variety for domestic use even after planters shifted to higher-yielding Asian rice (*O. sativa*) (Carney 2001; cf. Hawthorne 2010).

Many African societies reconfigured their lives, settlement and social structures, and production activities to face the new challenges of the Atlantic era. The Balanta communities evoked above, for example, moved from upland areas more vulnerable to attacks to riverine mangrove swamps suitable for paddy-rice farming, where they established household units within defensive villages surrounded by walls and entrenchments (Hawthorne 2001). Increased access to European imported iron helped develop an iron-edged blade plough. Age grades, the major units in Balanta sociopolitical organization and economic activities, coordinated mangrove clearance, dyke construction, and land desalinization. Thanks to such reorganization, the Balanta were able to maintain population growth in the face of the powerful and centralized slaving state of Kaabu even at the height of the Atlantic slave trade (cf. Linares 1987).

CONCLUDING REMARKS AND FUTURE DIRECTIONS

Over the past twenty years, archaeology has increasingly contributed fresh perspectives to historical debates over the fashioning of Atlantic Africa. From seminal studies focusing on European coastal enclaves and associated African settlements, research has expanded to examine portions of the continental interior and inland residential communities. This has been fuelled by new methodological orientations: the development of research agendas creatively combining rigorous excavations with regional survey. Their findings have enabled researchers to situate individual sites within broader settlement landscapes, and to investigate political linkages tying the coast to its hinterland and connecting towns with their countrysides. A particularly welcome trend has been a growing concern with the study of past village communities (Stahl 2004, 2007). Because African back-countries and peasant communities are traditionally poorly documented in written and oral records, archaeologies of village life are poised to illuminate one of the more obscure facets of the continent's global past, by exploring how non-elites and local peripheries actively contributed to the crafting of Atlantic Africa. Archaeological research has also added considerable time-depth to our historical portraits of global encounters on the continent, in part by examining African experiences both before and after the advent of Atlantic contacts.

Clearly, the research reviewed here provides solid foundations for future endeavours both in areas currently boasting long traditions of research (Bénin, Ghana, Mali, Senegal, Nigeria) and in those where research programmes are still little developed (Cape Verde, The Gambia, Guinea, Sierra Leone), if at all (Ivory Coast, Liberia). One of the most striking features of the geography of archaeological research on Atlantic Africa nevertheless remains its dramatic unevenness, itself an outcome of colonial legacies and current politics. It is thus ironic that Central Africa, the region most implicated in international slavery (and affected by it) (Miller 1988), is today among the most understudied archaeologically (but see Fromont 2009). Beyond repairing such omissions, where possible, we conclude by noting one final promising trend in the archaeology of the African Atlantic: the increasing rapprochement between scholars working in Africa and students of the African diaspora (Hauser and DeCorse 2003; Haviser and MacDonald 2005; Fennell 2007, 2011; Ogundiran and Falola 2007). While this work, too, has often been (understandably) limited by geography, its future lies in developing a truly 'oceanic' perspective that encompasses the historical geography of the Atlantic world as a whole, examines the temporality and flow of Atlantic circulations, and investigates processes of identity construction on Europe's imperial margins to help 'provincialize' the geographies of power underwriting world history and emphasize the inescapably global character of all societies caught in the emergence of capitalist modernity (Chakrabarty 2008; Trouillot 2003).

REFERENCES

ALPERS, E. A. (2009). *East Africa and the Indian Ocean*. Princeton, NJ: Markus Wiener.

AUSTEN, R. (2010). *Trans-Saharan Africa in World History*. Oxford: Oxford University Press.

BARRY, B. (1998). *Senegambia and the Atlantic Slave Trade*. Cambridge: Cambridge University Press.

BAUM, R. (1999). *Shrines of the Slave Trade: Diola Religion and Society in Precolonial Senegambia*. Oxford: Oxford University Press.

BROOKS, G. E. (1993). *Landlords and Strangers: Ecology, Society, and Trade in Western Africa, 1000–1630*. Boulder, Colo.: Westview Press.

—— (2003). *Eurafricans in Western Africa: Commerce, Social Status, Gender and Religious Observance from the Sixteenth to the Eighteenth Century*. Athens: Ohio University Press.

CARNEY, J. A. (2001). African rice in the Columbian exchange. *Journal of African History* 42: 377–96.

CHAKRABARTY, D. (2008). *Provincializing Europe: Postcolonial Thought and Historical Difference*. Princeton, NJ: Princeton University Press.

CURTIN, P. D. (1969). *The Atlantic Slave Trade: A Census*. Madison: University of Wisconsin Press.

—— (1975). *Economic Change in Precolonial Africa: Senegambia in the Era of the Slave Trade*. Madison: University of Wisconsin Press.

DE BARROS, P. (2001). The effects of the slave trade on the Bassar ironworking society of Togo. In DeCorse (2001a: 59–80).

DECORSE, C. R. (ed.) (2001a). *West Africa During the Atlantic Slave Trade: Archaeological Perspectives*. New York: Continuum.

—— (2001b). *An Archaeology of Elmina: Africans and Europeans on the Gold Coast, 1400–1900*. Washington, DC: Smithsonian Institution Press.

ELTIS, D. (2001). The volume and structure of the transatlantic slave trade: a reassessment. *William and Mary Quarterly* 58: 17–46.

FAGE, J. D. (1969). Slavery and the slave trade in the context of West African history. *Journal of African History* 10: 393–404.

FENNELL, C. (2007). *Crossroads and Cosmologies: Diasporas and Ethnogenesis in the New World.* Gainesville: University Press of Florida.

—— (2011). Early African America: archaeological studies of significance and diversity. *Journal of Archaeological Research* 19: 1–49.

FERGUSON, L. (1992). *Uncommon Ground: Archaeology and Early African America, 1650–1800.* Washington, DC: Smithsonian Institution Press.

FROMONT, C. (2009). Icônes chrétiennes ou symboles Kongo? L'art et la religion en Afrique centrale au temps de la Traite, XVIIème–XVIIIème siècles. *Cahiers des anneaux de la mémoire* 12: 47–60.

GIJANTO, L. (2011). Exchange, interaction, and change in local ceramic production the Niumi commercial center on the Gambia River. *Journal of Social Archaeology* 11: 21–48.

HAUSER, M., and DECORSE, C. R. (2003). Low-fired earthenwares in the African Diaspora: problems and prospects. *International Journal of Historical Archaeology* 7: 67–98.

HAVISER, J., and MACDONALD, K. C. (eds) (2005). *African Re-genesis: Confronting Social Issues in the Diaspora.* Walnut Creek, Calif.: Left Coast Press.

HAWTHORNE, W. (2001). Nourishing a stateless society during the slave trade: the rise of Balanta paddy-rice production in Guinea-Bissau. *Journal of African History* 42: 1–24.

—— (2003). *Planting Rice and Harvesting Slaves: Transformations Along the Guinea-Bissau Coast, 1400–1900.* Portsmouth: Heinemann.

—— (2010). From 'black rice' to 'brown': rethinking the history of risiculture in the seventeenth and eighteenth century Atlantic. *American Historical Review* 115: 151–63.

INIKORI, J. E., and ENGERMAN, S. (eds) (1992). *The Atlantic Slave Trade: Effects in Economies, Societies, and Peoples in Africa, the Americas, and Europe.* Durham, NC: Duke University Press.

KELLY, K. G. (1997). The archaeology of African–European interaction: investigating the social roles of trade, traders, and the use of space in the 17th and 18th century Hueda Kingdom, Republic of Bénin. *World Archaeology* 28: 77–95.

—— (2009). Controlling traders: Slave Coast strategies at Savi and Ouidah. In C. A. Williams (ed.), *Bridging the Early Modern Atlantic World.* Ashgate: University of Bristol Press, 186–212.

—— and NORMAN, N. (2007). Historical archaeologies of landscape in Atlantic Africa. In D. Hicks, L. Mcatackney, and G. Fairclough (eds), *Envisioning Landscape: Situations and Standpoints in Archaeology and Heritage.* Walnut Creek, Calif.: Left Coast Press, 173–93.

KLEIN, M. A. (1992). The impact of The Atlantic slave trade on the societies of the western Sudan. In Inikori And Engerman (1992: 25–47).

—— (1998). *Slavery And Colonial Rule In French West Africa.* Cambridge: Cambridge University Press.

—— (2001). The slave trade and decentralized societies. *Journal Of African History* 42: 49–65.

KNIGHT-BAYLAC, M. H. (1977). Gorée au XVIII siècle: l'appropriation du sol. *Revue Française d'Histoire d'Outre-Mer* 14: 33–59.

LARSON, P. (1999). *History and Memory in the Age of Enslavement: Becoming Merina in Highland Madagascar, 1770–1822.* Portsmouth, NH: Heinemann.

LA VIOLETTE, A., and FLEISHER, J. (2005). The archaeology of sub-Saharan urbanism: cities and their countrysides. In A. B. Stahl (ed.), *African Archaeology: A Critical Introduction*. Oxford: Blackwell, 327–52.

LAW, R. (2004). *Ouidah: The Social History of a West African Slaving 'Port,' 1727–1892*. Athens: Ohio University Press.

LINARES, O. F. (1987). Deferring to trade in slaves: the Jola of Casamance, Senegal, in historical perspective. *History in Africa* 14: 113–39.

LOVEJOY, P. (1982). The volume of the Atlantic slave trade: a synthesis. *Journal of African History* 23: 473–501.

—— (1989). The impact of the Atlantic slave trade on Africa: a review of the literature. *Journal of African History* 30: 365–94.

MACEACHERN, S. (1993). Selling the iron for their shackles: Wandala Montagnard interactions in northern Cameroon. *Journal of African History* 34: 247–70.

—— (2001). State formation and enslavement in the southern Lake Chad Basin. In C. R. DeCorse (ed.), *West Africa during the Atlantic Slave Trade: Archaeological Perspectives*. New York: Continuum, 131–51.

MARK, P. (2002). *'Portuguese' Style and Luso-African Identity: Precolonial Senegambia, Sixteenth–Nineteenth Centuries*. Indianapolis: Indiana University Press.

MILLER, J. (1988). *Way of Death: Merchant Capitalism and the Angolan Slave Trade, 1730–1830*. Madison: University of Wisconsin Press.

MITCHELL, P. J (2005). *African Connections: Archaeological Perspectives on Africa and the Wider World*. Walnut Creek, Calif.: AltaMira Press.

MONROE, J. C. (2007). Continuity, revolution or evolution on the Slave Coast of West Africa? Royal architecture and political order in precolonial Dahomey. *Journal of African History* 48: 349–73.

—— (2010). Power by design: architecture and politics in precolonial Dahomey. *Journal of Social Archaeology* 10: 367–97.

NORMAN, N. L. (2009). Hueda (Whydah) country and town: archaeological perspectives on the rise and collapse of an African kingdom. *International Journal of African Historical Studies* 42: 387–410.

—— and KELLY, K. G. (2004). Landscape politics: the serpent ditch and the rainbow in West Africa. *American Anthropologist* 106: 98–110.

OGUNDIRAN, A. (2002). Of small things remembered: beads, cowries and cultural translations of the Atlantic experience in Yorubaland. *International Journal of African Historical Studies* 35: 427–57.

—— and FALOLA, T. (eds) (2007). *Archaeology of Atlantic Africa and the African Diaspora*. Bloomington: Indiana University Press.

ORSER, C. E. (1996). *A Historical Archaeology of the Modern World*. New York: Plenum Press.

PRESTHOLDT, J. (2008). *Domesticating the World: African Consumerism and the Genealogies of Globalization*. Berkeley: University of California Press.

RICHARD, F. G. (2010). Re-charting Atlantic encounters: object trajectories and histories of value in the Siin (Senegal) and Senegambia. *Archaeological Dialogues* 17: 1–27.

—— (2012). Political transformations and cultural landscapes in the Senegambia: an alternative view from the Siin. In J. C. and A. Ogundiran (eds), *Power and Landscape in Atlantic West Africa: Archaeological Perspectives*. Cambridge: Cambridge University Press, 78–114.

RODNEY, W. (1966). African slavery and other forms of social oppression on the Upper Guinea Coast in the context of the Atlantic slave trade. *Journal of African History* 7: 431–43.

—— (1982). *How Europe Underdeveloped Africa*. Washington, DC: Howard University Press.

ROWLANDS, M. (1989). The archaeology of colonialism and constituting the African peasantry. In D. Miller, M. Rowlands, and C. Tilley (eds), *Domination and Resistance*. Boston: Allen & Unwin, 261–83.

SEARING, J. M. (1993). *West African Slavery and Atlantic Commerce: The Senegal River Valley, 1700–1860*. Cambridge: Cambridge University Press.

SHAW, R. (2002). *Memories of the Slave Trade: Ritual and the Historical Imagination in Sierra Leone*. Chicago: University of Chicago Press.

SØRENSEN, M. L. S., EVANS, C., and RICHTER, K. (2011). A place of history: archaeology and heritage at Cidade Velha, Cape Verde. In P. J. Lane and K. C. Macdonald (eds), *Comparative Dimensions of Slavery in Africa: Archaeology and Memory*. Oxford: Oxford University Press, 421–42.

STAHL, A. B. (2001). *Making History in Banda: Anthropological Visions of Africa's Past*. Cambridge: Cambridge University Press.

—— (2002). Colonial entanglements and the practices of taste: an alternative to logocentric approaches. *American Anthropologist* 104: 827–45.

—— (2004). Political economic mosaics: archaeology of the last two millennia in tropical sub-Saharan Africa. *Annual Review of Anthropology* 33: 145–72.

—— (2007). Entangled lives: the archaeology of daily life in the Gold Coast hinterlands, AD 1400–1900. In A. Ogundiran and T. Falola (eds), *Archaeology of Atlantic Africa and the African Diaspora*, Bloomington: Indiana University Press, 49–76.

—— and CRUZ, M. D. (1998). Men and women in a market economy: gender and craft production in west central Ghana, c. 1775–1995. In S. Kent (ed.), *Gender in African Prehistory*. Walnut Creek, Calif.: AltaMira Press, 205–26.

—— ——, NEFF, H., et al. (2008). Ceramic production, consumption and exchange in the Banda area, Ghana: insights from compositional analysis. *Journal of Anthropological Archaeology* 27: 363–81.

THIAW, I. (2000). L'impact de la traite des noirs dans le Haut Fleuve du Sénégal: archéologie des intéractions afro-européennes dans le Gajaaga et le Buundu aux XVIIIe et XIXe siècles. In D. Samb (ed.), *Saint-Louis et l'Esclavage*. Dakar: IFAN-Cheikh Anta Diop, 129–37.

—— (2008). Every house has a story: the archaeology of Gorée Island, Sénégal. In L. Sansone, E. Soumonni, and B. Barry (eds), *Africa, Brazil and the Construction of Trans-Atlantic Black Identities*. Trenton, NJ: Africa World Press, 45–62.

—— (2011). Slaves without shackles: an archaeology of everyday life on Gorée Island. In P. J. Lane and K. C. Macdonald (eds), *Comparative Dimensions of Slavery in Africa: Archaeology and Memory*. Oxford: Oxford University Press, 147–65.

THORNTON, J. (1992). *Africa and Africans in the Making of the Atlantic World, 1400–1680*. Cambridge: Cambridge University Press.

TROUILLOT, M.-R. (2003). *Global Transformations: Anthropology and the Modern World*. New York: Palgrave Macmillan.

WALLERSTEIN, I. (1974). *The Modern World System: Capitalist Agriculture and the Origins of the European World Economy in the Sixteenth Century*. New York: Academic Press.

WOLF, E. (1998). *Europe and the Peoples Without History*. Berkeley: University of California Press.

WOOD, R. W. (1967). An archaeological appraisal of early European settlements in the Senegambia. *Journal of African History* 8: 39–64.

CHAPTER 69

CONNECTING THE ARCHAEOLOGIES OF THE ATLANTIC WORLD

Africa and the African Diasporas

KENNETH G. KELLY

INTRODUCTION

THOUGH Africa has been the source of a series of diasporas from the moment the first hominins moved into Eurasia, the African diasporas of the Atlantic world find their origins in movement of people to the near shore islands of Bioko and the Canaries (Mitchell 2005) and the first voyages of European explorers along the West African coast. Even though the Portuguese who settled at Elmina in 1482 were unaware of the possibility of a trans-Atlantic trade, it did not take long before the reality of a world brought together by shared shores on the Atlantic became a reality. Although not exclusively associated with slavery, as sailors and others of African origin or descent also participated in the Iberian settlement of the Americas, the movement of Africans across the Atlantic was, until the very late 19th century, in very large part the consequence of the institution of chattel slavery. Furthermore, while archaeologies of the African diaspora typically focus on the trans-Atlantic world, there is a great need for these archaeologies to be grounded in detailed comparison with the archaeological record of Atlantic Africa (DeCorse 2001; Kelly 2004, 2011; Haviser and MacDonald 2006; Agorsah 2011).

Within a few years of Columbus' 1492 voyage, Africans were an integral part of the crews and cargos of the Spanish ships. By the first decades of the 16th century, Spanish colonial endeavours in the Caribbean were seeking out Africans to work in the mines of Hispaniola and incipient sugar plantations there and on Jamaica. That Africans met this demand resulted from several factors, including the extraordinarily high mortality suffered by the Caribbean's indigenous people because of disease and forced labour contributions and the ambivalence the Spanish professed at enslaving them, which was seen as contradicting the mission of propagating Christianity (Blackburn 1997).

The work of archaeologists, historians, and anthropologists who approach the Atlantic world from a diasporic perspective is uniquely informed by an appreciation of the importance of the contribution made by Africans and their descendants in creating the colonies and cultures of the 'new' world. Equally, it appreciates the overwhelmingly one-way movement of people (though not of ideas) and the challenging and violent context of what originated largely in plantation slavery. African diaspora archaeology has largely developed in the Americas as a way of acknowledging both the contributions to the colonizing venture, and the resistance and resilience manifested by Africans and their descendants in the face of race-based slavery. It has thus increasingly been characterized by a rich collaboration between archaeologists, anthropologists, folklorists, and others joined in a common goal of seeking to understand the degree to which Africans remembered their pasts and incorporated them in their daily practice (Leone et al. 2005; Fennell 2010). Ultimately informed by the Herskovitz/Frasier debates of the first half of the 20th century, which argued over the degree to which African 'continuities' could be expected to have endured in African American cultures (Price 2001; Price and Price 2003; Singleton 2006; Yelvington 2006), it has also been characterized by a search, whether explicit or implicit, for material traces of 'Africa' in the creation of the new, creole, cultures of the Atlantic world (e.g. Mintz and Price 1976). Since the Atlantic world brought together a very diverse array of people from different continents, and widely differing areas of those continents, a key feature remains an awareness of the importance these new arrangements played, and play, in the cultures surrounding the Atlantic (DeCorse 2001; Ogundiran and Falola 2007).

Spanish efforts to establish mines and plantations worked by enslaved Africans succeeded in some settings (mostly Hispaniola, Cuba, and some of the Caribbean's Central and South American shores), but by the second half of the 16th century interest was primarily focused on exploiting Spain's mainland colonies, especially Mexico and Peru. In the late 1500s, Portugal took on a more significant role in the African diaspora, with the establishment of sugar and other plantations and mines in Brazil (Blackburn 1997; Singleton and de Souza 2009). This process was greatly enhanced during the brief mid-17th century Dutch possession of Brazil's northeastern coast such that by 1700 Brazil was home to a very large enslaved African population, as well as some of the largest settlements of maroons, people who had fled life on the plantation for independence in *quilombos* of the interior. Palmares, the most famous and largest of these settlements, resisted multiple attacks and was only conquered in 1694 after an independent existence of at least 90 years (Orser 1994; Funari 1999).

The 17th century also saw English settlement of the mid-Atlantic region of North America, where Virginia pioneered the development of tobacco plantations (Deetz 1993; Morgan 1998), and the (mostly) English and French settlement of the now largely overlooked (by the Spanish) islands of the West Indies. English settlement of St Kitts (1624, with French settlers arriving a year later), Barbados (1627), and Nevis (1628) and French settlement of Martinique and Guadeloupe (1635) had profound impacts throughout Africa as these island colonies experimented with tobacco and other crops, eventually settling mostly on sugar after an influx of Dutch planters expelled from northeast Brazil (Blackburn 1997). From the mid-/late 17th century onward, the largely insatiable labour demands of the island sugar colonies and the tobacco and later rice and cotton colonies of North America was met by bringing captive Africans across the Atlantic from Senegal in the north to Angola in the south, and even extending into the Indian Ocean (Curtin 1969; Blackburn 1997; Slave Trade Database).

As a result the African diaspora grew substantially in scale. By the French Revolution of 1789, for example, St Domingue (present-day Haiti) was home to around half a million enslaved Africans, Jamaica to 250,000, and Guadeloupe, Martinique, and Barbados 80,000–100,000 each. Add a score or so of smaller Caribbean islands and we reach over one million. At the same time, Spanish America may have had as many as 2.5 million people of African heritage, Brazil over 1.2 million, and what was or became the United States a further million or more (Baranov 2000). All told, more than 5 million Africans and their descendants were living in the Atlantic world, out of over 8.6 million captives shipped involuntarily across the sea (Curtin 1969; Slave Trade Database). The trade continued to Cuba and Brazil in significant quantity, even after Britain (1807), the United States (1808), and other countries banned it, while smaller numbers of captives were brought to other areas of the Atlantic world; slavery finally ended only in 1865 in the United States, 1886 in Cuba, and 1888 in Brazil.

With populations of African origin of such size, and the cultural and demographic importance of descendant populations in many countries, it is unsurprising that interest developed in African-related sites in the diaspora (Posnansky 1984). Initially, the focus was simply to identify places where such peoples lived, whether in urban, rural, or (most commonly) plantation settings (Bullen and Bullen 1945; Ascher and Fairbanks 1971; Mathewson 1973; Moore 1985; Higman 1998). Attempts were also made to identify material traces of the African heritage of the captives, one of the first successful instances being Handler and Lange's (1978) identification of African artefacts and cultural practices (such as dental modification) in the Newton slave cemetery, Barbados. More commonly identified has been archaeological evidence of cultural practices influenced by the various African heritages of captive Africans that include housing, foodways, burial practices, ritual, and treatment of the body. Recent years have also seen archaeological interest in investigating the transformation of diasporic populations from bondage to freedom as the slave trade and slavery gradually declined through the 19th century (Leone 2005; Fennell 2010).

THE BUILT ENVIRONMENT OF THE AFRICAN DIASPORA

African antecedents are likely to have considerably influenced architectural practices, though housing was also influenced by poverty and expediency (Fig. 69.1). On plantation villages throughout the Caribbean, the general 17th/18th-century trend was for lightly built, rectangular structures, typically wattle and daub or lightly built wood, roofed with palm frond thatch or cane tops and trash (Armstrong 1990; Higman 1998). These structures were typically 3–5 m wide × 4–7 m long if single household dwellings, or approximately double that if 'double pen' houses that shared a common wall (Handler and Bergman 2009). Rare in the Caribbean, where cooking was generally done outside and heating was little needed, the latter are more common in the later period of North American slavery, perhaps to economize on chimney and fireplace construction (Armstrong 1990; Higman 1998; Wilkie and Farnsworth 2005; Handler and Bergman 2009).

The motivations behind the layout of particular slave villages are debated, with some evidence suggesting that little control was exercised beyond determining their general location

FIG. 69.1 Reconstructed slave house, Marie-Galante, Guadeloupe (photograph, Ken Kelly).

(typically on otherwise unproductive lands and close to the plantation core of owner or over-seer house, industrial buildings, and key crops or activities) (Higman 1988; Hauser and Hicks 2007). In some cases, the earliest villages may have followed English models, with an orderly row of houses facing the village 'street', perhaps to facilitate observation (Armstrong and Kelly 2000; Hicks 2007). Subsequently, as communities became self-reproducing, villages spread out to reflect internal social organization, with family or other groups living in adjacent clusters of houses and situated to take advantage of local topography (Higman 1998; Armstrong 1990; Kelly 2008).

Interestingly, certain African forms of housing are conspicuously lacking from the archaeological record. For example, while circular structures are reasonably common in many West African societies (Denyer 1978), there seems to be no evidence of circular slave housing, and non-rectangular housing among some Maroon groups in Brazil may be borrowed from local indigenous people. Similarly, except for the Cuban coffee plantation El Padre (Singleton and de Souza 2009), earthen-walled houses appear to be unknown in the Caribbean, though suitable clayey earth must have been present in some settings, such as interior Jamaica. Clay walls may be present at Parting Ways, near Plymouth, Massachusetts (Deetz 1996), but this is uncertain, and in Louisiana and South Carolina wall trenches excavated as foundations for earthen-walled structures that have been argued to be indicative of African practices (Ferguson 1992; Wheaton and Garrow 1985; MacDonald et al. 2006) may in fact be evidence of French construction techniques (Steen 1999).

As slavery 'matured', village layout and housing both changed. Some of the most significant changes responded to the growing pressure against slavery itself, both from within and from outside. While few uprisings succeeded on more than a limited scale, the constant perception of the threat of armed insurrection (made all the more real by the Haitian revolution of 1791–1804) led to increased efforts at surveillance and control of the lives of enslaved people (e.g. Delle 1998). This increased surveillance was manifested in a variety of ways, ranging from relocating villages from peripheral locations to establishing a rigid order that facilitated observation (Chapman 1991; Kelly 2008) and even constructing walls to enclose the village

(Singleton 2005). House construction was also modified, with houses (at least in the American southeast) being raised on piers to limit the ability of slaves to hide things in the floor (Samford 2007). Pressures from outside also led to transformations, with more durable houses of masonry replacing the lighter built houses of the Caribbean in an effort to create 'healthier' houses to 'ameliorate' the conditions of slavery, perhaps another impetus behind the raised structures of the American southeast, as they facilitated the circulation of air.

While direct analogies with African housing have proved elusive, a compelling and potentially productive route was developed in Deetz's (1996) application of structuralist principles to African American settings. Building upon earlier work (Bullens and Bullens 1945), he explored an African American setting outside the 'traditional' South at Parting Ways, Massachusetts, a small collection of houses attributed to African American veterans of the Revolutionary War (1774–1783). Following Vlach (1977), Deetz argued that differences between these houses and others in New England, especially in their basic dimensions, was due to the materialization of a different mental template of spatial organization and proxemics. Moreover, their smaller (12 ft; ~4 m) primary bay and linear arrangement of rooms may have drawn on West African, and specifically Yoruba, antecedents. As well as possible evidence for the employment of a clay-wall construction technique (see above), a cobble-paved area adjacent to the house sites had a large concentration of intentionally broken ceramics and glass that evoked 'African American ritual practices and their West African roots' (Deetz 1996: 207). Again drawing upon Vlach (1978), these deposits, clearly not associated with domestic disposal, have parallels with grave decoration practices in the American South.

DEM BELLY FULL: NOURISHING THE AFRICAN DIASPORA

Foodways are an aspect of African heritage that can be seen in the foods themselves (okra, sesame, rice, watermelon, pigeon peas, and yams) and in methods of preparation (gumbos, stews, pilaus, frying, etc.). An early observation on the prevalence of bowls in coastal Georgia slave village contexts led Otto (1984) to suggest that African-derived foodways, emphasizing preparation of soups and stews, and perhaps the communal sharing of bowls, were practised by people of African descent—a clear difference from the general pattern in Anglo-America for communal eating to be replaced by discrete place settings and a greater focus on individualism (Deetz 1996). Otto's observation has subsequently been identified in other settings of the African diaspora in North America and throughout the Caribbean (Armstrong 1990; Ferguson 1992; Franklin 2001; Wilkie and Farnsworth 2005), but it remains unclear how far the prevalence of bowls reflect an African-derived preference for certain foods, or consumption of slow-cooked liquid-based foods that required less attention when cooking as a result of poverty or excessive demands on labour (Fig. 69.2).

A similar question underlies much archaeozoological data from contexts associated with people of African descent, particularly those associated with slavery. In these settings, faunal remains frequently represent the less desirable portions of domesticated animals and tend to show extensive processing to extract maximum nutritional value. However, are highly

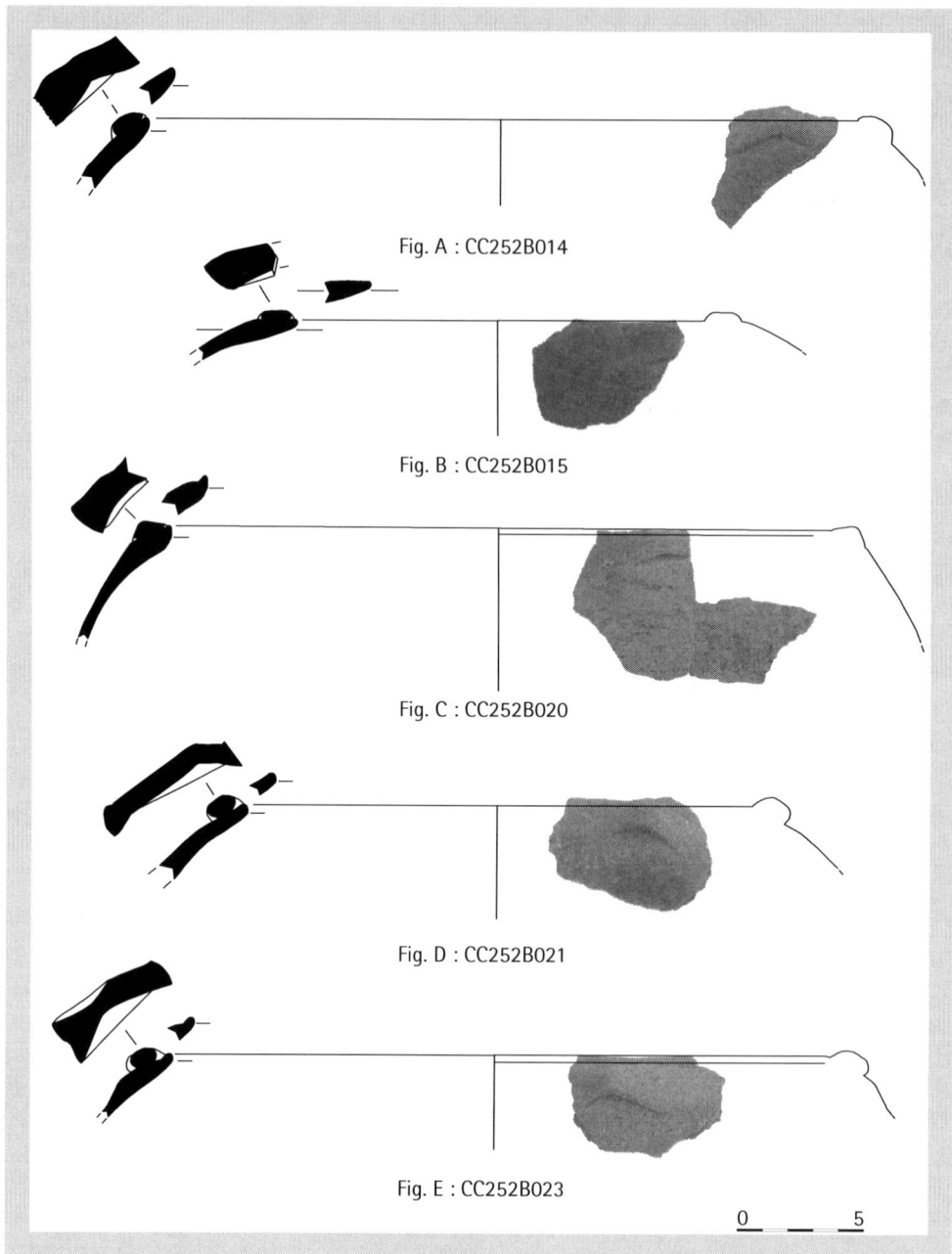

Fig. A : CC252B014

Fig. B : CC252B015

Fig. C : CC252B020

Fig. D : CC252B021

Fig. E : CC252B023

0 _ _ 5

FIG. 69.2 Low-fired earthenwares from Martinique (Ken Kelly and Franck Bigot).

processed or less desirable faunal remains the result of 'ethnic' preference or of restricted access to resources? Evidence for fishing, hunting, trapping, and gathering of wild resources also suggests that this pattern may be more complex than a simple indexical association of cultural preference (Crader 1990; Reitz et al. 1985; McKee 1987; Kipple 2001; Scott 2001). Given the small package size of some of these resources, there is a good argument for privation motivating people to augment their resources in any way possible (Young 1997; McKee 1999; Young et al. 2001). In a related study, Mullins (1999) explored the use of mass-marketed goods by 19th-century African Americans in Annapolis, arguing that they chose to purchase goods from national brands and through mail order to avoid unnecessary exposure to racist exploitation and unwelcoming environments.

Several researchers have recognized the importance of considering gardens and provision grounds in maintaining particular African American identities (Pulsipher 1994; Heath and Bennett 2000; Brown 2002). Such gardens were sources not just of food but also of medicines (Edwards-Ingram 2001), and areas that were structured for ritual protection (Benoit 2007). Ethnobotanical evidence would be an excellent addition to the data contributing to foodways and ethnomedicine, but very little relevant work has been conducted on African diaspora-related sites (Mrozowski et al. 2008). This remains one of the real gaps in African American archaeology studies of food and identity.

More positively, one of the most widely found archaeological aspects of foodways attributed to an explicit African heritage is the manufacture and use of low-fired earthenware pottery for cooking and eating (Hauser and DeCorse 2003). Pottery of this sort is widely found in the African diaspora, ranging from the West Indies (e.g. Jamaica, Cuba, Nevis, Martinique, and St Lucia, and probably also Haiti) (e.g. Handler 1963, 1964; Heath 1990, 1999; Hauser 2008; Kelly et al. 2008) to the United States (e.g. Ferguson 1988, 1992) and Brazil (Singleton and de Souza 2009). Researchers in the Caribbean were among the first to attribute contemporary hand-built ceramic traditions to African antecedents (e.g. Victor 1941; Handler 1964; Ebanks 1984), and when archaeologically recovered ceramics that bore similarities with these began to be recovered, it was a relatively simple step to assign them to African-derived production (e.g. Gartley 1979). Outside the Caribbean, where the direct historical method could not be applied, similar wares marrying hand-built manufacturing with 'European'-derived forms (flat bottoms, strap handles, etc.) were recovered in Virginia and named Colono-Indian ware to emphasize a hypothesized manufacture by native people for a colonial market (Noël-Hume 1962). But as these and similar ceramics began to be found in other parts of the southeast, particularly Lowcountry South Carolina, Ferguson (1980) suggested that it would be more accurate to acknowledge the likelihood that, in some contexts, African-descended people were probably the makers and users of this pottery, now termed Colono-ware. The recognition that these ceramics were used by enslaved Africans contributed to foodways studies by suggesting that the forms of the earthenware pots were related to particular kinds of cooking and eating, and that the pots themselves played a key role in maintaining a distinct identity, including the use of some smaller examples as medicine pots, as in West Africa (Ferguson 1992).

FLASH OF THE SPIRIT: RITUAL AND SPIRIT ACTIVITIES IN THE AFRICAN DIASPORA

African-derived spiritual activities are among the most interesting aspects of the archaeology of the African diaspora. A variety of ritual practices with complex African roots (some of which draw in practices from West and West Central Africa that might even include

Christianity from Kongo) are still vibrant throughout the Americas, including Brazilian Candomble, Cuban Santería, and Haitian Voudou (Ruppel et al. 2003; Leone et al. 2005; Fennell 2010). Yet archaeologically these activities have been remarkably elusive. Ideas about spirituality can potentially be seen in a variety of practices, ranging from treatment of the dead (Jamieson 1995; Blakey 1998) to personal ornamentation and actions engaged in to call upon assistance from the spirit realm. Among the earliest attempts to connect archaeological data with West and West Central African practices was Ferguson's (1992, 1999) research on a particular subset of Colono-ware pottery from South Carolina's Lowcountry that had 'cross' or 'X' marks incised on their bases and were, in some cases, recovered from river-bottom locations. Design and context can be explained by analogy with BaKongo and other West Central Africans for whom an intersecting vertical and horizontal line inscribed within a circle or arms curving around from the ends of the lines depict the world of the living separated from the world of the ancestors, and an *axis mundi* joining the two realms within the movement of the sun. Ferguson argued that some of these marked bowls might have been associated with offerings cast adrift on the Lowcountry's rivers. Such observations energized archaeologists to re-examine existing evidence and rethink how African-derived ritual activities might be manifest in diasporic contexts (Leone 2005; Fennell 2007).

Mid-19th-century finds from the Levi Jordan plantation near Houston, Texas, provide another example, this time interpreted as playing roles in activities ranging from charms and protection to curing (Brown and Cooper 1990; Fennell 2007). The Levi Jordan evidence suggests that otherwise mundane objects (mirror fragments, animal bones, red cloth, nails, shells, etc.) might, in particular contexts and combinations, result from ritual activities seeking to protect spaces from malevolent spirits or individuals or to cure certain ailments. Comparable assemblages (dating from the early 18th to early 20th centuries) have now been found in settings as diverse as New York (Ruppel et al. 2003), Maryland (Leone 2005), Louisiana, and the Bahamas (Wilkie and Farnsworth 2005). Items of personal decoration, particularly blue beads, may also have had ritual connotations, in this case expressing a widely held African derived belief in controlling malevolent spirits (Stine et al. 1996).

In the realm of mortuary treatment, the pioneering work of Handler and Lange (1978) in Barbados demonstrated that some individuals were interred with grave goods that indicated a continuity of African practices, such as the presence of waist beads. Waist or wrist beads were also seen in several burials from New York's African Burial Ground (Bianco et al. 2006), with the presence of filed teeth on one individual suggesting he was probably born somewhere in Africa itself (Handler 1994; Perry et al. 2006). Few other instances of beads in grave contexts are known in the African diaspora—surprisingly so given the vast quantities imported to Africa during the slave trade (Alpern 1995). Other aspects of grave treatment are also of interest. They include the presence at the Newton cemetery of one individual interpreted as having been a 'healer' from the goods accompanying him, including a necklace with animal teeth, cowrie shells, copper bracelets, and a clay pipe similar to some recovered in 17th/18th-century Ghanaian sites; a second individual was interpreted as a 'witch' as she was interred face down (Handler 1996, 1997). The principal challenge to identifying such African-derived spiritual practices in mortuary treatment come from the lack of large samples. Samples from Newton, the African Burial Ground, and the largely unreported Anse Ste Marguerite cemetery in Guadeloupe (Courtaud et al. 1999; Courtaud and Romon 2004) are among the few slavery-era cemetery collections to number more than a few individuals and to have been well excavated. This seriously limits our ability to generalize from behaviours that were probably only represented in a small proportion of the total inter-ments at any one location. Recent work drawing upon stable isotope analyses has been able to demonstrate specific regions of African origin for some individuals that, when combined with traditional artefact studies, should enable more nuanced and informed interpretations of the relation of African material culture and practices to African origin (Price et al. 2006; Schroeder et al. 2009) Other mortuary assemblages post-date slavery's abolition and, per-haps because of this, have virtually no discernible 'African' characteristics (Rankin-Hill 1997; McCarthy 2006).

Another aspect of African-derived mortuary behaviour is the practice of interring indi-viduals in settings other than formalized cemeteries, but this appears to be archaeologically documented only at Seville Plantation, Jamaica, where four graves were found buried in cof-fins below the floors of four different early (late 17th/early 18th century) houses in the slave village; at least one appeared to have been interred after the house had gone out of use (Armstrong and Fleishman 2003).

So what does it all mean?

The connections between African peoples and their diasporic cousins are strong today, and have been for some 400 years. It is not surprising that people forced into unimaginable cap-tivity, transportation, and slavery should draw upon items of their common, and individual, heritages as they sought to survive in the African diaspora. Archaeological research helps us to understand that process. However, it is important, and hopefully self-evident, that the complex social processes of creolization and ethnogenesis that resulted from adapting to new social, cultural, physical, and psychological environments are reflected in more than just the material remains of the past. As such, the African diaspora is too complex to be reduced to material remains. Its study necessarily draws upon multiple sources of evidence, and archaeological studies of the diasporic experience find their interpretive strength in the way in which they weave together these strands. What remains to be developed more fully is an analogous strength that builds increasingly sophisticated and complex bridges between the societies of the African continent and their offspring of the diaspora, such as has been pioneered by Agorsah (2011), Kelly (2004), and MacDonald et al. (2006).

References

AGORSAH, E. K. (2011). Archaeological perspectives on colonial slavery: placing Africa in African diaspora studies in the Caribbean. In P. J. Lane and K. C. Macdonald (eds), *Comparative Dimensions of Slavery in Africa: Archaeology and Memory*. Oxford: Oxford University Press, 199–221.

ALPERN, S. B. (1995). What Africans got for their slaves: a master list of European trade goods. *History in Africa* 22: 5–43.

ARMSTRONG, D. V. (1990). *The Old Village and the Great House: An Archaeological and Historical Examination of Drax Hall Plantation, St. Ann's Bay, Jamaica*. Urbana: University of Illinois Press.

ARMSTRONG, D. V. and FLEISCHMAN, M. (1994). *Analysis of Four Burials from African Jamaican House-Yard Contexts at Seville*. Syracuse, NY: Syracuse University Press.

—— (2003). House-yard burials of enslaved laborers in eighteenth-century Jamaica. *International Journal of Historical Archaeology* 7: 33–65.

—— and KELLY, K.G. (2000). Settlement patterns and the origin of African Jamaican society: Seville Plantation, St Ann's Bay, Jamaica. *Ethnohistory* 47: 369–97.

ASCHER, R., and FAIRBANKS, C. H. (1971). Excavation of a slave cabin: Georgia, U.S.A. *Historical Archaeology* 5: 3–17.

BARANOV, D. (2000). *The Abolition of Slavery in Brazil: The 'Liberation' of Africans through the Emancipation of Capital*. Westport, Conn.: Greenwood Press.

BENOIT, C. (2007). Gardens in the African diaspora: forging a Creole identity in the Caribbean and the U.S. In M. Conan and J. Quilter (eds), *Gardens and Cultural Change: A Pan-American Perspective*. Washington, DC: Dumbarton Oaks, 29–46.

BIANCO, B.A., DeCORSE, C. R., and HOWSON, J. (2006). Beads and other adornment. In W. R. Perry, J. Howson, and B. A. Bianco (eds), *New York African Burial Ground Archaeology Final Report*. Washington, DC: Howard University, 382–418.

BLACKBURN, R. (1997). *The Making of New World Slavery: From the Baroque to the Modern, 1492–1800*. London: Verso.

BLAKEY, M. L. (1998). The New York African Burial Ground Project: an examination of enslaved lives, a construction of ancestral ties. *Transforming Anthropology* 7: 53–8.

BROWN, K. L., and COOPER, D. C. (1990). Structural continuity in an African-American slave and tenant community. *Historical Archaeology* 24: 7–19.

BROWN, R. M. (2002). Walk in the *feenda*: West-Central Africans and the forest in the South Carolina–Georgia Lowcountry. In L. Heywood (ed.), *Central Africans and Cultural Transformations in the American Diaspora*. Cambridge: Cambridge University Press, 289–317.

BULLEN, R. P., and BULLEN, A. K. (1945). Black Lucy's Garden. *Bulletin of the Massachusetts Archaeological Society* 6: 17–28.

CHAPMAN, W. (1991). Slave villages in the Danish West Indies: changes of the late eighteenth and early nineteenth centuries. In T. Carter and B. L. Herman (eds), *Perspectives in Vernacular Architecture*, 4. Columbia: University of Missouri Press, 108–20.

COURTAUD, P., and ROMON, T. (2004). Le site d'Anse Sainte-Margeurite (Guadeloupe, Grande-Terre): présentation d'un cimetière d'époque coloniale. *Journal of Caribbean Archaeology* Special Publication 1: 58–67.

COURTAUD, P., DELPUECH, A., and ROMON, T. (1999). Archaeological investigations at colonial cemeteries on Guadeloupe: African slave burial sites or not? In J. Haviser (ed.), *African Sites Archaeology in the Caribbean*. Princeton, NJ: Markus Wiener, 277–90.

CRADER, D. C. (1990). Slave diet at Monticello. *American Antiquity* 55: 690–717.

CURTIN, P. (1969). *The Atlantic Slave Trade*. Madison: University of Wisconsin Press.

DeCORSE, C. R. (ed.). (2001). *West Africa During the Atlantic Slave Trade: Archaeological Perspectives*. Leicester: Leicester University Press.

DEETZ, J. (1993). *Flowerdew Hundred: The Archaeology of a Virginia Plantation, 1619–1864*. Charlottesville: University Press of Virginia.

—— (1996). *In Small Things Forgotten: An Archaeology of Early American Life*. New York: Anchor Books.

DELLE, J. A. (1998). *An Archaeology of Social Space: Analyzing Coffee Plantations in Jamaica's Blue Mountains*. New York: Plenum Press.

DENYER, S. (1978). *African Traditional Architecture*. London: Holmes & Meier.

EBANKS, R. (1984). Ma Lou, an Afro Jamaican pottery tradition. *Jamaica Journal* 17: 31–7.

EDWARDS-INGRAM, Y. (2001). African American medicine and the social relations of slavery. In C. E. Orser (ed.), *Race and the Archaeology of Identity*. Salt Lake City: University of Utah Press, 34–53.

FENNELL, C. C. (2007). *Crossroads and Cosmologies: Diasporas and Ethnogenesis in the New World*. Gainesville: University Press of Florida.

——(2010). Early African America: archaeological studies of significance and diversity. *Journal of Archaeological Research* 19: 1–49.

FERGUSON, L. (1980). Looking for the 'Afro' in Colono-Indian pottery. In R. Schuyler (ed.), *Archaeological Perspectives on Ethnicity in America: Afro-American and Asian American Culture History*. Farmingdale, NY: Baywood, 14–28.

——(1988). Review of *The Archaeology of Slavery and Plantation Life*, ed. Theresa Singleton. *American Antiquity* 53: 193–6.

——(1992). *Uncommon Ground: Archaeology and Early African America, 1650–1800*. Washington, DC: Smithsonian Institution Press.

FERGUSON, L. G. (1999). 'The cross is a magic sign': marks on eighteenth-century bowls from South Carolina. In T. A. Singleton (ed.), *'I, Too, Am America': Archaeological Studies of African-American Life*. Charlottesville: University Press of Virginia, 116–31.

FRANKLIN, M. (2001). The archaeological and symbolic dimensions of soul food: race, culture, and Afro-Virginian identity. In C. E. Orser (ed.), *Race, Material Culture and the Archaeology of Identity*. Salt Lake City: University of Utah Press, 88–107.

FUNARI, P. P. (1999). Maroon, race and gender: Palmares material culture and social relations at a runaway settlement. In P. P. Funari, M. Hall, and S. Jones (eds), *Historical Archaeology: Back from the Edge*. London: Routledge, 308–27.

GARTLEY, R. T. (1979). Afro-Cruzan pottery: a new style of colonial earthenware from St. Croix. *Journal of the Virgin Islands Archaeological Society* 8: 47–61.

HANDLER, J. (1963). A historical sketch of pottery manufacture in Barbados. *Journal of the Barbados Museum and Historical Society* 30: 129–53.

——(1964). Notes on pottery making in Antigua. *Man* 64: 184–5.

——(1994). Determining African birth from skeletal remains: a note on tooth mutilation. *Historical Archaeology* 28: 113–19.

——(1996). A prone burial from a plantation slave cemetery in Barbados, West Indies: possible evidence for an African-type witch or other negatively viewed person. *Historical Archaeology* 30: 76–86.

——(1997). An African-type healer/diviner and his grave goods: a burial from a plantation slave cemetery in Barbados, West Indies. *International Journal of Historical Archaeology* 1: 91–130.

—— and BERGMAN, S. (2009). Vernacular houses and domestic material culture on Barbadian sugar plantations, 1640–1838. *Journal of Caribbean History* 43: 1–39.

—— and LANGE, F. (1978). *Plantation Slavery in Barbados: An Archaeological and Historical Investigation*. Cambridge, Mass.: Harvard University Press.

HAUSER, M. W. (2008). *An Archaeology of Black Markets: Local Ceramics and Economies in Eighteenth-Century Jamaica*. Gainesville: University Press of Florida.

—— and DeCORSE, C. R. (2003). Low-fired earthenwares in the African diaspora: problems and prospects. *International Journal of Historical Archaeology* 7: 67–98.

—— and HICKS, D. (2007). Colonialism and landscape: power, materiality and scales of analysis in Caribbean historical archaeology. In D. Hicks, L. Mcatackney, and G. Fairclough (eds), *Envisioning Landscape: Situations and Standpoints in Archaeology and Heritage*. Walnut Creek, Calilf.: Left Coast Press, 251–74.

HAVISER, J., and MACDONALD, K. C. (eds) (2006). *African Re-genesis: Confronting Social Issues of the African Diaspora*. London: Routledge Press.

HEATH, B. J. (1990). 'Pots of earth': forms and functions of Afro-Caribbean ceramics. *Florida Journal of Anthropology* 16: 33–50.

—— (1999). Yabbas, monkeys, jugs, and jars: an historical context for African-Caribbean pottery on St. Eustatius. In T. A. Singleton (ed.), *'I, Too, am America': Archaeological Studies of African-American Life*. Charlottesville: University Press of Virginia, 196–220.

—— and BENNETT, A. (2000). 'The little spots allow'd them': the archaeological study of African-American yards. *Historical Archaeology* 34: 38–55.

HICKS, D. (2007). *'The Garden of the World:' An Historical Archaeology of Sugar Landscapes in the Eastern Caribbean*. Oxford: Archaeopress.

HIGMAN, B. W. (1988). *Jamaica Surveyed: Plantation Maps and Plans of the Eighteenth and Nineteenth Centuries*. Kingston: Institute of Jamaica.

—— (1998). *Montpelier, Jamaica: A Plantation Community in Slavery and Freedom, 1739–1912*. Kingston: University of the West Indies Press.

JAMIESON, R. W. (1995). Material culture and social death: African-American burial practices. *Historical Archaeology* 29: 39–58.

KELLY, K. G. (2004). The African diaspora starts here: historical archaeology in coastal West Africa. In P. Lane and A. Reid (eds), *African Historical Archaeologies*. New York: Kluwer Academic/Plenum, 219–41.

—— (2008). Plantation archaeology in the French West Indies. *Archéologiques Hors Série* 2: 55–69.

—— (2011). Archaeological perspectives on the Atlantic slave trade: contrasts in time and space in Bénin and Guinea. In P. J. Lane and K. C. Macdonald (eds), *Comparative Dimensions of Slavery in Africa: Archaeology and Memory*. Oxford: Oxford University Press, 125–46.

—— HAUSER, M., DESCANTES, C., and GLASCOCK, M. D. (2008). Cabotage or contraband: compositional analysis of French colonial ceramics. *Journal of Caribbean Archaeology* 8: 87–105.

KIPPLE, W. E. (2001). Sugar monoculture, bovid skeletal part frequencies, and stable carbon isotopes. *Journal of Archaeological Science* 28: 1191–8.

LEONE, M. P. (2005). *The Archaeology of Liberty in an American Capital: Excavations in Annapolis*. Berkeley: University of California Press.

—— LAROCHE, C. J., and BABIARZ, J. J. (2005). The archaeology of Black Americans in recent times. *Annual Review of Anthropology* 34: 575–98.

MACDONALD, K. C., MORGAN, D., and HANDLEY, F. (2006). The Cane River African Diaspora Archaeological Project: prospectus and initial results. In Haviser and MacDonald (2006: 123–44).

MATHEWSON, R. D. (1973). Archaeological analysis of material culture as a reflection of sub-cultural differentiation in 18th century Jamaica. *Jamaica Journal* 7: 25–9.

MCCARTHY, J. P. (2006). African community identity at the cemetery. In Haviser and MacDonald (2006: 176–83).

MCKEE, L. (1987). Delineating ethnicity from the garbage of early Virginians: faunal remains from the Kingsmill Plantation slave quarter. *American Archaeology* 6: 31–9.

—— (1999). Food supply and plantation social order: an archaeological perspective. In T. A. Singleton (ed.), *'I, Too, Am America': Archaeological Studies of African-American Life*. Charlottesville: University of Virginia Press, 218–39.

MITCHELL, P. J. (2005). *African Connections: Archaeological Perspectives on Africa and the Wider World*. Walnut Creek, Calif.: AltaMira Press.

MINTZ, S. W., and PRICE, R. (1976). *An Anthropological Approach to the Afro-American Past: A Caribbean Perspective*. Philadelphia: Institute for the Study of Human Issues.

MOORE, S. M. (1985). Social and economic status on the coastal plantation: an Archaeological Perspective. In T. A. Singleton (ed.), *The Archaeology of Slavery and Plantation Life*. San Diego, Calif.: Academic Press, 141–60.

MORGAN, P. D. (1998). *Slave Counterpoint*. Chapel Hill: University of North Carolina Press.

MROZOWSKI, S. A., FRANKLIN, M., and HUNT, L. (2008). Archaeobotanical analyses and interpretations of enslaved Virginian plant use at Rich Neck Plantation (44WB52). *American Antiquity* 73: 699–728.

MULLINS, P. R. (1999). *Race and Affluence: An Archaeology of African America and Consumer Culture*. New York: Kluwer Academic/Plenum.

NOEL-HUME, I. (1962). An Indian ware of the colonial period. *Quarterly Bulletin of the Archaeological Society of Virginia* 17: 2–14.

OGUNDIRAN, A., and FALOLA, T. (eds) (2007). *Archaeology of Atlantic Africa and the African Diaspora*. Bloomington: Indiana University Press.

ORSER, C. E. (1994). Towards a global historical archaeology: an example from Brazil. *Historical Archaeology* 28: 5–22.

OTTO, J. S. (1984). *Cannon's Point Plantation, 1794–1860: Living Conditions and Status Patterns in the Old South*. New York: Academic Press.

PERRY, W. R., HOWSON, J., and BIANCO, B. A. (eds). (2006). *New York African Burial Ground Archaeology Final Report*, vol. 1. Washington, DC: Howard University.

POSNANSKY, M. (1984). Towards an archaeology of the Black Diaspora. *Journal of Black Studies* 15: 195–202.

PRICE, R. (2001). The miracle of creolization: a retrospective. *New West Indian Guide/Nieuwe West-Indische Gids* 75: 35–64.

—— and PRICE, S. (2003). *The Root of Roots: Or, How Afro-American Anthropology Got Its Start*. Chicago: Prickly Paradigm Press.

PRICE, T. D., TIESLER, V., and BURTON, J. (2006). Early African diaspora in colonial Campeche, Mexico: strontium isotopic evidence. *American Journal of Physical Anthropology* 130: 485–90.

PULSIPHER, L. M. (1994). The landscapes and ideational roles of Caribbean slave gardens. In N. F. Miller and K. L. Gleason (eds), *The Archaeology of Garden and Field*. Philadelphia: University of Pennsylvania Press, 202–21.

RANKIN-HILL, L. M. (1997). *A Bio-history of 19th-Century Afro-Americans: The Burial Remains of a Philadelphia Cemetery*. Westport, Conn.: Bergin & Garvey.

REITZ, E. J., GIBBS, T., and RATHBUN, T. A. (1985). Archaeological evidence for subsistence on coastal plantations. In T. A. Singleton (ed.), *The Archaeology of Slavery and Plantation Life*. Orlando, Fla.: Academic Press, 163–91.

RUPPEL, T., NEUWIRTH, J., LEONE, M. P., and FRY, G.-M. (2003). Hidden in view: African spiritual spaces in North American landscapes. *Antiquity* 77: 321–35.

SAMFORD, P. M. (2007). *Subfloor Pits and the Archaeology of Slavery in Colonial Virginia*. Tuscaloosa: University of Alabama Press.

SCHROEDER, H., O'CONNELL, T. C., EVANS, J. A., SHULER, K. A., and HEDGES, R. E. M. (2009). Trans-Atlantic slavery: isotopic evidence for forced migration to Barbados. *American Journal of Physical Anthropology* 139: 547–57.

Scott, E. M. (2001). Food and social relations at Nina Plantation. *American Anthropologist* 103: 671–91.

Singleton, T. A. (2005). An archaeological study of slavery on a Cuban coffee plantation. In L. A. Curet, S. L. Dawdy, and G. La Rosa Corzo (eds), *Dialogues in Cuban Archaeology*. Tuscaloosa: University of Alabama Press, 181–99.

—— (2006). African diaspora archaeology in dialogue. In K. A. Yelvington (ed.), *Afro-Atlantic Dialogues: Anthropology in the Diaspora*. Santa Fe, NM: SAR Press, 249–87.

—— and de Souza, M. A. T. (2009). Archaeologies of the African diaspora: Brazil, Cuba, and the United States. In T. Majewski and D. Gaimester (eds), *International Handbook of Historical Archaeology*. New York: Springer, 449–69.

Slave Trade Database. http://www.slavevoyages.org/tast/index.faces

Steen, C. (1999). Stirring the ethnic stew in the South Carolina Backcountry: John de la Howe and Lethe Farm. In M. Franklin and G. Fesler (eds), *Historical Archaeology, Identity Formation, and the Interpretation of Ethnicity*. Williamsburg, Va.: Colonial Williamsburg Research Publication, 93–120.

Stine, L. F., Cabak, M. A., and Groover, M. (1996). Blue beads as African-American cultural symbols. *Historical Archaeology* 30: 49–75.

Victor, P. E. (1941). La poterie de Sainte-Anne. *Bulletin Agricole* 10: 1–54.

Vlach, J. M. (1977). Shotgun houses. *Natural History* 87: 50–7.

—— (1978). *The Afro-American Tradition in Decorative Arts*. Cleveland, OH: Cleveland Museum of Art.

Wheaton, T., and Garrow, P. (1985). Acculturation and the archaeological record in the Carolina Lowcountry. In T. A. Singleton (ed.), *The Archaeology of Slavery and Plantation Life*. San Diego, Calif.: Academic Press, 239–59.

Wilkie, L. A., and Farnsworth, P. (2005). *Sampling Many Pots: An Archaeology of Memory and Tradition at a Bahamian Plantation*. Gainesville: University Press of Florida.

Yelvington, K. A. (2006). Introduction. In K. A. Yelvington (ed.), *Afro-Atlantic Dialogues: Anthropology in the Diaspora*. Santa Fe, NM: SAR Press, 3–32.

Young, A. L. (1997). Risk management strategies among African American slaves at Locust Grove Plantation. *International Journal of Historical Archaeology* 1: 5–37.

—— Tuma, M., and Jenkins, C. (2001). The role of hunting to cope with risk at Saragossa Plantation, Natchez, Mississippi. *American Anthropologist* 103: 692–704.

CHAPTER 70

THE ARCHAEOLOGY OF COLONIAL ENCOUNTERS IN EASTERN AFRICA

SARAH CROUCHER

INTRODUCTION

THIS chapter offers an introduction to a dynamic and rapidly growing field in African archaeology. It covers a complex period of colonial history from the end of the 15th century, when the Portuguese first sailed along the East African coast, to the 1960s, when East African countries finally gained independence. Sandwiched between European periods of rule was that of the Omani sultanate, which ruled the coast and caravan routes with variable local powers from the 17th century until 1890, when Zanzibar became a British protectorate. These changing systems of rule interacted with local histories in which local African communities were increasingly engaged in the intensification of the caravan trade, especially enslaved persons and ivory, and the introduction of plantation agriculture.

An important debate for archaeologists working in later historical periods of East Africa, particularly those whose research clearly intersects with colonial histories, is the manner in which this should fit into broader archaeological discourse. Concern has been voiced with the label of 'historical archaeology' as an American-and European-based methodological and theoretical import, focused only on the periods of colonialism (Funari et al. 1999; Reid and Lane 2004; Schmidt 2006; Lane 2007; Schmidt and Walz 2007). In thinking about the archaeology of colonial periods in this region, it is important to be mindful of these debates, particularly since they raise the issue that within this period local oral histories can be ignored at the expense of privileging hegemonic histories which made their way into textual sources. This reminds us that it is vital to treat local oral sources on a par with textual sources (Schmidt, Ch. 3 above).

Labels aside, there are important reasons for the archaeology of colonial encounters in eastern Africa to be in dialogue with the wider field of historical archaeology. Africanist archaeologists may gain from thinking about historical archaeological work in wider contexts, particularly from recent studies that carefully balance historical sources with material data, resulting in explorations of the dynamics of colonial relations between a variety of rulers and ruled, and explore the complexities of changing identities as different groups came to be in contact and live with one another (Dawdy 2008; Voss 2008a; Richard 2010). Orser's (2010) review of the state of historical archaeology shows just how much the broader field has changed in drawing in wider contexts and non-traditional historical sources, along with many projects that place research squarely within the realm of local political situations (Hall 2000, 2008). Later archaeologies of Africa also have many important perspectives and critiques to offer a wider field, particularly where they explore novel forms of late Islamic colonialism, the impact of enslavement within East Africa, and the growth of new trading routes, all of which existed within a thriving East African indigenous cultural realm. The importance of working across different social scales ranging from local to global within later archaeologies has been widely recognized (Hall 2000; Voss 2008b; Orser 2010), and is equally important to endeavours in Eastern Africa, no matter what we name the field of study.

COLONIALISM AND POWER

The most obvious material forms of colonial encounters within eastern Africa are the forts and other structures constructed by those in power at different periods. Fort Jesus, Mombasa, the first to be investigated in any depth (Kirkman 1974), perhaps typifies the colonial histories of this region in that it was first constructed by the Portuguese during the 16th century, came under Omani control in the 17th century, and was used by the British during the late 19th and 20th centuries; it now hosts an important Kenyan museum and research centre. While the archaeology of such sites is important in mapping colonial landscapes of power and has often been the first stage of archaeological research on colonial Africa, as was also the case in West Africa (Osei-Tutu 2007), this archaeology has rightly been criticized for privileging only the clearest landmarks of colonial rulers, and provides little information about the vast majority of East Africans during the period the fort was used (Reid and Lane 2004). However, paying attention to these monuments does allow us to see the points at which colonizers attempted to assert their power through the creation of large structures, which must surely have seemed imposing to local populations, whatever the relations between those living and working within the forts and other local residents. Further examples analogous to Fort Jesus include Kilwa, Zanzibar, and Chake Chake, Pemba.

Smaller forts and other structures also help us to understand how colonial rulers attempted to impose power upon the landscape. A recent debate about the logic behind the location of Tongwe Fort as a demonstration of negotiations of power between Omani and local East African rulers (Lane 1993; Walz 2009) shows that thinking about these types of building can be instructive in understanding how colonizers were forced to work within local East African power dynamics, and how they were sometimes used by local rulers to increase the latter's power. Fortified structures were also a feature of indigenous East African communities, particularly in response to the intensification of slave raiding and caravan trading. Indigenous fortifications that appear to be a response to the upheavals of the colonial period have been documented archaeologically in several locations in eastern Africa, including western Tanzania (Wynne-Jones and Croucher 2007), Uganda (Sutton 2006), and both eastern (Kusimba 2004) and western Kenya (Scully 1969, 1979). This range of locations seems in and of itself to demonstrate the widespread nature of settlement changes as a deliberate response to intensified fighting and the upheavals often brought about by shifts in trading routes (Kusimba 2004; Wynne-Jones and Croucher 2007; see also Elzein, Ch. 66 above).

Non-fortified structures also testify to the growing landscape of imperial power. Although little studied in the region by archaeologists, these include prisons, hospitals, and mission sites. Within historical archaeology and other anthropological disciplines, a tradition exists of interpreting such institutions as part of the apparatus of imperial state power. Although an undeveloped field, archaeologies of sites such as the CMS Mission in Mombasa (Frankl 2008), mission sites along the caravan route (Wynne-Jones and Croucher 2007), and the multitude of other colonial institutions built by the Omanis, Portuguese, Germans, and British (Rhodes 2010) may help to elucidate the manner in which imperial powers attempted to assert control in varied ways across the region.

Settlement patterns

The period of colonial encounters in eastern Africa witnessed many changes in settlement patterns and locations. Archaeology is poised to make a strong contribution in interacting with historical records in demonstrating to what degree settlement and landscape change took place. Most historical evidence seems to point to dramatic shifts in settlement patterns and types, not for all East Africans, but for a significant number drawn into new urban centres, changing agrarian settlement—particularly plantations—and other new settlements, such as smaller halts or supply villages along caravan routes. Social composition in settlements may also have changed; for instance, women, children, and the elderly may have become a much larger proportion of year-round residents in Nyamwezi villages as a direct result of the participation of Nyamwezi men and women as caravan porters (Rockel 2006a, 2009). Such changes are as yet unexamined by archaeologists.

A number of studies are beginning to directly address to what degree and why settlement patterns changed in the region as a result of, or in relation to, colonial encounters. A major study has been that of the Historical Ecologies of East African Landscapes (HEEAL) project (Lane 2010), which has explored the relationship between ecological impacts of the intensification of the ivory trade in eastern Africa during the 19th century in relation to local cultures. One offshoot of this project has been the excavation of several sites along the Pangani River associated with the caravan trade (Biginagwa 2009). None of these sites appears to show any obvious earlier settlement below 17th and 18th century contexts, suggesting that these sites may partly have developed where they did as a result of the intensification of particular caravan routes. As an indirect consequence of the trade in enslaved Africans, Kusimba (2004, 2006) has also demonstrated that settlement patterns changed substantially in the Tsavo region of Kenya as residents moved to higher fortified sites as a defensive measure. Enslavement was also a key factor in the placement of *watoro* (maroon or runaway slave) settlements, one of which has been investigated on the Kenyan coast (see below). This type of fortification in response to fears of enslavement and slave-raiding activity also reminds us that we must be attuned to potential depopulation in some areas of East Africa during this period, and survey work should be mindful of any changes indicating abrupt settlement abandonment that might help us to understand areas severely impacted by colonial-era slave trading in East Africa. Plantations were also developed at several key areas, mostly under Omani control, particularly around Mombasa and Pangani and on Zanzibar (Cooper 1977; Glassman 1995; Croucher 2007a).

Colonial urbanism seems to have created a significant shift in the regional landscape. Many of the new towns along trade routes were relatively short-lived, showing the rapidity and scale with which economic and other factors altered the lives of East Africans (Rockel 2006b). Survey along the central caravan route in the area of Tabora and Ujiji, and later excavations at the settlement of Kasimbu, a suburb of Ujiji, produced scant evidence of earlier settlement directly in the areas of these predominantly 19th- and 20th-century urban centres (Wynne-Jones and Croucher 2007). In another area of direct Omani colonial control, on Zanzibar, major urban centres of the same date, particularly Zanzibar Stone Town, have been argued to be largely Omani-period cities, with some earlier Portuguese settlement in the area (Sheriff 2001–2). This pattern is also apparent at other key 19th-century urban sites, such as Pangani, and, of course, at later European colonial cities such as Nairobi and Dar es Salaam (Burton 2001–2). This is despite over a millennium of urban settlement on the coast and the continuation of key precolonial urban centres as major entrepôts within Omani and European colonial trade systems, particularly Kilwa, Mombasa, and Lamu (see La Violette, Ch. 62 above).

However, shifts in settlement and the intensification of urban centres should not be overemphasized at the risk of ignoring continuities in earlier settlement patterns and forms. In some cases, such as the Pangani region (Walz 2005) and along part of the southern Tanzanian coast (Pawlowicz 2009), indigenous patterns of settlement may have persisted, despite other social changes. Archaeologists working in this area of study have much to contribute to conversations outside of archaeology, particularly with those interested in preserving the built environment and landscape heritage of colonial periods in the region (Sheriff 1995; UNESCO 2005). A broad ranging survey of the urban centres dating to the British and German colonial periods of Tanga, Pangani, Bagamoyo, Zanzibar, Dar es Salaam, Chole (Mafia Island), Kilwa Kivinje, and Mombasa has been undertaken by Rhodes (2010), addressing the material aspects of colonial rule through specific buildings—*bomas*, caravanserais, post offices, forts, railway stations, markets, and various domestic buildings—and the layout of towns in regard to the systems of streets, orientation of the cities in relation to their port, railway, road, and market infrastructures, and the formation of specific residential areas (European/Indian/African). This study is broad-ranging and begins the process of taking a specifically historical archaeological perspective to these centres. As further urban-based studies are hopefully undertaken, an important aspect of an archaeological perspective in such investigations will be to figure these later colonial periods into long-term patterns, and in doing so to elucidate the reasons and outcomes of change and continuity at a settlement pattern scale.

ECONOMIC LIFE AND ARTEFACT STUDIES

The economic and productive realms of colonial Eastern Africa were similarly simultaneously in flux whilst retaining continuities with earlier periods. The most obvious example of this is the caravan trade. Historically we know that trade goods, particularly ivory and enslaved Africans, were traded at an intensity never seen before in this region (Alpers 1975; Rockel 2006a; Prestholdt 2008). As mentioned above, the HEEAL project (Biginagwa 2009; Lane 2010) is the most in-depth study to date of this intensifying trade, and sought to place this within the context of long-term environmental trends. A small amount of survey work was also carried out along the central caravan route, and has shown that alongside the growth of urban centres such as Ujiji, smaller indigenous settlements like Maswa's Fort grew up as local groups vied for dominance in local trading networks that linked into expanding global trade (Wynne-Jones and Croucher 2007). Settlements in western Tanzania and Tabora are comparable to those along the Pangani, possibly related to provisioning caravans and trading in ivory (Biginagwa 2009).

This caravan trade was not simply a local intensification of trade, but a complex mechanism of the relationship between Eastern Africa and global commerce that played out on a number of levels, including Europe and North America, as a result of the trade in ivory in particular (Shayt 1993; Malcarne 2001). Little work has yet been done on the social impact of intensifying economic relations between eastern Africa, the United States, and Europe, but work is beginning to address these connections as a social phenomenon. One way in which this global trade is increasingly understood is the use of mass-produced goods by East Africans and their importation into local systems of meaning. Large quantities of beads are found along some caravan route settlements (Biginagwa 2009; Wilson Marshall 2009), fitting historical descriptions of the importance of beads as trade goods to East Africans (Pallaver 2008), alongside cloth, an artefact that may prove harder for archaeologists to address. In studying the importation of mass-produced ceramics on Zanzibari plantations, one study has demonstrated the clear preferences for goods that fit into East African tastes (in this case relating to cuisine), and the manner in which this in turn affected production in European factories (Croucher 2011a). Future studies based on this type of commodity chain analysis may help us to understand how East African colonial trade relations were not simply a case of Africans buying up what few imported goods were available to them but, as in West Africa (Richard 2010), were the product of a complicated relationship between the desires of African consumers and the output of European producers (cf. Prestholdt 2008).

It is this type of relationship that alerts us to the growth of capitalism as an economic and social system in later colonial eastern Africa (particularly from the 19th century). The formation of plantations, producing only a monocrop output for regional and global markets, is one aspect of this, and in the process East African slavery was transformed into a system close to that of North American chattel slavery (Cooper 1979; Glassman 1995). Archaeological investigations of a clove plantation site on Pemba show how new spaces of capitalist labour—a clove plantation floor where planters could observe the work of their enslaved labourers—became sited alongside eastern African architectural forms, such as the stone-built plantation house at Mgoli (Croucher 2007a). In this example we see how the exigencies of capitalist production were brought into the social context of particular forms of colonial rule in eastern Africa. Omani colonial rule was not simply the same as European colonial rule, although it did share some of the same economic principles. But ideologies of Islam and social norms of eastern African society also shaped the way in which power became deployed within this colonial system. Archaeological examinations of the ways in which the eastern African context shaped specific iterations of colonialism are a key area in which archaeologists can, and do, contribute to wider debates.

Although capitalist trade increased in this period, it was not at the expense of local production. A curious fact of colonial Eastern Africa appears to be the persistence of earlier forms of local production, particularly in ceramic styles (Croucher and Wynne-Jones 2006; Biginagwa 2009). This phenomenon continues today along the East African coast (Wynne-Jones and Mapunda 2008). The social implications of such continuities alongside such widespread social change, particularly the massive immigration to regions in which ceramic style continuity has been demonstrated, are still under examination by archaeologists, but appear to show the way in which new identities, possibly along ethnic lines, may have been at least partially based on incorporating foreigners into local societies. This may, in part, be a continuation of the long-term fluidity of cultural incorporation on the East African coast, particularly at Swahili sites (Wynne-Jones and Mapunda 2008). Outside ceramics, little is known of local production, but the density of shell beads, alongside other objects such as clay pipes at sites along the Pangani (Biginagwa 2009), and the bead assembly area excavated at a Giriyama settlement in Kenya (Wilson Marshall 2009), seem to be early indications of widespread local production even as mass-produced goods became more widely available and commodification of goods intensified.

ENSLAVEMENT AND RESISTANCE

A vital area of research that is impossible to ignore in this chapter is the archaeology of enslavement and resistance in colonial Eastern Africa. Historically, it is irrefutable that enslavement drastically increased in scale from the 17th to the 19th centuries (Alpers 1975; Cooper 1977; Sheriff 1987). Enslavement can be difficult to document in the African archaeological record (Alexander 2001; Croucher 2004), but great strides have been made in the last decade to address this problem. A key study is that of Kusimba (2004, 2006) in Kenya's Tsavo region, where fortified settlements provide evidence of defensive measures taken in response to the fear of intense slave raiding. Runaway slave settlements (known in Swahili as *watoro*, comparable to maroon settlements in the Americas) have been studied by Wilson Marshall (2009), who documents the careful placement of a *watoro* community in Kenya, where the settlement had to balance contact with neighbouring communities—particularly through alliances with local Giriyama groups and with European missionaries—with distance from Swahili settlements where dangers of re-enslavement lay. Despite this, *watoro* settlements show material similarities with Swahili settlements, particularly in house forms. This supports historical arguments that enslaved East Africans attempted to demonstrate at least a veneer of cultural affiliation with Swahili and Omani owners in order to gain social status in coastal communities where plantation industries were located (Cooper 1977). As with the continuities of local production, this evidence seems to show that, as well as the exclusion of enslaved persons from full membership of colonial society through their increasing role as chattel slaves on plantations, eastern African colonial culture also allowed for a degree of acceptance of immigrants into new forms of East African identities shaped within this context.

Evidence of enslavement aside from resistance is harder to find. Survey work in plantation areas of Zanzibar yielded very few obvious sites associated with enslaved labourers, despite the fact that so many of these lived on the islands (Croucher 2004). This may partly be due to the lack of social memory of enslaved labourers, as their descendants have been fully incorporated into Zanzibari society. Nonetheless, the location of a Muslim graveyard and a single settlement site, said to be those of 19th-century plantation slaves, shows that sites associated with the enslaved do exist. A lime mortar house at the plantation site of Mgoli has also been interpreted as potentially being the home of a woman enslaved for relations of concubinage (Croucher 2007b, 2011b). Thus, archaeological evidence for enslaved segments of the East African colonial population exists, but may not always be as obvious as might be expected from its historically known scale.

FUTURE DIRECTIONS

The archaeology of colonial periods in eastern Africa looks certain to be a growing field within the region over coming years. It is clearly going to develop as a field that is heavily entwined with oral historical research and heritage discourse. UNESCO money to record sites of the slave route in the Indian Ocean region (UNESCO 2005) is likely to continue to have an impact in this area. On the Kenyan coast, at least one area has seen the 'remembrance' of a slave cave site in response to heightened heritage activity and tourist interest (Wynne-Jones and Walsh 2010). Cases such as this show that sites associated with the archaeology of colonial periods in the region continue to be part of an active dialogue concerning precisely what this history was, and how it fits with contemporary politics, communities, and identities today.

Historical archaeology in North America in particular has been at the forefront of grappling with issues of archaeological sites that remain important to community memory and identity, particularly with reference to the contestations of colonial histories (Wynne-Jones and Walsh 2010; see also Shepherd 2007; Weiss 2007 for South Africa). As we develop such programmes, we potentially have much to learn from issues raised in analogous contexts in other areas. Eastern African archaeology also seems poised to begin to force critical reflection on some of the often insular narratives of historical archaeology in other regions of the world, particularly in comparative discussions of the archaeology of enslavement, global trade, plantations, and maroon communities.

These different elements mean that the future of this field as it expands will be deeply rooted in local histories, helping to build heritage projects in the region, and using archaeology as a means of dialogue about the recent past with communities neighbouring projects. It will also have a global impact in forcing conversations in a field normally rooted in Atlantic worldviews to consider Indian Ocean perspectives.

REFERENCES

ALEXANDER, J. A. (2001). Islam, archaeology and slavery in Africa. *World Archaeology* 33: 44–60.
ALPERS, E. E. (1975). *Ivory and Slaves in East Central Africa*. Berkeley: University of California Press.

BIGINAGWA, T. J. (2009). Excavation of 19th-century caravan trade halts in north-eastern Tanzania: a preliminary report. *Nyame Akuma* 72: 52–60.

BURTON, A. (2001–2). Urbanism in Eastern Africa: an historical overview, c. 1750–2000. *Azania* 36–37: 1–28.

COOPER, F. (1977). *Plantation Slavery on the East Coast of Africa*. New Haven, Conn.: Yale University Press.

——(1979). The problem of slavery in African studies. *Journal of African History* 20: 103–25.

CROUCHER, S. K. (2004). Zanzibar clove plantation survey 2003: some preliminary findings. *Nyame Akuma* 62: 65–9.

——(2007a). Facing many ways: approaches to the archaeological landscapes of the East African coast. In D. Hicks, L. Mcatackney, and F. Fairclough (eds), *Envisioning Landscape: Situations and Standpoints in Archaeology and Heritage*. Walnut Creek, Calif.: Left Coast Press, 55–74.

——(2007b). Clove plantations on nineteenth-century Zanzibar: possibilities for gender archaeology in Africa. *Journal of Social Archaeology* 7: 302–24.

——(2011a). Exchange values: commodities, colonialism, and identity on 19th century Zanzibar. In S. K. Croucher and L. M. Weiss (eds), *Capitalism in Colonial Contexts: Postcolonial Historical Archaeologies*. New York: Springer, 165–92.

——(2011b). 'A concubine is still a slave': sexual relations and Omani colonial identities in nineteenth-century East Africa. In B. Voss and E. C. Casella (eds), *The Archaeology of Colonialism, Gender and Sexuality*. Cambridge: Cambridge University Press, 67–84.

——and WYNNE-JONES, S. (2006). People, not pots: locally produced ceramics and identity on the 19th-century East African coast. *International Journal of African Historical Studies* 39: 107–24.

DAWDY, S. L. (2008). *Building the Devil's Empire: French Colonial New Orleans*. Chicago: University of Chicago Press.

FRANKL, P. J. L. (2008). Mombasa Cathedral and the CMS Compound: the years of the East Africa Protectorate. *History in Africa* 35: 209–99.

FUNARI, P. P., HALL, M., and JONES, S. (eds) (1999). *Historical Archaeology: Back From the Edge*. New York: Routledge.

GLASSMAN, J. (1995). *Feasts and Riot: Revelry, Rebellion and Popular Consciousness on the Swahili Coast, 1856–1888*. London: James Currey.

HALL, M. (2000). *Archaeology and the Modern World: Colonial Transcripts in South Africa and the Chesapeake*. New York: Routledge.

——(2008). New subjectivities: capitalist, colonial subject and archaeologist. Review of 'Capitalism in colonial contexts', conference of the Society for Historical Archaeology, Albuquerque, Jan. 2008. *Archaeologies* 5: 3–17.

KIRKMAN, J. S. (1974). *Fort Jesus: A Portuguese Fortress on the East African Coast*. Oxford: Clarendon Press.

KUSIMBA, C. M. (2004). Archaeology of slavery in East Africa. *African Archaeological Review* 21: 59–87.

——(2006). Slavery and warfare in African chiefdoms. In E. N. Arkush and M. W. Allen (eds), *The Archaeology of Warfare: Prehistories of Raiding and Conquest*. Gainesville: University Press of Florida, 214–49.

LANE, P. J. (1993). Tongwe Fort. *Azania* 28: 133–41.

——(2007). Whither historical archaeology in Africa?. *Review of Archaeology* 28: 1–24.

——(2010). Developing landscape historical ecologies in Eastern Africa: an outline of current research and potential future directions. *African Studies* 69: 299–322.

MALCARNE, D. L. (2001). Ivoryton, Connecticut: the ivory industry and voluntary and involuntary migration in the late nineteenth century. *North American Archaeologist* 22: 283–95.

ORSER, C. E. (2010). Twenty-first century historical archaeology. *Journal of Archaeological Research* 18: 111–50.

OSEI-TUTU, B. (2007). Ghana's 'slave castles', tourism, and the social memory of the Atlantic slave trade. In A. Ogundiran and T. Falola (eds), *Archaeology of Atlantic Africa and the African Diaspora*. Bloomington: Indiana University Press, 185–98.

PALLAVER, K. (2008). 'A recognized currency in beads'. Glass beads as money in 19th-century East Africa: the central caravan road. In C. Eagleton and H. Fuller (eds), *Money in Africa*. London: British Museum Press, 20–29.

PAWLOWICZ, M. (2009). Archaeological exploration of the Mikindani region of the southern Tanzanian coast. *Nyame Akuma* 72: 41–51.

PRESTHOLDT, J. (2008). *Domesticating the World: African Consumerism and the Genealogies of Globalization*. Berkeley: University of California Press.

REID, A. M., and LANE, P. J. (2004). African historical archaeologies: an introductory consideration of scope and potential. In A. M. Reid and P. J. Lane (eds), *African Historical Archaeologies*. New York: Kluwer Academic/Plenum, 1–32.

RHODES, D. (2010). *Historical Archaeologies of Nineteenth-Century Colonial Tanzania: A Comparative Study*. Oxford: Archaeopress.

RICHARD, F. G. (2010). Recharting Atlantic encounters: object trajectories and histories of value in the Siin (Senegal) and Senegambia. *Archaeological Dialogues* 17: 1–27.

ROCKEL, S. J. (2006a). *Carriers of Culture: Labor on the Road in Nineteenth-Century East Africa*. Portsmouth: Heinemann.

——(2006b). Forgotten caravan towns in nineteenth-century Tanzania: Mbwamaji and Mpwapwa. *Azania* 41: 1–25.

——(2009). Slavery and freedom in nineteenth-century East Africa: the case of Waungwana caravan porters. *African Studies* 68: 87–109.

SCHMIDT, P. R. (2006). *Historical Archaeology in Africa: Representation, Social Memory and Oral Traditions*. Lanham, Md.: AltaMira Press.

——and WALZ, J. R. (2007). Re-representing African pasts through historical archaeology. *American Antiquity* 72: 53–70.

SCULLY, R. T. K. (1969). Fort sites of East Bukusu, Kenya. *Azania* 4: 105–14.

——(1979). Nineteenth century settlement sites and related oral traditions from the Bugoma area, western Kenya. *Azania* 14: 81–96.

SHAYT, D. H. (1993). Elephant under glass: the piano key bleach house of Deep River, Connecticut. *Industrial Archaeology* 19: 37–59.

SHEPHERD, N. (2007). Archaeology dreaming: post-apartheid urban imaginaries and the bones of the Prestwich Street dead. *Journal of Social Archaeology* 7: 3–28.

SHERIFF, A. (1987). *Slaves, Spices and Ivory in Zanzibar*. Athens: Ohio University Press.

——(1995). Introduction. In A. Sheriff (ed.), *The History and Conservation of Zanzibar Stone Town*. Athens: Ohio University Press, 1–7.

——(2001–2). The spatial dichotomy of Swahili towns: the case of Zanzibar in the nineteenth century *Azania* 36–7: 63–81.

SUTTON [published as SATON], J. (2006). Foweira on the Nile: camps, boat station and forts of the late nineteenth century. *Uganda Journal* 51: 38–44.

Unesco[S3] (United Nations Educational, Scientific And Cultural Organization) (2005). The slave route: trade in the Indian Ocean. http://portal.unesco.org/culture/en/ev,php-URL-ID=26960&URL_DO=DO_TOPIC&URL_SECTION=201.html Website accessed 20 Nov. 2010.

Voss, B. L. (2008a). *The Archaeology of Ethnogenesis: Race and Sexuality in Colonial San Francisco*. Berkeley: University of California Press.

——(2008b). Gender, race, and labor in the archaeology of the Spanish colonial Americas. *Current Anthropology* 49: 861–93.

Walz, J. R. (2005). Mombo and the Mkomazi Corridor: preliminary findings from lowland northeastern Tanzania. In B. B. B. Mapunda and P. Msemwa (eds), *Salvaging Tanzania's Cultural Heritage*. Dar es Salaam: University of Dar es Salaam Press, 198–213.

——(2009). Archaeologies of disenchantment. In P. R. Schmidt (ed.), *Postcolonial Archaeologies in Africa*. Santa Fe, NM: SAR Press, 21–38.

Weiss, L. M. (2007). Heritage-making and political identity. *Journal of Social Archaeology* 7: 413–31.

Wilson Marshall, L. (2009). Fugitive slave communities in 19th-century Kenya: a preliminary report on recent and historical research. *Nyame Akuma* 72: 21–9.

Wynne-Jones, S., and Croucher, S. K. (2007). The central caravan route of Tanzania: a preliminary archaeological reconnaissance. *Nyame Akuma* 67: 91–5

——and Mapunda, B. B. B. (2008). 'This is what pots look like here': ceramics, tradition and consumption on Mafia Island, Tanzania. *Azania* 43: 1–17.

——and Walsh, M. (2010). Heritage, tourism, and slavery at Shimoni: narrative and metanarrative on the East African coast. *History in Africa* 37: 247–73.

INDEX

Printed and bound by CPI Group (UK) Ltd, Croydon, CR0 4YY